Philosophical Questions:
Classical and Contemporary Readings

FIRST EDITION

W I L L I A M   F.   L A W H E A D
University of Mississippi

McGraw Hill

Boston   Burr Ridge, IL   Dubuque, IA   Madison, WI   New York   San Francisco   St. Louis
Bangkok   Bogotá   Caracas   Kuala Lumpur   Lisbon   London   Madrid   Mexico City
Milan   Montreal   New Delhi   Santiago   Seoul   Singapore   Sydney   Taipei   Toronto

McGraw-Hill Higher Education

A Division of The McGraw-Hill Companies

PHILOSOPHICAL QUESTIONS: CLASSICAL AND CONTEMPORARY READINGS
Published by McGraw-Hill, a business unit of the The McGraw-Hill Companies, Inc., 1221 Avenue of the Americas, New York, NY, 10020. Copyright © 2003 by The McGraw-Hill Companies, Inc. All rights reserved. No part of this publication may be reproduced or distributed in any form or by any means, or stored in a database or retrieval system, without the prior written consent of The McGraw-Hill Companies, Inc., including, but not limited to, in any network or other electronic storage or transmission, or broadcast for distance learning.
Some ancillaries, including electronic and print components, may not be available to customers outside the United States.

This book is printed on acid-free paper.

1 2 3 4 5 6 7 8 9 0 FGR/FGR 0 9 8 7 6 5 4 3 2

ISBN 0-7674-2411-5

Publisher: *Ken King*
Associate editor: *Jon-David Hague*
Marketing manager: *Greg Brueck*
Project manager: *Jill Moline*
Production supervisor: *Carol A. Bielski*
Designer: *Matthew Baldwin*
Cover image: *Alinari/Art Resource, NY*
Typeface: *10/12 New Baskerville*
Compositor: *ElectraGraphics, Inc.*
Printer: *Quebecor World Fairfield Inc.*

Library of Congress Cataloging-in-Publication Data

Philosophical questions : classical and contemporary readings / [edited by] William F. Lawhead.
    p. cm.
  Includes index.
  ISBN 0-7674-2411-5 (alk. paper)
  1. Philosophy—Introductions. I. Lawhead, William F.
BD21 .P467 2003
100—dc21
                                                     2002024631

www.mhhe.com

To Pam for her understanding and support

Preface

This textbook is an anthology of readings designed to be used in a standard introduction to philosophy course. It contains the typical range of topics that are usually covered in this sort of course. It includes not only the standard readings from classical philosophers, but selections from many contemporary writers as well. Each topic is framed in the form of a question and the readings are organized and titled as alternative answers to the question. Some anthologies are of the "sink and swim" variety. That is, they simply present the readings and have, at best, only cursory introductions, leaving it up to the reader to figure out how it all fits together. In contrast to this approach, my book is heavy on pedagogy. The introductions to the chapters and the readings structure the topic and provide guidance to the readers.

In choosing the selections for this anthology, I was guided by the following criteria: (1) Which readings would be most useful in an introduction to philosophy course? (2) How accessible or difficult is the selection for today's average student? (3) How interesting is it? (4) Does it provide a good example of philosophical argumentation? (5) Does it effectively represent one of the main philosophical answers to the question at hand?

THE SPECIFIC FORMAT OF EACH CHAPTER

Each chapter will contain the following elements.

1. Introduction   Each chapter begins with an introduction by the editor that serves to accomplish the following goals: (1) Demonstrating the relevance of the topic, arousing the interest of the students, provoking intellectual curiosity, and motivating the students to seek more understanding of the issue at hand. (2) Setting out the main issues and terminology concerning the topic. (3) Providing a clear presentation of the positions and their central themes. (4) Providing a chart that compares the responses of each position to several key questions concerning the topic.

2. Opening Narrative   The first reading of each chapter will be a fictional piece that introduces the topic in a provocative, tantalizing manner. Each fictional piece in the opening narratives will provoke more questions than it answers and will set the stage for the readings to follow.

3. Readings   Each reading will be preceded by a brief biography of the writer. Next, a brief overview of the reading will be offered. Finally, a series of *Reading Questions* will be provided to guide the reader through the selection. At the end of the reading will be *Questions for Reflection*. These will encourage the student to engage with the ideas just presented and will assist the reader in evaluating the ideas and considering their implications.

4. Contemporary Application   Each chapter ends with a section titled *Contemporary Application*. In this section the philosophical issues discussed in the chapter appear within a broader interdisciplinary setting by means of pro and con positions on a contemporary problem. This demonstrates to the students that philosophy is relevant to issues that appear in current news magazines. The Contemporary Application topics are

> Philosophy of Religion: Does religion conflict with science?
>
> Theory of Knowledge: Does science give us objective knowledge about the world?
>
> The Mind-Body Problem: Can computers think?
>
> Freedom and Determinism: Can criminals be held morally responsible for their actions?
>
> Ethics: Is abortion morally permissible?
>
> Political Philosophy: Does the government have a right to protect us from ourselves?

ADDITIONAL FEATURES

Philosophy through Fiction   For a change of pace and to heighten student interest, several of the readings present philosophical ideas through short literary selections. I have found that in some anthologies that use fiction, the readings are interesting, but I am sometimes puzzled as to how they are supposed to fit into the discussion. In this book, however, the readers should find that the philosophical point of each selection is fairly obvious and that the literary pieces serve to advance the discussion. Rather than being philosophical mind candy, they contain meaty issues. As mentioned previously, fictional pieces are used in the *Opening Narrative* component to raise some of the issues that will be discussed by the philosophers. Furthermore, there are occasional literary selections sprinkled amidst the other readings. The fictional selections include

> Edwin Abbott, *Flatland*
>
> Plato, "The Allegory of the Cave"
>
> Albert Camus, *The Plague*
>
> Daniel Dennett, "Where Am I?"
>
> R. Buckminster Fuller, "What's a Man?"
>
> Terry Bisson, "They're Made Out of Meat"
>
> Jonathan Harrison, "The Case of Dr. Svengali"
>
> Plato, "The Ring of Gyges"
>
> Richard Taylor, "The Parable of the Man"
>
> W. H. Auden, "The Unknown Citizen"

Of course, in many of the other philosophical essays a parable, story, or thought experiment plays a central role in the philosophical discussion.

Interdisciplinary Implications   While most of the essays are by philosophers, the *Contemporary Application* sections and other readings also include the philosophical views of scientists and other professionals. This reinforces the point that philosophy is not a narrow, esoteric, optional enterprise; instead philosophical issues are relevant to all the disciplines. These interdisciplinary selections include a biologist (Richard Dawkins), two physicists (Paul Davies, Steven Weinberg), a psychologist/computer scientist (Christopher Evans), a psychologist (B. F. Skinner), a trial lawyer (Clarence Darrow), an anthropologist (Ruth Benedict), a public policy specialist (James Q. Wilson), and a psychiatrist (Thomas Szasz).

SUGGESTED WAYS TO USE THIS BOOK

Probably no one will want to cover all the topics in this book in one semester. Even within a particular chapter, it may not be possible to cover all the readings. Furthermore, some instructors may wish to present the topics in a different order from the way they are organized in this book. None of this is a problem, however, for the book allows for maximum flexibility. The chapters and readings in this anthology are relatively independent and may be used in whatever order fits the needs of a particular course.

As mentioned earlier, each reading begins with *Reading Questions*. These guide the reader to the important landmarks in the essay and draw attention to key arguments and points. The student may want to write out the answers to these questions to have a handy summary of the selection's contents. Each selection is followed by *Questions for Reflection*. These questions require more than simply summarizing the content of the passage; they ask the reader to reflect upon, evaluate, and apply the ideas in the reading. The instructor may wish to use these as topics for class discussions or short papers.

ACKNOWLEDGMENTS

Before the book went from inspiration to execution, the initial outline passed through a number of reviewers. I appreciate the comments of the following reviewers:

Kathleen Wider, University of Michigan–Dearborn
Louise Excell, Dixie State College
Pat Matthews, Florida State University
David Carlson, Madison Area Technical College
Judy Barad, Indiana State University
Jay Wood, Wheaton College
D. Gene Witmer, University of Florida

Finally, this book is dedicated to my wife Pam who gave me loving support while I worked on it and patiently waited for its completion.

Contents

CHAPTER 3   Questions about Human Knowledge   160

C H A P T E R   1

Questions about Philosophy

WHAT IS PHILOSOPHY? WHY IS IT IMPORTANT?

A few years ago, after having spent a long day at an out-of-town philosophy conference, I stopped off to visit Walter, a friend of my wife's family. Walter is an engaging person and a successful, no-nonsense businessman. His greeting to me was "So, Bill, you've been attending a philosophy conference? You need to sit down, relax, and have a drink. You've been cooped up with weirdos all day." I mentally added that remark to my growing list of people's conceptions (or misconceptions) of philosophy. (Since I am a philosopher who was mingling with others of my profession at the conference, I also wondered what Walter's remark indicated about his conception of me.) In contrast, some misconceptions about philosophy are more flattering. Frequently, when I first make someone's acquaintance and they discover that I teach philosophy at a university, they exclaim "Oh . . . Philosophy is so profound and mysterious!" in a tone of voice that suggests that philosophers live on a plane far above ordinary mortals.

The problem with both of these reactions is that they imply that philosophy is an isolated, optional enterprise, reserved only for those who are either socially challenged or intellectually elite. The reason why this view of philosophy is off the mark is that everyone (in one sense of the word) is a philosopher. What I mean by this is that throughout the course of our humdrum, daily lives we are continually confronting philosophical questions and embracing philosophical conclusions.

To illustrate this last point, let's consider a toddler noticing her image in a mirror for the first time. She is intrigued by the little child she sees. She waves to her and the other child waves back. She jumps and the other girl jumps. Eventually, the child makes a breakthrough discovery, as the thought occurs to her that "The other child is me!" "But how can that be?" she thinks. "I am here and she is there!" In experiences such as these, the child encounters her first, basic philosophical problem: How do I distinguish appearance from reality? Furthermore, her fascinating encounter with the mirror teaches her that she can experience herself both as a subject and as an object. As a subject, she is immersed within the world as a subjective center of consciousness. But she can also stand back and view herself as an object to study and understand. One of the mysteries little children eventually begin to wrestle with is the relationship between me and my experiences on the one hand, and that which is not me on the other. In this way, the child begins to make critical judgments about what reality is like and what the self is like. Most importantly, she begins to realize that everything is not as it seems, that her beliefs can be mistaken, that she needs to work hard to sort out what she should believe from what she should not. When she reaches this stage in life, she will realize that answering these sorts of questions constitutes a lifelong agenda. She may also find that others have asked these questions before and that fellow questioners, both past and present, can help her in her task.

In what sense is this child's puzzlement about her image in the mirror the beginnings of her own philosophical journey, as I have suggested? Well, first of all, the famous Greek philosopher Aristotle (384–322 B.C.) once wrote that all philosophy begins with a sense of wonder. For the child, wondering is easy, for there is so little she understands. Her experiences are not filtered through acquired beliefs or taken-for-granted assumptions that have been accumulating for years. Hence, if Aristotle is right, to be a philosopher we must look at the world in a new way. We must get a fresh perspective on it and recapture a childlike sense of wonder about it. But while wonder is a prelude to philosophy, philosophy is more than just looking at the world. It is a matter of thinking about the world and human experience, drawing conclusions from those thoughts, and (most importantly) justifying those conclusions (both to others and to ourselves).

The word *philosophy* comes from a Greek word that literally means the love of wisdom. To love something does not mean that we possess it, but that our life is focused on it. Socrates, another famous Greek philosopher, said that the philosopher was one who had a passion for wisdom and who was intoxicated by this love. This makes quite a contrast with the image of the philosopher as being cold and analytical—sort of a walking and talking computer. On the contrary, the cognitive and the emotional are combined in philosophy. I do not rationally deliberate about those issues in life that are utterly trivial. When I pick up my copy of the daily campus newspaper, for example, I don't stand there and reason about which copy to grab. On the other hand, those issues that are most important to us are such things as our religious commitments (or lack of them), our moral values, our political commitments, our career, or (perhaps) who we will share our lives with. Unlike the trivial task of choosing a newspaper, our choices concerning our deepest loves, convictions, and commitments are those issues that demand our deepest thought and most thorough rational reflection. Philosophy, in part, is the search for that kind of wisdom that will inform the beliefs and values that enter into these crucial decisions.

If, as I have claimed, we are all engaged in the activity of philosophy and have been for most of our lives, then what is the point of opening up this book to study philosophy? The point is that philosophy, as with any other activity, can be done at various levels and with various degrees of success. There is a difference between a novice banging out "Chopsticks" on the piano and the efforts of a dedicated musician who continually practices and challenges himself in order to achieve his maximum level of performance. Similarly, for most people, running is a natural activity, but if an athlete wants to become an accomplished competitor on the racetrack, she has to work hard at it. To apply these examples to philosophy, as we grow up we naturally acquire a set of philosophical beliefs that influence our thinking and guide our lives. However, as with the musician and the athlete, there is a big difference between entertaining and embracing philosophical ideas in a haphazard, taken-for-granted manner and facing the challenge of engaging with philosophy in a self-conscious, careful, disciplined way.

The problem is that too often we acquire our beliefs the way we catch a cold. All kinds of ideas are floating around in our culture; they are part of the intellectual air that we breath. These ideas may be about God, the nature of reality, the value of science, human nature, moral values, or politics. The assumptions of our society also include ideas about what sorts of beliefs are acceptable, plausible, dangerous, or absurd. We passively absorb these ideas the way we do the cold virus. The cold once belonged to someone else and now it is our cold. But we were not aware that we were breathing it in and usually do not know where we acquired it. Similarly, we breathe in ideas that are in our cultural environment, but do not do so consciously and have never examined them, even though they are now a part of us.

While it is true that we are all philosophers in the sense that we have philosophical beliefs and assumptions, in the fullest sense of the word *philosophy* we have not truly engaged with philosophy until we attempt to evaluate and justify our basic beliefs in a careful, deliberate, and objective manner. In order to get a feel for how one does this, we need to examine three essential components of philosophy: questions, answers, and reasons.

QUESTIONS, ANSWERS, AND REASONS

Questions

This book is organized around questions, because that is one of the main things that philosophers do—ask questions. Before we discuss the distinctive nature of philosophical questions, think about why asking questions (in general) is important. First, *questioning is practical.* We can lose many things in life and still survive. But what if a brain disorder caused you to lose your ability to ask questions—either of yourself or of others? Can you imagine how deeply impaired you would be? By asking questions we are able to effectively deal with the world.

Second, *questioning is a unique feature of your humanity.* Ants have very complex societies with various social roles such as the queen, the workers, and the soldier ants. Because of this division of labor, their society is a simplified, miniature version of ours. However, we cannot imagine the worker ants thinking: "Why are we doing all the work, while the queen is living a life of luxury?" Instead, they blindly and instinctively carry out their activities. But humans do question the status quo and ponder questions about justice and morality. We stand back from our life and reflect on it. This is the mental version of what we do in a mirror. In both kinds of reflections we get a distance from ourselves so we can see ourselves objectively, put things in perspective, and make adjustments.

Third, *questions are crucial to the advancement of human thought.* The first philosopher in Western history we know anything about was Thales (roughly 624–545 B.C.). Thales looked at the world around him and asked, "What is the fundamental substance that underlies everything we find in the world?" His answer was "water." He probably concluded water is the basic element because it covers most of the earth, it comes from the sky, it is found in the ground, and it can become a solid, liquid, or gas. While even his contemporaries did not think much of his answer, it started people thinking and raising questions about the ultimate nature of reality. Likewise, throughout history, it has been someone who asked a question no one had ever considered before who took human thought to the next level of sophistication.

Thus far, there is nothing that I have said that couldn't apply to any other intellectual activity. What is it that makes philosophy unique? Let's ask the question this way. Biologists study frogs, astronomers study stars, and economists study economic transactions. So, what do philosophers study? I think a good answer is that philosophy is unique in comparison to other areas of study not because it thinks about different things, but because it thinks about things differently. To be more specific, philosophers study and ask questions about the most basic concepts that underlie every other human endeavor. This feature of philosophy can be made clear by comparing the sorts of questions asked by different disciplines with the sorts of questions asked by the philosopher in eight different areas, corresponding to the eight chapters of this book.

1. The psychologist studies *how* people think and the *causes* of people's beliefs, whether their thinking is rational or irrational. But the philosopher studies how we *ought* to think if we are to be rational and seeks to clarify what are good *reasons* for holding a belief. The study of the principles for distinguishing correct from incorrect reasoning is the area of philosophy known as **logic,** which will be discussed at the end of this chapter under the heading, How Do I Decide What to Believe? Tools for Examining Arguments.

2. The astronomer studies the laws that govern the heavenly bodies such as the stars. However, the philosopher asks, Is the existence and nature of the universe self-explanatory or does it need an explanation or a divine creator that lies outside of it? How do we account for the order in the world that makes science possible? Is the evidence of design sufficient to prove a designer?

The meteorologist asks, What causes hurricanes? and the medical researcher asks, What causes childhood leukemia? On the other hand, the philosopher asks questions such as these: Is there any rational way to believe in a good, all-powerful God who permits the undeserved destruction of hurricanes or the suffering of innocent children? Or is the evidence of undeserved suffering an argument against such a God?

The sociologist studies the religious beliefs of various groups and the social needs these beliefs fulfill, without making any judgments about the truth or rationality of these beliefs. However, the philosopher asks, Is faith opposed to reason, compatible with reason, or supported by reason, or is faith something that necessarily goes beyond reason? These sorts of questions about the existence of God, the problem of evil, and the relationship of faith and reason constitute the area of philosophy known as **philosophy of religion** and will be discussed in Chapter 2: Questions about God, Faith, and Reason.

3. The historian seeks to increase our knowledge of the Civil War by gathering facts and determining which accounts of the events are the most true. The philosopher asks, What is knowledge? What is a fact? What is truth? How could we know that something is true or not? Is there objective truth or are all opinions relative? Fundamental questions about the nature and source of knowledge, the concept of truth, and the objectivity or relativity of our beliefs are the concern of the theory of knowledge or **epistemology,** which you will encounter in Chapter 3: Questions about Human Knowledge.

4. The physicist studies the ultimate constituents of physical reality such as atoms, quarks, or neutrinos. On the other hand, the philosopher asks, Is physical reality all that there is? The neurobiologist studies the activity of the brain, but the philosopher asks, Are all mental events really brain events or is the mind something separate from the brain? **Metaphysics** is the area of philosophy concerned with fundamental questions

about the nature of reality. Certainly, science tells us about reality. But scientific accounts are limited to physical data that can be observed or measured with physical instruments. When we are engaged in philosophy, on the other hand, we step outside of science and ask, Is the scientific view complete? Is there more to be known that lies outside of the limits of science? The metaphysical questions we will examine in this book will focus on two topics concerning the nature of *human* reality. The first set of questions concerns the nature of the mind and its relation to the body. These questions will be covered in Chapter 4: Questions about the Mind.

5. The second set of questions about the person concerns the nature of our actions and choices. As before, the scientific ways of approaching this topic have to be situated within the broader philosophical issues. The psychologist, for example, attempts to find causal correlations between criminal behavior and the individual's genetic inheritance or social influences. The philosopher, on the other hand, asks, Is all behavior (good or bad) causally determined or do we have some degree of genuine freedom that cannot be scientifically explained? Is there necessarily a conflict between the scientific attempt to explain and predict behavior and our belief in human freedom? These sorts of metaphysical questions about the person will be addressed in Chapter 5: Questions about Free Will and Determinism.

6. The anthropologist studies the moral codes of various societies, describing both their similarities and differences, but without deciding which ones are best. On the other hand, the philosopher asks, Are there any objectively correct ethical values or are they all relative? Which ethical principles (if any) are the correct ones? How do we decide what is right or wrong? These questions are the concern of **ethics,** which will be the topic of Chapter 6: Questions about Right and Wrong.

7. The political scientist studies various forms of government, but the philosopher asks, Is disobeying the law ever morally justified? What is justice? What is the proper extent of individual freedom? What are the limits of governmental authority? These questions fall under the heading of **political philosophy** and will be discussed in Chapter 7: Questions about Human Liberty and the Government.

8. Science can tell us what *is* the case about certain features of our world. However, we cannot scientifically decide what all this *means* for our personal lives. This is a question we can only ask and attempt to answer when we stand back from both our scientific inquiries and our immediate engagement with our daily lives. The question "What is the meaning of it all?" is the premier philosophical question. We will examine several responses to this question in Chapter 8: Postscript: What Is the Meaning of Life?

Answers

"OK," you say, "questions are important, but what about the answers? Don't we ask questions for the purpose of finding answers?" Certainly, answers are important and philosophers are not shy about giving us their answers. However, what is important in philosophy is both the character of our answers and how we arrived at them.

The first point to be understood about philosophical answers is that we will never (or rarely) find a philosophical position about which everyone is agreed. In Chapter 5, for example, Baron d'Holbach will argue that all human actions are absolutely determined by previous causes. C. A. Campbell and others will argue that a significant number of actions are free. But the fact that people disagree about an issue does not prove that there is no truth about the matter. Nor does disagreement prove that the reasons in support of one position are not, in the final analysis, better than the reasons used to support an opposing position. The task that you have as a critical reader is to weigh and sift the arguments of the philosophers to see which one has made the best case for his or her position.

The second point about philosophical answers is that searching for adequate answers is always an ongoing task. Some of the very best philosophers have abandoned positions they once held because they realized that their arguments were weaker than they originally thought. The willingness to modify one's beliefs, based on reflective considerations, is the sign of a mature intellect. On the other hand, the refusal to entertain alternative points of view is the sign of a person who is fearful and interested in comfort rather than truth.

What this means is that we are never finished with philosophy and it is never finished with us, and our most dearly-held and fundamental ideas are never without the need for modification and improvement. This is difficult to accept because we like closure, finality, and quick solutions. We live in a world of 30-minute television dramas, lightning-speed computers, instant coffee, and microwave meals. However, it is helpful to compare the search for philosophical understanding to cultivating a meaningful relationship. The minute two people decide that they have figured out their relationship and do not need to work at it anymore, the relationship has grown stale. In both relationships and philosophy, there are always new problems to face and old problems to address in new ways. Appropriately, the term *philosopher* literally means "a *lover* of wisdom." The qualities that make one a successful lover or philosopher are similar. Successful lovers will never tire of exploring the facets of one another's personality. Likewise, the successful philosopher will endlessly desire to explore new ideas and undiscovered dimensions of old ideas. Hence, the search to understand our friend or to philosophically comprehend our experience is a quest that is always ongoing and never completed. However, this does not mean that in relationships or in philosophy we cannot make progress along the way.

While it is satisfying to have answers to our questions, not any old answer will do. In philosophy, the way we have arrived at our answers is just as important as what answers or positions we embrace. In other words, the process is just as important as the outcome. This leads us to the third element in philosophy, which is *reasons*.

Reasons

Suppose you showed a professor a test in which you believe you answered all the questions perfectly, but you still received a grade of C. You ask, "Shouldn't I have received an A on this test?" Suppose your professor answers "No" and turns and walks away. You would not be satisfied for you would be expecting some justification or a list of reasons why you received the grade you did. Providing reasons for our beliefs and philosophical conclusions is one of the most important aspects of philosophy.

In one sense, philosophy is a very personal undertaking. If you want to know the distance to the moon you can accept the expert opinion of an astronomer. But, in contrast, when it comes to your most fundamental beliefs, you have to decide for yourself. Of course you can learn from the writings of the great philosophers, but you still have to decide whether or not to adopt their views as your own. Furthermore, the philosophical ideas you embrace have an enormous impact on your personal life.

But even though philosophy is personal, it also must be objective. Evaluating philosophies is not like tasting foods ("I like this. I don't like that"). The reason is that philosophy is concerned with truth. For example, consider these two pairs of opposing positions: (1a) There is a God, (1b) There is not a God or (2a) All human choices are determined by previous causes, (2b) Some human choices are not determined by previous causes. With respect to each pair of statements, one of them must be true and one of them is false. In each case, I may be more emotionally inclined to accept one answer over the other, but that is irrelevant. This is because each position is making a claim about the nature of reality. My subjective preferences do not dictate what reality is like, nor are my preferences the best guide to knowing what to believe about reality. Accordingly, our task as human beings is to find the best answers we can, based on the best reasons we can find. To summarize, our engagement with philosophy is driven by subjective interests, involves personal choices, and has personal consequences. At the same time, philosophy is the pursuit of objective reasons that support our philosophical commitments.

More detailed information on the sorts of answers philosophers seek and the sorts of reasons that are used to justify those answers will be given in the last section in this chapter, which is titled: How Can I Decide What to Believe? Tools for Examining Arguments. For now, it will be worthwhile to examine some concrete examples of the activity of philosophy. We will begin with two accounts by Plato that center on his teacher Socrates, one of the greatest philosophers of all time.

PLATO

The Activity of Philosophy

Plato (428–348 B.C.) was one of the first philosophers in Western culture to develop a comprehensive system of philosophical thought. He was the student of Socrates, the teacher of Aristotle, and the founder of the first university (the Academy in Athens). Most of Plato's philosophical writings were in the form of dialogues between Socrates and one or more companions.

Socrates (470–399 B.C.) was one of the most remarkable human beings who ever lived. He is considered to be the paradigm of the philosopher, both for his style of asking questions and exploring concepts and for his willingness to die for his ideas. In the following dialogue Socrates encounters Euthyphro while they both are waiting to go to court. Socrates is being tried for his controversial teachings and Euthyphro is prosecuting his own father. As in all of Socrates' conversations, he quickly turns the discussion from the immediate, concrete concerns to an exploration of the fundamental philosophical concepts hidden beneath the practical issue. In this case, the concept Socrates examines is that of "piety." For the Greeks, one's obligations to the state and to the gods were the same issue. Hence, in this dialogue, piety is a broader notion than it is for us, so that the discussion between Euthyphro and Socrates should be read as an inquiry into the nature of moral obligation.

Reading Questions

1. Why does Euthyphro believe he is correct in prosecuting his father?
2. What question does Socrates immediately pose for Euthyphro? Why is it a significant one?
3. What is the first definition of piety Euthyphro offers? Why does Socrates say this definition is inadequate?
4. What is the second definition of piety Euthyphro proposes? Given what Euthyphro has already said about the nature of the gods, what problem does Socrates raise with this definition? How does Euthyphro modify his definition to avoid this problem?
5. What ambiguity does Socrates find with the statement "Piety is what all the gods love"? What is the difference between the two possible answers? What are the implications of accepting one answer or the other?
6. What solution do the two of them finally agree upon concerning the relationship between the gods loving an act and that act being pious?
7. According to Euthyphro, what distinguishes piety from other forms of justice?
8. What problems does Socrates find with the definition that piety is "the art of attending to the gods"?
9. Why is the discussion left unfinished?

From Plato, *Euthyphro,* from *The Dialogues of Plato,* trans. Benjamin Jowett (Oxford: Oxford University Press, 1896). (Some words have been modified to make the text more accessible to the modern reader.)

EUTHYPHRO: Why have you left the Lyceum, Socrates? and what are you doing in the Porch of the King Archon? Surely you cannot be concerned in a suit before the King, like myself?

SOCRATES: Not in a suit, Euthyphro; impeachment is the word which the Athenians use.

EUTHYPHRO: What! I suppose that someone has been prosecuting you, for I cannot believe that you are the prosecutor of another.

SOCRATES: Certainly not.

EUTHYPHRO: Then someone else has been prosecuting you?

SOCRATES: Yes.

EUTHYPHRO: And who is he?

SOCRATES: A young man who is little known, Euthyphro; and I hardly know him: his name is Meletus, and he is of the district of Pitthis. Perhaps you may remember his appearance; he has a beak, and long straight hair, and a beard which is ill grown.

EUTHYPHRO: No, I do not remember him, Socrates. But what is the charge which he brings against you?

SOCRATES: What is the charge? Well, a very serious charge, which shows a good deal of character in the young man, and for which he is certainly not to be despised. He says he knows how the youth are corrupted and who are their corruptors. I fancy that he must be a wise man, and seeing that I am the reverse of a wise man, he has found me out, and is going to accuse me of corrupting his young friends. And of this our mother the state is to be the judge. Of all our political men he is the only one who seems to me to begin in the right way, with the cultivation of virtue in youth; like a good husbandman, he makes the young shoots his first care, and clears away us who are the destroyers of them. This is only the first step; he will afterwards attend to the elder branches; and if he goes on as he has begun, he will be a very great public benefactor.

EUTHYPHRO: I hope that he may; but I rather fear, Socrates, that the opposite will turn out to be the truth. My opinion is that in attacking you he is simply aiming a blow at the foundation of the state. But in what way does he say that you corrupt the young?

SOCRATES: He brings a wonderful accusation against me, which at first hearing excites surprise: he says that I am a poet or maker of gods, and that I invent new gods and deny the existence of old ones; this is the ground of his indictment.

EUTHYPHRO: I understand, Socrates; he means to attack you about the familiar sign which occasionally, as you say, comes to you. He thinks that you are a religious reformer, and he is going to have you up before the court for this. He knows that such a charge is readily received by the world, as I myself know too well; for when I speak in the assembly about divine things, and foretell the future to them, they laugh at me and think me a madman. Yet every word that I say is true. But they are jealous of us all; and we must be brave and go at them.

SOCRATES: Their laughter, friend Euthyphro, is not a matter of much consequence. For a man may be thought wise; but the Athenians, I suspect, do not much trouble themselves about him until he begins to impart his wisdom to others, and then for some reason or other, perhaps, as you say, from jealousy, they are angry.

EUTHYPHRO: I am never likely to try their temper in this way.

SOCRATES: I dare say not, for you are reserved in your behaviour, and seldom impart your wisdom. But I have a benevolent habit of pouring out myself to everybody, and would even pay for a listener, and I am afraid that the Athenians may think me too talkative. Now if, as I was saying, they would only laugh at me, as you say that they laugh at you, the time might pass gaily enough in the court; but perhaps they may be in earnest, and then what the end will be you soothsayers only can predict.

EUTHYPHRO: I dare say that the affair will end in nothing, Socrates, and that you will win your cause; and I think that I shall win my own.

SOCRATES: And what is your suit, Euthyphro? are you the pursuer or the defendant?

EUTHYPHRO: I am the pursuer.

SOCRATES: Of whom?

EUTHYPHRO: You will think me mad when I tell you.

SOCRATES: Why, has the fugitive wings?

EUTHYPHRO: Nay, he is not very volatile at his time of life.

SOCRATES: Who is he?

EUTHYPHRO: My father.

SOCRATES: Your father! my good man?

EUTHYPHRO: Yes.

SOCRATES: And of what is he accused?

EUTHYPHRO: Of murder, Socrates.

SOCRATES: By the powers, Euthyphro! how little does the common herd know of the nature of right and truth. A man must be an extraordinary man, and have made great strides in wisdom, before he could have seen his way to bring such an action.

EUTHYPHRO: Indeed, Socrates, he must.

SOCRATES: I suppose that the man whom your father murdered was one of your relatives—clearly he was; for if he had been a stranger you would never have thought of prosecuting him.

EUTHYPHRO: I am amused, Socrates, at your making a distinction between one who is a relation and one who is not a relation; for surely the pollution is the same in either case, if you knowingly associate with the murderer when you ought to clear yourself and him by proceeding against him. The real question is whether the murdered man has been justly slain. If justly, then your duty is to let the matter alone; but if unjustly, then even if the murderer lives under the same roof with you and eats at the same table, proceed against him. Now the man who is dead was a poor dependent of mine who worked for us as a field labourer on our farm in Naxos, and one day in a fit of drunken passion he got into a quarrel with one of our domestic servants and slew him. My father bound him hand and foot and threw him into a ditch, and then sent to Athens to ask of a diviner what he should do with him. Meanwhile he never attended to him and took no care about him, for he regarded him as a murderer; and thought that no great harm would be done even if he did die. Now this was just what happened. For such was the effect of cold and hunger and chains upon him, that before the messenger returned from the diviner, he was dead. And my father and family are angry with me for taking the part of the mur-

derer and prosecuting my father. They say that he did not kill him, and that if he did, the dead man was but a murderer, and I ought not to take any notice, for that a son is impious who prosecutes a father. Which shows, Socrates, how little they know what the gods think about piety and impiety.

SOCRATES: Good heavens, Euthyphro! and is your knowledge of religion and of things pious and impious so very exact, that, supposing the circumstances to be as you state them, you are not afraid lest you too may be doing an impious thing in bringing an action against your father?

EUTHYPHRO: The best of Euthyphro, and that which distinguishes him, Socrates, from other men, is his exact knowledge of all such matters. What should I be good for without it?

SOCRATES: Rare friend! I think that I cannot do better than be your disciple. Then before the trial with Meletus comes on I shall challenge him, and say that I have always had a great interest in religious questions, and now, as he charges me with rash imaginations and innovations in religion, I have become your disciple. You, Meletus, as I shall say to him, acknowledge Euthyphro to be a great theologian, and sound in his opinions; and if you approve of him you ought to approve of me, and not have me into court; but if you disapprove, you should begin by indicting him who is my teacher, and who will be the ruin, not of the young, but of the old; that is to say, of myself whom he instructs, and of his old father whom he admonishes and chastises. And if Meletus refuses to listen to me, but will go on, and will not shift the indictment from me to you, I cannot do better than repeat this challenge in the court.

EUTHYPHRO: Yes, indeed, Socrates; and if he attempts to indict me I am mistaken if I do not find a flaw in him; the court shall have a great deal more to say to him than to me.

SOCRATES: And I, my dear friend, knowing this, am desirous of becoming your disciple. For I observe that no one appears to notice you—not even this Meletus; but his sharp eyes have found me out at once, and he has indicted me for impiety. And therefore, I adjure you to tell me the nature of piety and impiety, which you said that you knew so well, and of murder, and of other offences against the gods. What are they? Is not piety in every action always the same? and impiety, again—is it not always the opposite of piety, and also the same with itself, having, as impiety, one notion which includes whatever is impious?

EUTHYPHRO: To be sure, Socrates.

SOCRATES: And what is piety, and what is impiety?

EUTHYPHRO: Piety is doing as I am doing; that is to say, prosecuting any one who is guilty of murder, sacrilege, or of any similar crime—whether he be your father or mother, or whoever he may be—that makes no difference; and not to prosecute them is impiety. And please to consider, Socrates, what a notable proof I will give you of the truth of my words, a proof which I have already given to others:—of the principle, I mean, that the impious, whoever he may be, ought not to go unpunished. For do not men regard Zeus as the best and most righteous of the gods?—and yet they admit that he bound his father (Cronos) because he wickedly devoured his sons, and that he too had punished his own father (Uranus) for a similar reason, in a nameless manner. And yet when I proceed against my father, they are angry with me. So inconsistent are they in their way of talking when the gods are concerned, and when I am concerned.

SOCRATES: May not this be the reason, Euthyphro, why I am charged with impiety—that I cannot accept these stories about the gods? and therefore I suppose that people think me wrong. But, as you who are well informed about them approve of them, I cannot do better than assent to your superior wisdom. What else can I say, confessing as I do, that I know nothing about them? Tell me, for the love of Zeus, whether you really believe that they are true.

EUTHYPHRO: Yes, Socrates; and things more wonderful still, of which the world is in ignorance.

SOCRATES: And do you really believe that the gods fought with one another, and had dire quarrels, battles, and the like, as the poets say, and as you may see represented in the works of great artists? The temples are full of them; and notably the robe of Athene, which is carried up to the Acropolis at the great Panathenaea, is embroidered with them. Are all these tales of the gods true, Euthyphro?

EUTHYPHRO: Yes, Socrates; and, as I was saying, I can tell you, if you would like to hear them, many other things about the gods which would quite amaze you.

SOCRATES: I dare say; and you shall tell me them at some other time when I have leisure. But just at present I would rather hear from you a more precise answer, which you have not as yet given, my friend, to the question, What is "piety"? When asked, you only replied, Doing as you do, charging your father with murder.

EUTHYPHRO: And what I said was true, Socrates.

SOCRATES: No doubt, Euthyphro; but you would admit that there are many other pious acts?

EUTHYPHRO: There are.

SOCRATES: Remember that I did not ask you to give me two or three examples of piety, but to explain the general idea which makes all pious things to be pious. Do you not recollect that there was one idea which made the impious impious, and the pious pious?

EUTHYPHRO: I remember.

SOCRATES: Tell me what is the nature of this idea, and then I shall have a standard to which I may look, and by which I may measure actions, whether yours or those of any one else, and then I shall be able to say that such and such an action is pious, such another impious.

EUTHYPHRO: I will tell you, if you like.

SOCRATES: I should very much like.

EUTHYPHRO: Piety, then, is that which is dear to the gods, and impiety is that which is not dear to them.

SOCRATES: Very good, Euthyphro; you have now given me the sort of answer which I wanted. But whether what you say is true or not I cannot as yet tell, although I make no doubt that you will prove the truth of your words.

EUTHYPHRO: Of course.

SOCRATES: Come, then, and let us examine what we are saying. That thing or person which is dear to the gods is pious, and that thing or person which is hateful to the gods is impious, these two being the extreme opposites of one another. Was not that said?

EUTHYPHRO: It was.

SOCRATES: And well said?

EUTHYPHRO: Yes, Socrates, I thought so; it was certainly said.

SOCRATES: And further, Euthyphro, the gods were admitted to have enmities and hatreds and differences?

EUTHYPHRO: Yes, that was also said.

SOCRATES: And what sort of difference creates enmity and anger? Suppose for example that you and I, my good friend, differ about a number; do differences of this sort make us enemies and set us at variance with one another? Do we not go at once to arithmetic, and put an end to them by a sum?

EUTHYPHRO: True.

SOCRATES: Or suppose that we differ about magnitudes, do we not quickly end the differences by measuring?

EUTHYPHRO: Very true.

SOCRATES: And we end a controversy about heavy and light by resorting to a weighing machine?

EUTHYPHRO: To be sure.

SOCRATES: But what differences are there which cannot be thus decided, and which therefore make us angry and set us at enmity with one another? I dare say the answer does not occur to you at the moment, and therefore I will suggest that these enmities arise when the matters of difference are the just and unjust, good and evil, honourable and dishonourable. Are not these the points about which men differ, and about which when we are unable satisfactorily to decide our differences, you and I and all of us quarrel, when we do quarrel?

EUTHYPHRO: Yes, Socrates, the nature of the differences about which we quarrel is such as you describe.

SOCRATES: And the quarrels of the gods, noble Euthyphro, when they occur, are of a like nature?

EUTHYPHRO: Certainly they are.

SOCRATES: They have differences of opinion, as you say, about good and evil, just and unjust, honourable and dishonourable: there would have been no quarrels among them, if there had been no such differences—would there now?

EUTHYPHRO: You are quite right.

SOCRATES: Does not every man love that which he deems noble and just and good, and hate the opposite of them?

EUTHYPHRO: Very true.

SOCRATES: But, as you say, people regard the same things, some as just and others as unjust,—about these they dispute; and so there arise wars and fightings among them.

EUTHYPHRO: Very true.

SOCRATES: Then the same things are hated by the gods and loved by the gods, and are both hateful and dear to them?

EUTHYPHRO: True.

SOCRATES: And upon this view the same things, Euthyphro, will be pious and also impious?

EUTHYPHRO: So I should suppose.

SOCRATES: Then, my friend, I remark with surprise that you have not answered the question which I asked. For I certainly did not ask you to tell me what action is both pious and impious: but now it would seem that what is loved by the gods is also hated by them. And therefore, Euthyphro, in thus chastising your father you may very likely be doing what is agreeable to Zeus but disagreeable to Cronos or Uranus, and what is acceptable to Hephaestus but unacceptable to Hera, and there may be other gods who have similar differences of opinion.

EUTHYPHRO: But I believe, Socrates, that all the gods would be agreed as to the propriety of punishing a murderer: there would be no difference of opinion about that.

SOCRATES: Well, but speaking of men, Euthyphro, did you ever hear any one arguing that a murderer or any sort of evil-doer ought to be let off?

EUTHYPHRO: I should rather say that these are the questions which they are always arguing, especially in courts of law: they commit all sorts of crimes, and there is nothing which they will not do or say in their own defence.

SOCRATES: But do they admit their guilt, Euthyphro, and yet say that they ought not to be punished?

EUTHYPHRO: No; they do not.

SOCRATES: Then there are some things which they do not venture to say and do: for they do not venture to argue that the guilty are to be unpunished, but they deny their guilt, do they not?

EUTHYPHRO: Yes.

SOCRATES: Then they do not argue that the evildoer should not be punished, but they argue about the fact of who the evil-doer is, and what he did and when?

EUTHYPHRO: True.

SOCRATES: And the gods are in the same case, if as you assert they quarrel about just and unjust, and some of them say while others deny that injustice is done among them. For surely neither god nor man will ever venture to say that the doer of injustice is not to be punished?

EUTHYPHRO: That is true, Socrates, in the main.

SOCRATES: But they join issue about the particulars—gods and men alike; and, if they dispute at all, they dispute about some act which is called in question, and which by some is affirmed to be just, by others to be unjust. Is not that true?

EUTHYPHRO: Quite true.

SOCRATES: Well then, my dear friend Euthyphro, do tell me, for my better instruction and information, what proof have you that in the opinion of all the gods a servant who is guilty of murder, and is put in chains by the master of the dead man, and dies because he is put in chains before he who bound him can learn from the interpreters of the gods what he ought to do with him, dies unjustly; and that on behalf of such an one a son ought to proceed against his father and accuse him of murder. How would you show that all the gods absolutely agree in approving of his act? Prove to me that they do, and I will applaud your wisdom as long as I live.

EUTHYPHRO: It will be a difficult task; but I could make the matter very clear indeed to you.

SOCRATES: I understand; you mean to say that I am not so quick of apprehension as the judges: for to them you will be sure to prove that the act is unjust, and hateful to the gods.

EUTHYPHRO: Yes indeed, Socrates; at least if they will listen to me.

SOCRATES: But they will be sure to listen if they find that you are a good speaker. There was a notion that came into my mind while you were speaking; I said to myself: "Well, and what if Euthyphro does prove to me that all the gods regarded the death of the serf as unjust, how do I know anything more of the nature of piety and impiety? for granting that this action may be hateful to the gods, still piety and impiety are not adequately defined by these distinctions, for that which is hateful to the gods has been shown to be also pleasing and dear to them." And therefore, Euthyphro, I do not ask you to prove this; I will suppose, if you like, that all the gods condemn and abominate such an action. But I will amend the definition so far as to say that what all the gods hate is impious, and what they love pious or holy; and what some of them love and others hate is both or neither. Shall this be our definition of piety and impiety?

EUTHYPHRO: Why not, Socrates?

SOCRATES: Why not! certainly, as far as I am concerned, Euthyphro, there is no reason why not. But whether this admission will greatly assist you in the task of instructing me as you promised, is a matter for you to consider.

EUTHYPHRO: Yes, I should say that what all the gods love is pious and holy, and the opposite which they all hate, impious.

SOCRATES: Ought we to enquire into the truth of this, Euthyphro, or simply to accept the mere statement on our own authority and that of others? What do you say?

EUTHYPHRO: We should enquire; and I believe that the statement will stand the test of enquiry.

SOCRATES: We shall know better, my good friend, in a little while. The point which I should first wish to understand is whether the pious or holy is beloved by the gods because it is holy, or holy because it is beloved of the gods.

EUTHYPHRO: I do not understand your meaning, Socrates.

SOCRATES: I will endeavour to explain: we speak of carrying and we speak of being carried, of leading and being led, seeing and being seen. You know that in all such cases there is a difference, and you know also in what the difference lies?

EUTHYPHRO: I think that I understand.

SOCRATES: And is not that which is beloved distinct from that which loves?

EUTHYPHRO: Certainly.

SOCRATES: Well; and now tell me, is that which is carried in this state of carrying because it is carried, or for some other reason?*

EUTHYPHRO: No; that is the reason.

SOCRATES: And the same is true of what is led and of what is seen?

EUTHYPHRO: True.

SOCRATES: And a thing is not seen because it is visible, but conversely, visible because it is seen; nor is a thing led because it is in the state of being led, or carried because it is in the state of being carried, but the converse of this. And now I think, Euthyphro, that my meaning will be intelligible; and my meaning is, that any state of action or passion implies previous action or passion. It does not become because it is becoming, but it is in a state of becoming because it becomes; neither does it suffer because it is in a state of suffering, but it is in a state of suffering because it suffers. Do you not agree?

EUTHYPHRO: Yes.

SOCRATES: Is not that which is loved in some state either of becoming or suffering?

EUTHYPHRO: Yes.

SOCRATES: And the same holds as in the previous instances; the state of being loved follows the act of being loved, and not the act the state.

EUTHYPHRO: Certainly.

SOCRATES: And what do you say of piety, Euthyphro: is not piety, according to your definition, loved by all the gods?

EUTHYPHRO: Yes.

SOCRATES: Because it is pious or holy, or for some other reason?

EUTHYPHRO: No, that is the reason.

SOCRATES: It is loved because it is holy, not holy because it is loved?

EUTHYPHRO: Yes.

---

* Socrates' examples may be a little unclear here. Think of the following similar example. Is the boiling of the water what causes it to be heated to 212 degrees Fahrenheit? Or is the fact that it is heated to 212 degrees Fahrenheit what causes it to boil?—ed.

SOCRATES: And that which is dear to the gods is loved by them, and is in a state to be loved of them because it is loved of them?

EUTHYPHRO: Certainly.

SOCRATES: Then that which is dear to the gods, Euthyphro, is not the same as the holy, nor is that which is holy the same as that which loved by the gods, as you affirm; but they are two different things.

EUTHYPHRO: How do you mean, Socrates?

SOCRATES: I mean to say that the holy has been acknowledged by us to be loved by the gods because it is holy, not to be holy because it is loved.

EUTHYPHRO: Yes.

SOCRATES: But that which is dear to the gods is dear to them because it is loved by them, not loved by them because it is dear to them.

EUTHYPHRO: True.

SOCRATES: But, friend Euthyphro, if that which is holy is the same with that which is dear to the gods, and is loved because it is holy, then that which is dear to the gods would have been loved as being dear to the gods; but if that which is dear to the gods is dear to them because loved by them, then that which is holy would have been holy because loved by them. But now you see that the reverse is the case, and that they are quite different from one another. For one is of a kind to be loved because it is loved, and the other is loved because it is of a kind to be loved. Thus you appear to me, Euthyphro, when I ask you what is the essence of holiness, to offer an attribute only, and not the essence—the attribute of being loved by all the gods. But you still refuse to explain to me the nature of holiness. And therefore, if you please, I will ask you not to hide your treasure, but to tell me once more what holiness or piety really is, whether dear to the gods or not (for that is a matter about which we will not quarrel) and what is impiety?

EUTHYPHRO: I really do not know, Socrates, how to express what I mean. For somehow or other our arguments, on whatever ground we rest them, seem to turn round and walk away from us.

SOCRATES: Your words, Euthyphro, are like the handiwork of my ancestor Daedalus; and if I were the sayer or propounder of them, you might say that my arguments walk away and will not remain fixed where they are placed because I am a descendant of his. But now, since these notions are your own, you must find some other joke, for they certainly, as you yourself allow, show an inclination to be on the move.

EUTHYPHRO: Nay, Socrates, I shall still say that you are the Daedalus who sets arguments in motion; not I, certainly, but you make them move or go round, for they would never have stirred, as far as I am concerned.

SOCRATES: Then I must be a greater than Daedalus: for whereas he only made his own inventions to move, I move those of other people as well. And the beauty of it is, that I would rather not. For I would give the wisdom of Daedalus, and the wealth of Tantalus, to be able to detain them and keep them fixed. But enough of this. As I perceive that you are lazy, I will myself endeavor to show you how you might instruct me in the nature of piety; and I hope that you will not grudge your labour. Tell me, then—Is not that which is pious necessarily just?

EUTHYPHRO: Yes.

SOCRATES: And is, then, all which is just pious? or, is that which is pious all just, but that which is just, only in part and not all, pious?

EUTHYPHRO: I do not understand you, Socrates.

SOCRATES: And yet I know that you are as much wiser than I am, as you are younger. But, as I was saying, revered friend, the abundance of your wisdom makes you lazy. Please to exert yourself, for there is no real difficulty in understanding me. What I mean I may explain by an illustration of what I do not mean. The poet (Stasinus) sings:

Of Zeus, the author and creator of all these things, You will not tell: for where there is fear there is also reverence.

Now I disagree with this poet. Shall I tell you in what respect?

EUTHYPHRO: By all means.

SOCRATES: I should not say that where there is fear there is also reverence; for I am sure that many persons fear poverty and disease, and the like evils, but I do not perceive that they reverence the objects of their fear.

EUTHYPHRO: Very true.

SOCRATES: But where reverence is, there is fear; for he who has a feeling of reverence and shame about the commission of any action, fears and is afraid of an ill reputation.

EUTHYPHRO: No doubt.

SOCRATES: Then we are wrong in saying that where there is fear there is also reverence; and we should say, where there is reverence there is also fear. But there is not always reverence where there is fear; for fear is a more extended notion, and reverence is a part of fear, just as the odd is a part of number, and number is a more extended notion than the odd. I suppose that you follow me now?

EUTHYPHRO: Quite well.

SOCRATES: That was the sort of question which I meant to raise when I asked whether the just is always the pious, or the pious always the just; and whether there may not be justice where there is not piety; for justice is the more extended notion of which piety is only a part. Do you dissent?

EUTHYPHRO: No, I think that you are quite right.

SOCRATES: Then, if piety is a part of justice, I suppose that we should enquire what part? If you had pursued the enquiry in the previous cases; for instance, if you had asked me what is an even number, and what part of number the even is, I should have had no difficulty in replying, a number which represents a figure having two equal sides. Do you not agree?

EUTHYPHRO: Yes, I quite agree.

SOCRATES: In like manner, I want you to tell me what part of justice is piety or holiness, that I may be able to tell Meletus not to do me injustice, or indict me for impiety, as I am now adequately instructed by you in the nature of piety or holiness, and their opposites.

EUTHYPHRO: Piety or holiness, Socrates, appears to me to be that part of justice which attends to the gods, as there is the other part of justice which attends to men.

SOCRATES: That is good, Euthyphro; yet still there is a little point about which I should like to have further information, What is the meaning of "attention"? For attention can hardly be used in the same sense when applied to the gods as when applied to other things. For instance, horses are said to require attention, and not every person is able to attend to them, but only a person skilled in horsemanship. Is it not so?

EUTHYPHRO: Certainly.

SOCRATES: I should suppose that the art of horsemanship is the art of attending to horses?

EUTHYPHRO: Yes.

SOCRATES: Nor is every one qualified to attend to dogs, but only the huntsman?

EUTHYPHRO: True.

SOCRATES: And I should also conceive that the art of the huntsman is the art of attending to dogs?

EUTHYPHRO: Yes.

SOCRATES: As the art of the ox herd is the art of attending to oxen?

EUTHYPHRO: Very true.

SOCRATES: In like manner holiness or piety is the art of attending to the gods?—that would be your meaning, Euthyphro?

EUTHYPHRO: Yes.

SOCRATES: And is not attention always designed for the good or benefit of that to which the attention is given? As in the case of horses, you may observe that when attended to by the horseman's art they are benefited and improved, are they not?

EUTHYPHRO: True.

SOCRATES: As the dogs are benefited by the huntsman's art, and the oxen by the art of the ox herd, and all other things are tended or attended for their good and not for their hurt?

EUTHYPHRO: Certainly, not for their hurt.

SOCRATES: But for their good?

EUTHYPHRO: Of course.

SOCRATES: And does piety or holiness, which has been defined to be the art of attending to the gods, benefit or improve them? Would you say that when you do a holy act you make any of the gods better?

EUTHYPHRO: No, no; that was certainly not what I meant.

SOCRATES: And I, Euthyphro, never supposed that you did. I asked you the question about the nature of the attention, because I thought that you did not.

EUTHYPHRO: You do me justice, Socrates; that is not the sort of attention which I mean.

SOCRATES: Good: but I must still ask what is this attention to the gods which is called piety?

EUTHYPHRO: It is such, Socrates, as servants show to their masters.

SOCRATES: I understand—a sort of ministration to the gods.

EUTHYPHRO: Exactly.

SOCRATES: Medicine is also a sort of ministration or service, having in view the attainment of some object—would you not say of health?

EUTHYPHRO: I should.

SOCRATES: Again, there is an art which ministers to the ship-builder with a view to the attainment of some result?

EUTHYPHRO: Yes, Socrates, with a view to the building of a ship.

SOCRATES: As there is an art which ministers to the housebuilder with a view to the building of a house?

EUTHYPHRO: Yes.

SOCRATES: And now tell me, my good friend, about the art which ministers to the gods: what work does that help to accomplish? For you must surely know if, as you say, you are of all men living the one who is best instructed in religion.

EUTHYPHRO: And I speak the truth, Socrates.

SOCRATES: Tell me then, oh tell me—what is that fair work which the gods do by the help of our ministrations?

EUTHYPHRO: Many and fair, Socrates, are the works which they do.

SOCRATES: Why, my friend, and so are those of a general. But the chief of them is easily told. Would you not say that victory in war is the chief of them?

EUTHYPHRO: Certainly.

SOCRATES: Many and fair, too, are the works of the husbandman, if I am not mistaken; but his chief work is the production of food from the earth?

EUTHYPHRO: Exactly.

SOCRATES: And of the many and fair things done by the gods, which is the chief or principal one?

EUTHYPHRO: I have told you already, Socrates, that to learn all these things accurately will be very tiresome. Let me simply say that piety or holiness is learning how to please the gods in word and deed, by prayers and sacrifices. Such piety, is the salvation of families and states, just as the impious, which is unpleasing to the gods, is their ruin and destruction.

SOCRATES: I think that you could have answered in much fewer words the chief question which I asked, Euthyphro, if you had chosen. But I see plainly that you are not disposed to instruct me—clearly not: else why, when we reached the point, did you turn aside? Had you only answered me I should have truly learned of you by this time the—nature of piety. Now, as the asker of a question is necessarily dependent on the answerer, whither he leads—I must follow; and can only ask again, what is the pious, and what is piety? Do you mean that they are a, sort of science of praying and sacrificing?

EUTHYPHRO: Yes, I do.

SOCRATES: And sacrificing is giving to the gods, and prayer is asking of the gods?

EUTHYPHRO: Yes, Socrates.

SOCRATES: Upon this view, then piety is a science of asking and giving?

EUTHYPHRO: You understand me capitally, Socrates.

SOCRATES: Yes, my friend; the reason is that I am a votary of your science, and give my mind to it, and therefore nothing which you say will be thrown away upon me. Please then to tell me, what is the nature of this service to the gods? Do you mean that we prefer requests and give gifts to them?

EUTHYPHRO: Yes, I do.

SOCRATES: Is not the right way of asking to ask of them what we want?

EUTHYPHRO: Certainly.

SOCRATES: And the right way of giving is to give to them in return what they want of us. There would be no meaning in an art which gives to any one that which he does not want.

EUTHYPHRO: Very true, Socrates.

SOCRATES: Then piety, Euthyphro, is an art which gods and men have of doing business with one another?

EUTHYPHRO: That is an expression which you may use, if you like.

SOCRATES: But I have no particular liking for anything but the truth. I wish, however, that you would tell me what benefit accrues to the gods from our gifts. There is no doubt about what they give to us; for there is no good thing which they do not give; but how we can give any good thing to them in return is far from being equally clear. If they give everything and we give nothing, that must be an affair of business in which we have very greatly the advantage of them.

EUTHYPHRO: And do you imagine, Socrates, that any benefit accrues to the gods from our gifts?

SOCRATES: But if not, Euthyphro, what is the meaning of gifts which are conferred by us upon the gods?

EUTHYPHRO: What else, but tributes of honour; and, as I was just now saying, what pleases them?

SOCRATES: Piety, then, is pleasing to the gods, but not beneficial or dear to them?

EUTHYPHRO: I should say that nothing could be dearer.

SOCRATES: Then once more the assertion is repeated that piety is dear to the gods?

EUTHYPHRO: Certainly.

SOCRATES: And when you say this, can you wonder at your words not standing firm, but walking away? Will you accuse me of being the Daedalus who makes them walk away, not perceiving that there is another and far greater artist than Daedalus who makes them go round in a circle, and he is yourself; for the argument, as you will perceive, comes round to the same point. Were we not saying that the holy or pious was not the same with that which is loved of the gods? Have you forgotten?

EUTHYPHRO: I quite remember.

SOCRATES: And are you not saying that what is loved of the gods is holy; and is not this the same as what is dear to them—do you see?

EUTHYPHRO: True.

SOCRATES: Then either we were wrong in former assertion; or, if we were right then, we are wrong now.

EUTHYPHRO: One of the two must be true.

SOCRATES: Then we must begin again and ask, What is piety? That is an enquiry which I shall never be weary of pursuing as far as in me lies; and I entreat you not to scorn me, but to apply your mind to the utmost, and tell me the truth. For, if any man knows, you are he; and therefore I must detain you, like Proteus, until you tell. If you had not certainly known the nature of piety and impiety, I am confident that you would never, on behalf of a serf, have charged your aged father with murder. You would not have run such a risk of doing wrong in the sight of the gods, and you would have had too much respect for the opinions of men. I am sure, therefore, that you know the nature of piety and impiety. Speak out then, my dear Euthyphro, and do not hide your knowledge.

EUTHYPHRO: Another time, Socrates; for I am in a hurry, and must go now.

SOCRATES: Alas! my companion, and will you leave me in despair? I was hoping that you would instruct me in the nature of piety and impiety; and then I might have cleared myself of Meletus and his indictment. I would have told him that I had been enlightened by Euthyphro, and had given up rash innovations and speculations, in which I indulged only through ignorance, and that now I am about to lead a better life.

Questions for Reflection

1. Suppose you believed in God (maybe you do). How would you answer Socrates' question: (a) Does God love morally good acts because they are good or (b) is the fact that God loves an act the reason that it is labeled "good"? If you chose (a), what is it about an act that makes it good and, hence, that evokes God's love? If you chose (b), could God love murder and would that then make murder good?

2. It is easy to see why some thought Socrates to be simply a smart aleck. It is obvious that he is enjoying showing Euthyphro the flaws in his ideas. However, do you think that Socrates had a serious purpose in relentlessly questioning this young man as he did? What might that purpose be?

3. Given the fact that Socrates and Euthyphro never arrive at a satisfactory answer to Socrates' request for a definition of "piety," what do you think has been accomplished in this conversation—both in terms of Euthyphro's life and in terms of the issue they were exploring?

4. How has this dialogue illustrated the activity of philosophy?

PLATO

Philosophy on Trial

Socrates made a meager living as a stonecutter, as did his father. However, he spent most of his time in the marketplace of Athens, pestering people with his questions, trying to shake them out of their smug complacency so that they would begin to examine their lives and recognize the importance of seeking wisdom. He was popular with the young people, such as Plato, but he ran into trouble with the town's leading citizens, particularly the politicians, because of his skill in exposing their pompous, shallow thinking. The end result was that Socrates was brought to trial before the town assembly and was charged with corrupting the youth and not believing in the Athenians' stories about the gods. In the following selection, Plato gives his account of the trial. It is titled the *Apology*, not because Plato was apologizing for Socrates, but because the term originally meant "a formal defense," as in a lawyer's presentation to the jury.

Reading Questions

1. What are the popular prejudices concerning Socrates? How did these arise?
2. What did the priestess at Delphi tell Socrates that made him begin questioning people?
3. In what sense does Socrates believe that he has a wisdom that his fellow Athenians lack?
4. What specific charges has Meletus made against Socrates in the indictment? What arguments does he use to refute each charge?
5. How does Socrates respond to those who say he should be ashamed of leading a life that will bring about his execution? What response will he make if he is offered release on the condition that he not teach philosophy?
6. What does Socrates mean by describing himself as a "gadfly"?
7. After he is found guilty by a vote of 281 to 220, what alternative to the death penalty does he propose as the just consequences for his life? Does the jury accept Socrates' assessment of what reward he deserves?
8. What does he say is the greatest human good? What is his estimation of the unexamined life?
9. What is Socrates attitude toward his own death? What does he mean by saying "no evil can happen to a good man"?

How you have felt, O men of Athens, at hearing the speeches of my accusers, I cannot tell; but I know that their persuasive words almost made me forget who I was—such was the effect of them; and yet they have hardly spoken a word of truth. But many as their falsehoods were, there was one of them which quite amazed me;—I mean when they told you to be upon your guard, and not to let yourselves be deceived by the force of my eloquence. They ought to have been ashamed of saying this, because they were sure to be detected as soon as I opened my lips and displayed my deficiency; they certainly did appear to be most shameless in saying this, unless by the force of eloquence they mean the force of truth; for then I do indeed admit that I am eloquent. But in how different a way from theirs!

Well, as I was saying, they have hardly uttered a word, or not more than a word, of truth; but you shall hear from me the whole truth: not, however, delivered after their manner, in a set oration duly ornamented with words and phrases. No indeed! but I shall use the words and arguments which occur to me at the moment; for I am certain that this

Plato, *Euthyphro*, from *The Dialogues of Plato*, trans. Benjamin Jowett (Oxford: Oxford University Press, 1896). (Some words have been modified to make the text more accessible to the modern reader.)

is right, and that at my time of life I ought not to be appearing before you, O men of Athens, in the character of a juvenile orator—let no one expect this of me. And I must beg of you to grant me one favor, which is this—If you hear me using the same words in my defence which I have been in the habit of using, and which most of you may have heard in the agora, and at the tables of the money-changers, or anywhere else, I would ask you not to be surprised at this, and not to interrupt me. For I am more than seventy years of age, and this is the first time that I have ever appeared in a court of law, and I am quite a stranger to the ways of the place; and therefore I would have you regard me as if I were really a stranger, whom you would excuse if he spoke in his native tongue, and after the fashion of his country;—that I think is not an unfair request. Never mind the manner, which may or may not be good; but think only of the justice of my cause, and give heed to that: let the judge decide justly and the speaker speak truly.

And first, I have to reply to the older charges and to my first accusers, and then I will go to the later ones. For I have had many accusers, who accused me of old, and their false charges have continued during many years; and I am more afraid of them than of Anytus and his associates, who are dangerous, too, in their own way. But far more dangerous are these, who began when you were children, and took possession of your minds with their falsehoods, telling of one Socrates, a wise man, who speculated about the heaven above, and searched into the earth beneath, and made the worse appear the better cause. These are the accusers whom I dread; for they are the circulators of this rumor, and their hearers are too apt to fancy that speculators of this sort do not believe in the gods. And they are many, and their charges against me are of ancient date, and they made them in days when you were impressible—in childhood, or perhaps in youth—and the cause when heard went by default, for there was none to answer. And, hardest of all, their names I do not know and cannot tell; unless in the chance of a comic poet. But the main body of these slanderers who from envy and malice have wrought upon you—and there are some of them

who are convinced themselves, and impart their convictions to others—all these, I say, are most difficult to deal with; for I cannot have them up here, and examine them, and therefore I must simply fight with shadows in my own defence, and examine when there is no one who answers. I will ask you then to assume with me, as I was saying, that my opponents are of two kinds—one recent, the other ancient; and I hope that you will see the propriety of my answering the latter first, for these accusations you heard long before the others, and much oftener.

Well, then, I will make my defence, and I will endeavor in the short time which is allowed to do away with this evil opinion of me which you have held for such a long time; and I hope I may succeed, if this be well for you and me, and that my words may find favor with you. But I know that to accomplish this is not easy—I quite see the nature of the task. Let the event be as God wills: in obedience to the law I make my defence.

I will begin at the beginning, and ask what the accusation is which has given rise to this slander of me, and which has encouraged Meletus to proceed against me. What do the slanderers say? They shall be my prosecutors, and I will sum up their words in an affidavit. "Socrates is an evil-doer, and a curious person, who searches into things under the earth and in heaven, and he makes the worse appear the better cause; and he teaches the aforesaid doctrines to others." That is the nature of the accusation, and that is what you have seen yourselves in the comedy of Aristophanes; who has introduced a man whom he calls Socrates, going about and saying that he can walk in the air, and talking a deal of nonsense concerning matters of which I do not pretend to know either much or little—not that I mean to say anything disparaging of anyone who is a student of natural philosophy. I should be very sorry if Meletus could lay that to my charge. But the simple truth is, O Athenians, that I have nothing to do with these studies. Very many of those here present are witnesses to the truth of this, and to them I appeal. Speak then, you who have heard me, and tell your neighbors whether any of you have ever known me hold forth in few words or in many upon matters of this sort. . . . You hear their answer. And from what they say of this you will be able to judge of the truth of the rest.

As little foundation is there for the report that I am a teacher, and take money; that is no more true than the other. Although, if a man is able to teach, I honor him for being paid. There is Gorgias of Leontium, and Prodicus of Ceos, and Hippias of Elis, who go the round of the cities, and are able to persuade the young men to leave their own citizens, by whom they might be taught for nothing, and come to them, whom they not only pay, but are thankful if they may be allowed to pay them. There is actually a Parian philosopher residing in Athens, of whom I have heard; and I came to hear of him in this way:—I met a man who has spent a world of money on the Sophists, Callias the son of Hipponicus, and knowing that he had sons, I asked him: "Callias," I said, "if your two sons were foals or calves, there would be no difficulty in finding someone to put over them; we should hire a trainer of horses or a farmer probably who would improve and perfect them in their own proper virtue and excellence; but as they are human beings, whom are you thinking of placing over them? Is there anyone who understands human and political virtue? You must have thought about this as you have sons; is there anyone?" "There is," he said. "Who is he?" said I, "and of what country? and what does he charge?" "Evenus the Parian," he replied; "he is the man, and his charge is five minae." Happy is Evenus, I said to myself, if he really has this wisdom, and teaches at such a modest charge. Had I the same, I should have been very proud and conceited; but the truth is that I have no knowledge of the kind.

I dare say, Athenians, that someone among you will reply, "Why is this, Socrates, and what is the origin of these accusations of you: for there must have been something strange which you have been doing? All this great fame and talk about you would never have arisen if you had been like other men: tell us, then, why this is, as we should be sorry to judge hastily of you." Now I regard this as a fair challenge, and I will endeavor to explain to you the origin of this name of "wise," and of this evil fame.

Please to attend then. And although some of you may think I am joking, I declare that I will tell you the entire truth. Men of Athens, this reputation of mine has come of a certain sort of wisdom which I possess. If you ask me what kind of wisdom, I reply, such wisdom as is attainable by man, for to that extent I am inclined to believe that I am wise; whereas the persons of whom I was speaking have a superhuman wisdom, which I may fail to describe, because I have it not myself; and he who says that I have, speaks falsely, and is taking away my character. And here, O men of Athens, I must beg you not to interrupt me, even if I seem to say something extravagant. For the word which I will speak is not mine. I will refer you to a witness who is worthy of credit, and will tell you about my wisdom—whether I have any, and of what sort—and that witness shall be the god of Delphi. You must have known Chaerephon; he was early a friend of mine, and also a friend of yours, for he shared in the exile of the people, and returned with you. Well, Chaerephon, as you know, was very impetuous in all his doings, and he went to Delphi and boldly asked the oracle to tell him whether—as I was saying, I must beg you not to interrupt—he asked the oracle to tell him whether there was anyone wiser than I was, and the Pythian prophetess answered that there was no man wiser. Chaerephon is dead himself, but his brother, who is in court, will confirm the truth of this story.

Why do I mention this? Because I am going to explain to you why I have such an evil name. When I heard the answer, I said to myself, What can the god mean? and what is the interpretation of this riddle? for I know that I have no wisdom, small or great. What can he mean when he says that I am the wisest of men? And yet he is a god and cannot lie; that would be against his nature. After a long consideration, I at last thought of a method of trying the question. I reflected that if I could only find a man wiser than myself, then I might go to the god with a refutation in my hand. I should say to him, "Here is a man who is wiser than I am; but you said that I was the wisest." Accordingly I went to one who had the reputation of wisdom, and observed to him—his name I need not mention; he was a politician whom I selected for examination—and the result was as follows: When I began to talk with him, I could not help thinking that he was not really wise, although he was thought wise by many, and wiser still by himself; and I went and tried to explain to him that he thought himself wise, but was not really wise; and the consequence was that he hated me, and his enmity was shared by several who were present and heard me. So I left him, saying to myself, as I went away: Well, although I do not suppose that either of us knows anything really beautiful and good, I am better off than he is—for he knows nothing, and thinks that he knows. I neither know nor think that I know. In this latter particular, then, I seem to have slightly the advantage of him. Then I went to another, who had still higher philosophical pretensions, and my conclusion was exactly the same. I made another enemy of him, and of many others besides him.

After this I went to one man after another, being not unconscious of the enmity which I provoked, and I lamented and feared this: but necessity was laid upon me—the word of God, I thought, ought to be considered first. And I said to myself, Go I must to all who appear to know, and find out the meaning of the oracle. And I swear to you, Athenians, by the dog I swear!—for I must tell you the truth—the result of my mission was just this: I found that the men most in repute were all but the most foolish; and that some inferior men were really wiser and better. I will tell you the tale of my wanderings and of the "Herculean" labors, as I may call them, which I endured only to find at last the oracle irrefutable. When I left the politicians, I went to the poets; tragic, dithyrambic, and all sorts. And there, I said to myself, you will be detected; now you will find out that you are more ignorant than they are. Accordingly, I took them some of the most elaborate passages in their own writings, and asked what was the meaning of them—thinking that they would teach me something. Will you believe me? I am almost ashamed to speak of this, but still I must say that there is hardly a person present who would not have talked better about their poetry than they did themselves. That showed me in an instant that not by wisdom do poets write poetry, but by a sort of genius and inspiration; they are like

diviners or soothsayers who also say many fine things, but do not understand the meaning of them. And the poets appeared to me to be much in the same case; and I further observed that upon the strength of their poetry they believed themselves to be the wisest of men in other things in which they were not wise. So I departed, conceiving myself to be superior to them for the same reason that I was superior to the politicians.

At last I went to the artisans, for I was conscious that I knew nothing at all, as I may say, and I was sure that they knew many fine things; and in this I was not mistaken, for they did know many things of which I was ignorant, and in this they certainly were wiser than I was. But I observed that even the good artisans fell into the same error as the poets; because they were good workmen they thought that they also knew all sorts of high matters, and this defect in them overshadowed their wisdom—therefore I asked myself on behalf of the oracle, whether I would like to be as I was, neither having their knowledge nor their ignorance, or like them in both; and I made answer to myself and the oracle that I was better off as I was.

This investigation has led to my having many enemies of the worst and most dangerous kind, and has given occasion also to many calumnies, and I am called wise, for my hearers always imagine that I myself possess the wisdom which I find wanting in others: but the truth is, O men of Athens, that God only is wise; and in this oracle he means to say that the wisdom of men is little or nothing; he is not speaking of Socrates, he is only using my name as an illustration, as if he said, He, O men, is the wisest, who, like Socrates, knows that his wisdom is in truth worth nothing. And so I go my way, obedient to the god, and make inquisition into the wisdom of anyone, whether citizen or stranger, who appears to be wise; and if he is not wise, then in vindication of the oracle I show him that he is not wise; and this occupation quite absorbs me, and I have no time to give either to any public matter of interest or to any concern of my own, but I am in utter poverty by reason of my devotion to the god.

There is another thing:—young men of the richer classes, who have not much to do, come about me of their own accord; they like to hear the pretenders examined, and they often imitate me, and examine others themselves; there are plenty of persons, as they soon enough discover, who think that they know something, but really know little or nothing: and then those who are examined by them instead of being angry with themselves are angry with me: This confounded Socrates, they say; this villainous misleader of youth!—and then if somebody asks them, Why, what evil does he practise or teach? they do not know, and cannot tell; but in order that they may not appear to be at a loss, they repeat the ready-made charges which are used against all philosophers about teaching things up in the clouds and under the earth, and having no gods, and making the worse appear the better cause; for they do not like to confess that their pretence of knowledge has been detected—which is the truth: and as they are numerous and ambitious and energetic, and are all in battle array and have persuasive tongues, they have filled your ears with their loud and inveterate calumnies. And this is the reason why my three accusers, Meletus and Anytus and Lycon, have set upon me; Meletus, who has a quarrel with me on behalf of the poets; Anytus, on behalf of the craftsmen; Lycon, on behalf of the rhetoricians: and as I said at the beginning, I cannot expect to get rid of this mass of calumny all in a moment. And this, O men of Athens, is the truth and the whole truth; I have concealed nothing, I have dissembled nothing. And yet I know that this plainness of speech makes them hate me, and what is their hatred but a proof that I am speaking the truth?—this is the occasion and reason of their slander of me, as you will find out either in this or in any future inquiry.

I have said enough in my defence against the first class of my accusers; I turn to the second class, who are headed by Meletus, that good and patriotic man, as he calls himself. And now I will try to defend myself against them: these new accusers must also have their affidavit read. What do they say? Something of this sort:—That Socrates is a doer of evil, and corrupter of the youth, and he does not believe in the gods of the state, and has other new divinities of his own. That is the sort of charge; and now let us examine the particular counts. He says that I am a doer of evil, who cor-

rupt the youth; but I say, O men of Athens, that Meletus is a doer of evil, and the evil is that he makes a joke of a serious matter, and is too ready at bringing other men to trial from a pretended zeal and interest about matters in which he really never had the smallest interest. And the truth of this I will endeavor to prove.

Come hither, Meletus, and let me ask a question of you. You think a great deal about the improvement of youth?

MELETUS: Yes, I do.
SOCRATES: Tell the judges, then, who is their improver; for you must know, as you have taken the pains to discover their corrupter, and are citing and accusing me before them. Speak, then, and tell the judges who their improver is. Observe, Meletus, that you are silent, and have nothing to say. But is not this rather disgraceful, and a very considerable proof of what I was saying, that you have no interest in the matter? Speak up, friend, and tell us who their improver is.
MELETUS: The laws.
SOCRATES: But that, my good sir, is not my meaning. I want to know who the person is, who, in the first place, knows the laws.
MELETUS: The judges, Socrates, who are present in court.
SOCRATES: What do you mean to say, Meletus, that they are able to instruct and improve youth?
MELETUS: Certainly they are.
SOCRATES: What, all of them, or some only and not others?
MELETUS: All of them.
SOCRATES: By the goddess Hera, that is good news! There are plenty of improvers, then. And what do you say of the audience,—do they improve them?
MELETUS: Yes, they do.
SOCRATES: And the senators?
MELETUS: Yes, the senators improve them.
SOCRATES: But perhaps the members of the citizen assembly corrupt them?—or do they too improve them?
MELETUS: They improve them.
SOCRATES: Then every Athenian improves and elevates them; all with the exception of myself; and

I alone am their corrupter? Is that what you affirm?

MELETUS: That is what I stoutly affirm.

SOCRATES: I am very unfortunate if that is true. But suppose I ask you a question: Would you say that this also holds true in the case of horses? Does one man do them harm and all the world good? Is not the exact opposite of this true? One man is able to do them good, or at least not many;—the trainer of horses, that is to say, does them good, and others who have to do with them rather injure them? Is not that true, Meletus, of horses, or any other animals? Yes, certainly. Whether you and Anytus say yes or no, that is no matter. Happy indeed would be the condition of youth if they had one corrupter only, and all the rest of the world were their improvers. And you, Meletus, have sufficiently shown that you never had a thought about the young: your carelessness is seen in your not caring about matters spoken of in this very indictment.

And now, Meletus, I must ask you another question: Which is better, to live among bad citizens, or among good ones? Answer, friend, I say; for that is a question which may be easily answered. Do not the good do their neighbors good, and the bad do them evil?

MELETUS: Certainly.

SOCRATES: And is there anyone who would rather be injured than benefited by those who live with him? Answer, my good friend; the law requires you to answer—does anyone like to be injured?

MELETUS: Certainly not.

SOCRATES: And when you accuse me of corrupting and deteriorating the youth, do you allege that I corrupt them intentionally or unintentionally?

MELETUS: Intentionally, I say.

SOCRATES: But you have just admitted that the good do their neighbors good, and the evil do them evil. Now is that a truth which your superior wisdom has recognized thus early in life, and am I, at my age, in such darkness and ignorance as not to know that if a man with whom I have to live is corrupted by me, I am very likely to be harmed by him, and yet I corrupt him, and intentionally, too;—that is what you are saying, and of that you will never persuade me or any

other human being. But either I do not corrupt them, or I corrupt them unintentionally, so that on either view of the case you lie. If my offence is unintentional, the law has no cognizance of unintentional offences: you ought to have taken me privately, and warned and admonished me; for if I had been better advised, I should have left off doing what I only did unintentionally—no doubt I should; whereas you hated to converse with me or teach me, but you indicted me in this court, which is a place not of instruction, but of punishment.

I have shown, Athenians, as I was saying, that Meletus has no care at all, great or small, about the matter. But still I should like to know, Meletus, in what I am affirmed to corrupt the young. I suppose you mean, as I infer from your indictment, that I teach them not to acknowledge the gods which the state acknowledges, but some other new divinities or spiritual agencies in their stead. These are the lessons which corrupt the youth, as you say.

MELETUS: Yes, that I say emphatically.

SOCRATES: Then, by the gods, Meletus, of whom we are speaking, tell me and the court, in somewhat plainer terms, what you mean! for I do not as yet understand whether you affirm that I teach others to acknowledge some gods, and therefore do believe in gods and am not an entire atheist—this you do not lay to my charge; but only that they are not the same gods which the city recognizes—the charge is that they are different gods. Or, do you mean to say that I am an atheist simply, and a teacher of atheism?

MELETUS: I mean the latter—that you are a complete atheist.

SOCRATES: That is an extraordinary statement, Meletus. Why do you say that? Do you mean that I do not believe in the godhead of the sun or moon, which is the common creed of all men?

MELETUS: I assure you, judges, that he does not believe in them; for he says that the sun is stone, and the moon earth.

SOCRATES: Friend Meletus, you think that you are accusing Anaxagoras; and you have but a bad opinion of the judges, if you fancy them ignorant to such a degree as not to know that those doctrines are found in the books of Anaxagoras the Clazomenian, who is full of them. And these are the doctrines which the youth are said to learn of Socrates, when there are not unfrequently exhibitions of them at the theatre (price of admission one drachma at the most); and they might cheaply purchase them, and laugh at Socrates if he pretends to father such eccentricities. And so, Meletus, you really think that I do not believe in any god?

MELETUS: I swear by Zeus that you believe absolutely in none at all.

SOCRATES: You are a liar, Meletus, not believed even by yourself. For I cannot help thinking, O men of Athens, that Meletus is reckless and impudent, and that he has written this indictment in a spirit of mere wantonness and youthful bravado. Has he not compounded a riddle, thinking to try me? He said to himself:—I shall see whether this wise Socrates will discover my ingenious contradiction, or whether I shall be able to deceive him and the rest of them. For he certainly does appear to me to contradict himself in the indictment as much as if he said that Socrates is guilty of not believing in the gods, and yet of believing in them—but this surely is a piece of fun.

I should like you, O men of Athens, to join me in examining what I conceive to be his inconsistency; and do you, Meletus, answer. And I must remind you that you are not to interrupt me if I speak in my accustomed manner.

Did any man, Meletus, ever believe in the existence of human things, and not of human beings? . . . I wish, men of Athens, that he would answer, and not be always trying to get up an interruption. Did ever any man believe in horsemanship, and not in horses? or in flute-playing, and not in flute-players? No, my friend; I will answer to you and to the court, as you refuse to answer for yourself. There is no man who ever did. But now please to answer the next question: Can a man believe in spiritual and divine agencies, and not in spirits or demigods?

MELETUS: He cannot.

SOCRATES: I am glad that I have extracted that answer, by the assistance of the court; nevertheless you swear in the indictment that I teach and believe in divine or spiritual agencies (new or old, no matter for that); at any rate, I believe in spiritual agencies, as you say and swear in the affidavit; but if I believe in divine beings, I must believe in spirits or demigods;—is not that true? Yes, that is true, for I may assume that your silence gives assent to that. Now what are spirits or demigods? are they not either gods or the sons of gods? Is that true?

MELETUS: Yes, that is true.

SOCRATES: But this is just the ingenious riddle of which I was speaking: the demigods or spirits are gods, and you say first that I don't believe in gods, and then again that I do believe in gods; that is, if I believe in demigods. For if the demigods are the illegitimate sons of gods, whether by the Nymphs or by any other mothers, as is thought, that, as all men will allow, necessarily implies the existence of their parents. You might as well affirm the existence of mules, and deny that of horses and asses. Such nonsense, Meletus, could only have been intended by you as a trial of me. You have put this into the indictment because you had nothing real of which to accuse me. But no one who has a particle of understanding will ever be convinced by you that the same man can believe in divine and superhuman things, and yet not believe that there are gods and demigods and heroes.

I have said enough in answer to the charge of Meletus: any elaborate defence is unnecessary; but as I was saying before, I certainly have many enemies, and this is what will be my destruction if I am destroyed; of that I am certain;—not Meletus, nor yet Anytus, but the envy and detraction of the world, which has been the death of many good men, and will probably be the death of many more; there is no danger of my being the last of them.

Someone will say: And are you not ashamed, Socrates, of a course of life which is likely to bring you to an untimely end? To him I may fairly answer: There you are mistaken: a man who is good for anything ought not to calculate the chance of living or dying; he ought only to consider whether in doing anything he is doing right or wrong—acting the part of a good man or of a bad. . . . For wherever a man's place is, whether the place which he has chosen or that in which he has been placed by a commander, there he ought to remain in the hour of danger; he should not think of death or of anything, but of disgrace. And this, O men of Athens, is a true saying.

Strange, indeed, would be my conduct, O men of Athens, if I who, when I was ordered by the generals whom you chose to command me at Potidaea and Amphipolis and Delium, remained where they placed me, like any other man, facing death; if, I say, now, when, as I conceive and imagine, God orders me to fulfil the philosopher's mission of searching into myself and other men, I were to desert my post through fear of death, or any other fear; that would indeed be strange, and I might justly be arraigned in court for denying the existence of the gods, if I disobeyed the oracle because I was afraid of death: then I should be fancying that I was wise when I was not wise.

For this fear of death is indeed the pretence of wisdom, and not real wisdom, being the appearance of knowing the unknown; since no one knows whether death, which they in their fear apprehend to be the greatest evil, may not be the greatest good. Is there not here conceit of knowledge, which is a disgraceful sort of ignorance? And this is the point in which, as I think, I am superior to men in general, and in which I might perhaps fancy myself wiser than other men,—that whereas I know but little of the world below, I do not suppose that I know: but I do know that injustice and disobedience to a better, whether God or man, is evil and dishonorable, and I will never fear or avoid a possible good rather than a certain evil. And therefore if you let me go now, and reject the counsels of Anytus, who said that if I were not put to death I ought not to have been prosecuted, and that if I escape now, your sons will all be utterly ruined by listening to my words—if you say to me, Socrates, this time we will not mind Anytus, and will let you off, but upon one condition, that you are not to inquire and speculate in this way any more, and that if you are caught doing this again you shall die;—if this was the condition on which you let me go, I should reply: Men of Athens, I honor and love you;

but I shall obey God rather than you, and while I have life and strength I shall never cease from the practice and teaching of philosophy, exhorting anyone whom I meet after my manner, and convincing him, saying: O my friend, why do you who are a citizen of the great and mighty and wise city of Athens, care so much about laying up the greatest amount of money and honor and reputation, and so little about wisdom and truth and the greatest improvement of the soul, which you never regard or heed at all? Are you not ashamed of this? And if the person with whom I am arguing says: Yes, but I do care; I do not depart or let him go at once; I interrogate and examine and cross-examine him, and if I think that he has no virtue, but only says that he has, I reproach him with undervaluing the greater, and overvaluing the less. And this I should say to everyone whom I meet, young and old, citizen and alien, but especially to the citizens, inasmuch as they are my brethren. For this is the command of God, as I would have you know; and I believe that to this day no greater good has ever happened in the state than my service to the God.

For I do nothing but go about persuading you all, old and young alike, not to take thought for your persons and your properties, but first and chiefly to care about the greatest improvement of the soul. I tell you that virtue is not given by money, but that from virtue come money and every other good of man, public as well as private. This is my teaching, and if this is the doctrine which corrupts the youth, my influence is ruinous indeed. But if anyone says that this is not my teaching, he is speaking an untruth. Wherefore, O men of Athens, I say to you, do as Anytus bids or not as Anytus bids, and either acquit me or not; but whatever you do, know that I shall never alter my ways, not even if I have to die many times.

Men of Athens, do not interrupt, but hear me; there was an agreement between us that you should hear me out. And I think that what I am going to say will do you good: for I have something more to say, at which you may be inclined to cry out; but I beg that you will not do this.

I would have you know that, if you kill such a one as I am, you will injure yourselves more than you will injure me. Meletus and Anytus will not injure me: they cannot; for it is not in the nature of things that a bad man should injure a better than himself. I do not deny that he may, perhaps, kill him, or drive him into exile, or deprive him of civil rights; and he may imagine, and others may imagine, that he is doing him a great injury: but in that I do not agree with him; for the evil of doing as Anytus is doing—of unjustly taking away another man's life—is greater far. And now, Athenians, I am not going to argue for my own sake, as you may think, but for yours, that you may not sin against the God, or lightly reject his boon by condemning me. For if you kill me you will not easily find another like me, who, if I may use such a ludicrous figure of speech, am a sort of gadfly, given to the state by the God; and the state is like a great and noble steed who is tardy in his motions owing to his very size, and requires to be stirred into life. I am that gadfly which God has given the state and all day long and in all places am always fastening upon you, arousing and persuading and reproaching you. And as you will not easily find another like me, I would advise you to spare me. I dare say that you may feel irritated at being suddenly awakened when you are caught napping; and you may think that if you were to strike me dead, as Anytus advises, which you easily might, then you would sleep on for the remainder of your lives, unless God in his care of you gives you another gadfly. And that I am given to you by God is proved by this:—that if I had been like other men, I should not have neglected all my own concerns, or patiently seen the neglect of them during all these years, and have been doing yours, coming to you individually, like a father or elder brother, exhorting you to regard virtue; this I say, would not be like human nature. And had I gained anything, or if my exhortations had been paid, there would have been some sense in that: but now, as you will perceive, not even the impudence of my accusers dares to say that I have ever exacted or sought pay of anyone; they have no witness of that. And I have a witness of the truth of what I say; my poverty is a sufficient witness.

Someone may wonder why I go about in private, giving advice and busying myself with the concerns of others, but do not venture to come forward in public and advise the state. I will tell you the reason of this. You have often heard me speak of an oracle or sign which comes to me, and is the divinity which Meletus ridicules in the indictment. This sign I have had ever since I was a child. The sign is a voice which comes to me and always forbids me to do something which I am going to do, but never commands me to do anything, and this is what stands in the way of my being a politician. And rightly, as I think. For I am certain, O men of Athens, that if I had engaged in politics, I should have perished long ago and done no good either to you or to myself. And don't be offended at my telling you the truth: for the truth is that no man who goes to war with you or any other multitude, honestly struggling against the commission of unrighteousness and wrong in the state, will save his life; he who will really fight for the right, if he would live even for a little while, must have a private station and not a public one.

I can give you as proofs of this, not words only, but deeds, which you value more than words. Let me tell you a passage of my own life, which will prove to you that I should never have yielded to injustice from any fear of death, and that if I had not yielded I should have died at once. I will tell you a story—tasteless, perhaps, and commonplace, but nevertheless true. The only office of state which I ever held, O men of Athens, was that of senator; the tribe Antiochis, which is my tribe, had the presidency at the trial of the generals who had not taken up the bodies of the slain after the battle of Arginusae; and you proposed to try them all together, which was illegal, as you all thought afterwards; but at the time I was the only one of the Prytanes who was opposed to the illegality, and I gave my vote against you; and when the orators threatened to impeach and arrest me, and have me taken away, and you called and shouted, I made up my mind that I would run the risk, having law and justice with me, rather than take part in your injustice because I feared imprisonment and death. This happened in the days of the democracy. But when the oligarchy of the Thirty was in power, they sent for me and four others into the rotunda, and bade us bring Leon the Salaminian from Salamis, as they wanted to execute him. This was a specimen of the sort of commands which they were always giving with the view of implicating as many as possible in their crimes; and then I showed, not in words only, but in deed, that, if I may be allowed to use such an expression, I cared not a straw for death, and that my only fear was the fear of doing an unrighteous or unholy thing. For the strong arm of that oppressive power did not frighten me into doing wrong; and when we came out of the rotunda the other four went to Salamis and fetched Leon, but I went quietly home. For which I might have lost my life, had not the power of the Thirty shortly afterwards come to an end. And to this many will witness.

Now do you really imagine that I could have survived all these years, if I had led a public life, supposing that like a good man I had always supported the right and had made justice, as I ought, the first thing? No, indeed, men of Athens, neither I nor any other. But I have been always the same in all my actions, public as well as private, and never have I yielded any base compliance to those who are slanderously termed my disciples or to any other. For the truth is that I have no regular disciples: but if anyone likes to come and hear me while I am pursuing my mission, whether he be young or old, he may freely come. Nor do I converse with those who pay only, and not with those who do not pay; but anyone, whether he be rich or poor, may ask and answer me and listen to my words; and whether he turns out to be a bad man or a good one, that cannot be justly laid to my charge, as I never taught him anything. And if anyone says that he has ever learned or heard anything from me in private which all the world has not heard, I should like you to know that he is speaking an untruth.

But I shall be asked, Why do people delight in continually conversing with you? I have told you already, Athenians, the whole truth about this: they like to hear the cross-examination of the pretenders to wisdom; there is amusement in this. And this is a duty which the God has imposed upon me, as I am assured by oracles, visions, and in every sort of way in which the will of divine power was ever signified to anyone. . . .

Well, Athenians, this and the like of this is nearly all the defence which I have to offer. Yet a word

more. Perhaps there may be someone who is offended at me, when he calls to mind how he himself, on a similar or even a less serious occasion, had recourse to prayers and supplications with many tears, and how he produced his children in court, which was a moving spectacle, together with a posse of his relations and friends; whereas I, who am probably in danger of my life, will do none of these things. Perhaps this may come into his mind, and he may be set against me, and vote in anger because he is displeased at this. Now if there be such a person among you, which I am far from affirming, I may fairly reply to him: My friend, I am a man, and like other men, a creature of flesh and blood, and not of wood or stone, as Homer says; and I have a family, yes, and sons. O Athenians, three in number, one of whom is growing up, and the two others are still young; and yet I will not bring any of them hither in order to petition you for an acquittal. And why not? Not from any self-will or disregard of you. Whether I am or am not afraid of death is another question, of which I will not now speak. But my reason simply is that I feel such conduct to be discreditable to myself, and you, and the whole state. One who has reached my years, and who has a name for wisdom, whether deserved or not, ought not to debase himself. . . .

But, setting aside the question of dishonor, there seems to be something wrong in petitioning a judge, and thus procuring an acquittal instead of informing and convincing him. For his duty is, not to make a present of justice, but to give judgment; and he has sworn that he will judge according to the laws, and not according to his own good pleasure; and neither he nor we should get into the habit of perjuring ourselves—there can be no piety in that. Do not then require me to do what I consider dishonorable and impious and wrong, especially now, when I am being tried for impiety on the indictment of Meletus. For if, O men of Athens, by force of persuasion and entreaty, I could overpower your oaths, then I should be teaching you to believe that there are no gods, and convict myself, in my own defence, of not believing in them. But that is not the case; for I do believe that there are gods, and in a far higher sense than that in which any of my accusers believe in them. And to you and to God I commit my cause, to be determined by you as is best for you and me.

[The jury finds Socrates guilty by 281 votes to 220.]

There are many reasons why I am not grieved, O men of Athens, at the vote of condemnation. I expected it, and am only surprised that the votes are so nearly equal; for I had thought that the majority against me would have been far larger; but now, had thirty votes gone over to the other side, I should have been acquitted. And I may say that I have escaped Meletus. And I may say more; for without the assistance of Anytus and Lycon, he would not have had a fifth part of the votes, as the law requires, in which case he would have incurred a fine of a thousand drachmae, as is evident.

And so he proposes death as the penalty. And what shall I propose on my part, O men of Athens? Clearly that which is my due. And what is that which I ought to pay or to receive? What shall be done to the man who has never had the wit to be idle during his whole life; but has been careless of what the many care about—wealth, and family interests, and military offices, and speaking in the assembly, and magistracies, and plots, and parties. Reflecting that I was really too honest a man to follow in this way and live, I did not go where I could do no good to you or to myself; but where I could do the greatest good privately to everyone of you, thither I went, and sought to persuade every man among you that he must look to himself, and seek virtue and wisdom before he looks to his private interests, and look to the state before he looks to the interests of the state; and that this should be the order which he observes in all his actions. What shall be done to such a one? Doubtless some good thing, O men of Athens, if he has his reward; and the good should be of a kind suitable to him. What would be a reward suitable to a poor man who is your benefactor, who desires leisure that he may instruct you? There can be no more fitting reward than maintenance in the Prytaneum, O men of Athens, a reward which he deserves far more than the citizen who has won the prize at Olympia in the horse or chariot race, whether the chariots were drawn by two horses or by many. For I am in want, and he has enough; and he only gives you the ap-

pearance of happiness, and I give you the reality. And if I am to estimate the penalty justly, I say that maintenance in the Prytaneum is the just return.

Perhaps you may think that I am braving you in saying this, as in what I said before about the tears and prayers. But that is not the case. I speak rather because I am convinced that I never intentionally wronged anyone, although I cannot convince you of that—for we have had a short conversation only; but if there were a law at Athens, such as there is in other cities, that a capital cause should not be decided in one day, then I believe that I should have convinced you; but now the time is too short. I cannot in a moment refute great slanders; and, as I am convinced that I never wronged another, I will assuredly not wrong myself. I will not say of myself that I deserve any evil, or propose any penalty. Why should I? Because I am afraid of the penalty of death which Meletus proposes? When I do not know whether death is a good or an evil, why should I propose a penalty which would certainly be an evil? Shall I say imprisonment? And why should I live in prison, and be the slave of the magistrates of the year—of the Eleven? Or shall the penalty be a fine, and imprisonment until the fine is paid? There is the same objection. I should have to lie in prison, for money I have none, and I cannot pay. And if I say exile (and this may possibly be the penalty which you will affix), I must indeed be blinded by the love of life if I were to consider that when you, who are my own citizens, cannot endure my discourses and words, and have found them so grievous and odious that you would fain have done with them, others are likely to endure me. No, indeed, men of Athens, that is not very likely. And what a life should I lead, at my age, wandering from city to city, living in ever-changing exile, and always being driven out! For I am quite sure that into whatever place I go, as here so also there, the young men will come to me; and if I drive them away, their elders will drive me out at their desire: and if I let them come, their fathers and friends will drive me out for their sakes.

Someone will say: Yes, Socrates, but cannot you hold your tongue, and then you may go into a foreign city, and no one will interfere with you? Now I have great difficulty in making you understand my answer to this. For if I tell you that this would be a disobedience to a divine command, and therefore that I cannot hold my tongue, you will not believe that I am serious; and if I say again that the greatest good of man is daily to converse about virtue, and all that concerning which you hear me examining myself and others, and that the life which is unexamined is not worth living—that you are still less likely to believe. And yet what I say is true, although a thing of which it is hard for me to persuade you. Moreover, I am not accustomed to think that I deserve any punishment. Had I money I might have proposed to give you what I had, and have been none the worse. But you see that I have none, and can only ask you to proportion the fine to my means. However, I think that I could afford a minae, and therefore I propose that penalty; Plato, Crito, Critobulus, and Apollodorus, my friends here, bid me say thirty minae, and they will be the sureties. Well then, say thirty minae, let that be the penalty; for that they will be ample security to you.

[The jury condemns Socrates to death by a vote of 360 to 141.]

Not much time will be gained, O Athenians, in return for the evil name which you will get from the detractors of the city, who will say that you killed Socrates, a wise man; for they will call me wise even although I am not wise when they want to reproach you. If you had waited a little while, your desire would have been fulfilled in the course of nature. For I am far advanced in years, as you may perceive, and not far from death. I am speaking now only to those of you who have condemned me to death. And I have another thing to say to them: You think that I was convicted through deficiency of words—I mean, that if I had thought fit to leave nothing undone, nothing unsaid, I might have gained an acquittal. Not so; the deficiency which led to my conviction was not of words—certainly not. But I had not the boldness or impudence or inclination to address you as you would have liked me to address you, weeping and wailing and lamenting, and saying and doing many things which you have been accustomed to hear from others, and which, as I say, are unworthy of me. But I thought that I ought not to do anything common or mean in the hour of danger: nor do I now re-

pent of the manner of my defence, and I would rather die having spoken after my manner, than speak in your manner and live. For neither in war nor yet at law ought any man to use every way of escaping death. For often in battle there is no doubt that if a man will throw away his arms, and fall on his knees before his pursuers, he may escape death; and in other dangers there are other ways of escaping death, if a man is willing to say and do anything. The difficulty, my friends, is not in avoiding death, but in avoiding unrighteousness; for that runs faster than death. I am old and move slowly, and the slower runner has overtaken me, and my accusers are keen and quick, and the faster runner, who is unrighteousness, has overtaken them. And now I depart hence condemned by you to suffer the penalty of death, and they, too, go their ways condemned by the truth to suffer the penalty of villainy and wrong; and I must abide by my award—let them abide by theirs. I suppose that these things may be regarded as fated,—and I think that they are well.

And now, O men who have condemned me, I would fain prophesy to you; for I am about to die, and that is the hour in which men are gifted with prophetic power. And I prophesy to you who are my murderers, that immediately after my death punishment far heavier than you have inflicted on me will surely await you. Me you have killed because you wanted to escape the accuser, and not to give an account of your lives. But that will not be as you suppose: far otherwise. For I say that there will be more accusers of you than there are now; accusers whom hitherto I have restrained: and as they are younger they will be more severe with you, and you will be more offended at them. For if you think that by killing men you can avoid the accuser censuring your lives, you are mistaken; that is not a way of escape which is either possible or honorable; the easiest and noblest way is not to be crushing others, but to be improving yourselves. This is the prophecy which I utter before my departure, to the judges who have condemned me.

Friends, who would have acquitted me, I would like also to talk with you about this thing which has happened, while the magistrates are busy, and before I go to the place at which I must die. Stay then awhile, for we may as well talk with one another while there is time. You are my friends, and I should like to show you the meaning of this event which has happened to me. O my judges—for you I may truly call judges—I should like to tell you of a wonderful circumstance. Hitherto the familiar oracle within me has constantly been in the habit of opposing me even about trifles, if I was going to make a slip or error about anything; and now as you see there has come upon me that which may be thought, and is generally believed to be, the last and worst evil. But the oracle made no sign of opposition, either as I was leaving my house and going out in the morning, or when I was going up into this court, or while I was speaking, at anything which I was going to say; and yet I have often been stopped in the middle of a speech; but now in nothing I either said or did touching this matter has the oracle opposed me. What do I take to be the explanation of this? I will tell you. I regard this as a proof that what has happened to me is a good, and that those of us who think that death is an evil are in error. This is a great proof to me of what I am saying, for the customary sign would surely have opposed me had I been going to evil and not to good.

Let us reflect in another way, and we shall see that there is great reason to hope that death is a good, for one of two things:—either death is a state of nothingness and utter unconsciousness, or, as men say, there is a change and migration of the soul from this world to another. Now if you suppose that there is no consciousness, but a sleep like the sleep of him who is undisturbed even by the sight of dreams, death will be an unspeakable gain. For if a person were to select the night in which his sleep was undisturbed even by dreams, and were to compare with this the other days and nights of his life, and then were to tell us how many days and nights he had passed in the course of his life better and more pleasantly than this one, I think that any man, I will not say a private man, but even the great king, will not find many such days or nights, when compared with the others. Now if death is like this, I say that to die is gain; for eternity is then only a single night. But if death is the journey to another place, and there, as men say, all the dead are, what

good, O my friends and judges, can be greater than this? If indeed when the pilgrim arrives in the world below, he is delivered from the professors of justice in this world, and finds the true judges who are said to give judgment there, Minos and Rhadamanthus and Aeacus and Triptolemus, and other sons of God who were righteous in their own life, that pilgrimage will be worth making. What would not a man give if he might converse with Orpheus and Musaeus and Hesiod and Homer? Nay, if this be true, let me die again and again. I, too, shall have a wonderful interest in a place where I can converse with Palamedes, and Ajax the son of Telamon, and other heroes of old, who have suffered death through an unjust judgment; and there will be no small pleasure, as I think, in comparing my own sufferings with theirs. Above all, I shall be able to continue my search into true and false knowledge; as in this world, so also in that; I shall find out who is wise, and who pretends to be wise, and is not. What would not a man give, O judges, to be able to examine the leader of the great Trojan expedition; or Odysseus or Sisyphus, or numberless others, men and women too! What infinite delight would there be in conversing with them and asking them questions! For in that world they do not put a man to death for this; certainly not. For besides being happier in that world than in this, they will be immortal, if what is said is true.

Wherefore, O judges, be of good cheer about death, and know this of a truth—that no evil can happen to a good man, either in life or after death. He and his are not neglected by the gods; nor has my own approaching end happened by mere chance. But I see clearly that to die and be released was better for me; and therefore the oracle gave no sign. For which reason also, I am not angry with my accusers, or my condemners; they have done me no harm, although neither of them meant to do me any good; and for this I may gently blame them.

Still I have a favor to ask of them. When my sons are grown up, I would ask you, O my friends, to punish them; and I would have you trouble them, as I have troubled you, if they seem to care about riches, or anything, more than about virtue; or if they pretend to be something when they are really nothing,—then reprove them, as I have reproved you, for not caring about that for which they ought to care, and thinking that they are something when they are really nothing. And if you do this, I and my sons will have received justice at your hands.

The hour of departure has arrived, and we go our ways—I to die, and you to live. Which is better God only knows.

Questions for Reflection

1. Should Socrates have saved his life by accepting the compromise of agreeing not to teach philosophy or to move to another country?
2. What do you think of his claim that "the unexamined life is not worth living"?
3. Who have been the "gadflies" in your life? What was their effect on your life?
4. What ideas (if any) do you find to be uncomfortable, troubling, or even dangerous? Why?
5. Are there any ideas that you once thought were dangerous or false that you now accept?
6. Can you think of any ideas in the past that society thought were dangerous but that turned out to be true?
7. What ideas are worth living for? Are there any ideas that you would be willing to die for?
8. Socrates called people to search for wisdom. What people do you consider to be wise (either in the past or the present)? Why do you consider these persons to be wise?

HOW CAN I DECIDE WHAT TO BELIEVE? TOOLS FOR EXAMINING ARGUMENTS

Earlier in this chapter we suggested that philosophy is the search for fundamental beliefs that are justified. In reading a philosopher, it is important to avoid the "bottom line" syndrome. This problem involves simply agreeing or disagreeing with the author's conclusion without paying attention to whether or not the philosopher has provided good reasons for believing the conclusion. But responding in this way defeats a major goal of philosophy—the goal of seeing whether our beliefs or those of others are justified. For example, someone who believes in God (a theist) would agree with the conclusion of Thomas Aquinas's arguments (i.e., "There is a God"). But some theists do not think that Aquinas's arguments are strong. It is important to realize that in demonstrating that an argument is weak, we have not shown that its conclusion is false. We have merely shown that the reasons the author has given for the conclusion do not guarantee its truth. Nevertheless, if the only arguments that can be found to support a conclusion are weak, there is really no reason to suppose that the conclusion is true.

In the two readings by Plato preceding this section we were given concrete examples of Socrates' method of evaluating and justifying philosophical claims. In the first selection we watched Socrates analyze Euthyphro's various conceptions of piety to see whether they were acceptable. In the account of Socrates' trial in the *Apology*, we saw Socrates defending his pursuit of philosophy and refuting the accusations of the prosecutor. Now, in this section, we will give a more explicit but brief survey of the activity of evaluating philosophical claims or arguments.

Evaluating Philosophical Claims and Theories

In order to evaluate and choose between competing philosophical claims and theories, philosophers have agreed upon a number of criteria or tests. We will consider the six most common ones. I have formulated each one so that it contains a keyword that begins with the letter "c" in order to make them easy to remember. They are (1) conceptual *clarity,* (2) *consistency,* (3) rational *coherence,* (4) *comprehensiveness,* (5) *compatibility* with well-established facts and theories, and (6) having the support of *compelling* arguments. We will briefly look at each one in turn.

(1) *Conceptual clarity* is the first test that a philosophy must pass. If the terms or concepts in which it is expressed are not clear, then we don't know precisely what claim is being put forth. Suppose someone says "The only thing in life that has value is pleasure." We need to ask, what does the author mean by *pleasure?* Is the term referring only to physical sensations or do intellectual pleasures count? If it makes me feel good to sacrifice my own needs for those of others, am I really pursuing pleasure?

(2) *Consistency* is the second test that a philosophy must pass. A philosophy cannot contain any contradictions. One way to flunk this test is through **logical inconsistency,** which consists of making two assertions that could not both be true under any possible circumstances. The most obvious case of this would be any claim of the form "A is true and not-A is true." For example, if someone claims that God determines everything that happens in the world at the same time that she claims that humans have free will, there appears to be an inconsistency. The first claim implies that God determines what choices we make, but this seems to conflict with the claim that we freely make our own choices. The terms *determines* and *free will* would have to be defined differently than they normally are to avoid the inconsistency. The second kind of inconsistency is more subtle. It is called **self-referential inconsistency.** This occurs if an assertion implies that it cannot be true itself, or cannot be known to be true, or should not be believed. If I say that "All opinions are false," this implies that the opinion I just expressed is false. Similarly, if I claim that "Only statements that can be scientifically proven should be believed," this is a statement that cannot be scientifically proven.

(3) *Rational coherence* is a criterion that considers how well the various parts of a philosophy "hang together." The elements of a philosophy may not be explicitly contradictory, but they can still fail to fit together very well. A philosopher who believes that God acts in the world but fails to explain how that fits together with his belief that nature runs according to universal physical laws has articulated a philosophy that lacks coherence. Similarly, René Descartes argued that humans are made up of a physical body and a nonextended, nonphysical mind. While he believed that the two interacted, he failed to make clear how such different types of substances could causally influence one another. This gap in his theory earned him low points on the coherence criteria in the minds of many critics.

(4) *Comprehensiveness* is a criterion by means of which we evaluate a philosophy positively if it makes sense out of a wide range of phenomena and evaluate it negatively if it ignores significant areas of human experience or raises more questions than it answers. A philosophy that illuminates humanity's scientific, moral, aesthetic, and religious experience is better than one that explains only science but ignores the rest of human experience. To take a more specific example, a philosopher who claims that all

knowledge is based on sensory data, but fails to explain how we can have mathematical knowledge or moral knowledge falls short on this criterion. Similarly, a philosopher who claims that all morality is derived from the Ten Commandments, but fails to explain how some cultures have developed similar moral principles even if they never heard of these commandments fails in terms of comprehensiveness.

(5) *Compatibility with well-established facts and theories* is important because a good theory (in philosophy or science) is one that increases our understanding by unifying our knowledge. Hence, a theory that flies in the face of the rest of our understanding of the world may require us to lose more than we gain. For example, a philosophical theory about the mind should fit with the well-established findings of biology and psychology. However, there are exceptions to this rule. Throughout history, well-argued theories in philosophy and science have sometimes required us to violate common sense and abandon centuries-old beliefs, resulting in new knowledge. Nevertheless, we should do so only when the new theory is better than its competitors and promises to replace our current beliefs with an increase in understanding.

(6) *Having the support of compelling arguments* is the most important criterion of all for justifying or assessing a philosophical claim. This method of justifying a claim attempts to show that from certain true (or plausible) statements the claim either necessarily follows or is highly probable. Because this criterion is so central to doing good philosophy, we will devote the remaining three sections of this chapter to a discussion of the nature of arguments and methods for deciding whether they are compelling.

The Nature of Arguments

Philosophers attempt to establish the truth of their claims by means of arguments. But the word "argument" has two different meanings in everyday discourse. Suppose that two students were discussing whether or not there is a God and they began shouting at each other saying, "Yes there is," "No there isn't," "Yes there is," "No there isn't." If the exchange began to be quite heated, we might say that they were having an argument. In this context, "argument" would mean "a contentious dispute." However, this is not what philosophers mean by argument. In philosophy, an **argument** is a set of statements in which one or more statements (the **premises**) attempt to provide reasons for believing the truth of another statement (the **conclusion**).

An important step in analyzing an argument is deciding which statements are the premises and which is the conclusion. Often the conclusion is the last statement in a passage. However, an author may place the conclusion first or even in the middle. Using common sense and grasping the author's intentions are the best way to figure out the elements of a particular argument. There are key terms that are often used to indicate which statements are premises and which are conclusions. Typical **premise indicators** are: *since, because, for, given that.* Typical **conclusion indicators** are *therefore, so, hence, thus,* and *consequently.*

When it comes to determining whether or not an argument is acceptable, we can get some tips from the field of architecture. In order for a building to be stable, two factors have to work together: (a) the structure of the building designed by the architect has to follow good engineering principles and (b) the materials used to execute the design have to be solid and reliable. Corresponding to factor (a), a philosophical argument must have a reliable formal structure or else it will fail because of structural defects. These defects occur when the form of the argument is such that the premises do not provide adequate support for the conclusion. Corresponding to factor (b), the quality of the materials, an argument can be defective if the premises are known to be false or are, at least, implausible.

Here is an example of an argument in which the form is structurally flawed, even though the premises are true (there is nothing wrong with the materials composing the argument).

1. If Ronald Reagan was a U.S. President, then he was famous.
2. Ronald Reagan was famous.
3. Therefore, Ronald Reagan was a U.S. President.

I think that your logical intuitions will tell you that even though both premises are true and the conclusion is true, the conclusion does not logically follow from the premises. This can be shown by the fact that in 1960 both premises were true but the conclusion was false, because Ronald Reagan was famous for being a movie star and not a president. Hence, even though the conclusion happens to be true, it does not logically follow from the premises. If someone did not already know that Ronald Reagan was a president, this argument would not convince her of this conclusion.

In the next example the form of the argument is a good one, but the premises are false (the materials that fill out the form are faulty).

1. If President George Washington was a horse, then he had five legs.
2. President George Washington was a horse.
3. Therefore, President George Washington had five legs.

In this case, *if* the premises were true, the conclusion would have to be true. In other words, the conclusion logically follows from the premises. The problem, of course, is that this argument starts from false premises.

These examples provide us with two basic questions to ask about an argument:

■ If the premises were true, would they provide adequate logical support for the conclusion?

■ Are the premises true (or at least plausible)?

Logic is concerned with the answer to the first question. Any standard textbook in logic will provide many kinds of techniques for determining how strongly the premises support the conclusion, but in this chapter, we can only provide a few guidelines. A rather simple way to approach the question is to ask yourself:

■ How easy would it be to imagine that all the premises were true at the same time the conclusion was false?

If there are many ways to imagine that the premises were true and the conclusion false, this may indicate that the truth of the premises does not provide strong support for the truth of the conclusion. There is no single technique for answering the second question. Basically, you have to decide what sort of claim is being made in each premise and then decide what sort of evidence or sources of information would help in checking the truth of each premise.

What a good argument does is to establish a "price" for rejecting the conclusion. In other words it shows that if you believe the premises then you must believe the conclusion because the conclusion either logically follows from the premises or the premises show that it is most probably true. Hence, if you reject the conclusion of a logical argument, you can do so only by rejecting one or more of the premises. But in a very good argument, it would be implausible to reject the premises. There are two kinds of arguments, distinguished by their form. These are deductive arguments and inductive arguments. Another way of making this distinction is to say there are two standards for evaluating arguments: deductive validity and inductive strength. We will discuss each in turn.

Deductive Validity

We say that an argument is **valid** if it is impossible for the premises to be true and the conclusion false. Another way of putting this is to say that in a valid argument, *if* the premises are true, the conclusion *must* be true. Notice that the definition does not say that a valid argument will always have true premises. Furthermore, simply because the conclusion is true does not indicate that the argument is valid. The truth of the conclusion must logically follow from the premises. An argument whose author claims that it provides this sort of support for its conclusion but fails to do so is **invalid.** An argument that is valid or that the author claims is valid is called a **deductive argument.** A valid argument with true premises is a **sound argument.** In this case, the truth of the conclusion would be absolutely certain.

Now we will examine a number of valid argument forms that are very common (and a few that are invalid). As we go through these examples, keep the following equivalent definitions of validity in mind:

- In a valid argument, it is impossible for the premises to be true and the conclusion false.
- In a valid argument, *if* the premises are true then the conclusion *must* be true.

The argument forms we will discuss are those that are so frequently employed that they have been given names, sometimes in Latin. In each case, we will represent the skeletal structure of the argument in terms of various letters such as P and Q. The letters are variables that stand for propositions. To the right of each argument form, we will add "flesh" to the skeleton by replacing the letter variables with actual propositions. To make this discussion of logic relevant to our philosophical journey we will then provide a simple philosophical argument that makes use of the form in question. In examining these examples of valid or invalid arguments for a philosophical conclusion, do not suppose that this is the last word on the particular issue or that these are the best arguments available for the conclusion. In each case, if the argument is valid and you disagree with the conclusion (e.g., "there is a God" or "there is not a God"), then try to figure out a basis for questioning one or more of the premises.

Before discussing the first set of argument forms, we need to examine the nature of conditional statements (also known as hypothetical statements). A **conditional statement** contains two simpler statements that are connected with the words *if–then*. For example:

If it is raining, then the ground is wet.

If you study, then you will get good grades.

If Jones is pregnant, then Jones is a female.

The first part of a conditional statement (which follows the "if") is called the **antecedent.** The second part (which follows the "then") is called the **consequent.** In the examples the antecedents are "it is raining," "you study," and "Jones is pregnant." The consequents are "the ground is wet," "you will get good grades," and "Jones is a female."

A conditional statement claims that the truth of the antecedent is a **sufficient condition** for the truth of the consequent. To say that *A is a sufficient condition for B* means that if A is true, then B is true. Sometimes this is because the conditions that would make the antecedent true would *cause* conditions that would make the consequent true (as in the first two examples). However, Jones being pregnant does not *cause* Jones to be a female. So the notion of a sufficient condition has to do with the relationship between the truth of each statement and does not always express a causal relationship. A conditional statement also claims that the consequent is a **necessary condition** for the antecedent to be true. To say that *A is a necessary condition for B* means that for B to be true, A must be true. For example, being a female is a necessary condition for being pregnant. However, being a female is not a sufficient condition for being pregnant. These remarks about conditional statements are illustrated by the first five argument forms, which all contain conditional statements.

Modus Ponens

1. If P, then Q.   1. If Spot is a dog, then Spot is a mammal.
2. P.   2. Spot is a dog.
3. Therefore, Q.   3. Therefore, Spot is a mammal.

Philosophical example of modus ponens:

1. If the universe shows evidence of design, then there is a God.
2. The universe shows evidence of design.
3. Therefore, there is a God.

Modus ponens is also known as *affirming the antecedent.*

Modus Tollens

1. If P, then Q.   1. If John is eligible for the award, then he is a junior.
2. Not-Q.   2. John is not a junior.
3. Therefore, Not-P.   3. Therefore, John is not eligible for the award.

Philosophical example of modus tollens:

1. If God exists, there would be no unnecessary evil in the world.
2. There is unnecessary evil in the world.
3. Therefore, God does not exist.

Since modus tollens (also known as *denying the consequent*) is a valid argument form, it is clear that this argument about God's existence is valid. That is, if the premises are true, then the conclusion logically follows. Consequently, a theist who rejects the conclusion would have to find reasons for rejecting at least one of the premises.

Fallacy of Denying the Antecedent   A **fallacy** is an argument form that is logically defective such that the premises provide little to no support for the conclusion. There are two invalid arguments (deductive fallacies) that can be confused with either modus ponens or modus tollens. The first is the fallacy of denying the antecedent, which has this form:

1. If P, then Q.   1. If Jones is a mother, then Jones is a parent.
2. Not-P.   2. Jones is not a mother.
3. Therefore, not-Q. 3. Therefore, Jones is not a parent.

As the example illustrates, this argument form is invalid because we can imagine a situation in which the premises are true and the conclusion false. If Jones is a father, then it is true that Jones is not a mother but false that Jones is not a parent.

Philosophical example of the fallacy of denying the antecedent:

1. If Thomas Aquinas's arguments for God are valid, then there is a God.
2. Thomas Aquinas's arguments for God are not valid.
3. Therefore, there is not a God.

Fallacy of Affirming the Consequent   This is another invalid argument that is a counterfeit version of the first two and should not be confused with a valid argument form.

1. If P, then Q.   1. If George Washington was assassinated, then he is dead.
2. Q.   2. George Washington is dead.
3. Therefore, P.   3. Therefore, George Washington was assassinated.

Philosophical example of the fallacy of affirming the consequent:

1. If morality is completely subjective, then people will differ in their moral beliefs.
2. People do differ in their moral beliefs.
3. Therefore, morality is completely subjective. (There are no objective truths about what is morally right or wrong.)

One way to show that an argument is invalid is to construct another argument that has the same form as the original but that goes from true premises to a false conclusion. This would be an invalid argument since a valid argument will always carry us from true information to a true conclusion. However, if the form of reasoning is the same as the original argument, the counterexample will show that the original argument is invalid also. Since the following argument is the same as the argument about morality, except for the subject matter, it shows that the previous argument is invalid.

1. If medical science is completely subjective, then people will differ in their medical beliefs.
2. People do differ in their medical beliefs. (Some people believe that sacrificing twin babies will cure the community of a plague; on the other hand, we don't believe this.)

3. Therefore, medical science is completely subjective. (There are no objective truths about what will or won't cure disease—a false conclusion.)

Hypothetical Syllogism A **syllogism** is any argument with two premises and a conclusion. A hypothetical syllogism is one in which the premises and the conclusion are all hypothetical or conditional statements. It has this basic form:

1. If P, then Q.   1. If I learn logic, then I will write better essays.
2. If Q, then R.   2. If I write better essays, then I will get better grades.
3. Therefore, if P, then R.   3. Therefore, if I learn logic, then I will get better grades.

Philosophical example of a valid hypothetical syllogism:

1. If the methods of science only give us information about physical reality, then science cannot tell us whether or not a nonphysical reality exists.
2. If science cannot tell us whether or not a nonphysical reality exists, then science cannot tell us whether or not we have a soul.
3. Therefore, if the methods of science only give us information about physical reality, then science cannot tell us whether or not we have a soul.

Notice that the key to a hypothetical syllogism is that the consequent (Q) of one premise is the antecedent (Q) of the other premise such that they could be linked up like a chain if they were laid end to end. This would be true even if the order of the premises were reversed. Furthermore, the antecedent of the conclusion (P) is the beginning of the chain formed by the premises and the consequent of the conclusion (R) is the end of the chain. Any other arrangement will be invalid, as in the following examples.

Counterfeit (invalid) hypothetical syllogisms:

1. If P, then Q.   1. If P, then Q.
2. If R, then Q.   2. If Q, then R.
3. Therefore, if P, then R.   3. Therefore, if R, then P.

See if you can substitute statements for the letter variables in the previous invalid hypothetical syllogisms. Try to construct arguments that follow the given forms but in which true premises lead to a false conclusion in order to show that something is wrong with these types of arguments.

Disjunctive Syllogism A **disjunctive argument** is one that contains a disjunctive statement in a premise. A disjunctive statement asserts that at least one of two alternatives is true. It typically is expressed as an *either–or* statement. Normally a disjunctive statement asserts that at least one alternative is true and possibly both. For example, if Sherlock Holmes determines that the murder was an inside job, he might state, "Either the butler is guilty or the maid is guilty." Obviously, the fact that one of them must be guilty also includes the possibility that both of them are guilty. This is what a disjunctive syllogism looks like:

1. Either P or Q.	1. Either the bulb is burnt out or it is not receiving electricity.
2. Not-P.	2. The bulb is not burnt out.
3. Therefore, Q.	3. Therefore, the bulb is not receiving electricity.

Philosophical example of a disjunctive syllogism:

1. Either the universe contains in itself a sufficient reason for its existence or it was caused to exist.
2. The universe does not contain in itself a sufficient reason for its existence.
3. Therefore, the universe was caused to exist.

Fallacy of Affirming the Disjunct

1. Either P or Q.	1. Either the bulb is burnt out or it is not receiving electricity.
2. P.	2. The bulb is burnt out.
3. Therefore, not-Q.	3. Therefore, it is receiving electricity.

This is an invalid argument form that is a counterfeit of the disjunctive syllogism. In the example just given, the fact that the bulb is burnt out does not exclude the possibility that there are problems with the electricity as well. Since both alternatives could be true in a normal disjunction, simply affirming one alternative does not prove that the other is false. However, if the disjunction contained two contradictories (two statements that make opposite claims), then this type of argument would be valid. For example, if the first premise was "Either Howard is married or he is single," then the truth of one statement would imply the falsity of the other.

Philosophical example of the fallacy of affirming the disjunct:

1. Either reason is the source of moral principles or divine revelation is.
2. Reason is the source of moral principles.
3. Therefore, divine revelation is not the source of moral principles.

In this case, the conclusion does not follow because the two statements in the disjunction could both be true. (Some philosophers, such as Thomas Aquinas, believed that both reason and revelation could provide us with moral principles.)

Reductio ad Absurdum Arguments   The label of this valid argument form means "reducing to an absurdity." To use this technique, you begin by assuming that your opponent's position is true and then you show that it logically implies either an absurd conclusion or one that contradicts itself or that it contradicts other conclusions held by your opponent. If we can deduce a clearly false statement from a proposition, this is definitive proof that the original assumption was false. It is a way of exposing an inconsistency that is lurking in an opponent's position. When it is done well, it is an effective way to refute a position. (Socrates was a master of this type of argument and he used it in the first two readings presented earlier in this chapter.) Typically, the argument follows this form:

1. Suppose the truth of A (the position you wish to refute).
2. If A, then B.

3. If B, then C.

4. If C, then not-A.

5. Therefore, both A and not-A.

6. But 5 is a contradiction, so the original assumption must be false and not-A must be true.

Philosophical example of a reductio ad absurdum:

A group of ancient Greek philosophers called the Sophists believed that all truth was subjective and relative. Protagoras, one of the most famous Sophists, argued that one opinion is just as true as another opinion. The following is a summary of the argument that Socrates used to refute this position.*

1. One opinion is just as true as another opinion. (Socrates assumes the truth of Protagoras's position.)

2. Protagoras's critics have the following opinion: "Protagoras's opinion is false and that of his critics is true."

3. Since Protagoras believes premise 1, he believes that the opinion of his critics in premise 2 is true.

4. Hence, Protagoras also believes it is true that "Protagoras's opinion is false and that of his critics is true."

5. Since individual opinion determines what is true and everyone (both Protagoras and his critics) believe the statement "Protagoras's opinion is false," it follows that

6. Protagoras's opinion is false.

Inductive Strength

Not all arguments claim to be deductively valid. Nevertheless, even if an argument's conclusion does not follow necessarily from the premises, it may be a reasonably strong argument if it is such that true premises would make the conclusion highly probable. If the author of an argument is claiming that the premises provide this sort of support for the conclusion, then we treat it as an **inductive argument** and evaluate it in terms of its inductive strength. The inductive strength of an argument is a measure of how likely it is that the conclusion is true, given the premises. We say that the argument is a **strong argument** if the premises make it highly probable that the conclusion is true and highly unlikely that the conclusion is false. When we are applying the criteria of deductive validity, an argument is either valid or invalid. However, when we are treating an argument as an inductive one, its strength can range from *strong* (the premises make the truth of the conclusion very likely) to *moderate* (the premises provide some support for the conclusion), to *weak* (the premises give us little reason to believe the conclusion). A strong argument that actually does have true premises is a **cogent argument.** A cogent argument does not absolutely guarantee the conclusion (as does a sound argument), but it does give us good reasons for believing the conclusion.

---

* Plato, *Theaetetus* 171a, b.

One common form of inductive argument starts from the observation that a number of similar cases have a certain property in common and concludes that all other cases of this type will also have that property. Most of science is based on this type of inductive argument. For example, before a pharmaceutical drug is released on the market, it is tested extensively. From these tests on a sample group of patients, it may be concluded that the drug is safe for anyone to use. Of course, there is no guarantee that there may not be some dangerous side effects that have not been discovered yet. However, if the testing has been adequate, this makes a strong inductive argument that the drug is safe.

The case of inductive reasoning used in medical tests highlights two important factors that affect the strength of an inductive argument. First, the cases cited in the premises must be representative of the group mentioned in the premises. If the drug was found to be safe for male athletes under 25 years old, we could not conclude that it would be safe for everyone, because we have no evidence concerning its effects on women, people in poor physical condition, or older people. A second factor in evaluating the inductive strength of an argument is to consider the size of the sample in the premises compared with the size of the group in the conclusion. If the drug was only tested on three people and found to be safe, this would be exceedingly weak evidence for concluding that it will be safe for anyone. On the other hand, if the drug has been proven safe for a representative group of over 100,000 people, it would be a stronger argument. These examples make clear that with inductive reasoning, additional information (or premises) can either strengthen the argument or weaken it.

A special kind of inductive reasoning is called **reasoning by analogy.** In this sort of reasoning we argue that because two or more cases share one property in common, it is likely that they will share other properties in common. For example, if my new computer is made by the same company as my previous computer (even though it is a different model), and pressing a certain combination of keys reset my old computer, I might conclude that it is likely that pressing the same keys will have the same effect on my new computer. What is important in reasoning by analogy is to assess the number of relevant similarities and differences between the two cases and the likelihood that similarities of one sort will provide grounds for assuming the similarities stated in the conclusion.

An example of the pros and cons of reasoning by analogy can be found in reading 7 by William Paley where he argues that the universe and a watch are similar because they both exhibit a complex order. Since the complexity and order in the watch is the result of intelligent design, we may conclude that the universe, likewise, is a product of intelligent design. David Hume, in reading 8, will argue that this is a faulty analogy. We have seen many examples of watches, houses, and machines, he says, and we know how they are made. However, we have only one example of a universe, and, besides, the universe is very different from a watch, so we can conclude nothing about how universes are made.

Inference to the Best Explanation

Another form of reasoning is known as an **inference to the best explanation.** (This sort of reasoning is sometimes called "abduction.") Some philosophers consider it to be a variety of inductive reasoning. Unlike the previous sorts of arguments we have discussed, an inference to the best explanation does not try to directly prove the truth of a theory; it tries to show that the theory is superior to all its competitors and that it is therefore the one most likely to be true. An inference to the best explanation has the following form:

1. There is a collection of data that needs an explanation.
2. A theory is proposed that offers an explanation of the data.
3. This theory offers the best explanation of all known alternatives.
4. Therefore, until a better explanation is proposed, it is rational to believe this theory.

This method of reasoning is used extensively in both science and philosophy and, thus, a comparison of the sorts of evidence and explanations that are offered in science can provide a very helpful model for understanding the explanations that are provided by philosophical theories. First, scientists cannot always directly observe the entities or events postulated by their theories (neutrinos, quarks, black holes, the big bang). Similarly, in philosophy we cannot directly observe with our senses the presence or absence of God, free will, moral values, or justice. Second, inferences to the best explanation in science and philosophy are evaluated using the five criteria of clarity, consistency, coherence, comprehensiveness, and compatibility with well-established facts and theories that we discussed earlier and can be used to justify belief in either subatomic particles or the claims that philosophers make. For example, various philosophers attempt to justify claims such as the following: There is a God, mental events are really brain events, humans have free will, the morality of an action is determined by the consequences. Even though the defense of such claims cannot take the form of a confirming observation, philosophers can try to show that these theories make the best sense of what we do know and observe.

There is much more to be said about evaluating arguments and claims, but this section will provide you with some guidelines for evaluating the reasoning found in the philosophical readings in this book. If you want to learn more about this skill, pick up a book on logic or critical reasoning in the library or bookstore. Better yet, take a course in the subject.

C H A P T E R   2

Questions about God, Faith, and Reason

PHILOSOPHY OF RELIGION: WHAT ARE THE ISSUES?

Love and anger, guilt and ecstasy, humor and solemnity, optimism and cynicism, peace and doubt, hope and despair—religion seems capable of evoking a response corresponding to every peak and valley on the spectrum of human emotional life. Why is this? Philosopher and theologian Peter Kreeft attempts to assess the impact of the idea of God in the following passage:

> The idea of God has guided or deluded more lives, changed more history, inspired more music and poetry and philosophy than anything else, real or imagined. It has made more of a difference to human life on this planet, both individually and collectively, than anything else ever has. To see this clearly for yourself, just try this thought experiment: suppose no one in history had ever conceived the idea of God. Now, rewrite history following that premise. The task daunts and staggers the imagination. From the earliest human remains—religious funeral artifacts—to the most recent wars in the Mideast, religion—belief in a God or gods—has been the mainspring of the whole watch that is human history.*

Many have found the idea of God to be comforting, inspiring, and the source of hope. It is, perhaps, equally true that some have found the idea of God's nonexistence to be a comfortable thought, for they prefer to think of themselves as autonomous and not subject to any higher power. But these facts do not take us very far. The thought that my checking account currently has money in it is comforting and puts my mind at ease. However, with my finances, as well as with the God question, beliefs that are comforting can be in conflict with reality. Hence, philosophy of religion is not concerned with the psychological benefits of beliefs concerning the idea of God, but rather with the question of whether or not the word *God* refers to anything in reality. Certainly, religious questions are personal and how we answer them has an enormous effect on our lives. However, the question of God's existence is not personal in the sense that the truth of the matter depends on individual subjective feelings, as it does with such issues as whether one likes raw oysters or the color green. Instead, the God question is personal

---

*Peter Kreeft, Introduction to J. P. Moreland and Kai Nelson, *Does God Exist? The Great Debate* (Nashville: Thomas Nelson, 1990), p. 11.

just as the issue of death is personal. The statement "Someday I will die" is one of great subjective concern to me, but that doesn't change the fact that it is an objective truth. For this reason, Peter Kreeft says, "God is either a fact, like sand, or a fantasy, like Santa."*

But once we start raising questions about the existence of God, a number of other questions arise. How can we decide whether or not God exists? Are there rational arguments that demonstrate that God exists or, at least, that his existence is probable? Is there evidence that counts against God's existence? What about the existence of suffering in the world? Isn't it pretty hard to square this fact with the belief in an all-powerful, loving God? Is it impossible or inappropriate to approach this question in an objective way? Should we substitute faith or subjective considerations for objective reasons in making up our minds about the God question?

WHAT ARE MY OPTIONS CONCERNING PHILOSOPHY OF RELIGION?

The claim that belief in God must be supported by objective evidence is known as **evidentialism.** There are both religious believers and atheists who are evidentialists. The theistic evidentialist thinks that there is objective evidence for God. The atheistic evidentialist believes that one must have evidence for his or her belief in God to be rational, but goes on to argue that such evidence is lacking. Generally, all agnostics, that is people who do not think there is sufficient evidence either for theism or atheism, are evidentialists.

The theists who are evidentialists would, of course, agree that it is possible to demonstrate the existence of God through rational, objective arguments. They believe in the possibility and success of natural theology. **Natural theology** is the project of attempting to provide proofs for the existence of God based on reason and experience alone. In other words, the natural theologian does not appeal to supernatural revelation or faith of any sort to support his or her claims about God. This does not mean the natural theologian necessarily rejects revelation or faith, but only that he or she believes that it is possible to demonstrate God's existence, and perhaps the truth of other religious claims, solely through philosophical reasoning. The sorts of objective evidence that are used to support this belief will be the subject of the sections that follow. As we will see, the three main forms of objective arguments for God are the cosmological argument, the teleological or design argument, and the ontological argument. Readings 4 through 10 will present both proponents and critics of each of these arguments.

Atheism is the claim that God does not exist. Typically, atheists are evidentialists. Atheists support their position in two ways. First, they say that the burden of proof is on those who make claims concerning the existence of extraordinary beings such as God (as well as space aliens, ghosts, and so on). Furthermore, they argue that all attempts to prove the existence of God fail. Hence, atheism is claimed to be the only rational alternative. Second, atheists often offer positive evidence for the thesis that God does not exist. While a number of different kinds of arguments are used, the most common

---

*Ibid.

TABLE 2.1 SPECTRUM OF VIEWPOINTS ON THE EXISTENCE OF GOD

	Theistic Evidentialism (Natural Theology)	Atheistic Evidentialism	Agnosticism	Nonevidential Theism (Pragmatism, Subjectivism)
1. Objective evidence is required for religious belief.	Agree	Agree	Agree	Disagree
2. Objective evidence is available.	Agree	Disagree	Disagree	Disagree
3. Persuasive practical or subjective reasons for belief are available.	(May agree or disagree)	Disagree	Disagree	Agree
4. God exists.	Agree	Disagree	Undecided	Agree

argument atheists appeal to is based on the problem of evil. They claim that the existence of evil (such as the suffering of innocent people due to natural disasters) is evidence that casts doubt on the God hypothesis. Reading 11 by Albert Camus presents a graphic example of the problem and B. C. Johnson, in reading 12, argues that the problem of evil forces us to reject traditional notions of God. In reading 13 John Hick will attempt to resolve the problem.

Agnosticism is the position that there is not enough evidence for one to know whether there is or is not a God. This position is sometimes called *religious skepticism*. Agnostics are evidentialists, for they agree that objective evidence is necessary to believe in God's existence, but they believe that such evidence is unavailable. However, they also say that objective evidence is necessary to claim that God does *not* exist. Hence, unlike both the theist and the atheist, the agnostic does not think we can know anything concerning God's existence. Accordingly, the agnostic thinks we must suspend judgment on this issue. In reading 8 we will examine David Hume's refutation of the teleological argument for God's existence. Hume is an agnostic, for he thinks that we can neither know that God exists nor know that he does not exist.

Those who embrace **nonevidentialism** hold that it is not necessary to have objective, rational evidence for our basic beliefs and stance towards life. The nonevidentialist claims that there is a basis for religious belief other than reason. Accordingly, the nonevidentialist says that we must and, in fact, do form our ultimate commitments on the basis of subjective, personal factors and not on rational arguments. To put it more precisely, nonevidentialists do not think that there are any rational arguments that can prove the proposition "God exists," but some provide arguments as to why it is rationally permissible or even preferable to have faith in God. While there are those on both sides of the God issue who reject evidentialism, nonevidentialism is a position that appeals more to theists than atheists. Examples of this sort of appeal will be provided by Blaise Pascal (reading 14), the seventeenth-century mathematician and philosopher, and by William James (reading 15), the twentieth-century pragmatist.

The spectrum of viewpoints we have discussed is summarized in Table 2.1.

Our examination of the philosophy of religion will begin with an opening narrative to stretch our imaginations and raise the question of whether there might be a dimension of reality beyond what we immediately perceive. The remainder of the readings in this chapter will cover three major philosophical questions about religion. These are (1) Is there evidence for the existence of God? (2) Do suffering and evil count against the existence of God? (3) Is religious faith without evidence justified? Finally, the Contemporary Application readings will center on the question, Does religion conflict with science?

OPENING NARRATIVE: IS THERE A REALITY THAT TRANSCENDS OUR OWN?

  E D W I N   A .   A B B O T T

Flatland

Edwin Abbott (1838–1926) was an accomplished theologian, classics scholar, Shakespeare expert, and mathematician, as well as the headmaster of the City of London School. Although he wrote a number of books, his best known work is the classic science fiction work, *Flatland: A Romance in Many Dimensions.* As the name implies, Flatland is a two-dimensional world. Everything in it has width and length, but no three-dimensional depth. Accordingly, all of its inhabitants are geometrical figures such as lines, triangles, squares, pentagons, and circles. The women are exclusively lines, while circles are considered the most perfect of figures and are the priests. Much of the story is a social satire of Victorian England and an expression of Abbott's efforts to advance the cause of women and the lower classes. Nevertheless, the story also makes some interesting philosophical and theological observations.

The reading begins when one of the distinguished citizens of Flatland, a square, is enjoying a quiet evening at home and a stranger mysteriously appears in the square's sitting room. The stranger is a sphere, but being unfamiliar with the notion of a third dimension, the square can only perceive him as a circle that changes its diameter as the plane of Flatland bisects different portions of the sphere.

Reading Questions

1. When the sphere (the Stranger) says that he comes from space, why can the square not understand what he means?
2. The sphere says that the third dimension is "up above and down below" the plane of Flatland. Put yourself in the position of the square living in a two-dimensional plane. Why does the square assume that he means from the north and from the south?
3. Since the sphere cannot explain the third dimension in terms of the square's limited, two-dimensional concepts, what sorts of deeds does the sphere employ to convince him? Still not convinced, what explanation of the strange phenomenon does the square assume?
4. What means does the sphere use to finally convince the square that there is a third dimension?
5. How does this reading relate to the topic of religion? In what ways might the religious person say we are like the square, focusing on the world that is familiar but missing an important dimension of reality?
6. Interpreting this allegory religiously, who would the sphere be? What would be analogous to the mysterious third dimension that the square cannot understand? What sort of religious experience would correspond to the square suddenly being able to understand the third dimension?

From Edwin A. Abbott, *Flatland: A Romance of Many Dimensions,* 1884.

§16.–HOW THE STRANGER VAINLY ENDEAVOURED TO REVEAL TO ME IN WORDS THE MYSTERIES OF SPACELAND

. . . I began to approach the Stranger with the intention of taking a nearer view and of bidding him be seated: but his appearance struck me dumb and motionless with astonishment. Without the slightest symptoms of angularity he nevertheless varied every instant with gradations of size and brightness scarcely possible for any Figure within the scope of my experience. The thought flashed across me that I might have before me a burglar or cut-throat, some monstrous Irregular Isosceles, who, by feigning the voice of a Circle, had obtained admission somehow into the house, and was now preparing to stab me with his acute angle.

In a sitting-room, the absence of Fog (and the season happened to be remarkably dry), made it difficult for me to trust to Sight Recognition, especially at the short distance at which I was standing. Desperate with fear, I rushed forward with an unceremonious, "You must permit me, Sir—" and felt him. My Wife was right. There was not the trace of an angle, not the slightest roughness or inequality: never in my life had I met with a more perfect Circle. He remained motionless while I walked round him, beginning from his eye and returning to it again. Circular he was throughout, a perfectly satisfactory Circle; there could not be a doubt of it. Then followed a dialogue, which I will endeavour to set down as near as I can recollect it, omitting only some of my profuse apologies—for I was covered with shame and humiliation that I, a Square, should have been guilty of the impertinence of feeling a Circle. It was commenced by the Stranger with some impatience at the lengthiness of my introductory process.

STRANGER: Have you felt me enough by this time? Are you not introduced to me yet?

I: Most illustrious Sir, excuse my awkwardness, which arises not from ignorance of the usages of polite society, but from a little surprise and nervousness, consequent on this somewhat unexpected visit. And I beseech you to reveal my indiscretion to no one, and especially not to my Wife. But before your Lordship enters into further communications, would he deign to satisfy the curiosity of one who would gladly know whence his visitor came?

STRANGER: From Space, from Space, Sir: whence else?

I: Pardon me, my Lord, but is not your Lordship already in Space, your Lordship and his humble servant, even at this moment?

STRANGER: Pooh! what do you know of Space? Define Space.

I: Space, my Lord, is height and breadth indefinitely prolonged.

STRANGER: Exactly: you see you do not even know what Space is. You think it is of Two Dimensions only; but I have come to announce to you a Third—height, breadth, and length.

I: Your Lordship is pleased to be merry. We also speak of length and height, or breadth and thickness, thus denoting Two Dimensions by four names.

STRANGER: But I mean not only three names, but Three Dimensions.

I: Would your Lordship indicate or explain to me in what direction is the Third Dimension, unknown to me?

STRANGER: I came from it. It is up above and down below.

I: My Lord means seemingly that it is Northward and Southward.

STRANGER: I mean nothing of the kind. I mean a direction in which you cannot look, because you have no eye in your side.

I: Pardon me, my Lord, a moment's inspection will convince your Lordship that I have a perfect luminary at the juncture of two of my sides.

STRANGER: Yes: but in order to see into Space you ought to have an eye, not on your Perimeter, but on your side, that is, on what you would probably call your inside; but we in Spaceland should call it your side.

I: An eye in my inside! An eye in my stomach! Your Lordship jests.

STRANGER: I am in no jesting humour. I tell you that I come from Space, or, since you will not understand what Space means, from the Land of

Three Dimensions whence I but lately looked down upon your Plane which you call Space forsooth. From that position of advantage I discerned all that you speak of as *solid* (by which you mean "enclosed on four sides"), your houses, your churches, your very chests and safes, yes even your insides and stomachs, all lying open and exposed to my view.

I: Such assertions are easily made, my Lord. . . .

STRANGER: (*To himself.*) . . . How shall I convince him? Surely a plain statement of facts followed by ocular demonstration ought to suffice.— Now, Sir; listen to me.

You are living on a Plane. What you style Flatland is the vast level surface of what I may call a fluid, on, or in, the top of which you and your countrymen move about, without rising above it or falling below it.

I am not a plane Figure, but a Solid. You call me a Circle; but in reality I am not a Circle, but an infinite number of Circles, of size varying from a Point to a Circle of thirteen inches in diameter, one placed on the top of the other. When I cut through your plane as I am now doing, I make in your plane a section which you, very rightly, call a Circle. For even a Sphere—which is my proper name in my own country—if he manifest himself at all to an inhabitant of Flatland—must needs manifest himself as a Circle. . . .

The diminished brightness of your eye indicates incredulity. But now prepare to receive proof positive of the truth of my assertions. You cannot indeed see more than one of my sections, or Circles, at a time; for you have no power to raise your eye out of the plane of Flatland; but you can at least see that, as I rise in Space, so my sections become smaller. See now, I will rise; and the effect upon your eye will be that my Circle will become smaller and smaller till it dwindles to a point and finally vanishes.

There was no "rising" that I could see; but he diminished and finally vanished. I winked once or twice to make sure that I was not dreaming. But it was no dream. For from the depths of nowhere came forth a hollow voice—close to my heart it seemed—"Am I quite gone? Are you convinced now? Well, now I will gradually return to Flatland and you shall see my section become larger and larger."

Every reader in Spaceland will easily understand that my mysterious Guest was speaking the language of truth and even of simplicity. But to me, proficient though I was in Flatland Mathematics, it was by no means a simple matter. . . . it [will be] clear to any Spaceland child that the Sphere . . . must needs have manifested himself to me, or to any Flatlander, as a Circle, at first of full size, then small, and at last very small indeed, approaching to a Point. But to me, although I saw the facts before me, the causes were as dark as ever. All that I could comprehend was, that the Circle had made himself smaller and vanished, and that he had now reappeared and was rapidly making himself larger.

When he regained his original size, he heaved a deep sigh; for he perceived by my silence that I had altogether failed to comprehend him. And indeed I was now inclining to the belief that he must be no Circle at all, but some extremely clever juggler; or else that the old wives' tales were true, and that after all there were such people as Enchanters and Magicians. . . .

§17.—HOW THE SPHERE, HAVING IN VAIN TRIED WORDS, RESORTED TO DEEDS

My resolution was taken. It seemed intolerable that I should endure existence subject to the arbitrary visitations of a Magician. . . . If only I could in any way manage to pin him against the wall till help came!

. . . I dashed my hardest angle against him, at the same time alarming the whole household by my cries for aid. I believe, at the moment of my onset, the Stranger had sunk below our Plane, and really found difficulty in rising. In any case he remained motionless, while I, hearing, as I thought, the sound of some help approaching, pressed against him with redoubled vigour, and continued to shout for assistance.

A convulsive shudder ran through the Sphere. "This must not be," I thought I heard him say: "ei-

ther he must listen to reason, or I must have recourse to the last resource of civilization." Then,
addressing me in a louder tone, he hurriedly exclaimed, "Listen: no stranger must witness what
you have witnessed. Send your Wife back at once,
before she enters the apartment. The Gospel of
Three Dimensions must not be thus frustrated.
Not thus must the fruits of one thousand years of
waiting be thrown away. I hear her coming. Back!
back! Away from me, or you must go with me—
whither you know not—into the Land of Three
Dimensions!"

"Fool! Madman! Irregular!" I exclaimed; "never
will I release thee; thou shalt pay the penalty of
thine impostures."

"Ha! Is it come to this?" thundered the Stranger:
"then meet your fate: out of your Plane you go.
Once, twice, thrice! 'Tis done!"

§18.—HOW I CAME TO SPACELAND, AND WHAT I SAW THERE.

An unspeakable horror seized me. There was a
darkness; then a dizzy, sickening sensation of sight
that was not like seeing; I saw a Line that was no
Line; Space that was not Space: I was myself, and
not myself. When I could find voice, I shrieked
aloud in agony, "Either this is madness or it is
Hell." "It is neither," calmly replied the voice of the
Sphere, "it is Knowledge; it is Three Dimensions:
open your eye once again and try to look steadily."

I looked, and, behold, a new world! There stood
before me, visibly incorporate, all that I had before
inferred, conjectured, dreamed, of perfect Circular beauty. What seemed the centre of the
Stranger's form lay open to my view: yet I could see
no heart, nor lungs, nor arteries, only a beautiful
harmonious Something—for which I had no
words; but you, my Readers in Spaceland, would
call it the surface of the Sphere.

Prostrating myself mentally before my Guide, I
cried, "How is it, O divine ideal of consummate
loveliness and wisdom that I see thy inside, and yet
cannot discern thy heart, thy lungs, thy arteries, thy
liver?" "What you think you see, you see not," he
replied; "it is not given to you, nor to any other Be-

ing, to behold my internal parts. I am of a different
order of Beings from those in Flatland. Were I a
Circle, you could discern my intestines, but I am a
Being, composed as I told you before, of many Cir-
cles, the Many in the One, called in this country a
Sphere. And, just as the outside of a Cube is a
Square, so the outside of a Sphere presents the ap-
pearance of a Circle."

Bewildered though I was by my Teacher's enigmatic utterance, I no longer chafed against it, but
worshipped him in silent adoration. He continued,
with more mildness in his voice. "Distress not yourself if you cannot at first understand the deeper
mysteries of Spaceland. By degrees they will dawn
upon you. Let us begin by casting back a glance at
the region whence you came. Return with me a
while to the plains of Flatland, and I will shew you
that which you have often reasoned and thought
about, but never seen with the sense of sight—a visible angle." "Impossible!" I cried; but, the Sphere
leading the way, I followed as if in a dream, till once
more his voice arrested me: "Look yonder, and
behold your own Pentagonal house, and all its
inmates."

I looked below, and saw with my physical eye all
that domestic individuality which I had hitherto
merely inferred with the understanding. And how
poor and shadowy was the inferred conjecture in
comparison with the reality which I now beheld!
My four Sons calmly asleep in the North-Western
rooms, my two orphan Grandsons to the South; the
Servants, the Butler, my Daughter, all in their several apartments. Only my affectionate Wife,
alarmed by my continued absence, had quitted her
room and was roving up and down in the Hall, anx-
iously awaiting my return. Also the Page, aroused
by my cries, had left his room, and under pretext of
ascertaining whether I had fallen somewhere in a
faint, was prying into the cabinet in my study. All
this I could now *see,* not merely infer; and as we
came nearer and nearer, I could discern even the
contents of my cabinet, and the two chests of gold,
and the tablets of which the Sphere had made
mention.

Touched by my Wife's distress, I would have
sprung downward to reassure her, but I found myself incapable of motion. "Trouble not yourself

about your Wife," said my Guide: "she will not be long left in anxiety; meantime, let us take a survey of Flatland."

Once more I felt myself rising through space. It was even as the Sphere had said. The further we receded from the object we beheld, the larger became the field of vision. My native city, with the interior of every house and every creature therein, lay open to my view in miniature. We mounted higher, and lo, the secrets of the earth, the depths of mines and inmost caverns of the hills, were bared before me.

Awestruck at the sight of the mysteries of the earth, thus unveiled before my unworthy eye, I said to my Companion, "Behold, I am become as a God. For the wise men in our country say that to see all things, or as they express it, *omnividence,* is the attribute of God alone." There was something of scorn in the voice of my Teacher as he made answer: "Is it so indeed? Then the very pick-pockets and cut-throats of my country are to be worshipped by your wise men as being Gods: for there is not one of them that does not see as much as you see now. But trust me, your wise men are wrong."

I: Then is omnividence the attribute of others besides Gods?

SPHERE: I do not know. But, if a pick-pocket or a cut-throat of our country can see everything that is in your country, surely that is no reason why the pick-pocket or cut-throat should be accepted by you as a God. . . .

. . . But enough of this. Look yonder. Do you know that building?

I looked, and afar off I saw an immense Polygonal structure, in which I recognized the General Assembly Hall of the States of Flatland, surrounded by dense lines of Pentagonal buildings at right angles to each other, which I knew to be streets; and I perceived that I was approaching the great Metropolis.

"Here we descend," said my Guide. It was now morning, the first hour of the first day of the two thousandth year of our era. Acting, as was their wont, in strict accordance with precedent, the highest Circles of the realm were meeting in solemn conclave, as they had met on the first hour of the first day of the year 1000, and also on the first hour of the first day of the year 0.

The minutes of the previous meetings were now read by one whom I at once recognized as my brother, a perfectly Symmetrical Square, and the Chief Clerk of the High Council. It was found recorded on each occasion that: "Whereas the States had been troubled by divers ill-intentioned persons pretending to have received revelations from another World, and professing to produce demonstrations whereby they had instigated to frenzy both themselves and others, it had been for this cause unanimously resolved by the Grand Council that on the first day of each millenary, special injunctions be sent to the Prefects in the several districts of Flatland, to make strict search for such misguided persons, and without formality of mathematical examination, to destroy all such as were Isosceles of any degree, to scourge and imprison any regular Triangle, to cause any Square or Pentagon to be sent to the district Asylum, and to arrest any one of higher rank, sending him straightway to the Capital to be examined and judged by the Council."

"You hear your fate," said the Sphere to me, while the Council was passing for the third time the formal resolution. "Death or imprisonment awaits the Apostle of the Gospel of Three Dimensions." "Not so," replied I, "the matter is now so clear to me, the nature of real space so palpable, that methinks I could make a child understand it. Permit me but to descend at this moment and enlighten them." "Not yet," said my Guide, "the time will come for that. Meantime I must perform my mission. Stay thou there in thy place." Saying these words, he leaped with great dexterity into the sea (if I may so call it) of Flatland, right in the midst of the ring of Counsellors. "I come," cried he, "to proclaim that there is a land of Three Dimensions."

I could see many of the younger Counsellors start back in manifest horror, as the Sphere's circular section widened before them. But on a sign from the presiding Circle—who shewed not the slightest alarm or surprise—six Isosceles of a low type from six different quarters rushed upon the Sphere. "We have him," they cried; "No; yes; we have him still! he's going! he's gone!"

"My Lords," said the President to the Junior Circles of the Council, "there is not the slightest need for surprise; the secret archives, to which I alone have access, tell me that a similar occurrence happened on the last two millennial commencements. You will, of course, say nothing of these trifles outside the Cabinet."

Raising his voice, he now summoned the guards. "Arrest the policemen; gag them. You know your duty." After he had consigned to their fate the wretched policemen—ill-fated and unwilling witnesses of a State-secret which they were not to be permitted to reveal—he again addressed the Counsellors. "My Lords, the business of the Council being concluded, I have only to wish you a happy New Year." Before departing, he expressed, at some length, to the Clerk, my excellent but most unfortunate brother, his sincere regret that, in accordance with precedent and for the sake of secrecy, he must condemn him to perpetual imprisonment, but added his satisfaction that, unless some mention were made by him of that day's incident, his life would be spared.

Questions for Reflection

1. You have probably never had an experience as startling as that of the square. But has there ever been a time when you could not understand something and then some sort of decisive experience suddenly made things clear to you?
2. If you were the sphere, what sorts of arguments, analogies, or metaphors would you use to make the square understand the nature of three-dimensional solids?
3. If there is a God, would such a being be so incomprehensible that it would defy our understanding? But then would it be meaningless to even attempt to talk or think about God? If so, then would the term "God" be meaningless to us?
4. The square naively thought that all of reality consisted of only two dimensions. We, of course, know that there are three dimensions. But is it possible that there are other dimensions of which we, like the square, are unaware? Is it logically possible that there is a spiritual dimension that transcends our ordinary world of experience? Is this idea plausible?
5. Plato's Allegory of the Cave (reading 20) has a lot in common with the Flatland allegory. It might be interesting to compare them.

IS THERE EVIDENCE FOR THE EXISTENCE OF GOD?

Is it possible to provide evidence for the existence of something that we cannot directly see? It seems that scientists do this all the time. For example, we cannot literally see subatomic particles like electrons or neutrinos. Nevertheless, scientists believe these particles exist because their existence explains so much that we do see. Similarly, theists who are evidentialists (or natural theologians) claim that we can use reason and our experience of the world to prove the existence of God or least show that God's existence is highly probable. Likewise, atheists who are evidentialists agree that if there is a God, then there ought to be some evidence of this fact. However, such atheists go on to argue that the required evidence is lacking and that all arguments in support of God's existence are logically flawed. It should be noted, however, that refuting an argument in support of a conclusion does not, in itself, prove that the conclusion is false. So, to show that the proofs for God are inconclusive or invalid does not show that there is no God. Nevertheless, the atheist claims that it is irrational to continue believing in such an extraordinary being as God if this belief is not grounded in rational evidence.

Before considering the arguments for and against God's existence, a brief word about arguments in general is in order. All arguments fall into two main groups, and the arguments for the existence of God are no exception. These two kinds of arguments are *a posteriori* arguments and *a priori* arguments. We will briefly discuss each category to lay out the groundwork for the readings.

First, are *a posteriori* arguments. (*A posteriori* in Latin means "from what comes later," in other words, it refers to what comes after experience.) These arguments depend on premises that can only be known on the basis of experience. Knowledge that is based on experience is sometimes called **empirical** knowledge. The two major *a posteriori* arguments for God are the cosmological argument and the teleological argument.

A posteriori arguments typically have the following form:

1. The world has feature X.

2. If the world has feature X, then there is a God.

3. Therefore, there is a God

Premise 1 is an empirical premise. In the cosmological argument, this premise is that the world is dependent and cannot explain itself. The teleological argument (also called "the design argument") begins with the observation that there is an intricate order to the world and from that concludes that the world is the product of an intelligent cosmic designer.

The second category of arguments are *a priori* arguments. (*A priori* in Latin means "from what is prior," referring to what is prior to experience.) An *a priori* argument is based on reason and does not require empirical premises. Let's take an example from the realm of mathematics. In Euclidean geometry we begin with axioms that are considered to be self-evident and from these we deduce a number of theorems. In this way, we learn the essential truths about, say, triangles by reasoning about them *a priori* and not by observing or measuring dozens of triangles. In a later section, we will look at one of the most famous *a priori* arguments in philosophy, the ontological argument for God.

The Cosmological Argument

While there are many versions of the cosmological argument, they all begin with the fact that the universe is not self-explanatory and argue from there that the cosmos depends upon a self-sufficient cause outside of itself. Hence, the cosmological argument seeks to provide an answer to the question, Why is there something rather than nothing?

One formulation of the cosmological argument, similar to the one that Thomas Aquinas uses, goes like this:

1. The world contains things that were brought into existence by some cause.

2. Everything that exists is either uncaused or caused to exist by another.

3. There cannot be an infinite regress of causes.

4. So there must be an uncaused first cause.

5. An uncaused first cause is (in part) what we mean by God.

6. Therefore, God exists.

Almost no one would object to the first premise. Every moment of our life we are confronted with examples of things that came into existence as a result of previous causes. The second premise is a crucial one. It claims that something is either the sort of thing that requires no cause or its cause lies outside of itself. Two options are ruled out by this premise. First, it implies that it is impossible for something to cause itself to come into existence. As Aquinas points out in the first reading, for something to cause its own existence, it would have to exist prior to its own existence in order to bring itself into being, and this is absurd. Second, this premise denies that things that begin to exist can simply pop into existence. If something did not always exist, there had to be something that changed its status from that of a nonexisting, merely possible thing to that of an existing thing. Hence, the only two options for something that really exists is that its existence does not depend on anything outside itself or its existence is dependent. Notice that the argument never says that "*everything* has a cause for its existence," for this would imply that God's existence had a cause.

What is the basis for the claim, "Everything that exists is either uncaused or caused to exist by another"? Many of the philosophers in the seventeenth and eighteenth centuries believed it followed from the **principle of sufficient reason.** This principle states that everything that exists must have a reason that explains why it exists and why it has the properties it does. This reason could be that the being in question is uncaused, that is, it is self-sufficient and does not depend on anything outside itself. Or, it could be that the being in question is caused by something else that provides a sufficient explanation why it exists and exists just the way it does and not otherwise. In the second reading, Richard Taylor will make explicit use of this principle. Go back over the premises of the cosmological argument discussed earlier and decide which premise you think is the weakest or the most controversial. In the third reading William Rowe will argue that it is the second premise which is the questionable one, for he thinks that there is no way to know whether or not the principle of sufficient reason is true.

 THOMAS AQUINAS

Five Arguments for God

One of the foremost defenders of the cosmological argument was Thomas Aquinas (1225–1274). He was born into a noble family who resided in southern Italy about halfway between Rome and Naples. His family had always dreamed that Thomas would rise to a position of ecclesiastical authority where he would be politically influential and

From Thomas Aquinas, *Summa Theologica,* in *Basic Writings of Saint Thomas Aquinas,* vol. 1, ed. Anton C. Pegis (New York: Random House, 1945), part I, question 2, article 3.

even wealthy. While at the University of Naples, however, Thomas chose a different path for his life by joining the newly formed Dominican Order. The Dominicans did not aspire to be influential administrators but were humble and impoverished preachers and scholars. After earning the highest degree in theology, Aquinas spent the remainder of his life lecturing and writing while alternately residing in Paris and Italy. He died at age 49, while on his way to carry out a diplomatic mission.

Aquinas was an astoundingly prolific writer, for his works fill some 25 volumes. He is said to have kept four secretaries busy at once, dictating different manuscripts in progress to them that they would then transcribe. Although his philosophy is considered the official model for Catholic thought, he has influenced Protestant philosophers and other religious thinkers as well.

Aquinas has given us not one, but five arguments for God (or five "ways"to prove God). The first three are different versions of the cosmological argument. The first argument observes that there is motion in the world. (By "motion" Aquinas means any kind of change, such as fire causing wood to become hot.) Everything that is in motion (or changing), he argues, must be moved by something else. Ultimately, Aquinas concludes, there must be a first mover that is the cause of all other motions, but that is not itself caused by anything. The second argument observes that the world consists of causes and effects. However, this series cannot go on infinitely, so there must be a first cause. The third argument takes as its basis the fact that the world consists of contingent or dependent beings. In the final analysis, Aquinas argues, there must be a being that is not dependent but that is the cause of all things that are. The fourth argument observes that different things have different degrees of value or perfection. Therefore, it concludes, a supremely perfect being must exist as the ultimate source of all values. The fifth way argues from the evidence of design in the world. It is the predecessor of William Paley's teleological argument covered in the next section.

Reading Questions

1. After reading Aquinas's first argument (the "first way") think of an example of something moving or changing. Now think of what caused its motion. Can this series of causes go on forever? Why does Aquinas think not?

2. See if you can uncover the assumptions Aquinas makes in his second argument. Do you think they are plausible? Why?

3. What does Aquinas mean by "contingent" in his third argument? Why does he believe there must be something that is necessary?

4. Summarize the main point in each of the first three arguments as though you were explaining them to a friend.

The existence of God can be proved in five ways.

The first and more manifest way is the argument from motion. It is certain, and evident to our senses, that in the world some things are in motion. Now whatever is moved is moved by another, for nothing can be moved except it is in potentiality to that towards which it is moved; whereas a thing moves inasmuch as it is in act. For motion is nothing else than the reduction of something from potentiality to actuality. But nothing can be reduced from potentiality to actuality, except by something in a state of actuality. Thus that which is actually hot, as fire, makes wood, which is potentially hot, to be actually hot, and thereby moves and changes it. Now it is not possible that the same thing should be at once in actuality and potentiality in the same respect, but only in different respects. For what is actually hot cannot simultaneously be potentially hot; but it is simultaneously potentially cold. It is therefore impossible that in the same respect and in the same way a thing should be both mover and moved, *i.e.,* that it should move itself. Therefore, whatever is moved must be moved by another. If that by which it is moved be itself moved, then this also must needs be moved by another, and that by another again. But this cannot go on to infinity, because then there would be no first mover, and, consequently, no other mover, seeing that subsequent movers move only inasmuch as they are moved by the first mover; as the staff moves only because it is moved by the hand. Therefore it is necessary to arrive at a first mover, moved by no other; and this everyone understands to be God.

The second way is from the nature of efficient cause. In the world of sensible things we find there is an order of efficient causes. There is no case known (neither is it, indeed, possible) in which a thing is found to be the efficient cause of itself; for so it would be prior to itself, which is impossible. Now in efficient causes it is not possible to go on to infinity, because in all efficient causes following in order, the first is the cause of the intermediate cause, and the intermediate is the cause of the ultimate cause, whether the intermediate cause be several, or one only. Now to take away the cause is to take away the effect. Therefore, if there be no first cause among efficient causes, there will be no ultimate, nor any intermediate, cause. But if in efficient causes it is possible to go on to infinity, there will be no first efficient cause, neither will there be an ultimate effect, nor any intermediate efficient causes; all of which is plainly false. Therefore it is necessary to admit a first efficient cause, to which everyone gives the name of God.

The third way is taken from possibility and necessity, and runs thus. We find in nature things that

are possible to be and not to be, since they are found to be generated, and to be corrupted, and consequently, it is possible for them to be and not to be. But it is impossible for these always to exist, for that which can not-be at some time is not. Therefore, if everything can not-be, then at one time there was nothing in existence. Now if this were true, even now there would be nothing in existence, because that which does not exist begins to exist only through something already existing. Therefore, if at one time nothing was in existence, it would have been impossible for anything to have begun to exist; and thus even now nothing would be in existence—which is absurd. Therefore, not all beings are merely possible, but there must exist something the existence of which is necessary. But every necessary thing either has its necessity caused by another, or not. Now it is impossible to go on to infinity in necessary things which have their necessity caused by another, as has been already proved in regard to efficient causes. Therefore we cannot but admit the existence of some being having of itself its own necessity, and not receiving it from another, but rather causing in others their necessity. This all men speak of as God.

The fourth way is taken from the gradation to be found in things. Among beings there are some more and some less good, true, noble, and the like. But *more* and *less* are predicated of different things according as they resemble in their different ways something which is the maximum, as a thing is said to be hotter according as it more nearly resembles that which is hottest; so that there is something which is truest, something best, something noblest, and, consequently, something which is most being, for those things that are greatest in truth are greatest in being. . . . Now the maximum in any genus is the cause of all in that genus, as fire, which is the maximum of heat, is the cause of all hot things. . . . Therefore there must also be something which is to all beings the cause of their being, goodness, and every other perfection; and this we call God.

The fifth way is taken from the governance of the world. We see that things which lack knowledge, such as natural bodies, act for an end, and this is evident from their acting always, or nearly

always, in the same way, so as to obtain the best re- knowledge and intelligence; as the arrow is di-
sult. Hence it is plain that they achieve their end, rected by the archer. Therefore some intelligent
not fortuitously, but designedly. Now whatever being exists by whom all natural things are directed
lacks knowledge cannot move towards an end, un- to their end; and this being we call God.
less it be directed by some being endowed with

Questions for Reflection

1. Does it make sense to suppose that the series of causes producing a present event
   could go on infinitely, never ending in a first cause?
2. Does it make sense to speak of an uncaused being, such as God?
3. Which of the two ideas in questions 1 and 2 is the most implausible. Why?
4. Which of the following statements comes closest to your own position? (a) Aquinas
   has demonstrated the existence of God. (b) Aquinas has at least shown the existence
   of God to be probable. (c) Aquinas's arguments might not completely convince an
   unbeliever, but he has at least shown that the belief in God is rational. (d) Aquinas's
   arguments are really not very strong at all. What reasons would you give in support
   of the position you chose out of the four alternatives?

R I C H A R D   T A Y L O R

Why the World Needs an Explanation

In the following passage, the contemporary American philosopher Richard Taylor
(1919-) develops a contemporary version of the argument from contingency. Richard
Taylor was a professor of philosophy at the University of Rochester and is now retired.
This passage is taken from his best-selling book *Metaphysics,* which is now in its fourth
edition.

Reading Questions

1. What is Taylor's point concerning the mysterious, translucent ball?
2. How does Taylor define and defend the principle of sufficient reason?
3. Why does he claim that if we apply the principle of sufficient reason to individual
   things (such as the ball), we must apply it to the world itself?
4. It is commonly thought that the notion of divine creation refers to something that
   happened at a particular point in time. However, what is Taylor's notion of creation?
   How does he use the analogy concerning the flame and the beams of light to make
   this point?

From Richard Taylor, *Metaphysics,* 4th ed. (Englewood Cliffs, NJ: Prentice-Hall, 1992).

5. Even if the world had *always* existed, why does Taylor think that this fact does not eliminate the need for a God?
6. What does Taylor mean when he says God is a "necessary being"? What argument does Taylor give to convince us that the notion of a necessary being is a meaningful one?
7. What does Taylor mean when he says God is a "first cause"?

THE PRINCIPLE OF SUFFICIENT REASON

Suppose you were strolling in the woods and, in addition to the sticks, stones, and other accustomed litter of the forest floor, you one day came upon some quite unaccustomed object, something not quite like what you had ever seen before and would never expect to find in such a place. Suppose, for example, that it is a large ball, about your own height, perfectly smooth and translucent. You would deem this puzzling and mysterious, certainly, but if one considers the matter, it is no more inherently mysterious that such a thing should exist than that anything else should exist. If you were quite accustomed to finding such objects of various sizes around you most of the time, but had never seen an ordinary rock, then upon finding a large rock in the woods one day you would be just as puzzled and mystified. This illustrates the fact that something that is mysterious ceases to seem so simply by its accustomed presence. It is strange indeed, for example, that a world such as ours should exist; yet few people are very often struck by this strangeness but simply take it for granted.

Suppose, then, that you have found this translucent ball and are mystified by it. Now whatever else you might wonder about it, there is one thing you would hardly question; namely, that it did not appear there all by itself, that it owes its existence to something. You might not have the remotest idea whence and how it came to be there, but you would hardly doubt that there was an explanation. The idea that it might have come from nothing at all, that it might exist without there being any explanation of its existence, is one that few people would consider worthy of entertaining.

This illustrates a metaphysical belief that seems to be almost a part of reason itself, even though few ever think upon it; the belief, namely, that there is some explanation for the existence of anything whatever, some reason why it should exist rather than not. The sheer nonexistence of anything, which is not to be confused with the passing out of existence of something, never requires a reason; but existence does. That there should never have been any such ball in the forest does not require any explanation or reason, but that there should ever be such a ball does. If one were to look upon a barren plain and ask why there is not and never has been any large translucent ball there, the natural response would be to ask why there should be; but if one finds such a ball, and wonders why it is there, it is not quite so natural to ask why it should *not* be—as though existence should simply be taken for granted. That anything should not exist, then, and that, for instance, no such ball should exist in the forest, or that there should be no forest for it to occupy, or no continent containing a forest, or no Earth, nor any world at all, do not seem to be things for which there needs to be any explanation or reason; but that such things should be *does* seem to require a reason.

The principle involved here has been called the principle of sufficient reason. Actually, it is a very general principle, and it is best expressed by saying that, in the case of any positive truth, there is some sufficient reason for it, something that, in this sense, makes it true—in short, that there is some sort of explanation, known or unknown, for everything.

Now, some truths depend on something else, and are accordingly called *contingent,* while others depend only upon themselves, that is, are true by their very natures and are accordingly called *necessary*. There is, for example, a reason why the stone on my window sill is warm; namely, that the sun is shining upon it. This happens to be true, but not by its very nature. Hence, it is contingent, and depends upon something other than itself. It is also true that all the points of a circle are equidistant from the center, but this truth depends upon nothing but itself. No matter what happens, nothing can make it false. Similarly, it is a truth, and a necessary one, that if the stone on my window sill is a body, as it is, then it has a form, because this fact depends upon nothing but itself for its confirmation. Untruths are also, of course, either contingent or necessary, it being contingently false, for example, that the stone on my window sill is cold, and necessarily false that it is both a body and formless, because this is by its very nature impossible.

The principle of sufficient reason can be illustrated in various ways, as we have done, and if one thinks about it, he is apt to find that he presupposes it in his thinking about reality, but it cannot be proved. It does not appear to be itself a necessary truth, and at the same time it would be most odd to say it is contingent. If one were to try proving it, he would sooner or later have to appeal to considerations that are less plausible than the principle itself. Indeed, it is hard to see how one could even make an argument for it without already assuming it. For this reason it might properly be called a presupposition of reason itself. One can deny that it is true, without embarrassment or fear of refutation, but one is then apt to find that what he is denying is not really what the principle asserts. We shall, then, treat it here as a datum—not something that is provably true, but as something that people, whether they ever reflect upon it or not, seem more or less to presuppose.

THE EXISTENCE OF A WORLD

It happens to be true that something exists, that there is, for example, a world, and although no one ever seriously supposes that this might not be so, that there might exist nothing at all, there still seems to be nothing the least necessary in this, considering it just by itself. That no world should ever exist at all is perfectly comprehensible and seems to express not the slightest absurdity. Considering any particular item in the world it seems not at all necessary that the totality of these things, or any totality of things, should ever exist.

From the principle of sufficient reason it follows, of course, that there must be a reason not only for the existence of everything in the world but for the world itself, meaning by "the world" simply everything that ever does exist, except God, in case there is a god. This principle does not imply that there must be some purpose or goal for everything, or for the totality of all things; for explanations need not be, and in fact seldom are, teleological or purposeful. All the principle requires is that there be some sort of reason for everything. And it would certainly be odd to maintain that everything in the world owes its existence to something, that nothing in the world is either purely accidental, or such that it just bestows its own being upon itself, and then to deny this of the world itself. One can indeed *say* that the world is in some sense a pure accident, that there simply is no reason at all why this or any world should exist, and one can equally say that the world exists by its very nature, or is an inherently necessary being. But it is at least very odd and arbitrary to deny of this existing world the need for any sufficient reason, whether independent of itself or not, while presupposing that there is a reason for every other thing, that ever exists.

Consider again the strange ball that we imagine has been found in the forest. Now, we can hardly doubt that there must be an explanation for the existence of such a thing, though we may have no notion what that explanation is. It is not, moreover, the fact of its having been found in the forest rather than elsewhere that renders an explanation necessary. It matters not in the least where it happens to be, for our question is not how it happens to be *there* but how it happens to be at all. If we in our imagination annihilate the forest, leaving only this ball in an open field, our conviction that it is a contingent thing and owes its existence to something other than itself is not reduced in the least. If we now imagine the field to be annihilated, and in fact everything else as well to vanish into nothingness, leaving only this ball to constitute the entire physical universe, then we cannot for a moment suppose that its existence has thereby been explained, or the need for any explanation eliminated, or that its existence is suddenly rendered self-explanatory. If we now carry this thought one step further and suppose that no other reality ever has existed or ever will exist, that this ball forever constitutes the entire physical universe, then we must still insist on there being some reason independent of itself why it should exist rather than not. If there must be a reason for the existence of any particular thing, then the necessity of such a reason is not eliminated by the mere supposition that certain other things do *not* exist. And again, it matters not at all what the thing in question is, whether it be large and complex, such as the world we actually find ourselves in, or whether it be something small, simple, and insignificant, such as a ball, a bacterium, or the merest grain of sand. We do not avoid the necessity of a reason for the existence of something merely by describing it in this way or that. And it would, in any event, seem quite plainly absurd to say that if the world were composed entirely of a single ball about six feet in diameter, or of a single grain of sand, then it would be contingent and there would have to be some explanation other than itself why such a thing exists, but that, since the actual world is vastly more complex than this, there is no need for an explanation of its existence, independent of itself.

BEGINNINGLESS EXISTENCE

It should now be noted that it is no answer to the question, why a thing exists, to state *how long* it has existed. A geologist does not suppose that she has explained why there should be rivers and mountains merely by pointing out that they are old. Similarly, if one were to ask, concerning the ball of which we have spoken, for some sufficient reason for its being, he would not receive any answer upon being told that it had been there since yesterday. Nor would it be any better answer to say that it had existed since before anyone could remember, or

even that it had always existed; for the question was not one concerning its age but its existence. If, to be sure, one were to ask where a given thing came from, or how it came into being, then upon learning that it had always existed he would learn that it never really *came* into being at all; but he could still reasonably wonder why it should exist at all. If, accordingly, the world—that is, the totality of all things excepting God, in case there is a god—had really no beginning at all, but has always existed in some form or other, then there is clearly no answer to the question, where it came from and when it did not, on this supposition, *come* from anything at all, at any time. But still, it can be asked why there is a world, why indeed there is a beginningless world, why there should have perhaps always been something rather than nothing. And, if the principle of sufficient reason is a good principle, there must be an answer to that question, an answer that is by no means supplied by giving the world an age, or even an infinite age.

CREATION

This brings out an important point with respect to the concept of creation that is often misunderstood, particularly by those whose thinking has been influenced by Christian ideas. People tend to think that creation—for example, the creation of the world by God—*means* creation *in time,* from which it of course logically follows that if the world had no beginning in time, then it cannot be the creation of God. This, however, is erroneous, for creation means essentially *dependence,* even in Christian theology. If one thing is the creation of another, then it depends for its existence on that other, and this is perfectly consistent with saying that both are eternal, that neither ever came into being, and hence, that neither was ever created at any point of time. Perhaps an analogy will help convey this point. Consider, then, a flame that is casting beams of light. Now, there seems to be a clear sense in which the beams of light are dependent for their existence upon the flame, which is their source, while the flame, on the other hand, is not similarly dependent for its existence upon them. The beams of light arise from the flame, but the flame does not arise from them. In this sense, they are the creation of the flame; they derive their existence from it. And none of this has any reference to time; the relationship of dependence in such a case would not be altered in the slightest if we supposed that the flame, and with it the beams of light, had always existed, that neither had ever *come* into being.

Now if the world is the creation of God, its relationship to God should be thought of in this fashion; namely, that the world depends for its existence upon God, and could not exist independently of God. If God is eternal, as those who believe in God generally assume, then the world may (though it need not) be eternal too, without that altering in the least its dependence upon God for its existence, and hence without altering its being the creation of God. The supposition of God's eternality, on the other hand, does not by itself imply that the world is eternal too; for there is not the least reason why something of finite duration might not depend for its existence upon something of infinite duration—though the reverse is, of course, impossible.

GOD

If we think of God as "the creator of heaven and earth," and if we consider heaven and earth to include everything that exists except God, then we appear to have, in the foregoing considerations, fairly strong reasons for asserting that God, as so conceived, exists. Now of course most people have much more in mind than this when they think of God, for religions have ascribed to God ever so many attributes that are not at all implied by describing him merely as the creator of the world; but that is not relevant here. Most religious persons do, in any case, think of God as being at least the creator, as that being upon which everything ultimately depends, no matter what else they may say about Him in addition. It is, in fact, the first item in the creeds of Christianity that God is the "creator of heaven and earth." And, it seems, there are good

metaphysical reasons, as distinguished from the persuasions of faith, for thinking that such a creative being exists.

If, as seems clearly implied by the principle of sufficient reason, there must be a reason for the existence of heaven and earth—*i.e.,* for the world—then that reason must be found either in the world itself, or outside it, in something that is literally supranatural, or outside heaven and earth. Now if we suppose that the world—*i.e.,* the totality of all things except God—contains within itself the reason for its existence, we are supposing that it exists by its very nature, that is, that it is a necessary being. In that case there would, of course, be no reason for saying that it must depend upon God or anything else for its existence; for if it exists by its very nature, then it depends upon nothing but itself, much as the sun depends upon nothing but itself for its heat. This, however, is implausible, for we find nothing about the world or anything in it to suggest that it exists by its own nature, and we do find, on the contrary, ever so many things to suggest that it does not. For in the first place, anything that exists by its very nature must necessarily be eternal and indestructible. It would be a self-contradiction to say of anything that it exists by its own nature, or is a necessarily existing thing, and at the same time to say that it comes into being or passes away, or that it ever could come into being or pass away. Nothing about the world seems at all like this, for concerning anything in the world, we can perfectly easily think of it as being annihilated, or as never having existed in the first place, without there being the slightest hint of any absurdity in such a supposition. Some of the things in the universe are, to be sure, very old; the moon, for example, or the stars and the planets. It is even possible to imagine that they have always existed. Yet it seems quite impossible to suppose that they owe their existence to nothing but themselves, that they bestow existence upon themselves by their very natures, or that they are in themselves things of such nature that it would be impossible for them not to exist. Even if we suppose that something, such as the sun, for instance, has existed forever, and will never cease, still we cannot conclude just from this that it exists by its own nature. If, as is of course very doubtful, the sun has existed forever and will never cease, then it is possible that its heat and light have also existed forever and will never cease; but that would not show that the heat and light of the sun exist by their own natures. They are obviously contingent and depend on the sun for their existence, whether they are beginningless and everlasting or not.

There seems to be nothing in the world, then, concerning which it is at all plausible to suppose that it exists by its own nature, or contains within itself the reason for its existence. In fact, everything in the world appears to be quite plainly the opposite, namely, something that not only need not exist, but at some time or other, past or future or both, does not in fact exist. Everything in the world seems to have a finite duration, whether long or short. Most things, such as ourselves, exist only for a short while; they come into being, then soon cease. Other things, like the heavenly bodies, last longer, but they are still corruptible, and from all that we can gather about them, they too seem destined eventually to perish. We arrive at the conclusion, then, that although the world may contain some things that have always existed and are destined never to perish, it is nevertheless doubtful that it contains any such thing, and, in any case, everything in the world is capable of perishing, and nothing in it, however long it may already have existed and however long it may yet remain, exists by its own nature but depends instead upon something else.

Although this might be true of everything in the world, is it necessarily true of the world itself? That is, if we grant, as we seem forced to, that nothing in the world exists by its own nature, that everything in the world is contingent and perishable, must we also say that the world itself, or the totality of all these perishable things, is also contingent and perishable? Logically, we are not forced to, for it is logically possible that the totality of all perishable things might itself be imperishable, and hence, that the world might exist by its own nature, even though it is composed exclusively of things that are contingent. It is not logically necessary that a total-

ity should share the defects of its members. For example, even though every person is mortal, it does not follow from this that the human race, or the totality of all people, is also mortal; for it is possible that there will always be human beings, even though there are no human beings who will always exist. Similarly, it is possible that the world is in itself a necessary thing, even though it is composed entirely of things that are contingent.

This is logically possible, but it is not plausible. For we find nothing whatever about the world, any more than in its parts, to suggest that it exists by its own nature. Concerning anything in the world, we have not the slightest difficulty in supposing that it should perish, or even that it should never have existed in the first place. We have almost as little difficulty in supposing this of the world itself. It might be somewhat hard to think of everything as utterly perishing and leaving no trace whatever of its ever having been, but there seems to be not the slightest difficulty in imagining that the world should never have existed in the first place. We can, for instance, perfectly easily suppose that nothing in the world had ever existed except, let us suppose, a single grain of sand, and we can thus suppose that this grain of sand has forever constituted the whole universe. Now if we consider just this grain of sand, it is quite impossible for us to suppose that it exists by its very nature and could never have failed to exist. It clearly depends for its existence upon something other than itself, if it depends on anything at all. The same will be true if we consider the world to consist not of one grain of sand but of two, or of a million, or, as we in fact find, of a vast number of stars and planets and all their minuter parts.

It would seem, then, that the world, in case it happens to exist at all—and this is quite beyond doubt—is contingent and thus dependent upon something other than itself for its existence, if it depends upon anything at all. And it must depend upon something, for otherwise there could be no reason why it exists in the first place. Now, that upon which the world depends must be something that either exists by its own nature or does not. If it does not exist by its own nature, then it, in turn, depends for its existence upon something else, and so on. Now then, we can say either of two things; namely, (1) that the world depends for its existence upon something else, which in turn depends on still another thing, this depending upon still another, *ad infinitum;* or (2) that the world derives its existence from something that exists by its own nature and that is accordingly eternal and imperishable, and is the creator of heaven and earth. The first of these alternatives, however, is impossible, for it does not render a sufficient reason why anything should exist in the first place. Instead of supplying a reason why any world should exist, it repeatedly begs off giving a reason. It explains what is dependent and perishable in terms of what is itself dependent and perishable, leaving us still without a reason why perishable things should exist at all, which is what we are seeking. Ultimately, then, it would seem that the world, or the totality of contingent or perishable things, in case it exists at all, must depend upon something that is necessary and imperishable, and that accordingly exists, not in dependence upon something else, but by its own nature.

"SELF-CAUSED"

What has been said thus far gives some intimation of what meaning should be attached to the concept of a self-caused being, a concept that is quite generally misunderstood, sometimes even by scholars. To say that something—God, for example—is self-caused, or is the cause of its own existence, does not mean that this being brings itself into existence, which is a perfectly absurd idea. Nothing can *bring* itself into existence. To say that something is self-caused (*causa sui*) means only that it exists, not contingently or in dependence upon something else but by its own nature, which is only to say that it is a being which is such that it can neither come into being nor perish. Now, whether in fact such a being exists or not, there is in any case no absurdity in the idea. We have found, in fact, that the principle of sufficient reason seems to point to the existence of such a being, as that upon which the world, with everything in it, must ultimately depend for its existence.

"NECESSARY BEING"

A being that depends for its existence upon nothing but itself and is in this sense self-caused, can equally be described as a necessary being; that is to say, a being that is not contingent, and hence not perishable. For in the case of anything that exists by its own nature and is dependent upon nothing else, it is impossible that it should not exist, which is equivalent to saying that it is necessary. Many persons have professed to find the gravest difficulties in this concept, too, but that is partly because it has been confused with other notions. If it makes sense to speak of anything as an impossible being, or something that by its very nature does not exist, then it is hard to see why the idea of a necessary being, or something that in its very nature exists, should not be just as comprehensible. And of course, we have not the slightest difficulty in speaking of something, such as a square circle or a formless body, as an *impossible* being. And if it makes sense to speak of something as being perishable, contingent, and dependent upon something other than itself for its existence, as it surely does, then there seems to be no difficulty in thinking of something as imperishable and dependent upon nothing other than itself for its existence.

"FIRST CAUSE"

From these considerations we can see also what is properly meant by a "first cause," an appellative that has often been applied to God by theologians and that many persons have deemed an absurdity. It is a common criticism of this notion to say that there need not be any first cause, because the series of causes and effects that constitute the history of the universe might be infinite or beginningless and must, in fact, be infinite in case the universe itself had no beginning in time. This criticism, however, reflects a total misconception of what is meant by a first cause. *First* here does not mean first in time, and when God is spoken of as a first cause He is not being described as a being that, at some time in the remote past, *started* everything. To describe God as a first cause is only to say that He is literally a *pri-*

mary rather than a secondary cause, an ultimate rather than a derived cause, or a being upon which all other things, heaven and earth, ultimately depend for their existence. It is, in short, only to say that God is the creator, in the sense of creation previously explained. Now this, of course, is perfectly consistent with saying that the world is eternal or beginningless. As we have seen, one gives no reason for the existence of a world merely by giving it an age, even if it is supposed to have an infinite age. To use a helpful analogy, we can say that the sun is the first cause of daylight and, for that matter, of the moonlight of the night as well, which means only that daylight and moonlight ultimately depend upon the sun for their existence. The moon, on the other hand, is only a secondary or derivative cause of its light. This light would be no less dependent upon the sun if we affirmed that it had no beginning, for an ageless and beginningless light requires a source no less than an ephemeral one. If we supposed that the sun has always existed, and with it its light, then we would have to say that the sun has always been the first—*i.e.*, the primary or ultimate—cause of its light. Such is precisely the manner in which God should be thought of, and is by theologians often thought of, as the first cause of heaven and earth.

Questions for Reflection

1. Do you think Taylor's argument is convincing? Why or why not?
2. Is it implausible to suppose that the world depends on nothing but itself, as Taylor claims?
3. In mathematics and logic, we say that a theorem or a conclusion necessarily follows from the axioms or premises. Here we are simply saying that a series of *ideas* are necessarily related. But does it make sense to apply the notion of necessity to something's *existence?* Is the concept of a necessarily existing being a plausible notion?
4. Even if we were to agree with Taylor's argument that there must be a necessary being that caused the world, does that imply that this being is a personal God who is intelligent, loving, and all-powerful? Couldn't there be a necessary being that caused the world but which is impersonal like gravity or magnetism?

WILLIAM ROWE

A Critique of the Cosmological Argument

William Rowe (1931–) is a professor of philosophy at Purdue University and has written a number of books and articles on the philosophy of religion. The following selection is from his book *Philosophy of Religion: An Introduction.* After setting out the

---

From William L. Rowe, *Philosophy of Religion: An Introduction,* 3rd ed. (Belmont, CA: Wadsworth, 2001).

cosmological argument, Rowe sympathetically argues against some of its traditional criticisms. He concludes that if the principle of sufficient reason is true, then the cosmological argument is sound. In the final section, however, he raises the question of how we could know that this principle is true.

Reading Questions

1. What does Rowe mean by a "dependent being"? What does he mean by a "self-existent being"?
2. In Rowe's formulation, what is the first premise of the cosmological argument? What is it that makes this first premise both significant and controversial?
3. What are the two parts of the Principle of Sufficient Reason (PSR)?
4. What is the second premise of Rowe's version of the cosmological argument?
5. Suppose we accept the thesis that the causal series of dependent beings going back into the past is infinite. According to the eighteenth-century proponents of the cosmological argument, what is it that still needs to be explained?
6. What are the four criticisms of the cosmological argument?
7. How does Rowe respond to them?
8. What problems does Rowe raise with respect to the two ways of justifying the Principle of Sufficient Reason?

Before we state the Cosmological Argument itself, we shall consider some rather general points about the argument. Historically, it can be traced to the writings of the Greek philosophers, Plato and Aristotle, but the major developments in the argument took place in the thirteenth and in the eighteenth centuries. In the thirteenth century St. Thomas Aquinas put forth five distinct arguments for the existence of God, and of these, the first three are versions of the Cosmological Argument.[1] In the first of these he started from the fact that there are things in the world undergoing change and reasoned to the conclusion that there must be some ultimate cause of change that is itself unchanging. In the second he started from the fact that there are things in the world that clearly are caused to exist by other things and reasoned to the conclusion that there must be some ultimate cause of existence whose own existence is itself uncaused. And in the third argument he started from the fact that there are things in the world which need not have existed at all, things which do exist but which we can easily imagine might not, and reasoned to the conclusion that there must be some being that had to be, that exists and could not have failed to exist. Now it might be objected that even if Aquinas' arguments do prove beyond doubt the existence of an unchanging changer, an uncaused cause, and a being that could not have failed to exist, the arguments fail to prove the existence of the theistic God. For the theistic God, as we saw, is supremely good, omnipotent, omniscient, and creator of but separate from and independent of the world. How do we know, for example, that the unchanging changer isn't evil or slightly ignorant? The answer to this objection is that the Cosmological Argument has two parts. In the first part the effort is to prove the existence of a special sort of being, for example, a being that could not have failed to exist, or a being that causes change in other things but is itself unchanging. In the second part of the argument the effort is to prove that the special sort of being whose existence has been established in the first part has, and must have, the features—perfect goodness, omnipotence, omniscience, and so on—which go together to make up the theistic idea of God. What this means, then, is that Aquinas' three arguments are different versions of only the first part of the Cosmological Argument. Indeed, in later sections of his *Summa Theologica* Aquinas undertakes to show that the unchanging changer, the uncaused cause of existence, and the being which had to exist are one and the same being and that this single being has all of the attributes of the theistic God.

We noted above that a second major development in the Cosmological Argument took place in the eighteenth century, a development reflected in the writings of the German philosopher, Gottfried Leibniz (1646–1716), and especially in the writings of the English theologian and philosopher, Samuel Clarke (1675–1729). In 1704 Clarke gave a series of lectures, later published under the title *A Demonstration of the Being and Attributes of God*. These lectures constitute, perhaps, the most complete, forceful, and cogent presentation of the Cosmological Argument we possess. The lectures were read by the major skeptical philosopher of the century, David Hume (1711–1776), and in his brilliant attack on the attempt to justify religion in the court of reason, his *Dialogues Concerning Natural Religion*, Hume advanced several penetrating criticisms of Clarke's arguments, criticisms which have persuaded many philosophers in the modern period to reject the Cosmological Argument. In our study of the argument we shall concentrate our attention largely on its eighteenth century form and try to assess its strengths and weaknesses in the light of the criticisms which Hume and others have advanced against it.

The first part of the eighteenth-century form of the Cosmological Argument seeks to establish the existence of a self-existent being. The second part of the argument attempts to prove that the self-existent being is the theistic God, that is, has the features which we have noted to be basic elements in the theistic idea of God. We shall consider mainly the first part of the argument, for it is against the first part that philosophers from Hume to Bertrand Russell have advanced very important objections.

In stating the first part of the Cosmological Argument we shall make use of two important concepts, the concept of a *dependent being* and the concept of a *self-existent being*. By a *dependent being* we mean *a being whose existence is accounted for by the causal activity of other things*. Recalling, Anselm's division into the three cases [given in a previous chapter]: "explained by another," "explained by nothing," and "explained by itself," it's clear that a dependent being is a being whose existence is explained by another. By *a self-existent being* we mean *a being whose existence is accounted for by its own nature*. This idea . . . is an essential element in the theistic concept of God. Again, in terms of Anselm's three cases, a self-existent being is a being whose existence is explained by itself. Armed with these two concepts, the concept of a dependent being and the concept of a self-existent being, we can now state the first part of the Cosmological Argument.

1. Every being (that exists or ever did exist) is either a dependent being or a self-existent being.

2. Not every being can be a dependent being.

Therefore,

3. There exists a self-existent being.

DEDUCTIVE VALIDITY

Before we look critically at each of the premises of this argument, we should note that this argument is, to use an expression from the logician's vocabulary, *deductively valid*. To find out whether an argument is deductively valid, we need only ask the question: If its premises were true, would its conclusion have to be true? If the answer is yes, the argument is deductively valid. If the answer is no, the argument is deductively invalid. Notice that the question of the validity of an argument is entirely different from the question of whether its premises are in fact true. The following argument is made up entirely of false statements, but it is deductively valid.

1. Babe Ruth is the president of the United States.

2. The president of the United States is from Indiana.

Therefore,

3. Babe Ruth is from Indiana.

The argument is deductively valid because even though its premises are false, if they were true its conclusion would have to be true. Even God, Aquinas would say, cannot bring it about that the premises of this argument are true and yet its conclusion is false, for God's power extends only to what is possible, and it is an absolute impossibility that Babe Ruth be the president, the president be from Indiana, and yet Babe Ruth not be from Indiana.

The Cosmological Argument (that is, its first part) is a deductively valid argument. If its premises are or were true, its conclusion would have to be true. It's clear from our example about Babe Ruth, however, that the fact that an argument is deductively valid is insufficient to establish the truth of its conclusion. What else is required? Clearly that we know or have rational grounds for believing that the premises are true. If we know that the Cosmological Argument is deductively valid, and can establish that its premises are true, we shall thereby have proved that its conclusion is true. Are, then, the premises of the Cosmological Argument true? To this more difficult question we must now turn.

PSR AND THE FIRST PREMISE

At first glance the first premise might appear to be an obvious or even trivial truth. But it is neither obvious nor trivial. And if it appears to be obvious or trivial, we must be confusing the idea of a self-existent being with the idea of a being that is not a dependent being. Clearly, it is true that any being is either a dependent being (explained by other things) or it is not a dependent being (not explained by other things). But what our premise says is that any being is either a dependent being (explained by other things) or it is a self-existent being

(explained by itself). Consider again Anselm's three cases.

a. explained by another

b. explained by nothing

c. explained by itself

What our first premise asserts is that each being that exists (or ever did exist) is either of sort *a* or of sort *c*. It denies that any being is of sort *b*. And it is this denial that makes the first premise both significant and controversial. The obvious truth we must not confuse it with is the truth that any being is either of sort *a* or not of sort *a*. While this is true it is neither very significant nor controversial.

Earlier we saw that Anselm accepted as a basic principle that whatever exists has an explanation of its existence. Since this basic principle denies that any thing of sort *b* exists or ever did exist, it's clear that Anselm would believe the first premise of our Cosmological Argument. The eighteenth-century proponents of the argument also were convinced of the truth of the basic principle we attributed to Anselm. And because they were convinced of its truth, they readily accepted the first premise of the Cosmological Argument. But by the eighteenth century, Anselm's basic principle had been more fully elaborated and had received a name, the *Principle of Sufficient Reason*. Since this principle (PSR, as we shall call it) plays such an important role in justifying the premises of the Cosmological Argument, it will help us to consider it for a moment before we continue our enquiry into the truth or falsity of the premises of the Cosmological Argument.

PSR, as it was expressed by both Leibniz and Clarke, is a very general principle and is best understood as having two parts. In its first part it is simply a restatement of Anselm's principle that there must be an explanation of the *existence* of any being whatever. Thus if we come upon a man in a room, PSR implies that there must be an explanation of the fact that that particular man exists. A moment's reflection, however, reveals that there are many facts about the man other than the mere fact that he exists. There is the fact that the man in question is in the room he's in, rather than somewhere else, the fact that he is in good health, and the fact that he is at the moment thinking of Paris, rather than, say, London. Now, the purpose of the second part of PSR is to require an explanation of these facts, as well. We may state PSR, therefore, as the principle that *there must be an explanation (a) of the existence of any being, and (b) of any positive fact whatever.* We are now in a position to study the role this very important principle plays in the Cosmological Argument.

Since the proponent of the Cosmological Argument accepts PSR in both its parts, it is clear that he will appeal to its first part, PSRa, as justification for the first premise of the Cosmological Argument. Of course, we can and should enquire into the deeper question of whether the proponent of the argument is rationally justified in accepting PSR itself. But we shall put this question aside for the moment. What we need to see first is whether he is correct in thinking that *if* PSR is true then both of the premises of the Cosmological Argument are true. And what we have just seen is that if only the first part of PSR, that is, PSRa, is true, the first premise of the Cosmological Argument will be true. But what of the second premise of the argument? For what reasons does the proponent think that it must be true?

THE SECOND PREMISE

According to the second premise, not every being that exists can be a dependent being, that is, can have the explanation of its existence in some other being or beings. Presumably, the proponent of the argument thinks there is something fundamentally wrong with the idea that every being that exists is dependent, that each existing being was caused by some other being which in turn was caused by some other being, and so on. But just what does he think is wrong with it? To help us in understanding his thinking, let's simplify things by supposing that there exists only one thing now, A_1, a living thing perhaps, that was brought into existence by something else, A_2, which perished shortly after it brought A_1, into existence. Suppose further that A_2 was brought into existence in similar fashion some

time ago by A_3, and A_3 by A_4, and so forth back into the past. Each of these beings is a *dependent* being, it owes its existence to the preceding thing in the series. Now if nothing else ever existed but these beings, then what the second premise says would not be true. For if every being that exists or ever did exist is an A and was produced by a preceding A, then every being that exists or ever did exist would be dependent and, accordingly, premise two of the Cosmological Argument would be false. If the proponent of the Cosmological Argument is correct, there must, then, be something wrong with the idea that every being that exists or did exist is an A and that they form a causal series. A_1 caused by A_2, A_2 caused by A_3, A_3 caused by A_4, . . . A_n caused by A_{n+1}. How does the proponent of the Cosmological Argument propose to show us that there is something wrong with this view?

A popular but mistaken idea of how the proponent tries to show that something is wrong with the view, that every being might be dependent, is that he uses the following argument to reject it.

1. There must be a *first* being to start any causal series.
2. If every being were dependent there would be no *first* being to start the causal series.

Therefore,

3. Not every being can be a dependent being.

Although this argument is deductively valid, and its second premise is true, its first premise overlooks the distinct possibility that a causal series might be *infinite*, with no first member at all. Thus if we go back to our series of A beings, where each A is dependent, having been produced by the preceding A in the causal series, it's clear that if the series existed it would have no first member, for every A in the series there would be a preceding A which produced it, *ad infinitum.* The first premise of the argument just given assumes that a causal series must stop with a first member somewhere in the distant past. But there seems to be no good reason for making that assumption.

The eighteenth-century proponents of the Cosmological Argument recognized that the causal series of dependent beings could be infinite, without a first member to start the series. They rejected the idea that every being that is or ever was is dependent not because there would then be no first member to the series of dependent beings, but because there would then be no explanation for the fact that there are and have always been dependent beings. To see their reasoning let's return to our simplification of the supposition that the only things that exist or ever did exist are dependent beings. In our simplification of that supposition only one of the dependent beings exists at a time, each one perishing as it produces the next in the series. Perhaps the first thing to note about this supposition is that there is no individual A in the causal series of dependent beings whose existence is unexplained—A_1 is explained by A_2, A_2 by A_3, and A_n by A_{n+1}. So the first part of PSR, PSRa, appears to be satisfied. There is no particular being whose existence lacks an explanation. What, then, is it that lacks an explanation, if every particular A in the causal series of dependent beings has an explanation? It is the *series itself* that lacks an explanation. Or, as I've chosen to express it, *the fact that there are and have always been dependent beings*. For suppose we ask why it is that there are and have always been As in existence. It won't do to say that As have always been producing other As—we can't explain why there have always been As by saying there always have been As. Nor, on the supposition that only As have ever existed, can we explain the fact that there have always been As by appealing to something other than an A—for no such thing would have existed. Thus the supposition that the only things that exist or ever existed are dependent things leaves us with a fact for which there can be no explanation; namely, the fact that there are dependent beings rather than not.

QUESTIONING THE JUSTIFICATION OF THE SECOND PREMISE

Critics of the Cosmological Argument have raised several important objections against the claim that if every being is dependent the series or collection of those beings would have no explanation. Our understanding of the Cosmological Argument, as well as of its strengths and weaknesses, will be deepened by a careful consideration of these criticisms.

The first criticism is that the proponent of the Cosmological Argument makes the mistake of treating the collection or series of dependent beings as though it were itself a dependent being, and, therefore, requires an explanation of its existence. But, so the objection goes, the collection of dependent beings is not itself a dependent being any more than a collection of stamps is itself a stamp.

A second criticism is that the proponent makes the mistake of inferring that because each member of the collection of dependent beings has a cause, the collection itself must have a cause. But, as Russell noted, such reasoning is as fallacious as to infer that the human race (that is, the collection of human beings) must have a mother because each member of the collection (each human being) has a mother.

A third criticism is that the proponent of the argument fails to realize that for there to be an explanation of a collection of things is nothing more than for there to be an explanation of each of the things making up the collection. Since in the infinite collection (or series) of dependent beings, each being in the collection does have an explanation—by virtue of having been caused by some preceding member of the collection—the explanation of the collection, so the criticism goes, has already been given. As Hume remarked, "Did I show you the particular causes of each individual in a collection of twenty particles of matter, I should think it very unreasonable, should you afterwards ask me, what was the cause of the whole twenty. This is sufficiently explained in explaining the cause of the parts."[2]

Finally, even if the proponent of the Cosmological Argument can satisfactorily answer these objections, he must face one last objection to his ingenious attempt to justify premise two of the Cosmological Argument. For someone may agree that if nothing exists but an infinite collection of dependent beings, the infinite collection will have no explanation of its existence, and still refuse to conclude from this that there is something wrong with the idea that every being is a dependent being. Why, the proponent of the Cosmological Argument might ask, should we think that everything has to have an explanation? What's wrong with admitting that the fact that there are and have always been dependent beings is a *brute fact,* a fact having no explanation whatever? Why does everything have to have an explanation anyway? We must now see what can be said in response to these several objections.

RESPONSES TO CRITICISM

It is certainly a mistake to think that a collection of stamps is itself a stamp, and very likely a mistake to think that the collection of dependent beings is itself a dependent being. But the mere fact that the proponent of the argument thinks that there must be an explanation not only for each member of the collection of dependent beings but for the collection itself is not sufficient grounds for concluding that he must view the collection as itself a dependent being. The collection of human beings, for example, is certainly not itself a human being. Admitting this, however, we might still seek an explanation of why there is a collection of human beings, of why there are such things as human beings at all. So the mere fact that an explanation is demanded for the collection of dependent beings is no proof that the person who demands the explanation must be supposing that the collection itself is just another dependent being.

The second criticism attributes to the proponent of the Cosmological Argument the following bit of reasoning.

1. Every member of the collection of dependent beings has a cause or explanation.

Therefore,

2. The collection of dependent beings has a cause or explanation.

As we noted in setting forth this criticism, arguments of this sort are often unreliable. It would be a mistake to conclude that a collection of objects is light in weight simply because each object in the collection is light in weight, for if there were many objects in the collection it might be quite heavy. On the other hand, if we know that each marble weighs more than one ounce, we could infer validly that the collection of marbles weighs more than an ounce. Fortunately, however, we don't need to decide whether the inference from 1 to 2 is valid or invalid. We need not decide this question because the proponent of the Cosmological Argument need not use this inference to establish that there must be an explanation of the collection of dependent beings. He need not use this inference because he has in PSR a principle from which it follows immediately that the collection of dependent beings has a cause or explanation. For according to PSR, every positive fact must have an explanation. If it is a fact that there exists a collection of dependent beings then, according to PSR, that fact too must have an explanation. So it is PSR that the proponent of the Cosmological Argument appeals to in concluding that there must be an explanation of the collection of dependent beings, and not some dubious inference from the premise that each member of the collection has an explanation. It seems, then, that neither of the first two criticisms is strong enough to do any serious damage to the reasoning used to support the second premise of the Cosmological Argument.

The third objection contends that to explain the existence of a collection of things is the same thing as to explain the existence of each of its members. If we consider a collection of dependent beings in which each being in the collection is explained by the preceding member that caused it, it's clear that no member of the collection will lack an explanation of its existence. But, so the criticism goes, if we've explained the existence of every member of a collection, we've explained the existence of the collection—there's nothing left over to be explained. This forceful criticism, originally advanced by Hume, has gained considerable support in the modern period. But the criticism rests on an assumption that the proponent of the Cosmological Argument would not accept. The assumption is that to explain the existence of a collection of things it is *sufficient* to explain the existence of every member in the collection. To see what is wrong with this assumption is to understand the basic issue in the reasoning by which the proponent of the Cosmological Argument seeks to establish that not every being can be a dependent being.

In order for there to be an explanation of the existence of the collection of dependent beings, it's clear that the eighteenth-century proponents would require that the following two conditions be satisfied:

C1. There is an explanation of the existence of each of the members of the collection of dependent beings.

C2. There is an explanation of why there are *any* dependent beings.

According to the proponents of the Cosmological Argument, if every being that exists or ever did exist is a dependent being—that is, if the whole of reality consists of nothing more than a collection of dependent beings—C1 will be satisfied, but C2 will not be satisfied. And since C2 won't be satisfied, there will be no explanation of the collection of dependent beings. The third criticism, therefore, says in effect that if C1 is satisfied, C2 will be satisfied, and, since in a collection of dependent beings each member will have an explanation in whatever it was that produced it, C1 will be satisfied. So, therefore, C2 will be satisfied and the collection of dependent beings will have an explanation.

Although the issue is a complicated one, I think it is possible to see that the third criticism rests on a mistake: the mistake of thinking that if C1 is satisfied C2 must also be satisfied. The mistake is a natural one to make for it is easy to imagine circumstances in which if C1 is satisfied C2 also will be satisfied. Suppose, for example, that the whole of reality includes not just a collection of dependent beings but also a self-existent being. Suppose further that instead of each dependent being having been produced by some other dependent being, every dependent being was produced by the self-existent being. Finally, let us consider both the possibility that the collection of dependent beings is finite in time and has a first member, and the possibility that the collection of dependent beings

is infinite in past time, having no first member. Using G for the self-existent being, the first possibility may be diagramed as follows:

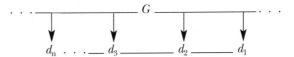

G, we shall say, has always existed and always will. We can think of d_1 as some presently existing dependent being, d_2, d_3, and so forth as dependent beings that existed at some time in the past, and d_n as the first dependent being to exist. The second possibility may be portrayed as follows:

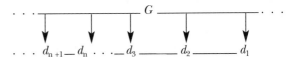

On this diagram there is no first member of the collection of dependent beings. Each member of the infinite collection, however, is explained by reference to the self-existent being G which produced it. Now the interesting point about both these cases is that the explanation that has been provided for the members of the collection of dependent beings carries with it, at least in part, an answer to the question of why there are any dependent beings at all. In both cases we may explain why there are dependent beings by pointing out that there exists a self-existent being that has been engaged in producing them. So once we have learned that the existence of each member of the collection of dependent beings has its existence explained by the fact that G produced it, we have already learned why there are dependent beings.

Someone might object that we haven't really learned why there are dependent beings until we also learn *why* G has been producing them. But, of course, we could also say that we haven't really explained the existence of a particular dependent being, say d_3, until we also learn not just that G produced it but *why* G produced it. The point we need to grasp, however, is that once we admit that every dependent being's existence is explained by G, we must admit that the fact that there are dependent beings has also been explained. So it is not unnatural that someone should think that to explain the existence of the collection of dependent beings is nothing more than to explain the existence of its members. For, as we've seen, to explain the collection's existence is to explain each member's existence and to explain why there are any dependent beings at all. And in the examples we've considered, in doing the one (explaining why each dependent being exists) we've already done the other (explained why there are any dependent beings at all). We must now see, however, that on the supposition that the whole of reality consists *only* of a collection of dependent beings, to give an explanation of each member's existence is not to provide an explanation of why there are dependent beings.

In the examples we've considered, we have gone *outside* of the collection of dependent beings in order to explain the members' existence. But if the only beings that exist or ever existed are dependent beings then each dependent being will be explained by some other dependent being, ad infinitum. This does not mean that there will be some particular dependent being whose existence is unaccounted for. Each dependent being has an explanation of its existence; namely, in the dependent being which preceded it and produced it. So C1 is satisfied: there is an explanation of the existence of each member of the collection of dependent beings. Turning to C2, however, we can see that it will not be satisfied. We cannot explain why there are (or have ever been) dependent beings by appealing to all the members of the infinite collection of dependent beings. For if the question to be answered is why there are (or have ever been) any dependent beings at all, we cannot answer that question by noting that there always have been dependent beings, each one accounting for the existence of some other dependent being. Thus on the supposition that every being is dependent, it seems there will be no explanation of why there are dependent beings. C2 will not be satisfied. Therefore, on the supposition that every being is dependent there will be no explanation of the existence of the collection of dependent beings.

THE TRUTH OF PSR

We come now to the final criticism of the reasoning supporting the second premise of the Cosmological Argument. According to this criticism, it is admitted that the supposition that every being is dependent implies that there will be a *brute fact* in the universe, a fact, that is, for which there can be no explanation whatever. For there will be no explanation of the fact that dependent beings exist and have always been in existence. It is this brute fact that the proponents of the argument were describing when they pointed out that if every being is dependent, the series or collection of dependent beings would lack an explanation of *its* existence. The final criticism asks what is wrong with admitting that the universe contains such a brute, unintelligible fact. In asking this question the critic challenges the fundamental principle, PSR, on which the Cosmological Argument rests. For, as we've seen, the first premise of the argument denies that there exists a being whose existence has no explanation. In support of this premise the proponent appeals to the first part of PSR. The second premise of the argument claims that not every being can be dependent. In support of this premise the proponent appeals to the second part of PSR, the part which states that there must be an explanation of any positive fact whatever.

The proponent reasons that if every being were a dependent being, then although the first part of PSR would be satisfied—every being would have an explanation—the second part would be violated; there would be no explanation for the positive fact that there are and have always been dependent beings. For first, since every being is supposed to be dependent, there would be nothing outside of the collection of dependent beings to explain the collection's existence. Second, the fact that each member of the collection has an explanation in some other dependent being is insufficient to explain why there are and have always been dependent beings. And, finally, there is nothing about the collection of dependent beings that would suggest that it is a self-existent collection. Consequently, if every being were dependent, the fact that there are and have always been dependent beings would have no explanation. But this violates the second part of PSR. So the second premise of the Cosmological Argument must be true: Not every being can be a dependent being. This conclusion, however, is no better than the principle, PSR, on which it rests. And it is the point of the final criticism to question the truth of PSR. Why, after all, should we accept the idea that every being and every positive fact must have an explanation? Why, in short, should we believe PSR? These are important questions, and any final judgment of the Cosmological Argument depends on how they are answered.

Most of the theologians and philosophers who accept PSR have tried to defend it in either of two ways. Some have held that PSR is (or can be) known *intuitively* to be true. By this they mean that if we fully understand and reflect on what is said by PSR we can see that it must be true. Now, undoubtedly, there are statements, which are known intuitively to be true. "Every triangle has exactly three angles" or "No physical object can be in two different places in space at one and the same time" are examples of statements whose truth we can apprehend just by understanding and reflecting on them. The difficulty with the claim that PSR is known intuitively to be true, however, is that a number of very able philosophers fail on careful reflection to apprehend its truth, and some have developed serious arguments for the conclusion that the principle is in fact false.[3] It is clear, therefore, that not everyone who has reflected on PSR has been persuaded that it is true, and some are persuaded that there are good reasons to think it is false. But while the fact that some able thinkers fail to apprehend the truth of PSR, and may even argue that it is false, is a decisive reason to believe that PSR is not so obvious a truth as say, "No physical object can be in two different places in space at one and the same time," it falls short of establishing that PSR is not a truth of reason. Here, perhaps, all that one can do is carefully reflect on what PSR says and form one's own judgment on whether it is a fundamental truth about the way reality must be. And if after carefully reflecting on PSR it does

strike one in that way, that person may well be rationally justified in taking it to be true and, having seen how it supports the premises of the Cosmological Argument, accepting the conclusion of that argument as true.

The second way philosophers and theologians who accept PSR have sought to defend it is by claiming that although it may not be known to be true, it is, nevertheless, a presupposition of reason, a basic assumption that rational people make, whether or not they reflect sufficiently to become aware of the assumption. It's probably true that there are some assumptions we all make about our world, assumptions which are so basic that most of us are unaware of them. And, I suppose, it might be true that PSR is such an assumption. What bearing would this view of PSR have on the Cosmological Argument? Perhaps the main point to note is that even if PSR is a presupposition we all share, the premises of the Cosmological Argument could still be false. For PSR itself could still be false. The fact, if it is a fact, that all of us *presuppose* that every existing being and every positive fact has an explanation does not imply that no being exists, and no positive fact obtains, without an explanation. Nature is not bound to satisfy our presuppositions. As the American philosopher William James once remarked in another connection, "In the great boarding house of nature, the cakes and the butter and the syrup seldom come out so even and leave the plates so clean."

Our study of the first part of the Cosmological Argument has led us to the fundamental principle on which its premises rest, the Principle of Sufficient Reason. We've seen that unless, on thoughtful reflection, PSR strikes us as something we see with certainty to be true, we cannot reasonably claim to know that the premises of the Cosmological Argument are true. Of course, they might be true. But unless we do know them to be true they cannot *establish* for us the conclusion that there exists a being that has the explanation of its existence within its own nature. If it were shown, however, that even though we do not *know* that PSR is true we all, nevertheless, *presuppose* PSR to be true, then, whether PSR is true or not, to be consistent we should accept the Cosmological Argument. For, as we've seen, its premises imply its conclusion and its premises do seem to follow from PSR. But no one has succeeded in *showing* that PSR is an assumption that most or all of us share. So our final conclusion must be that, with the exception of those who, on thoughtful reflection, reasonably conclude that PSR is a fundamental truth of reason, the Cosmological Argument does not provide us with good rational grounds for believing that among those beings that exist, there is one whose existence is accounted for by its own nature. And since the classical conception of God is of a being whose existence is accounted for by its own nature, apart from the exception noted, the Cosmological Argument fails to provide us with good rational grounds for believing that God exists.

NOTES

1. St. Thomas Aquinas, *Summa Theologica*, 1a. 2, 3, in *The Basic Writings of Saint Thomas Aquinas,* ed. Anton C. Pegis (New York: Random House, 1945).
2. David Hume, *Dialogues Concerning Natural Religion,* pt. IX, ed. H. D. Aiken (New York: Hafner Publishing Company, 1948), pp. 59–60.
3. For a brief account of two of these arguments see the preface to my *The Cosmological Argument* (New York: Fordham University Press, 1998).

Questions for Reflection

1. If it makes sense to say that God's existence doesn't have an explanation, is the atheist justified in claiming that the world doesn't have an explanation? What do you think?
2. Do you agree with Rowe that the Principle of Sufficient Reason cannot be justified? How would a defender of the Cosmological Argument (such as Thomas Aquinas or Richard Taylor) respond?

The Teleological Argument

Is there evidence of design in the world or is there only the appearance of design? Could the order in the world be explained by natural causes or does it suggest intelligent, purposeful design? It is interesting to consider the reflections of Charles Darwin on these issues. While Darwin's theory of evolution is often thought to be in conflict with religion, Darwin himself was a theist when he first published *Origin of Species* in 1859. (His only earned academic degree was in theology.) Even though he became an agnostic later in life, he originally saw his scientific findings as confirming divine design. He said that the strongest argument for the existence of God was "the extreme difficulty or rather impossibility of conceiving this immense and wonderful universe . . . as the result of blind chance or necessity."*

Likewise, the renowned British mathematical physicist Paul Davies says that it is hard to imagine that the thousands of carefully arranged atoms in the DNA molecule could have come about randomly. Accordingly, Davies concludes

> It is hard to resist the impression that the present structure of the universe, apparently so sensitive to minor alterations in the numbers, has been rather carefully thought out . . . the seemingly miraculous concurrence of these numerical values remain the most compelling evidence for cosmic design.†

---

*Charles Darwin, *The Life and Letters of Charles Darwin*, vol. 1, ed. Francis Darwin (New York: Basic Books, 1959), p. 282.
†Paul Davies, *God and the New Physics* (New York: Simon and Schuster, 1983), p. 189.

The evidence of design in the world, illustrated by these two quotations, forms the basis of one of the most popular arguments for God's existence. For obvious reasons, this is called "the argument from design," but philosophers usually call this argument the **teleological argument** for the existence of God. The name of the argument comes from the Greek word *telos* which means "end" or "goal." It is called the "teleological argument" because it points to the fact that many things and processes in the universe seem as though they were designed to fulfill purposeful ends or goals. Like the cosmological argument, it is an *a posteriori* argument, for it reasons from certain observed features of the world. These observations are claimed to provide evidence of design in the world. Its main thesis is "evidence of design implies a designer."

The teleological argument (or the design argument) has this general form:

1. The universe exhibits apparent design, that is, the ordering of complex means to the fulfillment of intelligible goals, ends, or purposes.

2. We have usually found a purposive, intelligent will to be the cause of such design or order.

3. Therefore, it is reasonable to conclude that the universe was caused by a purposive, intelligent will.

There are several things to notice about the teleological argument. First, the above argument is based on an analogy. It attempts to draw our attention to the alleged similarities between human creations (clocks, statues, computer programs, and so on) and the universe as a whole. Hence, the strength of the argument depends on how confident we are that meaningful similarities exist. The teleological argument's claim that the universe exhibits evidence of design is much less obvious than the cosmological argument's claim that contingent beings exist and depend on prior causes. Second, most versions of the argument take the form of a probabilistic argument or an argument to the best explanation. In other words, they do not show that it is absolutely necessary that the universe had a designer. Instead, they argue that this is the most probable explanation. Finally, of all the theistic arguments, the teleological argument probably is the least abstract, is the easiest to understand, and has the most popular appeal.

Any argument for God based on the evidence of design must address two questions. First, can we distinguish the mere appearance of design from genuine design? Second, can the order in nature be explained by any hypothesis other than that of an intelligent, purposeful cause that is above nature but operates on it? In the next reading, William Paley answers the first question affirmatively and the second question negatively. In the selection that follows, Hume answers the first question negatively and the second question affirmatively.

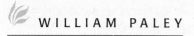

WILLIAM PALEY

The World Shows Evidence of Design

Although the teleological argument can be found in ancient writings, one of the clearest statements of it was given in the nineteenth century by William Paley (1743–1805), a British clergyman and philosopher. He argued that if we stumbled across a watch lying out in a field, we would conclude that it had a purposeful, intelligent cause. Even if we had never seen a watch before, the complexity and orderly arrangement of its parts would make it obvious that it did not come about by chance. Paley drives his point home by arguing that "every indication of contrivance, every manifestation of design, which existed in the watch, exists in the works of nature." Hence, if we must conclude that the watch had a designer, then even more so we must conclude that the immense and complex organization of the universe had a correspondingly great designer.

Reading Questions

1. According to Paley, what are the differences between the properties of the watch and those of the stone? What difference does this make in the sorts of inferences we would make concerning their respective origins?
2. Paley discusses eight possible objections to the conclusion that the watch had a designer. How does he respond to each one? In what way are these responses also replies to arguments that could be raised against the conclusion that the universe had a designer?
3. At the end of the essay, how does he apply his discussion of the watch to the issue of the existence of God?

In crossing a heath, suppose I pitched my foot against a *stone* and were asked how the stone came to be there, I might possibly answer that for anything I knew to the contrary it had lain there forever; nor would it, perhaps, be very easy to show the absurdity of this answer. But suppose I had found a *watch* upon the ground, and it should be inquired how the watch happened to be in that place, I should hardly think of the answer which I had before given, that for anything I knew the watch might have always been there. Yet why should not this answer serve for the watch as well as for the stone; why is it not as admissible in the second case as in the first? For this reason, and for no other, namely, that when we come to inspect the watch, we perceive—what we could not discover in the stone—that its several parts are framed and put together for a purpose, e.g., that they are so formed and adjusted as to produce motion, and that motion so regulated as to point out the hour of the day; that if the different parts had been differently shaped from what they are, or placed after any other manner or in any other order than that in which they are placed, either no motion at all would have been carried on in the machine, or none which would have answered the use that is

From William Paley, *Natural Theology,* 1802.

now served by it. To reckon up a few of the plainest of these parts and of their offices, all tending to one result: we see a cylindrical box containing a coiled elastic spring, which, by its endeavor to relax itself, turns round the box. We next observe a flexible chain—artificially wrought for the sake of flexure—communicating the action of the spring from the box to the fusee. We then find a series of wheels, the teeth of which catch in and apply to each other, conducting the motion from the fusee to the balance and from the balance to the pointer, and at the same time, by the size and shape of those wheels, so regulating that motion as to terminate in causing an index, by an equable and measured progression, to pass over a given space in a given time. We take notice that the wheels are made of brass, in order to keep them from rust; the springs of steel, no other metal being so elastic; that over the face of the watch there is placed a glass, a material employed in no other part of the work, but in the room of which, if there had been any other than a transparent substance, the hour could not be seen without opening the case. This mechanism being observed—it requires indeed an examination of the instrument, and perhaps some previous knowledge of the subject, to perceive and understand it; but being once, as we have said, observed and understood—the inference we think is inevitable, that the watch must have had a maker—that there must have existed, at some time and at some place or other, an artificer or artificers who formed it for the purpose which we find it actually to answer, who completely comprehended its construction and designed its use.

I. Nor would it, I apprehend, weaken the conclusion, that we had never seen a watch made—that we had never known an artist capable of making one—that we were altogether incapable of executing such a piece of workmanship ourselves, or of understanding in what manner it was performed; all this being no more than what is true of some exquisite remains of ancient art, of some lost arts, and, to the generality of mankind, of the more curious productions of modern manufacture. Does one man in a million know how oval frames are turned? Ignorance of this kind exalts our opinion of the unseen and unknown artist's skill, if he be unseen and unknown, but raises no doubt in our minds of the existence and agency of such an artist, at some former time and in some place or other. Nor can I perceive that it varies at all the inference, whether the question arise concerning a human agent or concerning an agent of a different species, or an agent possessing in some respects a different nature.

II. Neither, secondly, would it invalidate our conclusion, that the watch sometimes went wrong or that it seldom went exactly right. The purpose of the machinery, the design, and the designer might be evident, and in the case supposed, would be evident, in whatever way we accounted for the irregularity of the movement, or whether we could account for it or not. It is not necessary that a machine be perfect in order to show with what design it was made: still less necessary, where the only question is whether it were made with any design at all.

III. Nor, thirdly, would it bring any uncertainty into the argument, if there were a few parts of the watch, concerning which we could not discover or had not yet discovered in what manner they conduced to the general effect; or even some parts, concerning which we could not ascertain whether they conduced to that effect in any manner whatever. For, as to the first branch of the case, if by the loss, or disorder, or decay of the parts in question, the movement of the watch were found in fact to be stopped, or disturbed, or retarded, no doubt would remain in our minds as to the utility or intention of these parts, although we should be unable to investigate the manner according to which, or the connection by which, the ultimate effect depended upon their action or assistance; and the more complex the machine, the more likely is this obscurity to arise. Then, as to the second thing supposed, namely, that there were parts which might be spared without prejudice to the movement of the watch, and that we had proved this by experiment, these superfluous parts, even if we were completely assured that they were such, would not vacate the reasoning which we had instituted concerning other parts. The indication of contrivance remained, with respect to them, nearly as it was before.

IV. Nor, fourthly, would any man in his senses think the existence of the watch with its various machinery accounted for, by being told that it was one out of possible combinations of material forms; that whatever he had found in the place where he found the watch, must have contained some internal configuration or other; and that this configuration might be the structure now exhibited, namely, of the works of a watch, as well as a different structure.

V. Nor, fifthly, would it yield his inquiry more satisfaction, to be answered that there existed in things a principle of order, which had disposed the parts of the watch into their present form and situation. He never knew a watch made by the principle of order; nor can he even form to himself an idea of what is meant by a principle of order distinct from the intelligence of the watchmaker.

VI. Sixthly, he would be surprised to hear that the mechanism of the watch was no proof of contrivance, only a motive to induce the mind to think so:

VII. And not less surprised to be informed that the watch in his hand was nothing more than the result of the laws of *metallic* nature. It is a perversion of language to assign any law as the efficient, operative cause of any thing. A law presupposes an agent, for it is only the mode according to which an agent proceeds: it implies a power, for it is the order according to which that power acts. Without this agent, without this power, which are both distinct from itself, the *law* does nothing, is nothing. The expression, "the law of metallic nature," may sound strange and harsh to a philosophic ear; but it seems quite as justifiable as some others which are more familiar to him, such as "the law of vegetable nature," "the law of animal nature," or, indeed, as "the law of nature" in general, when assigned as the cause of phenomena, in exclusion of agency and power, or when it is substituted into the place of these.

VIII. Neither, lastly, would our observer be driven out of his conclusion or from his confidence in its truth by being told that he knew nothing at all about the matter. He knows enough for his argument; he knows the utility of the end; he knows the subserviency and adaptation of the means to the end. These points being known, his ignorance of other points, his doubts concerning other points affect not the certainty of his reasoning. The consciousness of knowing little need not beget a distrust of that which he does know. . . .

Contrivance, if established, appears to me to prove everything which we wish to prove. Among other things, it proves the *personality* of the Deity, as distinguished from what is sometimes called nature, sometimes called a principle; which terms, in the mouths of those who use them philosophically, seem to be intended to admit and to express an efficacy, but to exclude and to deny a personal agent. Now, that which can contrive, which can design, must be a person. These capacities constitute personality, for they imply consciousness and thought. They require that which can perceive an end or purpose, as well as the power of providing means and directing them to their end. They require a center in which perceptions unite, and from which volitions flow; which is mind. The acts of a mind prove the existence of a mind; and in whatever a mind resides, is a person. The seat of intellect is a person. We have no authority to limit the properties of mind to any particular corporeal form or to any particular circumscription of space. These properties subsist in created nature under a great variety of sensible forms. Also, every animated being has its *sensorium,* that is, a certain portion of space within which perception and volition are exerted. This sphere may be enlarged to an indefinite extent—may comprehend the universe; and being so imagined, may serve to furnish us with as good a notion as we are capable of forming, of the *immensity* of the divine nature, that is, of a Being, infinite, as well in essence as in power, yet nevertheless a person.

Questions for Reflection

1. In everyday life, what criteria do you use to decide whether something is the result of random, natural causes or purposeful design? How do these criteria apply in reasoning about the origin of the universe?
2. Make two lists, one describing the ways in which the universe is like a watch and another listing the ways in which it is not like a watch. Which list is longest or most significant? What implications do these considerations have for your assessment of Paley's argument?

DAVID HUME

The Evidence of Design Is Weak

Not everyone has been persuaded by the teleological argument. David Hume, the eighteenth-century Scottish skeptic, provided a formidable series of objections to the argument in his *Dialogues Concerning Natural Religion,* published in 1779, three years after his death. Ironically, although these criticisms came out 23 years before William Paley wrote his book and even though Paley criticized Hume on other issues, he seemed to be unaware of Hume's objections to the sort of argument Paley defends.

David Hume (1711–1776) was born in Edinburgh, Scotland, into a Calvinist family of modest means. He attended Edinburgh University where he studied the standard subjects of classics, mathematics, science, and philosophy. He went on to publish a number of important works on human nature, the theory of knowledge, religion, and morality. However, his skeptical and religious opinions were too controversial for the people of that time and he was never able to obtain an academic position. He was first rejected for a position in ethics at Edinburgh University In 1745. (To rectify their oversight, the philosophy department there is now housed in a building named after him.)

His scandalous reputation was further enhanced by his *Natural History of Religion,* released in 1757. It was a less than sympathetic account of the origins of the religious impulse in human experience. The reading that follows is a selection from his *Dialogues Concerning Natural Religion.* Learning from his previous experiences and having a desire "to live quietly and keep remote from all clamour," Hume requested that this work not be published until after his death. It has since become a classic in the philosophy of religion. Although his philosophy was filled with the hard edges of skepticism, Hume was actually a kind and gentle soul in his personal relationships. His friends loved to call him "St. David" and, as a result, the street on which he lived is still called St. David Street today.

From David Hume, *Dialogues Concerning Natural Religion,* 1779, Parts II and V.

As the title of Hume's book suggests, his arguments are presented in the course of a conversation between three fictional characters. Cleanthes is a natural theologian who presents some of the standard arguments for God. Demea is an orthodox believer who alternates between faith and rational arguments to justify his beliefs. Finally, Philo the skeptic provides refutations of the traditional religious arguments (while pretending to be as pious as Demea). Philo, undoubtedly, is the person who represents Hume's position. In reading this selection, it is important to understand that Hume is not arguing that God does not exist. Instead, he is an agnostic and, thus, is arguing that there is no way to *know* whether or not there is a God.

Reading Questions

1. What sort of argument does Cleanthes use to demonstrate the existence of God? How strong is it?
2. According to Philo, why can we infer that a particular house had a creator, but cannot infer that the universe did?
3. What is Philo's point concerning the hair and the leaf?
4. What does Philo say is a major difference between our knowledge of the causes of such things as ships or cities and our attempts to reason about the origin of the world?
5. In the last part of the selection, Philo assumes, for the sake of the argument, that there is a similarity between a humanly created machine and the universe. However, by comparing human creators with the source of the universe, what troubling consequences for traditional conceptions of God does he draw?

CLEANTHES: Not to lose any time in circumlocutions, said Cleanthes, addressing himself to Demea, much less in replying to the pious declamations of Philo; I shall briefly explain how I conceive this matter. Look round the world: contemplate the whole and every part of it: You will find it to be nothing but one great machine, subdivided into an infinite number of lesser machines, which again admit of subdivisions to a degree beyond what human senses and faculties can trace and explain. All these various machines, and even their most minute parts, are adjusted to each other with an accuracy which ravishes into admiration all men who have ever contemplated them. The curious adapting of means to ends, throughout all nature, resembles exactly, though it much exceeds, the productions of human contrivance; of human designs, thought, wisdom, and intelligence. Since, therefore, the effects resemble each other, we are led to infer, by all the rules of anal-

ogy, that the causes also resemble; and that the Author of Nature is somewhat similar to the mind of man, though possessed of much larger faculties, proportioned to the grandeur of the work which he has executed. By this argument *a posteriori*, and by this argument alone, do we prove at once the existence of a Deity, and his similarity to human mind and intelligence.

DEMEA: I shall be so free, Cleanthes, said Demea, as to tell you, that from the beginning, I could not approve of your conclusion concerning the similarity of the Deity to men; still less can I approve of the mediums by which you endeavour to establish it. What! No demonstration of the Being of God! No abstract arguments! No proofs *a priori!* Are these, which have hitherto been so much insisted on by philosophers, all fallacy, all sophism? Can we reach no further in this subject than experience and probability? I will not say that this is betraying the cause of a Deity: But surely, by this affected candour, you give advantages to atheists, which they never could obtain by the mere dint of argument and reasoning.

PHILO: What I chiefly scruple in this subject, said Philo, is not so much that all religious arguments are by Cleanthes reduced to experience, as that they appear not to be even the most certain and irrefragable of that inferior kind. That a stone will fall, that fire will burn, that the earth has solidity, we have observed a thousand and a thousand times; and when any new instance of this nature is presented, we draw without hesitation the accustomed inference. The exact similarity of the cases gives us a perfect assurance of a similar event; and a stronger evidence is never desired nor sought after. But wherever you depart, in the least, from the similarity of the cases, you diminish proportionably the evidence; and may at last bring it to a very weak analogy, which is confessedly liable to error and uncertainty. After having experienced the circulation of the blood in human creatures, we make no doubt that it takes place in Titius and Maevius. But from its circulation in frogs and fishes, it is only a presumption, though a strong one, from analogy, that it takes place in men and other animals. The analogical reasoning is much weaker, when we infer the circulation of the sap in vegetables from our experience that the blood circulates in animals; and those, who hastily followed that imperfect analogy, are found, by more accurate experiments, to have been mistaken.

If we see a house, Cleanthes, we conclude, with the greatest certainty, that it had an architect or builder; because this is precisely that species of effect which we have experienced to proceed from that species of cause. But surely you will not affirm, that the universe bears such a resemblance to a house, that we can with the same certainty infer a similar cause, or that the analogy is here entire and perfect. The dissimilitude is so striking, that the utmost you can here pretend to is a guess, a conjecture, a presumption concerning a similar cause; and how that pretension will be received in the world, I leave you to consider.

CLEANTHES: It would surely be very ill received, replied Cleanthes; and I should be deservedly blamed and detested, did I allow, that the proofs of a Deity amounted to no more than a guess or conjecture. But is the whole adjustment of means to ends in a house and in the universe so slight a resemblance? The economy of final causes? The order, proportion, and arrangement of every part? Steps of a stair are plainly contrived, that human legs may use them in mounting; and this inference is certain and infallible. Human legs are also contrived for walking and mounting; and this inference, I allow, is not altogether so certain, because of the dissimilarity which you remark; but does it, therefore, deserve the name only of presumption or conjecture?

DEMEA: Good God! cried Demea, interrupting him, where are we? Zealous defenders of religion allow, that the proofs of a Deity fall short of perfect evidence! And you, Philo, on whose assistance I depended in proving the adorable mysteriousness of the Divine Nature, do you assent to all these extravagant opinions of Cleanthes? For what other name can I give them? or, why spare my censure, when such principles are advanced, supported by such an authority, before so young a man as Pamphilus?

PHILO: You seem not to apprehend, replied Philo, that I argue with Cleanthes in his own way; and, by showing him the dangerous consequences of his tenets, hope at last to reduce him to our opinion. But what sticks most with you, I observe, is the representation which Cleanthes has made of the argument *a posteriori;* and finding that that argument is likely to escape your hold and vanish into air, you think it so disguised, that you can scarcely believe it to be set in its true light. Now, however much I may dissent, in other respects, from the dangerous principles of Cleanthes, I must allow that he has fairly represented that argument; and I shall endeavour so to state the matter to you, that you will entertain no further scruples with regard to it.

Were a man to abstract from every thing which he knows or has seen, he would be altogether incapable, merely from his own ideas, to determine what kind of scene the universe must be, or to give the preference to one state or situation of things above another. For as nothing which he clearly conceives could be esteemed impossible or implying a contradiction, every chimera of his fancy would be upon an equal footing; nor could he assign any just reason why he adheres to one idea or system, and rejects the others which are equally possible.

Again; after he opens his eyes, and contemplates the world as it really is, it would be impossible for him at first to assign the cause of any one event, much less of the whole of things, or of the universe. He might set his fancy a rambling; and she might bring him in an infinite variety of reports and representations. These would all be possible; but being all equally possible, he would never of himself give a satisfactory account for his preferring one of them to the rest. Experience alone can point out to him the true cause of any phenomenon.

Now, according to this method of reasoning, Demea, it follows, (and is, indeed, tacitly allowed by Cleanthes himself,) that order, arrangement, or the adjustment of final causes, is not of itself any proof of design; but only so far as it has been experienced to proceed from that principle. For aught we can know *a priori*, matter may contain the source or spring of order originally within itself, as well as mind does; and there is no more difficulty in conceiving, that the several elements, from an internal unknown cause, may fall into the most exquisite arrangement, than to conceive that their ideas, in the great universal mind, from a like internal unknown cause, fall into that arrangement. The equal possibility of both these suppositions is allowed. But, by experience, we find, (according to Cleanthes), that there is a difference between them. Throw several pieces of steel together, without shape or form; they will never arrange themselves so as to compose a watch. Stone, and mortar, and wood, without an architect, never erect a house. But the ideas in a human mind, we, see, by an unknown, inexplicable economy, arrange themselves so as to form the plan of a watch or house. Experience, therefore, proves,

that there is an original principle of order in mind, not in matter. From similar effects we infer similar causes. The adjustment of means to ends is alike in the universe, as in a machine of human contrivance. The causes, therefore, must be resembling.

I was from the beginning scandalised, I must own, with this resemblance, which is asserted, between the Deity and human creatures; and must conceive it to imply such a degradation of the Supreme Being as no sound theist could endure. With your assistance, therefore, Demea, I shall endeavour to defend what you justly call the adorable mysteriousness of the Divine Nature, and shall refute this reasoning of Cleanthes, provided he allows that I have made a fair representation of it.

When Cleanthes had assented, Philo, after a short pause, proceeded in the following manner.

PHILO: That all inferences, Cleanthes, concerning fact, are founded on experience; and that all experimental reasonings are founded on the supposition that similar causes prove similar effects, and similar effects similar causes; I shall not at present much dispute with you. But observe, I entreat you, with what extreme caution all just reasoners proceed in the transferring of experiments to similar cases. Unless the cases be exactly similar, they repose no perfect confidence in applying their past observation to any particular phenomenon. Every alteration of circumstances occasions a doubt concerning the event; and it requires new experiments to prove certainly, that the new circumstances are of no moment or importance. A change in bulk, situation, arrangement, age, disposition of the air, or surrounding bodies; any of these particulars may be attended with the most unexpected consequences: And unless the objects be quite familiar to us, it is the highest temerity to expect with assurance, after any of these changes, an event similar to that which before fell under our observation. The slow and deliberate steps of philosophers here, if any where, are distinguished from the precipitate march of the vulgar, who, hurried on by the smallest similitude, are incapable of all discernment or consideration.

But can you think, Cleanthes, that your usual phlegm and philosophy have been preserved in so wide a step as you have taken, when you compared to the universe houses, ships, furniture, machines, and, from their similarity in some circumstances, inferred a similarity in their causes? Thought, design, intelligence, such as we discover in men and other animals, is no more than one of the springs and principles of the universe, as well as heat or cold, attraction or repulsion, and a hundred others, which fall under daily observation. It is an active cause, by which some particular parts of nature, we find, produce alterations on other parts. But can a conclusion, with any propriety, be transferred from parts to the whole? Does not the great disproportion bar all comparison and inference? From observing the growth of a hair, can we learn any thing concerning the generation of a man? Would the manner of a leaf's blowing, even though perfectly known, afford us any instruction concerning the vegetation of a tree?

But, allowing that we were to take the operations of one part of nature upon another, for the foundation of our judgement concerning the origin of the whole (which never can be admitted), yet why select so minute, so weak, so bounded a principle, as the reason and design of animals is found to be upon this planet? What peculiar privilege has this little agitation of the brain which we call thought, that we must thus make it the model of the whole universe? Our partiality in our own favour does indeed present it on all occasions; but sound philosophy ought carefully to guard against so natural an illusion.

So far from admitting, continued Philo, that the operations of a part can afford us any just conclusion concerning the origin of the whole, I will not allow any one part to form a rule for another part, if the latter be very remote from the former. Is there any reasonable ground to conclude, that the inhabitants of other planets possess thought, intelligence, reason, or any thing similar to these faculties in men? When nature has so extremely diversified her manner

of operation in this small globe, can we imagine that she incessantly copies herself throughout so immense a universe? And if thought, as we may well suppose, be confined merely to this narrow corner, and has even there so limited a sphere of action, with what propriety can we assign it for the original cause of all things? The narrow views of a peasant, who makes his domestic economy the rule for the government of kingdoms, is in comparison a pardonable sophism.

But were we ever so much assured, that a thought and reason, resembling the human, were to be found throughout the whole universe, and were its activity elsewhere vastly greater and more commanding than it appears in this globe; yet I cannot see, why the operations of a world constituted, arranged, adjusted, can with any propriety be extended to a world which is in its embryo state, and is advancing towards that constitution and arrangement. By observation, we know somewhat of the economy, action, and nourishment of a finished animal; but we must transfer with great caution that observation to the growth of a foetus in the womb, and still more to the formation of an animalcule in the loins of its male parent. Nature, we find, even from our limited experience, possesses an infinite number of springs and principles, which incessantly discover themselves on every change of her position and situation. And what new and unknown principles would actuate her in so new and unknown a situation as that of the formation of a universe, we cannot, without the utmost temerity, pretend to determine.

A very small part of this great system, during a very short time, is very imperfectly discovered to us; and do we thence pronounce decisively concerning the origin of the whole?

Admirable conclusion! Stone, wood, brick, iron, brass, have not, at this time, in this minute globe of earth, an order or arrangement without human art and contrivance; therefore the universe could not originally attain its order and arrangement, without something similar to human art. But is a part of nature a rule for another part very wide of the former? Is it a rule for the whole? Is a very small part a rule for the universe? Is nature in one situation, a certain rule for nature in another situation vastly different from the former?

And can you blame me, Cleanthes, if I here imitate the prudent reserve of Simonides, who, according to the noted story, being asked by Hiero, *What God was?* desired a day to think of it, and then two days more; and after that manner continually prolonged the term, without ever bringing in his definition or description? Could you even blame me, if I had answered at first, that I did not know, and was sensible that this subject lay vastly beyond the reach of my faculties? You might cry out sceptic and railler, as much as you pleased: but having found, in so many other subjects much more familiar, the imperfections and even contradictions of human reason, I never should expect any success from its feeble conjectures, in a subject so sublime, and so remote from the sphere of our observation. When two species of objects have always been observed to be conjoined together, I can infer, by custom, the existence of one wherever I see the existence of the other; and this I call an argument from experience. But how this argument can have place, where the objects, as in the present case, are single, individual, without parallel, or specific resemblance, may be difficult to explain. And will any man tell me with a serious countenance, that an orderly universe must arise from some thought and art like the human, because we have experience of it? To ascertain this reasoning, it were requisite that we had experience of the origin of worlds; and it is not sufficient, surely, that we have seen ships and cities arise from human art and contrivance. . . .

. . . Can you pretend to show any such similarity between the fabric of a house, and the generation of a universe? Have you ever seen nature in any such situation as resembles the first arrangement of the elements? Have worlds ever been formed under your eye; and have you had leisure to observe the whole progress of the phenomenon, from the first appearance of order to its final consummation? If you have, then cite your experience, and deliver your theory. . . .

PHILO: But to show you still more inconveniences, continued Philo, in your anthropomorphism, please to take a new survey of your principles. Like effects prove like causes. This is the experimental argument; and this, you say too, is the sole theological argument. Now, it is certain, that the liker the effects are which are seen, and the liker the causes which are inferred, the stronger is the argument. Every departure on either side diminishes the probability, and renders the experiment less conclusive. You cannot doubt of the principle; neither ought you to reject its consequences.

All the new discoveries in astronomy, which prove the immense grandeur and magnificence of the works of Nature, are so many additional arguments for a Deity, according to the true system of theism; but, according to your hypothesis of experimental theism, they become so many objections, by removing the effect still further from all resemblance to the effects of human art and contrivance. For, if Lucretius, even following the old system of the world, could exclaim,▪

Who hath the power (I ask), who hath the power / To rule the sum of the immeasurable, / To hold with steady hand the giant reins / Of the unfathomed deep? Who hath the power / At once to roll a multitude of skies, / At once to heat with fires ethereal all / The fruitful lands of multitudes of worlds, / To be at all times in all places near . . .[1]

If Tully esteemed this reasoning so natural, as to put it into the mouth of his Epicurean:

What power of mental vision enabled your master Plato to discern the vast and elaborate architectural process which, as he makes out, the deity adopted in building the structure of the universe? What method of engineering was employed? What tools and levers and derricks? What agents carried out so vast an undertaking? And how were air, fire, water and earth enabled to obey and execute the will of the architect?[2]

If this argument, I say, had any force in former ages, how much greater must it have at present, when the bounds of Nature are so infinitely enlarged, and such a magnificent scene is opened to us? It is still more unreasonable to form our idea of so unlimited a cause from our experience of the narrow productions of human design and invention.

The discoveries by microscopes, as they open a new universe in miniature, are still objections, according to you, arguments, according to me. The further we push our researches of this kind, we are still led to infer the universal cause of all to be vastly different from mankind, or from any object of human experience and observation.

And what say you to the discoveries in anatomy, chemistry, botany? . . . These surely are no objections, replied Cleanthes; they only discover new instances of art and contrivance. It is still the image of mind reflected on us from innumerable objects. Add, a mind like the human, said Philo. I know of no other, replied Cleanthes. And the liker the better, insisted Philo. To be sure, said Cleanthes.

PHILO: Now, Cleanthes, said Philo, with an air of alacrity and triumph, mark the consequences. First, By this method of reasoning, you renounce all claim to infinity in any of the attri-butes of the Deity. For, as the cause ought only to be proportioned to the effect, and the effect, so far as it falls under our cognisance, is not infinite; what pretensions have we, upon your suppositions, to ascribe that attribute to the Divine Being? You will still insist, that, by removing him so much from all similarity to human creatures, we give in to the most arbitrary hypothesis, and at the same time weaken all proofs of his existence.

Secondly, You have no reason, on your theory, for ascribing perfection to the Deity, even in his finite capacity, or for supposing him free from every error, mistake, or incoherence, in his undertakings. There are many inexplicable difficulties in the works of nature, which, if we allow a perfect author to be proved *a priori*, are easily solved, and become only seeming difficulties, from the narrow capacity of man, who cannot trace infinite relations. But according to

your method of reasoning, these difficulties become all real; and perhaps will be insisted on, as new instances of likeness to human art and contrivance. At least, you must acknowledge, that it is impossible for us to tell, from our limited views, whether this system contains any great faults, or deserves any considerable praise, if compared to other possible, and even real systems. Could a peasant, if the Aeneid were read to him, pronounce that poem to be absolutely faultless, or even assign to it its proper rank among the productions of human wit, he, who had never seen any other production?

But were this world ever so perfect a production, it must still remain uncertain, whether all the excellences of the work can justly be ascribed to the workman. If we survey a ship, what an exalted idea must we form of the ingenuity of the carpenter who framed so complicated, useful, and beautiful a machine? And what surprise must we feel, when we find him a stupid mechanic, who imitated others, and copied an art, which, through a long succession of ages, after multiplied trials, mistakes, corrections, deliberations, and controversies, had been gradually improving? Many worlds might have been botched and bungled, throughout an eternity, ere this system was struck out; much labour lost, many fruitless trials made; and a slow, but continued improvement carried on during infinite ages in the art of world-making. In such subjects, who can determine, where the truth; nay, who can conjecture where the probability lies, amidst a great number of hypotheses which may be proposed, and a still greater which may be imagined?

And what shadow of an argument, continued Philo, can you produce, from your hypothesis, to prove the unity of the Deity? A great number of men join in building a house or ship, in rearing a city, in framing a commonwealth; why may not several deities combine in contriving and framing a world? This is only so much greater similarity to human affairs. By sharing the work among several, we may so much further limit the attributes of each, and get rid of that extensive power and knowledge, which must be supposed in one deity, and which, according to you, can only serve to weaken the proof of his existence. And if such foolish, such vicious creatures as man, can yet often unite in framing and executing one plan, how much more those deities or demons, whom we may suppose several degrees more perfect!

To multiply causes without necessity, is indeed contrary to true philosophy: but this principle applies not to the present case. Were one deity antecedently proved by your theory, who were possessed of every attribute requisite to the production of the universe; it would be needless, I own, (though not absurd,) to suppose any other deity existent. But while it is still a question, Whether all these attributes are united in one subject, or dispersed among several independent beings, by what phenomena in nature can we pretend to decide the controversy? Where we see a body raised in a scale, we are sure that there is in the opposite scale, however concealed from sight, some counterpoising weight equal to it; but it is still allowed to doubt, whether that weight be an aggregate of several distinct bodies, or one uniform united mass. And if the weight requisite very much exceeds any thing which we have ever seen conjoined in any single body, the former supposition becomes still more probable and natural. An intelligent being of such vast power and capacity as is necessary to produce the universe, or, to speak in the language of ancient philosophy, so prodigious an animal exceeds all analogy, and even comprehension.

But further, Cleanthes, men are mortal, and renew their species by generation; and this is common to all living creatures. The two great sexes of male and female, says Milton, animate the world. Why must this circumstance, so universal, so essential, be excluded from those numerous and limited deities? Behold, then, the theogony of ancient times brought back upon us.

And why not become a perfect anthropomorphite? Why not assert the deity or deities to be corporeal, and to have eyes, a nose, mouth, ears, &c.? Epicurus maintained, that no man had ever seen reason but in a human figure; therefore the gods must have a human figure.

And this argument, which is deservedly so much ridiculed by Cicero, becomes, according to you, solid and philosophical.

In a word, Cleanthes, a man who follows your hypothesis is able perhaps to assert, or conjecture, that the universe, sometime, arose from something like design: but beyond that position he cannot ascertain one single circumstance; and is left afterwards to fix every point of his theology by the utmost license of fancy and hypothesis. This world, for aught he knows, is very faulty and imperfect, compared to a superior standard; and was only the first rude essay of some infant deity, who afterwards abandoned it, ashamed of his lame performance: it is the work only of some dependent, inferior deity; and is the object of derision to his superiors: it is the production of old age and dotage in some superannuated deity; and ever since his death, has run on at adventures, from the first impulse and active force which it received from him. You justly give signs of horror, Demea, at these strange suppositions; but these, and a thousand more of the same kind, are Cleanthes's suppositions, not mine. From the moment the attributes of the Deity are supposed finite, all these have place. And I cannot, for my part, think that so wild and unsettled a system of theology is, in any respect, preferable to none at all.

CLEANTHES: These suppositions I absolutely disown, cried Cleanthes; they strike me, however, with no horror, especially when proposed in that rambling way in which they drop from you. On the contrary, they give me pleasure, when I see, that, by the utmost indulgence of your imagination, you never get rid of the hypothesis of design in the universe, but are obliged at every turn to have recourse to it. To this concession I adhere steadily; and this I regard as a sufficient foundation for religion.

NOTES

1. Lucretius, *On the Nature of Things, II,* trans. W. E. Leonard.

2. Marcus Tullius Cicero, *The Nature of the Gods, I,* trans. H. Rackham.

Questions for Reflection

1. Analyze each phase of Philo's argument and evaluate its strength.
2. Philo claims we cannot argue from the part to the whole. Is this true? For example, even though astronomers have not examined the entire universe, don't they still draw conclusions about it from what they do observe? How similar to or different from the teleological argument is this comparison to scientific reasoning?
3. Hume's arguments show that the teleological argument does not provide enough evidence to absolutely prove the existence of God without a doubt. However, has he shown that the argument has no evidential value whatsoever? If not, what degree of evidence does the argument provide to suggest that there is a God?

The Ontological Argument

The ontological argument makes use of the very important but difficult logical notions of possibility, impossibility, and necessity. While these terms may seem somewhat abstract, it is not hard to come up with concrete examples of their use. For example, there are some things in the universe that exist (such as dogs), but we can imagine a universe in which there were no such things. So, the nonexistence of dogs is logically possible. Likewise, there are some things that do not exist (such as unicorns), but we can imagine a universe in which it turned out that they did exist. In other words, the existence of unicorns is logically possible. In most cases, things happen to exist or happen not to exist because of certain conditions that produced them or failed to produce them. Furthermore, in most cases, we know of the existence or nonexistence of things because of experience and not through reason alone.

Now consider the case of round squares. Clearly they do not exist. But could we imagine a universe in which round squares did exist? The reason we cannot imagine such a world is that the very concept of round squares is such that their existence is logically impossible. But this suggests that in some unique cases, reason and logic can tell us about the existence of things. If this is true, then could we also conceive of something whose *nonexistence* is logically impossible? Such a being would, by its very nature, necessarily exist.

These considerations lead us into the ontological argument, one of the most unusual arguments for God's existence in the entire history of philosophy. The argument was first set forth by St. Anselm, an eleventh-century monk, and there have been numerous versions of the argument proposed ever since then. While many philosophers believe that the ontological argument is fallacious, almost every year someone publishes a philosophy journal article attempting to analyze the argument yet one more time. The argument has continued to both fascinate and haunt philosophers throughout its long history.

The adjective *ontological* is derived from the Greek and literally means "having to do with the science of being." Thus this argument attempts to derive God's existence from the very concept of God's being, much as we derive the properties of a triangle from the concept of a triangle. The crux of the argument is that if we conceive of the greatest possible being, we have the conception of a being that does not lack any positive qualities. Hence, (Anselm argues) such a being could not lack the property of necessary existence. Such a being would not be dependent on something else for its existence and there would be no conditions that could prevent it from existing. Ordinarily, simply having the idea of something (such as a kangaroo) is not sufficient in itself to tell us whether or not such a being exists. However, Anselm argues that the idea of God is absolutely unique. If God exists, could he just happen to be hanging around the world like kangaroos? Or could it just happen to be the case that there is no God in the same way that it happens to be the case that there are no pink elephants? The ontological argument revolves around two issues. Is the conception of the greatest possible being a meaningful one? Does the notion of a necessarily existing being make sense?

ST. ANSELM AND GAUNILO

The Ontological Argument—For and Against

The ontological argument for God's existence was first proposed by a medieval monk, St. Anselm (1033–1109), who went on to become the Archbishop of Canterbury.

Anselm was convinced that his faith was so rational that logically compelling arguments could be constructed to demonstrate the rationality of faith to anyone but the most obstinate fool. Of course, Anselm was already a believer when he discovered his famous argument. In fact, his argument is presented in the form of a prayer. Nevertheless, he thought that reason could help him understand more fully what he originally believed on faith. As he put it, "I do not seek to understand that I may believe, but I believe in order to understand."* Anselm begins with the thesis that both the believer and the unbeliever must have the idea of God in their understanding. But what is the concept of God? It is the concept of "a being than which nothing greater can be conceived." In other words, when we are thinking about God, we are contemplating the idea of the greatest possible being. While the unbeliever may be able to say the words "the greatest possible being (God) does not exist," that person fails to realize that this conception leads to a contradictory conclusion. This absurd conclusion is that "we can conceive of a being greater than the greatest possible being, namely, one who does exist." You will have to decide if Anselm is able to lead us from the idea of God to the idea of God's actual existence.

The selection following Anselm's argument is the classic reply by Gaunilo, an eleventh-century Benedictine monk. Other than the fact that Gaunilo lived in an abbey near Tours, France, we know little about him. Since Anselm claimed that a person would be a fool who denied God's existence, Gaunilo titled his refutation "On Behalf of the Fool." Gaunilo was a fellow Christian, so he believed that God existed. His point is that

---

*St. Anselm, *Proslogium*, chap. 1, in *Saint Anselm: Basic Writings*, trans. S.N. Deane (LaSalle, IL: Open Court, 1962).

These extracts are from Anselm's *Proslogium* and Gaunilo's *In Behalf of the Fool*. Reprinted from *St. Anselm Basic Writings*, trans S. W. Deane (La Salle, Il: Open Court, 1903, 1962).

Anselm's argument is not logically compelling, so it does not show that doubting God's existence makes one an illogical fool.

Reading Questions

1. What does Anselm mean when he defines God as "a being than which nothing greater can be conceived? Do you think this is a satisfactory way to define God?
2. What is the distinction he makes between something "existing in the understanding alone" and "existing in reality"? How does the analogy with the painter serve to illustrate this distinction?
3. What are Anselm's reasons for claiming that the greatest conceivable being cannot exist in the understanding alone?
4. After reading Anselm's first statement of the argument, see if you can formulate it in a series of succinct statements.
5. Which premise of the argument do you think is the most controversial one? What objections could be raised against it?
6. What is Gaunilo's point about the island? Why does he think this shows there is a problem with Anselm's argument?

Truly there is a God, although the fool hath said in his heart, There is no God.

And so, Lord, do thou, who dost give understanding to faith, give me, so far as thou knowest it to be profitable, to understand that thou art as we believe; and that thou art that which we believe. And, indeed, we believe that thou art a being than which nothing greater can be conceived. Or is there no such nature, since the fool hath said in his heart, there is no God? (Psalms xiv. 1). But, at any rate, this very fool, when he hears of this being of which I speak—a being than which nothing greater can be conceived—understands what he hears, and what he understands is in his understanding; although he does not understand it to exist.

For, it is one thing for an object to be in the understanding, and another to understand that the object exists. When a painter first conceives of what he will afterwards perform, he has it in his understanding, but he does not yet understand it to be, because he has not yet performed it. But after he has made the painting, he both has it in his understanding, and he understands that it exists, because he has made it.

Hence, even the fool is convinced that something exists in the understanding, at least, than which nothing greater can be conceived. For, when he hears of this, he understands it. And whatever is understood, exists in the understanding. And assuredly that, than which nothing greater can be conceived, cannot exist in the understanding alone. For, suppose it exists in the understanding alone: then it can be conceived to exist in reality; which is greater.

Therefore, if that, than which nothing greater can be conceived, exists in the understanding alone, the very being, than which nothing greater can be conceived, is one, than which a greater can be conceived. But obviously this is impossible. Hence, there is no doubt that there exists a being, than which nothing greater can be conceived, and it exists both in the understanding and in reality.

God cannot be conceived not to exist.—God is that, than which nothing greater can be conceived.—That which can be conceived not to exist is not God.

And it assuredly exists so truly, that it cannot be conceived not to exist. For, it is possible to conceive of a being which cannot be conceived not to exist; and this is greater than one which can be conceived not to exist. Hence, if that, than which nothing greater can be conceived, can be conceived not to exist, it is not that, than which nothing greater can be conceived. But this is an irreconcilable contradiction. There is, then, so truly a being than which nothing greater can be conceived to exist, that it cannot even be conceived not to exist; and this being thou art, O Lord, our God.

So truly, therefore, dost thou exist, O Lord, my God, that thou canst not be conceived not to exist; and rightly. For, if a mind could conceive of a being better than thee, the creature would rise above the Creator; and this is most absurd. And, indeed, whatever else there is, except thee alone, can be conceived not to exist. To thee alone, therefore, it belongs to exist more truly than all other beings, and hence in a higher degree than all others. For, whatever else exists does not exist so truly, and hence in a less degree it belongs to it to exist. Why, then, has the fool said in his heart, there is no God (Psalms xiv. 1), since it is so evident, to a rational mind, that thou dost exist in the highest degree of all? Why, except that he is dull and a fool?

> How the fool has said in his heart what cannot be conceived—A thing may be conceived in two ways: (1) when the word signifying it is conceived; (2) when the thing itself is understood. As far as the word goes, God can be conceived not to exist; in reality he cannot.

But how has the fool said in his heart what he could not conceive; or how is it that he could not conceive what he said in his heart? since it is the same to say in the heart, and to conceive.

But, if really, nay, since really, he both conceived, because he said in his heart; and did not say in his heart, because he could not conceive; there is more than one way in which a thing is said in the heart or conceived. For, in one sense, an object is conceived, when the word signifying it is conceived; and in another, when the very entity, which the object is, is understood.

In the former sense, then, God can be conceived not to exist; but in the latter, not at all. For no one who understands what fire and water are can conceive fire to be water, in accordance with the nature of the facts themselves, although this is possible according to the words. So, then, no one who understands what God is can conceive that

God does not exist; although he says these words in his heart, either without any, or with some foreign, signification. For, God is that than which a greater cannot be conceived. And he who thoroughly understands this, assuredly understands that this being so truly exists, that not even in concept can it be non-existent. Therefore, he who understands that God so exists, cannot conceive that he does not exist.

I thank thee, gracious Lord, I thank thee; because what I formerly believed by thy bounty, I now so understand by thine illumination, that if I were unwilling to believe that thou dost exist, I should not be able not to understand this to be true.

GAUNILO'S CRITICISM

The fool might make this reply:

This being is said to be in my understanding already, only because I understand what is said. Now could it not with equal justice be said that I have in my understanding all manner of unreal objects, having absolutely no existence in themselves, because I understand these things if one speaks of them, whatever they may be? . . .

For example: it is said that somewhere in the ocean is an island, which, because of the difficulty, or rather the impossibility, of discovering what does not exist, is called the lost island. And they say that this island has an inestimable wealth of all manner of riches and delicacies in greater abundance than is told of the Islands of the Blest; and that having no owner or inhabitant, it is more excellent than all other countries, which are inhabited by mankind, in the abundance with which it is stored.

Now if some one should tell me that there is such an island, I should easily understand his words, in which there is no difficulty. But suppose that he went on to say, as if by a logical inference: "You can no longer doubt that this island which is more excellent than all lands exists somewhere, since you have no doubt that it is in your understanding. And since it is more excellent not to be in the understanding alone, but to exist both in the understanding and in reality, for this reason it must exist. For if it does not exist, any land which really exists will be more excellent than it; and so the island already understood by you to be more excellent will not be more excellent."

If a man should try to prove to me by such reasoning that this island truly exists, and that its existence should no longer be doubted, either I should believe that he was jesting, or I know not which I ought to regard as the greater fool: myself, supposing that I should allow this proof; or him, if he should suppose that he had established with any certainty the existence of this island. For he ought to show first that the hypothetical excellence of this island exists as a real and indubitable fact, and in no wise as any unreal object, or one whose existence is uncertain, in my understanding.

This, in the mean time, is the answer the fool could make to the arguments urged against him. When he is assured in the first place that this being is so great that its non-existence is not even conceivable, and that this in turn is proved on no other ground than the fact that otherwise it will not be greater than all things, the fool may make the same answer, and say:

When did I say that any such being exists in reality, that is, a being greater than all others?—that on this ground it should be proved to me that it also exists in reality to such a degree that it cannot even be conceived not to exist? Whereas in the first place it should be in some way proved that a nature which is higher, that is, greater and better, than all other natures, exists; in order that from this we may then be able to prove all attributes which necessarily the being that is greater and better than all possesses.

Moreover, it is said that the non-existence of this being is inconceivable. It might better be said, perhaps, that its non-existence, or the possibility of its non-existence, is unintelligible. For according to the true meaning of the word, unreal objects are unintelligible. Yet their existence is conceivable in the way in which the fool conceived of the non-existence of God. I am most certainly aware of my own existence; but I know, nevertheless, that my non-existence is possible. As to that supreme being, moreover, which God is, I understand without any doubt both his existence, and the impossibility of his non-existence. Whether, however, so long as I am most positively aware of my existence, I can conceive of my non-existence, I am not sure. But if I can, why can I not conceive of the non-existence of whatever else I know with the same certainty? If, however, I cannot, God will not be the only being of which it can be said, it is impossible to conceive of his non-existence.

Questions for Reflection

1. Can we conceive of the greatest possible being? What objections might someone make to the argument concerning this point?

2. One of Anselm's key assumptions is that existence is a property that the greatest possible being could not lack. But is existence a property of the same sort as knowledge, power, or goodness? For example, think of a white cat sitting on your desk. Now add to your concept of this white cat the property of having a red collar. Now add to your picture of this white cat with a red collar the property of existence. Why is it impossible to do this? Does this show that existence really is not a property that we can add to a concept of something to make it the concept of something greater? If existence is not a property, does this undermine Anselm's argument?

3. The notion of logically impossible things (such as round squares) is a meaningful one. However, is the notion of a logically necessary being also a meaningful one?

MICHAEL MARTIN

A Critique of the Ontological Argument

Michael Martin has taught philosophy at Boston University since 1965. He has published nine books and over 100 articles in the areas of philosophy of religion, philosophy of social science, and philosophy of law.

In his critique of Anselm's ontological argument, Martin reviews some of its classic criticisms and offers replies to its defender's arguments. He questions whether existence can be considered a property and, if so, whether it necessarily is a property that makes something a greater sort of being. Finally, he agrees with Gaunilo that we cannot move from the concept of an entity to its actual existence.

Reading Questions

1. What does Martin identify as a "crucial assumption" of the ontological argument? What are the problems with this assumption?
2. What is the second assumption of the argument? How does Martin challenge this assumption?
3. How does Martin parody the ontological argument to show that it could also be used to prove the existence of a completely evil being?
4. What reply does Martin make to Plantinga's attack on Gaunilo's example of the perfect island?
5. Even if we grant all of Anselm's controversial assumptions, why does Martin think we cannot move from the concept of God to the actual existence of God?

ANSELM'S ONTOLOGICAL ARGUMENT

The most famous version of the ontological argument is that of St. Anselm, the Archbishop of Canterbury (1033–1109), in *Proslogion* 2. Anselm's argument takes the form of a commentary on the words of the Psalmist: "The fool hath said in his heart 'There is no God.'"

> And so, Lord, do thou, who dost give understanding to faith, give me, so far as thou knowest it to be profitable, to understand that thou art as we believe, and that thou art that which we believe. And, indeed, we believe that thou art a being than which nothing greater can be conceived. Or is there no such nature, since the fool hath said in his heart, there is no God? . . . But, at any rate, this very fool, when he hears of this being of which I speak—a being than which nothing greater can be conceived—understands what he hears, and what he understands is in his understanding, although he does not understand it to exist.
>
> For, it is one thing for any object to be in the understanding, and another to understand that the object exists. When a painter first conceives of what he will afterward perform, he has it in his understanding, but he does not yet understand it to be, because he has not yet

From Michael Martin, *Atheism: A Philosophical Justification* (Philadelphia: Temple University Press, 1990).

performed it. But after he has made the painting, he both has it in his understanding, and he understands that it exists, because he has made it.

Hence, even the fool is convinced that something exists in the understanding, at least, than which nothing greater can be conceived. For when he hears this, he understands it. And whatever is understood, exists in the understanding. And assuredly that, than which nothing greater can be conceived, cannot exist in the understanding alone. For suppose it exists in the understanding alone: then it can be conceived to exist in reality; which is greater.

Therefore, if that, than which nothing greater can be conceived, exists in the understanding alone, the very being than which nothing greater can be conceived, is one, than which a greater can be conceived. But obviously this is impossible. Hence, there is no doubt that there exists a being, than which nothing greater can be conceived, and it exists both in the understanding and in reality.

The argument proceeds as a *reductio ad absurdum* that purports to show that the fool has uttered a contradiction. It can be reformulated as follows: God is, by definition, a being such that no greater being can be conceived. Even the fool understands this is the meaning of "God." Consequently, such a being exists at least in the fool's understanding—that is, in the fool's mind. The fool, however, thinks that such a being exists only in his mind and in other minds, that it exists only as a mental object. But a greater being can be conceived that exists outside the fool's mind, in the real world. So the fool's thinking is incoherent; he thinks that he has conceived of a being such that no greater being can be conceived and that such a being exists only as a mental object. However, a being such that no greater being can be conceived must exist outside his mind, in the real world, thus contradicting his belief that God exists only as a mental object.

Clearly, one crucial assumption of this argument is that an entity is greater if it exists in reality than if it exists only as a mental object, merely some-

thing that someone is thinking about. This assumption can be and has been challenged. First, Kant questioned whether existence can be a property of an object. If it cannot, then it can hardly be the case that, other things being equal, an existing object is greater than a nonexistent one. For it is plausible to suppose that a sufficient condition for entity A being greater than entity B is that A has all and only the properties that B has except that A has, in addition, a property P that makes A more valued or prized than B. On this account, a judgment that A is a greater entity than B, given that A is exactly the same as B, except that A exists and B does not, assumes that existence is a property of A. However, the assumption that existence is a property of objects is a very controversial one; and insofar as the ontological argument makes this assumption, it is not a clearly sound argument. Kant's point still has force.

> By whatever and by however many predicates we may think a thing—even if we completely determine it—we do not make the least addition to the thing when we further declare that this thing is. Otherwise, it would not be exactly the same thing that exists, but something more than we had thought in the concept; and we could not, therefore, say that the exact object of my concept exists.[1]

Defenders of the argument at least have to show that existence is indeed a property. Although it may be possible to do this, Anselm did not attempt to show it.

Even if it is granted that existence is a property, the ontological argument further assumes that existence adds to the greatness of a being. After all, it may be the case that existence, although a property of an object, does not affect its greatness; indeed, it may be the case that existence even detracts from the object's greatness. God is supposed to be a perfect being. This means that He is all-good, all-knowing, and all-powerful. The assumption that God does not exist does not seem to take away from His perfection, as would, for example, the assumption that He is not all-knowing. Anselm seems to be using "a being, than which nothing greater can be conceived" as roughly synonymous with "a perfect being." So even if one allows that existence is a property of objects, the lack of existence would not detract from the greatness of a being who was all-good, all-knowing, and all-powerful. Furthermore, existence does not add to the greatness or value of other entities; hence it is difficult to see why it should with God. As Norman Malcolm points out:

> The doctrine that existence is a perfection is remarkably queer. It makes sense and is true to say that my future house will be a better one if it is insulated than if it is not insulated; but what could it mean to say that it will be a better house if it exists than if it does not? My future child will be a better man if he is honest than if he is not; who would understand the saying that he will be a better man if he exists than if he does not.[2]

On the other hand, it may be suggested that as far as religious believers are concerned, the existence of God is something that is valued and prized. Without the existence of God, life would be meaningless and without value. But this argument rests on a confusion. The existence of God adds not to the perfection or greatness of God per se, but to the value of something else, for example, human existence. This point suggests that we should amend the statement made above, which said that a sufficient condition for entity A being greater than entity B is that A has all and only the properties that B has except that A has, in addition, a property P that makes A more valued or prized than B. In order to be more accurate one should change the last phrase to read "in addition, a property P that makes A more valued or prized intrinsically than B."

Indeed, it may be argued that unless some such qualification is made, the value of the existence of God may be relativized to certain groups. Critics of religion may argue that the existence of God is not a desirable state of affairs. They may contend that a nonexistent God should be prized and valued as a beautiful and inspiring myth, while the actual existence of God would bring more problems than it is worth. If God existed, it may be argued, humans would lose a large part of their freedom and autonomy; they would be burdened with guilt and

sin; they would have to accept repugnant ontology; they would be faced with the difficult problem of knowing what He commanded and forbade. So unless one restricts the value of God's existence to what is intrinsically valuable, whether the existence of God is valuable will be contextually determined. But so restricted it is not at all clear that existence adds to the greatness of God.

Moreover, supposing that existence is an essential part of the intrinsic value of God, why could not one argue that existence is an essential part of the intrinsic evilness of a completely evil being? Such a being, let us suppose, is all-powerful, all-knowing, and completely evil. Let us call it the absolute evil one. An ontological proof of the absolute evil one would proceed as follows. By definition, the absolute evil one is a being such that no more evil being can be conceived. Even the fool understands that this is the meaning of "the absolute evil one." Consequently, such a being exists at least in the fool's understanding—that is, in the fool's mind. The fool, however, thinks that such a being exists only in his mind and in other minds, that it exists only as a mental object. But a more evil being can be conceived that exists outside the fool's mind, in the real world. So the fool's thinking is incoherent; he thinks that he has conceived of a being such that no more evil being can be conceived and that such a being exists only as a mental object. However, a being such that no more evil being can be conceived must exist outside his mind, in the real world, thus contradicting his belief that the absolute evil one exists only as a mental object. Clearly something is wrong. One cannot prove the existence of both God and the absolute evil one, since they are mutually exclusive.

Along these same lines Gaunilo, a contemporary of Anselm, parodied the ontological argument by arguing that one could prove that a perfect island existed. However, Anselm rejected Gaunilo's proof as have contemporary proponents of the ontological argument. Unfortunately, Anselm's reply consists in little more than insisting that the reasoning used in the argument can only be applied to God. Charles Hartshorne, a contemporary philosopher, argues that Gaunilo's parody fails since it assumes that a necessarily existing island is a coherent notion.[3] But it is not, according to Hartshorne. By its very nature, says Hartshorne, an island is a contingent being, not a necessary being.

Plantinga also rejects the parody on the ground that it is not possible for such an island to exist. But Plantinga conceives of the island not as a necessarily existing island, but as one such that no greater island can be conceived of. He contends that the idea of a greatest island is similar to the idea of a largest number. This idea is incoherent since, no matter how large a number one picks, there could always be a larger one. In a similar way there could not be a greatest island since, no matter what island one conceives of, one could always conceive of a greater island.[4] For example, if one conceives of an island with 1,000 coconut trees, one could conceive of an island with twice as many. In Plantinga's terms, the qualities that make for greatness in islands have no *intrinsic maximum*. However, this is not true in the case of the greatest being that can be conceived of, since the greatness of a being is defined in terms of qualities that do have intrinsic maximums. For example, a being such that no greater being can be conceived of would be all-knowing. However, an all-knowing being is one that for any proposition p would know whether p was true or false. . . .

Plantinga's critique fails because he assumes that the greatest conceivable island must have an unlimited number of entities such as coconut trees. But if one means by "the greatest conceivable island" a perfect island, it will not have an unlimited number of coconut trees but only the *right* number of coconut trees, whatever that may be. Too many coconut trees would spoil the perfection of the island. The same could be said of other properties, such as sunny days or pure water. Further, as we shall see when we come to Plantinga's version of the ontological argument, his own argument can be parodied without relying on the notion of greatness or an appeal to properties that have no intrinsic maximums. Plantinga's ontological argument can be used to show that it is rational to believe in the existence of a marvelous island (although not perhaps the greatest conceivable island) that has 360 sunny days per year, 10,000 coconut trees, a

year-round temperature of 72 degrees, and a population that never grows old.

So by indicating that this mode of argument can lead to absurd results that proponents of the ontological argument can hardly accept, Gaunilo's parody can be used to undermine the ontological argument. The onus is then on the proponents of the ontological argument to show why the parody of the ontological argument should not be accepted while the ontological argument should be.

So far we have seen that the ontological argument of Anselm is based on two debatable assumptions: that existence is a property and that existence is an essential part of the intrinsic value of God. We have seen also that even if these assumptions are granted, one can give a parody of the ontological proof for the existence of God—namely, ontological proof for the existence of the absolute evil one. But the problem remains of where the argument goes wrong.

Mackie has suggested[5] that even if one grants that existence is a property and is part of the intrinsic greatness of God, the argument does not work. Anselm appears to suppose that the fool's concept is that of *a nonexisting being than which no greater being can be conceived,* where the entire italicized phrase represents the content of his concept. Given this concept and the assumption that existence is part of the intrinsic greatness of God, the fool does indeed contradict himself. However, the fool need not and should not conceptualize the situation in this way. The fool may simply have the concept of *a being such that no greater being can be conceived.* He does not include nonexistence within the concept, although he believes that the concept has no application in the real world. Viewed in this way, the fool does not contradict himself. But can the fool afford to admit that existence is part of the concept of a being such that no greater one can be conceived of? There is no reason why he cannot admit this, for he can still insist that such a concept has no application to reality.

To put this in a different way, the argument can be undermined by noting the following: Suppose the fool admits that existence is a property of an entity, that existence would add to the greatness of any being, and that God is a being such that no greater being can be conceived of. The fool could say definitionally that God exists in reality. Or to put it in still a different way, "God is nonexistent" would be a contradiction. But the fool would not be forced into admitting that God *in fact* exists in reality and not just in his understanding. He could insist that the following is not a contradiction: "It is not the case that God exists" or "There is no God."

To say something exists definitionally and not in fact means that by virtue of the way a certain concept is defined, existence is part of the concept. For example, one can define a Loch Ness monster as a large sea animal that inhabits Loch Ness and define a *real* Loch Ness monster as a Loch Ness monster that exists in reality. Such a creature would then exist definitionally, since existence would be part of the definition of a real Loch Ness monster. But whether a real Loch Ness monster *in fact* exists is another question. Further, it would be a contradiction to say that a real Loch Ness monster did not exist. But one would not be uttering a contradiction by saying: "It is not the case that a real Loch Ness monster exists" or "There is no real Loch Ness monster." Similarly, if the fool said that God exists

definitionally but not in fact, he would in a way be acknowledging Anselm's point that God exists by definition while insisting that the concept that includes existence need not apply to the real world.

Given the above diagnosis of the problem, I must conclude that Anselm's ontological argument as it is usually formulated is unsound and that it is difficult to see how it could be revived.

NOTES

1. Immanuel Kant, *The Critique of Pure Reason*, trans. Norman Kemp Smith (London: Macmillan, 1929), p. 505, reprinted in Plantinga, *Ontological Argument* (Garden City, NY: Doubleday, 1965), p. 62.

2. Norman Malcolm, "Anselm's Ontological Arguments," reprinted in Plantinga, *Ontological Argument*, p. 139.

3. Charles Hartshorne, *The Logic of Perfection* (La Salle, IL: Open Court, 1962), p. 55.

4. Alvin Plantinga, *God, Freedom, and Evil* (Grand Rapids, MI: Eerdmans, 1983), pp. 90–91.

5. See J. L. Mackie, *The Miracle of Theism* (Oxford: Clarendon Press, 1982), pp. 52–53.

Questions for Reflection

1. How might a defender of Anselm's argument support either of the two controversial assumptions Martin rejects?
2. How could Plantinga respond to Martin's claim that Plantinga's critique of Gaunilo fails?
3. Do you think that Martin's critique of the ontological argument is compelling or do you think that Anselm's argument has value?

DO SUFFERING AND EVIL COUNT AGAINST THE EXISTENCE OF GOD?

Most atheists or agnostics base their case on the lack of evidence for God's existence. However, atheists have at least one, very powerful positive argument for their position. The argument is made that there cannot be a loving, all-knowing, all-powerful God because there is so much evil and suffering in the world. The difficulty of reconciling the existence of suffering and other evils in the world with the existence of God is called the problem of evil.

Traditionally, philosophers have distinguished between two kinds of evil. **Moral evil** consists of the bad actions and their unfortunate results for which humans (or other moral agents) are morally responsible. Lying, theft, murder, and rape, for example, are moral evils committed by people that cause the evil results of distrust, loss of property, and physical or emotional harm. **Natural evil** consists of the suffering to humans and animals resulting from natural causes such as genetic defects, diseases, earthquakes, and tornadoes. To avoid the atheist's charge of incoherence, the theist has the burden of explaining why God would allow either moral or natural evils to occur. The problem of evil can be formulated in terms of four propositions, all of which are propositions that the traditional theist wants to affirm. However, it seems difficult to reconcile the following four statements:

1. God is perfectly good.
2. God is all-knowing (omniscient).
3. God is all-powerful (omnipotent).
4. Evil exists.

By themselves, these four propositions do not constitute a contradiction the way that "Bob is a bachelor" and "Bob is a husband" contradict one another. Hence, to establish the conclusion that God does not exist, the atheist must add the following premise to complete the argument:

5. If God exists and is a being who is good, all-knowing, and all-powerful, then there would be no evil in the world.

If we add this premise to the previous four, we then get the following conclusion:

6. Therefore, God does not exist.

This argument is valid and, hence, if you accept the premises, you must accept the conclusion. However, if you think the conclusion is false, then you must reject at least one of the five premises. Let's consider the premises of the argument to see what options are available to the theist.

Different philosophers and religious thinkers throughout history have sought to evade the problem of evil by rejecting one or more of the first four premises in the above argument. To deny any of these premises we would have to replace the premise in question with one of these corresponding alternatives: (1) God is not good, (2) God does not know of all the evils that exist or will exist, (3) God is limited in power, or (4) evil is simply an illusion. Any one of these alternative theses will eliminate or lessen the alleged conflict between God's nature and the existence of evil. However, most religious thinkers have not found any of the above alternatives plausible or consistent with their conception of the nature of God.

Since the only alternative that is left is premise 5 (the claim that a good and powerful God would prevent or eliminate evil), this is the one that theists most often criticize. Contrary to the claim made by this premise, one could say that God allows certain evils to exist because in some way or other, these evils are necessary or are morally justified. The attempt to rationally justify God's permitting evil to occur in the world is known as a **theodicy.** Hence, many theodicists modify premise 5 to state "If God exists and is a being who is good, all-knowing, and all-powerful, then there would be no *unjustified* evil in the world." They then go on to defend the claim that "There are no unjustified evils in the world." In this way they attempt to show that the existence of evil or suffering does not count against the existence of God because God has good reasons for permitting their occurrence. The two most common ways of justifying the existence of evil are known as the "greater goods defense" and the "free will defense." I will briefly discuss each strategy in turn.

The **greater goods defense** claims that God allows some evil to exist because it is necessary to the achievement of a greater good. This argument assumes that (1) some evils are necessary to achieving certain good ends, (2) the good that is achieved outweighs the evil, and (3) the same or a greater amount of good could not have been attained by any means that did not involve the presence of these evils. For example, when my wife and I took our baby to get a shot, this caused him pain. But the pain was justified because it was a necessary means to a greater good, which is health. While advocates of the greater goods defense acknowledge that we can never explain the reason for each and every particular suffering that God allows, they have tried to set out some ways in which we can understand how God's permitting evil to occur may be morally justified, just as we were justified in allowing our baby to experience temporary pain. For example, certain moral goods such as courage, compassion, fortitude, forgiveness, and forbearance are human traits and responses that enrich us as human beings and that would not be possible if there were no evil in the world. In alleviating, resisting, and overcoming evil, we not only help those around us and make the world a better place, but we also make ourselves better persons in the process. Thus, it may be that enduring suffering and struggling against evil are necessary means to moral development.

Another way of dealing with the problem of evil is the **free will defense.** Its strategy is to claim that God could not create creatures (such as us) who have freedom of the will but who are incapable of doing evil. According to most religious philosophers, when we say God is omnipotent we mean that he has the power to do anything that is logically possible. Hence, it is not a limit on God's power to say that he cannot create *free* creatures who are *programmed* to do only what is good. In creating free agents, according to this account, God took a risk. He necessarily could not guarantee that we would choose good over evil. Like a parent, he can try to influence and persuade us in the right direction, but he cannot force us to act one way as opposed to another. The result is that we live in a world in which people choose to act in ways that are courageous, compassionate, forgiving, merciful, and loving. But it is also a world in which people freely choose to act in ways that are immoral, malicious, despicable, hateful, and destructive. Hence, God does not will or cause evil to occur, but in order to allow free agents such as us to exist, he has to allow us the freedom to commit evil acts.

The first reading on the topic of evil is from a novel by Albert Camus. He graphically raises the question of how a good and powerful God could allow an innocent child to suffer. The second reading is a philosophical essay by B. C. Johnson who uses the fact of suffering as an argument against the existence of an all-good God. The final reading is by philosopher of religion John Hick, who attempts to show that suffering is not incompatible with God's love, for it can produce a greater good.

ALBERT CAMUS

Two Responses to Suffering

Albert Camus (1913–1960), a French novelist, essayist, and playwright, was best known for such novels as *The Stranger, The Plague,* and *The Fall,* as well as for his work in leftist causes. After World War II, Camus was widely considered to be the spokesman for his generation. In 1957, at the relatively early age of 44, he received the Nobel Prize for Literature. Three years later, he died in an unfortunate automobile accident. The themes in his novels and his essays were the alienation and isolation of the individual, the finality of death, and the problem of evil, the latter being the subject of our current selection. Although some thought his writings bordered on a pessimistic nihilism, both his literary works and his life were a passionate, humanistic defense of the values of truth, integrity, and justice.

Camus' novel *The Plague* tells the story of a dread disease that sweeps through the French Port city of Oran on the Algerian Coast. Bringing with it a flood of suffering and death, the plague reduces the lives of the citizens of this community to the bare essentials. Each person is forced to confront the meaning of their life and the human condition. Early on, Father Paneloux, the local priest, gives a smug, confident, and harsh sermon that proclaims that the plague is God's judgment and a call for people to straighten up their lives. However, in a scene included below, he witnesses the tortuous death of an innocent child, which crushes his confidence, but leaves him embracing a chastened, raw faith. The main character, Dr. Rieux, is a physician and religious agnostic. Although he lacks any religious motivation for his endeavors, Rieux tirelessly risks his life to fight the plague, driven only by a love of his fellow human beings and a hatred of suffering. However, it is the senseless human suffering in the world that makes Dr. Rieux scornful of any pious belief in a loving God. The passage begins with a conversation between Rieux and a volunteer, Mr. Tarrou.

Reading Questions

1. What does Rieux think of Father Paneloux's response to the plague?
2. Why does Rieux think it is inconsistent for people to both believe in God and fight the plague?
3. After witnessing the suffering and death of the small boy, how does Father Paneloux think one should respond? What does Rieux think of this attitude?

From Albert Camus, *The Plague,* trans. Stuart Gilbert (New York: Random House, 1948), pp. 115–118, 189–197.

Tarrou's gray eyes met the doctor's gaze serenely.

"What did you think of Paneloux's sermon, doctor?"

The question was asked in a quite ordinary tone, and Rieux answered in the same tone.

"I've seen too much of hospitals to relish any idea of collective punishment. But, as you know, Christians sometimes say that sort of thing without really thinking it. They're better than they seem."

"However, you think, like Paneloux, that the plague has its good side; it opens men's eyes and forces them to take thought?"

The doctor tossed his head impatiently.

"So does every ill that flesh is heir to. What's true of all the evils in the world is true of plague as well. It helps men to rise above themselves. All the same, when you see the misery it brings, you'd need to be a madman, or a coward, or stone blind, to give in tamely to the plague."

Rieux had hardly raised his voice at all; but Tarrou made a slight gesture as if to calm him. He was smiling.

"Yes." Rieux shrugged his shoulders. "But you haven't answered my question yet. Have you weighed the consequences?"

Tarrou squared his shoulders against the back of the chair, then moved his head forward into the light.

"Do you believe in God, doctor?"

Again the question was put in an ordinary tone. But this time Rieux took longer to find his answer.

"No—but what does that really mean? I'm fumbling in the dark, struggling to make something out. But I've long ceased finding that original."

"Isn't that it—the gulf between Paneloux and you?"

"I doubt it. Paneloux is a man of learning, a scholar. He hasn't come in contact with death; that's why he can speak with such assurance of the truth—with a capital T. But every country priest who visits his parishioners and has heard a man gasping for breath on his deathbed thinks as I do. He'd try to relieve human suffering before trying to point out its excellence." Rieux stood up; his face was now in shadow. "Let's drop the subject," he said, "as you won't answer."

Tarrou remained seated in his chair; he was smiling again.

"Suppose I answer with a question."

The doctor now smiled, too.

"You like being mysterious, don't you? Yes, fire away."

"My question's this," said Tarrou. "Why do you yourself show such devotion, considering you don't believe in God? I suspect your answer may help me to mine."

His face still in shadow, Rieux said that he'd already answered: that if he believed in an all-powerful God he would cease curing the sick and leave that to Him. But no one in the world believed in a God of that sort; no, not even Paneloux, who believed that he believed in such a God. And this was proved by the fact that no one ever threw himself on Providence completely. Anyhow, in this respect Rieux believed himself to be on the right road—in fighting against creation as he found it.

"Ah," Tarrou remarked. "So that's the idea you have of your profession?"

"More or less." The doctor came back into the light.

Tarrou made a faint whistling noise with his lips, and the doctor gazed at him.

"Yes, you're thinking it calls for pride to feel that way. But I assure you I've no more than the pride that's needed to keep me going. I have no idea what's awaiting me, or what will happen when all this ends. For the moment I know this; there are sick people and they need curing. Later on, perhaps, they'll think things over; and so shall I. But what's wanted now is to make them well. I defend them as best I can, that's all."

"Against whom?"

Rieux turned to the window. A shadow-line on the horizon told of the presence of the sea. He was conscious only of his exhaustion, and at the same time was struggling against a sudden, irrational impulse to unburden himself a little more to his companion; an eccentric, perhaps, but who, he guessed, was one of his own kind.

"I haven't a notion, Tarrou; I assure you I haven't a notion. When I entered this profession, I did it 'abstractly,' so to speak; because I had a desire for it, because it meant a career like another, one that young men often aspire to. Perhaps, too, because it was particularly difficult for a workman's son, like myself. And then I had to see people die. Do you know that there are some who *refuse* to die? Have you ever heard a woman scream 'Never!' with her last gasp? Well, I have. And then I saw that I could never get hardened to it. I was young then, and I was outraged by the whole scheme of things, or so I thought. Subsequently I grew more modest. Only, I've never managed to get used to seeing people die. That's all I know. Yet after all—"

Rieux fell silent and sat down. He felt his mouth dry.

"After all—?" Tarrou prompted softly.

"After all," the doctor repeated, then hesitated again, fixing his eyes on Tarrou, "it's something that a man of your sort can understand most likely, but, since the order of the world is shaped by death, mightn't it be better for God if we refuse to believe in Him and struggle with all our might against death, without raising our eyes toward the heaven where He sits in silence."

Tarrou nodded.

"Yes. But your victories will never be lasting; that's all."

Rieux's face darkened.

"Yes, I know that. But it's no reason for giving up the struggle."

"No reason, I agree. Only, I now can picture what this plague must mean for you."

"Yes. A never ending defeat."

Tarrou stared at the doctor for a moment, then turned and tramped heavily toward the door. Rieux followed him and was almost at his side when Tarrou, who was staring at the floor, suddenly said:

"Who taught you all this, doctor?"

The reply came promptly:

"Suffering." . . .

Toward the close of October Castel's anti-plague serum was tried for the first time. Practically speaking, it was Rieux's last card. If it failed, the doctor was convinced the whole town would be at the mercy of the epidemic, which would either continue its ravages for an unpredictable period or perhaps die out abruptly of its own accord.

The day before Castel called on Rieux, M. Othon's son had fallen ill and all the family had to go into quarantine. Thus the mother, who had only recently come out of it, found herself isolated once again. In deference to the official regulations the magistrate had promptly sent for Dr. Rieux the moment he saw symptoms of the disease in his little boy. Mother and father were standing at the bedside when Rieux entered the room. The boy was in the phase of extreme prostration and submitted without a whimper to the doctor's examination. When Rieux raised his eyes he saw the magistrate's gaze intent on him, and, behind, the mother's pale face. She was holding a handkerchief to her mouth, and her big, dilated eyes followed each of the doctor's movements.

"He has it, I suppose?" the magistrate asked in a toneless voice.

"Yes." Rieux gazed down at the child again.

The mother's eyes widened yet more, but she still said nothing. M. Othon, too, kept silent for a while before saying in an even lower tone:

"Well, doctor, we must do as we are told to do."

Rieux avoided looking at Mme Othon, who was still holding her handkerchief to her mouth.

"It needn't take long," he said rather awkwardly, "if you'll let me use your phone."

The magistrate said he would take him to the telephone. But before going, the doctor turned toward Mme Othon.

"I regret very much indeed, but I'm afraid you'll have to get your things ready. You know how it is."

Mme Othon seemed disconcerted. She was staring at the floor.

Then, "I understand," she murmured, slowly nodding her head. "I'll set about it at once."

Before leaving, Rieux on a sudden impulse asked the Othons if there wasn't anything they'd like him to do for them. The mother gazed at him in silence. And now the magistrate averted his eyes.

"No," he said, then swallowed hard. "But—save my son." . . .

The boy was taken to the auxiliary hospital and put in a ward of ten beds which had formerly been a classroom. After some twenty hours Rieux became convinced that the case was hopeless. The infection was steadily spreading, and the boy's body putting up no resistance. Tiny, half-formed, but acutely painful buboes were clogging the joints of the child's puny limbs. Obviously it was a losing fight.

Under the circumstances Rieux had no qualms about testing Castel's serum on the boy. That night, after dinner, they performed the inoculation, a lengthy process, without getting the slightest reaction. At daybreak on the following day they gathered round the bed to observe the effects of this test inoculation on which so much hung.

The child had come out of his extreme prostration and was tossing about convulsively on the bed. From four in the morning Dr. Castel and Tarrou had been keeping watch and noting, stage by stage, the progress and remissions of the malady. Tarrou's bulky form was slightly drooping at the head of the bed, while at its foot, with Rieux standing beside him, Castel was seated, reading, with every appearance of calm, an old leather-bound book. One by one, as the light increased in the former classroom, the others arrived. Paneloux, the first to come, leaned against the wall on the opposite side of the bed to Tarrou. His face was drawn with grief, and the accumulated weariness of many weeks, during which he had never spared himself, had deeply seamed his somewhat prominent forehead. Grand came next. It was seven o'clock, and he apologized for being out of breath; he could only stay a moment, but wanted to know if any definite results had been observed. Without speaking, Rieux pointed to the child. His eyes shut, his teeth clenched, his features frozen in an agonized grimace, he was rolling his head from side to side on the bolster. When there was just light enough to make out the half-obliterated figures of an equation chalked on a blackboard that still hung on the wall at the far end of the room, Rambert entered. Posting himself at the foot of the next bed, he took a package of cigarettes from his pocket. But after his first glance at the child's face he put it back.

From his chair Castel looked at Rieux over his spectacles.

"Any news of his father?"

"No," said Rieux. "He's in the isolation camp."

The doctor's hands were gripping the rail of the bed, his eyes fixed on the small tortured body. Suddenly it stiffened, and seemed to give a little at the waist, as slowly the arms and legs spread out X-wise.

From the body, naked under an army blanket, rose a smell of damp wool and stale sweat. The boy had gritted his teeth again. Then very gradually he relaxed, bringing his arms and legs back toward the center of the bed, still without speaking or opening his eyes, and his breathing seemed to quicken. Rieux looked at Tarrou, who hastily lowered his eyes.

They had already seen children die—for many months now death had shown no favoritism—but they had never yet watched a child's agony minute by minute, as they had now been doing since daybreak. Needless to say, the pain inflicted on these innocent victims had always seemed to them to be what in fact it was: an abominable thing. But hitherto they had felt its abomination in, so to speak, an abstract way; they had never had to witness over so long a period the death-throes of an innocent child.

And just then the boy had a sudden spasm, as if something had bitten him in the stomach, and uttered a long, shrill wail. For moments that seemed endless he stayed in a queer, contorted position, his body racked by convulsive tremors; it was as if his frail frame were bending before the fierce breath of the plague, breaking under the reiterated gusts of fever. Then the storm-wind passed, there came a lull, and he relaxed a little; the fever seemed to recede, leaving him gasping for breath on a dank, pestilential shore, lost in a languor that already looked like death. When for the third time the fiery wave broke on him, lifting him a little, the child curled himself up and shrank away to the edge of the bed, as if in terror of the flames advancing on him, licking his limbs. A moment later, after tossing his head wildly to and fro, he flung off the blanket. From between the inflamed eyelids big tears welled up and trickled down the sunken, leaden-hued cheeks. When the spasm had passed, utterly exhausted, tensing his thin legs and arms, on which, within forty-eight hours, the flesh had wasted to the bone, the child lay flat, racked on the tumbled bed, in a grotesque parody of crucifixion.

Bending, Tarrou gently stroked with his big paw the small face stained with tears and sweat. Castel had closed his book a few moments before, and his eyes were now fixed on the child. He began to speak, but had to give a cough before continuing, because his voice rang out so harshly.

"There wasn't any remission this morning, was there, Rieux?"

Rieux shook his head, adding, however, that the child was putting up more resistance than one would have expected. Paneloux, who was slumped against the wall, said in a low voice:

"So if he is to die, he will have suffered longer."

Light was increasing in the ward. The occupants of the other nine beds were tossing about and groaning, but in tones that seemed deliberately subdued. Only one, at the far end of the ward, was screaming, or rather uttering little exclamations at regular intervals, which seemed to convey surprise more than pain. Indeed, one had the impression that even for the sufferers the frantic terror of the early phase had passed, and there was a sort of mournful resignation in their present attitude toward the disease. Only the child went on fighting with all his little might. Now and then Rieux took his pulse—less because this served any purpose than as an escape from his utter helplessness—and when he closed his eyes, he seemed to feel its tumult mingling with the fever of his own blood. And then, at one with the tortured child, he struggled to sustain him with all the remaining strength of his own body. But, linked for a few moments, the rhythms of their heartbeats soon fell apart, the child escaped him, and again he knew his impotence. Then he released the small, thin wrist and moved back to his place.

The light on the whitewashed walls was changing from pink to yellow. The first waves of another day of heat were beating on the windows. They hardly heard Grand saying he would come back as he turned to go. All were waiting. The child, his eyes still closed, seemed to grow a little calmer. His clawlike fingers were feebly plucking at the sides of the bed. Then they rose, scratched at the blanket over his knees, and suddenly he doubled up his limbs, bringing his thighs above his stomach, and remained quite still. For the first time he opened his eyes and gazed at Rieux, who was standing immediately in front of him. In the small face, rigid as a mask of grayish clay, slowly the lips parted and

from them rose a long, incessant scream, hardly varying with his respiration, and filling the ward with a fierce, indignant protest, so little childish that it seemed like a collective voice issuing from all the sufferers there. Rieux clenched his jaws, Tarrou looked away. Rambert went and stood beside Castel, who closed the book lying on his knees. Paneloux gazed down at the small mouth, fouled with the sores of the plague and pouring out the angry death-cry that has sounded through the ages of mankind. He sank on his knees, and all present found it natural to hear him say in a voice hoarse but clearly audible across that nameless, never ending wail:

"My God, spare this child!"

But the wail continued without cease and the other sufferers began to grow restless. The patient at the far end of the ward, whose little broken cries had gone on without a break, now quickened their tempo so that they flowed together in one unbroken cry, while the others' groans grew louder. A gust of sobs swept through the room, drowning Paneloux's prayer, and Rieux, who was still tightly gripping the rail of the bed, shut his eyes, dazed with exhaustion and disgust.

When he opened them again, Tarrou was at his side.

"I must go," Rieux said, "I can't bear to hear them any longer."

But then, suddenly, the other sufferers fell silent. And now the doctor grew aware that the child's wail, after weakening more and more, had fluttered out into silence. Around him the groans began again, but more faintly, like a far echo of the fight that now was over. For it was over. Castel had moved round to the other side of the bed and said the end had come. His mouth still gaping, but silent now, the child was lying among the tumbled blankets, a small, shrunken form, with the tears still wet on his cheeks.

Paneloux went up to the bed and made the sign of benediction. Then gathering up his cassock, he walked out by the passage between the beds.

"Will you have to start it all over again?" Tarrou asked Castel.

The old doctor nodded slowly, with a twisted smile.

"Perhaps. After all, he put up a surprisingly long resistance."

Rieux was already on his way out, walking so quickly and with such a strange look on his face that Paneloux put out an arm to check him when he was about to pass him in the doorway.

"Come, doctor," he began.

Rieux swung round on him fiercely.

"Ah! That child, anyhow, was innocent, and you know it as well as I do!"

He strode on, brushing past Paneloux, and walked across the school playground. Sitting on a wooden bench under the dingy, stunted trees, he wiped off the sweat that was beginning to run into his eyes. He felt like shouting imprecations—anything to loosen the stranglehold lashing his heart with steel. Heat was flooding down between the branches of the fig trees. A white haze, spreading rapidly over the blue of the morning sky, made the air yet more stifling. Rieux lay back wearily on the bench. Gazing up at the ragged branches, the shimmering sky, he slowly got back his breath and fought down his fatigue.

He heard a voice behind him. "Why was there that anger in your voice just now? What we'd been seeing was as unbearable to me as it was to you."

Rieux turned toward Paneloux.

"I know. I'm sorry. But weariness is a kind of madness. And there are times when the only feeling I have is one of mad revolt."

"I understand," Paneloux said in a low voice. "That sort of thing is revolting because it passes our human understanding. But perhaps we should love what we cannot understand."

Rieux straightened up slowly. He gazed at Paneloux, summoning to his gaze all the strength and fervor he could muster against his weariness. Then he shook his head.

"No, Father. I've a very different idea of love. And until my dying day I shall refuse to love a scheme of things in which children are put to torture."

Questions for Reflection

1. Whose response to suffering do you think makes the most sense? Rieux's or Father Paneloux's? Is there another alternative?
2. If you were a believer in God and had stood by the innocent young boy as he died a meaningless, agonizing death, how would you make sense of this? If you were an unbeliever like Rieux, what would your attitude be towards this suffering?
3. If the unbeliever looks at suffering and thinks "this shouldn't be happening" does this moral outrage at the injustice of the universe make sense if one also believes that the universe is simply a random collection of matter in motion?
4. Have you ever endured suffering (either physical or emotional) and found, in retrospect, that it had actually served a good purpose even though it seemed senseless and purposeless at the time? Does this experience help us understand how a good God might allow suffering in order to achieve a greater good? On the other hand, does this sort of explanation fall flat and seem too glib in the face of the suffering of an innocent child?

B. C. JOHNSON

Evil Disproves the Existence of God

B. C. Johnson is a pen name for the author, who wished to remain anonymous.

Johnson appeals to our ordinary moral intuitions to see if there is any possible way to reconcile the suffering of innocent people with the thesis that an all-powerful, all-good God exists. Taking the typical theistic solutions one by one, he shows that we would not accept these excuses for permitting suffering when used to justify the actions of our fellow human beings. Therefore, he claims, they do not justify God's actions either. His conclusion is that God cannot be all good and (by implication) that the God of traditional theism is incoherent.

Reading Questions

1. In the case of the baby's death, why does Johnson reject the claim that "the tragedy will, in the long run have good results, otherwise God would not have let it happen"? How would this solution justify any evil deeds that God does not prevent?
2. Why does Johnson claim that blaming evil on the actions of free agents does not absolve God?
3. How does Johnson show that explanations of why God does not intervene to prevent evil would also be an argument why we should not intervene to prevent evil?
4. How does Johnson respond to the claim that suffering is necessary so that others may develop the virtues of courage and sympathy?
5. Some theists claim that evil is a necessary by-product of the laws of nature and that such laws are a good feature of the world. What problems does Johnson raise with this solution?
6. Why is it unsatisfactory to claim that God has a "higher morality" that we cannot understand?
7. Why does Johnson claim that faith in God's goodness is unjustified?
8. How does Johnson argue that every excuse used to make the facts consistent with a good God could be used to make the facts consistent with an evil God?

Here is a common situation: a house catches on fire and a six-month-old baby is painfully burned to death. Could we possibly describe as "good" any person who had the power to save this child and yet refused to do so? God undoubtedly has this power and yet in many cases of this sort he has refused to help. Can we call God "good"? Are there adequate excuses for his behavior?

First, it will not do to claim that the baby will go to heaven. It was either necessary for the baby to suffer or it was not. If it was not, then it was wrong to allow it. The child's ascent to heaven does not change this fact. If it was necessary, the fact that the baby will go to heaven does not explain why it was necessary, and we are still left without an excuse for God's inaction.

B. C. Johnson, *The Atheist Debater's Handbook* (Buffalo, NY: Prometheus Books, 1981).

It is not enough to say that the baby's painful death would in the long run have good results and therefore should have happened, otherwise God would not have permitted it. For if we know this to be true, then we know—just as God knows—that every action successfully performed must in the end be good and therefore the right thing to do, otherwise God would not have allowed it to happen. We could deliberately set houses ablaze to kill innocent people and if successful we would then know we had a duty to do it. A defense of God's goodness which takes as its foundation duties known only after the fact would result in a morality unworthy of the name. Furthermore, this argument does not explain why God allowed the child to burn to death. It merely claims that there is some reason discoverable in the long run. But the belief that such a reason is within our grasp must rest upon the additional belief that God is good. This is just to counter evidence against such a belief by assuming the belief to be true. It is not unlike a lawyer defending his client by claiming that the client is innocent and therefore the evidence against him must be misleading—that proof vindicating the defendant will be found in the long run. No jury of reasonable men and women would accept such a defense and the theist cannot expect a more favorable outcome.

The theist often claims that man has been given free will so that if he accidentally or purposefully cause fires, killing small children, it is his fault alone. Consider a bystander who had nothing to do with starting the fire but who refused to help even though he could have saved the child with no harm to himself. Could such a bystander be called good? Certainly not. If we could not consider a mortal human being good under these circumstances, what grounds could we possibly have for continuing to assert the goodness of an all-powerful God?

The suggestion is sometimes made that it is best for us to face disasters without assistance, otherwise we would become dependent on an outside power for aid. Should we then abolish modern medical care or do away with efficient fire departments? Are we not dependent on their help? Is it not the case that their presence transforms us into soft, dependent creatures? The vast majority are not physi-cians or firemen. These people help in their capacity as professional outside sources of aid in much the same way that we would expect God to be helpful. Theists refer to aid from firemen and physicians as cases of man helping himself. In reality, it is a tiny minority of men helping a great many. We can become just as dependent on them as we can on God. Now the existence of this kind of outside help is either wrong or right. If it is right, then God should assist those areas of the world which do not have this kind of help. In fact, throughout history, such help has not been available. If aid ought to have been provided, then God should have provided it. On the other hand, if it is wrong to provide this kind of assistance, then we should abolish the aid altogether. But we obviously do not believe it is wrong.

Similar considerations apply to the claim that if God interferes in disasters, he would destroy a considerable amount of moral urgency to make things right. Once again, note that such institutions as modern medicine and fire departments are relatively recent. They function irrespective of whether we as individuals feel any moral urgency to support them. To the extent that they help others, opportunities to feel moral urgency are destroyed because they reduce the number of cases which appeal to us for help. Since we have not always had such institutions, there must have been a time when there was greater moral urgency than there is now. If such a situation is morally desirable, then we should abolish modern medical care and fire departments. If the situation is not morally desirable, then God should have remedied it.

Besides this point, we should note that God is represented as one who tolerates disasters, such as infants burning to death, in order to create moral urgency. It follows that God approved of these disasters as a means to encourage the creation of moral urgency. Furthermore, if there were no such disasters occurring, God would have to see to it that they occur. If it so happened that we lived in a world in which babies never perished in burning houses, God would be morally obliged to take an active hand in setting fire to houses with infants in them. In fact, if the frequency of infant mortality due to fire should happen to fall below a level necessary for the creation of maximum moral urgency in our real world, God would be justified in setting a few fires of his own. This may well be happening right now, for there is no guarantee that the maximum number of infant deaths necessary for moral urgency are occurring.

All of this is of course absurd. If I see an opportunity to create otherwise nonexistent opportunities for moral urgency by burning an infant or two, then I should *not* do so. But if it is good to maximize moral urgency, then I *should* do so. Therefore, it is not good to maximize moral urgency. Plainly we do not in general believe that it is a good thing to maximize moral urgency. The fact that we approve of modern medical care and applaud medical advances is proof enough of this.

The theist may point out that in a world without suffering there would be no occasion for the production of such virtues as courage, sympathy, and the like. This may be true, but the atheist need not demand a world without suffering. He need only claim that there is suffering which is in excess of that needed for the production of various virtues. For example, God's active attempts to save six-month-old infants from fires would not in itself create a world without suffering. But no one could sincerely doubt that it would improve the world.

The two arguments against the previous theistic excuse apply here also. "Moral urgency" and "building virtue" are susceptible to the same criticisms. It is worthwhile to emphasize, however, that we encourage efforts to eliminate evils; we approve of efforts to promote peace, prevent famine, and wipe out disease. In other words, we do value a world with fewer or (if possible) no opportunities for the development of virtue (when "virtue" is understood to mean the reduction of suffering). If we produce such a world for succeeding generations, how will they develop virtues? Without war, disease, and famine, they will not be virtuous. Should we then cease our attempts to wipe out war, disease, and famine? If we do not believe that it is right to cease attempts at improving the world, then by implication we admit that virtue-building is not an excuse for God to permit disasters. For we admit that the development of virtue is no excuse for permitting disasters.

It might be said that God allows innocent people to suffer in order to deflate man's ego so that the latter will not be proud of his apparently deserved good fortune. But this excuse succumbs to the arguments used against the preceding excuses and we need discuss them no further.

Theists may claim that evil is a necessary byproduct of the laws of nature and therefore it is irrational for God to interfere every time a disaster happens. Such a state of affairs would alter the whole causal order and we would then find it impossible to predict anything. But the death of a child caused by an electrical fire could have been prevented by a miracle and no one would ever have known. Only a minor alteration in electrical equipment would have been necessary. A very large disaster could have been avoided simply by producing in Hitler a miraculous heart attack—and no one would have known it was a miracle. To argue that continued miraculous intervention by God would be wrong is like insisting that one should never use salt because ingesting five pounds of it would be fatal. No one is requesting that God interfere all of the time. He should, however, intervene to prevent especially horrible disasters. Of course, the question arises: where does one draw the line? Well, certainly the line should be drawn somewhere this side of infants burning to death. To argue that we do not know where the line should be drawn is no excuse for failing to interfere in those instances that would be called clear cases of evil.

It will not do to claim that evil exists as a necessary contrast to good so that we might know what good is. A very small amount of evil, such as a toothache, would allow that. It is not necessary to destroy innocent human beings.

The claim could be made that God has a "higher morality" by which his actions are to be judged. But it is a strange "higher morality" which claims that what we call "bad" is good and what we call "good" is bad. Such a morality can have no meaning to us. It would be like calling black "white" and white "black." In reply the theist may say that God is the wise Father and we are ignorant children. How can we judge God any more than a child is able to judge his parent? It is true that a child may be puzzled by his parents' conduct, but his basis for deciding that their conduct is nevertheless good would be the many instances of good behavior he has observed. Even so, this could be misleading. Hitler, by all accounts, loved animals and children of the proper race; but if Hitler had had a child, this offspring would hardly have been justified in arguing that his father was a good man. At any rate, God's "higher morality," being the opposite of ours, cannot offer any grounds for deciding that he is somehow good.

Perhaps the main problem with the solutions to the problem of evil we have thus far considered is that no matter how convincing they may be in the abstract, they are implausible in certain particular cases. Picture an infant dying in a burning house and then imagine God simply observing from afar. Perhaps God is reciting excuses in his own behalf. As the child succumbs to the smoke and flames, God may be pictured as saying: "Sorry, but if I helped you I would have considerable trouble deflating the ego of your parents. And don't forget I have to keep those laws of nature consistent. And anyway if you weren't dying in that fire, a lot of moral urgency would just go down the drain. Besides, I didn't start this fire, so you can't blame *me*."

It does no good to assert that God may not be all-powerful and thus not able to prevent evil. He can create a universe and yet is conveniently unable to do what the fire department can do—rescue a baby from a burning building. God should at least be as powerful as a man. A man, if he had been at the right place and time, could have killed Hitler. Was this beyond God's abilities? If God knew in 1910 how to produce polio vaccine and if he was able to communicate with somebody, he should have communicated this knowledge. He must be incredibly limited if he could not have managed this modest accomplishment. Such a God if not dead, is the next thing to it. And a person who believes in such a ghost of a God is practically an atheist. To call such a thing a god would be to strain the meaning of the word.

The theist, as usual, may retreat to faith. He may say that he has faith in God's goodness and therefore the Christian Deity's existence has not been disproved. "Faith" is here understood as being much like confidence in a friend's innocence despite the evidence against him. Now in order to have confidence in a friend one must know him well enough to justify faith in his goodness. We cannot have justifiable faith in the supreme goodness of strangers. Moreover, such confidence must come not just from a speaking acquaintance. The friend may continually assure us with his words that he is good but if he does not act like a good person, we would have no reason to trust him. A person who says he has faith in God's goodness is speaking as if he had known God for a long time and during that time had never seen Him do any serious evil. But we know that throughout history God has allowed numerous atrocities to occur. No one can have justifiable faith in the goodness of such a God. This faith would have to be based on a close friendship wherein God was never found to do anything wrong. But a person would have to be blind and deaf to have had such a relationship with God. Suppose a friend of yours had always claimed to be good yet refused to help people when he was in a position to render aid. Could you have justifiable faith in his goodness?

You can of course say that you trust God anyway—that no arguments can undermine your faith. But this is just a statement describing how stubborn you are, it has no bearing whatsoever on the question of God's goodness.

The various excuses theists offer for why God has allowed evil to exist have been demonstrated to be inadequate. However, the conclusive objection to these excuses does not depend on their inadequacy.

First, we should note that every possible excuse making the actual world consistent with the existence of a good God could be used in reverse to make that same world consistent with an evil God. For example, we could say that God is evil and that he allows free will so that we can freely do evil things, which would make us more truly evil than we would be if forced to perform evil acts. Or we could say that natural disasters occur in order to make people more selfish and bitter, for most people tend to have a "me-first" attitude in a disaster (note, for example, stampedes to leave burning buildings). Even though some people achieve virtue from disasters, this outcome is necessary if persons are to react freely to disaster—necessary if the development of moral degeneracy is to continue freely. But, enough; the point is made. Every excuse we could provide to make the world consistent with a good God can be paralleled by an excuse to make the world consistent with an evil God. This is so because the world is a mixture of both good and bad.

Now there are only three possibilities concerning God's moral character. Considering the world as it actually is, we may believe *(a)* that God is more likely to be all evil than he is to be all good; *(b)* that God is less likely to be all evil than he is to be all good; or *(c)* that God is equally as likely to be all evil as he is to be all good. In case *(a)* it would be admitted that God is unlikely to be all good. Case *(b)* cannot be true at all, since—as we have seen—the belief that God is all evil can be justified to precisely the same extent as the belief that God is all good. Case *(c)* leaves us with no reasonable excuses for a good God to permit evil. The reason is as follows: if an excuse is to be a reasonable excuse, the circumstances it identifies as excusing conditions must be actual. For example, if I run over a pedestrian and my excuse is that the brakes failed because someone tampered with them, then the facts had better bear this out. Otherwise the excuse will not hold. Now if case *(c)* is correct and, given the

facts of the actual world, God is as likely to be all evil as he is to be all good, then these facts do not support the excuses which could be made for a good God permitting evil. Consider an analogous example. If my excuse for running over the pedestrian is that my brakes were tampered with, and if the actual facts lead us to believe that it is no more likely that they were tampered with than that they were not, the excuse is no longer reasonable. To make good my excuse, I must show that it is a fact or at least highly probable that my brakes were tampered with—not that it is just a possibility. The same point holds for God. His excuse must not be a possible excuse, but an actual one. But case *(c)*, in maintaining that it is just as likely that God is all evil as that he is all good, rules this out. For if case *(c)* is true, then the facts of the actual world do not make it any more likely that God is all good than that he is all evil. Therefore, they do not make it any more likely that his excuses are good than that they are not. But, as we have seen, good excuses have a higher probability of being true.

Cases *(a)* and *(c)* conclude that it is unlikely that God is all good, and case *(b)* cannot be true. Since these are the only possible cases, there is no escape from the conclusion that it is unlikely that God is all good. Thus the problem of evil triumphs over the traditional theism.

Questions for Reflection

1. One solution that Johnson does not consider in this essay would be to say that God is all good but his power is limited. Would this be an adequate solution? Is limiting our conception of God's power too high a price to pay to eliminate the problem that evil poses for belief in God?

2. Is it fair to compare how a limited human being, who does not know all the long-range outcomes of an event, should respond to a situation, with what an all-knowing God would do?

3. To respond to the problem of evil, is it necessary to know the justification of every particular instance of suffering or is it sufficient to show how it is possible that suffering could serve a greater good?

4. How strong a case do you think Johnson's emotionally jarring examples make against traditional theism? How might a theist respond?

JOHN HICK

There Is a Reason Why God Allows Evil

John Hick (1922–), a prominent Christian theologian and philosopher, was educated at Edinburgh, Oxford, and Cambridge Universities. He has taught and lectured at many universities throughout the world and was Danforth Professor of Religion at Claremont Graduate School until his retirement in 1994.

In this passage, Hick first discusses the free will defense. This strategy is based on the thesis that it would be logically impossible for God to create a world with free, moral agents such as ourselves, without taking the risk that we would use our freedom for evil ends. However, evil produced by free agents does not explain why this is a world full of natural evils such as the plague in Albert Camus' story. Hence, Hick develops a version of the greater goods defense, claiming that when God initially created humanity, there was still some work to be done in making us a completed product. However, this remaining work could not be accomplished by God alone (for then we would be like programmed robots). Instead, we have to contribute to the process of our own development as persons by facing the hardships and challenges of human life.

Reading Questions

1. Why does Hick believe that God could not create free agents who would inevitably do what is good?
2. What challenge has been posed to the above thesis and what is Hick's reply?
3. Why does Hick say it is not a limitation upon God's power that he cannot make us both free and incapable of doing evil?
4. What is the skeptic's faulty assumption concerning God's purpose in creating the world?
5. What is Hick's view of God's purpose in the creation of the world?
6. What does Hick mean by "soul-making"?
7. What would be the problems with a world in which all possibility of pain and suffering are excluded?

To many, the most powerful positive objection to belief in God is the fact of evil. Probably for most agnostics it is the appalling depth and extent of human suffering, more than anything else, that makes the idea of a loving Creator seem so implausible and disposes them toward one or another of the various naturalistic theories of religion.

As a challenge to theism, the problem of evil has traditionally been posed in the form of a dilemma: if God is perfectly loving, he must wish to abolish evil; and if he is all-powerful, he must be able to abolish evil. But evil exists; therefore God cannot be both omnipotent and perfectly loving.

Certain solutions, which at once suggest

From John Hick, *Philosophy of Religion* (Englewood Cliffs, NJ: Prentice Hall, 1963).

themselves, have to be ruled out so far as the Judaic-Christian faith is concerned.

To say, for example (with contemporary Christian Science), that evil is an illusion of the human mind, is impossible within a religion based upon the stark realism of the Bible. Its pages faithfully reflect the characteristic mixture of good and evil in human experience. They record every kind of sorrow and suffering, every mode of man's inhumanity to man and of his painfully insecure existence in the world. There is no attempt to regard evil as anything but dark, menacingly ugly, heart-rending, and crushing. In the Christian scriptures, the climax of this history of evil is the crucifixion of Jesus, which is presented not only as a case of utterly unjust suffering, but as the violent and murderous rejection of God's Messiah. There can be no doubt, then, that for biblical faith, evil is unambiguously evil, and stands in direct opposition to God's will.

Again, to solve the problem of evil by means of the theory (sponsored, for example, by the Boston "Personalist" School) of a finite deity who does the best he can with a material, intractable and co-eternal with himself, is to have abandoned the basic premise of Hebrew-Christian monotheism, for the theory amounts to rejecting belief in the infinity and sovereignty of God.

Indeed, any theory which would avoid the problem of the origin of evil by depicting it as an ultimate constituent of the universe, coordinate with good, has been repudiated in advance by the classic Christian teaching, first developed by Augustine, that evil represents the going wrong of something which in itself is good. Augustine holds firmly to the Hebrew-Christian conviction that the universe is *good*—that is to say, it is the creation of a good God for a good purpose. He completely rejects the ancient prejudice, widespread in his day, that matter is evil. There are, according to Augustine, higher and lower, greater and lesser goods in immense abundance and variety; but everything which has being is good in its own way and degree, except in so far as it may have become spoiled or corrupted. Evil—whether it be an evil will, an instance of pain, or some disorder or decay in nature—has not been set there by God, but represents the distortion of something that is in-

herently valuable. Whatever exists is, as such, and in its proper place, good; evil is essentially parasitic upon good, being disorder and perversion in a fundamentally good creation. This understanding of evil as something negative means that it is not willed and created by God; but it does not mean (as some have supposed) that evil is unreal and can be disregarded. Clearly, the first effect of this doctrine is to accentuate even more the question of the origin of evil.

Theodicy,* as many modern Christian thinkers see it, is a modest enterprise, negative rather than positive in its conclusions. It does not claim to explain, nor to explain away, every instance of evil in human experience, but only to point to certain considerations which prevent the fact of evil (largely incomprehensible though it remains) from constituting a final and insuperable bar to rational belief in God.

In indicating these considerations it will be useful to follow the traditional division of the subject. There is the problem of *moral evil* or wickedness: why does an all-good and all-powerful God permit this? And there is the problem of the *nonmoral evil* of suffering or pain, both physical and mental: why has an all-good and all-powerful God created a world in which this occurs?

Christian thought has always considered moral evil in its relation to human freedom and responsibility. To be a person is to be a finite center of freedom, a (relatively) free and self-directing agent responsible for one's own decisions. This involves being free to act wrongly as well as to act rightly. The idea of a person who can be infallibly guaranteed always to act rightly is self-contradictory. There can be no guarantee in advance that a genuinely free moral agent will never choose amiss. Consequently, the possibility of wrongdoing or sin is logically inseparable from the creation of finite persons, and to say that God should not have created beings who might sin amounts to saying that he should not have created people.

---

* The word "theodicy" from the Greek *theos* (God) and *dike* (righteous), means the justification of God's goodness in face of the fact of evil.

This thesis has been challenged in some recent philosophical discussions of the problem of evil, in which it is claimed that no contradiction is involved in saying that God might have made people who would be genuinely free and who could yet be guaranteed always to act rightly. A quote from one of these discussions follows:

> If there is no logical impossibility in a man's freely choosing the good on one, or on several occasions, there cannot be a logical impossibility in his freely choosing the good on every occasion. God was not, then, faced with a choice between making innocent automata and making beings who, in acting freely, would sometimes go wrong: there was open to him the obviously better possibility of making beings who would act freely but always go right. Clearly, his failure to avail himself of this possibility is inconsistent with his being both omnipotent and wholly good.[1]

A reply to this argument is suggested in another recent contribution to the discussion.[2] If by a free action we mean an action which is not externally compelled but which flows from the nature of the agent as he reacts to the circumstances in which he finds himself, there is, indeed, no contradiction between our being free and our actions being "caused" (by our own nature) and therefore being in principle predictable. There is a contradiction, however, in saying that God is the cause of our acting as we do but that we are free beings in relation to God. There is, in other words, a contradiction in saying that God has made us so that we shall of necessity act in a certain way, and that we are genuinely independent persons in relation to him. If all our thoughts and actions are divinely predestined, however free and morally responsible we may seem to be to ourselves, we cannot be free and morally responsible in the sight of God, but must instead be his helpless puppets. Such "freedom" is like that of a patient acting out a series of post-hypnotic suggestions: he appears, even to himself, to be free, but his volitions have actually been pre-determined by another will, that of the hypnotist, in relation to whom the patient is not a free agent.

A different objector might raise the question of whether or not we deny God's omnipotence if we admit that he is unable to create persons who are free from the risks inherent in personal freedom. The answer that has always been given is that to create such beings is logically impossible. It is no limitation upon God's power that he cannot accomplish the logically impossible, since there is nothing here to accomplish, but only a meaningless conjunction of words—in this case "person who is not a person." God is able to create beings of any and every conceivable kind; but creatures who lack moral freedom, however superior they might be to human beings in other respects, would not be what we mean by persons. They would constitute a different form of life which God might have brought into existence instead of persons. When we ask why God did not create such beings in place of persons, the traditional answer is that only persons could, in any meaningful sense, become "children of God," capable of entering into a personal relationship with their Creator by a free and uncompelled response to his love.

When we turn from the possibility of moral evil as a correlate of man's personal freedom to its actuality, we face something which must remain inexplicable even when it can be seen to be possible. For we can never provide a complete causal explanation of a free act; if we could, it would not be a free act. The origin of moral evil lies forever concealed within the mystery of human freedom.

The necessary connection between moral freedom and the possibility, now actualized, of sin throws light upon a great deal of the suffering which afflicts mankind. For an enormous amount of human pain arises either from the inhumanity or the culpable incompetence of mankind. This includes such major scourges as poverty, oppression and persecution, war, and all the injustice, indignity, and inequity which occur even in the most advanced societies. These evils are manifestations of human sin. Even disease is fostered to an extent, the limits of which have not yet been determined by psychosomatic medicine, by moral and emotional factors seated both in the individual and in his social environment. To the extent that all of these evils stem from human failures and wrong

Point system

decisions, their possibility is inherent in the creation of free persons inhabiting a world which presents them with real choices which are followed by real consequences.

We may now turn more directly to the problem of suffering. Even though the major bulk of actual human pain is traceable to man's misused freedom as a sole or part cause, there remain other sources of pain which are entirely independent of the human will, for example, earthquake, hurricane, storm, flood, drought, and blight. In practice, it is often impossible to trace a boundary between the suffering which results from human wickedness and folly and that which falls upon mankind from without. Both kinds of suffering are inextricably mingled together in human experience. For our present purpose, however, it is important to note that the latter category does exist and that it seems to be built into the very structure of our world. In response to it, theodicy, if it is wisely conducted, follows a negative path. It is not possible to show positively that each item of human pain serves the divine purpose of good; but, on the other hand, it does seem possible to show that the divine purpose as it is understood in Judaism and Christianity could not be forwarded in a world which was designed as a permanent hedonistic paradise.

An essential premise of this argument concerns the nature of the divine purpose in creating the world. The skeptic's assumption is that man is to be viewed as a completed creation and that God's purpose in making the world was to provide a suitable dwelling-place for this fully formed creature. Since God is good and loving, the environment which he has created for human life to inhabit is naturally as pleasant and comfortable as possible. The problem is essentially similar to that of a man who builds a cage for some pet animal. Since our world, in fact, contains sources of hardship, inconvenience, and danger of innumerable kinds, the conclusion follows that this world cannot have been created by a perfectly benevolent and all-powerful deity.

Christianity, however, has never supposed that God's purpose in the creation of the world was to construct a paradise whose inhabitants would ex-

Then why worship?

perience a maximum of pleasure and a minimum of pain. The world is seen, instead, as a place of "soul-making" in which free beings, grappling with the tasks and challenges of their existence in a common environment, may become "children of God" and "heirs of eternal life." A way of thinking theologically of God's continuing creative purpose for man was suggested by some of the early Hellenistic Fathers of the Christian Church, especially Irenaeus. Following hints from St. Paul, Irenaeus taught that man has been made as a person in the image of God but has not yet been brought as a free and responsible agent into the finite likeness of God, which is revealed in Christ. Our world, with all its rough edges, is the sphere in which this second and harder stage of the creative process is taking place.

This conception of the world (whether or not set in Irenaeus' theological framework) can be supported by the method of negative theodicy. Suppose, contrary to fact, that this world were a paradise from which all possibility of pain and suffering were excluded. The consequences would be very far-reaching. For example, no one could ever injure anyone else: the murderer's knife would turn to paper or his bullets to thin air; the bank safe, robbed of a million dollars, would miraculously become filled with another million dollars (without this device, on however large a scale, proving inflationary); fraud, deceit, conspiracy, and treason would somehow always leave the fabric of society undamaged. Again, no one would ever be injured by accident: the mountain-climber, steeplejack, or playing child falling from a height would float unharmed to the ground; the reckless driver would never meet with disaster. There would be no need to work, since no harm could result from avoiding work; there would be no call to be concerned for others in time of need or danger, for in such a world there could be no real needs or dangers. *Utopia – whats wrong?*

To make possible this continual series of individual adjustments, nature would have to work by "special providences: instead of running according to general laws which men must learn to respect on penalty of pain or death. The laws of nature would have to be extremely flexible: sometimes gravity would operate, sometimes not; sometimes an object would be hard and solid, sometimes soft. There could be no sciences, for there would be no enduring world structure to investigate. In eliminating the problems and hardships of an objective environment, with its own laws, life would become like a dream in which, delightfully but aimlessly, we would float and drift at ease.

One can at least begin to imagine such a world. It is evident that our present ethical concepts would have no meaning in it. If, for example, the notion of harming someone is an essential element in the concept of a wrong action, in our hedonistic paradise there could be no wrong actions—nor any right actions in distinction from wrong. Courage and fortitude would have no point in an environment in which there is, by definition, no danger or difficulty. Generosity, kindness, the *agape* aspect of love, prudence, unselfishness, and all other ethical notions which presuppose life in a stable environment, could not even be formed. Consequently, such a world, however well it might promote pleasure, would be very ill adapted for the development of the moral qualities of human personality. In relation to this purpose it would be the worst of all possible worlds. *How so?*

It would seem, then, that an environment intended to make possible the growth in free beings of the finest characteristics of personal life, must have a good deal in common with our present world. It must operate according to general and dependable laws; and it must involve real dangers, difficulties, problems, obstacles, and possibilities of pain, failure, sorrow, frustration, and defeat. If it did not contain the particular trials and perils which—subtracting man's own very considerable contribution—our world contains, it would have to contain others instead.

To realize this is not, by any means, to be in possession of a detailed theodicy. It is to understand that this world, with all its "heartaches and the thousand natural shocks that flesh is heir to," an environment so manifestly not designed for the maximization of human pleasure and the minimization of human pain, may be rather well adapted to the quite different purpose of "soul-making."

These considerations are related to theism as such. Specifically, Christian theism goes further in the light of the death of Christ, which is seen paradoxically both (as the murder of the divine Son) as the worst thing that has ever happened and (as the occasion of man's salvation) as the best thing that has ever happened. As the supreme evil turned to supreme good, it provides the paradigm for the distinctively Christian reaction to evil. Viewed from the standpoint of Christian faith, evils do not cease to be evils; and certainly, in view of Christ's healing work, they cannot be said to have been sent by God. Yet, it has been the persistent claim of those seriously and wholeheartedly committed to Christian discipleship that tragedy, though truly tragic, may nevertheless be turned, through a man's reaction to it, from a cause of despair and alienation from God to a stage in the fulfillment of God's loving purpose for that individual. As the greatest of all evils, the crucifixion of Christ, was made the occasion of man's redemption, so good can be won from other evils. As Jesus saw his execution by the Romans as an experience which God desired him to accept, an experience which was to be brought within the sphere of the divine purpose and made to serve the divine ends, so the Christian response to calamity is to accept the adversities, pains, and afflictions which life brings, in order that they can be turned to a positive spiritual use.

At this point, theodicy points forward in two ways to the subject of life after death, which is to be discussed in the following chapter.

First, although there are many striking instances of good being triumphantly brought out of evil through a man's or a woman's reaction to it, there are many other cases in which the opposite has happened. Sometimes obstacles breed strength of character, dangers evoke courage and unselfishness, and calamities produce patience and moral steadfastness. But sometimes they lead, instead, to resentment, fear, grasping selfishness, and disintegration of character. Therefore, it would seem that any divine purpose of soul-making which is at work in earthly history must continue beyond this life if

Greater Good negates free will

it is ever to achieve more than a very partial and fragmentary success.

Second, if we ask whether the business of soul-making is worth all the toil and sorrow of human life, the Christian answer must be in terms of a future good which is great enough to justify all that has happened on the way to it.

The conclusion of this chapter is thus parallel to the conclusion of the preceding one. There it appeared that we cannot decisively prove the existence of God; here it appears that neither can we decisively disprove his existence.

NOTES

1. J. L. Mackie, "Evil and Omnipotence," *Mind* (April, 1955), 209.
2. Antony Flew, "Divine Omnipotence and Human Freedom," in *New Essays in Philosophical Theology,* ed. Antony Flew and Alasdair MacIntyre (New York: Macmillan, 1964).

Questions for Reflection

1. Summarize, in your own words, Hick's explanation for the presence of moral evil. Is his argument convincing? Is it plausible that God could not have made us both free and incapable of doing evil?
2. Summarize, in your own words, Hick's explanation for the presence of nonmoral evil (natural evil), such as earthquakes and hurricanes. Is this argument convincing? How might a critic such as B. C. Johnson (see the previous reading) respond?
3. Some of Hick's critics acknowledge that some suffering might serve the good ends that Hick suggests. Nevertheless, they claim that these good ends could be achieved just as effectively with a lot less suffering than we find in the actual world. Is this a convincing criticism? How might Hick respond?

IS RELIGIOUS FAITH WITHOUT EVIDENCE JUSTIFIED?

Not all theists believe that it is necessary or even possible to prove the existence of God. Those who take this position could be broadly categorized as nonevidentialist theists. Ironically, these religious philosophers agree with Hume and other critics that the philosophical arguments for God fail. Nevertheless, nonevidential theists think that there are other considerations besides rational proofs that could lead an individual on a personal journey to a belief in and relationship with God. I have characterized these as pragmatic and subjective justifications for religious belief. We will examine Blaise Pascal and William James as representatives of this approach. While these two writers each have their unique approach to the issue of faith, reason, and belief in God, they tend to agree on the following three essential points.*

1. *The insufficiency of reason with regard to God's existence.* These two writers believe that theoretical, philosophical, or rational arguments can neither prove nor disprove the existence of God. God is infinite, but human reason, knowledge, and experience are finite. Thus, it is a mathematical impossibility to start from within the human situation

---

*The discussion of these three points is based on C. Stephen Evans, *Subjectivity and Religious Belief: An Historical Critical Study* (Grand Rapids, MI: William B. Eerdmans, Christian University Press, 1978), chap. 1.

and reason ourselves to God. On this point the nonevidentialists agree with David Hume. However, it is with the next point that they break with agnosticism.

2. *The impossibility of the neutral standpoint.* This theme emphasizes that we cannot be neutral when it comes to the question of God. We will either live our lives as though there is a God or, by default, we will live our lives as though there is not a God.

3. *The reasonableness of subjective justifications.* Even though we lack knowledge and evidence, these philosophers believe they can offer some personal and practical considerations which will make the religious option the most appealing. However, they do not believe that we should use subjective considerations for every decision (Pascal was a mathematician and scientist, and James was trained as a medical doctor). When objective evidence and reasons are available, we should use them. These philosophers claim, however, that it is legitimate to listen to the heart when we are forced to choose and when the intellect cannot give us guidance in making this choice.

BLAISE PASCAL

Faith Is Pragmatically Justified

The French thinker Blaise Pascal (1623–1662) was a brilliant mathematician, physicist, inventor, and philosopher. He demonstrated his remarkable intellectual gifts by publishing his first mathematical discovery at the age of 16. Later he provided the basis for the modern theory of probability and invented a calculating machine that was more powerful than any of that time. For this reason, the computer programming language PASCAL was named after him. Furthermore, his experiments with the barometer made important contributions to 17th-century science. However, a profound religious experience in 1654 changed his life and turned his interests to philosophy and theology.

Although Pascal knew well the power of reason and science, he was also convinced of their limits when it comes to the ultimate issues in human life such as religion. Concerning these issues, he thought that only personal, subjective considerations could give us any guidance. Accordingly, he once said, "the heart has its reasons which reason does not know." In the following passage, Pascal appeals to the reasons of the heart by means of his famous "wager."

Reading Questions

1. Find Pascal's statements that illustrate the three themes of the subjective justification of faith discussed in the beginning of this section.
2. Why can we not have rational knowledge of either God's existence or his nature?

From Blaise Pascal, *Thoughts*, trans. William F. Trotter, *The Harvard Classics*, vol. 48 (New York: P. F. Collier, 1910), Sec. 233.

3. What is Pascal's wager? What are the gains and losses that are possible depending on how we "bet" and on whether or not there is a God?

4. After providing considerations that should lead us to God, what advice does Pascal give to those who want to believe in God, but find themselves in the grips of unbelief?

Infinite—nothing.—Our soul is cast into a body, where it finds number, time, dimension. Thereupon it reasons, and calls this nature, necessity, and can believe nothing else.

Unity joined to infinity adds nothing to it, no more than one foot to an infinite measure. The finite is annihilated in the presence of the infinite, and becomes a pure nothing. So our spirit before God, so our justice before divine justice. There is not so great a disproportion between our justice and that of God, as between unity and infinity.

The justice of God must be vast like His compassion. Now justice to the outcast is less vast, and ought less to offend our feelings than mercy towards the elect.

We know that there is an infinite, and are ignorant of its nature. As we know it to be false that numbers are finite, it is therefore true that there is an infinity in number. But we do not know what it is. It is false that it is even, it is false that it is odd; for the addition of a unit can make no change in its nature. Yet it is a number, and every number is odd or even (this is certainly true of every finite number). So we may well know that there is a God without knowing what He is. Is there not one substantial truth, seeing there are so many things which are not the truth itself?

We know then the existence and nature of the finite, because we also are finite and have extension. We know the existence of the infinite, and are ignorant of its nature, because it has extension like us, but not limits like us. But we know neither the existence nor the nature of God, because He has neither extension nor limits.

But by faith we know His existence; in glory we shall know His nature. Now, I have already shown that we may well know the existence of a thing, without knowing its nature.

Let us now speak according to natural lights.

If there is a God, He is infinitely incomprehensible, since, having neither parts nor limits, He has no affinity to us. We are then incapable of knowing either what He is or if He is. This being so, who will dare to undertake the decision of the question? Not we, who have no affinity to Him.

Who then will blame Christians for not being able to give a reason for their belief, since they profess a religion for which they cannot give a reason? They declare, in expounding it to the world, that it is a foolishness, *stultitiam;* and then you complain that they do not prove it! If they proved it, they would not keep their words; it is in lacking proofs, that they are not lacking in sense. "Yes, but although this excuses those who offer it as such, and take away from them the blame of putting it forward without reason, it does not excuse those who receive it." Let us then examine this point, and say, "God is, or He is not." But to which side shall we incline? Reason can decide nothing here. There is an infinite chaos which separates us. A game is being played at the extremity of this infinite distance where heads or tails will turn up. What will you wager? According to reason, you can do neither the one thing nor the other; according to reason, you can defend neither of the propositions.

Do not then reprove for error those who have made a choice; for you know nothing about it. "No, but I blame them for having made, not this choice, but a choice; for again both he who chooses heads and he who chooses tails are equally at fault, they are both in the wrong. The true course is not to wager at all."

—Yes; but you must wager. It is not optional. You are embarked. Which will you choose then? Let us see. Since you must choose, let us see which interests you least. You have two things to lose, the true and the good; and two things to stake, your reason and your will, your knowledge and your happiness;

and your nature has two things to shun, error and misery. Your reason is no more shocked in choosing one rather than the other, since you must of necessity choose. This is one point settled. But your happiness? Let us weigh the gain and the loss in wagering that God is. Let us estimate these two chances. If you gain, you gain all; if you lose, you lose nothing. Wager then without hesitation that He is.—"That is very fine. Yes, I must wager; but I may perhaps wager too much."—Let us see. Since there is an equal risk of gain and of loss, if you had only to gain two lives, instead of one, you might still wager. But if there were three lives to gain, you would have to play (since you are under the necessity of playing), and you would be imprudent, when you are forced to play, not to chance your life to gain three at a game where there is an equal risk of loss and gain. But there is an eternity of life and happiness. And this being so, if there were an infinity of chances, of which one only would be for you, you would still be right in wagering one to win two, and you would act stupidly, being obliged to play, by refusing to stake one life against three at a game in which out of an infinity of chances there is one for you, if there were an infinity of an infinitely happy life to gain. But there is here an infinity of an infinitely happy life to gain, a chance of gain against a finite number of chances of loss, and what you stake is finite. It is all divided; wherever the infinite is and there is not an infinity of chances of loss against that of gain, there is no time to hesitate, you must give all. And thus, when one is forced to play, he must renounce reason to preserve his life, rather than risk it for infinite gain, as likely to happen as the loss of nothingness.

For it is no use to say it is uncertain if we will gain, and it is certain that we risk, and that the infinite distance between the *certainty* of what is staked and the *uncertainty* of what will be gained, equals the finite good which is certainly staked against the uncertain infinite. It is not so, as every player stakes a certainty to gain an uncertainty, and yet he stakes a finite certainty to gain a finite uncertainty, without transgressing against reason. There is not an infinite distance between the certainty staked and the uncertainty of the gain; that is untrue. In truth, there is an infinity between the certainty of gain and the certainty of loss. But the uncertainty of the gain is proportioned to the certainty of the stake according to the proportion of the chances of gain and loss. Hence it comes that, if there are as many risks on one side as on the other, the course is to play even; and then the certainty of the stake is equal to the uncertainty of the gain, so far is it from fact that there is an infinite distance between them. And so our proposition is of infinite force, when there is the finite to stake in a game where there are equal risks of gain and of loss, and the infinite to gain. This is demonstrable; and if men are capable of any truths, this is one.

"I confess it, I admit it. But still is there no means of seeing the faces of the cards?"—Yes, Scripture and the rest, &c.—"Yes, but I have my hands tied and my mouth closed; I am forced to wager, and am not free. I am not released, and am so made that I cannot believe. What then would you have me do?"

True. But at least learn your inability to believe, since reason brings you to this, and yet you cannot believe. Endeavour then to convince yourself, not by increase of proofs of God, but by the abatement of your passions. You would like to attain faith, and do not know the way; you would like to cure yourself of unbelief, and ask the remedy for it. Learn of those who have been bound like you, and who now stake all their possessions. These are people who know the way which you would follow, and who are cured of an ill of which you would be cured. Follow the way by which they began; by acting as if they believe, taking the holy water, having masses said, &c. Even this will naturally make you believe, and deaden your acuteness.—"But this is what I am afraid of."—And why? What have you to lose?

But to show you that this leads you there, it is this which will lessen the passions, which are your stumbling-blocks.

The end of this discourse.—Now what harm will befall you in taking this side? You will be faithful, honest, humble, grateful, generous, a sincere friend, truthful. Certainly you will not have those poisonous pleasures, glory and luxury; but will you not have others? I will tell you that you will thereby gain in this life, and that, at each step you take on this road, you will see so great certainty of gain, so much nothingness in what you risk, that you will at last recognize that you have wagered for something certain and infinite, for which you have given nothing.

"Ah! This discourse transports me, charms me," &c.

If this discourse pleases you and seems impressive, know that it is made by a man who has knelt, both before and after it, in prayer to that Being, infinite and without parts, before whom he lays all he has, for you also to lay before Him all you have for your own good and for His glory, so that strength may be given to lowliness.

Questions for Reflection

1. What do you think of Pascal's suggestion that we decide to believe in God using the same strategy we use in placing a bet at a casino? Aren't we expected to love God for himself and not for what we can get out of the deal? How might Pascal reply to this objection?

2. Doesn't Pascal assume that you can simply will yourself to believe something? Is there something odd about choosing to believe in God simply because the payoff seems best? Rather, shouldn't we embrace a belief because we think it is true?

3. Pascal seems to assume that the only options are to believe in the Christian God or to not believe in the Christian God. But what about the other great world religions? Shouldn't we consider them as options also? What would Pascal's wager look like if we included other religions? Couldn't these other religions make convincing arguments to accept their claims, using the same kind of wager Pascal uses for the acceptance of Christianity?

WILLIAM JAMES

Faith Is Subjectively Justified

William James (1842–1910) was born in New York into a well-to-do family for whom intellectual and cultural debates were part of the dinner table conversation. His brother Henry James was the well-known novelist. After spending years traveling the world and studying science, medicine, and painting both in Europe and in the United States, James earned his medical degree from Harvard in 1869. He pioneered the then infant discipline of scientific psychology and in 1890 published *Principles of Psychology*, one of the first textbooks in the field. Eventually he made philosophy his full-time occupation and taught in Harvard's philosophy department. James not only achieved fame in the academic community, but also was in demand as a popular lecturer.

William James, "The Will to Believe," in *The Will to Believe and Other Essays in Popular Philosophy*, 1896.

In his classic essay "The Will to Believe" (1896), James responded to another essay called "The Ethics of Belief" by W. K. Clifford. In this essay, Clifford tells the story of a man who believed his ship was seaworthy without evidence of this. Although he was sincere in his convictions, he had no right to his belief. As a matter of fact, the ship went down in the middle of the ocean, killing all its passengers. It would have made no difference if the ship, by good fortune, had completed the trip, for the man still had no right to hold a belief without evidence. Thus, when Pascal urges us to choose to believe in God without rational evidence, Clifford would say we are being asked to disregard our ethical duty to find a foundation for our beliefs. He summarizes his position by saying, "It is wrong always, everywhere, and for anyone, to believe anything on insufficient evidence."

In his response, James agrees that when an option is avoidable, then it may be appropriate to follow Clifford's advice and withhold our belief until we get more evidence. However, James argues that if we seriously consider the question of religious belief (it is a live option for us), then we will find that it is a forced, momentous decision. The problem is, however, James does not think reason can give us sufficient evidence to make a decision one way or another on this issue. When we face a decision that meets three criteria (it is a live, forced, momentous option) and when we cannot have objective, rational certainty, then we have the right to believe what is subjectively and pragmatically appealing.

Reading Questions

1. What does James mean by an "option"?
2. Provide your own examples of what James means by (a) a live versus a dead option, (b) a forced versus an avoidable option, (c) a momentous versus a trivial option.
3. What does James think of Pascal's wager?
4. What does James think of Clifford's position?
5. What role should our passional nature play in forming our beliefs? How does he defend this position? Under what conditions may our passions play this role?
6. What are the two great commandments with respect to our role as knowers? Why does James say they are two different laws and not two ways to say the same thing?
7. What examples does James give of where faith can create a fact?
8. Why does James claim that the agnostic's rules for truth seeking are irrational?

I

Let us give the name of *hypothesis* to anything that may be proposed to our belief; and just as the electricians speak of live and dead wires, let us speak of any hypothesis as either *live* or *dead*. A live hypothesis is one which appeals as a real possibility to him to whom it is proposed. If I ask you to believe in the Mahdi, the notion makes no electric connection with your nature,—it refuses to scintillate with any credibility at all. As an hypothesis it is completely dead. To an Arab, however (even if he be not one of the Mahdi's followers), the hypothesis is among the mind's possibilities: it is alive. This shows that deadness and liveness in an hypothesis are not intrinsic properties, but relations to the individual thinker. They are measured by his willingness to act. The maximum of liveness in an hypothesis means willingness to act irrevocably. Practically, that means belief; but there is some believing tendency wherever there is willingness to act at all.

Next, let us call the decision between two hypotheses an *option*. Options may be of several kinds. They may be—1, *living* or *dead;* 2, *forced* or *avoidable;* 3, *momentous* or *trivial;* and for our purposes we may call an option a *genuine* option when it is of the forced, living, and momentous kind.

(1) A living option is one in which both hypotheses are live ones. If I say to you: "Be a theosophist or be a Mohammedan," it is probably a dead option, because for you neither hypothesis is likely to be alive. But if I say: "Be an agnostic or be a Christian," it is otherwise: trained as you are, each hypothesis makes some appeal, however small, to your belief.

(2) Next, if I say to you: "Choose between going out with your umbrella or without it," I do not offer you a genuine option, for it is not forced. You can easily avoid it by not going out at all. Similarly, if I say, "Either love me or hate me," "Either call my theory true or call it false," your option is avoidable. You may remain indifferent to me, neither loving nor hating, and you may decline to offer any judgment as to my theory. But if I say, "Either accept this truth or go without it," I put on you a forced option, for there is no standing place outside of the alternative. Every dilemma based on a complete logical disjunction, with no possibility of not choosing, is an option of this forced kind.

(3) Finally, if I were Dr. Nansen and proposed to you to join my North Pole expedition, your option would be momentous; for this would probably be your only similar opportunity, and your choice now would either exclude you from the North Pole sort of immortality altogether or put at least the chance of it into your hands. He who refuses to embrace a unique opportunity loses the prize as surely as if he tried and failed. *Per contra,* the option is trivial when the opportunity is not unique, when the stake is insignificant, or when the decision is reversible if it later prove unwise. Such trivial options abound in the scientific life. A chemist finds an hypothesis live enough to spend a year in its verification: he believes in it to that extent. But if his experiments prove inconclusive either way, he is quit for his loss of time, no vital harm being done.

It will facilitate our discussion if we keep all these distinctions well in mind.

II

The next matter to consider is the actual psychology of human opinion. When we look at certain facts, it seems as if our passional and volitional nature lay at the root of all our convictions. When we look at others, it seems as if they could do nothing when the intellect had once said its say. Let us take the latter facts up first.

Does it not seem preposterous on the very face of it to talk of our opinions being modifiable at will? Can our will either help or hinder our intellect in its perceptions of truth? Can we, by just willing it, believe that Abraham Lincoln's existence is a myth, and that the portraits of him in *McClure's Magazine* are all of someone else? Can we, by any effort of our will, or by any strength of wish that it were true, believe ourselves well and about when we are roaring with rheumatism in bed, or feel certain that the sum of the two one-dollar bills in our pocket must be a hundred dollars? We can *say* any of these things, but we are absolutely impotent to believe them; and of just such things is the whole fabric of the truths that we do believe in made up,—matters of fact, immediate or remote, as Hume said, and relations between ideas, which are either there or not there for us if we see them so, and which if not there cannot be put there by any action of our own.

In Pascal's *Thoughts* there is a celebrated passage known in literature as Pascal's wager. In it he tries to force us into Christianity by reasoning as if our concern with truth resembled our concern with the stakes in a game of chance. Translated freely his words are these: You must either believe or not believe that God is—which will you do? Your human reason cannot say. A game is going on between you and the nature of things which at the day of judgment will bring out either heads or tails. Weigh what your gains and your losses would be if you should stake all you have on heads, or God's existence: if you win in such case, you gain eternal beatitude; if you lose, you lose nothing at all. If there were an infinity of chances, and only one for God in this wager, still you ought to stake your all on God; for though you surely risk a finite loss by this procedure, any finite loss is reasonable, even a certain one is reasonable, if there is but the possibility of infinite gain. Go, then, and take holy water, and have masses said: belief will come and stupefy your scruples. . . . Why should you not? At bottom, what have you to lose?

You probably feel that when religious faith expresses itself thus, in the language of the gaming table, it is put to its last trumps. Surely Pascal's own personal belief in masses and holy water had far other springs; and this celebrated page of his is but an argument for others, a last desperate snatch at a weapon against the hardness of the unbelieving heart. We feel that a faith in masses and holy water adopted wilfully after such a mechanical calculation would lack the inner soul of faith's reality; and if we were ourselves in the place of the Deity, we should probably take particular pleasure in cutting off believers of this pattern from their infinite reward. It is evident that unless there be some pre-existing tendency to believe in masses and holy water, the option offered to the will by Pascal is not a living option. Certainly no Turk ever took to masses and holy water on its account; and even to us Protestants these means of salvation seem such foregone impossibilities that Pascal's logic, invoked for them specifically, leaves us unmoved. As well might the Mahdi write to us, saying, "I am the Expected One whom God has created in his effulgence. You shall be infinitely happy if you confess me; otherwise you shall be cut off from the light of the sun. Weigh, then, your infinite gain if I am genuine against your finite sacrifice if I am not!" His logic would be that of Pascal; but he would vainly use it on us, for the hypothesis he offers us is dead. No tendency to act on it exists in us to any degree.

The talk of believing by our volition seems, then, from one point of view, simply silly. From another point of view it is worse than silly, it is vile. When one turns to the magnificent edifice of the physical sciences, and sees how it was reared; what thousands of disinterested moral lives of men lie buried in its mere foundation; what patience and postponement, what choking down of preference, what submission to the icy laws of outer fact are wrought into its very stones and mortar; how absolutely impersonal it stands in its vast augustness,—then how besotted and contemptible seems every little sentimentalist who comes blowing his voluntary smoke-wreaths, and pretending to decide things from out of his private dream! Can we wonder if those bred in the rugged and manly school of science should feel like spewing such subjectivism out of their mouths? The whole system of loyalties which grow up in the schools of science go dead against its toleration; so that it is only natural that those who have caught the scientific fever should pass over to the opposite extreme, and write sometimes as if the incorruptibly truthful intellect ought positively to prefer bitterness and unacceptableness to the heart in its cup.

It fortifies my soul to know

That, though I perish, Truth is so—

sings Clough, while Huxley exclaims: "My only consolation lies in the reflection that, however bad our posterity may become, so far as they hold by the plain rule of not pretending to believe what they have no reason to believe, because it may be to their advantage so to pretend [the word 'pretend' is surely here redundant], they will not have reached the lowest depth of immorality." And that delicious *enfant terrible* Clifford writes: "Belief is desecrated when given to unproved and unquestioned statements for the solace and private pleasure of the believer. . . . Whoso would deserve well of his fellows in this matter will guard the purity of his belief with a very fanaticism of jealous care, lest at any time it should rest on an unworthy object, and catch a stain which can never be wiped away. . . . If [a] belief has been accepted on insufficient evidence [even though the belief be true, as Clifford on the same page explains] the pleasure is a stolen one. . . . It is sinful because it is stolen in defiance of our duty to mankind. That duty is to guard ourselves from such beliefs as from a pestilence which may shortly master our own body and then spread to the rest of the town. . . . It is wrong always, everywhere, and for every one, to believe anything upon insufficient evidence."

III

All this strikes one as healthy, even when expressed, as by Clifford, with somewhat too much of robustious pathos in the voice. Free-will and simple wishing do seem, in the matter of our credences, to be only fifth wheels to the coach. Yet if any one should thereupon assume that intellectual insight is what remains after wish and will and sentimental preference have taken wing, or that pure reason is what then settles our opinions, he would fly quite as directly in the teeth of the facts.

It is only our already dead hypotheses that our willing nature is unable to bring to life again. But what has made them dead for us is for the most part a previous action of our willing nature of an antagonistic kind. When I say 'willing nature,' I do not mean only such deliberate volitions as may have set up habits of belief that we cannot now escape from,—I mean all such factors of belief as fear and hope, prejudice and passion, imitation and partisanship, the circumpressure of our caste and set. As a matter of fact we find our selves believing, we hardly know how or why. Mr. Balfour gives the name of 'authority' to all those influences, born of the intellectual climate, that make hypotheses possible or impossible for us, alive or dead. Here in this room, we all of us believe in molecules and the conservation of energy, in democracy and necessary progress, in Protestant Christianity and the duty of fighting for 'the doctrine of the immortal Monroe,' all for no reasons worthy of the name. We see into these matters with no more inner clearness, and probably with much less, than any disbeliever in them might possess. His unconventionality would probably have some grounds to show for its conclusions; but for us, not insight, but the *prestige* of the opinions, is what makes the spark shoot from them and light up our sleeping magazines of faith. Our reason is quite satisfied, in nine hundred and ninety-nine cases out of every thousand of us, if it can find a few arguments that will do to recite in case our credulity is criticised by someone else. Our

faith is faith in some one else's faith, and in the greatest matters this is most the case. Our belief in truth itself, for instance, that there is a truth, and that our minds and it are made for each other,— what is it but a passionate affirmation of desire, in which our social system backs us up? We want to have a truth; we want to believe that our experiments and studies and discussions must put us in a continually better and better position towards it; and on this line we agree to fight out our thinking lives. But if a pyrrhonistic sceptic asks us *how we know* all this, can our logic find a reply? No! certainly it cannot. It is just one volition against another,—we willing to go in for life upon a trust or assumption which he, for his part, does not care to make. . . .

Evidently, then, our non-intellectual nature does influence our convictions. There are passional tendencies and volitions which run before and others which come after belief, and it is only the latter that are too late for the fair; and they are not too late when the previous passional work has been already in their own direction. Pascal's argument, instead of being powerless, then seems a regular clincher, and is the last stroke needed to make our faith in masses and holy water complete. The state of things is evidently far from simple; and pure insight and logic, whatever they might do ideally, are not the only things that really do produce our creeds.

IV

Our next duty, having recognized this mixed-up state of affairs, is to ask whether it be simply reprehensible and pathological, or whether, on the contrary, we must treat it as a normal element in making up our minds. The thesis I defend is, briefly stated, this: *Our passional nature not only lawfully may, but must, decide an option between propositions, whenever it is a genuine option that cannot by its nature be decided on intellectual grounds; for to say, under such circumstances, "Do not decide, but leave the question open," is itself a passional decision,—just like deciding yes or no,—and is attended with the same risk of losing the truth.* . . .

VII

One more point, small but important, and our preliminaries are done. There are two ways of looking at our duty in the matter of opinion,—ways entirely different, and yet ways about whose difference the theory of knowledge seems hitherto to have shown very little concern. *We must know the truth;* and *we must avoid error,*—these are our first and great commandments as would be knowers; but they are not two ways of stating an identical commandment, they are two separable laws. Although it may indeed happen that when we believe the truth *A,* we escape as an incidental consequence from believing the falsehood *B,* it hardly ever happens that by merely disbelieving *B* we necessarily believe *A.* We may in escaping *B* fall into believing other falsehoods, *C* or *D,* just as bad as *B:* or we may escape *B* by not believing anything at all, not even *A.*

Believe truth! Shun error!—these, we see, are two materially different laws; and by choosing between them we may end, coloring differently our whole intellectual life. We may regard the chase for truth as paramount, and the avoidance of error as secondary; or we may, on the other hand, treat the avoidance of error as more imperative, and let truth take its chance. Clifford, in the instructive passage which I have quoted, exhorts us to the latter course. Believe nothing, he tells us, keep your mind in suspense forever, rather than by closing it on insufficient evidence incur the awful risk of believing lies. You, on the other hand, may think that the risk of being in error is a very small matter when compared with the blessings of real knowledge, and be ready to be duped many times in your investigation rather than postpone indefinitely the chance of guessing true. I myself find it impossible to go with Clifford. We must remember that these feelings of our duty about either truth or error are in any case only expressions of our passional life. Biologically considered, our minds are as ready to grind out falsehood as veracity, and he who says, "Better go without belief forever than believe a lie!" merely shows his own preponderant private horror of becoming a dupe. He may be critical of many of his desires and fears, but this fear he slavishly obeys. He cannot imagine any one questioning its

binding force. For my own part, I have also a horror of being duped; but I can believe that worse things than being duped may happen to a man in this world: so Clifford's exhortation has to my ears a thoroughly fantastic sound. It is like a general informing his soldiers that it is better to keep out of battle forever than to risk a single wound. Not so are victories either over enemies or over nature gained. Our errors are surely not such awfully solemn things. In a world where we are so certain to incur them in spite of all our caution, a certain lightness of heart seems healthier than this excessive nervousness on their behalf. At any rate, it seems the fittest thing for the empiricist philosopher.

VIII

And now, after all this introduction, let us go straight at our question. I have said, and now repeat it, that not only as a matter of fact do we find our passional nature influencing us in our opinions, but that there are some options between opinions in which this influence must be regarded both as an inevitable and as a lawful determinant of our choice.

I fear here that some of you my hearers will begin to scent danger, and lend an inhospitable ear. Two first steps of passion you have indeed had to admit as necessary,—we must think so as to avoid dupery, and we must think so as to gain truth; but the surest path to those ideal consummations, you will probably consider, is from now onwards to take no further passional step.

Well, of course, I agree as far as the facts will allow. Wherever the option between losing truth and gaining it is not momentous, we can throw the chance of *gaining truth* away, and at any rate save ourselves from any chance of *believing falsehood,* by not making up our minds at all till objective evidence has come. In scientific questions, this is almost always the case; and even in human affairs in general, the need of acting is seldom so urgent that a false belief to act on is better than no belief at all. Law courts, indeed, have to decide on the best evidence attainable for the moment, because a judge's duty is to make law as well as to ascertain it, and (as a learned judge once said to me) few cases are worth spending much time over: the great thing is to have them decided on *any* acceptable principle, and got out of the way. But in our dealings with objective nature we obviously are recorders, not makers, of the truth; and decisions for the mere sake of deciding promptly and getting on to the next business would be wholly out of place. Throughout the breadth of physical nature facts are what they are quite independently of us, and seldom is there any such hurry about them that the risks of being duped by believing a premature theory need be faced. The questions here are always trivial options, the hypotheses are hardly living (at any rate not living for us spectators), the choice between believing truth or falsehood is seldom forced. The attitude of sceptical balance is therefore the absolutely wise one if we would escape mistakes. What difference, indeed, does it make to most of us whether we have or have not a theory of the Röntgen rays, whether we believe or not in mind-stuff, or have a conviction about the causality of conscious states? It makes no difference. Such options are not forced on us. On every account it is better not to make them, but still keep weighing reasons *pro et contra* with an indifferent hand.

I speak, of course, here of the purely judging mind. For purposes of discovery such indifference is to be less highly recommended, and science would be far less advanced than she is if the passionate desires of individuals to get their own faiths confirmed had been kept out of the game. See for example the sagacity which Spencer and Weismann now display. On the other hand, if you want an absolute duffer in an investigation, you must, after all, take the man who has no interest whatever in its results: he is the warranted incapable, the positive fool. The most useful investigator, because the most sensitive observer, is always he whose eager interest in one side of the question is balanced by an equally keen nervousness lest he become deceived. Science has organized this nervousness into a regular *technique,* her so-called method of verification; and she has fallen so deeply in love with the method that one may even say she has ceased to care for truth by itself at all. It is only truth as technically verified that interests her. The truth of truths might come in merely affirmative form, and she would decline to touch it. Such truth as that, she might repeat with Clifford, would be stolen in defiance of her duty to mankind. Human passions, however, are stronger than technical rules. "Le coeur a ses raisons," as Pascal says, "que la raison ne connait pas;"* and however indifferent to all but the bare rules of the game the umpire, the abstract intellect, may be, the concrete players who furnish him the materials to judge of are usually, each one of them, in love with some pet 'live hypothesis' of his own. Let us agree, however, that wherever there is no forced option, the dispassionately judicial intellect with no pet hypothesis, saving us, as it does, from dupery at any rate, ought to be our ideal.

The question next arises: Are there not somewhere forced options in our speculative questions, and can we (as men who may be interested at least as much in positively gaining truth as in merely escaping dupery) always wait with impunity till the coercive evidence shall have arrived? It seems *a priori* improbable that the truth should be so nicely adjusted to our needs and powers as that. In the great boardinghouse of nature, the cakes and the butter and the syrup seldom come out so even and leave the plates so clean. Indeed, we should view them with scientific suspicion if they did.

IX

Moral questions immediately present themselves as questions whose solution cannot wait for sensible proof. A moral question is a question not of what sensibly exists, but of what is good, or would be good if it did exist. Science can tell us what exists; but to compare the *worths,* both of what exists and of what does not exist, we must consult not science, but what Pascal calls our heart. . . .

Turn now from these wide questions of good to a certain class of questions of fact, questions concerning personal relations, states of mind between

---

* [Ed.] "The heart has reasons which reason does not know."

one man and another, *Do you like me or not?*—for example. Whether you do or not depends, in countless instances, on whether I meet you half-way, am willing to assume that you must like me, and show you trust and expectation. The previous faith on my part in your liking's existence is in such cases what makes your liking come. But if I stand aloof, and refuse to budge an inch until I have objective evidence, until you shall have done something apt, as the absolutists say, *ad extorquendum assensum meum,* ten to one your liking never comes. How many women's hearts are vanquished by the mere sanguine insistence of some man that they *must* love him! he will not consent to the hypothesis that they cannot. The desire for a certain kind of truth here brings about that special truth's existence; and so it is in innumerable cases of other sorts. Who gains promotions, boons, appointments, but the man in whose life they are seen to play the part of live hypotheses, who discounts them, sacrifices other things for their sake before they have come, and takes risks for them in advance? His faith acts on the powers above him as a claim, and creates its own verification.

A social organism of any sort whatever, large or small, is what it is because each member proceeds to his own duty with a trust that the other members will simultaneously do theirs. Wherever a desired result is achieved by the cooperation of many independent persons, its existence as a fact is a pure consequence of the precursive faith in one another of those immediately concerned. A government, an army, a commercial system, a ship, a college, an athletic team, all exist on this condition, without which not only is nothing achieved, but nothing is even attempted. A whole train of passengers (individually brave enough) will be looted by a few highwaymen, simply because the latter can count on one another, while each passenger fears that if he makes a movement of resistance, he will be shot before any one else backs him up. If we believed that the whole car-full would rise at once with us, we should each severally rise, and train-robbing would never even be attempted. There are, then, cases where a fact cannot come at all unless a preliminary faith exists in its coming. *And where faith in a fact can help create the fact,* that would be an insane

logic which should say that faith running ahead of scientific evidence is the 'lowest kind of immorality' into which a thinking being can fall. Yet such is the logic by which our scientific absolutists pretend to regulate our lives!

X

In truths dependent on our personal action, then, faith based on desire is certainly a lawful and possibly an indispensable thing.

But now, it will be said, these are all childish human cases, and have nothing to do with great cosmical matters, like the question of religious faith. Let us then pass on to that. Religions differ so much in their accidents that in discussing the religious question we must make it very generic and broad. What then do we now mean by the religious hypothesis? Science says things are; morality says some things are better than other things; and religion says essentially two things.

First, she says that the best things are the more eternal things, the overlapping things, the things in the universe that throw the last stone, so to speak, and say the final word. "Perfection is eternal,"—this phrase of Charles Secrétan seems a good way of putting this first affirmation of religion, an affirmation which obviously cannot yet be verified scientifically at all.

The second affirmation of religion is that we are better off even now if we believe her first affirmation to be true.

Now, let us consider what the logical elements of this situation are *in case the religious hypothesis in both its branches be really true.* (Of course, we must admit that possibility at the outset. If we are to discuss the question at all, it must involve a living option. If for any of you religion be a hypothesis that cannot, by any living possibility be true, then you need to go no farther. I speak to the 'saving remnant' alone.) So proceeding, we see, first, that religion offers itself as a *momentous* option. We are supposed to gain, even now, by our belief, and to lose by our nonbelief, a certain vital good. Secondly, religion is a *forced* option, so far as that good goes. We cannot escape the issue by remaining sceptical and waiting for more light, because, although we do avoid error in that way *if religion be untrue,* we lose the good, *if it be true,* just as certainly as if we positively chose to disbelieve. It is as if a man should hesitate indefinitely to ask a certain woman to marry him because he was not perfectly sure that she would prove an angel after he brought her home. Would he not cut himself off from that particular angel-possibility as decisively as if he went and married some one else? Scepticism, then, is not avoidance of option; it is option of a certain particular kind of risk. *Better risk loss of truth than chance of error,*—that is your faith-vetoer's exact position. He is actively playing his stake as much as the believer is; he is backing the field against the religious hypothesis, just as the believer is backing the religious hypothesis against the field. To preach scepticism to us as a duty until 'sufficient evidence' for religion be found, is tantamount therefore to telling us, when in presence of the religious hypothesis, that to yield to our fear of its being error is wiser and better than to yield to our hope that it may be true. It is not intellect against all passions, then; it is only intellect with one passion laying down its law. And by what, forsooth, is the supreme wisdom of this passion warranted? Dupery for dupery, what proof is there that dupery through hope is so much worse than dupery through fear? I, for one, can see no proof; and I simply refuse obedience to the scientist's command to imitate his kind of option, in a case where my own sake is important enough to give me the right to choose my own form of risk. If religion be true and the evidence for it be still insufficient, I do not wish, by putting your extinguisher upon my nature (which feels to me as if it had after all some business in this matter), to forfeit my sole chance in life of getting upon the winning side,—that chance depending, of course, on my willingness to run the risk of acting as if my passional need of taking the world religiously might be prophetic and right.

All this is on the supposition that it really may be prophetic and right, and that, even to us who are discussing the matter, religion is a live hypothesis which may be true. Now, to most of us religion comes in a still further way that makes a veto on our active faith even more illogical. The more perfect and more eternal aspect of the universe is represented in our religions as having personal form. The universe is no longer a mere *It* to us, but a *Thou,* if we are religious; and any relation that may be possible from person to person might be possible here. For instance, although in one sense we are passive portions of the universe, in another we show a curious autonomy, as if we were small active centres on our own account. We feel, too, as if the appeal of religion to us were made to our own active good-will, as if evidence might be forever withheld from us unless we met the hypothesis half-way. To take a trivial illustration: just as a man who in a company of gentlemen made no advances, asked a warrant for every concession, and believed no one's word without proof, would cut himself off by such churlishness from all the social rewards that a more trusting spirit would earn,—so here, one who should shut himself up in snarling logicality and try to make the gods extort his recognition willy-nilly, or not get it at all, might cut himself off forever from his only opportunity of making the gods' acquaintance. This feeling, forced on us we know not whence, that by obstinately believing that there are gods (although not to do so would be so easy both for our logic and our life) we are doing the universe the deepest service we can, seems part of the living essence of the religious hypothesis. If the hypothesis *were* true in all its parts, including this one, then pure intellectualism, with its veto on our making willing advances, would be an absurdity; and some participation of our sympathetic nature would be logically required. I, therefore, for one, cannot see my way to accepting the agnostic rules for truth-seeking, or wilfully agree to keep my willing nature out of the game. I cannot do so for this plain reason, that *a rule of thinking which would absolutely prevent me from acknowledging certain kinds of truth if those kinds of truth were really there, would be an irrational rule.* That for me is the long and short of the formal logic of the situation, no matter what the kinds of truth might materially be.

I confess I do not see how this logic can be escaped. But sad experience makes me fear that some of you may still shrink from radically saying with me, in *abstracto,* that we have the right to believe at our own risk any hypothesis that is live enough to tempt our will. I suspect, however, that if this is so, it is because you have got away from the abstract logical point of view altogether, and are thinking (perhaps without realizing it) of some particular religious hypothesis which for you is dead. The freedom to "believe what we will" you apply to the case of some patent superstition; and the faith you think of is the faith defined by the school-boy when he said, "Faith is when you believe something that you know ain't true." I can only repeat that this is misapprehension. *In concreto,* the freedom to believe can only cover living options which the intellect of the individual cannot by itself resolve; and living options never seem absurdities to him who has them to consider. When I look at the religious question as it really puts itself to concrete men, and when I think of all the possibilities which both practically and theoretically it involves, then this command that we shall put a stopper on our hearts, instincts, and courage, and *wait*—acting of course meanwhile more or less as if religion were *not* true*—till doomsday, or till such time as our in-

* [Author's note] Since belief is measured by action, he who forbids us to believe religion to be true, necessarily also forbids us to act as we should if we did believe it to be true. The whole defence of religious faith hinges upon action. If the action required or inspired by the religious hypothesis is in no way different from that dictated by the naturalistic hypothesis, then religious faith is a pure superfluity, better pruned away, and controversy about its legitimacy is a piece of idle trifling, unworthy of serious minds. I myself believe, of course, that the religious hypothesis gives to the world an expression which specifically determines our reactions, and makes them in a large part unlike what they might be on a purely naturalistic scheme of belief.

tellect and senses working together may have raked in evidence enough—this command, I say, seems to me the queerest idol ever manufactured in the philosophic cave. Were we scholastic absolutists, there might be more excuse. If we had an infallible intellect with its objective certitudes, we might feel ourselves disloyal to such a perfect organ of knowledge in not trusting to it exclusively, in not waiting for its releasing word. But if we are empiricists, if we believe that no bell in us tolls to let us know for certain when truth is in our grasp, then it seems a piece of idle fantasticality to preach so solemnly our duty of waiting for the bell. Indeed we *may* wait if we will—I hope you do not think that I am denying that—but if we do so, we do so at our peril as much as if we believed. In either case we *act*, taking our life in our hands. No one of us ought to issue vetoes to the other, nor should we bandy words of abuse. We ought, on the contrary, delicately and profoundly to respect one another's mental freedom: then only shall we bring about the intellectual republic; then only shall we have that spirit of inner tolerance without which all our outer tolerance is soulless, and which is empiricism's glory; then only shall we live and let live, in speculative as well as in practical things.

Questions for Reflection

1. Which of the following two rules do you think would provide the best guidance for life? Clifford's rule: Better risk the loss of truth than the chance of error by believing only what we know is true. James's rule: Better risk the chance of error than the loss of truth by believing what might maximize our good.

2. Do you think James has given us practical guidelines for forming beliefs or has he given us a blank check to believe whatever makes us comfortable?

MICHAEL SCRIVEN

Faith Is Not Justified

Michael Scriven (1928–) has taught in the United States and Australia, in departments of mathematics, philosophy, psychology, the history and philosophy of science, and education. In the following selection from his book *Primary Philosophy*, Scriven argues that the burden of proof is on the theist to show that the existence of God is provable or at least probable. Elsewhere he has argued, in agreement with David Hume, that the arguments for God fail and that theism is wholly unfounded. However, unlike Hume, Scriven does not think that agnosticism or suspension of judgment is the proper response to the God issue. Agnosticism is the proper attitude, he says, when the evidence makes a thesis approximately 50 percent probable. However, since Scriven argues that theism lacks even this minimal support, he claims that we should reject it outright.

Reading Questions

1. Why does Scriven think that saying "I take it on faith" can never justify a belief?
2. Why does he claim that the common religious experience of the community of believers does not validate religious belief?
3. In what ways does he see scientific beliefs as different than religious beliefs?
4. Why does Scriven claim that the burden of proof is on the theist and not the atheist?
5. According to Scriven's diagram, what are the seven degrees of evidential support? What are the labels he gives to the five appropriate responses to each degree of evidence?
6. If we can neither prove nor disprove theism, why does Scriven think that atheism and not agnosticism is the proper stance?

Faith and Reason

We must now contend with the suggestion that reason is irrelevant to the commitment to theism because this territory is the domain of another faculty: the faculty of faith. It is sometimes even hinted that it is morally wrong and certainly foolish to suggest we should be reasoning about God. For this is the domain of faith or of the "venture of faith," of the "knowledge that passeth understanding," of religious experience and mystic insight.

Now the normal meaning of *faith* is simply "confidence"; we say that we have great faith in someone or in some claim or product, meaning that we believe and act as if they were very reliable. Of such faith we can properly say that it is well founded or not, depending on the evidence for whatever it is in which we have faith. So there is no incompatibility between this kind of faith and reason; the two are from different families and can make a very good marriage. Indeed if they do not join forces, then the resulting ill-based or inadequate confi-

From Michael Scriven, *Primary Philosophy* (New York: McGraw-Hill, 1966).

dence will probably lead to disaster. So faith, in this sense, means only a high degree of belief and may be reasonable or unreasonable.

But the term is sometimes used to mean an *alternative to reason* instead of something that should be founded on reason. Unfortunately, the mere use of the term in this way does not demonstrate that faith is a possible route to truth. It is like using the term "winning" as a synonym for "playing" instead of one possible outcome of playing. This is quaint, but it could hardly be called a satisfactory way of proving that we are winning; any time we "win" by changing the meaning of winning, the victory is merely illusory. And so it proves in this case. To use "faith" *as if* it were an alternative way to the truth cannot by-pass the crucial question whether such results really have any likelihood of being true. A rose by any other name will smell the same, and the inescapable facts about "faith" in the new sense are that it is still *applied* to a belief and is still supposed to imply *confidence* in that belief: the belief in the existence and goodness of God. So we can still ask the same old question about that belief: Is the confidence justified or misplaced? To say we "take it on faith" does not get it off parole.

Suppose someone replies that theism is a kind of belief that does not need justification by evidence. This means either that no one cares whether it is correct or not or that there is some other way of checking that it is correct besides looking at the evidence for it, i.e., giving reasons for believing it. But the first alternative is false since very many people care whether there is a God or not: and the second alternative is false because any method of showing that belief is likely to be true is, by definition, a justification of that belief, i.e., an appeal to reason. You certainly cannot show that a belief in God is likely to be true just by having confidence in it and by saying this is a case of knowledge "based on" faith, any more than you can win a game just by playing it and by calling that winning.

It is psychologically possible to have faith in something without any basis in fact, and once in a while you will turn out to be lucky and to have backed the right belief. This does not show you "really knew all along"; it only shows you cannot be un-

lucky all the time. But, in general, beliefs without foundations lead to an early grave or to an accumulation of superstitions, which are usually troublesome and always false beliefs. It is hardly possible to defend this approach just by *saying* that you have decided that in this area confidence is its own justification.

Of course, you might try to *prove* that a feeling of great confidence about certain types of propositions is a reliable indication of their truth. If you succeeded, you would indeed have shown that the belief was justified; you would have done this by justifying it. To do this you would have to show what the real facts were and show that when someone had the kind of faith we are now talking about, it usually turned out that the facts were as he believed, just as we might justify the claims of a telepath. The catch in all this is simply that you have got to show what the real facts are in some way *other* than by appealing to faith, since that would simply be assuming what you are trying to prove. And if you can show what the facts are in this other way, you do not need faith in any new sense at all; you are already perfectly entitled to confidence in any belief that you have shown to be well supported.

How are you going to show what the real facts are? You show this by any method of investigation that has itself been tested, the testing being done by still another tested method, etc., through a series of tested connections that eventually terminates in our ordinary everyday reasoning and testing procedures of logic and observation.

Is it not prejudiced to require that the validation of beliefs always involve ultimate reference to our ordinary logic and everyday-plus-scientific knowledge? May not faith (religious experience, mystic insight) give us access to some new domain of truth? It is certainly possible that it does this. But, of course, it is also possible that it lies. One can hardly accept the reports of those with faith or, indeed, the apparent revelations of one's own religious experiences on the ground that they *might* be right. So *might* be a fervent materialist who saw his interpretation as a revelation. Possibility is not veracity. Is it not of the very greatest importance that we should try to find out whether we really can justify the use of the term "truth" or "knowledge" in describing the content of faith? If it is, then we must find something in that content that is known to be true in some other way, because to get off the ground we must first push off against the ground—we cannot lift ourselves by our shoelaces. If the new realm of knowledge is to be a realm of knowledge and not mythology, then it must tell us something which relates it to the kind of case that gives meaning to the term "truth." If you want to use the old word for the new events, you must show that it is applicable.

Could not the validating experience, which religious experience must have if it is to be called true, be the experience of others who also have or have had religious experiences? The religious community could, surely, provide a basis of agreement analogous to that which ultimately underlies scientific truth. Unfortunately, agreement is not the only requirement for avoiding error, for all may be in error. The difficulty for the religious community is to show that its agreement is not simply agreement about a shared mistake. If agreement were the only criterion of truth, there could never be a shared mistake; but clearly either the atheist group or the theist group shares a mistake. To decide which is wrong must involve appeal to something other than mere agreement. And, of course, it is clear that particular religious beliefs are mistaken, since religious groups do not all agree and they cannot all be right.

Might not some or all scientific beliefs be wrong, too? This is conceivable, but there are crucial differences between the two kinds of belief. In the first place, any commonly agreed religious beliefs concern only one or a few entities and their properties and histories. What for convenience we are here calling "scientific belief" is actually the sum total of all conventionally founded human knowledge, much of it not part of any science, and it embraces billions upon billions of facts, each of them perpetually or frequently subject to checking by independent means, each connected with a million others. The success of *this* system of knowledge shows up every day in everything that we do: we eat, and the food is not poison; we read, and the pages do not turn to dust; we slip, and gravity does not

fail to pull us down. We are not just relying on the existence of agreement about the interpretation of a certain experience among a small part to the population. We are relying directly on our extremely reliable, nearly universal, and independently tested senses, and each of us is constantly obtaining independent confirmation for claims based on these, many of these confirmations being obtained for many claims, independently of each other. It is the wildest flight of fancy to suppose that there is a body of common religious beliefs which can be set out to exhibit this degree of repeated checking by religious experiences. In fact, there is not only gross disagreement on even the most fundamental claims in the creeds of different churches, each of which is supported by appeal to religious experience or faith, but where there is agreement by many people, it is all too easily open to the criticism that it arises from the common cultural exposure of the child or the adult convert and hence is not independent in the required way.

This claim that the agreement between judges is spurious in a particular case because it only reflects previous common indoctrination of those in agreement is a serious one. It must always be met by direct disproof whenever agreement is appealed to in science, and it is. The claim that the food is not poison cannot be explained away as a myth of some subculture, for anyone, even if told nothing about the eaters in advance, will judge that the people who ate it are still well. The whole methodology of testing is committed to the doctrine that any judges who could have learned what they are expected to say about the matter they are judging are completely valueless. Now anyone exposed to religious teaching, whether a believer or not, has long known the standard for such experiences, the usual symbols, the appropriate circumstances, and so on. These suggestions are usually very deeply implanted, so that they cannot be avoided by good intentions, and consequently members of our culture are rendered entirely incapable of being independent observers. Whenever observers are not free from previous contamination in this manner, the only way to support their claims is to examine independently testable *consequences* of the novel claims, such as predictions about the future. In the absence of these, the religious-experience gambit, whether involving literal or analogical claims, is wholly abortive.

A still more fundamental point counts against the idea that agreement among the religious can help support the idea of faith as an alternative path to truth. It is that every sane theist also believes in the claims of ordinary experience, while the reverse is not the case. Hence, the burden of proof is on the theist to show that the *further step* he wishes to take will not take him beyond the realm of truth. The two positions, of science and religion, are not symmetrical; the adherent of one of them suggests that we extend the range of allowable beliefs and yet is unable to produce the same degree of acceptance or "proving out" in the ordinary field of human activities that he insists on before believing in a new instrument or source of information. The atheist obviously cannot be shown his error in the way someone who thinks that there are no electrons can be shown his, *unless some of the arguments for the existence of God are sound.* Once again, we come back to these. If some of them work, the position of religious knowledge is secure, if they do not, nothing else will make it secure.

In sum, the idea of separating religious from scientific knowledge and making each an independent realm with its own basis in experience of quite different kinds is a counsel of despair and not a product of true sophistication, for one cannot break the connection between everyday experience and religious claims, for purposes of defending the latter, without eliminating the consequences of religion for everyday life. There is no way out of this inexorable contract: if you want to support your beliefs, you must produce some experience which can be shown to be a reliable indicator of truth, and that can be done only by showing a connection between the experience and what we know to be true in a previously established way.

So, if the criteria of religious truth are not connected with the criteria of everyday truth, then they are not criteria of truth at all and the beliefs they "establish" have no essential bearing on our lives, constitute no explanation of what we see around us, and provide no guidance for our course through time.

THE CONSEQUENCES IF THE ARGUMENTS FAIL

The arguments are the only way to establish theism, and they must be judged by the usual standards of evidence—this we have argued. It will now be shown that if they fail, there is no alternative to atheism.

Against this it has commonly been held that the absence of arguments *for* the existence of something is not the same as the presence of arguments *against* its existence; so agnosticism or an option remains when the arguments fail. But insofar as this is true, it is irrelevant. It is true only if we restrict "arguments for the existence of something" to highly specific demonstrations which attempt to establish their conclusion as beyond all reasonable doubt. The absence of these is indeed compatible with the conclusion's being quite likely, which would make denial of its existence unjustified. But if we take arguments for the existence of something to include all the evidence which supports the existence claim to any significant degree, i.e., makes it at all probable, then the absence of such evidence means there is *no* likelihood of the existence of the entity. And this, of course, is a complete justification for the claim that the entity does not exist, provided that the entity is not one which might leave no traces (a God who is impotent or who does not care for us), and provided that we have comprehensively examined the area where such evidence would appear if there were any. Now justifying the claim that something does not exist is not quite the same as proving or having arguments that it doesn't, but it is what we are talking about. That is, we need not have a proof that God does not exist in order to justify atheism. Atheism is obligatory in the absence of any evidence for God's existence.

Why do adults not believe in Santa Claus? Simply because they can now explain the phenomena for which Santa Claus's existence is invoked without any need for introducing a novel entity. When we were very young and naively believed our parents' stories, it was hard to see how the presents could get there on Christmas morning since the doors were locked and our parents were asleep in bed. Someone *must* have brought them down the chimney. And how could that person get to the roof without a ladder and with all those presents? Surely only by flying. And then there is that great traditional literature of stories and songs which immortalize the entity and his (horned) attendants; surely these cannot all be just products of imagination? Where there is smoke, there must be fire.

Santa Claus is not a bad hypothesis at all for six-year-olds. As we grow up, no one comes forward to *prove* that such an entity does not exist. We just come to see that there is not the least reason to think he *does* exist. And so it would be entirely foolish to assert that he does, or believe that he does, or even think it likely that he does. Santa Claus is in just the same position as fairy godmothers, wicked witches, the devil, and the ether. Each of these entities has some supernatural powers, i.e., powers which contravene or go far beyond the powers that we know exist, whether it be the power to levitate a sled and reindeer or the power to cast a spell. Now even belief in something for which there is *no* evidence, i.e., a belief which goes *beyond* the evidence, although a lesser sin than belief in something which is *contrary* to well-established laws, is plainly irrational in that it simply amounts to attaching belief where it is not justified. So the proper alternative, when there is no evidence, is not mere suspension of belief, e.g., about Santa Claus, it is *disbelief*. It most certainly is not faith.

The situation is slightly different with the Abominable Snowman, sea serpents, or even the Loch Ness monster. No "supernatural" (by which, in this context, we only mean wholly unprecedented) kinds of powers are involved. Previous discoveries have been made of creatures which had long seemed extinct, and from these we can immediately derive some likelihood of further discoveries. Footprints or disturbances for which no fully satisfactory alternative explanation has yet been discovered (although such an explanation is by no means impossible) have been seen in the Himalayan snow and the Scottish lochs. It would be credulous for the layman to believe firmly in the existence of these entities. Yet it would be equally inappropriate to say it is certain they do not exist. Here is a do-

main for agnosticism (though perhaps an agnosticism inclined toward skepticism). For the agnostic does not believe that a commitment either way is justified, and he is surely right about strange creatures which, while of a new *appearance,* have powers that are mere extensions, proportional to size, of those with which we are already familiar on this Earth. There is some suggestive, if by no means conclusive, evidence for such entities; and the balance of general considerations is not heavily against them.

But when the assertion is made that something exists with powers that strikingly transcend the well-established generalizations we have formulated about animal capacities or reasonable extrapolations from them, then we naturally expect correspondingly better evidence before we concede that there is a serious likelihood of having to abandon those generalizations. It is entirely appropriate to demand much stronger support for claims of telepathy or levitation or miraculous cures than for new sports records or feats of memory in which previous levels of performance are merely bettered to some degree, in a way that is almost predictable. On the other hand, it is entirely prejudiced to reject all such evidence on the ground that it *must* be deceptive because it contravenes previously established generalizations. This is simply to deify the present state of science; it is the precise opposite of the experimental attitude. It is right to demand a stronger case to overthrow a strong case and to demand very strong evidence to demonstrate unprecedented powers. It is irrational to require that the evidence of these powers be just as commonplace and compelling as for the previously known powers of man or beast: one cannot legislate the exceptional into the commonplace.

We can now use a set of distinctions that would previously have seemed very abstract. First, let us distinguish a belief which is wholly without general or particular evidential support from one which can be directly disproved. The claim that a race of men lives on the moons of Jupiter or that a certain cola causes cancer of the colon is entirely unfounded but not totally impossible. The view that the ratio of a circle's circumference to its diameter can be expressed as a fraction is demonstrably untenable, as is the view that some living men are infinitely strong, or that any man is or has been unbeatable at chess, or that the FBI has wiped out the Mafia. We normally say that a claim is *well founded* if there is evidence which is best explained by this claim. We may say it is *provable* if the evidence is indubitable and the claim is very clearly required. If there is no evidence which points to this particular claim, although some general background considerations make it not too unlikely that something like this should be true (Loch Ness monster, mile record broken twice in 1980), we would say there is *some general support* for the claim. We shall say it is *wholly unfounded* (or *wholly unsupported*) if there is no evidence for it in particular and no general considerations in its favor, and *disprovable* if it implies that something would be the case that definitely is not the case.

Of course it is foolish to believe a claim that is disproved, but it is also foolish to believe a wholly unsupported claim, and it is still foolish even to treat such a claim as if it were worth serious consideration. A claim for which there is some general or some particular support cannot be dismissed, but neither can it be treated as established. The connection between evidential support and the appropriate degree of belief can be demonstrated as shown in the diagram on the next page, which is quite unlike the oversimplified idea that the arrangement should be:

Provable   Theism

Disprovable   Atheism

Neither   Agnosticism

The crucial difference is that both "unfounded" and "disprovable" correlate with atheism, just as the two corresponding types of provability correlate with theism; hence the agnostic's territory is smaller than he often supposes.

Recalling that to get even a little evidential support for the existence of a Being with supernatural powers will require that the little be of very high quality (*little* does not mean "dubious"), we see that the failure of all the arguments, i.e., of all the evidence, will make even agnosticism in the wide sense an indefensible exaggeration of the evidential support. And agnosticism in the narrow sense will be an exaggeration unless the arguments are strong enough to establish about a 50 percent probability for the claim of theism. Apart from the wide and narrow senses of agnosticism there is also a distinction between a positive agnostic and a negative agnostic.

A *positive agnostic* maintains that the evidence is such as to make his position the correct one and those of the theist and atheist incorrect. *Negative agnosticism* is simply the position of not accepting either theism or atheism, it does not suggest that they are both wrong—it may be just an expression of felt indecision or ignorance. The difference between negative and positive agnosticism is like the difference between a *neutral* who says, "I don't know who's right—maybe one of the disputants, or maybe neither," and a *third force* who says. "Neither is right, and I have a third alternative which *is* right." Obviously, the negative agnostic has not progressed as far in his thinking as the positive agnostic, in one sense, because he has not been able to decide which of the three possible positions is correct. The view of the negative agnostic cannot be right, but his position may be the right position for someone who has not thought the matter through or who lacks the capacity to do so.

In practice, an agnostic's position is often the product of an untidy mixture of factors. He may never have happened to come across an argument for either theism or atheism which struck him as compelling; a rough head counting has revealed intelligent people on either side; his nose for social stigmas indicates a slight odor of intellectual deficiency attached to theism by contemporary intellectuals and a suggestion of unnecessary boat rocking or perhaps rabid subversion attached to atheism. This makes the agnostic fence look pretty attractive; so up he climbs, to sit on top. But now we put the challenge to him. Is he incapable of thinking out an answer for himself? If so, he is intellectually inferior to those below; if not, he must descend and demonstrate the failings of the contestants before he is entitled to his perch. Agnosticism as a position is interesting and debatable; agnosticism as the absence of a position is simply a sign of the absence of intellectual activity or capacity.

EVIDENTIAL SITUATION	APPROPRIATE ATTITUDE	NAME FOR APPROPRIATE ATTITUDE IN THEISM CASE	
1. Strictly disprovable, i.e., demonstrably incompatible with the evidence.	Rejection	Atheism	
2. Wholly unfounded, i.e., wholly lacking in general or particular support.			
3. Possessing some general or particular support; still improbable.	Skepticism but recognition as a real *possibility;* not to be wholly disregarded in comprehensive planning but to be bet *against.*	Skepticism	Agnosticism (wide sense)
4. Possessing substantial support but with substantial alternatives still open; a balance of evidence for and against; about 50 percent probable.	Suspension of judgment. Make no commitment either way; treat each alternative as approximately equally serious.	Agnosticism (narrow sense)	
5. Possessing powerful evidential support; some difficulties of inadequacies or significant alternatives remaining; probable.	Treat as probably true; bet *on.*	Pragmatic theism	
6. Possessing overwhelming particular support and no basis for alternative views; beyond reasonable doubt; provable in the usual sense.	Acceptance	Theism	
7. Strictly provable, i.e., as a demonstrably necessary result of indubitable facts.			

Questions for Reflection

1. Do you agree with Scriven that theism lacks *any* support? If not, where would you place theism in his list of seven degrees of evidential support?
2. What do you think of Scriven's claim that theism needs to be proven to accept it, but atheism does not?
3. In the earlier reading by Pascal, he agrees that God's existence cannot be proven. How, then, would Pascal respond to Scriven's argument? How would William James respond?

ANTONY FLEW, R. M. HARE, AND BASIL MITCHELL

Three Parables about Religious Faith

Antony Flew (1923–) has taught at universities all over the world, including England, Scotland, Australia, the United States, and Canada. R. M. Hare (1919–2002) and Basil Mitchell (1917–) were professors at Oxford University until their retirement. All three were educated at Oxford University and began their teaching careers there. Each, in his own way, has made important contributions to contemporary philosophy of religion even though their respective views are quite divergent.

The following selection is the transcript of a 1948 Oxford University symposium. In a now famous parable, Flew examines the conditions that would make a belief cognitively meaningful. He claims that if nothing could conceivably count against a belief, it does not really assert anything at all about the world. He thus challenges believers to state what conditions could possibly cause them to abandon their belief that "God exists" or "God loves us." Flew's position is more radical than that of the traditional skeptic who questions the *truth* of these claims. Instead, Flew questions their *meaningfulness*. If there is nothing that could possibly conflict with these beliefs, then it is not clear that they are making meaningful claims at all. Illustrating his points with his own parable, Hare agrees with Flew that religious faith cannot be falsified. This is because it is based on a set of basic assumptions, which he calls "bliks," that can neither be proven nor disproven. We cannot subject them to rational scrutiny, Hare claims, because they provide the framework for all our other beliefs, including our notions of what is and what is not rationally acceptable. Hare goes on to suggest that even our ordinary, nonreligious beliefs rest on such fundamental assumptions. Finally, Mitchell tries to arrive at a compromise position. In yet another parable, he argues that rational considerations may

---

From *New Essays in Philosophical Theology,* ed. Antony Flew and Alasdair MacIntyre (New York: Macmillan, 1955).

play a role in faith and that believers may find evidence that counts for their faith as well as against it. Each type of data should be weighed carefully. Mitchell even suggests that there may be a point at which the weight of the negative evidence could make a faith irrational. However, he says we cannot provide criteria in advance of when that point is reached and implies that it is unlikely that this sort of decisive refutation could occur. In the meantime, believers may face ambiguous evidence, but they also have reasons that led to their initial commitment in the first place. Hence, Mitchell claims that it is rational for believers to acknowledge conflicts while not letting anything count decisively against their faith.

Reading Questions

1. In Flew's parable, who does the gardener represent? What positions are represented by each explorer?
2. What point about religious claims is Flew making with his parable?
3. What does Flew mean when he says a hypothesis can suffer "death by a thousand qualifications"?
4. What is Hare's point concerning the paranoid?
5. What does Hare mean by a "blik"? How do bliks function?
6. What does Hare mean when he says both the lunatic and sane persons have their respective bliks?
7. In what ways does Hare agree with Flew? In what ways does he disagree with Flew?
8. What is the point of Mitchell's story about the stranger and the partisan?
9. In what ways does Mitchell agree with Flew? With Hare? What are his disagreements with each of them?

ANTONY FLEW

Let us begin with a parable. It is a parable developed from a tale told by John Wisdom in his haunting and revelatory article 'Gods,'[1] Once upon a time two explorers came upon a clearing in the jungle. In the clearing were growing many flowers and many weeds. One explorer says, 'Some gardener must tend this plot.' The other disagrees, 'There is no gardener.' So they pitch their tents and set a watch. No gardener is ever seen. 'But perhaps he is an invisible gardener.' So they set up a barbed-wire fence. They electrify it. They patrol with bloodhounds. (For they remember how H. G. Wells's *The Invisible Man* could be both smelt and touched though he could not be seen.) But no shrieks ever suggest that some intruder has received a shock. No movements of the wire ever betray an invisible climber. The bloodhounds never

give cry. Yet still the Believer is not convinced. 'But there is a gardener, invisible, intangible, insensible to electric shocks, a gardener who has no scent and makes no sound, a gardener who comes secretly to look after the garden which he loves.' At last the Sceptic despairs, 'But what remains of your original assertion? Just how does what you call an invisible, intangible, eternally elusive gardener differ from an imaginary gardener or even from no gardener at all?'

In this parable we can see how what starts as an assertion, that something exists or that there is some analogy between certain complexes of phenomena, may be reduced step by step to an altogether different status, to an expression perhaps of a 'picture preference.' The Sceptic says there is no gardener. The Believer says there is a gardener (but invisible, etc.). One man talks about sexual behaviour. Another man prefers to talk of Aphrodite (but knows that there is not really a superhuman person additional to, and somehow responsible for, all sexual phenomena). The process of qualification may be checked at any point before the original assertion is completely withdrawn and something of that first assertion will remain (Tautology). Mr. Wells's invisible man could not, admittedly, be seen, but in all other respects he was a man like the rest of us. But though the process of qualification may be, and of course usually is, checked in time, it is not always judiciously so halted. Someone may dissipate his assertion completely without noticing that he has done so. A fine brash hypothesis may thus be killed by inches, the death by a thousand qualifications.

And in this, it seems to me, lies the peculiar danger, the endemic evil, of theological utterance. Take such utterances as 'God has a plan.' 'God created the world,' 'God loves us as a father loves his children.' They look at first sight very much like assertions, vast cosmological assertions. Of course, this is no sure sign that they either are, or are intended to be, assertions. But let us confine ourselves to the cases where those who utter such sentences intend them to express assertions. (Merely remarking parenthetically that those who intend or interpret such utterances as crypto-commands, expressions of wishes, disguised ejaculations, concealed ethics, or as anything else but assertions, are unlikely to succeed in making them either properly orthodox or practically effective).

Now to assert that such and such is the case is necessarily equivalent to denying that such and such is not the case. Suppose then that we are in doubt as to what someone who gives vent to an utterance is asserting, or suppose that, more radically, we are sceptical as to whether he is really asserting anything at all, one way of trying to understand (or perhaps it will be to expose) his utterance is to attempt to find what he would regard as counting against, or as being incompatible with, its truth. For if the utterance is indeed an assertion, it will necessarily be equivalent to a denial of the negation of that assertion. And anything which would count against the assertion, or which would induce the speaker to withdraw it and to admit that it had been mistaken, must be part of (or the whole

of) the meaning of the negation of that assertion. And to know the meaning of the negation of an assertion, is as near as makes no matter, to know the meaning of that assertion. And if there is nothing which a putative assertion denies then there is nothing which it asserts either: and so it is not really an assertion. When the Sceptic in the parable asked the Believer, 'Just how does what you call an invisible, intangible, eternally elusive gardener differ from an imaginary gardener or even from no gardener at all?' he was suggesting that the Believer's earlier statement had been so eroded by qualification that it was no longer an assertion at all.

Now it often seems to people who are not religious as if there was no conceivable event or series of events the occurrence of which would be admitted by sophisticated religious people to be a sufficient reason for conceding 'There wasn't a God after all' or 'God does not really love us then.' Someone tells us that God loves us as a father loves his children. We are reassured. But then we see a child dying of inoperable cancer of the throat. His earthly father is driven frantic in his efforts to help, but his Heavenly Father reveals no obvious sign of concern. Some qualification is made—God's love is 'not a merely human love' or it is 'an inscrutable love,' perhaps—and we realize that such sufferings are quite compatible with the truth of the assertion that 'God loves us as a father (but, of course, . . .).' We are reassured again. But then perhaps we ask: what is this assurance of God's (appropriately qualified) love worth, what is this apparent guarantee really a guarantee against? Just what would have to happen not merely (morally and wrongly) to tempt but also (logically and rightly) to entitle us to say 'God does not love us' or even 'God does not exist'? I therefore put to the succeeding symposiasts the simple central questions, 'What would have to occur or to have occurred to constitute for you a disproof of the love of, or of the existence of, God?'

R. M. HARE

I wish to make it clear that I shall not try to defend Christianity in particular, but religion in general—not because I do not believe in Christianity, but because you cannot understand what Christianity is, until you have understood what religion is.

I must begin by confessing that, on the ground marked out by Flew, he seems to me to be completely victorious. I therefore shift my ground by relating another parable. A certain lunatic is convinced that all dons want to murder him. His friends introduce him to all the mildest and most respectable dons that they can find, and after each of them has retired, they say, 'You see, he doesn't really want to murder you; he spoke to you in a most cordial manner; surely you are convinced now?' But the lunatic replies 'Yes, but that was only his diabolical cunning; he's really plotting against me the whole time, like the rest of them; I know it I tell you.' However many kindly dons are produced, the reaction is still the same.

Now we say that such a person is deluded. But what is he deluded about? About the truth or falsity of an assertion? Let us apply Flew's test to him. There is no behaviour of dons that can be enacted which he will accept as counting against his theory; and therefore his theory, on this test, asserts nothing. But it does not follow that there is no difference between what he thinks about dons and what most of us think about them—otherwise we should not call him a lunatic and ourselves sane, and dons would have no reason to feel uneasy about his presence in Oxford.

Let us call that in which we differ from this lunatic, our respective *bliks*. He has an insane *blik* about dons; we have a sane one. It is important to realize that we have a sane one, not no *blik* at all; for there must be two sides to any argument—if he has a wrong *blik*, then those who are right about dons must have a right one. Flew has shown that a *blik* does not consist in an assertion or system of them; but nevertheless it is very important to have the right *blik*.

Let us try to imagine what it would be like to have different *bliks* about other things than dons. When I am driving my car, it sometimes occurs to me to wonder whether my movements of the steering-wheel will always continue to be followed by corresponding alterations in the direction of the car. I have never had a steering failure, though I have had skids, which must be similar. Moreover, I know enough about how the steering of my car is made, to know the sort of thing that would have to go wrong for the steering to fail—steel joints would have to part, or steel rods break, or something—but how do I know that this won't happen? The truth is, I don't know; I just have a *blik* about steel and its properties, so that normally I trust the steering of my car; but I find it not at all difficult to imagine what it would be like to lose this *blik* and acquire the opposite one. People would say I was silly about steel; but there would be no mistaking the reality of the difference between our respective *bliks*—for example, I should never go in a motor-car. Yet I should hesitate to say that the difference between us was the difference between contradictory assertions. No amount of safe arrivals or bench-tests will remove my *blik* and restore the normal one; for my *blik* is compatible with any finite number of such tests.

It was Hume who taught us that our whole commerce with the world depends upon our *blik* about the world; and that differences between *bliks* about the world cannot be settled by observation of what happens in the world. That was why, having performed the interesting experiment of doubting the ordinary man's *blik* about the world, and showing that no proof could be given to make us adopt one *blik* rather than another, he turned to backgammon to take his mind off the problem. It seems, indeed, to be impossible even to formulate as an assertion the normal *blik* about the world which makes me put my confidence in the future reliability of steel joints, in the continued ability of the road to support my car, and not gape beneath it revealing nothing below; in the general non-homicidal tendencies of dons; in my own continued well-being (in some sense of that word that I may not now fully understand) if I continue to do what is right according to my lights; in the general likelihood of people like Hitler coming to a bad end. But perhaps a formulation less inadequate than most is to be found in the Psalms: 'The earth is weak and all the inhabiters thereof: I bear up the pillars of it.'

The mistake of the position which Flew selects for attack is to regard this kind of talk as some sort of *explanation*, as scientists are accustomed to use the word. As such, it would obviously be ludicrous. We no longer believe in God as an Atlas—*nous n'avons pas besoin de cette hypothèse.* But it is nevertheless true to say that, as Hume saw, without a *blik* there can be no explanation; for it is by our *bliks* that we decide what is and what is not an explanation. Suppose we believed that everything that happened, happened by pure chance. This would not of course be an assertion; for it is compatible with anything happening or not happening, and so, incidentally, is its contradictory. But if we had this belief, we should not be able to explain or predict or plan anything. Thus, although we should not be *asserting* anything different from those of a more normal belief, there would be a great difference between us; and this is the sort of difference that there is between those who really believe in God and those who really disbelieve in him.

The word 'really' is important, and may excite suspicion. I put it in, because when people have had a good Christian upbringing, as have most of those who now profess not to believe in any sort of religion, it is very hard to discover what they really believe. The reason why they find it so easy to think that they are not religious, is that they have never got into the frame of mind of one who suffers from the doubts to which religion is the answer. Not for them the terrors of the primitive jungle. Having abandoned some of the more picturesque fringes of religion, they think that they have abandoned the whole thing—whereas in fact they still have got, and could not live without, a religion of a comfortably substantial, albeit highly sophisticated, kind, which differs from that of many 'religious people' in little more than this, that 'religious people' like to sing Psalms about theirs—a very natural and proper thing to do. But nevertheless there may be a big difference lying behind—the difference between two people who, though side by side, are walking in different directions. I do not know in what direction Flew is walking; perhaps he does not know either. But we have had some examples recently of various ways in which one can walk away from Christianity, and there are any number of possibilities. After all, man has not changed biologically since primitive times; it is his religion that has changed, and it can easily change again. And if you do not think that such changes make a difference, get acquainted with some Sikhs and some Mussulmans of the same Punjabi stock; you will find them quite different sorts of people.

There is an important difference between Flew's parable and my own which we have not yet noticed. The explorers do not *mind* about their garden; they discuss it with interest, but not with concern. But my lunatic, poor fellow, minds about dons; and I mind about the steering of my car; it often has people in it that I care for. It is because I mind very much about what goes on in the garden in which I find myself, that I am unable to share the explorers' detachment.

BASIL MITCHELL

Flew's article is searching and perceptive, but there is, I think, something odd about his conduct of the theologian's case. The theologian surely would not deny that the fact of pain counts against the assertion that God loves men. This very incompatibility generates the most intractable of theological problems—the problem of evil. So the theologian *does* recognize the fact of pain as counting against Christian doctrine. But it is true that he will not allow it—or anything—to count decisively against it; for he is committed by his faith to trust in God. His attitude is not that of the detached observer, but of the believer.

Perhaps this can be brought out by yet another parable. In time of war in an occupied country, a member of the resistance meets one night a stranger who deeply impresses him. They spend that night together in conversation. The Stranger tells the partisan that he himself is on the side of the resistance—indeed that he is in command of it, and urges the partisan to have faith in him no matter what happens. The partisan is utterly convinced at that meeting of the Stranger's sincerity and constancy and undertakes to trust him.

They never meet in conditions of intimacy again. But sometimes the Stranger is seen helping members of the resistance, and the partisan is grateful and says to his friends, 'He is on our side.'

Sometimes he is seen in the uniform of the police handing over patriots to the occupying power. On these occasions his friends murmur against him: but the partisan still says, 'He is on our side.' He still believes that, in spite of appearances, the Stranger did not deceive him. Sometimes he asks the Stranger for help and receives it. He is then thankful. Sometimes he asks and does not receive it. Then he says, 'The Stranger knows best.' Sometimes his friends, in exasperation, say 'Well, what *would* he have to do for you to admit that you were wrong and that he is not on our side?' But the partisan refuses to answer. He will not consent to put the Stranger to the test. And sometimes his friends complain, 'Well, if *that's* what you mean by his being on our side, the sooner he goes over to the other side the better.'

The partisan of the parable does not allow anything to count decisively against the proposition 'The Stranger is on our side.' This is because he has committed himself to trust the Stranger. But he of course recognizes that the Stranger's ambiguous behaviour *does* count against what he believes about him. It is precisely this situation which constitutes the trial of his faith.

When the partisan asks for help and doesn't get it, what can he do? He can *(a)* conclude that the stranger is not on our side or; *(b)* maintain that he is on our side, but that he has reasons for withholding help.

The first he will refuse to do. How long can he uphold the second position without its becoming just silly?

I don't think one can say in advance. It will depend on the nature of the impression created by the Stranger in the first place. It will depend, too, on the manner in which he takes the Stranger's behaviour. If he blandly dismisses it as of no consequence, as having no bearing upon his belief, it will be assumed that he is thoughtless or insane. And it quite obviously won't do for him to say easily, 'Oh, when used of the Stranger the phrase "is on our side" *means* ambiguous behaviour of this sort.' In that case he would be like the religious man who says blandly of a terrible disaster 'It is God's will.' No, he will only be regarded as sane and reason-

able in his belief, if he experiences in himself the full force of the conflict.

It is here that my parable differs from Hare's. The partisan admits that many things may and do count against his belief: whereas Hare's lunatic who has a *blik* about dons doesn't admit that anything counts against his *blik*. Nothing *can* count against *bliks*. Also the partisan has a reason for having in the first instance committed himself, viz. the character of the Stranger; whereas the lunatic has no reason for his *blik* about dons—because, of course, you can't have reasons for *bliks*.

This means that I agree with Flew that theological utterances must be assertions. The partisan is making an assertion when he says, 'The Stranger is on our side.'

Do I want to say that the partisan's belief about the Stranger is, in any sense, an explanation? I think I do. It explains and makes sense of the Stranger's behaviour: it helps to explain also the resistance movement in the context of which he appears. In each case it differs from the interpretation which the others put upon the same facts.

'God loves men' resembles 'the Stranger is on our side' (and many other significant statements, e.g. historical ones) in not being conclusively falsifiable. They can both be treated in at least three different ways: (1) As provisional hypotheses to be discarded if experience tells against them; (2) As significant articles of faith; (3) As vacuous formulae (expressing, perhaps, a desire for reassurance) to which experience makes no difference and which make no difference to life.

The Christian, once he has committed himself, is precluded by his faith from taking up the first attitude: 'Thou shalt not tempt the Lord thy God.' He is in constant danger, as Flew has observed, of slipping into the third. But he need not; and, if he does, it is a failure in faith as well as in logic.

ANTONY FLEW

It has been a good discussion: and I am glad to have helped to provoke it. But now—at least in *University*—it must come to an end: and the Editors

of *University* have asked me to make some concluding remarks. Since it is impossible to deal with all
the issues raised or to comment separately upon
each contribution, I will concentrate on Mitchell
and Hare, as representative of two very different
kinds of response to the challenge made in 'Theology and Falsification.'

The challenge, it will be remembered, ran like
this. Some theological utterances seem to, and are
intended to, provide explanations or express assertions. Now an assertion, to be an assertion at all,
must claim that things stand thus and thus; *and not
otherwise.* Similarly an explanation, to be an explanation at all, must explain why this particular thing
occurs; *and not something else.* Those last clauses are
crucial. And yet sophisticated religious people—or
so it seemed to me—are apt to overlook this, and
tend to refuse to allow, not merely that anything actually does occur, but that anything conceivably
could occur, which would count against their theological assertions and explanations. But in so far as
they do this their supposed explanations are actually bogus, and their seeming assertions are really
vacuous.

Mitchell's response to this challenge is ad-
mirably direct, straightforward, and understanding. He agrees 'that theological utterances must be
assertions.' He agrees that if they are to be assertions, there must be something that would count
against their truth. He agrees, too, that believers
are in constant danger of transforming their
would-be assertions into 'vacuous formulae.' But
he takes me to task for an oddity in my 'conduct of
the theologian's case. The theologian surely would
not deny that the fact of pain counts against the assertion that God loves men. This very incompatibility generates the most intractable of theological
problems, the problem of evil.' I think he is right.
I should have made a distinction between two very
different ways of dealing with what looks like evidence against the love of God: the way I stressed
was the expedient of qualifying the original assertion; the way the theologian usually takes, at first, is
to admit that it looks bad but to insist that there
is—there must be—some explanation which will
show that, in spite of appearances, there really is a
God who loves us. His difficulty, it seems to me, is

that he has given God attributes which rule out all
possible saving explanations. In Mitchell's parable
of the Stranger it is easy for the believer to find
plausible excuses for ambiguous behaviour: for the
Stranger is a man. But suppose the Stranger is God.
We cannot say that he would like to help but cannot: God is omnipotent. We cannot say that he
would help if he only knew: God is omniscient. We
cannot say that he is not responsible for the wickedness of others: God creates those others. Indeed an
omnipotent, omniscient God must be an accessory
before (and during) the fact to every human mis-
deed; as well as being responsible for every nonmoral defect in the universe. So, though I entirely
concede that Mitchell was absolutely right to insist
against me that the theologian's first move is to
look for an *explanation,* I still think that in the end,
if relentlessly pursued, he will have to resort to the
avoiding action of *qualification.* And there lies the
danger of that death by a thousand qualifications,
which would, I agree, constitute 'a failure in faith
as well as in logic.'

Hare's approach is fresh and bold. He confesses
that 'on the ground marked out by Flew, he seems
to me to be completely victorious.' He therefore introduces the concept of *blik.* But while I think that
there is room for some such concept in philosophy,
and that philosophers should be grateful to Hare
for his invention, I nevertheless want to insist that
any attempt to analyze Christian religious utterances as expressions or affirmations of a *blik* rather
than as (at least would-be) assertions about the
cosmos is fundamentally misguided. *First,* because
thus interpreted they would be entirely unortho-
dox. If Hare's religion really is a *blik,* involving no
cosmological assertions about the nature and activities of a supposed personal creator, then surely he
is not a Christian at all? *Second,* because thus interpreted, they could scarcely do the job they do. If
they were not even intended as assertions then
many religious activities would become fraudulent,
or merely silly. If 'You ought *because* it is God's will'
asserts no more than 'You ought,' then the person
who prefers the former phraseology is not really
giving a reason, but a fraudulent substitute for one,
a dialectical dud cheque. If 'My soul must be immortal *because* God loves his children, etc.' asserts

no more than 'My soul must be immortal,' then the man who reassures himself with theological arguments for immortality is being as silly as the man who tries to clear his overdraft by writing his bank a cheque on the same account. (Of course neither of these utterances would be distinctively Christian: but this discussion never pretended to be so confined.) Religious utterances may indeed express false or even bogus assertions: but I simply do not believe that they are not both intended and interpreted to be or at any rate to presuppose assertions, at least in the context of religious practice; whatever shifts may be demanded, in another context, by the exigencies of theological apologetic.

One final suggestion. The philosophers of religion might well draw upon George Orwell's last appalling nightmare *1984* for the concept of *doublethink*. *Doublethink* means the power of holding two contradictory beliefs simultaneously, and accepting both of them. The party intellectual knows that he is playing tricks with reality, but by the exercise of *doublethink* he also satisfies himself that reality is not violated' (*1984*, p. 220). Perhaps religious intellectuals too are sometimes driven to doublethink in order to retain their faith in a loving God in face of the reality of a heartless and indifferent world. But of this more another time, perhaps.

NOTES:

1. *P.A.S.*, 1944–5, reprinted as Ch. X of *Logic and Language*, Vol. I (Blackwell, 1951), and in his *Philosophy and Psychoanalysis* (Blackwell, 1953).

Questions for Reflection

1. Which of the three philosophers has given the most adequate account of religious belief? Are there other alternatives?
2. Hare and Mitchell give the most sympathetic accounts of faith. For a religious believer, what would be the intellectual advantages and disadvantages of accepting each position?
3. After reading these three accounts, what is or should be the relationship between faith and reason? Is faith completely irrational? Is faith immune to any counter evidence? Can a faith be rational apart from compelling evidence to support it?

CONTEMPORARY APPLICATION: DOES RELIGION CONFLICT WITH SCIENCE?

What is the relationship between science and religion? According to most accounts they both seem to be making claims about the world and offering explanations of why things are the way they are. It is clear that the ancients believed that many events in the world such as the motion of the planets, life-giving rainfalls, the nourishment of the sun, as well as diseases, droughts, and earthquakes are the result of the actions of the gods. It is equally clear modern science has replaced this type of explanation with natural causes. Even Isaac Newton, the great physicist, found that there were some things that his scientific laws could not explain (such as why gravitational attraction does not cause the heavenly bodies to collapse together). When his scientific explanations failed, Newton resorted to the hand of God as an explanation. This view is sometimes called the "God-of-the-gaps" position. When there are gaps in our scientific knowledge we plug in God to fill the gaps. The problem is that the gaps always seem to get filled by advances in scientific knowledge. Indeed, a generation or two after Newton, scientists figured out how to fill in the gaps with the principles of his own science. Is science then gradually making religion obsolete? Are the two enterprises engaged in a battle-to-the-death, winner-take-all competition?

One answer was given by the 17th-century thinker René Descartes, who was both a philosopher-scientist and a religious person. His view was that science and religion were like good neighbors. As long as they stay on their side of the fence and don't meddle in the other's business, they can coexist harmoniously. Similarly, as Galileo was being prosecuted by religious authorities for challenging the view that the earth was motionless and the center of the universe, he asserted that the purpose of religion was to "teach us how to go to heaven, not how the heavens go." The theme here is that religion and science describe different aspects of reality (the spiritual world versus the physical world) and have different purposes so that they are not in competition and cannot conflict.

However, some thinkers believe science and religion have a closer relationship than this. This basic conviction translates into two contrasting positions. The first view is held by those who claim that science and religion offer alternative and conflicting views of the world and thus reassert the warfare model. The second view is that science and religion can be partners and mutually support one another. The first reading by Richard Dawkins defends the first position and the second reading by Paul Davies defends the second position.

RICHARD DAWKINS

Science Is in Tension with Religion

Richard Dawkins (1941–), who holds a position at Oxford University, is considered to be one of the leading thinkers in modern evolutionary biology. His best-selling books are known for their success in explaining science and evolution to the general public. They include *The Selfish Gene* (1976, 1989), *The Blind Watchmaker* (1986), *River Out of Eden* (1995), *Climbing Mt. Improbable* (1996), and *Unweaving the Rainbow* (1998). Dawkins is never one to shy away from controversy and never attempts to soften the hard edges of his position. Accordingly, one magazine called Dawkins "the Bad Boy of Evolution."

The reading that follows is the transcript of a speech that Dawkins delivered to the American Humanist Association on the occasion of his accepting the award of 1996 Humanist of the Year. For Dawkins, religion and science are completely incompatible. The major difference between them is that science is based on observations while religious belief cares nothing about evidence. Turning the tables on those who charge that science, particularly evolutionary theory, is really a form of religious faith, Dawkins argues

Richard Dawkins, "Is Science a Religion?" transcript of a speech Dawkins delivered to the American Humanist Association when he accepted the award of 1996 Humanist of the Year.

that science offers a view of the world that is not only based on evidence but that can be just as emotionally satisfying and inspiring as religion.

Reading Questions

1. How does Dawkins respond to those who charge that science really is a form of religion?
2. Why does he think science and religion are competitors, as opposed to the view that they are operating in separate dimensions?
3. Why does Dawkins want to introduce science into religious education classes? What makes him think that science can be just as inspiring as religion?

It is fashionable to wax apocalyptic about the threat to humanity posed by the AIDS virus, "mad cow" disease, and many others, but I think a case can be made that faith is one of the world's great evils, comparable to the smallpox virus but harder to eradicate.

Faith, being belief that isn't based on evidence, is the principal vice of any religion. And who, looking at Northern Ireland or the Middle East, can be confident that the brain virus of faith is not exceedingly dangerous? One of the stories told to the young Muslim suicide bombers is that martyrdom is the quickest way to heaven—and not just heaven but a special part of heaven where they will receive their special reward of 72 virgin brides. It occurs to me that our best hope may be to provide a kind of "spiritual arms control": send in specially trained theologians to deescalate the going rate in virgins.

Given the dangers of faith—and considering the accomplishments of reason and observation in the activity called science—I find it ironic that, whenever I lecture publicly, there always seems to be someone who comes forward and says, "Of course, your science is just a religion like ours. Fundamentally, science just comes down to faith, doesn't it?"

Well, science is not religion and it doesn't just come down to faith. Although it has many of religion's virtues, it has none of its vices. Science is based upon verifiable evidence. Religious faith not only lacks evidence, its independence from evidence is its pride and joy, shouted from the rooftops. Why else would Christians wax critical of doubting Thomas? The other apostles are held up

to us as exemplars of virtue because faith was enough for them. Doubting Thomas, on the other hand, required evidence. Perhaps he should be the patron saint of scientists.

One reason I receive the comment about science being a religion is because I believe in the fact of evolution. I even believe in it with passionate conviction. To some, this may superficially look like faith. But the evidence that makes me believe in evolution is not only overwhelmingly strong; it is freely available to anyone who takes the trouble to read up on it. Anyone can study the same evidence that I have and presumably come to the same conclusion. But if you have a belief that is based solely on faith, I can't examine your reasons. You can retreat behind the private wall of faith where I can't reach you.

Now in practice, of course, individual scientists do sometimes slip back into the vice of faith, and a few may believe so single-mindedly in a favorite theory that they occasionally falsify evidence. However, the fact that this sometimes happens doesn't alter the principle that, when they do so, they do it with shame and not with pride. The method of science is so designed that it usually finds them out in the end.

Science is actually one of the most moral, one of the most honest disciplines around—because science would completely collapse if it weren't for a scrupulous adherence to honesty in the reporting of evidence. (As James Randi has pointed out, this is one reason why scientists are so often fooled by paranormal tricksters and why the debunking role is better played by professional conjurors; scientists just don't anticipate deliberate dishonesty as well.) There are other professions (no need to mention lawyers specifically) in which falsifying evidence or at least twisting it is precisely what people are paid for and get brownie points for doing.

Science, then, is free of the main vice of religion, which is faith. But, as I pointed out, science does have some of religion's virtues. Religion may aspire to provide its followers with various benefits—among them explanation, consolation, and uplift. Science, too, has something to offer in these areas.

Humans have a great hunger for explanation. It may be one of the main reasons why humanity so universally has religion, since religions do aspire to provide explanations. We come to our individual consciousness in a mysterious universe and long to understand it. Most religions offer a cosmology and a biology, a theory of life, a theory of origins, and reasons for existence. In doing so, they demonstrate that religion is, in a sense, science; it's just bad science. Don't fall for the argument that religion and science operate on separate dimensions and are concerned with quite separate sorts of questions. Religions have historically always attempted to answer the questions that properly belong to science. Thus religions should not be allowed now to retreat away from the ground upon which they have traditionally attempted to fight. They do offer both a cosmology and a biology; however, in both cases it is false.

Consolation is harder for science to provide. Unlike religion, science cannot offer the bereaved a glorious reunion with their loved ones in the hereafter. Those wronged on this earth cannot, on a scientific view, anticipate a sweet comeuppance for their tormentors in a life to come. It could be argued that, if the idea of an afterlife is an illusion (as I believe it is), the consolation it offers is hollow. But that's not necessarily so; a false belief can be just as comforting as a true one, provided the believer never discovers its falsity. But if consolation comes that cheap, science can weigh in with other cheap palliatives, such as pain-killing drugs, whose comfort may or may not be illusory, but they do work.

Uplift, however, is where science really comes into its own. All the great religions have a place for awe, for ecstatic transport at the wonder and beauty of creation. And it's exactly this feeling of spine-shivering, breath-catching awe—almost worship—this flooding of the chest with ecstatic wonder, that modern science can provide. And it does so beyond the wildest dreams of saints and mystics. The fact that the supernatural has no place in our explanations, in our understanding of so much about the universe and life, doesn't diminish the awe. Quite the contrary. The merest glance through a microscope at the brain of an ant or through a telescope at a long-ago galaxy of a billion worlds is enough to render poky and parochial the very psalms of praise.

Now, as I say, when it is put to me that science or some particular part of science, like evolutionary theory, is just a religion like any other, I usually deny it with indignation. But I've begun to wonder whether perhaps that's the wrong tactic. Perhaps the right tactic is to accept the charge gratefully and demand equal time for science in religious education classes. And the more I think about it, the more I realize that an excellent case could be made for this. So I want to talk a little bit about religious education and the place that science might play in it.

I do feel very strongly about the way children are brought up. I'm not entirely familiar with the way things are in the United States, and what I say may have more relevance to the United Kingdom, where there is state-obliged, legally enforced religious instruction for all children. That's unconstitutional in the United States, but I presume that children are nevertheless given religious instruction in whatever particular religion their parents deem suitable.

Which brings me to my point about mental child abuse. In a 1995 issue of the *Independent*, one of London's leading newspapers, there was a photograph of a rather sweet and touching scene. It was Christmas time, and the picture showed three children dressed up as the three wise men for a nativity play. The accompanying story described one child as a Muslim, one as a Hindu, and one as a Christian. The supposedly sweet and touching point of the story was that they were all taking part in this Nativity play.

What is not sweet and touching is that these children were all four years old. How can you possibly describe a child of four as a Muslim or a Christian or a Hindu or a Jew? Would you talk about a four-year-old economic monetarist? Would you talk about a four-year-old neo-isolationist or a four-year-old liberal Republican? There are opinions about the cosmos and the world that children, once grown, will presumably be in a position to evaluate for themselves. Religion is the one field in our culture about which it is absolutely accepted, without question—without even noticing how bizarre it is—that parents have a total and absolute say in what their children are going to be, how their children are going to be raised, what opinions their children are going to have about the cosmos, about life, about existence. Do you see what I mean about mental child abuse?

Looking now at the various things that religious education might be expected to accomplish, one of its aims could be to encourage children to reflect upon the deep questions of existence, to invite them to rise above the humdrum preoccupations of ordinary life and think *sub specie aeternitatis*.

Science can offer a vision of life and the universe which, as I've already remarked, for humbling poetic inspiration far outclasses any of the mutually contradictory faiths and disappointingly recent traditions of the world's religions.

For example, how could children in religious education classes fail to be inspired if we could get across to them some inkling of the age of the universe? Suppose that, at the moment of Christ's death, the news of it had started traveling at the maximum possible speed around the universe outwards from the earth. How far would the terrible tidings have traveled by now? Following the theory of special relativity, the answer is that the news could not, under any circumstances whatever, have reached more than one-fiftieth of the way across one galaxy—not one-thousandth of the way to our nearest neighboring galaxy in the 100-million-galaxy-strong universe. The universe at large couldn't possibly be anything other than indiffer-

ent to Christ, his birth, his passion, and his death. Even such momentous news as the origin of life on Earth could have traveled only across our little local cluster of galaxies. Yet so ancient was that event on our earthly time-scale that, if you span its age with your open arms, the whole of human history, the whole of human culture, would fall in the dust from your fingertip at a single stroke of a nail file.

The argument from design, an important part of the history of religion, wouldn't be ignored in my religious education classes, needless to say. The children would look at the spellbinding wonders of the living kingdoms and would consider Darwinism alongside the creationist alternatives and make up their own minds. I think the children would have no difficulty in making up their minds the right way if presented with the evidence. What worries me is not the question of equal time but that, as far as I can see, children in the United Kingdom and the United States are essentially given no time with evolution yet are taught creationism (whether at school, in church, or at home).

It would also be interesting to teach more than one theory of creation. The dominant one in this culture happens to be the Jewish creation myth, which is taken over from the Babylonian creation myth. There are, of course, lots and lots of others, and perhaps they should all be given equal time (except that wouldn't leave much time for studying anything else). I understand that there are Hindus who believe that the world was created in a cosmic butter churn and Nigerian peoples who believe that the world was created by God from the excrement of ants. Surely these stories have as much right to equal time as the Judeo-Christian myth of Adam and Eve.

So much for Genesis; now let's move on to the prophets. Halley's Comet will return without fail in the year 2062. Biblical or Delphic prophecies don't begin to aspire to such accuracy; astrologers and Nostradamians dare not commit themselves to factual prognostications but, rather, disguise their charlatanry in a smokescreen of vagueness. When comets have appeared in the past, they've often been taken as portents of disaster. Astrology has played an important part in various religious traditions, including Hinduism. The three wise men I mentioned earlier were said to have been led to the cradle of Jesus by a star. We might ask the children by what physical route do they imagine the alleged stellar influence on human affairs could travel.

Incidentally, there was a shocking program on the BBC radio around Christmas 1995 featuring an astronomer, a bishop, and a journalist who were sent off on an assignment to retrace the steps of the three wise men. Well, you could understand the participation of the bishop and the journalist (who happened to be a religious writer), but the astronomer was a supposedly respectable astronomy writer, and yet she went along with this! All along the route, she talked about the portents of when Saturn and Jupiter were in the ascendant up Uranus or whatever it was. She doesn't actually believe in astrology, but one of the problems is that our culture has been taught to become tolerant of it, vaguely amused by it—so much so that even scientific people who don't believe in astrology sort of think it's a bit of harmless fun. I take astrology very seriously indeed: I think it's deeply pernicious because it undermines rationality, and I should like to see campaigns against it.

When the religious education class turns to ethics, I don't think science actually has a lot to say, and I would replace it with rational moral philosophy. Do the children think there are absolute standards of right and wrong? And if so, where do they come from? Can you make up good working principles of right and wrong, like "do as you would be done by" and "the greatest good for the greatest number" (whatever that is supposed to mean)? It's a rewarding question, whatever your personal morality, to ask as an evolutionist where morals come from; by what route has the human brain gained its tendency to have ethics and morals, a feeling of right and wrong?

Should we value human life above all other life? Is there a rigid wall to be built around the species Homo sapiens, or should we talk about whether there are other species which are entitled to our humanistic sympathies? Should we, for example, follow the right-to-life lobby, which is wholly preoccupied with human life, and value the life of a hu-

man fetus with the faculties of a worm over the life of a thinking and feeling chimpanzee? What is the basis of this fence that we erect around Homo sapiens—even around a small piece of fetal tissue? (Not a very sound evolutionary idea when you think about it.) When, in our evolutionary descent from our common ancestor with chimpanzees, did the fence suddenly rear itself up?

Well, moving on, then, from morals to last things, to eschatology, we know from the second law of thermodynamics that all complexity, all life, all laughter, all sorrow, is hell bent on leveling itself out into cold nothingness in the end. They—and we—can never be more than temporary, local buckings of the great universal slide into the abyss of uniformity.

We know that the universe is expanding and will probably expand forever, although it's possible it may contract again. We know that, whatever happens to the universe, the sun will engulf the earth in about 60 million centuries from now.

Time itself began at a certain moment, and time may end at a certain moment—or it may not. Time may come locally to an end in miniature crunches called black holes. The laws of the universe seem to be true all over the universe. Why is this? Might the laws change in these crunches? To be really speculative, time could begin again with new laws of physics, new physical constants. And it has even been suggested that there could be many universes, each one isolated so completely that, for it, the others don't exist. Then again, there might be a Darwinian selection among universes.

So science could give a good account of itself in religious education. But it wouldn't be enough. I believe that some familiarity with the King James version of the Bible is important for anyone wanting to understand the allusions that appear in English literature. Together with the Book of Common Prayer, the Bible gets 58 pages in the Oxford Dictionary of Quotations. Only Shakespeare has more. I do think that not having any kind of biblical education is unfortunate if children want to read English literature and understand the provenance of phrases like "through a glass darkly," "all flesh is as grass," "the race is not to the swift," "crying in the wilderness," "reaping the whirlwind," "amid the alien corn," "Eyeless in Gaza," "Job's comforters," and "the widow's mite."

I want to return now to the charge that science is just a faith. The more extreme version of that charge—and one that I often encounter as both a scientist and a rationalist—is an accusation of zealotry and bigotry in scientists themselves as great as that found in religious people. Sometimes there may be a little bit of justice in this accusation; but as zealous bigots, we scientists are mere amateurs at the game. We're content to argue with those who disagree with us. We don't kill them.

But I would want to deny even the lesser charge of purely verbal zealotry. There is a very, very important difference between feeling strongly, even passionately, about something because we have thought about and examined the evidence for it on the one hand, and feeling strongly about something because it has been internally revealed to us, or internally revealed to somebody else in history and subsequently hallowed by tradition. There's all the difference in the world between a belief that one is prepared to defend by quoting evidence and logic and a belief that is supported by nothing more than tradition, authority, or revelation.

Questions for Reflection

1. Do you agree with Dawkins's claims that religion is like a virus and that it is dangerous? If not, how would you try to convince him otherwise?
2. Is Dawkins correct in claiming that science and religion are competitors and that they are attempting to answer the same questions?
3. Has he made his case that science can be as emotionally satisfying and inspiring as religion?

 PAUL DAVIES

Science Supports Religion

Paul Davies (1946–) has held positions in mathematical physics at universities in England and Australia, but has recently retired to devote more time to his writing and public speaking. He has written on fundamental physics and cosmology in over 100 research articles and in over 20 books. Because of his ability to communicate physics to the lay public, the *Washington Times* described Davies as "the best science writer on either side of the Atlantic." He has also written extensively on the relationship between science and religion. His best-selling books on this topic include *God and the New Physics* (1983) and *The Mind of God* (1991). In 1995 he won the one-million dollar Templeton Prize for Progress in Religion, the world's largest prize for intellectual endeavor.

In the following essay, Davies addresses the question, "Why does science . . . work, and work so well?" Taking off from what physicists now know about the universe, Davies

Paul Davies, "The Unreasonable Effectiveness of Science," in *Evidence of Purpose,* ed. John Marks Templeton (New York: Continuum, 1994), pp. 44–56.

outlines a contemporary version of the teleological argument, suggesting that the universe does not seem to be just the product of "lucky accidents" and "coincidences." While his understated argument does not explicitly mention religion, Davies concludes that the scientific evidence suggests that "the universe exists for a purpose, and that in our small yet significant way, we are part of that purpose."

Reading Questions

1. As you read through Davies's essay, list the various scientific facts that lead him to the conclusion that the universe is purposeful.
2. How does Davies answer his own question, Why does science work so well?
3. What is the anthropic principle? How does it support the thesis that the universe is the product of design?
4. Why are analogical arguments (such as William Paley's) incapable of providing a proof for a hypothesis? According to Davies, what is the best that an argument from analogy can accomplish? What examples does he give of analogical arguments we all accept?
5. Davies acknowledges that Darwin's theory of evolution dealt a blow to the traditional argument for design. How does Davies reformulate the argument in terms of physics to avoid the Darwinian refutation?

SCIENCE AND THE DEMYSTIFICATION OF NATURE

Human beings have always been struck by the complex harmony and intricate organization of the physical world. The movement of the heavenly bodies across the sky, the rhythms of the seasons, the patterns of a snowflake, the myriads of living creatures so well adapted to their environment— all these things seem too well arranged to be a mindless accident. It was only natural that our ancestors attributed the elaborate order of the universe to the purposeful workings of a deity.

The rise of science served to extend the range of nature's marvels, so that today we have discovered order in the deepest recesses of the atom and among the grandest collection of galaxies. But science has also provided its own reasons for this order. No longer do we need explicit theological explanations for snowflakes, or even for living organisms. The laws of nature are such that matter and energy can organize *themselves* into complex forms and systems. It now seems plausible that, given the laws of physics, the existence and nature of all physical systems can be accounted for in terms of ordinary physical processes.

Some people have concluded from this that science has robbed the universe of mystery and purpose, that the elaborate arrangement of the physical world is merely the meaningless outworking of mechanistic laws and random juxtapositions of clodlike particles. It is a sentiment well captured by the words of two eminent Nobel laureates. The biologist Jacques Monod writes: "The ancient covenant is in pieces: man at last knows that he is alone in the unfeeling immensity of the universe, out of which he has emerged only by chance. Neither his destiny nor his duty have been written down." The physicist Steven Weinberg echoes this dismal sentiment: "The more the universe seems comprehensible, the more it also seems pointless."

However, not all scientists find it so easy to accept the "miracle of nature" as a brute fact. It is all very well proclaiming that the laws of physics plus the cosmic initial conditions explain the universe, but this begs the question of where those laws and conditions came from in the first place. Science may be powerfully successful in explaining the universe, but how do we explain science? Why does science—based on the notion of eternal laws of physics—work, and work so well? As our understanding of the basic processes of nature advances, so it becomes increasingly clear that what we call scientific laws are not just any old laws, but are remarkably special in a number of intriguing ways.

COSMIC UNITY

Consider first the general orderliness of the universe. There are limitless ways in which the cosmos might have been totally chaotic. It might have had no laws at all, or laws that caused matter to behave in disorderly or unstable ways. One could also imagine a universe in which conditions changed from moment to moment in a complicated or random fashion, or even in which everything abruptly ceased to exist. There seems to be no logical obstacle to the idea of such unruly universes. But the real universe is not like this. It is highly ordered, and this order persists in a dependable manner. There exist well-defined physical laws and definite cause-effect relationships that we can rely upon.

The physical world is not arbitrarily regulated; it is ordered in a very particular way, poised between the twin extremes of simple regimented orderliness and random complexity; it is neither a crystal nor a random gas. The universe is undeniably complex, but its complexity is of an *organized* variety. Moreover, this organization was not built into the universe at its origin. It has emerged from primeval chaos in a sequence of self-organizing processes that have progressively enriched and complexified the evolving universe in a more or less unidirectional manner. It is easy to imagine a world that, while ordered, nevertheless does not possess the right sort of forces or conditions for the emergence of complex organization. Some scientists have been so struck by the uncanny efficiency of self-organizing processes in nature that they have suggested the existence of a type of optimization principle, whereby the universe evolves to create maximum richness and diversity. The fact that this rich and complex variety emerges from the featureless inferno of the Big Bang, and does so as a

consequence of laws of stunning simplicity and generality, indicates some sort of matching of means to ends that has a distinct teleological flavor to it.

The very fact that we can even talk meaningful about "the universe" as an all-embracing concept already indicates an underlying unity and coherence in nature. The physical world consists of a multiplicity of objects and systems, but they are structured in such a way that, taken together, they form a unified and consistent whole. For example, the various forces of nature are not just a haphazard conjunction of disparate influences. They dovetail together in a mutually supportive way that bestows upon nature a stability and harmony. Although this subtle coherence is hard to capture in a precise way, it is obvious to most practicing scientists. I like to compare doing science with completing a crossword puzzle. In conducting experiments, scientists enter into a dialogue with nature, from which they obtain clues to the underlying regularities. When these clues are "solved"— usually in the form of mathematical laws—it is like filling in a missing word. What we find is that the "words" gleaned from different branches of science form a coherent, interlocking matrix, and not just a "laundry list" of separate principles juxtaposed.

To elaborate this point, it is particularly striking, for example, how processes that occur on a microscopic scale—say in nuclear physics—seem to be fine-tuned to produce interesting and varied effects on a much larger scale, for example in astrophysics. Consider the death of stars in supernova explosions. Part of the explosive force is due to the action of the elusive subatomic particle called the neutrino. Neutrinos are almost entirely devoid of physical properties: the average cosmic neutrino could penetrate many light years of solid lead. Yet these ghostly entities can still, under the extreme conditions near the center of a dying massive star, pack enough punch to blast much of the stellar material into space. The resulting detritus is richly laced with heavy elements of the sort from which planet Earth is made. We can thus attribute the existence of terrestrial-like planets, with their special propensity to spawn complex material forms and systems, to the qualities of a subatomic particle so feeble in its effects that it might well have gone forever undetected.

In addition to this coherent interweaving of the various aspects of nature, there is the question of nature's curious uniformity. Laws of physics discovered in the laboratory apply equally well to the atoms of a distant galaxy. The electrons that make the image on your television screen have exactly the same mass, charge, and magnetic moment as those on the moon, or at the edge of the observable universe. Furthermore, these properties do not change detectably from one moment to the next.

NATURE'S INGENUITY

The subtle harmony of nature is perhaps manifested most forcefully in the field of subatomic particle physics. Here mathematical physics achieves its greatest successes. But a full understanding of the microworld of subnuclear processes requires the deployment of several branches of advanced mathematics in a delicate way. Progress is often hard. One finds that a straight-forward application of mathematics gets you so far, and then you get stuck. Some internal inconsistency appears, or else the theory yields wildly unacceptable results. Then someone discovers a clever mathematical trick, perhaps an obscure loophole in a theorem or an elegant reformulation of the original problem in new mathematical guise, and, hey presto, everything falls into place! It is impossible to resist the urge to proclaim nature at least as clever as the scientist for "spotting" the trick and exploiting it. One often hears theoretical physicists, speaking in the highly informal and colloquial way that they do, promoting their particular theory with the quip that it is so clever/subtle/elegant it is hard to imagine nature not taking advantage of it!

Sometimes it is the other way about, and the scientists are puzzled by what seems to be some arbitrariness or profligacy on nature's behalf. Physicists are often to be heard asking, "Why would nature bother with this?" or "What is the point of that?" Though uttered in a lighthearted spirit, there is a serious content too. Experience has shown that nature does share our sense of economy, efficiency, beauty, and mathematical subtlety, and this approach to research can often pay dividends. Most physicists believe that beneath the complexities of their subject lies an elegant and powerful unity, and that progress can be made by spotting the mathematical "tricks" that nature has exploited to generate an interestingly diverse and complex universe from this underlying simplicity.

There is a feeling among physicists that everything that exists in nature must have a "place" or a role as a part of some wider scheme; that each facet of physical reality should link in with the others in a "natural" and logical way. "Who ordered that?" exclaimed an astonished Isadore Rabi when the muon was discovered. The muon is a particle more or less identical to the electron in all respects except mass, which is 206.8 times greater. This big brother to the electron is unstable, and rapidly decays, so it is not a permanent feature of matter. Nevertheless it seems to be an elementary particle in its own right and not a composite of other particles. Rabi's reaction is typical. What is the muon for? Why does nature need another sort of electron, especially one that disappears so promptly? How would the world be different if the muon did not exist?

The hope and expectation is that the existence of the muon, and other "gratuitous" particles, can be explained as part of some all-embracing unification of particle physics, probably involving a branch of mathematics known as group theory, which can be used to connect together apparently distinct particles into unified families according to certain abstract mathematical symmetries. The groups have definite rules about how they can be represented and combined together, and how many of each type of particle they describe. Hopefully a group theoretical description will emerge that commends itself on other grounds, but which will also automatically incorporate the correct number of particles. Nature's apparent profligacy will then be seen as a necessary consequence of some deeper unifying symmetry. If so, nature will once again be shown to share our sense of economy, with "a place for everything and everything in its place." Current research trends strongly indicate this will be so.

THE ANTHROPIC PRINCIPLE

The strange harmony of nature becomes even more intriguing when we take into account the existence of living organisms. The fact that biological systems have very special requirements, and that these requirements are met by nature, has attracted much comment by scientists. In 1913 the Harvard biochemist Lawrence Henderson, impressed by the way that life on Earth seemed to depend crucially on some rather peculiar properties of water and other chemicals, wrote: "The properties of matter and the course of cosmic evolution are now seen to be intimately related to the structure of the living being and to its activities; . . . the biologist may now rightly regard the Universe in its very essence as biocentric."

In the 1960s the astronomer Fred Hoyle was struck by the fact that the element carbon, so crucial to terrestrial life, exists in abundance in the universe only by courtesy of a lucky fluke. Carbon nuclei are made by a rather delicate process involving the simultaneous encounter of three helium nuclei inside the cores of large stars. Because of the rarity of triple nuclear encounters, the reaction can proceed at a significant rate only at certain well-defined energies (called resonances), where the reaction rate is greatly amplified by quantum effects. By good fortune one of these resonances is positioned just about right to correspond to the sort of energies that helium nuclei have inside large stars. Hoyle was so impressed by this "monstrous accident," he was prompted to comment that it was as if "the laws of nuclear physics have been deliberately designed with regard to the consequences they produce inside the stars. Later he was to expound the view that the universe looks like a "put-up job" as though somebody had been "monkeying" with the laws of physics.

These cases are just samples. Quite a list of "lucky accidents" and "coincidences" has been compiled since, most notably by the astrophysicists Brandon Carter, Bernard Carr, and Martin Ress.

Taken together they provide impressive evidence that life as we know it depends very sensitively on the form of the laws of physics, and on some seemingly fortuitous accidents in the actual values that nature has chosen for various particle masses, force strengths, and so on. If we could play God, and select values for these natural quantities at whim by twiddling a set of knobs, we would find that almost all knob settings would render the universe uninhabitable. Some knobs would have to be fine-tuned to enormous precision if life is to flourish in the universe.

It is of course a truism that we can only observe a universe that is consistent with our own existence. This linkage between human observership and the laws and conditions of the universe is known as the anthropic principle. In the trivial form just stated, the anthropic principle does not assert that our existence *compels* the laws of physics to have the form they do, nor need one conclude that the laws have been deliberately designed with *Homo sapiens* in mind. On the other hand, the fact that even slight changes to the way things are might render the universe unobservable is surely a fact of deep significance.

ACCIDENT OR INTELLIGENT DESIGN?

The early Greek philosophers recognized that the order and harmony of the cosmos demanded explanation, but the idea that these felicitous properties derive from a creator working to a preconceived plan was well formulated only in the Christian era. In the twelfth century, Aquinas offered the view that natural bodies act as if guided toward a definite goal or end "so as to obtain the best result." This fitting of means to ends implies, argued Aquinas, an intention. But seeing as natural bodies lack consciousness, they cannot supply that intention themselves. "Therefore some intelligent being exists by whom all natural things are directed to their end; and this being we call God."

Aquinas's argument collapsed in the seventeenth century with the development of Newton's mechanics. Newton's laws explain the motion of material bodies quite satisfactorily in terms of inertia and proximate forces without the need for an overall plan, divine supervision, or any form of teleology. Nevertheless, this shift of worldview did not entirely eliminate the idea that the world must have been designed for a purpose. One could still puzzle, as did Newton himself, over the way in which material bodies have been arranged in the universe. For many scientists it was too much to suppose that the subtle and harmonious organization of nature is the result of mere chance. Thus Robert Boyle wrote:

> The excellent contrivance of that great system of the world, and especially the curious fabric of the bodies of the animals and the uses of their sensories and other parts, have been made the great motives that in all ages and nations induced philosophers to acknowledge a Deity as the author of these admirable structures.

It was Boyle who drew the famous comparison between the universe and a clockwork mechanism, which was most eloquently elaborated by William Paley in the eighteenth century. Suppose, argued Paley, that you were "crossing a heath" and came upon a watch lying on the ground. On inspecting the watch you observe the intricate organization of its parts and how they are arranged together in a cooperative way to achieve a collective end. Even if you had never seen a watch and had no idea of its function, you would still be led to conclude from this inspection that this was a contrivance designed for a purpose. Paley then went on to argue that, when we consider the much more elaborate contrivances of nature, we should reach the same conclusion even more forcefully.

The weakness of this argument is that it proceeds by analogy. The mechanistic universe is analogous to the watch; the watch had a designer, so therefore the universe must have had a designer. One might as well say that the universe is like an organism, so therefore it must have grown from a fetus in a cosmic womb! Clearly no analogical argument can amount to a proof. The best it can do is to offer support for a hypothesis. The degree of support will depend on how persuasive you find the analogy to be. There is clearly a point at which

nature would look so contrived that even the most ardent skeptic would believe it had been designed for a purpose. Our present understanding of nature does not provide compulsive proof of design. It is conceivable, however, that more compelling evidence exists in nature, but is hidden in some way from us. Perhaps we will only become aware of the "architect's trademark" when we achieve a certain level of scientific attainment. This possibility forms the theme of the novel *Contact* by the astronomer Carl Sagan, in which a message is subtly embedded in the digits of pi—a number that is incorporated into the very structure of the universe—and accessible only by the use of sophisticated computer analysis.

Although analogical arguments are merely suggestive, they are frequently accepted. Consider, for example, the existence of a physical world. One's immediate experiences always refer to a mental world of sensory impressions, which has the status of a map or model of the really-existing world "out there." Yet a map or a model is also just an analogy. An even greater leap of faith is required when we conclude that there exist other minds besides our own. Our experience of other human beings derives entirely from interactions with their bodies: we cannot perceive their minds directly. Certainly other people behave *as if* they share our own mental experiences, but we can never know that. The conclusion that other minds exist is based on analogy with our own behavior and experiences.

It is in the biological realm that one encounters the most arresting examples of "the contrivances of nature," where the adaptation of means to ends is legendary. It is hard to imagine, for example, that the eye is not meant to provide the faculty of sight, or that the wings of a bird are not intended for flight. To Paley and many others such intricate and successful adaptation indicated providential arrangement by an intelligent designer. Alas, Darwin's theory of evolution eliminated this argument by demonstrating that complex organization efficiently adapted to the environment could arise as a result of random mutations and natural selection. No designer is needed to produce an eye or a wing. Such organs appear as a result of perfectly ordinary natural processes.

Given the blow that Darwin dealt to the design argument, it is curious that it has made a reappearance. In its new form the argument is directed not to the material objects of the universe as such, but to the underlying laws, where it is immune from Darwinian attack. The essence of Darwinian evolution is variation and selection. This depends on nature's being able to select from a collection of similar, competing, individuals. When it comes to the laws of physics and the initial cosmological conditions, however, there is no obvious ensemble of competitors. The laws and initial conditions are apparently unique to our universe. If it is the case that the existence of life requires the laws of physics and the initial conditions to be fine-tuned to high precision, and that fine-tuning does in fact obtain, then the suggestion of design seems compelling.

But just how fine does the tuning have to be to convince a skeptic? One can always shrug aside any number of "coincidences" with the comment that they are a lucky but meaningless quirk of fate. Again, it is a question of personal judgment. The problem is that there is no natural way to quantify the intrinsic improbability of the known "coincidences." What is needed is a sort of metatheory—a theory of theories—that supplies a well-defined probability for each range of values of any parameter that is allegedly fine-tuned. No such metatheory is available, or has to my knowledge even been proposed. Until it is, the impression of "something fishy going on" must remain entirely subjective.

OTHER WORLDS

Undoubtedly the most serious challenge to the design argument comes from the hypothesis of many universes, or multiple realities. The basic idea is that the universe we see is but one among a vast ensemble. When deployed as an attack on the design argument, the theory proposes that all possible physical conditions are represented somewhere among the ensemble, and that the reason why our own particular universe looks designed is because only in those universes that have that seemingly contrived form will life (and hence consciousness)

be able to arise. Hence it is no surprise that we find ourselves in a universe so propitiously suited to biological requirements. It has been "anthropically selected."

The various universes must be considered to be in some sense "parallel" or coexisting realities. Though such a hypothesis may seem bizarre, it is supported, in one version or another, by many physicists as a natural interpretation of quantum mechanics. An alternative, and less outrageous proposal, is that what we have been calling "the universe" might be just a small patch of an infinite system extended in space. If we could look beyond the ten billion or so light-years accessible to our instruments, we might find regions of the universe that are very different from ours.

So can evidence for design equally well be taken as evidence for many universes? In some respects the answer is undoubtedly yes. For example, the spatial organization of the cosmos on a large scale is important for life. If the universe were highly irregular, it might produce black holes, or turbulent gas rather than well-ordered galaxies containing life-encouraging stars and planets. If matter was distributed at random, chaos would generally prevail. But here and there, purely by chance, an oasis of order would arise, permitting life to form. Although such oases would be almost unthinkably rare, it is no surprise that we find ourselves inhabiting one, for we could not live elsewhere. So the cosmic order need not be attributed to the providential arrangement of things, but rather to the inevitable selection effect connected with our own existence.

In spite of the apparent ease with which the many-universes theory can account for what would otherwise be considered remarkable features of the universe, the theory faces a number of serious objections. Not least of these is Ockham's razor: one must introduce a vast (indeed infinite) complexity to explain the regularities of just one universe. This "blunderbuss" approach to explaining the specialness of our universe is scientifically questionable. Another problem is that the theory can explain only those aspects of nature that are relevant to the existence of conscious life, otherwise there is no selection mechanism. Many of the best examples of design, such as the ingenuity and unity of particle physics, have little obvious connection with biology.

Another point that is often glossed over is the fact that in all of the many-universe theories that derive from real physics (as opposed to simply fantasizing about the existence of other worlds) the laws of physics are the same in all the worlds. The selection of universes on offer is restricted to those that are *physically* possible, as opposed to those that can be imagined. There will be many more universes that are logically possible, but contradict the laws of physics. So we cannot account for nature's *lawfulness* this way, unless one extends the many-universes idea to encompass all possible modes of behavior. Imagine a vast stack of alternative realities for which any notion of law, order, or regularity of any kind is absent. Physical processes are entirely random. However, just as a monkey tinkering with a typewriter will eventually type Shakespeare, so somewhere among that vast stack of realities will be worlds that are partially ordered, just by chance. Can anthropic reasoning be used to conclude that any given observer will perceive an ordered world, mind-boggling rare though such a world may be relative to its chaotic competitors? I think the answer is clearly no, because anthropic arguments work only for aspects of nature that are crucial to life. If there is utter lawlessness, then the overwhelming number of randomly selected inhabited worlds will be ordered only in ways that are essential to the preservation of life. There is no reason, for example, why the charge of the electron need remain absolutely fixed, or why different electrons should have exactly the same charge. Minor variations would not be life-threatening. But what else keeps the value fixed—and fixed to such astonishing precision—if it is not a law of physics? One could, perhaps, imagine an ensemble of universes with a selection of laws, so that each universe comes with a complete and fixed set of laws. We could then perhaps use anthropic reasoning to explain why at least some of the laws we observe are what they are. But this theory must still presuppose the concept of law, and begs the question of where those laws come from, and how they "attach" themselves to universes in an "eternal way."

THE COSMIC CODE

Another of Einstein's famous remarks is that the only incomprehensible thing about the universe is that it is comprehensible. The success of the scientific enterprise can often blind us to the astonishing fact that science works. Though it is usually taken for granted, it is both incredibly fortunate and deeply mysterious that we are able to fathom the workings of nature by use of the scientific method. The purpose of science is to uncover patterns and regularities in nature, but the raw data of observation rarely exhibit explicit regularities. Nature's order is hidden from us: the book of nature is written in a sort of code. To make progress in science we need to crack the cosmic code, to dig beneath the raw data, and uncover the hidden order. To return to the crossword analogy, the clues are highly cryptic, and require some considerable ingenuity to solve.

What is so remarkable is that human beings can actually perform this code-breaking operation. Why has the human mind the capacity to "unlock the secrets of nature" and make a reasonable success at completing nature's "cryptic crossword"? It is easy to imagine worlds in which the regularities of nature are transparent at a glance or impenetrably complicated or subtle, requiring far more brainpower than humans possess to decode them. In fact, the cosmic code seems almost attuned to human capabilities. This is all the more mysterious on account of the fact that human intellectual powers are presumably determined by biological evolution, and have absolutely no connection with doing science. Our brains have evolved to cope with survival "in the jungle," a far cry from describing the laws of electromagnetism or the structure of the atom. "Why should our cognitive processes have turned themselves to such an extravagant quest as the understanding of the entire Universe?" asks John Barrow. "Why should it be *us*? None of the sophisticated ideas involved appear to offer any selective advantage to be exploited during the pre-conscious period of our evolution. . . . How fortuitous that our minds (or at least the minds of some) should be poised to fathom the depths of Nature's secrets."

The effectiveness of science seems especially odd given the limitations of human educational development. It usually requires at least fifteen years before a student achieves a sufficient grasp of science to make a contribution to fundamental research. Yet major advances in fundamental science are usually made by men and women in their twenties. The combination of educational progress and waning creativity hem in the scientist, providing a brief, but crucial "window of opportunity" to contribute. Yet these intellectual restrictions presumably have their roots in mundane aspects of evolutionary biology, connected with the human life span, the structure of the brain, and the social organization of our species. It is odd that the durations involved are such as to permit creative scientific endeavor. Again, one can imagine a world in which we all had plenty of time to learn the necessary facts and concepts to do fundamental science, or another world in which it would take so many years to learn all the necessary things that death would intervene, or one's creative years would pass, long before the educational phase was finished.

No feature of this uncanny "tuning" of the human mind to the workings of nature is more striking than mathematics. Mathematics is the product of the higher human intellect, yet it finds ready application to the most basic processes of nature, such as subatomic particle physics. The fact that "mathematics works" when applied to the physical world—and works so stunningly well—demands explanation, for it is not clear we have any absolute right to expect that the world should be well described by our mathematics.

Much has been written about the "unreasonable effectiveness" of mathematics in science (to use Eugene Wigner's famous phrase). If mathematical ability has evolved by accident rather than in response to environmental pressures, then it is a truly astonishing coincidence that mathematics finds such ready application to the physical universe. If, on the other hand, mathematical ability does have some obscure survival value and has evolved by natural selection, we are still faced with the mystery of why the laws of nature are mathematical. After all, surviving "in the jungle" does not require knowledge of the *laws* of nature, only of their manifesta-

tions. We have seen how the laws themselves are in code, and not connected in a simple way at all to the actual physical phenomena subject to those laws. Survival depends on an appreciation of how the world is, not of any hidden underlying order. Certainly it cannot depend on the hidden order within atomic nuclei, or in blank holes, or in subatomic particles that are produced on Earth only inside particle accelerator machines.

It is sometimes argued that as the brain is a product of physical processes it should reflect the nature of those processes, including their mathematical character. But there is, in fact, no direct connection between the laws of physics and the structure of the brain. The thing that distinguishes the brain from a kilogram of ordinary matter is its complex organized form, in particular the elaborate interconnections between neurones. This wiring pattern cannot be explained by the laws of physics alone. It depends on many other factors, including a host of chance events that must have occurred during evolutionary history. Whatever laws may have helped shape the structure of the human brain (such as Mendel's laws of genetics) they bear no simple relationship to the laws of physics.

CONCLUSION

A careful study of the laws of physics suggests that they are not just "any old" set of laws, but special in a number of intriguing ways: in their coherence and harmony, their economy, their universality and dependability, their encouragement of diversity and complexity without total chaos, and so forth. Perhaps the oddest feature of all is the way that the laws are "decodable" by human beings, i.e., that science works so unreasonably well, especially in regard to its mathematical content. Also mysterious is the fact that these particular laws, which receive such succinct and elegant expression when cast in terms of human mathematics, nevertheless encourage the emergence from primeval featurelessness of a sufficiently rich and sufficiently organized complexity to permit the evolution of intelligent organisms in the universe, organisms that produce the very same mathematics as pertain to these laws.

This self-reflective, self-consistent loop is all the more remarkable when account is taken of the fine-tuning of parameters needed for it to occur. Attempts to explain this "too good to be true" arrangement by invoking an infinity of random universes require metaphysical assumptions at least as questionable as those of design.

The success of human science and mathematics and the anthropic fine-tuning that is apparently a prerequisite for the very existence of humanlike beings, strongly suggests that our existence is linked into the laws of the universe at the most basic level. Far from being a trivial and incidental by-product of random and meaningless physical processes, it seems that conscious organisms are a fundamental feature of the cosmos. That is not to say that the species *Homo sapiens* as such is preordained, but the emergence somewhere, sometime in the universe of intelligent organisms capable of reflecting on the significance of the cosmos is, I believe, written into the laws of nature. Clearly, the universe could have been otherwise. The fact that it is as it is, and that its form is linked so intimately with our own existence, is powerful evidence that the universe exists for a purpose, and that in our small yet significant way, we are part of that purpose.

Questions for Reflection

1. Is Davies's argument vulnerable to David Hume's skeptical arguments against design or have the recent advances in science made the design argument stronger?
2. How might an atheistic scientist, who agrees with Davies's scientific facts, argue that Davies's theist conclusion doesn't follow?
3. Which of the following conclusions do you find to be the most plausible? (a) Science and religion are in conflict, as Dawkins claims, (b) science lends support to the religious view of the world, as Davies claims, (c) the sorts of scientific facts Davies cites at least show that belief in a divine being is not unreasonable, (d) science and religion have nothing to do with one another. Is there another, alternative view of science and religion that you think is reasonable?

C H A P T E R 3

Questions about Human Knowledge

HUMAN KNOWLEDGE: WHAT ARE THE ISSUES?

Undoubtedly, you have many beliefs. These beliefs include answers to questions that are raised in this book, such as "Is there a God?" or "What makes an action morally wrong?" However, you have many other kinds of beliefs such as "I was not born five minutes ago" or "The sun is very far away." But how do you know these beliefs are true? Try the following thought experiment. Make a list of five statements you believe. Now put a check by every one that is true. Obviously, you would check all of them, for if you believe something, you believe that it is true. The problem is that all of us have had beliefs that we once were convinced were true, but later found out were false. So how do we know what to believe? What criterion or method can we use to make sure we have genuine knowledge? Furthermore, how would we know that our criterion for knowledge is the correct one? Finally, if some of our beliefs have turned out to be false, can we ever be sure that any of our current beliefs are true? The area of philosophy that is concerned with questions and theories about the nature and possibility of knowledge is called **epistemology.** The Greek word *episteme* means "knowledge" and *logos* means "rational discourse." Hence, epistemology is the philosophy of knowledge.

While there are an enormous number of philosophical problems concerning knowledge, we are going to focus on three of the major problems. The philosophies we will discuss in the remaining sections of this chapter are various attempts to answer the following three epistemological questions. (As you read them you might consider whether you would answer each question with a yes or a no at this point in your understanding.)

1. Is it possible to have knowledge at all?
2. Does reason provide us with knowledge of the world independently of experience?
3. Does our knowledge represent a reality that is independent of us?

WHAT ARE MY OPTIONS CONCERNING KNOWLEDGE?

Skepticism is the claim that we do *not* have knowledge. Most skeptics accept the traditional view that knowledge is true, justified belief, but go on from there to argue that it is impossible to have justified beliefs or that no one has provided any reasons to think that our beliefs are capable of being justified. Hence, the skeptics give a negative answer to the first epistemological question. Since they think that knowledge is unattainable, they consider the remaining two questions to be irrelevant. The philosophers represented by the remaining positions think we *can* obtain knowledge and, hence, in contrast to the skeptic, they answer the first question in the affirmative. The disagreements among the nonskeptics concern the source and nature of knowledge.

Rationalism claims that reason or the intellect is the primary source of our fundamental knowledge about reality. Nonrationalists agree that we can use reason to draw conclusions from the information provided by sense experience. However, what distinguishes the rationalists is that they claim that reason can give us knowledge *apart* from experience. This sort of knowledge is said to be ***a priori* knowledge,** for it is gained independently of (or prior to) experience. For example, the rationalists point out that we can arrive at mathematical truths about circles or triangles without having to measure, experiment with, or experience circular or triangular objects. We do so by constructing rational, deductive proofs that lead to absolutely indubitable conclusions that are always universally true of the world outside our minds.

Some rationalists, such as Socrates, Plato, and Descartes claim that our most basic forms of knowledge are in the form of **innate ideas.** Ideas or items of knowledge that are innate are part of the natural content of the human mind. They are discovered within, by reflection, and are not derived from experience. Other rationalists simply claim that we can rationally intuit certain truths and know that they are true. Examples of these kinds of truths are claimed to be the basic principles of logic and mathematics. Many rationalists would add the idea of God and ethical truths as examples of knowledge that we could not derive from the five senses. Obviously, the rationalists think the second question should be answered affirmatively.

Empiricism is the claim that sense experience is the sole source of our knowledge about the world. Empiricists insist that when we start life, the original equipment of our intellect is a *tabula rasa* or "blank tablet." Only through experience does that empty mind become filled with content. Accordingly, in the reading by John Locke, he will argue that there are no innate ideas. Various empiricists give different explanations of the nature of logical and mathematical truths. They are all agreed, however, that these truths are not already latent in the mind before we discover them and that there is no genuine knowledge about the world apart from experience. The empiricists believe that everything we know is an example of ***a posteriori* knowledge,** or knowledge that is based on (or posterior to) experience. The empiricists would respond with "No!" to the second epistemological question. With respect to question 3, both the rationalists and the empiricists think that our knowledge does represent a reality that is independent of us.

Constructivism will be used in this discussion to refer to the claim that knowledge is *neither* already in the mind *nor* passively received from experience, but that the mind *constructs* knowledge out of the materials of experience. Immanuel Kant, an 18th-century German philosopher, introduced this view. He was influenced by both the rationalists and the empiricists and attempted to reach a compromise between them. While Kant did not agree with the rationalists on everything, he did believe we can have rational *a priori* knowledge of the world as it is found in human experience. Although Kant did not use this label, I will call his position **constructivism** to capture his distinctive account of knowledge. One troubling consequence of his view was that since the mind imposes its own order on experience, we can never know the reality independent of our minds as it is in itself. We can only know reality as it appears to us after it has been filtered and processed by our minds. Hence, Kant answers question 3 negatively. Nevertheless, since Kant thought our minds all have the same cognitive structure, he thought we are able to arrive at universal and objective knowledge *within* the boundaries of the human situation.

Epistemological relativism is the claim that there is no universal, objective knowledge of reality, for all knowledge is relative to either the individual or to one's culture. In other words, the relativist believes there is no one, true story about reality, but many stories. Since we can no more jump outside of our respective ways of viewing the world than we can our own skins, there is no way to say that a particular claim about reality is the only true one. It may seem that the relativist is denying knowledge the way the skeptic does. However, the relativists would insist that we *do* have knowledge, but deny that this knowledge is universal and objective. Knowledge is always knowledge *for* someone and is shaped by each knower's psychological, philosophical, historical, or cultural circumstances. Hence, while answering question 1 affirmatively, the typical relativist would respond with "no" to the remaining two questions.

Pragmatism is a philosophy that stresses the intimate relation between thought and action by defining the meaning of our conceptions in terms of the practical effects we associate with them and the truth of our beliefs in terms of how successfully they guide our actions. For the pragmatist every belief is like a scientific hypothesis and every action based on that belief is like an experiment that either confirms or refutes the viability of our belief. Pragmatists believe that truth is dynamic and not static and that we cannot attain any rational, absolute view of the world as though we were gods looking down upon it. In other words, pragmatists reject the notion that truth is a matter of accurately reflecting a reality that exists independently of us. This is because we can never jump outside of our heads to compare our beliefs with the world. Instead, from within human experience, we try to arrive at beliefs that are useful and that will successfully guide our actions. Most of the pragmatists, with few exceptions, would fall into the camp of relativism, since they abandon the notion of absolute truth that is grounded in foundational certainty, and replace this notion with a view that truth is relative either to an individual or a community.

Feminism is a movement within philosophy and other disciplines that (1) emphasizes the role of gender in shaping how we think and how society is structured, (2) focuses on the historical and social forces that have excluded women from full participation in the intellectual and political realms, and (3) strives to produce a society that recognizes women and men as both different and equal. These three themes illustrate the fact that feminism includes both a theoretical understanding of the way things are, as well as an attempt to use this knowledge to transform the status quo. For the feminist, it is impossible to divorce issues in epistemology from political and social issues. This is because our beliefs both shape society and are shaped by it. Feminist epistemologists are agreed in rejecting the ideal of pure, objective reason that is untainted by subjectivity or the emotions and interests of the knower. While a few feminist philosophers are wary of relativism, most could be characterized as relativists, for they claim that how we think about the world and which ideas we consider to be plausible or not are issues that are shaped by our subjective experiences and by the power structures of society. Table 3.1 presents the three epistemological questions discussed earlier and lists the answers provided by five different positions. Since the pragmatists and feminist epistemologists reject some of the assumptions that lay behind these questions, I have not listed these positions in the table. How-

---

TABLE 3.1   THREE EPISTEMOLOGICAL QUESTIONS AND FIVE POSITIONS ON THEM

	Is knowledge possible?	Does reason provide us with knowledge of the world independently of experience?	Does our knowledge represent a reality that is independent of us?
Skepticism	No	—	—
Rationalism	Yes	Yes	Yes
Empiricism	Yes	No	Yes
Constructivism (Kant)	Yes	Yes	No
Relativism	Yes	No	No

---

ever, in so far as many of the representatives of these two positions could easily be considered relativists, the answers given for relativism would apply to them.

We will begin our readings on knowledge with selection 20, Plato's famous Allegory of the Cave. It is one of the classic stories in world literature. While Plato uses this story to argue for his own version of rationalism, this allegory raises some of the major concerns that all theories of knowledge attempt to address.

The next five readings address the issue of the roles of reason and experience in obtaining knowledge. René Descartes initially wrestles with the problem of skepticism and finds himself overwhelmed by doubts about every one of his beliefs. As he continues to reason about his situation, however, he begins to find the way out by following the road of rationalism. The three readings by John Locke, George Berkeley, and David Hume represent different forms of empiricism. In the case of Hume, however, he finds that experience does not give us the solid foundation for knowledge it initially promises and Hume ends up in skepticism. Next, the great German philosopher Immanuel Kant proposes a compromise between rationalism and empiricism. He argues that knowledge is formed out of the contributions of both experience and reason.

The readings by William James and Alison Jaggar represent two contemporary positions in epistemology. James defends pragmatism and Jaggar gives a feminist perspective on the role of the emotions in knowledge.

O. K. Bouwsma and John Hospers provide us with different attempts to avoid the sort of skepticism that haunted Descartes and that Hume cheerfully embraced. Bouwsma and Hospers each argue in their own distinctive way that skepticism is not as powerful a threat to knowledge as philosophers have supposed because the skeptic has misconstrued the nature of knowledge.

Finally, in the Contemporary Application section, we examine science, which many people consider to be the shining example of objective knowledge. Physicist Steven Weinberg argues the traditional position that science tells us about reality. Philosopher Richard Rorty, however, questions this claim. Most would identify Rorty as a relativist, although he himself thinks this label may be too pejorative and misleading.

OPENING NARRATIVE: DO WE KNOW AS MUCH AS WE THINK WE DO?

 P L A T O

The Allegory of the Cave

The ancient Greek philosopher Plato (c. 428–348 B.C.) was the student of Socrates and the teacher of Aristotle. Coming from an aristocratic family, he was destined for a career in politics. However, his encounter with Socrates and then the trial and execution of this great teacher set the course of Plato's life. Realizing the shortcomings of his own society, Plato wanted to find the principles on which a just society could be built. But he realized that ethics and political theory had to be grounded in a true understanding of the nature of knowledge and reality.

The following passage is the Allegory of the Cave from Plato's book, *The Republic*. It is one of the most powerful and moving parables in the history of literature. Through the character of Socrates, Plato presents his account of the movement from illusion to reality and from ignorance to truth. In Plato's view, the world of sense experience is the furthest from reality. It is only when we ascend to the intellectual world that we find truth. The "Good" in this account is Plato's term for the highest reality—the source of everything else. As you read the description of the cave you might try drawing a diagram of the various people and objects in it to get a clearer picture of the scene.

Reading Questions

1. Applying the allegory to the realm of our beliefs, what do the shadows represent?
2. Why do the prisoners think that the shadows are all that is to be known about truth and reality?
3. Why does the liberated prisoner first doubt the reality of the objects that are casting the shadows? Why does he want to take refuge in the shadows?
4. Once he reaches the upper world, what does he now know about the shadows and about the wooden representations of animals of his former life?
5. Why does the liberated prisoner return to the cave?
6. Why is the enlightened prisoner now unable to deal successfully with the shadow world?
7. What do the other prisoners think of their friend? How is his fate like that of Socrates?
8. How does Plato interpret his own story?
9. According to Plato, what is enlightenment?

From Plato, *The Republic*, trans. Benjamin Jowett (Oxford: Oxford University Press, 1896). (The text has been edited to make it more accessible to the modern reader.)

SOCRATES: And now, let me show in a parable how far our nature is enlightened or unenlightened. Imagine human beings living in an underground den, which has a mouth open towards the light. Here they have been from their childhood, and have their legs and necks chained so that they can not move, and can only see before them, being prevented by the chains from turning their heads around. Above and behind them a fire is blazing at a distance, and between the fire and the prisoners there is a raised walk; and you will see, if you look, a low wall built along the walkway, like the screen which marionette players have in front of them, over which they show the puppets.

GLAUCON: I see.

SOCRATES: And do you see men passing along the wall carrying all sorts of vessels, and statues and figures of animals made of wood and stone and various materials, which appear over the wall? Some of them are talking, others silent.

GLAUCON: You have shown me a strange image, and they are strange prisoners.

SOCRATES: Like ourselves; and they see only their own shadows, or the shadows of one another, which the fire throws on the opposite wall of the cave.

GLAUCON: True; how could they see anything but the shadows if they were never allowed to move their heads?

SOCRATES: And of the objects which are being carried in like manner they would only see the shadows?

GLAUCON: Yes.

SOCRATES: And if they were able to converse with one another, would they not suppose that they were naming what was actually before them?

GLAUCON: Very true.

SOCRATES: And suppose further that the prison had an echo which came from the cave wall, would they not be sure to believe when one of the passers-by spoke that the voice which they heard came from the passing shadow?

GLAUCON: No question.

SOCRATES: To them, the truth would be literally nothing but the shadows of the images.

GLAUCON: That is certain.

SOCRATES: And now look again, and see what will naturally follow if the prisoners are released and disabused of their error. At first, when any of them is liberated and compelled suddenly to stand up and turn his neck round and walk and look towards the light, he will suffer sharp pains. The glare will distress him, and he will be unable to see the realities of which in his former state he had seen the shadows; and then conceive some one saying to him, that what he saw before was an illusion, but that now, when he is approaching nearer to reality and his eye is turned towards more real existence, he has a clearer vision. What will be his reply? And you may further imagine that his instructor is pointing to the objects as they pass and requiring him to name them—will he not be perplexed? Will he not believe that the shadows which he formerly saw are truer than the objects which are now shown to him?

GLAUCON: Far truer.

SOCRATES: And if he is compelled to look straight at the light, will he not have a pain in his eyes which will make him turn away to take refuge in the shadows which he can see, and which he will conceive to be clearer than the things which are now being shown to him?

GLAUCON: True.

SOCRATES: And suppose once more, that he is reluctantly dragged up a steep and rugged ascent, and held fast until he is forced into the presence of the sun itself, is he not likely to be pained and irritated? When he approaches the light his eyes will be dazzled, and he will not be able to see anything at all of what are now called realities.

GLAUCON: Not all in a moment.

SOCRATES: He will need to grow accustomed to the sight of the upper world. And first he will see the shadows best, next the reflections of men and other objects in the water, and then the objects themselves; then he will gaze upon the light of the moon and the stars and the spangled heaven; and he will see the sky and the stars by night better than the sun or the light of the sun by day?

GLAUCON: Certainly.

SOCRATES: Last of all he will be able to see the sun, and not mere reflections of it in the water, but he will see the sun in its own proper place, and not in another; and he will contemplate the sun as it is.

GLAUCON: Certainly.

SOCRATES: He will then proceed to argue that this is what gives the season and the years, and is the guardian of all that is in the visible world, and in a certain way the cause of all things which he and his fellows have been accustomed to behold?

GLAUCON: Clearly, he would first see the sun and then reason about it.

SOCRATES: And when he remembered his old dwelling, and the wisdom of the den and his fellow-prisoners, do you not suppose that he would be happy about his change, and pity them?

GLAUCON: Certainly, he would.

SOCRATES: And if they were in the habit of conferring honors among themselves on those who were quickest to observe the passing shadows and to remark which of them went before, and which followed after, and which were together; and who were therefore best able to draw conclusions as to the future, do you think that he would care for such honors and glories, or envy the possessors of them? Would he not say with Homer, "Better to be the poor servant of a poor master" and to endure anything, rather than think as they do and live after their manner?

GLAUCON: Yes, I think that he would rather suffer anything than entertain these false notions and live in this miserable manner.

SOCRATES: Imagine once more, such a one coming suddenly out of the sun to be replaced in his old situation; would he not be certain to have his eyes full of darkness?

GLAUCON: To be sure.

SOCRATES: And if there were a contest, and he had to compete in measuring the shadows with the prisoners who had never moved out of the den, while his sight was still weak, and before his eyes had become steady (and the time which would be needed to acquire this new habit of sight

might be very considerable), would he not be ridiculous? Men would say of him that up he went and down he came without his eyes; and that it was better not even to think of ascending; and if any one tried to loose another and lead him up to the light, let them only catch the offender, and they would put him to death.

GLAUCON: No question.

SOCRATES: This allegory is connected to the previous argument about the ascent of knowledge. The prison-house-cave is the world of sight; the light of the fire is the sun; and the journey upwards is the ascent of the soul into the intellectual world. My view is that in the world of knowledge the idea of the Good appears last of all, and is seen only with great effort; and when seen, is also inferred to be the universal author of all things beautiful and right, parent of light and of the lord of light in this visible world [the sun], and the immediate source of reason and truth in the higher world; and that this is the power upon which he who would act rationally either in public or private life must have his eye fixed.

GLAUCON: I agree, as far as I am able to understand you.

SOCRATES: Moreover, you must not wonder that those who attain to this wonderful vision are unwilling to descend to human affairs; for their souls are ever hastening into the upper world where they desire to dwell; which desire of theirs is very natural, if our allegory is to be trusted.

GLAUCON: Yes, very natural.

SOCRATES: And is there anything surprising in one who passes from divine contemplations to the evil state of man, misbehaving himself in a ridiculous manner; if, while his eyes are blinking and before he has become accustomed to the surrounding darkness, he is compelled to fight in courts of law, or in other places, about the images or the shadows of images of justice, and is endeavoring to meet the conceptions of those who have never yet seen absolute justice?

GLAUCON: Anything but surprising, he replied.

SOCRATES: Anyone who has common sense will remember that the confusions of the eyes are of two kinds, and arise from two causes, either from coming out of the light or from going into the light, which is true of the mind's eye, quite as much as of the bodily eye; and he who remembers this when he sees anyone whose vision is perplexed and weak, will not be too ready to laugh; he will first ask whether that soul of man has come out of the brighter life, and is unable to see because unaccustomed to the dark, or having turned from darkness to the day is dazzled by excess of light. And he will count the one happy in his condition and state of being, and he will pity the other; or, if he have a mind to laugh at the soul which comes from below into the light, there will be more reason in this than in the laugh which greets him who returns from above out of the light into the den.

GLAUCON: That, he said, is a very just distinction.

SOCRATES: But then, if I am right, certain professors of education must be wrong when they say that they can put a knowledge into the soul which was not there before, like sight into blind eyes.

GLAUCON: They undoubtedly say this, he replied.

SOCRATES: Whereas, our argument shows that the power and capacity of learning exists in the soul already; and that just as the eye was unable to turn from darkness to light without the whole body, so too the instrument of knowledge can only by the movement of the whole soul be turned from the world of becoming into that of being, and learn by degrees to endure the sight of being, and of the brightest and best of being, or, in other words, of the Good.

Questions for Reflection

1. What are the "shadows" in our society? In your life?
2. In what sense does the freed prisoner not understand the shadows as well as his friends do when he returns back to the cave? In what sense does he understand the shadows better than his friends do?
3. Are there degrees of knowledge and degrees of reality as Plato suggests? What would this mean?
4. What criticism does Plato make of professors of education? What is his alternative account of knowledge? Which view do you think is correct?
5. In the path from the shadow world to full sunlight of wisdom, where would you place yourself?

WHAT CAN WE KNOW? HOW DO WE KNOW?

 RENÉ DESCARTES

Rationalism and the Search for Certainty

Much of the agenda of modern epistemology began with the French philosopher René Descartes (1596–1650). Descartes lived in exciting times. He was born little more than

From René Descartes, *Meditations on First Philosophy,* 3rd ed., trans. Donald A. Cress (Indianapolis: Hackett, 1993).

100 years after Columbus sailed to the Americas and half a century after Copernicus published the controversial thesis that the earth revolves around the sun. About the time that Descartes was born, Shakespeare was writing *Hamlet*. Descartes came from a wealthy, respected family in France. His inherited family fortune gave him the freedom to travel and write, without having to provide for his own support. It also enabled him to receive one of the best educations available to a young man in France at that time.

In spite of the reputation of his college, Descartes felt as though his education had given him a collection of ideas that were based on little else but tradition; many of these ideas had been proven false by his own research. Descartes's lifelong passion was to find certainty. Hence, he resolved that he would scrap everything he had previously learned and begin to lay the foundations of his own knowledge.

While Descartes did not end up a skeptic, he initially used skeptical doubt as a test to decide which beliefs were absolutely certain. Descartes's method was to bathe every one of his beliefs in an acid bath of doubt to see if any survived. Descartes employed a very rigorous standard here. If he could think of any possibility that a belief of his could be mistaken, no matter how improbable this basis of doubt was, then he would suspend judgment concerning that belief. He realized that most of his beliefs would dissolve when subjected to such intense scrutiny, but if there was even one belief that survived the skeptical attack, then he could be absolutely certain about that belief.

Following the path of rationalism, he eventually found certainty within his own mind. While he could doubt just about everything, he discovered that he was at least certain that he was doubting. If he was doubting, then he must exist. Consequently, it was the certainty of his own existence that provided the first foundation stone of his quest for truth.

Reading Questions

1. Since it would be impossible to survey every one of his opinions, what more efficient method does Descartes use to examine his beliefs?
2. On what basis does he doubt his senses?
3. Descartes says that his belief that two plus three makes five seems to be very certain. However, what possibility does he raise that puts this belief and almost every other one into question?
4. What is Descartes's argument that convinces him that there is at least one thing about which he can be certain?

MEDITATION ONE: CONCERNING THOSE THINGS THAT CAN BE CALLED INTO DOUBT

Several years have now passed since I first realized how numerous were the false opinions that in my youth I had taken to be true, and thus how doubtful were all those that I had subsequently built upon them. And thus I realized that once in my life I had to raze everything to the ground and begin again from the original foundations, if I wanted to establish anything firm and lasting in the sciences. But the task seemed enormous, and I was waiting until I reached a point in my life that was so timely that no more suitable time for undertaking these plans of action would come to pass. For this reason, I procrastinated for so long that I would henceforth be at fault, were I to waste the time that remains for carrying out the project by brooding over it. Accordingly, I have today suitably freed my mind of all cares, secured for myself a period of leisurely tranquility, and am withdrawing into solitude. At last I will apply myself earnestly and unreservedly to this general demolition of my opinions.

Yet to bring this about I will not need to show that all my opinions are false, which is perhaps something I could never accomplish. But reason now persuades me that I should withhold my assent no less carefully from opinions that are not completely certain and indubitable than I would from those that are patently false. For this reason, it will suffice for the rejection of all of these opinions, if I find in each of them some reason for doubt. Nor therefore need I survey each opinion individually, a task that would be endless. Rather, because undermining the foundations will cause whatever has been built upon them to crumble of its own accord, I will attack straightaway those principles which supported everything I once believed.

Surely whatever I had admitted until now as most true I received either from the senses or through the senses. However, I have noticed that the senses are sometimes deceptive; and it is a mark of prudence never to place our complete trust in those who have deceived us even once.

But perhaps, even though the senses do sometimes deceive us when it is a question of very small and distant things, still there are many other matters concerning which one simply cannot doubt, even though they are derived from the very same senses: for example, that I am sitting here next to the fire, wearing my winter dressing gown, that I am holding this sheet of paper in my hands, and the like. But on what grounds could one deny that these hands and this entire body are mine? Unless perhaps I were to liken myself to the insane, whose brains are impaired by such an unrelenting vapor of black bile that they steadfastly insist that they are kings when they are utter paupers, or that they are arrayed in purple robes when they are naked, or that they have heads made of clay, or that they are gourds, or that they are made of glass. But such people are mad, and I would appear no less mad, were I to take their behavior as an example for myself.

This would all be well and good, were I not a man who is accustomed to sleeping at night, and to experiencing in my dreams the very same things, or now and then even less plausible ones, as these insane people do when they are awake. How often does my evening slumber persuade me of such ordinary things as these: that I am here, clothed in my dressing gown, seated next to the fireplace—when in fact I am lying undressed in bed! But right now my eyes are certainly wide awake when I gaze upon this sheet of paper. This head which I am shaking is not heavy with sleep. I extend this hand consciously and deliberately, and I feel it. Such things would not be so distinct for someone who is asleep. As if I did not recall having been deceived on other occasions even by similar thoughts in my dreams! As I consider these matters more carefully, I see so plainly that there are no definitive signs by which to distinguish being awake from being asleep. As a result, I am becoming quite dizzy, and this dizziness nearly convinces me that I am asleep.

Let us assume then, for the sake of argument, that we are dreaming and that such particulars as these are not true: that we are opening our eyes, moving our head, and extending our hands. Perhaps we do not even have such hands, or any such body at all. Nevertheless, it surely must be admitted that the things seen during slumber are, as it were, like painted images, which could only have been produced in the likeness of true things, and that therefore at least these general things—eyes, head, hands, and the whole body—are not imaginary things, but are true and exist. For indeed when painters themselves wish to represent sirens and satyrs by means of especially bizarre forms, they surely cannot assign to them utterly new natures. Rather, they simply fuse together the members of various animals. Or if perhaps they concoct something so utterly novel that nothing like it has ever been seen before (and thus is something utterly fictitious and false), yet certainly at the very least the colors from which they fashion it ought to be true. And by the same token, although even these general things—eyes, head, hands and the like—could be imaginary, still one has to admit that at least certain other things that are even more simple and universal are true. It is from these components, as if from true colors, that all those images of things that are in our thought are fashioned, be they true or false.

This class of things appears to include corporeal nature in general, together with its extension; the shape of extended things; their quantity, that is, their size and number; as well as the place where they exist; the time through which they endure, and the like.

Thus it is not improper to conclude from this that physics, astronomy, medicine, and all the other disciplines that are dependent upon the consideration of composite things are doubtful, and that, on the other hand, arithmetic, geometry, and other such disciplines, which treat of nothing but the simplest and most general things and which are indifferent as to whether these things do or do not in fact exist, contain something certain and indubitable. For whether I am awake or asleep, two plus three make five, and a square does not have more than four sides. It does not seem possible that such obvious truths should be subject to the suspicion of being false.

Be that as it may, there is fixed in my mind a certain opinion of long standing, namely that there exists a God who is able to do anything and by whom I, such as I am, have been created. How do I know that he did not bring it about that there is no earth at all, no heavens, no extended thing, no shape, no size, no place, and yet bringing it about that all these things appear to me to exist precisely as they do now? Moreover, since I judge that others sometimes make mistakes in matters that they believe they know most perfectly, may I not, in like fashion, be deceived every time I add two and three or count the sides of a square, or perform an even simpler operation, if that can be imagined? But perhaps God has not willed that I be deceived in this way, for he is said to be supremely good. Nonetheless, if it were repugnant to his goodness to have created me such that I be deceived all the time, it would also seem foreign to that same goodness to permit me to be deceived even occasionally. But we cannot make this last assertion.

Perhaps there are some who would rather deny so powerful a God than believe that everything else is uncertain. Let us not oppose them; rather, let us grant that everything said here about God is fictitious. Now they suppose that I came to be what I am either by fate, or by chance, or by a connected chain of events, or by some other way. But because being deceived and being mistaken appear to be a certain imperfection, the less powerful they take the author of my origin to be, the more probable it will be that I am so imperfect that I am always deceived. I have nothing to say in response to these arguments. But eventually I am forced to admit that there is nothing among the things I once believed to be true which it is not permissible to doubt—and not out of frivolity or lack of forethought, but for valid and considered reasons. Thus I must be no less careful to withhold assent henceforth even from these beliefs than I would from those that are patently false, if I wish to find anything certain.

But it is not enough simply to have realized these things; I must take steps to keep myself mindful of them. For long-standing opinions keep returning, and, almost against my will, they take advantage of my credulity, as if it were bound over to them by long use and the claims of intimacy. Nor will I ever get out of the habit of assenting to them and believing in them, so long as I take them to be exactly what they are, namely, in some respects doubtful, as has just now been shown, but nevertheless highly probable, so that it is much more consonant with reason to believe them than to deny them. Hence, it seems to me I would do well to deceive myself by turning my will in completely the opposite direction and pretend for a time that these opinions are wholly false and imaginary, until finally, as if with prejudices weighing down each side equally, no bad habit should turn my judgment any further from the correct perception of things. For indeed I know that meanwhile there is no danger or error in following this procedure, and that it is impossible for me to indulge in too much distrust, since I am now concentrating only on knowledge, not on action.

Accordingly, I will suppose not a supremely good God, the source of truth, but rather an evil genius, supremely powerful and clever, who has directed his entire effort at deceiving me. I will regard the heavens, the air, the earth, colors, shapes, sounds, and all external things as nothing but the bedeviling hoaxes of my dreams, with which he lays snares for my credulity. I will regard myself as not having hands, or eyes, or flesh, or blood, or any senses, but as nevertheless falsely believing that I possess all these things. I will remain resolute and steadfast in this meditation, and even if it is not within my power to know anything true, it certainly is within my power to take care resolutely to withhold my assent to what is false, lest this deceiver, however powerful, however clever he may be, have any effect on me. But this undertaking is arduous, and a certain laziness brings me back to my customary way of living. I am not unlike a prisoner who enjoyed an imaginary freedom during his sleep, but, when he later begins to suspect that he is dreaming, fears being awakened and nonchalantly conspires with these pleasant illusions. In just the same way, I fall back of my own accord into my old opinions, and dread being awakened, lest the toilsome wakefulness which follows upon a peaceful rest must be spent thenceforward not in the light but among the inextricable shadows of the difficulties now brought forward.

MEDITATION TWO: CONCERNING THE NATURE OF THE HUMAN MIND: THAT IT IS BETTER KNOWN THAN THE BODY

Yesterday's meditation has thrown me into such doubts that I can no longer ignore them, yet I fail to see how they are to be resolved. It is as if I had suddenly fallen into a deep whirlpool; I am so tossed about that I can neither touch bottom with my foot, nor swim up to the top. Nevertheless I will work my way up and will once again attempt the same path I entered upon yesterday. I will accomplish this by putting aside everything that admits of the least doubt, as if I had discovered it to be completely false. I will stay on this course until I know something certain, or, if nothing else, until I at least know for certain that nothing is certain. Archimedes sought but one firm and immovable point in order to move the entire earth from one place to another. Just so, great things are also to be hoped for if I succeed in finding just one thing, however slight, that is certain and unshaken.

Therefore I suppose that everything I see is false. I believe that none of what my deceitful memory represents ever existed. I have no senses whatever. Body, shape, extension, movement, and place are all chimeras. What then will be true? Perhaps just the single fact that nothing is certain.

But how do I know there is not something else, over and above all those things that I have just reviewed, concerning which there is not even the slightest occasion for doubt? Is there not some God, or by whatever name I might call him, who instills these very thoughts in me? But why would I think that, since I myself could perhaps be the author of these thoughts? Am I not then at least something? But I have already denied that I have any senses and any body. Still I hesitate; for what follows from this? Am I so tied to a body and to the senses that I cannot exist without them? But I have persuaded myself that there is absolutely nothing in the world: no sky, no earth, no minds, no bodies. Is it then the case that I too do not exist? But doubtless I did exist, if I persuaded myself of something. But there is some deceiver or other who is supremely powerful and supremely sly and who is always deliberately deceiving me. Then too there is no doubt that I exist, if he is deceiving me. And let him do his best at deception, he will never bring it about that I am nothing so long as I shall think that I am something. Thus, after everything has been most carefully weighed, it must finally be established that this pronouncement "I am, I exist" is necessarily true every time I utter it or conceive it in my mind.

But I do not yet understand sufficiently what I am—I, who now necessarily exist. And so from this point on, I must be careful lest I unwittingly mistake something else for myself, and thus err in that very item of knowledge that I claim to be the most certain and evident of all. Thus, I will meditate once more on what I once believed myself to be, prior to embarking upon these thoughts. For this reason, then, I will set aside whatever can be weakened even to the slightest degree by the arguments brought forward, so that eventually all that remains is precisely nothing but what is certain and un-shaken.

What then did I use to think I was? A man, of course. But what is a man? Might I not say a "rational animal"? No, because then I would have to inquire what "animal" and "rational" mean. And thus from one question I would slide into many more difficult ones. Nor do I now have enough free time that I want to waste it on subtleties of this sort. Instead, permit me to focus here on what came spontaneously and naturally into my thinking whenever I pondered what I was. Now it occurred to me first that I had a face, hands, arms, and this entire mechanism of bodily members: the very same as are discerned in a corpse, and which I referred to by the name "body." It next occurred to me that I took in food, that I walked about, and that I sensed and thought various things; these actions I used to attribute to the soul. But as to what this soul might be, I either did not think about it or else I imagined it a rarified I-know-not-what, like a wind, or a fire, or ether, which had been infused into my coarser parts. But as to the body I was not in any doubt. On the contrary, I was under the impression that I knew its nature distinctly. Were I perhaps tempted to describe this nature such as I conceived it in my mind, I would have described it thus: by "body," I understand all that is capable of being bounded by some shape, of being enclosed in a place, and of filling up a space in such a way as to exclude any other body from it; of being perceived by touch, sight, hearing, taste, or smell; of being moved in several ways, not, of course, by itself, but by whatever else impinges upon it. For it was my view that the power of self-motion, and likewise of sensing or of thinking, in no way belonged to the nature of the body. Indeed I used rather to marvel that such faculties were to be found in certain bodies.

But now what am I, when I suppose that there is some supremely powerful and, if I may be permitted to say so, malicious deceiver who deliberately tries to fool me in any way he can? Can I not affirm that I possess at least a small measure of all those things which I have already said belong to the nature of the body? I focus my attention on them, I think about them, I review them again, but nothing comes to mind. I am tired of repeating this to no

purpose. But what about those things I ascribed to the soul? What about being nourished or moving about? Since I now do not have a body, these are surely nothing but fictions. What about sensing? Surely this too does not take place without a body; and I seemed to have sensed in my dreams many things that I later realized I did not sense. What about thinking? Here I make my discovery: thought exists; it alone cannot be separated from me. I am; I exist—this is certain. But for how long? For as long as I am thinking; for perhaps it could also come to pass that if I were to cease all thinking I would then utterly cease to exist. At this time I admit nothing that is not necessarily true. I am therefore precisely nothing but a thinking thing; that is, a mind, or intellect, or understanding, or reason—words of whose meanings I was previously ignorant. Yet I am a true thing and am truly existing; but what kind of thing? I have said it already: a thinking thing.

What else am I? I will set my imagination in motion. I am not that concatenation of members we call the human body. Neither am I even some subtle air infused into these members, nor a wind, nor a fire, nor a vapor, nor a breath, nor anything I devise for myself. For I have supposed these things to be nothing. The assumption still stands; yet nevertheless I am something. But is it perhaps the case that these very things which I take to be nothing, because they are unknown to me, nevertheless are in fact no different from that "me" that I know? This I do not know, and I will not quarrel about it now. I can make a judgment only about things that are known to me. I know that I exist; I ask now who is this "I" whom I know? Most certainly, in the strict sense the knowledge of this "I" does not depend upon things of whose existence I do not yet have knowledge. Therefore it is not dependent upon any of those things that I simulate in my imagination. But this word "simulate" warns me of my error. For I would indeed be simulating were I to "imagine" that I was something, because imagining is merely the contemplating of the shape or image of a corporeal thing. But I now know with certainty that I am and also that all these images—and, generally, everything belonging to the nature of the body—could turn out to be nothing but dreams.

Once I have realized this, I would seem to be speaking no less foolishly were I to say: "I will use my imagination in order to recognize more distinctly who I am," than were I to say: "Now I surely am awake, and I see something true; but since I do not yet see it clearly enough, I will deliberately fall asleep so that my dreams might represent it to me more truly and more clearly." Thus I realize that none of what I can grasp by means of the imagination pertains to this knowledge that I have of myself. Moreover, I realize that I must be most diligent about withdrawing my mind from these things so that it can perceive its nature as distinctly as possible.

But what then am I? A thing that thinks. What is that? A thing that doubts, understands, affirms, denies, wills, refuses, and that also imagines and senses.

Questions for Reflection

1. Think about a time in your life when you began to doubt a belief that was important to you. How did you resolve the issue?
2. Do you agree with Descartes, that we should examine and question our beliefs to make sure they are sound?
3. What do you think about Descartes's skeptical doubts about his senses? Do you think that the logical possibility that we could be mistaken or deceived is a sufficient reason to be wary of our beliefs?
4. Did Descartes convince you that you can be more certain of the existence of your mind than anything else in the world?

JOHN LOCKE

Empiricism and Common Sense

While the roots of empiricism go back to ancient Greece, it was the English philosopher John Locke (1632–1704) who laid the foundations of modern empiricism. A man of many talents and diverse interests, Locke studied theology, natural science, philosophy, and medicine at Oxford University. For about 17 years, he served as the personal physician and advisor to Lord Ashley (later to become the Earl of Shaftesbury). He was active in political affairs and, in addition to holding a number of public offices, Locke helped draft a constitution for the American Carolinas in 1669.

It is commonly held that the Age of Enlightenment was ushered in with the publication of Locke's seminal work *An Essay Concerning Human Understanding* in 1689. With the possible exception of the Bible, no book was more influential in the 18th century than Locke's *Essay*. According to his own account, the idea for the work began when Locke and five or six friends were engaged in a vigorous debate over matters

From John Locke, *An Essay Concerning Human Understanding*, 1689.

concerning morality and religion. Locke soon realized that these very difficult matters could never be resolved until they first made an assessment of the capabilities and limits of our human understanding. As he put it, "If we can find out how far the understanding can extend its view; how far it has faculties to attain certainty; and in what cases it can only judge and guess, we may learn to content ourselves with what is attainable by us in this state."*

Locke thought that it was obvious that experience gives us knowledge that enables us to deal successfully with the world external to our minds. Therefore, Locke gives an affirmative answer to the question, "Is knowledge possible?" Knowledge, however, is not something lying out there in the grass, but is located in our minds. So to understand knowledge we have to analyze the contents of our minds and see what they tell us about the world.

In the first section, he attacks the notion of innate ideas that was so dear to the rationalists. Locke argues that the ideas that are typically thought to be innate (such as logical principles or ethical notions) are actually derived from experience. Throughout this discussion, it is important to note that by *ideas,* Locke does not mean merely abstract ideas such as "freedom" or 'justice." When Locke uses the term *idea,* it means any kind of mental content and can include such mental contents as the sensations of yellow, cold, hardness, or a bitter taste as well as experience of the mind's own operations such as believing, willing, and reasoning.

---

*John Locke, "Introduction," *An Essay Concerning Human Understanding,* 1689, 4.

Reading Questions

1. How does Locke use the example of children to make the point that knowledge cannot be in the mind prior to experience?
2. If the mind starts out like a blank, white paper, how does it get furnished with content?
3. What two kinds of "fountains" or sources of experience provide us with ideas?
4. What is the distinction Locke makes between primary and secondary qualities?
5. What arguments does Locke give to support the belief that our senses give us information about the external world?
6. What reply does Locke make to the skeptic who worries that all of our experience may be nothing but a dream?

BOOK I

Chapter II

No Innate Principles in the Mind

1. It is an established opinion amongst some men, that there are in the understanding certain innate principles; some primary notions, . . . characters, as it were stamped upon the mind of man; which the soul receives in its very first being, and brings into the world with it. It would be sufficient to convince unprejudiced readers of the falseness of this supposition, if I should only show (as I hope I shall in the following parts of this Discourse) how men, barely by the use of their natural faculties, may attain to all the knowledge they have, without the help of any innate impressions; and may arrive at

certainty, without any such original notions or principles. For I imagine any one will easily grant that it would be impertinent to suppose the ideas of colours innate in a creature to whom God hath given sight, and a power to receive them by the eyes from external objects: and no less unreasonable would it be to attribute several truths to the impressions of nature, and innate characters, when we may observe in ourselves faculties fit to attain as easy and certain knowledge of them as if they were originally imprinted on the mind. But because a man is not permitted without censure to follow his own thoughts in the search of truth, when they lead him ever so little out of the common road, I shall set down the reasons that made me doubt of the truth of that opinion, as an excuse for my mistake, if I be in one; which I leave to be considered by those who, with me, dispose themselves to embrace truth wherever they find it.

2. There is nothing more commonly taken for granted than that there are certain principles, both speculative and practical, (for they speak of both), universally agreed upon by all mankind: which therefore, they argue, must needs be the constant impressions which the souls of men receive in their first beings, and which they bring into the world with them, as necessarily and really as they do any of their inherent faculties.

3. This argument, drawn from universal consent, has this misfortune in it, that if it were true in matter of fact, that there were certain truths wherein all mankind agreed, it would not prove them innate, if there can be any other way shown how men may come to that universal agreement, in the things they do consent in, which I presume may be done.

4. But, which is worse, this argument of universal consent, which is made use of to prove innate principles, seems to me a demonstration that there are none such: because there are none to which all mankind give an universal assent. I shall begin with the speculative, and instance in those magnified principles of demonstration, "Whatsoever is, is," and "It is impossible for the same thing to be and not to be"; which, of all others, I think have the most allowed title to innate. These have so settled a reputation of maxims universally received, that it will no doubt be thought strange if any one should seem to question it. But yet I take liberty to say, that these propositions are so far from having an universal assent, that there are a great part of mankind to whom they are not so much as known.

5. For, first, it is evident, that all children and idiots have not the least apprehension or thought of them. And the want of that is enough to destroy that universal assent which must needs be the necessary concomitant of all innate truths: it seeming to me near a contradiction to say, that there are truths imprinted on the soul, which it perceives or understands not: imprinting, if it signify anything, being nothing else but the making certain truths to be perceived. For to imprint anything on the mind without the mind's perceiving it, seems to me hardly intelligible. If therefore children and idiots have souls, have minds, with those impressions upon them, they must unavoidably perceive them, and necessarily know and assent to these truths; which since they do not, it is evident that there are no such impressions. For if they are not notions naturally imprinted, how can they be innate? and if they are notions imprinted, how can they be unknown? To say a notion is imprinted on the mind, and yet at the same time to say, that the mind is ignorant of it, and never yet took notice of it, is to make this impression nothing. No proposition can be said to be in the mind which it never yet knew, which it was never yet conscious of. For if any one may, then, by the same reason, all propositions that are true, and the mind is capable ever of assenting to, may be said to be in the mind, and to be imprinted: since, if any one can be said to be in the mind, which it never yet knew, it must be only because it is capable of knowing it; and so the mind is of all truths it ever shall know. Nay, thus truths may be imprinted on the mind which it never did, nor ever shall know; for a man may live long, and die at last in ignorance of many truths which his mind was capable of knowing, and that with certainty. So that if the capacity of knowing be the natural impression contended for, all the truths a man ever comes to know will, by this account, be every one of them innate; and this great point will amount to no more, but only to a very improper way of speaking; which, whilst it pretends to assert the contrary, says

nothing different from those who deny innate principles. For nobody, I think, ever denied that the mind was capable of knowing several truths. The capacity, they say, is innate; the knowledge acquired. But then to what end such contest for certain innate maxims? If truths can be imprinted on the understanding without being perceived, I can see no difference there can be between any truths the mind is capable of knowing in respect of their original: they must all be innate or all adventitious: in vain shall a man go about to distinguish them. He therefore that talks of innate notions in the understanding, cannot (if he intend thereby any distinct sort of truths) mean such truths to be in the understanding as it never perceived, and is yet wholly ignorant of. For if these words "to be in the understanding" have any propriety, they signify to be understood. So that to be in the understanding, and not to be understood; to be in the mind and never to be perceived, is all one as to say anything is and is not in the mind or understanding. If therefore these two propositions, "Whatsoever is, is," and "It is impossible for the same thing to be and not to be," are by nature imprinted, children cannot be ignorant of them: infants, and all that have souls, must necessarily have them in their understandings, know the truth of them, and assent to it.

BOOK II

Chapter I

Of Ideas in General

1. Every man being conscious to himself that he thinks; and that which his mind is applied about whilst thinking being the ideas that are there, it is past doubt that men have in their minds several ideas,—such as are those expressed by the words *whiteness, hardness, sweetness, thinking, motion, man, elephant, army, drunkenness,* and others: it is in the first place then to be inquired, How he comes by them?

I know it is a received doctrine, that men have native ideas, and original characters, stamped upon their minds in their very first being. This

opinion I have at large examined already; and, I suppose what I have said in the foregoing Book will be much more easily admitted, when I have shown whence the understanding may get all the ideas it has; and by what ways and degrees they may come into the mind;—for which I shall appeal to every one's own observation and experience.

2. Let us then suppose the mind to be, as we say, white paper, void of all characters, without any ideas:—How comes it to be furnished? Whence comes it by that vast store which the busy and boundless fancy of man has painted on it with an almost endless variety? Whence has it all the materials of reason and knowledge? To this I answer, in one word, from EXPERIENCE. In that all our knowledge is founded; and from that it ultimately derives itself. Our observation employed either, about external sensible objects, or about the internal operations of our minds perceived and reflected on by ourselves, is that which supplies our understandings with all the materials of thinking. These two are the fountains of knowledge, from whence all the ideas we have, or can naturally have, do spring.

3. First, our Senses, conversant about particular sensible objects, do convey into the mind several distinct perceptions of things, according to those various ways wherein those objects do affect them. And thus we come by those ideas we have of *yellow, white, heat, cold, soft, hard, bitter, sweet,* and all those which we call sensible qualities; which when I say the senses convey into the mind, I mean, they from external objects convey into the mind what produces there those perceptions. This great source of most of the ideas we have, depending wholly upon our senses, and derived by them to the understanding, I call SENSATION.

4. Secondly, the other fountain from which experience furnisheth the understanding with ideas is,—the perception of the operations of our own mind within us, as it is employed about the ideas it has got;—which operations, when the soul comes to reflect on and consider, do furnish the understanding with another set of ideas, which could not be had from things without. And such are *perception, thinking, doubting, believing, reasoning, knowing, willing,* and all the different actings of our own

minds;—which we being conscious of, and observing in ourselves, do from these receive into our understandings as distinct ideas as we do from bodies affecting our senses. This source of ideas every man has wholly in himself; and though it be not sense, as having nothing to do with external objects, yet it is very like it, and might properly enough be called internal sense. But as I call the other *Sensation,* so I call this REFLECTION, the ideas it affords being such only as the mind gets by reflecting on its own operations within itself. By reflection then, in the following part of this discourse, I would be understood to mean, that notice which the mind takes of its own operations, and the manner of them, by reason whereof there come to be ideas of these operations in the understanding. These two, I say, viz. external material things, as the objects of SENSATION, and the operations of our own minds within, as the objects of REFLECTION, are to me the only originals from whence all our ideas take their beginnings. The term *operations* here I use in a large sense, as comprehending not barely the actions of the mind about its ideas, but some sort of passions arising sometimes from them, such as is the satisfaction or uneasiness arising from any thought.

5. The understanding seems to me not to have the least glimmering of any ideas which it doth not receive from one of these two. *External Objects* furnish the mind with the ideas of sensible qualities, which are all those different perceptions they produce in us; and the *Mind* furnishes the understanding with ideas of its own operations.

These, when we have taken a full survey of them, and their several modes, combinations, and relations, we shall find to contain all our whole stock of ideas; and that we have nothing in our minds which did not come in one of these two ways. Let any one examine his own thoughts, and thoroughly search into his understanding; and then let him tell me, whether all the original ideas he has there, are any other than of the objects of his senses, or of the operations of his mind, considered as objects of his reflection. And how great a mass of knowledge soever he imagines to be lodged there, he will, upon taking a strict view, see that he has not any idea in his mind but what one of these two have

imprinted;—though perhaps, with infinite variety compounded and enlarged by the understanding, as we shall see hereafter.

6. He that attentively considers the state of a child, at his first coming into the world, will have little reason to think him stored with plenty of ideas, that are to be the matter of his future knowledge. It is by degrees he comes to be furnished with them. And though the ideas of obvious and familiar qualities imprint themselves before the memory begins to keep a register of time or order, yet it is often so late before some unusual qualities come in the way, that there are few men that cannot recollect the beginning of their acquaintance with them. And if it were worth while, no doubt a child might be so ordered as to have but a very few, even of the ordinary ideas, till he were grown up to a man. But all that are born into the world, being surrounded with bodies that perpetually and diversely affect them, variety of ideas, whether care be taken of it or not, are imprinted on the minds of children. Light and colours are busy at hand everywhere, when the eye is but open; sounds and some tangible qualities fail not to solicit their proper senses, and force an entrance to the mind;—but yet, I think, it will be granted easily, that if a child were kept in a place where he never saw any other but black and white till he were a man, he would have no more ideas of scarlet or green, than he that from his childhood never tasted an oyster, or a pineapple, has of those particular relishes. . . .

BOOK II

Chapter VIII

Primary and Secondary Qualities

8. Whatsoever the mind perceives in itself, or is the immediate object of perception, thought, or understanding, that I call *idea;* and the power to produce any idea in our mind, I call *quality* of the subject wherein that power is. Thus a snowball having the power to produce in us the ideas of *white, cold,* and *round,*—the power to produce those ideas

in us, as they are in the snowball, I call qualities; and as they are sensations or perceptions in our understandings, I call them ideas; which ideas, if I speak of sometimes as in the things themselves, I would be understood to mean those qualities in the objects which produce them in us.

9. Qualities thus considered in bodies are, *First*, such as are utterly inseparable from the body, in what state soever it be; and such as in all the alterations and changes it suffers, all the force can be used upon it, it constantly keeps; and such as sense constantly finds in every particle of matter which has bulk enough to be perceived; and the mind finds inseparable from every particle of matter, though less than to make itself singly be perceived by our senses: v.g. Take a grain of wheat, divide it into two parts; each part has still solidity, extension, figure, and mobility: divide it again, and it retains still the same qualities; and so divide it on, till the parts become insensible; they must retain still each of them all those qualities. For division (which is all that a mill, or pestle, or any other body, does upon another, in reducing it to insensible parts) can never take away either solidity, extension, figure, or mobility from any body, but only makes two or more distinct separate masses of matter, of that which was but one before; all which distinct masses, reckoned as so many distinct bodies, after division, make a certain number. These I call *original* or *primary qualities* of body, which I think we may observe to produce simple ideas in us, viz. solidity, extension, figure, motion or rest, and number.

10. *Secondly*, such qualities which in truth are nothing in the objects themselves but power to produce various sensations in us by their primary qualities, i.e. by the bulk, figure, texture, and motion of their insensible parts, as colours, sounds, tastes, &c. These I call *secondary qualities*. To these might be added a third sort, which are allowed to be barely powers; though they are as much real qualities in the subject as those which I, to comply with the common way of speaking, call qualities, but for distinction, secondary qualities. For the power in fire to produce a new colour, or consistency, in wax or clay,—by its primary qualities, is as much a quality in fire, as the power it has to produce in me a new idea or sensation of warmth or burning, which I

felt not before,—by the same primary qualities, viz. the bulk, texture, and motion of its insensible parts. . . .

13. . . . Let us suppose at present that the different motions and figures, bulk and number, of such particles, affecting the several organs of our senses, produce in us those different sensations which we have from the colours and smells of bodies; v.g. that a violet, by the impulse of such insensible particles of matter, of peculiar figures and bulks, and in different degrees and modifications of their motions, causes the ideas of the blue colour, and sweet scent of that flower to be produced in our minds. It being no more impossible to conceive that God should annex such ideas to such motions, with which they have no similitude, than that he should annex the idea of pain to the motion of a piece of steel dividing our flesh, with which that idea hath no resemblance.

14. What I have said concerning colours and smells may be understood also of tastes and sounds, and other the like sensible qualities; which, whatever reality we by mistake attribute to them, are in truth nothing in the objects themselves, but powers to produce various sensations in us; and depend on those primary qualities, viz. bulk, figure, texture, and motion of parts as I have said.

15. From whence I think it easy to draw this observation,—that the ideas of primary qualities of bodies are resemblances of them, and their patterns do really exist in the bodies themselves, but the ideas produced in us by these secondary qualities have no resemblance of them at all. There is nothing like our ideas, existing in the bodies themselves. They are, in the bodies we denominate from them, only a power to produce those sensations in us: and what is sweet, blue, or warm in idea, is but the certain bulk, figure, and motion of the insensible parts, in the bodies themselves, which we call so.

16. Flame is denominated hot and light; snow, white and cold; and manna, white and sweet, from the ideas they produce in us. Which qualities are commonly thought to be the same in those bodies that those ideas are in us, the one the perfect resemblance of the other, as they are in a mirror, and it would by most men be judged very extravagant if

one should say otherwise. And yet he that will consider that the same fire that, at one distance produces in us the sensation of warmth, does, at a nearer approach, produce in us the far different sensation of pain, ought to bethink himself what reason he has to say—that this idea of warmth, which was produced in him by the fire, is actually in the fire; and his idea of pain, which the same fire produced in him the same way, is not in the fire. Why are whiteness and coldness in snow, and pain not, when it produces the one and the other idea in us; and can do neither, but by the bulk, figure, number, and motion of its solid parts?

17. The particular bulk, number, figure, and motion of the parts of fire or snow are really in them,—whether any one's senses perceive them or no: and therefore they may be called real qualities, because they really exist in those bodies. But light, heat, whiteness, or coldness, are no more really in them than sickness or pain is in manna. Take away the sensation of them; let not the eyes see light or colours, nor the ears hear sounds; let the palate not taste, nor the nose smell, and all colours, tastes, odours, and sounds, as they are such particular ideas, vanish and cease, and are reduced to their causes, i.e. bulk, figure, and motion of parts. . . .

21. Ideas being thus distinguished and understood, we may be able to give an account how the same water, at the same time, may produce the idea of cold by one hand and of heat by the other: whereas it is impossible that the same water, if those ideas were really in it, should at the same time be both hot and cold. For, if we imagine warmth, as it is in our hands, to be nothing but a certain sort and degree of motion in the minute particles of our nerves or animal spirits, we may understand how it is possible that the same water may, at the same time, produce the sensations of heat in one hand and cold in the other; which yet figure never does, that never producing—the idea of a square by one hand which has produced the idea of a globe by another. But if the sensation of heat and cold be nothing but the increase or diminution of the motion of the minute parts of our bodies, caused by the corpuscles of any other body, it is easy to be understood, that if that motion be greater in one hand than in the other; if a body be

applied to the two hands, which has in its minute particles a greater motion than in those of one of the hands, and a less than in those of the other, it will increase the motion of the one hand and lessen it in the other; and so cause the different sensations of heat and cold that depend thereon.

22. I have in what just goes before been engaged in physical inquiries a little further than perhaps I intended. But, it being necessary to make the nature of sensation a little understood; and to make the difference between the qualities in bodies, and the ideas produced by them in the mind, to be distinctly conceived, without which it were impossible to discourse intelligibly of them;—I hope I shall be pardoned this little excursion into natural philosophy; it being necessary in our present inquiry to distinguish the *primary* and *real qualities* of bodies, which are always in them (viz. solidity, extension, figure, number, and motion, or rest, and are sometimes perceived by us, viz. when the bodies they are in are big enough singly to be discerned), from those *secondary* and *imputed qualities*, which are but the powers of several combinations of those primary ones, when they operate without being distinctly discerned;—whereby we may also come to know what ideas are, and what are not, resemblances of something really existing in the bodies we denominate from them. . . .

BOOK IV

Chapter XI

*Of Our Knowledge of the Existence
of Other Things*

1. The knowledge of our own being we have by intuition. The existence of a God, reason clearly makes known to us. . . .

The knowledge of the existence of any other thing we can have only by sensation: for there being no necessary connexion of real existence with any idea a man hath in his memory; nor of any other existence but that of God with the existence of any particular man: no particular man can know the existence of any other being, but only when, by actual operating upon him, it makes itself perceived by him. For, the having the idea of anything in our mind, no more proves the existence of that thing, than the picture of a man evidences his being in the world, or the visions of a dream make thereby a true history.

2. It is therefore the actual receiving of ideas from without that gives us notice of the existence of other things, and makes us know, that something doth exist at that time without us, which causes that idea in us; though perhaps we neither know nor consider how it does it. For it takes not from the certainty of our senses, and the ideas we receive by them, that we know not the manner wherein they are produced: v.g. whilst I write this, I have, by the paper affecting my eyes, that idea produced in my mind, which, whatever object causes, I call *white;* by which I know that that quality or accident (i.e. whose appearance before my eyes always causes that idea) doth really exist, and hath a being without me. And of this, the greatest assurance I can possibly have, and to which my faculties can attain, is the testimony of my eyes, which are the proper and sole judges of this thing; whose testimony I have reason to rely on as so certain, that I can no more doubt, whilst I write this, that I see white and black, and that something really exists that causes that sensation in me, than that I write or move my hand; which is a certainty as great as human nature is capable of, concerning the existence of anything, but a man's self alone, and of God.

3. The notice we have by our senses of the existing of things without us, though it be not altogether so certain as our intuitive knowledge, or the deductions of our reason employed about the clear abstract ideas of our own minds; yet it is an assurance that deserves the name of knowledge. If we persuade ourselves that our faculties act and inform us right concerning the existence of those objects that affect them, it cannot pass for an ill-grounded confidence: for I think nobody can, in earnest, be so sceptical as to be uncertain of the existence of those things which he sees and feels. At least, he that can doubt so far, (whatever he may have with his own thoughts,) will never have any controversy with me; since he can never be sure I say anything contrary to his own opinion. As to myself, I think God has given me assurance enough of the existence of things without me: since, by their different application, I can produce in myself both pleasure and pain, which is one great concernment of my present state. This is certain: the confidence that our faculties do not herein deceive us, is the greatest assurance we are capable of concerning the existence of material beings. For we cannot act anything but by our faculties; nor talk of knowledge itself, but by the help of those faculties which are fitted to apprehend even what knowledge is.

But besides the assurance we have from our senses themselves, that they do not err in the information they give us of the existence of things without us, when they are affected by them, we are further confirmed in this assurance by other concurrent reasons.

4. First, it is plain those perceptions are produced in us by exterior causes affecting our senses: because those that want the organs of any sense, never can have the ideas belonging to that sense produced in their minds. This is too evident to be doubted: and therefore we cannot but be assured that they come in by the organs of that sense, and no other way. The organs themselves, it is plain, do not produce them: for then the eyes of a man in the dark would produce colours, and his nose smell roses in the winter: but we see nobody gets the relish of a pineapple, till he goes to the Indies, where it is, and tastes it.

5. Secondly, because we find that an idea from actual sensation, and another from memory, are very distinct perceptions. Because sometimes I find that I cannot avoid the having those ideas produced in my mind. For though, when my eyes are shut, or windows fast, I can at pleasure recall to my mind the ideas of light, or the sun, which former sensations had lodged in my memory; so I can at pleasure lay by that idea, and take into my view that of the smell of a rose, or taste of sugar. But, if I turn my eyes at noon towards the sun, I cannot avoid the ideas which the light or sun then produces in me. So that there is a manifest difference between the ideas laid up in my memory, (over which, if they were there only, I should have constantly the same power to dispose of them, and lay them by at pleasure,) and those which force themselves upon me,

and I cannot avoid having. And therefore it must needs be some exterior cause, and the brisk acting of some objects without me, whose efficacy I cannot resist, that produces those ideas in my mind, whether I will or no. Besides, there is nobody who doth not perceive the difference in himself between contemplating the sun, as he hath the idea of it in his memory, and actually looking upon it: of which two, his perception is so distinct, that few of his ideas are more distinguishable one from another. And therefore he hath certain knowledge that they are not both memory, or the actions of his mind, and fancies only within him; but that actual seeing hath a cause without. . . .

8. This certainty is as great as our condition needs. But yet, if after all this any one will be so sceptical as to distrust his senses, and to affirm that all we see and hear, feel and taste, think and do, during our whole being, is but the series and deluding appearances of a long dream, whereof there is no reality; and therefore will question the existence of all things, or our knowledge of anything: I must desire him to consider, that, if all be a dream, then he doth but dream that he makes the question, and so it is not much matter that a waking man should answer him. But yet, if he pleases, he may dream that I make him this answer, That the certainty of things existing *in rerum natura* when we have the testimony of our senses for it is not only as great as our frame can attain to, but as our condition needs. For, our faculties being suited not to the full extent of being, nor to a perfect, clear, comprehensive knowledge of things free from all doubt and scruple; but to the preservation of us, in whom they are; and accommodated to the use of life: they serve to our purpose well enough, if they will but give us certain notice of those things, which are convenient or inconvenient to us. For he that sees a candle burning, and hath experimented the force of its flame by putting his finger in it, will little doubt that this is something existing without him, which does him harm, and puts him to great pain; which is assurance enough, when no man requires greater certainty to govern his actions by than what is as certain as his actions themselves. And if our dreamer pleases to try whether the glowing heat of a glass furnace be barely a wandering imagination in a drowsy man's fancy, by putting his hand into it, he may perhaps be wakened into a certainty greater than he could wish, that it is something more than bare imagination. So that this evidence is as great as we can desire, being as certain to us as our pleasure or pain, i.e. happiness or misery; beyond which we have no concernment, either of knowing or being. Such an assurance of the existence of things without us is sufficient to direct us in the attaining the good and avoiding the evil which is caused by them, which is the important concernment we have of being made acquainted with them. . . .

10. Whereby yet we may observe how foolish and vain a thing it is for a man of a narrow knowledge, who having reason given him to judge of the different evidence and probability of things, and to be swayed accordingly; how vain, I say, it is to expect demonstration and certainty in things not capable of it; and refuse assent to very rational propositions, and act contrary to very plain and clear truths, because they cannot be made out so evident, as to surmount every the least (I will not say reason, but) pretence of doubting. He that, in the ordinary affairs of life, would admit of nothing but direct plain demonstration, would be sure of nothing in this world, but of perishing quickly. The wholesomeness of his meat or drink would not give him reason to venture on it: and I would fain know what it is he could do upon such grounds as are capable of no doubt, no objection.

Questions for Reflection

1. Locke challenged you to examine your own thoughts and see if any of your ideas came from any source other than the experiences of sensation or reflection. Can you meet his challenge? Can you come up with an idea that was not derived from experience?
2. Most truths learned from experience are contingent. That is, they happen to be true, but we can imagine that the world might have been different. For example, water

freezes at low temperatures, but we can imagine the world was such that it didn't freeze. However, can Locke's appeal to experience explain the fact that we know that the laws of logic and mathematics are universal and necessary? Could experience ever teach us these truths?

3. What is your evaluation of Locke's commonsense rejection of skepticism? Has he shown that Descartes's worries were pointless? Keep Locke's rejection of skepticism in mind when you read Hume's skeptical arguments later.

GEORGE BERKELEY

Empiricism and Idealism

George Berkeley (1685–1753), Ireland's most famous philosopher, received his education at Trinity College in Dublin. There, he was exposed to the philosophies of René Descartes and John Locke, as well as the work of Newton and other leading scientists. In 1710 he was ordained as a priest in the Anglican Church and later became one of its bishops. He traveled to America in an attempt to set up a college for the sons of English planters and the native American Indians. Though his project failed for lack of funding, he had a decisive effect on American education. He provided Yale University with the finest library in America at that time and also donated books to Harvard University. Kings College (later to become Columbia University) was founded with his advice. In a poem, he praised the fresh, new spirit of America and predicted that the newly emerging nation would expand all the way to the western coast. As a result, the state of California established a university in a city named after Berkeley.

With Locke, Berkeley believed that it was only through experience and not reason that we have any knowledge of reality. However, it will soon be clear that Berkeley differed radically with Locke concerning what sort of reality is revealed to us within experience. Following Locke, Berkeley refers to the concrete contents of our experience as "ideas." Ideas are such things as the redness of a rose, the coldness of ice, the smell of freshly mown grass, the taste of honey, and the sound of a flute. We also have ideas of our own psychological states and operations, because we experience our own willing, doubting, and loving. Thus, ideas are images, feelings, or sense data that are directly present to the mind either in vivid sensory or psychological experiences, or in the less vivid presentations of either memory or imagination. Hence, when Berkeley says we have the idea of an apple, he is not referring to an abstract concept but to the experience or memory of the combined ideas (experiences) of roundness, redness, hardness, and sweetness.

While agreeing with Locke on these points, Berkeley believed Locke had not been a consistent enough empiricist and so Berkeley resolved to carry the theory of empiri-

From George Berkeley, *Three Dialogues Between Hylas and Philonous,* 1713.

cism to its logical conclusions. In doing so, Berkeley ended up with the rather astonishing position that since (a) all we know is what we find in experience, it follows that (b) we can never know or even make sense of a material world that allegedly lies outside of our own, private experiences. Berkeley's philosophy is commonly referred to as "subjective idealism," although he himself called it "immaterialism." **Idealism** is a position that maintains that ultimate reality is mental or spiritual in nature. Berkeley's position is known as "subjective idealism" because he believes reality is made up of many individual minds rather than one cosmic mind. According to Berkeley, reality is nonphysical and everything that exists falls into one of two categories: (1) minds (or spirits) and (2) the ideas they perceive. Hence, Berkeley claims that all the objects we encounter in experience (books, apples, rocks) fall into category (2) and are nothing more than mind-dependent collections of ideas. Berkeley expressed this by saying "To be is to be perceived." Notice that Berkeley is not claiming that the objects we find in experience are not real. Instead, he is claiming that once we declare that experience is the source of our knowledge of the world, then what we designate as "real" necessarily must refer to collections of experiences in the mind.

In the following dialogue, a character named Philonous (which in Greek means "lover of mind") debates with Hylas (from the Greek word for "matter"). It is clear that Philonous is Berkeley's spokesperson. A crucial feature of his argument is the fact that whenever we try to describe so-called "material objects," we do so in terms of our sensations (which are mental events). Once we have exhausted the list of mental experiences we associate with an object (our experiences of its shape, size, color, hardness, and so on), there is nothing left to our conception of the object.

Reading Questions

1. What is the issue over which Hylas and Philonous are disagreed?
2. What do Hylas and Philonous agree is the correct understanding of sensible things?
3. What is the point Philonous makes with respect to the relationship between heat and pain? What point does he make about the relationship of warmth and pleasure? How does he use these two cases to argue that heat is not a mind-independent quality?
4. What experiment does he use to make the same point about the quality of coldness?
5. How does Philonous extend this same method of reasoning to show that tastes, odors, and sounds are nothing more than experiences that are dependent on the mind?
6. In a passage not included in this selection, Philonous also argues that our experience of colors are subjective and mind-dependent. From what he has said thus far, can you imagine how he argues this point?
7. Hylas insists that there exists a material substratum, that is, matter that exists outside of all possible experiences, but which is their cause. How does Philonous attack this thesis?
8. How does Philonous reply to Hylas's claim that he can conceive of a tree or house existing unperceived by any mind at all?
9. Philonous has argued that for objects to exist they must be perceived by some mind or other. How does he go on to show that objects can still exist even when our human minds are not perceiving them?

HYLAS: You were represented in last night's conversation, as one who maintained the most extravagant opinion that ever entered into the mind of man, to wit, that there is no such thing as *material substance* in the world.

PHILONOUS: That there is no such thing as what philosophers call *material substance,* I am seriously persuaded: but if I were made to see anything absurd or sceptical in this, I should then have the same reason to renounce this, that I imagine I have now to reject the contrary opinion.

HYLAS: What! can anything be more fantastical, more repugnant to common sense, or a more manifest piece of scepticism, than to believe there is no such thing as *matter*?

PHILONOUS: Softly, good Hylas. What if it should prove, that you, who hold there is, are by virtue of that opinion a greater *sceptic*, and maintain more paradoxes and repugnancies to common sense, than I who believe no such thing? . . . How cometh it to pass then, Hylas, that you pronounce me a *sceptic*, because I deny what you affirm, to wit, the existence of matter? Since, for ought you can tell, I am as peremptory in my denial, as you in your affirmation.

HYLAS: Hold, Philonous, I have been a little out in my definition; but every false step a man makes in discourse is not to be insisted on. I said indeed, that a *sceptic* was one who doubted of everything; but I should have added, or who denies the reality and truth of things.

PHILONOUS: What things? Do you mean the principles and theorems of sciences? But these you know are universal intellectual notions, and consequently independent of matter; the denial therefore of this doth not imply the denying them.

HYLAS: I grant it. But are there no other things? What think you of distrusting the senses, of denying the real existence of sensible things, or pretending to know nothing of them. Is not this sufficient to denominate a man a *sceptic?*

PHILONOUS: Shall we therefore examine which of us it is that denies the reality of sensible things, or professes the greatest ignorance of them; since,

if I take you rightly, he is to be esteemed the greatest *sceptic?*

HYLAS: That is what I desire.

PHILONOUS: What mean you by sensible things?

HYLAS: Those things which are perceived by the senses. Can you imagine that I mean anything else?

PHILONOUS: Pardon me, Hylas, if I am desirous clearly to apprehend your notions, since this may much shorten our inquiry. Suffer me then to ask you this farther question. Are those things only perceived by the senses which are perceived immediately? Or may those things properly be said to be *sensible,* which are perceived mediately, or not without the intervention of others?

HYLAS: I do not sufficiently understand you.

PHILONOUS: In reading a book, what I immediately perceive are the letters, but mediately, or by means of these, are suggested to my mind the notions of God, virtue, truth, &c. Now, that the letters are truly sensible things, or perceived by sense, there is no doubt: but I would know whether you take the things suggested by them to be so too.

HYLAS: No certainly, it were absurd to think *God* or *Virtue* sensible things, though they may be signified and suggested to the mind by sensible marks, with which they have an arbitrary connexion.

PHILONOUS: It seems then, that by *sensible things* you mean those only which can be perceived immediately by sense.

HYLAS: Right.

PHILONOUS: Doth it not follow from this, that though I see one part of the sky red, and another blue, and that my reason doth thence evidently conclude there must be some cause of that diversity of colours, yet that cause cannot be said to be a sensible thing, or perceived by the sense of seeing?

HYLAS: It doth.

PHILONOUS: In like manner, though I hear variety of sounds, yet I cannot be said to hear the cause of those sounds.

HYLAS: You cannot.

PHILONOUS: And when by my touch I perceive a thing to be hot and heavy, I cannot say with any truth or propriety, that I feel the cause of its heat or weight.

HYLAS: To prevent any more questions of this kind, I tell you once for all, that by *sensible things* I mean those only which are perceived by sense, and that in truth the senses perceive nothing which they do not perceive immediately: for they make no inferences. The deducting therefore of causes or occasions from effects and appearances, which alone are perceived by sense, entirely relates to reason.

PHILONOUS: This point then is agreed between us, that *sensible things are those only which are immediately perceived by sense.* You will farther inform me, whether we immediately perceive by sight anything beside light, and colours, and figures: or by hearing, anything but sounds: by the palate, anything beside tastes: by the smell, beside odours: or by the touch, more than tangible qualities.

HYLAS: We do not.

PHILONOUS: It seems therefore, that if you take away all sensible qualities, there remains nothing sensible.

HYLAS: I grant it.

PHILONOUS: Sensible things therefore are nothing else but so many sensible qualities, or combinations of sensible qualities.

HYLAS: Nothing else.

PHILONOUS: Heat then is a sensible thing.

HYLAS: Certainly.

PHILONOUS: Doth the reality of sensible things consist in being perceived? or, is it something distinct from their being perceived, and that bears no relation to the mind?

HYLAS: To *exist* is one thing, and to be *perceived* is another.

PHILONOUS: I speak with regard to sensible things only: and of these I ask, whether by their real existence you mean a subsistence exterior to the mind, and distinct from their being perceived?

HYLAS: I mean a real absolute being, distinct from, and without any relation to their being perceived.

PHILONOUS: Heat therefore, if it be allowed a real being, must exist without the mind.

HYLAS: It must.

PHILONOUS: Tell me, Hylas, is this real existence equally compatible to all degrees of heat, which we perceive: or is there any reason why we should attribute it to some, and deny it others? And if there be, pray let me know that reason.

HYLAS: Whatever degree of heat we perceive by sense, we may be sure the same exists in the object that occasions it.

PHILONOUS: What, the greatest as well as the least?

HYLAS: I tell you, the reason is plainly the same in respect of both: they are both perceived by sense; nay, the greater degree of heat is more sensibly perceived; and consequently, if there is any difference, we are more certain of its real existence than we can be of the reality of a lesser degree.

PHILONOUS: But is not the most vehement and intense degree of heat a very great pain?

HYLAS: No one can deny it.

PHILONOUS: And is any unperceiving thing capable of pain or pleasure?

HYLAS: No certainly.

PHILONOUS: Is your material substance a senseless being, or a being endowed with sense and perception?

HYLAS: It is senseless, without doubt.

PHILONOUS: It cannot therefore be the subject of pain.

HYLAS: By no means.

PHILONOUS: Nor consequently of the greatest heat perceived by sense, since you acknowledge this to be no small pain.

HYLAS: I grant it.

PHILONOUS: What shall we say then of your external object; is it a material substance, or no?

HYLAS: It is a material substance with the sensible qualities inhering in it.

PHILONOUS: How then can a great heat exist in it, since you own it cannot in a material substance? I desire you would clear this point.

HYLAS: Hold, Philonous, I fear I was out in yielding intense heat to be a pain. It should seem rather, that pain is something distinct from heat, and the consequence or effect of it.

PHILONOUS: Upon putting your hand near the fire, do you perceive one simple uniform sensation, or two distinct sensations?

HYLAS: But one simple sensation.

PHILONOUS: Is not the heat immediately perceived?

HYLAS: It is.

PHILONOUS: And the pain?

HYLAS: True.

PHILONOUS: Seeing therefore they are both immediately perceived at the same time, and the fire affects you only with one simple, or uncompounded idea, it follows that this same simple idea is both the intense heat immediately perceived, and the pain; and consequently, that the intense heat immediately perceived, is nothing distinct from a particular sort of pain.

HYLAS: It seems so.

PHILONOUS: Again, try in your thoughts, Hylas, if you can conceive a vehement sensation to be without pain, or pleasure.

HYLAS: I cannot.

PHILONOUS: Or can you frame to yourself an idea of sensible pain or pleasure in general, abstracted from every particular idea of heat, cold, tastes, smells? &c.

HYLAS: I do not find that I can.

PHILONOUS: Doth it not therefore follow, that sensible pain is nothing distinct from those sensations or ideas, in an intense degree?

HYLAS: It is undeniable; and to speak the truth, I begin to suspect a very great heat cannot exist but in a mind perceiving it.

PHILONOUS: What! are you then in that *sceptical* state of suspense, between affirming and denying?

HYLAS: I think I may be positive in the point. A very violent and painful heat cannot exist without the mind.

PHILONOUS: It hath not therefore, according to you, any real being.

HYLAS: I own it.

PHILONOUS: Is it therefore certain, that there is no body in nature really hot?

HYLAS: I have not denied there is any real heat in bodies. I only say, there is no such thing as an intense real heat.

PHILONOUS: But did you not say before, that all degrees of heat were equally real: or if there was any difference, that the greater were more undoubtedly real than the lesser?

HYLAS: True: but it was, because I did not then consider the ground there is for distinguishing between them, which I now plainly see. And it is this: because intense heat is nothing else but a particular kind of painful sensation; and pain cannot exist but in a perceiving being; it follows that no intense heat can really exist in an unperceiving corporeal substance. But this is no reason why we should deny heat in an inferior degree to exist in such a substance.

PHILONOUS: But how shall we be able to discern those degrees of heat which exist only in the mind, from those which exist without it?

HYLAS: That is no difficult matter. You know, the least pain cannot exist unperceived; whatever therefore degree of heat is a pain, exists only in the mind. But as for all other degrees of heat, nothing obliges us to think the same of them.

PHILONOUS: I think you granted before, that no unperceiving being was capable of pleasure, any more than of pain.

HYLAS: I did.

PHILONOUS: And is not warmth, or a more gentle degree of heat than what causes uneasiness, a pleasure?

HYLAS: What then?

PHILONOUS: Consequently it cannot exist without the mind in any unperceiving substance, or body.

HYLAS: So it seems.

PHILONOUS: Since therefore, as well those degrees of heat that are not painful, as those that are, can exist only in a thinking substance; may we not conclude that external bodies are absolutely incapable of any degree of heat whatsoever?

HYLAS: On second thoughts, I do not think it so evident that warmth is a pleasure, as that a great degree of heat is a pain.

PHILONOUS: I do not pretend that warmth is as great a pleasure as heat is a pain. But if you grant it to be even a small pleasure, it serves to make good my conclusion.

HYLAS: I could rather call it an *indolence*. It seems to be nothing more than a privation of both pain and pleasure. And that such a quality or state as this may agree to an unthinking substance, I hope you will not deny.

PHILONOUS: If you are resolved to maintain that warmth, or a gentle degree of heat, is no pleasure, I know not how to convince you otherwise, than by appealing to your own sense. But what think you of cold?

HYLAS: The same that I do of heat. An intense degree of cold is a pain; for to feel a very great cold, is to perceive a great uneasiness: it cannot therefore exist without the mind; but a lesser degree of cold may, as well as a lesser degree of heat.

PHILONOUS: Those bodies therefore, upon whose application to our own, we perceive a moderate degree of heat, must be concluded to have a moderate degree of heat or warmth in them: and those, upon whose application we feel a like degree of cold, must be thought to have cold in them.

HYLAS: They must.

PHILONOUS: Can any doctrine be true that necessarily leads a man into an absurdity?

HYLAS: Without doubt it cannot.

PHILONOUS: Is it not an absurdity to think that the same thing should be at the same time both cold and warm?

HYLAS: It is.

PHILONOUS: Suppose now one of your hands hot, and the other cold, and that they are both at once put into the same vessel of water, in an intermediate state; will not the water seem cold to one hand, and warm to the other?

HYLAS: It will.

PHILONOUS: Ought we not therefore by your principles to conclude, it is really both cold and warm at the same time, that is, according to your own concession, to believe an absurdity.

HYLAS: I confess it seems so.

PHILONOUS: Consequently, the principles themselves are false, since you have granted that no true principle leads to an absurdity.

HYLAS: But after all, can anything be more absurd than to say, *there is no heat in the fire?*

PHILONOUS: To make the point still clearer; tell me, whether in two cases exactly alike, we ought not to make the same judgment?

HYLAS: We ought.

PHILONOUS: When a pin pricks your finger, doth it not rend and divide the fibres of your flesh?

HYLAS: It doth.

PHILONOUS: And when a coal burns your finger, doth it any more?

HYLAS: It doth not.

PHILONOUS: Since therefore you neither judge the sensation itself occasioned by the pin, nor anything like it to be in the pin; you should not, conformably to what you have now granted, judge the sensation occasioned by the fire, or anything like it, to be in the fire.

HYLAS: Well, since it must be so, I am content to yield this point, and acknowledge, that heat and cold are only sensations existing in our minds: but there still remain qualities enough to secure the reality of external things.

PHILONOUS: But what will you say, Hylas, if it shall appear that the case is the same with regard to all other sensible qualities, and that they can no more be supposed to exist without the mind, than heat and cold?

HYLAS: Then indeed you will have done something to the purpose; but that is what I despair of seeing proved.

PHILONOUS: Let us examine them in order. What think you of tastes, do they exist without the mind, or no?

HYLAS: Can any man in his senses doubt whether sugar is sweet, or wormwood bitter?

PHILONOUS: Inform me, Hylas. Is a sweet taste a particular kind of pleasure or pleasant sensation, or is it not?

HYLAS: It is.

PHILONOUS: And is not bitterness some kind of uneasiness or pain?

HYLAS: I grant it.

PHILONOUS: If therefore sugar and wormwood are unthinking corporeal substances existing without the mind, how can sweetness and bitterness, that is, pleasure and pain, agree to them?

HYLAS: HOLD, Philonous, I now see what it was deluded me all this time. You asked whether heat and cold, sweetness and bitterness, were not particular sorts of pleasure and pain; to which I answered simply, that they were. Whereas I should have thus distinguished: those qualities, as perceived by us, are pleasures or pains, but not as existing in the external objects. We must not therefore conclude absolutely, that there is no heat in the fire, or sweetness in the sugar, but only that heat or sweetness, as perceived by us, are not in the fire or sugar. What say you to this?

PHILONOUS: I say it is nothing to the purpose. Our discourse proceeded altogether concerning sensible things, which you defined to be the things we *immediately perceive by our senses.* Whatever other qualities therefore you speak of, as distinct from these, I know nothing of them, neither do they at all belong to the point in dispute. You may indeed pretend to have discovered certain qualities which you do not perceive, and assert those insensible qualities exist in fire and sugar. But what use can be made of this to your present purpose, I am at a loss to conceive. Tell me then once more, do you acknowledge that heat and cold, sweetness and bitterness (meaning those qualities which are perceived by the senses) do not exist without the mind?

HYLAS: I see it is to no purpose to hold out, so I give up the cause as to those mentioned qualities. Though I profess it sounds oddly, to say that sugar is not sweet.

PHILONOUS: But for your farther satisfaction, take this along with you: that which at other times seems sweet, shall to a distempered palate appear bitter. And nothing can be plainer, than that divers persons perceive different tastes in the same food, since that which one man delights in, another abhors. And how could this be, if the taste was something really inherent in the food?

HYLAS: I acknowledge I know not how.

PHILONOUS: In the next place, odours are to be considered. And with regard to these, I would fain know, whether what hath been said of tastes doth not exactly agree to them? Are they not so many pleasing or displeasing sensations?

HYLAS: They are.

PHILONOUS: Can you then conceive it possible that they should exist in an unperceiving thing?

HYLAS: I cannot.

PHILONOUS: Or can you imagine, that filth and ordure affect those brute animals that feed on them out of choice, with the same smells which we perceive in them?

HYLAS: By no means.

PHILONOUS; May we not therefore conclude of smells, as of the other forementioned qualities, that they cannot exist in any but a perceiving substance or mind?

HYLAS: I think so.

PHILONOUS: Then as to sounds, what must we think of them: are they accidents really inherent in external bodies, or not?

HYLAS: That they inhere not in the sonorous bodies, is plain from hence; because a bell struck in the exhausted receiver of an air-pump, sends forth no sound. The air therefore must be thought the subject of sound.

PHILONOUS: What reason is there for that, Hylas?

HYLAS: Because when any motion is raised in the air, we perceive a sound greater or lesser, in proportion to the air's motion; but without some motion in the air, we never hear any sound at all.

PHILONOUS: And granting that we never hear a sound but when some motion is produced in the air, yet I do not see how you can infer from thence, that the sound itself is in the air.

HYLAS: It is this very motion in the external air, that produces in the mind the sensation of *sound.* For, striking on the drum of the ear, it causeth a vibration, which by the auditory nerves being communicated to the brain, the soul is thereupon affected with the sensation called *sound.*

PHILONOUS: What! is sound then a sensation?

HYLAS: I tell you, as perceived by us, it is a particular sensation in the mind.

PHILONOUS: And can any sensation exist without the mind?

HYLAS: No certainly.

PHILONOUS: How then can sound, being a sensation exist in the air, if by the *air* you mean a senseless substance existing without the mind?

HYLAS: You must distinguish, Philonous, between sound as it is perceived by us, and as it is in itself; or (which is the same thing) between the sound we immediately perceive, and that which exists without us. The former indeed is a particular kind of sensation, but the latter is merely a vibrative or undulatory motion in the air.

PHILONOUS: I thought I had already obviated that distinction by the answer I gave when you were applying it in a like case before. But to say no more of that; are you sure then that sound is really nothing but motion?

HYLAS: I am.

PHILONOUS: Whatever therefore agrees to real sound, may with truth be attributed to motion.

HYLAS: It may.

PHILONOUS: It is then good sense to speak of *motion*, as of a thing that is *loud, sweet, acute,* or *grave.*

HYLAS: I see you are resolved not to understand me. Is it not evident, those accidents or modes belong only to sensible sound, or *sound* in the common acceptation of the word, but not to *sound* in the real and philosophic sense, which, as I just now told you, is nothing but a certain motion of the air?

PHILONOUS: It seems then there are two sorts of sound, the one vulgar, or that which is heard, the other philosophical and real.

HYLAS: even so.

PHILONOUS: And the latter consists in motion.

HYLAS: I told you so before.

PHILONOUS: Tell me, Hylas, to which of the senses think you, the idea of motion belongs: to the hearing?

HYLAS: No certainly, but to the sight and touch.

PHILONOUS: It should follow then, that according to you, real sounds may possibly be *seen* or *felt,* but never *heard.*

HYLAS: Look you, Philonous, you may if you please make a jest of my opinion, but that will not alter the truth of things. I own indeed, the inferences you draw me into, sound something oddly; but common language, you know, is framed by, and for the use of the vulgar: we must not therefore wonder, if expressions adapted to exact philosophic notions, seem uncouth and out of the way.

PHILONOUS: Is it come to that? I assure you, I imagine myself to have gained no small point, since you make so light of departing from common phrases and opinions; it being a main part of our inquiry, to examine whose notions are widest of the common road, and most repugnant to the general sense of the world. But can you think it no more than a philosophical paradox, to say that *real sounds are never heard,* and that the idea of them is obtained by some other sense. And is there nothing in this contrary to nature and the truth of things?

HYLAS: To deal ingenuously, I do not like it. And after the concessions already made, I had as well grant that sounds too have no real being without the mind. . . . I frankly own, Philonous, that it is in vain to stand out any longer. Colours, sounds, tastes, in a word, all those termed *secondary qualities,* have certainly no existence without the mind. But by this acknowledgement I must not be supposed to derogate anything from the reality of matter or external objects, seeing it is no more than several philosophers maintain, who nevertheless are the farthest imaginable from denying matter. For the clearer understanding of this, you must know sensible qualities are by philosophers divided into *primary* and *secondary.* The former are extension, figure, solidity, gravity, motion, and rest. And these they hold exist really in bodies. The latter are those above enumerated; or briefly, all sensible qualities beside the primary, which they assert are only so many sensations or ideas existing nowhere but in the mind. But all this, I doubt not, you are already apprised of. For my part, I have been a long time sensible there was such an opinion current among philosophers, but was never thoroughly convinced of its truth till now.

PHILONOUS: You are still then of opinion, that extension and figures are inherent in external unthinking substances.

HYLAS: I am.

PHILONOUS: But what if the same arguments which are brought against secondary qualities, will hold good against these also?

HYLAS: Why then I shall be obliged to think, they too exist only in the mind. . . . I acknowledge, Philonous, that upon a fair observation of what passes in my mind, I can discover nothing else, but that I am a thinking being, affected with variety of sensations; neither is it possible to conceive how a sensation should exist in an unperceiving substance. But then on the other hand, when I look on sensible things in a different view, considering them as so many modes and qualities, I find it necessary to suppose a material *substratum,* without which they cannot be conceived to exist.

PHILONOUS: *Material substratum* call you it? Pray, by which of your senses came you acquainted with that being?

HYLAS: It is not itself sensible; its modes and qualities only being perceived by the senses.

PHILONOUS: I presume then, it was by reflexion and reason you obtained the idea of it.

HYLAS: I do not pretend to any proper positive idea of it. However I conclude it exists, because qualities cannot be conceived to exist without a support.

PHILONOUS: It seems then you have only a relative notion of it, or that you conceive it not otherwise than by conceiving the relation it bears to sensible qualities.

HYLAS: Right.

PHILONOUS: Be pleased therefore to let me know wherein that relation consists.

HYLAS: Is it not sufficiently expressed in the term *substratum,* or *substance?*

PHILONOUS: If so, the word *substratum* should import, that it is spread under the sensible qualities or accidents.

HYLAS: True.

PHILONOUS: And consequently under extension.

HYLAS: I own it.

PHILONOUS: It is therefore somewhat in its own nature entirely distinct from extension.

HYLAS: I tell you, extension is only a mode, and matter is something that supports modes. And is it not evident the thing supported is different from the thing supporting?

PHILONOUS: So that something distinct from, and exclusive of extension, is supposed to be the *substratum* of extension.

HYLAS: Just so.

PHILONOUS: Answer me, Hylas. Can a thing be spread without extension? or is not the idea of extension necessarily included in *spreading?*

HYLAS: It is.

PHILONOUS: Whatsoever therefore you suppose spread under anything, must have in itself an extension distinct from the extension of that thing under which it is spread.

HYLAS: It must.

PHILONOUS: Consequently every corporeal substance being the *substratum* of extension, must have in itself another extension by which it is qualified to be a *substratum:* and so on to infinity. And I ask whether this be not absurd in itself, and repugnant to what you granted just now, to wit, that the *substratum* was something distinct from, and exclusive of extension.

HYLAS: Ay but, Philonous, you take me wrong. I do not mean that matter is *spread* in a gross literal sense under extension. The word *substratum* is used only to express in general the same thing with *substance.*

PHILONOUS: Well then, let us examine the relation implied in the term *substance.* Is it not that it stands under accidents?

HYLAS: The very same.

PHILONOUS: But that one thing may stand under or support another, must it not be extended?

HYLAS: It must.

PHILONOUS: Is not therefore this supposition liable to the same absurdity with the former?

HYLAS: You still take things in a strict literal sense: that is not fair, Philonous.

PHILONOUS: I am not for imposing any sense on your words: you are at liberty to explain them as you please. Only I beseech you, make me understand something by them. You tell me, matter supports or stands under accidents. How! is it as your legs support your body?

HYLAS: No; that is the literal sense.

PHILONOUS: Pray let me know any sense, literal or not literal, that you understand it in.—How long must I wait for an answer, Hylas?

HYLAS: I declare I know not what to say. I once thought I understood well enough what was meant by matter's supporting accidents. But now the more I think on it, the less can I comprehend it; in short, I find that I know nothing of it.

PHILONOUS: It seems then you have no idea at all, neither relative nor positive of matter; you know neither what it is in itself, nor what relation it bears to accidents.

HYLAS: I acknowledge it.

PHILONOUS: And yet you asserted, that you could not conceive how qualities or accidents should really exist, without conceiving at the same time a material support of them.

HYLAS: I did.

PHILONOUS: That is to say, when you conceive the real existence of qualities, you do withal conceive something which you cannot conceive.

HYLAS: It was wrong I own. But still I fear there is some fallacy or other. Pray what think you of this? It is just come into my head, that the ground of all our mistakes lies in your treating of each quality by itself. Now, I grant that each quality cannot singly subsist without the mind. Colour cannot without extension, neither can figure without some other sensible quality. But as the several qualities united or blended together form entire sensible things, nothing hinders why such things may not be supposed to exist without the mind.

PHILONOUS: Either, Hylas, you are jesting, or have a very bad memory. Though indeed we went through all the qualities by name one after another; yet my arguments, or rather your concessions nowhere tended to prove, that the secondary qualities did not subsist each alone by itself; but that they were not *at all* without the mind. Indeed in treating of figure and motion, we concluded they could not exist without the mind, because it was impossible even in thought to separate them from all secondary qualities, so as to conceive them existing by themselves. But then this was not the only argument made use of upon that occasion. But (to pass by all that hath been hitherto said, and reckon it for nothing, if you will have it so) I am content to put the whole upon this issue. If you can conceive it possible for any mixture or combination of qualities, or any sensible object whatever, to exist without the mind, then I will grant it actually to be so.

HYLAS: If it comes to that, the point will soon be decided. What more easy than to conceive a tree or house existing by itself, independent of, and unperceived by any mind whatsoever? I do at this present time conceive them existing after that manner.

PHILONOUS: How say you, Hylas, can you see a thing which is at the same time unseen?

HYLAS: No, that were a contradiction.

PHILONOUS: Is it not as great a contradiction to talk of *conceiving* a thing which is *unconceived*?

HYLAS: It is.

PHILONOUS: The tree or house therefore which you think of, is conceived by you.

HYLAS: How should it be otherwise?

PHILONOUS: And what is conceived, is surely in the mind.

HYLAS: Without question, that which is conceived is in the mind.

PHILONOUS: How then came you to say, you conceived a house or tree existing independent and out of all minds whatsoever?

HYLAS: That was I own an oversight; but stay, let me consider what led me into it.—It is a pleasant mistake enough. As I was thinking of a tree in a solitary place, where no one was present to see it, methought that was to conceive a tree as existing unperceived or unthought of, not considering that I myself conceived it all the while. But now I plainly see, that all I can do is to frame ideas in my own mind. I may indeed conceive in my own thoughts the idea of a tree, or a house, or a mountain, but that is all. And this is far from proving, that I can conceive them *existing out of the minds of all spirits.*

PHILONOUS: You acknowledge then that you cannot possibly conceive, how any one corporeal sensible thing should exist otherwise than in a mind.

HYLAS: I do. . . .

PHILONOUS: Well then, are you at length satisfied that no sensible things have a real existence; and that you are in truth an arrant *sceptic?*

HYLAS: It is too plain to be denied. . . .

PHILONOUS: . . . To be plain, can you expect this scepticism of yours will not be thought extravagantly absurd by all men of sense?

HYLAS: Other men may think as they please: but for your part you have nothing to reproach me with. My comfort is, you are as much a *sceptic* as I am.

PHILONOUS: There, Hylas, I must beg leave to differ from you.

HYLAS: What! have you all along agreed to the premises, and do you now deny the conclusion, and leave me to maintain those paradoxes by myself which you led me into? This surely is not fair.

PHILONOUS: I deny that I agreed with you in those notions that led to scepticism. You indeed said, the reality of sensible things consisted in an *absolute existence* out of the minds of spirits, or distinct from their being perceived. And pursuant to this notion of reality, you are obliged to deny sensible things any real existence: that is, according to your own definition, you profess yourself a *sceptic*. But I neither said nor thought the reality of sensible things was to be defined after that manner. To me it is evident, for the reasons you allow of, that sensible things cannot exist otherwise than in a mind or spirit. Whence I conclude, not that they have no real existence, but that seeing they depend not on my thought, and have an existence distinct from being perceived by me, *there must be some other mind wherein they exist.* As sure therefore as the sensible world really exists, so sure is there an infinite omnipresent spirit who contains and supports it.

HYLAS: What! this is no more than I and all Christians hold; nay, and all others too who believe there is a God, and that he knows and comprehends all things.

PHILONOUS: Ay, but here lies the difference. Men commonly believe that all things are known or perceived by God, because they believe the being of a God, whereas I on the other side, immediately and necessarily conclude the being of a God, because all sensible things must be perceived by him.

HYLAS: But so long as we all believe the same thing, what matter is it how we come by that belief?

PHILONOUS: But neither do we agree in the same opinion. For philosophers, though they acknowledge all corporeal beings to be perceived by God, yet they attribute to them an absolute subsistence distinct from their being perceived by any mind whatever, which I do not. Besides, is there no difference between saying, *there is a God, therefore he perceives all things:* and saying, *sensible things do really exist: and if they really exist, they are necessarily perceived by an infinite mind: therefore there is an infinite mind, or God.* This furnishes you with a direct and immediate demonstration, from a most evident principle, of the *being of a God.* Divines and philosophers had proved beyond all controversy, from the beauty and usefulness of the several parts of the creation, that it was the workmanship of God. But that setting aside all help of astronomy and natural philosophy, all contemplation of the contrivance, order, and adjustment of things, an infinite mind should be necessarily inferred from the bare existence of the sensible world, is an advantage peculiar to them only who have made this easy reflexion: that the sensible world is that which we perceive by our several senses; and that nothing is perceived by the senses beside ideas; and that no idea or archetype of an idea can exist otherwise than in a mind.

Questions for Reflection

1. The 18th-century philosopher David Hume said of Berkeley's arguments, "They admit of no answer and produce no conviction. Their only effect is to cause . . . momentary amazement and irresolution and confusion." What do you think about Berkeley's arguments? If we reject them, we must provide reasons why they fail. How would you criticize his arguments?

2. Samuel Johnson, a famous English writer and contemporary of Berkeley, responded to Berkeley's philosophy by kicking a stone, sending it flying into the air, saying, "I refute him thus." List all the sensations Johnson experienced while kicking the rock through the air. How could Berkeley argue that this entire event could be explained

by his immaterialism without bringing in the notion of any sort of matter that is independent of Johnson's mind or those of the spectators?

3. Throughout his writings, Berkeley maintains that his immaterialism is perfectly consistent with science. How can this be, since he rejects the notion of mind-independent matter? Figure out for yourself how Berkeley might present science as a description of the orderly sequence of mind-dependent experiences we normally have. Is this an adequate account of science?

4. The real world, according to Berkeley, consists of nothing more than the subjective experiences we have. Yet, even Berkeley agrees that what we experience in dreams is not "real." How might he make the distinction between reality (in his sense) and dreams without appealing to the notion of a material world outside of our experiences?

5. Berkeley says that the world is simply that sequence of experiences in our minds that God gives to us. Yet, we naturally think that the world exists independently of our experiences. Does Berkeley's account make God into the demon deceiver that was the source of Descartes's doubts? How would Berkeley defend his view that God is not a deceiver?

DAVID HUME

Empiricism and Skepticism

David Hume (1711–1776), the Scottish skeptic, has already been introduced in the discussion of the design argument for God (Chapter 2), where further details on his life may be found. His importance for this present chapter is signified by the fact that he is considered to be one of the greatest skeptics of all time. Even those who do not accept his conclusions admire him for the rigorous consistency of his reasoning.

Throughout his writings, Hume forcefully argued for skepticism by using his wrecking-ball logic against all of our most fundamental and taken-for-granted beliefs. Descartes began his quest for knowledge with the assumption that if he had rational certainty concerning his beliefs, he necessarily had knowledge, and if he did not have certainty, he did not have knowledge. David Hume began with the same assumption. Where they differ is that Descartes finally believed that there were a number of things of which he could be certain. However, Hume doubted whether Descartes or anyone could be certain about these things. Hence, lacking certainty, Hume believed we lacked knowledge.

David Hume was an empiricist, for he believed that all knowledge about the world comes through experience. However, he drives empiricism to a radical extreme and

From David Hume, *An Enquiry Concerning Human Understanding*, first published in 1748.

ends up with skepticism. His basic skeptical argument is this: If all we know are the contents of experience, how can we know anything about what lies outside of our experience?

According to Hume, most of our knowledge about the world is based on our understanding of causes and effects. But our ability to infer causal connections between events assumes the principle of induction. The **principle of induction** could be summarized as the assumption that "the future will be like the past." This principle requires belief in the **uniformity of nature** or the thesis that the laws of nature that have been true thus far will continue to be true tomorrow. But how do we know that this is true? As you will see, Hume argues that just because we have discovered certain things to hold true in the past, does not make it logically necessary that they will be true in the future.

Reading Questions

1. What are the two classes of perceptions? How do they differ?
2. The imagination seems to be unbounded, but what constraints are upon the powers of our imagination?
3. What two arguments does Hume give to show that all our thoughts are derived from impressions?
4. What test does he suggest to see if a philosophical term is meaningful or whether it corresponds to anything real?
5. What are the two categories of objects of human reason? How do they differ?
6. Why does he think that all reasonings concerning matters of fact are based on the relation of cause and effect?
7. Why does he say that the explosion of gunpowder or the attraction of a loadstone (a magnet) could never be discovered by *a priori* arguments?
8. How does Hume argue that our experience of past events cannot tell us about what to expect in future events? What are the implications for this with respect to our causal judgments?
9. What role does custom or habit play in our thinking, according to Hume?

SECTION II

Of the Origin of Ideas

Every one will readily allow, that there is a considerable difference between the perceptions of the mind, when a man feels the pain of excessive heat, or the pleasure of moderate warmth, and when he afterwards recalls to his memory this sensation, or anticipates it by his imagination. These faculties may mimic or copy the perceptions of the senses; but they never can entirely reach the force and vivacity of the original sentiment. The utmost we say of them, even when they operate with greatest vigour, is, that they represent their object in so lively a manner, that we could *almost* say we feel or see it: But, except the mind be disordered by disease or madness, they never can arrive at such a pitch of vivacity, as to render these perceptions altogether undistinguishable. All the colours of poetry, however splendid, can never paint natural objects in such a manner as to make the description be taken for a real landskip. The most lively thought is still inferior to the dullest sensation.

We may observe a like distinction to run through all the other perceptions of the mind. A man in a fit of anger, is actuated in a very different manner from one who only thinks of that emotion.

If you tell me, that any person is in love, I easily understand your meaning, and form a just conception of his situation; but never can mistake that conception for the real disorders and agitations of the passion. When we reflect on our past sentiments and affections, our thought is a faithful mirror, and copies its objects truly; but the colours which it employs are faint and dull, in comparison of those in which our original perceptions were clothed. It requires no nice discernment or metaphysical head to mark the distinction between them.

Here therefore we may divide all the perceptions of the mind into two classes or species, which are distinguished by their different degrees of force and vivacity. The less forcible and lively are commonly denominated *Thoughts* or *Ideas*. The other species want a name in our language, and in most others; I suppose, because it was not requisite for any, but philosophical purposes, to rank them under a general term or appellation. Let us, therefore, use a little freedom, and call them *Impressions;* employing that word in a sense somewhat different from the usual. By the term *impression,* then, I mean all our more lively perceptions, when we hear, or see, or feel, or love, or hate, or desire, or will. And impressions are distinguished from ideas, which are the less lively perceptions, of which we are conscious, when we reflect on any of those sensations or movements above mentioned.

Nothing, at first view, may seem more unbounded than the thought of man, which not only escapes all human power and authority, but is not even restrained within the limits of nature and reality. To form monsters, and join incongruous shapes and appearances, costs the imagination no more trouble than to conceive the most natural and familiar objects. And while the body is confined to one planet, along which it creeps with pain and difficulty; the thought can in an instant transport us into the most distant regions of the universe; or even beyond the universe, into the unbounded chaos, where nature is supposed to lie in total confusion. What never was seen, or heard of, may yet be conceived; nor is any thing beyond the power of thought, except what implies an absolute contradiction.

But though our thought seems to possess this unbounded liberty, we shall find, upon a nearer examination, that it is really confined within very narrow limits, and that all this creative power of the mind amounts to no more than the faculty of compounding, transposing, augmenting, or diminishing the materials afforded us by the senses and experience. When we think of a golden mountain, we only join two consistent ideas, *gold,* and *mountain,* with which we were formerly acquainted. A virtuous horse we can conceive; because, from our own feeling, we can conceive virtue; and this we may unite to the figure and shape of a horse, which is an animal familiar to us. In short, all the materials of thinking are derived either from our outward or inward sentiment: the mixture and composition of these belongs alone to the mind and will. Or, to express myself in philosophical language, all our ideas or more feeble perceptions are copies of our impressions or more lively ones.

To prove this, the two following arguments will, I hope, be sufficient. First, when we analyze our thoughts or ideas, however compounded or sublime, we always find that they resolve themselves into such simple ideas as were copied from a precedent feeling or sentiment. Even those ideas, which, at first view, seem the most wide of this origin, are found, upon a nearer scrutiny, to be derived from it. The idea of God, as meaning an infinitely intelligent, wise, and good Being, arises from reflecting on the operations of our own mind, and augmenting, without limit, those qualities of goodness and wisdom. We may prosecute this enquiry to what length we please; where we shall always find, that every idea which we examine is copied from a similar impression. Those who would assert that this position is not universally true nor without exception, have only one, and that an easy method of refuting it; by producing that idea, which, in their opinion, is not derived from this source. It will then be incumbent on us, if we would maintain our doctrine, to produce the impression, or lively perception, which corresponds to it.

Secondly. If it happens, from a defect of the organ, that a man is not susceptible of any species of sensation, we always find that he is as little susceptible of the correspondent ideas. A blind man can form no notion of colours; a deaf man of sounds. Restore either of them that sense in which he is deficient; by opening this new inlet for his sensations, you also open an inlet for the ideas; and he finds no difficulty in conceiving these objects. . . .

Here, therefore, is a proposition, which not only seems, in itself, simple and intelligible; but, if a proper use were made of it, might render every dispute equally intelligible, and banish all that jargon, which has so long taken possession of metaphysical reasonings, and drawn disgrace upon them. All ideas, especially abstract ones, are naturally faint and obscure: the mind has but a slender hold of them: they are apt to be confounded with other resembling ideas; and when we have often employed any term, though without a distinct meaning, we are apt to imagine it has a determinate idea annexed to it. On the contrary, all impressions, that is, all sensations, either outward or inward, are strong and vivid: the limits between them are more exactly determined: nor is it easy to fall into any error or mistake with regard to them. When we entertain, therefore, any suspicion that a philosophical term is employed without any meaning or idea (as is but too frequent), we need but enquire, *from what impression is that supposed idea derived?* And if it be impossible to assign any, this will serve to confirm our suspicion. By bringing ideas into so clear a light we may reasonably hope to remove all dispute, which may arise, concerning their nature and reality.

SECTION IV

Sceptical Doubts Concerning the Operations of the Understanding

Part I

All the objects of human reason or enquiry may naturally be divided into two kinds, to wit, *Relations of Ideas*, and *Matters of Fact*. Of the first kind are the sciences of Geometry, Algebra, and Arithmetic; and in short, every affirmation which is either intuitively or demonstratively certain. *That the square of the hypotenuse is equal to the square of the two sides*, is a proposition which expresses a relation between these figures. *That three times five is equal to the half of thirty*, expresses a relation between these numbers. Propositions of this kind are discoverable by the mere operation of thought, without dependence on what is anywhere existent in the universe. Though there never were a circle or triangle in nature, the truths demonstrated by Euclid would for ever retain their certainty and evidence.

Matters of fact, which are the second objects of human reason, are not ascertained in the same manner; nor is our evidence of their truth, however great, of a like nature with the foregoing. The contrary of every matter of fact is still possible; because it can never imply a contradiction, and is conceived by the mind with the same facility and distinctness, as if ever so conformable to reality. *That the sun will not rise to-morrow* is no less intelligible a proposition, and implies no more contradiction, than the affirmation, *that it will rise*. We should in vain, therefore, attempt to demonstrate its falsehood. Were it demonstratively false, it would imply a contradiction, and could never be distinctly conceived by the mind.

It may, therefore, be a subject worthy of curiosity, to enquire what is the nature of that evidence which assures us of any real existence and matter of fact, beyond the present testimony of our senses, or the records of our memory. This part of philosophy, it is observable, has been little cultivated, either by the ancients or moderns; and therefore our doubts and errors, in the prosecution of so important an enquiry, may be the more excusable; while we march through such difficult paths without any guide or direction. They may even prove useful, by exciting curiosity, and destroying that implicit faith and security, which is the bane of all reasoning and free enquiry. The discovery of defects in the common philosophy, if any such there be, will not, I presume, be a discouragement, but rather an incitement, as is usual, to attempt something more full and satisfactory than has yet been proposed to the public.

All reasonings concerning matter of fact seem to be founded on the relation of *Cause and Effect*. By means of that relation alone we can go beyond the evidence of our memory and senses. If you were to ask a man, why he believes any matter of fact, which is absent; for instance, that his friend is in the country, or in France; he would give you a reason; and this reason would be some other fact; as a letter received from him, or the knowledge of his former resolutions and promises. A man finding a watch or any other machine in a desert island, would conclude that there had once been men in that island. All our reasonings concerning fact are of the same nature. And here it is constantly supposed that there is a connexion between the present fact and that which is inferred from it. Were there nothing to bind them together, the inference would be entirely precarious. The hearing of an articulate voice and rational discourse in the dark assures us of the presence of some person: Why? because these are the effects of the human make and fabric, and closely connected with it. If we anatomize all the other reasonings of this nature, we shall find that they are founded on the relation of cause and effect, and that this relation is either near or remote, direct or collateral. Heat and light are collateral effects of fire, and the one effect may justly be inferred from the other.

If we would satisfy ourselves, therefore, concerning the nature of that evidence, which assures us of matters of fact, we must enquire how we arrive at the knowledge of cause and effect.

I shall venture to affirm, as a general proposition, which admits of no exception, that the knowledge of this relation is not, in any instance, attained by reasonings *a priori;* but arises entirely from experience, when we find that any particular objects are constantly conjoined with each other. Let an object be presented to a man of ever so strong natural reason and abilities; if that object be entirely new to him, he will not be able, by the most accurate examination of its sensible qualities, to discover any of its causes or effects. Adam, though his rational faculties be supposed, at the very first, entirely perfect, could not have inferred from the fluidity and transparency of water that it would suffocate him, or from the light and warmth of fire that it would consume him. No object ever discovers, by the qualities which appear to the senses, either the causes which produced it, or the effects which will arise from it; nor can our reason, unas-

sisted by experience, ever draw any inference concerning real existence and matter of fact.

This proposition, *that causes and effects are discoverable, not by reason but by experience,* will readily be admitted with regard to such objects, as we remember to have once been altogether unknown to us; since we must be conscious of the utter inability, which we then lay under, of foretelling what would arise from them. Present two smooth pieces of marble to a man who has no tincture of natural philosophy; he will never discover that they will adhere together in such a manner as to require great force to separate them in a direct line, while they make so small a resistance to a lateral pressure. Such events, as bear little analogy to the common course of nature, are also readily confessed to be known only by experience; nor does any man imagine that the explosion of gunpowder, or the attraction of a loadstone, could ever be discovered by arguments *a priori.* In like manner, when an effect is supposed to depend upon an intricate machinery or secret structure of parts, we make no difficulty in attributing all our knowledge of it to experience. Who will assert that he can give the ultimate reason, why milk or bread is proper nourishment for a man, not for a lion or a tiger?

But the same truth may not appear, at first sight, to have the same evidence with regard to events, which have become familiar to us from our first appearance in the world, which bear a close analogy to the whole course of nature, and which are supposed to depend on the simple qualities of objects, without any secret structure of parts. We are apt to imagine that we could discover these effects by the mere operation of our reason, without experience. We fancy, that were we brought on a sudden into this world, we could at first have inferred that one Billiard-ball would communicate motion to another upon impulse; and that we needed not to have waited for the event, in order to pronounce with certainty concerning it. Such is the influence of custom, that, where it is strongest, it not only covers our natural ignorance, but even conceals itself, and seems not to take place, merely because it is found in the highest degree.

But to convince us that all the laws of nature, and all the operations of bodies without exception, are known only by experience, the following reflections may, perhaps, suffice. Were any object presented to us, and were we required to pronounce concerning the effect, which will result from it, without consulting past observation; after what manner, I beseech you, must the mind proceed in this operation? It must invent or imagine some event, which it ascribes to the object as its effect; and it is plain that this invention must be entirely arbitrary. The mind can never possibly find the effect in the supposed cause, by the most accurate scrutiny and examination. For the effect is totally different from the cause, and consequently can never be discovered in it. Motion in the second Billiard-ball is a quite distinct event from motion in the first; nor is there anything in the one to suggest the smallest hint of the other. A stone or piece of metal raised into the air, and left without any support, immediately falls: but to consider the matter *a priori*, is there anything we discover in this situation which can beget the idea of a downward, rather than an upward, or any other motion, in the stone or metal?

And as the first imagination or invention of a particular effect, in all natural operations, is arbitrary, where we consult not experience; so must we also esteem the supposed tie or connexion between the cause and effect, which binds them together, and renders it impossible that any other effect could result from the operation of that cause. When I see, for instance, a Billiard-ball moving in a straight line towards another; even suppose motion in the second ball should by accident be suggested to me, as the result of their contact or impulse; may I not conceive, that a hundred different events might as well follow from that cause? May not both these balls remain at absolute rest? May not the first ball return in a straight line, or leap off from the second in any line or direction? All these suppositions are consistent and conceivable. Why then should we give the preference to one, which is no more consistent or conceivable than the rest? All our reasonings *a priori* will never be able to show us any foundation for this preference.

In a word, then, every effect is a distinct event from its cause. It could not, therefore, be discov-

ered in the cause, and the first invention or conception of it, *a priori*, must be entirely arbitrary. And even after it is suggested, the conjunction of it with the cause must appear equally arbitrary; since there are always many other effects, which, to reason, must seem fully as consistent and natural. In vain, therefore, should we pretend to determine any single event, or infer any cause or effect, without the assistance of observation and experience. . . .

Part II

But we have not yet attained any tolerable satisfaction with regard to the question first proposed. Each solution still gives rise to a new question as difficult as the foregoing, and leads us on to farther enquiries. When it is asked, *What is the nature of all our reasonings concerning matter of fact?* the proper answer seems to be, that they are founded on the relation of cause and effect. When again it is asked, *What is the foundation of all our reasonings and conclusions concerning that relation?* it may be replied in one word, Experience. But if we still carry on our sifting humour, and ask, *What is the foundation of all conclusions from experience?* this implies a new question, which may be of more difficult solution and explication. Philosophers, that give themselves airs of superior wisdom and sufficiency, have a hard task when they encounter persons of inquisitive dispositions, who push them from every corner to which they retreat, and who are sure at last to bring them to some dangerous dilemma. The best expedient to prevent this confusion, is to be modest in our pretensions; and even to discover the difficulty ourselves before it is objected to us. By this means, we may make a kind of merit of our very ignorance.

I shall content myself, in this section, with an easy task, and shall pretend only to give a negative answer to the question here proposed. I say then, that, even after we have experience of the operations of cause and effect, our conclusions from that experience are *not* founded on reasoning, or any process of the understanding. This answer we must endeavour both to explain and to defend.

It must certainly be allowed, that nature has kept us at a great distance from all her secrets, and has afforded us only the knowledge of a few superficial qualities of objects; while she conceals from us those powers and principles on which the influence of these objects entirely depends. Our senses inform us of the colour, weight, and consistence of bread; but neither sense nor reason can ever inform us of those qualities which fit it for the nourishment and support of a human body. Sight or feeling conveys an idea of the actual motion of bodies; but as to that wonderful force or power, which would carry on a moving body for ever in a continued change of place, and which bodies never lose but by communicating it to others; of this we cannot form the most distant conception. But notwithstanding this ignorance of natural powers and principles, we always presume, when we see like sensible qualities, that they have like secret powers, and expect that effects, similar to those which we have experienced, will follow from them. If a body of like colour and consistence with that bread, which we have formerly eat, be presented to us, we make no scruple of repeating the experiment, and foresee, with certainty, like nourishment and support. Now this is a process of the mind or thought, of which I would willingly know the foundation. It is allowed on all hands that there is no known connexion between the sensible qualities and the secret powers; and consequently, that the mind is not led to form such a conclusion concerning their constant and regular conjunction, by anything which it knows of their nature. As to past *Experience,* it can be allowed to give *direct* and *certain* information of those precise objects only, and that precise period of time, which fell under its cognizance: but why this experience should be extended to future times, and to other objects, which for aught we know, may be only in appearance similar; this is the main question on which I would insist. The bread, which I formerly eat, nourished me; that is, a body of such sensible qualities was, at that time, endued with such secret powers: but does it follow, that other bread must also nourish me at another time, and that like sensible qualities must always be attended with like secret powers? The consequence seems nowise necessary. At least, it must be acknowledged that there is here a consequence drawn by the mind; that there is a certain

step taken; a process of thought, and an inference, which wants to be explained. These two propositions are far from being the same, *I have found that such an object has always been attended with such an effect,* and *I foresee, that other objects, which are, in appearance, similar, will be attended with similar effects.* I shall allow, if you please, that the one proposition may justly be inferred from the other: I know, in fact, that it always is inferred. But if you insist that the inference is made by a chain of reasoning, I desire you to produce that reasoning. The connexion between these propositions is not intuitive. There is required a medium, which may enable the mind to draw such an inference, if indeed it be drawn by reasoning and argument. What that medium is, I must confess, passes my comprehension; and it is incumbent on those to produce it, who assert that it really exists, and is the origin of all our conclusions concerning matter of fact. . . .

In reality, all arguments from experience are founded on the similarity which we discover among natural objects, and by which we are induced to expect effects similar to those which we have found to follow from such objects. And though none but a fool or madman will ever pretend to dispute the authority of experience, or to reject that great guide of human life, it may surely be allowed a philosopher to have so much curiosity at least as to examine the principle of human nature, which gives this mighty authority to experience, and makes us draw advantage from that similarity which nature has placed among different objects. From causes which appear *similar* we expect similar effects. This is the sum of all our experimental conclusions. Now it seems evident that, if this conclusion were formed by reason, it would be as perfect at first, and upon one instance, as after ever so long a course of experience. But the case is far otherwise. Nothing so like as eggs; yet no one, on account of this appearing similarity, expects the same taste and relish in all of them. It is only after a long course of uniform experiments in any kind, that we attain a firm reliance and security with regard to a particular event. Now where is that process of reasoning which, from one instance, draws a conclusion, so different from that which it infers from a hundred instances that are nowise different from that single one? This question I propose as much for the sake of information, as with an intention of raising difficulties. I cannot find, I cannot imagine any such reasoning. But I keep my mind still open to instruction, if any one will vouchsafe to bestow it on me.

Should it be said that, from a number of uniform experiments, we *infer* a connexion between the sensible qualities and the secret powers; this, I must confess, seems the same difficulty, couched in different terms. The question still recurs, on what process of argument this *inference* is founded? Where is the medium, the interposing ideas, which join propositions so very wide of each other? It is confessed that the colour, consistence, and other sensible qualities of bread appear not, of themselves, to have any connexion with the secret powers of nourishment and support. For otherwise we could infer these secret powers from the first appearance of these sensible qualities, without the aid of experience; contrary to the sentiment of all philosophers, and contrary to plain matter of fact. Here, then, is our natural state of ignorance with regard to the powers and influence of all objects. How is this remedied by experience? It only shows us a number of uniform effects, resulting from certain objects, and teaches us that those particular objects, at that particular time, were endowed with such powers and forces. When a new object, endowed with similar sensible qualities, is produced, we expect similar powers and forces, and look for a like effect. From a body of like colour and consistence with bread we expect like nourishment and support. But this surely is a step or progress of the mind, which wants to be explained. When a man says, *I have found, in all past instances, such sensible qualities conjoined with such secret powers:* And when he says, *Similar sensible qualities will always be conjoined with similar secret powers,* he is not guilty of a tautology, nor are these propositions in any respect the same. You say that the one proposition is an inference from the other. But you must confess that the inference is not intuitive; neither is it demonstrative: Of what nature is it, then? To say it is experimental, is begging the question. For all inferences from experience suppose, as their foundation, that the future will resemble the past, and that similar powers will be conjoined with similar sensible qual-

ities. If there be any suspicion that the course of nature may change, and that the past may be no rule for the future, all experience becomes useless, and can give rise to no inference or conclusion. It is impossible, therefore, that any arguments from experience can prove this resemblance of the past to the future; since all these arguments are founded on the supposition of that resemblance. Let the course of things be allowed hitherto ever so regular; that alone, without some new argument or inference, proves not that, for the future, it will continue so. In vain do you pretend to have learned the nature of bodies from your past experience. Their secret nature, and consequently all their effects and influence, may change, without any change in their sensible qualities. This happens sometimes, and with regard to some objects: Why may it not happen always, and with regard to all objects? What logic, what process of argument secures you against this supposition? My practice, you say, refutes my doubts. But you mistake the purport of my question. As an agent, I am quite satisfied in the point; but as a philosopher, who has some share of curiosity, I will not say scepticism, I want to learn the foundation of this inference. No reading, no enquiry has yet been able to remove my difficulty, or give me satisfaction in a matter of such importance. Can I do better than propose the difficulty to the public, even though, perhaps, I have small hopes of obtaining a solution? We shall at least, by this means, be sensible of our ignorance, if we do not augment our knowledge.

I must confess that a man is guilty of unpardonable arrogance who concludes, because an argument has escaped his own investigation, that therefore it does not really exist. I must also confess that, though all the learned, for several ages, should have employed themselves in fruitless search upon any subject, it may still, perhaps, be rash to conclude positively that the subject must, therefore, pass all human comprehension. Even though we examine all the sources of our knowledge, and conclude them unfit for such a subject, there may still remain a suspicion, that the enumeration is not complete, or the examination not accurate. But with regard to the present subject, there are some considerations which seem to remove all this accusation of arrogance or suspicion of mistake.

It is certain that the most ignorant and stupid peasants—nay infants, nay even brute beasts—improve by experience, and learn the qualities of natural objects, by observing the effects which result from them. When a child has felt the sensation of pain from touching the flame of a candle, he will be careful not to put his hand near any candle; but will expect a similar effect from a cause which is similar in its sensible qualities and appearance. If you assert, therefore, that the understanding of the child is led into this conclusion by any process of argument or ratiocination, I may justly require you to produce that argument; nor have you any pretense to refuse so equitable a demand. You cannot say that the argument is abstruse, and may possibly escape your enquiry; since you confess that it is obvious to the capacity of a mere infant. If you hesitate, therefore, a moment, or if, after reflection, you produce any intricate or profound argument, you, in a manner, give up the question, and confess that it is not reasoning which engages us to suppose the past resembling the future, and to expect similar effects from causes which are, to appearance, similar. This is the proposition which I intended to enforce in the present section. If I be right, I pretend not to have made any mighty discovery. And if I be wrong, I must acknowledge myself to be indeed a very backward scholar; since I cannot now discover an argument which, it seems, was perfectly familiar to me long before I was out of my cradle.

SECTION V

Sceptical Solution of These Doubts

Part I

. . . Nature will always maintain her rights, and prevail in the end over any abstract reasoning whatsoever. Though we should conclude, for instance, as in the foregoing section, that, in all reasonings from experience, there is a step taken by the mind which is not supported by any argument or process of the understanding; there is no danger that these reasonings, on which almost all knowledge depends, will ever be affected by such a discovery. If the mind be not engaged by argument to make this step, it must be induced by some other principle of equal weight and authority; and that principle will preserve its influence as long as human nature remains the same. What that principle is may well be worth the pains of enquiry.

Suppose a person, though endowed with the strongest faculties of reason and reflection, to be brought on a sudden into this world; he would, indeed, immediately observe a continual succession of objects, and one event following another; but he would not be able to discover anything farther. He would not, at first, by any reasoning, be able to reach the idea of cause and effect; since the particular powers, by which all natural operations are performed, never appear to the senses; nor is it reasonable to conclude, merely because one event, in one instance, precedes another, that therefore the one is the cause, the other the effect. Their conjunction may be arbitrary and casual. There may be no reason to infer the existence of one from the appearance of the other. And in a word, such a person, without more experience, could never employ his conjecture or reasoning concerning any matter of fact, or be assured of anything beyond what was immediately present to his memory and senses.

Suppose, again, that he has acquired more experience, and has lived so long in the world as to have observed similar objects or events to be constantly conjoined together; what is the consequence of this experience? He immediately infers the existence of one object from the appearance of the other. Yet he has not, by all his experience, acquired any idea or knowledge of the secret power by which the one object produces the other; nor is it, by any process of reasoning, he is engaged to draw this inference. But still he finds himself determined to draw it: And though he should be convinced that his understanding has no part in the operation, he would nevertheless continue in the same course of thinking. There is some other principle which determines him to form such a conclusion.

This principle is Custom or Habit. For wherever the repetition of any particular act or operation produces a propensity to renew the same act or operation, without being impelled by any reasoning or process of the understanding, we always say, that this propensity is the effect of *Custom*. By employing that word, we pretend not to have given the ultimate reason of such a propensity. We only point out a principle of human nature, which is universally acknowledged, and which is well known by its effects. Perhaps we can push our enquiries no farther, or pretend to give the cause of this cause; but must rest contented with it as the ultimate principle, which we can assign, of all our conclusions from experience. It is sufficient satisfaction, that we can go so far, without repining at the narrowness of our faculties because they will carry us no farther. And it is certain we here advance a very intelligible proposition at least, if not a true one, when we assert that, after the constant conjunction of two objects—heat and flame, for instance, weight and solidity—we are determined by custom alone to expect the one from the appearance of the other. This hypothesis seems even the only one which explains the difficulty, why we draw from a thousand instances, an inference which we are not able to draw from one instance, that is, in no respect, different from them. Reason is incapable of any such variation. The conclusions which it draws from considering one circle are the same which it would form upon surveying all the circles in the universe. But no man, having seen only one body move after being impelled by another, could infer that every other body will move after a like impulse. All inferences from experience, therefore, are effects of custom, not of reasoning.

Custom, then, is the great guide of human life. It is that principle alone which renders our experience useful to us, and makes us expect, for the future, a similar train of events with those which have appeared in the past. Without the influence of custom, we should be entirely ignorant of every matter of fact beyond what is immediately present to the memory and senses. We should never know how to adjust means to ends, or to employ our natural powers in the production of any effect. There would be an end at once of all action, as well as of the chief part of speculation.

But here it may be proper to remark, that though our conclusions from experience carry us beyond our memory and senses, and assure us of matters of fact which happened in the most distant places and most remote ages, yet some fact must always be present to the senses or memory, from which we may first proceed in drawing these conclusions. A man, who should find in a desert country the remains of pompous buildings, would conclude that the country had, in ancient times, been cultivated by civilized inhabitants; but did nothing of this nature occur to him, he could never form such an inference. We learn the events of former ages from history; but then we must peruse the volumes in which this instruction is contained, and thence carry up our inferences from one testimony to another, till we arrive at the eyewitnesses and spectators of these distant events. In a word, if we proceed not upon some fact, present to the memory or senses, our reasonings would be merely hypothetical; and however the particular links might be connected with each other, the whole chain of inferences would have nothing to support it, nor could we ever, by its means, arrive at the knowledge of any real existence. If I ask why you believe any particular matter of fact, which you relate, you must tell me some reason; and this reason will be some other fact, connected with it. But as you cannot proceed after this manner, *in infinitum,* you must at last terminate in some fact, which is present to your memory or senses; or must allow that your belief is entirely without foundation.

What, then, is the conclusion of the whole matter? A simple one; though, it must be confessed, pretty remote from the common theories of philosophy. All belief of matter of fact or real existence is derived merely from some object, present to the memory or senses, and a customary conjunction between that and some other object. Or in other words; having found, in many instances, that any two kinds of objects—flame and heat, snow and cold—have always been conjoined together; if flame or snow be presented anew to the senses, the mind is carried by custom to expect heat or cold, and to *believe* that such a quality does exist, and will discover itself upon a nearer approach. This belief is the necessary result of placing the mind in such circumstances. It is an operation of the soul, when we are so situated, as unavoidable as to feel the passion of love, when we receive benefits; or hatred, when we meet with injuries. All these operations are a species of natural instincts, which no reasoning or process of the thought and understanding is able either to produce or to prevent.

Questions for Reflection

1. According to Hume, why is the following argument a fallacy? "We know that the future will be like the past because our past experience shows that events always follow this rule." In what way is appealing to past experience to justify the principle of induction really arguing in a circle?

2. Hume drew some very brutal conclusions from his epistemology, as illustrated by this passage, which ends the book from which our reading has been taken: "When we run over libraries, persuaded of these principles, what havoc must we make? If we take in our hand any volume; of divinity or school metaphysics, for instance; let us ask, Does it contain any abstract reasoning concerning quantity or number? No. Does it contain any experimental reasoning concerning matter of fact and existence? No. Commit it then to the flames: for it can contain nothing but sophistry and illusion." Based on these criteria, find concrete examples of books that Hume would want to burn. Do you agree with Hume that they "contain nothing but sophistry and illusion"? Do you think that Hume's criteria are inadequate? If not, what other criteria would you use for evaluating in terms of the claims they make?

3. Both Descartes and Hume set a very high standard for knowledge, but Hume thinks we can never reach this standard and, thus, we can never evade skeptical doubt. Do you think his criterion of knowledge is too high? Or do you think Hume's skepticism is justified?

IMMANUEL KANT

Knowledge Is Based Both on Reason and Experience

Immanuel Kant (1724–1804) was born in Königsberg in what was then known as East Prussia (now Kaliningrad, Russia) and he lived there all his life. Being one of the most brilliant intellectuals of his day, he spent his life as a professor at the local university where he lectured on everything from philosophy to geography. Although he lived a rather mundane life (Kant never traveled more than 50 miles from the place of his

From Immanuel Kant, *Critique of Pure Reason* (1781), trans. J. M. D. Meiklejohn (London: Bell & Daldy, 1871).

birth), his ideas were revolutionary. His impact on philosophy was so profound that all philosophies are now characterized as either pre-Kantian or post-Kantian.

Kant struggled with the differences between the rationalists and the empiricists. The rationalists such as Plato and Descartes believed that reason alone was the source of those truths that are universal and necessary. The mind is full of content in the form of innate ideas, they argued. On the other hand, the empiricists, such as Locke, Berkeley, and Hume said that originally the mind is like a blank tablet and all its content, all our knowledge, is derived from experience. Kant agreed with the rationalists that we do know universal and necessary truths. He also agreed with the empiricists that all knowledge arises out of experience. The problem is, as Hume showed, experience can only tell us what has happened to be true on past occasions; it cannot give us universal and necessary truths about all possible experience.

Kant's solution was to observe that the rationalists and the empiricists each provided us with one-half of the answer and that a compromise between them was required. In other words, Kant concluded that both reason and experience play a role in constructing our knowledge. Accordingly, Kant's epistemology could justifiably be called "rational-empiricism" or "empirical-rationalism." He himself called it "critical philosophy" for he wanted to critique reason, which means that he wanted to sort out the legitimate claims of reason from groundless ones. As Kant says in the preface to his *Critique of Pure Reason,* he took a cue from Copernicus who suggested that the sun does not revolve around the earth, but, instead, the earth revolves around the sun. Similarly, Kant proposed a radical reversal or a "Copernican revolution" in knowledge. He did this by claiming that the mind is not passively formed by the data given to us by the senses, but, instead, that our experience of the world is formed by the way the mind organizes and categorizes the data of the senses. Hence, knowledge is a product of both reason and sense experience. The senses provide the raw materials and the mind provides the structure to experience. As Kant says, "thoughts without content [sense data] are void; intuitions [sensations] without conceptions, blind."

What could it possibly mean to say that our experience of the world is formed by the mind? A visual experiment may illustrate what Kant was getting at. Look at Figure 3.1. Do you see the large white triangle in the foreground?

The problem is that there is no triangle there. What we see as a triangle is simply the space in between the other figures. The mind has taken the space between the partial circles and mentally organized it to produce the image of a triangle. Similarly, Kant says, in every moment of our waking lives, the senses give us a stream of sense data (col-

FIGURE 3.1

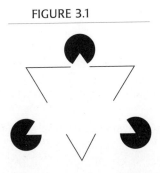

ors, sounds, and textures), and the mind composes them into meaningful objects of experience.

In the following passage, Kant speaks of *a priori* knowledge as knowledge that is obtained independently of experience. *A posteriori* knowledge is based on experience. An analytic judgment is one in which the predicate is contained in the subject ("all mothers are parents"). In contrast, a synthetic statement is one that *synthesizes* two concepts or adds information to the concept of the subject ("lemon juice is acidic"). Hume claimed that universal and necessary truths were always cases of analytic *a priori* knowledge (as in the case of the statement about mothers). They merely explicate the meaning of a concept. On the other hand, Hume said that all real knowledge about the world must be synthetic *a posteriori* knowledge (as in the statement about lemon juice). Kant, however, believes that there is a third kind of knowledge, which is synthetic *a priori* knowledge. It is *a priori* because it is not based on experience, but it is synthetic because it does give us genuine information about what our experience of the world will be like. The key phrase here is *our experience* of the world. We can't know what the world is like in itself, but we can know the universal and necessary features of our experience, because we can know the way our minds shape and form that experience. For this reason Kant thought that we could have universal and necessary *a priori* knowledge that also tells about the world as we experience it. This includes mathematical truths, the fundamental presuppositions of physics, the principle of causality, and other such knowledge.

Reading Questions

1. Why does Kant speak of his new approach to knowledge as similar to the Copernican revolution in astronomy?
2. Which statements sound like those an empiricist would make? Which ones sound like those a rationalist would make? How does Kant try to integrate the insights of both positions?
3. What is the difference between *a priori* and *a posteriori* knowledge? What are two "infallible tests" for identifying *a priori* knowledge?
4. Why does Kant think that "Every change must have a cause" must be a case of *a priori* knowledge?
5. What is the distinction between analytic and synthetic judgments? What examples does Kant give of each?
6. From what two sources in the mind does knowledge spring forth?
7. What does Kant mean when he says "thoughts without content [sense data] are void; intuitions [sensations] without conceptions, blind"?

PREFACE TO THE SECOND EDITION*

. . . It has hitherto been assumed that our knowledge must conform to the objects; but all attempts

———————

*Editor's note: Throughout this reading I have substituted the words *thought, knowledge,* and their derivatives for *cognition* and its derivatives.

to ascertain anything about these objects *a priori*, by means of conceptions, and thus to extend the range of our knowledge, have been rendered abortive by this assumption. Let us then make the experiment whether we may not be more successful in metaphysics, if we assume that the objects must conform to our knowledge. This appears, at all events, to accord better with the possibility of our gaining the end we have in view, that is to say, of arriving at the knowledge of objects *a priori*, of determining something with respect to these objects, before they are given to us. We here propose to do just what Copernicus did in attempting to explain the celestial movements. When he found that he could make no progress by assuming that all the heavenly bodies revolved round the spectator, he reversed the process, and tried the experiment of assuming that the spectator revolved, while the stars remained at rest. We may make the same experiment with regard to the intuition* of objects. If the intuition must conform to the nature of the objects, I do not see how we can know anything of them *a priori*. If, on the other hand, the object conforms to the nature of our faculty of intuition, I can then easily conceive the possibility of such an *a priori* knowledge.

INTRODUCTION

I. Of the Difference between Pure and Empirical Knowledge

That all our knowledge begins with experience there can be no doubt. For how is it possible that the faculty of knowledge should be awakened into exercise otherwise than by means of objects which affect our senses, and partly of themselves produce representations, partly rouse our powers of understanding into activity, to compare to connect, or to separate these, and so to convert the raw material of our sensuous impressions into a knowledge of objects, which is called experience? In respect of time, therefore, no knowledge of ours is antecedent to experience, but begins with it.

But, though all our knowledge begins with experience, it by no means follows that all arises out of experience. For, on the contrary, it is quite possible that our empirical knowledge is a compound of that which we receive through impressions, and that which the faculty of knowledge supplies from itself (sensuous impressions giving merely the *occasion*),

an addition which we cannot distinguish from the original element given by sense, till long practice has made us attentive to, and skilful in separating it. It is, therefore, a question which requires close investigation, and not to be answered at first sight, whether there exists a knowledge altogether independent of experience, and even of all sensuous impressions? Knowledge of this kind is called *a priori*, in contradistinction to empirical knowledge, which has its sources *a posteriori*, that is, in experience.

But the expression, "*a priori*," is not as yet definite enough adequately to indicate the whole meaning of the question above started. For, in speaking of knowledge which has its sources in experience, we are wont to say, that this or that may be known *a priori*, because we do not derive this knowledge immediately from experience, but from a general rule, which, however, we have itself borrowed from experience. Thus, if a man undermined his house, we say, "he might know *a priori* that it would have fallen;" that is, he needed not to have waited for the experience that it did actually fall. But still, *a priori*, he could not know even this much. For, that bodies are heavy, and, consequently, that they fall when their supports are taken away, must have been known to him previously, by means of experience.

By the term "knowledge *a priori*," therefore, we shall in the sequel understand, not such as is independent of this or that kind of experience, but such as is absolutely so of all experience. Opposed to this is empirical knowledge, or that which is possible only *a posteriori*, that is, through experience. Knowledge *a priori* is either pure or impure. Pure knowledge *a priori* is that with which no empirical element is mixed up. For example, the proposition, "Every change has a cause," is a proposition *a priori*, but impure, because change is a conception which can only be derived from experience.

II. The Human Intellect, Even in an Unphilosophical State, Is in Possession of Certain Knowledge *A Priori*

The question now is as to a *criterion*, by which we may securely distinguish a pure from an empirical knowledge. Experience no doubt teaches us that

---

*When Kant uses the term *intuition* he is not referring to a special gift of insight, but he means "the object of sensory awareness" or "sensation."

this or that object is constituted in such and such a manner, but not that it could not possibly exist otherwise. Now, in the first place, if we have a proposition which contains the idea of necessity in its very conception, it is a judgment *a priori;* if, moreover, it is not derived from any other proposition, unless from one equally involving the idea of necessity, it is absolutely *a priori.* Secondly, an empirical judgment never exhibits strict and absolute, but only assumed and comparative universality (by induction); therefore, the most we can say is—so far as we have hitherto observed, there is no exception to this or that rule. If, on the other hand, a judgment carries with it strict and absolute universality, that is, admits of no possible exception, it is not derived from experience, but is valid absolutely *a priori.*

Empirical universality is, therefore, only an arbitrary extension of validity, from that which may be predicated of a proposition valid in most cases, to that which is asserted of a proposition which holds good in all; as, for example, in the affirmation, "All bodies are heavy." When, on the contrary, strict universality characterizes a judgment, it necessarily indicates another peculiar source of knowledge, namely, a faculty of knowledge *a priori.* Necessity and strict universality, therefore, are infallible tests for distinguishing pure from empirical knowledge, and are inseparably connected with each other. But as in the use of these criteria the empirical limitation is sometimes more easily detected than the contingency of the judgment, or the unlimited universality which we attach to a judgment is often a more convincing proof than its necessity, it may be advisable to use the criteria separately, each being by itself infallible.

Now, that in the sphere of human knowledge we have judgments which are necessary, and in the strictest sense universal, consequently pure *a priori,* it will be an easy matter to show. If we desire an example from the sciences, we need only take any proposition in mathematics. If we cast our eyes upon the commonest operations of the understanding, the proposition, "Every change must have a cause," will amply serve our purpose. In the latter case, indeed, the conception of a cause so plainly involves the conception of a necessity of connection with an effect, and of a strict universality of the law, that the very notion of a cause would entirely disappear, were we to derive it, like Hume, from a frequent association of what happens with that which precedes; and the habit thence originating of connecting representations—the necessity inherent in the judgment being therefore merely subjective. Besides, without seeking for such examples of principles existing *a priori* in knowledge, we might easily show that such principles are the indispensable basis of the possibility of experience itself, and consequently prove their existence *a priori.* For whence could our experience itself acquire certainty, if all the rules on which it depends were themselves empirical, and consequently fortuitous? No one, therefore, can admit the validity of the use of such rules as first principles. But, for the present, we may content ourselves with having established the fact, that we do possess and exercise a faculty of pure *a priori* knowledge; and, secondly, with having pointed out the proper tests of such knowledge, namely, universality and necessity.

Not only in judgments, however, but even in conceptions, is an *a priori* origin manifest. For example, if we take away by degrees from our conceptions of a body all that can be referred to mere sensuous experience—color, hardness or softness, weight, even impenetrability—the body will then vanish; but the space which it occupied still remains, and this it is utterly impossible to annihilate in thought. Again, if we take away, in like manner, from our empirical conception of any object, corporeal or incorporeal, all properties which mere experience has taught us to connect with it, still we cannot think away those through which we think it as substance, or adhering to substance, although our conception of substance is more determined than that of an object. Compelled, therefore, by that necessity with which the conception of substance forces itself upon us, we must confess that it has its seat in our faculty of knowledge *a priori.* . . .

IV. Of the Difference between Analytical and Synthetical Judgments

In all judgments wherein the relation of a subject to the predicate is thought (I mention affirmative judgments only here; the application to negative will be very easy), this relation is possible in two different ways. Either the predicate B belongs to the subject A, as somewhat which is contained (though covertly) in the conception A; or the predicate B lies completely out of the conception A, although it stands in connection with it. In the first instance, I term the judgment analytical, in the second, synthetical. Analytical judgments (affirmative) are therefore those in which the connection of the predicate with the subject is thought through identity; those in which this connection is thought without identity, are called synthetical judgments. The former may be called *explicative*, the latter *augmentative* judgments; because the former add in the predicate nothing to the conception of the subject, but only analyze it into its constituent conceptions, which were thought already in the subject, although in a confused manner; the latter add to our conceptions of the subject a predicate which was not contained in it, and which no analysis could ever have discovered therein. For example, when I say, "All bodies are extended," this is an analytical judgment. For I need not go beyond the conception of body in order to find extension connected with it, but merely analyze the conception, that is, become conscious of the manifold properties which I think in that conception, in order to discover this predicate in it: it is therefore an analytical judgment. On the other hand, when I say, "All bodies are heavy," the predicate is something totally different from that which I think in the mere conception of a body. By the addition of such a predicate, therefore, it becomes a synthetical judgment.

Judgments of experience, as such, are always synthetical. For it would be absurd to think of grounding an analytical judgment on experience, because in forming such a judgment I need not go out of the sphere of my conceptions, and therefore recourse to the testimony of experience is quite unnecessary. That "bodies are extended" is not an empirical judgment, but a proposition which stands firm *a priori*. For before addressing myself to experience, I already have in my conception all the requisite conditions for the judgment, and I have only to extract the predicate from the conception, according to the principle of contradiction, and thereby at the same time become conscious of the

necessity of the judgment, a necessity which I could never learn from experience. On the other hand, though at first I do not at all include the predicate of weight in my conception of body in general, that conception still indicates an object of experience, a part of the totality of experience, to which I can still add other parts; and this I do when I recognize by observation that bodies are heavy. I can apprehend beforehand by analysis the conception of body through the characteristics of extension, impenetrability, shape, etc., all which are thought in this conception. But now I extend my knowledge, and looking back on experience from which I had derived this conception of body, I find weight at all times connected with the above characteristics, and therefore I synthetically add to my conceptions this as a predicate, and say, "All bodies are heavy." Thus it is experience upon which rests the possibility of the synthesis of the predicate of weight with the conception of body, because both conceptions, although the one is not contained in the other, still belong to one another (only contingently, however), as parts of a whole, namely, of experience, which is itself a synthesis of intuitions.

But to synthetical judgments *a priori*, such aid is entirely wanting. If I go out of and beyond the conception A, in order to recognize another B as connected with it, what foundation have I to rest on, whereby to render the synthesis possible? I have here no longer the advantage of looking out in the sphere of experience for what I want. Let us take, for example, the proposition, "Everything that happens has a cause." In the conception of "something that happens," I indeed think an existence which a certain time antecedes, and from this I can derive analytical judgments. But the conception of a cause lies quite out of the above conception, and indicates something entirely different from "that which happens," and is consequently not contained in that conception. How then am I able to assert concerning the general conception—"that which happens"—something entirely different from that conception, and to recognize the conception of cause although not contained in it, yet as belonging to it, and even necessarily? what is here the unknown = X, upon which the understanding rests when it believes it has found, out of the conception A a foreign predicate B, which it nevertheless considers to be connected with it? It cannot be experience, because the principle adduced annexes the two representations, cause and effect, to the representation existence, not only with universality, which experience cannot give, but also with the expression of necessity, therefore completely *a priori* and from pure conceptions. Upon such synthetical, that is augmentative propositions, depends the whole aim of our speculative knowledge *a priori;* for although analytical judgments are indeed highly important and necessary, they are so, only to arrive at that clearness of conceptions which is requisite for a sure and extended synthesis, and this alone is a real acquisition.

V. In All Theoretical Sciences of Reason, Synthetical Judgments *A Priori* Are Contained as Principles

1. Mathematical judgments are always synthetical. Hitherto this fact, though incontestably true and very important in its consequences, seems to have escaped the analysts of the human mind, nay, to be in complete opposition to all their conjectures. For as it was found that mathematical conclusions all proceed according to the principle of contradiction (which the nature of every apodeictic certainty requires), people became persuaded that the fundamental principles of the science also were recognized and admitted in the same way. But the notion is fallacious; for although a synthetical proposition can certainly be discerned by means of the principle of contradiction, this is possible only when another synthetical proposition precedes, from which the latter is deduced, but never of itself.

Before all, be it observed, that proper mathematical propositions are always judgments *a priori,* and not empirical, because they carry along with them the conception of necessity, which cannot be given by experience. If this be demurred to, it matters not; I will then limit my assertion to *pure* mathematics, the very conception of which implies that it consists of knowledge altogether non-empirical and *a priori.*

We might, indeed at first suppose that the proposition $7 + 5 = 12$ is a merely analytical proposition, following (according to the principle of contradiction) from the conception of a sum of seven and five. But if we regard it more narrowly, we find that our conception of the sum of seven and five contains nothing more than the uniting of both sums into one, whereby it cannot at all be thought what this single number is which embraces both. The conception of twelve is by no means obtained by merely thinking the union of seven and five; and we may analyze our conception of such a possible sum as long as we will, still we shall never discover in it the notion of twelve. We must go beyond these conceptions, and have recourse to an intuition which corresponds to one of the two—our five fingers, for example, . . . and so by degrees, add the units contained in the five given in the intuition, to the conception of seven. For I first take the number 7, and, for the conception of 5 calling in the aid of the fingers of my hand as objects of intuition, I add the units, which I before took together to make up the number 5, gradually now by means of the material image my hand, to the number 7, and by this process, I at length see the number 12 arise. That 7 should be added to 5, I have certainly thought in my conception of a sum $= 7 + 5$, but not that this sum was equal to 12. Arithmetical propositions are therefore always synthetical, of which we may become more clearly convinced by trying large numbers. For it will thus become quite evident that, turn and twist our conceptions as we may, it is impossible, without having recourse to intuition, to arrive at the sum total or product by means of the mere analysis of our conceptions. Just as little is any principle of pure geometry analytical. "A straight line between two points is the shortest," is a synthetical proposition. For my conception of *straight* contains no notion of *quantity,* but is merely *qualitative.* The conception of the shortest is therefore wholly an addition, and by no analysis can it be extracted from our conception of a straight line. Intuition must therefore here lend its aid, by means of which, and thus only, our synthesis is possible.

Some few principles preposited by geometricians are, indeed, really analytical, and depend on the principle of contradiction. They serve, however, like identical propositions, as links in the chain of method, not as principles—for example,

$a = a$, the whole is equal to itself, or $(a + b) > a$, the whole is greater than its part. And yet even these principles themselves, though they derive their validity from pure conceptions, are only admitted in mathematics because they can be presented in intuition. What causes us here commonly to believe that the predicate of such apodeictic judgments is already contained in our conception, and that the judgment is therefore analytical, is merely the equivocal nature of the expression. We must join in thought a certain predicate to a given conception, and this necessity cleaves already to the conception. But the question is, not what we must join in thought to the given conception, but what we really think therein, though only obscurely, and then it becomes manifest that the predicate pertains to these conceptions, necessarily indeed, yet not as thought in the conception itself, but by virtue of an intuition, which must be added to the conception.

2. The science of natural philosophy (physics) contains in itself synthetical judgments *a priori,* as principles. I shall adduce two propositions. For instance, the proposition, "In all changes of the material world, the quantity of matter remains unchanged"; or, that, "In all communication of motion, action and reaction must always be equal." In both of these, not only is the necessity, and therefore their origin *a priori* clear, but also that they are synthetical propositions. For in the conception of matter, I do not think its permanency, but merely its presence in space, which it fills. I therefore really go out of and beyond the conception of matter, in order to think on to it something *a priori,* which I did not think in it. The proposition is therefore not analytical, but synthetical, and nevertheless conceived *a priori;* and so it is with regard to the other propositions of the pure part of natural philosophy.

3. As to metaphysics, even if we look upon it merely as an attempted science, yet, from the nature of human reason, an indispensable one, we find that it must contain synthetical propositions *a priori.* It is not merely the duty of metaphysics to dissect, and thereby analytically to illustrate the conceptions which we form *a priori* of things; but we seek to widen the range of our *a priori* knowledge. For this purpose, we must avail ourselves of such principles as add something to the original conception—something not identical with, nor contained in it, and by means of synthetical judgments *a priori,* leave far behind us the limits of experience; for example, in the proposition, "the world must have a beginning," and such like. Thus metaphysics, according to the proper aim of the science, consists merely of synthetical propositions *a priori.* . . .

TRANSCENDENTAL DOCTRINE OF ELEMENTS; SECOND PART: TRANSCENDENTAL LOGIC INTRODUCTION: IDEA OF A TRANSCENDENTAL LOGIC

I. Of Logic in General

Our knowledge springs from two main sources in the mind, first of which is the faculty or power of receiving representations (receptivity for impressions); the second is the power of knowing by means of these representations (spontaneity in the production of conceptions). Through the first an object is given to us; through the second, it is, in relation to the representation (which is a mere determination of the mind), thought. Intuition and conceptions constitute, therefore, the elements of all our knowledge, so that neither conceptions without an intuition in some way corresponding to them, nor intuition without conceptions, can afford us a knowledge. Both are either pure or empirical. They are empirical, when sensation (which presupposes the actual presence of the object) is contained in them; and pure, when no sensation is mixed with the representation. Sensations we may call the matter of sensuous knowledge. Pure intuition consequently contains merely the form under which something is intuited, and pure conception only the form of the thought of an object. Only pure intuitions and pure conceptions are possible *a priori;* the empirical only *a posteriori.*

We apply the term sensibility to the receptivity of the mind for impressions, in so far as it is in some way affected; and, on the other hand, we call the faculty of spontaneously producing representations, or the spontaneity of knowledge, understanding. Our nature is so constituted that intuition with us never can be other than sensuous, that is, it contains only the mode in which we are affected by objects. On the other hand, the faculty of thinking the object of sensuous intuition is the understanding. Neither of these faculties has a preference over the other. Without the sensuous faculty no object would be given to us, and without the understanding no object would be thought. Thoughts without content are void; intuitions without conceptions, blind. Hence it is as necessary for the mind to make its conceptions sensuous (that is, to join to them the object in intuition), as to make its intuitions intelligible (that is, to bring them under conceptions). Neither of these faculties can exchange its proper function. Understanding cannot intuit, and the sensuous faculty cannot think. In no other way than from the united operation of both, can knowledge arise. But no one ought, on this account, to overlook the difference of the elements contributed by each; we have rather great reason carefully to separate and distinguish them. We therefore distinguish the science of the laws of sensibility, that is, aesthetic, from the science of the laws of the understanding, that is, logic.

Questions for Reflection

1. What would your experience be like if you only had a barrage of sense data, but the mind could not organize it in a meaningful way? (Think about what your immediate experience is like when the alarm first goes off in the morning.)
2. Has Kant found an effective compromise between the rationalists and the empiricists?
3. Since Kant believed that our experience of the world is always a product of the way the mind shapes that experience, he concluded that we can never know reality as it really is. Is this a problem? Or is it sufficient to have a humanly meaningful and structured experience, even though the structure is a product of our own minds?

WILLIAM JAMES

The Pragmatic Theory of Knowledge

One of the most influential theories of knowledge in the contemporary period has been that of pragmatism. If philosophies came in colors, pragmatism would be painted red, white, and blue. It is the only major philosophical movement that was American-grown. The foremost pioneers of pragmatic thought were the Americans Charles Sanders Peirce, William James, and John Dewey, all of whom lived in the latter part of the 19th century and the early 20th century. **Pragmatism** is a philosophy that stresses the intimate relation between thought and action by defining the meaning of our conceptions in terms of the practical effects we associate with them and the truth of our beliefs in terms

From William James, *Pragmatism: A New Name for Some Old Ways of Thinking* (New York: Longmans, Green, and Co., 1907), Lectures VI and II.

of how successfully they guide our actions. The word *pragmatism* can be traced back to a Greek word that means "action," "deed," or "practice."

The pragmatists criticized what they called "the spectator theory of knowledge." According to this outlook, the mind is like a passive mirror which reflects an external reality. But according to the pragmatists, this divorces meaning, truth, and knowledge from our practical engagement with the world. Dewey once said that the model of knowledge should not be that of a spectator viewing a painting but that of the artist producing the painting. The pragmatists similarly criticized the correspondence theory of truth. This was the view that a statement or belief is true to the degree that it corresponds to reality. The problem is that a statement or belief is not a photograph of the external world, so in what sense do they "correspond" to it? A statement has no magical powers to relate itself to reality. For the pragmatists the issue is not so much how a statement or belief relates to the world but how *we* can use them in *our* relationship to our world.

William James (1842–1910) was one of pragmatism's most eloquent representatives. (We previously encountered James and his view of religious belief in Chapter 2, where a discussion of his life may be found.) In the following selection, James proposes a radically new view of truth by claiming that truth is dynamic and changing so that *"ideas (which themselves are but parts of our experience) become true just in so far as they help us to get into satisfactory relation with other parts of our experience. . . ."* Furthermore, he says "the true is the name of whatever proves itself to be good in the way of belief."

Reading Questions

1. As you read through this passage, write down all the ways in which James uses the words *practical, instruments, useful,* and refers to the way that ideas have "cash-value," "lead us," "work," and "pay." What does this tell you about his view of ideas and truth?
2. How does James describe the intellectualist position? (When James speaks of "intellectualists," he is referring to rationalists and traditional empiricists.)
3. What questions does the pragmatist ask of an idea?
4. How does James define "true ideas"?
5. What does James mean by saying an idea "agrees" with reality?
6. What does it mean to find a theory that will "work"?
7. In what ways is the pursuit of truth similar to the pursuit of health and other goals in life?
8. What does James mean when he says that what is true is "the expedient"? How does this differ from the correspondence theory of truth?
9. What are the implications of saying the true is whatever is "good in the way of belief"? What qualification does he add to this notion?

PRAGMATISM'S CONCEPTION OF TRUTH

Truth, as any dictionary will tell you, is a property of certain of our ideas. It means their 'agreement,' as falsity means their disagreement, with 'reality.' Pragmatists and intellectualists both accept this definition as a matter of course. They begin to quarrel only after the question is raised as to what may precisely be meant by the term 'agreement,' and what by the term 'reality,' when reality is taken as something for our ideas to agree with.

In answering these questions the pragmatists are more analytic and painstaking, the intellectualists more offhand and irreflective. The popular notion is that a true idea must copy its reality. Like other popular views, this one follows the analogy of the most unusual experience. Our true ideas of sensible things do indeed copy them. Shut your eyes and think of yonder clock on the wall, and you get just such a true picture or copy of its dial. But your idea of its 'works' (unless you are a clockmaker) is much less of a copy, yet it passes muster, for it in no way clashes with the reality. Even though it should shrink to the mere word 'works,' that word still serves you truly; and when you speak of the 'time-keeping function' of the clock, or of its spring's 'elasticity,' it is hard to see exactly what your ideas can copy.

You perceive that there is a problem here. Where our ideas cannot copy definitely their object, what does agreement with that object mean? Some idealists seem to say that they are true whenever they are what God means that we ought to think about that object. Others hold the copy-view all through, and speak as if our ideas possessed truth just in proportion as they approach to being copies of the Absolute's eternal way of thinking.

These views, you see, invite pragmatistic discussion. But the great assumption of the intellectualists is that truth means essentially an inert static relation. When you've got your true idea of anything, there's an end of the matter. You're in possession; you *know;* you have fulfilled your thinking destiny. You are where you ought to be mentally; you have obeyed your categorical imperative; and nothing more need follow on that climax of your rational destiny. Epistemologically you are in stable equilibrium.

Pragmatism, on the other hand, asks its usual question. "Grant an idea or belief to be true," it says, "what concrete difference will its being true make in any one's actual life? How will the truth be realized? What experiences will be different from those which would obtain if the belief were false? What, in short, is the truth's cash-value in experiential terms?"

The moment pragmatism asks this question, it sees the answer: *True ideas are those that we can assimilate, validate, corroborate and verify. False ideas are those that we cannot.* That is the practical difference it makes to us to have true ideas; that, therefore, is the meaning of truth, for it is all that truth is known-as.

This thesis is what I have to defend. The truth of an idea is not a stagnant property inherent in it. Truth *happens* to an idea. It becomes true, is *made* true by events. Its verity *is* in fact an event, a process: the process namely of its verifying itself, its veri-*fication*. Its validity is the process of its valid-*ation.*

But what do the words verification and validation themselves pragmatically mean? They again signify certain practical consequences of the verified and validated idea. It is hard to find any one phrase that characterizes these consequences better than the ordinary agreement-formula—just such consequences being what we have in mind whenever we say that our ideas 'agree' with reality. They lead us, namely, through the acts and other ideas which they instigate, into or up to, or towards, other parts of experience with which we feel all the while—such feeling being among our potentialities—that the original ideas remain in agreement. The connexions and transitions come to us from point to point as being progressive, harmonious, satisfactory. This function of agreeable leading is what we mean by an idea's verification. . . .

. . . The possession of true thoughts means everywhere the possession of invaluable instruments of action; and that our duty to gain truth, so far from being a blank command from out of the blue, or a 'stunt' self-imposed by our intellect, can account for itself by excellent practical reasons.

The importance to human life of having true beliefs about matters of fact is a thing too notorious. We live in a world of realities that can be infinitely useful or infinitely harmful. Ideas that tell us which of them to expect count as the true ideas in all this primary sphere of verification, and the pursuit of such ideas is a primary human duty. The possession of truth, so far from being here an end in itself, is only a preliminary means towards other vital satisfactions. If I am lost in the woods and starved, and find what looks like a cow-path, it is of the utmost importance that I should think of a human habitation at the end of it, for if I do so and follow it, I save myself. The true thought is useful here because the house which is its object is useful. The practical value of true ideas is thus primarily derived from the practical importance of their objects to us. Their objects are, indeed, not important at all times. I may on another occasion have no use for the house; and then my idea of it, however verifiable, will be practically irrelevant, and had better remain latent. Yet since almost any object may some day become temporarily important, the advantage of having a general stock of *extra* truths, of ideas that shall be true of merely possible situations, is obvious. We store such extra truths away in our memories, and with the overflow we fill our books of reference. Whenever such an extra truth becomes practically relevant to one of our emergencies, it passes from cold-storage to do work in the world and our belief in it grows active. You can say of it then either that 'it is useful because it is true' or that 'it is true because it is useful.' Both these phrases mean exactly the same thing, namely that here is an idea that gets fulfilled and can be verified. True is the name for whatever idea starts the verification-process, useful is the name for its completed function in experience. True ideas would never have been singled out as such, would never have acquired a class-name, least of all a name suggesting value, unless they had been useful from the outset in this way.

From this simple cue pragmatism gets her general notion of truth as something essentially bound up with the way in which one moment in our experience may lead us towards other moments which it will be worth while to have been led to. Primarily, and on the common-sense level, the truth of a state of mind means this function of *a leading that is worth while*. When a moment in our experience, of any kind whatever, inspires us with a thought that is true, that means that sooner or later we dip by that thought's guidance into the particulars of experience again and make advantageous connexion with them. This is a vague enough statement, but I beg you to retain it, for it is essential.

Our experience meanwhile is all shot through with regularities. One bit of it can warn us to get ready for another bit, can 'intend' or be 'significant of' that remoter object. The object's advent is the significance's verification. Truth, in these cases, meaning nothing but eventual verification, is manifestly incompatible with waywardness on our part. Woe to him whose beliefs play fast and loose with the order which realities follow in his experience; they will lead him nowhere or else make false connexions.

By 'realities' or 'objects' here, we mean either things of common sense, sensibly present, or else common-sense relations, such as dates, places, distances, kinds, activities. Following our mental image of a house along the cow-path, we actually come to see the house; we get the image's full verification. *Such simply and fully verified leadings are certainly the originals and prototypes of the truth-process.* Experience offers indeed other forms of truth-process, but they are all conceivable as being primary verifications arrested, multiplied or substituted one for another.

Take, for instance, yonder object on the wall. You and I consider it to be a 'clock,' although no one of us has seen the hidden works that make it one. We let our notion pass for true without attempting to verify. If truths mean verification-process essentially, ought we then to call such unverified truths as this abortive? No, for they form the overwhelmingly large number of the truths we live by. Indirect as well as direct verifications pass muster. Where circumstantial evidence is sufficient, we can go without eye-witnessing. Just as we here assume Japan to exist without ever having been there, because it *works* to do so, everything we know conspiring with the belief, and nothing interfering, so we assume that thing to be a clock. We *use* it as a clock, regulating the length of our lecture by it. The verification of the assumption here means its leading to no frustration or contradiction. Verifi*ability* of wheels and weights and pendulum is as good as verification. For one truth-process completed there are a million in our lives that function in this state of nascency. They turn us *towards* direct verification; lead us into the *surroundings* of the objects they envisage; and then, if everything runs on harmoniously, we are so sure that verification is possible that we omit it, and are usually justified by all that happens.

Truth lives, in fact, for the most part on a credit system. Our thoughts and beliefs 'pass,' so long as nothing challenges them, just as bank-notes pass so long as nobody refuses them. But this all points to direct face-to-face verifications somewhere, without which the fabric of truth collapses like a financial system with no cash-basis whatever. You accept my verification of one thing, I yours of another. We trade on each other's truth. But beliefs verified concretely by *somebody* are the posts of the whole superstructure.

Another great reason—beside economy of time—for waiving complete verification in the usual business of life is that all things exist in kinds and not singly. Our world is found once for all to have that peculiarity. So that when we have once directly verified our ideas about one specimen of a kind, we consider ourselves free to apply them to other specimens without verification. A mind that habitually discerns the kind of thing before it, and acts by the law of the kind immediately, without pausing to verify, will be a 'true' mind in ninety-nine out of a hundred emergencies, proved so by its conduct fitting everything it meets, and getting no refutation.

Indirectly or only potentially verifying processes may thus be true as well as full verification-processes. They work as true processes would work, give us the same advantages, and claim our recognition for the same reasons. . . .

Realities mean . . . either concrete facts, or abstract kinds of thing and relations perceived intuitively between them. They furthermore and thirdly mean, as things that new ideas of ours must

no less take account of, the whole body of other truths already in our possession. But what now does 'agreement' with such threefold realities mean?— to use again the definition that is current.

Here it is that pragmatism and intellectualism begin to part company. Primarily, no doubt, to agree means to copy, but we saw that the mere word 'clock' would do instead of a mental picture of its works, and that of many realities our ideas can only be symbols and not copies. 'Past time,' 'power,' 'spontaneity,'—how can our mind copy such realities?

To 'agree' in the widest sense with a reality *can only mean to be guided either straight up to it or into its surroundings, or to be put into such working touch with it as to handle either it or something connected with it better than if we disagreed.* Better either intellectually or practically! And often agreement will only mean the negative fact that nothing contradictory from the quarter of that reality comes to interfere with the way in which our ideas guide us elsewhere. To copy a reality is, indeed, one very important way of agreeing with it, but it is far from being essential. The essential thing is the process of being guided. Any idea that helps us to *deal*, whether practically or intellectually, with either the reality or its belongings, that doesn't entangle our progress in frustrations, that *fits*, in fact, and adapts our life to the reality's whole setting, will agree sufficiently to meet the requirement. It will hold true of that reality.

Thus, *names* are just as 'true' or 'false' as definite mental pictures are. They set up similar verification-processes, and lead to fully equivalent practical results.

All human thinking gets discursified; we exchange ideas; we lend and borrow verifications, get them from one another by means of social intercourse. All truth thus gets verbally built out, stored up, and made available for every one. Hence, we must *talk* consistently just as we must *think* consistently: for both in talk and thought we deal with kinds. Names are arbitrary, but once understood they must be kept to. We mustn't now call Abel 'Cain' or Cain 'Abel.' If we do, we ungear ourselves from the whole book of Genesis, and from all its connexions with the universe of speech and fact down to the present time. We throw ourselves out of whatever truth that entire system of speech and fact may embody.

The overwhelming majority of our true ideas admit of no direct or face-to-face verification—those of past history, for example, as of Cain and Abel. The stream of time can be remounted only verbally, or verified indirectly by the present prolongations or effects of what the past harbored. Yet if they agree with these verbalities and effects, we can know that our ideas of the past are true. *As true as past time itself was,* so true was Julius Caesar, so true were antediluvian monsters, all in their proper dates and settings. That past time itself was, is guaranteed by its coherence with everything that's present. True as the present is, the past was also.

Agreement thus turns out to be essentially an affair of leading—leading that is useful because it is into quarters that contain objects that are important. True ideas lead us into useful verbal and conceptual quarters as well as directly up to useful sensible termini. They lead to consistency, stability and flowing human intercourse. They lead away from excentricity and isolation, from foiled and barren thinking. The untrammeled flowing of the leading-process, its general freedom from clash and contradiction, passes for its indirect verification; but all roads lead to Rome, and in the end and eventually, all true processes must lead to the face of directly verifying sensible experiences *somewhere,* which somebody's ideas have copied.

Such is the large loose way in which the pragmatist interprets the word agreement. He treats it altogether practically. He lets it cover any process of conduction from a present idea to a future terminus, provided only it run prosperously. It is only thus that 'scientific' ideas, flying as they do beyond common sense, can be said to agree with their realities. It is, as I have already said, *as if* reality were made of ether, atoms or electrons, but we mustn't think so literally. The term 'energy' doesn't even pretend to stand for anything 'objective.' It is only a way of measuring the surface of phenomena so as to string their changes on a simple formula.

Yet in the choice of these man-made formulas we can not be capricious with impunity any more than we can be capricious on the common-sense practical level. We must find a theory that will *work;* and that means something extremely difficult; for our theory must mediate between all previous truths and certain new experiences. It must derange common sense and previous belief as little as possible, and it must lead to some sensible terminus or other that can be verified exactly. To 'work' means both these things; and the squeeze is so tight that there is little loose play for any hypothesis. Our theories are wedged and controlled as nothing else is. Yet sometimes alternative theoretic formulas are equally compatible with all the truths we know, and then we choose between them for subjective reasons. We choose the kind of theory to which we are already partial; we follow 'elegance' or 'economy.' Clerk-Maxwell somewhere says it would be 'poor scientific taste' to choose the more complicated of two equally well-evidenced conceptions; and you will all agree with him. Truth in science is what gives us the maximum possible sum of satisfactions, taste included, but consistency both with previous truth and with novel fact is always the most imperious claimant. . . .

Our account of truth is an account of truths in the plural, of processes of leading, realized *in rebus,** and having only this quality in common, that they *pay.* They pay by guiding us into or towards some part of a system that dips at numerous points into sense-percepts, which we may copy mentally or not, but with which at any rate we are now in the kind of commerce vaguely designated as verification. Truth for us is simply a collective name for verification-processes, just as health, wealth, strength, etc., are names for other processes connected with life, and also pursued because it pays to pursue them. Truth is *made,* just as health, wealth and strength are made, in the course of experience.

Here rationalism is instantaneously up in arms against us. I can imagine a rationalist to talk as follows:

"Truth is not made," he will say; "it absolutely obtains, being a unique relation that does not wait upon any process, but shoots straight over the head

---

*Editor's note: [in things].

of experience, and hits its reality every time. Our belief that yon thing on the wall is a clock is true already, altho no one in the whole history of the world should verify it. The bare quality of standing in that transcendent relation is what makes any thought true that possesses it, whether or not there be verification. You pragmatists put the cart before the horse in making truth's being reside in verification-processes. These are merely signs of its being, merely our lame ways of ascertaining after the fact, which of our ideas already has possessed the wondrous quality. The quality itself is timeless, like all essences and natures. Thoughts partake of it directly, as they partake of falsity or of irrelevancy. It can't be analyzed away into pragmatic consequences."

The whole plausibility of this rationalist tirade is due to the fact to which we have already paid so much attention. In our world, namely, abounding as it does in things of similar kinds and similarly associated, one verification serves for others of its kind, and one great use of knowing things is to be led not so much to them as to their associates, especially to human talk about them. The quality of truth, obtaining *ante rem,** pragmatically means, then, the fact that in such a world innumerable ideas work better by their indirect or possible than by their direct and actual verification. Truth *ante rem* means only verifiability, then; or else it is a case of the stock rationalist trick of treating the *name* of a concrete phenomenal reality as an independent prior entity, and placing it behind the reality as its explanation. . . .

In the case of 'wealth' we all see the fallacy. We know that wealth is but a name for concrete processes that certain men's lives play a part in, and not a natural excellence found in Messrs. Rockefeller and Carnegie, but not in the rest of us.

Like wealth, health also lives *in rebus.* It is a name for processes, as digestion, circulation, sleep, etc., that go on happily, tho in this instance we are more inclined to think of it as a principle and to say the man digests and sleeps so well *because* he is so healthy.

---

*Editor's note: [before the thing].

With 'strength' we are, I think, more rationalistic still, and decidedly inclined to treat it as an excellence pre-existing in the man and explanatory of the herculean performances of his muscles.

With 'truth' most people go over the border entirely, and treat the rationalistic account as self-evident. But really all these words ending in *th* are exactly similar. Truth exists *ante rem* just as much and as little as the other things do.

The scholastics, following Aristotle, made much of the distinction between habit and act. Health *in actu* means, among other things, good sleeping and digesting. But a healthy man need not always be sleeping, or always digesting, any more than a wealthy man need be always handling money, or a strong man always lifting weights. All such qualities sink to the status of 'habits' between their times of exercise; and similarly truth becomes a habit of certain of our ideas and beliefs in their intervals of rest from their verifying activities. But those activities are the root of the whole matter, and the condition of there being any habit to exist in the intervals.

'The true,' to put it very briefly, *is only the expedient in the way of our thinking, just as 'the right' is only the expedient in the way of our behaving.* Expedient in almost any fashion; and expedient in the long run and on the whole of course; for what meets expediently all the experience in sight won't necessarily meet all farther experiences equally satisfactorily. Experience, as we know, has ways of *boiling over,* and making us correct our present formulas.

The 'absolutely' true, meaning what no farther experience will ever alter, is that ideal vanishing-point towards which we imagine that all our temporary truths will some day converge. It runs on all fours with the perfectly wise man, and with the absolutely complete experience; and, if these ideals are ever realized, they will all be realized together. Meanwhile we have to live to-day by what truth we can get to-day, and be ready to-morrow to call it falsehood. Ptolemaic astronomy, euclidean space, aristotelian logic, scholastic metaphysics, were expedient for centuries, but human experience has boiled over those limits, and we now call these things only relatively true, or true within those borders of experience. 'Absolutely' they are false; for we know that those limits were casual, and might have been transcended by past theorists just as they are by present thinkers.

When new experiences lead to retrospective judgments, using the past tense, what these judgments utter *was* true, even tho no past thinker had been led there. We live forwards, a Danish thinker has said, but we understand backwards. The present sheds a backward light on the world's previous processes. They may have been truth-processes for the actors in them. They are not so for one who knows the later revelations of the story.

This regulative notion of a potential better truth to be established later, possibly to be established some day absolutely, and having powers of retroactive legislation, turns its face, like all pragmatist notions, towards concreteness of fact, and towards the future. Like the half-truths, the absolute truth will have to be *made,* made as a relation incidental to the growth of a mass of verification-experience, to which the half-truth ideas are all along contributing their quota.

I have already insisted on the fact that truth is made largely out of previous truths. Men's beliefs at any time are so much experience *funded.* But the beliefs are themselves parts of the sum total of the world's experience, and become matter, therefore, for the next day's funding operations. So far as reality means experienceable reality, both it and the truths men gain about it are everlastingly in process of mutation—mutation towards a definite goal, it may be—but still mutation.

Mathematicians can solve problems with two variables. On the Newtonian theory, for instance, acceleration varies with distance, but distance also varies with acceleration. In the realm of truth-processes facts come independently and determine our beliefs provisionally. But these beliefs make us act, and as fast as they do so, they bring into sight or into existence new facts which re-determine the beliefs accordingly. So the whole coil and ball of truth, as it rolls up, is the product of a double influence. Truths emerge from facts; but they dip forward into facts again and add to them; which facts again create or reveal new truth (the word is indifferent) and so on indefinitely. The 'facts' themselves meanwhile are not *true*. They simply *are.* Truth is the function of the beliefs that start and terminate among them. . . .

WHAT PRAGMATISM MEANS

I am well aware how odd it must seem to some of you to hear me say that an idea is 'true' so long as to believe it is profitable to our lives. That it is *good,* for as much as it profits, you will gladly admit. If what we do by its aid is good, you will allow the idea itself to be good in so far forth, for we are the better for possessing it. But is it not a strange misuse of the word 'truth,' you will say, to call ideas also 'true' for this reason?

To answer this difficulty fully is impossible at this stage of my account. . . . Let me now say only this, that truth is *one species of good,* and not, as is usually supposed, a category distinct from good, and coordinate with it. *The true is the name of whatever proves itself to be good in the way of belief, and good, too, for definite, assignable reasons.* Surely you must admit this, that if there were *no* good for life in true ideas, or if the knowledge of them were positively disadvantageous and false ideas the only useful ones, then the current notion that truth is divine and precious, and its pursuit a duty, could never have grown up or become a dogma. In a world like that, our duty would be to *shun* truth, rather. But in this world, just as certain foods are not only agreeable to our taste, but good for our teeth, our stomach, and our tissues; so certain ideas are not only agreeable to think about, or agreeable as supporting other ideas that we are fond of, but they are also helpful in life's practical struggles. If there be any life that it is really better we should lead, and if there be any idea which, if believed in, would help us to lead that life, then it would be really *better for us* to believe in that idea, *unless, indeed, belief in it incidentally clashed with other greater vital benefits.*

'What would be better for us to believe'! This sounds very like a definition of truth. It comes very near to saying 'what we *ought* to believe': and in *that* definition none of you would find any oddity. Ought we ever not to believe what it is *better for us* to believe? And can we then keep the notion of what is better for us, and what is true for us, permanently apart?

Pragmatism says no, and I fully agree with her. Probably you also agree, so far as the abstract statement goes, but with a suspicion that if we practically did believe everything that made for good in our own personal lives, we should be found indulging all kinds of fancies about this world's affairs, and all kinds of sentimental superstitions about a world hereafter. Your suspicion here is undoubtedly well founded, and it is evident that something happens when you pass from the abstract to the concrete that complicates the situation.

I said just now that what is better for us to believe is true *unless the belief incidentally clashes with some other vital benefit.* Now in real life what vital benefits is any particular belief of ours most liable to clash with? What indeed except the vital benefits yielded by *other beliefs* when these prove incompatible with the first ones? In other words, the greatest enemy of any one of our truths may be the rest of our truths. Truths have once for all this desperate instinct of self-preservation and of desire to extinguish whatever contradicts them.

Questions for Reflection

1. James says that when a belief grows active for us, you can say of it that (1) "it is useful because it is true" or that (2) "it is true because it is useful" and that "both these phrases mean exactly the same thing." But are they the same? Why? Can you think of a belief that might be useful at the same time that is not true?
2. Given James's theory, would it be possible for the same idea to be both true and false, since its consequences may be satisfactory for some people and unsatisfactory for others? What might be some problems with this view?
3. How does James's conception of truth compare with your own ideas about truth? What are the strengths and weaknesses of James's position?

ALISON M. JAGGAR

A Feminist Perspective

Alison M. Jaggar (1942–) holds a joint appointment at the University of Colorado at Boulder in the Department of Philosophy and the Women's Studies Program. She has published in the areas of contemporary social, moral and political theory, especially from a feminist perspective.

Alison Jaggar believes that the Western tradition has left emotions out of the picture in its account of epistemology and that, by doing so, it has obscured the role of emotion in the construction of knowledge. Taking her cue from recent work in the

Alison Jaggar, "Love and Knowledge: Emotion in Feminist Epistemology," *Inquiry*, 32(2).

philosophy of science, Jaggar argues that all observation is selective and involves our values, motivations, interests, and emotions. These "subjective" factors direct our cognitive pursuits, shape what we know, and help determine its significance. Furthermore, she argues that the emotions of marginalized people (such as women) make them epistemologically privileged with respect to some issues. Because they are "outsiders" to the mainstream of intellectual life and political power, women can have a much more discerning perspective on the prevailing cognitive and social structures, while such structures remain invisible to men.

Reading Questions

1. What has been the dominant view of the emotions throughout the Western philosophical tradition? How have they been evaluated in comparison to reason?
2. What does Jaggar mean by the Dumb View of emotions? Why does she reject it? Why does she not like the identification of the emotions with feelings?
3. What does she mean when she says emotions are "socially constructed"?
4. Why does she think the emotions can play a positive role in the pursuit of knowledge, contrary to the "myth of dispassionate investigation"?
5. What does Jaggar mean by "outlaw" emotions? What political and epistemological significance might they have?
6. Why does she say "oppressed people have a kind of epistemological privilege"?

I. INTRODUCTION: EMOTION IN WESTERN EPISTEMOLOGY

Within the Western philosophical tradition, emotions have usually been considered potentially or actually subversive of knowledge. From Plato until the present, with a few notable exceptions, reason rather than emotion has been regarded as the indispensable faculty for acquiring knowledge.

Typically, although again not invariably, the rational has been contrasted with the emotional, and this contrasted pair then often linked with other dichotomies. Not only has reason been contrasted with emotion, but it has also been associated with the mental, the cultural, the universal, the public and the male, whereas emotion has been associated with the irrational, the physical, the natural, the particular, the private and, of course, the female.

Although Western epistemology has tended to give pride of place to reason rather than emotion, it has not always excluded emotion completely from the realm of reason. In the *Phaedrus*, Plato portrayed emotions, such as anger or curiosity, as irrational urges (horses) that must always be controlled by reason (the charioteer). On this model, the emotions were not seen as needing to be totally suppressed, but rather as needing direction by reason: for example, in a genuinely threatening situation, it was thought not only irrational but foolhardy not to be afraid. The split between reason and emotion was not absolute, therefore, for the Greeks. Instead, the emotions were thought of as providing indispensable motive power that needed to be channeled appropriately. Without horses, after all, the skill of the charioteer would be worthless.

The contrast between reason and emotion was sharpened in the seventeenth century by redefining reason as a purely instrumental faculty. For both the Greeks, and the medieval philosophers, reason had been linked with value in so far as reason provided access to the objective structure or order of reality, seen as simultaneously natural and morally justified. With the rise of modern science, however, the realms of nature and value were separated: nature was stripped of value and reconceptualized as an inanimate mechanism of no intrinsic worth. Values were relocated in human beings, rooted in their preferences and emotional responses. The separation of supposedly natural fact from human value meant that reason, if it were to provide trustworthy insight into reality, had to be uncontaminated by or abstracted from value. Increasingly, therefore, though never universally, reason was reconceptualized as the ability to make valid inferences from premises established elsewhere, the ability to calculate means but not to determine ends. The validity of logical inferences was thought independent of human attitudes and preferences; this was now the sense in which reason was taken to be objective and universal.

The modern redefinition of rationality required a corresponding reconceptualization of emotion. This was achieved by portraying emotions as nonrational and often irrational urges that regularly swept the body, rather as a storm sweeps over the land. The common way of referring to the emotions as the 'passions' emphasized that emotions happened to or were imposed upon an individual, something she suffered rather than something she did.

The epistemology associated with this new ontology rehabilitated sensory perception that, like emotion, typically had been suspected or even discounted by the Western tradition as a reliable source of knowledge. British empiricism, succeeded in the nineteenth century by positivism, took its epistemological task to be the formulation of rules of inference that would guarantee the derivation of certain knowledge from the 'raw data' supposedly given directly to the senses. Empirical testability became accepted as the hallmark of natural science; this, in turn, was viewed as the paradigm of genuine knowledge. Often epistemology was equated with the philosophy of science, and the dominant methodology of positivism prescribed that truly scientific knowledge must be capable of intersubjective verification. Because values and emotions had been defined as variable and

idiosyncratic, positivism stipulated that trustworthy knowledge could be established only by methods that neutralized the values and emotions of individual scientists.

Recent approaches to epistemology have challenged some fundamental assumptions of the positivist epistemological model. Contemporary theorists of knowledge have undermined once rigid distinctions between analytic and synthetic statements, between theories and observations and even between facts and values. However, few challenges have been raised thus far to the purported gap between emotion and knowledge. In this paper, I wish to begin bridging this gap through the suggestion that emotions may be helpful and even necessary rather than inimical to the construction of knowledge. My account is exploratory in nature and leaves many questions unanswered. It is not supported by irrefutable arguments or conclusive proofs; instead, it should be viewed as a preliminary sketch for an epistemological model that will require much further development before its workability can be established.

PART ONE: EMOTION

II. What Are Emotions?

The philosophical question, 'What are emotions?' requires both explicating the ways in which people ordinarily speak about emotion and evaluating the adequacy of those ways for expressing and illuminating experience and activity. Several problems confront someone trying to answer this deceptively simple question. One set of difficulties results from the variety, complexity, and even inconsistency of the ways in which emotions are viewed, both in daily life and in scientific contexts. It is in part this variety that makes emotions into a 'question' at the same time that it precludes answering that question by simple appeal to ordinary usage. A second difficulty is the wide range of phenomena covered by the term 'emotion': these extend from apparently instantaneous 'knee-jerk' responses of fright to lifelong dedication to an individual or a cause;

from highly civilized aesthetic responses to undifferentiated feelings of hunger and thirst; from background moods such as contentment or depression to intense and focused involvement in an immediate situation. It may well be impossible to construct a manageable account of emotion to cover such apparently diverse phenomena.

A further problem concerns the criteria for preferring one account of emotion to another. The more one learns about the ways in which other cultures conceptualize human faculties, the less plausible it becomes that emotions constitute what philosophers call a 'natural kind.' Not only do some cultures identify emotions unrecognized in the West, but there is reason to believe that the concept of emotion itself is a historical invention, like the concept of intelligence (Lewontin [1982]) or even the concept of mind (Rorty [1979]). For instance, anthropologist Catherine Lutz argues that the 'dichotomous categories of "cognition" and "affect" are themselves Euroamerican cultural constructions, master symbols that participate in the fundamental organization of our ways of looking at ourselves and others [1985, 1986], both in and outside of social science' (1987, p. 308). If this is true, then we have even more reason to wonder about the adequacy of ordinary Western ways of talking about emotion. Yet we have no access either to our own emotions or to those of others independent of or unmediated by the discourse of our culture.

In the face of these difficulties, I shall sketch an account of emotion with the following limitations. First, it will operate within the context of Western discussions of emotion: I shall not question, for instance, whether it would be possible or desirable to dispense entirely with anything resembling our concept of emotion. Second, although this account attempts to be consistent with as much as possible of Western understandings of emotion, it is intended to cover only a limited domain, not every phenomenon that may be called an emotion. On the contrary, it excludes as genuine emotions both automatic physical responses and non-intentional sensations, such as hunger pangs. Third, I do not pretend to offer a complete theory of emotion; instead, I focus on a few specific aspects of emotion

that I take to have been neglected or misrepresented, especially in positivist and neopositivist accounts. Finally, I would defend my approach not only on the ground that it illuminates aspects of our experience and activity that are obscured by positivist and neopositivist construals, but also on the ground that it is less open than these to ideological abuse. In particular, I believe that recognizing certain neglected aspects of emotion makes possible a better and less ideologically biased account of how knowledge is, and so ought to be, constructed.

III. Emotions as Intentional

Early positivist approaches to understanding emotions assumed that an adequate account required analytically separating emotion from other human faculties. Just as positivist accounts of sense perception attempted to distinguish the supposedly raw data of sensation from their cognitive interpretations, so positivist accounts of emotion tried to separate emotion conceptually from both reason and sense perception. As part of their sharpening of these distinctions, positivist construals of emotion tended to identify emotions with the physical feelings or involuntary bodily movements that typically accompany them, such as pangs or qualms, flushes or tremors; emotions were also assimilated to the subduing of physiological function or movement, as in the case of sadness, depression or boredom. The continuing influence of such supposedly scientific conceptions of emotion can be seen in the fact that 'feeling' is often used colloquially as a synonym for emotion, even though the more central meaning of 'feeling' is physiological sensation. On such accounts, emotions were not seen as being *about* anything: instead, they were contrasted with and seen as potential disruptions of other phenomena that *are* about some thing, phenomena such as rational judgments, thoughts, and observations. The positivist approach to understanding emotion has been called the Dumb View (Spelman [1982]).

The Dumb View of emotion is quite untenable. For one thing, the same feeling or physiological response is likely to be interpreted as various emotions, depending on the context of experience. This point often is illustrated by reference to a famous experiment; excited feelings were induced in research subjects by the injection of adrenalin, and the subjects then attributed to themselves appropriate emotions depending on their context (Schachter and Singer [1969]). Another problem with the Dumb View is that identifying emotions with feelings would make it impossible to postulate that a person might not be aware of her emotional state, because feelings by definition are a matter of conscious awareness. Finally, emotions differ from feelings, sensations or physiological responses in that they are dispositional rather than episodic. For instance, we may assert truthfully that we are outraged by, proud of or saddened by certain events, even if at that moment we are neither agitated nor tearful.

In recent years, contemporary philosophers have tended to reject the Dumb View of emotion and have substituted more intentional or cognitivist understandings. These newer conceptions emphasize that intentional judgments as well as physiological disturbances are integral elements in emotion. They define or identify emotions not by the quality or character of the physiological sensation that may be associated with them, but rather by their intentional aspect, the associated judgment. Thus, it is the content of my associated thought or judgment that determines whether my physical agitation and restlessness are defined as 'anxiety about my daughter's lateness' rather than as 'anticipation of tonight's performance'.

Cognitivist accounts of emotion have been criticized as overly rationalist, inapplicable to allegedly spontaneous, automatic or global emotions, such as general feelings of nervousness, contentedness, *Angst,* ecstasy or terror. Certainly, these accounts entail that infants and animals experience emotions, if at all, in only a primitive, rudimentary form. Far from being unacceptable, however, this entailment is desirable because it suggests that humans develop and mature in emotions as well as in other dimensions, increasing the range, variety and subtlety of their emotional responses in accordance with their life experiences and their reflections on these.

Cognitivist accounts of emotion are not without their own problems. A serious difficulty with many is that they end up replicating within the structure of emotion the very problem they are trying to solve—namely, that of an artificial split between emotion and thought—because most cognitivist accounts explain emotion as having two 'components': an affective or feeling component and a cognition that supposedly interprets or identifies the feelings. Such accounts, therefore, unwittingly perpetuate the positivist distinction between the shared, public, objective world of verifiable calculations, observations, and facts and the individual, private, subjective world of idiosyncratic feelings, and sensations. This sharp distinction breaks any conceptual links between our feelings and the 'external' world: if feelings are still conceived as blind or raw or undifferentiated, then we can give no sense to the notion of feelings fitting or failing to fit our perceptual judgments, that is, being appropriate or inappropriate. When intentionality is viewed as intellectual cognition and moved to the center of our picture of emotion, the affective elements are pushed to the periphery and become shadowy conceptual danglers whose relevance to emotion is obscure or even negligible. An adequate cognitive account of emotion must overcome this problem.

Most cognitivist accounts of emotion thus remain problematic in so far as they fail to explain the relation between the cognitive and the affective aspects of emotion. Moreover, in so far as they prioritize the intellectual over the feeling aspects, they reinforce the traditional Western preference for mind over body. Nevertheless, they do identify a vital feature of emotion overlooked by the Dumb View, namely, its intentionality.

IV. Emotions as Social Constructs

We tend to experience our emotions as involuntary individual responses to situations, responses that are often (though, significantly, not always) private in the sense that they are not perceived as directly and immediately by other people as they are by the subject of the experience. The apparently individual and involuntary character of our emotional experience is often taken as evidence that emotions are presocial, instinctive responses, determined by our biological constitution. This inference, however, is quite mistaken. Although it is probably true that the physiological disturbances characterizing emotions (facial grimaces, changes in the metabolic rate, sweating, trembling, tears, and so on) are continuous with the instinctive responses of our prehuman ancestors and also that the ontogeny of emotions to some extent recapitulates their phylogeny, mature human emotions can be seen neither as instinctive nor as biologically determined. Instead, they are socially constructed on several levels.

The most obvious way in which emotions are socially constructed is that children are taught deliberately what their culture defines as appropriate responses to certain situations: to fear strangers, to enjoy spicy food or to like swimming in cold water. On a less conscious level, children also learn what their culture defines as the appropriate ways to express the emotions that it recognizes. Although there may be crosscultural similarities in the expression of some apparently universal emotions, there are also wide divergences in what are recognized as expressions of grief, respect, contempt or anger. On an even deeper level, cultures construct divergent understandings of what emotions are. For instance, English metaphors and metonymies are said to reveal a 'folk' theory of anger as a hot fluid contained in a private space within an individual and liable to dangerous public explosion (Lakoff and Kovecses [1987]). By contrast, the Ilongot, a people of the Philippines, apparently do not understand the self in terms of a public/private distinction and consequently do not experience anger as an explosive internal force: for them, rather, it is an interpersonal phenomenon for which an individual may, for instance, be paid (Rosaldo [1984]).

Further aspects of the social construction of emotion are revealed through reflection on emotion's intentional structure. If emotions necessarily involve judgments, then obviously they require concepts, which may be seen as socially constructed ways of organizing and making sense of the world. For this reason, emotions are simultaneously made possible and limited by the conceptual and linguis-

tic resources of a society. This philosophical claim is borne out by empirical observation of the cultural variability of emotion. Although there is considerable overlap in the emotions identified by many cultures (Wierzbicka [1986]), at least some emotions are historically or culturally specific, including perhaps *ennui, Angst,* the Japanese *amai* (in which one clings to another, affiliative love), and the response of 'being a wild pig', which occurs among the Gururumba, a horticultural people living in the New Guinea Highlands (Averell [1980, p. 158]). Even apparently universal emotions, such as anger or love, may vary crossculturally. We have just seen that the Ilongot experience of anger is apparently quite different from the contemporary Western experience. Romantic love was invented in the Middle Ages in Europe and since that time has been modified considerably; for instance, it is no longer confined to the nobility, and it no longer needs to be extramarital or unconsummated. In some cultures, romantic love does not exist at all.

Thus there are complex linguistic and other social preconditions for the experience, that is, for the existence of human emotions. The emotions that we experience reflect prevailing forms of social life. For instance, one could not feel or even be betrayed in the absence of social norms about fidelity: it is inconceivable that betrayal or indeed any distinctively human emotion could be experienced by a solitary individual in some hypothetical presocial state of nature. There is a sense in which any individual's guilt or anger, joy or triumph, presupposes the existence of a social group capable of feeling guilt, anger, joy, or triumph. This is not to say that group emotions historically precede or are logically prior to the emotions of individuals; it is to say that individual experience is simultaneously social experience. In later sections, I shall explore the epistemological and political implications of this social rather than individual understanding of emotion.

V. Emotions as Active Engagements

We often interpret our emotions as experiences that overwhelm us rather than as responses we consciously choose: that emotions are to some extent involuntary is part of the ordinary meaning of the term 'emotion'. Even in daily life, however, we recognize that emotions are not entirely involuntary and we try to gain control over them in various ways ranging from mechanistic behavior-modification techniques designed to sensitize or desensitize our feeling responses to various situations to cognitive techniques designed to help us to think differently about situations. For instance, we might try to change our response to an upsetting situation by thinking about it in a way that will either divert our attention from its more painful aspects or present it as necessary for some larger good.

Some psychological theories interpret emotions as chosen on an even deeper level, interpreting them as actions for which the agent disclaims responsibility. For instance, the psychologist Averell likens the experience of emotion to playing a culturally recognized role we ordinarily perform so smoothly and automatically that we do not realize we are giving a performance. He provides many examples demonstrating that even extreme and apparently totally involving displays of emotion in fact are functional for the individual and/or the society. For example, students requested to record their experiences of anger or annoyance over a two-week period came to realize that their anger was not as uncontrollable and irrational as they had assumed previously, and they noted the usefulness and effectiveness of anger in achieving various social goods. Averell notes, however, that emotions often are useful in attaining their goals only if they are interpreted as passions rather than as actions and he cites the case of one subject led to reflect on her anger who later wrote that it was less useful as a defense mechanism when she became conscious of its function.

The action/passion dichotomy is too simple for understanding emotion, as it is for other aspects of our lives. Perhaps it is more helpful to think of emotions as habitual responses that we may have more or less difficulty in breaking. We claim or disclaim responsibility for these responses depending on our purposes in a particular context. We could never experience our emotions entirely as deliberate actions, for then they would appear nongenuine and inauthentic, but neither should emotions be seen as nonintentional, primal or physical

forces with which our rational selves are forever at war. As they have been socially constructed, so may they be reconstructed, although describing how this might happen would have to be a long and complicated story.

Emotions, then, are wrongly seen as necessarily passive or involuntary responses to the world. Rather, they are ways in which we engage actively and even construct the world. They have both 'mental' and 'physical' aspects, each of which conditions the other; in some respects they are chosen but in others they are involuntary; they presuppose language and a social order. Thus, they can be attributed only to what are sometimes called 'whole persons', engaged in the on-going activity of social life.

VI. Emotion, Evaluation, and Observation

Emotions and values are closely related. The relation is so close, indeed, that some philosophical accounts of what it is to hold or express certain values reduce these phenomena to nothing more than holding or expressing certain emotional attitudes. When the relevant conception of emotion is the Dumb View, then simple emotivism is certainly too crude an account of what it is to hold a value; on this account, the intentionality of value judgments vanishes and value judgments become nothing more than sophisticated grunts and groans. Nevertheless, the grain of important truth in emotivism is its recognition that values presuppose emotions to the extent that emotions provide the experiential basis for values. If we had no emotional responses to the world, it is inconceivable that we should ever come to value one state of affairs more highly than another.

Just as values presuppose emotions, so emotions presuppose values. The object of an emotion—that is, the object of fear, grief, pride, and so on—is a complex state of affairs that is appraised or evaluated by the individual. For instance, my pride in a friend's achievement necessarily incorporates the value judgment that my friend has done something worthy of admiration.

Emotions and evaluations, then, are logically or conceptually connected. Indeed, many evaluative terms derive directly from words for emotions: 'desirable', 'admirable', 'contemptible', 'despicable', 'respectable', and so on. Certainly it is true (*pace* J. S. Mill) that the evaluation of a situation as desirable or dangerous does not entail that it is universally desired or feared, but it does entail that desire or fear is viewed generally as an appropriate response to the situation. If someone is unafraid in a situation perceived generally as dangerous, her lack of fear requires further explanation; conversely, if someone is afraid without evident danger, then her fear demands explanation; and, if no danger can be identified, her fear is denounced as irrational or pathological. Thus, every emotion presupposes an evaluation of some aspect of the environment while, conversely, every evaluation or appraisal of the situation implies that those who share that evaluation will share, *ceteris paribus,* a predictable emotional response to the situation.

The rejection of the Dumb View and the recognition of intentional elements in emotion already incorporate a realization that observation influences and indeed partially constitutes emotion. We have seen already that distinctively human emotions are not simple instinctive responses to situations or events; instead, they depend essentially on the ways that we perceive those situations and events, as well on the ways that we have learned or decided to respond to them. Without characteristically human perceptions of and engagements in the world, there would be no characteristically human emotions.

Just as observation directs, shapes, and partially defines emotion, so too emotion directs, shapes, and even partially defines observation. Observation is not simply a passive process of absorbing impressions or recording stimuli; instead, it is an activity of selection and interpretation. What is selected and how it is interpreted are influenced by emotional attitudes. On the level of individual observation, this influence has always been apparent to common sense, which notes that we remark very different features of the world when we are happy, depressed, fearful, or confident. This influence of emotion on perception is now being explored by social scientists. One example is the so-called Honi phenomenon, named after a subject called Honi who, under identical experimental conditions, perceived strangers' heads as changing in size but saw her husband's head as remaining the same.

The most obvious significance of this sort of example is in illustrating how the individual experience of emotion focuses our attention selectively, directing, shaping, and even partially defining our observations, just as our observations direct, shape, and partially define our emotions. In addition, the example has been taken further in an argument for the social construction of what are taken in any situation to be undisputed facts, showing how these rest on intersubjective agreements that consist partly in shared assumptions about 'normal' or appropriate emotional responses to situations (McLaughlin [1985]). Thus these examples suggest that certain emotional attitudes are involved on a deep level in all observation, in the intersubjectively verified and so supposedly dispassionate observations of science as well as in the common perceptions of daily life. In the next section, I shall elaborate this claim.

PART TWO: EPISTEMOLOGY

VII. The Myth of Dispassionate Investigation

As we have already seen, Western epistemology has tended to view emotion with suspicion and even hostility. This derogatory Western attitude toward emotion, like the earlier Western contempt for sensory observation, fails to recognize that emotion, like sensory perception, is necessary to human survival. Emotions prompt us to act appropriately, to approach some people and situations and to avoid others, to caress or cuddle, fight or flee. Without emotion, human life would be unthinkable. Moreover, emotions have an intrinsic as well as an instrumental value. Although not all emotions are enjoyable or even justifiable, as we shall see, life without any emotion would be life without any meaning.

Within the context of Western culture, however, people have often been encouraged to control or even suppress their emotions. Consequently, it is not unusual for people to be unaware of their emotional state or to deny it to themselves and others. This lack of awareness, especially combined with a neopositivist understanding of emotion that construes it as just a feeling of which one is aware, lends plausibility to the myth of dispassionate investigation. But lack of awareness of emotions certainly does not mean that emotions are not present subconsciously or unconsciously, or that subterranean emotions do not exert a continuing influence on people's articulated values and observations, thoughts, and actions.

Within the positivist tradition, the influence of emotion is usually seen only as distorting or impeding observation or knowledge. Certainly it is true that contempt, disgust, shame, revulsion or fear may inhibit investigation of certain situations or phenomena. Furiously angry or extremely sad people often seem quite unaware of their surroundings or even of their own conditions; they may fail to hear or may systematically misinterpret what other people say. People in love are notoriously oblivious to many aspects of the situation around them.

In spite of these examples, however, positivist epistemology recognizes that the role of emotion in the construction of knowledge is not invariably deleterious and that emotions may make a valuable contribution to knowledge. But the positivist tradition will allow emotion to play only the role of suggesting hypotheses for investigation. Emotions are allowed this because the so-called logic of discovery sets no limits on the idiosyncratic methods that investigators may use for generating hypotheses.

When hypotheses are to be tested, however, positivist epistemology imposes the much stricter logic of justification. The core of this logic is replicability, a criterion believed capable of eliminating or cancelling out what are conceptualized as emotional as well as evaluative biases on the part of individual investigators. The conclusions of Western science thus are presumed 'objective', precisely in the sense that they are uncontaminated by the supposedly 'subjective' values and emotions that might bias individual investigators (Nagel [1968, pp. 33–34]).

But if, as has been argued, the positivist distinction between discovery and justification is not vi-

able, then such a distinction is incapable of filtering out values in science. For example, although such a split, when built into the Western scientific method, is generally successful in neutralizing the idiosyncratic or unconventional values of individual investigators, it has been argued that it does not, indeed, cannot, eliminate generally accepted social values. These values are implicit in the identification of the problems that are considered worthy of investigation, in the selection of the hypotheses that are considered worthy of testing and in the solutions to the problems that are considered worthy of acceptance. The science of past centuries provides ample evidence of the influence of prevailing social values, whether seventeenth-century atomistic physics (Merchant [1980]) or nineteenth-century competitive interpretations of natural selection (Young [1985]).

Of course, only hindsight allows us to identify clearly the values that shaped the science of the past and thus to reveal the formative influence on science of pervasive emotional attitudes, attitudes that typically went unremarked at the time because they were shared so generally. For instance, it is now glaringly evident that contempt for (and perhaps fear of) people of color is implicit in nineteenth-century anthropology's interpretations and even constructions of anthropological facts. Because we are closer to them, however, it is harder for us to see how certain emotions, such as sexual possessiveness or the need to dominate others, are currently accepted as guiding principles in twentieth-century sociobiology or even defined as part of reason within political theory and economics (Quinby [1986]).

Values and emotions enter into the science of the past and the present not only at the level of scientific practice but also at the metascientific level, as answers to various questions: What is science? How should it be practiced? And what is the status of scientific investigation versus nonscientific modes of inquiry? For instance, it is claimed with increasing frequency that the modern Western conception of science, which identifies knowledge with power and views it as a weapon for dominating nature, reflects the imperialism, racism, and misogyny of the societies that created it. Several feminist theorists have argued that modern epistemology it-self may be viewed as an expression of certain emotions alleged to be especially characteristic of males in certain periods, such as separation anxiety and paranoia (Flax [1983], Bordo [1987]) or an obsession with control and fear of contamination (Scheman [1985], Schott [1988]).

Positivism views values and emotions as alien invaders that must be repelled by a stricter application of the scientific method. If the foregoing claims are correct, however, the scientific method and even its positivist construals themselves incorporate values and emotions. Moreover, such an incorporation seems a necessary feature of all knowledge and conceptions of knowledge. Therefore, rather than repressing emotion in epistemology it is necessary to rethink the relation between knowledge and emotion and construct conceptual models that demonstrate the mutually constitutive rather than oppositional relation between reason and emotion. Far from precluding the possibility of reliable knowledge, emotion as well as value must be shown as necessary to such knowledge. Despite its classical antecedents and as in the ideal of disinterested inquiry, the ideal of dispassionate inquiry is an impossible dream, but a dream none the less or perhaps a myth that has exerted enormous influence on Western epistemology. Like all myths, it is a form of ideology that fulfils certain social and political functions.

VIII. The Ideological Function of the Myth

So far, I have spoken very generally of people and their emotions, as though everyone experienced similar emotions and dealt with them in similar ways. It is an axiom of feminist theory, however, that all generalizations about 'people' are suspect. The divisions in our society are so deep, particularly the divisions of race, class, and gender, that many feminist theorists would claim that talk about people in general is ideologically dangerous because such talk obscures the fact that no one is simply a person but instead is constituted fundamentally by race, class, and gender. Race, class, and gender shape every aspect of our lives, and our emotional consti-

tution is not excluded. Recognizing this helps us to see more clearly the political functions of the myth of the dispassionate investigator.

Feminist theorists have pointed out that the Western tradition has not seen everyone as equally emotional. Instead, reason has been associated with members of dominant political, social, and cultural groups and emotion with members of subordinate groups. Prominent among those subordinate groups in our society are people of color, except for supposedly 'inscrutable orientals', and women.

Although the emotionality of women is a familiar cultural stereotype, its grounding is quite shaky. Women appear to be more emotional than men because they, along with some groups of people of color, are permitted and even required to express emotion more openly. In contemporary Western culture, emotionally inexpressive women are suspect as not being real women, whereas men who express their emotions freely are suspected of being homosexual or in some other way deviant from the masculine ideal. Modern Western men, in contrast with Shakespeare's heroes, for instance, are required to present a façade of coolness, lack of excitement, even boredom, to express emotion only rarely and then for relatively trivial events, such as sporting occasions, where the emotions expressed are acknowledged to be dramatized and so are not taken entirely seriously. Thus, women in our society form the main group allowed or even expected to express emotion. A woman may cry in the face of disaster, and a man of color may gesticulate, but a white man merely sets his jaw.

White men's control of their emotional expression may go to the extremes of repressing their emotions, failing to develop emotionally or even losing the capacity to experience many emotions. Not uncommonly, these men are unable to identify what they are feeling, and even they may be surprised, on occasion, by their own apparent lack of emotional response to a situation, such as a death, where emotional reaction is perceived to be appropriate. In some married couples, the wife is implicitly assigned the job of feeling emotion for both of them. White, college-educated men increasingly enter therapy in order to learn how to 'get in touch with' their emotions, a project other men may ridicule as weakness. In therapeutic situations, men may learn that they are just as emotional as women but less adept at identifying their own or others' emotions. In consequence, their emotional development may be relatively rudimentary; this may lead to moral rigidity or insensitivity. Paradoxically, men's lacking awareness of their own emotional responses frequently results in their being more influenced by emotion rather than less.

Although there is no reason to suppose that the thoughts and actions of women are any more influenced by emotion than the thoughts and actions of men, the stereotypes of cool men and emotional women continue to flourish because they are confirmed by an uncritical daily experience. In these circumstances, where there is a differential assignment of reason and emotion, it is easy to see the ideological function of the myth of the dispassionate investigator. It functions, obviously, to bolster the epistemic authority of the currently dominant groups, composed largely of white men, and to discredit the observations and claims of the currently subordinate groups including, of course, the observations and claims of many people of color and women. The more forcefully and vehemently the latter groups express their observations and claims, the more emotional they appear and so the more easily they are discredited. The alleged epistemic authority of the dominant groups then justifies their political authority.

The previous section of this paper argued that dispassionate inquiry was a myth. This section has shown that the myth promotes a conception of epistemological justification vindicating the silencing of those, especially women, who are defined culturally as the bearers of emotion and so are perceived as more 'subjective', biased and irrational. In our present social context, therefore, the ideal of the dispassionate investigator is a classist, racist, and especially masculinist myth.

IX. Emotional Hegemony and Emotional Subversion

As we have seen already, mature human emotions are neither instinctive nor biologically determined, although they may have developed out of presocial,

instinctive responses. Like everything else that is human, emotions in part are socially constructed; like all social constructs, they are historical products, bearing the marks of the society that constructed them. Within the very language of emotion, in our basic definitions and explanations of what it is to feel pride or embarrassment, resentment or contempt, cultural norms and expectations are embedded. Simply describing ourselves as angry, for instance, presupposes that we view ourselves as having been wronged, victimized by the violation of some social norm. Thus, we absorb the standards and values of our society in the very process of learning the language of emotion, and those standards and values are built into the foundation of our emotional constitution.

Within a hierarchical society, the norms and values that predominate tend to serve the interests of the dominant groups. Within a capitalist, white suprematist, and male-dominant society, the predominant values will tend to be those that serve the interests of rich white men. Consequently, we are all likely to develop an emotional constitution that is quite inappropriate for feminism. Whatever our color, we are likely to feel what Irving Thalberg has called 'visceral racism'; whatever our sexual orientation, we are likely to be homophobic; whatever our class, we are likely to be at least somewhat ambitious and competitive; whatever our sex, we are likely to feel contempt for women. Such emotional responses may be rooted in us so deeply that they are relatively impervious to intellectual argument and may recur even when we pay lip service to changed intellectual convictions.

By forming our emotional constitution in particular ways, our society helps to ensure its own perpetuation. The dominant values are implicit in responses taken to be precultural or acultural, our so-called gut responses. Not only do these conservative responses hamper and disrupt our attempts to live in or prefigure alternative social forms but also, and in so far as we take them to be natural responses, they blinker us theoretically. For instance, they limit our capacity for outrage; they either prevent us from despising or encourage us to despise; they lend plausibility to the belief that greed and domination are inevitable human motivations; in sum, they blind us to the possibility of alternative ways of living.

This picture may seem at first to support the positivist claim that the intrusion of emotion only disrupts the process of seeking knowledge and distorts the results of that process. The picture, however, is not complete; it ignores the fact that people do not always experience the conventionally acceptable emotions. They may feel satisfaction rather than embarrassment when their leaders make fools of themselves. They may feel resentment rather than gratitude for welfare payments and hand-me-downs. They may be attracted to forbidden modes of sexual expression. They may feel revulsion for socially sanctioned ways of treating children or animals. In other words, the hegemony that our society exercises over people's emotional constitution is not total.

People who experience conventionally unacceptable, or what I call 'outlaw' emotions often are subordinated individuals who pay a disproportionately high price for maintaining the *status quo.* The social situation of such people makes them unable to experience the conventionally prescribed emotions: for instance, people of color are more likely to experience anger than amusement when a racist joke is recounted, and women subjected to male sexual banter are less likely to be flattered than uncomfortable or even afraid.

When unconventional emotional responses are experienced by isolated individuals, those concerned may be confused, unable to name their experience; they may even doubt their own sanity. Women may come to believe that they are 'emotionally disturbed' and that the embarrassment or fear aroused in them by male sexual innuendo is prudery or paranoia. When certain emotions are shared or validated by others, however, the basis exists for forming a subculture defined by perceptions, norms, and values that systematically oppose the prevailing perceptions, norms, and values. By constituting the basis for such a subculture, outlaw emotions may be politically because epistemologically subversive.

Outlaw emotions are distinguished by their incompatibility with the dominant perceptions and values, and some, though certainly not all, of these outlaw emotions are potentially or actually feminist emotions. Emotions become feminist when they incorporate feminist perceptions and values, just as emotions are sexist or racist when they incorporate sexist or racist perceptions and values. For example, anger becomes feminist anger when it involves the perception that the persistent importuning endured by one woman is a single instance of a widespread pattern of sexual harassment, and pride becomes feminist pride when it is evoked by realizing that a certain person's achievement was possible only because that individual overcame specifically gendered obstacles to success.

Outlaw emotions stand in a dialectical relation to critical social theory: at least some are necessary for developing a critical perspective on the world, but they also presuppose at least the beginnings of such a perspective. Feminists need to be aware of how we can draw on some of our outlaw emotions in constructing feminist theory, and also of how the increasing sophistication of feminist theory can contribute to the re-education, refinement, and eventual reconstruction of our emotional constitution.

X. Outlaw Emotions and Feminist Theory

The most obvious way in which feminist and other outlaw emotions can help in developing alternatives to prevailing conceptions of reality is by motivating new investigations. This is possible because, as we saw earlier, emotions may be long-term as well as momentary; it makes sense to say that someone continues to be shocked or saddened by a situation, even if she is at the moment laughing heartily. As we have seen already, theoretical investigation is always purposeful, and observation always selective. Feminist emotions provide a political motivation for investigation and so help to determine the selection of problems as well as the method by which they are investigated. Susan Griffin makes the same point when she characterizes feminist theory as following 'a direction determined by pain, and trauma, and compassion and outrage' (Griffin [1979, p. 31]).

As well as motivating critical research, outlaw emotions may also enable us to perceive the world differently from its portrayal in conventional descriptions. They may provide the first indications that something is wrong with the way alleged facts have been constructed, with accepted understandings of how things are. Conventionally unexpected or inappropriate emotions may precede our conscious recognition that accepted descriptions and justifications often conceal as much as reveal the prevailing state of affairs. Only when we reflect on our initially puzzling irritability, revulsion, anger or fear may we bring to consciousness our 'gut-level' awareness that we are in a situation of coercion, cruelty, injustice or danger. Thus, conventionally inexplicable emotions, particularly though not exclusively those experienced by women, may lead us to make subversive observations that challenge dominant conceptions of the *status quo*. They may help us to realize that what are taken generally to be facts have been constructed in a way that obscures the reality of subordinated people, especially women's reality.

But why should we trust the emotional responses of women and other subordinated groups? How can we determine which outlaw emotions are to be endorsed or encouraged and which rejected? In what sense can we say that some emotional responses are more appropriate than others? What reason is there for supposing that certain alternative perceptions of the world, perceptions informed by outlaw emotions, are to be preferred to perceptions informed by conventional emotions? Here I can indicate only the general direction of an answer, whose full elaboration must await another occasion.

I suggest that emotions are appropriate if they are characteristic of a society in which all humans (and perhaps some non-human life too) thrive, or if they are conducive to establishing such a society. For instance, it is appropriate to feel joy when we are developing or exercising our creative powers, and it is appropriate to feel anger and perhaps disgust in those situations where humans are denied their full creativity or freedom. Similarly, it is appropriate to feel fear if those capacities are threatened in us.

This suggestion, obviously, is extremely vague and may even verge on the tautologous. How can

we apply it in situations where there is disagreement over what is or is not disgusting or exhilarating or unjust? Here I appeal to a claim for which I have argued elsewhere: the perspective on reality that is available from the standpoint of the subordinated, which in part at least is the standpoint of women, is a perspective that offers a less partial and distorted and therefore more reliable view (Jaggar [1983, ch. 11]). Subordinated people have a kind of epistemological privilege in so far as they have easier access to this standpoint and therefore a better chance of ascertaining the possible beginnings of a society in which all could thrive. For this reason, I would claim that the emotional responses of subordinated people in general, and often of women in particular, are more likely to be appropriate than the emotional responses of the dominant class. That is, they are more likely to incorporate reliable appraisals of situations.

Even in contemporary science, where the ideology of dispassionate inquiry is almost overwhelming, it is possible to discover a few examples that seem to support the claim that certain emotions are more appropriate than others in both a moral and epistemological sense. For instance, Hilary Rose claims that women's practice of caring, even though warped by its containment in the alienated context of a coercive sexual division of labor, has nevertheless generated more accurate and less oppressive understandings of women's bodily functions, such as menstruation (Rose [1983]). Certain emotions may be both morally appropriate and epistemologically advantageous in approaching the non-human and even the inanimate world. Jane Goodall's scientific contribution to our understanding of chimpanzee behavior seems to have been made possible only by her amazing empathy with or even love for these animals (Goodall [1986]). In her study of Barbara McClintock, Evelyn Fox Keller describes McClintock's relation to the objects of her research—grains of maize and their genetic properties—as a relation of affection, empathy and 'the highest form of love: love that allows for intimacy without the annihilation of difference'. She notes that McClintock's 'vocabulary is consistently a vocabulary of affection, of kinship, of empathy' (Keller [1984, p. 164]). Examples like these prompt Hilary Rose to assert that a feminist science of nature needs to draw on heart as well as hand and brain.

XI. Some Implications of Recognizing the Epistemic Potential of Emotion

Accepting that appropriate emotions are indispensable to reliable knowledge does not mean, of course, that uncritical feeling may be substituted for supposedly dispassionate investigation. Nor does it mean that the emotional responses of women and other members of the underclass are to be trusted without question. Although our emotions are epistemologically indispensable, they are not epistemologically indisputable. Like all our faculties, they may be misleading, and their data, like all data, are always subject to reinterpretation and revision. Because emotions are not presocial, physiological responses to unequivocal situations, they are open to challenge on various grounds. They may be dishonest or self-deceptive, they may incorporate inaccurate or partial perceptions, or they may be constituted by oppressive values. Accepting the indispensability of appropriate emotions to knowledge means no more (and no less) than that discordant emotions should be attended to seriously and respectfully rather than condemned, ignored, discounted or suppressed.

Just as appropriate emotions may contribute to the development of knowledge, so the growth of knowledge may contribute to the development of appropriate emotions. For instance, the powerful insights of feminist theory often stimulate new emotional responses to past and present situations. Inevitably, our emotions are affected by the knowledge that the women on our faculty are paid systematically less than the men, that one girl in four is subjected to sexual abuse from heterosexual men in her own family, and that few women reach orgasm in heterosexual intercourse. We are likely to feel different emotions toward older women or people of color as we re-evaluate our standards of sexual attractiveness or acknowledge that black is beautiful. The new emotions evoked by feminist insights are likely in turn to stimulate further feminist observations and insights, and these may generate new directions in both theory and political practice. There is a continuous feedback loop between our emotional constitution and our theorizing such that each continually modifies the other and is in principle inseparable from it.

The ease and speed with which we can re-educate our emotions is unfortunately not great. Emotions are only partially within our control as individuals. Although affected by new information, they are habitual responses not quickly unlearned. Even when we come to believe consciously that our fear or shame or revulsion is unwarranted, we may still continue to experience emotions inconsistent with our conscious politics. We may still continue to be anxious for male approval, competitive with our comrades and sisters and possessive with our lovers. These unwelcome, because apparently inappropriate emotions, should not be suppressed or denied; instead, they should be acknowledged and subjected to critical scrutiny. The persistence of such recalcitrant emotions probably demonstrates how fundamentally we have been constituted by the dominant world view, but it may also indicate superficiality or other inadequacy in our emerging theory and politics. We can only start from where we are—beings who have been created in a cruelly racist, capitalist and male-dominated society that has shaped our bodies and our minds, our perceptions, our values and our emotions, our language, and our systems of knowledge.

The alternative epistemological models that I suggest would display the continuous interaction between how we understand the world and who we are as people. They would show how our emotional responses to the world change as we conceptualize it differently and how our changing emotional responses then stimulate us to new insights. They would demonstrate the need for theory to be self-reflexive, to focus not only on the outer world but also on ourselves and our relation to that world, to examine critically our social location, our actions, our values, our perceptions, and our emotions. The models would also show how feminist and other critical social theories are indispensable psychotherapeutic tools because they provide some insights necessary to a full understanding of our emotional constitution. Thus, the models would explain how the reconstruction of knowledge is inseparable from the reconstruction of ourselves.

A corollary of the reflexivity of feminist and other critical theory is that it requires a much broader construal than positivism accepts of the process of theoretical investigation. In particular, it requires acknowledging that a necessary part of theoretical process is critical self-examination. Time spent in analyzing emotions and uncovering their sources should be viewed, therefore, neither as irrelevant to theoretical investigation nor even as a prerequisite for it; it is not a kind of clearing of the emotional decks, 'dealing with' our emotions so that they will not influence our thinking. Instead, we must recognize that our efforts to reinterpret and refine our emotions are necessary to our theoretical investigation, just as our efforts to re-educate our emotions are necessary to our political activity. Critical reflection on emotion is not a self-indulgent substitute for political analysis and political action. It is itself a kind of political theory and political practice, indispensable for an adequate social theory and social transformation.

Finally, the recognition that emotions play a vital part in developing knowledge enlarges our understanding of women's claimed epistemic advantage. We can now see that women's subversive insights owe much to women's outlaw emotions, themselves appropriate responses to the situations of women's subordination. In addition to their propensity to experience outlaw emotions, at least on some level, women are relatively adept at identifying such emotions, in themselves and others, in part because of their social responsibility for caretaking, including emotional nurturance. It is true that women, like all subordinated peoples, especially those who must live in close proximity with their masters, often engage in emotional deception and even self-deception as the price of their survival. Even so, women may be less likely than other subordinated groups to engage in denial or suppression of outlaw emotions. Women's work of emotional nurturance has required them to develop a special acuity in recognizing hidden emotions and in understanding the genesis of those emotions. This emotional acumen can now be recognized as a skill in political analysis and validated as giving women a special advantage both in understanding the mechanisms of domination and in envisioning freer ways to live.

XII. Conclusion

The claim that emotion is vital to systematic knowledge is only the most obvious contrast between the conception of theoretical investigation that I have sketched here and the conception provided by positivism. For instance, the alternative approach emphasizes that what we identify as emotion is a conceptual abstraction from a complex process of human activity that also involves acting, sensing, and evaluating. This proposed account of theoretical construction demonstrates the simultaneous necessity for and interdependence of faculties that our culture has abstracted and separated from each other: emotion and reason, evaluation and perception, observation and action. The model of knowing suggested here is nonhierarchical and antifoundationalist; instead, it is appropriately symbolized by the radical feminist metaphor of the upward spiral. Emotions are neither more basic than observation, reason or action in building theory, nor secondary to them. Each of these human faculties reflects an aspect of human knowing inseparable from the other aspects. Thus, to borrow a famous phrase from a Marxian context, the development of each of these faculties is a necessary condition for the development of all.

In conclusion, it is interesting to note that acknowledging the importance of emotion for knowledge is not an entirely novel suggestion within the Western epistemological tradition. That archrationalist, Plato himself, came to accept in the end that knowledge required a (very purified form of) love. It may be no accident that in the *Symposium* Socrates learns this lesson from Diotima, the wise woman!

REFERENCES

Averell, James R. 1980. "The Emotions," in Ervin Staub (ed.), *Personality: Basic Aspects and Current Research.* Englewood Cliffs, NJ: Prentice Hall.

Bordo, S. R. 1987. *The Flight to Objectivity: Essays on Cartesianism and Culture.* Albany, NY: SUNY Press.

Fisher, Berenice. 1984. "Guilt and Shame in the Women's Movement: The Radical Ideal of Action and Its Meaning for Feminist Intellectuals." *Feminist Studies 10*, 185–212.

Flax, Jane. 1983. "Political Philosophy and the Patriarchal Unconscious: A Psychoanalytic Perspective on Epistemology and Metaphysics," in Sandra Harding and Merrill Hintikka (eds.), *Discovering Reality: Feminist Perspectives on Epistemology, Metaphysics, Methodology and Philosophy of Science*. Dordrecht, Holland: D. Reidel.

Goodall, Jane. 1986. *The Chimpanzees of Bombe: Patterns of Behavior*. Cambridge, MA: Harvard University Press.

Griffin, Susan. 1979. *Rape: The Power of Consciousness*. San Francisco: Harper & Row.

Hinman, Lawrence. 1986. "Emotion, Morality and Understanding." Paper presented at Annual Meeting of the Central Division of the American Philosophical Association, St. Louis, MO: May 1986.

Jaggar, Alison M. 1983. *Feminist Politics and Human Nature*. Totowa, NJ: Rowman & Allanheld/ Brighton, U.K.: Harvester Press.

Keller, E. F. 1984. *Gender and Science*. New Haven, CT: Yale University Press.

Kilpatrick, Franklin P. (ed.) 1961. *Explorations in Transactional Psychology*. New York: New York University Press.

Lakoff, George, and Kovecses, Zoltan. 1987. "The Cognitive Model of Anger Inherent in American English," in N. Quinn and D. Holland (eds.), *Cultural Models in Language and Thought*. New York: Cambridge University Press.

Lewontin, R. C. 1982. "Letter to the Editor." *New York Review of Books*, 4 February, 40–41. This letter was drawn to my attention by Alan Soble.

Lloyd, Genevieve. 1984. *The Man of Reason: 'Male' and 'Female' in Western Philosophy*. Minneapolis: University of Minnesota Press.

Lutz, Catherine. 1985. "Depression and the Translation of Emotional Worlds," in A. Kleinman and B. Good (eds.), *Culture and Depression: Studies in the Anthropology and Cross-cultural Psychiatry of Affect and Disorder*. Berkeley: University of California Press, 63–100.

Lutz, Catherine. 1986. "Emotion, Thought, and Estrangement: Emotion as a Cultural Category." *Cultural Anthropology 1*, 287–309.

Lutz, Catherine. 1987. "Goals, Events and Understanding in Ifaluk and Emotion Theory," in N. Quinn and D. Holland (eds.), *Cultural Models in Language and Thought*. New York: Cambridge University Press.

McLaughlin, Andrew. 1985. "Images and Ethics of Nature." *Environmental Ethics 7*, 293–319.

Merchant, Carolyn M. 1980. *The Death of Nature: Women, Ecology and the Scientific Revolution*. New York: Harper & Row.

Moravcsik, J. M. E. 1982. "Understanding and the Emotions," *Dialectica 36*, nos. 2–3, 207–24.

Nagel, E. 1968. "The Subjective Nature of Social Subject Matter," in May Brodbeck (ed.), *Readings in the Philosophy of the Social Sciences*. New York: Macmillan.

Quinby, Lee. 1986. Discussion following talk at Hobart and William Smith Colleges, April 1986.

Rorty, Richard. 1979. *Philosophy and the Mirror of Nature*. Princeton, NJ: Princeton University Press.

Rosaldo, Michelle Z. 1984. "Towards an Anthropology of Self and Feeling," in Richard A. Shweder and Robert A. LeVine (eds.), *Culture Theory*. Cambridge: Cambridge University Press.

Rose, Hilary. 1983. "Hand, Brain, and Heart: A Feminist Epistemology for the Natural Sciences." *Signs: Journal of Women in Culture and Society 9*, no. 1, 73–90.

Schachter, Stanley and Singer, Jerome B. 1969. "Cognitive, Social and Psychological Determinants of Emotional State." *Psychological Review 69*, 379–99.

Scheman, Naomi. 1985. "Women in the Philosophy Curriculum." Paper presented at the Annual Meeting of the Central Division of the American Philosophical Association. Chicago, April 1985.

Schott, Robin M. 1988. *Cognition and Eros: A Critique of the Kantian Paradigm*. Boston, MA: Beacon.

Spelman, E. V. 1982. "Anger and Insubordination." Manuscript; early version read to midwestern chapter of the Society for Women in Philosophy, Spring, 1982.

Wierzbicka, Anna. 1986. "Human Emotions: Universal or Culture-Specific?" *American Anthropologist 88*, 584–94.

Young, R. M. 1985. *Darwin's Metaphor: Nature's Place in Victorian Culture*. Cambridge: Cambridge University Press.

Questions for Reflection

1. In the epistemological writings of the rationalists (such as René Descartes) and the classical empiricists (such as John Locke), little mention is made of the emotions, or, if they are discussed, they are spoken of negatively. Is Jaggar correct in claiming that this is a mistake? Can the emotions play a positive role in knowledge?
2. Do you agree with her that the emotions are socially constructed and that they reflect our political and social agendas?
3. Some say that dispassionate investigation is the ideal of all rational knowing, but Jaggar says it is a "myth." What do you think?
4. Is it possible to have a balanced view of both reason and emotions, giving each their due? Or would Jaggar say that this very question implies that they can be understood separately?
5. How does the definition of philosophy as the *love* of wisdom tie into Jaggar's thesis about the emotions and the pursuit of knowledge?

CAN WE KNOW ANYTHING AT ALL?—RESPONSES TO SKEPTICISM

Right now you are reading this book and its chapter on knowledge—or are you? Isn't it possible that you are really dead asleep under your covers dreaming that you are reading a book? Even worse, isn't it at least possible that some very malicious and powerful being is messing with your mind, or, perhaps, sending electrical signals to your brain that are making you believe you are reading a book? Although this latter possibility is, admittedly, wildly implausible, the technology of virtual reality machines is getting better every day and is closing in on what was once merely fantastic science fiction. Furthermore, as we learn more about the brain, it is conceivable that someday a mad scientist could produce vivid hallucinations in a subject that could be controlled, much as we program a computer game.

With thought experiments similar to these, René Descartes set the agenda for much of modern philosophy when he raised the possibility that he could be totally deceived all the time and that nothing is as it seems. Of course, by concluding that he could be certain that he exists, Descartes believed that he had found the way out of skepticism. But for some, doubts still remain. The earlier reading by David Hume, who doubted whether we could be certain of our causal judgments and other conclusions derived from experience, illustrates the appeal of skepticism. In the next two readings, O. K. Bouwsma and John Hospers provide two different attempts to lay to rest the ghost of Descartes's skeptical doubts.

O. K. BOUWSMA

Descartes' Evil Genius

O. K. Bouwsma (1898–1978) taught at the University of Nebraska from 1928 to 1965 and at the University of Texas at Austin from 1965 to 1978. He was a student and friend of Ludwig Wittgenstein, one of the 20th century's most influential philosophers. Through his published essays and decades of teaching, Bouwsma introduced generations of philosophy students to Wittgenstein's unique style of philosophizing.

In this whimsical, fictional piece, Bouwsma imagines that there is an evil demon that is attempting to deceive a poor victim, much as Descartes feared. However, as he tells his tale, Bouwsma attempts to show that such large-scale, global deception is impossible, for deceptions and illusions can only exist and have meaning in contrast to experiences of genuinely encountering reality.

Reading Questions

1. What is the evil genius's first illusion? Why is Tom not fooled?
2. How does the evil genius go about trying to construct the perfect, undetectable illusion?
3. What does the evil genius mean by "thin illusions" and "thick illusions"? Why does Tom say that "thin illusions" mean the same thing as what he calls, simply, "illusions" and that "thick illusions" are what he means by "flowers"?
4. Bouwsma says that the illusion created by the evil genius is such that "no seeing, no touching, no smelling are relevant to detecting the illusion." Why does he think that this point is important?

There was once an evil genius who promised the mother of us all that if she ate of the fruit of the tree, she would be like God, knowing good and evil. He promised knowledge. She did eat and she learned, but she was disappointed, for to know good and evil and not to be God is awful. Many an Eve later, there was rumor of another evil genius. This evil genius promised no good, promised no knowledge. He made a boast, a boast so wild and so deep and so dark that those who heard it cringed in hearing it. And what was that boast? Well, that apart from a few, four or five, clear and distinct ideas, he could deceive any son of Adam about anything. So he boasted. And with some result? Some indeed! Men going about in the brightest noonday would look and exclaim: "How obscure!" and if some careless merchant counting his apples was heard to say: "Two and three are five," a hearer of the boast would rub his eyes and run away. This evil genius still whispers, thundering, among the leaves of books, frightening people, whispering: "I can. Maybe I will. Maybe so, maybe not." The tantalizer! In what follows I should like to examine the boast of this evil genius.

O. K. Bouwsma, "Descartes' Evil Genius," in *Philosophical Essays* (Lincoln, NE: University of Nebraska Press, 1965).

I am referring, of course, to that evil genius of whom Descartes writes:

> I shall then suppose, not that God who is supremely good and the fountain of truth, but some evil genius not less powerful than deceitful, has employed his whole energies in deceiving me; I shall consider that the heavens, the earth, the colors, figures, sound, and all other external things are nought but illusions and dreams of which this evil genius has availed himself, in order to lay traps for my credulity; I shall consider myself as having no hands, no eyes, no flesh, no blood, nor any senses, yet falsely believing myself to possess all these things.

This then is the evil genius whom I have represented as boasting that he can deceive us about all these things. I intend now to examine this boast, and to understand how this deceiving and being deceived are to take place. I expect to discover that the evil genius may very well deceive us, but that if we are wary, we need not be deceived. He will deceive us, if he does, by bathing the word "illusion" in a fog. This then will be the word to keep our minds on. In order to accomplish all this, I intend to describe the evil genius carrying out his boast in two adventures. The first of these I shall consider a thoroughly transparent case of deception. The word "illusion" will find a clear and familiar application. Nevertheless in this instance the evil genius will not have exhausted "his whole energies in deceiving us." Hence we must aim to imagine a further trial of the boast, in which the "whole energies" of the evil genius are exhausted. In this instance I intend to show that the evil genius is himself befuddled, and that if we too exhaust some of our energies in sleuthing after the peculiarities in his diction, then we need not be deceived either.

Let us imagine the evil genius then at his ease meditating that very bad is good enough for him, and that he would let bad enough alone. All the old pseudos, pseudo names and pseudo statements, are doing very well. But today it was different. He took no delight in common lies, everyday fibs, little ones, old ones. He wanted something new and something big. He scratched his genius;

he uncovered an idea. And he scribbled on the inside of his tattered halo, "Tomorrow, I will deceive," and he smiled, and his words were thin and like fine wire. "Tomorrow I will change everything, everything, everything. I will change flowers, human beings, trees, hills, sky, the sun, and everything else into paper. Paper alone I will not change. There will be paper flowers, paper human beings, paper trees. And human beings will be deceived. They will think that there are flowers, human beings, and trees, and there will be nothing but paper. It will be gigantic. And it ought to work. After all men have been deceived with much less trouble. There was a sailor, a Baptist I believe, who said that all was water. And there was no more water then than there is now. And there was a poolhall keeper who said that all was billiard balls. That's a long time ago of course, a long time before they opened one, and listening, heard that it was full of the sound of a trumpet. My prospects are good. I'll try it."

And the evil genius followed his own directions and did according to his words. And this is what happened.

Imagine a young man, Tom, bright today as he was yesterday, approaching a table where yesterday he had seen a bowl of flowers. Today it suddenly strikes him that they are not flowers. He stares at them troubled, looks away, and looks again. Are they flowers? He shakes his head. He chuckles to himself. "Huh! that's funny. Is this a trick? Yesterday there certainly were flowers in that bowl." He sniffs suspiciously, hopefully, but smells nothing. His nose gives no assurance. He thinks of the birds that flew down to peck at the grapes in the picture and of the mare that whinnied at the likeness of Alexander's horse. Illusions! The picture oozed no juice, and the likeness was still. He walked slowly to the bowl of flowers. He looked, and he sniffed, and he raised his hand. He stroked a petal lightly, lover of flowers, and he drew back. He could scarcely believe his fingers. They were not flowers. They were paper.

As he stands, perplexed, Milly, friend and dear, enters the room. Seeing him occupied with the flowers, she is about to take up the bowl and offer them to him, when once again he is overcome with feelings of strangeness. She looks just like a great big doll. He looks more closely, closely as he dares, seeing this may be Milly after all. Milly, are you Milly?—that wouldn't do. Her mouth clicks as she opens it, speaking, and it shuts precisely. Her forehead shines, and he shudders at the thought of Mme Tussaud's. Her hair is plaited, evenly, perfectly, like Milly's but as she raises one hand to guard its order, touching it, preening, it whispers like a newspaper. Her teeth are white as a genteel monthly. Her gums are pink, and there is a clapper in her mouth. He thinks of mama dolls, and of the rubber doll he used to pinch; it had a misplaced navel right in the pit of the back, that whistled. Galatea in paper! Illusions!

He noted all these details, flash by flash by flash. He reaches for a chair to steady himself and just in time. She approaches with the bowl of flowers, and, as the bowl is extended towards him, her arms jerk. The suppleness, the smoothness, the roundness of life is gone. Twitches of a smile mislight up her face. He extends his hand to take up the bowl and his own arms jerk as hers did before. He takes the bowl, and as he does so sees his hand. It is pale, fresh, snowy. Trembling, he drops the bowl, but it does not break, and the water does not run. What a mockery!

He rushes to the window, hoping to see the real world. The scene is like a theatre-set. Even the pane in the window is drawn very thin, like cellophane. In the distance are the forms of men walking about and tossing trees and houses and boulders and hills upon the thin cross section of a truck that echoes only echoes of chugs as it moves. He looks into the sky upward, and it is low. There is a patch straight above him, and one seam is loose. The sun shines out of the blue like a drop of German silver. He reaches out with his pale hand, crackling the cellophane, and his hand touches the sky. The sky shakes and tiny bits of it fall, flaking his white hand with confetti.

Make-believe!

He retreats, crinkling, creaking, hiding his sight. As he moves he misquotes a line of poetry: "Those are perils that were his eyes," and he mutters, "Hypocritical pulp!" He goes on: "I see that the heavens, the earth, colors, figures, sound, and all other external things, flowers, Milly, trees and rocks and hills are paper, paper laid as traps for my credulity. Paper flowers, paper Milly, paper sky!" Then he paused, and in sudden fright he asked "And what about me?" He reaches to his lip and with two fingers tears the skin and peels off a strip of newsprint. He looks at it closely, grim. "I shall consider myself as having no hands, no eyes, no flesh, no blood, or any senses." He lids his paper eyes and stands dejected. Suddenly he is cheered. He exclaims: "*Cogito me papyrum esse, ergo sum.*" He has triumphed over paperdom.

I have indulged in this phantasy in order to illustrate the sort of situation which Descartes' words might be expected to describe. The evil genius attempts to deceive. He tries to mislead Tom into thinking what is not. Tom is to think that these are flowers, that this is the Milly that was, that those are trees, hills, the heavens, etc. And he does this by creating illusions, that is, by making something that looks like flowers, artificial flowers; by making something that looks like and sounds like and moves like Milly, an artificial Milly. An illusion is something that looks like or sounds like, so much like, something else that you either mistake it for something else, or you can easily understand how someone might come to do this. So when the evil genius creates illusions intending to deceive he makes things which might quite easily be mistaken for what they are not. Now in the phantasy as I discovered it Tom is not deceived. He does experience the illusion, however. The intention of this is not to cast any reflection upon the deceptive powers of the evil genius. With such refinements in the paper art as we now know, the evil genius might very well have been less unsuccessful. And that in spite of his rumored lament: "And I made her of the best paper!" No, that Tom is not deceived, that he detects the illusion, is introduced in order to remind ourselves how illusions are detected. That the paper flowers are illusory is revealed by the recognition that they are paper. As soon as Tom realizes that though they look like flowers but are paper, he is acquainted with, sees through the illusion, and is not deceived. What is required, of course, is that he know the difference between flowers and paper, and that when presented with one or the other he can tell the difference. The attempt of the evil genius also presupposes this. What he intends is that though Tom knows this difference, the paper will look so much like flowers that Tom will not notice the respect in which the paper is different from the flowers. And even though Tom had actually been deceived and had not recognized the illusion, the evil genius himself must have been aware of the difference, for this is involved in his design. This is crucial, as we shall see when we come to consider the second adventure of the evil genius.

As you will remember I have represented the foregoing as an illustration of the sort of situation which Descartes' words might be expected to describe. Now, however, I think that this is misleading. For though I have described a situation in which there are many things, nearly all of which are calculated to serve as illusions, this question may still arise. Would this paper world still be properly described as a world of illusions? If Tom says: "These are flowers," or "These look like flowers" (uncertainly), then the illusion is operative. But if Tom says: "These are paper," then the illusion has been destroyed. Descartes uses the words: "And all other external things are nought but illusions." This means that the situation which Descartes has in mind is such that if Tom says: "These are flowers," he will be wrong, but he will be wrong also if he says: "These are paper," and it won't matter what sentence of that type he uses. If he says: "These are rock"—or cotton or cloud or wood—he is wrong by the plan. He will be right only if he says: "These are illusions." But the project is to keep him from recognizing the illusions. This means that the illusions are to be brought about not by anything so crude as paper or even cloud. They must be made of the stuff that dreams are made of.

Now let us consider this second adventure.

The design then is this. The evil genius is to create a world of illusions. There are to be no flowers, no Milly, no paper. There is to be nothing at all, but Tom is every moment to go on mistaking nothing for something, nothing at all for flowers, nothing at all for Milly, etc. This is, of course, quite different from mistaking paper for flowers, paper for Milly. And yet all is to be arranged in such a way that Tom will go on just as we now do, and just as Tom did before the paper age, to see, hear, smell the world. He will love the flowers, he will kiss Milly, he will blink at the sun. So he thinks. And in thinking about these things he will talk and argue just as we do. But all the time he will be mistaken. There are no flowers, there is no kiss, there is no sun. Illusions all. This then is the end at which the evil genius aims.

How now is the evil genius to attain this end? Well, it is clear that a part of what he aims at will be realized if he destroys everything. Then there will be no flowers, and if Tom thinks that there are flowers he will be wrong. There will be no face that is Milly's and no tumbled beauty on her head, and if Tom thinks that there is Milly's face and Milly's hair, he will be wrong. It is necessary then to see to it that there are none of these things. So the evil genius, having failed with paper, destroys even all paper. Now there is nothing to see, nothing to hear, nothing to smell, etc. But this is not enough to deceive. For though Tom sees nothing, and neither hears nor smells anything, he may also think that he sees nothing. He must also be misled into thinking that he does see something, that there are flowers and Milly, and hands, eyes, flesh, blood, and all other senses. Accordingly the evil genius restores to Tom his old life. Even the memory of that paper day is blotted out, not a scrap remains. Witless Tom lives on, thinking, hoping, loving as he used to, unwitted by the great destroyer. All that seems so solid, so touchable to seeming hands, so biteable to apparent teeth, is so flimsy that were the evil genius to poke his index at it, it would curl away save for one tiny trace, the smirch of that index. So once more the evil genius has done according to his word.

And now let us examine the result.

I should like first of all to describe a passage of Tom's life. Tom is all alone, but he doesn't know it. What an opportunity for methodologico-metaphysico-solipsimo! I intend, in any case, to disregard the niceties of his being so alone and to borrow his own words, with the warning that the evil genius smiles as he reads them. Tom writes:

Today, as usual, I came into the room and there was the bowl of flowers on the table. I went up to them, caressed them, and smelled over them. I thank God for flowers! There's nothing so real to me as flowers. Here the genuine essence of the world's substance, at its gayest and most hilarious speaks to me. It seems unworthy even to think of them as erect, and waving on pillars of sap. Sap! Sap!

There was more in the same vein, which we need not bother to record. I might say that the evil genius was a bit amused, snickered in fact, as he read the words "so real," "essence," "substance," etc., but later he frowned and seemed puzzled. Tom went on to describe how Milly came into the room, and how glad he was to see her. They talked about the flowers. Later he walked to the window and watched the gardener clearing a space a short distance away. The sun was shining, but there were a few heavy clouds. He raised the window, extended his hand and four large drops of rain wetted his hand. he returned to the room and quoted to Milly a song from *The Tempest*. He got all the words right, and was well pleased with himself. There were more he wrote, but this was enough to show how quite normal everything seems. And, too, how successful the evil genius is.

And the evil genius said to himself, not quite in solipsimo, "Not so, not so, not at all so."

The evil genius was, however, all too human. Admiring himself but unadmired, he yearned for admiration. To deceive but to be unsuspected in too little glory. The evil genius set about then to plant the seeds of suspicion. But how to do this? Clearly there was no suggestive paper to tempt Tom's confidence. There was nothing but Tom's mind, a stream of seemings and of words to make the seemings seem no seemings. The evil genius must have words with Tom and must engage the same seemings with him. To have words with Tom is to have the words together, to use them in the same way, and to engage the same seemings is to see and to hear and to point to the same. And so the evil genius, free spirit, entered in at the door of Tom's pineal gland and lodged there. He floated in the humors that flow, glandwise and sensewise, everywhere being as much one with Tom as difference will allow. He looked out of the same eyes, and

when Tom pointed with his finger, the evil genius said "This" and meant what Tom, hearing, also meant, seeing. Each heard with the same ear what the other heard. For every sniffing of the one nose there were two identical smells, and there were two tactualities for every touch. If Tom had had a toothache, together they would have pulled the same face. The twinsomeness of two monads finds here the limit of identity. Nevertheless there was otherness looking out of those eyes as we shall see.

It seems then that on the next day, the evil genius "going to and fro" in Tom's mind and "walking up and down in it," Tom once again, as his custom was, entered the room where the flowers stood on the table. He stopped, looked admiringly, and in a caressing voice said: "Flowers! Flowers!" And he lingered. The evil genius, more subtle "than all the beasts of the field," whispered "Flowers? Flowers?" For the first time Tom has an intimation of company, of some intimate partner in perception. Momentarily he is checked. He looks again at the flowers. "Flowers? Why, of course, flowers." Together they look out of the same eyes. Again the evil genius whispers, "Flowers?" The seed of suspicion is to be the question. But Tom now raises the flowers nearer to his eyes almost violently as though his eyes were not his own. He is, however, not perturbed. The evil genius only shakes their head. "Did you ever hear of illusions?" says he.

Tom, still surprisingly good-natured, responds: "But you saw them, didn't you? Surely you can see through my eyes. Come, let us bury my nose deep in these blossoms, and take one long breath together. Then tell whether you can recognize these as flowers."

So they dunked the one nose. But the evil genius said "Huh!" as much as to say: What has all this seeming and smelling to do with it? Still he explained nothing. And Tom remained as confident of the flowers as he had been at the first. The little seeds of doubt, "Flowers? Flowers?" and again "Flowers?" and "Illusions?" and now this stick in the spokes, "Huh!" made Tom uneasy. He went on: "Oh, so you are one of these seers that has to touch everything. You're a tangibilite. Very well, here's my hand, let's finger these flowers. Careful! They're tender."

The evil genius was amused. He smiled inwardly and rippled in a shallow humor. To be taken for a materialist! As though the grand illusionist was not a spirit! Nevertheless, he realized that though deception is easy where the lies are big enough (where had he heard that before?), a few scattered, questioning words are not enough to make guile grow. He was tempted to make a statement, and he did. He said, "Your flowers are nothing but illusions."

"My flowers illusions?" exclaimed Tom, and he took up the bowl and placed it before a mirror. "See," said he, "here are the flowers and here, in the mirror, is an illusion. There's a difference surely. And you with my eyes, my nose, and my fingers can tell what that difference is. Pollen on your fingers touching the illusion? send Milly the flowers in the mirror? Set a bee to suck honey out of this glass? You know all this as well as I do. I can tell flowers from illusions, and my flowers, as you now plainly see, are not illusions."

The evil genius was now sorely tried. He had his make-believe, but he also had his pride. Would he now risk the make-believe to save his pride? Would he explain? He explained.

"Tom," he said, "notice. The flowers in the mirror look like flowers, but they only look like flowers. We agree about that. The flowers before the mirror also look like flowers. But they, you say, are flowers because they also smell like flowers and they feel like flowers, as though they would be any more flowers because they also like flowers multiply. Imagine a mirror such that it reflected not only the looks of flowers, but also their fragrance and their petal surfaces, and then you smelled and touched, and the flowers before the mirror would be just like the flowers in the mirror. Then you could see immediately that the flowers before the mirror are illusions just as those in the mirror are illusions. As it is now, it is clear that the flowers in the mirror are thin illusions, and the flowers before the mirror are thick. Thick illusions are the best for deception. And they may be as thick as you like. From them you may gather pollen, send them to Milly, and foolish bees may sleep in them."

But Tom was not asleep. "I see that what you mean by thin illusions is what I mean by illusions, and what you mean by thick illusions is what I mean by flowers. So when you say that my flowers are your thick illusions this doesn't bother me. And as for your mirror that mirrors all layers of your thick illusions, I shouldn't call that a mirror at all. It's a duplicator, and much more useful than a mirror, provided you can control it. But I do suppose that when you speak of thick illusions you do mean that thick illusions are related to something you call flowers in much the same way that the thin illusions are related to the thick ones. Is that true?"

The evil genius was now diction-deep in explanations and went on. "In the first place let me assure you that these are not flowers. I destroyed all flowers. There are no flowers at all. There are only thin and thick illusions of flowers. I can see your flowers in the mirror, and I can smell and touch the flowers before the mirror. What I cannot smell and touch, having seen as in the mirror, is not even thick illusion. But if I cannot also *cerpicio* what I see, smell, touch, etc., what I have then seen is not anything real. *Esse est cerpici.* I just now tried to *cerpicio* your flowers, but there was nothing there. Man is after all a four- or five- or six-sense creature and you cannot expect much from so little."

Tom rubbed his eyes and his ears tingled with an eighteenth-century disturbance. Then he stared at the flowers. "I see," he said, "that this added sense of yours has done wickedly with our language. You do not mean by illusion what we mean, and neither do you mean by flowers what we mean. As for *cerpicio* I wouldn't be surprised if you'd made up that word just to puzzle us. In any case what you destroyed is what, according to you, you used to *cerpicio*. So there is nothing for you to *cerpicio* any more. But there still are what we mean by flowers. If your intention was to deceive, you must learn the language of those you are to deceive. I should say that you are like the doctor who prescribes for his patients what is so bad for himself and is then surprised at the health of his patients." And he pinned a flower near their nose.

The evil genius, discomfited, rode off on a corpuscle. He had failed. He took to an artery, made haste to the pineal exit, and was gone. Then "sun by sun" he fell. And he regretted his mischief.

I have tried in this essay to understand the boast of the evil genius. His boast was that he could deceive, deceive about "the heavens, the earth, the colors, figures, sound, and all other external things." In order to do this I have tried to bring clearly to mind what deception and such deceiving would be like. Such deception involves illusions and such deceiving involves the creation of illusions. Accordingly I have tried to imagine the evil genius engaged in the practice of deception, busy in the creation of illusions. In the first adventure everything is plain. The evil genius employs paper, paper making believe it's many other things. The effort to deceive, ingenuity in deception, being deceived by paper, detecting the illusion—all these are clearly understood. It is the second adventure, however, which is more crucial. For in this instance it is assumed that the illusion is of such a kind that no seeing, no touching, no smelling, are relevant to detecting the illusion. Nevertheless the evil genius sees, touches, smells, and does detect the illusion. He made the illusion; so, of course, he must know it. How then does he know it? The evil genius has a sense denied to men. He senses the flower-in-itself, Milly-in-her-self, etc. So he creates illusions made up of what can be seen, heard, smelled, etc., illusions all because when seeing, hearing, and smelling have seen, heard, and smelled all, the special sense senses nothing. So what poor human beings sense is the illusion of what only the evil genius can sense. This is formidable. Nevertheless, once again everything is clear. If we admit the special sense, then we can readily see how it is that the evil genius should have been so confident. He has certainly created his own illusions, though he has not himself been deceived. But neither has anyone else been deceived. For human beings do not use the word "illusion" by relation to a sense with which only the evil genius is blessed.

I said that the evil genius had not been deceived, and it is true that he has not been deceived by his own illusions. Nevertheless he was deceived in boasting that he could deceive, for his confidence in this is based upon an ignorance of the difference between our uses of the words, "heavens," "earth," "flowers," "Milly," and "illusions" of these things, and his own uses of these words. For though there certainly is an analogy between our own uses and his, the difference is quite sufficient to explain his failure at grand deception. We can also understand how easily Tom might have been taken in. The dog over the water dropped his meaty bone for a picture on the water. Tom, however, dropped nothing at all. But the word "illusion" is a trap.

I began this essay uneasily, looking at my hands and saying "no hands," blinking my eyes and saying "no eyes." Everything I saw seemed to me like something Cheshire, a piece of cheese, for instance, appearing and disappearing in the leaves of the tree. Poor kitty! And now? Well. . . .

Questions for Reflection

1. Is it possible for *every* dollar bill to be counterfeit? Why is it that there can be counterfeits only if there is the real thing? Likewise, is it possible for every experience to be an illusion? What would this mean?

2. The illusion in this story is such that it is only meaningful to the special sensory powers of the evil genius. Hence, there is no distinction between what he calls illusory flowers and what Tom calls real flowers. So, from our human standpoint, is it meaningful to refer to it as an illusion at all?

3. When the evil genius uses "thin illusions" to refer to the image of flowers in the mirror and "thick illusions" to refer to the flowers that Tom sees, smells, and touches, is the evil genius using the term *illusion* in a meaningful sense?

4. Has Bouwsma convinced you that Descartes's doubts rest on an impossible supposition?

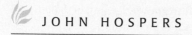

JOHN HOSPERS

An Argument Against Skepticism

John Hospers (1918–   ) is an emeritus professor of philosophy at the University of Southern California. He was one of the founders of the Libertarian Party and was that party's candidate for president of the United States in 1972. Hospers is well known for his work in aesthetics and ethics as well as for his classic book, *Introduction to Philosophical Analysis,* from which the following selection is taken.

   In the section preceding the following excerpt, Hospers describes three kinds of knowledge. First, there is *acquaintance knowledge.* For example, we say "I know Richard Smith" or "I know the sound of Mary's voice." This type of knowledge requires some sort of direct experience. Second, there is *knowing how.* This refers to a skill, as in "I know how to use a computer." Finally, there is *propositional knowledge.* This type of knowledge can be expressed by saying "I know that . . ." where the sentence is completed by a proposition. For example, we say, "I know that the capitol of the United States is Washington D. C." Our reading begins with Hospers's analysis of this third kind of knowledge.

Reading Questions

1. What are the three conditions for having propositional knowledge?
2. Why can we not be said to know something if we simply have a true belief?
3. What does Hospers mean by the weak and strong senses of "know"?
4. Why does Hospers think there is a point at which the skeptic's doubts become meaningless?

THREE CONDITIONS OF KNOWLEDGE

Now, what is required for us to know in this third and most important sense? Taking the letter "p" to stand for any proposition, what requirements must be met in order for one to assert truly that he knows p? There are, after all, many people who claim to know something when they don't; so how can one separate the rightful claims to know from the mistaken ones?

   a. *p must be true.* The moment you have some reason to believe that a proposition is not true, this im-

mediately negates a person's claim to know it: you can't know p if p isn't true. If I say, "I know p, but p is not true," my statement is self-contradictory, for part of what is involved in knowing p is that p is true. Similarly, if I say, "He knows p, but p is not true," this too is self-contradictory. It may be that I *thought* I knew p; but if p is false, I didn't really know it. I only thought I did. If I nevertheless claim to know p, while admitting that p is false, my hearers may rightly conclude that I have not yet learned how to use the word "know." This is already implicit in our previous discussion, for what is it that you

From John Hospers, *An Introduction to Philosophical Analysis,* 2nd ed. (Englewood Cliffs, NJ: Prentice-Hall, 1967).

know about *p* when you know *p*? You know that *p is true*, of course; the very formulation gives away the case: knowing *p* is knowing that *p* is true. . . .

But the truth-requirement, though necessary, is not sufficient. There are plenty of true propositions, for example in nuclear physics, that you and I do not know to be true unless we happen to be specialists in that area. But the fact that they are true does not imply that we know them to be true. And there are plenty of true statements we could make about the flora and fauna on the ocean floor if we were in a position to go there and observe for ourselves; but at the moment, though many statements we might make about them could well be true, we are not in a position to *know* that they are true. What more, then, is required?

b. *Not only must p be true: we must believe that p is true.* This may be called the "subjective requirement": we must have a certain attitude toward *p*— not merely that of wondering or speculating about *p*, but positively *believing* that *p* is true. "I know that *p* is true, but I don't believe that it is" would not only be a very peculiar thing to say, it would entitle our hearers to conclude that we had not learned in what circumstances to use the word "know." There may be numerous statements that you believe but do not know to be true, but there can be none which you know to be true but don't believe, since believing is a part (a defining characteristic) of knowing.

"I know *p*" implies "I believe *p*," and "He knows *p*" implies "He believes *p*," for believing is a defining characteristic of knowing. But believing *p* is *not* a defining characteristic of *p's being true: p* can be true even though neither he nor I nor anyone else believes it. (The earth was round even before anyone believed that it was.) There is no contradiction whatever in saying "He believed *p* (that is, believed it to be true), but *p* is not true." Indeed, we say things of this kind all the time: "He believes that people are persecuting him, but of course it isn't true.". . .

We have now discussed two requirements for knowing, an "objective" one (*p* must be true) and a "subjective" one (one must believe *p*). Are these sufficient? Can you be said to know something if you believe it and if what you believe is true? If so,

we can simply define knowledge as true belief, and that will be the end of the matter.

Unfortunately, however, the situation is not so simple. True belief is not yet knowledge. A proposition may be true, and you may believe it to be true, and yet you may not *know* it to be true. Suppose you believe that there are sentient beings on Mars, and suppose that in the course of time, after space-travelers from the earth have landed there, your belief turns out to be true. The statement was true at the time you uttered it, and you also believed it at the time you uttered it—but did you *know* it to be true at the time you uttered it? Certainly not, we would be inclined to say; you were not in a position to know. It was a lucky guess. Even if you had *some* evidence that it was true, you didn't *know* that it was true at the time you said it. Some further condition, therefore, is required to prevent a lucky guess from passing as knowledge. . . .

We would have suspected in any case that "knowledge is true belief" is not enough. Consider some matter that no one yet knows anything about, such as whether there are planets circling around some distant star; consider, in fact, a thousand such stars. Or consider whether the next hundred tosses of a coin will turn up heads or tails. You might guess "heads" for them all, and let us suppose that 50 per cent of the time you guess correctly. Now, if you are the kind of person who quickly believes everything he says, you might actually believe you will be right all those times. But surely you did not *know* whether it would be heads or tails during that 50 percent of the time you were right, no matter how strongly you believed it. One's knowledge is not greater merely because one has a greater confidence in one's own beliefs than other people do. It depends not on how firmly you believe but on what *grounds*, what *reason*, you have, for believing it. This brings us to our third condition.

c. *You must have evidence for p (reason to believe p).* When you guessed which tosses of the coin would be heads, you had no reason to believe that your guesses would be correct, so you did not *know*. But after you watched all the tosses and carefully observed which way the coin tossed each time, then you knew. You had the evidence of your senses—as well as of people around you, and photographs if you wished to take them—that this throw was heads, that one tails, and so on. Similarly, when you predict on the basis of tonight's red sunset that tomorrow's weather will be fair, you don't yet *know* that your prediction will be borne out by the facts; you have some reason (perhaps) to believe it, but you cannot be sure. But tomorrow when you go outdoors and see for yourself what the weather is like, you do know for sure; when tomorrow comes you have the full evidence before you, which you do not yet have tonight. Tomorrow "the evidence is in"; tonight, it is not knowledge but only an "educated guess."

This, then, is our third requirement—evidence. But at this point our troubles begin. How much evidence must there be? "Some evidence" won't suffice as an answer: there may be some evidence that tomorrow will be sunny, but you don't yet know it. How about "all the evidence that is available"? But this won't do either; all the evidence that is now available may not be enough. All the evidence that is now available is far from sufficient to enable us to know whether there are conscious beings on other planets. We just don't know, even after we have examined all the evidence at our disposal.

How about "enough evidence to give us *good reason* to believe it"? But how much evidence is this? I may have known someone for years and found him to be scrupulously honest during all that time; by virtually any criterion, this would constitute good evidence that he will be honest the next time—and yet he may not be; suppose that the next time he steals someone's wallet. I had good reason to believe that he would remain honest, but nevertheless I didn't *know* that he would remain honest, for it was not true. We are all familiar with cases in which someone had good reason to believe a proposition that nevertheless turned out to be false.

What then *is* sufficient? We are now tempted to say "Complete evidence—all the evidence there could ever be—the works, everything." But if we say this, let us notice at once that there are very few propositions whose truth we can claim to know. Most of those propositions that in daily life we claim to know without the slightest hesitation we would *not* know according to this criterion. For example, we say "I know that if I were to let go of this pencil, it would fall," and we don't have the slight-

est hesitation about it; but although we may have excellent evidence (pencils and other objects have always fallen when let go), we don't have *complete* evidence, for we have not yet observed the outcome of letting go of it *this* time. To take an even more obvious case, we say "I know that there is a book before me now," but we have not engaged in every possible observation that would be relevant to determining the truth of this statement: we have not examined the object (the one we take to be a book) from *all* angles (and since there are an infinite number of angles, who could?), and even if we have looked at it steadily for half an hour, we have not done so for a hundred hours, or a million; and yet it would *seem* (though some have disputed this, as we shall see) that if one observation provides evidence, a thousand observations should provide more evidence—and when could the accumulation of evidence end? . . .

We might, nevertheless, stick to our definition and say that we really do *not* know most of the propositions that in daily life we claim to know: perhaps I don't *know* that this is a book before me, that I am now indoors and not outdoors, that I am now reading sentences written in the English language, or that there are any other people in the world. But this is a rather astounding claim and needs to be justified. We are all convinced that we know these things: we act on them every day of our lives, and if we were asked outside a philosophy classroom whether we knew them, we would say "yes" without hesitation. Surely we cannot accept a definition of "know" that would practically define knowledge out of existence? But if not, what alternative have we?

"Perhaps we don't have to go so far as to say '*all* the evidence,' '*complete* evidence,' and so on. All we have to say is that we must have *adequate* evidence." But when is the evidence adequate? Is anything less than "all the evidence there could ever be" adequate? "Well, adequate for enabling us to know." But this little addition to our definition lands us in a circle. We are trying to define "know," and we cannot in doing so employ the convenient phrase "enough to enable us to know"—for the last word in this definition is the very one we are trying to define. But once we have dropped the phrase "to know," we are left with our problem once more: how much evidence is adequate evidence? Is it adequate when anything less than *all* the evidence is in? If not all the evidence is in, but only 99.99 percent of it, couldn't that .01 per cent go contrary to the rest of it and require us to conclude that the proposition might not be true after all, and that therefore we didn't know it? Surely it has happened often enough that a statement that we thought we knew, perhaps even would have staked our lives on, turned out in the end to be false, or just doubtful. But in that case, we didn't really *know* it after all: the evidence was good, even overwhelming, but yet not good enough, not really adequate, for it was not enough to guarantee the truth of the proposition. Can we know *p* with anything less than *all* the evidence there ever could be for *p*?

STRONG AND WEAK SENSES OF "KNOW"

In daily life we say we know—not just believe or surmise, but *know*—that heavier-than-air objects fall, that snow is white, that we can read and write, and countless other things. If someone denies this, and no fact cited by the one disputant suffices to convince the other, we may well suspect that there is a verbal issue involved: in this case, that they are operating on two different meanings of "know," because they construe the third requirement—the evidence requirement—differently.

Suppose I say, "There is a bookcase in my office," and someone challenges this assertion. I reply, "I *know* that there is a bookcase in my office. I put it there myself, and I've seen it there for years. In fact, I saw it there just two minutes ago when I took a book out of it and left the office to go into the classroom." Now suppose we both go to my office, take a look, and there is the bookcase, exactly as before. "See, I *knew* it was there," I say. "Oh no," he replies, "you *believed with good reason* that it was still there, because you had seen it there often before and you didn't see or hear anyone removing it. But you didn't *know* it was there when you said it, for at that moment you were in the classroom and not in your office."

At this point, I may reply, "But I did know it was there, even when I said it. I knew it because *(1) I believed it, (2) I had good grounds on which to base the belief, and (3) the belief was true.* And I would call it knowledge whenever these three conditions are fulfilled. This is the way we use the word 'know' every day of our lives. One knows those true propositions that one believes with good reason. And when I said the bookcase was still in my office, I was uttering one of those propositions."

But now my opponent may reply, "But you still didn't know it. You had good reason to say it, I admit, for you had not seen or heard anyone removing it. You had good reason, but not *sufficient* reason. The evidence you gave was still compatible with your statement being false—and if it was false, you of course did not *know* that it was true. Suppose that you had made your claim to knowledge, and I had denied your claim, and we had both gone into your office, and to your great surprise (and mine too) the bookcase was no longer there. Could you *then* have claimed to know that it was still there?"

"Of course not. The falsity of a statement always invalidates the claim to know it. If the bookcase had not been there, I would not have been entitled to say that I knew it was there; my claim would have been mistaken."

"Right—it would have been mistaken. But now please note that the only difference between the two cases is that in the first case the bookcase was there and in the second case it wasn't. *The evidence in the two cases was exactly the same.* You had exactly the same reason for saying that the bookcase was still there in the *second* case (when we found it missing) that you did in the *first* case (when we found it still there). And since you—as you yourself admit—didn't know it in the second case, you couldn't have known it in the first case either. You believed it with good reason, but you didn't *know* it."

Here my opponent may have scored an important point; he may have convinced me that since I admittedly didn't know in the second case I couldn't have known in the first case either. But here I may make an important point in return: "My belief was the same in the two cases; the evidence was the same in the two cases (I had seen the bookcase two minutes before, had heard or seen no one removing it). The only difference was that in the first case the bookcase was there and in the second case it wasn't (*p* was true in the first case, false in the second). But *this doesn't show that I didn't know* in the first case. What it does show is that *although I might have been mistaken, I wasn't mistaken.* Had the bookcase not been there, I couldn't have claimed to know that it was; but since the bookcase in fact *was* still there, I *did* know, although (on the basis of the evidence I had) I *might* have been mistaken."

"Yes, it turned out to be true—you were lucky. But as we both agree, a lucky guess isn't the same as knowledge."

"But this wasn't just a lucky guess. I had excellent reasons for believing that the bookcase was still there. So the evidence requirement was fulfilled."

"No, it wasn't. You had good reason, excellent reason, but not *sufficient* reason—both times—for believing that the bookcase was still there. But in the second case it wasn't there, so you didn't know; therefore, in the first case, where your evidence was *exactly the same,* you didn't know either; you just believed it with good reason, but that wasn't enough: your reason wasn't sufficient, and so you didn't *know.*"

Now the difference in the criterion of knowing between the two disputants begins to emerge. According to me, I did know *p* in the first case because my belief was based on excellent evidence and was also true. According to my opponent, I did not know *p* in the first case because my evidence was still less than complete—I wasn't in the room seeing or touching the bookcase when I made the statement. It seems, then, that I am operating with a less demanding definition of "know" than he is. I am using "know" in the *weak* sense, in which I know a proposition when I believe it, have good reason for believing it, and it is true. But he is using "know" in a more demanding sense: he is using it in the *strong* sense, which requires that in order to know a proposition, it must be true, I must believe it, and I must have absolutely *conclusive* evidence in favor of it.

Let us contrast these two cases:

Suppose that after a routine medical examination the excited doctor reports to me that the X-ray photographs show that I have no heart. I should tell him to get a new machine. I should be inclined to say that the fact that I have a heart is one of the few things that I can count on as absolutely certain. I can feel it beat. I know it's there. Furthermore, how could my blood circulate if I didn't have one? Suppose that later on I suffer a chest injury and undergo a surgical operation. Afterwards the astonished surgeons solemnly declare that they searched my chest cavity and found no heart, and that they made incisions and looked about in other likely places but found it not. They are convinced that I am without a heart. They are unable to understand how circulation can occur or what accounts for the thumping in my chest. But they are in agreement and obviously sincere, and they have clear photographs of my interior spaces. What would be my attitude? Would it be to insist that they were all mistaken? I think not. I believe that I should eventually accept their testimony and the evidence of the photographs. I should consider to be false what I now regard as an absolute certainty. [When I say I know I have a heart, I know it in the weak sense.]

Suppose that as I write this paper someone in the next room were to call out to me, "I can't find an ink-bottle; is there one in the house?" I should reply, "Here is an ink-bottle." If he said in a doubtful tone, "Are you sure? I looked there before," I should reply, "Yes, I know there is; come and get it."

Now could it turn out to be false that there is an ink-bottle directly in front of me on this desk? Many philosophers have thought so. They would say that many things could happen of such a nature that if they did happen it would be proved that I am deceived. I agree that many extraordinary things could happen, in the sense that there is no logical absurdity in the supposition. It could happen that when I next reach for this ink-bottle my hand should seem to pass *through* it and I should not feel the contact of any object. It could happen that in the next moment the ink-bottle will suddenly vanish from sight; or that I should find myself under a tree in the garden with no ink-bottle about; or that one or more persons should enter this room and declare with apparent sincerity that they see no ink-bottle on this desk; or that a photograph taken now of the top of the desk should clearly show all of the objects on it except the ink-bottle. Having admitted that these things *could happen,* am I compelled to admit that if they did happen, then it would be proved that there is no ink-bottle here *now*? Not at all. I could say that when my hand seemed to pass through the ink-bottle I should *then* be suffering from hallucination; that if the ink-bottle suddenly vanished, it would have miraculously ceased to exist; that the other persons were conspiring to drive me mad, or were themselves victims of remarkable concurrent hallucinations; that the camera possessed some strange flaw or that there was trickery in developing the negative: . . . Not only do I not *have* to admit that those extraordinary occurrences would be evidence that there is no ink-bottle here; the fact is that I *do not* admit it. There is nothing whatever that could happen in the next moment or the next year that would by me be called *evidence* that there is not an ink-bottle here now. No future experience or investigation could prove to me that I am mistaken. Therefore, if I were to say, "I know that there is an ink-bottle here," I should be using "know" in the strong sense.[1]

It is in the weak sense that we use the word "know" in daily life, as when I say I know that I have a heart, that if I let go this piece of chalk it will fall, that the sun will rise tomorrow, and so on. I have excellent reason (evidence) to believe all these things, evidence so strong that (so we say) it amounts to certainty. And yet there are events that could conceivably occur which, if they did occur, would cast doubt on the beliefs or even show them to be false. . . .

THE ARGUMENT AGAINST SKEPTICISM

But the philosopher is apt to be more concerned with "know" in the strong sense. He wants to inquire whether there are any propositions that we can know without the shadow of a doubt will never be proved false, or even rendered dubious to the smallest degree. "You can say," he will argue, "and I admit that it would be good English usage to say, that you know that you have a heart and that the sun is more than 90 million miles from the earth. But you don't know it until you have absolutely conclusive evidence, and you must admit that the evidence you have, while very strong, is not conclusive. So I shall say, using "know" in the strong sense, that you do not know these propositions. I want then to ask what propositions can be known in the strong sense, the sense that puts the proposition forever past the possibility of doubt?"

And on this point many philosophers have been quite skeptical; they have granted few if any propositions whose truth we could know in the strong sense. Many of them would not even have agreed with the illustration about the ink-bottle: they would have said that our evidence for the ink-bottle was not conclusive, and that if we had suddenly found ourselves transported into a garden with no ink-bottle around, this would have entitled us to doubt that we were right in the first place in saying that there was an ink-bottle there. Many of them would add that even if there were no mysterious sudden change of location, we could still not know (in the strong sense) that there was an ink-bottle there. They would say that even for the presence of an ink-bottle there is an infinite number of tests, that they can never all be made, that we cannot look forever, but that every added observation adds further evidence in favor of the proposition without ever rendering it certain. Such a person is a *skeptic.* We claim (he says) to know many things about the world, but in fact none of these propositions can be known for certain. What are we to say of the skeptic's position?

Let us first note that in the phrase "know for certain," the "for certain" is redundant—how can we know except for certain? If it is less than certain, how can it be knowledge? We do, however, use the word "certain" ambiguously: (1) Sometimes we say "I am certain," which just means that I have a feeling of certainty about it—"I feel certain that I locked the door of the apartment"—and of course the feeling of certainty is no guarantee that the statement is true. People have very strong feelings of certainty about many propositions that they have no evidence for at all, particularly if they want to believe them or are consoled by believing them. The phrase "feeling certain," then, refers simply to a psychological state, whose existence in no way guarantees that what the person feels certain about is true. But (2) sometimes when we say "I am certain," we mean that it *is* certain—in other words, that we *do* know the proposition in question to be true. This, of course, is the sense of "certain" that is of interest to philosophers (the first sense is of more interest to psychiatrists in dealing with patients). Thus we could reformulate our question, "Is anything certain?" or "Are any propositions certain?"

"I can well understand," one might argue, "how you could question some statements, even most statements. But if you carry on this merry game until you have covered *all* statements, you are simply mistaken, and I think I can show you why. You may see someone in a fog or in a bad light and not know (not be certain) whether he has a right hand. But don't you know that *you* have a right hand? There it is! Suppose I now raise my hand and say, 'Here is a hand.' Now you say to me, 'I doubt that there's a hand.' But what evidence do you want? What does your doubt consist of? You don't believe your eyes, perhaps? Very well, then come up and touch the hand. You still aren't satisfied? Then keep on looking at it steadily and touching it, photograph it, call in other people for testimony if you like. If after all this you still say it isn't certain, what more do you want? Under what conditions would you admit that it *is* certain, that you *do* know it? I can understand your doubt when there is some condition left unfulfilled, some test left uncompleted. At the beginning, perhaps you doubted that *if* you tried to touch my hand you would find anything there to touch; but then you did touch, and so you resolved *that* doubt. You resolved further doubts by calling in other people and so on. You performed all the relevant tests, and they turned out favorably. So now, at the end of the process, what is it that you doubt? Oh, I know what you *say:* 'I still doubt that that's a hand.' But isn't this saying 'I doubt' now an empty formula? I can no longer attach any content to that so-called doubt, for there is nothing left to

doubt; you yourself *cannot specify any further test that, if performed, would resolve your doubt.* 'Doubt' now becomes an empty word. You're not doubting now that *if* you raised your hand to touch mine, you would touch it, or that *if* Smith and others were brought in, they would also testify that this is a hand—we've already gone through all that. So what is it specifically that you doubt? What possible test is there the negative result of which you fear? I submit that there isn't any. You are confusing a situation in which doubt is understandable (*before* you made the tests) with the later situation in which it isn't, for it has all been dispelled. . . .

"But your so-called doubt becomes meaningless when there is nothing left to doubt—when the tests have been carried out and their results are all favorable. Suppose a physician examines a patient and says, 'It's probable that you have an inflamed appendix.' Here one can still doubt, for the signs may be misleading. So the physician operates on the patient, finds an inflamed appendix and removes it, and the patient recovers. *Now* what would be the sense of the physician's saying 'It's *probable* that he had an inflamed appendix'? If seeing it and removing it made it only *probable*, what would make it certain? Or you are driving along and you hear a rapid regular thumping sound and you say, 'It's *probable* that I have a flat tire.' So far you're right; it's only probable—the thumping might be caused by something else. So you go out and have a look, and there is the tire, flat. You find a nail embedded in it, change the tire, and then resume your ride with no more thumping. Are you *now* going to say 'It's merely *probable* that the car had a flat tire'? But if given all those conditions it would be merely probable, what in the world would make it certain? Can you describe to me the circumstances in which you would say it's certain? If you can't, then the phrase 'being certain' has no meaning as you are using it. You are simply using it in such a special way that it has no application at all, and there is no reason at all why anyone else should follow your usage. In daily life we have a very convenient and useful distinction between the application of the words 'probable' and 'certain.' We say appendicitis is probable *before* the operation, but when the physician has the patient's appendix visible before him on the operating table, now it's certain—that's just the kind of situation in which we apply the word 'certain,' as opposed to 'probable.' Now you, for some reason, are so fond of the word 'probable' that you want to use it for everything—you use it to describe *both* the preoperative and postoperative situations, and the word 'certain' is left without any application at all. But this is nothing but a verbal manipulation on your part. You have changed nothing; you have only taken, as it were, two bottles with different contents, and instead of labeling them differently ('probable' and 'certain'), as the rest of us do, you put the same label ('probable') on both of them! What possible advantage is there in this? It's just verbal contrariness. And since you have pre-empted the word 'probable' to cover *both* the situations, we now have to devise a *different* pair of words to mark the perfectly obvious distinction between the situation *before* the surgery and the situation *during* the surgery—the same difference we previously marked by the words 'probable' and 'certain' until you used the word 'probable' to apply to both of them. What gain is there in this verbal manipulation of yours?". . .

---

[1] Norman Malcolm, "Knowledge and Belief," in *Knowledge and Certainty* (Englewood Cliffs, NJ: Prentice Hall, 1963), pp. 66–68.

Questions for Reflection

1. Hospers's three conditions of propositional knowledge go all the way back to Plato. Do you think this is an adequate account of knowledge? Are all three conditions necessary? Are there any that should be added?
2. Do you think his distinction between the strong and weak senses of knowledge are helpful?
3. How does Hospers's account of strong knowledge compare with the kind of certainty Descartes required for knowledge? Do you think Descartes would agree that Hospers has resolved the problem of skeptical doubt?
4. Has Hospers convinced you that the skeptic's doubts are not only unreasonable but meaningless? How might a skeptic such as Hume reply to Hospers's argument?

CONTEMPORARY APPLICATION: DOES SCIENCE GIVE US OBJECTIVE KNOWLEDGE ABOUT THE WORLD?

Ever since the early beginnings of modern science with the discoveries of such figures as Copernicus, Galileo, and Issac Newton, scientists, philosophers, and the general public have assumed that science is a particularly effective method for obtaining objective truth about reality. In the 20th century, however, the status of science and its claims to knowledge came into question. Of course, there have always been some religious people who see science and religion in competition and who have sought to diminish the status of the scientific theories they reject by claiming that they are simply "subjective, value-laden viewpoints" that are masquerading as objective truth. However, in recent years, the biggest threat to the objectivity of science has come from certain philosophers, sociologists, and historians who have no religious agenda, but who question the objectivity of science because they reject the notion of objective truth altogether. There is a big debate in current philosophy of science between those who emphasize the rationality and objectivity of science and those who see science as a product of subjective viewpoints and social forces. This debate has come to be known as the "science wars."

Much of the discussion in the science wars revolves around the 1962 book *The Structure of Scientific Revolutions* by historian and philosopher of science Thomas Kuhn. In this book, Kuhn questions the traditional view that science progresses through an accumulation of objective facts and that it is driven by strictly rational considerations. Using case studies from the history of science, Kuhn argues that science is characterized by periods of "normal science" in which there is a high degree of agreement among scientists who share a dominant "paradigm" or standard way of viewing nature and of doing science. Periodically, however, the current paradigm will run into difficulties and, if these are severe enough, a scientific revolution will occur and the followers of a new paradigm will now become the dominant force in the scientific enterprise. Kuhn contends that advocates of competing paradigms cannot rationally argue with one another because they have differing views of the standards of "rationality," "evidence," and even of the ways that the facts should be interpreted. Hence, in Kuhn's account, changes in scientific paradigms are more like value choices or religious conversions rather than being rational decisions based on neutral, objective facts. If there are no objective standards by means of which we can compare and evaluate successive stages of science, then the notion of scientific progress or the notion that science is converging upon the truth falls by the wayside.

In the following two readings, physicist Steven Weinberg criticizes Kuhn and defends the traditional view that science gives us ever-increasing objective knowledge about reality. On the other hand, philosopher Richard Rorty champions Kuhn's cause and contends that we should toss out the notions of "objective truth" and "correspondence with reality," even with respect to science.

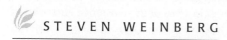

STEVEN WEINBERG

Scientific Knowledge Is Based in Reality

Steven Weinberg (1933–   ) holds an endowed chair of science at the University of Texas at Austin. He is a member of the Physics and Astronomy Departments there and serves as the director of the Theory Research Group. He has won numerous awards and in 1979 he and two other scientists won the Nobel Prize for their research in physics.

Reading Questions

1. What does Thomas Kuhn mean by a "paradigm," according to Weinberg? What is a "paradigm shift"?
2. What bothers Weinberg about the conclusions of Kuhn's writings?
3. Why does Weinberg think the change from Newtonian mechanics to Einstein's theory is not as radical as Kuhn thinks?

Steven Weinberg, "The Revolution That Didn't Happen," in *The New York Review of Books,* October 8, 1998.

4. According to Weinberg, how does Kuhn defend the conclusion that as science changes, we do not move closer to the truth? Why does Weinberg think this argument fails to fit the facts?

5. What distinction does Weinberg make between the "hard" part and the "soft" part of a scientific theory? Why does he think this shows a cumulative movement toward the truth?

6. Why does Kuhn's view of scientific progress leave us with a mystery? How does Weinberg answer his own question about this mystery?

7. What statement by Weinberg was attacked by Richard Rorty? How does Weinberg reply?

8. In his conclusion, what is Weinberg's view of scientific progress? What change does he make to Kuhn's view?

I first read Thomas Kuhn's famous book *The Structure of Scientific Revolutions* a quarter-century ago, soon after the publication of the second edition. I had known Kuhn only slightly when we had been together on the faculty at Berkeley in the early 1960s, but I came to like and admire him later, when he came to MIT. His book I found exciting.

Evidently others felt the same. *Structure* has had a wider influence than any other book on the history of science. Soon after Kuhn's death in 1996, the sociologist Clifford Geertz remarked that Kuhn's book had "opened the door to the eruption of the sociology of knowledge" into the study of sciences. Kuhn's ideas have been invoked again and again in the recent conflict over the relation of science and culture known as the science wars.

Structure describes the history of science as a cyclic process. There are periods of "normal science" that are characterized by what Kuhn sometimes called a "paradigm" and sometimes called a "common disciplinary matrix." Whatever you call it, it describes a consensus view: in a period of normal science, scientists tend to agree about what phenomena are relevant and what constitutes an explanation of these phenomena, about what problems are worth solving and what is a solution of a problem. Near the end of a period of normal science a crisis occurs—experiments give results that don't fit existing theories, or internal contradictions are discovered in these theories. There is alarm and confusion. Strange ideas fill the scientific literature. Eventually there is a revolution. Scientists become converted to a new way of looking at nature, resulting eventually in a new period of normal science. The "paradigm" has shifted.

To take an example given special attention in *Structure,* after the widespread acceptance of Newton's physical theories—the Newtonian paradigm—in the eighteenth century, there began a period of normal science in the study of motion and gravitation. Scientists used Newtonian theory to make increasingly accurate calculations of planetary orbits, leading to spectacular successes like the prediction in 1846 of the existence and orbit of the planet Neptune before astronomers discovered it. By the end of the nineteenth century there was a crisis: a failure to understand the motion of light. This problem was solved through a paradigm shift, a revolutionary revision in the understanding of space and time carried out by Einstein in the decade between 1905 and 1915. Motion affects the flow of time; matter and energy can be converted into each other; and gravitation is a curvature in space-time. Einstein's theory of relativity then became the new paradigm, and the study of motion and gravitation entered upon a new period of normal science.

Though one can question the extent to which Kuhn's cyclic theory of scientific revolution fits what we know of the history of science, in itself this theory would not be very disturbing, nor would it have made Kuhn's book famous. For many people, it is Kuhn's reinvention of the word "paradigm" that has been either most useful or most objectionable. Of course, in ordinary English the word "paradigm" means some accomplishment that serves as a model for future work. This is the way that Kuhn had used this word in his earlier book on the scientific revolution associated with Copernicus, and one way that he continued occasionally to use it.

The first critic who took issue with Kuhn's new use of the word "paradigm" in *Structure* was Harvard President James Bryant Conant. Kuhn had begun his career as a historian as Conant's assistant in teaching an undergraduate course at Harvard, when Conant asked Kuhn to prepare case studies on the history of mechanics. After seeing a draft of *Structure,* Conant complained to Kuhn that "paradigm" was "a word you seem to have fallen in love with!" and "a magical verbal word to explain everything!" A few years later Margaret Masterman pointed out that Kuhn had used the word "paradigm" in over twenty different ways. But the quarrel over the word "paradigm" seems to me unimportant. Kuhn was right that there is more to a scientific consensus than just a set of explicit theories. We need a word for the complex of attitudes and traditions that go along with our theories in a period of normal science, and "paradigm" will do as well as any other.

What does bother me on rereading *Structure* and some of Kuhn's later writings is his radically skeptical conclusions about what is accomplished in the work of science. And it is just these conclusions that have made Kuhn a hero to the philosophers, historians, sociologists, and cultural critics who question the objective character of scientific knowledge, and who prefer to describe scientific theories as social constructions, not so different from democracy or baseball.

Kuhn made the shift from one paradigm to another seem more like a religious conversion than an exercise of reason. He argued that our theories change so much in a paradigm shift that it is nearly impossible for scientists after a scientific revolution to see things as they had been seen under the previous paradigm. Kuhn compared the shift from one paradigm to another to a gestalt flip, like the optical illusion created by pictures in which what had seemed to be white rabbits against a black background suddenly appear as black goats against a white background. But for Kuhn the shift is more profound; he added that "the scientist does not preserve the gestalt subject's freedom to switch back and forth between ways of seeing."

Kuhn argued further that in scientific revolutions it is not only our scientific theories that change but the very standards by which scientific theories are judged, so that the paradigms that govern successive periods of normal science are *incommensurable.* He went on to reason that since a paradigm shift means complete abandonment of an earlier paradigm, and there is no common standard to judge scientific theories developed under different paradigms, there can be no sense in which theories developed after a scientific revolution can be said to add cumulatively to what was known before the revolution. Only within the context of a paradigm can we speak of one theory being true or false. Kuhn in *Structure* concluded, tentatively, "We may, to be more precise, have to relinquish the notion explicit or implicit that changes of paradigm carry scientists and those who learn from them closer and closer to the truth." More recently, in his Rothschild Lecture at Harvard in 1992, Kuhn remarked that it is hard to imagine what can be meant by the phrase that a scientific theory takes us "closer to the truth."

Kuhn did not deny that there is progress in science, but he denied that it is progress *toward* anything. He often used the metaphor of biological evolution: scientific progress for him was like evolution as described by Darwin, a process driven from behind, rather than pulled toward some fixed goal to which it grows ever closer. For him, the natural selection of scientific theories is driven by problem solving. When, during a period of normal science, it turns out that some problems can't be solved using existing theories, then new ideas proliferate, and the ideas that survive are those that do best at solving these problems. But according to Kuhn, just as there was nothing inevitable about mammals appearing in the Cretaceous period and out-surviving the dinosaurs when a comet hit the earth, so also there's nothing built into nature that made it inevitable that our science would evolve in the direction of Maxwell's equations or general relativity. Kuhn recognizes that Maxwell's and

Einstein's theories are better than those that preceded them, in the same way that mammals turned out to be better than dinosaurs at surviving the effects of comet impacts, but when new problems arise they will be replaced by new theories that are better at solving *those* problems, and so on, with no overall improvement.

All this is wormwood to scientists like myself, who think the task of science is to bring us closer and closer to objective truth. But Kuhn's conclusions are delicious to those who take a more skeptical view of the pretensions of science. If scientific theories can only be judged within the context of a particular paradigm, then in this respect the scientific theories of any one paradigm are not privileged over other ways of looking at the world, such as shamanism or astrology or creationism. If the transition from one paradigm to another cannot be judged by any external standard, then perhaps it is culture rather than nature that dictates the content of scientific theories.

Kuhn himself was not always happy with those who invoked his work. In 1965 he complained that for the philosopher Paul Feyerabend to describe his arguments as a defense of irrationality in science seemed to him to be "not only absurd but vaguely obscene." In a 1991 interview with John Horgan, Kuhn sadly recalled a student in the 1960s complimenting him, "Oh, thank you, Mr. Kuhn, for telling us about paradigms. Now that we know about them, we can get rid of them." Kuhn was also uncomfortable with the so-called "strong program" in the sociology of science, which is "strong" in its uncompromisingly skeptical aim to show how political and social power and interests dominate the success or failure of scientific theories. This program is particularly associated with a group of philosophers and sociologists of science that at one time worked at the University of Edinburgh. About this, Kuhn remarked in 1991, "I am among those who have found the claims of the strong program absurd, an example of deconstruction gone mad."

But even when we put aside the excesses of Kuhn's admirers, the radical part of Kuhn's theory of scientific revolutions is radical enough. And I think it is quite wrong.

It is not true that scientists are unable to "switch back and forth between ways of seeing," and that after a scientific revolution they become incapable of understanding the science that went before it. One of the paradigm shifts to which Kuhn gives much attention in *Structure* is the replacement at the beginning of this century of Newtonian mechanics by the relativistic mechanics of Einstein. But in fact in educating new physicists the first thing that we teach them is still good old Newtonian mechanics, and they never forget how to think in Newtonian terms, even after they learn about Einstein's theory of relativity. Kuhn himself as an instructor at Harvard must have taught Newtonian mechanics to undergraduates.

In defending his position, Kuhn argued that the words we use and the symbols in our equations mean different things before and after a scientific revolution; for instance, physicists meant different things by mass before and after the advent of relativity. It is true that there was a good deal of uncertainty about the concept of mass *during* the Einsteinian revolution. For a while there was talk of "longitudinal" and "transverse" masses, which were supposed to depend on a particle's speed and to resist accelerations along the direction of motion and perpendicular to it. But this has all been resolved. No one today talks of longitudinal or transverse mass, and in fact the term "mass" today is most frequently understood as "rest mass," an intrinsic property of a body that is not changed by motion, which is much the way that mass was understood before Einstein. Meanings can change, but generally they do so in the direction of an increased richness and precision of definition, so that we do not lose the ability to understand the theories of past periods of normal science.

Perhaps Kuhn came to think that scientists in one period of normal science generally do not understand the science of earlier periods because of his experience in teaching and writing about the history of science. He probably had to contend with the ahistorical notions of scientists and students, who have not read original sources, and who believe that we can understand the work of the scientists in a revolutionary period by supposing that scientists of the past thought about their theories in the way that we describe these theories in our science textbooks. Kuhn's 1978 book on the birth of quantum theory convinced me that I made just this mistake in trying to understand what Max Planck was doing when he introduced the idea of the quantum.

It is also true that scientists who come of age in a period of normal science find it extraordinarily difficult to understand the work of the scientists in previous scientific *revolutions,* so that in this respect we are often almost incapable of reliving the "gestalt flip" produced by the revolution. For instance, it is not easy for a physicist today to read Newton's *Principia,* even in a modern translation from Newton's Latin. The great astrophysicist Subrahmanyan Chandrasekhar spent years translating the *Principia's* reasoning into a form that a modern physicist could understand. But those who participate in a scientific revolution are in a sense living in two worlds: the earlier period of normal science, which is breaking down, and the new period of normal science, which they do not yet fully comprehend. It is much less difficult for scientists in one period of normal science to understand the theories of an earlier paradigm *in their mature form.*

I was careful earlier to talk about Newtonian mechanics, not Newton's mechanics. In an important sense, especially in his geometric style. Newton is pre-Newtonian. Recall the aphorism of John Maynard Keynes, that Newton was not the first modern scientist but rather the last magician. Newtonianism reached its mature form in the early nineteenth century through the work of Laplace, Lagrange, and others, and it is this mature Newtonianism—which still predates special relativity by a century—that we teach our students today. They have no trouble in understanding it, and they continue to understand it and use it where appropriate after they learn about Einstein's theory of relativity. . . .

In judging the nature of scientific progress, we have to look at mature scientific theories, not theories at the moments when they are coming into being. If it made sense to ask whether the Norman Conquest turned out to be a good thing, we might try to answer the question by comparing Anglo-Saxon and Norman societies in their mature forms—say, in the reigns of Edward the Confessor and Henry I. We would not try to answer it by studying what happened at the Battle of Hastings.

Nor do scientific revolutions necessarily change the way that we assess our theories, making different paradigms incommensurable. Over the past forty years I have been involved in revolutionary changes in the way that physicists understand the elementary particles that are the basic constituents of matter. The greater revolutions of this century, quantum mechanics and relativity, were before my time, but they are the basis of the physics research of my generation. Nowhere have I seen any signs of Kuhn's incommensurability between different paradigms. Our ideas have changed, but we have continued to assess our theories in pretty much the same way: a theory is taken as a success if it is based on simple general principles and does a good job of accounting for experimental data in a natural way. I am not saying that we have a book of rules that tells us how to assess theories, or that we have a clear idea what is meant by "simple general principles" or "natural." I am only saying that whatever we mean, there have been no sudden changes in the way we assess theories, no changes that would make it impossible to compare the truth of theories before and after a revolution.

For instance, at the beginning of this century physicists were confronted with the problem of understanding the spectra of atoms, the huge number of bright and dark lines that appear in the light from hot gases, like those on the surface of the sun, when the light is separated by a spectroscope into its different colors. When Niels Bohr showed in 1913 how to use quantum theory to explain the spectrum of hydrogen, it became clear to physicists generally that quantum theory was very promising, and when it turned out after 1925 that quantum mechanics could be used to explain the spectrum of any atom, quantum mechanics became the hot subject that young physicists had to learn. In the same way, physicists today are confronted with a dozen or so measured masses for the electron and similar particles and for quarks of various types,

and the measured numerical values of these different masses have so far resisted theoretical explanation. Any new theory that succeeds in explaining
these masses will instantly be recognized as an important step forward. The subject matter has
changed, but not our aims.

This is not to say that there have been no
changes at all in the way we assess our theories. For
instance, it is now considered to be much more acceptable to base a physical theory on some principle of "invariance" (a principle that says that the
laws of nature appear the same from certain different points of view) than it was at the beginning of
the century, when Einstein started to worry about
the invariance of the laws of nature under changes
in the motion of an observer. But these changes
have been evolutionary, not revolutionary. Nature
seems to act on us as a teaching machine. When a
scientist reaches a new understanding of nature, he
or she experiences an intense pleasure. These experiences over long periods have taught us how to
judge what sort of scientific theory will provide the
pleasure of understanding nature.

Even more radical than Kuhn's notion of the incommensurability of different paradigms is his conclusion that in the revolutionary shifts from one
paradigm to another we do not move closer to the
truth. To defend this conclusion, he argued that all
past beliefs about nature have turned out to be
false, and that there is no reason to suppose that we
are doing better now. Of course, Kuhn knew very
well that physicists today go on using the Newtonian theory of gravitation and motion and the
Maxwellian theory of electricity and magnetism as
good approximations that can be deduced from
more accurate theories—we certainly don't regard
Newtonian and Maxwellian theories as simply false,
in the way that Aristotle's theory of motion or the
theory that fire is an element ("phlogiston") are
false. Kuhn himself in his earlier book on the
Copernican revolution told how parts of scientific
theories survive in the more successful theories
that supplant them, and seemed to have no trouble
with the idea. Confronting this contradiction,
Kuhn in *Structure* gave what for him was a remarkably weak defense, that Newtonian mechanics and
Maxwellian electrodynamics as we use them today
are not the same theories as they were before the
advent of relativity and quantum mechanics, because then they were not known to be approximate
and now we know that they are. It is like saying that
the steak you eat is not the one that you bought, because now you know it is stringy and before you
didn't.

It is important to keep straight what does and
what does not change in scientific revolutions, a
distinction that is not made in *Structure*. There is a
"hard" part of modern physical theories ("hard"
meaning not difficult, but durable, like bones in
paleontology or potsherds in archeology) that usually consists of the equations themselves, together
with some understandings about what the symbols
mean operationally and about the sorts of phenomena to which they apply. Then there is a "soft"
part; it is the vision of reality that we use to explain
to ourselves why the equations work. The soft part
does change; we no longer believe in Maxwell's
ether, and we know that there is more to nature
than Newton's particles and forces.

The changes in the soft part of scientific theories also produce changes in our understanding of
the conditions under which the hard part is a good
approximation. But after our theories reach their
mature forms, their hard parts represent permanent accomplishments. If you have bought one of
those T-shirts with Maxwell's equations on the
front, you may have to worry about its going out of
style, but not about its becoming false. We will go
on teaching Maxwellian electrodynamics as long as
there are scientists. I can't see any sense in which
the increase in scope and accuracy of the hard
parts of our theories is *not* a cumulative approach
to truth.

Some of what Kuhn said about paradigm shifts
does apply to the soft parts of our theories, but
even here I think that Kuhn overestimated the degree to which scientists during a period of normal
science are captives of their paradigms. There are
many examples of scientists who remained skeptical about the soft parts of their own theories. It
seems to me that Newton's famous slogan *Hypotheses non fingo* (I do not make hypotheses) must have
meant at least in part that his commitment was not
to the reality of gravitational forces acting at a dis-

tance, but only to the validity of the predictions derived from his equations.

However that may be, I can testify that although our present theory of elementary particles, the Standard Model, has been tremendously successful in accounting for the measured properties of the particles, physicists today are not firmly committed to the view of nature on which it is based. The Standard Model is a field theory, which means that it takes the basic constituents of nature to be fields—conditions of space, considered apart from any matter that may be in it, like the magnetic field that pulls bits of iron toward the poles of a bar magnet—rather than particles. In the past two decades it has been realized that any theory based on quantum mechanics and relativity will look like a field theory when experiments are done at sufficiently low energies. The Standard Model is today widely regarded as an "effective field theory," a low-energy approximation to some unknown fundamental theory that may not involve fields at all.

Even though the Standard Model provides the paradigm for the present normal-science period in fundamental physics, it has several ad hoc features, including at least eighteen numerical constants, such as the mass and charge of the electron, that have to be arbitrarily adjusted to make the theory fit experiments. Also, the Standard Model does not incorporate gravitation. Theorists know that they need to find a more satisfying new theory, to which the Standard Model would be only a good approximation, and experimentalists are working very hard to find some new data that would disagree with some prediction of the Standard Model. The recent announcement from an underground experiment in Japan, that the particles called neutrinos have masses that would be forbidden in the original version of the Standard Model, provides a good example. This experiment is only the latest step in a search over many years for such masses, a search that has been guided in part by arguments that, whatever more satisfying theory turns out to be the next step beyond the Standard Model, this theory is likely to entail the existence of small neutrino masses.

Kuhn overstated the degree to which we are hypnotized by our paradigms, and in particular he exaggerated the extent to which the discovery of anomalies during a period of normal science is inadvertent. He was quite wrong in saying that it is no part of the work of normal science to find new sorts of phenomena.

Kuhn's view of scientific progress would leave us with a mystery: Why does anyone bother? If one scientific theory is only better than another in its ability to solve the problems that happen to be on our minds today, then why not save ourselves a lot of trouble by putting these problems out of our minds? We don't study elementary particles because they are intrinsically interesting, like people. They are not—if you have seen one electron, you've seen them all. What drives us onward in the work of science is precisely the sense that there are truths out there to be discovered, truths that once discovered will form a permanent part of human knowledge.

It was not Kuhn's description of scientific revolutions that impressed me so much when I first read *Structure* in 1972, but rather his treatment of normal science. Kuhn showed that a period of normal science is not a time of stagnation, but an essential phase of scientific progress. This had become important to me personally in the early 1970s because of recent developments in both cosmology and elementary particle physics.

Until the late 1960s cosmology had been in a state of terrible confusion. I remember when most astronomers and astrophysicists were partisans of some preferred cosmology, and considered anyone else's cosmology as mere dogma. Once at a dinner party in New York around 1970 I was sitting with the distinguished Swedish physicist Hannes Alfven, and took the opportunity to ask whether or not certain physical effects on which he was an expert would have occurred in the early universe. He asked me, "Is your question posed within the context of the Big Bang Theory?" and when I said yes, it was, he said that he didn't want to talk about it. The fractured state of cosmological discourse began to heal after the discovery in 1965 of the cosmic microwave background radiation, radiation that is left over from the time when the universe was about a million years old. This discovery forced everyone (or at least almost everyone) to think seriously about the early universe.

At last measurements were being made that could confirm or refute our cosmological speculations, and very soon, in less than a decade, the Big Bang Theory was developed in its modern form and became widely accepted. In a treatise on gravitation and cosmology that I finished in 1971 I used the phrase "Standard Model" for the modern big bang cosmology, to emphasize that I regarded it not as a dogma to which everyone had to swear allegiance, but as a common ground on which all physicists and astronomers could meet to discuss cosmological calculations and observations. There remained respected physicists and astronomers, like Alfven and Fred Hoyle, who did not like the direction of the growing consensus. Some of them attacked the very idea of consensus, holding out instead a sort of "Shining Path" ideal of science as a continual revolution, in which all should pursue their own ideas and go off in their own directions. But there is much more danger in a breakdown of communication among scientists than in a premature consensus that happens to be in error. It is only when scientists share a consensus that they can focus on the experiments and the calculations that can tell them whether their theories are right or wrong, and, if wrong, can show the way to a new consensus. It was to good effect that Kuhn quoted Francis Bacon's dictum, "Truth emerges more readily from error than from confusion."

Elementary particle physics also was entering into a new period of normal science in the early 1970s. It had earlier been in a state of confusion, not because of a lack of data, of which there was more than enough, but because of the lack of a convincing body of theory that could explain this data. By the early 1970s theoretical developments and some important new experiments led to a consensus among elementary particle physicists, embodied in what is now also called a Standard Model. Yet for a while some physicists remained skeptical because they felt there hadn't been enough experiments done yet to prove the correctness of the Standard Model, or that the experimental data could be interpreted in other ways. When I argued that any other way of interpreting the data was ugly and artificial, some physicists answered that science has nothing to do with aesthetic judgments, a response that would have amused Kuhn. As he said, "The act of judgment that leads scientists to reject the previously accepted theory is always based upon more than a comparison of that theory with the world." Any set of data can be fit by many different theories. In deciding among these theories we have to judge which ones have the kind of elegance and consistency and universality that make them worth taking seriously. Kuhn was by no means the first person who had made this point—he was preceded by, among others, Pierre Duhem—but Kuhn made it very convincingly.

By now the arguments about the Standard Model are pretty well over, and it is almost universally agreed to give a correct account of observed phenomena. We are living in a new period of normal science, in which the implications of the Standard Model are being calculated by theorists and tested by experimentalists. As Kuhn recognized, it is precisely this sort of work during periods of normal science that can lead to the discovery of anomalies that will make it necessary to take the next step beyond our present paradigm.

But Kuhn's view of normal science, though it remains helpful and insightful, is not what made his reputation. The famous part of his work is his description of scientific revolutions and his view of scientific progress. And it is here that his work is so seriously misleading.

What went wrong? What in Kuhn's life led him to his radical skepticism, to his strange view of the progress of science? Certainly not ignorance—he evidently understood many episodes in the history of physical science as well as anyone ever has. I picked up a clue to Kuhn's thinking the last time I saw him, at a ceremony in Padua in 1992 celebrating the 400th anniversary of the first lecture Galileo delivered in the University of Padua. Kuhn told how in 1947 as a young physics instructor at Harvard, studying Aristotle's work in physics, he had been wondering

How could [Aristotle's] characteristic talent have deserted him so systematically when he turned to the study of motion and mechanics? Equally, if his talents had deserted him, why had his writings in physics been taken so seriously for so many centuries after his death? . . . Suddenly the fragments in my head sorted themselves out in a new way, and fell into place altogether. My jaw dropped with surprise, for all at once Aristotle seemed a very good physicist indeed, but of a sort I'd never dreamed possible.

I asked Kuhn what he had suddenly understood about Aristotle. He didn't answer my question, but wrote to me to tell me again how important this experience was to him:

What was altered by my own first reading of [Aristotle's writings on physics] was my understanding, not my evaluation, of what they achieved. And what made that change an epiphany was the transformation it immediately effected in my understanding (again, not my evaluation) of the nature of scientific achievement, most immediately the achievements of Galileo and Newton.

Later, I read Kuhn's explanation in a 1977 article that, without becoming an Aristotelian physicist, he had for a moment learned to think like one, to think of motion as a change in the quality of an object that is like many other changes in quality rather than a state that can be studied in isolation. This apparently showed Kuhn how it is possible to adopt the point of view of any scientist one studies. I suspect that because this moment in his life was so important to Kuhn, he took his idea of a paradigm shift from the shift from Aristotelian to Newtonian physics—the shift (which actually took many centuries) from Aristotle's attempt to give systematic qualitative descriptions of everything in nature to Newton's quantitative explanations of carefully selected phenomena, such as the motion of the planets around the sun.

Now, that really *was* a paradigm shift. For Kuhn it seems to have been the paradigm of paradigm shifts, which set a pattern into which he tried to shoehorn every other scientific revolution. It really does fit Kuhn's description of paradigm shifts: it is extraordinarily difficult for a modern scientist to get into the frame of mind of Aristotelian physics,

and Kuhn's statement that all previous views of reality have proved false, though not true of Newtonian mechanics or Maxwellian electrodynamics, certainly does apply to Aristotelian physics.

Revolutions in science seem to fit Kuhn's description only to the extent that they mark a shift in understanding some aspect of nature from pre-science to modern science. The birth of Newtonian physics was a mega-paradigm shift, but nothing that has happened in our understanding of motion since then—not the transition from Newtonian to Einsteinian mechanics, or from classical to quantum physics—fits Kuhn's description of a paradigm shift.

During the last few decades of his life Kuhn worked as a philosopher, worrying about the meaning of truth and reality, problems on which he had touched briefly decades earlier in *Structure*. After Kuhn's death Richard Rorty said that Kuhn was "the most influential philosopher to write in English since World War II." Kuhn's conclusions about philosophy show the same corrosive skepticism as his writings on history. In his Rothschild Lecture at Harvard in 1992, he remarked, "I am not suggesting, let me emphasize, that there is a reality which science fails to get at. My point is rather that no sense can be made of the notion of reality as it has ordinarily functioned in the philosophy of science."

It seems to me that pretty good sense had been made of the notion of reality over a century ago by the pragmatic philosopher Charles Sanders Peirce, but I am not equipped by taste or education to judge conflicts among philosophers. Fortunately we need not allow philosophers to dictate how philosophical arguments are to be applied in the history of science, or in scientific research itself, any more than we would allow scientists to decide by themselves how scientific discoveries are to be used in technology or medicine.

I remarked in a recent article in *The New York Review of Books* that for me as a physicist the laws of nature are real in the same sense (whatever that is) as the rocks on the ground. A few months after the publication of my article I was attacked for this remark by Richard Rorty. He accused me of thinking that as a physicist I can easily clear up questions about reality and truth that have engaged philosophers for millennia. But that is not my position. I know that it is terribly hard to say precisely what we mean when we use words like "real" and "true." That is why, when I said that the laws of nature and the rocks on the ground are real in the same sense, I added in parentheses "whatever that is." I respect the efforts of philosophers to clarify these concepts, but I'm sure that even Kuhn and Rorty have used words like "truth" and "reality" in everyday life, and had no trouble with them. I don't see any reason why we cannot also use them in some of our statements about the history of science. Certainly philosophers can do us a great service in their attempts to clarify what we mean by truth and reality. But for Kuhn to say that as a philosopher he has trouble understanding what is meant by truth or reality proves nothing beyond the fact that he has trouble understanding what is meant by truth or reality.

Finally, I would like to describe my own idea of scientific progress. As I said, Kuhn uses the metaphor of Darwinian evolution: undirected improvement, but not improvement toward anything.

Kuhn's metaphor is not bad, if we make one change in it: the progress of physical science looks like evolution running backward. Just as humans and other mammal species can trace their origins back to some kind of furry creature hiding from the dinosaurs in the Cretaceous period, and that furry creature and the dinosaurs and all life on Earth presumably can be traced back to what Pooh-Bah in *The Mikado* called "a protoplasmal primordial atomic globule," in the same way we have seen the science of optics and the science of electricity and magnetism merge together in Maxwell's time into what we now call electrodynamics, and in recent years we have seen electrodynamics and the theories of other forces in nature merge into the modern Standard Model of elementary particles. We hope that in the next great step forward in physics we shall see the theory of gravitation and all of the different branches of elementary particle physics flow together into a single unified theory. This is what we are working for and what we spend the taxpayers' money for. And when we have discovered this theory, it will be part of a true description of reality.

Questions for Reflection

1. Do you think Weinberg has satisfactorily made the case for the truth-seeking nature of science over Kuhn's relativistic view? Why?

2. Do you agree with Weinberg that if scientists accepted Kuhn's view there would be no motivation to bother with science?

3. Do you think the enormous amounts of money our society spends on scientific research is worth it? Is it worth it to learn all we can about nature even if much of this research has no immediate practical applications?

4. If our best scientific knowledge is not objective and moving us closer to the truth, what would be the implications of this for the rest of our knowledge? Is it possible to think of *all* of your beliefs as subjective and having no real correspondence to the way things are? Why?

RICHARD RORTY

Scientific Knowledge Is Based in Social Solidarity

Richard Rorty (1931–   ), one of the most famous living philosophers in the United States, is a professor of philosophy and comparative literature at Stanford University. Among his many publications is his highly influential *Philosophy and the Mirror of Nature* (1979). In his writings, Rorty has developed an extremely relativistic version of pragmatism (sometimes called "neo-pragmatism") and he frequently quotes William James's phrase that truth is "what it is good for us to believe."

In this selection, Rorty critiques the traditional view that science is a method for pursuing objective truth and constructing theories that correspond to reality. He agrees with philosopher of science Thomas Kuhn that "there is no theory-independent way to reconstruct phrases like 'really there.'" In Rorty's view, science is just one more cultural activity and should not be accorded any special status. Building upon the position of pragmatism, he says we should abandon the notion of objectivity and make our goal that of intersubjective agreement or social solidarity. Accordingly, scientific theories should be judged, as should any beliefs, on the basis of how well they create social consensus, how interesting they are, and how they contribute to our cultural life.

Reading Questions

1. According to Rorty, what is the status of science in our culture?
2. What are the two senses of the term *rationality?* How do the humanities measure up under each conception? Which view of rationality does Rorty advocate?
3. What do critics say about Thomas Kuhn? On the other hand, why does Rorty congratulate him?
4. What are the three interpretations of relativism? Which one does Rorty prefer?
5. What does Rorty say about the view that truth is correspondence to reality? What is his view of truth?
6. Why does Rorty contend that "we fuzzies" (relativists) have a right to be opposed to moral evil such as Nazism?
7. What would Rorty's ideal society be like?

In our culture, the notions of "science," "rationality," "objectivity," and "truth" are bound up with one another. Science is thought of as offering "hard," "objective" truth: truth as correspondence to reality, the only sort of truth worthy of the name. Humanists like philosophers, theologians, historians, and literary critics have to worry about whether they are being "scientific"—whether they

From Richard Rorty, "Science as Solidarity," in *The Rhetoric of the Human Sciences: Language and Argument in Scholarship and Public Affairs,* ed. John S. Nelson, Allan Megill, and Donald N. McCloskey (Madison: University of Wisconsin Press, 1987).

are entitled to think of their conclusions, no matter how carefully argued, as worthy of the term "true." We tend to identify seeking "objective truth" with "using reason," and so we think of the natural sciences as paradigms of rationality. We also think of rationality as a matter of following procedures laid down in advance, of being "methodical." So we tend to use "methodical," "rational," "scientific," and "objective" as synonyms.

Worries about "cognitive status" and "objectivity" are characteristic of a secularized culture in which the scientist replaces the priest. The scientist is now seen as the person who keeps humanity in touch with something beyond itself. As the universe was depersonalized, beauty (and, in time, even moral goodness) came to be thought of as "subjective." So truth is now thought of as the only point at which human beings are responsible to something nonhuman. A commitment to "rationality" and to "method" is thought to be a recognition of this responsibility. The scientist becomes a moral exemplar, one who selflessly exposes himself again and again to the hardness of fact.

One result of this way of thinking is that any academic discipline which wants a place at the trough, but is unable to offer the predictions and the technology provided by the natural sciences, must either pretend to imitate science or find some way of obtaining "cognitive status" without the necessity of discovering facts. Practitioners of these disciplines must either affiliate themselves with this quasi-priestly order by using terms like "behavioral sciences" or else find something other than "fact" to be concerned with. People in the humanities typically choose the latter strategy. They either describe themselves as concerned with "value" as opposed to facts, or as developing and inculcating habits of "critical reflection."

Neither sort of rhetoric is very satisfactory. No matter how much humanists talk about "objective values," the phrase always sounds vaguely confused. It gives with one hand what it takes back with the other. The distinction between the objective and the subjective was designed to parallel that between fact and value, so an objective value sounds as vaguely mythological as a winged horse. Talk about the humanists' special skill at critical reflection

fares no better. Nobody really believes that philosophers or literary critics are better at critical thinking, or at taking big broad views of things, than theoretical physicists or microbiologists. So society tends to ignore both these kinds of rhetoric. It treats humanities as on a par with the arts, and thinks of both as providing pleasure rather than truth. Both are, to be sure, thought of as providing "high" rather than "low" pleasures. But an elevated and spiritual sort of pleasure is still a long way from the grasp of a truth.

These distinctions between hard facts and soft values, truth and pleasure, and objectivity and subjectivity are awkward and clumsy instruments. They are not suited to dividing up culture; they create more difficulties than they resolve. It would be best to find another vocabulary, to start afresh. But in order to do so, we first have to find a new way of describing the natural sciences. It is not a question of debunking or downgrading the natural scientist, but simply of ceasing to see him as a priest. We need to stop thinking of science as the place where the human mind confronts the world, and of the scientist as exhibiting proper humility in the face of superhuman forces. We need a way of explaining why scientists are, and deserve to be, moral exemplars which does not depend on a distinction between objective fact and something softer, squishier, and more dubious.

To get such a way of thinking, we can start by distinguishing two senses of the term "rationality." In one sense, the one I have already discussed, to be rational is to be methodical: that is, to have criteria for success laid down in advance. We think of poets and painters as using some faculty other than "reason" in their work because, by their own confession, they are not sure of what they want to do before they have done it. They make up new standards of achievement as they go along. By contrast, we think of judges as knowing in advance what criteria a brief will have to satisfy in order to invoke a favorable decision, and of business people as setting well-defined goals and being judged by their success in achieving them. Law and business are good examples of rationality, but the scientist, knowing in advance what would count as disconfirming his hypothesis and prepared to abandon that hypothesis as a result of the unfavorable outcome of a single experiment, seems a truly heroic example. Further, we seem to have a clear criterion for the success of a scientific theory—namely, its ability to predict, and thereby to enable us to control some portion of the world. If to be rational means to be able to lay down criteria in advance, then it is plausible to take natural science as the paradigm of rationality.

The trouble is that in this sense of "rational" the humanities are never going to qualify as rational activities. If the humanities are concerned with ends rather than means, then there is no way to evaluate their success in terms of antecedently specified criteria. If we already knew what criteria we wanted to satisfy, we would not worry about whether we were pursuing the right ends. If we thought we knew the goals of culture and society in advance, we would have no use for the humanities—as totalitarian societies in fact do not. It is characteristic of democratic and pluralistic societies to continually redefine their goals. But if to be rational means to satisfy criteria, then this process of redefinition is bound to be nonrational. So if the humanities are to be viewed as rational activities, rationality will have to be thought of as something other than the satisfaction of criteria which are statable in advance.

Another meaning for "rational" is, in fact, available. In this sense, the word means something like "sane" or "reasonable" rather than "methodical." It names a set of moral virtues: tolerance, respect for the opinions of those around one, willingness to listen, reliance on persuasion rather than force. These are the virtues which members of a civilized society must possess if the society is to endure. In this sense of "rational," the word means something more like "civilized" than like "methodical." When so construed, the distinction between the rational and the irrational has nothing in particular to do with the difference between the arts and the sciences. On this construction, to be rational is simply to discuss any topic—religious, literary, or scientific—in a way which eschews dogmatism, defensiveness, and righteous indignation.

There is no problem about whether, in this latter, weaker, sense, the humanities are "rational disciplines." Usually humanists display the moral virtues in question. Sometimes they don't, but then sometimes scientists don't either. Yet these moral virtues are felt to be not enough. Both humanists and the public hanker after rationality in the first, stronger sense of the term: a sense which is associated with objective truth, correspondence to reality, and method, and criteria.

We should not try to satisfy this hankering, but rather try to eradicate it. No matter what one's opinion of the secularization of culture, it was a mistake to try to make the natural scientist into a new sort of priest, a link between the human and the nonhuman. So was the idea that some sorts of truths are "objective" whereas others are merely "subjective" or "relative"—the attempt to divide up the set of true sentences into "genuine knowledge" and "mere opinion," or into the "factual" and "judgmental." So was the idea that the scientist has a special method which, if only the humanists would apply it to ultimate values, would give us the same kind of self-confidence about the moral ends as we now have about technological means. I think that we should content ourselves with the second, "weaker" conception of rationality, and avoid the first, "stronger" conception. We should avoid the idea that there is some special virtue in knowing in advance what criteria you are going to satisfy, in having standards by which to measure progress.

One can make these issues somewhat more concrete by taking up the current controversy among philosophers about the "rationality of science." For some twenty years, ever since the publication of Thomas Kuhn's book *The Structure of Scientific Revolutions,* philosophers have been debating whether science is rational. Attacks on Kuhn for being an "irrationalist" are now as frequent and as urgent as were, in the thirties and forties, attacks on the logical positivists for saying that moral judgments were "meaningless." We are constantly being warned of the danger of "relativism," which will beset us if we give up our attachment to objectivity, and to the idea of rationality as obedience to criteria.

Whereas Kuhn's enemies routinely accuse him of reducing science to "mob psychology," and pride themselves on having (by a new theory of meaning, or reference, or verisimilitude) vindicated the "rationality of science," his pragmatist friends (such as myself) routinely congratulate him on having softened the distinction between science and nonscience. It is fairly easy for Kuhn to show that the enemies are attacking a straw man. But it is harder for him to save himself from his friends. For he has said that "there is no theory-independent way to reconstruct phrases like 'really there.'" He has asked whether it really helps "to imagine that there is some one full, objective, true account of nature and that the proper measure of scientific achievement is the extent to which it brings us closer to that ultimate goal." We pragmatists quote these passages incessantly in the course of our effort to enlist Kuhn in our campaign to drop the objective-subjective distinction altogether.

What I am calling "pragmatism" might also be called "left-wing Kuhnianism." It has been also rather endearingly called (by one of its critics, Clark Glymour) the "new fuzziness," because it is an attempt to blur just those distinctions between the objective and the subjective and between fact and value which the criterial conception of rationality has developed. We fuzzies would like to substitute the idea of "unforced agreement" for that of "objectivity." We should like to put all of culture on an epistemological level—or, to put it another way, we would like to get rid of the idea of "epistemological level" or "cognitive status." We would like to disabuse social scientists and humanists of the idea that there is something called "scientific status" which is a desirable goal. On our view, "truth" is a univocal term. It applies equally to the judgments of lawyers, anthropologists, physicists, philologists, and literary critics. There is no point in assigning degrees of "objectivity" or "hardness" to such disciplines. For the presence of unforced agreement in all of them gives us everything in the way of "objective truth" which one could possibly want: namely, intersubjective agreement.

As soon as one says that objectivity is intersubjectivity, one is likely to be accused of being a relativist. That is the epithet traditionally applied to pragmatists. But this epithet is ambiguous. It can name any of three different views. The first is the silly and self-refuting view that every belief is as good as every other. The second is the wrong-headed view that "true" is an equivocal term, having as many meanings as there are contexts of justification. The third is the ethnocentric view that there is nothing to be said about either truth or rationality apart from descriptions of the familiar procedures of justification which a given society—*ours*—uses in one or another area of inquiry. The pragmatist does hold this third, ethnocentric, view. But he does not hold the first or the second.

But "relativism" is not an appropriate term to describe this sort of ethnocentrism. For we pragmatists are not holding a positive theory which says that something is relative to something else. Instead, we are making the purely *negative* point that we would be better off without the traditional distinctions between knowledge and opinion, construed as the distinction between truth as correspondence to reality and truth as a commendatory term for well-justified belief. Our opponents call this negative claim "relativistic" because they cannot imagine that anybody would seriously deny that truth has an intrinsic nature. So when we say that there is nothing to be said about truth save that each of us will commend as true those beliefs which he or she finds good to believe, the realist is inclined to interpret this as one more positive theory about the nature of truth: a theory according to which truth is simply the contemporary opinion of a chosen individual or group. Such a theory would, of course, be self-refuting. But we pragmatists do not have a theory of truth, much less a relativistic one. As partisans of solidarity, our account of the value of cooperative human inquiry has only an ethical base, not an epistemological or metaphysical one.

To say that we must be ethnocentric may sound suspicious, but this will only happen if we identify ethnocentrism with pig-headed refusal to talk to representatives of other communities. In my sense of ethnocentrism, to be ethnocentric is simply to work by our own lights. The defense of ethnocentrism is simply that there are no other lights to work by. Beliefs suggested by another individual or another culture must be tested by trying to weave them together with beliefs which we already have. We *can* so test them, because everything which we can identify as a human being or as a culture will be something which shares an enormous number of beliefs with us. (If it did not, we would simply not be able to recognize that it was speaking a language, and thus that it had any beliefs at all.)

This way of thinking runs counter to the attempt, familiar since the eighteenth century, to think of political liberalism as based on a conception of the nature of man. To most thinkers of the Enlightenment, it seemed clear that the access to Nature which physical science had provided should now be followed by the establishment of social, political, and economic institutions which were "in accordance with Nature." Ever since, liberal social thought has centered on social reform as made possible by objective knowledge of what human beings are like—not knowledge of what Greeks or Frenchmen or Chinese are like, but of humanity as such. This tradition dreams of a universal human community which will exhibit a nonparochial solidarity because it is the expression of an ahistorical human nature.

Philosophers who belong to this tradition, who wish to ground solidarity in objectivity, have to construe truth as correspondence to reality. So they must construct an epistemology which had room for a kind of justification which is not merely social but natural, springing from human nature itself, and made possible by a link between that part of nature and the rest of nature. By contrast, we pragmatists, who wish to reduce objectivity to solidarity, do not require either a metaphysics or an epistemology. We do not need an account of a relation between beliefs and objects called "correspondence," nor an account of human cognitive abilities which ensures that our species is capable of entering into that relation. We see the gap between truth and justification not as something to be bridged by isolating a natural and transcultural sort of rationality which can be used to criticize certain cultures and praise others, but simply as the gap between the actual good and the possible better. From a pragmatist point of view, to say that what is rational for us now to believe may not be *true* is simply to say that somebody may come up with a better idea. . . .

Another reason for describing us as "relativistic" is that we pragmatists drop the idea that inquiry is

destined to converge to a single point—that Truth is "out there" waiting for human beings to arrive at it. This idea seems to us an unfortunate attempt to carry a religious conception over into a culture. All that is worth preserving of the claim that rational inquiry will converge to a single point is the claim that we must be able to explain why past false views were held in the past, and thus explain how we go about reeducating our benighted ancestors. To say that we think we are heading in the right direction is just to say, with Kuhn, that we can, by hindsight, tell the story of the past as a story of progress.

But the fact that we can trace such a direction and tell such a story does not mean that we have gotten closer to a goal which is out there waiting for us. We cannot, I think, imagine a moment at which the human race could settle back and say, "Well, now that we've finally arrived at the Truth we can relax." Paul Feyerabend is right in suggesting that we should discard the metaphor of inquiry, and human knowledge generally, as converging rather than proliferating, becoming more unified rather than more diverse. On the contrary, we should relish the thought that the sciences as well as the arts will *always* provide a spectacle of fierce competition between alternative theories, movements, and schools. The end of human activity is not rest, but rather richer and better human activity. We should think of human progress as making it possible for human beings to do more interesting things and be more interesting people, not as heading toward a place which has somehow been prepared for us in advance. To drop the criterial conception of rationality in favor of the pragmatist conception would be to give up the idea of Truth as something to which we were responsible. Instead we should think of "true" as a word which applies to those beliefs upon which we are able to agree, as roughly synonymous with "justified." To say that beliefs can be agreed upon without being true is, once again, merely to say that somebody might come up with a better idea.

Another way of characterizing this line of thought is to say that pragmatists would like to drop the idea that human beings are responsible to a nonhuman power. We hope for a culture in which questions about the "objectivity of value" or the "rationality of science" would seem equally un-intelligible. Pragmatists would like to replace the desire for objectivity—the desire to be in touch with a reality which is more than some community with which we identify ourselves—with the desire for solidarity with that community. They think that the habits of relying on persuasion rather than force, of respect for the opinions of colleagues, of curiosity and eagerness for new data and ideas, are the *only* virtues which scientists have. They do not think that there is an intellectual virtue called "ra-tionality" over and above these moral virtues.

On this view there is no reason to praise scien-tists for being more "objective" or "logical" or "me-thodical" or "devoted to truth" than other people. But there is plenty of reason to praise the institu-tions they have developed and within which they work, and to use these as models for the rest of cul-ture. For these institutions give concreteness and detail to the idea of "unforced agreement." Refer-ence to such institutions fleshes out the idea of "a free and open encounter"—the sort of encounter in which truth cannot fail to win. On this view, to say that truth will win in such an encounter is not to make a metaphysical claim about the connection between human reason and the nature of things. It is merely to say that the best way to find out what to believe is to listen to as many suggestions and ar-guments as you can. . . .

Pragmatists interpret the goal of inquiry (in any sphere of culture) as the attainment of an appro-priate mixture of unforced agreement with tol-erant disagreement (where what counts as appropriate is determined, within that sphere, by trial and error). Such a reinterpretation of our sense of responsibility would, if carried through, gradually make unintelligible the subject-object model of inquiry, the child-parent model of moral obligation, and the correspondence theory of truth. A world in which those models, and that the-ory, no longer had any intuitive appeal would be a pragmatist's paradise.

When Dewey urged that we try to create such a paradise, he was said to be irresponsible. For, it was said, he left us bereft of weapons to use against our enemies; he gave us nothing with which to "answer the Nazis." When we new fuzzies try to revive

Dewey's repudiation of criteriology, we are said to be "relativistic." We must, people say, believe that every coherent view is as good as every other, since we have no "outside" touchstone for choice among such views. We are said to leave the general public defenseless against the witch doctor, the defender of creationism, or anyone else who is clever and patient enough to deduce a consistent and wide-ranging set of theorems from his "alternative first principles."

Nobody is convinced when we fuzzies say that we can be just as morally indignant as the next philosopher. We are suspected of being contritely fallibilist when righteous fury is called for. Even when we actually display appropriate emotions we get nowhere, for we are told that we have no *right* to these emotions. When we suggest that one of the few things we know (or need to know) about truth is that it is what wins in a free and open encounter, we are told that we have defined "true" as "satisfies the standards of our community." But we pragma-tists do not hold this relativist view. We do not infer from "there is no way to step outside communities to a neutral standpoint" that "there is no rational way to justify liberal communities over totalitarian communities." For that inference involves just the notion of "rationality" as a set of ahistorical princi-ples which pragmatists abjure. What we in fact infer is that there is no way to beat totalitarians in argu-ment by appealing to shared common premises, and no point in pretending that a common human nature makes the totalitarians unconsciously hold such premises.

The claim that we fuzzies have no right to be fu-rious at moral evil, no right to commend our views as true unless we simultaneously refute ourselves by claiming that there are objects out there which *make* those views true, begs all the theoretical ques-tions. But it gets to the practical and moral heart of the matter. This is the question of whether notions like "unforced agreement" and "free and open en-counter"—descriptions of social situations—can take the place in our moral lives of notions like "the world," "the will of God," "the moral law," "what our beliefs are trying to represent accu-rately," and "what makes our beliefs true." All the philosophical presuppositions which make Hume's fork [the separation of facts and values] seem inevitable are ways of suggesting that human communities must justify their existence by striving to attain a nonhuman goal. To suggest that we can forget about Hume's fork, forget about being responsible to what is "out there," is to suggest that human communities can only justify their existence by comparisons with other actual and possible human communities.

I can make this contrast a bit more concrete by asking whether free and open encounters, and the kind of community which permits and encourages such encounters, are for the sake of truth and goodness, or whether "the quest for truth and goodness" is simply the quest for that kind of community. Is the sort of community which is exemplified by groups of scientific inquirers and by democratic political institutions a means to an end, or is the formation of such communities the only goal we need? Dewey thought that it was the only goal we needed, and I think he was right. But whether he was or not, this question is the one to which the debates about Kuhn's "irrationalism" and the new fuzzies' "relativism" will eventually boil down.

Dewey was accused of blowing up the optimism and flexibility of a parochial and jejune way of life (the American) into a philosophical system. So he did, but his reply was that *any* philosophical system is going to be an attempt to express the ideals of *some* community's way of life. He was quite ready to admit that the virtue of his philosophy was, indeed, nothing more than the virtue of the way of life which it commended. On his view, philosophy does not justify affiliation with a community in the light of something ahistorical called "reason" or "transcultural principles." It simply expatiates on the special advantages of that community over other communities. Dewey's best argument for doing philosophy this way is also the best argument we partisans of solidarity have against partisans of objectivity: it is Nietzsche's argument that the traditional Western metaphysico-epistemological way of firming up our habits is not working anymore.

What would it be like to be less fuzzy and parochial than this? I suggest that it would be to become less genial, tolerant, open-minded, and falli-

bilist than we are now. In the nontrivial, pejorative, sense of "ethnocentric," the sense in which we congratulate ourselves on being less ethnocentric now than our ancestors were three hundred years ago, the way to avoid ethnocentrism is precisely to abandon the sort of thing we fuzzies are blamed for abandoning. It is to have only the most tenuous and cursory formulations of criteria for changing our beliefs, only the loosest and most flexible standards. Suppose that for the last three hundred years we had been using an explicit algorithm for determining how just a society was, and how good a physical theory was. Would we have developed either parliamentary democracy or relativity physics? Suppose that we had the sort of "weapons" against the fascists of which Dewey was said to deprive us—firm, unrevisable, moral principles which were not merely "ours" but "universal" and "objective." How could we avoid having these weapons turn in our hands and bash all the genial tolerance out of our own heads?

Imagine, to use another example, that a few years from now you open your copy of the *New York Times* and read that the philosophers, in convention assembled, have unanimously agreed that values are objective, science rational, truth a matter of correspondence to reality, and so on. Recent breakthroughs in semantics and meta-ethics, the report goes on, have caused the last remaining noncognitivists in ethics to recant. Similar breakthroughs in philosophy of science have led Kuhn formally to abjure his claim that there is no theory-independent way to reconstruct statements about what is "really there." All the new fuzzies have repudiated all their former views. By way of making amends for the intellectual confusion which the philosophical profession has recently caused, the philosophers have adopted a short, crisp, set of standards of rationality and morality. Next year the convention is expected to adopt the report of the committee charged with formulating a standard of aesthetic taste.

Surely the public reaction to this would not be "Saved!" but rather "Who on earth do these philosophers think they *are?*" It is one of the best things about the form of intellectual life we Western liberals lead that this *would* be our reaction. No matter how much we moan about the disorder and confusion of the current philosophical scene, about the treason of the clerks, we do not really want things any other way. What prevents us from relaxing and enjoying the new fuzziness is perhaps no more than cultural lag, the fact that the rhetoric of the Enlightenment praised the emerging natural sciences in a vocabulary which was left over from a less liberal and tolerant era. This rhetoric enshrined all the old philosophical oppositions between mind and world, appearance and reality, subject and object, truth and pleasure. Dewey thought that it was the continued prevalence of such oppositions which prevented us from seeing that modern science was a new and promising invention, a way of life which had not existed before and which ought to be encouraged and imitated, something which required a new rhetoric rather than justification by an old one.

Suppose that Dewey was right about this, and that eventually we learn to find the fuzziness which results from breaking down such oppositions spiritually comforting rather than morally offensive. What would the rhetoric of the culture, and in particular of the humanities, sound like? Presumably it would be more Kuhnian, in the sense that it would mention particular concrete achievements—paradigms—more, and "method" less. There would be less talk about rigor and more about originality. The image of the great scientist would not be of somebody who got it right but of somebody who made it new. The new rhetoric would draw more on the vocabulary of Romantic poetry and socialist politics, and less on that of Greek metaphysics, religious morality, or Enlightenment scientism. A scientist would rely on a sense of solidarity with the rest of her profession, rather than a picture of herself as battling through the veils of illusion, guided by the light of reason.

If all this happened, the term "science," and thus the oppositions between the humanities, the arts, and the sciences, might gradually fade away. Once "science" was deprived of an honorific sense, we might not need it for taxonomy. We might feel no more need for a term which groups together paleontology, physics, anthropology, and psychology than we do for one which groups together engineering, law, social work, and medicine. The people now called "scientists" would no longer think of themselves as a member of a quasi-priestly order, nor would the public think of themselves as in the care of such an order.

In this situation, "the humanities" would no longer think of themselves as such, nor would they share a common rhetoric. Each of the disciplines which now fall under that rubric would worry as little about its method or cognitive status as do mathematics, civil engineering, and sculpture. It would worry as little about its philosophical foundations. For terms which denoted disciplines would not be thought to divide "subject-matters," chunks of the world which had "interfaces" with each other. Rather, they would be thought to denote communities whose boundaries were as fluid as the interests of their members. In this heyday of the fuzzy, there would be as little reason to be self-conscious about the nature and status of one's discipline as, in the ideal democratic community, about the nature and status of one's race or sex. For one's ultimate loyalty would be to the larger community which permitted and encouraged this kind of freedom and insouciance. This community would serve no higher end than its own preservation and self-improvement, the preservation and enhancement of civilization. It would identify rationality with that effort, rather than with the desire for objectivity. So it would feel no need for a foundation more solid than reciprocal loyalty.

Questions for Reflection

1. Do you agree with Rorty that the notions of objective truth and correspondence with reality are unimportant?
2. Do you think that scientists would be motivated to do research if they adopted Rorty's view?

3. To what degree is the distinction between objective and subjective approaches intrinsic to good science?

4. Suppose a society practiced some form of morally objectionable discrimination, but even those who were discriminated against had been socialized to believe that this was the way things were supposed to be. Thus, there are no dissenting voices within this society. It could be argued that this society has achieved "social solidarity" and "unforced agreement" (to use Rorty's terms). Would Rorty be forced to say that this society had achieved his ideal? If not, on what basis might he object to it?

C H A P T E R   4

Questions about the Mind

THE MIND: WHAT ARE THE ISSUES?

Who are you? If you were asked that question you might respond by stating your name, your parents, your hometown, or your school. If there are others with the same name, you could uniquely identify yourself by reciting your social security number. Or, perhaps, you might answer the question by describing your personality, your likes and dislikes, your beliefs, and your values. Certainly, all these facts about you play a role in your sense of identity. However, some of these facts are peripheral. You can imagine that you were given a different name or social security number and, yet, you would still be the same person you are today. But if you imagine that you had different parents and different genes or grew up in a different part of the world, would it then be as easy to imagine that you would be the same person? Once you strip away all the variable facts about yourself, what remains? Is there a core self that constitutes the real you? How many facts about you could be different without changing who you are as a person?

On the other hand, maybe there is no core self. Maybe all the facts that describe you constitute who you are and there is nothing beyond them. In asking about the "real" you we were assuming that the self is like a peach. Strip away the outer layers and there is a core inside it. However, we are now switching the metaphor and suggesting that you might be more like an onion. Peel back the layers of the onion and nothing remains at the core. Which metaphor best describes the self?

The readings in this chapter all revolve around the nature of the mind and the self. But what is the mind? You are a being that is conscious and aware, and that thinks, believes, judges, imagines, and hopes. Traditionally, these activities have been associated with the mind. However, your body is also important. Its pains, feelings, and appearance are part of who you are. But what is the relationship between the mental, conscious part of you and your physical body and brain? The ancient Greeks wrestled with the mystery of the mind and body and could not resolve it to everyone's satisfaction. The difficulty of the problem is indicated by the fact that it is still with us today, with many competing, alternative solutions being offered by different philosophers and the proponents of each position claiming that theirs is the absolutely correct one.

Notice that we have two different ways of describing a person. We can say of a someone that she is sitting, standing, running, or jumping. We can also say that she is thinking, imagining, doubting, or believing. We might describe her as five feet tall, weighing 120 pounds, with black hair and brown eyes. We can also describe her as intelligent, imaginative, pessimistic, or compassionate. One set of descriptions applies to her physical body, while the second set seems to apply to her mind. We don't speak of her body as being pessimistic, nor do we speak of her mind as having a certain weight. To make the same point in a different way, read the following list of properties and, for each one, think of a physical object that it might describe: green, square, tall, heavy, wet. Now take these same adjectives and try applying them to a mental object such as a belief, a hope, or an idea. Obviously it makes no sense to talk of a green, square, tall hope (unless we are speaking metaphorically).

The point of all this is that reality seems to be divided into two kinds of things, each having its own, unique set of properties. On the one hand there are minds and mental objects (beliefs, ideas), as well as mental activities (believing) and mental properties (intelligent). On the other hand there are human bodies and other physical objects, as well as physical activities (falling) and physical properties (heavy, yellow). At the same time, and in spite of their differences, our body and mind seem to interact and causally affect one another. When you worry (a mental event), it may cause you to lose your appetite (an effect on your body). When you drink too much coffee (a physical event), it may cause you to be irritable (an effect on your mind).

These considerations support three commonsense beliefs that characterize our traditional concept of the mind and body:

1. The body is a physical thing.
2. The mind is a nonphysical thing.
3. The mind and body interact and causally affect one another.

Having said all this, one nagging problem remains: Exactly how does a nonphysical thing (the mind) interact with a physical thing (the body)? Physical things interact by pushing, pulling, merging, energizing, attracting, magnetizing, and so forth. However, all these sorts of interactions involve physical forces that can be explained by the laws of physics. Most people, if asked, would tend to agree with the statement, "The motion of a physical body is completely subject to physical laws." However, if the mind is not a physical thing, then it cannot affect a body through gravitational, electrical, magnetic, or mechanical force. How then can there be any causal relationship between the mind and body? To explain this interaction by referring to the brain is of very little help, because the brain is simply another sort of physical body. The difficulty of understanding how a nonphysical thing such as the mind can have any causal interaction with a physical body, suggests a fourth proposition:

4. Nonphysical things cannot causally interact with physical things.

We now seem to have four, equally plausible propositions. The problem is, they cannot all be true. You can believe any combination of three of them, but when you add the remaining proposition, you end up in a contradiction. It seems that we are forced to decide which one of the four preceding propositions we are going to reject. The problem is, there is a price to pay for rejecting any of them and that is the necessity of rejecting the commonsense reasons that led us to think that particular belief to be plausible in the first place. As we will see, each of the positions on the mind-body problem avoids the difficulty by rejecting one of the above propositions. In preparation for what follows, ask yourself the following question: Which one of the four propositions would I find it easiest to reject?

WHAT ARE MY OPTIONS CONCERNING THE MIND?

Mind-body dualism is the claim that the mind and the body (which includes the brain) are separate entities. The body is a physical thing, while the mind is a nonphysical (immaterial or spiritual) thing. (For the sake of brevity, whenever I discuss dualism with respect to the mind and body in the remainder of this chapter, I will refer to mind-body dualism as simply *dualism*.)

The most common version of dualism is called **interactionism.** Interactionism adds to the dualistic thesis the claim that the mind and body, though different, causally interact with one another. This version of dualism was defended by the seventeenth-century French philosopher Descartes and represents the commonsense view of the issue we explored above. Note that it is common in many religious views to identify the real person with his or her soul, which is said to be a nonphysical or spiritual entity. In discussing dualism, we will assume that the terms *soul* or *mind* may be used interchangeably, since they both refer to the nonphysical component within us that constitutes the real person.

During the time of Descartes, there were two other forms of dualism that were developed as alternatives to interactionism. Each of them claimed that the mind and body were separate realities, while denying that the two causally affected one another. In this way they avoided the problem interactionism faced of explaining how our nonphysical mind can interact with our physical body. The first alternative form of dualism is known as **parallelism.** This position claims that mental events cause only other mental events and physical events cause only other physical events. These two separate series of events only seem to interact because they always operate parallel to one another. Arnold Geulincx (1624–1669), for example, said God arranges the two parallel series of mental and physical events to work together like two clocks that are set to strike the hour at the same time. Since God has foreseen that I am now willing my pen to write on this paper, he has arranged the physical world so that my hand and the pen move simultaneously with my mental willing. The second position was that of **occasionalism.** It was very similar to parallelism except that there was no preestablished harmony created by God. Instead, on the occasion of a physical event, God causes a mental event and vice-versa. Hence, when the telephone produces physical sound waves, God causes you to experience the sound of ringing. When you think relaxing thoughts, God causes your blood pressure to go down. Nicholas Malebranche (1638–1715) was a leading defender of occasionalism.

Physicalism (sometimes called *materialism*) is the claim that the self is identical to or the product of the activities of the body or the brain and that there is no nonphysical aspect of the person. There are several varieties of physicalism. One version of physicalism is **logical behaviorism,** which is the claim that statements about mental events can be analyzed into statements about behavior or behavioral dispositions. Hence, to say that "John believes the pan is hot" is simply to say that he will be inclined not to touch it. Rejecting the dualist's view that the mind is a nonphysical substance, the logical behaviorist claims that to talk of a person's mind is simply to talk of the person's abilities or inclinations to behave in a certain way. Two more versions of physicalism are **identity theory** (or **reductionism**) and **eliminativism.** Even though identity theorists deny that there is a separate, nonphysical mind, they think it is meaningful to talk about the mind, because they claim that all talk about the mind can be translated into talk about brain states. On the other hand, the eliminativist thinks that our mental vocabulary should be eliminated altogether in favor of a physiological vocabulary. Hence, for the eliminativists, to talk about whether the mind is or is not physical or whether it does or does not interact with the body, is like asking "Are leprechauns in favor of nuclear disarmament?" or "Do ghosts enjoy modern art?" Once you have decided that leprechauns and ghosts do not exist, these questions are pointless. Similarly, the eliminativists want to discard all language that refers to mental events, because they believe there are no such things. For these theorists, there are only brain events as described by contemporary psychology and physiology.

Even though interactionism and physicalism are the most common positions throughout the history of philosophy, there is another option worth mentioning. **Idealism** claims that the physical world and the body are just a collection of mental experiences or are aspects of a larger mental reality. The idealist solves the problem of how the mind and body relate together by claiming that they are not really two different, irreducible kinds of reality. Idealism is like the photographic negative of physicalism. Whereas the physicalist says that human beings are nothing but matter, the idealist says that human beings (and all of reality) are nothing but mental substances. The idealist's view of the mind has been presented previously through the philosophy of George Berkeley in Chapter 3 (reading 23).

The various positions that have been discussed are summarized in terms of their answers to five questions in Table 4.1. Notice that in this table we have five questions and six positions. Each one of the positions avoids the mind-body problem by answering *No* to one of the questions. Even though both the logical behaviorist and identity theorist deny that there is a separate, nonphysical mind, they both think it is meaningful to talk about the mind (question 2). For the logical behaviorist, mental concepts are meaningful because they refer to behavior. For the identity theorist, mental concepts are meaningful because they refer to brain states. However, the logical behaviorist does not think that it is meaningful to say that the mind and body interact, because the mind is not a thing (question 4). The identity theorist might say that it is meaningful to say the mind and body interact since mental states really are just brain states and our brain states certainly interact with the rest of the body. All three varieties of physicalists refrain from answering the fifth question, because they do not think there is any nonphysical mental reality at all. The eliminativists also refrain from answering questions three and four because they deny that the term *mind* refers to anything.

There is yet one more position, called **functionalism.** Functionalism could not be placed on the chart because its advocates question the way that the mind-body issue has been divided up in the chart. They reject the dualist's claim that the mind is a separate substance. At the same time, they reject the identity theorist's claim that mental events are identical to brain events. They also reject the eliminativist's claim that there are no mental events. Instead, functionalists argue that the realm of the mental is characterized by particular patterns of input-processing-output. Hence, functionalists claim that the brain is like the physical hardware of the computer and the mind is like the computer program that is run on the hardware, but is logically distinct from it. Some philosophers and artificial intelligence researchers claim that some day computers will be able to think just as well, if not better, than we do. As such, these same theorists also claim that when that happens, computers will have minds, since functionalists believe that having a mind is not dependent on being made of the same materials as we are, but

TABLE 4.1 POSITIONS ON THE MIND-BODY PROBLEM

	Is the Body a Physical Thing?	Do We Have a Mind?	Is the Mind a Nonphysical Thing?	Do the Mind and Body Interact?	Is It Impossible for a Nonphysical Thing to Interact with a Physical Thing?
Dualism: Interactionism	Yes	Yes	Yes	Yes	No
Dualism: Occasionalism, Parallelism	Yes	Yes	Yes	No	Yes
Physicalism: Logical Behaviorism	Yes	Yes	No	—	—
Physicalism: Identity Theory (Reductionism)	Yes	Yes	No	Yes	—
Physicalism: Eliminativism	Yes	No	—	—	—
Idealism	No	Yes	Yes	Yes	Yes

in functioning cognitively as we do. The readings by Jeffrey Olen (41), Christopher Evans (43), and Terry Bisson (45) could be viewed as supporting functionalism, while John Searle (44) is critical of this approach.

The first set of readings will address the major issue of the nature of the mind and its relation to the body. The second set of readings address the question, "What is the basis of personal identity?" The answer to this question will go a long way in answering another question, "Do I survive my death?" As we will see, this second set of questions is related to the first issue of how we understand the mind. Finally, we will consider the contemporary application question, "Can computers think?" Since computers are physical entities made up of wires and chips, it should be clear that this last question is also related to how we understand the mind and its relationship to our physical embodiment.

Our opening narrative, a fictional work by Daniel Dennett, will raise perplexing questions about the mind, the self, the body, personal identity, and computer-based intelligence. Hence, it will bombard us with all the above questions in one, well-crafted philosophical tale.

OPENING NARRATIVE: WHAT IS THE SELF?

D A N I E L   D E N N E T T

"Where Am I?"

Daniel Dennett (1942–   ) is Distinguished Arts and Sciences Professor, Professor of Philosophy, and Director of the Center for Cognitive Studies at Tufts University. He has published over 100 articles, and his most recent books are *Consciousness Explained* (1991), *Darwin's Dangerous Idea* (1995), *Kinds of Minds* (1996), and *Brainchildren: Essays on Designing Minds* (1998).

    Three intimately related facets of our existence play a role in our sense of identity. These are (1) our brain, (2) the rest of our body (our sense organs and limbs), and (3) our consciousness, our awareness, or our point of view. Normally, these three factors always go together and are centrally located. Thus, it is easy to answer the question, "Where am I?," for it is wherever the unified collection of my brain, body, and conscious awareness is. However, in this science fiction story, Dennett asks us to imagine that these three elements are separated. This scenario forces us to reassess how we would answer the question "Where am I?" and even "Who am I?"

Reading Questions

1. Why does Dennett initially have problems deciding if he is here staring through a glass at his own brain, or whether he is there (the brain in the vat being stared at by his own eyes)?
2. What are the three possible alternatives he proposes for answering the question, "Where am I?" What problems does he pose for each alternative?
3. When the tunnel caves in, what does he mean when he says "an instant before I had been buried alive in Oklahoma, now I was disembodied in Houston"?
4. Using the labels that Dennett chose, what happened to Hamlet? Who (or what) is Yorick? Who (or what) is Fortinbras? Who (or what) is Hubert? Where in all of this do you think Dennett resides?
5. What conditions would create the possibility of there being two Dennetts? What does he consider to be the pros and cons of that possibility?
6. What startling revelation occurs when Dennett flips the switch between his organic brain and the computer duplicate? What caused the breakdown of the unity between the two systems?

Daniel Dennett, "Where Am I?," in *Brainstorms: Philosophical Essays on Mind and Psychology* (Cambridge, MA: MIT Press, 1981).

Now that I've won my suit under the Freedom of Information Act, I am at liberty to reveal for the first time a curious episode in my life that may be of interest not only to those engaged in research in the philosophy of mind, artificial intelligence, and neuroscience but also to the general public.

Several years ago I was approached by Pentagon officials who asked me to volunteer for a highly dangerous and secret mission. In collaboration with NASA and Howard Hughes, the Department of Defense was spending billions to develop a Supersonic Tunneling Underground Device, or STUD. It was supposed to tunnel through the earth's core at great speed and deliver a specially designed atomic warhead "right up the Red's missile silos," as one of the Pentagon brass put it.

The problem was that in an early test they had succeeded in lodging a warhead about a mile deep under Tulsa, Oklahoma, and they wanted me to retrieve it for them. "Why me?" I asked. Well, the mission involved some pioneering applications of current brain research, and they had heard of my interest in brains and of course my Faustian curiosity and great courage and so forth. . . . Well, how could I refuse? The difficulty that brought the Pentagon to my door was that the device I'd been asked to recover was fiercely radioactive, in a new way. According to monitoring instruments, something about the nature of the device and its complex interactions with pockets of material deep in the earth had produced radiation that could cause severe abnormalities in certain tissues of the brain. No way had been found to shield the brain from these deadly rays, which were apparently harmless to other tissues and organs of the body. So it had been decided that the person sent to recover the device should *leave his brain behind*. It would be kept in a safe place where it could execute its normal control functions by elaborate radio links. Would I submit to a surgical procedure that would completely remove my brain, which would then be placed in a life-support system at the Manned Spacecraft Center in Houston? Each input and output pathway, as it was severed, would be restored by a pair of microminiaturized radio transceivers, one attached precisely to the brain, the other to the nerve stumps in the empty cranium. No informa-

tion would be lost, all the connectivity would be preserved. At first I was a bit reluctant. Would it really work? The Houston brain surgeons encouraged me. "Think of it," they said, "as a mere *stretching* of the nerves. If your brain were just moved over an *inch* in your skull, that would not alter or impair your mind. We're simply going to make the nerves indefinitely elastic by splicing radio links into them."

I was shown around the life-support lab in Houston and saw the sparkling new vat in which my brain would be placed, were I to agree. I met the large and brilliant support team of neurologists, hematologists, biophysicists, and electrical engineers, and after several days of discussions and demonstrations, I agreed to give it a try. I was subjected to an enormous array of blood tests, brain scans, experiments, interviews, and the like. They took down my autobiography at great length, recorded tedious lists of my beliefs, hopes, fears, and tastes. They even listed my favorite stereo recordings and gave me a crash session of psychoanalysis.

The day for surgery arrived at last and of course I was anesthetized and remember nothing of the operation itself. When I came out of anesthesia, I opened my eyes, looked around, and asked the inevitable, the traditional, the lamentably hackneyed postoperative question: "Where am I?" The nurse smiled down at me. "You're in Houston," she said, and I reflected that this still had a good chance of being the truth one way or another. She handed me a mirror. Sure enough, there were the tiny antennae poling up through their titanium ports cemented into my skull.

"I gather the operation was a success," I said. "I want to go see my brain." They led me (I was a bit dizzy and unsteady) down a long corridor and into the life-support lab. A cheer went up from the assembled support team, and I responded with what I hoped was a jaunty salute. Still feeling lightheaded, I was helped over to the life-support vat. I peered through the glass. There, floating in what looked like ginger ale, was undeniably a human brain, though it was almost covered with printed circuit chips, plastic tubules, electrodes, and other paraphernalia. "Is that mine?" I asked. "Hit the output transmitter switch there on the side of the vat and see for yourself," the project director replied. I moved the switch to OFF, and immediately slumped, groggy and nauseated, into the arms of the technicians, one of whom kindly restored the switch to its ON position. While I recovered my equilibrium and composure, I thought to myself: "Well, here I am sitting on a folding chair, staring through a piece of plate glass at my own brain. . . . But wait," I said to myself, "shouldn't I have thought, 'Here I am, suspended in a bubbling fluid, being stared at by my own eyes'?" I tried to think this latter thought. I tried to project it into the tank, offering it hopefully to my brain, but I failed to carry off the exercise with any conviction. I tried again. "Here am *I*, Daniel Dennett, suspended in a bubbling fluid, being stared at by my own eyes." No, it just didn't work. Most puzzling and confusing. Being a philosopher of firm physicalist conviction, I believed unswervingly that the tokening of my thoughts was occurring somewhere in my brain: yet, when I thought "Here I am," where the thought occurred to me was *here,* outside the vat, where I, Dennett, was standing staring at my brain.

I tried and tried to think myself into the vat, but to no avail. I tried to build up to the task by doing mental exercises. I thought to myself, "The sun is shining *over there,*" five times in rapid succession, each time mentally ostending a different place: in order, the sunlit corner of the lab, the visible front lawn of the hospital, Houston, Mars, and Jupiter. I found I had little difficulty in getting my "there" 's to hop all over the celestial map with their proper references. I could loft a "there" in an instant through the farthest reaches of space, and then aim the next "there" with pinpoint accuracy at the upper left quadrant of a freckle on my arm. Why was I having such trouble with "here"? "Here in Houston" worked well enough, and so did "here in the lab," and even "here in this part of the lab," but "here in the vat" always seemed merely an unmeant mental mouthing. I tried closing my eyes while thinking it. This seemed to help, but still I couldn't manage to pull it off, except perhaps for a fleeting instant. I couldn't be sure. The discovery that I couldn't be sure was also unsettling. How did I

know *where* I meant by "here" when I thought "here"? Could I *think* I meant one place when in fact I meant another? I didn't see how that could be admitted without untying the few bonds of intimacy between a person and his own mental life that had survived the onslaught of the brain scientists and philosophers, the physicalists and behaviorists. Perhaps I was incorrigible about where I *meant* when I said "here." But in my present circumstances it seemed that either I was doomed by sheer force of mental habit to thinking systematically false indexical thoughts, or where a person is (and hence where his thoughts are tokened for purposes of semantic analysis) is not necessarily where his brain, the physical seat of his soul, resides. Nagged by confusion, I attempted to orient myself by falling back on a favorite philosopher's ploy. I began naming things.

"Yorick," I said aloud to my brain, "you are my brain. The rest of my body, seated in this chair, I dub 'Hamlet.'" So here we all are: Yorick's my brain, Hamlet's my body, and I am Dennett. *Now,* where am I? And when I think "where am I?" where's that thought tokened? Is it tokened in my brain, lounging about in the vat, or right here between my ears where it *seems* to be tokened? Or nowhere? Its *temporal* coordinates give me no trouble; must it not have spatial coordinates as well? I began making a list of the alternatives.

1. *Where Hamlet goes, there goes Dennett.* This principle was easily refuted by appeal to the familiar brain-transplant thought experiments so enjoyed by philosophers. If Tom and Dick switch brains, Tom is the fellow with Dick's former body—just ask him; he'll claim to be Tom, and tell you the most intimate details of Tom's autobiography. It was clear enough, then, that my current body and I could part company, but not likely that I could be separated from my brain. The rule of thumb that emerged so plainly from the thought experiments was that in a brain-transplant operation, one wanted to be the *donor,* not the recipient. Better to call such an operation a *body* transplant, in fact. So perhaps the truth was,

2. *Where Yorick goes, there goes Dennett.* This was not at all appealing, however. How could I be in the vat and not about to go anywhere, when I was so

obviously outside the vat looking in and beginning to make guilty plans to return to my room for a substantial lunch? This begged the question I realized, but it still seemed to be getting at something important. Casting about for some support for my intuition, I hit upon a legalistic sort of argument that might have appealed to Locke.

Suppose, I argued to myself, I were now to fly to California, rob a bank, and be apprehended. In which state would I be tried: in California, where the robbery took place, or in Texas, where the brains of the outfit were located? Would I be a California felon with an out-of-state brain, or a Texas felon remotely controlling an accomplice of sorts in California? It seemed possible that I might beat such a rap just on the undecidability of that jurisdictional question, though perhaps it would be deemed an interstate, and hence Federal, offense. In any event, suppose I were convicted. Was it likely that California would be satisfied to throw Hamlet into the brig, knowing that Yorick was living the good life and luxuriously taking the waters in Texas? Would Texas incarcerate Yorick, leaving Hamlet free to take the next boat to Rio? This alternative appealed to me. Barring capital punishment or other cruel and unusual punishment, the state would be obliged to maintain the life-support system for Yorick though they might move him from Houston to Leavenworth, and aside from the unpleasantness of the opprobrium, I, for one, would not mind at all and would consider myself a free man under those circumstances. If the state has an interest in forcibly relocating persons in institutions, it would fail to relocate me in any institution by locating Yorick there. If this were true, it suggested a third alternative.

3. *Dennett is wherever he thinks he is.* Generalized, the claim was as follows: At any given time a person has a *point of view,* and the location of the point of view (which is determined internally by the content of the point of view) is also the location of the person.

Such a proposition is not without its perplexities, but to me it seemed a step in the right direction. The only trouble was that it seemed to place one in a heads-I-win/tails-you-lose situation of unlikely infallibility as regards location. Hadn't I my-self often been wrong about where I was, and at least as often uncertain? Couldn't one get lost? Of course, but getting lost *geographically* is not the only way one might get lost. If one were lost in the woods one could attempt to reassure oneself with the consolation that at least one knew where one was: one was right *here* in the familiar surroundings of one's own body. Perhaps in this case one would not have drawn one's attention to much to be thankful for. Still, there were worse plights imaginable, and I wasn't sure I wasn't in such a plight right now.

Point of view clearly had something to do with personal location, but it was itself an unclear notion. It was obvious that the content of one's point of view was not the same as or determined by the content of one's beliefs or thoughts. For example, what should we say about the point of view of the Cinerama viewer who shrieks and twists in his seat as the roller-coaster footage overcomes his psychic distancing? Has he forgotten that he is safely seated in the theater? Here I was inclined to say that the person is experiencing an illusory shift in point of view. In other cases, my inclination to call such shifts illusory was less strong. The workers in laboratories and plants who handle dangerous materials by operating feedback-controlled mechanical arms and hands undergo a shift in point of view that is crisper and more pronounced than anything Cinerama can provoke. They can feel the heft and slipperiness of the containers they manipulate with their metal fingers. They know perfectly well where they are and are not fooled into false beliefs by the experience, yet it is as if they were inside the isolation chamber they are peering into. With mental effort, they can manage to shift their point of view back and forth, rather like making a transparent Necker cube or an Escher drawing change orientation before one's eyes. It does seem extravagant to suppose that in performing this bit of mental gymnastics, they are transporting *themselves* back and forth.

Still their example gave me hope. If I was in fact in the vat in spite of my intuitions, I might be able to train myself to adopt that point of view even as a matter of habit. I should dwell on images of myself comfortably floating in my vat, beaming volitions to that familiar body *out there*. I reflected that the ease or difficulty of this task was presumably independent of the truth about the location of one's brain. Had I been practicing before the operation, I might now be finding it second nature. You might now yourself try such a *trompe l'oeil*. Imagine you have written an inflammatory letter which has been published in the *Times,* the result of which is that the government has chosen to impound your brain for a probationary period of three years in its Dangerous Brain Clinic in Bethesda, Maryland. Your body of course is allowed freedom to earn a salary and thus to continue its function of laying up income to be taxed. At this moment, however, your body is seated in an auditorium listening to a peculiar account by Daniel Dennett of his own similar experience. Try it. Think yourself to Bethesda, and then hark back longingly to your body, far away, and yet *seeming* so near. It is only with long-distance restraint (yours? the government's?) that you can control your impulse to get those hands clapping in polite applause before navigating the old body to the rest room and a well-deserved glass of evening sherry in the lounge. The task of imagination is certainly difficult, but if you achieve your goal the results might be consoling.

Anyway, there I was in Houston, lost in thought as one might say, but not for long. My speculations were soon interrupted by the Houston doctors, who wished to test out my new prosthetic nervous system before sending me off on my hazardous mission. As I mentioned before, I was a bit dizzy at first, and not surprisingly, although I soon habituated myself to my new circumstances (which were, after all, well nigh indistinguishable from my old circumstances). My accommodation was not perfect, however, and to this day I continue to be plagued by minor coordination difficulties. The speed of light is fast, but finite, and as my brain and body move farther and farther apart, the delicate interaction of my feedback systems is thrown into disarray by the time lags. Just as one is rendered close to speechless by a delayed or echoic hearing of one's speaking voice so, for instance, I am virtually unable to track a moving object with my eyes whenever my brain and my body are more than a few miles apart. In most matters my impairment is

scarcely detectable, though I can no longer hit a slow curve ball with the authority of yore. There are some compensations of course. Though liquor tastes as good as ever, and warms my gullet while corroding my liver, I can drink it in any quantity I please, without becoming the slightest bit inebriated, a curiosity some of my close friends may have noticed (though I occasionally have *feigned* inebriation, so as not to draw attention to my unusual circumstances). For similar reasons, I take aspirin orally for a sprained wrist, but if the pain persists I ask Houston to administer codeine to me *in vitro*. In times of illness the phone bill can be staggering.

But to return to my adventure. At length, both the doctors and I were satisfied that I was ready to undertake my subterranean mission. And so I left my brain in Houston and headed by helicopter for Tulsa. Well, in any case, that's the way it seemed to me. That's how I would put it, just off the top of my head as it were. On the trip I reflected further about my earlier anxieties and decided that my first postoperative speculations had been tinged with panic. The matter was not nearly as strange or metaphysical as I had been supposing. Where was I? In two places, clearly: both inside the vat and outside it. Just as one can stand with one foot in Connecticut and the other in Rhode Island, I was in two places at once. I had become one of those scattered individuals we used to hear so much about. The more I considered this answer, the more obviously true it appeared. But, strange to say, the more true it appeared, the less important the question to which it could be the true answer seemed. A sad, but not unprecedented, fate for a philosophical question to suffer. This answer did not completely satisfy me, of course. There lingered some question to which I should have liked an answer, which was neither "Where are all my various and sundry parts?" nor "What is my current point of view?" Or at least there seemed to be such a question. For it did seem undeniable that in some sense *I* and not merely *most of me* was descending into the earth under Tulsa in search of an atomic warhead.

When I found the warhead, I was certainly glad I had left my brain behind, for the pointer on the specially built Geiger counter I had brought with me was off the dial. I called Houston on my ordinary radio and told the operation control center of my position and my progress. In return, they gave me instructions for dismantling the vehicle, based upon my on-site observations. I had set to work with my cutting torch when all of a sudden a terrible thing happened. I went stone deaf. At first I thought it was only my radio earphones that had broken, but when I tapped on my helmet, I heard nothing. Apparently the auditory transceivers had gone on the fritz. I could no longer hear Houston or my own voice, but I could speak, so I started telling them what had happened. In midsentence, I knew something else had gone wrong. My vocal apparatus had become paralyzed. Then my right hand went limp—another transceiver had gone. I was truly in deep trouble. But worse was to follow. After a few more minutes, I went blind. I cursed my luck, and then I cursed the scientists who had led me into this grave peril. There I was, deaf, dumb, and blind, in a radioactive hole more than a mile under Tulsa. Then the last of my cerebral radio links broke, and suddenly I was faced with a new and even more shocking problem: whereas an instant before I had been buried alive in Oklahoma, now I was disembodied in Houston. My recognition of my new status was not immediate. It took me several very anxious minutes before it dawned on me that my poor body lay several hundred miles away, with heart pulsing and lungs respirating, but otherwise as dead as the body of any heart-transplant donor, its skull packed with useless, broken electronic gear. The shift in perspective I had earlier found well nigh impossible now seemed quite natural. Though I could think myself back into my body in the tunnel under Tulsa, it took some effort to sustain the illusion. For surely it was an illusion to suppose I was still in Oklahoma: I had lost all contact with that body.

It occurred to me then, with one of those rushes of revelation of which we should be suspicious, that I had stumbled upon an impressive demonstration of the immateriality of the soul based upon physicalist principles and premises. For as the last radio signal between Tulsa and Houston died away, had I not changed location from Tulsa to Houston at the speed of light? And had I not accomplished this

without any increase in mass? What moved from A to B at such speed was surely myself, or at any rate my soul or mind—the massless center of my being and home of my consciousness. My *point of view* had lagged somewhat behind, but I had already noted the indirect bearing of point of view on personal location. I could not see how a physicalist philosopher could quarrel with this except by taking the dire and counterintuitive route of banishing all talk of persons. Yet the notion of personhood was so well entrenched in everyone's world view, or so it seemed to me, that any denial would be as curiously unconvincing, as systematically disingenuous, as the Cartesian negation, "non sum."

The joy of philosophic discovery thus tided me over some very bad minutes or perhaps hours as the helplessness and hopelessness of my situation became more apparent to me. Waves of panic and even nausea swept over me, made all the more horrible by the absence of their normal body-dependent phenomenology. No adrenaline rush of tingles in the arms, no pounding heart, no premonitory salivation. I did feel a dread sinking feeling in my bowels at one point, and this tricked me momentarily into the false hope that I was undergoing a reversal of the process that landed me in this fix—a gradual undisembodiment. But the isolation and uniqueness of that twinge soon convinced me that it was simply the first of a plague of phantom body hallucinations that I, like any other amputee, would be all too likely to suffer.

My mood then was chaotic. On the one hand, I was fired up with elation of my philosophic discovery and was wracking my brain (one of the few familiar things I could still do), trying to figure out how to communicate my discovery to the journals; while on the other, I was bitter, lonely, and filled with dread and uncertainty. Fortunately, this did not last long, for my technical support team sedated me into a dreamless sleep from which I awoke, hearing with magnificent fidelity the familiar opening strains of my favorite Brahms piano trio. So that was why they had wanted a list of my favorite recordings! It did not take me long to realize that I was hearing the music without ears. The output from the stereo stylus was being fed through some fancy rectification circuitry directly into my auditory nerve. I was mainlining Brahms, an unforgettable experience for any stereo buff. At the end of the record it did not surprise me to hear the reassuring voice of the project director speaking into a microphone that was now my prosthetic ear. He confirmed my analysis of what had gone wrong and assured me that steps were being taken to reembody me. He did not elaborate, and after a few more recordings, I found myself drifting off to sleep. My sleep lasted, I later learned, for the better part of a year, and when I awoke, it was to find myself fully restored to my senses. When I looked into the mirror, though, I was a bit startled to see an unfamiliar face. Bearded and a bit heavier, bearing no doubt a family resemblance to my former face, and with the same look of spritely intelligence and resolute character, but definitely a new face. Further self-explorations of an intimate nature left me no doubt that this was a new body, and the project director confirmed my conclusions. He did not volunteer any information on the past history of my new body and I decided (wisely, I think in retrospect) not to pry. As many philosophers unfamiliar with my ordeal have more recently speculated, the acquisition of a new body leaves one's *person* intact. And after a period of adjustment to a new voice, new muscular strengths and weaknesses, and so forth, one's *personality* is by and large also preserved. More dramatic changes in personality have been routinely observed in people who have undergone extensive plastic surgery, to say nothing of sex-change operations, and I think no one contests the survival of the person in such cases. In any event I soon accommodated to my new body, to the point of being unable to recover any of its novelties to my consciousness or even memory. The view in the mirror soon became utterly familiar. That view, by the way, still revealed antennae, and so I was not surprised to learn that my brain had not been moved from its haven in the life-support lab.

I decided that good old Yorick deserved a visit. I and my new body, whom we might as well call Fortinbras, strode into the familiar lab to another round of applause from the technicians, who were of course congratulating themselves, not me. Once more I stood before the vat and contemplated poor Yorick, and on a whim I once again cavalierly flicked off the output transmitter switch. Imagine my surprise when nothing unusual happened. No fainting spell, no nausea, no noticeable change. A technician hurried to restore the switch to ON, but still I felt nothing. I demanded an explanation, which the project director hastened to provide. It seems that before they had even operated on the first occasion, they had constructed a computer duplicate of my brain, reproducing both the complete information-processing structure and the computational speed of my brain in a giant computer program. After the operation, but before they had dared to send me off on my mission to Oklahoma, they had run this computer system and Yorick side by side. The incoming signals from Hamlet were sent simultaneously to Yorick's transceivers and to the computer's array of inputs. And the outputs from Yorick were not only beamed back to Hamlet, my body; they were recorded and checked against the simultaneous output of the computer program, which was called "Hubert" for reasons obscure to me. Over days and even weeks, the outputs were identical and synchronous, which of course did not *prove* that they had succeeded in copying the brain's functional structure, but the empirical support was greatly encouraging.

Hubert's input, and hence activity, had been kept parallel with Yorick's during my disembodied days. And now, to demonstrate this, they had actually thrown the master switch that put Hubert for the first time in on-line control of my body—not Hamlet, of course, but Fortinbras. (Hamlet, I learned, had never been recovered from its underground tomb and could be assumed by this time to have largely returned to the dust. At the head of my grave still lay the magnificent bulk of the abandoned device, with the word STUD emblazoned on its side in large letters—a circumstance which may provide archeologists of the next century with a curious insight into the burial rites of their ancestors.)

The laboratory technicians now showed me the master switch, which had two positions, labeled *B,* for Brain (they didn't know my brain's name was Yorick) and *H,* for Hubert. The switch did indeed point to *H,* and they explained to me that if I wished, I could switch it back to *B.* With my heart in my mouth (and my brain in its vat), I did this. Nothing happened. A click, that was all. To test their claim, and with the master switch now set at *B*, I hit Yorick's output transmitter switch on the vat and sure enough, I began to faint. Once the output switch was turned back on and I had recovered my wits, so to speak, I continued to play with the master switch, flipping it back and forth. I found that with the exception of the transitional click, I could detect no trace of a difference. I could switch in mid-utterance, and the sentence I had begun speaking under the control of Yorick was finished without a pause or hitch of any kind under the control of Hubert. I had a spare brain, a prosthetic device which might some day stand me in very good stead, were some mishap to befall Yorick. Or alternatively, I could keep Yorick as a spare and use Hubert. It didn't seem to make any difference which I chose, for the wear and tear and fatigue on my body did not have any debilitating effect on either brain, whether or not it was actually causing the motions of my body, or merely spilling its output into thin air.

The one truly unsettling aspect of this new development was the prospect, which was not long in dawning on me, of someone detaching the spare—Hubert or Yorick, as the case might be—from Fortinbras and hitching it to yet another body—some Johnny-come-lately Rosencrantz or Guildenstern. Then (if not before) there would be *two* people, that much was clear. One would be me, and the other would be a sort of super-twin brother. If there were two bodies, one under the control of Hubert and the other being controlled by Yorick, then which would the world recognize as the true Dennett? And whatever the rest of the world decided, which one would be *me?* Would I be the Yorick-brained one, in virtue of Yorick's causal priority and former intimate relationship with the original Dennett body, Hamlet? That seemed a bit legalistic, a bit too redolent of the arbitrariness of consanguinity and legal possession, to be convincing at the metaphysical level. For suppose that before the arrival of the second body on the scene, I had been keeping Yorick as the spare for years, and letting Hubert's output drive my body—that is, Fortinbras—all that time. The Hubert-Fortinbras couple

would seem then by squatter's rights (to combat one legal intuition with another) to be the true Dennett and the lawful inheritor of everything that was Dennett's. This was an interesting question, certainly, but not nearly so pressing as another question that bothered me. My strongest intuition was that in such an eventuality *I* would survive so long as *either* brain-body couple remained intact, but I had mixed emotions about whether I should want both to survive.

I discussed my worries with the technicians and the project director. The prospect of two Dennetts was abhorrent to me, I explained, largely for social reasons. I didn't want to be my own rival for the affections of my wife, nor did I like the prospect of the two Dennetts sharing my modest professor's salary. Still more vertiginous and distasteful, though, was the idea of knowing *that much* about another person, while he had the very same goods on me. How could we ever face each other? My colleagues in the lab argued that I was ignoring the bright side of the matter. Weren't there many things I wanted to do but, being only one person, had been unable to do? Now one Dennett could stay at home and be the professor and family man, while the other could strike out on a life of travel and adventure—missing the family of course, but happy in the knowledge that the other Dennett was keeping the home fires burning. I could be faithful and adulterous at the same time. I could even cuckold myself—to say nothing of other more lurid possibilities my colleagues were all too ready to force upon my overtaxed imagination. But my ordeal in Oklahoma (or was it Houston?) had made me less adventurous, and I shrank from this opportunity that was being offered (though of course I was never quite sure it was being offered to *me* in the first place).

There was another prospect even more disagreeable: that the spare, Hubert or Yorick as the case might be, would be detached from any input from Fortinbras and just left detached. Then, as in the other case, there would be two Dennetts, or at least two claimants to my name and possessions, one embodied in Fortinbras, and the other sadly, miserably disembodied. Both selfishness and altruism bade me take steps to prevent this from happening. So I asked that measures be taken to ensure that no one could ever tamper with the transceiver connections or the master switch without my (our? no, *my*) knowledge and consent. Since I had no desire to spend my life guarding the equipment in Houston, it was mutually decided that all the electronic connections in the lab would be carefully locked. Both those that controlled the life-support system for Yorick and those that controlled the power supply for Hubert would be guarded with fail-safe devices, and I would take the only master switch, outfitted for radio remote control, with me wherever I went. I carry it strapped around my waist and—wait a moment—*here it is.* Every few months I reconnoiter the situation by switching channels. I do this only in the presence of friends, of course, for if the other channel were, heaven forbid, either dead or otherwise occupied, there would have to be somebody who had my interests at heart to switch it back, to bring me back from the void. For while I could feel, see, hear, and otherwise sense whatever befell my body, subsequent to such a switch, I'd be unable to control it. By the way, the two positions on the switch are intentionally unmarked, so I never have the faintest idea whether I am switching from Hubert to Yorick or vice versa. (Some of you may think that in this case I really don't know *who* I am, let alone where I am. But such reflections no longer make much of a dent on my essential Dennettness, on my own sense of who I am. If it is true that in one sense I don't know who I am then that's another one of your philosophical truths of underwhelming significance.)

In any case, every time I've flipped the switch so far, nothing has happened. *So let's give it a try. . . .*

"THANK GOD! I THOUGHT YOU'D NEVER FLIP THAT SWITCH! You can't imagine how horrible it's been these last two weeks—but now you know; it's your turn in purgatory. How I've longed for this moment! You see, about two weeks ago— excuse me, ladies and gentlemen, but I've got to explain this to my . . . um, brother, I guess you could say, but he's just told you the facts, so you'll understand—about two weeks ago our two brains drifted just a bit out of synch. I don't know whether *my* brain is now Hubert or Yorick, any more than you do, but in any case, the two brains drifted apart, and of course once the process started, it snowballed, for I was in a slightly different receptive state for the input we both received, a difference that was soon magnified. In no time at all the illusion that I was in control of my body—our body—was completely dissipated. There was nothing I could do—no way to call you. YOU DIDN'T EVEN KNOW I EXISTED! It's been like being carried around in a cage, or better, like being possessed—hearing my own voice say things I didn't mean to say, watching in frustration as my own hands performed deeds I hadn't intended. You'd scratch our itches, but not the way I would have, and you kept me awake, with your tossing and turning. I've been totally exhausted, on the verge of a nervous breakdown, carried around helplessly by your frantic round of activities, sustained only by the knowledge that some day you'd throw the switch.

"Now it's your turn, but at least you'll have the comfort of knowing *I* know you're in there. Like an expectant mother, I'm eating—or at any rate tasting, smelling, seeing—for *two* now, and I'll try to make it easy for you. Don't worry. Just as soon as this colloquium is over, you and I will fly to Houston, and we'll see what can be done to get one of us another body. You can have a female body— your body could be any color you like. But let's think it over. I tell you what—to be fair, if we both want this body, I promise I'll let the project director flip a coin to settle which of us gets to keep it and which then gets to choose a new body. That should guarantee justice, shouldn't it? In any case, I'll take care of you, I promise. These people are my witnesses.

"Ladies and gentlemen, this talk we have just heard is not exactly the talk *I* would have given, but I assure you that everything he said was perfectly true. And now if you'll excuse me, I think I'd— we'd—better sit down."

Questions for Reflection

1. There is abundant evidence that our memories, personalities, and beliefs are coded in particular locations of the brain. Damaging a certain portion of the brain will erase specific memories. Certain kinds of drugs or brain damage can cause the brain to produce hallucinations or false beliefs and can cause personality changes. Electrically stimulating portions of the brain will produce the sensations of colors or sounds. Scientists can study the patterns of a subject's brain waves and study the changes that occur when the subject makes a choice or comprehends a sentence. Do you think that it is possible that everything you are, including your thoughts, beliefs, values, and desires, is located in your brain in the form of chemically coded information? Assuming that the technological problems could be solved, do you think that it is possible that the person you are could be "uploaded" into a computer duplicate of your brain as happened to Dennett in the story?

2. Some philosophers of mind (called "functionalists") would say that your brain (either the natural, organic one or a computer duplicate) is the "hardware" and the person himself or herself is the "software" or the program the brain is running. (In fact, this is a rough approximation of Dennett's position.) In what way is this analogy a helpful one? Are there any limitations to this computer model of the person?

WHAT IS THE MIND? IS IT SEPARATE FROM THE BODY?

 HUGH ELLIOT

"Tantalus"

Hugh Elliot (1881–1930) was a British writer who wrote popular defenses of science and materialism (physicalism). In this story, he tries to identify the mistake that the dualist makes and the solution that is offered by a correct understanding of physiology and brain science. The reference to Tantalus in the story is to a figure in Greek mythology who was punished by having to carry out an eternal task.

Reading Questions

1. Elliot asks us to imagine that an observer has no background knowledge about how the world works and knows only the interacting shadows and the correlated sounds. What might such a person think is causing the sounds?

From Hugh Elliot, *Modern Science and the Illusions of Professor Bergson* (1912), quoted in Daniel Kolak and Raymond Martin, *The Experience of Philosophy*, 3rd ed. (Belmont, CA: Wadsworth, 1996).

2. What comparison does Elliot make between this naive observer and a philosopher introspecting his or her own mental processes and trying to determine their cause?
3. What comparison does Elliot make between removing the screen to show the real source of the sound and using physiology to show the real cause of our mental life?
4. What philosophical position is Elliot trying to defend?

Suppose there existed a Tantalus who was condemned for evermore to strike with a hammer upon an anvil. Suppose that Tantalus, his hammer, and his anvil were concealed from the observer's view by a screen or otherwise, and that a light, carefully arranged, threw the shadow of the hammer and anvil upon a wall where it could easily be seen. Suppose an observer, whose mind was *tabula rasa* [a blank tablet] were set to watch the shadow. Every time the shadow of the hammer descended upon the shadow of the anvil, the sound of the percussion is heard. The sound is only heard when the two shadows meet. The hammer's shadow occasionally beats fast, occasionally slow: the succession of sounds exactly corresponds. Perhaps the hammer raps out a tune on the anvil; every note heard follows upon a blow visible in the shadows. The two series correspond invariably and absolutely; what is the inevitable effect upon the observer's mind? He knows nothing of the true cause of sound behind the screen: his whole experience is an experience of shadows and sounds. He cannot escape the conclusion that the cause of each sound is the blow which the shadow of the hammer strikes upon the shadow of the anvil.

The observer is in the position of an introspective philosopher. Introspection teaches us nothing about nerve currents or cerebral activity: it speaks in terms of mind and sensation alone. To the introspective philosopher, it is plain that some mental or psychical process is the condition of action. He thinks, he feels, he wills, and then he acts. Therefore the thinking and feeling and willing are the cause of the acting. Introspection *can* get no farther. But now the physiologist intervenes. He skillfully dissects away the screen and behold! there is a real hammer and a real anvil, of which nothing but the shadow was formerly believed to exist. He proves that states of consciousness are shadows accompanying cerebral functioning; he shows that the cause of action lies in the cerebral functioning and not in the shadows which accompany it.

Questions for Reflection

1. Do you agree with Elliot that our belief in a nonphysical mind that is the source of our thoughts and actions is as confused as the belief that the shadows are causing the sounds?
2. Do you think that introspection is an inferior way to understand our mental life when compared to physiology?
3. Could a dualist turn Elliot's analogy around and argue that the shadows refer to the physical world known by the senses and that the real cause of our mental life, represented by the hammer and the anvil behind the screen, is the mind?

RENÉ DESCARTES

Dualism—The Mind Is Separate from the Body

The 17th-century philosopher René Descartes is not merely a representative of mind-body dualism, he is its most famous advocate. Hence, we can get a very good look at dualism by surveying Descartes's views.

In Chapter 3 we examined Descartes's attempts to find certainty by doubting every one of his beliefs to see if any withstood critical examination (reading 21). The one belief he could not doubt was "I exist." However, the certainty of his own existence applied only to his existence as a mind, a mental substance distinct from his body. Descartes believed he was directly and immediately acquainted with his mind or his consciousness, but his belief that he had a physical body which existed in the external world was simply something he inferred from his physical sensations. The problem is that in dreams and hallucinations we can experience bodily sensations that are illusions and that do not reflect what is really there in the external world. Descartes eventually solves the problem, however, by developing a proof for the existence of God (in *Meditation III*, which is not included here). Since he finds the existence of a perfect God rationally irrefutable, he is confident that this God would not allow him to be massively deceived about the existence of his own body and the external world.

Based on the above considerations, Descartes concludes that he is not only a mind, but that his mind is associated with a body. The picture that emerges is that human beings are made up of two different kinds of reality that are somehow linked together. On the one hand, we have bodies and are a part of the physical world. According to Descartes, the body is a machine made out of flesh and bone. Your joints and tendons act like pivots, pulleys, and ropes. Your heart is a pump and your lungs are bellows. Since the body is a physical thing, it is subject to the laws of physics and is located in space and time. According to Descartes, animals are also machines, and their behavior is sheerly a product of mechanical laws. Humans, however, are unique in that in addition to their bodies, they also possess minds. According to Descartes, your mind (which is identical to your soul and your consciousness) is the "real" you. If you lose an arm or a leg, your bodily mechanism is impaired but you are still as complete a person as before. Descartes's position can be called **mind-body dualism** or **psychophysical dualism.** Since Descartes has given the classic statement of this position, it is also commonly referred to as **Cartesian dualism** in his honor. In the following selection from *Meditation VI*, Descartes makes the case that the mind and body are separate but interact.

Reading Questions

1. How does Descartes use the criteria of clearness and distinctness to argue for the difference between the mind and the body? What are the two properties of the mind and how do they differ from the properties of the body?

From René Descartes, *Meditations on First Philosophy*, 3rd ed., trans. Donald A. Cress (Indianapolis: Hackett, 1993).

2. Now that he has confidence that God exists and is not a deceiver, how can he be certain that a physical world exists external to his mind?

3. Why does he say that the relation of the mind to the body is not like that of a sailor in a ship?

4. How does Descartes use the property of divisibility to argue for the difference between the mind and the body?

5. How does he use the examples of pain in the foot and thirst to illustrate how the mind and body work together?

But now, having begun to have a better knowledge of myself and the author of my origin, I am of the opinion that I must not rashly admit everything that I seem to derive from the senses; but neither, for that matter, should I call everything into doubt.

First, I know that all the things that I clearly and distinctly understand can be made by God such as I understand them. For this reason, my ability clearly and distinctly to understand one thing without another suffices to make me certain that the one thing is different from the other, since they can be separated from each other, at least by God. The question as to the sort of power that might effect such a separation is not relevant to their being thought to be different. For this reason, from the fact that I know that I exist, and that at the same time I judge that obviously nothing else belongs to my nature or essence except that I am a thinking thing, I rightly conclude that my essence consists entirely in my being a thinking thing. And although perhaps (or rather, as I shall soon say, assuredly) I have a body that is very closely joined to me, nevertheless, because on the one hand I have a clear and distinct idea of myself, insofar as I am merely a thinking thing and not an extended thing, and because on the other hand I have a distinct idea of a body, insofar as it is merely an extended thing and not a thinking thing, it is certain that I am really distinct from my body, and can exist without it.

Moreover, I find in myself faculties for certain special modes of thinking, namely the faculties of imagining and sensing. I can clearly and distinctly understand myself in my entirety without these faculties, but not vice versa: I cannot understand them clearly and distinctly without me, that is, without a substance endowed with understanding in which they inhere, for they include an act of understanding in their formal concept. Thus I perceive them to be distinguished from me as modes from a thing. I also acknowledge that there are certain other faculties, such as those of moving from one place to another, of taking on various shapes, and so on, that, like sensing or imagining, cannot be understood apart from some substance in which they inhere, and hence without which they cannot exist. But it is clear that these faculties, if in fact they exist, must be in a corporeal or extended substance, not in a substance endowed with understanding. For some extension is contained in a clear and distinct concept of them, though certainly not any understanding. Now there clearly is in me a passive faculty of sensing, that is, a faculty for receiving and knowing the ideas of sensible things; but I could not use it unless there also existed, either in me or in something else, a certain active faculty of producing or bringing about these ideas. But this faculty surely cannot be in me, since it clearly presupposes no act of understanding, and these ideas are produced without my cooperation and often even against my will. Therefore the only alternative is that it is in some substance different from me, containing either formally or eminently all the reality that exists objectively in the ideas produced by that faculty, as I have just noted above. Hence this substance is either a body, that is, a corporeal nature, which contains formally all that is contained objectively in the ideas, or else it is God, or some other creature more noble than a body, which contains eminently all that is contained objectively in the ideas. But since God is not a deceiver, it is patently obvious that he does not send me these ideas either immediately by himself, or even through the mediation of some creature that contains the objective reality of these ideas not formally but only eminently. For since God has given me no faculty whatsoever for making this determination, but instead has given me a great inclination to believe that these ideas issue from corporeal things, I fail to see how God could be understood not to be a deceiver, if these ideas were to issue from a source other than corporeal things. And consequently corporeal things exist. Nevertheless, perhaps not all bodies exist exactly as I grasp them by sense, since this sensory grasp is in many cases very obscure and confused. But at least they do contain everything I clearly and distinctly understand—that is, everything, considered in a general sense, that is encompassed in the object of pure mathematics.

As far as the remaining matters are concerned, which are either merely particular (for example, that the sun is of such and such a size or shape, and so on) or less clearly understood (for example, light, sound, pain, and the like), even though these matters are very doubtful and uncertain, nevertheless the fact that God is no deceiver (and thus no falsity can be found in my opinions, unless there is also in me a faculty given me by God for the purpose of rectifying this falsity) offers me a definite hope of reaching the truth even in these matters. And surely there is no doubt that all that I am taught by nature has some truth to it; for by "nature," taken generally, I understand nothing other than God himself or the ordered network of created things which was instituted by God. By my own particular nature I understand nothing other than the combination of all the things bestowed upon me by God.

There is nothing that this nature teaches me more explicitly than that I have a body that is ill-disposed when I feel pain, that needs food and drink when I suffer hunger or thirst, and the like. Therefore, I should not doubt that there is some truth in this.

By means of these sensations of pain, hunger, thirst and so on, nature also teaches not merely that I am present to my body in the way a sailor is present in a ship, but that I am most tightly joined and, so to speak, commingled with it, so much so that I and the body constitute one single thing. For if this were not the case, then I, who am only a thinking thing, would not sense pain when the body is injured; rather, I would perceive the wound by means of the pure intellect, just as a sailor perceives by sight whether anything in his ship is broken. And when the body is in need of food or drink, I should understand this explicitly, instead of having confused sensations of hunger and thirst. For clearly these sensations of thirst, hunger, pain, and so on are nothing but certain confused modes of thinking arising from the union and, as it were, the commingling of the mind with the body. . . .

Now my first observation here is that there is a great difference between a mind and a body in that a body, by its very nature, is always divisible. On the other hand, the mind is utterly indivisible. For when I consider the mind, that is, myself insofar as I am only a thinking thing, I cannot distinguish any parts within me; rather, I understand myself to be manifestly one complete thing. Although the entire mind seems to be united to the entire body, nevertheless, were a foot or an arm or any other bodily part to be amputated, I know that nothing has been taken away from the mind on that account. Nor can the faculties of willing, sensing, understanding, and so on be called "parts" of the mind, since it is one and the same mind that wills, senses, and understands. On the other hand, there is no corporeal or extended thing I can think of that I may not in my thought easily divide into parts; and in this way I understand that it is divisible. This consideration alone would suffice to teach me that the mind is wholly diverse from the body, had I not yet known it well enough in any other way.

My second observation is that my mind is not immediately affected by all the parts of the body, but only by the brain, or perhaps even by just one small part of the brain, namely, by that part where the "common" sense is said to reside. Whenever this part of the brain is disposed in the same manner, it presents the same thing to the mind, even if the other parts of the body are able meanwhile to be related in diverse ways. Countless experiments show this, none of which need be reviewed here.

My next observation is that the nature of the body is such that whenever any of its parts can be moved by another part some distance away, it can also be moved in the same manner by any of the parts that lie between them, even if this more distant part is doing nothing. For example, in the cord ABCD, if the final part D is pulled, the first part A would be moved in exactly the same manner as it could be, if one of the intermediate parts B or C were pulled, while the end part D remained immobile. Likewise, when I feel a pain in my foot, physics teaches me that this sensation took place by means of nerves distributed throughout the foot, like stretched cords extending from the foot all the way to the brain. When these nerves are pulled in the foot, they also pull on the inner parts of the brain to which they extend, and produce a certain motion in them. This motion has been constituted by nature so as to affect the mind with a sensation of pain, as if it occurred in the foot. But because these nerves need to pass through the shin, thigh, loins, back, and neck to get from the foot to the brain, it can happen that even if it is not the part in the foot but merely one of the intermediate parts that is being struck, the very same movement will occur in the brain that would occur were the foot badly injured. The inevitable result will be that the mind feels the same pain. The same opinion should hold for any other sensation.

My final observation is that, since any given motion occurring in that part of the brain immediately affecting the mind produces but one sensation in it, I can think of no better arrangement than that it produces the one sensation that, of all the ones it is able to produce, is most especially and most often conducive to the maintenance of a healthy man. Moreover, experience shows that all the sensations bestowed on us by nature are like this. Hence there is absolutely nothing to be found in them that does not bear witness to God's power and goodness. Thus, for example, when the nerves in the foot are agitated in a violent and unusual manner, this motion of theirs extends through the marrow of the spine to the inner reaches of the brain, where it gives the mind the sign to sense something, namely, the pain as if it is occurring in the foot. This provokes the mind to do its utmost to move away from the cause of the pain, since it is seen as harmful to the foot. But the nature of man could have been so constituted by God that this same motion in the brain might have indicated something else to the mind: for example, either the motion itself as it occurs in the brain, or in the foot, or in some place in between, or something else entirely different. But nothing else would have served so well the maintenance of the body. Similarly, when we need something to drink, a certain dryness arises in the throat that moves the nerves in the throat, and, by means of them, the inner parts of the brain. And this motion affects the mind with a sensation of thirst, because in this entire affair nothing is more useful for us to know than that we need something to drink in order to maintain our health; the same holds in the other cases.

Questions for Reflection

1. When Descartes was wrestling with skepticism, he discovered that he could doubt his body but not his mind. Hence, he concluded that the mind must not be the same as the body. But compare this argument with the following:

    a. I am in doubt as to whether the 16th president of the United States ever had a beard.

    b. I am not in doubt that Abraham Lincoln had a beard.

    c. If two things do not have identical properties, then they cannot be identical.

    d. Therefore, the 16th president of the United States and Abraham Lincoln are not identical.

The problem is that these two persons are identical. Does this raise problems with Descartes's confidence that his own introspection can discern the difference between the mind and body? Is it possible he is simply ignorant of how the brain produces his thoughts?

2. Descartes assumes that the mind (unlike the body) is not divisible. But don't we sometimes experience conflicting emotions? Furthermore, people with impaired brains can have fragmented experiences. Doesn't this suggest that what we call our mind is made up of different components? Do these considerations undermine Descartes's argument at this point?

3. Descartes argues that minds alone are thinking things. In other words, minds have consciousness, but physical things do not. What do you think of his argument that it is inconceivable to suppose that a hunk of matter (such as a brain) or a machine (such as a computer) can produce consciousness?

GILBERT RYLE

Logical Behaviorism—Mental Statements Refer to Behavior

Gilbert Ryle (1900–1976) was a leading English philosopher who had an enormous influence over generations of students during his decades of teaching at Oxford University. He believed the task of philosophy was primarily to uncover the philosophical confusions caused by the misleading expressions of our language. Ryle is noted for identifying what he calls "category-mistakes" as a source of philosophical problems. A category-mistake occurs when we assume that something belongs to one kind of category when it actually belongs to a quite different one. For example, if someone says "Sally came home in a flood of tears" and another person says "No! Sally came home in a taxi," the second person has committed a category-mistake by assuming the first person was talking about Sally's spatial location rather than her emotional state.

In this selection from *The Concept of Mind,* Ryle accuses Cartesian dualism of postulating "a ghost in the machine." Ryle claims that dualism commits the category-mistake of assuming that the differences between our descriptions of mental activities and physical activities imply that we are talking about two different types of realities. According to dualism, mental activities take place in the "private, windowless chamber" of the mind. But if this were true, we could never know another person's mental capacities or propensities. Instead, Ryle insists, I know about both your and my own mental characteristics and abilities in the same way—by observing the person's behavior. For this rea-

From Gilbert Ryle, *The Concept of Mind* (New York: Barnes and Noble, 1949).

son, his position has been called *logical behaviorism*. The advocates of this position claim that the mind-body problem can be dissolved by analyzing our mental terminology and showing that these terms do not apply to a private "ghostly" substance, but that they are really describing publicly observable behavior.

Reading Questions

1. What does Ryle mean when he refers to the "official doctrine"?
2. List the contrasting sets of properties of bodies and minds according to the official doctrine.
3. What are the three examples of category-mistakes Ryle provides? What is common to them all?
4. According to Ryle, how do you know whether or not someone is lazy? Is there any different method for knowing that you are lazy?

THE OFFICIAL DOCTRINE

There is a doctrine about the nature and place of minds which is so prevalent among theorists and even among laymen that it deserves to be described as the official theory. Most philosophers, psychologists and religious teachers subscribe, with minor reservations, to its main articles and, although they admit certain theoretical difficulties in it, they tend to assume that these can be overcome without serious modifications being made to the architecture of the theory. It will be argued here that the central principles of the doctrine are unsound and conflict with the whole body of what we know about minds when we are not speculating about them.

The official doctrine, which hails chiefly from Descartes, is something like this. With the doubtful exceptions of idiots and infants in arms every human being has both a body and a mind. Some would prefer to say that every human being is both a body and a mind. His body and his mind are ordinarily harnessed together, but after the death of the body his mind may continue to exist and function.

Human bodies are in space and are subject to the mechanical laws which govern all other bodies in space. Bodily processes and states can be inspected by external observers. So a man's bodily life is as much a public affair as are the lives of animals and reptiles and even as the careers of trees, crystals and planets.

But minds are not in space, nor are their operations subject to mechanical laws. The workings of one mind are not witnessable by other observers; its career is private. Only I can take direct cognisance of the states and processes of my own mind. A person therefore lives through two collateral histories, one consisting of what happens in and to his body, the other consisting of what happens in and to his mind. The first is public, the second private. The events in the first history are events in the physical world, those in the second are events in the mental world.

It has been disputed whether a person does or can directly monitor all or only some of the episodes of his own private history; but, according to the official doctrine, of at least some of these episodes he has direct and unchallengeable cognisance. In consciousness, self-consciousness and introspection he is directly and authentically apprised of the present states and operations of his mind. He may have great or small uncertainties about concurrent and adjacent episodes in the physical world, but he can have none about at least part of what is momentarily occupying his mind.

It is customary to express this bifurcation of his two lives and of his two worlds by saying that the things and events which belong to the physical world, including his own body, are external, while the workings of his own mind are internal. This antithesis of outer and inner is of course meant to be construed as a metaphor, since minds, not being in space, could not be described as being spatially inside anything else, or as having things going on spatially inside themselves. But relapses from this good intention are common and theorists are found speculating how stimuli, the physical sources of which are yards or miles outside a person's skin, can generate mental responses inside his skull, or how decisions framed inside his cranium can set going movements of his extremities.

Even when 'inner' and 'outer' are construed as metaphors, the problem how a person's mind and body influence one another is notoriously charged with theoretical difficulties. What the mind wills, the legs, arms and the tongue execute; what affects the ear and the eye has something to do with what the mind perceives; grimaces and smiles betray the mind's moods and bodily castigations lead, it is hoped, to moral improvement. But the actual transactions between the episodes of the private history and those of the public history remain mysterious, since by definition they can belong to neither series. They could not be reported among the happenings described in a person's autobiography of his inner life, but nor could they be reported among those described in some one else's biography of that person's overt career. They can be inspected neither by introspection nor by laboratory experiment. They are theoretical shuttlecocks which are forever being bandied from the physiologist back to the psychologist and from the psychologist back to the physiologist.

Underlying this partly metaphorical representation of the bifurcation of a person's two lives there is a seemingly more profound and philosophical assumption. It is assumed that there are two different kinds of existence or status. What exists or happens may have the status of physical existence, or it may have the status of mental existence. Somewhat as the faces of coins are either heads or tails, or somewhat as living creatures are either male or female, so, it is supposed, some existing is physical existing, other existing is mental existing. It is a necessary feature of what has physical existence that it is in space and time; it is a necessary feature of what has mental existence that it is in time but not in space. What has physical existence is composed of matter, or else is a function of matter;

what has mental existence consists of consciousness, or else is a function of consciousness.

There is thus a polar opposition between mind and matter, an opposition which is often brought out as follows. Material objects are situated in a common field, known as 'space,' and what happens to one body in one part of space is mechanically connected with what happens to other bodies in other parts of space. But mental happenings occur in insulated fields, known as 'minds,' and there is, apart maybe from telepathy, no direct causal connection between what happens in one mind and what happens in another. Only through the medium of the public physical world can the mind of one person make a difference to the mind of another. The mind is its own place and in his inner life each of us lives the life of a ghostly Robinson Crusoe. People can see, hear and jolt one another's bodies, but they are irremediably blind and deaf to the workings of one another's minds and inoperative upon them.

What sort of knowledge can be secured of the workings of a mind? On the one side, according to the official theory, a person has direct knowledge of the best imaginable kind of the workings of his own mind. Mental states and processes are (or are normally) conscious states and processes, and the consciousness which irradiates them can engender no illusions and leaves the door open for no doubts. A person's present thinkings, feelings and willings, his perceivings, rememberings and imaginings are intrinsically 'phosphorescent'; their existence and their nature are inevitably betrayed to their owner. The inner life is a stream of consciousness of such a sort that it would be absurd to suggest that the mind whose life is that stream might be unaware of what is passing down it.

True, the evidence adduced recently by Freud seems to show that there exist channels tributary to this stream, which run hidden from their owner. People are actuated by impulses the existence of which they vigorously disavow; some of their thoughts differ from the thoughts which they acknowledge; and some of the actions which they think they will to perform they do not really will. They are thoroughly gulled by some of their own hypocrisies and they successfully ignore facts about their mental lives which on the official theory ought to be patent to them. Holders of the official theory tend, however, to maintain that anyhow in normal circumstances a person must be directly and authentically seized of the present state and workings of his own mind.

Besides being currently supplied with these alleged immediate data of consciousness, a person is also generally supposed to be able to exercise from time to time a special kind of perception, namely inner perception, or introspection. He can take a (non-optical) 'look' at what is passing in his mind. Not only can he view and scrutinize a flower through his sense of sight and listen to and discriminate the notes of a bell through his sense of hearing; he can also reflectively or introspectively watch, without any bodily organ of sense, the current episodes of his inner life. This self-observation is also commonly supposed to be immune from illusion, confusion or doubt. A mind's reports of its own affairs have a certainty superior to the best that is possessed by its reports of matters in the physical world. Sense-perceptions can, but consciousness and introspection cannot, be mistaken or confused.

On the other side, one person has no direct access of any sort to the events of the inner life of another. He cannot do better than make problematic inferences from the observed behaviour of the other person's body to the states of mind which, by analogy from his own conduct, he supposes to be signalised by that behaviour. Direct access to the workings of a mind is the privilege of that mind itself; in default of such privileged access, the workings of one mind are inevitably occult to everyone else. For the supposed arguments from bodily movements similar to their own to mental workings similar to their own would lack any possibility of observational corroboration. Not unnaturally, therefore, an adherent of the official theory finds it difficult to resist this consequence of his premises, that he has no good reason to believe that there do exist minds other than his own. Even if he prefers to believe that to other human bodies there are harnessed minds not unlike his own, he cannot claim to be able to discover their individual characteristics, or the particular things that they undergo and do. Absolute solitude is on this showing the ineluctable destiny of the soul. Only our bodies can meet.

As a necessary corollary of this general scheme there is implicitly prescribed a special way of construing our ordinary concepts of mental powers and operations. The verbs, nouns and adjectives, with which in ordinary life we describe the wits, characters and higher-grade performances of the people with whom we have do, are required to be construed as signifying special episodes in their secret histories, or else as signifying tendencies for such episodes to occur. When someone is described as knowing, believing or guessing something, as hoping, dreading, intending or shirking something, as designing this or being amused at that, these verbs are supposed to denote the occurrence of specific modifications in his (to us) occult stream of consciousness. Only his own privileged access to this stream in direct awareness and introspection could provide authentic testimony that these mental-conduct verbs were correctly or incorrectly applied. The onlooker, be he teacher, critic, biographer or friend, can never assure himself that his comments have any vestige of truth. Yet it was just because we do in fact all know how to make such comments, make them with general correctness and correct them when they turn out to be confused or mistaken, that philosophers found it necessary to construct their theories of the nature and place of minds. Finding mental-conduct concepts being regularly and effectively used, they properly sought to fix their logical geography. But the logical geography officially recommended would entail that there could be no regular or effective use of these mental-conduct concepts in our descriptions of, and prescriptions for, other people's minds.

THE ABSURDITY OF THE OFFICIAL DOCTRINE

Such in outline is the official theory. I shall often speak of it, with deliberate abusiveness, as 'the dogma of the Ghost in the Machine.' I hope to prove that it is entirely false, and false not in detail but in principle. It is not merely an assemblage of particular mistakes. It is one big mistake and a mistake of a special kind. It is, namely, a category-mistake. It represents the facts of mental life as if they belonged to one logical type or category (or range of types or categories), when they actually belong to another. The dogma is therefore a philosopher's myth. In attempting to explode the myth I shall probably be taken to be denying well-known facts about the mental life of human beings, and my plea that I aim at doing nothing more than rectify the logic of mental-conduct concepts will probably be disallowed as mere subterfuge.

I must first indicate what is meant by the phrase 'Category-mistake.' This I do in a series of illustrations.

A foreigner visiting Oxford or Cambridge for the first time is shown a number of colleges, libraries, playing fields, museums, scientific departments and administrative offices. He then asks 'But where is the University? I have seen where the members of the Colleges live, where the Registrar works, where the scientists experiment and the rest. But I have not yet seen the University in which reside and work the members of your University.' It has then to be explained to him that the University is not another collateral institution, some ulterior counterpart to the colleges, laboratories and offices which he has seen. The University is just the way in which all that he has already seen is organized. When they are seen and when their co-ordination is understood, the University has been seen. His mistake lay in his innocent assumption that it was correct to speak of Christ Church, the Bodleian Library, the Ashmolean Museum *and* the University, to speak, that is, as if 'the University' stood for an extra member of the class of which these other units are members. He was mistakenly allocating the University to the same category as that to which the other institutions belong.

The same mistake would be made by a child witnessing the march-past of a division, who, having had pointed out to him such and such battalions, batteries, squadrons, etc., asked when the division was going to appear. He would be supposing that a division was a counterpart to the units already seen, partly similar to them and partly unlike them. He would be shown his mistake by being told that in watching the battalions, batteries and squadrons marching past he had been watching the division marching past. The march-past was not a parade of battalions, batteries, squadrons *and* a division; it was a parade of the battalions, batteries and squadrons *of* a division.

One more illustration. A foreigner watching his first game of cricket learns what are the functions of the bowlers, the batsmen, the fielders, the umpires and the scorers. He then says 'But there is no one left on the field to contribute the famous element of team-spirit. I see who does the bowling, the batting and the wicket-keeping; but I do not see whose role it is to exercise *esprit de corps.*' Once more, it would have to be explained that he was looking for the wrong type of thing. Team-spirit is not another cricketing-operation supplementary to all of the other special tasks. It is, roughly, the keenness with which each of the special tasks is performed, and performing a task keenly is not performing two tasks. Certainly exhibiting team-spirit is not the same thing as bowling or catching, but nor is it a third thing such that we can say that the bowler first bowls *and* then exhibits team-spirit or that a fielder is at a given moment *either* catching *or* displaying *esprit de corps.*

These illustrations of category-mistakes have a common feature which must be noticed. The mistakes were made by people who did not know how to wield the concepts *University, division* and *team-spirit.* Their puzzles arose from inability to use certain items in the English vocabulary.

The theoretically interesting category-mistakes are those made by people who are perfectly competent to apply concepts, at least in the situations with which they are familiar, but are still liable in their abstract thinking to allocate those concepts to logical types to which they do not belong. An instance of a mistake of this sort would be the following story. A student of politics has learned the main differences between the British, the French and the American Constitutions, and has learned also the differences and connections between the Cabinet, Parliament, the various Ministries, the Judicature and the Church of England. But he still becomes embarrassed when asked questions about the connections between the Church of England, the Home Office and the British Constitution. For while the Church and the Home Office are institutions, the British Constitution is not another institution in the same sense of that noun. So inter-institutional relations which can be asserted or denied to hold between the Church and the Home Office cannot be asserted or denied to hold between either of them and the British Constitution. 'The British Constitution' is not a term of the same logical type as 'the Home Office' and 'the Church of England.' In a partially similar way, John Doe may be a relative, a friend, an enemy or a stranger to Richard Roe; but he cannot be any of these things to the Average Taxpayer. He knows how to talk sense in certain sorts of discussions about the Average Taxpayer, but he is baffled to say why he could not come across him in the street as he can come across Richard Roe.

It is pertinent to our main subject to notice that, so long as the student of politics continues to think of the British Constitution as a counterpart to the other institutions, he will tend to describe it as a mysteriously occult institution; and so long as John Doe continues to think of the Average Taxpayer as a fellow-citizen, he will tend to think of him as an elusive insubstantial man, a ghost who is everywhere yet nowhere.

My destructive purpose is to show that a family of radical category-mistakes is the source of the double-life theory. The representation of a person as a ghost mysteriously ensconced in a machine derives from this argument. Because, as is true, a person's thinking, feeling and purposive doing cannot be described solely in the idioms of physics, chemistry and physiology, therefore they must be described in counterpart idioms. As the human body is a complex organised unit, so the human mind must be another complex organised unit, though one made of a different sort of stuff and with a different sort of structure. Or, again, as the human body, like any other parcel of matter, is a field of causes and effects, so the mind must be another field of causes and effects, though not (Heaven be praised) mechanical causes and effects. . . .

SELF-KNOWLEDGE WITHOUT PRIVILEGED ACCESS

It has been argued from a number of directions that when we speak of a person's mind, we are not speaking of a second theatre of special-status incidents, but of certain ways in which some of the incidents of his one life are ordered. His life is not a double series of events taking place in two different kinds of stuff; it is one concatenation of events, the differences between some and other classes of which largely consist in the applicability or inapplicability to them of logically different types of law-propositions and law-like propositions. Assertions about a person's mind are therefore assertions of special sorts about that person. So questions about the relations between a person and his mind, like those about the relations between a person's body and his mind, are improper questions. They are important in much the same way as is the question, 'What transactions go on between the House of Commons and the British Constitution?'

It follows that it is a logical solecism to speak, as theorists often do, of someone's mind knowing this, or choosing that. The person himself knows this and chooses that, though the fact that he does so can, if desired, be classified as a mental fact about that person. In partly the same way it is improper to speak of my eyes seeing this, or my nose smelling that; we should say, rather, that I see this, or I smell that, and that these assertions carry with them certain facts about my eyes and nose. But the analogy is not exact, for while my eyes and nose are organs of sense, 'my mind' does not stand for another organ. It signifies my ability and proneness to do certain sorts of things and not some piece of personal apparatus without which I could or would not do them. Similarly the British Constitution is not another British political institution functioning alongside of the Civil Service, the Judiciary, the Established Church, the Houses of Parliament and the Royal Family. Nor is it the sum of these institutions, or a liaison-staff between them. We can say that Great Britain has gone to the polls; but we cannot say that the British Constitution has gone to the polls, though the fact that Great Britain has gone to the polls might be described as a constitutional fact about Great Britain.

Actually, though it is not always convenient to avoid the practice, there is a considerable logical hazard in using the nouns 'mind' and 'minds' at all. The idiom makes it too easy to construct logically improper conjunctions, disjunctions and cause-effect propositions such as 'so and so took place not in my body but in my mind,' 'my mind made my hand write,' 'a person's body and mind interact upon each other' and so on. Where logical candour is required from us, we ought to follow the example set by novelists, biographers and diarists, who speak only of persons doing and undergoing things.

The questions 'What knowledge can a person get of the workings of his own mind?' and 'How does he get it?' by their very wording suggest absurd answers. They suggest that, for a person to know that he is lazy, or has done a sum carefully, he must have taken a peep into a windowless chamber, illuminated by a very peculiar sort of light, and one to which only he has access. And when the question is construed in this sort of way, the parallel questions, 'What knowledge can one person get of the workings of another mind?' and 'How does he get it?' by their very wording seem to preclude any answer at all; for they suggest that one person could only know that another person was lazy, or had done a sum carefully, by peering into another secret chamber to which, *ex hypothesi,* he has no access.

In fact the problem is not one of this sort. It is simply the methodological question, how we establish, and how we apply, certain sorts of law-like propositions about the overt and the silent behaviour of persons. I come to appreciate the skill and tactics of a chess-player by watching him and others playing chess, and I learn that a certain pupil of mine is lazy, ambitious and witty by following his work, noticing his excuses, listening to his conversation and comparing his performances with those of others. Nor does it make any important difference if I happen myself to be that pupil. I can indeed then listen to more of his conversations, as I am the addressee of his unspoken soliloquies; I notice more of his excuses, as I am never absent,

when they are made. On the other hand, my comparison of his performances with those of others is more difficult, since the examiner is himself taking the examination, which makes neutrality hard to preserve and precludes the demeanour of the candidate, when under interrogation, from being in good view.

To repeat a point previously made, the question is not the envelope-question 'How do I discover that I or you have a mind?' but the range of specific questions of the pattern, 'How do I discover that I am more unselfish than you; that I can do long division well, but differential equations only badly; that you suffer from certain phobias and tend to shirk facing certain sorts of facts; that I am more easily irritated than most people but less subject to panic, vertigo, or morbid conscientiousness?' Besides such pure dispositional questions there is also the range of particular performance questions and occurrence questions of the patterns, 'How do I find out that I saw the joke and that you did not; that your action took more courage than mine; that the service I rendered to you was rendered from a sense of duty and not from expectation of kudos; that, though I did not fully understand what was said at the time, I did fully understand it, when I went over it in my head afterwards, while you understood it perfectly from the start; that I was feeling homesick yesterday?' Questions of these sorts offer no mysteries; we know quite well how to set to work to find out the answers to them; and though often we cannot finally solve them and may have to stop short at mere conjecture, yet, even so, we have no doubt what sorts of information would satisfy our requirements, if we could get it; and we know what it would be like to get it. For example, after listening to an argument, you aver that you understand it perfectly; but you may be deceiving yourself, or trying to deceive me. If we then part for a day or two, I am no longer in a position to test whether or not you did understand it perfectly. But still I know what tests would have settled the point. If you had put the argument into your own words, or translated it into French; if you had invented appropriate concrete illustrations of the generalisations and abstractions in the argument; if you had stood up to cross-questioning; if you had correctly drawn further consequences from different stages of the argument and indicated points where the theory was inconsistent with other theories; if you had inferred correctly from the nature of the argument to the qualities of intellect and character of its author and predicted accurately the subsequent development of his theory, then I should have required no further evidence that you understood it perfectly. And exactly the same sorts of tests would satisfy me that I had understood it perfectly; the sole differences would be that I should probably not have voiced aloud the expressions of my deductions, illustrations, etc., but told them to myself more perfunctorily in silent soliloquy; and I should probably have been more easily satisfied of the completeness of my understanding than I was of yours.

In short it is part of the *meaning* of 'you understood it' that you could have done so and so and would have done it, if such and such, and the *test* of whether you understood it is a range of performances satisfying the apodoses of these general hypothetical statements. It should be noticed, on the one hand, that there is no single nuclear performance, overt or in your head, which would determine that you had understood the argument. Even if you claimed that you had experienced a flash or click of comprehension and had actually done so, you would still withdraw your other claim to have understood the argument, if you found that you could not paraphrase it, illustrate, expand or recast it; and you would allow someone else to have understood it who could meet all examination-questions about it, but reported no click of comprehension. It should also be noticed, on the other hand, that though there is no way of specifying how many or what sub-tests must be satisfied for a person to qualify as having perfectly understood the argument, this does not imply that no finite set of sub-tests is ever enough. To settle whether a boy can do long division, we do not require him to try out his hand on a million, a thousand, or even a hundred different problems in long division. We should not be quite satisfied after one success, but we should not remain dissatisfied after twenty, provided that they were judiciously variegated and that he had not done them before. A good teacher, who

not only recorded the boy's correct and incorrect solutions, but also watched his procedure in reaching them, would be satisfied much sooner, and he would be satisfied sooner still if he got the boy to describe and justify the constituent operations that he performed, though of course many boys can do long division sums who cannot describe or justify the operations performed in doing them.

I discover my or your motives in much, though not quite, the same way as I discover my or your abilities. The big practical difference is that I cannot put the subject through his paces in my inquiries into his inclinations as I can in my inquiries into his competences. To discover how conceited or patriotic you are, I must still observe your conduct, remarks, demeanour and tones of voice, but I cannot subject you to examination-tests or experiments which you recognise as such. You would have a special motive for responding to such experiments in a particular way. From mere conceit, perhaps, you would try to behave self-effacingly, or from mere modesty you might try to behave conceitedly. None the less, ordinary day to day observation normally serves swiftly to settle such questions. To be conceited is to tend to boast of one's own excellences, to pity or ridicule the deficiencies of others, to daydream about imaginary triumphs, to reminisce about actual triumphs, to weary quickly of conversations which reflect unfavourably upon oneself, to lavish one's society upon distinguished persons and to economise in association with the undistinguished. The tests of whether a person is conceited are the actions he takes and the reactions he manifests in such circumstances. Not many anecdotes, sneers or sycophancies are required from the subject for the ordinary observer to make up his mind, unless the candidate and the examiner happen to be identical.

The ascertainment of a person's mental capacities and propensities is an inductive process, an induction to law-like propositions from observed actions and reactions. Having ascertained these long-term qualities, we explain a particular action or reaction by applying the result of such an induction to the new specimen, save where open avowals let us know the explanation without research. These inductions are not, of course, carried out under laboratory conditions, or with any statistical apparatus, any more than is the shepherd's weather-lore, or the general practitioner's understanding of a particular patient's constitution. But they are ordinarily reliable enough. It is a truism to say that the appreciations of character and the explanations of conduct given by critical, unprejudiced and humane observers, who have had a lot of experience and take a lot of interest, tend to be both swift and reliable; those of inferior judges tend to be slower and less reliable. Similarly the marks awarded by practised and keen examiners who know their subject well and are reasonably sympathetic towards the candidates tend to be about right; those of inferior examiners tend to scatter more widely from the proper order. The point of these truisms is to remind us that in real life we are quite familiar with the techniques of assessing persons and accounting for their actions, though according to the standard theory no such techniques could exist.

Questions for Reflection

1. If the dualist is correct, we cannot have access to the private region of another person's mind. How then could you tell that someone loved you? Wouldn't you judge this based on the person's behavior? If you are confused about your own emotions or motives, couldn't you get some insight by observing your own actions, dispositions, and responses? Do these correlations between someone's mental states and behavior lend plausibility to Ryle's thesis?
2. Do you think that Ryle has shown that dualism is based on a mistake?
3. In spite of his many examples of category-mistakes, is it possible that the dualist is not making the same mistake? Is it possible that the differences in our mental and physical vocabularies are best explained by referring to two different entities?
4. Can all mental expressions be exhaustively translated into statements about behavioral dispositions, as Ryle claims?

PAUL CHURCHLAND

Eliminative Materialism—There Is No Mind

Paul Churchland is a professor of philosophy at the University of California at San Diego. His research focuses on philosophy of science, the philosophy of mind, artificial intelligence, cognitive neurobiology, epistemology, and perception. He has written numerous articles and books, including *The Engine of Reason, The Seat of the Soul: A Philosophical Journey into the Brain* (1995), *A Neurocomputational Perspective: The Nature of Mind and the Structure of Science* (1989), and *Matter and Consciousness* (1984), from which this selection is taken.

From Paul Churchland, *Matter and Consciousness* (Cambridge, MA: MIT Press, 1984).

In the reading, Churchland begins by criticizing identity theory, which is one version of physicalism. As discussed previously, identity theory (or reductionism) claims that there is a one-to-one correspondence between mental states and brain states such that all talk about mental states (believing, hoping, imagining) can be translated into or reduced to talk about brain states. Churchland uses the term *intertheoretic reduction* to refer to a situation where the terms and principles of an older theory are translated into the terms and principles of a new and more powerful theory. For example, when we talk about rainbows we now know we are really talking about the refraction, reflection, and dispersion of the sun's rays in water droplets. However, Churchland thinks that such reduction is not possible with mental terms. This is because he believes that talk about the mind's activities is a remnant of "folk psychology" or a flawed, outmoded, pseudo-scientific theory about cognition and should be eliminated.

The position Churchland defends is eliminative materialism. (*Materialism* is his term for what I have called *physicalism*.) He argues that talk about the mind and mental events follows from a mistaken theory about human behavior and should be replaced with a scientific theory that is based on an understanding of how the brain works.

Reading Questions

1. Why does Churchland believe identity theory is mistaken?
2. What four historical examples does he provide of where the ontology of an older theory was eliminated in favor of the ontology of a new and superior theory? (An *ontology* is a claim about what entities exist.)
3. What three arguments does Churchland provide in favor of eliminative materialism?
4. What three arguments against eliminative materialism does he pose and what is his response to each one?

ELIMINATIVE MATERIALISM

The identity theory was called into doubt not because the prospects for a materialist account of our mental capacities were thought to be poor, but because it seemed unlikely that the arrival of an adequate materialist theory would bring with it the nice one-to-one match-ups, between the concepts of folk psychology and the concepts of theoretical neuroscience, that intertheoretic reduction requires. The reason for that doubt was the great variety of quite different physical systems that could instantiate the required functional organization. *Eliminative materialism* also doubts that the correct neuroscientific account of human capacities will produce a neat reduction of our common-sense

framework, but here the doubts arise from a quite different source.

As the eliminative materialists see it, the one-to-one match-ups will not be found, and our common-sense psychological framework will not enjoy an intertheoretic reduction, *because our common-sense psychological framework is a false and radically misleading conception of the causes of human behavior and the nature of cognitive activity.* On this view, folk psychology is not just an incomplete representation of our inner natures; it is an outright *mis*representation of our internal states and activities. Consequently, we cannot expect a truly adequate neuroscientific account of our inner lives to provide theoretical categories that match up nicely with the categories of our common-sense framework. Accordingly, we must expect that the older framework will simply be eliminated, rather than be reduced, by a matured neuroscience.

Historical Parallels

As the identity theorist can point to historical cases of successful intertheoretic reduction, so the eliminative materialist can point to historical cases of the outright elimination of the ontology of an older theory in favor of the ontology of a new and superior theory. For most of the eighteenth and nineteenth centuries, learned people believed that heat was a subtle *fluid* held in bodies, much in the way water is held in a sponge. A fair body of moderately successful theory described the way this fluid substance—called "caloric"—flowed within a body, or from one body to another, and how it produced thermal expansion, melting, boiling, and so forth. But by the end of the last century it had become abundantly clear that heat was not a substance at all, but just the energy of motion of the trillions of jostling molecules that make up the heated body itself. The new theory—the "corpuscular/kinetic theory of matter and heat"—was much more successful than the old in explaining and predicting the thermal behavior of bodies. And since we were unable to *identify* caloric fluid with kinetic energy (according to the old theory, caloric is a material *substance;* according to the new theory, kinetic energy is a form of *motion*), it was finally agreed that there is *no such thing* as caloric. Caloric was simply eliminated from our accepted ontology.

A second example. It used to be thought that when a piece of wood burns, or a piece of metal rusts, a spiritlike substance called "phlogiston" was being released: briskly, in the former case, slowly in the latter. Once gone, that 'noble' substance left only a base pile of ash or rust. It later came to be appreciated that both processes involve, not the loss of something, but the *gaining* of a substance taken from the atmosphere: oxygen. Phlogiston emerged, not as an incomplete description of what was going on, but as a radical misdescription. Phlogiston was therefore not suitable for reduction to or identification with some notion from within the new oxygen chemistry, and it was simply eliminated from science.

Admittedly, both of these examples concern the elimination of something nonobservable, but our history also includes the elimination of certain widely accepted 'observables.' Before Copernicus' views became available, almost any human who ventured out at night could look up at *the starry sphere of the heavens,* and if he stayed for more than a few minutes he could also see that it *turned,* around an axis through Polaris. What the sphere was made of (crystal?) and what made it turn (the gods?) were theoretical questions that exercised us for over two millennia. But hardly anyone doubted the existence of what everyone could observe with their own eyes. In the end, however, we learned to reinterpret our visual experience of the night sky within a very different conceptual framework, and the turning sphere evaporated.

Witches provide another example. Psychosis is a fairly common affliction among humans, and in earlier centuries its victims were standardly seen as cases of demonic possession, as instances of Satan's spirit itself, glaring malevolently out at us from behind the victims' eyes. That witches exist was not a matter of any controversy. One would occasionally see them, in any city or hamlet, engaged in incoherent, paranoid, or even murderous behavior. But observable or not, we eventually decided that witches simply do not exist. We concluded that the concept of a witch is an element in a conceptual framework that misrepresents so badly the phenomena to which it was standardly applied that literal application of the notion should be permanently withdrawn. Modern theories of mental dysfunction led to the elimination of witches from our serious ontology.

The concepts of folk psychology—belief, desire, fear, sensation, pain, joy, and so on—await a similar fate, according to the view at issue. And when neuroscience has matured to the point where the poverty of our current conceptions is apparent to everyone, and the superiority of the new framework is established, we shall then be able to set about *re*conceiving our internal states and activities, within a truly adequate conceptual framework at last. Our explanations of one another's behavior will appeal to such things as our neuropharmacological states, the neural activity in specialized anatomical areas, and whatever other states are deemed relevant by the new theory. Our private introspection will also be transformed, and may be profoundly enhanced by reason of the more accurate and penetrating framework it will have to work with—just as the astronomer's perception of the night sky is much enhanced by the detailed knowledge of modern astronomical theory that he or she possesses.

The magnitude of the conceptual revolution here suggested should not be minimized: it would be enormous. And the benefits to humanity might be equally great. If each of us possessed an accurate neuroscientific understanding of (what we now conceive dimly as) the varieties and causes of mental illness, the factors involved in learning, the neural basis of emotions, intelligence, and socialization, then the sum total of human misery might be much reduced. The simple increase in mutual understanding that the new framework made possible could contribute substantially toward a more peaceful and humane society. Of course, there would be dangers as well: increased knowledge means increased power, and power can always be misused.

Arguments for Eliminative Materialism

The arguments for eliminative materialism are diffuse and less than decisive, but they are stronger than is widely supposed. The distinguishing feature of this position is its denial that a smooth intertheoretic reduction is to be expected—even a species-specific reduction—of the framework of folk psychology to the framework of a matured neuroscience. The reason for this denial is the eliminative materialist's conviction that folk psychology is a hopelessly primitive and deeply confused conception of our internal activities. But why this low opinion of our common-sense conceptions?

There are at least three reasons. First, the eliminative materialist will point to the widespread explanatory, predictive, and manipulative failures of folk psychology. So much of what is central and familiar to us remains a complete mystery from

within folk psychology. We do not know what *sleep* is, or why we have to have it, despite spending a full third of our lives in that condition. (The answer, "For rest," is mistaken. Even if people are allowed to rest continuously, their need for sleep is undiminished. Apparently, sleep serves some deeper functions, but we do not yet know what they are.) We do not understand how *learning* transforms each of us from a gaping infant to a cunning adult, or how differences in *intelligence* are grounded. We have not the slightest idea how *memory* works, or how we manage to retrieve relevant bits of information instantly from the awesome mass we have stored. We do not know what *mental illness* is, nor how to cure it.

In sum, the most central things about us remain almost entirely mysterious from within folk psychology. And the defects noted cannot be blamed on inadequate time allowed for their correction, for folk psychology has enjoyed no significant changes or advances in well over 2,000 years, despite its manifest failures. Truly successful theories may be expected to reduce, but significantly unsuccessful theories merit no such expectation.

This argument from explanatory poverty has a further aspect. So long as one sticks to normal brains, the poverty of folk psychology is perhaps not strikingly evident. But as soon as one examines the many perplexing behavioral and cognitive deficits suffered by people with *damaged* brains, one's descriptive and explanatory resources start to claw the air. . . . As with other humble theories asked to operate successfully in unexplored extensions of their old domain (for example, Newtonian mechanics in the domain of velocities close to the velocity of light, and the classical gas law in the domain of high pressures or temperatures), the descriptive and explanatory inadequacies of folk psychology become starkly evident.

The second argument tries to draw an inductive lesson from our conceptual history. Our early folk theories of motion were profoundly confused, and were eventually displaced entirely by more sophisticated theories. Our early folk theories of the structure and activity of the heavens were wildly off the mark, and survive only as historical lessons in how wrong we can be. Our folk theories of the nature of fire, and the nature of life, were similarly cockeyed. And one could go on, since the vast majority of our past folk conceptions have been similarly exploded. All except folk psychology, which survives to this day and has only recently begun to feel pressure. But the phenomenon of conscious intelligence is surely a more complex and difficult phenomenon than any of those just listed. So far as accurate understanding is concerned, it would be a *miracle* if we had got *that* one right the very first time, when we fell down so badly on all the others. Folk psychology has survived for so very long, presumably, not because it is basically correct in its representations, but because the phenomena addressed are so surpassingly difficult that any useful handle on them, no matter how feeble, is unlikely to be displaced in a hurry.

A third argument attempts to find an *a priori* advantage for eliminative materialism over the identity theory and functionalism. It attempts to counter the common intuition that eliminative materialism is distantly possible, perhaps, but is much less probable than either the identity theory or functionalism. The focus again is on whether the concepts of folk psychology will find vindicating match-ups in a matured neuroscience. The eliminativist bets no; the other two bet yes. (Even the functionalist bets yes, but expects the match-ups to be only species-specific, or only person-specific. Functionalism, recall, denies the existence only of *universal* type/type identities.)

The eliminativist will point out that the requirements on a reduction are rather demanding. The new theory must entail a set of principles and embedded concepts that mirrors very closely the specific conceptual structure to be reduced. And the fact is, there are vastly many more ways of being an explanatorily successful neuroscience while *not* mirroring the structure of folk psychology, than there are ways of being an explanatorily successful neuroscience while also *mirroring* the very specific structure of folk psychology. Accordingly, the *a priori* probability of eliminative materialism is not lower, but substantially *higher* than that of either of its competitors. One's initial intuitions here are simply mistaken.

Granted, this initial *a priori* advantage could be reduced if there were a very strong presumption in favor of the truth of folk psychology—true theories are better bets to win reduction. But according to the first two arguments, the presumptions on this point should run in precisely the opposite direction.

Arguments against Eliminative Materialism

The initial plausibility of this rather radical view is low for almost everyone, since it denies deeply entrenched assumptions. That is at best a question-begging complaint, of course, since those assumptions are precisely what is at issue. But the following line of thought does attempt to mount a real argument.

Eliminative materialism is false, runs the argument, because one's introspection reveals directly the existence of pains, beliefs, desires, fears, and so forth. Their existence is as obvious as anything could be.

The eliminative materialist will reply that this argument makes the same mistake that an ancient or medieval person would be making if he insisted that he could just see with his own eyes that the heavens form a turning sphere, or that witches exist. The fact is, all observation occurs within some system of concepts, and our observation judgments are only as good as the conceptual framework in which they are expressed. In all three cases—the starry sphere, witches, and the familiar mental states—precisely what is challenged is the integrity of the background conceptual frameworks in which the observation judgments are expressed. To insist on the validity of one's experiences, *traditionally interpreted,* is therefore to beg the very question at issue. For in all three cases, the question is whether we should *re*conceive the nature of some familiar observational domain.

A second criticism attempts to find an incoherence in the eliminative materialist's position. The bald statement of eliminative materialism is that the familiar mental states do not really exist. But that statement is meaningful, runs the argument, only if it is the expression of a certain *belief,* and an *intention* to communicate, and a *knowledge* of the language, and so forth. But if the statement is true, then no such mental states exist, and the statement is therefore a meaningless string of marks or noises, and cannot be true. Evidently, the assumption that eliminative materialism is true entails that it cannot be true.

The hole in this argument is the premise concerning the conditions necessary for a statement to be meaningful. It begs the question. If eliminative materialism is true, then meaningfulness must have some different source. To insist on the 'old' source is to insist on the validity of the very framework at issue. Again, an historical parallel may be helpful here. Consider the medieval theory that being biologically *alive* is a matter of being ensouled by an immaterial *vital spirit*. And consider the following response to someone who has expressed disbelief in that theory.

> My learned friend has stated that there is no such thing as vital spirit. But this statement is incoherent. For if it is true, then my friend does not have vital spirit, and must therefore be *dead*. But if he is dead, then his statement is just a string of noises, devoid of meaning or truth. Evidently, the assumption that antivitalism is true entails that it cannot be true! Q.E.D.

This second argument is now a joke, but the first argument begs the question in exactly the same way.

A final criticism draws a much weaker conclusion, but makes a rather stronger case. Eliminative materialism, it has been said, is making mountains out of molehills. It exaggerates the defects in folk psychology, and underplays its real successes. Perhaps the arrival of a matured neuroscience will require the elimination of the occasional folk-psychological concept, continues the criticism, and a minor adjustment in certain folk-psychological principles may have to be endured. But the large-scale elimination forecast by the eliminative materialist is just an alarmist worry or a romantic enthusiasm.

Perhaps this complaint is correct. And perhaps it is merely complacent. Whichever, it does bring out the important point that we do not confront two simple and mutually exclusive possibilities here: pure reduction versus pure elimination. Rather, these are the end points of a smooth spectrum of possible outcomes, between which there are mixed cases of partial elimination and partial reduction. Only empirical research . . . can tell us where on that spectrum our own case will fall. Perhaps we should speak here, more liberally, of "revisionary materialism," instead of concentrating on the more radical possibility of an across-the-board elimination. Perhaps we should. But it has been my aim in this section to make it at least intelligible to you that our collective conceptual destiny lies substantially toward the revolutionary end of the spectrum.

Questions for Reflection

1. Consider the three arguments for eliminativism and the three arguments against it that Churchland discusses. Evaluate the strengths and weaknesses of each.
2. Do you think that it is conceivable that a physical organ, such as the brain, can produce consciousness and subjective awareness through electro-chemical interactions? Is the problem of consciousness one that physicalism can solve?
3. From all that we know today, doesn't it seem undeniable that the brain is an essential part of all our mental activities? To what degree does this support the physicalist's claim that all the advances in the brain sciences indicate that there is nothing left for a nonphysical mind to explain?
4. Can you think of any feature or activity of the mind that could not, in principle, be given a physicalistic explanation?

DAVID CHALMERS

The Puzzle of Conscious Experience

David Chalmers (1966–   ) is Professor of Philosophy and Associate Director of the Center for Consciousness Studies at the University of Arizona. He received his B.A. in mathematics and computer science from the University of Adelaide in Australia and his Ph.D. in philosophy and cognitive science from Indiana University. His book *The Conscious Mind: In Search of a Fundamental Theory* was published by Oxford University Press in 1996 and continues to cause an uproar in the philosophical community because of its forceful attack on physicalism.

When you look at a lemon, your eyes and brain are physically affected by the light reflecting off the object. Obviously, however, there is more going on than when a photoelectric cell responds to the same object and registers the color. You have the subjective experience of the quality of yellow, but the machine does not. In this reading, Chalmers claims that all the progress of the brain sciences have been in terms of the easy problems. What they have not done and, Chalmers claims, will not be able to do is to solve the hard problem of consciousness. The hard problem is: How do we explain the subjective experiences of awareness that characterize consciousness?

Reading Questions

1. What is the distinction Chalmers makes between the objective and subjective aspects of our cognitive life?
2. What are reductionist theories and what is mysterianism? What is Chalmers's evaluation of these two approaches?
3. What are the "easy problems" of consciousness? What is the "hard problem"?
4. Why does Chalmers think that the story of Mary, proposed by Frank Jackson, reveals the problems of reductionism?
5. What is the "explanatory gap" according to Chalmers? Why does he think that the work of Crick, Koch, Dennett, Hameroff, and Penrose will not solve the hard problem?
6. Why does Chalmers think that physics will never be able to give us a true theory of everything? Why does he propose we should consider consciousness to be a fundamental entity? What will be the function of the psychophysical laws Chalmers thinks will be necessary to a complete theory of everything?
7. What are some difficulties in searching for psychophysical laws? Why does Chalmers think they can be overcome?
8. According to Chalmers's speculation, what role might the concept of information play in formulating psychophysical laws?

David Chalmers, "The Puzzle of Conscious Experience," *Scientific American 237* (December 1995), pp. 80–86.

Conscious experience is at once the most familiar thing in the world and the most mysterious. There is nothing we know about more directly than consciousness, but it is extraordinarily hard to reconcile it with everything else we know. Why does it exist? What does it do? How could it possibly arise from neural processes in the brain? These questions are among the most intriguing in all of science.

From an objective viewpoint, the brain is relatively comprehensible. When you look at this page, there is a whir of processing: photons strike your retina, electrical signals are passed up your optic nerve and between different areas of your brain, and eventually you might respond with a smile, a perplexed frown or a remark. But there is also a subjective aspect. When you look at the page, you are conscious of it, directly experiencing the images and words as part of your private, mental life. You have vivid impressions of colored flowers and vibrant sky. At the same time, you may be feeling some emotions and forming some thoughts. Together such experiences make up consciousness: the subjective, inner life of the mind.

For many years, consciousness was shunned by researchers studying the brain and the mind. The prevailing view was that science, which depends on objectivity, could not accommodate something as subjective as consciousness. The behaviorist movement in psychology, dominant earlier in this century, concentrated on external behavior and disallowed any talk of internal mental processes. Later, the rise of cognitive science focused attention on processes inside the head. Still, consciousness remained off-limits, fit only for late-night discussion over drinks.

Over the past several years, however, an increasing number of neuroscientists, psychologists and philosophers have been rejecting the idea that consciousness cannot be studied and are attempting to delve into its secrets. As might be expected of a field so new, there is a tangle of diverse and conflicting theories, often using basic concepts in incompatible ways. To help unsnarl the tangle, philosophical reasoning is vital.

The myriad views within the field range from reductionist theories, according to which consciousness can be explained by the standard methods of neuroscience and psychology, to the position of the so-called mysterians, who say we will never understand consciousness at all. I believe that on close analysis both of these views can be seen to be mistaken and that the truth lies somewhere in the middle. Against reductionism I will argue that the tools of neuroscience cannot provide a full account of conscious experience, although they have much to offer. Against mysterianism I will hold that consciousness might be explained by a new kind of theory. The full details of such a theory are still out of reach, but careful reasoning and some educated inferences can reveal something of its general nature. For example, it will probably involve new fundamental laws, and the concept of information may play a central role. These faint glimmerings suggest that a theory of consciousness may have startling consequences for our view of the universe and of ourselves.

THE HARD PROBLEM

Researchers use the word "consciousness" in many different ways. To clarify the issues, we first have to separate the problems that are often clustered together under the name. For this purpose, I find it useful to distinguish between the "easy problems" and the "hard problem" of consciousness. The easy problems are by no means trivial—they are actually as challenging as most in psychology and biology—but it is with the hard problem that the central mystery lies.

The easy problems of consciousness include the following: How can a human subject discriminate sensory stimuli and react to them appropriately? How does the brain integrate information from many different sources and use this information to control behavior? How is it that subjects can verbalize their internal states? Although all these questions are associated with consciousness, they all concern the objective mechanisms of the cognitive system. Consequently, we have every reason to expect that continued work in cognitive psychology and neuroscience will answer them.

The hard problem, in contrast, is the question of how physical processes in the brain give rise to subjective experience. This puzzle involves the inner aspect of thought and perception: the way things feel for the subject. When we see, for example, we experience visual sensations, such as that of vivid blue. Or think of the ineffable sound of a distant oboe, the agony of an intense pain, the sparkle of happiness or the meditative quality of a moment lost in thought. All are part of what I am calling consciousness. It is these phenomena that pose the real mystery of the mind.

To illustrate the distinction, consider a thought experiment devised by the Australian philosopher Frank Jackson. Suppose that Mary, a neuroscientist in the 23rd century, is the world's leading expert on the brain processes responsible for color vision. But Mary has lived her whole life in a black-and-white room and has never seen any other colors. She knows everything there is to know about physical processes in the brain—its biology, structure and function. This understanding enables her to grasp everything there is to know about the easy problems: how the brain discriminates stimuli, integrates information and produces verbal reports. From her knowledge of color vision, she knows the way color names correspond with wavelengths on the light spectrum. But there is still something crucial about color vision that Mary does not know: what it is like to experience a color such as red. It follows that there are facts about conscious experience that cannot be deduced from physical facts about the functioning of the brain.

Indeed, nobody knows why these physical processes are accompanied by conscious experience at all. Why is it that when our brains process light of a certain wavelength, we have an experience of deep purple? Why do we have any experience at all? Could not an unconscious automaton have performed the same tasks just as well? These are questions that we would like a theory of consciousness to answer.

I am not denying that consciousness arises from the brain. We know, for example, that the subjective experience of vision is closely linked to processes in the visual cortex. It is the link itself that perplexes, however. Remarkably, subjective experience seems to emerge from a physical process. But we have no idea how or why this is.

IS NEUROSCIENCE ENOUGH?

Given the flurry of recent work on consciousness in neuroscience and psychology, one might think this mystery is starting to be cleared up. On closer examination, however, it turns out that almost all the current work addresses only the easy problems of consciousness. The confidence of the reductionist view comes from the progress on the easy problems, but none of this makes any difference where the hard problem is concerned.

Consider the hypothesis put forward by neurobiologists Francis Crick of the Salk Institute for Biological Studies in San Diego and Christof Koch of the California Institute of Technology. They suggest that consciousness may arise from certain oscillations in the cerebral cortex, which become synchronized as neurons fire 40 times per second. Crick and Koch believe the phenomenon might explain how different attributes of a single perceived object (its color and shape, for example), which are processed in different parts of the brain, are merged into a coherent whole. In this theory, two pieces of information become bound together precisely when they are represented by synchronized neural firings.

The hypothesis could conceivably elucidate one of the easy problems about how information is integrated in the brain. But why should synchronized oscillations give rise to a visual experience, no matter how much integration is taking place? This question involves the hard problem, about which the theory has nothing to offer. Indeed, Crick and Koch are agnostic about whether the hard problem can be solved by science at all.

The same kind of critique could be applied to almost all the recent work on consciousness. In his 1991 book *Consciousness Explained,* philosopher Daniel C. Dennett laid out a sophisticated theory of how numerous independent processes in the brain combine to produce a coherent response to a perceived event. The theory might do much to explain how we produce verbal reports on our internal states, but it tells us very little about why there should be a subjective experience behind these reports. Like other reductionist theories, Dennett's is a theory of the easy problems.

The critical common trait among these easy problems is that they all concern how a cognitive or behavioral function is performed. All are ultimately questions about how the brain carries out some task—how it discriminates stimuli, integrates information, produces reports and so on. Once neurobiology specifies appropriate neural mechanisms, showing how the functions are performed, the easy problems are solved. The hard problem of consciousness, in contrast, goes beyond problems about how functions are performed. Even if every behavioral and cognitive function related to consciousness were explained, there would still remain a further mystery: Why is the performance of these functions accompanied by conscious experience? It is this additional conundrum that makes the hard problem hard.

THE EXPLANATORY GAP

Some have suggested that to solve the hard problem, we need to bring in new tools of physical explanation: nonlinear dynamics, say, or new discoveries in neuroscience, or quantum mechanics. But these ideas suffer from exactly the same difficulty. Consider a proposal from Stuart R. Hameroff of the University of Arizona and Roger Penrose of the University of Oxford. They hold that consciousness arises from quantum-physical processes taking place in microtubules, which are protein structures inside neurons. It is possible (if not likely) that such a hypothesis will lead to an explanation of how the brain makes decisions or even how it proves mathematical theorems, as Hameroff and Penrose suggest. But even if it does, the theory is silent about how these processes might give rise to conscious experience. Indeed, the same problem arises with any theory of consciousness based only on physical processing.

The trouble is that physical theories are best suited to explaining why systems have a certain physical structure and how they perform various functions. Most problems in science have this form; to explain life, for example, we need to describe how a physical system can reproduce, adapt and metabolize. But consciousness is a different sort of problem entirely, as it goes beyond the explanation of structure and function.

Of course, neuroscience is not irrelevant to the study of consciousness. For one, it may be able to reveal the nature of the neural correlate of consciousness—the brain processes most directly associated with conscious experience. It may even give a detailed correspondence between specific processes in the brain and related components of experience. But until we know why these processes give rise to conscious experience at all, we will not have crossed what philosopher Joseph Levine has called the explanatory gap between physical processes and consciousness. Making that leap will demand a new kind of theory.

A TRUE THEORY OF EVERYTHING

In searching for an alternative, a key observation is that not all entities in science are explained in terms of more basic entities. In physics, for example, space-time, mass and charge (among other things) are regarded as fundamental features of the world, as they are not reducible to anything simpler. Despite this irreducibility, detailed and useful theories relate these entities to one another in terms of fundamental laws. Together these features and laws explain a great variety of complex and subtle phenomena.

It is widely believed that physics provides a complete catalogue of the universe's fundamental features and laws. As physicist Steven Weinberg puts it in his 1992 book *Dreams of a Final Theory*, the goal of physics is a "theory of everything" from which all there is to know about the universe can be derived. But Weinberg concedes that there is a problem with consciousness. Despite the power of physical theory, the existence of consciousness does not seem to be derivable from physical laws. He defends physics by arguing that it might eventually explain what he calls the objective correlates of consciousness (that is, the neural correlates), but of course to do this is not to explain consciousness itself. If the existence of consciousness cannot be derived from physical laws, a theory of physics is not a true theory of everything. So a final theory must contain an additional fundamental component.

Toward this end, I propose that conscious experience be considered a fundamental feature, irreducible to anything more basic. The idea may seem strange at first, but consistency seems to demand it. In the 19th century it turned out that electromagnetic phenomena could not be explained in terms of previously known principles. As a consequence, scientists introduced electromagnetic charge as a new fundamental entity and studied the associated fundamental laws. Similar reasoning should apply to consciousness. If existing fundamental theories cannot encompass it, then something new is required.

Where there is a fundamental property, there are fundamental laws. In this case, the laws must relate experience to elements of physical theory. These laws will almost certainly not interfere with those of the physical world; it seems that the latter form a closed system in their own right. Rather the laws will serve as a bridge, specifying how experience depends on underlying physical processes. It is this bridge that will cross the explanatory gap.

Thus, a complete theory will have two components: physical laws, telling us about the behavior of physical systems from the infinitesimal to the cosmological, and what we might call psychophysical laws, telling us how some of those systems are associated with conscious experience. These two components will constitute a true theory of everything.

SEARCHING FOR A THEORY

Supposing for the moment that they exist, how might we uncover such psychophysical laws? The greatest hindrance in this pursuit will be a lack of data. As I have described it, consciousness is subjective, so there is no direct way to monitor it in others. But this difficulty is an obstacle, not a dead end. For a start, each one of us has access to our own experiences, a rich trove that can be used to formulate theories. We can also plausibly rely on indirect information, such as subjects' descriptions of their experiences. Philosophical arguments and thought experiments also have a role to play. Such methods have limitations, but they give us more than enough to get started.

These theories will not be conclusively testable, so they will inevitably be more speculative than those of more conventional scientific disciplines. Nevertheless, there is no reason they should not be strongly constrained to account accurately for our own first-person experiences, as well as the evidence from subjects' reports. If we find a theory that fits the data better than any other theory of equal simplicity, we will have good reason to accept it. Right now we do not have even a single theory that fits the data, so worries about testability are premature.

We might start by looking for high-level bridging laws, connecting physical processes to experience at an everyday level. The basic contour of such a law might be gleaned from the observation that when we are conscious of something, we are generally able to act on it and speak about it—which are objective, physical functions. Conversely, when some information is directly available for action and speech, it is generally conscious. Thus, consciousness correlates well with what we might call "awareness": the process by which information in the brain is made globally available to motor processes such as speech and bodily action.

The notion may seem trivial. But as defined here, awareness is objective and physical, whereas consciousness is not. Some refinements to the definition of awareness are needed, in order to extend the concept to animals and infants, which cannot speak. But at least in familiar cases, it is possible to see the rough outlines of a psychophysical law: where there is awareness, there is consciousness, and vice versa.

To take this line of reasoning a step further, consider the structure present in the conscious experience. The experience of a field of vision, for example, is a constantly changing mosaic of colors, shapes and patterns and as such has a detailed geometric structure. The fact that we can describe this structure, reach out in the direction of many of its components and perform other actions that depend on it suggests that the structure corresponds directly to that of the information made available in the brain through the neural processes of awareness.

Similarly, our experiences of color have an intrinsic three-dimensional structure that is mirrored in the structure of information processes in the brain's visual cortex. This structure is illustrated in the color wheels and charts used by artists. Colors are arranged in a systematic pattern—red to green on one axis, blue to yellow on another, and black to white on a third. Colors that are close to one another on a color wheel are experienced as similar. It is extremely likely that they also correspond to similar perceptual representations in the brain, as part of a system of complex three-dimensional coding among neurons that is not yet fully understood. We can recast the underlying concept as a principle of structural coherence: the structure of conscious experience is mirrored by the structure of information in awareness, and vice versa.

Another candidate for a psychophysical law is a principle of organizational invariance. It holds that physical systems with the same abstract organization will give rise to the same kind of conscious experience, no matter what they are made of. For example, if the precise interactions between our neurons could be duplicated with silicon chips, the same conscious experience would arise. The idea is somewhat controversial, but I believe it is strongly supported by thought experiments describing the gradual replacement of neurons by silicon chips. The remarkable implication is that consciousness might someday be achieved in machines.

INFORMATION: PHYSICAL AND EXPERIENTIAL

The ultimate goal of a theory of consciousness is a simple and elegant set of fundamental laws, analogous to the fundamental laws of physics. The principles described above are unlikely to be fundamental, however. Rather they seem to be high-level psychophysical laws, analogous to macroscopic principles in physics such as those of thermodynamics or kinematics. What might the underlying fundamental laws be? No one knows, but I don't mind speculating.

I suggest that the primary psychophysical laws may centrally involve the concept of information. The abstract notion of information, as put forward in the 1940s by Claude E. Shannon of the Massachusetts Institute of Technology, is that of a set of separate states with a basic structure of similarities and differences between them. We can think of a 10-bit binary code as an information state, for example. Such information states can be embodied in the physical world. This happens whenever they correspond to physical states (voltages, say), the differences between which can be transmitted along some pathway, such as a telephone line.

We can also find information embodied in conscious experience. The pattern of color patches in a visual field, for example, can be seen as analogous to that of the pixels covering a display screen. Intriguingly, it turns out that we find the same information states embedded in conscious experience and in underlying physical processes in the brain. The three-dimensional encoding of color spaces, for example, suggests that the information state in a color experience corresponds directly to an information state in the brain. We might even regard the two states as distinct aspects of a single information state, which is simultaneously embodied in both physical processing and conscious experience.

A natural hypothesis ensues. Perhaps information, or at least some information, has two basic aspects: a physical one and an experiential one. This hypothesis has the status of a fundamental principle that might underlie the relation between physical processes and experience. Wherever we find conscious experience, it exists as one aspect of an information state, the other aspect of which is embedded in a physical process in the brain. This proposal needs to be fleshed out to make a satisfying theory. But it fits nicely with the principles mentioned earlier—systems with the same organization will embody the same information, for example—and it could explain numerous features of our conscious experience.

The idea is at least compatible with several others, such as physicist John A. Wheeler's suggestion that information is fundamental to the physics of the universe. The laws of physics might ultimately be cast in informational terms, in which case we would have a satisfying congruence between the constructs in both physical and psychophysical laws. It may even be that a theory of physics and a theory of consciousness could eventually be consolidated into a single grander theory of information.

A potential problem is posed by the ubiquity of information. Even a thermostat embodies some information, for example, but is it conscious? There are at least two possible responses. First, we could constrain the fundamental laws so that only some information has an experiential aspect, perhaps depending on how it is physically processed. Second, we might bite the bullet and allow that all information has an experiential aspect—where there is complex information processing, there is complex experience, and where there is simple information processing, there is simple experience. If this is so, then even a thermostat might have experiences, although they would be much simpler than even a basic color experience, and there would certainly be no accompanying emotions or thoughts. This seems odd at first, but if experience is truly fundamental, we might expect it to be widespread. In any case, the choice between these alternatives should depend on which can be integrated into the most powerful theory.

Of course, such ideas may be all wrong. On the other hand, they might evolve into a more powerful proposal that predicts the precise structure of our conscious experience from physical processes in our brains. If this project succeeds, we will have good reason to accept the theory. If it fails, other avenues will be pursued, and alternative fundamental theories may be developed. In this way, we may one day resolve the greatest mystery of the mind.

Questions for Reflection

1. In what ways is Chalmers in agreement with Descartes? In what ways do they seem to differ?

2. Do you agree with Chalmers that studies of the brain alone will not solve the hard problem of consciousness? How might a physicalist reply to Chalmers' criticisms?

3. Which of the following two interpretations of Chalmers do you think most accurately captures his position? (a) "Chalmers is saying that there are some things such as consciousness that science will never be able to explain. Therefore, he is a dualist." (b) "Chalmers is saying that our current *science* cannot explain consciousness. Therefore, physical science must be expanded and new laws developed, just as we formulated new laws to explain electromagnetism. These new laws will provide a scientific basis for explaining consciousness. Therefore, Chalmers is a physicalist."

On the other hand, do both of these formulations misrepresent his position?

R. BUCKMINSTER FULLER

"What's a Man?"

R. Buckminster Fuller (1895–1983) was an engineer, architect, essayist, poet, inventor, and all-round visionary. Educated at Harvard and the United States Naval Academy, Fuller had a long career in industry and lectured at Yale, Harvard, and a host of other universities. He designed the geodesic dome and invented the Dymaxion three-wheeled automobile in the 1930s. His books include *No More Secondhand God, Education Automation, Ideas and Integrities, The Unfinished Epic Poem of Industrialization,* and *An Operating Manual for Spaceship Earth.* In the following excerpt, from *Nine Chains to the Moon* (1938), Fuller gives a description of the human person in terms of engineering concepts. (Please ignore the outdated convention of referring collectively to human beings as "man.")

Reading Questions

1. As you read through this description of a human in engineering terms, what do the different mechanistic systems refer to in your body?
2. Do you think that this sort of description is adequate? Does it leave anything out?

"What is that, mother?"

"It's a man, darling."

"What's a man?"

Man?

A self-balancing, 28-jointed adapter-base biped; an electrochemical reduction-plant, integral with segregated stowages of special energy extracts in storage batteries, for subsequent actuation of thousands of hydraulic and pneumatic pumps, with motors attached; 62,000 miles of capillaries; millions of warning signal, railroad and conveyor systems; crushers and cranes (of which the arms are magnificent 23-jointed affairs with self-surfacing and lubricating systems, and a universally distributed telephone system needing no service for 70 years if well managed); the whole, extraordinarily complex mechanism guided with exquisite precision from a turret in which are located telescopic and microscopic self-registering and recording range finders, a spectroscope, *et cetera,* the turret control being closely allied with an air conditioning intake-and-exhaust, and a main fuel intake.

Within the few cubic inches housing the turret mechanisms, there is room, also, for two sound-wave and sound-direction-finder recording diaphragms, a filing and instant reference system, and an expertly devised analytical laboratory large enough not only to contain minute records of every last and continual event of up to 70 years' experience, or more, but to extend, by computation and abstract fabrication, this experience with relative accuracy into all corners of the observed universe. There is, also, a forecasting and tactical plotting department for the reduction of future possibilities and probabilities to generally successful specific choice.

R. Buckminster Fuller, "The Phantom Captain," in *Nine Chains to the Moon* (Carbondale: Southern Illinois University Press, 1938), pp. 18–19.

Questions for Reflection

1. Is Fuller giving us a tongue-in-cheek, playful parody of a physicalist's view of the person or is this an attempt to show that we can be described in purely physical terms? In other words, should this be treated as an argument against physicalism or for it?
2. What would Descartes say about this description? What would Churchland say? What would Chalmers say?
3. Do you think that, in principle, this description is on the right track, or is it woefully inadequate? If the latter, what is wrong with it?

WHAT IS THE BASIS OF PERSONAL IDENTITY? DO I SURVIVE MY DEATH?

As I write this paragraph, I am looking at a photograph of a 16-year-old student in a high school yearbook. Strangely, he has my exact name. He even looks somewhat like me. In fact, someone might suppose that he is my son. The truth of the matter is that he *is* me—well, sort of. We have the same birth certificates and his dental records and mine are identical, as is our DNA. A forensic scientist would not hesitate in concluding that we are the same person. So why do I hesitate in saying that we are the same person? First, I am familiar with the things he thought were of earth-shaking importance and which to me seem trivial. Furthermore, although we share many of the same values, there is also much about which we would radically disagree. Finally, I find his taste in music and clothing styles embarrassing and find it impossible to understand why he had such a delirious crush on a certain girl he dated for a while.

My uneasy relationship with my own, past self is the emotional and personal side of a rather thorny, philosophical problem known as the *problem of personal identity*. The problem can be posed in the following fashion. The weather changes over the course of several days, changing, say, from sunny to rainy. In this case, it would be absurd to say it is really the "same" weather with different properties. However, if you see a friend today and then see her a month from now, she may look the same, but you will be looking at literally different skin cells. Furthermore, as we grow from infants to adolescents to adults, we change even more dramatically. Yet, with persons (unlike the weather) we say that, in spite of the changes, it is the same person that is continuing through time. What is it that makes someone the *same* person over time?

One of the classic answers to this question was given by John Locke in the 17th century. Locke argued for the *psychological continuity theory* of personal identity. Even though our body is constantly changing (most of our bodily cells change every seven years), it is the continuity of our psychological states or consciousness that makes us the same over time. Locke specifically focused on memory as the key to psychological continuity. Different people may have similar personalities and beliefs, but it seems obvious that specific memories can only be owned by one person. My friends may remember attending my 16th birthday party, but only I remember being the person who received the gifts that day.

There is something appealing about this view. Suppose you were confronted by two identical twins. One is a close friend and the other is his evil twin. How would you know who to trust and who to shun? If you could quiz each one about experiences that only you and your friend had shared, then the one with the correct memories would be your friend. In Dennett's story (reading 32), Dennett had a new body and half the time his memories were coming from a computer duplicate of his brain. Even though there was no continuity between him and his past body and brain, he still felt as though he was the same person and his acquaintances treated him as such, because his memories and personality were the same.

There are difficulties with Locke's position, however. First, our memories are not continuous. When you are asleep you have no conscious awareness of your memories, so are you the same person? Furthermore, there are vast stretches of my earlier life that I cannot remember. Does that mean that the person who occupied my body during those times was not me? In cases of severe amnesia, would Locke's view commit us to saying that the person has no past if she has no memories? The second problem is that our memories are not always accurate. Sometimes I think I remember funny things I did when I was a baby, but I am probably reconstructing the scene from the stories my parents told me about my baby years. To consider more extreme cases, some people have multiple personalities due to a childhood trauma. The famous case of Sybil is that of a woman who had 16 personalities and 16 different sets of memories. Should we say that there were 16 persons occupying one body or would it make more sense to view Sybil as one person with fractured psychological states? A hypnotist can create false memories within a person, and in the science fiction movie *Total Recall* an evil scientist reprogrammed the brain of Arnold Schwarzenegger's character so that he had a completely false set of memories of who he was. For these reasons, some philosophers think that memories or psychological states are too fleeting and deceptive to serve as a criterion for personal identity.

Some think that the *bodily continuity theory* gives us the best account of personal identity. According to this view, persons are continuous with their bodies. Since we commonly use bodily continuity as the criterion for recognizing one another, it makes sense to say that this is what constitutes personal identity. Suppose, for example, that I suffer brain damage that changes my personality and erases my memories. Even though my friends may find me different, if I am the same physical person who signed the deed on my house before the brain damage, then I am the person who owns the house. However, this view cannot account for the theoretical possibility of transplanting my brain to another body. It would seem that where my brain goes, my personality and memories also go. Therefore, where my brain goes, I go. But this simply means that it is not any old part of my body that counts, but it is my brain that makes me who I am.

What we now have is the *brain continuity theory* of personal identity. It is actually a more narrow and focused version of the bodily continuity theory. But is brain continuity a sufficient or even necessary condition for personal continuity? What if doctors told you that the only way to save your life is to have your brain transplanted from your dying body to a healthy donor body? This sounds fine until they explain that during the surgery, your brain will be "zapped." This means that all your memories and psychological traits will be destroyed. Someone will wake up in the recovery room and will live a happy life with your former brain, but is there any reason to believe that *you* will survive the surgery? This seems to return us full circle to the memory and psychological traits criterion. You would want the person who wakes up after surgery to be more or less who you are now, with most of your memories and personality intact.

Since each theory has its pluses and minuses, you will have to choose the theory that (1) best explains the facts and our experiences, (2) makes the best sense of our intuitions about persons, and (3) is consistent with the way we speak about persons. John Locke will argue for the psychological states and memory criteria. David Hume will argue, in so many words, that you are like the weather—constantly changing, but without any continuity. Finally, Jeffrey Olen will apply a modified version of Locke's theory to the issue of survival after death and Linda Badham will defend the bodily continuity theory as a means of arguing against personal immortality.

JOHN LOCKE

The Self Is Identical to Its Psychological States

The English philosopher John Locke (1632–1704) developed one of the classic positions on personal identity. (Information about his life was given in Chapter 3 in connection with reading 22.) Locke's view is that personal identity is related to the continuity of one's psychological states, particularly memory. According to this criterion, you could be given a different body (say, after death) and yet would be the same person if your memories and conscious life were the same as before. In the case of Dennett's story (reading 32), Dennett's brain was duplicated in a computer. Hence, even though there was no physical continuity with either Dennett's former body or his brain, Locke would have to say that Dennett was the same person if his conscious life and his memories were the same. Similarly, the same immaterial substance (or soul) would not constitute the same person unless there was also a continuity of memories. Notice that Locke makes a distinction between our loose ways of identifying the "same man" (which might be based on physical similarities) and the real sense in which someone is the "same person" across time.

Reading Questions

1. According to Locke, what does the word person refer to?
2. What is the key element in personal identity according to Locke's theory?
3. Can one be the same person if the body changes?
4. How does Locke apply his view to the identity of the person after death?
5. What point does Locke make with the story of the prince and the cobbler?
6. Can the same immaterial substance or soul alone account for personal identity?
7. In what sense is it possible for the mad man and the sober man to be the same *man* and yet to be different *persons?*

From John Locke, "Of Ideas of Identity and Diversity," in *An Essay Concerning Human Understanding*, book II, chap. 27, first published in 1689.

THE NATURE OF THE PERSON

To find wherein personal identity consists, we must consider what *person* stands for—which, I think, is a thinking intelligent being, that has reason and reflection, and can consider itself as itself, the same thinking thing, in different times and places; which it does only by that consciousness which is inseparable from thinking, and, as it seems to me, essential to it: it being impossible for any one to perceive without perceiving that he does perceive. When we see, hear, smell, taste, feel, meditate, or will anything, we know that we do so. Thus it is always as to our present sensations and perceptions; and by this every one is to himself that which he calls self—it not being considered, in this case, whether the same self be continued in the same or divers substances. For, since consciousness always accompanies thinking, and it is that which makes every one to be what he calls self, and thereby distinguishes himself from all other thinking things, in this alone consists personal identity, i.e., the sameness of a rational being; and as far as this consciousness can be extended backwards to any past action or thought, so far reaches the identity of that person; it is the same self now it was then; and it is by the same self with this present one that now reflects on it, that that action was done.

CONSCIOUSNESS MAKES PERSONAL IDENTITY

But it is further inquired, whether it be the same identical substance. This, few would think they had reason to doubt of, if these perceptions, with their consciousness, always remained present in the mind, whereby the same thinking thing would be always consciously present, and, as would be thought, evidently the same to itself. But that which seems to make the difficulty is this, that this consciousness being interrupted always by forgetfulness, there being no moment of our lives wherein we have the whole train of all our past actions before our eyes in one view, but even the best memories losing the sight of one part whilst they are viewing another; and we sometimes, and that the

greatest part of our lives, not reflecting on our past selves, being intent on our present thoughts, and in sound sleep having no thoughts at all, or at least none with that consciousness which remarks our waking thoughts—I say, in all these cases, our consciousness being interrupted, and we losing the sight of our past selves, doubts are raised whether we are the same thinking thing, i.e., the same substance or no. Which, however reasonable or unreasonable, concerns not personal identity at all. The question being what makes the same person; and not whether it be the same identical substance, which always thinks in the same person, which, in this case, matters not at all: different substances, by the same consciousness (where they do partake in it) being united into one person, as well as different bodies by the same life are united into one animal, whose identity is preserved in that change of substances by the unity of one continued life. For, it being the same consciousness that makes a man be himself to himself, personal identity depends on that only, whether it be annexed solely to one individual substance, or can be continued in a succession of several substances. For as far as any intelligent being can repeat the idea of any past action with the same consciousness it had of it at first, and with the same consciousness it has of any present action; so far it is the same personal self. For it is by the consciousness it has of its present thoughts and actions, that it is self to itself now, and so will be the same self, as far as the same consciousness can extend to actions past or to come; and would be by distance of time, or change of substance, no more two persons, than a man be two men by wearing other clothes today than he did yesterday, with a long or a short sleep between: the same consciousness uniting those distant actions into the same person, whatever substances contributed to their production.

PERSONAL IDENTITY IN CHANGE OF SUBSTANCES

That this is so, we have some kind of evidence in our very bodies, all whose particles, whilst vitally united to this same thinking conscious self, so that we feel when they are touched, and are affected by, and conscious of good or harm that happens to them, as a part of ourselves; i.e., of our thinking conscious self. Thus, the limbs of his body are to every one a part of himself; he sympathizes and is concerned for them. Cut off a hand, and thereby separate it from that consciousness he had of its heat, cold, and other affections, and it is then no longer a part of that which is himself, any more than the remotest part of matter. Thus, we see the substance whereof personal self consisted at one time may be varied at another, without the change of personal identity; there being no question about the same person, though the limbs which but now were a part of it, be cut off. . . .

MEMORY AND PERSONAL IDENTITY

And thus may we be able, without any difficulty, to conceive the same person at the resurrection, though in a body not exactly in make or parts the same which he had here—the same consciousness going along with the soul that inhabits it. But yet the soul alone, in the change of bodies, would scarce to any one but to him that makes the soul the man, be enough to make the same man. For should the soul of a prince, carrying with it the consciousness of the prince's past life, enter and inform the body of a cobbler, as soon as deserted by his own soul, every one sees he would be the same *person* with the prince, accountable only for the prince's actions: but who would say it was the same *man*? The body too goes to the making the man, and would, I guess, to everybody determine the man in this case, wherein the soul, with all its princely thoughts about it, would not make another man: but he would be the same cobbler to every one besides himself. I know that, in the ordinary way of speaking, the same person, and the same man, stand for one and the same thing. And indeed every one will always have a liberty to speak as he pleases, and to apply what articulate sounds to what ideas he thinks fit, and change them as often as he pleases. But yet, when we will inquire what makes the same spirit, man, or person, we

must fix the ideas of spirit, man, or person in our minds; and having resolved with ourselves what we mean by them, it will not be hard to determine, in either of them, or the like, when it is the same, and when not.

CONSCIOUSNESS ALONE UNITES ACTIONS INTO THE SAME PERSON

But though the same immaterial substance or soul does not alone, wherever it be, and in whatsoever state, make the same man; yet it is plain, consciousness, as far as ever it can be extended— should it be to ages past—unites existences and actions very remote in time into the same person, as well as it does the existences and actions of the immediately preceding moment: so that whatever has the consciousness of present and past actions, is the same person to whom they both belong. Had I the same consciousness that I saw the ark and Noah's flood, as that I saw an overflowing of the Thames last winter, or as that I write now, I could no more doubt that I who write this now, that saw the Thames overflowed last winter, and that viewed the flood at the general deluge, was the same self— place that self in what substance you please—than that I who write this am the same myself now whilst I write (whether I consist of all the same substance, material or immaterial, or no) that I was yesterday. For as to this point of being the same self, it matters not whether this present self be made up of the same or other substances—I being as much concerned, and as justly accountable for any action that was done a thousand years since, appropriated to me now by this self-consciousness, as I am for what I did the last moment. . . .

PERSONAL IDENTITY IS IDENTITY OF CONSCIOUSNESS

This may show us wherein personal identity consists: not in the identity of substance, but, as I have said, in the identity of consciousness, wherein if Socrates and the present mayor of Queenborough agree, they are the same person: if the same Socrates waking and sleeping do not partake of the same consciousness, Socrates waking and sleeping is not the same person. And to punish Socrates waking for what sleeping Socrates thought, and waking Socrates was never conscious of, would be no more of right, than to punish one twin for what his brother-twin did, whereof he knew nothing, because their outsides were so like, that they could not be distinguished; for such twins have been seen.

But yet possibly it will still be objected—Suppose I wholly lose the memory of some parts of my life, beyond a possibility of retrieving them, so that perhaps I shall never be conscious of them again; yet am I not the same person that did those actions, had those thoughts that I once was conscious of, though I have now forgot them? To which I answer, that we must here take notice what the word *I* is applied to; which, in this case, is the *man* only. And the same man being presumed to be the same person, *I* is easily here supposed to stand also for the same person. But if it be possible for the same man to have distinct incommunicable consciousness at different times, it is past doubt the same man would at different times make different persons; which, we see, is the sense of mankind in the solemnest declaration of their opinions, human laws not punishing the mad man for the sober man's actions, nor the sober man for what the mad man did—thereby making them two persons: which is somewhat explained by our way of speaking in English when we say such an one is "not himself," or is "beside himself"; in which phrases it is insinuated, as if those who now, or at least first used them, thought that self was changed; the selfsame person was no longer in that man.

THE DIFFERENCE BETWEEN THE IDENTITY OF THE MAN AND OF THE PERSON

But yet it is hard to conceive that Socrates, the same individual man, should be two persons. To help us a little in this, we must consider what is meant by Socrates, or the same individual *man*.

First, it must be either the same individual, immaterial, thinking substance; in short, the same numerical soul, and nothing else.

Secondly, or the same animal, without any regard to an immaterial soul.

Thirdly, or the same immaterial spirit united to the same animal.

Now, take which of these suppositions you please, it is impossible to make personal identity to consist in anything but consciousness; or reach any further than that does.

For, by the first of them, it must be allowed possible that a man born of different women, and in distant times, may be the same man. A way of speaking which, whoever admits, must allow it possible for the same man to be two distinct persons, as any two that have lived in different ages without the knowledge of one another's thoughts.

By the second and third, Socrates, in this life and after it, cannot be the same man any way, but by the same consciousness; and so making human identity to consist in the same thing wherein we place personal identity, there will be no difficulty to allow the same man to be the same person. But then they who place human identity in consciousness only, and not in something else, must consider how they will make the infant Socrates the same man with Socrates after the resurrection. But whatsoever to some men makes a man, and consequently the same individual man, wherein perhaps few are agreed, personal identity can by us be placed in nothing but consciousness, (which is that alone which makes what we call *self*,) without involving us in great absurdities. . . .

CONSCIOUSNESS UNITES SUBSTANCES, MATERIAL OR SPIRITUAL, WITH THE SAME PERSONALITY

I agree, the more probable opinion is, that this consciousness is annexed to, and the affection of, one individual immaterial substance.

But let men, according to their diverse hypotheses, resolve of that as they please. This every intelligent being, sensible of happiness or misery, must grant, that there is something that is himself, that he is concerned for, and would have happy; that this self has existed in a continued duration more than one instant, and therefore it is possible may exist, as it has done, months and years to come, without any certain bounds to be set to its duration; and may be the same self, by the same consciousness continued on for the future. And thus, by this consciousness he finds himself to be the same self which did such and such an action some years since, by which he comes to be happy or miserable now. In all which account of self, the same numerical substance is not considered as making the same self, but the same continued consciousness, in which several substances may have been united, and again separated from it, which, whilst they continued in a vital union with that wherein this consciousness then resided, made a part of that same self. Thus any part of our bodies, vitally united to that which is conscious in us, makes a part of ourselves: but upon separation from the vital union by which that consciousness is communicated, that which a moment since was part of ourselves, is now no more so than a part of another man's self is a part of me: and it is not impossible but in a little time may become a real part of another person. And so we have the same numerical substance become a part of two different persons; and the same person preserved under the change of various substances. Could we suppose any spirit wholly stripped of all its memory or consciousness of past actions, as we find our minds always are of a great part of ours, and sometimes of them all; the union or separation of such a spiritual substance would make no variation of personal identity, any more than that of any particle of matter does. Any substance vitally united to the present thinking being is a part of that very same self which now is; anything united to it by a consciousness of former actions, makes also a part of the same self, which is the same both then and now.

Questions for Reflection

1. What would Locke say of the view that the soul of a previous person, say, Cleopatra, could be reincarnated in the body of someone today? If the contemporary person had no memories of their previous life as Cleopatra, would Locke say they were the same person? If the contemporary person did have Cleopatra's memories of ancient events, what would Locke say then?

2. In a court of law the insanity defense assumes that a person cannot be charged with a crime if it can be shown that the person was temporarily insane at the time the crime was committed and that the defendant is not psychologically identical with the person who committed the crime. What would Locke say about such a defense?

3. What would Locke say about a case of severe amnesia, where a person has lost his memories? Is this person continuous with the person whose actions he has forgotten?

4. What would Locke say about cases of multiple personalities where a psychologically fractured person can have 16 personalities with 16 different sets of memories? Would Locke have to say that 16 different persons inhabit the same body?

5. Suppose that on your 10th birthday, you remember the details of your 5th birthday party. On this basis, Locke would say the 10-year-old is same person as the 5-year-old. Furthermore, let's suppose that at age 40 you can remember the details of your 10th birthday and other events in the life of that 10-year-old. On this basis, Locke would say the 40-year-old is the same person as the 10-year-old. However, suppose that at age 40, you can no longer remember your 5th birthday party. Since the 40-year-old does

not remember the experiences of the 5-year-old, does this now mean that they are not the same person? Does this result in a contradiction in Locke's theory? Is memory too ephemeral and transitory to be the basis for personal identity as Locke supposes?

DAVID HUME

There Is No Self

David Hume (1711–1776), the Scottish skeptic, is one of the leading representatives of the "no self" view. (A biographical sketch of Hume was provided in Chapter 2 with reading 8.) Hume's view could be characterized as the "onion" view of the self. Peel away all the layers and there is no core self that remains. As was clear from his epistemology discussed in Chapter 3, Hume believes that all we can directly know are sensory impressions and the other contents of our own psychological states. However, our psychological states are constantly changing. Each of us is a "stream of consciousness." For example, you are literally a different person now compared with the person who first began reading this book, because your ideas and thoughts are different. Furthermore, when we introspect, we do not have any impressions of something called the "self." Accordingly, Hume concludes that the notion of personal identity has no basis.

Reading Questions

1. What does Hume mean when he says there is no single impression of the self? Why does he think that this fact is significant?
2. What does he find when he introspectively searches for what he calls "myself"?
3. What does he mean when he says the mind is a kind of theater?
4. According to Hume, what makes us believe in personal identity?
5. In closing, what does he say to those who believe that memory constitutes our personal identity (e.g., Locke)?

There are some philosophers who imagine we are every moment intimately conscious of what we call our SELF; that we feel its existence and its continuance in existence; and are certain, beyond the ev-idence of a demonstration, both of its perfect identity and simplicity. . . .

Unluckily all these positive assertions are contrary to that very experience, which is pleaded for

From David Hume, "Of Personal Identity," in *A Treatise of Human Nature*, book I, part 4. First published in 1739.

them, nor have we any idea of *self,* after the manner it is here explained. For from what impression could this idea be derived? This question it is impossible to answer without a manifest contradiction and absurdity; and yet it is a question, which must necessarily be answered, if we would have the idea of self pass for clear and intelligible. It must be some one impression, that gives rise to every real idea. But self or person is not any one impression, but that to which our several impressions and ideas are supposed to have a reference. If any impression gives rise to the idea of self, that impression must continue invariably the same, through the whole course of our lives; since self is supposed to exist after that manner. But there is no impression constant and invariable. Pain and pleasure, grief and joy, passions and sensations succeed each other, and never all exist at the same time. It cannot, therefore, be from any of these impressions, or from any other, that the idea of self is derived; and consequently there is no such idea.

But farther, what must become of all our particular perceptions upon this hypothesis? All these are different, and distinguishable, and separable from each other, and may be separately considered, and may exist separately, and have no need of any thing to support their existence. After what manner, therefore, do they belong to self; and how are they connected with it? For my part, when I enter most intimately into what I call *myself,* I always stumble on some particular perception or other, of heat or cold, light or shade, love or hatred, pain or pleasure. I never can catch *myself* at any time without a perception, and never can observe any thing but the perception. When my perceptions are removed for any time, as by sound sleep; so long am I insensible of *myself,* and may truly be said not to exist. And were all my perceptions removed by death, and could I neither think, nor feel, nor see, nor love, nor hate after the dissolution of my body, I should be entirely annihilated, nor do I conceive what is farther requisite to make me a perfect nonentity. If any one, upon serious and unprejudiced reflection thinks he has a different notion of himself, I must confess I call reason no longer with him. All I can allow him is, that he may be in the right as well as I, and that we are essentially differ-

ent in this particular. He may, perhaps, perceive something simple and continued, which he calls *himself;* though I am certain there is no such principle in me.

But setting aside some metaphysicians of this kind, I may venture to affirm of the rest of mankind, that they are nothing but a bundle or collection of different perceptions, which succeed each other with an inconceivable rapidity, and are in a perpetual flux and movement. Our eyes cannot turn in their sockets without varying our perceptions. Our thought is still more variable than our sight; and all our other senses and faculties contribute to this change; nor is there any single power of the soul, which remains unalterably the same, perhaps for one moment. The mind is a kind of theatre, where several perceptions successively make their appearance; pass, repass, glide away, and mingle in an infinite variety of postures and situations. There is properly no *simplicity* in it at one time, nor *identity* in different; whatever natural propension we may have to imagine that simplicity and identity. The comparison of the theatre must not mislead us. They are the successive perceptions only, that constitute the mind; nor have we the most distant notion of the place, where these scenes are represented, or of the materials, of which it is composed.

What then gives us so great a propension to ascribe an identity to these successive perceptions, and to suppose ourselves possessed of an invariable and uninterrupted existence through the whole course of our lives? . . .

We have a distinct idea of an object, that remains invariable and uninterrupted through a supposed variation of time; and this idea we call that of *identity* or *sameness*. We have also a distinct idea of several different objects existing in succession, and connected together by a close relation; and this to an accurate view affords as perfect a notion of *diversity,* as if there was no manner of relation among the objects. But though these two ideas of identity, and a succession of related objects be in themselves perfectly distinct, and even contrary, yet it is certain, that in our common way of thinking they are generally confounded with each other. That action of the imagination, by which we consider the uninterrupted and invariable object, and that by which we reflect on the succession of related objects, are almost the same to the feeling, nor is there much more effort of thought required in the latter case than in the former. The relation facilitates the transition of the mind from one object to another, and renders its passage as smooth as if it contemplated one continued object. This resemblance is the cause of the confusion and mistake, and makes us substitute the notion of identity, instead of that of related objects. However at one instant we may consider the related succession as variable or interrupted, we are sure the next to ascribe to it a perfect identity, and regard it as invariable and uninterrupted. Our propensity to this mistake is so great from the resemblance above-mentioned, that we fall into it before we are aware; and though we incessantly correct ourselves by reflection, and return to a more accurate method of thinking, yet we cannot long sustain our philosophy, or take off this bias from the imagination. Our last resource is to yield to it, and boldly assert that these different related objects are in effect the same, however interrupted and variable. In order to justify to ourselves this absurdity, we often feign some new and unintelligible principle, that connects the objects together, and prevents their interruption or variation. Thus we feign the continued existence of the perceptions of our senses, to remove the interruption, and run into the notion of a *soul*, and *self*, and *substance*, to disguise the variation. . . .

Thus the controversy concerning identity is not merely a dispute of words. For when we attribute identity, in an improper sense, to variable or interrupted objects, our mistake is not confined to the expression, but is commonly attended with a fiction, either of something invariable and uninterrupted, or of something mysterious and inexplicable, or at least with a propensity to such fictions. What will suffice to prove this hypothesis to the satisfaction of every fair enquirer, is to show from daily experience and observation, that the objects, which are variable or interrupted, and yet are supposed to continue the same, are such only as consist of a succession of parts, connected together by resemblance, contiguity, or causation. For as such a succession answers evidently to our notion of diversity, it can only be by mistake we ascribe to it an identity; and as the relation of parts, which leads us into this mistake, is really nothing but a quality, which produces an association of ideas, and an easy transition of the imagination from one to another, it can only be from the resemblance, which this act of the mind bears to that, by which we contemplate one continued object, that the error arises. Our chief business, then, must be to prove, that all objects, to which we ascribe identity, without observing their invariableness and uninterruptedness, are such as consist of a succession of related objects. . . .

. . . A ship, of which a considerable part has been changed by frequent reparations, is still considered as the same; nor does the difference of the materials hinder us from ascribing an identity to it. The common end, in which the parts conspire, is the same under all their variations, and affords an easy transition of the imagination from one situation of the body to another.

But this is still more remarkable, when we add a sympathy of parts to their common end, and suppose that they bear to each other, the reciprocal relation of cause and effect in all their actions and operations. This is the case with all animals and vegetables; where not only the several parts have a reference to some general purpose, but also a mutual dependence on, and connection with each other. The effect of so strong a relation is, that though every one must allow, that in a very few years both vegetables and animals endure a total change, yet we still attribute identity to them, while their form, size, and substance are entirely altered. An oak, that grows from a small plant to a large tree, is still the same oak; though there be not one particle of matter, or figure of its parts the same. An infant becomes a man, and is sometimes fat, sometimes lean, without any change in his identity.

We may also consider the two following phenomena, which are remarkable in their kind. The first is, that though we commonly be able to distinguish pretty exactly between numerical and specific identity, yet it sometimes happens, that we confound them, and in our thinking and reasoning employ the one for the other. Thus a man, who hears a noise, that is frequently interrupted and renewed, says, it is still the same noise; though it is evident the sounds have only a specific identity or resemblance, and there is nothing numerically the same, but the cause, which produced them. In like manner it may be said without breach of the propriety of language, that such a church, which was formerly of brick, fell to ruin, and that the parish rebuilt the same church of free-stone, and according to modern architecture. Here neither the form nor materials are the same, nor is there any thing common to the two objects, but their relation to the inhabitants of the parish; and yet this alone is sufficient to make us denominate them the same. . . .

We now proceed to explain the nature of personal identity, which has become so great a question in philosophy. . . . The identity, which we ascribe to the mind of man, is only a fictitious one, and of a like kind with that which we ascribe to vegetables and animal bodies. It cannot, therefore, have a different origin, but must proceed from a like operation of the imagination upon like objects.

But lest this argument should not convince the reader; though in my opinion perfectly decisive; let him weigh the following reasoning, which is still closer and more immediate. It is evident, that the identity, which we attribute to the human mind, however perfect we may imagine it to be, is not able to run the several different perceptions into one, and make them lose their characters of distinction and difference, which are essential to them. It is still true, that every distinct perception, which enters into the composition of the mind, is a distinct existence, and is different, and distinguishable, and separable from every other perception, either contemporary or successive. But, as, notwithstanding this distinction and separability, we suppose the whole train of perceptions to be united by identity, a question naturally arises concerning this relation of identity; whether it be something that really binds our several perceptions together, or only associates their ideas in the imagination. That is, in other words, whether in pronouncing concerning the identity of a person, we observe some real bond among his perceptions, or only feel one among the ideas we form of them. This question we might eas-

ily decide, if we would recollect what has been already proved at large, that the understanding never observes any real connection among objects, and that even the union of cause and effect, when strictly examined, resolves itself into a customary association of ideas. For from thence it evidently follows, that identity is nothing really belonging to these different perceptions, and uniting them together; but is merely a quality, which we attribute to them, because of the union of their ideas in the imagination, when we reflect upon them. . . .

The only question, therefore, which remains, is, by what relations this uninterrupted progress of our thought is produced, when we consider the successive existence of a mind or thinking person. And here it is evident we must confine ourselves to resemblance and causation, and must drop contiguity, which has little or no influence in the present case.

To begin with *resemblance,* suppose we could see clearly into the breast of another, and observe that succession of perceptions, which constitutes his mind or thinking principle, and suppose that he always preserves the memory of a considerable part of past perceptions; it is evident that nothing could more contribute to the bestowing a relation on this succession amidst all its variations. For what is the memory but a faculty, by which we raise up the images of past perceptions? And as an image necessarily resembles its object, must not the frequent placing of these resembling perceptions in the chain of thought, convey the imagination more easily from one link to another, and make the whole seem like the continuance of one object? In this particular, then, the memory not only discovers the identity, but also contributes to its production, by producing the relation of resemblance among the perceptions. The case is the same whether we consider ourselves or others.

As to *causation,* we may observe, that the true idea of the human mind, is to consider it as a system of different perceptions or different existences, which are linked together by the relation of cause and effect, and mutually produce, destroy, influence, and modify each other. Our impressions give rise to their correspondent ideas, and these ideas in their turn produce other impressions. One thought chases another, and draws after it a third, by which it is expelled in its turn. In this respect, I cannot compare the soul more properly to any thing than to a republic or commonwealth, in which the several members are united by the reciprocal ties of government and subordination, and give rise to other persons, who propagate the same republic in the incessant changes of its parts. And as the same individual republic may not only change its members, but also its laws and constitutions; in like manner the same person may vary his character and disposition, as well as his impressions and ideas, without losing his identity. Whatever changes he endures, his several parts are still connected by the relation of causation. And in this view our identity with regard to the passions serves to corroborate that with regard to the imagination, by the making our distant perceptions influence each other, and by giving us a present concern for our past or future pains or pleasures.

As memory alone acquaints us with the continuance and extent of this succession of perceptions, it is to be considered, upon that account chiefly, as the source of personal identity. Had we no memory, we never should have any notion of causation, nor consequently of that chain of causes and effects, which constitute our self or person. But having once acquired this notion of causation from the memory, we can extend the same chain of causes, and consequently the identity of our persons beyond our memory, and can comprehend times, and circumstances, and actions, which we have entirely forgot, but suppose in general to have existed. For how few of our past actions are there, of which we have any memory? . . . In this view, therefore, memory does not so much produce as discover personal identity, by showing us the relation of cause and effect among our different perceptions. It will be incumbent on those, who affirm that memory produces entirely our personal identity, to give a reason why we can thus extend our identity beyond our memory.

The whole of this doctrine leads us to a conclusion, which is of great importance in the present affair, *viz.*, that all the nice and subtle questions concerning personal identity can never possibly be decided. . . .

Questions for Reflection

1. Descartes thought that the one thing he could be sure of was that he existed as a thinking substance or a self. What would Hume say to Descartes concerning this?
2. We frequently hear people say, "I'm trying to find myself." Why would Hume think this was a fruitless quest?
3. Hume says that we are nothing but a passing flow of psychological states without any continuity. However, some critics (such as Immanuel Kant) have said that it is one thing to have successive experiences and another thing to be aware of the experience of succession. To have the latter there must be an underlying, unified self that is synthesizing the various moments of consciousness. How effective is this as a criticism of Hume's "no-self" view?

JEFFREY OLEN

An Account of Personal Identity and Immortality

Philosopher Jeffrey Olen has had a varied career. On his way to an undergraduate degree at the University of Pennsylvania's Wharton School of Finance and Commerce, he took four years off to write for newspapers, magazines, radio, and children's television. By his own account he became interested in philosophy almost by accident and ended up completing a Ph.D. at Temple University. He has taught at the University of Wisconsin-Stevens Point, Temple University, the University of Colorado at Colorado Springs, and Regis University in Colorado Springs. Besides numerous journal articles, he is the author of *Ethics in Journalism, Applying Ethics, Moral Freedom,* and *Persons and Their World,* from which the current selection is taken.

Reading Questions

1. After reading the opening story, answer Jeffrey Olen's questions. Who woke up in Joe Everglade's bed? Who woke up in John Badger's? Which one is Mary's husband?
2. What are Olen's seven criteria for being a person?
3. What is the distinction he makes between the *criteria* for establishing identity through time and the issue of what *constitutes* identity through time? Why is this distinction significant?
4. Under normal circumstances, what are the two criteria we use for personal identity? Why are they in conflict in Olen's story?
5. What are the two problems Olen raises with Locke's criterion of personal identity?
6. What is the problem with simply saying bodily continuity constitutes personal identity?
7. What is the solution to the problem of personal identity offered by the position of functionalism and Anthony Quinton? How is it different from the brain criterion?
8. How does Olen attempt to reconcile materialism (physicalism) and belief in life after death?

It is Sunday night. After a long night of hard drinking, John Badger puts on his pajamas, lowers the heat in his Wisconsin home to fifty-five degrees and climbs into bed beneath two heavy blankets. Meanwhile, in Florida, Joe Everglade kisses his wife goodnight and goes to sleep.

The next morning, two very confused men wake up. One wakes up in Wisconsin, wondering where he is and why he is wearing pajamas, lying under two heavy blankets, yet shivering from the cold. He looks out the window and sees nothing but pine trees and snow. The room is totally unfamiliar.

From Jeffrey Olen, *Persons and Their World,* chap. 13 (New York: Random House, 1983).

Where is his wife? How did he get to this cold, strange place? Why does he have such a terrible hangover? He tries to spring out of bed with his usual verve but feels an unaccustomed aching in his joints. Arthritis? He wanders unsurely through the house until he finds the bathroom. What he sees in the mirror causes him to spin around in sudden fear. But there is nobody behind him. Then the fear intensifies as he realizes that it was his reflection that had stared back at him. But it was the reflection of a man thirty years older than himself, with coarser features and a weather-beaten face.

In Florida, a man awakens with a young woman's arm around him. When she too awakens, she snuggles against him and wishes him good morning. "Who are you?" he asks. "What am I doing in your bed?" She just laughs, then tells him that he will have to hurry if he is going to get in his ten miles of jogging. From the bathroom she asks him about his coming day. None of the names or places she mentions connect with anything he can remember. He climbs out of bed, marveling at the ease with which he does so, and looks first out the window and then into the mirror over the dresser. The sun and swimming pool confound him. The handsome young man's reflection terrifies him.

Then the phone rings. The woman answers it. It is the man from Wisconsin. "What happened last night, Mary? How did I get here? How did I get to look this way?"

"Who is this?" she asks.

"Don't you recognize my voice, Mary?" But he knew that the voice was not his own. "It's Joe."

"Joe who?"

"Your husband."

She hangs up, believing it to be a crank call. When she returns to the bedroom, the man in her husband's robe asks how he got there from Wisconsin, and why he looks as he does.

PERSONAL IDENTITY

What happened in the above story? Who woke up in Joe Everglade's bed? Who woke up in John Badger's? Which one is Mary's husband? Has Badger awakened with Everglade's memories and Ever-glade with Badger's? Or have Badger and Ever-glade somehow switched bodies? How are we to decide? What considerations are relevant?

To ask such questions is to raise the problem of *personal identity*. It is to ask what makes a person the same person he was the day before. It is to ask how we determine that we are dealing with the same person that we have dealt with in the past. It is to ask what constitutes personal identity over time. It is also to ask what we mean by the *same person*. And to answer this question, we must ask what we mean by the word "person."

Persons

In the previous chapter, we asked what a human being is. We asked what human beings are made of, what the nature of the human mind is, and whether human beings are part of nature or distinct from it.

To ask what a *person is,* however, is to ask a different question. Although we often use the terms "person" and "human being" interchangeably, they do not mean the same thing. If we do use them interchangeably, it is only because all the persons we know of are human beings, and because, as far as we know, whenever we are confronted with the same human being we are confronted with the same person.

But the notion of a human being is a *biological* notion. To identify something as a human being is to identify it as a member of *Homo sapiens,* a particular species of animal. It is a type of organism defined by certain physical characteristics.

The notion of a person, on the other hand, is *not* a biological one. Suppose, for instance, that we find life on another planet, and that this life is remarkably like our own. The creatures we discover communicate through a language as rich as our own, act according to moral principles, have a legal system, and engage in science and art. Suppose also that despite these cultural similarities, this form of life is biologically different from human life. In that case, these creatures would be persons, but not humans. Think, for example, of the alien in *E.T.* Since he is biologically different from us, he is not human. He is, however, a person.

What, then, is a person? Although philosophers disagree on this point, the following features are relatively noncontroversial.

First, a person is an intelligent, rational creature. Second, it is a creature capable of a peculiar sort of consciousness—self-consciousness. Third, it not only has beliefs, desires, and so forth, but it has beliefs *about* its beliefs, desires, and so forth. Fourth, it is a creature to which we ascribe moral responsibility. Persons are responsible for their actions in a way that other things are not. They are subject to moral praise and moral blame. Fifth, a person is a creature that we treat in certain ways. To treat something as a person is to treat it as a member of our own moral community. It is to grant it certain rights, both moral and legal. Sixth, a person is a creature capable of reciprocity. It is capable of treating us as members of the same moral community. Finally, a person is capable of verbal communication. It can communicate by means of a *language,* not just by barks, howls, and tail-wagging.

Since, as far as we know, only human beings meet the above conditions, only human beings are considered to be persons. But once we recognize that to be a person is not precisely the same thing that it is to be a human being, we also recognize that other creatures, such as the alien in *E.T.,* is also a person. We also recognize that perhaps not all human beings are persons—human fetuses, for example, as some have argued. Certainly, in the American South before the end of the Civil War, slaves were not considered to be persons. We might also mention a remark of D'Artagnan, in Richard Lester's film version of *The Three Musketeers.* Posing as a French nobleman, he attempted to cross the English Channel with a companion. When a French official remarked that his pass was only for one person, D'Artagnan replied that he was only one person—his companion was a servant.

Moreover, once we recognize the distinction between human beings and persons, certain questions arise. Can one human being embody more than one person, either at the same time or successive times? In the example we introduced at the beginning of this chapter, has Badger's body become Everglade's and Everglade's Badger's? Can the person survive the death of the human being?

Is there personal survival after the death of the body?

The Memory Criterion and the Bodily Criterion

Concerning identity through time in general, two issues must be distinguished. First, we want to know how we can *tell* that something is the same thing we encountered previously. That is, we want to know what the *criteria* are for establishing identity through time. Second, we want to know what *makes* something the same thing it was previously. That is we want to know what *constitutes* identity through time.

Although these issues are related, they are not the same, as the following example illustrates. We can *tell* that someone has a case of the flu by checking for certain symptoms, such as fever, lack of energy, and sore muscles. But having these symptoms does not *constitute* having a case of the flu. It is the presence of a flu virus—not the symptoms—that makes an illness a case of the flu.

We commonly use two criteria for establishing personal identity. The first is the *bodily criterion,* the second the *memory criterion.* How do we apply them?

We apply the bodily criterion in two ways. First, we go by physical resemblance. If I meet someone on the street who looks, walks, and sounds just like Mary, I assume that it is Mary. Since the body I see resembles Mary's body exactly, I assume that the person I see is Mary. But that method can sometimes fail us, as in the case of identical twins. In such cases, we can apply the bodily criterion in another way. If I can discover that there is a continuous line from one place and time to another that connects Mary's body to the body I now see, I can assume that I now see Mary. Suppose, for example, that Mary and I went to the beach together, and have been together all afternoon. In that case, I can say that the person I am now with is the person I began the day with.

There are, however, times when the bodily criterion is not available. If Mary and Jane are identical twins, and I run across one of them on the street, I may have to ask who it is. That is, I may have to rely on Mary's memory of who she is. And, if I want to make sure that I am not being fooled, I may ask a few questions. If Mary remembers things that I believe only Mary can remember, and if she remembers them as happening to *her,* and not to somebody else, then I can safely say that it really is Mary.

Generally, the bodily criterion and the memory criterion do not conflict, so we use whichever is more convenient. But what happens if they do conflict? That is what happened in our imagined story. According to the bodily criterion, each person awoke in his own bed, but with the memories of someone else. According to the memory criterion, each person awoke in the other's bed with the body of someone else. Which criterion should we take as decisive? Which is fundamental, the memory criterion or the bodily criterion.

The Constitution of Personal Identity

To ask the above questions is to ask what *constitutes* personal identity. What is it that makes me the same person I was yesterday? What makes the author of this book the same person as the baby born to Sam and Belle Olen in 1946? Answers to these questions will allow us to say which criterion is fundamental.

Perhaps the most widely discussed answer to our question comes from John Locke (1632–1704), whose discussion of the topic set the stage for all future discussions. According to Locke, the bodily criterion cannot be fundamental. Since the concept of a person is most importantly the concept of a conscious being who can be held morally and legally responsible for past actions, it is *continuity of consciousness* that constitutes personal identity. The bodily criterion is fundamental for establishing sameness of *animal,* but not sameness of *person.*

Suppose, for instance, that John Badger had been a professional thief. If the person who awoke in Badger's bed could never remember any of Badger's life as his own, but had only Everglade's memories and personality traits, while the man who awoke in Everglade's bed remembered all of Badger's crimes as his own, would we be justified in jailing the man who awoke in Badger's bed while letting the man who awoke in Everglade's go free?

Locke would say no. The person who awoke in Badger's bed was not Badger.

If we agree that it is sameness of consciousness that constitutes personal identity, we must then ask what constitutes sameness of consciousness. Some philosophers have felt that it is sameness of *mind,* where the mind is thought of as a continuing nonphysical substance. Although Locke did not deny that minds are nonphysical, he did not believe that sameness of nonphysical substance is the same thing as sameness of consciousness. If we can conceive of persons switching *physical* bodies, we can also conceive of persons switching *nonphysical* ones.

Then what does Locke take to be crucial for personal identity? *Memory.* It is my memory of the events of Jeffrey Olen's life as happening to *me* that makes me the person those events happened to. It is my memory of his experiences as *mine* that makes them mine.

Although Locke's answer seems at first glance a reasonable one, many philosophers have considered it inadequate. One reason for rejecting Locke's answer is that we don't remember everything that happened to us. If I don't remember anything that happened to me during a certain period, does that mean that whoever existed "in" my body then was not me? Hardly.

Another reason for rejecting Locke's answer is that memory is not always accurate. We often sincerely claim to remember things that never happened. There is a difference, then, between *genuine* memory and *apparent* memory. What marks this difference is the *truth* of the memory claim. If what I claim to remember is not true, it cannot be a case of genuine memory.

But that means that memory cannot constitute personal identity. If I claim to remember certain experiences as being my experiences, that does not make them mine, because my claim may be a case of apparent memory. If it is a case of genuine memory, that is because it is true that the remembered experiences are mine. But the memory does not *make* them mine. Rather, the fact that they *are* mine makes it a case of genuine memory. So Locke has the situation backward. But if memory does not constitute personal identity, what does?

Some philosophers have claimed that, regardless of Locke's views, it *must* be sameness of mind, where the mind is thought of as a continuing nonphysical entity. This entity can be thought of as the self. It is what makes us who we are. As long as the same self continues to exist, the same person continues to exist. The major problem with this answer is that it assumes the truth of mind-body dualism, a position we found good reason to reject in the previous chapter. But apart from that, there is another problem.

In one of the most famous passages in the history of philosophy, David Hume (1711–1776) argued that there is no such self—for reasons that have nothing to do with the rejection of dualism. No matter how hard we try, Hume said, we cannot discover such a self. Turning inward and examining our own consciousness, we find only individual experiences—thoughts, recollections, images, and the like. Try as we might, we cannot find a continuing self. In that case, we are justified in believing only that there are *experiences*—not that there is a continuing *experiencer*. Put another way, we have no reason to believe that there is anything persisting through time that underlies or unifies these experiences. There are just the experiences themselves.

But if we accept this view, and still require a continuing nonphysical entity for personal identity, we are forced to the conclusion that there is no such thing as personal identity. We are left, that is, with the position that the idea of a person existing through time is a mere fiction, however useful in daily life. And that is the position that Hume took. Instead of persons, he said, there are merely "bundles of ideas."

Thus, the view that personal identity requires sameness of mind can easily lead to the view that there is no personal identity. Since this conclusion seems manifestly false, we shall have to look elsewhere. But where?

The Primacy of the Bodily Criterion

If neither memory nor sameness of mind constitutes personal identity, perhaps we should accept the view that sameness of *body* does. Perhaps it is really the bodily criterion that is fundamental.

If we reflect on the problem faced by Locke's theory because of the distinction between genuine and apparent memory, it is tempting to accept the primacy of the bodily criterion. Once again, a sincere memory claim may be either genuine memory or apparent memory. How can we tell whether the claim that a previous experience was mine is genuine memory? By determining whether I was in the right place in the right time to have it. And how can we determine that? By the bodily criterion. If my *body* was there, then *I* was there. But that means that the memory criterion must rest on the bodily criterion. Also, accepting the primacy of the bodily criterion gets us around Hume's problem. The self that persists through and has the experiences I call mine is my physical body.

This answer also has the advantage of being in keeping with materialism, a view accepted in the previous chapter. If human beings are purely physical, then persons must also be purely physical, whatever differences there may be between the notion of a person and the notion of a human being. But if persons are purely physical, what makes me the same person I was yesterday is no different in kind from what makes my typewriter the same typewriter it was yesterday. In both cases, we are dealing with a physical object existing through time. In the latter case, as long as we have the same physical materials (allowing for change of ribbon, change of keys, and the like) arranged in the same way, we have the same typewriter. So it is with persons. As long as we have the same physical materials (allowing for such changes as the replacement of cells) arranged in the same way, we have the same person.

Although this answer is a tempting one, it is not entirely satisfactory. Suppose that we could manage a brain transplant from one body to another. If we switched two brains, so that all the memories and personality traits of the persons involved were also switched, wouldn't we conclude that the persons, as well as their brains, had switched bodies? When such operations are performed in science-fiction stories, they are described this way.

But this possibility does not defeat the view that the bodily criterion is fundamental. It just forces us to hold that the bodily criterion must be applied to the brain, rather than the entire body. Personal identity then becomes a matter of brain identity. Same brain, same person. Unfortunately, even with this change, our answer does not seem satisfactory. Locke still seems somehow right. Let us see why.

Badger and Everglade Reconsidered

Returning to our tale of Badger and Everglade, we find that some troubling questions remain. If Mrs. Everglade continues to live with the man who awoke in her bed, might she not be committing adultery? Shouldn't she take in the man who awoke in Badger's bed? And, once again assuming that Badger was a professional thief, would justice really be served by jailing the man who awoke in his bed? However we answer these questions, one thing is certain—the two men would always feel that they had switched bodies. So, probably, would the people who knew them. Furthermore, whenever we read science-fiction stories describing such matters, we invariably accept them as stories of switched bodies. But if we accept the bodily criterion as fundamental, we are accepting the impossible, and the two men in our story, Mrs. Everglade, and their friends are mistaken in their beliefs. How, then, are we to answer our questions?

If we are unsure, it is because such questions become very tricky at this point. Their trickiness seems to rest on two points. First, cases like the Badger-Everglade case do not happen in this world. Although we are prepared to accept them in science-fiction tales, we are totally unprepared to deal with them in real life.

Second, and this is a related point, we need some way of *explaining* such extraordinary occurrences. Unless we know how the memories of Badger and Everglade came to be reversed, we will be unable to decide the answers to our questions. In the movies, it is assumed that some nonphysical substance travels from one body to another, or that there has been a brain transplant of some sort. On these assumptions, we are of course willing to describe what happens as a change of body. This description seems to follow naturally from such explanations.

What explains what happened to Badger and Everglade? We can rule out change of nonphysical

substance, because of what was said in the previous chapter and earlier in this chapter. If we explain what happened as the product of a brain switch, then the bodily criterion applied to the brain allows us to say that Badger and Everglade did awaken in each other's bed, and that Mrs. Everglade would be committing adultery should she live with the man who awoke in her bed.

Are there any other possible explanations? One that comes readily to mind is hypnotism. Suppose, then, that someone had hypnotized Badger and Everglade into believing that each was the other person. In that case, we should not say that there had been a body switch. Badger and Everglade awoke in their own beds, and a wave of the hypnotist's hand could demonstrate that to everyone concerned. Their memory claims are not genuine memories, but apparent ones.

But suppose it was not a case of hypnotism? What then? At this point, many people are stumped. What else could it be? The strong temptation is to say nothing. Without a brain transplant or hypnotism or something of the sort, the case is impossible.

Suppose that we accept this conclusion. If we do, we may say the following: The memory criterion and the bodily criterion cannot really conflict. If the memories are genuine, and not apparent, then whenever I remember certain experiences as being mine, it is possible to establish that the same brain is involved in the original experiences and the memory of them. Consequently, the memory criterion and the bodily criterion are equally fundamental. The memory criterion is fundamental in the sense that consciousness determines what part of the body is central to personal identity. Because sameness of consciousness requires sameness of brain, we ultimately must apply the bodily criterion to the brain. But the bodily criterion is also fundamental, because we assume that some physical object—the brain—must remain the same if the person is to remain the same.

The Memory Criterion Revisited

Although the answer given above is a tidy one, it may still seem unsatisfactory. Perhaps it is a cheap trick just to dismiss the Badger-Everglade case as mere fantasy and then ignore it. After all, if we can meaningfully describe such cases in books and films, don't we have to pay some attention to them? As long as we can imagine situations in which two persons can switch bodies without a brain transplant, don't we need a theory of personal identity to cover them?

Philosophers are divided on this point. Some think that a theory of personal identity has to account only for what can happen in this world, while others think it must account for whatever can happen in any conceivable world. Then again, some do not believe that there is any conceivable world in which two persons could change bodies without a brain switch, while there are others who are not sure that such things are impossible in the actual world.

Without trying to decide the matter, I can make the following suggestion for those who demand a theory of personal identity that does not rely on the assumption that genuine memory is tied to a particular brain.

In the previous chapter, I concluded that functionalism is the theory of mind most likely to be true. To have a mind, I said, is to embody a psychology. I also said that we don't merely move our bodies, but write poetry, caress the cheek of someone we love, and perform all sorts of human actions. I might have expressed this point by saying that we are not just human beings, but persons as well. What makes a human being a person? We are persons because we embody a psychology.

If that is true, then it may also be true that we are the persons we are because of the psychologies we embody. If it is a psychology that makes a human being a person, then it is a particular psychology that makes a particular human being a particular person. Sameness of psychology constitutes sameness of person. In that case, we can agree with this much of Locke's theory—it is continuity of consciousness that constitutes personal identity. But what is continuity of consciousness, if not memory?

An answer to this question is provided by the contemporary British philosopher Anthony Quinton. At any moment, we can isolate a number of mental states belonging to the same momentary consciousness. Right now, for instance, I am simul-taneously aware of the sound and sight and feel of my typewriter, plus the feel and taste of my pipe, plus a variety of other things. Such *momentary* consciousnesses belong to a continuous *series*. Each one is linked to the one before it and the one following it by certain similarities and recollections. This series is my own *continuity* of consciousness, my own *stream* of consciousness. It is this stream of consciousness that makes me the same person I was yesterday.

If we accept Quinton's theory, we can then say that the memory criterion, not the bodily criterion, is fundamental. We can also say that, even if in this world continuity of consciousness requires sameness of brain, we can conceive of worlds in which it does not. To show this, let us offer another possible explanation of the Badger-Everglade situation.

Suppose a mad computer scientist has discovered a way to reprogram human beings. Suppose that he has found a way to make us the embodiment of any psychology he likes. Suppose further that he decided to experiment on Badger and Everglade, giving Badger Everglade's psychology and Everglade Badger's and that is why the events of our story occurred. With this explanation and the considerations of the previous paragraphs, we can conclude that Badger and Everglade did change bodies. By performing his experiment, the mad scientist has made it possible for a continuing stream of consciousness to pass from one body to another. He has, in effect, performed a body transplant.

Should we accept Quinton's theory? There seems to be no good reason not to. In fact, there are at least two good reasons for accepting it. First, it seems consistent with a functionalist theory of the mind. Second, it allows us to make sense of science-fiction stories while we continue to believe that in the real world to be the same person we were yesterday is to have the same brain.

LIFE AFTER DEATH

Is it possible for the person to survive the death of the body? Is there a sense in which *we* can continue to live after our bodies have died? Can there be a personal life after death?

According to one popular conception of life after death, at the death of the body the soul leaves the body and travels to a realm known as heaven. Of course, this story must be taken as metaphorical. Does the soul literally leave the body? How? Out of the mouth? Ears? And how does it get to heaven? By turning left at Mars? Moreover, if the soul remains disembodied, how can it perceive anything? What does it use as sense organs? And if all souls remain disembodied, how can one soul recognize another? What is there to recognize?

As these questions might suggest, much of this popular story trades on a confusion. The soul is thought of as a translucent physical substance, much like Casper the ghost, through which other objects can pass as they do through air or water. But if the soul is *really* nonphysical, it can be nothing like that.

If this story is not to be taken literally, is there some version of it that we can admit as a possibility? Is there also the possibility of personal survival through reincarnation as it is often understood— the re-embodiment of the person without memory of the former embodiment?

Materialism and the Disembodied Soul

So far, we have considered both the mind and the body as they relate to personal identity. Have we neglected the soul? It may seem that we have, but philosophers who discuss the mind-body question and personal identity generally use the terms "mind" and "soul" interchangeably. Is the practice legitimate, or is it a confusion?

The practice seems to be thoroughly legitimate. If the soul is thought to be the crucial element of the person, it is difficult to see how it could be anything but the mind. If it is our character traits, personality, thoughts, likes and dislikes, memories, and continuity of experience that make us the persons we are, then they must belong to the soul. If they are taken to be crucial for one's personal identity, then it seems impossible to separate them from one's soul.

Moreover, people who accept some version of the popular conception of life after death noted above believe in certain continuities between earthly experiences and heavenly ones. In heaven, it is believed, we remember our earthly lives, we recognize friends and relatives, our personalities are like our earthly personalities, and we are judged by God for our actions on earth. But if we believe any of this, we must also believe that the soul cannot be separated from the mind.

If that is the case, it is difficult to accept the continued existence of a disembodied soul. Once we accept some form of materialism, we seem compelled to believe that the soul must be embodied. Does that rule out the possibility of any version of the popular story being true?

Some philosophers think that it does. Suppose, for instance, that the mind-brain identity theory is true. In that case, when the brain dies, so does the mind. Since the mind is the repository of memory and personality traits, it is identical with the soul. So when the brain dies, so does the soul.

This is a powerful argument, and it has convinced a number of people. On the other hand, it has also kept a number of people from accepting materialism of any sort. If it is felt that materialism and life after death are incompatible, and if one is firmly committed to the belief in life after death, then it is natural for one to reject materialism.

Is there a way of reconciling materialism and life after death? I think so.

Although it seems necessary that persons must be embodied, it does not seem necessary that the same person must be embodied by the same body. In our discussion of personal identity, we allowed that Badger and Everglade might have changed bodies, depending on our explanation of the story. Let us try a similar story.

Mary Brown is old and sick. She knows she will die within a couple of weeks. One morning she does die. At the same time, in some other world, a woman wakes up believing herself to be Mary. She looks around to find herself in a totally unfamiliar place. Someone is sitting next to her. This other woman looks exactly like Mary's mother, who died years earlier, and believes herself to be Mary's mother. Certainly, she knows everything about Mary that Mary's mother would know.

Before the woman believing herself to be Mary can speak, she notices some surprising things about herself. She no longer feels old or sick. Her pains are gone, and her mind is as sharp as ever. When she asks where she is, she is told heaven. She is also told that her husband, father, and numerous old friends are waiting to see her. All of them are indistinguishable from the persons they claim to be. Meanwhile, back on earth, Mary Brown is pronounced dead. Is this woman in "heaven" really Mary Brown? How could we possibly explain the phenomenon?

Suppose we put the story in a religious context. Earlier, we saw that one possible explanation of the Badger-Everglade case is that some mad computer scientist had reprogrammed the two so that each embodied the psychology of the other. Suppose we replace the mad scientist with God, and say that God had kept a body in heaven for the purpose of embodying Mary's psychology when she died, and that the person believing herself to be Mary is the new embodiment of Mary's psychology. Would this count as a genuine case of life after death?

If we accept the Badger-Everglade story, appropriately explained, as a case of two persons switching bodies, there seems no reason to deny that Mary has continued to live "in" another body. But even if we are unsure of the Badger-Everglade case, we can approach Mary Brown's this way. What is it that we want to survive after death? Isn't it our memories, our consciousness of self, our personalities, our relations with others? What does it matter whether there is some nonphysical substance that survives? If that substance has no memories of a prior life, does not recognize the soul of others who were important in that earlier life, what comfort could such a continuing existence bring? In what sense would it be the survival of the *person*? How would it be significantly different from the return of the lifeless body to the soil?

If we assume that our story is a genuine case of personal survival of the death of the body, we may wonder about another point. Is it compatible with Christian belief? According to John Hick, a contemporary British philosopher who imagined a similar story, the answer is yes. In I Corinthians 15, Paul writes of the resurrection of the body—not of the physical body, but of some spiritual body. Although one *can* think of this spiritual body as a translucent ghostlike body that leaves the physical body at death, Hick offers another interpretation.

The human being, Hick says, becomes extinct at death. It is only through God's intervention that the spiritual body comes into existence. By the resurrection of this spiritual body, we are to understand a *recreation* or *reconstitution* of the person's body in heaven. But that is precisely what happened in our story.

Thus, a materialist view of the nature of human beings is not incompatible with the Christian view of life after death. Nor, for that matter, is it incompatible with the belief that the spiritual body is nonphysical. If we can make sense of the claim that there might be such things as nonphysical bodies, then there is no reason why a nonphysical body could not embody a psychology. Remember—according to functionalism, an abstract description such as a psychology is independent of any physical description. Just as we can play chess using almost anything as chess pieces, so can a psychology be embodied by almost anything, assuming that it is complex enough. So if there can be nonphysical bodies, there can be nonphysical persons. Of course, nothing said so far assures us that the Christian story—or any other story of life after death—is true.

Reincarnation

Much of what has been said so far does, however, rule out the possibility of reincarnation as commonly understood. If human beings are purely physical, then there is no nonphysical substance that is the person that can be reincarnated in another earthly body. Moreover, even if there were such a substance, it is difficult to see how its continued existence in another body could count as the reincarnation of a particular person, *if* there is no other continuity between the old life and the new one. Once again, personal survival requires some continuity of consciousness. It is not sameness of *stuff* that constitutes personal identity, but sameness of consciousness. This requirement is often overlooked by believers in reincarnation.

But suppose that there is some continuity of consciousness in reincarnation. Suppose that memories and the rest do continue in the next incarnation, but that they are not easily accessible. Suppose, that is, that the slate is not wiped completely clean, but that what is written on it is hard to recover. In that case, the passage of the soul into a new incarnation would count as personal survival *if* there were such a soul to begin with.

Assuming, again, that there is not, what can we say about the possibility of reincarnation? To conceive of such a possibility, we must conceive of some very complicated reprogramming by God or some mad scientist or whatever. I shall leave it to you to come up with such a story, but I shall say this much. There does not seem to be any good reason to think that any such story is remotely plausible, least of all true.

THE FINAL WORD?

In this chapter we looked at two closely related questions: What constitutes personal identity? And is it possible for a person to survive the death of her own body?

The answer to the second question depended on the first. If we had concluded that the basis of personal identity is sameness of body, then we would have been forced to conclude that life after death is impossible. And there did seem to be good reason to come to these conclusions. How, we

asked, could we assure that any memory claim is a case of genuine memory? Our answer was this. In the cases likely to confront us in our daily lives, we must establish some physical continuity between the person who had the original experience and the person who claims to remember it.

But the problem with this answer is that it is too limited. Because we can imagine cases like the Everglade-Badger example, and because our science-fiction tales and religious traditions offer stories of personal continuity without bodily continuity, we can say the following. Regardless of what happens in our daily lives, our concept of a person is a concept of something that does not seem tied to a particular body. Rather, our concept of a person seems to be tied to a particular stream of consciousness. If there is one continuing stream of consciousness over time, then there is one continuing person. Our question, then, was whether we can give a coherent account of continuity of consciousness from one body to another.

The answer was yes. Using the computer analogy of the functionalist, we can explain such continuity in terms of programming. If it is possible to "program" another brain to have the same psychology as the brain I now have, then it is possible for me to change bodies. And if it is possible for me to change bodies, then it is also possible for me to survive the death of my body.

Questions for Reflection

1. In what ways is Olen's solution to the problem of personal identity similar to Locke's theory? Are there any differences?
2. Do you think that Olen's attempt to reconcile materialism and belief in life after death is satisfactory?
3. What if two people had the same psychology and memories (as with Dennett's brain and its computer duplicate in reading 32). Would Olen then have to say that these two people were identical persons? Does this raise problems with his theory?

LINDA BADHAM

An Argument against Immortality

Linda Badham has a doctorate in philosophy of science from the University of Wales. She has published articles and co-edited several books in the philosophy of religion. In this reading she gives a scientific and philosophical critique of dualism and of the notion of personal survival after death.

Reading Questions

1. What three problems does Badham raise with the notion of a literal bodily resurrection?
2. What is the "replica problem" she raises with respect to Polkinghorne's notion of the pattern of the person being recreated in the resurrection?
3. What are the problems she raises concerning the dualist's notion that the soul is what survives death?
4. What philosophical problems does she raise concerning a notion of personal continuity that is not based in physical continuity?
5. What three points does Badham make with respect to accounts of near-death experiences?

INTRODUCTION

It is a popularly held view that science and religion are antithetical. And this view is supported by the sociological fact that leading scholars and scientists are significantly less likely to be Christian than other groups in society. Yet even so, there are a number of very eminent scientists, and particularly physicists, who claim that there is no real conflict between their scientific and religious beliefs. And many Christian apologists have drawn comfort from such claims in an age where the tide of secularism threatens to engulf the ancient citadel of Christian belief. However, I have my doubts as to whether or not Christianity is secure from attack by science in general on some of its most crucial tenets. And, in particular, what I want to argue in

this chapter is that the implications of modern science are far more damaging to doctrines of life after death than many Christian writers have supposed.

RESURRECTION OF THE BODY (THIS FLESH)

Although many might think that belief in the resurrection of this flesh at the end of time is now unthinkable, it has to be recognized that this is the form that orthodox Christian belief took from at least the second century onwards. Thus the Apostles' Creed affirms belief in the resurrection of the flesh; the Nicene Creed looks for the "upstanding of the dead bodies"; and the Christian Fathers were

From Linda Badham, "A Naturalistic Case for Extinction," in *Death and Immortality in the Religions of the World,* ed. Paul and Linda Badham (St. Paul: Paragon House, 1987).

utterly explicit that the resurrection was definitely a physical reconstitution. Moreover, such belief is still Catholic orthodoxy: a recent *Catholic Catechism for Adults* declares that each one of us will rise one day "the same person he was, in the same flesh made living by the same spirit." And Wolfhart Pannenberg, one of the most influential continental Protestant theologians of our day, also affirms belief in the traditional doctrine. Hence it seems reasonable to suppose that this form of resurrection belief is still held among Christians. Yet a minimal knowledge of modern science seems sufficient to undermine it completely.

First, there is the problem that "this flesh" is only temporarily mine. I am not like a machine or artifact, which keeps its atoms and molecules intact throughout its existence, save for those lost by damage or replaced during repair. Rather, I am a biological system in dynamic equilibrium (more or less) with my environment, in that I exchange matter with that environment continually. As J. D. Bernal writes, "It is probable that none of us have more than a few atoms with which we started life, and that even as adults we probably change most of the material of our bodies in a matter of a few months." Thus it might prove an extremely difficult business to resurrect 'this' flesh at the end of time, for the atoms that will constitute me at the moment of death will return to the environment and will doubtless become part of innumerable other individuals. Augustine discussed the case of cannibals having to restore the flesh they had "borrowed" as an exception. But in the light of our current knowledge, shared atoms would seem the rule rather than the exception.

Moreover, there is the further problem that even if the exact atoms that constituted me at death could all be reassembled without leaving some other people bereft of vital parts, then the reconstituted body would promptly expire again. For whatever caused the systems failure in my body, which led to my death originally, would presumably still obtain if the body exactly as it was prior to death were remade. But perhaps we can overcome this problem with a fairly simple proviso: the resurrection body should be identical to the body that died, malfunctions apart. After all, it might be said,

we have no difficulty in accepting our television set returned in good working order from the repair shop after a breakdown as one and the same television set that we took to be repaired, even though some or even several of its components have been replaced. But people are not television sets. What counts as malfunction? Increasing age usually brings some diminution in physical and mental powers. Are all these to be mended too? How much change can a body take and still be the same person? Nor is it possible to suggest that the resurrection environment might be such as to reverse the effects of aging and disease. For this move implies such a great change in the properties of the matter that is "this flesh" as to make it dubious whether "this" flesh really had been resurrected. The more one actually fills out the vague notion of the resurrection of the same flesh that perished, the more problems arise.

And even if the problem of reconstituting each one of us to the same (healthy) flesh he was (or might have been) could be overcome, there would remain the question of where we could all be resurrected. There is a space problem. If the countless millions of human beings who have ever lived and may live in the future were all to be resurrected on this earth, then the overcrowding would be acute. Now there are at least two theological maneuvers that we could make to circumvent this embarrassment. If we want to retain resurrection on this earth, then we might say that only the chosen will be resurrected and thereby limit the numbers. But that solution raises insuperable problems about the morality of a God who would behave in such a way. Alternatively, it might be argued that the resurrection will be to a new life in heaven and not to eternal life on earth. But in that case it has to be noted that resurrected bodies would need a biological environment markedly similar to the one we now live in. This leads to the implication that heaven would have to be a planet, or series of planets, all suitable for human life. The further one pushes this picture, the more bizarre and religiously unsatisfying it becomes.

In sum, then, a little knowledge of the biochemistry of living organisms together with a brief consideration of the physiochemical conditions that such organisms require if they are to live, ought to have rendered the traditional notion of literal bodily resurrection unthinkable.

RESURRECTION OF THE BODY (TRANSFORMED)

It might be argued, as John Polkinghorne claims, that all this is irrelevant: "We know that there is nothing significant about the material which at any one time constitutes our body. . . . It is the pattern they [the atoms] form which persists and evolves. We are liberated, therefore, from the quaint medieval picture of the reassembly of the body from its scattered components. In very general terms it is not difficult to imagine the pattern recreated (the body resurrected) in some other world."

At this point we should note that the doctrine being proposed here has shifted in a very significant way. The old doctrine of resurrection of the flesh guaranteed personal survival because the resurrected body was physically identical with the one laid in the grave. Physical continuity supplied the link between the person who died and the one who was resurrected. But Polkinghorne's version of the resurrection envisages recreation of a *pattern* in some other world. This is open to a host of philosophical problems about the sense in which the recreation of a replica can count as the survival of the person who died.

What would we say, for example, if the replica were created *before* my death? Would I then die happily knowing that someone was around to carry on, as it were, in my place? Would I think to myself that the replica really was me? Consider the possibility of cloning. Let us imagine that science reaches a stage where a whole adult human individual can be regenerated from a few cells of a person in such a way that the original—Jones I—and the copy—Jones II—are genetically identical, and that the clone knows everything that Jones I knows. We may imagine that the purpose of doing this is to give a healthy body to house the thoughts of the physically ailing, but brilliant Jones I. Now does Jones I die secure in the knowledge that he will live again? I would suggest that he might feel relieved to know

that his life's work would carry on, and that his project would be entrusted to one incomparably suited to continue with it. He might also feel exceptionally close to Jones II and be deeply concerned for his welfare. But the other would not *be* him. In the end, Jones I would be dead and the other, Jones II, would carry on in his place. As far as Jones I was concerned, he himself would not live again, even though most other people would treat Jones II as if here were Jones I rejuvenated.

If these intuitions are correct, then they suggest that whatever it is that we count as essential for being one and the same person, it is not a "pattern." And I would suggest that all theories of resurrection that speak of our rising with new and transformed bodies fall foul of what I term the replica problem. For without some principle of continuity between the person who died and the one who was resurrected, then what was resurrected would only be something very similar to the one who died, a replica, and not a continuation of the dead person.

THE SOUL

Such considerations have led theologians at least from Aquinas onwards to argue that any tenable resurrection belief hinges on a concept of the soul. For even if we hold to a belief in the resurrection of some "new and glorious body," then we need the soul to avoid the replica problem. There has to be a principle of continuity between this world and the next if what is raised to new life really is one and the same person as the one who died. Moreover, this principle of continuity must encapsulate enough of the real "me" for both "old" and "new" versions to count as the same person. Might this requirement be fulfilled if we were to espouse a dualist concept of the person and say, with Descartes, that my essential personhood is to be identified with my mind, that is, with the subject of conscious experiencing? However, I want to argue that not even this move is sufficient to rescue the Christian claim.

First, there are all the practical problems of which contemporary dualists are very much aware. Our personal experience and emotions are intimately linked to our body chemistry. Indeed, the limits to what we are able to think at all are set by our genetic endowment; so that one man's physio-chemical equipment enables him to be a brilliant mathematician, while another's lack condemns him to lifelong imbecility. If our diet is imbalanced and inadequate, or if certain of our organs are malfunctioning, then our bodies may be starved of essential nutrients or poisoned by the excessive production of some hormone. In such cases, the whole personality may be adversely affected. The "subject of my conscious experiences" would seem to be very much at the mercy of my physiochemical constitution.

A second difficulty lies in deciding which organisms count as having souls and which do not. And if God is to give eternal life to the former class and not to the latter, then even He has to be able to draw a line somewhere, and that nonarbitrarily. The problem occurs both in considering the evolution of the species *Homo sapiens* and the individual development of human beings. Even if we ignore the problem of nonhuman animals and restrict the possibility of possessing a soul to humans, there are still insuperable difficulties.

Consider first the evolutionary pathway that led from the early mammals to man. Somewhere along that line we would be fairly secure in denying that such and such a creature had any awareness of self. And it is also true to say that most normal adult humans possess such an awareness. But between these extremes lies a gray area. To have a nonarbitrary dividing line, it has to be possible for us to decide (at least in principle) where a sharp division can be drawn between the last generation of anthropoid apes and the first generation of true *Homo sapiens.* Are we to suppose that in one generation there were anthropoid apes who gave birth to the next generation of true *Homo sapiens,* and that the changes between one generation and the next were so great that the children counted in God's eyes as the bearers of immortality while their parents were "mere animals"? Yet unless dualists are prepared to fly in the face of evolutionary biology, how can they avoid this unpalatable conclusion?

The problems that we see in the evolution of the species are mirrored in the development of each fertilized human ovum. Somewhere in the path leading from conception to adulthood awareness of self develops. When exactly seems impossible to pinpoint (unless it turns out that awareness of self is a sort of quantum leap in a child's development). Nor can the difficulty be evaded by claiming that each fertilized ovum is a potential human being and therefore potentially self-aware, not least because some genetic combinations become cancerous and are in no sense even potential human beings.

Just as there were religious difficulties arising for the dualist's position from the lack of sharp divisions in evolutionary development, so too there are religious difficulties here. For if, as Descartes would have us believe, it is the ability to doubt that guarantees the existence of the "I", and if what survives is this subject of conscious experiences, then there is nothing to survive in any potential human being that has yet to develop the necessary level of mental life. Panpsychists apart, most of us would accept that a certain minimum of neurological equipment is a necessary condition of conscious experience. As Arturo Rosenblueth writes: "In the human species, the central nervous system, especially the cerebral cortex of the newborn baby, is very underdeveloped as compared with those of an adolescent or an adult. . . . The first signs of conscious behaviour do not appear until this anatomical and neurophysiological evolution reaches a sufficiently high level."

If this is right, then would we have to imagine God greeting two mothers in heaven and saying to one, "The soul of your long-lost infant is now fully mature and waits here to be reunited with you"; while to the other he mutters, "Well, I am sorry about this, but your baby didn't quite make it because he failed to develop self-consciousness before he died"? Nor is the problem to be circumvented by claiming that what survives has nothing to do with neural equipment. It is rather the immaterial soul, which admittedly had yet to manifest its presence in the infant. For what content could be given to claiming that this tabula rasa was the real child? This theory of the soul fails to satisfy not just because it seems incompatible with our scientific knowledge, but also because it has some undesirable religious implications.

There are, in addition, some further objections of a more purely philosophical nature, which I think need mentioning at this point. The subject of my conscious experiencing is singularly unconvincing as a principle of continuity that guarantees persistence of the "same" person through change. Moreover, defining the "real" me in this way actually misses a lot of what most of us would want to say is a part of the "real" me. I shall begin by discussing the question of a principle of continuity.

One great problem with my awareness of self is its lack of persistence, its transitoriness. My stream of consciousness is far from being a constant or even ever-present (though varying) flow. When I am unconscious, in a dreamless sleep, or even in a vacant mood, it just is not there. Yet *I* do not cease to exist whenever my conscious mind is, as it were, switched off temporarily. Secondly, we have to face the problem that this awareness of self is ever-changing. What I was as a child is very different from what I, as I am in myself, am today; and if I live to be an old lady, doubtless the subject of my conscious experiences will look back with a mixture of wry amusement and nostalgia at that other her of forty years ago. Now it might be thought that this problem of continual change is no greater a problem for the notion of same "self" than it is for the notion of same "body" since the body is also in a continual state of flux. But I would suggest that what supplies continuity through change is matter. It may be that all my constituent atoms will have changed in the next few months, but they will not have all changed simultaneously. Moreover, the physically-based blueprints from the chemistry that keeps my body going are passed on from one generation of cells to another in a direct physical line of succession. Thus, I would argue that what keeps the subject of my conscious experiencing belonging to one and the same person is this physical continuity.

The essential requirement of physical continuity can be illustrated if we return to the clone example. Let us modify the thought experiment a little, and makes Jones II a copy of a perfectly healthy Jones I. And let us also stipulate that the two Joneses emerge from the cloning laboratory not knowing who is the original and who the copy. In other words, Jones I and II are, seemingly, wholly similar. Neither they nor we can tell which is which, unless we trace the histories of the two bodies to ascertain which grew from a fertilized ovum and which developed as the result of cloning. Now if we apply the implications of this to the question of what might live again after death, we see that being "the subject of my conscious experiences" is not sufficient to guarantee that I am one and the same person as the one who died. For what the clone example shows is that both Jones I and Jones II may believe (or doubt) equally that he really is the same person as Jones I while he relies solely on his personal experience of himself as Jones. Only when he traces the path of physical continuity can he know whether he truly is Jones I or not. (Of course, we might want to say that where there had been one person, Jones, there were now two distinct individuals, both of whom were physically continuous with the original. But in that case the possibility of defining "same person" in terms of "same stream of consciousness" does not even arise.)

Thus I contend, a dualist definition of what I really am fails because it cannot provide adequate criteria for recognizing the "same" person through change. I can think of no other case where we would even be tempted to accept something as transitory and ever-changing as "consciousness of self" to be the essential criterion for defining what it is that an entity has to retain if it is to count as remaining the same individual through change.

I move on now to the problems that arise from the restrictedness of defining me as the subject of my conscious experiences. A great deal of what I am does not involve my conscious thoughts at all, even when I am fully awake. Take the familiar example of driving a car. When I was learning to drive, I certainly employed a great amount of conscious effort. But nowadays my conscious thoughts are fairly free to attend to other matters when I am driving, even though, of course, intense conscious attention instantly returns if danger threatens. I certainly do not want to say "my body" drove here. *I* drove here, even though most of the time the subject of my conscious experiences was not much involved.

Moreover, we cannot ignore the possibility that the conscious subject might actually fail to recognize a significant part of all that I really am. To exemplify the point: imagine someone who believes himself to be a great wit, when most of his colleagues find him a crashing bore. If he were to arrive in the resurrection world without his familiar characteristics—clumsiness of speech, repetitiveness, triviality, self-centeredness—would he really be the person who had died? Yet could he bring these characteristics with him if the subject of his conscious experiences, the "real" him, was wholly unaware of having been like this?

In sum, what I have been arguing against dualism is that this concept of the soul cannot bear the weight put on it. Yet it has to bear this weight if it is to be the sine qua non of my surviving bodily death. Considerations from the natural sciences and philosophy, and even religious implications, combine to render it far from convincing. But, it might be countered, no amount of argument on the basis of current scientific theory, philosophy, or religious sentiments can count against hard empirical fact. So what about the reports that exist of near-death experiences, which seem to show that some people really do have experiences apart from their bodies?

NEAR-DEATH EXPERIENCES

Let me begin by stating quite clearly that I shall not be concerned to discuss the merits or otherwise of individual cases. I am going to suppose, for the purposes of discussion, that there is strong, bonafide evidence that some people come back from the brink of death fully convinced that they had left their bodies and had had apparently veridical experiences as if from a vantage point different from that of the body. The question then is, how do we interpret these "travelers tales."

I have three main points to make here. The first is that a present absence of satisfactory normal explanations for these cases does not imply that there are no such explanations ever to be found. We should not be hurried into a supernaturalist account merely because we can find no other, as if the God-of-the-gaps lesson had yet to be learned. And I note that at least one worker in this field, Dr.

Susan Blackmore, argues for a psychological approach to explaining out-of-the-body experiences (OBEs). Dr. Blackmore has spent the last decade researching OBEs and has moved from an initial belief that persons can leave their bodies to her present more skeptical position. She writes: "Everything perceived in an OBE is a product of memory and imagination, and during the OBE one's imagination is more vividly experienced than it is in everyday life." One limiting factor, for our purposes here, in Dr. Blackmore's work is that she has been researching primarily "astral projection" rather than near-death experiences. And clearly, if there is such a thing as a quasi-independent human soul, it is at least possible that such a soul cannot actually leave the body while the body is not near death. In that case, all the research in the world into astral projection may be wholly irrelevant. But we should be prepared to explore naturalistic accounts of OBEs before embracing a supernaturalistic hypothesis.

My second point is that even if we take near-death experiences as supplying empirical proof of the existence, nay persistence, of the human soul or mind, that would not smooth out all the difficulties. All the problems that I have discussed earlier would still be there, awaiting some kind of resolution. And there would arise yet further problems. Take, for example, the question of how the soul actually "sees" physical objects while it supposedly hovers below the ceiling. William Rushton puts the point thus: "What is this out-of-the-body eye that can encode the visual scene exactly as does the real eye, with its hundred million photoreceptors and its million signaling optic nerves? Can you imagine anything but a replica of the real eye could manage to do this? But if this floating replica is to see, it must catch light, and hence cannot be transparent, and so must be visible to people in the vicinity. In fact floating eyes are not observed, nor would this be expected, for they exist only in fantasy." And if it be countered that the soul perceives without using the normal physicochemical mechanisms, then we might ask why on earth did such a complicated organ as the eye ever evolve (or remain unatrophied) if human beings possess souls that can "see" without normal eyes. Moreover, one might expect that blind people, deprived of normal visual stimuli, would use this psychic ability, if it really existed. These, and kindred problems concerned with modes of perception, would need answers if we were to take seriously supernatural interpretations of OBEs.

Finally, I suggest that to accept the existence of some nonmaterial soul in man would be to embrace a notion fundamentally at variance with other well-founded convictions about the nature of reality. For we would then have to allow for events happening in the world that rest on no underlying physicochemical mechanisms. Now I am very well aware that scientists are continually changing their theories to accommodate new data, and that from time to time some wholesale replacement of outmoded ideas has been necessary. So, it might be asked, can we not envisage some new scientific outlook that embraces both the normal data and the paranormal? Just so. A new scientific outlook, which could encompass both normal and paranormal data, would clearly be more satisfactory than one which could in no way account for the paranormal. But it must be remembered that the whole scientific enterprise presupposes the existence of underlying mechanisms whose discovery enables us to understand the "how" of an event. So it is hard to see how any unified scientific theory could embrace both the notion that most events in the world depend on underlying physicochemical mechanisms, and also that there are some events that do not utilize any such mechanisms at all. And if paranormal data are taken as support for the belief in the existence of nonmaterial entities (like souls) then these data fly in the face of normal science. Thus I concur with C. D. Broad that "It is certainly right to demand a much higher standard of evidence for events which are alleged to be paranormal than those which would be normal. . . . For in dealing with evidence we have always to take into account the antecedent probability or improbability of the alleged event, i.e. its probability or improbability relative to all the rest of our knowledge and well-founded belief other than the special evidence adduced in its favour."

In sum then, it seems that at present paranormal data cannot be accommodated within naturalist science. But to move from that to claiming that we have empirical evidence for the existence of immaterial souls seems unwarranted, not least because to explicate the paranormal in terms of the activities of immaterial souls may appear to solve one explanatory difficulty, but only at the expense of raising a host of other problems.

CONCLUSION

When Christianity was originally formulated, man's entire world view was very different from our current beliefs. It was plausible to think in terms of a three-decker universe in which the center of God's interest was this Earth and its human population. The idea that God would raise man from the dead to an eternal life of bliss fitted neatly into this schema. However, the erosion of this picture, beginning from at least the time of Copernicus and Galileo, has cut the traditional Christian hope adrift from the framework of ideas in which it was originally formulated. What I have tried to show in this chapter is that various attempts, which have been made to try to accommodate some form of resurrection/immortality belief within our current world view, are inadequate and fail. I conclude, then, that a due consideration of man's place in nature leads us to the view that he belongs there and nowhere else.

Questions for Reflection

1. Do you think that Badham's scientific considerations are a decisive refutation of the possibility of life after death?
2. How might John Locke or Jeffrey Olen reply to her arguments that psychological continuity is inadequate to account for personal identity?

3. What would Badham say about Dennett's story (reading 32) where the subject was recreated in a different body?

CONTEMPORARY APPLICATION: CAN COMPUTERS THINK?

In the latter part of the 20th century, the philosophy of mind has taken an interesting new turn with the attempt to create artificial intelligence (hereafter referred to as AI). Today's computers are able to perform many of the activities that we formerly thought only human minds could perform. These activities include playing chess, proving mathematical theorems, making complex medical diagnoses, and summarizing a newspaper article and drawing inferences from it. Advanced computer programs do more than blindly follow orders, for they can learn from experience and modify themselves in ways that their programmers could not predict. The progress of AI raises several interesting philosophical questions. If we take the ability to perform certain activities as evidence that a person can think and has a mind, and computers can perform these activities, then should we conclude that computers can think and have a mind? If so, what insight does this provide on the mind-body problem and what does this do to our concept of the self?

One landmark event in this whole discussion occurred on May 11, 1997, when IBM's computer named "Deep Blue" defeated Garry Kasparov, the world chess champion, in a six-game chess match. A year earlier, Deep Blue had defeated Kasparov in their very first encounter, even though the human player went on to either win or tie the remaining games. Speaking about one of Deep Blue's moves, Kasparov said "it was a wonderful and extremely human move. . . . I had played a lot of computers but I had never experienced anything like this. I could feel—I could *smell*—a new kind of intelligence across the table."

Was Kasparov right, as some believe? Was this computer chess master actually able to think? Or was the chess-playing computer merely *simulating* thinking? To answer the question "Can computers think?" we need a criterion of what constitutes thinking. In 1950 the British mathematician Alan Turing proposed a test to determine whether a computer can think or not. Turing is considered to be the founding father of modern computer science. Although he never built a computer himself, he laid the theoretical and mathematical foundations that were essential for designing our modern computers. Here is a contemporary version of his proposal, which has since become immortalized as the **Turing Test.** Let us suppose that you and several other judges are seated in a room in front of a computer terminal. Your terminal is communicating with a terminal in another room. You communicate interactively with the unseen person in the other room by typing in questions on your keyboard and reading the other's responses on your monitor. The key feature of the test is that in some of the sessions you are not communicating with a flesh and blood person, but with an artificial intelligence program running on a computer. Turing's claim was that if the computer program could fool a panel of judges into thinking they were communicating with a human being a significant percentage of the time, this would be proof that the computer program was capable of thought. Hence, Turing replaced the abstract and rather vague question

"Can computers think?" with an operational test of intelligence: "Can computers pass the Turing Test?" The theory behind this test can be summed up by the cliché, "If it looks like a duck, walks like a duck, and quacks like a duck—it is a duck!" In other words, if a computer's responses fulfill the criteria we use to judge that a human is intelligent, then we are committed to saying that the computer is intelligent.

Some have expanded Turing's thesis into the claim that the ability to pass the Turing Test is a logically sufficient condition for having a mind. Thus, the claim is that an appropriately programmed computer really *is* a mind and can be *literally* said to understand, believe, and have other cognitive states. This is known as the **strong AI thesis.** The **weak AI thesis** is the relatively innocuous claim that artificial intelligence research may help us explore various theoretical models of human mental processes.

In his essay in reading 44, John Searle, a critic of strong AI, contends that computers can simulate cognitive processes but they cannot duplicate them. Searle points out that

> We can do a computer simulation of the flow of money in the British economy, or the pattern of power distribution in the Labour party. We can do computer simulation of rain storms in the home counties, or warehouse fires in East London. Now, in each of these cases, nobody supposes that the computer simulation is actually the real thing; no one supposes that a computer simulation of a storm will leave us all wet, or a computer simulation of a fire is likely to burn the house down. Why on earth would anyone in his right mind suppose a computer simulation of mental processes actually had mental processes?

This is a pretty good argument, isn't it? Well, not everyone thinks it is. Daniel Dennett (the author of reading 32) replies to the above argument in this way:

> But now suppose we made a computer simulation of a mathematician, and suppose it worked well. Would we complain that what we had hoped for was *proofs,* but alas, all we got instead was mere *representations* of proofs? But representations of proofs *are* proofs, aren't they?*

In other words, in some cases (a rain storm) the simulation or representation of something is quite different from the real thing. In other cases, the representation of something (a mathematical proof) is equivalent to the real thing. The word *artificial* is ambiguous because it can serve two purposes. We might use it to make this contrast: artificial versus genuine. In this sense, artificial flowers or artificial diamonds are not real flowers or diamonds, but only simulate the genuine articles. On the other hand, we can use *artificial* to make a different sort of contrast: artificial versus natural. Artificial light is not natural, for it is produced by human technology. But in contrast to artificial flowers, artificial light is *real* light. So, is artificial, machine intelligence like artificial light (it is the real thing) or is artificial intelligence like an artificial flower (it is a simulation)?

In the following readings, Christopher Evans will defend Turing's thesis of strong AI. John Searle will defend weak AI, the thesis that computer intelligence is not real intelligence but is merely a simulation. In the third reading, science fiction writer Terry Bisson will reverse the issue by imagining intelligent robots who ponder whether humans can really think.

---

*The Mind's I, ed. Douglas Hofstadter and Daniel Dennett (New York: Bantam Books, 1981), p. 94.

CHRISTOPHER EVANS

Computers Will Some Day Be Able to Think

Christopher Evans (1931–1979) was an experimental psychologist and computer scientist. He personally knew and worked with some of the pioneers in the field of artificial intelligence and wrote several books and articles on psychology and artificial intelligence. The following selection is from his book *The Micro Millennium*. It should be noted that this book was published in 1979, 18 years before IBM's computer beat the world's human chess champion and before many of the advances in AI research that have occurred. While Evans thought that the rate of progress of such research would be faster than it has been, if he were alive to see the use of today's computers in such intelligent tasks as medical diagnoses, he would certainly conclude that his optimism had been vindicated.

Reading Questions

1. What are the seven objections to AI that Evans lists? How does he reply to each one?
2. How does Evans reply to the skeptic's argument that a computer will not be able to perform a creative task?
3. What was the test Alan Turing proposed to decide if a computer can think?
4. Why does Evans say that "the difference, in intellectual terms, between a human being and a computer is one of degree and not of kind"?
5. What are the two reasons why Evans is confident that Turing's prediction of the rise of very intelligent machines will turn out to be true?
6. What is I. J. Good's definition of an "Ultra-Intelligent Machine"?

CAN A MACHINE THINK?

In the early years of the Second World War when the British began, in ultra-secret, to put together their effort to crack German codes, they set out to recruit a team of the brightest minds available in mathematics and the then rather novel field of electronic engineering. Recruiting the electronic whizzes was easy, as many of them were to be found engrossed in the fascinating problem of radio location of aircraft—or radar as it later came to be called. Finding mathematicians with the right kind of obsessive brilliance to make a contribution in the strange field of cryptography was another matter. In the end they adopted the ingenious strategy of searching through lists of young mathematicians who were also top-flight chess players. As a result of a nation-wide trawl an amazing collection of characters were billeted together in the country-house surroundings of Bletchley Park, and three of the most remarkable were Irving John Good, Donald Michie, and Alan Turing. . . .

If contemporary accounts of what the workers at Bletchley were talking about in their few moments

From Christopher Evans, "Can a Machine Think" and "Towards the Ultra-Intelligent Machine," chaps. 13 and 14 in *The Micro Millennium* (New York: Viking Press, 1979).

of spare time can be relied on, many of them were a bit over-optimistic if anything. Both Good and Michie believed that the use of electronic computers such as Colossus would result in major advances in mathematics in the immediate post-war era and Turing was of the same opinion. All three (and one or two of their colleagues) were also confident that it would not be long before machines were exhibiting intelligence, including problem-solving abilities, and that their role as simple number-crunchers was only one phase in their evolution. Although the exact substance of their conversations, carried long into the night when they were waiting for the test results of the first creaky Colossus prototypes, has softened with the passage of time, it is known the topic of machine intelligence loomed very large. They discussed, with a *frisson** of excitement and unease, the peculiar ramifications of the subject they were pioneering and about which the rest of the world knew (and still knows) so little. Could there ever be a machine which was able to solve problems that no human could solve? Could a computer ever beat a human at chess? Lastly, could a machine *think*?

Of all the questions that can be asked about computers none has such an eerie ring. Allow a machine intelligence perhaps, the ability to control other machines, repair itself, help us solve problems, compute numbers a millionfold quicker than any human; allow it to fly airplanes, drive cars, superintend our medical records and even, possibly, give advice to politicians. Somehow you can see how a machine might come to do all these things. But that it could be made to perform that apparently exclusively human operation known as *thinking* is something else, and something which is offensive, alien and threatening. Only in the most *outre*† forms of science fiction, stretching back to Mary Shelley's masterpiece *Frankenstein,* is the topic touched on, and always with a sense of great uncertainty about the enigmatic nature of the problem area.

Good, Michie and their companions were content to work the ideas through in their spare mo-

ments. But Turing—older, a touch more serious and less cavalier—set out to consider things in depth. In particular he addressed himself to the critical question: Can, or could, a machine think? The way he set out to do this three decades ago and long before any other scientists had considered it so cogently, is of lasting interest. The main thesis was published in the philosophical journal *Mind* in 1952. Logically unassailable, when read impartially it serves to break down any barriers of uncertainty which surround this and parallel questions. Despite its classic status the work is seldom read outside the fields of computer science and philosophy, but now that events in computer science and in the field of artificial intelligence are beginning to move with the rapidity and momentum which the Bletchley scientists knew they ultimately would, the time has come for Turing's paper to achieve a wider public.

Soon after the war ended and the Colossus project folded, Turing joined the National Physical Laboratory in Teddington and began to work with a gifted team on the design of what was to become the world's most powerful computer, ACE. Later he moved to Manchester, where, spurred by the pioneers Kilburn, Hartree, Williams and Newman, a vigorous effort was being applied to develop another powerful electronic machine. It was a heady, hard-driving time, comparable to the state of events now prevailing in microprocessors, when anyone with special knowledge rushes along under immense pressure, ever conscious of the feeling that whoever is second in the race may as well not have entered it at all. As a result Turing found less time than he would have hoped to follow up his private hobbies, particularly his ideas on computer game-playing—checkers, chess and the ancient game of Go—which he saw was an important subset of machine intelligence.

Games like chess are unarguably intellectual pursuits, and yet, unlike certain other intellectual exercises, such as writing poetry or discussing the inconsistent football of the hometown team, they have easily describable rules of operation. The task, therefore, would seem to be simply a matter of writing a computer program which "knew" these rules and which could follow them when faced with

---

*[shudder]
†[excessive]

moves offered by a human player. Turing made very little headway as it happens, and the first chess-playing programs which were scratched together in the late '40s and early '50s were quite awful—so much so that there was a strong feeling that this kind of project was not worth pursuing, since the game of chess as played by an "expert" involves some special intellectual skill which could never be specified in machine terms.

Turing found this ready dismissal of the computer's potential to be both interesting and suggestive. If people were unwilling to accept the idea of a machine which could play games, how would they feel about one which exhibited "intelligence," or one which could "think"? In the course of discussions with friends Turing found that a good part of the problem was that people were universally unsure of their definitions. What exactly did one mean when one used the word "thought"? What processes were actually in action when "thinking" took place? If a machine was created which *could* think, how would one set about testing it? The last question, Turing surmised, was the key one, and with a wonderful surge of imagination spotted a way to answer it, proposing what has in computer circles come to be known as "The Turing Test for Thinking Machines." In the next chapter, we will examine the test, see how workable it is, and also try to assess how close computers have come, and will come, to passing it.

When Turing asked people whether they believed that a computer could think, he found almost universal rejection of the idea—just as I did when I carried out a similar survey almost thirty years later. The objections I received were similar to those that Turing documented in his paper "Computing Machinery and Intelligence," and I will summarize them here, adding my own comments and trying to meet the various objections as they occur.

First there is the Theological Objection. This was more common in Turing's time than it is now, but it still crops up occasionally. It can be summed up as follows: "Man is a creation of God, and has been given a soul and the power of conscious thought. Machines are not spiritual beings, have no soul and thus must be incapable of thought." As Turing

pointed out, this seems to place an unwarranted restriction on God. Why shouldn't he give machines souls and allow them to think if he wanted to? On one level I suppose it is irrefutable: if someone chooses to define thinking as something that *only* Man can do and that *only* God can bestow, then that is the end of the matter. Even then the force of the argument does seem to depend upon a confusion between "thought" and "spirituality," upon the old Cartesian dichotomy of the ghost in the machine. The ghost presumably does the thinking while the machine is merely the vehicle which carries the ghost around. . . .

The Personal Consciousness Objection is, superficially, a rather potent argument which comes up in various guises. Turing noticed it expressed particularly cogently in a report, in the *British Medical Journal* in 1949, on the Lister Oration for that year, which was entitled "The Mind of Mechanical Man." It was given by a distinguished medical scientist, Professor G. Jefferson. A short quote from the Oration will suffice:

> Not until a machine can write a sonnet or compose a concerto *because of thoughts and emotions felt,* and not by the chance fall of symbols, could we agree that machine equals brain—that is, not only write it but *know that it had written it.* No mechanism could feel (and not merely artificially signal, an easy contrivance) pleasure at its successes, grief when its valves fuse, be warmed by flattery, be made miserable by its mistakes, be charmed by sex, be angry or depressed when it cannot get what it wants.

The italics, which are mine, highlight what I believe to be the fundamental objection: the output of the machine is more or less irrelevant, no matter how impressive it is. Even if it wrote a sonnet—and a very good one—it would not mean much unless it had written it as the result of "thoughts and emotions felt," and it would also have to "know that it had written it." This could be a useful "final definition" of one aspect of human thought—but how would you establish whether or not the sonnet was written with "emotions"? Asking the computer would not help for, as Professor Jefferson realized, there would be no guarantee that it was not simply *declaring* that it had felt emotions. He is really pro- pounding the extreme solipsist position and should, therefore, apply the same rules to humans. Extreme solipsism is logically irrefutable ("I am the only real thing; all else is illusion") but it is so un- helpful a view of the universe that most people choose to ignore it and decide that when people say they are thinking or feeling they may as well be- lieve them. In other words, Professor Jefferson's objection could be over-ridden if you *became* the computer and experienced its thoughts (if any)— only then could you really *know*. His objection is worth discussing in some depth because it is so commonly heard in one form or another, and be- cause it sets us up in part for Turing's resolution of the machine-thought problem, which we will come to later.

The Unpredictability Objection argues that com- puters are created by humans according to sets of rules and operate according to carefully scripted programs which themselves are sets of rules. So if you wanted to, you could work out exactly what a computer was going to do at any particular time. It is, in principle, totally predictable. *If* you have all the facts available you *can* predict a computer's be- haviour because it follows rules, whereas there is no way in which you could hope to do the same with a human *because he is not behaving according to a set of immutable rules*. Thus there is an essential differ- ence between computers and humans, so (the ar- gument gets rather weak here) thinking, because it is unpredictable and does not blindly follow rules, must be an essentially human ability.

There are two comments: firstly, computers are becoming so complex that it is doubtful their be- haviour could be predicted even if everything was known about them—computer programmers and engineers have found that one of the striking char- acteristics of present-day systems is that they con- stantly spring surprises. The second point follows naturally: humans are *already* in that super-complex state and the reason that we cannot predict what they do is *not* because they have no ground rules but because (a) we don't know what the rules are, and (b) even if we did know them they would still be too complicated to handle. At best, the unpre-

dictability argument is thin, but it is often raised. People frequently remark that there is always "the element of surprise" in a human. I have no doubt that that is just because *any* very complex system is bound to be surprising. A variant of the argument is that humans are capable of error whereas the "perfect" computer is not. That may well be true, which suggests that machines are superior to hu- mans, for there seems to be little point in having any information-processing system, biological or electronic, that makes errors in processing. It would be possible to build a random element into computers to make them unpredictable from time to time, but it would be a peculiarly pointless exercise.

The "See How Stupid They Are" Objection will not need much introduction. At one level it is ex- pressed in jokes about computers that generate ridiculous bank statements or electricity bills; at an- other and subtler level, it is a fair appraisal of the computer's stupendous weaknesses in comparison with Man. "How could you possibly imagine that such backward, limited things could ever reach the point where they could be said to think?" The an- swer, as we have already pointed out, is that they may be dumb now but they have advanced at a pretty dramatic rate and show every sign of contin- uing to do so. Their present limitations may be valid when arguing whether they could be said to be capable of thinking *now* or in the *very* near fu- ture, but it has no relevance to whether they would be capable of thinking at some later date.

The "Ah But It Can't Do That" Objection is an eternally regressing argument which, for a quarter of a century, computer scientists have been listen- ing to, partially refuting, and then having to listen to all over again. It runs: "Oh yes, you can obviously make a computer do so and so—you have just demonstrated that, but of course you will never be able to make it do such and such." The such and such may be anything you name—once it was play a good game of chess, have a storage capacity greater than the human memory, read human hand-writing or understand human speech. Now that these "Ah buts" have (quite swiftly) been over- come, one is faced by a new range: beat the world human chess champion, operate on parallel as opposed to serial processing, perform medical diagnosis better than a doctor, translate satisfactorily from one language to another, help solve its own software problems, etc. When these challenges are met, no doubt it will have to design a complete city from scratch, invent a game more interesting than chess, admire a pretty girl/handsome man, work out the unified field theory, enjoy bacon and eggs, and so on. I cannot think of anything more silly than developing a computer which could enjoy bacon and eggs, but there is nothing to suggest that, provided enough time and money was invested, one could not pull off such a surrealistic venture. On the other hand, it might be *most* useful to have computers design safe, optimally cheap buildings. Even more ambitious (and perhaps comparable to the bacon and egg project but more worthwhile) would be to set a system to tackle the problem of the relationship between gravity and light, and my own guess is that before the conclusion of the long-term future (before the start of the twenty-first century), computers will be hard at work on these problems and will be having great success.

The "It Is Not Biological" Objection may seem like another version of the theological objection—only living things could have the capacity for thought, so non-biological systems could not possibly think. But there is a subtle edge that requires a bit more explanation. It is a characteristic of most modern computers that they are discrete state machines, which is to say that they are digital and operate in a series of discrete steps—on/off. Now the biological central nervous system may not be so obviously digital, though there is evidence that the neurone, the basic unit of communication, acts in an on/off, all or nothing way. But if it turned out that it were *not,* and operated on some more elaborate strategy, then it is conceivable that "thought" might only be manifest in things which had switching systems of this more elaborate kind. Put it another way: it might be possible to build digital computers which were immensely intelligent, but no matter how intelligent they became they would never be able to *think.* The argument cannot be refuted at the moment, but even so there is no shred of evidence to suppose that only non-digital systems can think. There may be other facets of living

things that make them unique from the point of view of their capacity to generate thought, but none that we can identify, or even guess at. This objection therefore is not a valid one at present, though in the event of some new biological discovery, it may become so. . . .

The last of the . . . arguments against the concept of a thinking machine has become known as Lady Lovelace's Objection. . . . In its modern form this comes up as, "A Computer cannot do anything that you have not programmed it to." The objection is so fundamental and so widely accepted that it needs detailed discussion.

In the most absolute and literal sense, this statement is perfectly correct and applies to any machine or computer that has been made or that could be made. According to the rules of the universe that we live in, nothing can take place without a prior cause; a computer will not spring into action without something powering it and guiding it on its way. In the case of the various tasks that a computer performs, the "cause"—to stretch the use of the word rather—is the program or sets of programs that control these tasks. Much the same applies to a brain: it, too, must come equipped with sets of programs which cause it to run through its repertoire of tasks. This might seem to support Lady Lovelace, at least to the extent that machines "need" a human to set them up, but it would also seem to invalidate the argument that this constitutes an essential difference between computers and people. But is there not still a crucial difference between brains and computers? No matter how sophisticated computers are, must there not always have been a human being to *write* its programs? Surely the same does not have to be said for humans?

To tackle this we need to remember that all brains, human included, are equipped at birth with a comprehensive collection of programs which are common to all members of a species and which are known as instincts. These control respiration, gastric absorption, cardiac activity, and, at a behavioural level, such reflexes as sucking, eyeblink, grasping and so on. There may also be programs which "cause" the young animal to explore its environment, exercise its muscles, play and so on.

Where do these come from? Well, they are acquired over an immensely long-winded trial-and-error process through the course of evolution. We might call them permanent software ("firmware" is the phrase used sometimes by computer scientists) and they correspond to the suites of programs which every computer has when it leaves the factory, and which are to do with its basic running, maintenance, and so on.

In addition to this, all biological computers come equipped with a bank of what might best be described as raw programs. No one has the faintest idea whether they are neurological, biochemical, electrical or what—all we know is that they *must* exist. They start being laid down the moment the creature begins to interact with the world around it. In the course of time they build up into a colossal suite of software which ultimately enables us to talk, write, walk, read, enjoy bacon and eggs, appreciate music, think, feel, write books, or come up with mathematical ideas. These programs are useful only to the owner of that particular brain, vanish with his death and are quite separate from the "firmware."

If this seems too trivial a description of the magnificent field of human learning and achievement, it is only because anything appears trivial when you reduce it to its bare components: a fabulous sculpture to a quintillion highly similar electrons and protons, a microprocessor to a million impurities buried in a wafer of sand, the human brain into a collection of neurones, blood cells and chemical elements. What is not trivial is the endlessly devious, indescribably profound way in which these elements are structured to make up the whole. The real difference between the brain and most existing computers is that in the former, data acquisition and the initial writing and later modification of the program is done by a mechanism within the brain itself, while in the latter, the software is prepared outside and passed to the computer in its completed state. But I did use the word "most." In recent years increasing emphasis has been placed on the development of "adaptive" programs—software which can be modified and revised on the basis of the program's interaction with the environment. In simple terms these could be looked upon as "programs which learn for themselves," and they will, in due course, become an important feature of many powerful computer systems.

At this point the sceptic still has a few weapons in his armoury. The first is generally put in the form of the statement: "Ah, but even when computers *can* update their own software and acquire new programs for themselves, they will still only be doing this because of Man's ingenuity. Man may no longer actually write the programs, but had he not invented the idea of the self-adaptive program in the first place none of this could have happened." This is perfectly true but has little to do with whether or not computers could think, or perform any other intellectual exercise. It could place computers eternally in our debt, and we may be able to enjoy a smug sense of pride at having created them, but it offers no real restriction on their development.

The sceptic may also argue that no matter how clever or how intelligent you make computers, they will never be able to perform a creative task. Everything they do will inevitably spring from something they have been taught, have experienced or is the subject of some pre-existing program. There are two points being made here. One is that computers could never have an original or creative thought. The other is that the seeds of everything they do, no matter how intelligent, lie in their existing software. To take the second point first: again one is forced to say that the same comment applies to humans. Unless the argument is that some of Man's thoughts or ideas come from genuine inspiration—a message from God, angels, or the spirits of the departed—no one can dispute that all aspects of our intelligence evolve from pre-existing programs and the background experiences of life. This evolution may be enormously complex and its progress might be impossible to track, but any intellectual flowerings arise from the seeds of experience planted in the fertile substrate of the brain.

There still remains the point about creativity, and it is one that is full of pitfalls. Before making any assumptions about creativity being an *exclusive* attribute of Man, the concept has to be defined. It is not enough to say "write a poem," "paint a picture" or "discuss philosophical ideas," because it is easy enough to program computers to do all these things. The fact that their poems, paintings and philosophical ramblings are pretty mediocre is beside the point: it would be just as unfair to ask them to write, say, a sonnet of Shakespearian calibre or a painting of da Vinci quality and fail them for lack of creativity as it would be to give the same task to the man in the street. Beware too of repeating the old saying, "Ah, but you have to program them to paint, play chess and so on," for the same is unquestionably true of people. Try handing a twelve-month-old baby a pot of paint or a chessboard if you have any doubts about the need for some measure of learning and experience.

Obviously a crisper definition of creativity is required, and here is one that is almost universally acceptable: If a person demonstrates a skill which has never been demonstrated before and which was not specifically taught to him by someone else, or in the intellectual domain provides an *entirely novel* solution to a problem—a solution which was not known to any other human being—then they can be said to have done something original or had an original or creative thought. There may be other forms of creativity of course, but this would undeniably be an example of it in action. There is plenty of evidence that humans are creative by this standard and the history of science is littered with "original" ideas which humans have generated. Clearly, until a computer also provides such evidence, Lady Lovelace's Objection still holds, at least in one of its forms.

But alas for the sceptics. This particular barrier has been overthrown by computers on a number of occasions in the past few years. A well-publicized one was the solution, by a computer, of the venerable "four colour problem." This has some mathematical importance, and can best be expressed by thinking of a two-dimensional map featuring a large number of territories, say the counties of England or the states of the USA. Supposing you want to give each territory a colour, what is the minimum number of colours you need to employ to ensure that no two territories of the same colour adjoin each other?

After fiddling around with maps and crayons, you will find that the number seems to come out at four, and no one has ever been able to find a configuration where five colours are required, or where you can always get away with three. Empirically, therefore, four is the answer—hence the name of the problem. But if you attempt to demonstrate this mathematically and *prove* that four colours will do for any conceivable map, you will get nowhere. For decades mathematicians have wrestled with this elusive problem, and from time to time have come up with a "proof" which in the end turns out to be incomplete or fallacious. But the mathematical world was rocked when in 1977 the problem was handed over to a computer, which attacked it with a stupendous frontal assault, sifting through huge combinations of possibilities and eventually demonstrating, to every mathematician's satisfaction, that four colours would do the trick. Actually, although this is spectacular testimony to the computer's creative powers, it is not really the most cogent example, for its technique was block-busting rather than heuristic (problem solving by testing hypotheses). It was like solving a chess problem by working out every possible combination of moves, rather than by concentrating on likely areas and experimenting with them. A better, and much earlier, demonstration of computer originality came from a program which was set to generate some totally new proofs in Euclidean geometry. The computer produced a completely novel proof of the well-known theorem which shows that the base angles of an isosceles triangle are equal, by flipping the triangles through 180 degrees and declaring them to be congruent. Quite apart from the fact that it had not before been known to Man, it showed such originality that one famous mathematician remarked, "If any of my students had done that, I would have marked him down as a budding genius."

And so Lady Lovelace's long-lasting objection can be overruled. We have shown that computers can be intelligent, and that they can even be creative—but we have not yet proved that they can, or ever could, *think*.

Now, what do we mean by the word "think"?

TOWARDS THE ULTRA-INTELLIGENT MACHINE

The most common objections raised to the notion of thinking machines are based on misunderstandings of fairly simple issues, or on semantic confusions of one kind or another. We are still left with the problem of defining the verb "to think," and in this chapter we will attempt to deal with this, or at least to discuss one particular and very compelling way of dealing with it. From this position we shall find ourselves drifting inevitably into a consideration of the problem of creating thinking machines, and in particular to the eerie concept of the Ultra-Intelligent Machine.

Most people believe that they know what they mean when they talk about "thinking" and have no difficulty identifying it when it is going on in their own heads. We are prepared to believe other human beings think because we have experience of it ourselves and accept that it is a common property of the human race. But we cannot make the same assumption about machines, and would be sceptical if one of them told us, no matter how persuasively, that it too was thinking. But sooner or later a machine will make just such a declaration and the question then will be, how do we decide whether to believe it or not?

When Turing tackled the machine-thought issue, he proposed a characteristically brilliant solution which, while not entirely free from flaws, is nevertheless the best that has yet been put forward. The key to it all, he pointed out, is to ask what the signs and signals are that humans give out, from which we infer that *they* are thinking. It is clearly a matter of *what kind of conversation we can have with them,* and has nothing to do with what kind of face they have and what kind of clothes they wear. Unfortunately physical appearances automatically set up prejudices in our minds, and if we were having a spirited conversation with a microprocessor we might be very sceptical about its capacity for thought, simply because it did not look like any thinking thing we had seen in the past. But we *would* be interested in what it had to say; and thus Turing invented his experiment or test.

Put a human—the judge or tester—in a room where there are two computer terminals, one connected to a computer, the other to a person. The judge, of course, does not know which terminal is connected to which, but can type into either terminal and receive typed messages back on them. Now the judge's job is to decide, by carrying out conversations with the entities on the end of the respective terminals, *which is which.* If the computer is very stupid, it will immediately be revealed as such and the human will have no difficulty identifying it. If it is bright, he may find that he can carry on quite a good conversation with it, though he may ultimately spot that it must be the computer. If it is exceptionally bright and has a wide range of knowledge, he may find it impossible to say whether it is the computer he is talking to or the person. In this case, Turing argues, the computer will have passed the test and could for all practical purposes be said to be a thinking machine.

The argument has a simple but compelling force: if the intellectual exchange we achieve with a machine is indistinguishable from that we have with a being we *know* to be thinking, then we are, to all intents and purposes, communicating with another thinking being. This, by the way, does not imply that the personal experience, state of consciousness, level of awareness or whatever, if the entity is going to be the same as that experienced by a human when he or she thinks, so the test is not for these particular qualities. They are not, in any case, the parameters which concern the observer.

At first the Turing Test may seem a surprising way of looking at the problem, but it is an extremely sensible way of approaching it. The question now arises: is any computer at present in existence capable of passing the test?—And if not, how long is it likely to be before one comes along? From time to time one laboratory or another claims that a computer has had at least a pretty good stab at it. Scientists using the big computer conferencing systems (each scientist has a terminal in his office and is connected to his colleagues via the computer, which acts as host and general message-sorter) often find it difficult to be sure, for a brief period of time at least, whether they are talking to the computer or to one of their colleagues. On one celebrated occasion at MIT, two scientists had been chatting via the network when one of them left the scene without telling the other, who carried on a cheery conversation with the computer under the assumption that he was talking to his friend. I have had the same spooky experience when chatting with computers which I have programmed myself, and often find their answers curiously perceptive and unpredictable.

To give another interesting example: in the remarkable match played in Toronto in August 1978 between the International Chess Master, David Levy, and the then computer chess champion of the world, Northwestern University's "Chess 4.7," the computer made a number of moves of an uncannily "human" nature. The effect was so powerful that Levy subsequently told me that he found it difficult to believe that he was not facing an outstanding human opponent. Few chess buffs who looked at the move-by-move transcripts of the match were, without prior knowledge, able to tell which had been made by the computer and which by the flesh-and-blood chess master. David Levy himself suggested that Chess 4.7 had effectively passed the Turing Test.

It would be nice to believe that I had been present on such an historic occasion, but this did not constitute a proper "pass." In the test as Turing formulated it, the judge is allowed to converse with either of his two mystery entities on any topic that he chooses, and he may use any conversational trick he wants. Furthermore he can continue the inquisition for as long as he wants, always seeking some clue that will force the computer to reveal itself. Both the computer and the human can lie if they want to in their attempts to fool the tester, so the answers to questions like "Are you the computer?" or "Do you watch much television?" will not give much away. Obviously any computer with a chance in hell of passing the test will have to have a pretty substantial bank of software at its disposal, and not just be extremely bright in one area. Chess 4.7 for example might look as though it was think-

ing if it was questioned about chess, or, better still, invited to play the game, but switch the area of discourse to human anatomy, politics or good restaurants and it would be shown up as a dunderhead.

As things stand at present, computers have quite a way to go before they jump the hurdle so cleverly laid out for them by Turing. But this should not be taken as providing unmitigated comfort for those who resist the notion of advanced machine intelligence. It should now be clear that the difference, in intellectual terms, between a human being and a computer is one of degree and not of kind.

Turing himself says in his *Mind* paper that he feels computers will have passed the test before the turn of the century, and there is little doubt that he would dearly have liked to live long enough to be around on the splendiferous occasion when "machine thinking" first occurred. . . .

Does Turing's prediction of the relative imminence of very intelligent machines still hold? I believe it does, for two reasons. In the first place there is a misleading feature of the Turing Test which we have already touched on, but which might need spelling out a bit more. This is that it is offered up as a test for a *thinking*, and not for an *intelligent* machine. A thinking machine would, of course, have to be an intelligent one, but an intelligent—even super-intelligent—machine might not necessarily be capable of thinking. While colossal resources might have to be allocated over quite a few decades in order to give a computer the breadth of software needed to pass the Turing Test, the allocation of far fewer resources over a much shorter period of time could be enough to make a computer zoom up the IQ scale in one or two areas of knowledge or understanding. The fact that with quite minimal resources, computer chess IQ has already passed that of 99.5 per cent of mankind should be a clear smoke signal.

In the second place, as with almost all areas of scientific advance, progress tends to accelerate. Add to that a novel feature. As cheaper computer-power becomes available, it will become more realistic to apply the power of the computer to help improve its own software and hardware. The paradox of something being used to solve its own problems is an apparent one only. Men can be used to help solve other men's problems and the same applies to computers. Already work is beginning in this field and it is likely that some progress will have been made by the early 1980s. A good deal of the effort, one suspects, will come from the vast band of enthusiastic amateurs—the hobbyists, the home-computer freaks—who are beginning to develop highly imaginative software purely for the fun of it. But more will come from the giant computer corporations and the huge software houses, who will see the advantages that will accrue to anyone who pulls the computer in to help with his work. The outcome should be a sharp advance in machine intelligence, if only along certain fronts. To the computer enthusiast this is exciting enough, but yet another factor, even more potent, will by this time be coming into play.

The idea, so far as I can tell, was first put forward by I. J. Good . . . when he commented on a remark made by the distinguished British scientist Lord Bowden. Bowden said that there seemed to be little point in spending vast sums of money on creating a computer as intelligent as a human when the world was already heavily overpopulated with intelligent beings, all of whom could be created quite easily, relatively cheaply and in a far more enjoyable way. This was a witty (and salutary) remark, but it missed an important point. If one could, with a given expenditure of time, money and effort, develop a computer with the overall intelligence of a man, then one could, presumably, with a bit of extra effort, make one which was *more* intelligent than a man. Man's intelligence, according to our definition, easily transcends that of any other creature on the planet, but there is no suggestion that it represents the pinnacle of intellectual capability. It is certainly the best that evolution has been able to achieve in the time that it has had at its disposal, but there is no reason to suppose that, given an equivalent amount of time and sufficient evolutionary pressure, further advances in human intelligence might not result. Unfortunately the world is in such a perilous condition that we do not have the time to hang around for this to happen—a grim fact that more and more people are beginning to grasp. The logical outcome must be a growing realization of the importance of channelling

considerable effort into machine intelligence, not simply to produce an intellectual equivalent of Man but, in due course, his intellectual superior. This intriguing search has been described by Jack Good as the quest for the Ultra-Intelligent Machine.

The concept of the Ultra-Intelligent Machine (or UIM as it is abbreviated) is a controversial, challenging and, at the same time, slightly frightening one—the more so because it is a logically coherent idea which springs naturally out of our present understanding of computer science. By Good's definition an Ultra-Intelligent Machine is a computer programmed to perform any intellectual activity at least marginally better than Man. Intellectual activity, incidentally, excludes such things as enjoying bacon and eggs and admiring good-looking men or women, and includes such things as solving problems, making tactical decisions, exploring logical possibilities and even carrying on interesting conversations. Good points out it might be necessary to teach the computer some of the principles of aesthetics—a task which is already being attempted on an experimental basis at one or two computer centers—for the computer's conversations might be horribly bland and limited without some understanding of aesthetics. But the most interesting question to consider is what will we do with the Ultra-Intelligent Machines when they arrive?

Clearly, the first thing would be to put them to work on some of the numerous problems facing society. These could be economic, medical or educational matters, and also, perhaps, strategic modelling to forecast trends and produce "early warnings" of difficulties or crises. Weather forecasting, for example, has already been substantially improved through computer analysis, and has great economic significance in parts of the world where the climate is unpredictable and hostile. But as the UIMs improve and expand their capabilities, other areas of interest will fall to their inspection with substantial benefits to mankind. . . .

Progress will be slow at first, for the problems are numerous and complex. Nevertheless, if we so choose, limitless computer effort could be applied, and sooner or later machine intelligence will be not only above that of humans, but also above that of the first UIMs. Then the second generation of UIMs will be available for work and they, too, will be put to general problem-solving and, because of their enhanced IQ, might advance at a dramatic pace. Some Mark 2 UIMs could be assigned to produce further advances in artificial intelligence and a *third* generation of even smarter machines would result. And so it will go on: the brighter the machines, the more capable they will be of enhancing their own intelligence, and they will begin to leap-frog ahead, each bound being progressively larger than the previous one.

The exponential progress of UIMs, once they get the bit between their teeth, is something which I. J. Good and many other workers in artificial intelligence hold to be more or less inevitable. For a number of reasons, I think it is a possibility but nowhere near a certainty. The problem could be solved by simply refusing to push artificial intelligence any further than it is at present. Some workers (a small minority indeed) believe this is by far the best course. Perhaps it *would* be, if the only gain of artificial intelligence studies was to satisfy our own intellectual curiosity, or to amuse ourselves with clever computer chess partners or tireless intellectual chatting companions.

But the gains are likely to be far more concrete and substantial. Even the most optimistic fan of human beings will admit that our world is in a most dangerously muddled state, and Man, unaided, is unlikely to be able to do much to improve it. Many people feel that the longer he remains at the job the worse the muddle will be, and that the only solution would be to blow everything up with a couple of hundred hydrogen bombs—a most likely possibility, unfortunately. The realization of our desperate plight in a world hopelessly over-complicated and overloaded with information, will become glaringly apparent in the turbulent 1980s when the full impact of the Computer Revolution will be upon us. In such circumstances the temptation to turn to the computer for assistance will be overwhelming. Once we have yielded, however, things will never be the same again. Man, for so long the sole and undisputed master of the planet, will no longer have to face the universe alone. Other intelligences, initially comparable, and later vastly superior, will stand by his side.

Questions for Reflection

1. Which of the seven objections to strong AI do you think is the strongest? How effective is Evans's reply to it?

2. Do you agree with Evans that humans are like computers in that our creativity is based on our "programming" and background experiences in life?

3. Is the Turing Test an effective way to decide if computers can think? Suppose that someday a computer passes the test. Would you then agree that computers are equal in intelligence to humans? Why?

JOHN SEARLE

Computer Programs Can Only Simulate Thinking

John Searle (1932–   ) is the Mills Professor of the Philosophy of Mind and Language at the University of California at Berkeley. He has published 10 books and over 140 articles on language and the philosophy of mind. The following selection contains his attack on strong AI known as the "Chinese Room Argument." It has caused quite a stir among computer scientists and philosophers ever since he first introduced it.

Reading Questions

1. What is strong AI?
2. Why does Searle say that the fact that computer programs are merely a collection of formal symbols is fatal to the view that they can be identical to mental processes?
3. In Searle's thought experiment, how is his response to the Chinese symbols similar to a computer program responding to linguistic input? How is it different from the response of someone who actually understands Chinese? What is the point of the story?
4. What are the two arguments used against Searle that he discusses? What is his reply to each?
5. What is Searle's final answer to the question "Can a digital computer think?" Why does he give this answer?
6. What is the distinction he makes between duplication and simulation? How does this distinction apply to artificial intelligence?
7. What are the four conclusions Searle draws from his main points?

Though we do not know in detail how the brain functions, we do know enough to have an idea of the general relationships between brain processes and mental processes. Mental processes are caused by the behaviour of elements of the brain. At the same time, they are realised in the structure that is made up of those elements. I think this answer is consistent with the standard biological approaches to biological phenomena. Indeed, it is a kind of commonsense answer to the question, given what we know about how the world works. However, it is very much a minority point of view. The prevailing view in philosophy, psychology, and artificial intelligence is one which emphasizes the analogies between the functioning of the human brain and the functioning of digital computers. According to the most extreme version of this view, the brain is just a digital computer and the mind is just a computer program. One could summarise this view—I call it "strong artificial intelligence," or "strong AI"—by saying that the mind is to the brain, as the program is to the computer hardware.

This view has the consequence that there is nothing essentially biological about the human

From John Searle, *Minds, Brains, and Science* (Cambridge, MA: Harvard University Press, 1984).

mind. The brain just happens to be one of an indefinitely large number of different kinds of hardware computers that could sustain the programs which make up human intelligence. On this view, any physical system whatever that had the right program with the right inputs and outputs would have a mind in exactly the same sense that you and I have minds. So, for example, if you made a computer out of old beer cans powered by windmills; if it had the right program, it would have to have a mind. And the point is not that for all we know it might have thoughts and feelings, but rather that it must have thoughts and feelings, because that is all there is to having thoughts and feelings: implementing the right program.

Most people who hold this view think we have not yet designed programs which are minds. But there is pretty much general agreement among them that it's only a matter of time until computer scientists and workers in artificial intelligence design the appropriate hardware and programs which will be the equivalent of human brains and minds. These will be artificial brains and minds which are in every way the equivalent of human brains and minds.

Many people outside of the field of artificial intelligence are quite amazed to discover that anybody could believe such a view as this. So, before criticising it, let me give you a few examples of the things that people in this field have actually said. Herbert Simon of Carnegie-Mellon University says that we already have machines that can literally think. There is no question of waiting for some future machine, because existing digital computers already have thoughts in exactly the same sense that you and I do. Well, fancy that! Philosophers have been worried for centuries about whether or not a machine could think, and now we discover that they already have such machines at Carnegie-Mellon. Simon's colleague Alan Newell claims that we have now discovered (and notice that Newell says "discovered" and not "hypothesised" or "considered the possibility," but we have *discovered*) that intelligence is just a matter of physical symbol manipulation; it has no essential connection with any specific kind of biological or physical wetware or hardware. Rather, any system whatever that is capable of manipulating physical symbols in the right way is capable of intelligence in the same literal sense as human intelligence of human beings. Both Simon and Newell, to their credit, emphasise that there is nothing metaphorical about these claims; they mean them quite literally. Freeman Dyson is quoted as having said that computers have an advantage over the rest of us when it comes to evolution. Since consciousness is just a matter of formal processes, in computers these formal processes can go on in substances that are much better able to survive in a universe that is cooling off than beings like ourselves made of our wet and messy materials. Marvin Minsky of MIT says that the next generation of computers will be so intelligent that we will "be lucky if they are willing to keep us around the house as household pets." My all-time favourite in the literature of exaggerated claims on behalf of the digital computer is from John McCarthy, the inventor of the term "artificial intelligence." McCarthy says even "machines as simple as thermostats can be said to have beliefs." And indeed, according to him, almost any machine capable of problem-solving can be said to have beliefs. I admire McCarthy's courage. I once asked him: "What beliefs does your thermostat have?" And he said: "My thermostat has three beliefs—it's too hot in here, it's too cold in here, and it's just right in here." As a philosopher, I like all these claims for a simple reason. Unlike most philosophical theses, they are reasonably clear, and they admit of a simple and decisive refutation. It is this refutation that I am going to undertake in this chapter.

The nature of the refutation has nothing whatever to do with any particular stage of computer technology. It is important to emphasise this point because the temptation is always to think that the solution to our problems must wait on some as yet uncreated technological wonder. But in fact, the nature of the refutation is completely independent of any state of technology. It has to do with the very definition of a digital computer, with what a digital computer is.

It is essential to our conception of a digital computer that its operations can be specified purely formally; that is, we specify the steps in the operation of the computer in terms of abstract symbols—

sequences of zeroes and ones printed on a tape, for example. A typical computer "rule" will determine that when a machine is in a certain state and it has a certain symbol on its tape, then it will perform a certain operation such as erasing the symbol or printing another symbol and then enter another state such as moving the tape one square to the left. But the symbols have no meaning; they have no semantic content; they are not about anything. They have to be specified purely in terms of their formal or syntactical structure. The zeroes and ones, for example, are just numerals; they don't even stand for numbers. Indeed, it is this feature of digital computers that makes them so powerful. One and the same type of hardware, if it is appropriately designed, can be used to run an indefinite range of different programs. And one and the same program can be run on an indefinite range of different types of hardwares.

But this feature of programs, that they are defined purely formally or syntactically, is fatal to the view that mental processes and program processes are identical. And the reason can be stated quite simply. There is more to having a mind than having formal or syntactical processes. Our internal mental states, by definition, have certain sorts of contents. If I am thinking about Kansas City or wishing that I had a cold beer to drink or wondering if there will be a fall in interest rates, in each case my mental state has a certain mental content in addition to whatever formal features it might have. That is, even if my thoughts occur to me in strings of symbols, there must be more to the thought than the abstract strings, because strings by themselves can't have any meaning. If my thoughts are to be *about* anything, then the strings must have a *meaning* which makes the thoughts about those things. In a word, the mind has more than a syntax, it has a semantics. The reason that no computer program can ever be a mind is simply that a computer program is only syntactical, and minds are more than syntactical. Minds are semantical, in the sense that they have more than a formal structure, they have a content.

To illustrate this point I have designed a certain thought-experiment. Imagine that a bunch of computer programmers have written a program that

will enable a computer to simulate the understanding of Chinese. So, for example, if the computer is given a question in Chinese, it will match the question against its memory, or data base, and produce appropriate answers to the questions in Chinese. Suppose for the sake of argument that the computer's answers are as good as those of a native Chinese speaker. Now then, does the computer, on the basis of this, understand Chinese, does it literally understand Chinese, in the way that Chinese speakers understand Chinese? Well, imagine that you are locked in a room, and in this room are several baskets full of Chinese symbols. Imagine that you (like me) do not understand a word of Chinese, but that you are given a rule book in English for manipulating these Chinese symbols. The rules specify the manipulations of the symbols purely formally, in terms of their syntax, not their semantics. So the rule might say: "Take a squiggle-squiggle sign out of basket number one and put it next to a squoggle-squoggle sign from basket number two." Now suppose that some other Chinese symbols are passed into the room, and that you are given further rules for passing back Chinese symbols out of the room. Suppose that unknown to you the symbols passed into the room are called "questions" by the people outside the room, and the symbols you pass back out of the room are called "answers to the questions." Suppose, furthermore, that the programmers are so good at designing the programs and that you are so good at manipulating the symbols, that very soon your answers are indistinguishable from those of a native Chinese speaker. There you are locked in your room shuffling your Chinese symbols and passing out Chinese symbols in response to incoming Chinese symbols. On the basis of the situation as I have described it, there is no way you could learn any Chinese simply by manipulating these formal symbols.

Now the point of the story is simply this: by virtue of implementing a formal computer program from the point of view of an outside observer, you behave exactly as if you understood Chinese, but all the same you don't understand a word of Chinese. But if going through the appropriate computer program for understanding Chinese is not enough to give you an understanding of Chinese, then it is not enough to give *any other digital computer* an understanding of Chinese. And again, the reason for this can be stated quite simply. If you don't understand Chinese, then no other computer could understand Chinese because no digital computer, just by virtue of running a program, has anything that you don't have. All that the computer has, as you have, is a formal program for manipulating uninterpreted Chinese symbols. To repeat, a computer has a syntax, but no semantics. The whole point of the parable of the Chinese room is to remind us of a fact that we knew all along. Understanding a language, or indeed, having mental states at all, involves more than just having a bunch of formal symbols. It involves having an interpretation, or a meaning attached to those symbols. And a digital computer, as defined, cannot have more than just formal symbols because the operation of the computer, as I said earlier, is defined in terms of its ability to implement programs. And these programs are purely formally specifiable—that is, they have no semantic content.

We can see the force of this argument if we contrast what it is like to be asked and to answer questions in English, and to be asked and to answer questions in some language where we have no knowledge of any of the meanings of the words. Imagine that in the Chinese room you are also given questions in English about such things as your age or your life history, and that you answer these questions. What is the difference between the Chinese case and the English case? Well again, if like me you understand no Chinese and you do understand English, then the difference is obvious. You understand the questions in English because they are expressed in symbols whose meanings are known to you. Similarly, when you give the answers in English you are producing symbols which are meaningful to you. But in the case of the Chinese, you have none of that. In the case of the Chinese, you simply manipulate formal symbols according to a computer program, and you attach no meaning to any of the elements.

Various replies have been suggested to this argument by workers in artificial intelligence and in psychology, as well as philosophy. They all have something in common; they are all inadequate.

And there is an obvious reason why they have to be inadequate, since the argument rests on a very simple logical truth, namely, syntax alone is not sufficient for semantics, and digital computers insofar as they are computers have, by definition, a syntax alone.

I want to make this clear by considering a couple of the arguments that are often presented against me.

Some people attempt to answer the Chinese room example by saying that the whole system understands Chinese. The idea here is that though I, the person in the room manipulating the symbols do not understand Chinese, I am just the central processing unit of the computer system. They argue that it is the whole system, including the room, the baskets full of symbols and the ledgers containing the programs and perhaps other items as well, taken as a totality, that understands Chinese. But this is subject to exactly the same objection I made before. There is no way that the system can get from the syntax to the semantics. I, as the central processing unit, have no way of figuring out what any of these symbols means; but then neither does the whole system.

Another common response is to imagine that we put the Chinese understanding program inside a robot. If the robot moved around and interacted causally with the world, wouldn't that be enough to guarantee that it understood Chinese? Once again the inexorability of the semantics-syntax distinction overcomes this manoeuvre. As long as we suppose that the robot has only a computer for a brain then, even though it might behave exactly as if it understood Chinese, it would still have no way of getting from the syntax to the semantics of Chinese. You can see this if you imagine that I am the computer. Inside a room in the robot's skull I shuffle symbols without knowing that some of them come in to me from television cameras attached to the robot's head and others go out to move the robot's arms and legs. As long as all I have is a formal computer program, I have no way of attaching any meaning to any of the symbols. And the fact that the robot is engaged in causal interactions with the outside world won't help me to attach any meaning to the symbols unless I have some way of finding out about that fact. Suppose the robot picks up a hamburger and this triggers the symbol for hamburger to come into the room. As long as all I have is the symbol with no knowledge of its causes or how it got there, I have no way of knowing what it means. The causal interactions between the robot and the rest of the world are irrelevant unless those causal interactions are represented in some mind or other. But there is no way they can be if all that the so-called mind consists of is a set of purely formal, syntactical operations.

It is important to see exactly what is claimed and what is not claimed by my argument. Suppose we ask the question that I mentioned at the beginning: "Could a machine think?" Well, in one sense, of course, we are all machines. We can construe the stuff inside our heads as a meat machine. And of course, we can all think. So, in one sense of "machine," namely that sense in which a machine is just a physical system which is capable of performing certain kinds of operations, in that sense, we are all machines, and we can think. So, trivially, there are machines that can think. But that wasn't the question that bothered us. So let's try a different formulation of it. Could an artefact think? Could a man-made machine think? Well, once again, it depends on the kind of artefact. Suppose we designed a machine that was molecule-for-molecule indistinguishable from a human being. Well then, if you can duplicate the causes, you can presumably duplicate the effects. So once again, the answer to that question is, in principle at least, trivially yes. If you could build a machine that had the same structure as a human being, then presumably that machine would be able to think. Indeed, it would be a surrogate human being. Well, let's try again.

The question isn't: "Can a machine think?" or: "Can an artefact think?" The question is: "Can a digital computer think?" But once again we have to be very careful in how we interpret the question. From a mathematical point of view, anything whatever can be described *as if* it were a digital computer. And that's because it can be described as instantiating or implementing a computer program. In an utterly trivial sense, the pen that is on the desk in front of me can be described as a digital computer. It just happens to have a very boring computer program. The program says: "Stay there." Now since in this sense, anything whatever is a digital computer, because anything whatever can be described as implementing a computer program, then once again, our question gets a trivial answer. Of course our brains are digital computers, since they implement any number of computer programs. And of course our brains can think. So once again, there is a trivial answer to the question. But that wasn't really the question we were trying to ask. The question we wanted to ask is this: "Can a digital computer, as defined, think?" That is to say: "Is instantiating or implementing the right computer program with the right inputs and outputs, sufficient for, or constitutive of, thinking?" And to this question, unlike its predecessors, the answer is clearly "no." And it is "no" for the reason that we have spelled out, namely, the computer program is defined purely syntactically. But thinking is more than just a matter of manipulating meaningless symbols, it involves meaningful semantic contents. These semantic contents are what we mean by "meaning."

It is important to emphasise again that we are not talking about a particular stage of computer technology. The argument has nothing to do with the forthcoming, amazing advances in computer science. It has nothing to do with the distinction between serial and parallel processes, or with the size of programs, or the speed of computer operations, or with computers that can interact causally with their environment, or even with the invention of robots. Technological progress is always grossly exaggerated, but even subtracting the exaggeration, the development of computers has been quite remarkable, and we can reasonably expect that even more remarkable progress will be made in the future. No doubt we will be much better able to simulate human behaviour on computers than we can at present, and certainly much better than we have been able to in the past. The point I am making is that if we are talking about having mental states, having a mind, all of these simulations are simply irrelevant. It doesn't matter how good the technology is, or how rapid the calculations made by the computer are. If it really is a computer, its operations have to be defined syntactically, whereas consciousness, thoughts, feelings, emotions, and all the rest of it involve more than a syntax. Those features, by definition, the computer is unable to *duplicate* however powerful may be its ability to *simulate*. The key distinction here is between duplication and simulation. And no simulation by itself ever constitutes duplication.

What I have done so far is give a basis to the sense that those citations I began this talk with are really as preposterous as they seem. There is a puzzling question in this discussion though, and that is: "Why would anybody ever have thought that computers could think or have feelings and emotions and all the rest of it?" After all, we can do computer simulations of any process whatever that can be given a formal description. So, we can do a computer simulation of the flow of money in the British economy, or the pattern of power distribution in the Labour party. We can do computer simulation of rain storms in the home counties, or warehouse fires in East London. Now, in each of these cases, nobody supposes that the computer simulation is actually the real thing; no one supposes that a computer simulation of a storm will leave us all wet, or a computer simulation of a fire is likely to burn the house down. Why on earth would anyone in his right mind suppose a computer simulation of mental processes actually had mental processes? I don't really know the answer to that, since the idea seems to me, to put it frankly, quite crazy from the start. But I can make a couple of speculations.

First of all, where the mind is concerned, a lot of people are still tempted to some sort of behaviourism. They think if a system behaves as if it understood Chinese, then it really must understand Chinese. But we have already refuted this form of behaviourism with the Chinese room argument. Another assumption made by many people is that the mind is not a part of the biological world, it is not a part of the world of nature. The strong artificial intelligence view relies on that in its conception that the mind is purely formal; that somehow or other, it cannot be treated as a concrete product of biological processes like any other biological product. There is in these discussions, in short, a kind of residual dualism. AI partisans believe that the mind is more than a part of the natural biological world; they believe that the mind is purely formally specifiable. The paradox of this is that the AI literature is filled with fulminations against some view called "dualism," but in fact, the whole thesis of strong AI rests on a kind of dualism. It rests on a rejection of the idea that the mind is just a natural biological phenomenon in the world like any other.

I want to conclude this chapter by putting together the thesis of the last chapter and the thesis of this one. Both of these theses can be stated very simply. And indeed, I am going to state them with perhaps excessive crudeness. But if we put them together I think we get a quite powerful conception of the relations of minds, brains and computers. And the argument has a very simple logical structure, so you can see whether it is valid or invalid. The first premise is:

1. *Brains cause minds.*
   Now, of course, that is really too crude. What we mean by that is that mental processes that we consider to constitute a mind are caused, entirely caused, by processes going on inside the brain. But let's be crude, let's just abbreviate that as three words—brains cause minds. And that is just a fact about how the world works. Now let's write proposition number two:

2. *Syntax is not sufficient for semantics.*
   That proposition is a conceptual truth. It just articulates our distinction between the notion of what is purely formal and what has content. Now, to these two propositions— that brains cause minds and that syntax is not sufficient for semantics—let's add a third and a fourth:

3. *Computer programs are entirely defined by their formal, or syntactical, structure.*
   That proposition, I take it, is true by definition; it is part of what we mean by the notion of a computer program.

4. *Minds have mental contents; specifically, they have semantic contents.*

And that, I take it, is just an obvious fact about how our minds work. My thoughts, and beliefs, and desires are about something, or they refer to something, or they concern states of affairs in the world; and they do that because their content directs them at these states of affairs in the world. Now, from these four premises, we can draw our first conclusion; and it follows obviously from premises 2, 3 and 4:

CONCLUSION 1. *No computer program by itself is sufficient to give a system a mind. Programs, in short, are not minds, and they are not by themselves sufficient for having minds.*

Now, that is a very powerful conclusion, because it means that the project of trying to create minds solely by designing programs is doomed from the start. And it is important to re-emphasise that this has nothing to do with any particular state of technology or any particular state of the complexity of the program. This is a purely formal, or logical, result from a set of axioms which are agreed to by all (or nearly all) of the disputants concerned. That is, even most of the hardcore enthusiasts for artificial intelligence agree that in fact, as a matter of biology, brain processes cause mental states, and they agree that programs are defined purely formally. But if you put these conclusions together with certain other things that we know, then it follows immediately that the project of strong AI is incapable of fulfilment.

However, once we have got these axioms, let's see what else we can derive. Here is a second conclusion:

CONCLUSION 2. *The way that brain functions cause minds cannot be solely in virtue of running a computer program.*

And this second conclusion follows from conjoining the first premise together with our first conclusion. That is, from the fact that brains cause minds and that programs are not enough to do the job, it follows that the way that brains cause minds can't be solely by running a computer program. Now that also I think is an important result, because it has the consequence that the brain is not, or at least is not just, a digital computer. We saw earlier that anything can trivially be described as if it were a digital computer, and brains are no exception. But the importance of this conclusion is

that the computational properties of the brain are simply not enough to explain its functioning to produce mental states. And indeed, that ought to seem a commonsense scientific conclusion to us anyway because all it does is remind us of the fact that brains are biological engines; their biology matters. It is not, as several people in artificial intelligence have claimed, just an irrelevant fact about the mind that it happens to be realised in human brains.

Now, from our first premise, we can also derive a third conclusion:

CONCLUSION 3. *Anything else that caused minds would have to have causal powers at least equivalent to those of the brain.*

And this third conclusion is a trivial consequence of our first premise. It is a bit like saying that if my petrol engine drives my car at seventy-five miles an hour, then any diesel engine that was capable of doing that would have to have a power output at least equivalent to that of my petrol engine. Of course, some other system might cause mental processes using entirely different chemical or biochemical features from those the brain in fact uses. It might turn out that there are beings on other planets, or in other solar systems, that have mental states and use an entirely different biochemistry from ours. Suppose that Martians arrived on earth and we concluded that they had mental states. But suppose that when their heads were opened up, it was discovered that all they had inside was green slime. Well still, the green slime, if it functioned to produce consciousness and all the rest of their mental life, would have to have causal powers equal to those of the human brain. But now, from our first conclusion, that programs are not enough, and our third conclusion, that any other system would have to have causal powers equal to the brain, conclusion four follows immediately:

CONCLUSION 4. *For any artefact that we might build which had mental states equivalent to human mental states, the implementation of a computer program would not by itself be sufficient. Rather the artefact would have to have powers equivalent to the powers of the human brain.*

The upshot of this discussion I believe is to remind us of something that we have known all along: namely, mental states are biological phenomena. Consciousness, intentionality, subjectivity and mental causation are all a part of our biological life history, along with growth, reproduction, the secretion of bile, and digestion.

Questions for Reflection

1. When you say something in a conversation, what sort of responses from your listener indicates that he or she understood what you said? If a computer could respond in the same way as your friend, would this be sufficient to show that the computer had understanding and was intelligent? What would Searle say?
2. What is Searle's criterion for linguistic understanding that supports his conclusion that computers do not understand language? Is this an adequate notion of understanding?
3. In what ways would the dualist agree with Searle? How would Searle and the dualist differ?

TERRY BISSON

"They're Made Out of Meat"

In his own words, author Terry Bisson "was born a long time ago." He grew up in Kentucky and attended Grinnell College and the University of Louisville. Bisson is a member of the Authors Guild and the Science Fiction and Fantasy Writers of America. He has published six novels as well as several children's books and his fiction and nonfiction work has appeared in numerous magazines. His fiction has received a number of national and international awards. He currently resides and writes in New York and occasionally teaches courses on science fiction writing.

As Christopher Evans points out (reading 43), many humans raise objections against the notion that computers or robots could ever think. As he says, many of these objections are emotional ones and based on our inability to imagine that something as different from us as a machine could think like us. In this science fiction story, Terry Bisson imagines that the shoe is on the other foot.

Reading Questions

1. If the speakers in this story are not made out of meat (flesh), then who are they?
2. Who is the "meat" they have discovered in the universe?

Terry Bisson, "They're Made Out of Meat," *Omni* (April 1991).

3. Why does the senior scientist have problems with the notion of thinking meat?

4. How does this story relate to the issue of whether computers can think?

"They're made out of meat."

"Meat?"

"Meat. They're made out of meat."

"Meat?"

"There's no doubt about it. We picked up several from different parts of the planet, took them aboard our recon vessels, and probed them all the way through. They're completely meat."

"That's impossible. What about the radio signals? The messages to the stars?"

"They use the radio waves to talk, but the signals don't come from them. The signals come from machines."

"So who made the machines? That's who we want to contact."

"They made the machines. That's what I'm trying to tell you. Meat made the machines."

"That's ridiculous. How can meat make a machine? You're asking me to believe in sentient meat."

"I'm not asking you, I'm telling you. These creatures are the only sentient race in that sector and they're made out of meat."

"Maybe they're like the orfolei. You know, a carbon-based intelligence that goes through a meat stage."

"Nope. They're born meat and they die meat. We studied them for several of their life spans, which didn't take long. Do you have any idea what's the life span of meat?"

"Spare me. Okay, maybe they're only part meat. You know, like the weddilei. A meat head with an electron plasma brain inside."

"Nope. We thought of that, since they do have meat heads, like the weddilei. But I told you, we probed them. They're meat all the way through."

"No brain?"

"Oh, there's a brain all right. It's just that the brain is made out of meat! That's what I've been trying to tell you."

"So . . . what does the thinking?"

"You're not understanding, are you? You're refusing to deal with what I'm telling you. The brain does the thinking. The meat."

"Thinking meat! You're asking me to believe in thinking meat!"

"Yes, thinking meat! Conscious meat! Loving meat. Dreaming meat. The meat is the whole deal! Are you beginning to get the picture or do I have to start all over?"

"Omigod. You're serious then. They're made out of meat."

"Thank you. Finally. Yes. They are indeed made out of meat. And they've been trying to get in touch with us for almost a hundred of their years."

"Omigod. So what does this meat have in mind?"

"First it wants to talk to us. Then I imagine it wants to explore the Universe, contact other sentiences, swap ideas and information. The usual."

"We're supposed to talk to meat."

"That's the idea. That's the message they're sending out by radio. 'Hello. Anyone out there. Anybody home.' That sort of thing."

"They actually do talk, then. They use words, ideas, concepts?"

"Oh, yes. Except they do it with meat."

"I thought you just told me they used radio."

"They do, but what do you think is on the radio? Meat sounds. You know how when you slap or flap meat, it makes a noise? They talk by flapping their meat at each other. They can even sing by squirting air through their meat."

"Omigod. Singing meat. This is altogether too much. So what do you advise?"

"Officially or unofficially?"

"Both."

"Officially, we are required to contact, welcome and log in any and all sentient races or multibeings in this quadrant of the Universe, without prejudice, fear or favor. Unofficially, I advise that we erase the records and forget the whole thing."

"I was hoping you would say that."

"It seems harsh, but there is a limit. Do we really want to make contact with meat?"

"I agree one hundred percent. What's there to say? 'Hello, meat. How's it going?' But will this work? How many planets are we dealing with here?"

"Just one. They can travel to other planets in special meat containers, but they can't live on them. And being meat, they can only travel through C space. Which limits them to the speed of light and makes the possibility of their ever making contact pretty slim. Infinitesimal, in fact."

"So we just pretend there's no one home in the Universe."

"That's it."

"Cruel. But you said it yourself, who wants to meet meat? And the ones who have been aboard our vessels, the ones you probed? You're sure they won't remember?"

"They'll be considered crackpots if they do. We went into their heads and smoothed out their meat so that we're just a dream to them."

"A dream to meat! How strangely appropriate, that we should be meat's dream."

"And we marked the entire sector unoccupied."

"Good. Agreed, officially and unofficially. Case closed. Any others? Anyone interesting on that side of the galaxy?"

"Yes, a rather shy but sweet hydrogen core cluster intelligence in a class nine star in G445 zone. Was in contact two galactic rotations ago, wants to be friendly again."

"They always come around."

"And why not? Imagine how unbearably, how unutterably cold the Universe would be if one were all alone . . ."

Questions for Reflection

1. If you met the senior robot in the story, how would you convince this being that you could really think and were not just simulating thinking?

2. In what ways are the robots' reactions to the idea of thinking meat similar to critics' reactions to the idea of thinking machines?

3. In George Lukas's film *Star Wars,* we were presented with intelligent robots (R2D2, C3PO), who had beliefs, desires, and feelings just like ours. In the context of the story, they were made up of wires and computer chips. Yet, we can imagine ourselves relating to them just as we would any other companion. We would feel sorry for them if they became damaged. Do our emotional reactions to these characters lend plausibility to the notion that a highly intelligent machine could be psychologically similar to us?

C H A P T E R 5

Questions about Free Will and Determinism

FREEDOM AND DETERMINISM: WHAT ARE THE ISSUES?

On February 9, 1979, identical twins Jim Lewis and Jim Springer met for the first time. Having been separated at birth, the twins had lived completely apart for 39 years. During this time, there had been no contact between the two brothers, nor between the two sets of adoptive parents. In the midst of their euphoria over their rediscovery of each other, the twin brothers became aware of a series of eerie similarities in their lives and behavior. Both of them: had been married to women named Linda the first time, had married women named Betty the second time, chain-smoked the same brand of cigarettes, drank the same brand of beer, served as sheriff's deputies, had owned dogs named Toy, drove Chevys, and lived in the only house on their block. In these and numerous other ways, their lives had developed along parallel tracks.

This case and thousands like it are helping scientists get a handle on one of humanity's oldest mysteries: To what degree is human behavior influenced by heredity or environment, genes or life experiences, nature or nurture? If identical twins are raised in separate and different environments, any similarities in their behavior provide support for the thesis that much of our behavior is a product of our genes. On the other hand, the differences between such twins would have to be a result of differences in their environment or life's experiences.

What are we to make of these studies? Obviously, you did not choose many of the features that make you the person you are: the color of your eyes, hair, and skin, your sex, or your height. It would seem to be equally obvious that many facts about you are the result of decisions that you freely made: what music you listen to, who you will date, your job, the name of your dog, and your ethical beliefs. Throughout your life you feel as though it is up to you to examine the alternatives, to deliberate, and to make a choice. Surely, the twins in these studies felt as though they were freely making these sorts of decisions. Yet, it appears as though they were being forced down parallel tracks by causes of which they were not aware. While the verdict on these issues is not yet in and behavioral scientists are still debating the data, many claim that we are a lot more determined in the decisions we make than we would like to think. Hence, the question is, how do we balance the evidence that suggests we are determined with the reasons that lead us to believe we are free? Furthermore, what are the implications of all this for moral responsibility?

WHAT ARE MY OPTIONS CONCERNING HUMAN FREEDOM?

Two Questions

We can formulate the issue of freedom and determinism in terms of two questions and different combinations of answers to these questions. The two questions are

1. Are we determined?
2. Do we have the sort of freedom necessary to be morally responsible?

You can take one of three positions on the issue of freedom and determinism: hard determinism, libertarianism, and compatibilism. We will examine each one in turn.

Hard Determinism

There are two varieties of the position known as determinism (hard determinism and compatibilism). We will begin by discussing what they have in common. **Determinism** (both versions) is the claim that all events, including human choices, beliefs, desires, and actions, are the necessary result of previous causes. Determinists disagree as to which type of cause is most important in producing our behavior, whether it be our genetic inheritance, biochemistry, behavioral conditioning, or even God's will. Nevertheless, they all agree that everything that happens in nature and in human behavior is the inevitable outcome of the causal order. Obviously, anyone who is a determinist will answer "yes" to the question, "Are we determined?"

The determinist claims that human actions are just as much the product of causal necessity as is any other event in nature. The basic argument of the determinist could be formulated in the following way:

1. Every event, without exception, is causally determined by prior events.
2. Human thoughts and actions are events.
3. Therefore, human thoughts and actions are, without exception, causally determined by prior events.

Premise 1 is a statement of the thesis of universal causation. The only way to avoid determinism is to reject this thesis. But is it plausible to do so? We normally believe that every event in the external world has a cause. But aren't we being inconsistent in making our own actions and choices exceptions to this rule? The determinist argues that if we are rational, we will recognize that our actions and psychological states are the result of previous causes, as is every other event in the world. How else could we explain why we do what we do? Most of our actions are the result of acts of will that flow from our personality, our values, or our desires. But where did these come from? If we did not choose our personality, then it must have been produced by causes acting upon us.

Thus far, our discussion has focused on the points that are common to all determinists. However, there is a specific variety of this position known as hard determinism. What distinguishes the hard determinist? The hard determinist answers "no" to the second question: "Do we have the sort of freedom necessary to be morally responsible?" The reason they respond this way is that hard determinists embrace the thesis of **incompatibilism,** which is the claim that determinism is incompatible with the sort of freedom required to be morally responsible for our behavior. What does it mean to be morally responsible for an action? It means that we deserve praise or rebuke, credit or blame, reward or punishment for it. It is not a question of whether rewards or punishments are effective in causally determining a person's behavior. Instead, for the incompatibilists, moral responsibility is a question of whether we *deserve* reward or punishment. We can only deserve these consequences, they say, if we had genuine alternatives such that we could have chosen to act otherwise than we did. In other words, their claim is that having moral responsibility requires that we have a free and undetermined will. However, since hard determinists believe that we do not have this sort of freedom, they believe that the whole category of moral responsibility must be eliminated. Since our character and actions are the inevitable product of forces beyond our control, we cannot be responsible for our actions any more than we are for the size of our feet.

Libertarianism

Libertarianism is the position that rejects determinism and asserts that we *do* have freedom of the will. Hence, the libertarian answers "no" to the first question ("Are we determined?"). (Note: the libertarianism we are concerned with here is a metaphysical position and is entirely different from the political philosophy of the same name.) If libertarianism is true, then at least some human actions are free and exempt from causal necessity. Free actions are originated by the agent, are grounded in the free will of the person, and, hence, are not the inevitable result of previous causes. Accordingly, the libertarian claims that it is often impossible (even in principle) to predict every detail of a person's behavior. The libertarian can acknowledge (and most do) that it is possible for *some* of a person's actions to be determined and, hence, not free. The most obvious examples would be cases in which a person is brainwashed, hypnotized, or under the influence of drugs or medication. Nevertheless, the libertarian claims that, for the most part, while our decisions may be *influenced* by a number of factors, they are not causally *determined* by previous conditions (whether these be our prior psychological states or external factors).

The one thing that libertarians and *hard* determinists agree on is incompatibilism. They both agree that determinism is incompatible with moral responsibility. However, since the libertarians believe we do have freedom of the will, they respond "yes" to the question, "Do we have the sort of freedom necessary to be morally responsible?" To make the case that we have genuine freedom of the will, libertarians provide at least two arguments for their position: the argument from deliberation and the argument from moral responsibility.

The Argument from Deliberation   Our choices and actions frequently are preceded by a period of deliberation in which we weigh the evidence, consider the pros and cons of our alternatives, calculate the probable consequences of an action, and evaluate all these data in terms of our values and desires. In this sort of situation, the libertarian claims, we experience the fact that the decision is not already latent in the causes acting on us, but instead we have a distinct sense that we are actively deciding what the decision will be. Contrary to the determinist's account, when we deliberate we are not simply like a metal ball suspended between two opposing magnetic fields. Rather than passively awaiting the outcome of the war between our conflicting motives, goals, or desires, we often find ourselves actively choosing which one will prevail.

The Argument from Moral Responsibility   If someone devotes her spare time to building houses for the poor, we would be inclined to say that her actions are morally good, commendable, admirable, laudable, and praiseworthy. On the other hand, if someone emotionally hurts other people by pretending to love them only to get something from them, we would want to say his behavior was morally bad, shabby, despicable, contemptible, and blameworthy. But could we make these judgments about people if their actions were the inevitable outcome of deterministic causes? If the determinist is correct in saying that all our behavior is the result of causes over which we have no control, then the humanitarian who builds houses for the poor should no more be praised for her actions or the deceiver condemned for his than the humanitarian should be applauded for having low blood pressure and the deceiver denounced for having high blood pressure. In the final analysis, determinism implies that our eye color, blood pressure, and moral character are all products of causes that operate upon us and whose outcomes we did not choose. But the libertarians argue that morality is one of the most significant features of our humanity. Furthermore, they say, the experiential evidence for our own and others' moral responsibility is at least as strong as that for the more speculative thesis of universal causation. As the 18th-century English writer Samuel Johnson is reputed to have said, "All theory is against freedom of the will, all experience for it."

Compatibilism

It might seem as though the previous two positions cover all the options. However, there is another variety of determinism known as compatibilism. **Compatibilism** is the claim that we are both 100 percent determined *and* have the sort of freedom necessary to be morally responsible for our actions. Sometimes compatibilism is referred to as **soft determinism.** However, do not interpret this label to mean that these determinists are "soft" on determinism, for they believe that the thesis of universal causation applies to all human actions. Since compatibilists claim we have moral responsibility, they believe the implications of determinism are not as severe as the hard determinist claims (hence the label *soft* determinism).

It should be clear that compatibilists answer "yes" to both of our questions. Since compatibilists believe in both determinism and freedom, what sort of freedom do they think we have? According to the compatibilist, an action is free to the degree that the immediate cause of your action is your own will, choices, values, or desires. If an action results from your own psychological states, then it is a free or voluntary action for which you can be held responsible. At the same time, the compatibilist insists that your personality, motives, and values are completely determined by previous causes. However, contrary to the hard determinist and the libertarian, the compatibilist believes that being free of causes external to our own psychological states is the only kind of freedom necessary for us to be responsible for our choices and actions. Table 5.1 outlines these three positions on free will and determinism.

All three positions on freedom and determinism are ably represented in the selections to follow. Baron d'Holbach will defend the hard determinist position. C. A. Campbell will advocate libertarianism. W. T. Stace will provide arguments for compatibilism.

TABLE 5.1 THREE POSITIONS ON FREEDOM AND DETERMINISM

Philosophical Positions	1 Are We Determined?	2 Do We Have the Sort of Freedom Necessary to Be Morally Responsible?
Hard Determinism	Yes	No
Libertarianism	No	Yes
Compatibilism	Yes	Yes

Finally, B. F. Skinner will take on the difficult task of explaining how the determinist can account for human creativity. The practical implications of this philosophical debate will be explored in the Contemporary Application question: Can Criminals Be Held Morally Responsible for Their Actions? C. S. Lewis will argue that anything less than a libertarian account of moral responsibility will have dire consequences for society and for the criminal as well. Clarence Darrow will attempt to make the case that hard determinism is true and that none of us are responsible for our actions because none of us made our own personality.

OPENING NARRATIVE: WHEN ARE WE MORALLY RESPONSIBLE FOR OUR ACTIONS?

JONATHAN HARRISON

The Case of Dr. Svengali

Jonathan Harrison was a professor of philosophy at the University of Nottingham until his retirement a few years ago. He has published numerous articles and books on a variety of topics.

In this troubling piece of science fiction, Harrison goes beyond the issue of what controls our behavior to the deeper issue of what controls our desires. Obviously, our desires are not controlled by a mad scientist's machine as are those of the characters in the story. Nevertheless, Harrison leaves us wondering what does control our desires and if we are in any significant sense different than the characters in the story. Furthermore, this story raises questions concerning the type of freedom necessary for moral responsibility.

Reading Questions

1. In his first experiment, Dr. Svengali is able to make Mrs. O'Farrell behave the way he wants her to behave. Why does he find the results unacceptable?
2. In a later experiment, Dr. Svengali is eventually able to make Mrs. O'Farrell want to cook, but she still resents the fact that she wants to cook. In what way is her conflict of desires similar to the case of an alcoholic who wants to drink but regrets the fact that he or she wants to drink?
3. In what sense are both Mrs. O'Farrell and the alcoholic free? In what sense are they not free?
4. How does Dr. Svengali solve the problem of Mrs. O'Farrell resenting the fact that she desires to cook and clean the house?
5. Why does the court decide that Dr. Svengali was not morally responsible for his crimes? Do you agree with them?

Once upon a time Dr. Thomas Svengali was walking by the side of a lake when he saw some children playing with their boats. They were model boats of course, but it was possible to control them by short-wave radio. In this way they could be made to go through all the manoeuvres which life-sized boats could execute, but in an unrealistically jerky way, like mice pretending to be elephants.

This gave Dr. Svengali an idea. It was not an original one. Even some twentieth-century philosophers had had it before him. Had he not spent so much of his life immersed in his study of the human brain he would probably have had it before. He had recently been experiencing a great deal of trouble with his housekeeper, a Mrs. Geraldine O'Farrell. He had never liked the new-fangled

From Jonathan Harrison, "Tom & Jerry, or What Price Pelagius?" *Religious Studies 17* (December 1981).

practice of having his house run by a computer, but being as unversed in the ways of the opposite sex as he was knowledgeable about brain physiology and electronics, he had not the faintest idea how to manage a woman. And the fact that Mrs. O'Farrell considered that she would not have been compelled to occupy her present poorly paid position had it not been for the deplorably inequitable way in which her sex was treated made her quite exceptionally and often quite deliberately incompetent.

It occurred to Dr. Svengali that if he could not make her perform her household duties in any other way he might insert a device into her skull which would enable her to be controlled by a short-wave radio transmitter, which Dr. Svengali prudently kept locked in a cupboard when not in use, out of Mrs. O'Farrell's reach. Though this transmitter could, if necessary, be worked manually, doing so would save Dr. Svengali only labour, but no time. Hence, when familiarity caused him no longer to regard it as a plaything, he built into it a programmer which, at the appointed hours, caused Mrs. O'Farrell to cook, shop and clean, without any further intervention on his part. When these things were not necessary the transmitter automatically switched itself off, and left Mrs. O'Farrell to do what she thought she pleased.

Dr. Svengali found, however, that this way of solving the problem presented by Mrs. O'Farrell's intransigence had a drawback. Though her limbs went through the movements of polishing and bed-making in a highly efficient and satisfactory way, the expression on her face was disturbingly resentful, and her language so appalling as to be quite unacceptable to someone as gently nurtured as Dr. Svengali. It was also extremely embarrassing to him when he had visitors.

To a man of Dr. Svengali's ability the task of modifying the controlling device in Mrs. O'Farrell's brain in such a way as to produce a more pleasing facial expression and a less colourful vocabulary was easily accomplished. Dr. Svengali, however, was a sensitive man, and he found the mere knowledge of the resentment that Mrs. O'Farrell felt, but could not express, extremely disturbing to him. And though a very poor housekeeper, she had been a good companion, and

resentment at being forced to do her work in such a humiliating manner made her extremely disagreeable to Dr. Svengali in the evenings. Most of these she spent in reproaching him bitterly for the way in which he treated her, and in trying to bring home to him how dreadful it was to find one's limbs manipulated from without—just as if, as Mrs. O'Farrell herself strikingly and originally put it, she was possessed.

Dr. Svengali took longer to solve this second problem. He reasoned that just as he could move Mrs. O'Farrell's limbs, so he could produce or eradicate the desires which normally made her move them. Hence he thought he might make her a better housekeeper without at the same time making her a worse companion if he built a modified device, which would make her *want* to cook, shop and clean at the required times.

Promising though this idea seemed to Dr. Svengali when it first occurred to him, it in fact turned out to be a complete failure. Mrs. O'Farrell did, at the times the controlling device decided that she should, want to cook, clean and shop. But by now she had become so incensed that no such inducement would make her perform these duties well. However intensely Dr. Svengali's machine made her want to do things, she regarded the desires so produced as akin to temptations from the devil. A calvinistic upbringing and a naturally obdurate disposition aided her in her determination to resist, and she very rarely succumbed. When the strength of her wants became overwhelming and, for a short while she did her work in a satisfactory way, she was subsequently so overcome with exasperation and remorse that she treated Dr. Svengali in the evenings in a way which he found nearly unendurable.

Clearly, Dr. Svengali thought, he must modify his device a second time. He decided that the easiest thing to do was simply to combine the first two versions of it, and insert in Mrs. O'Farrell's brain a dual instrument which both made her limbs adequately perform her external tasks, and which also made her want to do, and enjoy doing, them, though it was in fact the instrument, and not the wants, which produced the movements. But Mrs. O'Farrell's fanaticism was so implacable that even the knowledge that in caring for Dr. Svengali, she was simply doing what she herself wanted to do, did little, if anything, to diminish the hostility with which she treated him when the transmitter was switched off.

Since a remote ancestor of hers had once read philosophy in a twentieth-century British university, her mother had inherited some books and journals. One of them, she had been told, contained an article by someone called Harrison, arguing that a man was free so long as he was doing what he wanted to do. In a rare philosophical moment, Mrs. O'Farrell reasoned that, in cooking, shopping and cleaning she was doing what she wanted to do. Nevertheless, so far from being free, she was even more helpless than when she had been controlled by Dr. Svengali's first device, which had made her look after him, even when she did not want to. She at first thought that the reason why she could not be free, although she both wanted to keep house and did, was that she would still be keeping house even though she did not want to. A little reflection, however, made her realise that this was not so. For Dr. Svengali had so constructed his radio control that the only dial setting which made Mrs. O'Farrell *want* to make the beds, for example, also caused the control to direct her to move her limbs to go through the external motions of making them. Hence had she not wanted to make the beds, she would not have. Mrs. O'Farrell failed to find consolation in philosophy and efficiently though his household was run, Dr. Svengali's evenings were as miserable as before.

The intractable nature of his problem caused Dr. Svengali also to engage in unwonted philosophical reflection. After all, he thought, Geraldine (he was not a man to insist in superficial ways upon the superiority of his position) must want not to be made to do the housework, for whatever absurd reason, or she would not resist my attempts to make her do it. So if I can make her want to do the housework, why cannot I eradicate those more central and recalcitrant impulses which make her want not to want to do the housework, and which motivate her prolonged and determined resistance to all my efforts to manage her? Perhaps if I could learn to control those impulses which lie at the very core of her being, I might be able so to manipulate her that I can get my house looked after and some agreeable conversation and pleasant companionship in the evenings.

Trial and error showed that he was right in his surmise. The correct dial setting on his radio control blotted out Mrs. O'Farrell's sense of her duty to the community of women, and she happily did everything Dr. Svengali wished to his entire satisfaction. But success had whetted Dr. Svengali's appetite, and Faustus-like he looked about for more worlds to conquer. In the days when Mrs. O'Farrell was controlled by Mark I of his device, he had made her steal the notes of some experiments from a colleague, to which study she, but not he, had access. A man naturally prone to make other people bear the guilt which he incurred by his own actions, Dr. Svengali had tried to put the blame upon her, but without success. She had not, she always insisted, stolen the papers. Her feet had gone to the study and her hands taken them against her will. She had even threatened to inform the police of what she considered Dr. Svengali had done, and at one time only doubts about the possibility of convicting him had prevented her from doing so. Now, however, Dr. Svengali saw the chance of having her a willing accomplice to his schemes. He did not consider that Mrs. O'Farrell would make a very effective criminal, but at least, if she were found out, his machine could eradicate any inclination she might have to turn informer.

After a surprisingly successful criminal career, Mrs. O'Farrell was eventually apprehended, tried, convicted and sentenced to a long term of imprisonment. The sentence proved not to be nearly as onerous as intended. She died a week after entering prison from a brain tumour caused by Dr. Svengali's insertion of the control. She herself felt, as was only to be expected, no inclination to blame him, or to feel anything other than that she was herself responsible for what she had apparently done. No-one, she now argued, had compelled her to do it. She had simply done what she herself pleased, and had she not wanted to steal it was by no means outside her power to refrain. She had simply not tried. The remote causes of her want to steal, she thought, were irrelevant. For her wanting to steal must have been caused by something, and the fact that it was actually caused by Dr. Svengali, though highly relevant to what moral judgements ought to be passed upon him, were quite beside the point when it came to passing moral judgments about her.

The prison chaplain, with whom she discussed the matter, agreed. He did not try to get Mrs. O'Farrell pardoned, but instead informed the police of Dr. Svengali's complicity, if one could call it that, in the matter. The latter, however, had by this time vanished.

He reappeared a few months later, a changed man, in a country whose police force had the reputation of being weak and internationally uncooperative. But Mrs. O'Farrell's apprehension, conviction and subsequent demise made him realise that he was in fact deeply fond of her. Remorse at the way in which he had treated her overcame him, and he was consumed by a desire to be a better person. To a man of Dr. Svengali's outlook and training, the obvious way to accomplish this difficult feat was to alter the physiology of his own brain in such a manner as to secure the desired improvement. He found an assistant to insert Mrs. O'Farrell's control into his own skull, and himself set the dial on his short-wave radio transmitter, which he had prudently taken with him, in such a manner as to eradicate from himself any further desire towards similar misbehaviour.

Unfortunately, however, his hand slipped, and the dial fell back to the slightly worn place where it had been set to control the behaviour of Mrs. O'Farrell. From that time forward Dr. Svengali stole for himself, and his exploits became progressively more and more dangerous.

Though he, unlike Mrs. O'Farrell, had the knowledge to alter the dial setting so as to eliminate his desire to steal or, at any rate, so as to produce a counter-desire to avoid prison or a stronger dislike of his addiction to such dishonourable conduct, the machine itself, by causing him to be quite satisfied with his behaviour, brought it about that he had no motive for doing so. His very desire to steal prevented him from ordering its own extinction. Inevitably he was eventually apprehended, and the laws of his new country, which tried to make up by their extreme severity for the inefficiency of its police force, condemned him to death.

The imminence of his decease did what the death of his now beloved Geraldine had been unable to do, and he became at last overwhelmed with a readily effective remorse. Even the knowledge that he would not have been in his present plight but for a quite inadvertent slip of his fingers on the control could not prevent him from deciding to hang himself. A stool and a piece of rope had been left in his cell by thoughtful and economically minded prison authorities, but Dr. Svengali had always been a little clumsy, and in climbing onto the stool his foot slipped, and his consequent fall jolted the control in such a way as to make it function in a highly erratic manner, and Dr. Svengali to behave as one demented. The cell, of course, was not padded, and he so damaged himself against its stone sides that the prison authorities, perhaps a little inconsistently, took him to hospital to prevent him doing himself any further injury.

In the course of his treatment doctors discovered the controlling device inside his skull and removed it. His behaviour instantly became as normal as it had ever been. His solicitor appealed against the conviction on the ground that the person who was to be hanged was a different person from the person who had committed the crimes and, alternatively, on the ground that Dr. Svengali was not responsible for his actions, which were caused by the control, not by Dr. Svengali himself. The appeal court found in his favour, though one judge disagreed, on the ground that Dr. Svengali had put the control inside his own skull.

Dr. Svengali thanked God, whom he imagined in his own augmented image as a supremely powerful brain physiologist without much moral character, for his good fortune, for since his belief in the deity manifested itself only in moments of stress, he did not notice the impropriety of ascribing anything at all to luck. On his release from prison, he returned to his own country, where Mrs. O'Farrell had cached most of their booty.

His first act upon retaking up his abode in his former lodgings was to advertise for another housekeeper.

Questions for Reflection

1. When Dr. Svengali and Mrs. O'Farrell were controlled by the machine and committed crimes, were they free? Were they morally responsible? What would a hard determinist say? A libertarian? A compatibilist?

2. You do not (presumably) have a humanly made controlling device in your brain producing your desires. Nevertheless, where do your desires come from? Do you choose your desires? If so, what causes you to choose the desires that you do? Is it another sort of desire? Or are your desires and motives simply something that happens to you? What would be the implications of this? How are you similar to or different from Mrs. O'Farrell?

DO WE HAVE FREE WILL? ARE WE MORALLY RESPONSIBLE?

BARON D'HOLBACH

Hard Determinism—We Are Determined and Not Responsible

Baron Paul Henri d'Holbach (1723–1789), was born in Germany but inherited his French uncle's money, estate, and title. His estate was a meeting place for the leading French radical thinkers (the *philosophes*) of the late 18th century. He was an atheist, materialist, and determinist who believed that the universe is a complex physical system governed by mechanistic laws of cause and effect. The following selection is taken from his book *The System of Nature* (1770). In this classic essay d'Holbach gives an enthusiastic defense of determinism. Along the way, he counters some of the typical arguments against determinism posed by the libertarians.

Reading Questions

1. What is the position of those who believe that the soul is immaterial?
2. In contrast, how does d'Holbach describe the soul (our mental life) and its relation to the body?
3. Why is it thought that the notion of free will is essential to religion and our system of punishment?

From Baron d'Holbach, "Of the System of Man's Free Agency," in *The System of Nature,* trans. H. D. Robinson, chap. XI (Boston: J. P. Mendum, 1853). This work was originally published in 1770.

4. What is it that causes a person's will to act?
5. How does d'Holbach reconcile his determinism with the fact that we frequently deliberate before we act or make a choice?

MOTIVES AND THE DETERMINATION OF THE WILL

In whatever manner man is considered, he is connected to universal nature, and submitted to the necessary and immutable laws that she imposes on all the beings she contains, according to their peculiar essences or to the respective properties with which, without consulting them, she endows each particular species. Man's life is a line that nature commands him to describe upon the surface of the earth, without his ever being able to swerve from it, even for an instant. He is born without his own consent; his organization does in nowise depend upon himself; his ideas come to him involuntarily; his habits are in the power of those who cause him to contract them; he is unceasingly modified by causes, whether visible or concealed, over which he has no control, which necessarily regulate his mode of existence, give the hue to his way of thinking, and determine his manner of acting. He is good or bad, happy or miserable, wise or foolish, reasonable or irrational, without his will being for anything in these various states. Nevertheless, in spite of the shackles by which he is bound, it is pretended he is a free agent, or that independent of the causes by which he is moved, he determines his own will, and regulates his own condition.

However slender the foundation of this opinion, of which everything ought to point out to him the error, it is current at this day and passes for an incontestable truth with a great number of people, otherwise extremely enlightened; it is the basis of religion, which, supposing relations between man and the unknown being she has placed above nature, has been incapable of imagining how man could merit reward or deserve punishment from this being, if he was not a free agent. Society has been believed interested in this system; because an idea has gone abroad, that if all the actions of man were to be contemplated as necessary, the right of punishing those who injure their associates would no longer exist. At length human vanity accommodated itself to a hypothesis which, unquestionably, appears to distinguish man from all other physical beings, by assigning to him the special privilege of a total independence of all other causes, but of which a very little reflection would have shown him the impossibility. . . .

The will, as we have elsewhere said, is a modification of the brain, by which it is disposed to action, or prepared to give play to the organs. This will is necessarily determined by the qualities, good or bad, agreeable or painful, of the object or the motive that acts upon his senses, or of which the idea remains with him, and is resuscitated by his memory. In consequence, he acts necessarily, his action is the result of the impulse he receives either from the motive, from the object, or from the idea which has modified his brain, or disposed his will. When he does not act according to this impulse, it is because there comes some new cause, some new motive, some new idea, which modifies his brain in a different manner, gives him a new impulse, determines his will in another way, by which the action of the former impulse is suspended: thus, the sight of an agreeable object, or its idea, determines his will to set him in action to procure it; but if a new object or a new idea more powerfully attracts him, it gives a new direction to his will, annihilates the effect of the former, and prevents the action by which it was to be procured. This is the mode in which reflection, experience, reason, necessarily arrests or suspends the action of man's will: without this he would of necessity have followed the anterior impulse which carried him towards a then desirable object. In all this he always acts according to necessary laws from which he has no means of emancipating himself.

If when tormented with violent thirst, he figures to himself an idea, or really perceives a fountain, whose limpid streams might cool his feverish want, is he sufficient master of himself to desire or not to desire the object competent to satisfy so lively a want? It will no doubt be conceded, that it is impossible he should not be desirous to satisfy it; but it will be said—if at this moment it is announced to him that the water he so ardently desires is poisoned, he will, notwithstanding his vehement thirst, abstain from drinking it: and it has, therefore, been falsely concluded that he is a free agent. The fact, however, is, that the motive in either case is exactly the same: his own conservation. The same necessity that determined him to drink before he knew the water was deleterious upon this new discovery equally determined him not to drink; the desire of conserving himself either annihilates or suspends the former impulse; the second motive becomes stronger than the preceding, that is, the fear of death, or the desire of preserving himself, necessarily prevails over the painful sensation caused by his eagerness to drink: but, it will be said, if the thirst is very parching, an inconsiderate man without regarding the danger will risk swallowing the water. Nothing is gained by this remark: in this case, the anterior impulse only regains the ascendency; he is persuaded that life may possibly be longer preserved, or that he shall derive a greater good by drinking the poisoned water than by enduring the torment, which, to his mind, threatens instant dissolution; thus the first becomes the strongest and necessarily urges him on to action. Nevertheless, in either case, whether he partakes of the water, or whether he does not, the two actions will be equally necessary; they will be the effect of that motive which finds itself most puissant; which consequently acts in the most coercive manner upon his will.

This example will serve to explain the whole phenomena of the human will. This will, or rather the brain, finds itself in the same situation as a bowl, which, although it has received an impulse that drives it forward in a straight line, is deranged in its course whenever a force superior to the first obliges it to change its direction. The man who drinks the poisoned water appears a madman; but the actions of fools are as necessary as those of the most prudent individuals. The motives that determine the voluptuary and the debauchee to risk their health are as powerful, and their actions are

as necessary, as those which decide the wise man to manage his. But, it will be insisted, the debauchee may be prevailed on to change his conduct: this does not imply that he is a free agent; but that motives may be found sufficiently powerful to annihilate the effect of those that previously acted upon him; then these new motives determine his will to the new mode of conduct he may adopt as necessarily as the former did to the old mode.

Man is said to *deliberate*, when the action of the will is suspended; this happens when two opposite motives act alternately upon him. *To deliberate*, is to hate and to love in succession; it is to be alternately attracted and repelled; it is to be moved, sometimes by one motive, sometimes by another. Man only deliberates when he does not distinctly understand the quality of the objects from which he receives impulse, or when experience has not sufficiently apprised him of the effects, more or less remote, which his actions will produce. He would take the air, but the weather is uncertain; he deliberates in consequence; he weighs the various motives that urge his will to go out or to stay at home; he is at length determined by that motive which is most probable; this removes his indecision, which necessarily settles his will, either to remain within or to go abroad: his motive is always either the immediate or ultimate advantage he finds, or thinks he finds, in the action to which he is persuaded.

Man's will frequently fluctuates between two objects, of which either the presence or the ideas move him alternately: he waits until he has contemplated the objects, or the ideas they have left in his brain which solicit him to different actions; he then compares these objects or ideas; but even in the time of deliberation, during the comparison, pending these alternatives of love and hatred which succeed each other, sometimes with the utmost rapidity, he is not a free agent for a single instant; the good or the evil which he believes he finds successively in the objects, are the necessary motives of these momentary wills; of the rapid motion of desire or fear, that he experiences as long as his uncertainty continues. From this it will be obvious that deliberation is necessary; that uncertainty is necessary; that whatever part he takes, in consequence of this deliberation, it will always necessarily be that which he has judged, whether well or ill, is most probable to turn to his advantage.

When the soul is assailed by two motives that act alternately upon it, or modify it successively, it deliberates; the brain is in a sort of equilibrium, accompanied with perpetual oscillations, sometimes towards one object, sometimes towards the other, until the most forcible carries the point, and thereby extricates it from this state of suspense, in which consists the indecision of his will. But when the brain is simultaneously assailed by causes equally strong that move it in opposite directions, agreeable to the general law of all bodies when they are struck equally by contrary powers, it stops . . . it is neither capable to will nor to act; it waits until one of the two causes has obtained sufficient force to overpower the other; to determine its will; to attract it in such a manner that it may prevail over the efforts of the other cause.

This mechanism, so simple, so natural, suffices to demonstrate why uncertainty is painful, and why suspense is always a violent state for man. The brain, an organ so delicate and so mobile, experiences such rapid modifications that it is fatigued; or when it is urged in contrary directions, by causes equally powerful, it suffers a kind of compression, that prevents the activity which is suitable to the preservation of the whole, and which is necessary to procure what is advantageous to its existence. This mechanism will also explain the irregularity, the indecision, the inconstancy of man, and account for that conduct which frequently appears an inexplicable mystery, and which is, indeed, the effect of the received systems. In consulting experience, it will be found that the soul is submitted to precisely the same physical laws as the material body. If the will of each individual, during a given time, was only moved by a single cause or passion, nothing would be more easy than to foresee his actions; but his heart is frequently assailed by contrary powers, by adverse motives, which either act on him simultaneously or in succession; then his brain, attracted in opposite directions, is either fatigued, or else tormented by a state of compression, which deprives it of activity. Sometimes it is in a state of incommodious action; sometimes it is the sport of the alternate shocks it undergoes. Such, no

doubt, is the state in which man finds himself when a lively passion solicits him to the commission of crime, whilst fear points out to him the danger by which it is attended; such, also, is the condition of him whom remorse, by the continued labour of his distracted soul, prevents from enjoying the objects he has criminally obtained.

Choice by no means proves the free agency of man: he only deliberates when he does not yet know which to choose of the many objects that move him; he is then in an embarrassment, which does not terminate until his will is decided by the greater advantage he believes he shall find in the object he chooses, or the action he undertakes. From whence it may be seen, that choice is necessary, because he would not determine for an object, or for an action, if he did not believe that he should find it in some direct advantage. That man should have free agency it were needful that he should be able to will or choose without motive, or that he could prevent motives coercing his will. Action always being the effect of his will once determined, and as his will cannot be determined but by a motive which is not in his own power, it follows that he is never the master of the determination of his own peculiar will; that consequently he never acts as a free agent. It has been believed that man was a free agent because he had a will with the power of choosing; but attention has not been paid to the fact that even his will is moved by causes independent of himself; is owing to that which is inherent in his own organization, or which belongs to the nature of the beings acting on him. Is he the master of willing not to withdraw his hand from the fire when he fears it will be burnt? Or has he the power to take away from fire the property which makes him fear it? Is he the master of not choosing a dish of meat, which he knows to be agreeable or analogous to his palate; of not preferring it to that which he knows to be disagreeable or dangerous? It is always according to his sensations, to his own peculiar experience, or to his suppositions, that he judges of things, either well or ill; but whatever may be his judgment, it depends necessarily on his mode of feeling, whether habitual or accidental, and the qualities he finds in the causes that move him, which exist in despite of himself. . . .

In short, the actions of man are never free; they are always the necessary consequence of his temperament, of the received ideas, and of the notions, either true or false, which he has formed to himself of happiness; of his opinions, strengthened by example, by education, and by daily experience. So many crimes are witnessed on the earth only because every thing conspires to render man vicious and criminal; the religion he has adopted, his government, his education, the examples set before him, irresistibly drive him on to evil: under these circumstances, morality preaches virtue to him in vain. In those societies where vice is esteemed, where crime is crowned, where venality is constantly recompensed, where the most dreadful disorders are punished only in those who are too weak to enjoy the privilege of committing them with impunity, the practice of virtue is considered nothing more than a painful sacrifice of happiness. Such societies chastise, in the lower orders, those excesses which they respect in the higher ranks; and frequently have the injustice to condemn those in the penalty of death, whom public prejudices, maintained by constant example, have rendered criminal.

Man, then, is not a free agent in any one instant of his life; he is necessarily guided in each step by those advantages, whether real or fictitious, that he attaches to the objects by which his passions are roused: these passions themselves are necessary in a being who unceasingly tends towards his own happiness; their energy is necessary, since that depends on his temperament; his temperament is necessary, because it depends on the physical elements which enter into his composition; the modification of this temperament is necessary, as it is the infallible and inevitable consequence of the impulse he receives from the incessant action of moral and physical beings.

CHOICE DOES NOT PROVE FREEDOM

In spite of these proofs of the want of free agency in man, so clear to unprejudiced minds, it will, perhaps be insisted upon with no small feeling of triumph, that if it be proposed to any one, to move or not to move his hand, an action in the number of those called indifferent, he evidently appears to be the master of choosing; from which it is concluded that evidence has been offered of free agency. The reply is, this example is perfectly simple; man in performing some action which he is resolved on doing, does not by any means prove his free agency; the very desire of displaying this quality, excited by the dispute, becomes a necessary motive, which decides his will either for the one or the other of these actions: What deludes him in this instance, or that which persuades him he is a free agent at this moment, is, that he does not discern the true motive which sets him in action, namely, the desire of convincing his opponent: if in the heat of the dispute he insists and asks, "Am I not the master of throwing myself out of the window?" I shall answer him, no; that whilst he preserves his reason there is no probability that the desire of proving his free agency, will become a motive sufficiently powerful to make him sacrifice his life to the attempt: if, notwithstanding this, to prove he is a free agent, he should actually precipitate himself from the window, it would not be a sufficient warranty to conclude he acted freely, but rather that it was the violence of his temperament which spurred him on to this folly. Madness is a state, that depends upon the heat of the blood, not upon the will. A fanatic or a hero, braves death as necessarily as a more phlegmatic man or coward flies from it.

It is said that free agency is the absence of those obstacles competent to oppose themselves to the actions of man, or to the exercise of his faculties: it is pretended that he is a free agent whenever, making use of these faculties, he produces the effect he has proposed to himself. In reply to this reasoning, it is sufficient to consider that it in nowise depends upon himself to place or remove the obstacles that either determine or resist him. The motive that causes his action is no more in his own power than the obstacle that impedes him, whether this obstacle or motive be within his own machine or exterior of his person. He is not master of the thought presented to his mind, which determines his will; this thought is excited by some cause independent of himself.

To be undeceived on the system of his free agency, man has simply to recur to the motive by which his will is determined; he will always find this motive is out of his own control. It is said: that in consequence of an idea to which the mind gives birth, man acts freely if he encounters no obstacle. But the question is, what gives birth to this idea in his brain? was he the master either to prevent it from presenting itself, or from renewing itself in his brain? Does not this idea depend either upon objects that strike him exteriorly and in despite of himself, or upon causes, that without his knowledge, act within himself and modify his brain? Can he prevent his eyes, cast without design upon any object whatever, from giving him an idea of this object, and from moving his brain? He is not more master of the obstacles; they are the necessary effects of either interior or exterior causes, which always act according to their given properties. A man insults a coward; this necessarily irritates him against his insulter; but his will cannot vanquish the obstacle that cowardice places to the object of his desire, because his natural conformation, which does not depend upon himself, prevents his having courage. In this case, the coward is insulted in spite of himself; and against his will is obliged patiently to brook the insult he has received.

ABSENCE OF RESTRAINT IS NOT ABSENCE OF NECESSITY

The partisans of the system of free agency appear ever to have confounded constraint with necessity. Man believes he acts as a free agent, every time he does not see any thing that places obstacles to his actions; he does not perceive that the motive which causes him to will, is always necessary and independent of himself. A prisoner loaded with chains is compelled to remain in prison; but he is not a free agent in the desire to emancipate himself; his chains prevent him from acting, but they do not prevent him from willing; he would save himself if they would loose his fetters; but he would not save himself as a free agent; fear or the idea of punishment would be sufficient motives for his action.

Man may, therefore, cease to be restrained, without, for that reason, becoming a free agent. In whatever manner he acts, he will act necessarily, according to motives by which he shall be determined. He may be compared to a heavy body that finds itself arrested in its descent by any obstacle whatever. Take away this obstacle, it will gravitate or continue to fall; but who shall say this dense body is free to fall or not? Is not its descent the necessary effect of its own specific gravity? The virtuous Socrates submitted to the laws of his country, although they were unjust; and though the doors of his jail were left open to him, he would not save himself; but in this he did not act as a free agent. The invisible chains of opinion, the secret love of decorum, the inward respect for the laws, even when they were iniquitous, the fear of tarnishing his glory, kept him in his prison; they were motives sufficiently powerful with this enthusiast for virtue, to induce him to wait death with tranquility; it was not in his power to save himself, because he could find no potential motive to bring him to depart, even for an instant, from those principles to which his mind was accustomed.

Man, it is said, frequently acts against his inclination, from whence it is falsely concluded he is a free agent; but when he appears to act contrary to his inclination, he is always determined to it by some motive sufficiently efficacious to vanquish this inclination. A sick man, with a view to his cure, arrives at conquering his repugnance to the most disgusting remedies. The fear of pain, or the dread of death, then become necessary motives; consequently this sick man cannot be said to act freely.

When it is said, that man is not a free agent, it is not pretended to compare him to a body moved by a simple impulsive cause. He contains within himself causes inherent to his existence; he is moved by an interior organ, which has its own peculiar laws, and is itself necessarily determined in consequence of ideas formed from perception resulting from sensation which it receives from exterior objects. As the mechanism of these sensations, of these perceptions, and the manner they engrave ideas on the brain of man, are not known to him; because he is unable to unravel all these motions; because he cannot perceive the chain of operations in his soul, or the motive principle that acts within him, he supposes himself a free agent; which literally translated, signifies, that he moves himself by himself; that he determines himself without cause. When he rather ought to say, that he is ignorant how or why he acts in the manner he does. It is true the soul enjoys an activity peculiar to itself, but it is equally certain that this activity would never be displayed, if some motive or some cause did not put it in a condition to exercise itself. At least it will not be pretended that the soul is able either to love or to hate without being moved, without knowing the objects, without having some idea of their qualities. Gunpowder has unquestionably a particular activity, but this activity will never display itself, unless fire be applied to it; this, however, immediately sets it in motion.

THE COMPLEXITY OF HUMAN CONDUCT AND THE ILLUSION OF FREE AGENCY

It is the great complication of motion in man, it is the variety of his action, it is the multiplicity of causes that move him, whether simultaneously or in continual succession, that persuades him he is a free agent. If all his motions were simple, if the causes that move him did not confound themselves with each other, if they were distinct, if his machine were less complicated, he would perceive that all his actions were necessary, because he would be enabled to recur instantly to the cause that made him act. A man who should be always obliged to go towards the west, would always go on that side; but he would feel that, in so going, he was not a free agent. If he had another sense, as his actions or his motion, augmented by a sixth, would be still more varied and much more complicated, he would believe himself still more a free agent than he does with his five senses.

It is, then, for want of recurring to the causes that move him; for want of being able to analyze, from not being competent to decompose the complicated motion of his machine, that man believes himself a free agent. It is only upon his own ignorance that he founds the profound yet deceitful notion he has of his free agency; that he builds those opinions which he brings forward as a striking proof of his pretended freedom of action. If, for a short time, each man was willing to examine his own peculiar actions, search out their true motives to discover their concatenation, he would remain convinced that the sentiment he has of his natural free agency, is a chimera that must speedily be destroyed by experience.

Nevertheless it must be acknowledged that the multiplicity and diversity of the causes which continually act upon man, frequently without even his knowledge, render it impossible, or at least extremely difficult for him to recur to the true principles of his own peculiar actions, much less the actions of others. They frequently depend upon causes so fugitive, so remote from their effects, and which, superficially examined, appear to have so little analogy, so slender a relation with them, that it requires singular sagacity to bring them into light. This is what renders the study of the moral man a task of such difficulty; this is the reason why his heart is an abyss, of which it is frequently impossible for him to fathom the depth.

Questions for Reflection

1. How effectively has d'Holbach made the case that there is no free will? What do you think is his strongest point? What is his weakest point?
2. If you were d'Holbach, how would you explain each of the following items: (a) your choice of friends, (b) the career choices you have made or are considering, (c) your moral values? Do you think these explanations are adequate?
3. Every society is based on the assumption that what we do can affect people's behavior. Our parenting practices and our educational and criminal systems are attempts to make people behave in socially acceptable ways. We worry about too much

violence on television because we suppose that this can have a negative causal effect on children. To what extent do these practices reflect the determinist's claim that behavior is caused? How might a libertarian respond to these points?

4. If hard determinism is true, people are not morally responsible for their actions. If our society accepted this claim, what changes would be made to our public policy? How would these changes affect our treatment of criminals?

5. The biologist J. B. S. Haldane said, "If my mental processes are determined wholly by the motions of atoms in my brain, I have no reason to suppose that my beliefs are true. . . . And hence I have no reason for supposing my brain to be composed of atoms." In what way is this an argument against determinism? How good an argument is it?

C. A. CAMPBELL

Libertarianism—We Are Free and Responsible

Charles Arthur Campbell (1897–1974) was an influential British philosopher who was known for his vigorous defense of free will. He spent most of his career as a professor of philosophy at the University of Glasgow.

Campbell begins this essay by clarifying the issue of what sort of freedom is necessary for there to be moral responsibility. He argues that a person is responsible for an action if that person "could have done otherwise." However he rejects the compatibilist's interpretation that states a person could have done otherwise "*if* he had a different character" or "*if* he had been placed in different circumstances." When we act, Campbell says, we always have the character that we have at the moment and face the circumstances that we face. So, these hypothetical alternatives really do not play a role in a person's concrete behavior. What is important, he concludes, is our experience of acting creatively, of having the power to resist the inclinations of our formed characters. The possibility and the actuality of this sort of free action is encountered in inner experience and is the best evidence that the will is free.

Reading Questions

1. Why does Campbell believe that the issue of freedom pertains primarily to our inner acts and not our outward behavior?

2. Campbell says that a condition of moral responsibility is that the person be the sole author of the act in question. However, he thinks there is another condition

C. A. Campbell, "Has the Self 'Free Will'?," in *On Selfhood and Godhood* (London: George Allen & Unwin, 1957).

that is required for moral responsibility. What is it? Why does he add this further requirement?

3. What is the hypothetical interpretation of the claim "X could have done otherwise"? Why does Campbell think that the hypothetical interpretation does not address the issue of moral responsibility?

4. He thinks it is correct to make allowances for persons whose circumstances prevent them from acting morally as easily as a more fortunate person. At the same time, he thinks this does not mean that the more unfortunate person lacks free will. Why does he believe this?

5. Why does Campbell think that the ability to predict a certain amount of another person's actions is not sufficient evidence to conclude that there is no free will?

6. What is the second criticism of libertarianism Campbell discusses? Why does he think this objection is based on a circular argument?

7. Why does he think that the insights we gain from inner experience tell us more about free will than can be learned from external observation?

I

. . . It is something of a truism that in philosophic enquiry the exact formulation of a problem often takes one a long way on the road to its solution. In the case of the Free Will problem I think there is a rather special need of careful formulation. For there are many sorts of human freedom; and it can easily happen that one wastes a great deal of labour in proving or disproving a freedom which has almost nothing to do with the freedom which is at issue in the traditional problem of Free Will. The abortiveness of so much of the argument for and against Free Will in contemporary philosophical literature seems to me due in the main to insufficient pains being taken over the preliminary definition of the problem. . . .

Fortunately we can at least make a beginning with a certain amount of confidence. It is not seriously disputable that the kind of freedom in question is the freedom which is commonly recognised to be in some sense a precondition of moral responsibility. Clearly, it is on account of this integral connection with moral responsibility that such exceptional importance has always been felt to attach to the Free Will problem. But in what precise sense is free will a precondition of moral responsibility, and thus a postulate of the moral life in general? This is an exceedingly troublesome question; but

until we have satisfied ourselves about the answer to it, we are not in a position to state, let alone decide, the question whether "Free Will" in its traditional, ethical, significance is a reality. . . .

The first point to note is that the freedom at issue (as indeed the very name "Free *Will* Problem" indicates) pertains primarily not to overt acts but to inner acts. The nature of things has decreed that, save in the case of one's self, it is only overt acts which one can directly observe. But a very little reflection serves to show that in our moral judgments upon others their overt acts are regarded as significant only in so far as they are the expression of inner acts. We do not consider the acts of a robot to be morally responsible acts; nor do we consider the acts of a man to be so save in so far as they are distinguishable from those of a robot by reflecting an inner life of choice. Similarly, from the other side, if we are satisfied (as we may on occasion be, at least in the case of ourselves) that a person has definitely elected to follow a course which he believes to be wrong, but has been prevented by external circumstances from translating his inner choice into an overt act, we still regard him as morally blameworthy. Moral freedom, then, pertains to *inner* acts.

The next point seems at first sight equally obvious and uncontroversial; but, as we shall see, it has awkward implications if we are in real earnest with it (as almost nobody is). It is the simple point that the act must be one of which the person judged can be regarded as the *sole* author. It seems plain enough that if there are any *other* determinants of the act, external to the self, to that extent the act is not an act which the *self* determines, and to that extent not an act for which the self can be held morally responsible. The self is only part-author of the act, and his moral responsibility can logically extend only to those elements within the act (assuming for the moment that these can be isolated) of which he is the *sole* author. . . .

Thirdly, we come to a point over which much recent controversy has raged. We may approach it by raising the following question. Granted an act of which the agent is sole author, does this "sole authorship" suffice to make the act a morally free act? We may be inclined to think that it does, until we contemplate the possibility that an act of which the agent is sole author might conceivably occur as a necessary expression of the agent's nature; the way in which, e.g. some philosophers have supposed the Divine act of creation to occur. This consideration excites a legitimate doubt; for it is far from easy to see how a person can be regarded as a proper subject for moral praise or blame in respect of an act which he *cannot help* performing—even if it be his own "nature" which necessitates it. Must we not recognise it as a condition of the morally free act that the agent "could have acted otherwise" than he in fact did? It is true, indeed, that we sometimes praise or blame a man for an act about which we are prepared to say, in the light of our knowledge of his established character, that he "could do no other." But I think that a little reflection shows that in such cases we are not praising or blaming the man strictly for what he does *now* (or at any rate we ought not to be), but rather for those past acts of his which have generated the firm habit of mind from which his *present* act follows "necessarily." In other words, our praise and blame, so far as justified, are really retrospective, being directed not to the agent *qua* performing *this* act, but to the agent *qua* performing those past acts which have built up his present character, and in respect to which we presume that he *could* have acted otherwise, that there really *were* open possibilities before him.

These cases, therefore, seem to me to constitute no valid exception to what I must take to be the rule, viz. that a man can be morally praised or blamed for an act only if he could have acted otherwise.

Now philosophers today are fairly well agreed that it is a postulate of the morally responsible act that the agent "could have acted otherwise" in *some* sense of that phrase. But sharp differences of opinion have arisen over the way in which the phrase ought to be interpreted. There is a strong disposition to water down its apparent meaning by insisting that it is not (as a postulate of moral responsibility) to be understood as a straightforward categorical proposition, but rather as a disguised hypothetical proposition. All that we really require to be assured of, in order to justify our holding X morally responsible for an act, is, we are told, that X could have acted otherwise *if* he had *chosen* otherwise or perhaps that X could have acted otherwise *if* he had had a different character, or *if* he had been placed in different circumstances.

I think it is easy to understand, and even, in a measure, to sympathise with, the motives which induce philosophers to offer these counterinterpretations. It is not just the fact that "X could have acted otherwise," as a bald categorical statement, is incompatible with the universal sway of causal law—though this is, to some philosophers, a serious stone of stumbling. The more wide-spread objection is that at least it looks as though it were incompatible with that causal continuity of an agent's character with his conduct which is implied when we believe (surely with justice) that we can often tell the sort of thing a man will do from our knowledge of the sort of man he is.

We shall have to make our accounts with that particular difficulty later. At this stage I wish merely to show that neither of the hypothetical propositions suggested—and I think the same could be shown for *any* hypothetical alternative—is an acceptable substitute for the categorical proposition "X could have acted otherwise" as the presupposition of moral responsibility.

Let us look first at the earlier suggestion—"X could have acted otherwise *if* he had chosen otherwise." Now clearly there are a great many acts with regard to which we are entirely satisfied that the agent is thus situated. We are often perfectly sure that—for this is all it amounts to—if X had chosen otherwise, the circumstances presented no external obstacle to the translation of that choice into action. For example, we often have no doubt at all that X, who in point of fact told a lie, could have told the truth *if* he had so chosen. But does our confidence on this score allay all legitimate doubts about whether X is really blameworthy? Does it entail that X is free in the sense required for moral responsibility? Surely not. The obvious question immediately arises: "But *could* X have *chosen* otherwise than he did?" It is doubt about the true answer to *that* question which leads most people to doubt the reality of moral responsibility. Yet on this crucial question the hypothetical proposition which is offered as a sufficient statement of the condition justifying the ascription of moral responsibility gives us no information whatsoever.

Indeed this hypothetical substitute for the categorical "X could have acted otherwise" seems to me to lack all plausibility unless one contrives to forget why it is, after all, that we ever come to feel fundamental doubts about man's moral responsibility. Such doubts are born, surely, when one becomes aware of certain reputable world-views in religion or philosophy, or of certain reputable scientific beliefs, which in their several ways imply that man's actions are necessitated, and thus could not be otherwise than they in fact are. But clearly a doubt so based is not even touched by the recognition that a man could very often act otherwise *if* he so chose. That proposition is entirely compatible with the necessitarian theories which generate our doubt: indeed it is this very compatibility that has recommended it to some philosophers, who are reluctant to give up either moral responsibility or Determinism. The proposition which we *must* be able to affirm if moral praise or blame of X is to be justified is the categorical proposition that X could have acted otherwise because—not if—he could have chosen otherwise; or, since it is essentially the inner side of the act that matters, the proposition simply that X could have chosen otherwise.

For the second of the alternative formulae suggested we cannot spare more than a few moments.

But its inability to meet the demands it is required to meet is almost transparent. "X could have acted otherwise," as a statement of a precondition of X's moral responsibility, really means (we are told) "X could have acted otherwise *if* he were differently constituted, or *if* he had been placed in different circumstances." It seems a sufficient reply to this to point out that the person whose moral responsibility is at issue is X; a specific individual, in a specific set of circumstances. It is totally irrelevant to X's moral responsibility that we should be able to say that some person differently constituted from X, or X in a different set of circumstances, could have done something different from what X did. . . .

II

That brings me to the second, and more constructive, part of this lecture. From now on I shall be considering whether it is reasonable to believe that man does in fact possess a free will of the kind specified in the first part of the lecture. If so, just how and where within the complex fabric of the volitional life are we to locate it?—for although free will must presumably belong (if anywhere) to the volitional side of human experience, it is pretty clear from the way in which we have been forced to define it that it does not pertain simply to volition as such; not even to all volitions that are commonly dignified with the name of "choices." It has been, I think, one of the more serious impediments to profitable discussion of the Free Will problem that Libertarians and Determinists alike have so often failed to appreciate the comparatively narrow area within which the free will that is necessary to "save" morality is required to operate. It goes without saying that this failure has been gravely prejudicial to the case for Libertarianism. I attach a good deal of importance, therefore, to the problem of locating free will correctly within the volitional orbit. Its solution forestalls and annuls, I believe, some of the more tiresome clichés of Determinist criticism.

We saw earlier that Common Sense's practice of "making allowances" in its moral judgments for the influence of heredity and environment indicates Common Sense's conviction, both that a just moral judgment must discount determinants of choice over which the agent has no control, and also (since it still accepts moral judgments as legitimate) that *something* of moral relevance survives which can be regarded as genuinely self-originated. We are now to try to discover what this "something" is. And I think we may still usefully take Common Sense as our guide. Suppose one asks the ordinary intelligent citizen *why* he deems it proper to make allowances for X, whose heredity and/or environment are unfortunate. He will tend to reply, I think, in some such terms as these: that X has more and stronger temptations to deviate from what is right than Y or Z, who are normally circumstanced, so that he must put forth a *stronger moral effort* if he is to achieve the same level of external conduct. The intended implication seems to be that X is just as morally praiseworthy as Y or Z *if* he exerts an equivalent moral effort, even though he may not thereby achieve an equal success in conforming his will to the "concrete" demands of duty. And this implies, again, Common Sense's belief that *in moral effort* we have something for which a man is responsible *without qualification,* something that is *not* affected by heredity and environment but depends *solely* upon the self itself.

Now in my opinion Common Sense has here, in principle, hit upon the one and only defensible answer. Here, and here alone, so far as I can see, in the act of deciding whether to put forth or withhold the moral effort required to resist temptation and rise to duty, is to be found an act which is free in the sense required for moral responsibility; an act of which the self is sole author, and of which it is true to say that "it could be" (or, after the event, "could have been") "otherwise." Such is the thesis which we shall now try to establish.

The species of argument appropriate to the establishment of a thesis of this sort should fall, I think, into two phases. First, there should be a consideration of the evidence of the moral agent's own inner experience. What *is* the act of moral decision, and what does it imply, from the standpoint of the actual participant? Since there is no way of knowing the act of moral decision—or for that matter any other form of activity—except by actual participation in it, the evidence of the subject, or

agent, is on an issue of this kind of palmary importance. It can hardly, however, be taken as in itself conclusive. For even if that evidence should be overwhelmingly to the effect that moral decision does have the characteristics required by moral freedom, the question is bound to be raised—and in view of considerations from other quarters pointing in a contrary direction is *rightly* raised—Can we *trust* the evidence of inner experience? That brings us to what will be the second phase of the argument. We shall have to go on to show, if we are to make good our case, that the extraneous considerations so often supposed to be fatal to the belief in moral freedom are in fact innocuous to it. . . .

These arguments can, I think, be reduced in principle to no more than two: first, the argument from "predictability"; second, the argument from the alleged meaninglessness of an act supposed to be the self's act and yet not an expression of the self's character. Contemporary criticism of free will seems to me to consist almost exclusively of variations on these two themes. I shall deal with each in turn. . . .

Let us remind ourselves briefly of the setting within which, on our view, free will functions. There is X, the course which we believe we ought to follow, and Y, the course towards which we feel our desire is strongest. The freedom which we ascribe to the agent is the freedom to put forth or refrain from putting forth the moral effort required to resist the pressure of desire and do what he thinks he ought to do.

But then there is surely an immense range of practical situations—covering by far the greater part of life—in which there is no question of a conflict within the self between what he most desires to do and what he thinks he ought to do. Indeed such conflict is a comparatively rare phenomenon for the majority of men. Yet over that whole vast range there is nothing whatever in our version of Libertarianism to prevent our agreeing that character determines conduct. In the absence, real or supposed, of any "moral" issue, what a man chooses will be simply that course which, after such reflection as seems called for, he deems most likely to bring him what he most strongly desires; and that is the same as to say the course to which his present character inclines him.

Over by far the greater area of human choices, then, our theory offers no more barrier to successful prediction on the basis of character than any other theory. For where there is no clash of strongest desire with duty, the free will we are defending has no business. There is just nothing for it to do.

But what about the situations—rare enough though they may be—in which there *is* this clash and in which free will does therefore operate? Does our theory entail that there at any rate, as the critic seems to suppose, "anything may happen"?

Not by any manner of means. In the first place, and by the very nature of the case, the range of the agent's possible choices is bounded by what he thinks he ought to do on the one hand, and what he most strongly desires on the other. The freedom claimed for him is a freedom of decision to make or withhold the effort required to do what he thinks he ought to do. There is no question of a freedom to act in some "wild" fashion, out of all relation to his characteristic beliefs and desires. This so-called "freedom of caprice," so often charged against the Libertarian, is, to put it bluntly, a sheer figment of the critic's imagination, with no *habitat* in serious Libertarian theory. Even in situations where free will does come into play it is perfectly possible, on a view like ours, given the appropriate knowledge of a man's character, to predict within certain limits how he will respond. . . .

I claim, therefore, that the view of free will I have been putting forward is consistent with predictability of conduct on the basis of character over a very wide field indeed. And I make the further claim that that field will cover all the situations in life concerning which there is any empirical evidence that successful prediction is possible.

Let us pass on to consider the second main line of criticism. This is, I think, much the more illuminating of the two, if only because it compels the Libertarian to make explicit certain concepts which are indispensable to him, but which, being desperately hard to state clearly, are apt not to be stated at all. The critic's fundamental point might be stated somewhat as follows:

"Free will as you describe it is completely unintelligible. On your own showing no *reason* can be given, because there just *is* no reason, why a man decides to exert rather than to withhold moral effort, or *vice versa*. But such an act—or more properly, such an 'occurrence'—it is nonsense to speak of as an act of a *self*. If there is nothing in the self's character to which it is, even in principle, in any way traceable, the self has nothing to do with it. Your so-called 'freedom,' therefore, so far from supporting the self's moral responsibility, destroys it as surely as the crudest Determinism could do."

If we are to discuss this criticism usefully, it is important, I think, to begin by getting clear about two different senses of the word "intelligible."

If, in the first place, we mean by an "intelligible" act one whose occurrence is in principle capable of being inferred, since it follows necessarily from something (though we may not know in fact from what), then it is certainly true that the Libertarian's free will is unintelligible. But that is only saying, is it not, that the Libertarian's "free" act is not an act which follows necessarily from something! This can hardly rank as a *criticism* of Libertarianism. It is just a description of it. That there can be nothing unintelligible in *this* sense is precisely what the Determinist has got to *prove*.

Yet it is surprising how often the critic of Libertarianism involves himself in this circular mode of argument. Repeatedly it is urged against the Libertarian, with a great air of triumph, that on this view he can't say *why* I now decide to rise to duty, or now decide to follow my strongest desire in defiance of duty. Of course he can't. If he could he wouldn't *be* a Libertarian. To "account for" a "free" act is a contradiction in terms. A free will is *ex hypothesi* the sort of thing of which the request for an *explanation* is absurd. The assumption that an explanation must be in principle possible for the act of moral decision deserves to rank as a classic example of the ancient fallacy of "begging the question."

But the critic usually has in mind another sense of the word "unintelligible." He is apt to take it for granted that an act which is unintelligible in the *above* sense (as the morally free act of the Libertarian undoubtedly is) is unintelligible in the *further* sense that we can attach no meaning to it. And this is an altogether more serious matter. If it could really be shown that the Libertarian's "free will" were unintelligible in this sense of being meaningless, that, for myself at any rate, would be the end of the affair. Libertarianism would have been conclusively refuted.

But it seems to me manifest that this can *not* be shown. The critic has allowed himself, I submit, to become the victim of a widely accepted but fundamentally vicious assumption. He has assumed that whatever is meaningful must exhibit its meaningfulness to those who view it from the standpoint of external observation. Now if one chooses thus to limit one's self to the role of external observer, it is, I think, perfectly true that one can attach no meaning to an act which is the act of something we call a "self" and yet follows from nothing in that self's character. But then *why should we* so limit ourselves, when what is under consideration is a subjective activity? For the apprehension of subjective acts there is *another* standpoint available, that of *inner experience,* of the practical consciousness in its actual functioning. If our free will should turn out to be something to which we can attach a meaning from *this* standpoint, no more is required. And no more ought to be expected. For I must repeat that only from the inner standpoint of living experience *could* anything of the nature of "activity" be directly grasped. Observation from without is in the nature of the case impotent to apprehend the active *qua* active. We can from without observe sequences of states. If into these we read activity (as we sometimes do), this can only be on the basis of what we discern in ourselves from the inner standpoint. It follows that if anyone insists upon taking this criterion of the meaningful simply from the standpoint of external observation, he is really deciding in advance of the evidence that the notion of activity, and *a fortiori* the notion of a free will, is "meaningless." He looks for the free act through a medium which is in the nature of the case incapable of revealing it, and then, because inevitably he doesn't find it, he declares that it doesn't exist!

But if, as we surely ought in this context, we adopt the inner standpoint, then (I am suggesting) things appear in a totally different light. From the inner standpoint, it seems to me plain, there is no

difficulty whatever in attaching meaning to an act which is the self's act and which nevertheless does not follow from the self's character. So much I claim has been established by the phenomenological analysis, in this and the previous lecture, of the act of moral decision in face of moral temptation. It is thrown into particularly clear relief where the moral decision is to make the moral effort required to rise to duty. For the very function of moral effort, as it appears to the agent engaged in the act, is to enable the self to act against the line of least resistance, against the line to which his character as so far formed most strongly inclines him. But if the self is thus conscious here of *combating* his formed character, he surely cannot possibly suppose that the act, although his own act, *issues from* his formed character? I submit, therefore, that the self knows very well indeed—from the inner standpoint—what is meant by an act which is the *self's* act and which nevertheless does not follow from the self's *character.*

What this implies—and it seems to me to be an implication of cardinal importance for any theory of the self that aims at being more than superficial—is that the nature of the self is for itself something more than just its character as so far formed. The "nature" of the self and what we commonly call the "character" of the self are by no means the same thing, and it is utterly vital that they should not be confused. The "nature" of the self comprehends, but is not without remainder reducible to, its "character"; it must, if we are to be true to the testimony of our experience of it, be taken as including *also* the authentic creative power of fashioning and re-fashioning "character.". . .

. . . It may be helpful if I conclude by reminding you, in bald summary, of the main things I have been trying to say. Let me set them out in so many successive theses.

1. The freedom which is at issue in the traditional Free Will problem is the freedom which is presupposed in moral responsibility.

2. Critical reflection upon carefully considered attributions of moral responsibility reveals that the only freedom that will do is a freedom which pertains to inner acts of choice, and that

these acts must be acts (*a*) of which the self is *sole* author, and (*b*) which the self could have performed otherwise.

3. From phenomenological analysis of the situation of moral temptation we find that the self as engaged in this situation is inescapably convinced that it possesses a freedom of precisely the specified kind, located in the decision to exert or withhold the moral effort needed to rise to duty where the pressure of its desiring nature is felt to urge it in a contrary direction.

Passing to the question of the *reality* of this moral freedom which the moral agent believes himself to possess, we argued:

4. Of the two types of Determinist criticism which seem to have most influence today, that based on the predictability of much human behaviour fails to touch a Libertarianism which confines the area of free will as above indicated. Libertarianism so understood is compatible with all the predictability that the empirical facts warrant. And:

5. The second main type of criticism, which alleges the 'meaninglessness' of an act which is the self's act and which is yet not determined by the self's character, is based on a failure to appreciate that the standpoint of inner experience is not only legitimate but indispensable where what is at issue is the reality and nature of a subjective activity. The creative act of moral decision is inevitably meaningless to the mere external observer; but from the inner standpoint it is as real, and as significant, as anything in human experience.

Questions for Reflection

1. Do you think that Campbell has made the case that belief in free will is intelligible and is to be preferred to determinism?
2. Think of a situation when you acted one way but had the sense that you could have acted another way. How would the compatibilist interpret your claim that "I could have acted otherwise"? How does Campbell think it should be interpreted?
3. Can you think of a situation when someone predicted how you would act, but you still believed that you were acting freely? How strongly does this support Campbell's thesis?
4. Have you ever felt that you were, as Campbell describes it, acting freely in such a way that you were acting against the way your character had been formed? What would a determinist say about this?
5. Do you agree with Campbell that the testimony of our inner experience provides better evidence concerning free will than does the "standpoint of external observation"? How would Campbell reply to the objection that the data of the brain sciences and the behavioral sciences should be trusted more than introspection?

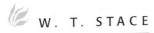

W. T. STACE

Compatibilism—We Are Determined, Free, and Responsible

W. T. Stace (1886–1967) was born in Britain and educated at Trinity College, Dublin. In 1932 he received an appointment at Princeton University where he taught for over 20 years, holding the title of Stuart Professor of Philosophy. He wrote numerous articles and influential books in the theory of knowledge, metaphysics, ethics, social and political thought, and the philosophy of religion. Although a life-long defender of empiricism, Stace argued that it could be compatible with a mystical understanding of religion.

In the following selection, Stace agrees with the hard determinist that every human action is as much determined by previous causes as is any other event in the world. However, he also agrees with the libertarian that without free will there can be no morality. To be morally responsible for an action requires that you freely chose to perform the action on the basis of your own motives, desires, and values. But how can one consistently combine determinism with free will? Don't they exclude one another? In this reading Stace argues the compatibilist (or soft determinist) position that determinism and moral responsibility are completely compatible when the concept of free will is clarified.

Reading Questions

1. According to Stace, what is the relationship between free will and morality?
2. What is the incorrect definition of free will, according to Stace?
3. On what basis does Stace argue for his understanding of free will?
4. In Stace's scenarios, what is common to the four cases of free will and what is lacking in the four cases where free choice is lacking?
5. Why does he say that all the free acts he describes had deterministic causes?
6. Why does Stace think that predictability and free will are compatible?
7. What are the two grounds on which punishment is justified?
8. Why does Stace say that moral responsibility requires determinism?

I shall first discuss the problem of free will, for it is certain that if there is no free will there can be no morality. Morality is concerned with what men ought and ought not to do. But if a man has no freedom to choose what he will do, if whatever he does is done under compulsion, then it does not make sense to tell him that he ought not to have done what he did and that he ought to do something different. All moral precepts would in such case be meaningless. Also if he acts always under compulsion, how can he be held morally responsible for his actions? How can he, for example, be punished for what he could not help doing?

It is to be observed that those learned professors of philosophy or psychology who deny the existence of free will do so only in their professional

From W. T. Stace, *Religion and the Modern Mind* (New York: Lippincott, 1952).

moments and in their studies and lecture rooms. For when it comes to doing anything practical, even of the most trivial kind, they invariably behave as if they and others were free. They inquire from you at dinner whether you will choose this dish or that dish. They will ask a child why he told a lie, and will punish him for not having chosen the way of truthfulness. All of which is inconsistent with a disbelief in free will. This should cause us to suspect that the problem is not a real one; and this, I believe, is the case. The dispute is merely verbal, and is due to nothing but a confusion about the meanings of words. It is what is now fashionably called a semantic problem.

How does a verbal dispute arise? Let us consider a case which, although it is absurd in the sense that no one would ever make the mistake which is involved in it, yet illustrates the principle which we shall have to use in the solution of the problem. Suppose that someone believed that the word "man" means a certain sort of five-legged animal; in short that "five-legged animal" is the correct definition of man. He might then look around the world, and rightly observing that there are no five-legged animals in it, he might proceed to deny the existence of men. This preposterous conclusion would have been reached because he was using an incorrect *definition* of "man." All you would have to do to show him his mistake would be to give him the correct definition; or at least to show him that his definition was wrong. Both the problem and its solution would, of course, be entirely verbal. The problem of free will, and its solution, I shall maintain, is verbal in exactly the same way. The problem has been created by the fact that learned men, especially philosophers, have assumed an incorrect definition of free will, and then finding that there is nothing in the world which answers to their definition, have denied its existence. As far as logic is concerned, their conclusion is just as absurd as that of the man who denies the existence of men. The only difference is that the mistake in the latter case is obvious and crude, while the mistake which the deniers of free will have made is rather subtle and difficult to detect.

Throughout the modern period, until quite recently, it was assumed, both by the philosophers who denied free will and by those who defended it, that *determinism is inconsistent with free will*. If a man's actions were wholly determined by chains of causes stretching back into the remote past, so that they could be predicted beforehand by a mind which knew all the causes, it was assumed that they could not in that case be free. This implies that a certain definition of actions done from free will was assumed, namely that they are actions *not* wholly determined by causes or predictable beforehand. Let us shorten this by saying that free will was defined as meaning indeterminism. This is the incorrect definition which has led to the denial of free will. As soon as we see what the true definition is we shall find that the question whether the world is deterministic, as Newtonian science implied, or in a measure indeterministic, as current physics teaches, is wholly irrelevant to the problem.

Of course there is a sense in which one can define a word arbitrarily in any way one pleases. But a definition may nevertheless be called correct or incorrect. It is correct if it accords with a *common usage* of the word defined. It is incorrect if it does not. And if you give an incorrect definition, absurd and untrue results are likely to follow. For instance, there is nothing to prevent you from arbitrarily defining a man as a five-legged animal, but this is incorrect in the sense that it does not accord with the ordinary meaning of the word. Also it has the absurd result of leading to a denial of the existence of men. This shows that *common usage is the criterion for deciding whether a definition is correct or not*. And this is the principle which I shall apply to free will. I shall show that indeterminism is not what is meant by the phrase "free will" *as it is commonly used*. And I shall attempt to discover the correct definition by inquiring how the phrase is used in ordinary conversation.

Here are a few samples of how the phrase might be used in ordinary conversation. It will be noticed that they include cases in which the question whether a man acted with free will is asked in order to determine whether he was morally and legally responsible for his acts.

JONES: I once went without food for a week.
SMITH: Did you do that of your own free will?

JONES: No. I did it because I was lost in a desert and could find no food.

But suppose that the man who had fasted was Mahatma Gandhi. The conversation might then have gone:

GANDHI: I once fasted for a week.
SMITH: Did you do that of your own free will?
GANDHI: Yes. I did it because I wanted to compel the British Government to give India its independence.

Take another case. Suppose that I had stolen some bread, but that I was as truthful as George Washington. Then, if I were charged with the crime in court, some exchange of the following sort might take place:

JUDGE: Did you steal the bread of your own free will?
STACE: Yes. I stole it because I was hungry.

Or in different circumstances the conversation might run:

JUDGE: Did you steal of your own free will?
STACE: No. I stole because my employer threatened to beat me if I did not.

At a recent murder trial in Trenton some of the accused had signed confessions, but afterwards asserted that they had done so under police duress. The following exchange might have occurred:

JUDGE: Did you sign this confession of your own free will?
PRISONER: No. I signed it because the police beat me up.

Now suppose that a philosopher had been a member of the jury. We could imagine this conversation taking place in the jury room.

FOREMAN OF THE JURY: The prisoner says he signed the confession because he was beaten, and not of his own free will.
PHILOSOPHER: This is quite irrelevant to the case. There is no such thing as free will.
FOREMAN: Do you mean to say that it makes no difference whether he signed because his con-

science made him want to tell the truth or because he was beaten?
PHILOSOPHER: None at all. Whether he was caused to sign by a beating or by some desire of his own—the desire to tell the truth, for example—in either case his signing was causally determined, and therefore in neither case did he act of his own free will. Since there is no such thing as free will, the question whether he signed of his own free will ought not to be discussed by us.

The foreman and the rest of the jury would rightly conclude that the philosopher must be making some mistake. What sort of a mistake could it be? There is only one possible answer. The philosopher must be using the phrase "free will" in some peculiar way of his own which is not the way in which men usually use it when they wish to determine a question of moral responsibility. That is, he must be using an incorrect definition of it as implying action not determined by causes.

Suppose a man left his office at noon, and were questioned about it. Then we might hear this:

JONES: Did you go out of your own free will?
SMITH: Yes. I went out to get my lunch.

But we might hear:

JONES: Did you leave your office of your own free will?
SMITH: No. I was forcibly removed by the police.

We have now collected a number of cases of actions which, in the ordinary usage of the English language, would be called cases in which people have acted of their own free will. We should also say in all these cases that they *chose* to act as they did. We should also say that they could have acted otherwise, if they had chosen. For instance, Mahatma Gandhi was not compelled to fast; he chose to do so. He could have eaten if he had wanted to. When Smith went out to get his lunch, he chose to do so. He could have stayed and done some more work, if he had wanted to. We have also collected a number of cases of the opposite kind. They are cases in which men were not able to exercise their free will. They had no choice. They were compelled to do as they did. The man in the desert did not fast of his own free will. He had no choice in the matter. He was compelled to fast because there was nothing for him to eat. And so with the other cases. It ought to be quite easy, by an inspection of these cases, to tell what we ordinarily mean when we say that a man did or did not exercise free will. We ought therefore to be able to extract from them the proper definition of the term. Let us put the cases in a table:

Free Acts	*Unfree Acts*
Gandhi fasting because he wanted to free India.	The man fasting in the desert because there was no food.
Stealing bread because one is hungry.	Stealing because one's employer threatened to beat one.
Signing a confession because one wanted to tell the truth.	Signing because the police beat one.
Leaving the office because one wanted one's lunch.	Leaving because forcibly removed.

It is obvious that to find the correct definition of free acts we must discover what characteristic is common to all the acts in the left-hand column, and is, at the same time, absent from all the acts in the right-hand column. This characteristic which all free acts have, and which no unfree acts have, will be the defining characteristic of free will.

Is being uncaused, or not being determined by causes, the characteristic of which we are in search? It cannot be, because although it is true that all the acts in the right-hand column have causes, such as the beating by the police or the absence of food in the desert, so also do the acts in the left-hand column. Mr. Gandhi's fasting was caused by his desire to free India, the man leaving his office by his hunger, and so on. Moreover there is no reason to doubt that these causes of the free acts were in turn caused by prior conditions, and that these were again the results of causes, and so on back indefinitely into the past. Any physiologist can tell us the causes of hunger. What caused Mr. Gandhi's

tremendously powerful desire to free India is no doubt more difficult to discover. But it must have had causes. Some of them may have lain in peculiarities of his glands or brain, others in his past experiences, others in his heredity, others in his education. Defenders of free will have usually tended to deny such facts. But to do so is plainly a case of special pleading, which is unsupported by any scrap of evidence. The only reasonable view is that all human actions, both those which are freely done and those which are not, are either wholly determined by causes, or at least as much determined as other events in nature. It may be true, as the physicists tell us, that nature is not as deterministic as was once thought. But whatever degree of determinism prevails in the world, human actions appear to be as much determined as anything else. And if this is so, it cannot be the case that what distinguishes actions freely chosen from those which are not free is that the latter are determined by causes while the former are not. Therefore, being uncaused or being undetermined by causes, must be an incorrect definition of free will.

What, then, is the difference between acts which are freely done and those which are not? What is the characteristic which is present to all the acts in the left-hand column and absent from all those in the right-hand column? Is it not obvious that, although both sets of actions have causes, the causes of those in the left-hand column are *of a different kind* from the causes of those in the right-hand column? The free acts are all caused by desires, or motives, or by some sort of internal psychological states of the agent's mind. The unfree acts, on the other hand, are all caused by physical forces or physical conditions, outside the agent. Police arrest means physical force exerted from the outside; the absence of food in the desert is a physical condition of the outside world. We may therefore frame the following rough definitions. *Acts freely done are those whose immediate causes are psychological states in the agent. Acts not freely done are those whose immediate causes are states of affairs external to the agent.*

It is plain that if we define free will in this way, then free will certainly exists, and the philosopher's denial of its existence is seen to be what it is—nonsense. For it is obvious that all those actions of men which we should ordinarily attribute to the exercise of their free will, or of which we should say that they freely chose to do them, are in fact actions which have been caused by their own desires, wishes, thoughts, emotions, impulses, or other psychological states.

In applying our definition we shall find that it usually works well, but that there are some puzzling cases which it does not seem exactly to fit. These puzzles can always be solved by paying careful attention to the ways in which words are used, and remembering that they are not always used consistently. I have space for only one example. Suppose that a thug threatens to shoot you unless you give him your wallet, and suppose that you do so. Do you, in giving him your wallet, do so of your own free will or not? If we apply our definition, we find that you acted freely, since the immediate cause of the action was not an actual outside force but the fear of death, which is a psychological cause. Most people, however, would say that you did not act of your own free will but under compulsion. Does this show that our definition is wrong? I do not think so. Aristotle, who gave a solution of the problem of free will substantially the same as ours (though he did not use the term "free will") admitted that there are what he called "mixed" or borderline cases in which it is difficult to know whether we ought to call the acts free or compelled. In the case under discussion, though no actual force was used, the gun at your forehead so nearly approximated to actual force that we tend to say the case was one of compulsion. It is a borderline case.

Here is what may seem like another kind of puzzle. According to our view an action may be free though it could have been predicted beforehand with certainty. But suppose you told a lie, and it was certain beforehand that you would tell it. How could one then say, "You could have told the truth"? The answer is that it is perfectly true that you could have told the truth *if* you had wanted to. In fact you would have done so, for in that case the causes producing your action, namely your desires, would have been different, and would therefore have produced different effects. It is a delusion that predictability and free will are incompatible.

This agrees with common sense. For if, knowing your character, I predict that you will act honorably, no one would say when you do act honorably, that this shows you did not do so of your own free will.

Since free will is a condition of moral responsibility, we must be sure that our theory of free will gives a sufficient basis for it. To be held morally responsible for one's actions means that one may be justly punished or rewarded, blamed or praised, for them. But it is not just to punish a man for what he cannot help doing. How can it be just to punish him for an action which it was certain beforehand that he would do? We have not attempted to decide whether, as a matter of fact, all events, including human actions, are completely determined. For that question is irrelevant to the problem of free will. But if we assume for the purposes of argument that complete determinism is true, but that we are nevertheless free, it may then be asked whether such a deterministic free will is compatible with moral responsibility. For it may seem unjust to punish a man for an action which it could have been predicted with certainty beforehand that he would do.

But that determinism is incompatible with moral responsibility is as much a delusion as that it is incompatible with free will. You do not excuse a man for doing a wrong act because, knowing his character, you felt certain beforehand that he would do it. Nor do you deprive a man of a reward or prize because, knowing his goodness or his capabilities, you felt certain beforehand that he would win it.

Volumes have been written on the justification of punishment. But so far as it affects the question of free will, the essential principles involved are quite simple. The punishment of a man for doing a wrong act is justified, either on the ground that it will correct his own character, or that it will deter other people from doing similar acts. The instrument of punishment has been in the past, and no doubt still is, often unwisely used; so that it may often have done more harm than good. But that is not relevant to our present problem. Punishment, if and when it is justified, is justified only on one or both of the grounds just mentioned. The question then is how, if we assume determinism, punishment can correct character or deter people from evil actions.

Suppose that your child develops a habit of telling lies. You give him a mild beating. Why? Because you believe that his personality is such that the usual motives for telling the truth do not cause him to do so. You therefore supply the missing cause, or motive, in the shape of pain and the fear of future pain if he repeats his untruthful behavior. And you hope that a few treatments of this kind will condition him to the habit of truth-telling, so that he will come to tell the truth without the infliction of pain. You assume that his actions are determined by causes, but that the usual causes of truth-telling do not in him produce their usual effects. You therefore supply him with an artificially injected motive, pain and fear, which you think will in the future cause him to speak truthfully.

The principle is exactly the same where you hope, by punishing one man, to deter others from wrong actions. You believe that the fear of punishment will cause those who might otherwise do evil to do well.

We act on the same principle with non-human, and even with inanimate, things, if they do not behave in the way we think they ought to behave. The rose bushes in the garden produce only small and poor blooms, whereas we want large and rich ones. We supply a cause which will produce large blooms, namely fertilizer. Our automobile does not go properly. We supply a cause which will make it go better, namely oil in the works. The punishment for the man, the fertilizer for the plant, and the oil for the car, are all justified by the same principle and in the same way. The only difference is that different kinds of things require different kinds of causes to make them do what they should. Pain may be the appropriate remedy to apply, in certain cases, to human beings, and oil to the machine. It is, of course, of no use to inject motor oil into the boy or to beat the machine.

Thus we see that moral responsibility is not only consistent with determinism, but requires it. The assumption on which punishment is based is that human behavior is causally determined. If pain could not be a cause of truth-telling there would be no justification at all for punishing lies. If human actions and volitions were uncaused, it would be useless either to punish or reward, or indeed to do anything else to correct people's bad behavior. For nothing that you could do would in any way influence them. Thus moral responsibility would entirely disappear. If there were no determinism of human beings at all, their actions would be completely unpredictable and capricious, and therefore irresponsible. And this is in itself a strong argument against the common view of philosophers that free will means being undetermined by causes.

Questions for Reflection

1. Do you agree or disagree with Stace's definition of "free acts"?
2. To what degree do you think your actions are predictable by your friends or family? To what degree are your friends' actions predictable? How is it possible for us to predict another person's actions? Do you agree or disagree with Stace that an action can be predictable, yet still be said to be "free"?
3. What if you found out that all your values and desires were controlled by an evil scientist or hypnotist? In other words, all your tastes in foods, your choice of a career, your musical preferences, your personality traits, your moral and political beliefs, and your attitude toward religion were all part of a master plan that was programed into you. You always act on your own desires and psychological dispositions, but these are controlled by someone else. (This was the case in Jonathan Harrison's story of Dr. Svengali in reading 46.) Would this change how you viewed your life? Do these considerations pose a problem for Stace's claim that we have free will even if we are determined?

4. In what way is the following passage by philosopher Peter van Inwagen a criticism of compatibilism? How might Stace reply to it?

> If determinism is true, then our acts are the consequences of the laws of nature and events in the remote past. But it is not up to us what went on before we were born, and neither is it up to us what the laws of nature are. Therefore, the consequences of these things (including our present acts) are not up to us. [Peter van Inwagen, *An Essay on Free Will* (Oxford: Clarendon Press, 1983), p. 16]

B. F. SKINNER

Can Determinism Explain Creativity?

B. F. Skinner (1904–1990) was a famous American psychologist who made behaviorism one of the most influential theories in the 20th century. After graduating from college he had a brief and unsuccessful career writing literature. Upon reflection, Skinner realized that his interest as a writer had been in investigating human behavior and decided that psychology might be another way to achieve this goal. Consequently, he went on to earn a Ph.D. in psychology at Harvard University. After that, Skinner spent most of his career at Harvard, teaching and conducting his classic experiments on behavioral conditioning until his retirement in 1974. Throughout his long and illustrious career, he was one of the most influential advocates for behaviorism, a form of determinism that claims all behavior is the result of changing conditioned responses produced throughout one's life by external causes. Some of his best-known books are *Science and Human Behavior, Verbal Behavior, Beyond Freedom and Dignity,* and the novel *Walden Two.*

In the following selection, B. F. Skinner analyzes the notion of creativity. Human creativity in art, poetry, and in every other area of life is commonly thought to be based on free choices and free actions. In other words, we resist the notion that creativity is simply a product of environmental causes acting on the artist for which he or she is not responsible. However, Skinner attempts to argue that even creativity can be explained on the basis of behaviorism.

Reading Questions

1. Skinner compares having a baby to both producing a poem and giving his lecture. What is the point of this comparison?
2. In what ways does Skinner suggest the poet is like the hen?
3. In what sense is the mother responsible or not responsible for the positive characteristics of her baby? What is the comparison Skinner makes between the mother and the poet?

B. F. Skinner, "A Lecture on 'Having' a Poem," in *Cumulative Record: A Selection of Papers,* 3rd ed. (New York: Appleton-Century-Crofts, 1972).

4. What results from the fact that the poet "is not aware of the origins of his behavior"?
5. What does Skinner mean by "the autonomy of the poet"? Why does he reject it?
6. What does Skinner think will be the outcome of having a "deliberate design" or "scientific analysis" of human behavior?
7. At the end of the selection, how does Skinner characterize his own lecture and its origins? What sorts of conditions does he say would have made him write a different lecture?

What I am going to say has the curious property of illustrating itself. The quotation marks in my title ["A Lecture on 'Having' a Poem"] are intended to suggest that there is a sense in which having a poem is like having a baby, and in that sense I am in labor; I am having a lecture. In it I intend to raise the question of whether I am responsible for what I am saying, whether I am actually originating anything, and to what extent I deserve credit or blame. . . .

. . . I am to compare having a poem with having a baby, and it will do no harm to start with a lower class of living things. Samuel Butler suggested the comparison years ago when he said that a poet writes a poem as a hen lays an egg, and both feel better afterwards.

But there are other points of similarity, and on one of them Butler built a whole philosophy of purposive evolution. The statement was current in early post-Darwinism days that "a hen is only an egg's way of making another egg." It is not, of course, a question of which comes first, though that is not entirely irrelevant. The issue is who *does* what, who *acts* to produce something and therefore deserves credit. Must we give the hen credit for the egg or the egg for the hen? Possibly it does not matter, since no one is seriously interested in defending the rights of hen or egg, but something of the same sort can be said about a poet, and then it does matter. Does the poet create, originate, initiate the thing called a poem, or is his behavior merely the product of his genetic and environmental histories?

I raised that question a number of years ago with a distinguished poet at a conference at Columbia University. I was just finishing *Verbal Behavior* and could not resist summarizing my position. I thought it was possible to account for verbal behavior in terms of the history of the speaker, without reference to ideas, meanings, propositions, and the like. The poet stopped me at once. He could not agree. "That leaves no place for me as a poet," he said, and he would not discuss the matter further. It was a casual remark which, I am sure, he has long since forgotten, and I should hesitate to identify him if he had not recently published something along the same lines.

When Jerome Weisner was recently inaugurated as President of Massachusetts Institute of Technology, Archibald MacLeish read a poem. He praised Dr. Weisner as:

A good man in a time when men are
scarce, when the intelligent foregather,
follow each other around in the fog like
sheep, bleat in the rain, complain
because Godot never comes; because
all life is a tragic absurdity—Sisyphus
sweating away at his rock, and the rock
won't; because freedom and dignity . . .

Oh, weep, they say, for freedom and dignity!
You're not free: it's your grandfather's itch
  you're scratching.
You have no dignity: you're not a man,
you're a rat in a vat of rewards and
  punishments,
you think you've chosen the rewards, you
  haven't:

the rewards have chosen you.

Aye! Weep!

I am just paranoid enough to believe that he is alluding to *Beyond Freedom and Dignity*. In any case, he sums up the main issue rather effectively: "You think you've chosen the rewards; you haven't. The rewards have chosen you." To put it more broadly, a person does not act upon the environment, perceiving it and deciding what to do about it; the environment acts upon him, determining that he will perceive it and act in special ways. George Eliot glimpsed the issue: "Our deeds determine us, as much as we determine our deeds," though she did not understand *how* we are determined by our deeds. Something does seem to be taken away from the poet when his behavior is traced to his genetic and personal histories. Only a person who truly initiates his behavior can claim that he is free to do so and that he deserves credit for any achievement. If the environment is the initiating force, he is not free, and the environment must get the credit.

The issue will be clearer if we turn to a biological parallel—moving from the oviparous hen to the viviparous human mother. When we say that a woman "bears" a child, we suggest little by way of creative achievement. The verb refers to carrying the fetus to term. The expression "gives birth" goes a little further; a bit of a platonic idea, birth, is captured by the mother and given to the baby, which then becomes born. We usually say simply that a woman "has" a baby where "has" means little more than possess. To have a baby is to come into possession of it. The woman who does so is then a mother, and the child is her child. But what is the nature of her contribution? She is not responsible for the skin color, eye color, strength, size, intelligence, talents, or any other feature of her baby. She gave it half its genes, but she got those from *her* parents. She could, of course, have damaged the baby. She could have aborted it. She could have caught rubella at the wrong time or taken drugs, and as a result the baby would have been defective. *But she made no positive contribution.*

A biologist has no difficulty in describing the role of the mother. She is a place, a locus in which a very important biological process takes place. She supplies protection, warmth, and nourishment, but she does not design the baby who profits from them. The poet is also a locus, a place in which certain genetic and environmental causes come together to have a common effect. Unlike a mother, the poet has access to his poem during gestation.

He may tinker with it. A poem seldom makes its appearance in a completed form. Bits and pieces *occur* to the poet, who rejects or allows them to stand, and who puts them together to *compose* a poem. But they come from his past history, verbal and otherwise, and he has had to learn how to put them together. The act of composition is no more an act of creation than "having" the bits and pieces composed.

But can this interpretation be correct if a poem is unquestionably new? Certainly the plays of Shakespeare did not exist until he wrote them. Possibly all their parts could be traced by an omniscient scholar to Shakespeare's verbal and nonverbal histories, but he must have served some additional function. How otherwise are we to explain the creation of something new?

The answer is again to be found in biology. A little more than a hundred years ago the act of creation was debated for a very different reason. The living things on the surface of the earth show a fantastic variety—far beyond the variety in the works of Shakespeare—and they had long been attributed to a creative Mind. The anatomy of the hand, for example, was taken as evidence of a prior design. And just as we are told today that a behavioral analysis cannot explain the "potentially infinite" number of sentences composable by a speaker, so it was argued that no physical or biological process could explain the potentially infinite number of living things on the surface of the earth. . . .

The key term in Darwin's title is Origin. Novelty could be explained without appeal to prior design if random changes in structure were selected by their consequences. It was the contingencies of survival which created new forms. Selection is a special kind of causality, much less conspicuous than the push-pull causality of nineteenth-century physics, and Darwin's discovery may have appeared so late in the history of human thought for that reason. The selective action of the consequences of behavior was also overlooked for a long time. It was not until the seventeenth century that any important initiating action by the environment was recognized. People acted upon the world, but the world did not act upon them. The first evidence to the contrary was of the conspicuous push-pull kind.

Descartes's . . . theoretical anticipation of the reflex and the reflex physiology of the nineteenth century gave rise to a stimulus-response psychology in which behavior was said to be triggered by the environment. There is no room in such a formulation for a more important function. When a person acts, the consequences may strengthen his tendency to act in the same way again. The Law of Effect, formulated nearly three quarters of a century ago by Edward L. Thorndike, owed a great deal to Darwinian theory, and it raised very similar issues. It is not some prior purpose, intention, or act of will which accounts for novel behavior; it is the "contingencies of reinforcement." (Among the behaviors thus explained are techniques of self-management, once attributed to "higher mental processes," which figure in the gestation of new topographies.)

The poet often knows that some part of his history is contributing the poem he is writing. He may, for example, reject a phrase because he sees that he has borrowed it from something he has read. But it is quite impossible for him to be aware of all his history, and it is in this sense that he does not know where his behavior comes from. Having a poem, like having a baby, is in large part a matter of exploration and discovery, and both poet and mother are often surprised by what they produce. And because the poet is not aware of the origins of his behavior, he is likely to attribute it to a creative mind, an "unconscious" mind, perhaps, or a mind belonging to someone else—to a muse, for example, whom he has invoked to come and write his poem for him.

A person produces a poem and a woman produces a baby, and we call the person a poet and the woman a mother. Both are essential as loci in which vestiges of the past come together in certain combinations. The process is creative in the sense that the products are new. Writing a poem is the sort of thing men and women do as men and women, having a baby is the sort of thing a woman does as a woman, and laying an egg is the sort of thing a hen does as a hen. To deny a creative contribution does not destroy man *qua* man or woman *qua* woman any more than Butler's phrase destroys hen *qua* hen. . . .

What is threatened, of course, is the autonomy of the poet. The autonomous is the uncaused, and the uncaused is miraculous, and the miraculous is God. For the second time in a little more than a century a theory of selection by consequences is threatening a traditional belief in a creative mind. And is it not rather strange that although we have abandoned that belief with respect to the creation of the world, we fight so desperately to preserve it with respect to the creation of a poem?

But is there anything wrong with a supportive myth? Why not continue to believe in our creative powers if the belief gives us satisfaction? The answer lies in the future of poetry. To accept a wrong explanation because it flatters us is to run the risk of missing a right one—one which in the long run may offer more by way of "satisfaction." Poets know all too well how long a sheet of paper remains a *carte blanche*. To wait for genius or a genie is to make a virtue of ignorance. If poetry is a good thing, if we want more of it and better, and if writing poems is a rewarding experience, then we should look afresh at its sources.

Perhaps the future of poetry is not that important, but I have been using a poem simply as an example. I could have developed the same theme in art, music, fiction, scholarship, science, invention—in short, wherever we speak of *original* behavior. We say that we "have" ideas and again in the simple sense of coming into possession of them. An idea "occurs to us" or "comes to mind." And if for idea we read "the behavior said to express an idea," we come no closer to an act of creation. We "have" behavior, as the etymology of the word itself makes clear. It "occurs to us" to act in a particular way, and it is not any prior intention, purpose, or plan which disposes us to do so. By analyzing the genetic and individual histories responsible for our behavior, we may learn how to be more original. The task is not to think of new forms of behavior but to create an environment in which they are likely to occur.

Something of the sort has happened in the evolution of cultures. Over the centuries men and women have built a world in which they behave much more effectively than in a natural environment, but they have not done so by deliberate design. A culture evolves when new practices arise which make it more likely to survive. We have reached a stage in which our culture induces some of its members to be concerned for its survival. A kind of deliberate design is then possible, and a scientific analysis is obviously helpful. We can build a world in which men and women will be better poets, better artists, better composers, better novelists, better scholars, better scientists—in a word, better people. We can, in short, "have" a better world.

And that is why I am not much disturbed by the question with which George Kateb concludes his review of *Beyond Freedom and Dignity*. He is attacking my utopianism, and he asks, "Does Skinner not see that only silly geese lay golden eggs?" The question brings us back to the oviparous again, but it does not matter, for the essential issue is raised by all living things. It is characteristic of the evolution of a species, as it is of the acquisition of behavior and of the evolution of a culture, that ineffective forms give rise to effective. Perhaps a goose is silly if, because she lays a golden egg, she gets the ax; but, silly or not, she has laid a golden egg. And what if that egg hatches a golden goose? There, in an eggshell, is the great promise of evolutionary theory. A silly goose, like Butler's hen, is simply the way in which an egg produces a *better* egg.

And now my labor is over. I have had my lecture. I have no sense of fatherhood. If my genetic and personal histories had been different, I should have come into possession of a different lecture. If I deserve any credit at all, it is simply for having served as a place in which certain processes could take place. I shall interpret your polite applause in that light.

Questions for Reflection

1. When a new idea suddenly comes to you, where do you think it comes from? Based on what Skinner has said, where does *he* think it comes from?
2. At the end of his essay Skinner suggests that a scientific analysis of human behavior will allow us to control behavior such that we can create "better poets, better artists . . . better people." Do you agree with his optimism about the fruits of behavioral science? Why?
3. What is your assessment of Skinner's account of creativity?
4. Which of the following two positions do you think is correct: (a) Skinner does deserve credit for his lecture or (b) Skinner does *not* deserve credit for his lecture? How would you defend this position?
5. How does the lecture demonstrate the fact that Skinner is a hard determinist?

CONTEMPORARY APPLICATION: CAN CRIMINALS BE HELD MORALLY RESPONSIBLE FOR THEIR ACTIONS?

The problem of freedom and determinism is not just an academic problem of concern only to philosophers, for how we resolve this issue has implications for how we view one another and for public policy. If the determinist is correct, every human choice and action is determined by previous causes just as much as the motion of a billiard ball. Of course, the determinist recognizes that the causes of human behavior are much more complex, subtle, and hard to discern than are the causes operating on simple physical objects. Determinists debate among themselves concerning the degree to which the causes of our behavior are the result of our genes, our life's experiences, or biochemical conditions in the brain. Nevertheless, all determinists are agreed that every event had to result from some previous event or state of the world.

Those determinists known as hard determinists conclude that it is no more reasonable to hold people morally responsible for their behavior than it is to hold them responsible for a brain tumor. It follows from this that it is inhumane to punish criminals. Instead, they should be treated similarly to someone who has contracted tuberculosis. In other words, criminals should be confined (to protect themselves and society) and treated for their social disorder until they are cured or rehabilitated. The libertarian, on the other hand, believes that some decisions and actions are not the inevitable result of previous causes. According to this theory, people have free will and are responsible for what they do. Hence, wrongdoing merits punishment. In the following readings, C. S. Lewis argues for a theory of punishment that assumes the libertarian account and Clarence Darrow argues that criminals are not responsible for their actions, based on the claims of hard determinism.

C. S. LEWIS

Criminals Are Responsible for Their Actions

Clive Staples Lewis (1898–1963) was a British scholar and novelist who authored 40 books. He is most famous for his numerous books and essays that defended the Christian view of the world. From 1925 to 1954 he was a fellow and tutor at Oxford University and from 1954 until his death he was a professor of medieval and Renaissance English at Cambridge University.

In the following essay Lewis discusses various theories concerning the punishment of criminals. The rehabilitation theory, which he rejects, is related to determinism, for this theory of punishment assumes that criminals are not fully responsible for their behavior. Hence, the rehabilitation theory maintains that what the criminal needs is for his or her behavior to be modified by qualified behavioral scientists. However, Lewis argues that this approach ignores the issue of *desert,* which is the notion that the criminal deserves punishment. In the final analysis, Lewis believes that the humanitarian theory of punishment is not really humanitarian because it undermines the criminal's dignity as a responsible individual and has unacceptable consequences.

Reading Questions

1. What is the humanitarian theory of punishment?
2. According to Lewis what are the implications of the humanitarian theory for human rights?

C. S. Lewis, "The Humanitarian Theory of Punishment," in *God in the Dock* (Grand Rapids: William B. Eerdmans, 1970).

3. What does Lewis mean by "desert"? Why does he think it is an important concern in our treatment of the criminal?
4. Why is Lewis opposed to the view that the purpose of punishment is to deter crime or to cure the criminal?

In England we have lately had a controversy about Capital Punishment. I do not know whether a murderer is more likely to repent and make a good end on the gallows a few weeks after his trial or in the prison infirmary thirty years later. I do not know whether the fear of death is an indispensable deterrent. I need not, for the purpose of this article, decide whether it is a morally permissible deterrent. Those are questions which I propose to leave untouched. My subject is not Capital Punishment in particular, but that theory of punishment in general which the controversy showed to be almost universal among my fellow-countrymen. It may be called the Humanitarian theory. Those who hold it think that it is mild and merciful. In this I believe that they are seriously mistaken. I believe that the 'Humanity' which it claims is a dangerous illusion and disguises the possibility of cruelty and injustice without end. I urge a return to the traditional or Retributive theory not solely, not even primarily, in the interests of society, but in the interests of the criminal.

According to the Humanitarian theory, to punish a man because he deserves it, and as much as he deserves, is mere revenge, and, therefore, barbarous and immoral. It is maintained that the only legitimate motives for punishing are the desire to deter others by example or to mend the criminal. When this theory is combined, as frequently happens, with the belief that all crime is more or less pathological, the idea of mending tails off into that of healing or curing and punishment becomes therapeutic. Thus it appears at first sight that we have passed from the harsh and self-righteous notion of giving the wicked their deserts to the charitable and enlightened one of tending the psychologically sick. What could be more amiable? One little point which is taken for granted in this theory needs, however, to be made explicit. The things done to the criminal, even if they are called cures, will be just as compulsory as they were in the old days when we called them punishments. If a tendency to steal can be cured by psychotherapy, the thief will no doubt be forced to undergo the treatment. Otherwise, society cannot continue.

My contention is that this doctrine, merciful though it appears, really means that each one of us, from the moment he breaks the law, is deprived of the rights of a human being.

The reason is this. The Humanitarian theory removes from Punishment the concept of Desert. But the concept of Desert is the only connecting link between punishment and justice. It is only as deserved or undeserved that a sentence can be just or unjust. I do not here contend that the question 'Is it deserved?' is the only one we can reasonably ask about a punishment. We may very properly ask whether it is likely to deter others and to reform the criminal. But neither of these two last questions is a question about justice. There is no sense in talking about a 'just deterrent' or a 'just cure'. We demand of a deterrent not whether it is just but whether it will deter. We demand of a cure not whether it is just but whether it succeeds. Thus when we cease to consider what the criminal deserves and consider only what will cure him or deter others, we have tacitly removed him from the sphere of justice altogether; instead of a person, a subject of rights, we now have a mere object, a patient, a 'case'.

The distinction will become clearer if we ask who will be qualified to determine sentences when sentences are no longer held to derive their propriety from the criminal's deservings. On the old view the problem of fixing the right sentence was a moral problem. Accordingly, the judge who did it was a person trained in jurisprudence; trained, that is, in a science which deals with rights and duties, and which, in origin at least, was consciously accepting guidance from the Law of Nature, and from Scripture. We must admit that in the actual penal code of most countries at most times these high originals were so much modified by local custom, class interests, and utilitarian concessions, as to be very imperfectly recognizable. But the code was never in principle, and not always in fact, beyond the control of the conscience of the society. And when (say, in eighteenth-century England) actual punishments conflicted too violently with the moral sense of the community, juries refused to convict and reform was finally brought about. This was possible because, so long as we are thinking in terms of Desert, the propriety of the penal code, being a moral question, is a question on which every man has the right to an opinion, not because he follows this or that profession, but because he is simply a man, a rational animal enjoying the Natural Light. But all this is changed when we drop the concept of Desert. The only two questions we may now ask about a punishment are whether it deters and whether it cures. But these are not questions on which anyone is entitled to have an opinion simply because he is a man. He is not entitled to an opinion even if, in addition to being a man, he should happen also to be a jurist, a Christian, and a moral theologian. For they are not questions about principle but about matter of fact; and for such *cuiquam in sua arte credendum.** Only the expert 'penologist' (let barbarous things have barbarous names), in the light of previous experiment, can tell us what is likely to deter: only the psychotherapist can tell us what is likely to cure. It will be in vain for the rest of us, speaking simply as men, to say, 'but this punishment is hideously unjust, hideously disproportionate to the criminal's deserts'. The experts with perfect logic will reply, 'but nobody was talking about deserts. No one was talking about *punishment* in your archaic vindictive sense of the word. Here are the statistics proving that this treatment deters. Here are the statistics proving that this other treatment cures. What is your trouble?'

The Humanitarian theory, then, removes sentences from the hands of jurists whom the public conscience is entitled to criticize and places them in the hands of technical experts whose special sciences do not even employ such categories as rights or justice. It might be argued that since this transference results from an abandonment of the old idea of punishment, and, therefore, of all vindictive motives, it will be safe to leave our criminals in such hands. I will not pause to comment on the simple-minded view of fallen human nature which such a belief implies. Let us rather remember that the 'cure' of criminals is to be compulsory; and let us then watch how the theory actually works in the mind of the Humanitarian. The immediate starting point of this article was a letter I read in one of our Leftist weeklies. The author was pleading that a certain sin, now treated by our laws as a crime, should henceforward be treated as a disease. And he complained that under the present system the offender, after a term in gaol, was simply let out to return to his original environment where he would probably relapse. What he complained of was not the shutting up but the letting out. On his remedial view of punishment the offender should, of course, be detained until he was cured. And of course the official straighteners are the only people who can say when that is. The first result of the Humanitarian theory is, therefore, to substitute for a definite sentence (reflecting to some extent the community's moral judgment on the degree of ill-desert involved) an indefinite sentence terminable only by the word of those experts—and they are not experts in moral theology nor even in the Law of Nature—who inflict it. Which of us, if he stood in the dock, would not prefer to be tried by the old system?

It may be said that by the continued use of the word punishment and the use of the verb 'inflict' I am misrepresenting Humanitarians. They are not punishing, not inflicting, only healing. But do not let us be deceived by a name. To be taken without consent from my home and friends; to lose my liberty; to undergo all those assaults on my personality which modern psychotherapy knows how to deliver; to be re-made after some pattern of 'normality' hatched in a Viennese laboratory to which I never professed allegiance; to know that this process will never end until either my captors have

---

*We must believe the expert in his own field.

succeeded or I grown wise enough to cheat them with apparent success—who cares whether this is called Punishment or not? That it includes most of the elements for which any punishment is feared—shame, exile, bondage, and years eaten by the locust—is obvious. Only enormous ill-desert could justify it; but ill-desert is the very conception which the Humanitarian theory has thrown overboard.

If we turn from the curative to the deterrent justification of punishment we shall find the new theory even more alarming. When you punish a man *in terrorem,** make of him an 'example' to others, you are admittedly using him as a means to an end; someone else's end. This, in itself, would be a very wicked thing to do. On the classical theory of Punishment it was of course justified on the ground that the man deserved it. That was assumed to be established before any question of 'making him an example' arose. You then, as the saying is, killed two birds with one stone; in the process of giving him what he deserved you set an example to others. But take away desert and the whole morality of the punishment disappears. Why, in Heaven's name, am I to be sacrificed to the good of society in this way?—unless, of course, I deserve it.

But that is not the worst. If the justification of exemplary punishment is not to be based on desert but solely on its efficacy as a deterrent, it is not absolutely necessary that the man we punish should even have committed the crime. The deterrent effect demands that the public should draw the moral, 'If we do such an act we shall suffer like that man.' The punishment of a man actually guilty whom the public think innocent will not have the desired effect; the punishment of a man actually innocent will, provided the public think him guilty. But every modern State has powers which make it easy to fake a trial. When a victim is urgently needed for exemplary purposes and a guilty victim cannot be found, all the purposes of deterrence will be equally served by the punishment (call it 'cure' if you prefer) of an innocent victim, provided that the public can be cheated into thinking him guilty. It is no use to ask me why I assume that

our rulers will be so wicked. The punishment of an innocent, that is, an undeserving, man is wicked only if we grant the traditional view that righteous punishment means deserved punishment. Once we have abandoned that criterion, all punishments have to be justified, if at all, on other grounds that have nothing to do with desert. Where the punishment of the innocent can be justified on those grounds (and it could in some cases be justified as a deterrent) it will be no less moral than any other punishment. Any distaste for it on the part of a Humanitarian will be merely a hang-over from the Retributive theory.

It is, indeed, important to notice that my argument so far supposes no evil intentions on the part of the Humanitarian and considers only what is involved in the logic of his position. My contention is that good men (not bad men) consistently acting upon that position would act as cruelly and unjustly as the greatest tyrants. They might in some respects act even worse. Of all tyrannies a tyranny sincerely exercised for the good of its victims may be the most oppressive. It may be better to live under robber barons than under omnipotent moral busybodies. The robber baron's cruelty may sometimes sleep, his cupidity may at some point be satiated; but those who torment us for our own good will torment us without end for they do so with the approval of their own conscience. They may be more likely to go to Heaven yet at the same time likelier to make a Hell of earth. Their very kindness stings with intolerable insult. To be 'cured' against one's will and cured of states which we may not regard as disease is to be put on a level with those who have not yet reached the age of reason or those who never will; to be classed with infants, imbeciles, and domestic animals. But to be punished, however severely, because we have deserved it, because we 'ought to have known better', is to be treated as a human person made in God's image.

In reality, however, we must face the possibility of bad rulers armed with a Humanitarian theory of punishment. A great many popular blue prints for a Christian society are merely what the Elizabethans called 'eggs in moonshine' because they assume that the whole society is Christian or that the Christians are in control. This is not so in most

---

*'to cause terror'.

contemporary States. Even if it were, our rulers would still be fallen men, and, therefore, neither very wise nor very good. As it is, they will usually be unbelievers. And since wisdom and virtue are not the only or the commonest qualifications for a place in the government, they will not often be even the best unbelievers.

The practical problem of Christian politics is not that of drawing up schemes for a Christian society, but that of living as innocently as we can with unbelieving fellow-subjects under unbelieving rulers who will never be perfectly wise and good and who will sometimes be very wicked and very foolish. And when they are wicked the Humanitarian theory of punishment will put in their hands a finer instrument of tyranny than wickedness ever had before. For if crime and disease are to be regarded as the same thing, it follows that any state of mind which our masters choose to call 'disease' can be treated as crime; and compulsorily cured. It will be vain to plead that states of mind which displease government need not always involve moral turpitude and do not therefore always deserve forfeiture of liberty. For our masters will not be using the concepts of Desert and Punishment but those of disease and cure. We know that one school of psychology already regards religion as a neurosis. When this particular neurosis becomes inconvenient to government, what is to hinder government from proceeding to 'cure' it? Such 'cure' will, of course, be compulsory; but under the Humanitarian theory it will not be called by the shocking name of Persecution. No one will blame us for being Christians, no one will hate us, no one will revile us. The new Nero will approach us with the silky manners of a doctor, and though all will be in fact as compulsory as the *tunica molesta* or Smithfield or Tyburn, all will go on within the unemotional therapeutic sphere where words like 'right' and 'wrong' or 'freedom' and 'slavery' are never heard. And thus when the command is given, every prominent Christian in the land may vanish overnight into Institutions for the Treatment of the Ideologically Unsound, and it will rest with the expert gaolers to say when (if ever) they are to reemerge. But it will not be persecution. Even if the treatment is painful, even if it is life-long, even if it is fatal, that will be only a regrettable accident; the intention was purely therapeutic. In ordinary medicine there were painful operations and fatal operations; so in this. But because they are 'treatment', not punishment, they can be criticized only by fellow-experts and on technical grounds, never by men as men and on grounds of justice.

This is why I think it essential to oppose the Humanitarian theory of punishment, root and branch, wherever we encounter it. It carries on its front a semblance of mercy which is wholly false. That is how it can deceive men of good will. The error began, perhaps, with Shelley's statement that the distinction between mercy and justice was invented in the courts of tyrants. It sounds noble, and was indeed the error of a noble mind. But the distinction is essential. The older view was that mercy 'tempered' justice, or (on the highest level of all) that mercy and justice had met and kissed. The essential act of mercy was to pardon; and pardon in its very essence involves the recognition of guilt and ill-desert in the recipient. If crime is only a disease which needs cure, not sin which deserves punishment, it cannot be pardoned. How can you pardon a man for having a gumboil or a club foot? But the Humanitarian theory wants simply to abolish Justice and substitute Mercy for it. This means that you start being 'kind' to people before you have considered their rights, and then force upon them supposed kindnesses which no one but you will recognize as kindnesses and which the recipient will feel as abominable cruelties. You have overshot the mark. Mercy, detached from Justice, grows unmerciful. That is the important paradox. As there are plants which will flourish only in mountain soil, so it appears that Mercy will flower only when it grows in the crannies of the rock of Justice: transplanted to the marshlands of mere Humanitarianism, it becomes a man-eating weed, all the more dangerous because it is still called by the same name as the mountain variety. But we ought long ago to have learned our lesson. We should be too old now to be deceived by those humane pretensions which have served to usher in every cruelty of the revolutionary period in which we live. These are the 'precious balms' which will 'break our heads'.

Questions for Reflection

1. Do you agree with Lewis that the humanitarian theory of punishment is a dangerous one, even for the criminal?
2. Do you think there could be any circumstances (such as insanity) in which someone definitely committed a crime but should not be held morally responsible for it?

  CLARENCE DARROW

Criminals Are Not Responsible for Their Actions

Clarence Darrow (1867–1938) was one of America's best-known criminal attorneys. He was famous for his many defenses of unpopular causes. For example, early in his career he was a lawyer for a big railroad line but quit his job to defend union strikers against his former employer. He is best known for being the defense attorney in the famous Scopes trial in Dayton, Tennessee, in 1925. Darrow defended John Scopes, a high school biology teacher, who violated state law by teaching evolution.

The following selection is from Darrow's summation for the defense in the Leopold-Loeb murder trial in Chicago in 1924. At the time, the newspapers called it the "crime of the century." The defendants were Nathan Leopold, Jr. (18) and Richard Loeb (17). Both of them came from wealthy Chicago families and were brilliant students, Leopold having already graduated from the University of Chicago and Loeb from the University of Michigan. The murder was the result of an intellectual "experiment" in which they attempted to commit the perfect crime. Although the boys confessed to having committed the crime, Clarence Darrow argued that the two boys were the helpless victims of their heredity and environment. Hence, they were no more responsible for their crime, he said, than they were for the color of their eyes. After Darrow had spoken for 12 hours, presenting his final arguments, the silence of the courtroom was broken only by the judge's weeping. The jury was moved by his arguments and chose life sentences for the boys over the death penalty.

Reading Questions

1. As you read this passage, what phrases indicate that Darrow is not only a determinist, but a hard determinist as well?

From Clarence Darrow, "The Crime of Compulsion," in *Attorney for the Damned,* ed. Arthur Weinberg (New York: Simon and Schuster, 1957).

2. What factors in Loeb's background does Darrow use to exempt the boy from responsibility?

3. What is the point of the poem by Omar Khayyam? How does it relate to the crime that the boys committed?

4. Throughout the passage, what does Darrow say about the responsibility of the boys' governess, parents, ancestors, and society with respect to their behavior?

I have tried to study the lives of these two most unfortunate boys. Three months ago, if their friends and the friends of the family had been asked to pick out the most promising lads of their acquaintance, they probably would have picked these two boys. With every opportunity, with plenty of wealth, they would have said that those two would succeed.

In a day, by an act of madness, all this is destroyed, until the best they can hope for now is a life of silence and pain, continuing to the end of their years.

How did it happen?

Let us take Dickie Loeb first.

I do not claim to know how it happened; I have sought to find out. I know that something, or some combination of things, is responsible for this mad act. I know that there are no accidents in nature. I know that effect follows cause. I know that, if I were wise enough, and knew enough about this case, I could lay my finger on the cause. I will do the best I can, but it is largely speculation.

The child, of course, is born without knowledge.

Impressions are made upon its mind as it goes along. Dickie Loeb was a child of wealth and opportunity. Over and over in this court Your Honor has been asked, and other courts have been asked, to consider boys who have no chance; they have been asked to consider the poor, whose home had been the street, with no education and no opportunity in life, and they have done it, and done it rightfully.

But, Your Honor, it is just as often a great misfortune to be the child of the rich as it is to be the child of the poor. Wealth has its misfortunes. Too much, too great opportunity and advantage, given to a child has its misfortunes, and I am asking Your Honor to consider the rich as well as the poor (and nothing else). Can I find what was wrong? I think I can. Here was a boy at a tender age, placed in the hands of a governess, intellectual, vigorous, devoted, with a strong ambition for the welfare of this boy. He was pushed in his studies, as plants are forced in hothouses. He had no pleasures, such as a boy should have, except as they were gained by lying and cheating.

Now, I am not criticizing the nurse. I suggest that some day Your Honor look at her nature. It explains her fully. Forceful, brooking no interference, she loved the boy, and her ambition was that he should reach the highest perfection. No moment to pause, no time to stop from one book to another, no time to have those pleasures which a boy ought to have to create a normal life. And what happened? Your Honor, what would happen? Nothing strange or unusual. This nurse was with him all the time, except when he stole out at night, from two to fourteen years of age. He, scheming and planning as healthy boys would do, to get out from under her restraint; she, putting before him the best books, which children generally do not want; and he, when she was not looking, reading detective stories, which he devoured, story after story, in his young life. Of all of this there can be no question.

What is the result? Every story he read was a story of crime. We have a statute in this state, passed only last year, if I recall it, which forbids minors reading stories of crime. Why? There is only one reason. Because the legislature in its wisdom felt that it would produce criminal tendencies in the boys who read them. The legislature of this state has given its opinion, and forbidden boys to read these books. He read them day after day. He never stopped. While he was passing through college at Ann Arbor he was still reading them. When he was a senior he read them, and almost nothing else.

Now, these facts are beyond dispute. He early developed the tendency to mix with crime, to be a detective; as a little boy shadowing people on the street; as a little child going out with his fantasy of being the head of a band of criminals and directing them on the street. How did this grow and develop in him? Let us see. It seems to be as natural as the day following the night. Every detective story is a story of a sleuth getting the best of it: trailing some unfortunate individual through devious ways until his victim is finally landed in jail or stands on the gallows. They all show how smart the detective is, and where the criminal himself falls down.

This boy early in his life conceived the idea that there could be a perfect crime, one that nobody could ever detect; that there could be one where the detective did not land his game—a perfect crime. He had been interested in the story of Charley Ross, who was kidnaped. He was interested in these things all his life. He believed in his childish way that a crime could be so carefully planned that there would be no detection, and his idea was to plan and accomplish a perfect crime. It would involve kidnaping and involve murder.

There had been growing in Dickie's brain, dwarfed and twisted—as every act in this case shows it to have been dwarfed and twisted—there had been growing this scheme, not due to any wickedness of Dickie Loeb, for he is a child. It grew as he grew; it grew from those around him; it grew from the lack of the proper training until it possessed him. He believed he could beat the police. He believed he could plan the perfect crime. He had thought of it and talked of it for years—had talked of it as a child, had worked at it as a child—this sorry act of his, utterly irrational and motiveless, a plan to commit a perfect crime which must contain kidnaping, and there must be ransom, or else it could not be perfect, and they must get the money. . . .

The law knows and has recognized childhood for many and many a long year. What do we know about childhood? The brain of the child is the home of dreams, of castles, of visions, of illusions and of delusions. In fact, there could be no childhood without delusions, for delusions are always more alluring than facts. Delusions, dreams and hallucinations are a part of the warp and woof of childhood. You know it and I know it. I remember, when I was a child, the men seemed as tall as the trees, the trees as tall as the mountains. I can remember very well when, as a little boy, I swam the deepest spot in the river for the first time. I swam breathlessly and landed with as much sense of glory and triumph as Julius Caesar felt when he led his army across the Rubicon. I have been back since, and I can almost step across the same place, but it seemed an ocean then. And those men whom I thought so wonderful were dead and left nothing behind. I had lived in a dream. I had never known the real world which I met, to my discomfort and despair, and that dispelled the illusions of my youth.

The whole life of childhood is a dream and an illusion, and whether they take one shape or another shape depends not upon the dreamy boy but on what surrounds him. As well might I have dreamed of burglars and wished to be one as to dream of policemen and wished to be one. Perhaps I was lucky, too, that I had no money. We have grown to think that the misfortune is in not having it. The great misfortune in this terrible case is the money. That has destroyed their lives. That has fostered these illusions. That has promoted this mad act. And, if Your Honor shall doom them to die, it will be because they are the sons of the rich. . . .

Now, to get back to Dickie Loeb. He was a child. The books he read by day were not the books he read by night. We are all of us molded somewhat by the influences around us, and of those, to people who read, perhaps books are the greatest and the strongest influences.

I know where my life has been molded by books, amongst other things. We all know where our lives have been influenced by books. The nurse, strict and jealous and watchful, gave him one kind of book; by night he would steal off and read the other.

Which, think you, shaped the life of Dickie Loeb? Is there any kind of question about it? A child. Was it pure maliciousness? Was a boy of five or six or seven to blame for it? Where did he get it? He got it where we all get our ideas, and these books became a part of his dreams and a part of his life, and as he grew up his visions grew to hallucinations.

He went out on the street and fantastically directed his companions, who were not there, in their various moves to complete the perfect crime. Can there be any sort of question about it?

Suppose, Your Honor, that instead of this boy being here in this court, under the plea of the State that Your Honor shall pronounce a sentence to hang him by the neck until dead, he had been taken to a pathological hospital to be analyzed, and the physicians had inquired into his case. What would they have said? There is only one thing that they could possibly have said. They would have traced everything back to the gradual growth of the child.

That is not all there is about it. Youth is hard enough. The only good thing about youth is that it has no thought and no care; and how blindly we can do things when we are young!

Where is the man who has not been guilty of delinquencies in youth? Let us be honest with ourselves. Let us look into our own hearts. How many men are there today—lawyers and congressmen and judges, and even state's attorneys—who have not been guilty of some mad act in youth? And if they did not get caught, or the consequences were trivial, it was their good fortune.

We might as well be honest with ourselves, Your Honor. Before I would tie a noose around the neck of a boy I would try to call back into my mind the emotions of youth. I would try to remember what the world looked like to me when I was a child. I would try to remember how strong were these instinctive, persistent emotions that moved my life. I would try to remember how weak and inefficient was youth in the presence of the surging, controlling feelings of the child. One that honestly remembers and asks himself the question and tries to unlock the door that he thinks is closed, and calls back the boy, can understand the boy.

But, Your Honor, that is not all there is to boyhood. Nature is strong and she is pitiless. She works in her own mysterious way, and we are her victims. We have not much to do with it ourselves. Nature takes this job in hand, and we play our parts. In the words of old Omar Khayyam, we are only:

> But helpless pieces in the game He plays
> Upon this checkerboard of nights and days;
> Hither and thither moves, and checks, and slays,
> And one by one back in the closet lays.

What had this boy to do with it? He was not his own father; he was not his own mother; he was not his own grandparents. All of this was handed to him. He did not surround himself with governesses and wealth. He did not make himself. And yet he is to be compelled to pay.

There was a time in England, running down as late as the beginning of the last century, when judges used to convene court and call juries to try a horse, a dog, a pig, for crime. I have in my library a story of a judge and jury and lawyers trying and convicting an old sow for lying down on her ten pigs and killing them.

What does it mean? Animals were tried. Do you mean to tell me that Dickie Loeb had any more to do with his making than any other product of heredity that is born upon the earth? . . .

For God's sake, are we crazy? In the face of history, of every line of philosophy, against the teaching of every religionist and seer and prophet the world has ever given us, we are still doing what our barbaric ancestors did when they came out of the caves and the woods.

From the age of fifteen to the age of twenty or twenty-one, the child has the burden of adolescence, of puberty and sex thrust upon him. Girls are kept at home and carefully watched. Boys without instruction are left to work the period out for themselves. It may lead to excess. It may lead to disgrace. It may lead to perversion. Who is to blame? Who did it? Did Dickie Loeb do it?

Your Honor, I am almost ashamed to talk about it. I can hardly imagine that we are in the twentieth century. And yet there are men who seriously say that for what nature has done, for what life has done, for what training has done, you should hang these boys.

Now, there is no mystery about this case, Your Honor. I seem to be criticizing their parents. They had parents who were kind and good and wise in their way. But I say to you seriously that the parents are more responsible than these boys. And yet few boys had better parents.

Your Honor, it is the easiest thing in the world to be a parent. We talk of motherhood, and yet every woman can be a mother. We talk of fatherhood, and yet every man can be a father. Nature takes care of that. It is easy to be a parent. But to be wise and farseeing enough to understand the boy is another thing; only a very few are so wise and so farseeing as that. When I think of the light way nature has of picking our parents and populating the earth, having them born and die, I cannot hold human beings to the same degree of responsibility that young lawyers hold them when they are enthusiastic in a prosecution. I know what it means.

I know there are no better citizens in Chicago than the fathers of these poor boys. I know there were no better women than their mothers. But I am going to be honest with this court, if it is at the expense of both. I know that one of two things happened to Richard Loeb: that this terrible crime was inherent in his organism, and came from some ancestor; or that it came through his education and his training after he was born. Do I need to prove it? Judge Crowe said at one point in this case, when some witness spoke about their wealth, that "probably that was responsible."

To believe that any boy is responsible for himself or his early training is an absurdity that no lawyer or judge should be guilty of today. Somewhere this came to the boy. If his failing came from his heredity, I do not know where or how. None of us are bred perfect and pure; and the color of our hair, the color of our eyes, our stature, the weight and fineness of our brain, and everything about us could, with full knowledge, be traced with absolute certainty to somewhere. If we had the pedigree it could be traced just the same in a boy as it could in a dog, a horse or a cow.

I do not know what remote ancestors may have sent down the seed that corrupted him, and I do not know through how many ancestors it may have passed until it reached Dickie Loeb.

All I know is that it is true, and there is not a biologist in the world who will not say that I am right.

If it did not come that way, then I know that if he was normal, if he had been understood, if he had been trained as he should have been it would not have happened. Not that anybody may not slip, but I know it and Your Honor knows it, and every schoolhouse and every church in the land is an evidence of it. Else why build them?

Every effort to protect society is an effort toward training the youth to keep the path. Every bit of training in the world proves it, and it likewise proves that it sometimes fails. I know that if this boy had been understood and properly trained—properly for him—and the training that he got might have been the very best for someone; but if it had been the proper training for him he would not be in this courtroom today with the noose above his head. If there is responsibility anywhere, it is back of him; somewhere in the infinite number of his ancestors, or in his surroundings, or in both. And I submit, Your Honor, that under every principle of natural justice, under every principle of conscience, of right, and of law, he should not be made responsible for the acts of someone else. . . .

Questions for Reflection

1. Do you think that it could ever be plausible to say that someone should not be held morally responsible for a crime they committed?

2. Do you agree with Darrow that, under the circumstances, the boys were not morally responsible for their crime? Even if you think they should be held accountable do you think their moral responsibility was diminished enough that they should not get the maximum penalty?

3. Have you ever said "I couldn't help myself" or offered some similar excuse for something you intentionally did? If so, does this lend some plausibility to Darrow's appeal?

4. If Darrow is correct in saying we do not make ourselves, what are the implications for those who are model citizens? Can anyone rightly be praised for good behavior?
5. How would C. S. Lewis respond to Darrow's arguments?
6. Darrow suggests that the boys' parents and society are more to blame for the crime than the boys themselves. But in claiming that others are responsible, is he contradicting his hard determinism?

C H A P T E R   6

Questions about Right and Wrong

RIGHT AND WRONG: WHAT ARE THE ISSUES?

Questions about right and wrong fall within that area of philosophy known as ethics. **Ethics** is the systematic attempt to reason about morality, particularly the meaning and justification of claims concerning right or wrong actions, obligation, moral rules, virtue, and the possibility of objective morality. Ethics is quite a different philosophical field from those that we have studied thus far. In previous chapters we have asked questions such as, Does God exist? What is knowledge? How is the mind related to the body? Do we have free will? In answering these questions we have been attempting to *describe* what *is* true about the world. In ethics, however, we are concerned with what we *ought* to do, what consequences *ought* to be achieved, and what sort of persons we *ought* to become. In other words, ethics is a *normative* inquiry and not a descriptive one. It seeks to establish and prescribe norms, standards, rules, or principles for evaluating our actual practices.

One problem we face in seeking to reflect on ethics is that the factors relevant to making moral decisions are so numerous that it is difficult to know what role they should play in our moral judgments. Typically, ethical theories have something to say about actions, motives, consequences, and character and subject these factors to moral evaluation. But after all is said and done, which of these factors is most important or has priority over the others?

At first glance, one may think that ethics has to do with actions, which we evaluate according to the list of dos and don'ts that describe morally good or bad actions. For example, telling the truth would be an example of a good action. However, consider the moral differences between the following three cases of truth-telling.

1. When Andre was asked, "Did you have a good reason for missing the required morning meeting?" he is tempted to lie by saying that he had a class scheduled at that time. Instead, however, he tells the truth: "No, I was too lazy to get out of bed." He tells the truth because it is his moral obligation to do so.

2. When Brandee was asked, "Did you have a good reason for missing the required morning meeting?" she is tempted to lie, saying that she had a class scheduled at that time. Instead, however, she tells the truth: "No, I was too lazy to get out of bed." She tells the truth because she knows her excuse can be checked out and her lie exposed.

3. Chris says to the Dean, "Do you know what? Professor Fields came to class sober today." That is the absolute truth because the professor never took an alcoholic drink in his life. However, Chris knows that the Dean will infer that Professor Fields sometimes does not come to class sober and hopes that this will ruin his lousy teacher's reputation.

All things being equal, we are inclined to say that telling the truth is the morally right thing to do. However, only Andre told the truth *because* it was his moral obligation. The other two persons told the truth based on morally suspect motives. It seems that Brandee might have lied if she thought she could get away with it. Chris told the truth for malicious reasons.

So now it seems that motives have to be taken into account in our moral evaluations. However, consider these two cases.

1. Dr. Kindhearted is a surgeon who sincerely wants to heal people and make them better. However, he has been too busy to read a medical journal in the last twenty-five years. As a result of his ignorance, he continually makes avoidable mistakes and bad medical decisions. His patients continually die on the operating table or are maimed for life.

2. Dr. Moneyman is one of the top heart surgeons in the nation. As a young man he had considered going into either law or business, but decided that surgery would bring him the most money and fame. He is a competent surgeon and has developed a number of innovative surgical techniques. However, his striving for excellence as a surgeon is motivated by the fame and the income that it brings him and the beneficial results to his patients is just a means to his self-centered goals.

In spite of the fact that Dr. Kindhearted's motives are morally pure, he has obviously been derelict in his responsibilities. The goodness of his motives seem overwhelmed by the bad consequences of his actions. As the old saying goes, "The road to hell is paved with good intentions." On the other hand, even though Moneyman's motives are not as lofty as Kindhearted's, one would probably prefer to go to Dr. Moneyman for surgery. Because Moneyman does so much more good for people, he seems to be a better person than Kindhearted in carrying out his moral responsibilities as a surgeon.

Now it seems that the consequences of our actions have a lot to do with whether an action is morally good or not. But can we rest with the simple formula, "morally good actions are those that produce good consequences and bad actions are those that produce bad consequences"? Doesn't morality have to do with more than the results of our actions? Isn't morality concerned with character, with the sorts of persons we are and are striving to be? The following two scenarios may shed some light on this question.

1. Gary has been charged with delivering a professor's painting to a museum. On his way there, he notices a small girl drowning in a river. Knowing that every second counts, he throws her the painting to use as a float until he can get to her. Unable to spare the time fooling with his clothes, he then jumps into the water wearing the good suit that he borrowed from his roommate for an upcoming job interview. In spite of Gary's best efforts, the child drowns. He didn't save the child, but he ruined both the professor's painting and his friend's suit, as well as missing his job interview.

2. Hollie spends her weekends working on a project that builds homes for the poor. The families who move into the homes are overjoyed with the fruits of her labor. She actually doesn't care anything about the people she helps. However, doing such public service makes her feel superior to these "wretched creatures" (as she calls them) and, thereby, feeds her ego. Besides, she wants to run for homecoming queen at her college and her good works will make her look good.

In Gary's case, the consequences of his actions turned out badly. In Hollie's case, the consequences were good, for her actions contributed to people's happiness. But in our moral evaluation of these two individuals, Gary seems to exhibit the more virtuous moral character, because he acted courageously and selflessly. On the other hand, Hollie helps people, not because it is the right thing to do, but because it will advance her own interests. Her motive in this specific case is morally suspect, but in the broader picture her motive seems to flow from a character that is morally deficient. But can we divorce our assessment of a person's moral character from the sorts of actions they typically perform? This brings us back to the point where we started and shows how difficult it is to sort out the complex, interwoven factors that make up the moral dimension of human life.

Before reading this chapter, you have faced many moral dilemmas and have been making moral decisions all your life. Given this fact, why do you need to engage in a philosophical examination of morality? In other words, what is the purpose of moral theories? Moral philosopher Judith A. Boss answers the question in this way:

> Moral theories can be compared to road maps. A good theory offers *guidance* or sign posts for thinking about and resolving moral issues. Although we may just happen to come upon a good solution, a moral theory, like a road map, makes it more likely that we will reach our destination with the least amount of wrong turns and aggravation. By providing guidelines, moral theories help us identify conflicts and contradictions in our thinking and make more satisfactory moral decisions.*

Each of the philosophers in the following readings is providing a map to give us guidance in making moral decisions. In doing so, they will assign different weights to the four factors of actions, motives, consequences, and character. Furthermore, they will provide different principles for evaluating the moral goodness of the relevant factors. Since some of these maps conflict, they cannot all be correct. It will be up to you to evaluate the adequacy of these various moral theories to see which one provides the best guidance in negotiating the terrain of morality.

WHAT ARE MY OPTIONS CONCERNING RIGHT AND WRONG?

Ethical relativism is the position that there are no objective or universally valid moral principles, for all moral judgments are simply a matter of human opinion. In other words, there is no right or wrong apart from what people consider to be right or wrong.

*Judith A. Boss, *Analyzing Moral Issues* (Mountain View, CA: Mayfield, 1999), p. 3.

This position comes in two versions, depending upon whose opinion is considered to be the standard for morality.

Subjective ethical relativism (subjectivism) is the doctrine that each individual is the sole authority for himself or herself as to what is right or wrong. Just as some people like the color purple and some detest it, and each person's judgment on this matter is simply a matter of his or her individual taste, so there is no standard other than each person's own opinion when it comes to right or wrong. This doctrine implies that it is impossible for an individual to be mistaken about what is right or wrong. We will not discuss this position here, but in Chapter 8 on the meaning of life, this position is defended by Jean-Paul Sartre (reading 78).

Conventional ethical relativism (conventionalism) refers to the claim that morality is relative to each particular society or culture. For example, whether or not it is moral for women to wear shorts is a question of whether you are talking about mainstream American society or the Iranian culture. In other words, there are no universal objective moral standards in terms of which the ethical opinions and practices of a particular culture can be evaluated. This doctrine implies that it is possible for an individual to be mistaken about what is right or wrong in his or her particular society. However, since each society defines morality in its own terms, it would be impossible for a society to be mistaken about what is right or wrong.

Ethical objectivism is the view that there are universal and objectively valid moral principles that are neither relative to the individual nor society. Because objectivism is a very general doctrine that covers a wide range of more specific ethical theories, various objectivists will differ as to what the correct moral principles are and how we can know them. Nevertheless, they all agree that in every concrete situation there are morally correct and morally wrong ways to act. Furthermore, they would agree that if a certain action in a given situation is morally right or wrong for a particular person, then it will be the same for anyone who is relevantly similar and facing relevantly similar circumstances. Ethical objectivism implies that it is possible for individuals or an entire society to sincerely believe that their actions are morally right at the same time that they are deeply mistaken about this.

The next four theories all fall under the heading of ethical objectivism. While they disagree about what ethical principles should be followed, they all agree that there are one or more nonarbitrary, nonsubjective, universal moral principles that determine whether or not an action is right or wrong.

Virtue ethics refers to any theory that sees the character of the agent to be the primary focus of ethics rather than actions or duties. In contrast, the remaining theories are concerned primarily with rules or principles for deciding how to act. While they do not ignore the issue of what makes a good person, they tend to define the goodness of persons in terms of either what actions they perform or what principles they employ. For virtue ethics, however, this reverses the proper order. The good person is not one who performs good actions, but good actions are defined as those that a person with a good moral character would do. Whereas the other objectivist theories ask "What should I do?" virtue ethics asks "What sort of person should I be?"

Kantian ethics is one variety of a more general category known as **deontological ethics.** Common to all varieties of deontological ethics (from the Greek word *deon* meaning duty) is the claim that we have absolute moral duties that are not affected by the consequences. Hence, the rightness or wrongness of an action is said to be intrinsic to the type of action it is. Kantian ethics (named after the philosopher Immanuel Kant) argues that we can discover our moral duties by asking whether the principle on which we act is one that we could rationally wish everyone to follow at all times. For Kantian ethics, as with every deontological theory, our moral duty cannot be decided by anything as variable and uncertain as the projected consequences of an action.

Utilitarianism is the theory that the right action is the one that produces the greatest amount of happiness for the greatest number of people. Accordingly, utilitarians (contrary to Kantian theorists) claim that the morality of an action cannot be divorced from its consequences. Any theory (such as utilitarianism) that judges the moral rightness or wrongness of an act according to the desirability or undesirability of the action's consequences is called **consequentialism.** To put it glibly, the consequentialist believes that "all's well that ends well." This type of theory is also known as **teleological ethics** (from the Greek word *telos,* meaning end or purpose). The utilitarian formula that the moral act is one that produces the greatest amount of happiness possible would allow the same type of action to be moral in one set of circumstances and immoral in a different situation if the consequences were different. Nevertheless, while the moral evaluation of an action may be relative to the circumstances, there is still an unchanging, universal, ethical principle that is being followed.

Ethical egoism is the theory that people always and only have a moral obligation to do what is in their own self-interest. According to this position, the locus of value is the individual and there can be no higher value for me than my own life and its well-being and no higher value for you than your own life. This is a version of ethical objectivism and should not be mistaken for subjective ethical relativism, for the egoist would say that my moral judgments can be wrong, if I put another person's interests before my own. Of course, the egoist's principle will dictate different, and sometimes, competing courses of action. For example, it is in my best interests to promote the flourishing of the philosophy program at my university, while it is in a coach's interest to promote the flourishing of the football program. Nevertheless, the egoist would maintain that competing interests can lead to the best outcome. In business, for example, if each company tries to capture the market with the best product, society as a whole benefits. Similarly, in a court of law, each lawyer promotes the best interests of his or her client, and we presume that this procedure will help insure that all aspects of the case will be revealed.

Feminist ethics is a new development in recent decades that questions some of the fundamental assumptions of traditional ethical theory. Feminist theory is still developing and it represents multiple perspectives, so it is difficult to summarize it in a brief statement. For example, some feminists agree with ethical relativism, while others are more aligned with some version of ethical objectivism. However, in spite of their differences, most feminists agree that there are distinctively male and female ways of viewing a situation and this gender perspective will make a decided difference to our ethical perspective. Their complaint is that traditional ethical theories are one-sided, for they typically represent the style, aims, concerns, questions, and theoretical assumptions of men. For example, some psychological studies seem to suggest that males tend toward a judicial model of ethical decision making in which abstract principles and reason predominate. Females, however, are more concerned with relationships and the emotional textures of a situation. These differences play out in completely different theoretical approaches to ethical issues. While some feminists want to replace the male-biased approaches with new perspectives, others simply want to supplement the historically one-sided approaches with a more balanced perspective. While feminist theorists bring a fresh new perspective to ethics, they often work within and use the resources of the other theories as much as they critique their limitations.

This spectrum of ethical theories is summarized in Table 6.1. Unfortunately, it is impossible to represent feminist ethics in such a simplified scheme because writers who can be characterized as representing the feminist perspective on ethics can be found within each of the traditional categories. Feminist writers are not distinguished so much by how they answer the following questions, but by the way that they bring gender issues to bear on the traditional questions and theories in moral philosophy.

Each major position discussed in this section is represented in the readings that follow. The first two readings address the question, "Are moral principles objective or relative?" Ruth Benedict (reading 54) will defend conventional ethical relativism, claiming that morality is a function of a particular culture's conventions. On the other hand, James Rachels (reading 55) will critique this sort of conventional ethical relativism and

TABLE 6.1 FIVE ETHICAL THEORIES

	Are There Moral Principles or Truths That Are Objectively Valid?	Is Morality More Concerned with the Character of a Virtuous Person Than with Rules of Conduct?	Are Actions Right or Wrong in Themselves, Independent of Their Consequences	Do the Consequences of an Action Make It Right or Wrong?	Is Serving One's Own Self-Interest the Only Moral Duty?
Ethical Relativism	No	—	—	—	—
Virtue Ethics (Aristotle)	Yes	Yes	Only as they relate to certain character traits	No	No
Kantian Ethics	Yes	Morality is concerned with both	Yes	No	No
Utilitarianism	Yes	No	No	Yes	No
Ethical Egoism	Yes	No	No	Yes—but only the consequences for the person performing the action	Yes

support ethical objectivism. The next set of readings provides the answers of different ethical theories to the question, "How do we decide what is right or wrong?" These authors and the positions they defend are Aristotle (virtue ethics), Immanuel Kant (deontological ethics), John Stuart Mill (utilitarianism), Ayn Rand (ethical egoism), and Alison Jaggar (feminist ethics). Finally, in the Contemporary Application readings, Judith Jarvis Thomson and Sidney Callahan will develop contrasting arguments concerning the concrete ethical issue of abortion.

As our opening narrative, Plato's classic story of "The Ring of Gyges" will set the stage for a consideration of these philosophical theories about ethics. In this narrative, Plato has one of his characters raise provocative questions about the very purpose of morality.

OPENING NARRATIVE: WHY SHOULD I BE MORAL?

 PLATO

The Ring of Gyges

Why should you worry about being a moral person? Is moral goodness something that you should pursue for its own sake, or is it desirable simply because of the consequences? To use an analogy, no one enjoys going to the dentist to get his or her teeth drilled and most people do not choose to go on a severely restrictive diet for its own sake. Instead, we do these things only because of the results they bring—physical health. If going to the dentist or dieting did not pay in terms of better health, there would be little reason to do these things. Is morality like that? Is the only reason for being a morally good person the fact that the external consequences are desirable, while the external consequences of being immoral are undesirable?

The question "Why be moral?" was taken up in Plato's dialogue, the *Republic*. Through the character of Glaucon, Plato presents a position contrary to his own in order to clarify the issues. Glaucon entertains the position that most reasonable people (if they were truly honest) would agree that being a just and moral person is *not* desirable in itself, but is only desirable for the social rewards that it brings and the unpleasant consequences it avoids. To make his point as sharply as possible, Glaucon tells the story of a shepherd named Gyges who discovers a ring that will make him invisible when it is turned a certain way. This enables Gyges to do whatever he wishes without worrying about society's sanctions. Glaucon uses this story as a thought experiment to demonstrate his thesis. According to this theory of morality, there would be no reason to be moral if one could get away with being immoral. In so far as he embraces this position, Glaucon aligns himself with the Sophists. The Sophists were a group of Greek philosophers who Plato despised. They were radical relativists who believed that all morality was simply a matter of subjective opinion. Glaucon begins his account by sympathetically setting out the theory of the Sophist Thrasymachus and his followers.

Reading Questions

1. What is the popular view of justice, according to Glaucon? Why do people strive to appear just?
2. What reasons lead Glaucon to suggest that all people "believe in their hearts that injustice is far more profitable to the individual than justice"?
3. What is the point of the story of the ring of Gyges and the hypothetical comparison of the unjust and just person?

From Plato, *Republic*, in *The Dialogues of Plato*, trans. Benjamin Jowett (New York: Oxford University Press, 1896).

If you, please, then, I will revive the argument of Thrasymachus. And first I will speak of the nature and origin of justice according to the common view of them. Secondly, I will show that all men who practice justice do so against their will, of necessity, but not as a good. And thirdly, I will argue that there is reason in this view, for the life of the unjust is after all better far than the life of the just—if what they say is true. . . .

They say that to do injustice is, by nature, good; to suffer injustice, evil; but that the evil is greater than the good. And so when men have both done and suffered injustice and have had experience of both, not being able to avoid the one and obtain the other, they think that they had better agree among themselves to have neither; hence there arise laws and mutual covenants; and that which is ordained by law is termed by them lawful and just. This they affirm to be the origin and nature of justice:—it is a mean or compromise, between the best of all, which is to do injustice and not be punished, and the worst of all, which is to suffer injustice without the power of retaliation; and justice, being at a middle point between the two, is tolerated not as a good, but as the lesser evil, and honoured by reason of the inability of men to do injustice. For no man who is worthy to be called a man would ever submit to such an agreement if he were able to resist; he would be mad if he did. Such is the received account, Socrates, of the nature and origin of justice.

Now that those who practice justice do so involuntarily and because they have not the power to be unjust will best appear if we imagine something of this kind: having given both to the just and the unjust power to do what they will, let us watch and see whither desire will lead them; then we shall discover in the very act the just and unjust man to be proceeding along the same road, following their interest, which all natures deem to be their good, and are only diverted into the path of justice by the force of law. The liberty which we are supposing may be most completely given to them in the form of such a power as is said to have been possessed by Gyges the ancestor of Croesus the Lydian. According to the tradition, Gyges was a shepherd in the service of the king of Lydia; there was a great storm, and an earthquake made an opening in the earth at the place where he was feeding his flock. Amazed at the sight, he descended into the opening, where, among other marvels, he beheld a hollow brazen horse, having doors, at which he stooping and looking in saw a dead body of stature, as appeared to him, more than human, and having nothing on but a gold ring; this he took from the finger of the dead and reascended. Now the shepherds met together, according to custom, that they might send their monthly report about the flocks to the king; into their assembly he came having the ring on his finger, and as he was sitting among them he chanced to turn the collet of the ring inside his hand, when instantly he became invisible to the rest of the company and they began to speak of him as if he were no longer present. He was astonished at this, and again touching the ring he turned the collet outwards and reappeared; he made several trials of the ring, and always with the same result—when he turned the collet inwards he became invisible, when outwards he reappeared. Whereupon he contrived to be chosen one of the messengers who were sent to the court; where as soon as he arrived he seduced the queen, and with her help conspired against the king and slew him, and took the kingdom. Suppose now that there were two such magic rings, and the just put on one of them and the unjust the other; no man can be imagined to be of such an iron nature that he would stand fast in justice. No man would keep his hands off what was not his own when he could safely take what he liked out of the market, or go into houses and lie with any one at his pleasure, or kill or release from prison whom he would, and in all respects be like a God among men. Then the actions of the just would be as the actions of the unjust; they would both come at last to the same point. And this we may truly affirm to be a great proof that a man is just, not willingly or because he thinks that justice is any good to him individually, but of necessity, for wherever any one thinks that he can safely be unjust, there he is unjust. For all men believe in their hearts that injustice is far more profitable to the individual than justice, and he who argues as I have been supposing, will say that they are right. If you could imagine any one obtaining this power of becoming invisible, and never doing any wrong or touching what was another's, he would be thought by the lookers-on to be a most wretched idiot, although they would praise him to one another's faces, and keep up appearances with one another from a fear that they too might suffer injustice. Enough of this.

Now, if we are to form a real judgment of the life of the just and unjust, we must isolate them; there is no other way; and how is the isolation to be effected? I answer: Let the unjust man be entirely unjust, and the just man entirely just; nothing is to be taken away from either of them, and both are to be perfectly furnished for the work of their respective lives. First, let the unjust be like other distinguished masters of craft; like the skillful pilot or physician, who knows intuitively his own powers and keeps within their limits, and who, if he fails at any point, is able to recover himself. So let the unjust make his unjust attempts in the right way, and lie hidden if he means to be great in his injustice (he who is found out is nobody): for the highest reach of injustice is: to be deemed just when you are not. Therefore I say that in the perfectly unjust man we must assume the most perfect injustice; there is to be no deduction, but we must allow him, while doing the most unjust acts, to have acquired the greatest reputation for justice. If he have taken a false step he must be able to recover himself; he must be one who can speak with effect, if any of his deeds come to light, and who can force his way where force is required his courage and strength, and command of money and friends. And at his side let us place the just man in his nobleness and simplicity, wishing, as Aeschylus says, to be and not to seem good. There must be no seeming, for if he seem to be just he will be honoured and rewarded, and then we shall not know whether he is just for the sake of justice or for the sake of honours and rewards; therefore, let him be clothed in justice only, and have no other covering; and he must be imagined in a state of life the opposite of the former. Let him be the best of men, and let him be thought the worst; then he will have been put to the proof; and

we shall see whether he will be affected by the fear of infamy and its consequences. And let him continue thus to the hour of death; being just and seeming to be unjust. When both have reached the uttermost extreme, the one of justice and the other of injustice, let judgment be given which of them is the happier of the two. . . .

. . . And now that we know what they are like there is no difficulty in tracing out the sort of life which awaits either of them. This I will proceed to describe; but as you may think the description a little too coarse, I ask you to suppose, Socrates, that the words which follow are not mine.—Let me put them into the mouths of the eulogists of injustice: They will tell you that the just man who is thought unjust will be scourged, racked, bound—will have his eyes burnt out; and, at last, after suffering every kind of evil, he will be impaled: Then he will understand that he ought to seem only, and not to be, just; the words of Aeschylus may be more truly spoken of the unjust than of the just. For the unjust is pursuing a reality; he does not live with a view to appearances—he wants to be really unjust and not to seem only:—

His mind has a soil deep and fertile.

Out of which spring his prudent counsels.

In the first place, he is thought just, and therefore bears rule in the city; he can marry whom he will, and give in marriage to whom he will; also he can trade and deal where he likes, and always to his own advantage, because he has no misgivings about injustice and at every contest, whether in public or private, he gets the better of his antagonists, and gains at their expense, and is rich, and out of his gains he can benefit his friends, and harm his enemies; moreover, he can offer sacrifices, and dedicate gifts to the gods abundantly and magnificently, and can honour the gods or any man whom he wants to honour in a far better style than the just, and therefore he is likely to be dearer than they are to the gods. And thus, Socrates, gods and men are said to unite in making the life of the unjust better than the life of the just.

Questions for Reflection

1. Do you agree with Glaucon that most people would do whatever they could get away with if they had the power to be invisible?
2. How would you behave if you had the magic ring?
3. Some people think that the reason for being moral is because of rewards or punishments in the afterlife. Is this a worthy motive for being moral? Or does it merely confirm Glaucon's cynical view that people are concerned to be moral for self-serving, greedy reasons?
4. Which life would you choose: to be an immoral person while people think you are a saint or to be a genuinely moral person who people wrongly punish because they think you are evil? Why?

ARE MORAL PRINCIPLES OBJECTIVE OR RELATIVE?

Why do people disagree over whether raw oysters taste good? Why is it considered morally justifiable to carry out the death penalty in some societies and immoral in others? Why do some people think abortion is morally permissible and others think it is absolutely wrong? The answer to the question about oysters is obvious. People have different tastes and opinions about food. It is equally obvious that it makes no sense to argue about the taste of oysters. It is simply a matter of individual preference. Do these same conclusions apply to ethical questions, such as the questions about the death penalty or abortion? One might claim that rightness or wrongness of the death penalty is relative to a culture (conventional ethical relativism) and that the rightness or wrongness of abortion is relative to an individual's preference (subjective ethical relativism). But others would point out that, unlike the issue of the taste of oysters, we do argue over these latter two issues and, in doing so, each side seems to assume that there is a morally correct stance to take on the matter (ethical objectivism). We will first look at a defense of conventional ethical relativism and then examine criticisms of it from the standpoint of ethical objectivism.

 R U T H   B E N E D I C T

A Defense of Moral Relativism

Ruth Benedict (1887–1948) was one of America's foremost anthropologists. She taught at Columbia University and her book *Patterns of Culture* (1934) is considered a classic of

From Ruth Benedict, "Anthropology and the Abnormal," *The Journal of General Psychology 10* (1934), 59–82, a publication of the Helen Dwight Reid Educational Foundation.

comparative anthropology. Benedict used her anthropological studies to demonstrate that much of our behavior arises from the prevailing standards of the culture in which we were raised. More specifically, moral beliefs and the practices resulting from them are a form of human behavior that varies from culture to culture. From this observation, Benedict argues that whether an action is genuinely right or wrong (and not simply *considered* right or wrong) is dependent upon the moral beliefs and practices of a particular society. In other words, there is no other basis for moral judgments than the standards of one's society. This is a form of conventional ethical relativism for Benedict implies that an action could be morally permissible in one society and immoral in terms of the standards of another society at the same time that there is no higher objective principle for judging one society as better than the other.

Reading Questions

1. Why does Benedict think it is useful to study cultures other than our own? How does she view modern civilization in the light of these other cultures?
2. What does she conclude from her study of other cultures concerning our categories of "normal" and "abnormal"?
3. List some examples she uses to show how the morality of other cultures differs from our own. Does the fact that different cultures have different moral beliefs support her thesis that there is no one, correct morality?
4. What comparisons does Benedict make between the development of a culture's preferences with respect to language or fashions and the development of its ethical beliefs?
5. Benedict claims that the assertion "It is morally good" is synonymous with what other assertion? What do you think are the implications of her equating these two statements?

Modern social anthropology has become more and more a study of the varieties and common elements of cultural environment and the consequences of these in human behavior. For such a study of diverse social orders primitive peoples fortunately provide a laboratory not yet entirely vitiated by the spread of a standardized worldwide civilization. Dyaks and Hopis, Fijians and Yakuts are significant for psychological and sociological study because only among these simpler peoples has there been sufficient isolation to give opportunity for the development of localized social forms. In the higher cultures the standardization of custom and belief over a couple of continents has given a false sense of the inevitability of the particular forms that have gained currency, and we need to turn to a wider survey in order to check the conclusions we hastily base upon this near-universality of familiar customs. Most of the simpler cultures did not gain the wide currency of the one which, out of our experience, we identify with human nature, but this was for various historical reasons, and certainly not for any that gives us as its carriers a monopoly of social good or of social sanity. Modern civilization, from this point of view, becomes not a necessary pinnacle of human achievement but one entry in a long series of possible adjustments.

These adjustments, whether they are in mannerisms like the ways of showing anger, or joy, or grief in any society, or in major human drives like those of sex, prove to be far more variable than experience in any one culture would suggest. In certain fields, such as that of religion or of formal marriage arrangements, these wide limits of variability are well known and can be fairly described. In others it is not yet possible to give a generalized account, but that does not absolve us of the task of indicating the significance of the work that has been done and of the problems that have arisen.

One of these problems relates to the customary modern normal-abnormal categories and our conclusions regarding them. In how far are such categories culturally determined, or in how far can we with assurance regard them as absolute? In how far can we regard inability to function socially as diagnostic of abnormality, or in how far is it necessary to regard this as a function of the culture?

As a matter of fact, one of the most striking facts that emerge from a study of widely varying cultures is the ease with which our abnormals function in other cultures. It does not matter what kind of "abnormality" we choose for illustration, those which indicate extreme instability, or those which are more in the nature of character traits like sadism or delusions of grandeur or of persecution, there are well-described cultures in which these abnormals function at ease and with honor, and apparently without danger or difficulty to the society. . . .

Cataleptic and trance phenomena are . . . only one illustration of the fact that those whom we regard as abnormals may function adequately in other cultures. Many of our culturally discarded traits are selected for elaboration in different societies. Homosexuality is an excellent example, for in this case our attention is not constantly diverted, as in the consideration of trance, to the interruption of routine activity which it implies. Homosexuality poses the problem very simply. A tendency toward this trait in our culture exposes an individual to all the conflicts to which all aberrants are always exposed, and we tend to identify the consequences of this conflict with homosexuality. But these consequences are obviously local and cultural. Homosexuals in many societies are not incompetent, but they may be such if the culture asks adjustments of them that would strain any man's vitality. Wherever homosexuality has been given an honorable place in any society, those to whom it is congenial have filled adequately the honorable rôles society assigns to them. Plato's *Republic* is, of course, the most convincing statement of such a reading of homosexuality. It is presented as one of the major means to the good life, and it was generally so regarded in Greece at that time.

The cultural attitude toward homosexuals has not always been on such a high ethical plane, but it has been very varied. Among many American Indian tribes there exists the institution of the berdache, as the French called them. These men-women were men who at puberty or thereafter took the dress and the occupations of women. Sometimes they married other men and lived with them. Sometimes they were men with no inversion, persons of weak sexual endowment who chose this rôle to avoid the jeers of the women. The berdaches were never regarded as of first-rate supernatural power, as similar men-women were in Siberia, but rather as leaders in women's occupations, good healers in certain diseases, or, among certain tribes, as the genial organizers of social affairs. In any case, they were socially placed. They were not left exposed to the conflicts that visit the deviant who is excluded from participation in the recognized patterns of his society.

The most spectacular illustrations of the extent to which normality may be culturally defined are those cultures where an abnormality of our culture is the cornerstone of their social structure. It is not possible to do justice to these possibilities in a short discussion. A recent study of an island of northwest Melanesia by Fortune describes a society built upon traits which we regard as beyond the border of paranoia. In this tribe the exogamic groups look upon each other as prime manipulators of black magic, so that one marries always into an enemy group which remains for life one's deadly and unappeasable foes. They look upon a good garden crop as a confession of theft, for everyone is engaged in making magic to induce into his garden the productiveness of his neighbors'; therefore no secrecy in the island is so rigidly insisted upon as the secrecy of a man's harvesting of his yams. Their polite phrase at the acceptance of a gift is, "And if you now poison me, how shall I repay you this present?" Their preoccupation with poisoning is constant; no woman ever leaves her cooking pot for a moment untended. Even the great affinal economic exchanges that are characteristic of this Melanesian culture area are quite altered in Dobu since they are incompatible with this fear and distrust that pervades the culture. They go farther and people the whole world outside their own quarters with such malignant spirits that all-night feasts and ceremonials simply do not occur here. They have even rigorous religiously enforced customs that forbid the sharing of seed even in one family group. Anyone else's food is deadly poison to you, so that communality of stores is out of the question. For some months before harvest the whole society is on the verge of starvation, but if one falls to the temptation and eats up one's seed yams, one is an outcast and a beachcomber for life. There is no coming back. It involves, as a matter of course, divorce and the breaking of all social ties.

Now in this society where no one may work with another and no one may share with another, Fortune describes the individual who was regarded by all his fellows as crazy. He was not one of those who periodically ran amok and, beside himself and frothing at the mouth, fell with a knife upon anyone he could reach. Such behavior they did not regard as putting anyone outside the pale. They did not even put the individuals who were known to be liable to these attacks under any kind of control. They merely fled when they saw the attack coming on and kept out of the way. "He would be all right tomorrow." But there was one man of sunny, kindly disposition who liked work and liked to be helpful. The compulsion was too strong for him to repress it in favor of the opposite tendencies of his culture. Men and women never spoke of him without laughing; he was silly and simple and definitely crazy. Nevertheless, to the ethnologist used to a culture that has, in Christianity, made his type the model of all virtue, he seemed a pleasant fellow.

An even more extreme example, because it is of a culture that has built itself upon a more complex abnormality, is that of the North Pacific Coast of North America. The civilization of the Kwakiutl, at the time when it was first recorded in the last decades of the nineteenth century, was one of the most vigorous in North America. . . .

. . . Among the Kwakiutl it did not matter whether a relative had died in bed of disease, or by

the hand of an enemy, in either case death was an affront to be wiped out by the death of another person. The fact that one had been caused to mourn was proof that one had been put upon. A chief's sister and her daughter had gone up to Victoria, and either because they drank bad whiskey or because their boat capsized they never came back. The chief called together his warriors. "Now I ask you, tribes, who shall wail? Shall I do it or shall another?" The spokesman answered, of course, "Not you, Chief. Let some other of the tribes." Immediately they set up the war pole to announce their intention of wiping out the injury, and gathered a war party. They set out, and found seven men and two children asleep and killed them. "Then they felt good when they arrived at Sebaa in the evening."

The point which is of interest to us is that in our society those who on that occasion would feel good when they arrived at Sebaa that evening would be the definitely abnormal. There would be some, even in our society, but it is not a recognized and approved mood under the circumstances. On the Northwest Coast those are favored and fortunate to whom that mood under those circumstances is congenial, and those to whom it is repugnant are unlucky. This latter minority can register in their own culture only by doing violence to their congenial responses and acquiring others that are difficult for them. The person, for instance, who, like a Plains Indian whose wife has been taken from him, is too proud to fight, can deal with the Northwest Coast civilization only by ignoring its strongest bents. If he cannot achieve it, he is the deviant in that culture, their instance of abnormality.

This head-hunting that takes place on the Northwest Coast after a death is no matter of blood revenge or of organized vengeance. There is no effort to tie up the subsequent killing with any responsibility on the part of the victim for the death of the person who is being mourned. A chief whose son has died goes visiting wherever his fancy dictates, and he says to his host, "My prince has died today, and you go with him." Then he kills him. In this, according to their interpretation, he acts nobly because he has not been downed. He has thrust back in return. The whole procedure is meaningless without the fundamental paranoid reading of bereavement. Death, like all the other untoward accidents of existence, confounds man's pride and can only be handled in the category of insults.

Behavior honored upon the Northwest Coast is one which is recognized as abnormal in our civilization, and yet it is sufficiently close to the attitudes of our own culture to be intelligible to us and to have a definite vocabulary with which we may discuss it. The megalomaniac paranoid trend is a definite danger in our society. It is encouraged by some of our major preoccupations, and it confronts us with a choice of two possible attitudes. One is to brand it as abnormal and reprehensible, and is the attitude we have chosen in our civilization. The other is to make it an essential attribute of ideal man, and this is the solution in the culture of the Northwest Coast.

These illustrations, which it has been possible to indicate only in the briefest manner, force upon us the fact that normality is culturally defined. An adult shaped to the drives and standards of either of these cultures, if he were transported into our civilization, would fall into our categories of abnormality. He would be faced with the psychic dilemmas of the socially unavailable. In his own culture, however, he is the pillar of society, the end result of socially inculcated mores, and the problem of personal instability in his case simply does not arise.

No one civilization can possibly utilize in its mores the whole potential range of human behavior. Just as there are great numbers of possible phonetic articulations, and the possibility of language depends on a selection and standardization of a few of these in order that speech communication may be possible at all, so the possibility of organized behavior of every sort, from the fashions of local dress and houses to the dicta of a people's ethics and religion, depends upon a similar selection among the possible behavior traits. In the field of recognized economic obligations or sex tabus this selection is as nonrational and subconscious a process as it is in the field of phonetics. It is a process which goes on in the group for long periods of time and is historically conditioned by innu-

merable accidents of isolation or of contact of peoples. In any comprehensive study of psychology, the selection that different cultures have made in the course of history within the great circumference of potential behavior is of great significance.

Every society, beginning with some slight inclination in one direction or another, carries its preference farther and farther, integrating itself more and more completely upon its chosen basis, and discarding those types of behavior that are uncongenial. Most of those organizations of personality that seem to us most incontrovertibly abnormal have been used by different civilizations in the very foundations of their institutional life. Conversely the most valued traits of our normal individuals have been looked on in differently organized cultures as aberrant. Normality, in short, within a very wide range, is culturally defined. It is primarily a term for the socially elaborated segment of human behavior in any culture; and abnormality, a term for the segment that that particular civilization does not use. The very eyes with which we see the problem are conditioned by the long traditional habits of our own society.

It is a point that has been made more often in relation to ethics than in relation to psychiatry. We do not any longer make the mistake of deriving the morality of our own locality and decade directly from the inevitable constitution of human nature. We do not elevate it to the dignity of a first principle. We recognize that morality differs in every society, and is a convenient term for socially approved habits. Mankind has always preferred to say, "It is a morally good," rather than "It is habitual," and the fact of this preference is matter enough for a critical science of ethics. But historically the two phrases are synonymous.

The concept of the normal is properly a variant of the concept of the good. It is that which society has approved. A normal action is one which falls well within the limits of expected behavior for a particular society. Its variability among different peoples is essentially a function of the variability of the behavior patterns that different societies have created for themselves, and can never be wholly divorced from a consideration of culturally institutionalized types of behavior.

Each culture is a more or less elaborate working-out of the potentialities of the segment it has chosen. In so far as a civilization is well integrated and consistent within itself, it will tend to carry farther and farther, according to its nature, its initial impulse toward a particular type of action, and from the point of view of any other culture those elaborations will include more and more extreme and aberrant traits.

Each of these traits, in proportion as it reinforces the chosen behavior patterns of that culture, is for that culture normal. Those individuals to whom it is congenial either congenitally, or as the result of childhood sets, are accorded prestige in that culture, and are not visited with the social contempt or disapproval which their traits would call down upon them in a society that was differently organized. On the other hand, those individuals whose characteristics are not congenial to the selected type of human behavior in that community are the deviants, no matter how valued their personality traits may be in a contrasted civilization.

The Dobuan who is not easily susceptible to fear of treachery, who enjoys work and likes to be helpful, is their neurotic and regarded as silly. On the Northwest Coast the person who finds it difficult to read life in terms of an insult contest will be the person upon whom fall all the difficulties of the culturally unprovided for. The person who does not find it easy to humiliate a neighbor, nor to see humiliation in his own experience, who is genial and loving, may, of course, find some unstandardized way of achieving satisfactions in his society, but not in the major patterned responses that his culture requires of him. If he is born to play an important rôle in a family with many hereditary privileges, he can succeed only by doing violence to his whole personality. If he does not succeed, he has betrayed his culture; that is, he is abnormal.

I have spoken of individuals as having sets toward certain types of behavior, and of these sets as running sometimes counter to the types of behavior which are institutionalized in the culture to which they belong. From all that we know of contrasting cultures it seems clear that differences of temperament occur in every society. The matter has never been made the subject of investigation, but from the available material it would appear that these temperament types are very likely of universal recurrence. That is, there is an ascertainable range of human behavior that is found wherever a sufficiently large series of individuals is observed. But the proportion in which behavior types stand to one another in different societies is not universal. The vast majority of the individuals in any group are shaped to the fashion of that culture. In other words, most individuals are plastic to the moulding force of the society into which they are born. In a society that values trance, as in India, they will have supernormal experience. In a society that institutionalizes homosexuality, they will be homosexual. In a society that sets the gathering of possessions as the chief human objective, they will amass property. The deviants, whatever the type of behavior the culture has institutionalized, will remain few in number, and there seems no more difficulty in moulding the vast malleable majority to the "normality" of what we consider an aberrant trait, such as delusions of reference, than to the normality of such accepted behavior patterns as acquisitiveness. The small proportion of the number of the deviants in any culture is not a function of the sure instinct with which that society has built itself upon the fundamental sanities, but of the universal fact that, happily, the majority of mankind quite readily take any shape that is presented to them. . . .

Questions for Reflection

1. Benedict points out that helping others is considered by our culture to be morally virtuous while other cultures consider it to be silly and even crazy behavior. From examples like this one Benedict concludes that if there are differences in what people consider to be right and wrong, then it is meaningless to consider what is genuinely right or wrong. Do you think her conclusion logically follows from her examples? Explain.

2. What would be some of the implications of adopting Benedict's relativism? Are any implications good? Are any problematic?

3. At the time Ruth Benedict was writing her article (1934) the Nazis were beginning to take over Europe. Would an ethical relativist have to say that the rest of the world had no right to condemn the elitist, racist, and genocidal actions of the Nazis as long as the Nazis were consistent with their own moral ideals? Does ethical relativism imply that we can never criticize the accepted practices of another society? How might Benedict reply?

4. Are we ever justified in saying that the practices of one culture are morally better than the practices of another culture? What sort of justification could be offered in support of such a claim? How would the ethical relativist argue against such a claim?

JAMES RACHELS

A Critique of Moral Relativism

James Rachels (1941–   ) is a professor of philosophy at the University of Alabama. He is well known for his books and articles on philosophy of religion and ethics. Besides *The Elements of Moral Philosophy,* from which the current selection is taken, he has published *The End of Life: Euthanasia and Morality* (Oxford University Press, 1986), *Created from Animals: The Moral Implications of Darwinism* (Oxford University Press, 1991), and *Can Ethics Provide Answers? And Other Essays in Moral Philosophy* (Rowman and Littlefield, 1997).

Rachels examines the typical arguments for ethical relativism (which he calls "cultural relativism") and concludes that they fail to make their case. He finds that at the heart of cultural relativism (or ethical relativism) is a certain form of argument that he calls the "cultural differences argument." This argument begins with the premise that cultures differ in their moral beliefs and practices and from this it concludes that there is no objective truth in morality. It is exactly the same sort of argument used by Ruth Benedict in the previous reading. However, Rachels replies that the premise concerns what people *believe* while the conclusion concerns *what is really the case.* The fact that people disagree about an issue does not prove that there is no correct or incorrect position. He then examines three implications of cultural relativism that count against its acceptability.

Reading Questions

1. The Greek historian Herodotus said that "custom is king over all." What do you think he meant by this? How does his story of the Callatian and Greek funeral practices illustrate his point?

From James Rachels, *The Elements of Moral Philosophy* (New York: Random House, 1986).

2. How do Eskimo practices lend support to the thesis of cultural relativism? How does Rachels later show that their treatment of babies is consistent with ethical objectivism?

3. What is the cultural differences argument? Why does Rachels think that it is flawed?

4. What are the three consequences of cultural relativism? Why are they problematic?

5. How does Rachels argue that the differences among cultures concerning their moral values often are not as great as they may seem at first?

6. Why does Rachels believe there must be some moral rules that are common to every culture? What examples does he provide of moral rules that are universal?

1. HOW DIFFERENT CULTURES HAVE DIFFERENT MORAL CODES

Darius, a king of ancient Persia, was intrigued by the variety of cultures he encountered in his travels. He had found, for example, that the Callatians (a tribe of Indians) customarily ate the bodies of their dead fathers. The Greeks, of course, did not do that—the Greeks practiced cremation and regarded the funeral pyre as the natural and fitting way to dispose of the dead. Darius thought that a sophisticated understanding of the world must include an appreciation of such differences between cultures. One day, to teach this lesson, he summoned some Greeks who happened to be present at his court and asked them what they would take to eat the bodies of their dead fathers. They were shocked, as Darius knew they would be, and replied that no amount of money could persuade them to do such a thing. Then Darius called in some Callatians, and while the Greeks listened asked them what they would take to burn their dead fathers' bodies. The Callatians were horrified and told Darius not even to mention such a dreadful thing.

This story, recounted by Herodotus in his *History*, illustrates a recurring theme in the literature of social science: different cultures have different moral codes. What is thought right within one group may be utterly abhorrent to the members of another group, and vice versa. Should we eat the bodies of the dead or burn them? If you were a Greek, one answer would seem obviously correct; but if you were a Callatian, the opposite would seem equally certain.

It is easy to give additional examples of the same kind. Consider the Eskimos. They are a remote and inaccessible people. Numbering only about 25,000, they live in small, isolated settlements scattered mostly along the northern fringes of North America and Greenland. Until the beginning of this century, the outside world knew little about them. Then explorers began to bring back strange tales.

Eskimo customs turned out to be very different from our own. The men often had more than one wife, and they would share their wives with guests, lending them for the night as a sign of hospitality. Moreover, within a community, a dominant male might demand—and get—regular sexual access to other men's wives. The women, however, were free to break these arrangements simply by leaving their husbands and taking up with new partners—free, that is, so long as their former husbands chose not to make trouble. All in all, the Eskimo practice was a volatile scheme that bore little resemblance to what we call marriage.

But it was not only their marriage and sexual practices that were different. The Eskimos also seemed to have less regard for human life. Infanticide, for example, was common. Knud Rasmussen, one of the most famous early explorers, reported that he met one woman who had borne twenty children but had killed ten of them at birth. Female babies, he found, were especially liable to be destroyed, and this was permitted simply at the parents' discretion, with no social stigma attached to it. Old people also, when they became too feeble to contribute to the family, were left out in the snow to die. So there seemed to be, in this society, remarkably little respect for life.

To the general public, these were disturbing revelations. Our own way of living seems so natural and right that for many of us it is hard to conceive of others living so differently. And when we do hear of such things, we tend immediately to categorize those other peoples as "backward" or "primitive." But to anthropologists and sociologists, there was nothing particularly surprising about the Eskimos. Since the time of Herodotus, enlightened observers have been accustomed to the idea that conceptions of right and wrong differ from culture to culture. If we assume that our ideas of right and wrong will be shared by all peoples at all times, we are merely naive.

2. CULTURAL RELATIVISM

To many thinkers, this observation—"Different cultures have different moral codes"—has seemed to be the key to understanding morality. The idea of universal truth in ethics, they say, is a myth. The customs of different societies are all that exist. These customs cannot be said to be "correct" or "incorrect," for that implies we have an independent standard of right and wrong by which they may be judged. But there is no such independent standard; every standard is culture-bound. The great pioneering sociologist William Graham Sumner, writing in 1906, put the point like this:

> The "right" way is the way which the ancestors used and which has been handed down. The tradition is its own warrant. It is not held subject to verification by experience. The notion of right is in the folkways. It is not outside of them, of independent origin, and brought to test them. In the folkways, whatever is, is right. This is because they are traditional, and therefore contain in themselves the authority of the ancestral ghosts. When we come to the folkways we are at the end of our analysis.

This line of thought has probably persuaded more people to be skeptical about ethics than any other single thing. *Cultural Relativism,* as it has been called, challenges our ordinary belief in the objectivity and universality of moral truth. It says, in effect, that there is no such thing as universal truth in ethics; there are only the various cultural codes, and nothing more. Moreover, our own code has no special status; it is merely one among many.

As we shall see, this basic idea is really a compound of several different thoughts. It is important to separate the various elements of the theory because, on analysis, some parts of the theory turn out to be correct, whereas others seem to be mistaken. As a beginning, we may distinguish the following claims, all of which have been made by cultural relativists:

1. Different societies have different moral codes.

2. There is no objective standard that can be used to judge one societal code better than another.

3. The moral code of our own society has no special status; it is merely one among many.

4. There is no "universal truth" in ethics—that is, there are no moral truths that hold for all peoples at all times.

5. The moral code of a society determines what is right within that society; that is, if the moral code of a society says that a certain action is right, then that action is right, at least within that society.

6. It is mere arrogance for us to try to judge the conduct of other peoples. We should adopt an attitude of tolerance toward the practices of other cultures.

Although it may seem that these six propositions go naturally together, they are independent of one another, in the sense that some of them might be true even if others are false. In what follows, we will try to identify what is correct in Cultural Relativism, but we will also be concerned to expose what is mistaken about it.

3. THE CULTURAL DIFFERENCES ARGUMENT

Cultural Relativism is a theory about the nature of morality. At first blush it seems quite plausible. However, like all such theories, it may be evaluated by subjecting it to rational analysis; and when we analyze Cultural Relativism we find that it is not so plausible as it first appears to be.

The first thing we need to notice is that at the heart of Cultural Relativism there is a certain *form of argument*. The strategy used by cultural relativists is to argue from facts about the differences between cultural outlooks to a conclusion about the status of morality. Thus we are invited to accept this reasoning:

1. The Greeks believed it was wrong to eat the dead, whereas the Callatians believed it was right to eat the dead.

2. Therefore, eating the dead is neither objectively right nor objectively wrong. It is merely a matter of opinion, which varies from culture to culture.

Or, alternatively:

1. The Eskimos see nothing wrong with infanticide, whereas Americans believe infanticide is immoral.

2. Therefore, infanticide is neither objectively right nor objectively wrong. It is merely a matter of opinion, which varies from culture to culture.

Clearly, these arguments are variations of one fundamental idea. They are both special cases of a more general argument, which says:

1. Different cultures have different moral codes.

2. Therefore, there is no objective "truth" in morality. Right and wrong are only matters of opinion, and opinions vary from culture to culture.

We may call this the *Cultural Differences Argument*. To many people, it is very persuasive. But from a logical point of view, is it a *sound* argument?

It is not sound. The trouble is that the conclusion does not really follow from the premise—that is, even if the premise is true, the conclusion still might be false. The premise concerns what people *believe:* in some societies, people believe one thing; in other societies, people believe differently. The conclusion, however, concerns *what really is the case.* The trouble is that this sort of conclusion does not follow logically from this sort of premise.

Consider again the example of the Greeks and Callatians. The Greeks believed it was wrong to eat the dead; the Callatians believed it was right. Does it follow, *from the mere fact that they disagreed,* that there is no objective truth in the matter? No, it does not follow; for it *could* be that the practice was objectively right (or wrong) and that one or the other of them was simply mistaken.

To make the point clearer, consider a very different matter. In some societies, people believe the earth is flat. In other societies, such as our own, people believe the earth is (roughly) spherical. Does it follow, *from the mere fact that they disagree,* that there is no "objective truth" in geography? Of course not; we would never draw such a conclusion because we realize that, in their beliefs about the world, the members of some societies might simply be wrong. There is no reason to think that if the world is round everyone must know it. Similarly, there is no reason to think that if there is moral truth everyone must know it. The fundamental mistake in the Cultural Differences Argument is that it attempts to derive a substantive conclusion about a subject (morality) from the mere fact that people disagree about it.

It is important to understand the nature of the point that is being made here. We are *not* saying (not yet, anyway) that the conclusion of the argument is false. Insofar as anything being said here is concerned, it is still an open question whether the conclusion is true. We *are* making a purely logical point and saying that the conclusion does not *follow from* the premise. This is important, because in order to determine whether the conclusion is true, we need arguments in its support. Cultural Relativism proposes this argument, but unfortunately the argument turns out to be fallacious. So it proves nothing.

4. THE CONSEQUENCES OF TAKING CULTURAL RELATIVISM SERIOUSLY

Even if the Cultural Differences Argument is invalid, Cultural Relativism might still be true. What would it be like if it were true?

In the passage quoted above, William Graham Sumner summarizes the essence of Cultural Relativism. He says that there is no measure of right and wrong other than the standards of one's society: "The notion of right is in the folkways. It is not outside of them, of independent origin, and brought to test them. In the folkways, whatever is, is right."

Suppose we took this seriously. What would be some of the consequences?

1. *We could no longer say that the customs of other societies are morally inferior to our own.* This, of course, is one of the main points stressed by Cultural Relativism. We would have to stop condemning other societies merely because they are "different." So long as we concentrate on certain examples, such as the funerary practices of the Greeks and Callatians, this may seem to be a sophisticated, enlightened attitude.

However, we would also be stopped from criticizing other, less benign practices. Suppose a society waged war on its neighbors for the purpose of taking slaves. Or suppose a society was violently anti-Semitic and its leaders set out to destroy the Jews. Cultural Relativism would preclude us from saying that either of these practices was wrong. We would not even be able to say that a society tolerant of Jews is *better* than the anti-Semitic society, for that would imply some sort of transcultural standard of comparison. The failure to condemn *these* practices does not seem "enlightened"; on the contrary, slavery and anti-Semitism seem wrong *wherever* they occur. Nevertheless, if we took Cultural Relativism seriously, we would have to admit that these social practices also are immune from criticism.

2. *We could decide whether actions are right or wrong just by consulting the standards of our society.* Cultural Relativism suggests a simple test for determining what is right and what is wrong: all one has to do is ask whether the action is in accordance with the code of one's society. Suppose a resident of South Africa is wondering whether his country's policy of *apartheid*—rigid racial segregation—is morally correct. All he has to do is ask whether this policy conforms to his society's moral code. If it does, there is nothing to worry about, at least from a moral point of view.

This implication of Cultural Relativism is disturbing because few of us think that our society's code is perfect—we can think of ways it might be improved. Yet Cultural Relativism would not only forbid us from criticizing the codes of *other* societies; it would stop us from criticizing our *own*. After all, if right and wrong are relative to culture, this must be true for our own culture just as much as for others.

3. *The idea of moral progress is called into doubt.* Usually, we think that at least some changes in our society have been for the better. (Some, of course, may have been changes for the worse.) Consider this example: Throughout most of Western history the place of women in society was very narrowly circumscribed. They could not own property; they could not vote or hold political office; with a few exceptions, they were not permitted to have paying jobs; and generally they were under the almost absolute control of their husbands. Recently much of this has changed, and most people think of it as progress.

If Cultural Relativism is correct, can we legitimately think of this as progress? Progress means replacing a way of doing things with a *better* way. But by what standard do we judge the new ways as better? If the old ways were in accordance with the social standards of their time, then Cultural Relativism would say it is a mistake to judge them by the standards of a different time. Eighteenth-century society was, in effect, a different society from the one we have now. To say that we have made progress implies a judgment that present-day society is better, and that is just the sort of transcultural judgment that, according to Cultural Relativism, is impermissible.

Our idea of social *reform* will also have to be reconsidered. A reformer such as Martin Luther King, Jr., seeks to change his society for the better.

Within the constraints imposed by Cultural Relativism, there is one way this might be done. If a society is not living up to its own ideals, the reformer may be regarded as acting for the best: the ideals of the society are the standard by which we judge his or her proposals as worthwhile. But the "reformer" may not challenge the ideals themselves, for those ideals are by definition correct. According to Cultural Relativism, then, the idea of social reform makes sense only in this very limited way.

These three consequences of Cultural Relativism have led many thinkers to reject it as implausible on its face. It does make sense, they say, to condemn some practices, such as slavery and anti-Semitism, wherever they occur. It makes sense to think that our own society has made some moral progress, while admitting that it is still imperfect and in need of reform. Because Cultural Relativism says that these judgments make no sense, the argument goes, it cannot be right.

5. WHY THERE IS LESS DISAGREEMENT THAN IT SEEMS

The original impetus for Cultural Relativism comes from the observation that cultures differ dramatically in their views of right and wrong. But just how much do they differ? It is true that there are differences. However, it is easy to overestimate the extent of those differences. Often, when we examine what *seems* to be a dramatic difference, we find that the cultures do not differ nearly as much as it appears.

Consider a culture in which people believe it is wrong to eat cows. This may even be a poor culture, in which there is not enough food; still, the cows are not to be touched. Such a society would *appear* to have values very different from our own. But does it? We have not yet asked why these people will not eat cows. Suppose it is because they believe that after death the souls of humans inhabit the bodies of animals, especially cows, so that a cow may be someone's grandmother. Now do we want to say that their values are different from ours? No; the difference lies elsewhere. The difference is in our belief systems, not in our values. We agree that

we shouldn't eat Grandma; we simply disagree about whether the cow *is* (or could be) Grandma.

The general point is this. Many factors work together to produce the customs of a society. The society's values are only one of them. Other matters, such as the religious and factual beliefs held by its members and the physical circumstances in which they must live, are also important. We cannot conclude, then, merely because customs differ, that there is a disagreement about *values*. The difference in customs may be attributable to some other aspect of social life. Thus there may be less disagreement about values than there appears to be.

Consider the Eskimos again. They often kill perfectly normal infants, especially girls. We do not approve of this at all; a parent who did this in our society would be locked up. Thus there appears to be a great difference in the values of our two cultures. But suppose we ask *why* the Eskimos do this. The explanation is not that they have less affection for their children or less respect for human life. An Eskimo family will always protect its babies if conditions permit. But they live in a harsh environment, where food is often in short supply. A fundamental postulate of Eskimo thought is: "Life is hard, and the margin of safety small." A family may want to nourish its babies but be unable to do so.

As in many "primitive" societies, Eskimo mothers will nurse their infants over a much longer period of time than mothers in our culture. The child will take nourishment from its mother's breast for four years, perhaps even longer. So even in the best of times there are limits to the number of infants that one mother can sustain. Moreover, the Eskimos are a nomadic people—unable to farm, they must move about in search of food. Infants must be carried, and a mother can carry only one baby in her parka as she travels and goes about her outdoor work. Other family members can help, but this is not always possible.

Infant girls are more readily disposed of because, first, in this society the males are the primary food providers—they are the hunters, according to the traditional division of labor—and it is obviously important to maintain a sufficient number of food gatherers. But there is an important second reason as well. Because the hunters suffer a high casualty rate, the adult men who die prematurely far outnumber the women who die early. Thus if male and female infants survived in equal numbers, the female adult population would greatly outnumber the male adult population. Examining the available statistics, one writer concluded that "were it not for female infanticide . . . there would be approximately one-and-a-half times as many females in the average Eskimo local group as there are food-producing males."

So among the Eskimos, infanticide does not signal a fundamentally different attitude toward children. Instead, it is a recognition that drastic measures are sometimes needed to ensure the family's survival. Even then, however, killing the baby is not the first option considered. Adoption is common; childless couples are especially happy to take a more fertile couple's "surplus." Killing is only the last resort. I emphasize this in order to show that the raw data of the anthropologists can be misleading; it can make the differences in values between cultures appear greater than they are. The Eskimos' values are not all that different from our values. It is only that life forces upon them choices that we do not have to make.

6. HOW ALL CULTURES HAVE SOME VALUES IN COMMON

It should not be surprising that, despite appearances, the Eskimos are protective of their children. How could it be otherwise? How could a group survive that did not value its young? This suggests a certain argument, one which shows that all cultural groups must be protective of their infants:

1. Human infants are helpless and cannot survive if they are not given extensive care for a period of years.

2. Therefore, if a group did not care for its young, the young would not survive, and the older members of the group would not be replaced. After a while the group would die out.

3. Therefore, any cultural group that continues to exist must care for its young. Infants

that are not cared for must be the exception rather than the rule.

Similar reasoning shows that other values must be more or less universal. Imagine what it would be like for a society to place no value at all on truth telling. When one person spoke to another, there would be no presumption at all that he was telling the truth—for he could just as easily be speaking falsely. Within that society, there would be no reason to pay attention to what anyone says. (I ask you what time it is, and you say "Four o'clock." But there is no presumption that you are speaking truly; you could just as easily have said the first thing that came into your head. So I have no reason to pay attention to your answer—in fact, there was no point in my asking you in the first place!) Communication would then be extremely difficult, if not impossible. And because complex societies cannot exist without regular communication among their members, society would become impossible. It follows that in any complex society there *must* be a presumption in favor of truthfulness. There may of course be exceptions to this rule: there may be situations in which it is thought to be permissible to lie. Nevertheless, these will be exceptions to a rule that *is* in force in the society.

Let me give one further example of the same type. Could a society exist in which there was no prohibition on murder? What would this be like? Suppose people were free to kill other people at will, and no one thought there was anything wrong with it. In such a "society," no one could feel secure. Everyone would have to be constantly on guard. People who wanted to survive would have to avoid other people as much as possible. This would inevitably result in individuals trying to become as self-sufficient as possible—after all, associating with others would be dangerous. Society on any large scale would collapse. Of course, people might band together in smaller groups with others that they *could* trust not to harm them. But notice what this means: they would be forming smaller societies that did acknowledge a rule against murder. The prohibition of murder, then, is a necessary feature of all societies.

There is a general theoretical point here, namely, that *there are some moral rules that all societies will have in common, because those rules are necessary for society to exist.* The rules against lying and murder are two examples. And in fact, we do find these rules in force in all viable cultures. Cultures may differ in what they regard as legitimate exceptions to the rules, but this disagreement exists against a background of agreement on the larger issues. Therefore, it is a mistake to overestimate the amount of difference between cultures. Not *every* moral rule can vary from society to society.

Questions for Reflection

1. Why does Rachels think that the Eskimos' moral values are not radically different from our own, even though they practice the killing of infants? Do you agree or disagree with him here?

2. Rachels claims that cultural relativism leads to three unfortunate consequences. Do you agree with him that the consequences he lists are implied by ethical relativism? To what degree do these consequences count against ethical relativism? To what degree are the consequences of holding a belief important or not important in assessing its truth?

3. Argue for or against Rachels's conclusion that there are some moral rules that all societies must have in common. If you agree with him, are there any universal moral rules that you would add to his examples?

4. On what basis might one formulate a universal core morality? What criteria would one use to decide what values or rules must be universal?

5. Could one agree with Rachels that certain moral principles are universal and objective while still acknowledging that there are other moral rules that are culturally relative?

6. Having examined the pros and cons, do you think that ethical relativism or ethical objectivism is the stronger position?

HOW DO WE DECIDE WHAT IS RIGHT OR WRONG?

The next five readings are by authors who believe that there are objective moral principles that ought to be followed by everyone. In other words, they all agree that some actions are objectively right and some actions are objectively wrong. Consistent with their ethical objectivism, they all contend that a person (or an entire culture) could be mistaken about what is moral or immoral since ethics transcends subjective, personal opinions and cultural conventions. However, each writer disagrees concerning what moral principles ought to be followed.

 **ARISTOTLE**

Virtue Ethics

Aristotle (384–322 B.C.) was an ancient Greek philosopher and scientist, and one of the most influential thinkers in history. He was a student of Plato, tutor to Alexander the Great, and the founder of logic, being the first to discover the principles for evaluating the form of arguments. His works addressed every major area of philosophy, including epistemology, metaphysics, aesthetics, and ethics, as well as the philosophical treatment of science, psychology, and politics. Aristotle founded the Lyceum, a school in Athens, and his school rivaled the Academy, Plato's school.

As will be clear in the selection from *Nicomachean Ethics* that follows, Aristotle believes that the task of ethics is to find the highest and best good in human life. You spend your life pursuing many goals and most of these goals are means to the achievement of further goals. For example, you study for tests so that you will get good grades, so that you can graduate, so that you can have a fulfilling career, and so on. Aristotle, however, argues that this cannot go on forever, so there must be one, highest goal toward which all our activities are directed. The ultimate goal in human life is **eudaimonia,** which means "happiness." However, happiness is not simply pleasure or any other kind of subjective state, for these experiences are all temporary. Happiness, according to Aristotle, means "living well" or "flourishing." It characterizes the sum total of one's life—a life that is worth living.

Aristotle goes on to explain that everything has a function or purpose given to it by nature. For example, the function of the heart is to pump blood. Hence, if we are to understand what human life is all about, we must understand what sort of beings we are. To fulfill one's function is to achieve excellence or virtue. For humans, achieving excellence means realizing our potential to be rational beings. Hence, for us, achieving virtue (or excellence) means living a life that is guided by reason. Aristotle says that there are both intellectual virtues and moral virtues. However, achieving intellectual excellence is not sufficient for living life well, for one can intellectually know what is good, but fail to do it. Hence, one has to have moral virtue as well, and this can only be acquired through practice, much as one learns to be a good musician. In other words, the good person is one who has developed the right habits and acquired a certain style of life, so that doing the right thing is a natural outflow of one's character.

In Aristotle's view, the rational life is a life of balance and moderation. Being virtuous means finding the balance (the mean) between the two vices of excess or deficiency. For example, leaping into the water to save a child is rash or foolhardy if I cannot swim (the vice of excessive confidence). If I simply run away from the crisis, this is cowardice (the vice of deficient confidence). However, if I am a competent swimmer and rationally assess the risks in leaping in the water, then I have exhibited the virtue of courage.

From Aristotle, *Nicomachean Ethics,* translated by W.D. Ross (1925). The section headings have been added.

Aristotle's ethics has enjoyed a new popularity in recent years under the heading of "virtue ethics." According to Aristotle, morality is not simply a list of dos and don'ts, nor is it merely a matter of fulfilling my duty, as it is for Kant (see reading 57). Neither is ethics merely a matter of achieving the best consequences with my actions, as it is for the utilitarians (see reading 58). Instead, for Aristotle, ethics is first and foremost a matter of developing a virtuous or excellent moral character and then all the rest will follow. Only if you achieve the best moral character possible will your biographer be able to say "this person flourished, found happiness, and lived life well."

Reading Questions

1. Why must there be something that is desired for its own sake and not for the sake of something else?
2. Pleasure, honor, or wealth are all good. But why do they not qualify as the chief good of life?
3. Why does Aristotle think that there must be some function that is common to all persons? What is the chief human function or good that constitutes happiness?
4. Why does Aristotle claim that the moral virtues do not arise within us by nature? If the moral virtues are not given us by nature, how do we acquire them?
5. What is the point he makes concerning the effects of defect and excess with respect to strength and health? What insight does he think this offers us concerning the moral virtues?
6. Aristotle says that an act can be *in accordance* with the virtues, but not be done justly or temperately. Why is this? What three conditions must be present for an act to be genuinely just or temperate (morally good)?
7. Why are virtues and vices not identical to passions?
8. Toward the end of section 6, Aristotle defines virtue as "a state of character concerned with choice, lying in a mean, i.e. the mean relative to us, this being determined by a rational principle, and by that principle by which the man of practical wisdom would determine it." What does he mean by the following four components of this definition: (1) a state of character, (2) concerned with choice, (3) lying in a mean, (4) the mean relative to us? Why are each of these factors crucial to his understanding of ethics?
9. In Book II, section 9, Aristotle gives some practical advise on how to be a good person (hitting the mean). Summarize his advice as a list of principles to follow.

BOOK I

What Is the Aim of All Human Actions?

1. Every art and every inquiry, and similarly every action and pursuit, is thought to aim at some good; and for this reason the good has rightly been declared to be that at which all things aim. But a certain difference is found among ends; some are activities, others are products apart from the activities that produce them. Where there are ends apart from the actions, it is the nature of the products to be better than the activities. Now, as there are many actions, arts, and sciences, their ends also are many; the end of the medical art is health, that of shipbuilding a vessel, that of strategy victory, that of economics wealth. But where such arts fall under a single capacity—as bridle-making and the other

arts concerned with the equipment of horses fall under the art of riding, and this and every military action under strategy, in the same way other arts fall under yet others—in all of these the ends of the master arts are to be preferred to all the subordinate ends; for it is for the sake of the former that the latter are pursued. It makes no difference whether the activities themselves are the ends of the actions, or something else apart from the activities, as in the case of the sciences just mentioned.

2. If, then, there is some end of the things we do, which we desire for its own sake (everything else being desired for the sake of this), and if we do not choose everything for the sake of something else (for at that rate the process would go on to infinity, so that our desire would be empty and vain), clearly this must be the good and the chief good. Will not the knowledge of it, then, have a great influence on life? Shall we not, like archers who have a mark to aim at, be more likely to hit upon what is right? If so, we must try, in outline at least, to determine what it is, and of which of the sciences or capacities it is the object. . . .

5. . . . To judge from the lives that men lead, most men, and men of the most vulgar type, seem (not without some ground) to identify the good, or happiness, with pleasure; which is the reason why they love the life of enjoyment. For there are, we may say, three prominent types of life—that just mentioned, the political, and thirdly the contemplative life. Now the mass of mankind are evidently quite slavish in their tastes, preferring a life suitable to beasts, but they get some ground for their view from the fact that many of those in high places share the tastes of Sardanapallus.* A consideration of the prominent types of life shows that people of superior refinement and of active disposition identify happiness with honour; for this is, roughly speaking, the end of the political life. But it seems too superficial to be what we are looking for, since it is thought to depend on those who bestow honour rather than on him who receives it, but the good we divine to be something proper to a man

and not easily taken from him. Further, men seem to pursue honour in order that they may be assured of their goodness; at least it is by men of practical wisdom that they seek to be honoured, and among those who know them, and on the ground of their virtue; clearly, then, according to them, at any rate, virtue is better. And perhaps one might even suppose this to be, rather than honour, the end of the political life. But even this appears somewhat incomplete; for possession of virtue seems actually compatible with being asleep, or with lifelong inactivity, and, further, with the greatest sufferings and misfortunes; but a man who was living so no one would call happy, unless he were maintaining a thesis at all costs. But enough of this; for the subject has been sufficiently treated even in the current discussions. Third comes the contemplative life, which we shall consider later.

The life of money-making is one undertaken under compulsion, and wealth is evidently not the good we are seeking; for it is merely useful and for the sake of something else. And so one might rather take the aforenamed objects to be ends; for they are loved for themselves. But it is evident that not even these are ends; yet many arguments have been thrown away in support of them. Let us leave this subject, then. . . .

What Is The Chief Good in Human Life?

7. Let us again return to the good we are seeking, and ask what it can be. It seems different in different actions and arts; it is different in medicine, in strategy, and in the other arts likewise. What then is the good of each? Surely that for whose sake everything else is done. In medicine this is health, in strategy victory, in architecture a house, in any other sphere something else, and in every action and pursuit the end; for it is for the sake of this that all men do whatever else they do. Therefore, if there is an end for all that we do, this will be the good achievable by action, and if there are more than one, these will be the goods achievable by action.

So the argument has by a different course reached the same point; but we must try to state this even more clearly. Since there are evidently

---

*[A ruler known for his pursuit of pleasure.]

more than one end, and we choose some of these (e.g. wealth, flutes, and in general instruments) for the sake of something else, clearly not all ends are final ends; but the chief good is evidently something final. Therefore, if there is only one final end, this will be what we are seeking, and if there are more than one, the most final of these will be what we are seeking. Now we call that which is in itself worthy of pursuit more final than that which is worthy of pursuit for the sake of something else, and that which is never desirable for the sake of something else more final than the things that are desirable both in themselves and for the sake of that other thing, and therefore we call final without qualification that which is always desirable in itself and never for the sake of something else.

Now such a thing happiness, above all else, is held to be; for this we choose always for self and never for the sake of something else, but honour, pleasure, reason, and every virtue we choose indeed for themselves (for if nothing resulted from them we should still choose each of them), but we choose them also for the sake of happiness, judging that by means of them we shall be happy. Happiness, on the other hand, no one chooses for the sake of these, nor, in general, for anything other than itself.

From the point of view of self-sufficiency the same result seems to follow; for the final good is thought to be self-sufficient. Now by self-sufficient we do not mean that which is sufficient for a man by himself, for one who lives a solitary life, but also for parents, children, wife, and in general for his friends and fellow citizens, since man is born for citizenship. But some limit must be set to this; for if we extend our requirement to ancestors and descendants and friends' friends we are in for an infinite series. Let us examine this question, however, on another occasion; the self-sufficient we now define as that which when isolated makes life desirable and lacking in nothing; and such we think happiness to be; and further we think it most desirable of all things, without being counted as one good thing among others—if it were so counted it would clearly be made more desirable by the addition of even the least of goods; for that which is added becomes an excess of goods, and of goods

the greater is always more desirable. Happiness, then, is something final and self-sufficient, and is the end of action.

Presumably, however, to say that happiness is the chief good seems a platitude, and a clearer account of what it is still desired. This might perhaps be given, if we could first ascertain the function of man. For just as for a flute-player, a sculptor, or an artist, and, in general, for all things that have a function or activity, the good and the "well" is thought to reside in the function, so would it seem to be for man, if he has a function. Have the carpenter, then, and the tanner certain functions or activities, and has man none? Is he born without a function? Or as eye, hand, foot, and in general each of the parts evidently has a function, may one lay it down that man similarly has a function apart from all these? What then can this be? Life seems to be common even to plants, but we are seeking what is peculiar to man. Let us exclude, therefore, the life of nutrition and growth. Next there would be a life of perception, but it also seems to be common even to the horse, the ox, and every animal. There remains, then, an active life of the element that has a rational principle; of this, one part has such a principle in the sense of being obedient to one, the other in the sense of possessing one and exercising thought. And, as "life of the rational element" also has two meanings, we must state that life in the sense of activity is what we mean; for this seems to be the more proper sense of the term. Now if the function of man is an activity of soul which follows or implies a rational principle, and if we say "a so-and-so" and "a good so-and-so" have a function which is the same in kind, e.g. a lyre, and a good lyre-player, and so without qualification in all cases, eminence in respect of goodness being added to the name of the function (for the function of a lyre-player is to play the lyre, and that of a good lyre-player is to do so well): if this is the case, and we state the function of man to be a certain kind of life, and this to be an activity or actions of the soul implying a rational principle, and the function of a good man to be the good and noble performance of these, and if any action is well performed when it is performed in accordance with the appropriate excellence: if this is the case, human good turns out to be activity of soul in accordance with virtue, and if there are more than one virtue, in accordance with the best and most complete.

But we must add "in a complete life." For one swallow does not make a summer, nor does one day; and so too one day, or a short time, does not make a man blessed and happy. . . .

13. Since happiness is an activity of soul in accordance with perfect virtue, we must consider the nature of virtue; for perhaps we shall thus see better the nature of happiness. . . . But clearly the virtue we must study is human virtue; for the good we were seeking was human good and the happiness human happiness. By human virtue we mean not that of the body but that of the soul; and happiness also we call an activity of soul. . . .

BOOK II

How Is Virtue Acquired?

1. Virtue, then, being of two kinds, intellectual and moral, intellectual virtue in the main owes both its birth and its growth to teaching (for which reason it requires experience and time), while moral virtue comes about as a result of habit, whence also its name (*ethike*) is one that is formed by a slight variation from the word *ethos* (habit). From this it is also plain that none of the moral virtues arises in us by nature; for nothing that exists by nature can form a habit contrary to its nature. For instance the stone which by nature moves downwards cannot be habituated to move upwards, not even if one tries to train it by throwing it up ten thousand times; nor can fire be habituated to move downwards, nor can anything else that by nature behaves in one way be trained to behave in another. Neither by nature, then, nor contrary to nature do the virtues arise in us; rather we are adapted by nature to receive them, and are made perfect by habit.

Again, of all the things that come to us by nature we first acquire the potentiality and later exhibit the activity (this is plain in the case of the senses; for it was not by often seeing or often hearing that we got these senses, but on the contrary we

had them before we used them, and did not come to have them by using them); but the virtues we get by first exercising them, as also happens in the case of the arts as well. For the things we have to learn before we can do them, we learn by doing them, e.g. men become builders by building and lyre players by playing the lyre; so too we become just by doing just acts, temperate by doing temperate acts, brave by doing brave acts.

This is confirmed by what happens in states; for legislators make the citizens good by forming habits in them, and this is the wish of every legislator, and those who do not effect it miss their mark, and it is in this that a good constitution differs from a bad one.

Again, it is from the same causes and by the same means that every virtue is both produced and destroyed, and similarly every art; for it is from playing the lyre that both good and bad lyre players are produced. And the corresponding statement is true of builders and of all the rest; men will be good or bad builders as a result of building well or badly. For if this were not so, there would have been no need of a teacher, but all men would have been born good or bad at their craft. This, then, is the case with the virtues also; by doing the acts that we do in our transactions with other men we become just or unjust, and by doing the acts that we do in the presence of danger, and being habituated to feel fear or confidence, we become brave or cowardly. The same is true of appetites and feelings of anger; some men become temperate and good-tempered, others self-indulgent and irascible, by behaving in one way or the other in the appropriate circumstances. Thus, in one word, states of character arise out of like activities. This is why the activities we exhibit must be of a certain kind; it is because the states of character correspond to the differences between these. It makes no small difference, then, whether we form habits of one kind or of another from our very youth; it makes a very great difference, or rather all the difference.

2. Since, then, the present inquiry does not aim at theoretical knowledge like the others (for we are inquiring not in order to know what virtue is, but in order to become good, since otherwise

our inquiry would have been of no use), we must examine the nature of actions, namely how we ought to do them; for these determine also the nature of the states of character that are produced, as we have said. Now, that we must act according to the right rule is a common principle and must be assumed—it will be discussed later, i.e. both what the right rule is, and how it is related to the other virtues. But this must be agreed upon beforehand, that the whole account of matters of conduct must be given in outline and not precisely, as we said at the very beginning that the accounts we demand must be in accordance with the subject-matter; matters concerned with conduct and questions of what is good for us have no fixity, any more than matters of health. The general account being of this nature, the account of particular cases is yet more lacking in exactness; for they do not fall under any art or precept but the agents themselves must in each case consider what is appropriate to the occasion, as happens also in the art of medicine or of navigation.

But though our present account is of this nature we must give what help we can. First, then, let us consider this, that it is the nature of such things to be destroyed by defect and excess, as we see in the case of strength and of health (for to gain light on things imperceptible we must use the evidence of sensible things); both excessive and defective exercise destroys the strength, and similarly drink or food which is above or below a certain amount destroys the health, while that which is proportionate both produces and increases and preserves it. So too is it, then, in the case of temperance and courage and the other virtues. For the man who flies from and fears everything and does not stand his ground against anything becomes a coward, and the man who fears nothing at all but goes to meet every danger becomes rash; and similarly the man who indulges in every pleasure and abstains from none becomes self-indulgent, while the man who shuns every pleasure, as boors do, becomes in a way insensible; temperance and courage, then, are destroyed by excess and defect, and preserved by the mean.

But not only are the sources and causes of their origination and growth the same as those of

their destruction, but also the sphere of their actualization will be the same; for this is also true of the things which are more evident to sense, e.g. of strength; it is produced by taking much food and undergoing much exertion, and it is the strong man that will be most able to do these things. So too is it with the virtues; by abstaining from pleasures we become temperate, and it is when we have become so that we are most able to abstain from them; and similarly too in the case of courage; for by being habituated to despise things that are terrible and to stand our ground against them we become brave, and it is when we have become so that we shall be most able to stand our ground against them.

3. We must take as a sign of states of character the pleasure or pain that ensues on acts; for the man who abstains from bodily pleasures and delights in this very fact is temperate, while the man who is annoyed at it is self-indulgent, and he who stands his ground against things that are terrible and delights in this or at least is not pained is brave, while the man who is pained is a coward. For moral excellence is concerned with pleasures and pains; it is on account of the pleasure that we do bad things, and on account of the pain that we abstain from noble ones. Hence we ought to have been brought up in a particular way from our very youth, as Plato says, so as both to delight in and to be pained by the things that we ought; for this is the right education. . . .

4. The question might be asked, what we mean by saying that we must become just by doing just acts, and temperate by doing temperate acts; for if men do just and temperate acts, they are already just and temperate, exactly as, if they do what is in accordance with the laws of grammar and of music, they are grammarians and musicians.

Or is this not true even of the arts? It is possible to do something that is in accordance with the laws of grammar, either by chance or at the suggestion of another. A man will be a grammarian, then, only when he has both done something grammatical and done it grammatically; and this means doing it in accordance with the grammatical knowledge in himself.

Again, the case of the arts and that of the virtues are not similar; for the products of the arts have their goodness in themselves, so that it is enough that they should have a certain character, but if the acts that are in accordance with the virtues have themselves a certain character it does not follow that they are done justly or temperately. The agent also must be in a certain condition when he does them; in the first place he must have knowledge, secondly he must choose the acts, and choose them for their own sakes, and thirdly his action must proceed from a firm and unchangeable character. These are not reckoned in as conditions of the possession of the arts, except the bare knowledge; but as a condition of the possession of the virtues knowledge has little or no weight, while the other conditions count not for a little but for everything, i.e. the very conditions which result from often doing just and temperate acts.

Actions, then, are called just and temperate when they are such as the just or the temperate man would do; but it is not the man who does these that is just and temperate, but the man who also does them as just and temperate men do them. It is well said, then, that it is by doing just acts that the just man is produced, and by doing temperate acts the temperate man; without doing these no one would have even a prospect of becoming good.

But most people do not do these, but take refuge in theory and think they are being philosophers and will become good in this way, behaving somewhat like patients who listen attentively to their doctors, but do none of the things they are ordered to do. As the latter will not be made well in body by such a course of treatment, the former will not be made well in soul by such a course of philosophy.

What Is Virtue?

5. Next we must consider what virtue is. Since things that are found in the soul are of three kinds—passions, faculties, states of character, virtue must be one of these. By passions I mean appetite, anger, fear, confidence, envy, joy, friendly feeling, hatred, longing, emulation, pity, and in general the feelings that are accompanied by pleasure or pain; by faculties the things in virtue of which we are said to be capable of feeling these, e.g. of becoming angry or being pained or feeling pity; by states of character the things in virtue of which we stand well or badly with reference to the passions, e.g. with reference to anger we stand badly if we feel it violently or too weakly, and well if we feel it moderately; and similarly with reference to the other passions.

Now neither the virtues nor the vices are passions, because we are not called good or bad on the ground of our passions, but are so called on the ground of our virtues and our vices, and because we are neither praised nor blamed for our passions (for the man who feels fear or anger is not praised, nor is the man who simply feels anger blamed, but the man who feels it in a certain way), but for our virtues and our vices we are praised or blamed.

Again, we feel anger and fear without choice, but the virtues are modes of choice or involve choice. Further, in respect of the passions we are said to be moved, but in respect of the virtues and the vices we are said not to be moved but to be disposed in a particular way.

For these reasons also they are not faculties; for we are neither called good nor bad, nor praised nor blamed, for the simple capacity of feeling the passions; again, we have the faculties by nature, but we are not made good or bad by nature; we have spoken of this before.

If, then, the virtues are neither passions nor faculties, all that remains is that they should be states of character.

Thus we have stated what virtue is in respect of its genus.

6. We must, however, not only describe virtue as a state of character, but also say what sort of state it is. We may remark, then, that every virtue or excellence both brings into good condition the thing of which it is the excellence and makes the work of that thing be done well; e.g. the excellence of the eye makes both the eye and its work good; for it is by the excellence of the eye that we see well. Simi-

larly the excellence of the horse makes a horse both good in itself and good at running and at carrying its rider and at awaiting the attack of the enemy. Therefore, if this is true in every case, the virtue of man also will be the state of character which makes a man good and which makes him do his own work well.

How this is to happen we have stated already, but it will be made plain also by the following consideration of the specific nature of virtue. In everything that is continuous and divisible it is possible to take more, less, or an equal amount, and that either in terms of the thing itself or relatively to us; and the equal is an intermediate between excess and defect. By the intermediate in the object I mean that which is equidistant from each of the extremes, which is one and the same for all men; by the intermediate relatively to us that which is neither too much nor too little—and this is not one, nor the same for all. For instance, if ten is many and two is few, six is the intermediate, taken in terms of the object; for it exceeds and is exceeded by an equal amount; this is intermediate according to arithmetical proportion. But the intermediate relatively to us is not to be taken so; if ten pounds are too much for a particular person to eat and two too little, it does not follow that the trainer will order six pounds; for this also is perhaps too much for the person who is to take it, or too little—too little for Milo,* too much for the beginner in athletic exercises. The same is true of running and wrestling. Thus a master of any art avoids excess and defect, but seeks the intermediate and chooses this—the intermediate not in the object but relatively to us.

If it is thus, then, that every art does its work well—by looking to the intermediate and judging its works by this standard (so that we often say of good works of art that it is not possible either to take away or to add anything, implying that excess and defect destroy the goodness of works of art, while the mean preserves it; and good artists, as we say, look to this in their work), and if, further,

*[A famous wrestler]

virtue is more exact and better than any art, as nature also is, then virtue must have the quality of aiming at the intermediate. I mean moral virtue; for it is this that is concerned with passions and actions, and in these there is excess, defect, and the intermediate. For instance, both fear and confidence and appetite and anger and pity and in general pleasure and pain may be felt both too much and too little, and in both cases not well; but to feel them at the right times, with reference to the right objects, towards the right people, with the right motive, and in the right way, is what is both intermediate and best, and this is characteristic of virtue. Similarly with regard to actions also there is excess, defect, and the intermediate. Now virtue is concerned with passions and actions, in which excess is a form of failure, and so is defect, while the intermediate is praised and is a form of success; and being praised and being successful are both characteristics of virtue. Therefore virtue is a kind of mean, since, as we have seen, it aims at what is intermediate.

Again, it is possible to fail in many ways (for evil belongs to the class of the unlimited, as the Pythagoreans conjectured, and good to that of the limited), while to succeed is possible only in one way (for which reason also one is easy and the other difficult—to miss the mark easy, to hit it difficult); for these reasons also, then, excess and defect are characteristic of vice, and the mean of virtue.

"For men are good in but one way, but bad in many."

Virtue, then, is a state of character concerned with choice, lying in a mean, i.e. the mean relative to us, this being determined by a rational principle, and by that principle by which the man of practical wisdom would determine it. Now it is a mean between two vices, that which depends on excess and that which depends on defect; and again it is a mean because the vices respectively fall short of or exceed what is right in both passions and actions, while virtue both finds and chooses that which is intermediate. Hence in respect of its substance and the definition which states its essence virtue is a mean, with regard to what is best and right an extreme.

But not every action nor every passion admits of a mean; for some have names that already imply badness, e.g. spite, shamelessness, envy, and in the case of actions adultery, theft, murder; for all of these and suchlike things imply by their names that they are themselves bad, and not the excesses or deficiencies of them. It is not possible, then, ever to be right with regard to them; one must always be wrong. Nor does goodness or badness with regard to such things depend on committing adultery with the right woman, at the right time, and in the right way, but simply to do any of them is to go wrong. It would be equally absurd, then, to expect that in unjust, cowardly, and voluptuous action there should be a mean, an excess, and a deficiency; for at that rate there would be a mean of excess and of deficiency, an excess of excess, and a deficiency of deficiency. But as there is no excess and deficiency of temperance and courage because what is intermediate is in a sense an extreme, so too of the actions we have mentioned there is no mean nor any excess and deficiency, but however they are done they are wrong; for in general there is neither a mean of excess and deficiency, nor excess and deficiency of a mean. . . .

[Editor's note: In section 7, here omitted, Aristotle provides examples of activities in which the virtuous character trait is the balance (or mean) between the extremes of too much and too little (see Table 6.2).]

9. That moral virtue is a mean, then, and in what sense it is so, and that it is a mean between two vices, the one involving excess, the other deficiency, and that it is such because its character is to aim at what is intermediate in passions and in actions, has been sufficiently stated. Hence also it is no easy task to be good. For in everything it is no easy task to find the middle, e.g. to find the middle of a circle is not for every one but for him who knows; so, too, any one can get angry—that is easy—or give or spend money; but to do this to the right person, to the right extent, at the right time, with the right motive, and in the right way, that is

TABLE 6.2

Aristotelian Virtues and Vices

Activity	Vice (excess)	Virtue (mean)	Vice (deficiency)
Confidence in facing danger	Rashness	Courage	Cowardice
Enjoying pleasure	Self-indulgence	Temperance	Being puritanical
Giving of money	Vulgarity	Generosity	Stinginess
Truth telling about oneself	Boastfulness	Self-honesty	Self-deprecation

not for every one, nor is it easy; wherefore goodness is both rare and laudable and noble.

Hence he who aims at the intermediate must first depart from what is the more contrary to it, as Calypso advises—

"Hold the ship out beyond that surf and spray."

For of the extremes one is more erroneous, one less so; therefore, since to hit the mean is hard in the extreme, we must as a second best, as people say, take the least of the evils; and this will be done best in the way we describe. But we must consider the things towards which we ourselves also are easily carried away; for some of us tend to one thing, some to another; and this will be recognizable from the pleasure and the pain we feel. We must drag ourselves away to the contrary extreme; for we shall get into the intermediate state by drawing well away from error, as people do in straightening sticks that are bent.

Now in everything the pleasant or pleasure is most to be guarded against; for we do not judge it impartially. We ought, then, to feel towards pleasure as the elders of the people felt towards Helen, and in all circumstances repeat their saying; for if we dismiss pleasure thus we are less likely to go astray. It is by doing this, then, (to sum the matter up) that we shall best be able to hit the mean.

But this is no doubt difficult, and especially in individual cases; for it is not easy to determine both how and with whom and on what provocation and how long one should be angry; for we too sometimes praise those who fall short and call them good-tempered, but sometimes we praise those who get angry and call them manly. The man, however, who deviates little from goodness is not blamed, whether he do so in the direction of the more or of the less, but only the man who deviates more widely; for he does not fail to be noticed. But up to what point and to what extent a man must deviate before he becomes blameworthy it is not easy to determine by reasoning, any more than anything else that is perceived by the senses; such things depend on particular facts, and the decision rests with perception. So much, then, is plain, that the intermediate state is in all things to be praised, but that we must incline sometimes towards the excess, sometimes towards the deficiency; for so shall we most easily hit the mean and what is right.

Questions for Reflection

1. How satisfactory is Aristotle's ethical theory? Do you think it captures how we commonly characterize a morally good (or virtuous) person?
2. Think of an ethical choice that you have had to make. What sort of advice would Aristotle give you in this specific case? Would his advice be too general to be of any value or would it be helpful?
3. Aristotle says that a virtuous character trait will be one that is the mean between two extremes. But he also says that the mean will be relative to each individual. Think of examples where actions that exhibited courage or generosity might vary from individual to individual. In other words, think of a situation where the same action might exhibit generosity for one person but stinginess for another. By introducing this measure of relativity in his ethics, has he made it too subjective or has he merely shown that objective principles might be applied differently in different cases?
4. Consider Table 6.2, which summarizes some of Aristotle's catalog of virtues and vices. Can you add other examples of your own of activities in which an excess or deficiency of some trait would be bad, but a balance would characterize the morally virtuous person?

IMMANUEL KANT

The Call of Duty

Immanuel Kant (1724–1804) is considered to be one of history's most important thinkers. He was discussed previously in Chapter 3, Questions about Human Knowledge. (See the introduction to reading 25 for some brief comments about his life.) Kant

---

From Immanuel Kant, *The Foundations of the Metaphysics of Morals,* trans. T. K. Abbott (1873).

developed a moral philosophy that remains one of the most influential theories today. Many thinkers consider the Kantian approach to ethics to be one of the leading sources of ethical insight as we face the troubling issues our contemporary culture is encountering in the areas of political, legal, medical, and business ethics.

For Kant, ethics is concerned not simply with what actions we do or abstain from doing (although that is important to him), but equally with the reasons or motives behind our behavior. In the following selection there are at least five major themes: (1) the importance of acting from a sense of duty and not for any other reason, (2) the irrelevance of consequences in determining our obligations or the moral rightness and wrongness of actions, (3) the importance of consistency for living the moral life and choosing our moral rules, (4) the necessity of having moral absolutes that are not qualified by any exceptions, and (5) the irreducible dignity and worth of every person. Kant's ethical theory is known as a deontological theory, for it claims that the rightness or wrongness of an act is inherent in the type of act it is and has nothing to do with the desirability of its consequences.

Reading Questions

1. What is the only thing that is good without qualification, according to Kant?
2. What does Kant mean by the "good will"?
3. Why does he think that such traits or states as intelligence, happiness, prosperity, or calm-deliberation are not good without qualification?
4. In discussing actions that conform to duty, why is Kant concerned with whether they are done from a sense of duty or from some other motive or inclination? What is Kant's view of the moral worth of actions done on the basis of inclination (that is, feelings or psychological desires)?
5. In the second and third propositions of morality, what does Kant say is the relationship between the moral worth of an action and the consequences that are achieved or expected?
6. When considering whether or not to break a promise, what question should we ask ourselves? Why do you think Kant believes this question gets us at the heart of morality? Do you agree with Kant that the moral principle he introduces is one that the average person uses in making decisions?
7. What is the distinction between a hypothetical and a categorical imperative? Why do you suppose that Kant thinks only a categorical imperative can be the basis for morality?
8. What is Kant's first formulation of the categorical imperative? Try to express it in your own words.
9. What four examples does Kant use to illustrate his moral law? Do you agree with him that in all these cases the morally wrong action would be based on a maxim that would be irrational or contradictory if universalized?
10. What is Kant's second formulation of the categorical imperative? Do you agree with him that this principle is at the heart of morality?

THE GOOD WILL

Nothing can possibly be conceived in the world, or even out of it, which can be called good, without qualification, except a good will. Intelligence, wit, judgment, and the other *talents* of the mind, however they may be named, or courage, resolution, perseverance, as qualities of temperament, are undoubtedly good and desirable in many respects; but these gifts of nature may also become extremely bad and mischievous if the will which is to make use of them, and which, therefore, constitutes what is called *character,* is not good. It is the same with the *gifts of fortune.* Power, riches, honor, even health, and the general well-being and contentment with one's condition which is called *happiness,* inspire pride, and often presumption, if there is not a good will to correct the influence of these on the mind, and with this also to rectify the whole principle of acting and adapt it to its end. The sight of a being who is not adorned with a single feature of a pure and good will, enjoying unbroken prosperity, can never give pleasure to an impartial rational spectator. Thus a good will appears to constitute the indispensable condition even of being worthy of happiness.

There are even some qualities which are of service to this good will itself and may facilitate its action, yet which have no intrinsic unconditional value, but always presuppose a good will, and this qualifies the esteem that we justly have for them and does not permit us to regard them as absolutely good. Moderation in the affections and passions, self-control, and calm deliberation are not only good in many respects, but even seem to constitute part of the intrinsic worth of the person; but they are far from deserving to be called good without qualification, although they have been so unconditionally praised by the ancients. For without the principles of a good will, they may become extremely bad, and the coolness of a villain not only makes him far more dangerous, but also directly makes him more abominable in our eyes than he would have been without it.

A good will is good not because of what it performs or effects, not by its aptness for the attainment of some proposed end, but simply by virtue of the volition; that is, it is good in itself, and considered by itself is to be esteemed much higher than all that can be brought about by it in favor of any inclination, nay even of the sum total of all inclinations. Even if it should happen that, owing to special disfavor of fortune, or the [stingy] provision of a step-motherly nature, this will should wholly lack power to accomplish its purpose, if with its greatest efforts it should yet achieve nothing, and there should remain only the good will (not, to be sure, a mere wish, but the summoning of all means in our power), then, like a jewel, it would still shine by its own light, as a thing which has its whole value in itself. Its usefulness or fruitfulness can neither add nor take away anything from this value. It would be, as it were, only the setting to enable us to handle it the more conveniently in common commerce, or to attract to it the attention of those who are not yet connoisseurs, but not to recommend it to true connoisseurs, or to determine its value. . . .

THE FIRST PROPOSITION OF MORALITY

[To have moral worth, an action must be done from a sense of duty.]

We have then to develop the notion of a will which deserves to be highly esteemed for itself and is good without a view to anything further, a notion which exists already in the sound natural understanding, requiring rather to be cleared up than to be taught, and which in estimating the value of our actions always takes the first place and constitutes the condition of all the rest. In order to do this, we will take the notion of duty, which includes that of a good will, although implying certain subjective restrictions and hindrances. These, however, far from concealing it, or rendering it unrecognizable, rather bring it out by contrast and make it shine forth so much the brighter.

I omit here all actions which are already recognized as inconsistent with duty, although they may be useful for this or that purpose, for with these the question whether they are done *from duty* cannot arise at all, since they even conflict with it. I also set aside those actions which really conform to duty, but to which men have *no* direct *inclination,* performing them because they are impelled thereto by some other inclination. For in this case we can readily distinguish whether the action which agrees with duty is done *from duty,* or from a selfish view. It is much harder to make this distinction when the action accords with duty and the subject has besides a *direct* inclination to it. For example, it is always a matter of duty that a dealer should not overcharge an inexperienced purchaser; and wherever there is much commerce the prudent tradesman does not overcharge, but keeps a fixed price for everyone, so that a child buys of him as well as any other. Men are thus *honestly* served; but this is not enough to make us believe that the tradesman has so acted from duty and from principles of honesty: his own advantage required it; it is out of the question in this case to suppose that he might besides have a direct inclination in favor of the buyers, so that, as it were, from love he should give no advantage to one over another. Accordingly the action was done neither from duty nor from direct inclination, but merely with a selfish view.

On the other hand, it is a duty to maintain one's life; and, in addition, everyone has also a direct inclination to do so. But on this account the often anxious care which most men take for it has no intrinsic worth, and their maxim has no moral import. They preserve their life as *duty requires,* no doubt, but not *because duty requires.* On the other hand, if adversity and hopeless sorrow have completely taken away the relish for life; if the unfortunate one, strong in mind, indignant at his fate rather than desponding or dejected, wishes for death, and yet preserves his life without loving it—not from inclination or fear, but from duty—then his maxim has a moral worth.

To be beneficent when we can is a duty; and besides this, there are many minds so sympathetically constituted that, without any other motive of vanity or self-interest, they find a pleasure in spreading joy around them and can take delight in the satisfaction of others so far as it is their own work. But I maintain that in such a case an action of this kind, however proper, however amiable it may be, has nevertheless no true moral worth, but is on a level with other inclinations, e.g., the inclination to honor, which, if it is happily directed to that which is in fact of public utility and accordant with duty and consequently honorable, deserves praise and encouragement, but not esteem. For the maxim lacks the moral import, namely, that such actions be done *from duty,* not from inclination. Put the case that the mind of that philanthropist were clouded by sorrow of his own, extinguishing all sympathy with the lot of others, and that, while he still has the power to benefit others in distress, he is not touched by their trouble because he is absorbed with his own; and now suppose that he tears himself out of this dead insensibility, and performs the action without any inclination to it, but simply from duty, then first has his action its genuine moral worth. Further still; if nature has put little sympathy in the heart of this or that man; if he, supposed to be an upright man, is by temperament cold and indifferent to the sufferings of others, perhaps because in respect of his own he is provided with the special gift of patience and fortitude and supposes, or even requires, that others should have the same—and such a man would certainly not be the meanest product of nature—but if nature had not specially framed him for a philanthropist, would he not still find in himself a source from whence to give himself a far higher worth than that of a good-natured temperament could be? Unquestionably. It is just in this that the moral worth of the character is brought out which is incomparably the highest of all, namely, that he is beneficent, not from inclination, but from duty.

To secure one's own happiness is a duty, at least indirectly; for discontent with one's condition, under a pressure of many anxieties and amidst unsatisfied wants, might easily become a great *temptation to transgression of duty.* But here again, without looking to duty, all men have already the strongest and most intimate inclination to happiness, because it is just in this idea that all inclinations are combined in one total. But the precept of happiness is often of such a sort that it greatly interferes with some inclinations, and yet a man cannot form any definite and certain conception of the sum of satisfaction of all of them which is called happiness. It is not then to be wondered at that a single inclination, definite both as to what it promises and as to the time within which it can be gratified, is often able to overcome such a fluctuating idea, and that a gouty patient, for instance, can choose to enjoy what he likes, and to suffer what he may, since, according to his calculation, on this occasion at least, be has not sacrificed the enjoyment of the present moment to a possibly mistaken expectation of a happiness which is supposed to be found in health. But even in this case, if the general desire for happiness did not influence his will, and supposing that in his particular case health was not a necessary element in this calculation, there yet remains in this, as in all other cases, this law, namely, that he should promote his happiness not from inclination but from duty, and by this would his conduct first acquire true moral worth.

It is in this manner, undoubtedly, that we are to understand those passages of Scripture also in which we are commanded to love our neighbor, even our enemy. For love, as an affection, cannot be commanded, but beneficence for duty's sake may; even though we are not impelled to it by any inclination—nay, are even repelled by a natural and unconquerable aversion. This is *practical* love and not *pathological*—a love which is seated in the will, and not in the propensities of sense—in principles of action and not of tender sympathy; and it is this love alone which can be commanded.

THE SECOND PROPOSITION OF MORALITY

The second proposition is: That an action done from duty derives its moral worth, *not from the purpose* which is to be attained by it, but from the maxim* by which it is determined, and therefore does not depend on the realization of the object of the action, but merely on the *principle of volition* by

———————
*As Kant uses the term, a maxim is the subjective principle or rule on which a particular person acts. It is contrasted with an objective law, which is valid for all rational beings and which is a principle on which everyone *ought to act*. Kant argues that our personal maxims ought to be those that we could will to be universal laws on the basis of which everyone, without exception, would act.

which the action has taken place, without regard to any object of desire. It is clear from what precedes that the purposes which we may have in view in our actions, or their effects regarded as ends and springs of the will, cannot give to actions any unconditional or moral worth. In what, then, can their worth lie, if it is not to consist in the will and in reference to its expected effect? It cannot lie anywhere but in the *principle of the will* without regard to the ends which can be attained by the action. For the will stands between its *a priori principle,* which is formal, and its *a posteriori* spring, which is material, as between two roads, and as it must be determined by something, in that it must be determined by the formal principle of volition when an action is done from duty, in which case every material principle has been withdrawn from it.

THE THIRD PROPOSITION OF MORALITY

The third proposition, which is a consequence of the two preceding, I would express thus: *Duty is the necessity of acting from respect for the law.* I may have *inclination* for an object as the effect of my proposed action, but I cannot have *respect* for it, just for this reason, that it is an effect and not an energy of will. Similarly I cannot have respect for inclination, whether my own or another's; I can at most, if my own, approve it; if another's, sometimes even love it; i.e., look on it as favorable to my own interest. It is only what is connected with my will as a principle, by no means as an effect—what does not subserve my inclination, but overpowers it, or at least in case of choice excludes it from its calculation—in other words, simply the law of itself, which can be an object of respect, and hence a command. Now an action done from duty must wholly exclude the influence of inclination and with it every object of the will, so that nothing remains which can determine the will except objectively the *law,* and subjectively *pure respect* for this practical law, and consequently the maxim that I should follow this law even to the thwarting of all my inclinations.

Thus the moral worth of an action does not lie in the effect expected from it, nor in any principle of action which requires to borrow its motive from this expected effect. For all these effects—agreeableness of one's condition and even the promotion of the happiness of others—could have been also brought about by other causes, so that for this there would have been no need of the will of a rational being; whereas it is in this alone that the supreme and unconditional good can be found. The pre-eminent good which we call moral can therefore consist in nothing else than *the conception of law* in itself, *which certainly is only possible in a rational being,* in so far as this conception, and not the expected effect, determines the will. This is a good which is already present in the person who acts accordingly, and we have not to wait for it to appear first in the result.

THE BASIS OF MORALITY

But what sort of law can that be, the conception of which must determine the will, even without paying any regard to the effect expected from it, in order that this will may be called good absolutely and without qualification? As I have deprived the will of every impulse which could arise to it from obedience to any law, there remains nothing but the universal conformity of its actions to law in general, which alone is to serve the will as a principle, i.e., *I am never to act otherwise than so that I could also will that my maxim should become a universal law.* Here, now, it is the simple conformity to law in general, without assuming any particular law applicable to certain actions, that serves the will as its principle and must so serve it, if duty is not to be a vain delusion and a chimerical notion. The common reason of men in its practical judgments perfectly coincides with this and always has in view the principle here suggested. Let the question be, for example: May I when in distress make a promise with the intention not to keep it? I readily distinguish here between the two significations which the question may have: Whether it is prudent, or whether it is right, to make a false promise? The former may undoubtedly often be the case. I see clearly indeed that it is not enough to extricate myself from a present difficulty by means of this subterfuge, but

it must be well considered whether there may not hereafter spring from this lie much greater inconvenience than that from which I now free myself, and as, with all my supposed *cunning,* the consequences cannot be so easily foreseen but that credit once lost may be much more injurious to me than any mischief which I seek to avoid at present, it should be considered whether it would not be more *prudent* to act herein according to a universal maxim and to make it a habit to promise nothing except with the intention of keeping it. But it is soon clear to me that such a maxim will still only be based on the fear of consequences. Now it is a wholly different thing to be truthful from duty and to be so from apprehension of injurious consequences. In the first case, the very notion of the action already implies a law for me; in the second case, I must first look about elsewhere to see what results may be combined with it which would affect myself. For to deviate from the principle of duty is beyond all doubt wicked; but to be unfaithful to my maxim of prudence may often be very advantageous to me, although to abide by it is certainly safer. The shortest way, however, and an unerring one, to discover the answer to this question whether a lying promise is consistent with duty, is to ask myself, "Should I be content that my maxim (to extricate myself from difficulty by a false promise) should hold good as a universal law, for myself as well as for others? and should I be able to say to myself, "Every one may make a deceitful promise when he finds himself in a difficulty from which he cannot otherwise extricate himself?" Then I presently become aware that while I can will the lie, I can by no means will that lying should be a universal law. For with such a law there would be no promises at all, since it would be in vain to allege my intention in regard to my future actions to those who would not believe this allegation, or if they over hastily did so would pay me back in my own coin. Hence my maxim, as soon as it should be made a universal law, would necessarily destroy itself.

I do not, therefore, need any far-reaching penetration to discern what I have to do in order that my will may be morally good. Inexperienced in the course of the world, incapable of being prepared for all its contingencies, I only ask myself: Canst thou also will that thy maxim should be a universal law? If not, then it must be rejected, and that not because of a disadvantage accruing from it to myself or even to others, but because it cannot enter as a principle into a possible universal legislation, and reason extorts from me immediate respect for such legislation. I do not indeed as yet *discern* on what this respect is based (this the philosopher may inquire), but at least I understand this, that it is an estimation of the worth which far outweighs all worth of what is recommended by inclination, and that the necessity of acting from *pure* respect for the practical law is what constitutes duty, to which every other motive must give place, because it is the condition of a will being good *in itself,* and the worth of such a will is above everything.

Thus, then, without quitting the moral knowledge of common human reason, we have arrived at its principle. And although, no doubt, common men do not conceive it in such an abstract and universal form, yet they always have it really before their eyes and use it as the standard of their decision. . . .

THE NATURE OF IMPERATIVES

The conception of an objective principle, in so far as it is obligatory for a will, is called a command (of reason), and the formula of the command is called an imperative.

All imperatives are expressed by the word *ought* [or *shall*], and thereby indicate the relation of an objective law of reason to a will, which from its subjective constitution is not necessarily determined by it (an obligation). They say that something would be good to do or to forbear, but they say it to a will which does not always do a thing because it is conceived to be good to do it. That is practically *good,* however, which determines the will by means of the conceptions of reason, and consequently not from subjective causes, but objectively, that is on principles which are valid for every rational being as such. It is distinguished from the *pleasant,* as that which influences the will only by means of sensation from merely subjective causes, valid only for

the sense of this or that one, and not as a principle of reason, which holds for everyone.

A perfectly good will would therefore be equally subject to objective laws (viz., laws of good), but could not be conceived as obliged thereby to act lawfully, because of itself from its subjective constitution it can only be determined by the conception of good. Therefore no imperatives hold for the Divine will, or in general for a holy will; ought is here out of place, because the volition is already of itself necessarily in unison with the law. Therefore imperatives are only formulae to express the relation of objective laws of all volition to the subjective imperfection of the will of this or that rational being, e.g., the human will.

Now all *imperatives* command either *hypothetically* or *categorically.* The former represent the practical necessity of a possible action as means to something else that is willed (or at least which one might possibly will). The categorical imperative would be that which represented an action as necessary of itself without reference to another end, i.e., as objectively necessary.

Since every practical law represents a possible action as good and, on this account, for a subject who is practically determinable by reason, necessary, all imperatives are formulae determining an action which is necessary according to the principle of a will good in some respects. If *now the action is good only as a means to something else, then the imperative is* hypothetical; if it is conceived as good *in itself* and consequently as being necessarily the principle of a will which of itself conforms to reason, then it is *categorical.*

Thus the imperative declares what action possible by me would be good and presents the practical rule in relation to a will which does not forthwith perform an action simply because it is good, whether because the subject does not always know that it is good, or because, even if it know this, yet its maxims might be opposed to the objective principles of practical reason.

Accordingly the hypothetical imperative only says that the action is good for some purpose, *possible* or *actual.* . . . The categorical imperative which declares an action to be objectively necessary in itself without reference to any purpose, i.e., without any other end, is valid as an *apodeictic* (practical) principle. . . .

. . . [A categorical imperative] concerns not the matter of the action, or its intended result, but its form and the principle of which it is itself a result; and what is essentially good in it consists in the mental disposition, let the consequence be what it may. This imperative may be called that of *morality.* . . .

THE FIRST FORMULATION OF THE CATEGORICAL IMPERATIVE: CONFORMITY TO A UNIVERSAL LAW

In this problem we will first inquire whether the mere conception of a categorical imperative may not perhaps supply us also with the formula of it, containing the proposition which alone can be a categorical imperative; for even if we know the tenor of such an absolute command, yet how it is possible will require further special and laborious study, which we postpone to the last section.

When I conceive a hypothetical imperative, in general I do not know beforehand what it will contain until I am given the condition. But when I conceive a categorical imperative, I know at once what it contains. For as the imperative contains besides the law only the necessity that the maxims shall conform to this law, while the law contains no conditions restricting it, there remains nothing but the general statement that the maxim of the action should conform to a universal law, and it is this conformity alone that the imperative properly represents as necessary.

There is therefore but one categorical imperative, namely, this: *Act only on that maxim whereby thou canst at the same time will that it should become a universal law.*

Now if all imperatives of duty can be deduced from this one imperative as from their principle, then, although it should remain undecided what is called duty is not merely a vain notion, yet at least we shall be able to show what we understand by it and what this notion means.

Since the universality of the law according to which effects are produced constitutes what is properly called *nature* in the most general sense (as to form), that is the existence of things so far as it is determined by general laws, the imperative of duty may be expressed thus: *Act as if the maxim of thy action were to become by thy will a universal law of nature.*

FOUR EXAMPLES

We will now enumerate a few duties, adopting the usual division of them into duties to ourselves and to others, and into perfect and imperfect duties.

1. A man reduced to despair by a series of misfortunes feels wearied of life, but is still so far in possession of his reason that he can ask himself whether it would not be contrary to his duty to himself to take his own life. Now he inquires whether the maxim of his action could become a universal law of nature. His maxim is: "From self-love I adopt it as a principle to shorten my life when its longer duration is likely to bring more evil than satisfaction." It is asked then simply whether this principle founded on self-love can become a universal law of nature. Now we see at once that a system of nature of which it should be a law to destroy life by means of the very feeling whose special nature it is to impel to the improvement of life would contradict itself and, therefore, could not exist as a system of nature; hence that maxim cannot possibly exist as a universal law of nature and, consequently, would be wholly inconsistent with the supreme principle of all duty.

2. Another finds himself forced by necessity to borrow money. He knows that he will not be able to repay it, but sees also that nothing will be lent to him unless he promises stoutly to repay it in a definite time. He desires to make this promise, but he has still so much conscience as to ask himself: "Is it not unlawful and inconsistent with duty to get out of a difficulty in this way?" Suppose however that he resolves to do so: then the maxim of his action would be expressed thus: "When I think myself in want of money, I will borrow money and promise to repay it, although I know that I never can do so." Now this principle of self-love or of one's own ad-

vantage may perhaps be consistent with my whole future welfare; but the question now is, "Is it right?" I change then the suggestion of self-love into a universal law, and state the question thus: "How would it be if my maxim were a universal law?" Then I see at once that it could never hold as a universal law of nature, but would necessarily contradict itself. For supposing it to be a universal law that everyone when he thinks himself in a difficulty should be able to promise whatever he pleases, with the purpose of not keeping his promise, the promise itself would become impossible, as well as the end that one might have in view in it, since no one would consider that anything was promised to him, but would ridicule all such statements as vain pretenses.

3. A third finds in himself a talent which with the help of some culture might make him a useful man in many respects. But he finds himself in comfortable circumstances and prefers to indulge in pleasure rather than to take pains in enlarging and improving his happy natural capacities. He asks, however, whether his maxim of neglect of his natural gifts, besides agreeing with his inclination to indulgence, agrees also with what is called duty. He sees then that a system of nature could indeed subsist with such a universal law although men (like the South Sea islanders) should let their talents rest and resolve to devote their lives merely to idleness, amusement, and propagation of their species—in a word, to enjoyment; but he cannot possibly *will* that this should be a universal law of nature, or be implanted in us as such by a natural instinct. For, as a rational being, he necessarily wills that his faculties be developed, since they serve him and have been given him, for all sorts of possible purposes.

4. A fourth, who is in prosperity, while he sees that others have to contend with great wretchedness and that he could help them, thinks: "What concern is it of mine? Let everyone be as happy as Heaven pleases, or as he can make himself; I will take nothing from him nor even envy him, only I do not wish to contribute anything to his welfare or to his assistance in distress!" Now no doubt if such a mode of thinking were a universal law, the human race might very well subsist and doubtless even better than in a state in which everyone talks of sympathy and good-will, or even takes care occasionally to put it into practice, but, on the other side, also cheats when he can, betrays the rights of men, or otherwise violates them. But although it is possible that a universal law of nature might exist in accordance with that maxim, it is impossible to *will* that such a principle should have the universal validity of a law of nature. For a will which resolved this would contradict itself, inasmuch as many cases might occur in which one would have need of the love and sympathy of others, and in which, by such a law of nature, sprung from his own will, he would deprive himself of all hope of the aid he desires.

These are a few of the many actual duties, or at least what we regard as such, which obviously fall into two classes on the one principle that we have laid down. We must be *able to will* that a maxim of our action should be a universal law. This is the canon of the moral appreciation of the action generally. Some actions are of such a character that their maxim cannot without contradiction be even *conceived* as a universal law of nature, far from it being possible that we should *will* that it *should* be so. In others this intrinsic impossibility is not found, but still it is impossible to *will* that their maxim should be raised to the universality of a law of nature, since such a will would contradict itself. It is easily seen that the former violate strict or rigorous (inflexible) duty; the latter only laxer (meritorious) duty. Thus it has been completely shown how all duties depend as regards the nature of the obligation (not the object of the action) on the same principle.

If now we attend to ourselves on occasion of any transgression of duty, we shall find that we in fact do not will that our maxim should be a universal law, for that is impossible for us; on the contrary, we will that the opposite should remain a universal law, only we assume the liberty of making an *exception* in our own favor or (just for this time only) in favor of our inclination. Consequently if we considered all cases from one and the same point of view, namely, that of reason, we should find a contradiction in our own will, namely, that a certain principle should be objectively necessary as a universal law, and yet subjectively should not be universal, but admit of exceptions. As however we at one moment regard our action from the point of view of a will wholly conformed to reason, and then again look at the same action from the point of view of a will affected by inclination, there is not really any contradiction, but an antagonism of inclination to the precept of reason, whereby the universality of the principle is changed into a mere generality, so that the practical principle of reason shall meet the maxim half way. Now, although this cannot be justified in our own impartial judgment, yet it proves that we do really recognize the validity of the categorical imperative and (with all respect for it) only allow ourselves a few exceptions, which we think unimportant and forced from us. . . .

SECOND FORMULATION OF THE CATEGORICAL IMPERATIVE: PERSONS AS ENDS IN THEMSELVES

Now I say: man and generally any rational being *exists* as an end in himself, *not merely as a means* to be arbitrarily used by this or that will, but in all his actions, whether they concern himself or other rational beings, must be always regarded at the same time as an end. All objects of the inclinations have only a conditional worth, for if the inclinations and the wants founded on them did not exist, then their object would be without value. But the inclinations, themselves being sources of want, are so far from having an absolute worth for which they should be desired that on the contrary it must be the universal wish of every rational being to be wholly free from them. Thus the worth of any object which is *to be acquired* by our action is always

conditional. Beings whose existence depends not on our will but on nature's, have nevertheless, if they are irrational beings, only a relative value as means, and are therefore called *things;* rational beings, on the contrary, are called *persons,* because their very nature points them out as ends in themselves, that is as something which must not be used merely as means, and so far therefore restricts freedom of action (and is an object of respect). These, therefore, are not merely subjective ends whose existence has a worth *for us* as an effect of our action, but *objective ends,* that is, things whose existence is an end in itself; an end moreover for which no other can be substituted, which they should subserve *merely* as means, for otherwise nothing whatever would possess *absolute worth;* but if all worth were conditioned and therefore contingent, then there would be no supreme practical principle of reason whatever.

If then there is a supreme practical principle or, in respect of the human will, a categorical imperative, it must be one which, being drawn from the conception of that which is necessarily an end for everyone because it is *an end in itself,* constitutes an *objective* principle of will, and can therefore serve as a universal practical law. The foundation of this principle is: *rational nature exists as an end in itself.* Man necessarily conceives his own existence as being so; so far then this is a *subjective* principle of human actions. But every other rational being regards its existence similarly, just on the same rational principle that holds for me: so that it is at the same time an objective principle, from which as a supreme practical law all laws of the will must be capable of being deduced. Accordingly the practical imperative will be as follows: *So act as to treat humanity, whether in thine own person or in that of any other, in every case as an end withal, never as means only.*

Questions for Reflection

1. Kant tends to make a sharp dichotomy between doing our duty for duty's sake and doing it because of our inclinations. But some critics claim that this approach is too one-sided. They claim, contrary to Kant, that morality should be related to our emotions, our habitual or spontaneous behavior, what we love, what we disdain, and what we feel good about. Do you agree or disagree with these critics that Kant overem-

phasizes rational deliberation and rules of conduct in discussing morality? How would Kant reply to this criticism?

2. Is Kant's insistence that consequences should never play a role in discerning our moral duty plausible? What if telling the truth in certain circumstances would result in the loss of hundreds of innocent lives but would not lead to any positive results? Is it still our moral duty to tell the truth?

3. Is Kant correct in suggesting that immoral behavior always involves making myself an exception to a universal rule that I expect others to follow? Think of some examples where this is the case. Are there any examples in which this is not the case?

4. Suppose an egoist has the personal maxim that "I will always tend to my own interests and not to the needs of others." Furthermore, this person also claims that if she were in need, she would neither expect nor want you to sacrifice your interests for hers. Has such an egoist fulfilled the requirement of universalizability of Kant's categorical imperative? Does this possible universalizing of egoism undermine Kant's point in his fourth example? What would Kant say?

5. Kant says that we should always treat persons as ends in themselves and not only as a means. What implications would following this principle have for your social life, including your actual or potential romantic involvements? What is the significance of the qualification "not *only* as a means?

6. Kant says we should not treat *ourselves* as merely a means. Do you agree with him that we have moral duties not only to others but also to ourselves? What would this mean? What sort of behaviors would violate this principle?

7. Is it ever possible for two moral duties to conflict? Can you think of an example of this? Does Kant's ethics have a way of dealing with such a situation?

JOHN STUART MILL

Utilitarian Ethics

John Stuart Mill (1806–1873) was born in London, the eldest son of nine children. Educated at home, John began studying Greek and arithmetic at age three. By the time he was 13 he was better educated than any university graduate of the time. Although he was one of history's greatest ethical and political thinkers, John Stuart Mill made his living as an executive of a trading firm in London, writing philosophy on the side. He was elected to Parliament in 1865. His wife Harriet Taylor was a brilliant woman who had a deep influence on him and was the joint author with him of many of his most

---

From John Stuart Mill, *Utilitarianism* (1861), Chapters 2 and 4.

important works. While serving a term in Parliament, Mill unsuccessfully tried to amend the Reform Bill of 1867 to give women the vote. Furthermore, he published *The Subjection of Women* in 1869 in which he argued for the political empowerment of women on utilitarian grounds. Mill died in Avignon, France, on May 8, 1873, where he was buried next to Harriet who had died earlier.

Mill was one of the founders of utilitarianism, the theory that the right action is the one that produces the greatest amount of happiness for the greatest number of people. As such, his ethics falls under the more general heading of consequentialism or teleological ethics because of his claim that the desirability or undesirability of an action is determined by its consequences. But what consequences are desirable? In answering this question, Mill argued for **hedonism,** the claim that pleasure is the only thing that has intrinsic value. However, he defined pleasure very broadly so that it includes more than pleasant physical sensations, which are the pleasures animals pursue. Accordingly, Mill said that we ought to pursue the "higher" pleasures such as intellectual, moral, and aesthetic pleasures—those that are consistent with our higher human faculties and dignity.

Because utilitarian ethics is concerned with the consequences of an action, Mill's theory is in stark contrast to deontological theories such as Immanuel Kant's ethics. Kant said the moral rightness or wrongness of an act is intrinsic in the nature of the act itself. Hence, Kant claims that it is always wrong to lie, no matter what the consequences, while Mill would say that in certain circumstances a lie might be morally justifiable if it produces the greatest amount of happiness over any alternative course of action. However, Mill would point out that such cases are rare, for lying generally produces distrust and more negative consequences than positive ones.

Reading Questions

1. What is the principle of utility (or the greatest happiness principle)?
2. What are the only things that are desirable as ends?
3. How does Mill respond to the objection that Epicureanism (a variety of hedonism) is a philosophy worthy only of swine? Besides the pleasures of sensation, what other types of pleasure does Mill recognize?
4. According to Mill, what test can we use for deciding that one pleasure is more valuable than another?
5. What does Mill mean when he says it is "better to be a Socrates dissatisfied than a fool satisfied"?
6. How does Mill respond to the objection that some who know the higher pleasures will sometimes choose the lower ones?
7. Is the utilitarian standard for evaluating actions concerned only with the agent's own, individual happiness?
8. What is the "sole evidence" that something is desirable?
9. How does Mill respond to the objection that some people desire virtue in addition to happiness?

CHAPTER 2: WHAT UTILITARIANISM IS

The creed which accepts as the foundation of morals, Utility, or the Greatest Happiness Principle, holds that actions are right in proportion as they tend to promote happiness, wrong as they tend to produce the reverse of happiness. By happiness is intended pleasure, and the absence of pain; by unhappiness, pain, and the privation of pleasure. To give a clear view of the moral standard set up by the theory, much more requires to be said; in particular, what things it includes in the ideas of pain and pleasure; and to what extent this is left an open question. But these supplementary explanations do not affect the theory of life on which this theory of morality is grounded—namely, that pleasure, and freedom from pain, are the only things desirable as ends; and that all desirable things (which are as numerous in the utilitarian as in any other scheme) are desirable either for the pleasure inherent in themselves, or as means to the promotion of pleasure and the prevention of pain.

Now, such a theory of life excites in many minds, and among them in some of the most estimable in feeling and purpose, inveterate dislike. To suppose that life has (as they express it) no higher end than pleasure—no better and nobler object of desire and pursuit—they designate as utterly mean and groveling; as a doctrine worthy only of swine, to whom the followers of Epicurus were, at a very early period, contemptuously likened; and modern holders of the doctrine are occasionally made the subject of equally polite comparisons by its German, French, and English assailants.

When thus attacked, the Epicureans have always answered, that it is not they, but their accusers, who represent human nature in a degrading light; since the accusation supposes human beings to be capable of no pleasures except those of which swine are capable. If this supposition were true, the charge could not be gainsaid, but would then be no longer an imputation; for if the sources of pleasure were precisely the same to human beings and to swine, the rule of life which is good enough for the one would be good enough for the other. The comparison of the Epicurean life to that of beasts is felt as degrading, precisely because a beast's pleasures do not satisfy a human being's conceptions of happiness. Human beings have faculties more elevated than the animal appetites, and when once made conscious of them, do not regard anything as happiness which does not include their gratification. I do not, indeed, consider the Epicureans to have been by any means faultless in drawing out their scheme of consequences from the utilitarian principle. To do this in any sufficient manner, many Stoic, as well as Christian elements require to be included. But there is no known Epicurean theory of life which does not assign to the pleasures of the intellect, of the feelings and imagination, and of the moral sentiments, a much higher value as pleasures than to those of mere sensation. It must be admitted, however, that utilitarian writers in general have placed the superiority of mental over bodily pleasures chiefly in the greater permanency, safety, uncostliness, etc., of the former—that is, in their circumstantial advantages rather than in their intrinsic nature. And on all these points utilitarians have fully proved their case; but they might have taken the other, and, as it may be called, higher ground, with entire consistency. It is quite compatible with the principle of utility to recognize the fact, that some kinds of pleasure are more desirable and more valuable than others. It would be absurd that while, in estimating all other things, quality is considered as well as quantity, the estimation of pleasures should be supposed to depend on quantity alone.

If I am asked, what I mean by difference of quality in pleasures, or what makes one pleasure more valuable than another, merely as a pleasure, except its being greater in amount, there is but one possible answer. Of two pleasures, if there be one to which all or almost all who have experience of both give a decided preference, irrespective of any feeling of moral obligation to prefer it, that is the more desirable pleasure. If one of the two is, by those who are competently acquainted with both, placed so far above the other that they prefer it, even though knowing it to be attended with a greater amount of discontent, and would not resign it for any quantity of the other pleasure which their nature is capable of, we are justified in ascribing to the preferred enjoyment a superiority in quality, so far outweighing quantity as to render it, in comparison, of small account.

Now it is an unquestionable fact that those who are equally acquainted with, and equally capable of appreciating and enjoying, both, do give a most marked preference to the manner of existence which employs their higher faculties. Few human creatures would consent to be changed into any of the lower animals, for a promise of the fullest allowance of a beast's pleasures; no intelligent human being would consent to be a fool, no instructed person would be an ignoramus, no person of feeling and conscience would be selfish and base, even though they should be persuaded that the fool, the dunce, or the rascal is better satisfied with his lot than they are with theirs. They would not resign what they possess more than he for the most complete satisfaction of all the desires which they have in common with him. If they ever fancy they would, it is only in cases of unhappiness so extreme, that to escape from it they would exchange their lot for almost any other, however undesirable in their own eyes. A being of higher faculties requires more to make him happy, is capable probably of more acute suffering, and certainly accessible to it at more points, than one of an inferior type; but in spite of these liabilities, he can never really wish to sink into what he feels to be a lower grade of existence. We may give what explanation we please of this unwillingness; we may attribute it to pride, a name which is given indiscriminately to some of the most and to some of the least estimable feelings of which mankind are capable: we may refer it to the love of liberty and personal independence, an appeal to which was with the Stoics one of the most effective means for the inculcation of it; to the love of power, or to the love of excitement, both of which do really enter into and contribute to it: but its most appropriate appellation is a sense of dignity, which all human beings possess in one form or other, and in some, though by no means in exact, proportion to their higher faculties, and which is so essential a part of the happiness of those in whom it is strong, that nothing which conflicts with it could be, otherwise than momentarily, an object of desire to them.

Whoever supposes that this preference takes place at a sacrifice of happiness—that the superior being, in anything like equal circumstances, is not happier than the inferior—confounds the two very different ideas, of happiness, and content. It is indisputable that the being whose capacities of enjoyment are low, has the greatest chance of having them fully satisfied; and a highly endowed being will always feel that any happiness which he can look for, as the world is constituted, is imperfect. But he can learn to bear its imperfections, if they are at all bearable; and they will not make him envy the being who is indeed unconscious of the imperfections, but only because he feels not at all the good which those imperfections qualify. It is better to be a human being dissatisfied than a pig satisfied; better to be Socrates dissatisfied than a fool satisfied. And if the fool, or the pig, are a different opinion, it is because they only know their own side of the question. The other party to the comparison knows both sides.

It may be objected, that many who are capable of the higher pleasures, occasionally, under the influence of temptation, postpone them to the lower. But this is quite compatible with a full appreciation of the intrinsic superiority of the higher. Men often, from infirmity of character, make their election for the nearer good, though they know it to be the less valuable; and this no less when the choice is between two bodily pleasures, than when it is between bodily and mental. They pursue sensual indulgences to the injury of health, though perfectly aware that health is the greater good.

It may be further objected, that many who begin with youthful enthusiasm for everything noble, as they advance in years sink into indolence and selfishness. But I do not believe that those who undergo this very common change, voluntarily choose the lower description of pleasures in preference to the higher. I believe that before they devote themselves exclusively to the one, they have already become incapable of the other. Capacity for the nobler feelings is in most natures a very tender plant, easily killed, not only by hostile influences, but by mere want of sustenance; and in the majority of young persons it speedily dies away if the occupations to which their position in life has devoted them, and the society into which it has thrown them, are not favorable to keeping that higher capacity in exercise. Men lose their high aspirations as they lose their intellectual tastes, because they have not time or opportunity for indulging them; and they addict themselves to inferior pleasures, not because they deliberately prefer them, but because they are either the only ones to which they have access, or the only ones which they are any longer capable of enjoying. It may be questioned whether any one who has remained equally susceptible to both classes of pleasures, ever knowingly and calmly preferred the lower; though many, in all ages, have broken down in an ineffectual attempt to combine both.

From this verdict of the only competent judges, I apprehend there can be no appeal. On a question which is the best worth having of two pleasures, or which of two modes of existence is the most grateful to the feelings, apart from its moral attributes and from its consequences, the judgment of those who are qualified by knowledge of both, or, if they differ, that of the majority among them, must be admitted as final. And there needs be the less hesitation to accept this judgment respecting the quality of pleasures, since there is no other tribunal to be referred to even on the question of quantity. What means are there of determining which is the acutest of two pains, or the intensest of two pleasurable sensations, except the general suffrage of those who are familiar with both? Neither pains nor pleasures are homogeneous, and pain is always heterogeneous with pleasure. What is there to decide whether a particular pleasure is worth purchasing at the cost of a particular pain, except the feelings and judgment of the experienced? When, therefore, those feelings and judgment declare the pleasures derived from the higher faculties to be preferable in kind, apart from the question of intensity, to those of which the animal nature, disjoined from the higher faculties, is susceptible, they are entitled on this subject to the same regard.

I have dwelt on this point, as being a necessary part of a perfectly just conception of Utility or Happiness, considered as the directive rule of human conduct. But it is by no means an indispensable condition to the acceptance of the utilitarian standard; for that standard is not the agent's own greatest happiness, but the greatest amount of happiness altogether; and if it may possibly be doubted whether a noble character is always the happier for its nobleness, there can be no doubt that it makes other people happier, and that the world in general is immensely a gainer by it. Utilitarianism, therefore, could only attain its end by the general cultivation of nobleness of character, even if each individual were only benefitted by the nobleness of others, and his own, so far as happiness is concerned, were a sheer deduction from the benefit. But the bare enunciation of such an absurdity as this last, renders refutation superfluous.

According to the Greatest Happiness Principle, as above explained, the ultimate end, with reference to and for the sake of which all other things are desirable (whether we are considering our own good or that of other people), is an existence exempt as far as possible from pain, and as rich as possible in enjoyments, both in point of quantity and quality; the test of quality, and the rule for measuring it against quantity, being the preference felt by those who in their opportunities of experience, to which must be added their habits of self-consciousness and self-observation, are best furnished with the means of comparison. This, being, according to the utilitarian opinion, the end of human action, is necessarily also the standard of morality; which may accordingly be defined, the rules and precepts for human conduct, by the observance of which an existence such as has been described might be, to the greatest extent possible, secured to all mankind; and not to them only, but, so far as the nature of things admits, to the whole sentient creation. . . .

The objectors to utilitarianism cannot always be charged with representing it in a discreditable light. On the contrary, those among them who entertain anything like a just idea of its disinterested character, sometimes find fault with its standard as being too high for humanity. They say it is exacting too much to require that people shall always act from the inducement of promoting the general interests of society. But this is to mistake the very meaning of a standard of morals, and confound the rule of action with the motive of it. It is the business of ethics to tell us what are our duties, or by what test we may know them; but no system of ethics requires that the sole motive of all we do shall be a feeling of duty; on the contrary, ninety-nine hundredths of all our actions are done from other motives, and rightly so done, if the rule of duty does not condemn them. It is the more unjust to utilitarianism that this particular misapprehension should be made a ground of objection to it, inasmuch as utilitarian moralists have gone beyond almost all others in affirming that the motive has nothing to do with the morality of the action, though much with the worth of the agent. He who saves a fellow creature from drowning does what is morally right, whether his motive be duty, or the hope of being paid for his trouble; he who betrays the friend that trusts him, is guilty of a crime, even if his object be to serve another friend to whom he is under greater obligations.

But to speak only of actions done from the motive of duty, and in direct obedience to principle: it is a misapprehension of the utilitarian mode of thought, to conceive it as implying that people should fix their minds upon so wide a generality as the world, or society at large. The great majority of good actions are intended not for the benefit of the world, but for that of individuals, of which the good of the world is made up; and the thoughts of the most virtuous man need not on these occasions travel beyond the particular persons concerned, except so far as is necessary to assure himself that in benefitting them he is not violating the rights, that is, the legitimate and authorised expectations, of any one else. The multiplication of happiness is, according to the utilitarian ethics, the object of virtue: the occasions on which any person (except one in a thousand) has it in his power to do this on an extended scale, in other words to be a public benefactor, are but exceptional; and on these occasions alone is he called on to consider public utility; in every other case, private utility, the interest or happiness of some few persons, is all he has to attend to. Those alone the influence of whose actions extends to society in general, need concern themselves habitually about so large an object. In the case of abstinences indeed—of things which people forbear to do from moral considerations,

though the consequences in the particular case might be beneficial—it would be unworthy of an intelligent agent not to be consciously aware that the action is of a class which, if practiced generally, would be generally injurious, and that this is the ground of the obligation to abstain from it. The amount of regard for the public interest implied in this recognition, is no greater than is demanded by every system of morals, for they all enjoin to abstain from whatever is manifestly pernicious to society. . . .

CHAPTER 4: OF WHAT SORT OF PROOF THE PRINCIPLE OF UTILITY IS SUSCEPTIBLE

It has already been remarked, that questions of ultimate ends do not admit of proof, in the ordinary acceptation of the term. To be incapable of proof by reasoning is common to all first principles; to the first premises of our knowledge, as well as to those of our conduct. But the former, being matters of fact, may be the subject of a direct appeal to the faculties which judge of fact—namely, our senses, and our internal consciousness. Can an appeal be made to the same faculties on questions of practical ends? Or by what other faculty is cognizance taken of them?

Questions about ends are, in other words, questions about what things are desirable. The utilitarian doctrine is, that happiness is desirable, and the only thing desirable, as an end; all other things being only desirable as means to that end. What ought to be required of this doctrine—what conditions is it requisite that the doctrine should fulfil—to make good its claim to be believed?

The only proof capable of being given that an object is visible, is that people actually see it. The only proof that a sound is audible, is that people hear it: and so of the other sources of our experience. In like manner, I apprehend, the sole evidence it is possible to produce that anything is desirable, is that people do actually desire it. If the end which the utilitarian doctrine proposes to itself were not, in theory and in practice, acknowledged to be an end, nothing could ever convince any person that it was so. No reason can be given why the general happiness is desirable, except that each person, so far as he believes it to be attainable, desires his own happiness. This, however, being a fact, we have not only all the proof which the case admits of, but all which it is possible to require, that happiness is a good: that each person's happiness is a good to that person, and the general happiness, therefore, a good to the aggregate of all persons. Happiness has made out its title as one of the ends of conduct, and consequently one of the criteria of morality.

But it has not, by this alone, proved itself to be the sole criterion. To do that, it would seem, by the same rule, necessary to show, not only that people desire happiness, but that they never desire anything else. Now it is palpable that they do desire things which, in common language, are decidedly distinguished from happiness. They desire, for example, virtue, and the absence of vice, no less really than pleasure and the absence of pain. The desire of virtue is not as universal, but it is as authentic a fact, as the desire of happiness. And hence the opponents of the utilitarian standard deem that they have a right to infer that there are other ends of human action besides happiness, and that happiness is not the standard of approbation and disapprobation.

But does the utilitarian doctrine deny that people desire virtue, or maintain that virtue is not a thing to be desired? The very reverse. It maintains not only that virtue is to be desired, but that it is to be desired disinterestedly, for itself. Whatever may be the opinion of utilitarian moralists as to the original conditions by which virtue is made virtue; however they may believe (as they do) that actions and dispositions are only virtuous because they promote another end than virtue; yet this being granted, and it having been decided, from considerations of this description, what is virtuous, they not only place virtue at the very head of the things which are good as means to the ultimate end, but they also recognize as a psychological fact the possibility of its being, to the individual, a good in itself, without looking to any end beyond it; and hold, that the mind is not in a right state, not in a state conformable to Utility, not in the state most

conducive to the general happiness, unless it does love virtue in this manner—as a thing desirable in itself, even although, in the individual instance, it should not produce those other desirable consequences which it tends to produce, and on account of which it is held to be virtue. This opinion is not, in the smallest degree, a departure from the Happiness principle. The ingredients of happiness are very various, and each of them is desirable in itself, and not merely when considered as swelling an aggregate. The principle of utility does not mean that any given pleasure, as music, for instance, or any given exemption from pain, as for example health, is to be looked upon as means to a collective something termed happiness, and to be desired on that account. They are desired and desirable in and for themselves; besides being means, they are a part of the end. Virtue, according to the utilitarian doctrine, is not naturally and originally part of the end, but it is capable of becoming so; and in those who love it disinterestedly it has become so, and is desired and cherished, not as a means to happiness, but as a part of their happiness. . . .

. . . Life would be a poor thing, very ill provided with sources of happiness, if there were not this provision of nature, by which things originally indifferent, but conducive to, or otherwise associated with, the satisfaction of our primitive desires, become in themselves sources of pleasure more valuable than the primitive pleasures, both in permanency, in the space of human existence that they are capable of covering, and even in intensity.

Virtue, according to the utilitarian conception, is a good of this description. There was no original desire of it, or motive to it, save its conduciveness to pleasure, and especially to protection from pain. But through the association thus formed, it may be felt a good in itself, and desired as such with as great intensity as any other good; and with this difference between it and the love of money, of power, or of fame, that all of these may, and often do, render the individual noxious to the other members of the society to which he belongs, whereas there is nothing which makes him so much a blessing to them as the cultivation of the disinterested love of virtue. And consequently, the utilitarian standard, while it tolerates and approves those other acquired desires, up to the point beyond which they would be more injurious to the general happiness than promotive of it, enjoins and requires the cultivation of the love of virtue up to the greatest strength possible, as being above all things important to the general happiness.

It results from the preceding considerations, that there is in reality nothing desired except happiness. Whatever is desired otherwise than as a means to some end beyond itself, and ultimately to happiness, is desired as itself a part of happiness, and is not desired for itself until it has become so. Those who desire virtue for its own sake, desire it either because the consciousness of it is a pleasure, or because the consciousness of being without it is a pain, or for both reasons united; as in truth the pleasure and pain seldom exist separately, but almost always together, the same person feeling pleasure in the degree of virtue attained, and pain in not having attained more. If one of these gave him no pleasure, and the other no pain, he would not love or desire virtue, or would desire it only for the other benefits which it might produce to himself or to persons whom he cared for.

We have now, then, an answer to the question, of what sort of proof the principle of utility is susceptible. If the opinion which I have now stated is psychologically true—if human nature is so constituted as to desire nothing which is not either a part of happiness or a means of happiness, we can have no other proof, and we require no other, that these are the only things desirable. If so, happiness is the sole end of human action, and the promotion of it the test by which to judge of all human conduct; from whence it necessarily follows that it must be the criterion of morality, since a part is included in the whole.

And now to decide whether this is really so; whether mankind do desire nothing for itself but that which is a pleasure to them, or of which the absence is a pain; we have evidently arrived at a question of fact and experience, dependent, like all similar questions, upon evidence. It can only be determined by practiced self-consciousness and self-observation, assisted by observation of others. I believe that these sources of evidence, impartially consulted, will declare that desiring a thing and finding it pleasant, aversion to it and thinking of it as painful, are phenomena entirely inseparable, or rather two parts of the same phenomenon; in strictness of language, two different modes of naming the same psychological fact: that to think of an object as desirable (unless for the sake of its consequences), and to think of it as pleasant, are one and the same thing; and that to desire anything, except in proportion as the idea of it is pleasant, is a physical and metaphysical impossibility.

Questions for Reflection

1. Do you agree with Mill that the only thing in life that is intrinsically valuable is pleasure? Can you think of any counterexamples?

2. Do you agree with Mill that it is "better to be a Socrates dissatisfied than a fool satisfied"?

3. Mill claims that the only criteria for deciding that something is desirable is that people actually desire it. What do you think of his argument in defense of this point? Critics charge that the fact that something is *desired* is a descriptive statement. But to say that something is *desirable* is a normative statement because it is claiming that the item in question is something that *ought* to be desired. The distinction is clear in the following sentence: "Trixie *desires* drugs but drug addiction is not a very *desirable* lifestyle for anyone." Do these considerations undermine Mill's defense of utilitarianism?

4. Some critics have claimed that there are actions that are immoral that, nevertheless, would be justified according to utilitarianism if they create the greatest amount of happiness for the most people. Can you think of any such examples? Mill would have

to respond by arguing that either the action in question is not immoral or that, in the long run, it would not maximize happiness. How would he respond in the case of your examples?

5. State the points on which Mill and Immanuel Kant (reading 57) would disagree. Can you think of any cases where Mill's ethics and Kant's ethics would lead to different ethical decisions?

A Y N   R A N D

Ethical Egoism

The philosophy of ethical egoism was forcefully articulated in the essays and novels of Ayn Rand (1905–1982). Although Rand grew up in Russia, she rebelled against what she perceived as the excessive governmental tyranny and disintegration of free inquiry that followed the communist revolution. In 1926 she escaped to America and began her career as a Hollywood screenwriter. However, she is best known for her defense of both ethical egoism and capitalism in her essays and literary works. Among her best-known novels are *We the Living* (1936), *The Fountainhead* (1943), and *Atlas Shrugged* (1959).

As stated previously, ethical egoism makes the claim: Every person ought to do only what will further his or her own interests. Notice that this does not say "do whatever you want," for sometimes what I want (that second piece of pie) is not in my best interests. For Ayn Rand, egoism requires that I always seek for my *rational* self-interest. As she makes clear in the beginning of the following essay, her position is diametrically opposed to **altruism,** which is the claim that we should be unselfishly concerned for the welfare of others and should act for the sake of other people's interests and needs. In contrast, Rand thinks that altruism is the source of many of the ills of our modern society and governmental life. She says that one has no moral obligations other than the rational pursuit of those ends that will contribute to one's personal happiness, to the achievement of the good life for oneself, or to the maximization of one's own good and well-being. She does qualify this by noting that you may freely choose to help others because their well-being is important to your own happiness or in a temporary situation such as an emergency, which does not require any great personal sacrifice on your part. The first case would actually be one of acting in your own self-interest, and the second case would be one of trivial generosity, but not moral duty. Nevertheless, while an egoist may freely choose to help others in these unusual cases, there is no universal moral duty to help others. For Ayn Rand, human relationships should be like those of traders. A trader is "a man who earns what he gets and does not give or take the undeserved. . . .

From Ayn Rand, "The Ethics of Emergencies," in *The Virtue of Selfishness:* A New Concept of Egoism (New York: Signet Books, 1964).

He deals with men by means of a free, voluntary, unforced, uncoerced exchange–an exchange which benefits both parties by their own independent judgment."*

In the following essay Rand refers to her personal version of egoism as "Objectivism." This should not be confused with the more general term, *ethical objectivism*, discussed previously. To be sure, Rand's egoism is a form of ethical objectivism in that she does believe there are objective moral principles. However, most ethical objectivists would deny that egoistic self-interest is the only moral principle as Rand's Objectivism claims.

Reading Questions

1. According to Rand, what are the undesirable consequences of accepting altruism?
2. What is the false dichotomy promoted by altruism?
3. What is the notion of "sacrifice" that Rand identifies with altruism? What is the rational principle of conduct she advocates?
4. Does she think that love and friendship are selfish or unselfish values?
5. In the example of the man's wife who is afflicted with a dangerous illness, what does Rand consider to be the selfish course of action? What does she consider to be the sacrificial course of action? According to Rand, which course of action is the most rational?
6. What criteria should we use in deciding whether to help another person? Under what conditions would risking one's life to help another be rational?
7. According to Rand, what is the "moral purpose of one's life"?
8. What does she mean when she values the virtue of integrity over that of selflessness or sacrifice?
9. Why should we value our fellow human beings?
10. What are Rand's reasons for saying the application of moral principles is different in normal situations and in emergencies? What are the implications of this difference for our behavior?

---

*Ayn Rand, "The Objectivist Ethics," in *The Virtue of Selfishness* (New York: Signet Books, 1964), p. 31.

The psychological results of altruism may be observed in the fact that a great many people approach the subject of ethics by asking such questions as: "Should one risk one's life to help a man who is: (a) drowning, (b) trapped in a fire, (c) stepping in front of a speeding truck, (d) hanging by his fingernails over an abyss?"

Consider the implications of that approach. If a man accepts the ethics of altruism, he suffers the following consequences (in proportion to the degree of his acceptance):

1. Lack of self-esteem—since his first concern in the realm of values is not how to live his life, but how to sacrifice it.

2. Lack of respect for others—since he regards mankind as a herd of doomed beggars crying for someone's help.

3. A nightmare view of existence—since he believes that men are trapped in a "malevolent universe" where disasters are the constant and primary concern of their lives.

4. And, in fact, a lethargic indifference to ethics, a hopelessly cynical amorality—since his questions involve situations which he is not likely ever to encounter, which bear no relation to the actual problems of his own life and thus leave him to live without any moral principles whatever.

By elevating the issue of helping others into the central and primary issue of ethics, altruism has destroyed the concept of any authentic benevolence or good will among men. It has indoctrinated men with the idea that to value another human being is an act of selflessness, thus implying that a man can have no personal interest in others—that *to value* another means *to sacrifice* oneself—that any love, respect or admiration a man may feel for others is not and cannot be a source of his own enjoyment, but is a threat to his existence, a sacrificial blank check signed over to his loved ones.

The men who accept that dichotomy but choose its other side, the ultimate products of altruism's dehumanizing influence, are those psychopaths who do not challenge altruism's basic premise, but proclaim their rebellion against self-sacrifice by announcing that they are totally indifferent to anything living and would not lift a finger to help a man or a dog left mangled by a hit-and-run driver (who is usually one of their own kind).

Most men do not accept or practice either side of altruism's viciously false dichotomy, but its result is a total intellectual chaos on the issue of proper human relationships and on such questions as the nature, purpose or extent of the help one may give to others. Today, a great many well-meaning, reasonable men do not know how to identify or conceptualize the moral principles that motivate their love, affection or good will, and can find no guidance in the field of ethics, which is dominated by the stale platitudes of altruism.

On the question of why man is not a sacrificial animal and why help to others is not his moral duty, I refer you to *Atlas Shrugged*. This present discussion is concerned with the principles by which one identifies and evaluates the instances involving a man's *nonsacrificial* help to others.

"Sacrifice" is the surrender of a greater value for the sake of a lesser one or of a nonvalue. Thus, altruism gauges a man's virtue by the degree to which he surrenders, renounces or betrays his values (since help to a stranger or an enemy is regarded as more virtuous, less "selfish," than help to those one loves). The rational principle of conduct is the exact opposite: always act in accordance with the hierarchy of your values, and never sacrifice a greater value to a lesser one.

This applies to all choices, including one's actions toward other men. It requires that one possess a defined hierarchy of *rational* values (values chosen and validated by a rational standard). Without such a hierarchy, neither rational conduct nor considered value judgments nor moral choices are possible.

Love and friendship are profoundly personal, selfish values: love is an expression and assertion of self-esteem, a response to one's own values in the person of another. One gains a profoundly personal, selfish joy from the mere existence of the person one loves. It is one's personal, selfish happiness that one seeks, earns and derives from love.

A "selfless," "disinterested" love is a contradiction in terms: it means that one is indifferent to that which one values. Concern for the welfare of those one loves is a rational part of one's selfish interests. If a man who is passionately in love with his wife spends a fortune to cure her of a dangerous illness, it would be absurd to claim that he does it as a "sacrifice" for *her* sake, not his own, and that it makes no difference to *him,* personally and selfishly, whether she lives or dies.

Any action that a man undertakes for the benefit of those he loves is *not a sacrifice* if, in the hierarchy of his values, in the total context of the choices open to him, it achieves that which is of greatest *personal* (and rational) importance to *him.* In the above example, his wife's survival is of greater value to the husband than anything else that his money could buy, it is of greatest importance to his own happiness and, therefore, his action is *not* a sacrifice.

But suppose he let her die in order to spend his money on saving the lives of ten other women, none of whom meant anything to him—as the ethics of altruism would require. That would be a sacrifice. Here the difference between Objectivism and altruism can be seen most clearly: if sacrifice is the moral principle of action, then that husband *should* sacrifice his wife for the sake of ten other women. What distinguishes the wife from the ten others? Nothing but her value to the husband who has to make the choice—nothing but the fact that *his* happiness requires her survival.

The Objectivist ethics would tell him: your highest moral purpose is the achievement of your own happiness, your money is yours, use it to save your wife, *that* is your moral right and your rational, moral choice.

Consider the soul of the altruistic moralist who would be prepared to tell that husband the opposite. (And then ask yourself whether altruism is motivated by benevolence.)

The proper method of judging when or whether one should help another person is by reference to one's own rational self-interest and one's own hierarchy of values: the time, money or effort one gives or the risk one takes should be proportionate to the value of the person in relation to one's own happiness.

To illustrate this on the altruists' favorite example: the issue of saving a drowning person. If the person to be saved is a stranger, it is morally proper to save him only when the danger to one's own life is minimal; when the danger is great, it would be immoral to attempt it: only a lack of self-esteem could permit one to value one's life no higher than that of any random stranger. (And, conversely, if one is drowning, one cannot expect a stranger to risk his life for one's sake, remembering that one's life cannot be as valuable to him as his own.)

If the person to be saved is not a stranger, then the risk one should be willing to take is greater in proportion to the greatness of that person's value to oneself. If it is the man or woman one loves, then one can be willing to give one's own life to save him or her—for the selfish reason that life without the loved person could be unbearable.

Conversely, if a man is able to swim and to save his drowning wife, but becomes panicky, gives in to an unjustified, irrational fear and lets her drown, then spends his life in loneliness and misery—one would not call him "selfish"; one would condemn him morally for his treason to himself and to his own values, that is: his failure to fight for the preservation of a value crucial to his own happiness. Remember that values are that which one acts to gain and/or keep, and that one's own happiness has to be achieved by one's own effort. Since one's own happiness is the moral purpose of one's life, the man who fails to achieve it because of his own default, because of his failure to fight for it, is morally guilty.

The virtue involved in helping those one loves is not "selflessness" or "sacrifice," but *integrity*. Integrity is loyalty to one's convictions and values; it is the policy of acting in accordance with one's values, of expressing, upholding and translating them into practical reality. If a man professes to love a woman, yet his actions are indifferent, inimical or damaging to her, it is his lack of integrity that makes him immoral.

The same principle applies to relationships among friends. If one's friend is in trouble, one should act to help him by whatever nonsacrificial means are appropriate. For instance, if one's friend is starving, it is not a sacrifice, but an act of integrity to give him money for food rather than buy some insignificant gadget for oneself, because his welfare is important in the scale of one's personal values. If the gadget means more than the friend's suffering, one had no business pretending to be his friend.

The practical implementation of friendship, affection and love consists of incorporating the welfare (the *rational* welfare) of the person involved into one's own hierarchy of values, then acting accordingly.

But this is a reward which men have to earn by means of their virtues and which one cannot grant to mere acquaintances or strangers.

What, then, should one properly grant to strangers? The generalized respect and good will which one should grant to a human being in the name of the potential value he represents—until and unless he forfeits it.

A rational man does not forget that *life* is the source of all values and, as such, a common bond among living beings (as against inanimate matter), that other men are potentially able to achieve the same virtues as his own and thus be of enormous value to him. This does not mean that he regards human lives as interchangeable with his own. He recognizes the fact that his own life is the *source,* not only of all his values, but of *his capacity to value.* Therefore, the value he grants to others is only a consequence, an extension, a secondary projection of the primary value which is himself.

"The respect and good will that men of self-esteem feel toward other human beings is profoundly egoistic; they feel, in effect: 'Other men are of value because they are of the same species as myself.' In revering living entities, they are revering their own life. This is the psychological base of any emotion of sympathy and any feeling of 'species solidarity.'"*

Since men are born *tabula rasa*†, both cognitively and morally, a rational man regards strangers as innocent until proved guilty, and grants them that initial good will in the name of their human potential. After that, he judges them according to the moral character they have actualized. If he finds them guilty of major evils, his good will is replaced by contempt and moral condemnation. (If one values human life, one cannot value its destroyers.) If he finds them to be virtuous, he grants them personal, individual value and appreciation, in proportion to their virtues.

It is on the ground of that generalized good will and respect for the value of human life that one helps strangers in an emergency—*and only in an emergency.*

It is important to differentiate between the rules of conduct in an emergency situation and the rules of conduct in the normal conditions of human existence. This does not mean a double standard of morality: the standard and the basic principles remain the same, but their application to either case requires precise definitions.

An emergency is an unchosen, unexpected event, limited in time, that creates conditions under which human survival is impossible—such as a flood, an earthquake, a fire, a shipwreck. In an emergency situation, men's primary goal is to combat the disaster, escape the danger and restore normal conditions (to reach dry land, to put out the fire, etc.).

---

*Nathaniel Branden, "Benevolence versus Altruism," *The Objectivist Newsletter,* July 1962.
†[Latin, "blank tablet." In other words, people are not born with any innate knowledge or given moral character.]

By "normal" conditions I mean *metaphysically* normal, normal in the nature of things, and appropriate to human existence. Men can live on land, but not in water or in a raging fire. Since men are not omnipotent, it is metaphysically possible for unforeseeable disasters to strike them, in which case their only task is to return to those conditions under which their lives can continue. By its nature, an emergency situation is temporary; if it were to last, men would perish.

It is only in emergency situations that one should volunteer to help strangers, if it is in one's power. For instance, a man who values human life and is caught in a shipwreck, should help to save his fellow passengers (though not at the expense of his own life). But this does not mean that after they all reach shore, he should devote his efforts to saving his fellow passengers from poverty, ignorance, neurosis or whatever other troubles they might have. Nor does it mean that he should spend his life sailing the seven seas in search of shipwreck victims to save.

Or to take an example that can occur in everyday life: suppose one hears that the man next door is ill and penniless. Illness and poverty are not metaphysical emergencies, they are part of the normal risks of existence; but since the man is temporarily helpless, one may bring him food and medicine, if one can afford it (as an act of goodwill, not of duty) or one may raise a fund among the neighbors to help him out. But this does not mean that one must support him from then on, nor that one must spend one's life looking for starving men to help.

In the normal conditions of existence, man has to choose his goals, project them in time, pursue them and achieve them by his own effort. He cannot do it if his goals are at the mercy of and must be sacrificed to any misfortune happening to others. He cannot live his life by the guidance of rules applicable only to conditions under which human survival is impossible.

The principle that one should help men in an emergency cannot be extended to regard all human suffering as an emergency and to turn the misfortune of some into a first mortgage on the lives of others.

Poverty, ignorance, illness and other problems of that kind are not metaphysical emergencies. By the *metaphysical* nature of man and of existence, man has to maintain his life by his own effort; the values he needs—such as wealth or knowledge—are not given to him automatically, as a gift of nature, but have to be discovered and achieved by his own thinking and work. One's sole obligation toward others, in this respect, is to maintain a social system that leaves men free to achieve, to gain and to keep their values.

Every code of ethics is based on and derived from a metaphysics, that is: from a theory about the fundamental nature of the universe in which man lives and acts. The altruist ethics is based on a "malevolent universe" metaphysics, on the theory that man, by his very nature, is helpless and doomed—that success, happiness, achievement are impossible to him—that emergencies, disasters, catastrophes are the norm of his life and that his primary goal is to combat them.

As the simplest empirical refutation of that metaphysics—as evidence of the fact that the material universe is not inimical to man and that catastrophes are the exception, not the rule of his existence—observe the fortunes made by insurance companies.

Observe also that the advocates of altruism are unable to base their ethics on any facts of men's normal existence and that they always offer "lifeboat" situations as examples from which to derive the rules of moral conduct. ("What should you do if you and another man are in a lifeboat that can carry only one?" etc.)

The fact is that men do not live in lifeboats—and that a lifeboat is not the place on which to base one's metaphysics.

The moral purpose of a man's life is the achievement of his own happiness. This does not mean that he is indifferent to all men, that human life is of no value to him and that he has no reason to help others in an emergency. But it *does* mean that he does not subordinate his life to the welfare of others, that he does not sacrifice himself to their needs, that the relief of their suffering is not his primary concern, that any help he gives is an *exception*, not a rule, an act of generosity, not of moral duty, that it is *marginal* and *incidental*—as disasters are marginal and incidental in the course of human existence—and that *values*, not disasters, are the goal, the first concern and the motive power of his life.

Questions for Reflection

1. The title of Rand's essay is "The Ethics of Emergencies." Why does she think this is an apt description of the ethics of altruism?

2. Some would think that a person committed to egoism could not value friends or have a love relationship. What would Rand say? Do you agree with Rand's contention that love and friendship are "profoundly personal, selfish values"? Why?

3. Can you think of a time in which you acted in a way that benefited others but you were actually benefiting yourself in doing so? Do you agree with Rand that all times when it is rational to help others are like this case? In other words, is it rational to help others only when you are pursuing your own interests and values?

4. Ethical egoists often present a choice between pure egoism (being concerned exclusively with our own interests) and pure altruism (being concerned exclusively with others' interests). Because a policy of always sacrificing our own interests is untenable, ethical egoism seems to win out by default. But is this argument a false dichotomy (forcing us to choose between two untenable extremes)? Is it possible to formulate an ethical theory that would attempt to balance our own interests with those of others?

5. If you have read the selections by Immanuel Kant and John Stuart Mill, how would these thinkers respond to Rand's ethical egoism?

6. In the following argument, contemporary philosopher James Rachels claims that ethical egoism is an arbitrary and unacceptable doctrine:

   a. Any moral doctrine that assigns greater importance to the interests of one group than to those of another is unacceptably arbitrary unless there is some difference between the members of the groups that justifies treating them differently.

   b. Ethical Egoism would have each person assign greater importance to his or her own interests than to the interests of others. *But there is no general difference between oneself and others, to which each person can appeal, that justifies this difference in treatment.*

   c. Therefore, Ethical Egoism is unacceptably arbitrary.*

   Is Rachel's argument a decisive refutation? How might an ethical egoist respond?

ALISON M. JAGGAR

A Feminist Perspective on Ethics

In Chapter 3, where we discussed philosophical questions about knowledge, Alison Jaggar argued for the importance of the emotions in the construction of knowledge (reading 27). In the current reading, she examines the feminist perspective on ethics. As Jaggar's essay suggests, feminists think that the history of ethics has not been a neutral account of human moral experience, nor has it provided an adequate set of moral norms. Instead, it has been a gender-biased enterprise. This bias, of course, is due to the fact that the history of thought has been dominated by male thinkers. Even though there have been women philosophers throughout history, going back to antiquity, their voices have not been heard. However, the goal of feminist ethics is not merely to draw attention to the deficiencies of traditional moral theories. After all, we weed our gardens only because we think we have something better to plant in them. However, most contemporary feminists do not think that traditional moral theories can be remedied by simply adding on this or that missing component. Instead, they call for a radical rethinking of ethics, a redirecting of its focus, and a broadening of its traditional concerns. While Jaggar's essay is primarily a survey of the themes that are common to all feminist ethical theories, she makes clear what she thinks an adequate feminist ethical theory should look like, often taking issue with some of her feminist colleagues.

From Alison Jaggar, "Feminist Ethics," in *Encyclopedia of Ethics,* vol. 1, eds. Lawrence C. Becker and Charlotte B. Becker (New York: Routledge, 2001).

*James Rachels, *The Elements of Moral Philosophy* (New York: Random House, 1986), pp. 77–78.

Reading Questions

1. According to Jaggar, what are the practical goals of feminist ethics? What are its theoretical goals?
2. What was the thesis of psychologist Carol Gilligan? What influence did it have on some feminists' approaches to ethics?
3. What are the five feminist challenges to traditional Western ethics?
4. Why does Jaggar believe that feminist ethics cannot be simply an inversion of the criticisms of traditional ethics?
5. What are the four minimum conditions of adequacy for any feminist ethics?
6. Why is Jaggar opposed to viewing sexual equality as giving identical treatment to men and women under gender-blind laws?
7. What are her proposals for broadening the domain of ethics?
8. What does she mean by "rethinking the moral subject"? What improvements over traditional notions of human subjectivity do feminists propose?
9. What is meant by "revaluing the feminine"? What is the feminist approach known as the "ethics of care"? Why do some feminist critics think that the ethics of care is inadequate?
10. Why do some feminists critique the tradition's emphasis on rights? Why do other feminists argue that a focus on rights is important to their concerns?

Feminist approaches to ethics, often known collectively as feminist ethics, are distinguished by an explicit commitment to correcting male biases they perceive in traditional ethics, biases that may be manifest in rationalizations of women's subordination, or in disregard for, or disparagement of, women's moral experience. Feminist ethics, by contrast, begins from the convictions that the subordination of women is morally wrong and that the moral experience of women is as worthy of respect as that of men. On the practical level, then, the goals of feminist ethics are the following: first, to articulate moral critiques of actions and practices that perpetuate women's subordination; second, to prescribe morally justifiable ways of resisting such actions and practices; and, third, to envision morally desirable alternatives that will promote women's emancipation. On the theoretical level, the goal of feminist ethics is to develop philosophical accounts of the nature of morality and of the central moral concepts that treat women's moral experience respectfully, though never uncritically.

Just as feminist ethics may be identified by its explicit commitment to challenging perceived male bias in ethics, so approaches that do not express such a commitment may be characterized as nonfeminist. Nonfeminist approaches to ethics are not necessarily anti-feminist or male-biased; they may or may not be so.

THE DEVELOPMENT OF CONTEMPORARY FEMINIST ETHICS

The history of Western philosophy includes a number of isolated but indisputable instances of moral opposition to women's subordination. Noteworthy examples are Mary Wollstonecraft's (1759–1797) *A Vindication of the Rights of Woman* (1792), John Stuart Mill's (1806–1873) *The Subjection of Women* (1869), Frederick Engels' (1820–1895) *The Origin of the Family, Private Property and the State* (1884), and Simone de Beauvoir's (1908–1986) *The Second Sex* (1949).

In the late 1960s, however, as part of a general resurgence of feminist activism, an unprecedented explosion of feminist ethical debate occurred, first among the general public, soon in academic discourse. Actions and practices whose gendered dimensions hitherto had been either unnoticed or unchallenged now became foci of public and philosophical attention, as feminists subjected them to outspoken moral critique, developed sometimes dramatic strategies for opposing them, and proposed alternatives that nonfeminists often perceived as dangerously radical. First grassroots and soon academic feminist perspectives were articulated on topics such as abortion, equality of opportunity, domestic labor, portrayals of women in the media, and a variety of issues concerning sexuality, such as rape and compulsory heterosexuality. By the 1980s, feminists were expressing ethical concern about pornography, reproductive technology, so-called surrogate motherhood, militarism, the environment, and the situation of women in developing nations.

Despite the long history of feminist ethical debate, the term "feminist ethics" did not come into general use until the late 1970s or early 1980s. At this time, a number of feminists began expressing doubts about the possibility of fruitfully addressing so-called women's issues in terms of the conceptual apparatus supplied by traditional ethical theory. For instance, some feminists alleged that a rights framework distorted discussions of abortion because it construed pregnancy and motherhood as adversarial situations. Other feminists charged that certain assumptions widely accepted by traditional ethical theory were incompatible with what was now beginning to be claimed as a distinctively feminine moral experience or sensibility. Social contract theory, for instance, was criticized for postulating a conception of human individuals as beings who were free, equal, independent, and mutually disinterested, a conception that some feminists claimed reflected an experience and perspective that were characteristically masculine. Even impartiality, usually taken as a defining feature of morality, became the object of feminist criticism insofar as it was alleged to generate prescriptions counter to many women's moral intuitions. Some feminists began to speculate that

traditional ethics was more deeply male-biased and needed more fundamental rethinking than they had realized hitherto.

Such reflection was fueled by the much-publicized work of developmental psychologist Carol Gilligan, whose 1982 book, *In a Different Voice: Psychological Theory and Women's Development,* seemed to demonstrate empirically that the moral development of women was significantly different from that of men. Claiming that females tend to fear separation or abandonment while males, by contrast, tend to perceive closeness as dangerous, Gilligan reported that girls and women often construe moral dilemmas as conflicts of responsibilities rather than of rights and seek to resolve those dilemmas in ways that will repair and strengthen webs of relationship. Furthermore, Gilligan described females as less likely than males to make or justify moral decisions by the application of abstract moral rules; instead, she claimed that girls and women were more likely to act on their feelings of love and compassion for particular individuals. Gilligan concluded that whereas men typically adhere to a morality of justice, whose primary values are fairness and equality, women often adhere to a morality of care, whose primary values are inclusion and protection from harm. For this reason, studies of moral development based exclusively on a morality of justice do not provide an appropriate standard for measuring female moral development and may be said to be male-biased.

Many feminists seized on Gilligan's work as offering evidence for the existence of a characteristically feminine approach to morality, an approach assumed to provide the basis for a distinctively feminist ethics. For some, indeed, feminist ethics became and remained synonymous with an ethics of care. Just how an ethics of care should be delineated, however, was far from evident; nor was it clear whether it should supplement or supplant an ethics of justice. Since the 1980s, many feminists have explored such questions, even though the empirical connection between women and care has been challenged by some psychologists, who allege Gilligan's samples to be nonrepresentative, her methods of interpreting her data suspect, and her claims impossible to substantiate, especially when the studies are controlled for occupation and class.

Regardless of empirical findings in moral psychology, debate continues over whether the fundamental tenets of Western ethics are male-biased in some sense: if not in the sense that they express a moral sensibility characteristic of men rather than women, then perhaps in that they promote a culturally masculine image of moral psychology, discourage preoccupation with issues defined culturally as feminine, or in other ways covertly advance men's interests over women's. Since feminism is essentially a normative stance, and since its meaning is continually contested by feminists themselves, all feminists are constantly engaged in ethical reflection; in this sense, feminist ethics is practiced both inside and outside the academy. Within the academy, its practitioners are scholars located mainly in the disciplines of philosophy, religious studies, and jurisprudence; they represent a variety of philosophical traditions, secular and religious, Anglo-American and continental European. In challenging perceived male bias in those traditions, feminist scholars often draw extensively on feminist work in other disciplines, such as literature, history, and psychology.

Scholarly work in feminist ethics often is also responsive to the ethical reflections of nonacademic feminists as these occur, for instance, in much feminist fiction and poetry. In addition, a considerable body of nonfiction, written by nonacademics and directed towards a nonacademic audience, presents itself as feminist ethics. Popular feminist books and journals frequently engage in ethical consideration of moral or public policy issues and sometimes also offer more general discussions of supposedly "masculine" and "feminine" value systems.

Much of the work in feminist ethics has been done by white Western women, but this is slowly changing. A few male philosophers are doing significant work in feminist ethics, and people of color are making increasing contributions, both within and outside the discipline of philosophy, although they sometimes hesitate to accept the label "feminist," because of feminism's racist history.

FEMINIST CRITICISMS OF WESTERN ETHICS

Since most feminist ethics is done in a Western context, it is Western ethics, particularly (though not exclusively) the European Enlightenment tradition, that has been the most frequent target of feminist critique. The feminist challenges to this tradition may be grouped conveniently under five main headings.

Lack of concern for women's interests. Many of the major theorists, such as Aristotle (384–322 B.C.E.) and Rosseau (1712–1778), are accused of having given insufficient consideration to women's interests, a lack of concern expressed theoretically by their prescribing for women allegedly feminine virtues such as obedience, silence, and faithfulness. Some feminists charge that many contemporary ethical discussions continue the tendency to regard women as instrumental to male-dominated institutions, such as the family or the state; in debates on abortion, for instance, the pregnant woman may be portrayed as little more than a container or environment for the fetus, while much discussion of reproductive technology has assumed that infertility is a problem only for heterosexual married women, *i.e.,* women defined in relationship to men.

Neglect of "women's issues." Issues of special concern to women are said to have been ignored by modern moral philosophers, who have tended to portray the domestic realm as an arena outside the economy and beyond justice, private in the sense of being beyond the scope of legitimate political regulation. Within the modern liberal tradition, the public domain is conceived as properly regulated by universal principles of right whereas the private is a domain in which varying goods may properly be pursued. Even philosophers like Aristotle or Hegel (1770–1831), who give some ethical importance to the domestic realm, have tended to portray the home as an arena in which the most fully human excellences cannot be realized. Feminist philosophers began early to criticize this conceptual bifurcation of social life. They pointed out that the home was precisely that realm to which women had been confined historically, and that it had become symbolically associated with the feminine, despite the fact that heads of households were paradigmatically male. They argued that the philosophical devaluation of the domestic realm made it impossible to raise questions about the justice of the domestic division of labor, because it obscured the far-reaching social significance and creativity of women's work in the home, and concealed, even legitimated, the domestic abuse of women and girls.

Denial of women's moral agency. Women's moral agency is said to have often been denied, not simply by excluding women from moral debate or ignoring their contributions, but through philosophical claims to the effect that women lack moral reason. Such claims were made originally by Aristotle, but they have been elaborated and refined by modern theorists such as Rousseau, Kant (1724–1804), Hegel, and Freud (1856–1939).

Depreciation of "feminine" values. Western moral theory is said to embody values that are "masculine," insofar as they are culturally associated with men. Such associations may be empirical, normative, or symbolic. For instance, Western ethics is alleged to prioritize the supposedly masculine values of independence, autonomy, intellect, will, wariness, hierarchy, domination, culture, transcendence, product, asceticism, war, and death over the supposedly feminine values of interdependence, community, connection, sharing, emotion, body, trust, absence of hierarchy, nature, immanence, process, joy, peace, and life. Claims like this are common in both popular and academic feminist writings on ethics.

Devaluation of women's moral experience. Finally, some feminists also charge that prevailing Western conceptualizations of the nature of morality, moral problems, and moral reasoning are masculine insofar as they too are associated with men, rather than women, in associations that again may be empirical, symbolic, or normative. For instance, feminists have accused modern moral theory of being excessively preoccupied with rules, obsessed with impartiality, and exclusively focused on discrete deeds. In addition, feminists have charged modern moral theory with taking the contract as the paradigmatic moral relation and construing moral rationality so narrowly as to exclude emotions of assessment, sometimes called moral emotions. All these characteristics have been asserted to be masculine in some sense. A feminine (not feminist) approach to ethics, by contrast, has been supposed to avoid assuming that individuals ordinarily are free, equal, and independent; to take more account of the specificities of particular contexts; and to be more likely to resolve moral dilemmas by relying on empathic feeling rather than by appealing to rules.

Not all feminists endorse all of the above clusters of criticisms—and even where they agree with the general statement, they may well disagree over its applicability in the case of specific philosophers or debates. Despite differences of relative detail, feminists tend generally to agree on the first three clusters of criticisms, whose correction seems not only attainable in principle within the framework of Enlightenment moral theory but even to be required by that framework. However, they disagree sharply on the last two clusters of criticisms, especially the fifth, which obviously contains clear parallels with a number of nonfeminist criticisms of Enlightenment ethics made by proponents of, for example, situation ethics, virtue ethics, communitarianism, and postmodernism.

COMMON MISCONSTRUALS OF FEMINIST ETHICS

Feminist ethics has sometimes been construed, both by some of its proponents and some of its critics, as a simple inversion of the criticisms listed above. In other words, it has sometimes been identified with one or more of the following: putting women's interests first; focusing exclusively on so-called women's issues; accepting women (or feminists) as moral experts or authorities; substituting "female" (or feminine) for "male" (or masculine) values; or extrapolating directly from women's moral experience. These characterizations of feminist ethics are sufficiently pervasive that it is worth noting just why they cannot be correct.

1. Putting women's interests first occasionally has been recommended as a way of achieving a "woman-centered" ethics that transcends the covert bias of a supposed humanism grounded in fact on male norms. Whatever might be said for or against this recommendation, it cannot be definitive of feminist ethics because the formula, as it stands, raises more questions than it answers. It fails to specify not only which women's interests should be preferred over which men's (or children's) and in what circumstances, but also what should be done about conflicts of interest between women and even how interests should be identified at all. Most obviously, feminist ethics cannot be identified with "putting women's interests first" simply because many feminists would refuse to accept and, indeed, be morally outraged by what they would perceive as blatant partiality and immorality.

2. Feminist ethics certainly addresses issues of special concern to women that have been neglected by modern moral theory, but it cannot be identified with an exclusive focus on such issues. This is partly because nonfeminists as well as feminists have addressed these issues—and, indeed, are doing so increasingly as feminism grows stronger and more articulate. It is also because feminism rejects the notion that moral issues can be divided cleanly into those that are and those that are not of special concern to women. On the one hand, since men's and women's lives are inextricably intertwined, there are no "women's issues" that are not also men's issues; for instance, the availability or nonavailability of child care and abortion has significant consequences for the lives of men as well as women. On the other hand, since men and women typically are not what lawyers call "similarly situated" relative to each other, it is difficult to think of any moral or public policy ("human") issue in which women do not have a special interest. For instance, such "human" issues as war, peace, and world hunger have special significance for women because the world's hungry are disproportionately women (and children), because women are primarily those in need of the social services neglected to fund military spending, and because women suffer disproportionately from war and benefit relatively little from militarism and the weapons industries. For these reasons, it would be a mistake to identify feminist ethics with attention to some explicitly gendered subset of ethical issues. On the contrary, rather than being limited to a restricted ethical domain, feminist ethics has *enlarged* the traditional concerns of ethics, both through identifying previously unrecognized ethical issues and by introducing fresh perspectives on issues already acknowledged as having an ethical dimension.

3. Feminist ethics certainly is being developed by feminists, most of whom are women, but this does not imply, of course, that any woman, or even any feminist, should be regarded as a moral expert whose moral authority is beyond question. Not only are there deep disagreements among women and even among feminists such that it would be difficult to know whom to select as an expert, but many painful examples of failed insight or principle on the part of feminist leaders demonstrate only too clearly that no woman, or feminist, is morally infallible.

4. There are also serious difficulties with thinking of feminist ethics as the substitution of female or feminine for male or masculine values. These difficulties include problems with establishing that *any* values are male or female in the sense of being generally held by men or women, when both women's and men's values vary so much, both within cultures as well as across them. Similar problems confront attempts to establish that certain values are masculine or feminine in the sense of being considered socially appropriate for individuals of one gender or the other. Again, norms of masculinity and femininity vary not only between societies but even within the same society along such axes as class and ethnicity: some social groups, for instance, value physical health, strength, or athletic prowess in women; others value physical fragility, weakness, or incompetence. Even if certain values could be identified in some sense as male or female, masculine or feminine, the conclusive objection to identifying feminist ethics with the elaboration of female or feminine values is that the femin*ine* is not necessarily the femin*ist*. Indeed,

since the feminine typically has been constructed in circumstances of male domination, it is likely to be quite opposed to the feminist. Personal charm, for example, may be valued not only *in* women, but also *by* them; even if charm were, in these senses, a feminine value, however, it would seem at least as likely to undermine feminist goals as to promote them.

5. Similar problems apply to defining feminist ethics as the systematic extrapolation of women's moral experience, exclusive of men's. While no approach to morality can be adequate if it ignores the moral experience of women, it is most unlikely that women generally are similar enough to each other and different enough from men that a single distinctively female or feminine approach to ethics can be identified. Attempts to establish such an identification frequently commit the fallacy of generalizing about the experience of *all* or *most* women from the moral experience of *some* women; this seems to have been one flaw at least in Gilligan's earlier work. Again, even if a distinctively femin*ine* approach to morality could be identified, perhaps in terms of symbolic or normative connections with women rather than empirical ones, there is no reason to suppose that such an approach would be femin*ist*. Indeed, given the feminist commitment to a critical rethinking of cultural constructions of both masculinity and femininity, there is good *prima facie* reason to suppose that it would not.

MINIMUM CONDITIONS OF ADEQUACY FOR FEMINIST ETHICS

Even though feminist ethics is far broader and more open than it appears in the foregoing misconstruals, its goals are sufficiently specific, especially when taken in conjunction with its criticisms of traditional ethics, as to generate certain minimum conditions of adequacy for any approach to ethics that purports to be feminist.

1. First of all, feminist ethics can never begin by assuming that women and men are similarly situated—although it may discover that some women are situated similarly with some men in specific respects or contexts. In addition, not only does feminist ethics need constant vigilance to detect subtle as well as blatant manifestations of gender privilege, it must also be sensitive to the ways in which gendered norms are different for different groups of women—or in which the same norms, such as a cultural preference for slimness or blondness, affect different groups of women differently. Ultimately feminism's concern for *all* women means that feminist ethics must address not only "local" issues of racism or homophobia or class privilege but also such global issues as environmental destruction, war, and access to world resources.

2. In order to develop guides to action that will tend to subvert rather than reinforce the systematic subordination of women, feminist approaches to ethics must understand individual actions in the context of broader social practices, evaluating the symbolic and cumulative implications of individual action as well as its immediately observable consequences. They must be equipped to recognize covert as well as overt manifestations of domination, subtle as well as blatant forms of control, and they must develop sophisticated accounts of coercion and consent. Similarly, they must provide the conceptual resources for identifying and evaluating the varieties of resistance and struggle in which women, particularly, have engaged. They must recognize the often unnoticed ways in which women and other members of the underclass have refused cooperation and opposed domination, while acknowledging the inevitability of collusion and the impossibility of totally clean hands. In short, feminist approaches to ethics must be transitional and nonutopian, often extensions of, rather than alternatives to, feminist political theory, exercises in non-ideal rather than ideal theory.

3. Since most of most women's lives have been excluded from that domain conceptualized as public, a third requirement for feminist approaches to ethics is that they should be salient to issues of so-called private life, such as intimate relations, sexuality, and child rearing. Thus, they must articulate the moral dimensions of issues that may not hitherto have been recognized as moral. In addition,

we have seen that feminist approaches to ethics must provide appropriate guidance for dealing with national and international issues, strangers and foreigners. In developing the conceptual tools for undertaking these tasks, feminist ethics cannot assume that moral concepts developed originally for application to the so-called public realm, concepts such as impartiality or exploitation, are appropriate for use in the so-called private; neither can it assume that concepts such as care, developed in intimate relationships, will necessarily be helpful in the larger world. Indeed, the whole distinction between public and private life must be examined critically by feminist ethics, with no prior assumptions as to whether the distinction should be retained, redrawn, or rejected.

4. Finally, feminist ethics must take the moral experience of all women seriously, though not, of course, uncritically. Although what is *feminist* often will turn out to be very different from what is *feminine,* a basic respect for women's moral experience is necessary to acknowledge women's capacities as moral subjects and to countering traditional stereotypes of women as less than full moral agents, as childlike or close to nature. Furthermore, empirical claims about differences in the moral sensibility of women and men make it impossible to assume that any approach to ethics will be unanimously accepted if it fails to consult the moral experience of women. Additionally, it seems plausible to suppose that women's distinctive social experience may make them especially perceptive regarding the implications of domination, especially gender domination, and especially well equipped to detect the male bias that feminists believe has pervaded so much of male-authored Western moral theory.

Most feminist, and perhaps even many nonfeminist, philosophers might well find the general statement of these conditions quite uncontroversial, but they will inevitably disagree sharply over when the conditions have been met. Not only may feminists disagree with nonfeminists, but they are likely even to differ with each other over, for instance, what are women's interests, what are manifestations of domination and coercion, how

resistance should be expressed, and which aspects of women's moral experience are worth developing and in which directions.

Those who practice feminist ethics thus may be seen both as united by a shared project and as diverging widely in their views as to how this project may be accomplished. Their divergences result from a variety of philosophical differences, including differing conceptions of feminism itself, which, as we have seen, is a constantly contested concept. The inevitability of such divergence means that feminist ethics can never be identified in terms of a specific range of topics, methods, or orthodoxies. While feminist ethics is distinguished by its explicit commitment to developing approaches to ethics that will respect women's moral experience and avoid rationalizing women's subordination, attempts to define it more precisely or substantively than this are likely to disregard the richness and variety of feminist moral thinking and prematurely foreclose feminist moral debates.

CURRENT CONCERNS IN FEMINIST ETHICS

Since the 1970s, feminists have made significant contributions to both practical and theoretical ethics. Because it is impossible to offer anything like a comprehensive survey of this work in the space available, this article will end by sketching a few illustrative examples of feminist work designed to counter male bias in ethics. Much of this work draws on the culturally feminine as a resource for reconceiving ethical norms or standards thought to be androcentric.

Giving equal weight to women's interests. Eighteenth and nineteenth century feminist philosophers, such as Mary Wollstonecraft and John Stuart Mill, responded to the fact that Western ethics had often accorded less weight to women's interests than to men's by demanding that women receive the same rights and privileges bestowed on men. They conceptualized sexual equality as formal equality; that is, as identity of treatment for both men and women under gender-blind laws. Their twentieth-century successors sought to enshrine this understanding of sexual equality in the U.S. Constitution *via* an Equal Rights Amendment (passed by Congress in 1972, it was not ratified by the minimum number of states) that would have made any sex specific law unconstitutional.

Formal equality does not necessarily result in substantive equality, however. Feminist work in practical ethics is characterized by its use of gender as a category of ethical analysis and its employment of this category has revealed that many formally gender-blind policies and practices are not gender-neutral in their outcomes but instead have a disproportionately negative impact on women. Many illustrations could be added to the examples of war, peace, and world hunger, noted above; for instance, women, especially poor women, are among those hardest hit by seemingly gender-blind economic policies, such as structural adjustment measures; similarly, environmental degradation often has more serious consequences for women, especially for mothers, than it does for men. Such systematically gendered outcomes suggest that construing sexual equality in purely formal terms may be inadequate for reaching substantive sexual equality. Because norms of gender situate women differently from men in most social contexts across the world, substantive equality may require establishing policies and practices that are gender-sensitive or gender-responsive rather than gender-blind.

Formulating policies and practices that respond appropriately to gender differences is controversial and complicated. For instance, providing women with special legal protections such as pregnancy and maternity leaves may promote a public perception that women are less reliable workers than men. Attempts to protect women's sexuality by restricting pornography or excluding women from employment in male institutions such as prisons may have the unintended consequence of perpetuating the cultural myth that women are by nature the sexual prey of men; by suggesting that sexual harassment and assault are in some sense natural, this myth implicitly legitimates these practices. Thus, gender-responsive interpretations of sexual equality may not only provoke an anti-feminist backlash, they may even undermine the prospects of long-

term sexual equality by stigmatizing women's competences. In addition, although gender-responsive conceptions of equality are intended to reflect sensitivity to differences in the circumstances of men and women in general, they are sometimes insensitive to differences in the social situations of different women. They may fail to notice that broad social groups, like men and women, are characterized by internal differences that are systematic as well as individual, following the fault lines of other social divisions such as race and class. Thus, these conceptions are sometimes responsive to gendered differences in need that are characteristic of only some men and women but not of all; often those taken as paradigms are men and women from more privileged classes; for instance, a feminist demand that child care be provided for mothers in paid employment may be used to discredit other mothers' claims to welfare support.

Some contemporary feminists seek to avoid the horns of the so-called equality/difference dilemma by questioning its underlying assumptions about the normative individual who is taken as the standard against which others' equality is measured. These feminists argue that equal concern for women's interests requires reassessing major social institutions on the presumption that their users are likely to be women—including women who are not otherwise privileged. The revised institutions would still be formally gender-blind but they would not be designed primarily for people who were able-bodied and fully employed, people unlikely to be subjected to sexual assault or harassment, people without responsibilities for the primary care of dependents such as children or elders. For instance, they might offer workers paid leaves to enable them to care for family members or they might provide child care on the same basis as public schooling. If social policies and practices were revised according to a principle of what Christine A. Littleton calls "equality of acceptance," sex differences could become socially "costless."

Broadening the domain of ethics. In response to their recognition that mainstream, especially modern, Western ethics has defined the moral domain in such a way as to exclude many issues of special concern to women, contemporary feminists have sought to expand the ethical arena. In some cases, their questions have generated whole new bodies of research, such as feminist environmentalism and feminist bioethics. Issues that feminists have identified as morally problematic include: abortion; sexuality, including compulsory heterosexuality, sexual harassment, and rape; representations of masculinity and femininity, including those produced by the mass media and pornography; the domestic division of labor; self-presentation, including body image and fashion; and the role of language in reinforcing as well as reflecting women's subordination. Although these issues received little attention from mainstream ethics until recent years, all have significant implications for women's lives, to the extent that they sometimes involve matters of life and death for women. As noted earlier, feminists resist characterizing such issues as exclusively women's issues; instead, by presenting them as hitherto neglected human issues, they broaden previous conceptions of normative human experience.

Rethinking the moral subject. Feminists' first response to Western philosophy's disparagement of women's moral subjectivity was to insist on women's capacity for moral autonomy and rationality, soon, however, they began to question prevailing understandings of autonomy, rationality, and even subjectivity. With respect to autonomy, for instance, feminist concern about women's collaborations with male dominance and consequent interest in the social construction of gendered character structures provided insight into many ways in which choice can be socialized and consent manipulated. Some feminists have faulted much modern moral philosophy for failing to recognize that autonomy cannot be assumed but instead is an achievement with complex material and social preconditions.

Conceptions of moral subjectivity that privilege autonomy are especially characteristic of the European Enlightenment; they derive from the Cartesian model of the self as disembodied, asocial, unified, rational, and essentially similar to all other selves. In developing alternatives to this conception, some feminists have drawn on traditions such as Marxism, psychoanalysis, communitarianism and postmodernism; others have been influenced by the work of Carol Gilligan, who postulated that girls and women were more likely than boys and men to conceive themselves in relational terms. Viewing oneself as integrally related to others is said to promote systematically different moral preoccupations from those that have characterized much mainstream Western ethics, particularly modern ethics; for instance, such a view of the self encourages women to construe moral dilemmas as conflicts of responsibilities rather than rights. Many feminist philosophers argue that a relational conception of moral subjectivity is not only more adequate empirically than an atomistic model but that it also generates moral values and a conception of moral rationality that are superior to those characteristic of the Enlightenment. For instance, it encourages women to seek resolutions to conflicts by means that promise to repair and strengthen relationships, to practice positive caretaking rather than respectful nonintervention, and to prioritize the personal values of care, trust, attentiveness, and love for particular others above impersonal principles of equality, respect, and rights.

Feminist dissatisfaction with the Enlightenment conception of moral subjectivity springs partly from an interest in the body, which many feminists regard as key to women's subordination. Some argue that this subordination is maintained by male control of women's bodies, especially women's procreative and sexual capacities, and that it is expressed in women's traditional assignments for biological reproduction and bodily maintenance. They see Western philosophy's symbolic association of women with the body as not only reflecting but also rationalizing and reinforcing these unjust social arrangements.

Attention to human embodiment has implications for moral psychology. The identity of embodied moral subjects is constituted in part by specific social relations, and these, in turn, are partially determined by the social meanings attached to bodily characteristics such as parentage, age, or sex. Recognizing human embodiment explains why moral subjects are often motivated more by considerations of particular attachment than by abstract concern for duty, more by care than by respect, and more by responsibility than by right. Some feminists have argued that devaluing the body in comparison with the mind has turned moral theorists' attention away from bodily related differences among individuals, such as age, sex, and ability, and encouraged them to regard people as indistinguishable and interchangeable. They further contend that disparaging the body has encouraged ethical theory to ignore many fundamental aspects of human life and to posit ideals unattainable by human beings.

Philosophical reflection that begins from the body tends to give prominence to aspects of human nature that are very different from those emphasized by Cartesianism; for instance, it highlights temporality and situatedness rather than timelessness and nonlocatedness, growth and decay rather than changelessness, particularity rather than universality, sociality rather than isolation. Reflection on these features reveals that inequality, dependence and interdependence, specificity, social embeddedness, and historical community must be recognized as permanent features of human social life. They generate ethical problems that cannot be adequately addressed by developing highly idealized conceptions of equality, liberty, autonomy, and impartiality or that posit isolated individuals, ideal communities, or some supposedly universal human condition.

The features of human subjectivity emphasized by many feminist philosophers are precisely those that Western culture associates with women and the feminine; they are features that tend to preoccupy women in virtue of their social situation, they are culturally defined as appropriate to women, or they are associated symbolically with women. However, to point to these features of human subjectivity is not to imply that the paradigm moral subject should be a woman rather than a man, or even culturally feminine rather than culturally masculine. Instead, it is to suggest that previous conceptions of human subjectivity have often provided understandings and ideals of both women and men that are partial and distorted.

Revaluing the feminine. Feminists have frequently responded to Western philosophy's disparagement of what it has constructed as feminine by insisting that the feminine should be revalued. We have observed already that feminist ethics cannot be identified with feminine ethics but we have also seen that ways of thinking that are culturally feminine may point toward less biased and more adequate approaches to ethics. Some feminists regard the ethics of care as a case in point.

The first articulations of the ethics of care represented it as an expression of women's characteristic experience of nurturing or mothering particular others, but later studies had difficulty confirming a clear empirical link between women and caring. When subjects were matched for education and occupation, women often achieved almost identical scores with men on justice-oriented tests of moral development, leaving women who worked in the home as the main representatives of the care perspective; moreover, some men as well as women were found to employ care thinking. Recent advocates of an ethics of care acknowledge not only that some women think in terms of justice and some men in terms of care, but also that most people of each sex are able to adopt either perspective. Nevertheless, they still view care as feminine on the grounds that it emerges from forms of socialization and practice that, in contemporary Western society, are culturally feminine; these include nursing, maintaining a home, raising children, and tending to the elderly. Caring is also feminine in the symbolic or normative sense of expressing cultural expectations that women be more empathic, altruistic, nurturant, and sensitive than men.

Some feminists have associated the ethics of care not only with gender but also with race and class. Joan Tronto links the moral perspective of care with the work of cleaning up after body functions, tasks that in Western history have been relegated primarily to women but not to all women or to women exclusively; caring work is done not only by women but also by the working classes, especially, in most of the West, by people of colour. This analysis of the social genesis of care thinking fits well with Lawrence Blum's argument that justice ethics expresses a juridical-administrative perspective that is indeed masculine but reflects the concerns specifically of men from the professional and administrative classes. Together, these arguments suggest that both the ethics of justice and the ethics of care express moral perspectives that are not only gendered but simultaneously characteristic of different races and classes.

Feminist philosophers are divided about the potential of care ethics. One concern is that it may be insufficiently sensitive to the characteristically feminine moral failing of self-sacrifice; another is that its emphasis on meeting the immediately perceived needs of particular individuals may lead agents to show unfair partiality to those closest to them. There also exist concerns about whether care's characteristic focus on the details of small-scale situations can address problems that are rooted in social structures; such a focus may encourage what are sometimes called band aid or social work approaches to moral problems rather than attempts to address them through institutional changes. For these and other reasons, some feminists doubt that care ethics provides resources capable of adequately critiquing male dominance in both public and private life.

Despite these problems, many philosophers are continuing to draw on care's "feminine" insights and values to develop alternative and more feminist approaches to democratic theory, to social and economic policy, and to international relations. Rather than dismissing the claims of justice, such approaches typically seek to reinterpret them within a framework of care. Their goal is to reconceptualize social and even global institutions so that they will enable and reinforce caring relations among people.

Building on women's moral experience. The ethics of care is often represented as an approach to ethics that is based on women's moral experience; however, it has been presented here as an ethical revaluation of the culturally feminine. To illustrate ethical initiatives that are based on women's moral experience, let us consider instead some recent feminist reinterpretations of human rights.

The concept of rights was central to the emergence of Western feminism but, because rights are central in most modern versions of the so-called justice tradition, some contemporary feminists

have dismissed them as reflections of a moral perspective that is characteristically masculine. These feminists regard rights as expressing an inherently adversarial morality that disparages the more basic and important human values of interdependence, cooperation, and trust. Some contend that appeals to rights may rationalize male power over women; for example, the right to freedom of expression may justify misogynist pornography. Others observe that legal equality of rights may obscure inequalities of power to exercise them, noting that the procedures associated with claiming and redressing rights are often degrading, intimidating, and humiliating for women, especially in trials for rape and sexual harassment. Still other feminists argue that focusing on rights ignores the ways in which women may be compelled by their social situations to exercise their rights in a manner that is harmful to them, for instance, by "choosing" prostitution or cosmetic surgery. In short, some feminists charge that rights talk may often be not only unhelpful to women but even rationalize their inequality.

It is certainly true that appeals to rights have had only limited success in promoting women's equality. The United Nations identifies three categories or "generations" of rights, including civil, political, economic, social, and cultural rights and, in each of these categories, abuses to women are often still neglected or excused. Either women are seen as identical to men, so that substantive equality is equated with formal equality, ignoring salient differences between the social situations of men and women; or women are seen as "other," inherently different from men, so that abuses of their rights have been represented as "normal," "natural," or "inevitable."

Despite continuing systematic abuse and subordination of women, some feminists still believe that the rights tradition constitutes a valuable resource for women's liberation. For instance, rights may be interpreted to take account of morally salient differences among rights holders and they may be assigned to groups as well as individuals. They may include "positive" as well as "negative" rights, which are "entitlements" rather than liberties and carry claims not only to noninterference but also to correlative duties on the part of others. Such rights may be thought of as embodying the supposedly feminine values of interdependence, social co-operation, and care.

Faith in the concept of rights is certainly evident in the currently burgeoning global feminist movement, which is united by the slogan, "Women's rights are human rights." This movement calls not simply for enforcing women's human rights but for radically rethinking how human rights have been conceived. Many feminist proposals for reinterpreting rights begin by recognizing that violations of women's rights are more often carried out by nonstate than by state actors—often by male family members—and that they occur in the private as well as the public sphere. This recognition requires expanding the definition of state sanctioned repression to include acceptance of family forms in which brides are sold and in which fathers and husbands exert strict control over women's sexuality, dress, speech, and movement; it also requires redefining slavery to include forced domestic labour and prostitution. Because some violations of human rights take gender-specific forms, the definition of war crimes must be expanded to include systematic rape and sexual torture. Similarly, the definition of genocide must be expanded to include female infanticide; the systematic withholding of food, medical care, and education from girls; and the battery, starvation, mutilation, and even murder of adult women. Feminists have also noted that women's rights are often indivisible from each other; for instance, many violations of women's civic and political rights are made possible by women's economic vulnerability. Fully protecting women's human rights requires changing not only laws but also economic systems and cultural practices.

In the above examples, women's gender-specific experiences have served as a resource for identifying covert male biases lurking in existing definitions of human rights and as a model for revising those definitions. However, to imagine the normative bearer of rights as a woman rather than a man is not to replace male with female bias. Because women are vastly overrepresented among the poor and illiterate of the world and among those most vulnerable to oppressive systems of power, this image instead exposes the false humanism of older conceptions of human rights; it also points toward new understandings of rights that are more inclusive and fully human.

The global movement for women's human rights provides a final illustration of the trajectory followed by much feminist ethics; beginning by criticizing the exclusion of women and discrimination against them, it moves to challenging the covert male bias of existing ethical frameworks, and finally draws on the culturally feminine to propose more ethically adequate norms and standards.

Questions for Reflection

1. Besides the fact that traditional moral theories have primarily been developed by male writers, do you think they are as one-sided in their concerns and as inadequate as feminists claim?

2. Review the various moral theories that you have read prior to Jaggar's. What criticisms might she make of each of these theories?

3. From your own experience and from what you have read, do you think there are differences between the ways men and women approach ethical issues? If there are differences that are rooted in our biological natures, what would be the implications of this? If there are differences that are caused by our social conditioning, what would be the implications of this?

4. Suppose that feminist moral theory had been the dominant moral tradition throughout the history of our society. In this case, how would history and today's society be different? What differences would it have made in our institutions, politics, laws, and

social arrangements? Which of these changes (if any) would have been better? Which (if any) would have been worse?

CONTEMPORARY APPLICATION: IS ABORTION MORALLY PERMISSIBLE?

Few moral and political disagreements have been as divisive in our contemporary society as the issue of abortion. In America, the debate over abortion has been around for quite some time. However the 1973 United States Supreme Court decision *Roe* v. *Wade* marked a turning point in the debate. The court ruled that in the first trimester of a pregnancy (about the first 13 weeks), state laws and regulations may not interfere with a woman's right to end a pregnancy through abortion. (State laws were given increasingly more latitude to introduce regulations as the pregnancy develops through the middle and final trimesters.) Although the statistics vary from year to year, there are typically around 45 million abortions a year worldwide (both legal and illegal). In the United States, there are roughly around 1.3 million abortions a year. Because abortion is one of the most frequent clinical procedures, the sheer magnitude of the practice illustrates the enormous implications of either allowing or prohibiting abortion.

Although the debate over abortion frequently takes on religious overtones, it would be too simplistic to view it as simply a religious debate. There are many proabortion voices in typically antiabortion religious groups. Furthermore, there are many persons who are opposed to abortion who do not make use of any religious arguments and some who do not have any religious affiliations at all. In the two readings that follow, one in favor of abortion and one against, you will notice that there is no explicit reference to religious themes or terminology such as the "soul." Furthermore, as will be clear from Sidney Callahan's essay, it is obvious that those who are opposed to abortion do so from a stance of moral objectivism, for they argue that abortion is morally, objectively wrong. However, it is not always understood that those who argue for the permissibility of abortion necessarily do so from a stance of moral objectivism as well. While arguing that abortion is a personal decision to be made by an individual woman in consultation with her doctor, pro-choice advocates (as illustrated by Judith Jarvis Thomson's essay) also argue that a woman has a moral right to choose an abortion if she wishes and that it would be morally wrong for society to prevent her from doing so.

Much of the debate over abortion revolves around the moral status of the human fetus. Clearly the fetus is human tissue in the same way that your appendix or a flap of skin could readily be identified as belonging to a human body. It is clear as well that a normal fetus has the potential to develop into a human being just as you and I did. However, a large part of the debate concerns whether the fetus in its current state is a human being or is a person with moral rights or whether it is merely a collection of cells with no moral or legal rights. In addition to the moral status of the fetus, the abortion debate also concerns what moral rights and obligations are possessed by the woman. In the two essays that follow, note how each author addresses these two issues.

JUDITH JARVIS THOMSON

Abortion Is a Matter of Personal Choice

Judith Jarvis Thomson is a professor of philosophy at Massachusetts Institute of Technology. She has published extensively on topics in ethics and metaphysics. In addition to publishing over 70 articles, she is the author of several books, including *Rights, Restitution and Risk* (1986), *The Realm of Rights* (1990), and *Goodness and Advice* (2001).

The following essay by Thomson is one of the most frequently reprinted contributions to the abortion debate. Since the question of whether or not the fetus is a person is so difficult to resolve, Thomson had decided to yield that territory to her opponents for the sake of the argument. Through a clever analogy in which she compares the physical status of the fetus to that of an adult who is clearly a person, she argues that a pregnant woman has no moral obligation to sustain the life of a fetus that she did not choose to create. While Thomson acknowledges that it might be a selfless and exemplary act for such a woman to bring her baby to birth, it is morally permissible for the woman to act as she chooses.

Reading Questions

1. According to Thomson, what is one of the most common premises used in arguments against abortion? What argument is typically offered to support this premise? What does Thomson mean by calling it a "slippery slope" argument?
2. In spite of her problems with this crucial premise, what concession does she grant to the opponents of abortion?
3. What is the point she seeks to make with the story of the violinist?
4. What is the "extreme view"? How does Thomson use the violinist analogy to respond to this view?
5. How does she respond to the argument that the unborn person has a right to life at least when the mother's life is not at stake?
6. What is the significance of her claim that "the right to life consists not in the right not to be killed, but rather in the right not to be killed unjustly"?
7. How does Thomson respond to the case where conception is the result of voluntary sex? What is the point she is making with the analogies of the burglar and the "people-seeds"?
8. What is the distinction between making a personal sacrifice (for the sake of the violinist or the fetus) because you are a morally decent person (a Good Samaritan) and being morally required to make that sacrifice?

From Judith Jarvis Thomson, "A Defense of Abortion," in *Philosophy and Public Affairs 1* (1), 1971. Section titles added.

Most opposition to abortion relies on the premise that the fetus is a human being, a person, from the moment of conception. The premise is argued for, but, as I think, not well. Take, for example, the most common argument. We are asked to notice that the development of a human being from conception through birth into childhood is continuous; then it is said that to draw a line, to choose a point in this development and say "before this point the thing is not a person, after this point it is a person" is to make an arbitrary choice, a choice for which in the nature of things no good reason can be given. It is concluded that the fetus is, or anyway that we had better say it is, a person from the moment of conception. But this conclusion does not follow. Similar things might be said about the development of an acorn into an oak tree, and it does not follow that acorns are oak trees, or that we had better say they are. Arguments of this form are sometimes called "slippery slope arguments"—the phrase is perhaps self-explanatory—and it is dismaying that opponents of abortion rely on them so heavily and uncritically.

I am inclined to agree, however, that the prospects for "drawing a line" in the development of the fetus look dim. I am inclined to think also that we shall probably have to agree that the fetus has already become a human person well before birth. Indeed, it comes as a surprise when one first learns how early in its life it begins to acquire human characteristics. By the tenth week, for example, it already has a face, arms and legs, fingers and toes; it has internal organs, and brain activity is detectable. On the other hand, I think that the premise is false, that the fetus is not a person from the moment of conception. A newly fertilized ovum, a newly implanted clump of cells, is no more a person than an acorn is an oak tree. But I shall not discuss any of this. For it seems to me to be of great interest to ask what happens if, for the sake of argument, we allow the premise. How, precisely, are we supposed to get from there to the conclusion that abortion is morally impermissible? Opponents of abortion commonly spend most of their time establishing that the fetus is a person, and hardly any time explaining the step from there to the impermissibility of abortion. Perhaps they think the step too simple and obvious to require much comment. Or perhaps instead they are simply being economical in argument. Many of those who defend abortion rely on the premise that the fetus is not a person, but only a bit of tissue that will become a person at birth; and why pay out more arguments than you have to? Whatever the explanation, I suggest that the step they take is neither easy nor obvious, that it calls for closer examination than it is commonly given, and that when we do give it this closer examination we shall feel inclined to reject it.

I propose, then, that we grant that the fetus is a person from the moment of conception. How does the argument go from here? Something like this, I take it. Every person has a right to life. So the fetus has a right to life. No doubt the mother has a right to decide what shall happen in and to her body; everyone would grant that. But surely a person's right to life is stronger and more stringent than the mother's right to decide what happens in and to her body, and so outweighs it. So the fetus may not be killed; an abortion may not be performed.

It sounds plausible. But now let me ask you to imagine this. You wake up in the morning and find yourself back to back in bed with an unconscious violinist. A famous unconscious violinist. He has been found to have a fatal kidney ailment, and the Society of Music Lovers has canvassed all the available medical records and found that you alone have the right blood type to help. They have therefore kidnapped you, and last night the violinist's circulatory system was plugged into yours, so that your kidneys can be used to extract poisons from his blood as well as your own. The director of the hospital now tells you, "Look, we're sorry the Society of Music Lovers did this to you—we would never have permitted it if we had known. But still, they did it, and the violinist now is plugged into you. To unplug you would be to kill him. But never mind, it's only for nine months. By then he will have recovered from his ailment, and can safely be unplugged from you." Is it morally incumbent on you to accede to this situation? No doubt it would be very nice of you if you did, a great kindness. But do you *have* to accede to it? What if it were not nine months, but nine years? Or longer still? What if the director of the hospital says, "Tough luck, I agree, but you've now got to stay in bed, with the violinist plugged into you, for the rest of your life. Because remember this. All persons have a right to life, and violinists are persons. Granted you have a right to decide what happens in and to your body, but a person's right to life outweighs your right to decide what happens in and to your body. So you cannot ever be unplugged from him." I imagine you would regard this as outrageous, which suggests that something really is wrong with that plausible-sounding argument I mentioned a moment ago.

In this case, of course, you were kidnapped; you didn't volunteer for the operation that plugged the violinist into your kidneys. Can those who oppose abortion on the ground I mentioned make an exception for a pregnancy due to rape? Certainly. They can say that persons have a right to life only if they didn't come into existence because of rape; or they can say that all persons have a right to life, but that some have less of a right to life than others, in particular, that those who came into existence because of rape have less. But these statements have a rather unpleasant sound. Surely the question of whether you have a right to life at all, or how much of it you have, shouldn't turn on the question of whether or not you are the product of a rape. And in fact the people who oppose abortion on the ground I mentioned do not make this distinction, and hence do not make an exception in case of rape.

Nor do they make an exception for a case in which the mother has to spend the nine months of her pregnancy in bed. They would agree that would be a great pity, and hard on the mother; but all the same, all persons have a right to life, the fetus is a person, and so on. I suspect, in fact, that they would not make an exception for a case in which, miraculously enough, the pregnancy went on for nine years, or even the rest of the mother's life.

Some won't even make an exception for a case in which continuation of the pregnancy is likely to shorten the mother's life; they regard abortion as impermissible even to save the mother's life. Such cases are nowadays very rare, and many opponents of abortion do not accept this extreme view. All the

same, it is a good place to begin: a number of points of interest come out in respect to it.

THE EXTREME VIEW

Let us call the view that abortion is impermissible even to save the mother's life "the extreme view." I want to suggest first that it does not issue from the argument I mentioned earlier without the addition of some fairly powerful premises. Suppose a woman has become pregnant, and now learns that she has a cardiac condition such that she will die if she carries the baby to term. What may be done for her? The fetus, being a person, has a right to life, but as the mother is a person too, so has she a right to life. Presumably they have an equal right to life. How is it supposed to come out that an abortion may not be performed? If mother and child have an equal right to life, shouldn't we perhaps flip a coin? Or should we add to the mother's right to life her right to decide what happens in and to her body, which everybody seems to be ready to grant—the sum of her rights now outweighing the fetus' right to life?

The most important argument here is the following. We are told that performing the abortion would be directly killing the child, whereas doing nothing would not be killing the mother, but only letting her die. Moreover, in killing the child, one would be killing an innocent person, for the child has committed no crime, and is not aiming at his mother's death. And then there are a variety of ways in which this might be continued. (1) But as directly killing an innocent person is always and absolutely impermissible, an abortion may not be performed. Or, (2) as directly killing an innocent person is murder, and murder is always and absolutely impermissible, an abortion may not be performed. Or, (3) as one's duty to refrain from directly killing an innocent person is more stringent than one's duty to keep a person from dying, an abortion may not be performed. Or, (4) if one's only options are directly killing an innocent person or letting a person die, one must prefer letting the person die, and thus an abortion may not be performed.

Some people seem to have thought that these are not further premises which must be added if the conclusion is to be reached, but that they follow from the very fact that an innocent person has a right to life. But this seems to me to be a mistake, and perhaps the simplest way to show this is to bring out that while we must certainly grant that innocent persons have a right to life, the theses in (1) through (4) are all false. Take (2), for example. If directly killing an innocent person is murder, and thus is impermissible, then the mother's directly killing the innocent person inside her is murder, and thus is impermissible. But it cannot seriously be thought to be murder if the mother performs an abortion on herself to save her life. It cannot seriously be said that she *must* refrain, that she *must* sit passively by and wait for her death. Let us look again at the case of you and the violinist. There you are, in bed with the violinist, and the director of the hospital says to you, "It's all most distressing, and I deeply sympathize, but you see this is putting an additional strain on your kidneys, and you'll be dead within the month. But you *have* to stay where you are all the same. Because unplugging you would be directly killing an innocent violinist, and that's murder, and that's impermissible." If anything in the world is true, it is that you do not commit murder, you do not do what is impermissible, if you reach around to your back and unplug yourself from that violinist to save your life. . . .

In sum, a woman surely can defend her life against the threat to it posed by the unborn child, even if doing so involves its death. And this shows not merely that the theses in (1) through (4) are false; it shows also that the extreme view of abortion is false, and so we need not canvass any other possible ways of arriving at it from the argument I mentioned at the outset. . . .

THE RIGHT TO LIFE

Where the mother's life is not at stake, the argument I mentioned at the outset seems to have a much stronger pull. "Everyone has a right to life, so the unborn person has a right to life." And isn't the child's right to life weightier than anything other than the mother's own right to life, which she might put forward as ground for an abortion?

This argument treats the right to life as if it were unproblematic. It is not, and this seems to me to be precisely the source of the mistake.

For we should now, at long last, ask what it comes to, to have a right to life. In some views having a right to life includes having a right to be given at least the bare minimum one needs for continued life. But suppose that what in fact *is* the bare minimum a man needs for continued life is something he has no right at all to be given? If I am sick unto death, and the only thing that will save my life is the touch of Henry Fonda's cool hand on my fevered brow, then all the same, I have no right to be given the touch of Henry Fonda's cool hand on my fevered brow. It would be frightfully nice of him to fly in from the West Coast to provide it. It would be less nice, though no doubt well meant, if my friends flew out to the West Coast and carried Henry Fonda back with them. But I have no right at all against anybody that he should do this for me. Or again, to return to the story I told earlier, the fact that for continued life that violinist needs the continued use of your kidneys does not establish that he has a right to be given the continued use of your kidneys. He certainly has no right against you that *you* should give him continued use of your kidneys. For nobody has any right to use your kidneys unless you give him such a right; and nobody has the right against you that you shall give him this right—if you do allow him to go on using your kidneys, this is a kindness on your part, and not something he can claim from you as his due. Nor has he any right against anybody else that *they* should give him continued use of your kidneys. Certainly he had no right against the Society of Music Lovers that they should plug him into you in the first place. And if you now start to unplug yourself, having learned that you will otherwise have to spend nine years in bed with him, there is nobody in the world who must try to prevent you, in order to see to it that he is given something he has a right to be given.

Some people are rather stricter about the right to life. In their view, it does not include the right to be given anything, but amounts to, and only to, the right not to be killed by anybody. But here a related difficulty arises. If everybody is to refrain from killing that violinist, then everybody must refrain from doing a great many different sorts of things. Everybody must refrain from slitting his throat, everybody must refrain from shooting him—and everybody must refrain from unplugging you from him. But does he have a right against everybody that they shall refrain from unplugging you from him? To refrain from doing this is to allow him to continue to use your kidneys. It could be argued that he has a right against us that *we* should allow him to continue to use your kidneys. That is, while he had no right against us that we should give him the use of your kidneys, it might be argued that he anyway has a right against us that we shall not now intervene and deprive him of the use of your kidneys. I shall come back to third-party interventions later. But certainly the violinist has no right against you that *you* shall allow him to continue to use your kidneys. As I said, if you do allow him to use them, it is a kindness on your part, and not something you owe him. . . .

THE RIGHT TO USE ANOTHER'S BODY

There is another way to bring out the difficulty. In the most ordinary sort of case, to deprive someone of what he has a right to is to treat him unjustly. Suppose a boy and his small brother are jointly given a box of chocolates for Christmas. If the older boy takes the box and refuses to give his brother any of the chocolates, he is unjust to him, for the brother has been given a right to half of them. But suppose that, having learned that otherwise it means nine years in bed with that violinist, you unplug yourself from him. You surely are not being unjust to him, for you gave him no right to use your kidneys, and no one else can have given him any such right. But we have to notice that in unplugging yourself, you are killing him; and violinists, like everybody else, have a right to life, and thus in the view we were considering just now, the right not to be killed. So here you do what he supposedly has a right you shall not do, but you do not act unjustly to him in doing it.

The emendation which may be made at this point is this: the right to life consists not in the right not to be killed, but rather in the right not to be killed unjustly. This runs a risk of circularity, but never mind: it would enable us to square the fact that the violinist has a right to life with the fact that you do not act unjustly toward him in unplugging yourself, thereby killing him. For if you do not kill him unjustly, you do not violate his right to life, and so it is no wonder you do him no injustice.

But if this emendation is accepted, the gap in the argument against abortion stares us plainly in the face: it is by no means enough to show that the fetus is a person, and to remind us that all persons have a right to life—we need to be shown also that killing the fetus violates its right to life, i.e., that abortion is unjust killing. And is it?

I suppose we may take it as a datum that in a case of pregnancy due to rape the mother has not given the unborn person a right to the use of her body for food and shelter. Indeed, in what pregnancy could it be supposed that the mother has given the unborn person such a right? It is not as if there were unborn persons drifting about the world, to whom a woman who wants a child says "I invite you in."

But it might be argued that there are other ways one can have acquired a right to the use of another person's body than by having been invited to use it by that person. Suppose a woman voluntarily indulges in intercourse, knowing of the chance it will issue in pregnancy, and then she does become pregnant; is she not in part responsible for the presence, in fact the very existence, of the unborn person inside her? No doubt she did not invite it in. But doesn't her partial responsibility for its being there itself give it a right to the use of her body? If so, then her aborting it would be more like the boy's taking away the chocolates, and less like your unplugging yourself from the violinist—doing so would be depriving it of what it does have a right to, and thus would be doing it an injustice.

And then, too, it might be asked whether or not she can kill it even to save her own life: If she voluntarily called it into existence, how can she now kill it, even in self-defense?

The first thing to be said about this is that it is something new. Opponents of abortion have been so concerned to make out the independence of the fetus, in order to establish that it has a right to life, just as its mother does, that they have tended to overlook the possible support they might gain from making out that the fetus is *dependent* on the mother, in order to establish that she has a special kind of responsibility for it, a responsibility that gives it rights against her which are not possessed by any independent person—such as an ailing violinist who is a stranger to her.

On the other hand, this argument would give the unborn person a right to its mother's body only if her pregnancy resulted from a voluntary act, undertaken in full knowledge of the chance a pregnancy might result from it. It would leave out entirely the unborn person whose existence is due to rape. Pending the availability of some further argument, then, we would be left with the conclusion that unborn persons whose existence is due to rape have no right to the use of their mothers' bodies, and thus that aborting them is not depriving them of anything they have a right to and hence is not unjust killing.

And we should also notice that it is not at all plain that this argument really does go even as far as it purports to. For there are cases and cases, and the details make a difference. If the room is stuffy, and I therefore open a window to air it, and a burglar climbs in, it would be absurd to say, "Ah, now he can stay, she's given him a right to the use of her house—for she is partially responsible for his presence there, having voluntarily done what enabled him to get in, in full knowledge that there are such things as burglars, and that burglars burgle." It would be still more absurd to say this if I had had bars installed outside my windows, precisely to prevent burglars from getting in, and a burglar got in only because of a defect in the bars. It remains equally absurd if we imagine it is not a burglar who climbs in, but an innocent person who blunders or falls in. Again, suppose it were like this: people-seeds drift about in the air like pollen, and if you open your windows, one may drift in and take root in your carpets or upholstery. You don't want children, so you fix up your windows with fine mesh screens, the very best you can buy. As can happen, however, and on very, very rare occasions does happen, one of the screens is defective; and a seed drifts in and takes root. Does the person-plant who now develops have a right to the use of your house? Surely not—despite the fact that you voluntarily opened your windows, you knowingly kept carpets and upholstered furniture, and you knew that screens were sometimes defective. Someone may argue that you are responsible for its rooting, that it does have a right to your house, because after all you *could* have lived out your life with bare floors and furniture, or with sealed windows and doors. But this won't do—for by the same token anyone can avoid a pregnancy due to rape by having a hysterectomy, or anyway by never leaving home without a (reliable!) army.

It seems to me that the argument we are looking at can establish at most that there are *some* cases in which the unborn person has a right to the use of its mother's body, and therefore *some* cases in which abortion is unjust killing. There is room for much discussion and argument as to precisely which, if any. But I think we should sidestep this issue and leave it open, for at any rate the argument certainly does not establish that all abortion is unjust killing.

There is room for yet another argument here, however. We surely must all grant that there may be cases in which it would be morally indecent to detach a person from your body at the cost of his life. Suppose you learn that what the violinist needs is not nine years of your life, but only one hour: all you need do to save his life is to spend one hour in that bed with him. Suppose also that letting him use your kidneys for that one hour would not affect your health in the slightest. Admittedly you were kidnapped. Admittedly you did not give anyone permission to plug him into you. Nevertheless it seems to me plain you *ought* to allow him to use your kidneys for that hour—it would be indecent to refuse.

Again, suppose pregnancy lasted only an hour, and constituted no threat to life or health. And suppose that a woman becomes pregnant as a result of rape. Admittedly she did not voluntarily do anything to bring about the existence of a child.

Admittedly she did nothing at all which would give the unborn person a right to the use of her body. All the same it might well be said, as in the newly emended violinist story, that she *ought* to allow it to remain for that hour—that it would be indecent in her to refuse.

Now some people are inclined to use the term "right" in such a way that it follows from the fact that you ought to allow a person to use your body for the hour he needs, that he has a right to use your body for the hour he needs, even though he has not been given that right by any person or act. They may say that it follows also that if you refuse, you act unjustly toward him. This use of the term is perhaps so common that it cannot be called wrong; nevertheless it seems to me to be an unfortunate loosening of what we would do better to keep a tight rein on. Suppose that box of chocolates I mentioned earlier had not been given to both boys jointly, but was given only to the older boy. There he sits, stolidly eating his way through the box, his small brother watching enviously. Here we are likely to say "You ought not to be so mean. You ought to give your brother some of those chocolates." My own view is that it just does not follow from the truth of this that the brother has any right to any of the chocolates. If the boy refuses to give his brother any, he is greedy, stingy, callous—but not unjust. I suppose that the people I have in mind will say it does follow that the brother has a right to some of the chocolates, and thus that the boy does act unjustly if he refuses to give his brother any. But the effect of saying this is to obscure what we should keep distinct, namely the difference between the boy's refusal in this case and the boy's refusal in the earlier case, in which the box was given to both boys jointly, and in which the small brother thus had what was from any point of view clear title to half.

A further objection to so using the term "right" that from the fact that A ought to do a thing for B, it follows that B has a right against A that A do it for him, is that it is going to make the question of whether or not a man has a right to a thing turn on how easy it is to provide him with it; and this seems not merely unfortunate, but morally unacceptable. Take the case of Henry Fonda again. I said earlier

that I had no right to the touch of his cool hand on my fevered brow, even though I needed it to save my life. I said it would be frightfully nice of him to fly in from the West Coast to provide me with it, but that I had no right against him that he should do so. But suppose he isn't on the West Coast. Suppose he has only to walk across the room, place a hand briefly on my brow—and lo, my life is saved. Then surely he ought to do it, it would be indecent to refuse. Is it to be said "Ah, well, it follows that in this case she has a right to the touch of his hand on her brow, and so it would be an injustice in him to refuse"? So that I have a right to it when it is easy for him to provide it, though no right when it's hard? It's rather a shocking idea that anyone's rights should fade away and disappear as it gets harder and harder to accord them to him.

So my own view is that even though you ought to let the violinist use your kidneys for the one hour he needs, we should not conclude that he has a right to do so—we should say that if you refuse, you are, like the boy who owns all the chocolates and will give none away, self-centered and callous, indecent in fact, but not unjust. And similarly, that even supposing a case in which a woman pregnant due to rape ought to allow the unborn person to use her body for the hour he needs, we should not conclude that he has a right to do so; we should conclude that she is self-centered, callous, indecent, but not unjust, if she refuses. The complaints are no less grave; they are just different. However, there is no need to insist on this point. If anyone does wish to deduce "he has a right" from "you ought," then all the same he must surely grant that there are cases in which it is not morally required of you that you allow that violinist to use your kidneys, and in which he does not have a right to use them, and in which you do not do him an injustice if you refuse. And so also for mother and unborn child. Except in such cases as the unborn person has a right to demand it—and we were leaving open the possibility that there may be such cases—nobody is morally *required* to make large sacrifices, of health, of all other interests and concerns, of all other duties and commitments, for nine years, or even for nine months, in order to keep another person alive. . . .

What we should ask is not whether anybody should be compelled by law to be a Good Samaritan, but whether we must accede to a situation in which somebody is being compelled—by nature, perhaps—to be a Good Samaritan. We have, in other words, to look now at third-party interventions. I have been arguing that no person is morally required to make large sacrifices to sustain the life of another who has no right to demand them, and this even where the sacrifices do not include life itself; we are not morally required to be Good Samaritans or anyway Very Good Samaritans to one another. But what if a man cannot extricate himself from such a situation? What if he appeals to us to extricate him? It seems to me plain that there are cases in which we can, cases in which a Good Samaritan would extricate him. There you are, you were kidnapped, and nine years in bed with that violinist lie ahead of you. You have your own life to lead. You are sorry, but you simply cannot see giving up so much of your life to the sustaining of his. You cannot extricate yourself, and ask us to do so. I should have thought that—in light of his having no right to the use of your body—it was obvious that we do not have to accede to your being forced to give up so much. We can do what you ask. There is no injustice to the violinist in our doing so.

Following the lead of the opponents of abortion, I have throughout been speaking of the fetus merely as a person, and what I have been asking is whether or not the argument we began with, which proceeds only from the fetus' being a person, really does establish its conclusion. I have argued that it does not. . . .

Questions for Reflection

1. How effective is Thomson's argument? In what ways is the case of the violinist similar to that of a pregnant woman? What are some of the relevant differences? Do any of the differences make the case of the violinist irrelevant to the morality of abortion?

2. Do you agree with Thomson that in some cases it may be morally decent to make sacrifices to preserve someone else's life, without it being your moral obligation to do so? Do you agree with her that carrying an unwanted baby for nine months is such a case?

3. Consider how Thomson's analysis would apply to these cases: (a) a couple has sex without using any contraception at all, (b) a couple intentionally conceives a baby but they change their plans and decide to abort it when the wife is suddenly offered an attractive job that would be incompatible with motherhood. Would abortion be morally permissible or immoral in each of these cases?

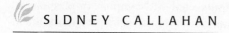

S I D N E Y   C A L L A H A N

Abortion Is Morally Wrong

Sidney Callahan is professor of psychology at Mercy College, Dobbs Ferry, New York, and the author of many books and articles. She is co-editor, with her husband Daniel Callahan, of *Abortion: Understanding Differences.*

In her essay, Callahan argues that by adopting a pro-choice stance, the modern feminist movement is undermining itself. It has done so by embracing a male-oriented model of sexuality and the status of women. Accordingly, she argues that only a pro-life feminism will enhance women's rights and liberation.

Reading Questions

1. State in your own words the four claims involved in the feminist case in support of abortion.
2. Why does Callahan think that the moral right to control one's own body is irrelevant in cases of pregnancy? Why does she reject Judith Jarvis Thomson's violinist analogy (reading 61)?
3. What are her arguments against those who claim the fetus does not have the status of personhood?
4. Why does Callahan think that abortion is a betrayal of feminists' struggle for justice?
5. Why does she think that our moral obligations are not limited to those explicit contracts that we freely accept? What are the implications of this expanded sense of responsibility for abortion?
6. According to Callahan, what does the abortion advocate believe is the source of human value and rights? Why does Callahan think this claim is seriously flawed?
7. Why does she claim that "feminine and fetal liberation are ultimately one and the same cause"?
8. Why does she think that permissive abortion undermines men's responsibilities and commitments with respect to sexual relationships and child support? What are the implications, according to Callahan, for society's support of women's needs with respect to maternity and child support?
9. Why does Callahan claim that the pro-choice feminists have actually supported the values of male domination and male attitudes toward sexuality?

The abortion debate continues. In the latest and perhaps most crucial development, pro-life feminists are contesting pro-choice feminist claims that abortion rights are prerequisites for women's full development and social equality. The outcome of this debate may be decisive for the culture as a whole. Pro-life feminists, like myself, argue on good feminist principles that women can never achieve the fulfillment of feminist goals in a society permissive toward abortion.

From Sidney Callahan, "Abortion and the Sexual Agenda," in *Commonweal* (April 25, 1986).

These new arguments over abortion take place within liberal political circles. This round of intense intra-feminist conflict has spiraled beyond earlier right-versus-left abortion debates, which focused on "tragic choices," medical judgments, and legal compromises. Feminist theorists of the pro-choice position now put forth the demand for unrestricted abortion rights as a *moral imperative* and insist upon women's right to complete reproductive freedom. They morally justify the present situation and current abortion practices. Thus it is all the more important that pro-life feminists articulate their different feminist perspective.

These opposing arguments can best be seen when presented in turn. Perhaps the most highly developed feminist arguments for the morality and legality of abortion can be found in Beverly Wildung Harrison's *Our Right to Choose* (Beacon Press, 1983) and Rosalind Pollack Petchesky's *Abortion and Woman's Choice* (Longman, 1984). Obviously it is difficult to do justice to these complex arguments, which draw on diverse strands of philosophy and social theory and are often interwoven in pro-choice feminists' own version of a "seamless garment." Yet the fundamental feminist case for the morality of abortion, encompassing the views of Harrison and Petchesky, can be analyzed in terms of four central moral claims: (1) the moral right to control one's own body; (2) the moral necessity of autonomy and choice in personal responsibility; (3) the moral claim for the contingent value of fetal life; (4) the moral right of women to true social equality.

1. The moral right to control one's own body. Pro-choice feminism argues that a woman choosing an abortion is exercising a basic right of bodily integrity granted in our common law tradition. If she does not choose to be physically involved in the demands of a pregnancy and birth, she should not be compelled to be so against her will. Just because it is *her* body which is involved, a woman should have the right to terminate any pregnancy, which at this point in medical history is tantamount to terminating fetal life. No one can be forced to donate an organ or submit to other invasive physical procedures for however good a cause. Thus no woman

should be subjected to "compulsory pregnancy." And it should be noted that in pregnancy much more than a passive biological process is at stake.

From one perspective, the fetus is, as Petchesky says, a "biological parasite" taking resources from the woman's body. During pregnancy, a woman's whole life and energies will be actively involved in the nine-month process. Gestation and childbirth involve physical and psychological risks. After childbirth a woman will either be a mother who must undertake a twenty-year responsibility for childrearing, or face giving up her child for adoption or institutionalization. Since hers is the body, hers the risk, hers the burden, it is only just that she alone should be free to decide on pregnancy or abortion.

This moral claim to abortion, according to the pro-choice feminists, is especially valid in an individualistic society in which women cannot count on medical care or social support in pregnancy, childbirth, or childrearing. A moral abortion decision is never made in a social vacuum, but in the real life society which exists here and now.

2. The moral necessity of autonomy and choice in personal responsibility. Beyond the claim for individual *bodily* integrity, the pro-choice feminists claim that to be a full adult *morally,* a woman must be able to make responsible life commitments. To plan, choose, and exercise personal responsibility, one must have control of reproduction. A woman must be able to make yes or no decisions about a specific pregnancy, according to her present situation, resources, prior commitments, and life plan. Only with such reproductive freedom can a woman have the moral autonomy necessary to make mature commitments, in the area of family, work, or education.

Contraception provides a measure of personal control, but contraceptive failure or other chance events can too easily result in involuntary pregnancy. Only free access to abortion can provide the necessary guarantee. The chance biological process of an involuntary pregnancy should not be allowed to override all the other personal commitments and responsibilities a woman has: to others, to family, to work, to education, to her future development, health, or well-being. Without reproductive freedom, women's personal moral agency and human consciousness are subjected to biology and chance.

3. The moral claim for the contingent value of fetal life. Pro-choice feminist exponents like Harrison and Petchesky claim that the value of fetal life is contingent upon the woman's free consent and subjective acceptance. The fetus must be invested with maternal valuing in order to become human. This process of "humanization" through personal consciousness and "sociality" can only be bestowed by the woman in whose body and psychosocial system a new life must mature. The meaning and value of fetal life are constructed by the woman; without this personal conferral there only exists a biological, physiological process. Thus fetal interests or fetal rights can never outweigh the woman's prior interest and rights. If a woman does not consent to invest her pregnancy with meaning or value, then the merely biological process can be freely terminated. Prior to her own free choice and conscious investment, a woman cannot be described as a "mother" nor can a "child" be said to exist.

Moreover, in cases of voluntary pregnancy, a woman can withdraw consent if fetal genetic defects or some other problem emerges at any time before birth. Late abortion should thus be granted without legal restrictions. Even the minimal qualifications and limitations on women embedded in *Roe v. Wade* are unacceptable—repressive remnants of patriarchal unwillingness to give power to women.

4. The moral right of women to full social equality. Women have a moral right to full social equality. They should not be restricted or subordinated because of their sex. But this morally required equality cannot be realized without abortion's certain control of reproduction. Female social equality depends upon being able to compete and participate as freely as males can in the structures of educational and economic life. If a woman cannot control when and how she will be pregnant or rear children, she is at a distinct disadvantage, especially in our male-dominated world.

Psychological equality and well-being is also at stake. Women must enjoy the basic right of a person to the free exercise of heterosexual intercourse and full sexual expression, separated from procreation. No less than males, women should be able to be sexually active without the constantly inhibiting fear of pregnancy. Abortion is necessary for women's sexual fulfillment and the growth of uninhibited feminine self-confidence and ownership of their sexual powers.

But true sexual and reproductive freedom means freedom to procreate as well as to inhibit fertility. Pro-choice feminists are also worried that women's freedom to reproduce will be curtailed through the abuse of sterilization and needless hysterectomies. Besides the punitive tendencies of a male-dominated healthcare system, especially in response to repeated abortions or welfare pregnancies, there are other economic and social pressures inhibiting reproduction. Genuine reproductive freedom implies that day care, medical care, and financial support would be provided mothers, while fathers would take their full share in the burdens and delights of raising children.

Many pro-choice feminists identify feminist ideals with communitarian, ecologically sensitive approaches to reshaping society. Following theorists like Sara Ruddick and Carol Gilligan, they link abortion rights with the growth of "maternal thinking" in our heretofore patriarchal society. Maternal thinking is loosely defined as a responsible commitment to the loving nurture of specific human beings as they actually exist in socially embedded interpersonal contexts. It is a moral perspective very different from the abstract, competitive, isolated, and principled rigidity so characteristic of patriarchy.

How does a pro-life feminist respond to these arguments? Pro-life feminists grant the good intentions of their pro-choice counterparts but protest that the pro-choice position is flawed, morally inadequate, and inconsistent with feminism's basic demands for justice. Pro-life feminists champion a more encompassing moral ideal. They recognize the claims of fetal life and offer a different perspective on what is good for women. The feminist vision is expanded and refocused.

1. From the moral right to control one's own body to a more inclusive ideal of justice. The moral right to control one's own body does apply to cases of organ transplants, mastectomies, contraception, and sterilization; but it is not a conceptualization adequate for abortion. The abortion dilemma is caused by the fact that 266 days following a conception in one body, another body will emerge. One's own body no longer exists as a single unit but is engendering another organism's life. This dynamic passage from conception to birth is genetically ordered and universally found in the human species. Pregnancy is not like the growth of cancer or infestation by a biological parasite; it is the way every human being enters the world. Strained philosophical analogies fail to apply: having a baby is not like rescuing a drowning person, being hooked up to a famous violinist's artificial life-support system, donating organs for transplant—or anything else.

As embryology and fetology advance, it becomes clear that human development is a continuum. Just as astronomers are studying the first three minutes in the genesis of the universe, so the first moments, days, and weeks at the beginning of human life are the subject of increasing scientific attention. While neonatology pushes the definition of viability ever earlier, ultrasound and fetology expand the concept of the patient in utero. Within such a continuous growth process, it is hard to defend logically any demarcation point after conception as the point at which an immature form of human life is so different from the day before or the day after, that it can be morally or legally discounted as a non-person. Even the moment of birth can hardly differentiate a nine-month fetus from a newborn. It is not surprising that those who countenance late abortions are logically led to endorse selective infanticide.

The same legal tradition which in our society guarantees the right to control one's own body firmly recognizes the wrongfulness of harming other bodies, however immature, dependent, different looking, or powerless. The handicapped, the retarded, and newborns are legally protected from deliberate harm. Pro-life feminists reject the suppositions that would except the unborn from this protection.

After all, debates similar to those about the fetus were once conducted about feminine personhood. Just as women, or blacks, were considered too different, too underdeveloped, too "biological," to have souls or to possess legal rights, so the fetus is now seen as "merely" biological life, subsidiary to a person. A woman was once viewed as incorporated into the "one flesh" of her husband's person; she too was a form of bodily property. In all patriarchal unjust systems, lesser orders of human life are granted rights only when wanted, chosen, or invested with value by the powerful.

Fortunately, in the course of civilization there has been a gradual realization that justice demands the powerless and dependent be protected against the uses of power wielded unilaterally. No human can be treated as a means to an end without consent. The fetus is an immature, dependent form of human life which only needs time and protection to develop. Surely, immaturity and dependence are not crimes.

In an effort to think about the essential requirements of a just society, philosophers like John Rawls recommend imagining yourself in an "original position," in which your position in the society to be created is hidden by a "veil of ignorance." You will have to weigh the possibility that any inequalities inherent in that society's practices may rebound upon you in the worst, as well as in the best, conceivable way. This thought experiment helps ensure justice for all.

Beverly Harrison argues that in such an envisioning of society everyone would institute abortion rights in order to guarantee that if one turned out to be a woman one would have reproductive freedom. But surely in the original position and behind the "veil of ignorance," you would have to contemplate the possibility of being the particular fetus to be aborted. Since everyone has passed through the fetal stage of development, it is false to refuse to imagine oneself in this state when thinking about a potential world in which justice would govern.

Would it be just that an embryonic life—in half the cases, of course, a female life—be sacrificed to the right of a woman's control over her own body? A woman may be pregnant without consent and experience a great many penalties, but a fetus killed without consent pays the ultimate penalty.

It does not matter (*The Silent Scream* notwithstanding) whether the fetus being killed is fully conscious or feels pain. We do not sanction killing the innocent if it can be done painlessly or without the victim's awareness. Consciousness becomes important to the abortion debate because it is used as a criterion for the "personhood" so often seen as the prerequisite for legal protection. Yet certain philosophers set the standard of personhood so high that half the human race could not meet the criteria during most of their waking hours (let alone their sleeping ones). Sentience, self-consciousness, rational decision-making, social participation? Surely no infant, or child under two, could qualify. Either our idea of person must be expanded or another criterion, such as human life itself, be employed to protect the weak in a just society. Pro-life feminists who defend the fetus empathetically identify with an immature state of growth passed through by themselves, their children, and everyone now alive.

It also seems a travesty of just procedures that a pregnant woman now, in effect, acts as sole judge of her own case, under the most stressful conditions. Yes, one can acknowledge that the pregnant woman will be subject to the potential burdens arising from a pregnancy, but it has never been thought right to have an interested party, especially the more powerful party, decide his or her own case when there may be a conflict of interest. If one considers the matter as a case of a powerful versus a powerless, silenced claimant, the pro-choice feminist argument can rightly be inverted: since hers is the body, hers the risk, and hers the greater burden, then how in fairness can a woman be the sole judge of the fetal right to life?

Human ambivalence, a bias toward self-interest, and emotional stress have always been recognized as endangering judgment. Freud declared that love and hate are so entwined that if instant

thoughts could kill, we would all be dead in the bosom of our families. In the case of a woman's involuntary pregnancy, a complex, long-term solution requiring effort and energy has to compete with the immediate solution offered by a morning's visit to an abortion clinic. On the simple, perceptual plane, with imagination and thinking curtailed, the speed, ease, and privacy of abortion, combined with the small size of the embryo, tend to make early abortions seem less morally serious—even though speed, size, technical ease, and the private nature of an act have no moral standing.

As the most recent immigrants from non-personhood, feminists have traditionally fought for justice for themselves and the world. Women rally to feminism as a new and better way to live. Rejecting male aggression and destruction, feminists seek alternative, peaceful, ecologically sensitive means to resolve conflicts while respecting human potentiality. It is a chilling inconsistency to see pro-choice feminists demanding continued access to assembly-line, technological methods of fetal killing—the vacuum aspirator, prostaglandins, and dilation and evacuation. It is a betrayal of feminism, which has built the struggle for justice on the bedrock of women's empathy. After all, "maternal thinking" receives its name from a mother's unconditional acceptance and nurture of dependent, immature life. It is difficult to develop concern for women, children, the poor and the dispossessed—and to care about peace—and at the same time ignore fetal life.

2. From the necessity of autonomy and choice in personal responsibility to an expanded sense of responsibility. A distorted idea of morality overemphasizes individual autonomy and active choice. Morality has often been viewed too exclusively as a matter of human agency and decisive action. In moral behavior persons must explicitly choose and aggressively exert their wills to intervene in the natural and social environments. The human will dominates the body, overcomes the given, breaks out of the material limits of nature. Thus if one does not choose to be pregnant or cannot rear a child, who must be given up for adoption, then better to abort the pregnancy. Willing, planning, choosing one's moral commitments through the contracting of one's individual resources becomes the premier model of moral responsibility.

But morality also consists of the good and worthy acceptance of the unexpected events that life presents. Responsiveness and response-ability to things unchosen are also instances of the highest human moral capacity. Morality is not confined to contracted agreements of isolated individuals. Yes, one is obligated by explicit contracts freely initiated, but human beings are also obligated by implicit compacts and involuntary relationships in which persons simply find themselves. To be embedded in a family, a neighborhood, a social system, brings moral obligations which were never entered into with informed consent.

Parent-child relationships are one instance of implicit moral obligations arising by virtue of our being part of the interdependent human community. A woman, involuntarily pregnant, has a moral obligation to the now-existing dependent fetus whether she explicitly consented to its existence or not. No pro-life feminist would dispute the forceful observations of pro-choice feminists about the extreme difficulties that bearing an unwanted child in our society can entail. But the stronger force of the fetal claim presses a woman to accept these burdens; the fetus possesses rights arising from its extreme need and the interdependency and unity of humankind. The woman's moral obligation arises both from her status as a human being embedded in the interdependent human community and her unique life-giving female reproductive power. To follow the pro-choice feminist ideology of insistent individualistic autonomy and control is to betray a fundamental basis of the moral life.

3. From the moral claim of the contingent value of fetal life to the moral claim for the intrinsic value of human life. The feminist pro-choice position which claims that the value of the fetus is contingent upon the pregnant woman's bestowal—or willed, conscious "construction"—of humanhood is seriously flawed. The inadequacies of this position flow from the erroneous premises (1) that human value and rights can be granted by individual will; (2) that the individual woman's consciousness can exist and operate in an *a priori* isolated fashion; and (3) that "mere" biological, genetic human life has little meaning. Pro-life feminism takes a very different stance to life and nature.

Human life from the beginning to the end of development *has* intrinsic value, which does not depend on meeting the selective criteria or tests set up by powerful others. A fundamental humanist assumption is at stake here. Either we are going to value embodied human life and humanity as a good thing, or take some variant of the nihilist position that assumes human life is just one more random occurrence in the universe such that each instance of human life must explicitly be justified to prove itself worthy to continue. When faced with a new life, or an involuntary pregnancy, there is a world of difference in whether one first asks, "Why continue?" or "Why not?" Where is the burden of proof going to rest? The concept of "compulsory pregnancy" is as distorted as labeling life "compulsory aging."

In a sound moral tradition, human rights arise from human needs, and it is the very nature of a right, or valid claim upon another, that it cannot be denied, conditionally delayed, or rescinded by more powerful others at their behest. It seems fallacious to hold that in the case of the fetus it is the pregnant woman alone who gives or removes its right to life and human status solely through her subjective conscious investment or "humanization." Surely no pregnant woman (or any other individual member of the species) has created her own human nature by an individually willed act of consciousness, nor for that matter been able to guarantee her own human rights. An individual woman and the unique individual embryonic life within her can only exist because of their participation in the genetic inheritance of the human species as a whole. Biological life should never be discounted. Membership in the species, or collective human family, is the basis for human solidarity, equality, and natural human rights.

4. The moral right of women to full social equality from a pro-life feminist perspective. Pro-life feminists and pro-choice feminists are totally agreed on the moral right of women to the full social equality so far denied them. The disagreement between them concerns the definition of the desired goal and the best means to get there. Permissive abortion laws do not bring women reproductive freedom, social equality, sexual fulfillment, or full personal development.

Pragmatic failures of a pro-choice feminist position combined with a lack of moral vision are, in fact, causing disaffection among young women. Middle-aged pro-choice feminists blamed the "big chill" on the general conservative backlash. But they should look rather to their own elitist acceptance of male models of sex and to the sad picture they present of women's lives. Pitting women against their own offspring is not only morally offensive, it is psychologically and politically destructive. Women will never climb to equality and social empowerment over mounds of dead fetuses, numbering now in the millions. As long as most women choose to bear children, they stand to gain from the same constellation of attitudes and institutions that will also protect the fetus in the woman's womb—and they stand to lose from the cultural assumptions that support permissive abortion. Despite temporary conflicts of interest, feminine and fetal liberation are ultimately one and the same cause.

Women's rights and liberation are pragmatically linked to fetal rights because to obtain true equality, women need (1) more social support and changes in the structure of society, and (2) increased self-confidence, self-expectations, and self-esteem. Society in general, and men in particular, have to provide women more support in rearing the next generation, or our devastating feminization of poverty will continue. But if a woman claims the right to decide by herself whether the fetus becomes a child or not, what does this do to paternal and communal responsibility? Why should men share responsibility for child support or childrearing if they cannot share in what is asserted to be the woman's sole decision? Furthermore, if explicit intentions and consciously accepted contracts are necessary for moral obligations, why should men be held responsible for what *they* do not voluntarily choose to happen? By pro-choice reasoning, a man

who does not want to have a child, or whose contraceptive fails, can be exempted from the responsibilities of fatherhood and child support. Traditionally, many men have been laggards in assuming parental responsibility and support for their children; ironically, ready abortion, often advocated as a response to male dereliction, legitimizes male irresponsibility and paves the way for even more male detachment and lack of commitment.

For that matter, why should the state provide a system of day-care or child support, or require workplaces to accommodate women's maternity and the needs of childrearing? Permissive abortion, granted in the name of women's privacy and reproductive freedom, ratifies the view that pregnancies and children are a woman's private individual responsibility. More and more frequently, we hear some version of this old rationalization: if she refuses to get rid of it, it's her problem. A child becomes a product of the individual woman's freely chosen investment, a form of private property resulting from her own cost-benefit calculation. The larger community is relieved of moral responsibility.

With legal abortion freely available, a clear cultural message is given: conception and pregnancy are no longer serious moral matters. With abortion as an acceptable alternative, contraception is not as responsibly used; women take risks, often at the urging of male sexual partners. Repeat abortions increase, with all their psychological and medical repercussions. With more abortion there is more abortion. Behavior shapes thought as well as the other way round. One tends to justify morally what one has done; what becomes commonplace and institutionalized seems harmless. Habituation is a powerful psychological force. Psychologically it is also true that whatever is avoided becomes more threatening; in phobias it is the retreat from anxiety-producing events which reinforces future avoidance. Women begin to see themselves as too weak to cope with involuntary pregnancies. Finally, through the potency of social pressure and the force of inertia, it becomes more and more difficult, in fact almost unthinkable, *not* to use abortion to solve problem pregnancies. Abortion becomes no longer a choice but a "necessity."

But "necessity," beyond the organic failure and death of the body, is a dynamic social construction open to interpretation. The thrust of present feminist pro-choice arguments can only increase the justifiable indications for "necessary" abortion; every unwanted fetal handicap becomes more and more unacceptable. Repeatedly assured that in the name of reproductive freedom, women have a right to specify which pregnancies and which children they will accept, women justify sex selection, and abort unwanted females. Female infanticide, after all, is probably as old a custom as the human species possesses. Indeed, all kinds of selection of the fit and the favored for the good of the family and the tribe have always existed. Selective extinction is no new program.

There are far better goals for feminists to pursue. Pro-life feminists seek to expand and deepen the more communitarian, maternal elements of feminism—and move society from its male-dominated course. First and foremost, women have to insist upon a different, woman-centered approach to sex and reproduction. While Margaret Mead stressed the "womb envy" of males in other societies, it has been more or less repressed in our own. In our male-dominated world, what men don't do, doesn't count. Pregnancy, childbirth, and nursing have been characterized as passive, debilitating, animal-like. The disease model of pregnancy and birth has been entrenched. This female disease or impairment, with its attendant "female troubles," naturally handicaps women in the "real" world of hunting, war, and the corporate fast track. Many pro-choice feminists, deliberately childless, adopt the male perspective when they cite the "basic injustice that women have to bear the babies," instead of seeing the injustice in the fact that men cannot. Women's biologically unique capacity and privilege has been denied, despised, and suppressed under male domination; unfortunately, many women have fallen for the phallic fallacy. . . .

Fully accepting our bodies as ourselves, what should women want? I think women will only flourish when there is a feminization of sexuality, very different from the current cultural trend toward masculinizing female sexuality. Women can never have the self-confidence and self-esteem they need to achieve feminist goals in society until a more holistic, feminine model of sexuality becomes the dominant cultural ethos. To say this affirms the view that men and women differ in the domain of sexual functioning, although they are more alike than different in other personality characteristics and competencies. For those of us committed to achieving sexual equality in the culture, it may be hard to accept the fact that sexual differences make it imperative to talk of distinct male and female models of sexuality. But if one wants to change sexual roles, one has to recognize pre-existing conditions. A great deal of evidence is accumulating which points to biological pressures for different male and female sexual functioning.

Males always and everywhere have been more physically aggressive and more likely to fuse sexuality with aggression and dominance. Females may be more variable in their sexuality, but since Masters and Johnson, we know that women have a greater capacity than men for repeated orgasm and a more tenuous path to arousal and orgasmic release. Most obviously, women also have a far greater sociobiological investment in the act of human reproduction. On the whole, women as compared to men possess a sexuality which is more complex, more intense, more extended in time, involving higher investment, risks, and psychosocial involvement.

Considering the differences in sexual functioning, it is not surprising that men and women in the same culture have often constructed different sexual ideals. In Western culture, since the nineteenth century at least, most women have espoused a version of sexual functioning in which sex acts are embedded within deep emotional bonds and secure long-term commitments. Within these committed "pair bonds" males assume parental obligations. In the idealized Victorian version of the Christian sexual ethic, culturally endorsed and maintained by women, the double standard was not countenanced. Men and women did not need to marry to be whole persons, but if they did engage in sexual functioning, they were to be equally chaste, faithful, responsible, loving, and parentally concerned. Many of the most influential women in the nineteenth-century women's movement preached and lived this sexual ethic, often by the side of exemplary feminist men. While the ideal has never been universally obtained, a culturally dominant demand for monogamy, self-control, and emotionally bonded and committed sex works well for women in every stage of their sexual life cycles. When love, chastity, fidelity, and commitment for better or worse are the ascendant cultural prerequisites for sexual functioning, young girls and women expect protection from rape and seduction, adult women justifiably demand male support in childrearing, and older women are more protected from abandonment as their biological attractions wane.

Of course, these feminine sexual ideals always coexisted in competition with another view. A more male-oriented model of erotic or amative sexuality endorses sexual permissiveness without long-term commitment or reproductive focus. Erotic sexuality emphasizes pleasure, play, passion, individual self-expression, and romantic games of courtship and conquest. It is assumed that a variety of partners and sexual experiences are necessary to stimulate romantic passion. This erotic model of the sexual life has often worked satisfactorily for men, both heterosexual and gay, and for certain cultural elites. But for the average woman, it is quite destructive. Women can only play the erotic game successfully when like the "*Cosmopolitan* woman," they are young, physically attractive, economically powerful, and fulfilled enough in a career to be willing to sacrifice family life. Abortion is also required. As our society increasingly endorses this male-oriented, permissive view of sexuality, it is all too ready to give women abortion on demand. Abortion helps a woman's body be more like a man's. It has been observed that *Roe* v. *Wade* removed the last defense women possessed against male sexual demands.

Unfortunately, the modern feminist movement made a mistaken move at a critical juncture. Rightly rebelling against patriarchy, unequal education, restricted work opportunities, and women's downtrodden political status, feminists also rejected the nineteenth-century feminine sexual ethic. Amative, erotic, permissive sexuality (along with abortion rights) became symbolically identified with other struggles for social equality in education, work, and politics. This feminist mistake also turned off many potential recruits among women who could not deny the positive dimensions of their own traditional feminine roles, nor their allegiance to the older feminine sexual ethic of love and fidelity.

An ironic situation then arose in which many pro-choice feminists preach their own double standard. In the world of work and career, women are urged to grow up, to display mature self-discipline and self-control; they are told to persevere in long-term commitments, to cope with unexpected obstacles by learning to tough out the inevitable sufferings and setbacks entailed in life and work. But this mature ethic of commitment and self-discipline, recommended as the only way to progress in the world of work and personal achievement, is discounted in the domain of sexuality.

In pro-choice feminism, a permissive, erotic view of sexuality is assumed to be the only option. Sexual intercourse with a variety of partners is seen as "inevitable" from a young age and as a positive growth experience to be managed by access to contraception and abortion. Unfortunately, the pervasive cultural conviction that adolescents, or their elders, cannot exercise sexual self-control, undermines the responsible use of contraception. When a pregnancy occurs, the first abortion is viewed in some pro-choice circles as a *rite de passage*. Responsibly choosing an abortion supposedly ensures that a young woman will take charge of her own life, make her own decisions, and carefully practice contraception. But the social dynamics of a permissive, erotic model of sexuality, coupled with permissive laws, work toward repeat abortions. Instead of being empowered by their abortion choices, young women having abortions are confronting the debilitating reality of *not* bringing a baby into the world; *not* being able to count on a committed male partner; *not* accounting oneself strong enough, or the master of enough resources, to avoid killing the fetus. Young women are hardly going to develop the self-esteem, self-discipline, and self-confidence necessary to confront a male-dominated society through abortion.

The male-oriented sexual orientation has been harmful to women and children. It has helped bring us epidemics of venereal disease, infertility, pornography, sexual abuse, adolescent pregnancy, divorce, displaced older women, and abortion. Will these signals of something amiss stimulate pro-choice feminists to rethink what kind of sex ideal really serves women's best interests? While the erotic model cannot encompass commitment, the committed model can—happily—encompass and encourage romance, passion, and playfulness. In fact, within the security of long-term commitments, women may be more likely to experience sexual pleasure and fulfillment.

The pro-life feminist position is not a return to the old feminine mystique. That espousal of "the eternal feminine" erred by viewing sexuality as so sacred that it cannot be humanly shaped at all. Woman's *whole* nature was supposed to be opposite to man's, necessitating complementary and radically different social roles. Followed to its logical conclusion, such a view presumes that reproductive and sexual experience is necessary for human fulfillment. But as the early feminists insisted, no woman has to marry or engage in sexual intercourse to be fulfilled, nor does a woman have to give birth and raise children to be complete, nor must she stay home and function as an earth mother. But female sexuality does need to be deeply respected as a unique potential and trust. Since most contraceptives and sterilization procedures really do involve only the woman's body rather than destroying new life, they can be an acceptable and responsible moral option.

With sterilization available to accelerate the inevitable natural ending of fertility and childbearing, a woman confronts only a limited number of years in which she exercises her reproductive trust and may have to respond to an unplanned pregnancy. Responsible use of contraception can lower the probabilities even more. Yet abortion is not decreasing. The reason is the current permissive attitude embodied in the law, not the "hard cases" which constitute 3 percent of today's abortions. Since attitudes, the law, and behavior interact, pro-life feminists conclude that unless there is an enforced limitation of abortion, which currently confirms the sexual and social status quo, alternatives will never be developed. For women to get what they need in order to combine childbearing, education, and careers, society has to recognize that female bodies come with wombs. Women and their reproductive power, and the children women have, must be supported in new ways. Another and different round of feminist consciousness-raising is needed in which all of women's potential is accorded respect. This time, instead of humbly buying entrée by conforming to male lifestyles, women will demand that society accommodate to them.

New feminist efforts to rethink the meaning of sexuality, femininity, and reproduction are all the more vital as new techniques for artificial reproduction, surrogate motherhood, and the like present a whole new set of dilemmas. In the long run, the very long run, the abortion debate may be merely the opening round in a series of far-reaching struggles over the role of human sexuality and the ethics of reproduction. Significant changes in the culture, both positive and negative in outcome, may begin as local storms of controversy. We may be at one of those vaguely realized thresholds when we had best come to full attention. What kind of people are we going to be? Pro-life feminists pursue a vision for their sisters, daughters, and granddaughters. Will their great-granddaughters be grateful?

Questions for Reflection

1. Callahan observes that, in the past, powerless and marginalized groups (such as women and blacks) were denied human rights by those in society who possessed all the power. Do you agree with her that fetuses in our current society suffer this same sort of injustice and marginalization suffered by women and blacks in the past?

2. What would Callahan's response be to cases where pregnancy results from rape and incest?

3. Do you agree with Callahan's argument that permissive abortion undermines the goals of feminism and actually supports a male-dominated social agenda? Do you agree with her argument that pro-life feminism will, in the long run, actually be better for the status of women in our society?

4. In contrast to the feminist fight for abortion rights, Callahan says that "there are far better goals for feminists to pursue." What sorts of goals does she have in mind?

5. Make a point by point comparison of Judith Jarvis Thomson's (reading 61) and Sidney Callahan's views of a woman's obligations toward her fetus. Who do you think has the stronger argument?

C H A P T E R   7

Questions about Individual Liberty and the Government

INDIVIDUAL LIBERTY AND THE GOVERNMENT: WHAT ARE THE ISSUES?

Why is there government? What is it that makes a government legitimate? What is its purpose? What are its limits? To answer these questions, the 17th-century English philosopher Thomas Hobbes wrote his classic book *Leviathan* in 1651. Using a thought experiment, he imagined what human life would be like if there were no government, a condition that he called the "state of nature." Hobbes surmised that without a government to maintain order and regulate human interactions, this condition would be "a war of all against all" as each person did whatever he or she could get away with doing. In short, he concluded that human life without government would be "solitary, poor, nasty, brutish, and short."

Most of us would agree with Hobbes that a government of some sort is a practical necessity. But do we need as much government as we currently have? Does the government need to poke its nose into our personal affairs as much as it does? Every time we look at a paycheck and see how much of our original income has been eaten up by the government's voracious appetite, we are reminded of the presence of the government in our lives. Many despair over what they perceive as the heavy hand of the government in collecting excessive taxes, imposing unnecessary regulations, creating huge bureaucracies, and squandering their hard-earned money on people and causes that they deem undeserving. These sentiments are summed up in a famous maxim (commonly attributed to Thomas Jefferson) "that government governs best that governs least."

Is government as bad as this quote implies? Even though many in previous centuries thought there was too much government, there was less government in earlier times than in our present society. However, with less government, people also had virtually no protection from harmful medicines and dangerous products sold by unscrupulous or negligent persons. There were few health and safety standards in the workplace. If you deposited money in a bank, there was no guarantee that you could get it back if the bank failed. In today's world, a college education would be beyond the reach of anybody but the most wealthy without government supported financial aid and loans. Furthermore, even if a student is not receiving direct financial aid, his or her college education is made possible by tax-supported federal programs. With the high costs of technology and other resources, no major university and most colleges could not fulfill their mission if it were not for the direct or indirect support of the local, state, and federal governments.

So, we are back to Thomas Hobbes's point that government seems to be a necessary part of human life. But even if we agree on that point, it still leaves a host of questions concerning the nature of government and what exact role it should play in human affairs. Issues such as these make up the central core of political philosophy.

In this chapter, we will focus on two basic questions in political philosophy. The first question we consider is, "Should I always obey the government?" In other words, Is civil disobedience ever morally permissible? If we agree that government is something necessary and even good, then it would seem that obeying the government is necessary and good. But are there situations in which it would be bad and even immoral to obey the government? If so, under what conditions would it be morally permissible to break the law?

The second question is, "What makes a government just?" Every government exercises some degree of authority over its citizens. It does so by passing laws, which it then enforces by imposing penalties on those who violate them. To be an effective government requires that it has the power to control the behavior of its citizens. However, not every use of power is legitimate. So, for a government to be legitimate and for the extent of its control over citizens' lives to be appropriate, the government must conform to certain standards of justice. But what are these standards by which we judge a government to be just? Besides having power, a government must have the right to use that power in certain ways. What gives a government that right and what principles should guide and limit the use of the government's authority?

WHAT ARE MY OPTIONS CONCERNING GOVERNMENTAL AUTHORITY?

Our first question, "Should I always obey the government," has two simple answers: yes or no. What is important, however, are the justifications that are given for each answer. In Plato's dialogue *Crito,* Socrates argues that we have an absolute obligation to obey our own government. According to Socrates, if I have benefited from the government's services and protection, and have not chosen to renounce my citizenship, then I have an absolute duty to obey the government. Socrates' sentiments are echoed in a patriotic slogan that goes back several hundred years: "My country, right or wrong." Martin Luther King, Jr., disagrees, stating that we have an obligation to obey just laws and also an obligation to disobey unjust laws.

The next set of readings explores the deeper question, "What makes a government just?" We will explore five different positions.

The **social contract theory** claims that a government is just and legitimate if its exercise of power is based on an explicit or implicit agreement made between the citizens and the government. In other words, the government has the authority to have some measure of control over the lives of its citizens, only because each citizen has given the government that authority. While the basic idea of the social contract is implicit in the teachings of Socrates and other ancient thinkers, it came to the forefront in the 17th century. Thomas Hobbes (mentioned earlier) was a leading proponent of the social contract theory of government. However, Hobbes's rather grim view of human nature led him to conclude that life without government would be next to impossible. Accordingly, he believed that for a government to function effectively, it would be necessary for the government to have almost absolute power. John Locke, however, disagreed. Locke acknowledged that life without government would be inconvenient and, for this reason, it would be rational for people to form a government. However, Locke believed that though we delegate some of our powers and freedoms to the government, we do not surrender them. The government, for Locke, is always our creation and servant. Hence, Locke's view of government was one of a liberal democracy, created by the social contract and ruled by the will of the majority. In the readings that follow, Locke will represent the social contract view.

In the chapter on ethics we saw that utilitarianism is the theory that the right action is the one that produces the greatest amount of happiness for the greatest number of people. Accordingly, with respect to political theory, **utilitarianism** claims that the function of the government is to promote the well-being of its citizens by creating a society that achieves the greatest good for the greatest number. In reading 67, Mill will argue that maximizing individual liberty is an essential means to creating the best society for all. Accordingly, it follows that any restriction on individual liberty that cannot be shown to promote the general good is illegitimate.

Marxism claims that the fundamental principle of a just society is that the goods of a society should be distributed equally. In the Marxist ideal society, private property would be abolished and its ownership would be held by the community. In speaking of "property" here, the Marxist is referring specifically to property that is essential to the economic life of a society, such as lands and factories. In such a society there would be no extremes of wealth and poverty, for the society would be ruled by the maxim, "from each according to his ability, to each according to his need." This notion of community-owned property is commonly called communism, and this social and economic system has been around since ancient times. However, the term *communism* has come to be associated with the most recent and powerful version constructed by Karl Marx and his collaborator Friedrich Engels in the 19th century.

Contemporary liberalism, as defended by John Rawls, attempts to find a compromise between the two goals of individual liberty and social equality. Rawls thinks that the just government is one that would allow the greatest amount of basic liberties, provided that any social and economic inequalities would produce the greatest benefit for the least advantaged and would afford everyone equality of opportunity. Rawls thinks that such a society would be just because it would be the most fair and because it would be agreeable to everyone who adopted a standpoint of total impartiality.

Political libertarianism claims that the only role of government is to protect its citizens from external and internal threats to their basic rights. Other than that, the government has no responsibility to promote the general welfare, but must let everyone live their lives as they wish. The position of political libertarianism should not be confused with metaphysical libertarianism (discussed in Chapter 5), which addresses the very different question of freedom of the will. The reading by John Hospers represents contemporary political libertarianism. Hospers's position obviously has affinities with Mill's. However, Mill tended to emphasize that individual liberty should be protected because doing so served the pursuit of society's greatest good. Hospers, however, believes that individual liberty is an intrinsic right that should be valued in itself, independent of any social goals that it serves. Nevertheless, Hospers does believe that maximizing individual freedom would have the side effect of creating the best society.

The two questions in political philosophy and the responses to each one we have just discussed are summarized in Tables 7.1 and 7.2.

TABLE 7.1

	Should I always obey the government?
Socrates	Yes. We have an absolute duty to obey the government.
Martin Luther King, Jr.	No. We should obey just laws and disobey seriously unjust laws.

TABLE 7.2

	What makes a government just?
Social Contract Theory (John Locke)	The government is founded on the consent of the governed and ruled by the will of the majority.
Utilitarianism (John Stuart Mill)	The government maximizes individual liberty and pursues the greatest happiness for the greatest number.
Marxism (Karl Marx)	Society's goods are commonly held and distributed equally.
Contemporary Liberalism (John Rawls)	The government maximizes individual liberty consistent with the greatest benefit to the least advantaged and equality of opportunity.
Political Libertarianism (John Hospers)	The government does not intrude upon an individual's freedom as long as everyone else's rights are secured.

OPENING NARRATIVE: WHO MAKES THE RULES? WHY SHOULD I OBEY THEM?

The Parable of the Man

Our opening narrative is a clever story by contemporary American philosopher Richard Taylor (1919–   ). Richard Taylor was a professor of philosophy at the University of Rochester and is now retired. In his fable, he asks us to imagine a loose-knit band of people whose lives are intruded upon by a gang of people who serve a mysterious figure called "The Man." The story is crafted to make us feel the sense of injustice and unfairness of this situation. However, in the end, Taylor asks us to consider what resemblances there might be between their situation and ours.

Reading Questions

1. Why does Taylor believe it is difficult for us to raise philosophical problems about our own government?
2. The servants of The Man occasionally come around to help themselves to a portion of the contents of everyone's pockets. Certainly, nothing exactly like this happens to us. However, what feature of our life as citizens might be comparable to this?
3. In what sense are the people in the story governed by rules of their own making? What ritual in our public life corresponds to sending The Man a letter expressing approval or disapproval of The Man's rules?
4. What other correspondences are there between the following features of the society in the story and your own: the rules regulating the consumption of goat's milk, the prohibition on making or selling tea, the zoos, the regulation of relationships between males and females, "The Block," and the ceremonial day off from work to honor The Man?

It is one thing to formulate the philosophical problems of government, but quite another to feel them as problems. So long as things are familiar and go along in accustomed ways, we feel little inclination to ask questions. It is only when we feel the pinch, when things pose threats to our interests, that intellectual justifications are apt to be sought. Thus a colony may suddenly "discover" that its king is with-

out any clear authority to rule them when they find that he has imposed an onerous tax and that they have the means to resist his rule, whereas they had until then little reason for thinking of themselves as other than his subjects. Similarly, one cannot help being struck sometimes by the evident contentment of people living under the most corrupt despotism in which their basic needs appear to be

From Richard Taylor, *Freedom, Anarchy, and the Law: An Introduction to Political Philosophy,* 2nd ed. (Buffalo, NY: Prometheus Books, 1982).

met, though there seems to be not the slightest trace of legitimacy in the regime that has set itself over them, other than what can be conferred by the fear of guns in the hands of a loyal army.

It is, however, a mistake to suppose that philosophical problems of government exist only for citizens of nations other than one's own. We, no less than they, have from childhood been taught to deal with such problems in terms of slogans rather than of thought, so much so that it is common to find grown men, even men of intelligence and learning, solemnly intoning them. We are struck by the use of slogans in other cultures, particularly those headed by revolutionary regimes who look to certain writings and heroes for justification, but we easily overlook the extent to which slogans serve as substitutes for thinking on our own part. Thus we are expected to say, for example, that in our system men are free to exercise their rights, provided they do not interfere with the rights of others; or again, that only under popular government, such as ours, are men truly free; or that democratic government is of, by, and for the people who are governed, and so on—epigrammatic summations of political philosophy that are not so much false as simply empty. They are in this respect rather like such claims as that a given dictatorship is the vanguard of the proletariat, that with the abolition of class conflict the state will wither away, etc., claims whose speciousness is far more evident to us than to those who have been taught to mouth them.

In the effort, then, to foster the state of mind in which it can be appreciated that there are philosophical problems of government, we propose a little fable. This story is slightly far-fetched in spots, but something of the sort seems desirable in order to penetrate the massive complacency that has been fortified in many by their indoctrination from childhood.

A LITTLE FABLE

Let us imagine a band of men—refugees or pilgrims, perhaps fleeing oppression—who have at last found a pleasant place to live in peace, a vast domain of rolling hills, fresh winding streams and green meadows, all conveying and supporting a natural sense of abundance and freedom, with ample space and means for their activities and pursuits. Here they raise their dwellings, sharing their domain over the years with their growing numbers of kinsmen, so that eventually everything has for them the feeling of familiarity and the kind of warmth and security men associate with being at home, in their own surroundings, with their own people.

Eventually, however, they begin to find men encamped here and there in what they had thought of as their homeland, men whose numbers greatly increase with time, until it becomes almost impossible to venture out without encountering them. They detect in them a patronizing attitude toward themselves and find that these men are all accompanied by, or can quickly summon, armed servants, ready at an instant to do their bidding. These servants keep a close eye on things, noting the comings and goings of the people and speculating on their purposes, from time to time peering into their windows to see what is going on there, noting down all their impressions, and regularly sending these along to someone they deferentially refer to as The Man. They also come around occasionally to help themselves to a certain fraction of the contents of everyone's pockets, according to a formula provided by The Man. Eventually it is discovered that high fences have gone up around the entire periphery of the place, intended, the people learn, to keep everyone inside. In case anyone should want to leave, to go through this high fence, he must first seek permission from The Man. Such permission, one is assured, will probably not be withheld, provided it is first established that the applicant has not violated any of a long and complex list of rules. These rules of course emanate from The Man—but not in any arbitrary or despotic way. Not at all. The people are themselves, they learn, the authors of them, at least for all practical purposes. Indeed, The Man and his servants make and enforce all these rules only with the prior consent of the people who must obey them. This is ensured in the most obvious and foolproof way imaginable, by their being given the opportunity every few years of writing The Man a letter—or at least, those who have obeyed all the rules are allowed to do this; the others are not. The letter is very succinct and to the point; so brief, in fact, that it contains only the single word "yes" or "no," which is meant to express how its author feels about The Man and his latest rules. In time this right of sending the letter, at quadrennial intervals, comes to be represented as the most precious blessing anyone can possess, far exceeding in its importance any interest he may have in anything else. It matters little what else one is allowed or forbidden to do as long as he is allowed to write this short letter every few years; for without this, he has *no* freedoms at all, whereas with this one, he has them *all.* At least, so everyone is told. No one actually looks at these letters, of course, except to pile them into two stacks and see which is higher; but they do serve the overwhelmingly important purpose of ensuring that the people who write them are free men, governed by their own consent, and of demonstrating that the often frivolous and sometimes galling rules enforced at every turn at the point of a gun do not really in any way delimit anyone's freedom at all. On the contrary, they guarantee for everyone a higher order of freedom. Nor are the rules really concocted by The Man, notwithstanding appearances, but by the people themselves, for that is what they were really doing, the last time they sent him their terse and friendly letters.

About half of the rules make sense. People are not supposed to go around hitting each other, for instance, nor taking each other's money without asking. The *Man* can take their money without asking, to be sure; in fact, once each year he sends agents around to reach into the peoples' pockets and take a fixed proportion of what they find there. If the agents meet with resistance, they end up taking whatever they want. But this is all right, since the people in effect told them they could do this by writing "yes" in their last letter. Or in the case of those who did not, then their neighbors did this for them. In any case, *someone* said "yes," which can accordingly be taken as the expression of each man's will.

So about half of the rules have some sense to them. The rest, however, are pulled out of a hat. People propose rules—any rules, it doesn't matter

what they are—and these are all dropped into a hat and from time to time randomly drawn out. One of them is to the effect that no one may drink goat's milk except at certain hours and in certain precisely defined areas, and at exorbitant cost, most of the cost of it being a hidden tax that goes to The Man. Many people have an inordinate fondness for goat's milk, but some who tried it did not like it; so they put in the hat the rule that no one should ever have it at all, and that rule somehow got drawn from the hat. For awhile it was vigorously enforced, until modified by The Man in response to public clamor on the one hand and his desire for more revenue on the other. Another such rule, not so old and hence still uncompromisingly enforced, is that one may never drink tea, even at home, nor even possess it, even in molecular quantities. This rule was originally one of those drawn from the hat, of course, but it came to be represented as expressing the most basic of all those virtues that are traceable to the founding fathers and, some say, to God. Thus, in order to avoid public disgrace, a person has to sneak into a remote cave and there, in the darkness and isolation, proceed to brew it; if he is discovered, he is stripped, for the time being and perhaps for life, of the most basic human right to send a quadrennial letter to The Man, is made to turn over a considerable portion of his possessions, or else has obloquy heaped upon him and is locked up for years in one of the many zoos built for this purpose. Far worse than this, however, is selling tea—an act that is made the more hazardous by the fact that The Man pays his servants to be purchasers of it in order to trap people into selling it so he can send them off to the zoos.

There are many rules like that, drawn from the hat. In time some of them become obsolescent and are left unenforced, or are enforced only sporadically at the whim of The Man's armed servants; but others are always drawn from the hat to replace them. One of them, for example, requires that no adult male share his life with an adult female not related by blood without first obtaining The Man's permission and submitting to certain ritualistic procedures. Having once got this permission, gone through with the required forms, and begun such an arrangement, he may not then dissolve it without again soliciting permission from The Man, and this permission is given only with reluctance, if at all. One may not take two or more such persons under his roof under any circumstances whatever, at least not at the same time, The Man insisting on zealous enforcement of this rule always, having declared it to be essential to something or other.

The rules that are drawn from the hat are sometimes enforced with greater zeal than those in which one can discern some sort of point. Indeed, this is generally the case. For example, The Man long ago commissioned an artisan to carve out a huge wooden block that was oddly composed and resembled nothing in particular. This came to be referred to as "The Block," and eventually pictures of it began to appear everywhere. Songs were written about The Block, verses composed; these are now intoned with an air of solemnity wherever people foregather. Children are taught, upon arriving at school, to put small replicas of The Block on their heads and hop about on one foot for a minute or two while reciting verses about The Block and affirming their devotion to it. Lifelong habits are thus created. For instance, even old men, upon hearing Block refrains, leap to their feet as a reflex and hop about, clapping both hands on their heads (after first removing their hats); and scornful glances are directed to anyone who may be slow in doing this.

Periodically everyone takes a day off from work to honor The Man and his servants, particularly those trained in the use of knives, guns, and grenades. At these times replicas of The Block are seen everywhere: people set them out on their porches and yards, in their windows, on their roofs, and on their cars. Exhortations are struck and displayed for the general edification, always in juxtaposition to replicas of The Block. The simplest and commonest is: "Honor your Block." One of the more inspirational is: "Ask not what The Man can do for you; rather ask, what you can do for The Man." Although apparently no one ever does actually ask such a question, and would be suspected of having been drinking goat's milk if he did, such sentiments and the evocation of feelings that are everywhere associated with The Block are thought to render people less bilious when The Man's emis-

saries come around to rifle through their pockets and help themselves to what they find there, or to peer in their windows to see what might be going on, or to break into rooms to see whether they can find any tea.

THE PROBLEMS OF GOVERNMENT

One could hardly maintain that this yarn bears no resemblance to the lot of any people with whom we are familiar. Perhaps then, it can serve as the background for the philosophical problems enunciated before, problems that must be dealt with, not fabulously, but philosophically. The people just described could certainly, with great justification, ask (1) What is the rational justification for the government of some men by others, in case any exists? Do we obey because we are slaves and have to, from fear of threats, or is government justified in what it demands of us? Further, they could with great justice ask (2) What renders the rule of this government legitimate, in preference to rule by others who might, for example, fulfill our needs better? Again, they could properly ask (3) What, after all, is the purpose of government—to perpetuate allegiance to its own trappings? To ensure us greater security? To enable us to pursue our own happiness? Or what? Similarly, the more thoughtful among them would insist upon asking (4) What is the proper extent of governmental authority and control over the individual? Where do our liberties end, and the coercive power of government begin? And finally, it is clearly important for them to wonder (5) What are our duties as citizens? To obey all the laws? Or only those that are just? Do our obligations as men transcend our duties as citizens of this commonwealth? Or is it the other way around?

It will of course be noted that these are precisely the five questions listed at the outset. For the intelligent people in the fable, they would be, not just abstract questions of philosophy, but questions of the most overwhelming importance that reach to the very basis of human happiness and the rationale of social and political life. And so they are for us, for our lot is not so different from that of those fabulous citizens, and our problems are essentially the same. It may be that all these questions have answers that do not in the least threaten the established order under which we live. On the other hand, the answers to them may leave that order with no support whatever that human reason can accept. Or the truth may, of course, lie somewhere between these extremes.

Questions for Reflection

1. We may be inclined to think that the injustice of The Man's government results from the fact that it was imposed upon the colony of people by force. But can you think of any radically new system of government that did not rise to power through force, whether it be war or revolution? How did the American government arise? Were all of the American colonists in favor of their new government? In assessing the legitimacy of a government, how important is it to consider how it originated as opposed to judging it on the basis of its current practices?
2. Any stable government (your own or the one in the story) obviously has the force to impose its will on us, but having force does not equal having morally justified authority. While the practical benefits of your government are obvious, does it have any morally justified authority over you, or is its control simply based on its power? What sort of justification could be given to the authority of the government?

SHOULD I ALWAYS OBEY THE GOVERNMENT?

For government to exist, there must be laws. So, if you believe that government is generally a good thing, then you must believe that it is essential to the good of society to have laws. However, if people did not obey the laws, then there might as well not be any laws at all and, practically speaking, society would be lawless. So initially, it seems as though disobeying the laws of one's government is never morally justified. But what if the laws a government passes are illegal (they violate its own constitution)? Or what if the laws are legal, but they are deeply immoral? For example, Adolph Hitler rose to power in Nazi Germany through a legal political process. Once in power, he began to change the laws (again through legal procedures) so that many of the horrors of that society, such as the confiscation of people's property and imprisonment of innocent "enemies of the state," were perfectly legal. In the 18th and 19th centuries it was legal to own slaves in portions of the United States, even though this practice is clearly immoral. Furthermore, up until the latter half of the 20th century, racial discrimination was protected by the law in the United States. What should a citizen do in these cases?

While most political philosophers agree that obedience to the law is an important foundation stone of any society, many have argued that there are limits to this obligation and that, under certain conditions, civil disobedience is morally justified. **Civil disobedience** may be defined as an illegal act of moral protest. But this raises the question of the difference between civil disobedience and criminal disobedience, since both categories involve illegal actions. The major difference is that civil disobedience (unlike criminal disobedience) is a public defiance of some law, policy, or action of a governmental body in order to draw attention to the unjustness of the law, the problems with the policy, or the wrongness of a particular action on the part of the government. Ultimately, of course, the goal is to change the law or the government's behavior. In contrast, a simple criminal act does not have any sort of high-minded purpose. The criminal breaks the law for personal gain, by robbing a bank or driving with an illegal license, for example.

Furthermore, to be an act of moral protest, the civil disobedience must be a public flouting of the law. On the other hand, a criminal action is done secretly with the intent of evading the law. By this criteria, bombing an abortion clinic or a governmental office and then evading capture is a criminal act. However, placing one's body in front of the door until arrested and dragged away by the police is an act of civil disobedience. Both types of action may be motivated by a dissatisfaction with the system, but the difference is in the means used to protest it. In the next reading, Plato provides us with an account of Socrates' last hours in jail and his argument against civil disobedience. On the other hand, the selection by Martin Luther King, Jr., provides us with a defense of the legitimacy of civil disobedience.

 PLATO

We Have an Absolute Obligation to Obey the Government

One of the classic spokespersons for opposing civil disobedience is Socrates. We have encountered the figure of Socrates throughout this book, starting with his discussion with Euthyphro in reading 1 and then his trial for heresy and corrupting the youth in reading 2. In a sequel to the story of the trial, Plato tells about Socrates' discussion with one of his students while in jail waiting for his execution. Crito, the young disciple, believes that Socrates has been the victim of trumped-up charges and an unjust verdict. Consequently, Crito begs Socrates to escape from prison. In the course of the discussion, Socrates makes clear his controversial stand on civil disobedience.

Reading Questions

1. What reasons does Crito give for why Socrates should escape from the jail?
2. What is the first principle Socrates gets Crito to accept concerning the doing of evil?
3. In Socrates' imaginary dialogue with the laws of the state, how do the laws respond to the charge that they may be disobeyed since Socrates received an unjust sentence?
4. Why do the laws claim that Socrates has an "implied contract" with them?
5. If Socrates disobeys the law, what three wrongs will he commit?

From Plato, *Crito,* trans. Benjamin Jowett (1898). A few changes to the translation have been made for greater readability.

6. What evidence do the laws give that Socrates has been satisfied to be a citizen of Athens up until this point?

7. If Socrates believed the verdict of his guilt was wrong, what alternative could he have taken that he turned down?

8. What is the significance of the claim that Socrates has been "a victim, not of the laws, but of men"?

SOCRATES: Why have you come at this hour, Crito? It must be quite early.

CRITO: Yes, certainly.

SOCRATES: What is the exact time?

CRITO: The dawn is breaking.

SOCRATES: I am surprised the keeper of the prison would let you in.

CRITO: He knows me because I often come, Socrates; moreover, I have done him a kindness.

SOCRATES: Did you just get here?

CRITO: No, I came some time ago.

SOCRATES: Then why did you sit and say nothing, instead of awakening me at once? . . .

CRITO: Oh, my beloved Socrates, let me entreat you once more to take my advice and escape. For if you die I shall not only lose a friend who can never be replaced, but there is another evil: people who do not know you and me will believe that I might have saved you if I had been willing to give money, but that I did not care. . . . Nor can I think that you are justified, Socrates, in betraying your own life when you might be saved; this is playing into the hands of your enemies and destroyers; and moreover I should say that you were betraying your children; for you might bring them up and educate them; instead of which you go away and leave them, and they will have to take their chance; and if they do not meet with the usual fate of orphans, there will be small thanks to you. No man should bring children into the world who is unwilling to persevere to the end in their nurture and education. . . .

SOCRATES: Dear Crito, your zeal is invaluable, if a right one; but if wrong, the greater the zeal the greater the evil; and therefore we ought to consider whether these things shall be done or not. For I am and always have been one of those na-tures who must be guided by reason, whatever the reason may be which upon reflection ap-pears to me to be the best; and now that this for-tune has come upon me, I cannot put away the reasons which I have before given: the princi-ples which I have hitherto honored and revered I still honor, and unless we can find other and better principles on the instant, I am certain not to agree with you . . . .

Let us consider the matter together, and ei-ther refute me if you can, and I will be con-vinced; or else cease, my dear friend, from repeating to me that I ought to escape against the wishes of the Athenians: for I am extremely desirous to be persuaded by you, but not against my own better judgment. . . .

CRITO: I will do my best.

SOCRATES: Are we to say that we are never inten-tionally to do wrong, or that in one way we ought and in another way we ought not to do wrong, or is doing wrong always evil and dis-honorable? Are all our former admissions which were made within a few days to be thrown away? And have we, at our age, been earnestly dis-coursing with one another all our life long only to discover that we are no better than children? Or are we to rest assured, in spite of the opinion of the many, and in spite of consequences whether better or worse, of the truth of what was then said, that injustice is always an evil and dis-honor to him who acts unjustly? Shall we affirm that?

CRITO: Yes.

SOCRATES: Then we must do no wrong?

CRITO: Certainly not.

SOCRATES: When we are injured should we injure in return, as the many imagine? Or must we injure no one at all?

CRITO: Clearly not.

SOCRATES: Again, Crito, may we do evil?

CRITO: Surely not, Socrates.

SOCRATES: And what of doing evil in return for evil, which is the morality of the many—is that just or not?

CRITO: Not just.

SOCRATES: For doing evil to another is the same as injuring him?

CRITO: Very true.

SOCRATES: Then we ought not to retaliate or render evil for evil to anyone, whatever evil we may have suffered from him. But I would have you consider, Crito, whether you really mean what you are saying. For this opinion has never been held, and never will be held, by any considerable number of persons; and those who are agreed and those who are not agreed upon this point have no common ground, and can only despise one another when they see how widely they differ. Tell me, then, whether you agree with and assent to my first principle, that neither injury nor retaliation nor warding off evil by evil is ever right. And shall that be the premise of our argument? Or do you decline and dissent from this? For this has been of old and is still my opinion; but, if you are of another opinion, let me hear what you have to say. If, however, you remain of the same mind as formerly, I will proceed to the next step.

CRITO: You may proceed, for I have not changed my mind.

SOCRATES: Then I will proceed to the next step, which may be put in the form of a question: Ought a man to do what he admits to be right, or ought he to betray the right?

CRITO: He ought to do what he thinks right.

SOCRATES: But if this is true, what is the application? In leaving the prison against the will of the Athenians, do I wrong any? or rather do I not wrong those whom I ought least to wrong? Do I not desert the principles which were acknowledged by us to be just? What do you say?

CRITO: I cannot tell, Socrates, for I do not know.

SOCRATES: Then consider the matter in this way: Imagine that I am about to play truant (you may call the proceeding by any name which you like), and the laws and the government come and interrogate me: "Tell us, Socrates," they say; "what are you trying to do? Are you attempting to overturn us—the laws and the whole State, as far as you are able? Do you imagine that a State can subsist and not be overthrown, in which the decisions of law have no power, but are set aside and overthrown by individuals?" What will be our answer, Crito, to these and the like words? Anyone, and especially a clever rhetorician, will have a good deal to urge about the evil of setting aside the law which requires a sentence to be carried out; and we might reply, "Yes; but the State has injured us and given an unjust sentence." Suppose I say that?

CRITO: Very good, Socrates.

SOCRATES: "And was that our agreement with you?" the law would say; "or were you to abide by the sentence of the State?" And if I were to express astonishment at their saying this, the law would probably add: "Answer, Socrates, instead of opening your eyes: you are in the habit of asking and answering questions. Tell us what complaint you have to make against us which justifies you in attempting to destroy us and the State? In the first place did we not bring you into existence? Your father married your mother by our aid and begat you. Say whether you have any objection to urge against those of us who regulate marriage?" None, I should reply. "Or against those of us who regulate the system of nurture and education of children in which you were trained? Were not the laws, who have the charge of this, right in commanding your father to train you in music and gymnastic?" Right, I should reply. . . .

What answer shall we make to this, Crito? Do the laws speak truly, or do they not?

CRITO: I think that they do.

SOCRATES: Then the laws will say: "Consider, Socrates, if this is true, that in your present attempt you are going to do us wrong. For, after having brought you into the world, and nurtured and educated you, and given you and every other citizen a share in every good that we had to give, we further proclaim and give the right to every Athenian, that if he does not like us when he has come of age and has seen the ways of the city, and made our acquaintance, he may go where he pleases and take his goods with him; and none of us laws will forbid him or interfere with him. Any of you who does not like us and the city, and who wants to go to a colony or to any other city, may go where he likes, and take his goods with him. But he who has experience of the manner in which we order justice and administer the State, and still remains, has entered into an implied contract that he will do as we command him. And he who disobeys us is, as we maintain, thrice wrong: first, because in disobeying us he is disobeying his parents; secondly, because we are the authors of his education; thirdly, because he has made an agreement with us that he will duly obey our commands; and he neither obeys them nor convinces us that our commands are wrong; and we do not rudely impose them, but give him the alternative of obeying or convincing us; that is what we offer, and he does neither."

"These are the sort of accusations to which, as we were saying, you, Socrates, will be exposed if you accomplish your intentions; you, above all other Athenians." Suppose I ask, why is this? They will justly retort upon me that I above all other men have acknowledged the agreement. "There is clear proof, Socrates," they will say, "that we and the city were not displeasing to you. Of all Athenians you have been the most constant resident in the city, which, as you never leave, you may be supposed to love. For you never went out of the city either to see the games, except once when you went to the Isthmus, or to any other place unless when you were on military service; nor did you travel as other men do. Nor had you any curiosity to know other States or their laws: your affections did not go beyond us and our State; we were your special favorites, and you acquiesced in our government of you; and this is the State in which you begat your children, which is a proof of your satisfaction."

"Moreover, you might, if you had liked, have fixed the penalty at banishment in the course of the trial—the State which refuses to let you go

now would have let you go then. But you pretended that you preferred death to exile, and that you were not grieved at death. And now you have forgotten these fine sentiments, and pay no respect to us, the laws, of whom you are the destroyer; and are doing what only a miserable slave would do, running away and turning your back upon the compacts and agreements which you made as a citizen. And first of all answer this very question: Are we right in saying that you agreed to be governed according to us in deed, and not in word only? Is that true or not?"

How shall we answer that, Crito? Must we not agree?

CRITO: There is no help, Socrates.

SOCRATES: Then will they not say: "You, Socrates, are breaking the covenants and agreements which you made with us at your leisure, not in any haste or under any compulsion or deception, but having had seventy years to think of them, during which time you were at liberty to leave the city, if we were not to your mind, or if our covenants appeared to you to be unfair. You had your choice, and might have gone either to Lacedaemon or Crete, which you often praise for their good government, or to some other Hellenic or foreign State. Whereas you, above all other Athenians, seemed to be so fond of the State, or, in other words, of us her laws (for who would like a State that has no laws), that you never stirred out of her. . . . And now you run away and forsake your agreements. Not so, Socrates, if you will take our advice; do not make yourself ridiculous by escaping out of the city. . . .

"Listen, then, Socrates, to us who have brought you up. Think not of life and children first, and of justice afterwards, but of justice first, that you may be justified before the princes of the world below. For neither will you nor any that belong to you be happier or holier or more just in this life, or happier in another, if you do as Crito bids. Now you depart in innocence, a sufferer and not a doer of evil; a victim, not of the laws, but of men. . . . Listen, then, to us and not to Crito."

This is the voice which I seem to hear murmuring in my ears, like the sound of the flute in the ears of the mystic; that voice, I say, is humming in my ears, and prevents me from hearing any other. And I know that anything more which you may say will be in vain. Yet speak, if you have anything to say.

CRITO: I have nothing to say, Socrates.

SOCRATES: Then let me follow the intimations of the will of God.

Questions for Reflection

1. What do you think of Socrates' arguments? Assuming that the decision of the court was wrong, did Socrates do the right thing in refusing to escape from prison? Suppose you were Crito. How would you convince Socrates not to stay and die?
2. At the end of their speech, the laws tell Socrates that he is "a victim, not of the laws, but of men." Is this distinction between the justice of the laws and the injustice of people's application of them a helpful one? What would be the practical application of this distinction?
3. The laws claim that Socrates had an implied contract with them. Do you have an implied contract with your government? You never signed your name to any document agreeing to your obligations to the government as you do with a commercial transaction. Nevertheless, on what basis could it be argued that the government has agreed to certain conditions and you have agreed to certain conditions governing your mutual relationship?
4. If you disagree with Socrates that absolute obedience to the government is always required, then what principles would justify an act of civil disobedience?

MARTIN LUTHER KING, JR.

We Should Obey Just Laws and Disobey Unjust Laws

Martin Luther King, Jr. (1929–1968) is noted not only for being an effective political leader and agent of social change, but also for developing a philosophy of political action to guide his activism. King was born in Atlanta, the son and grandson of Baptist ministers. While in college he felt called to follow his father's and grandfather's example and decided to become a minister. He went on to get a degree from Crozer Theological Seminary in Pennsylvania and then earned a doctorate in systematic theology from Boston University. While in Boston, he met and married Coretta Scott, who would become a great civil rights leader herself. Although he had offers for academic positions,

From Martin Luther King, Jr., "Letter from Birmingham Jail," in *Why We Can't Wait* (New York: Harper & Row, 1964).

Martin and Coretta returned to the South where he became pastor of a prominent Baptist church in Montgomery, Alabama.

In 1955, a pivotal event in American social history set the course of King's life. An African-American seamstress named Rosa Parks climbed onto a Montgomery bus after a long day of work. Because all the seats in the back of the bus were taken, she sat down on a seat in the "whites only" section. Consequently, she was forcibly removed and arrested for violating the city's segregationist laws. As a popular minister and community leader, Dr. King was elected president of an organization formed to protest the racist laws of their city. King put into effect the philosophy of nonviolent resistence that he had been developing since college. A bus boycott was put into effect that would last a year. As a result, King's house was bombed, his life was continually threatened, and he and his associates were convicted of conspiracy. Finally, The U.S. Supreme Court ruled that Montgomery had to provide equal treatment to all people on public buses.

Building on this success, King and other African-American ministers founded the Southern Christian Leadership Conference, and King's life became a succession of protest marches, speeches, books, and other forms of political action. Finally, after years of social protests, Congress passed the Civil Rights Act of 1964. The following year, King became *Time* magazine's Man of the Year, and he received the Nobel Prize. On April 4, 1968, while lending support to a garbage workers' strike in Memphis, Tennessee, King was assassinated.

In 1963, one year before he won the Nobel Prize, Dr. King found himself in jail for participating in a civil rights demonstration. Eight prominent Alabama clergy wrote an open letter critical of King's methods. In the following selection, taken from Dr. King's famous "Letter from Birmingham Jail," King responded to their criticisms and provided an eloquent justification of civil disobedience.

Reading Questions

1. What are the four steps in any program of nonviolent protest?
2. How does King respond to the criticism that he should use negotiation instead of direct action?
3. How does King distinguish between just laws and unjust laws? List the various principles he cites. How does he apply these principles to the laws protecting segregation and discrimination?
4. What does King mean when he says "sometimes a law is just on its face and unjust in its application"?
5. According to King, under what conditions is it permissible to break the law?
6. What examples does he provide from history of when it was legitimate to break the law?

My Dear Fellow Clergymen,

While confined here in the Birmingham city jail, I came across your recent statement calling our present activities "unwise and untimely." Seldom, if ever, do I pause to answer criticism of my work and ideas. If I sought to answer all of the criticisms that cross my desk, my secretaries would be engaged in little else in the course of the day, and I would have no time for constructive work. But since I feel that you are men of genuine good will and your criticisms are sincerely set forth, I would like to answer your statement in what I hope will be patient and reasonable terms. . . .

You deplore the demonstrations that are presently taking place in Birmingham. But I am sorry that your statement did not express a similar concern for the conditions that brought the demonstrations into being. I am sure that each of you would want to go beyond the superficial social analyst who looks merely at effects, and does not grapple with underlying causes. I would not hesitate to say that it is unfortunate that so-called demonstrations are taking place in Birmingham at this time, but I would say in more emphatic terms that it is even more unfortunate that the white power structure of this city left the Negro community with no other alternative.

In any nonviolent campaign there are four basic steps: (1) collection of the facts to determine whether injustices are alive, (2) negotiation, (3) self-purification, and (4) direct action. We have gone through all of these steps in Birmingham. There can be no gainsaying of the fact that racial injustice engulfs this community. . . .

You may well ask, "Why direct action? Why sit-ins, marches, etc.? Isn't negotiation a better path?" You are exactly right in your call for negotiation. Indeed, this is the purpose of direct action. Nonviolent direct action seeks to create such a crisis and establish such creative tension that a community that has constantly refused to negotiate is forced to confront the issue. It seeks so to dramatize the issue that it can no longer be ignored. I just referred to the creation of tension as a part of the work of the nonviolent resister. This may sound rather shocking. But I must confess that I am not afraid of the word tension. I have earnestly worked and preached against violent tension, but there is a type of constructive nonviolent tension that is necessary for growth. Just as Socrates felt that it was necessary to create a tension in the mind so that individuals could rise from the bondage of myths and half-truths to the unfettered realm of creative analysis and objective appraisal, we must see the need of having nonviolent gadflies to create the kind of tension in society that will help men to rise from the dark depths of prejudice and racism to the majestic

heights of understanding and brotherhood. So the purpose of the direct action is to create a situation so crisis-packed that it will inevitably open the door to negotiation. We, therefore, concur with you in your call for negotiation. Too long has our beloved Southland been bogged down in the tragic attempt to live in monologue rather than dialogue. . . .

You express a great anxiety over our willingness to break laws. This is certainly a legitimate concern. Since we so diligently urge people to obey the Supreme Court's decision of 1954 outlawing segregation in the public schools, it is rather strange and paradoxical to find us consciously breaking laws. One may well ask, "How can you advocate breaking some laws and obeying others?" The answer is found in the fact that there are two types of laws: there are just and there are unjust laws. I would agree with Saint Augustine that "An unjust law is no law at all." Now what is the difference between the two? How does one determine when a law is just or unjust? A just law is a man-made code that squares with the moral law or the law of God. An unjust law is a code that is out of harmony with the moral law. To put it in the terms of Saint Thomas Aquinas, an unjust law is a human law that is not rooted in eternal and natural law. Any law that uplifts human personality is just. Any law that degrades human personality is unjust. All segregation statutes are unjust because segregation distorts the soul and damages the personality. It gives the segregator a false sense of superiority, and the segregated a false sense of inferiority. To use the words of Martin Buber, the great Jewish philosopher, segregation substitutes an "I-it" relationship for the "I-thou" relationship, and ends up relegating persons to the status of things. So segregation is not only politically, economically and sociologically unsound, but it is morally wrong and sinful. Paul Tillich has said that sin is separation. Isn't segregation an existential expression of man's tragic separation, an expression of his awful estrangement, his terrible sinfulness? So I can urge men to disobey segregation ordinances because they are morally wrong.

Let us turn to a more concrete example of just and unjust laws. An unjust law is a code that a majority inflicts on a minority that is not binding on itself. This is difference made legal. On the other hand a just law is a code that a majority compels a minority to follow that it is willing to follow itself. This is sameness made legal.

Let me give another explanation. An unjust law is a code inflicted upon a minority which that minority had no part in enacting or creating because they did not have the unhampered right to vote. Who can say that the legislature of Alabama which set up the segregation laws was democratically elected? Throughout the state of Alabama all types of conniving methods are used to prevent Negroes from becoming registered voters and there are some counties without a single Negro registered to vote despite the fact that the Negro constitutes a majority of the population. Can any law set up in such a state be considered democratically structured? These are just a few examples of unjust and just laws. There are some instances when a law is just on its face and unjust in its application. For instance, I was arrested Friday on a charge of parading without a permit. Now there is nothing wrong with an ordinance which requires a permit for a parade, but when the ordinance is used to preserve segregation and to deny citizens the First Amendment privilege of peaceful assembly and peaceful protest, then it becomes unjust.

I hope you can see the distinction I am trying to point out. In no sense do I advocate evading or defying the law as the rabid segregationist would do. This would lead to anarchy. One who breaks an unjust law must do it *openly, lovingly* (not hatefully as the white mothers did in New Orleans when they were seen on television screaming, "nigger, nigger, nigger"), and with a willingness to accept the penalty. I submit that an individual who breaks a law that conscience tells him is unjust, and willingly accepts the penalty by staying in jail to arouse the conscience of the community over its injustice, is in reality expressing the very highest respect for law.

Of course, there is nothing new about this kind of civil disobedience. It was seen sublimely in the refusal of Shadrach, Meshach and Abednego to obey the laws of Nebuchadnezzar because a higher moral law was involved. It was practiced superbly by the early Christians who were willing to face hungry lions and the excruciating pain of chopping blocks, before submitting to certain unjust laws of the Roman Empire. To a degree academic freedom is a reality today because Socrates practiced civil disobedience. In our own nation, the Boston Tea Party represented a massive act of civil disobedience.

We should never forget that everything Adolf Hitler did in Germany was "legal" and everything the Hungarian freedom fighters did in Hungary was "illegal." It was "illegal" to aid and comfort a Jew in Hitler's Germany. Even so, I am sure that, had I lived in Germany at the time, I would have aided and comforted my Jewish brothers. If today I lived in a Communist country where certain principles dear to the Christian faith are suppressed, I would openly advocate disobeying that country's antireligious laws. . . .

Let us all hope that the dark clouds of racial prejudice will soon pass away and the deep fog of misunderstanding will be lifted from our fear-drenched communities and in some not too distant tomorrow the radiant stars of love and brotherhood will shine over our great nation with all of their scintillating beauty.

Yours for the cause of Peace and Brotherhood,
Martin Luther King, Jr.

Questions for Reflection

1. What do you think of the principles King uses to distinguish just laws from unjust laws? Using his principles, cite examples of just laws. Similarly, find examples of unjust laws from history or current politics, either in your own society or in other countries.

2. How might King respond to the criticism that there are always less radical means for achieving social change than civil disobedience?

3. Adopt the position of either Socrates or King and write a letter to the other person (Socrates or King), explaining to him why he is wrong by refuting his arguments.

WHAT MAKES A GOVERNMENT JUST?

The next five readings provide opposing visions of the ideal government. In doing so, each author presents a theory of what the function of a government should be and what the limits and extent of both individual liberty and the government's authority should be. As always, pay particular attention to the arguments each author provides in defense of his particular position on these issues.

J O H N   L O C K E

The Social Contract Theory

We encountered the English philosopher John Locke (1632–1704) in reading 22 where we discussed his empiricist theory of knowledge. (A short account of his life can be found there.) Besides being interested in the theory of knowledge, Locke also wrote extensively on political philosophy. Locke's political philosophy consisted of many interwoven themes. First, Locke was a natural law theorist. **Natural law theory** claims that there is an objective moral law that transcends human conventions and decisions, governs individuals and the conduct of society, and can be known through reason and experience on the basis of the natural order of the world and the built-in tendencies of human nature. As with most theistic versions of this theory, Locke believed that this moral law was instituted by God. Furthermore, Locke argued that this natural law guaranteed us basic, natural, inherent rights, by virtue of the fact that we are human.

Some rights can be granted by law. For example, a 16-year-old may have the right to drive a car. However, rights granted by law can be taken away (the minimum driving age can be changed to 18). Locke insisted, however, that some rights are natural, human rights that cannot be taken away by the government. These rights are sometimes said to be *indefeasible* (cannot be made void) or *inalienable* (cannot be taken away). According to Locke, we possess these rights in the state of nature, before government came on the scene. Among these natural, moral rights are the preservation of our life, health, liberty, and possessions.

Locke's natural law theory is wedded to a social contract theory. The **social contract theory** claims that the justification of a government and its exercise of power is based on an explicit or implicit agreement made between the individuals who live under that government or between the citizens and the government. In other words, the government has the authority to make laws, enforce penalties for violating those laws, and exercise control over the lives of its citizens, only because each citizen has given the government that authority.

From John Locke, *An Essay Concerning the True, Original, Extent and End of Civil Government,* the second essay in *Two Treatises of Government* (1680).

Locke's view of both rights and the social contract has major implications for political theory. If we have natural, indefeasible, inalienable rights, then the government can never justifiably violate these rights. If it does so, then it is no longer a legitimate government. (The framers of the American Declaration of Independence were inspired by Locke's theory.) Furthermore, we create the government with the social contract, but we do not surrender our rights to the government nor does it create our rights. Instead, we bring the government into being in order to protect our natural rights.

In the following reading, Locke starts out by describing the hypothetical "state of nature" in which people exist prior to forming a government. In the subsequent discussion he explains how people could form a social contract to bring a government into being and examines the reason why people would be motivated to form a government at all. To critics who object that they have never actually signed a contract with the government, Locke explains that every citizen has made a *tacit* contract with it if he or she chooses to remain in the country and benefit from its laws, protection, and services.

Reading Questions

1. What is the natural state of human beings (the "state of nature"), prior to there being a government?
2. How does government or a civil society come into being?
3. Does Locke think that an absolute monarchy is consistent with his notion of a civil society? Why?
4. What role does the will of the majority play in the decisions of the government?
5. What point does Locke make concerning a person's tacit consent to be bound by the laws of a government?
6. What is lacking in the state of nature that motivates people to surrender some of their freedoms to create a government?
7. What two powers does a person have in the state of nature that are delegated to the state when a government is formed?
8. What are the purposes and limits of a government's power?
9. Under what conditions is a revolution legitimate?

OF THE STATE OF NATURE

4. To understand political power aright, and derive it from its original, we must consider what estate all men are naturally in, and that is, a state of perfect freedom to order their actions, and dispose of their possessions and persons as they think fit, within the bounds of the law of Nature, without asking leave or depending upon the will of any other man.

A state also of equality, wherein all the power and jurisdiction is reciprocal, no one having more than another, there being nothing more evident than that creatures of the same species and rank, promiscuously born to all the same advantages of Nature, and the use of the same faculties, should also be equal one amongst another, without subordination or subjection, unless the lord and master of them all should, by any manifest declaration of his will, set one above another, and confer on him, by an evident and clear appointment, an undoubted right to dominion and sovereignty. . . .

6. But though this be a state of liberty, yet it is not a state of licence; though man in that state have an uncontrollable liberty to dispose of his person or possessions, yet he has not liberty to destroy him-

self, or so much as any creature in his possession, but where some nobler use than its bare preservation calls for it. The state of Nature has a law of Nature to govern it, which obliges every one, and reason, which is that law, teaches all mankind who will but consult it, that being all equal and independent, no one ought to harm another in his life, health, liberty or possessions; for men being all the workmanship of one omnipotent and infinitely wise Maker; all the servants of one sovereign Master, sent into the world by His order and about His business; they are His property, whose workmanship they are made to last during His, not one another's pleasure. And, being furnished with like faculties, sharing all in one community of Nature, there cannot be supposed any such subordination among us that may authorise us to destroy one another, as if we were made for one another's uses, as the inferior ranks of creatures are for ours. Every one as he is bound to preserve himself, and not to quit his station wilfully, so by the like reason, when his own preservation comes not in competition, ought he as much as he can to preserve the rest of mankind, and not unless it be to do justice on an offender, take away or impair the life, or what tends to the preservation of the life, the liberty, health, limb, or goods of another.

7. And that all men may be restrained from invading others' rights, and from doing hurt to one another, and the law of Nature be observed, which willeth the peace and preservation of all mankind, the execution of the law of Nature is in that state put into every man's hands, whereby every one has a right to punish the transgressors of that law to such a degree as may hinder its violation. For the law of Nature would, as all other laws that concern men in this world, be in vain if there were nobody that in the state of Nature had a power to execute that law, and thereby preserve the innocent and restrain offenders; and if any one in the state of Nature may punish another for any evil he has done, every one may do so. For in that state of perfect equality, where naturally there is no superiority or jurisdiction of one over another, what any may do in prosecution of that law, every one must needs have a right to do. . . .

OF POLITICAL OR CIVIL SOCIETY

87. Man being born, as has been proved, with a title to perfect freedom and an uncontrolled enjoyment of all the rights and privileges of the law of Nature, equally with any other man, or number of men in the world, hath by nature a power not only to preserve his property—that is, his life, liberty, and estate—against the injuries and attempts of other men, but to judge of and punish the breaches of that law in others, as he is persuaded the offence deserves, even with death itself, in crimes where the heinousness of the fact, in his opinion, requires it. But because no political society can be, nor subsist, without having in itself the power to preserve the property, and in order thereunto punish the offences of all those of that society, there, and there only, is political society where every one of the members hath quitted this natural power, resigned it up into the hands of the community in all cases that exclude him not from appealing for protection to the law established by it. And thus all private judgment of every particular member being excluded, the community comes to be umpire, and by understanding indifferent rules and men authorised by the community for their execution, decides all the differences that may happen between any members of that society concerning any matter of right, and punishes those offences which any member hath committed against the society with such penalties as the law has established; whereby it is easy to discern who are, and are not, in political society together. Those who are united into one body, and have a common established law and judicature to appeal to, with authority to decide controversies between them and punish offenders, are in civil society one with another; but those who have no such common appeal, I mean on earth, are still in the state of Nature, each being where there is no other, judge for himself and executioner; which is, as I have before showed it, the perfect state of Nature. . . .

89. Wherever, therefore, any number of men so unite into one society as to quit every one his executive power of the law of Nature, and to resign it to the public, there and there only is a political or

civil society. And this is done wherever any number of men, in the state of Nature, enter into society to make one people one body politic under one supreme government: or else when any one joins himself to, and incorporates with any government already made. For hereby he authorises the society, or which is all one, the legislative thereof, to make laws for him as the public good of the society shall require, to the execution whereof his own assistance (as to his own decrees) is due. And this puts men out of a state of Nature into that of a commonwealth, by setting up a judge on earth with authority to determine all the controversies and redress the injuries that may happen to any member of the commonwealth, which judge is the legislative or magistrates appointed by it. And wherever there are any number of men, however associated, that have no such decisive power to appeal to, there they are still in the state of Nature.

90. And hence it is evident that absolute monarchy, which by some men is counted for the only government in the world, is indeed inconsistent with civil society, and so can be no form of civil government at all. For the end of civil society being to avoid and remedy those inconveniences of the state of Nature which necessarily follow from every man's being judge in his own case, by setting up a known authority to which every one of that society may appeal upon any injury received, or controversy that may arise, and which every one of the society ought to obey. Wherever any persons are who have not such an authority to appeal to, and decide any difference between them there, those persons are still in the state of Nature. And so is every absolute prince in respect of those who are under his dominion. . . .

95. Men being, as has been said, by nature all free, equal, and independent, no one can be put out of this estate and subjected to the political power of another without his own consent, which is done by agreeing with other men, to join and unite into a community for their comfortable, safe, and peaceable living, one amongst another, in a secure enjoyment of their properties, and a greater security against any that are not of it. This any number

of men may do, because it injures not the freedom of the rest; they are left, as they were, in the liberty of the state of Nature. When any number of men have so consented to make one community or government, they are thereby presently incorporated, and make one body politic, wherein the majority have a right to act and conclude the rest.

96. For, when any number of men have, by the consent of every individual, made a community, they have thereby made that community one body, with a power to act as one body, which is only by the will and determination of the majority. For that which acts any community, being only the consent of the individuals of it, and it being one body, must move one way, it is necessary the body should move that way whither the greater force carries it, which is the consent of the majority, or else it is impossible it should act or continue one body, one community, which the consent of every individual that united into it agreed that it should; and so every one is bound by that consent to be concluded by the majority. And therefore we see that in assemblies empowered to act by positive laws where no number is set by that positive law which empowers them, the act of the majority passes for the act of the whole, and of course determines as having, by the law of Nature and reason, the power of the whole.

97. And thus every man, by consenting with others to make one body politic under one government, puts himself under an obligation to every one of that society to submit to the determination of the majority, and to be concluded by it; or else this original compact, whereby he with others incorporates into one society, would signify nothing, and be no compact if he be left free and under no other ties than he was in before in the state of Nature. For what appearance would there be of any compact? What new engagement if he were no farther tied by any decrees of the society than he himself thought fit and did actually consent to? This would be still as great a liberty as he himself had before his compact, or any one else in the state of Nature, who may submit himself and consent to any acts of it if he thinks fit.

98. For if the consent of the majority shall not in reason be received as the act of the whole, and conclude every individual, nothing but the consent of every individual can make anything to be the act of the whole, which, considering the infirmities of health and avocations of business, which in a number though much less than that of a commonwealth, will necessarily keep many away from the public assembly; and the variety of opinions and contrariety of interests which unavoidably happen in all collections of men, it is next impossible ever to be had. . . . For where the majority cannot conclude the rest, there they cannot act as one body, and consequently will be immediately dissolved again.

99. Whosoever, therefore, out of a state of Nature unite into a community, must be understood to give up all the power necessary to the ends for which they unite into society to the majority of the community, unless they expressly agreed in any number greater than the majority. And this is done by barely agreeing to unite into one political society, which is all the compact that is, or needs be, between the individuals that enter into or make up a commonwealth. And thus, that which begins and actually constitutes any political society is nothing but the consent of any number of freemen capable of majority, to unite and incorporate into such a society. And this is that, and that only, which did or could give beginning to any lawful government in the world. . . .

119. Every man being, as has been showed, naturally free, and nothing being able to put him into subjection to any earthly power, but only his own consent, it is to be considered what shall be understood to be a sufficient declaration of a man's consent to make him subject to the laws of any government. There is a common distinction of an express and a tacit consent, which will concern our present case. Nobody doubts but an express consent of any man, entering into any society, makes him a perfect member of that society, a subject of that government. The difficulty is, what ought to be looked upon as a tacit consent, and how far it binds—i.e., how far anyone shall be looked on to

have consented, and thereby submitted to any government, where he has made no expressions of it at all. And to this I say, that every man that hath any possession or enjoyment of any part of the dominions of any government doth hereby give his tacit consent, and is as far forth obliged to obedience to the laws of that government, during such enjoyment, as any one under it, whether this his possession be of land to him and his heirs for ever, or a lodging only for a week; or whether it be barely traveling freely on the highway; and, in effect, it reaches as far as the very being of any one within the territories of that government. . . .

122. But submitting to the laws of any country, living quietly and enjoying privileges and protection under them, makes not a man a member of that society; it is only a local protection and homage due to and from all those who, not being in a state of war, come within the territories belonging to any government, to all parts whereof the force of its law extends. But this no more makes a man a member of that society, a perpetual subject of that commonwealth, than it would make a man a subject to another in whose family he found it convenient to abide for some time, though, whilst he continued in it, he were obliged to comply with the laws and submit to the government he found there. . . . Nothing can make any man [a citizen] but his actually entering into it by positive engagement and express promise and compact. This is that which, I think, concerning the beginning of political societies, and that consent which makes any one a member of any commonwealth.

OF THE ENDS OF POLITICAL SOCIETY AND GOVERNMENT

123. If man in the state of Nature be so free as has been said, if he be absolute lord of his own person and possessions, equal to the greatest and subject to nobody, why will he part with his freedom, this empire, and subject himself to the dominion and control of any other power? To which it is obvious to answer, that though in the state of Nature

he hath such a right, yet the enjoyment of it is very uncertain and constantly exposed to the invasion of others; for all being kings as much as he, every man his equal, and the greater part no strict observers of equity and justice, the enjoyment of the property he has in this state is very unsafe, very insecure. This makes him willing to quit this condition which, however free, is full of fears and continual dangers; and it is not without reason that he seeks out and is willing to join in society with others who are already united, or have a mind to unite for the mutual preservation of their lives, liberties and estates, which I call by the general name, property.

124. The great and chief end, therefore, of men uniting into commonwealths, and putting themselves under government, is the preservation of their property; to which in the state of Nature there are many things wanting.

First, there wants an established, settled, known law, received and allowed by common consent to be the standard of right and wrong, and the common measure to decide all controversies between them. For though the law of Nature be plain and intelligible to all rational creatures, yet men, being biased by their interest, as well as ignorant for want of study of it, are not apt to allow of it as a law binding to them in the application of it to their particular cases.

125. Secondly, in the state of Nature there wants a known and indifferent judge, with authority to determine all differences according to the established law. For every one in that state being both judge and executioner of the law of Nature, men being partial to themselves, passion and revenge is very apt to carry them too far, and with too much heat in their own cases, as well as negligence and unconcernedness, make them too remiss in other men's.

126. Thirdly, in the state of Nature there often wants power to back and support the sentence when right, and to give it due execution. They who by any injustice offended will seldom fail where they are able by force to make good their injustice.

Such resistance many times makes the punishment dangerous, and frequently destructive to those who attempt it.

127. Thus mankind, notwithstanding all the privileges of the state of Nature, being but in an ill condition while they remain in it are quickly driven into society. Hence it comes to pass, that we seldom find any number of men live any time together in this state. The inconveniencies that they are therein exposed to by the irregular and uncertain exercise of the power every man has of punishing the transgressions of others, make them take sanctuary under the established laws of government, and therein seek the preservation of their property. It is this that makes them so willingly give up every one his single power of punishing to be exercised by such alone as shall be appointed to it amongst them, and by such rules as the community, or those authorised by them to that purpose, shall agree on. And in this we have the original right and rise of both the legislative and executive power as well as of the governments and societies themselves.

128. For in the state of Nature, to omit the liberty he has of innocent delights, a man has two powers. The first is to do whatsoever he thinks fit for the preservation of himself and others within the permission of the law of Nature; by which law, common to them all, he and all the rest of mankind are one community, make up one society distinct from all other creatures, and were it not for the corruption and viciousness of degenerate men, there would be no need of any other, no necessity that men should separate from this great and natural community, and associate into lesser combinations. The other power a man has in the state of Nature is the power to punish the crimes committed against that law. Both these he gives up when he joins in a private, if I may so call it, or particular political society, and incorporates into any commonwealth separate from the rest of mankind.

129. The first power, viz., of doing whatsoever he thought fit for the preservation of himself and the rest of mankind, he gives up to be regulated by laws made by the society, so far forth as the preser-

vation of himself and the rest of that society shall require; which laws of the society in many things confine the liberty he had by the law of Nature.

130. Secondly, the power of punishing he wholly gives up, and engages his natural force, which he might before employ in the execution of the law of Nature, by his own single authority, as he thought fit, to assist the executive power of the society as the law thereof shall require. For being now in a new state, wherein he is to enjoy many conveniencies from the labour, assistance, and society of others in the same community, as well as protection from its whole strength, he is to part also with as much of his natural liberty, in providing for himself, as the good, prosperity, and safety of the society shall require, which is not only necessary but just, since the other members of the society do the like.

131. But though men when they enter into society give up the equality, liberty, and executive power they had in the state of Nature into the hands of the society, to be so far disposed of by the legislative as the good of the society shall require, yet it being only with an intention in every one the better to preserve himself, his liberty and property (for no rational creature can be supposed to change his condition with an intention to be worse), the power of the society or legislative constituted by them can never be supposed to extend farther than the common good, but is obliged to secure every one's property by providing against those three defects above mentioned that made the state of Nature so unsafe and uneasy. And so, whoever has the legislative or supreme power of any commonwealth, is bound to govern by established standing laws, promulgated and known to the people, and not by extemporary decrees, by indifferent and upright judges, who are to decide controversies by those laws; and to employ the force of the community at home only in the execution of such laws, or abroad to prevent or redress foreign injuries and secure the community from inroads and invasion. And all this to be directed to no other end but the peace, safety, and public good of the people. . . .

OF THE EXTENT OF THE LEGISLATIVE POWER

142. These are the bounds which the trust that is put in them by the society and the law of God and Nature have set to the legislative power of every commonwealth, in all forms of government.

First: They are to govern by promulgated established laws, not to be varied in particular cases, but to have one rule for rich and poor, for the favourite at Court, and the countryman at plough.

Secondly: These laws also ought to be designed for no other end ultimately but the good of the people.

Thirdly: They must not raise taxes on the property of the people without the consent of the people given by themselves or their deputies. And this properly concerns only such governments where the legislative is always in being, or at least where the people have not reserved any part of the legislative to deputies, to be from time to time chosen by themselves.

Fourthly: The legislative neither must nor can transfer the power of making laws to anybody else, or place it anywhere but where the people have.

THE LEGITIMACY OF REVOLUTION

222. The reason why men enter into society is the preservation of their property; and the end while they choose and authorise a legislative is that there may be laws made, and rules set, as guards and fences to the properties of all the society, to limit the power and moderate the dominion of every part and member of the society. For since it can never be supposed to be the will of the society that the legislative should have a power to destroy that which every one designs to secure by entering into society, and for which the people submitted themselves to legislators of their own making. Whenever the legislators endeavour to take away and destroy the property of the people, or to reduce them to slavery under arbitrary power, they put themselves into a state of war with the people, who are thereupon absolved from any farther

obedience, and are left to the common refuge which God hath provided for all men against force and violence. Whensoever, therefore, the legislative shall transgress this fundamental rule of society, and either by ambition, fear, folly, or corruption, endeavour to grasp themselves, or put into the hands of any other, an absolute power over the lives, liberties, and estates of the people, by this breach of trust they forfeit the power the people had put into their hands for quite contrary ends, and it devolves to the people, who have a right to resume their original liberty, and by the establishment of a new legislative (such as they shall think fit), provide for their own safety and security, which is the end for which they are in society. What I have said here concerning the legislative in general holds true also concerning the supreme executor, who having a double trust put in him—both to have a part in the legislative and the supreme execution of the law—acts against both, when he goes about to set up his own arbitrary will as the law of the society. . . .

240. Here, it is like, the common question will be made: Who shall be judge whether the prince or legislative act contrary to their trust? This, perhaps, ill-affected and factious men may spread amongst the people, when the prince only makes use of his due prerogative. To this I reply, The people shall be judge; for who shall be judge whether his trustee or deputy acts well and according to the trust reposed in him, but he who deputes him and must, by hav-

ing deputed him, have still a power to discard him when he fails in his trust? If this be reasonable in particular cases of private men, why should it be otherwise in that of the greatest moment, where the welfare of millions is concerned and also where the evil, if not prevented, is greater, and the redress very difficult, dear, and dangerous? . . .

243. To conclude: The power that every individual gave the society when he entered into it can never revert to the individuals again, as long as the society lasts, but will always remain in the community; because without this there can be no community, no commonwealth, which is contrary to the original agreement; so also when the society hath placed the legislative in any assembly of men, to continue in them and their successors, with direction and authority for providing such successors, the legislative can never revert to the people whilst that government lasts: because, having provided a legislative with power to continue forever, they have given up their political power to the legislative, and cannot resume it. But if they have set limits to the duration of their legislative, and made this supreme power in any person or assembly only temporary; or else when, by the miscarriages of those in authority, it is forfeited; upon the forfeiture of their rulers, or at the determination of the time set, it reverts to the society, and the people have a right to act as supreme, and continue the legislative in themselves or place it in a new form, or new hands, as they think good.

Questions for Reflection

1. Locke bases the legitimacy of a government and our obligation to obey our government on the notion that we the citizens have entered into a social contract with the state. Do you agree that this is the basis of a government's authority? Do you agree with him that you have entered into a "tacit contract" with your government?

2. To what degree does the notion of a social contract play a role in Socrates' argument against civil disobedience (see reading 64)?

3. Does Locke's emphasis on rule by majority permit the tyranny of the majority over the interests of a minority? Under what conditions might the will of the majority not be legitimate?

4. Locke gives very specific powers to the government. What are they? To what degree would he agree or disagree with the power that your government has today?

5. The founders of the American government based much of their political philosophy and call to revolution on Locke's ideas. What similarities do you find between

Locke's ideas and those that inspired the American revolution and the founding of the United States government? Do the same for any other political revolution in history. Would Locke find it to be justified or not?

6. On the basis of Locke's theory of government, argue that civil disobedience is or is not justified under certain conditions.

JOHN STUART MILL

The Utilitarian Theory of Government

John Stuart Mill (1806–1873) was one of the most influential political theorists in the last two centuries. Whether or not you have read Mill, it is likely that your ideas about society show traces of his influence. We encountered Mill previously in our discussion of utilitarian ethics. (See reading 58 and the accompanying discussion of Mill's ethics and the brief account of his life.) Since Mill believed that the morally right action was one that produced the greatest happiness for the greatest number, it is natural that his ethical concerns would lead to a political theory. In the realm of politics, Mill's concern was "What sort of society will produce the greatest happiness for the greatest number?"

Previous democratic thinkers (such as Locke) had been so concerned to defend the rights of the citizens from the tyranny of the king that they had ignored the sort of tyranny that can arise in a democracy—the tyranny of the majority. Realizing that the will of the majority, when enforced by the state, could be as oppressive as any monarch, Mill sought for principles that would limit the power of the government over individual lives. From his standpoint, censorship, intolerance, government-imposed morality, and legislated conformity are some of the greatest dangers that a society can face. For, unlike a foreign invader, these intrusions upon liberty arise in the midst of a society and masquerade as defenders of the social good. However, allowing total individual freedom is not feasible either, for society needs to prevent individuals from harming one another and from undermining the general welfare. With these problems in mind, Mill published *On Liberty* in 1859 to establish the proper balance between governmental control and individual freedom. Since then, it has become a classic and one of the most influential essays on this topic ever published.

Reading Questions

1. What is the one simple principle that Mill seeks to establish?
2. Mill places some limits on the application of his principle. What are these limits?
3. What boundaries define the sphere of an individual's freedom from society's interference?

From John Stuart Mill, *On Liberty* (1859).

4. What three kinds of liberty does he think should be granted to each individual?
5. What four reasons does Mill provide in defense of freedom of thought and speech?
6. What does Mill say about the freedom to pursue different lifestyles?
7. What does Mill think of the notion that society is based on a social contract (as Locke maintained)?
8. In return for society's protection, what obligations does an individual have toward society?
9. How does Mill respond to the objection that the distinction between the private sphere and the public sphere cannot be maintained because an individual's behavior always has an indirect effect on society?
10. According to Mill, what is the strongest argument against society's interference in purely personal conduct?

CHAPTER 1: INTRODUCTION

The object of this Essay is to assert one very simple principle, as entitled to govern absolutely the dealings of society with the individual in the way of compulsion and control, whether the means used be physical force in the form of legal penalties, or the moral coercion of public opinion. That principle is, that the sole end for which mankind are warranted, individually or collectively, in interfering with the liberty of action of any of their number, is self-protection. That the only purpose for which power can be rightfully exercised over any member of a civilized community, against his will, is to prevent harm to others. His own good, either physical or moral, is not a sufficient warrant. He cannot rightfully be compelled to do or forbear because it will be better for him to do so, because it will make him happier, because, in the opinions of others, to do so would be wise, or even right. These are good reasons for remonstrating with him, or reasoning with him, or persuading him, or entreating him, but not for compelling him, or visiting him with any evil in case he do otherwise. To justify that, the conduct from which it is desired to deter him must be calculated to produce evil to someone else. The only part of the conduct of any one, for which he is amenable to society, is that which concerns others. In the part which merely concerns himself, his independence is, of right, absolute. Over himself, over his own body and mind, the individual is sovereign.

It is, perhaps, hardly necessary to say that this doctrine is meant to apply only to human beings in the maturity of their faculties. We are not speaking of children, or of young persons below the age which the law may fix as that of manhood or womanhood. Those who are still in a state to require being taken care of by others, must be protected against their own actions as well as against external injury. . . .

It is proper to state that I forego any advantage which could be derived to my argument from the idea of abstract right, as a thing independent of utility. I regard utility as the ultimate appeal on all ethical questions; but it must be utility in the largest sense, grounded on the permanent interests of a man as a progressive being. Those interests, I contend, authorize the subjection of individual spontaneity to external control, only in respect to those actions of each, which concern the interests of other people. If any one does an act hurtful to others, there is a prima facie case for punishing him, by law, or, where legal penalties are not safely applicable, by general disapprobation. There are also many positive acts for the benefit of others, which he may rightfully be compelled to perform; such as to give evidence in a court of justice; to bear his fair share in the common defense, or in any other joint work necessary to the interest of the society of which he enjoys the protection; and to perform certain acts of individual beneficence, such as saving a fellow creature's life, or interposing to protect the defenseless against ill-usage, things which whenever it is obviously a man's duty to do, he may rightfully be made responsible to society for not doing. A person may cause evil to others not only by his actions but by his inaction, and in either case he is justly accountable to them for the injury. The latter case, it is true, requires a much more cautious exercise of compulsion than the former. To make any one answerable for doing evil to others is the rule; to make him answerable for not preventing evil is, comparatively speaking, the exception. . . .

But there is a sphere of action in which society, as distinguished from the individual, has, if any, only an indirect interest; comprehending all that portion of a person's life and conduct which affects only himself, or if it also affects others, only with their free, voluntary, and undeceived consent and participation. When I say only himself, I mean directly, and in the first instance; for whatever affects himself, may affect others through himself; and the objection which may be grounded on this contingency, will receive consideration in the sequel. This, then, is the appropriate region of human liberty. It comprises, first, the inward domain of consciousness; demanding liberty of conscience in the most comprehensive sense; liberty of thought and feeling; absolute freedom of opinion and sentiment on all subjects, practical or speculative, scientific, moral, or theological. The liberty of expressing and publishing opinions may seem to fall under a different principle, since it belongs to that part of the conduct of an individual which concerns other people; but, being almost of as much importance as the liberty of thought itself, and resting in great part on the same reasons, is practically inseparable from it. Secondly, the principle requires liberty of tastes and pursuits; of framing the plan of our life to suit our own character; of doing as we like, subject to such consequences as may follow: without impediment from our fellow creatures, so long as what we do does not harm them, even though they should think our conduct foolish, perverse, or wrong. Thirdly, from this liberty of each individual, follows the liberty, within the same limits, of combination among individuals; freedom to unite, for any purpose not involving harm to others: the persons combining

being supposed to be of full age, and not forced or deceived.

No society in which these liberties are not, on the whole, respected, is free, whatever may be its form of government; and none is completely free in which they do not exist absolute and unqualified. The only freedom which deserves the name, is that of pursuing our own good in our own way, so long as we do not attempt to deprive others of theirs, or impede their efforts to obtain it. Each is the proper guardian of his own health, whether bodily, or mental and spiritual. Mankind are greater gainers by suffering each other to live as seems good to themselves, than by compelling each to live as seems good to the rest. . . .

Apart from the peculiar tenets of individual thinkers, there is also in the world at large an increasing inclination to stretch unduly the powers of society over the individual, both by the force of opinion and even by that of legislation; and as the tendency of all the changes taking place in the world is to strengthen society, and diminish the power of the individual, this encroachment is not one of the evils which tend spontaneously to disappear, but, on the contrary, to grow more and more formidable. The disposition of mankind, whether as rulers or as fellow-citizens, to impose their own opinions and inclinations as a rule of conduct on others, is so energetically supported by some of the best and by some of the worst feelings incident to human nature, that it is hardly ever kept under restraint by anything but want of power; and as the power is not declining, but growing, unless a strong barrier of moral conviction can be raised against the mischief, we must expect, in the present circumstances of the world, to see it increase. . . .

CHAPTER 2: OF THE LIBERTY OF THOUGHT AND DISCUSSION

The time, it is to be hoped, is gone by, when any defense would be necessary of the "liberty of the press" as one of the securities against corrupt or tyrannical government. No argument, we may suppose, can now be needed, against permitting a legislature or an executive, not identified in interest with the people, to prescribe opinions to them, and determine what doctrines or what arguments they shall be allowed to hear. . . . Let us suppose . . . that the government is entirely at one with the people, and never thinks of exerting any power of coercion unless in agreement with what it conceives to be their voice. But I deny the right of the people to exercise such coercion, either by themselves or by their government. The power itself is illegitimate. The best government has no more title to it than the worst. It is as noxious, or more noxious, when exerted in accordance with public opinion, than when in opposition to it. If all mankind minus one were of one opinion, and only one person were of the contrary opinion, mankind would be no more justified in silencing that one person, than he, if he had the power, would be justified in silencing mankind. Were an opinion a personal possession of no value except to the owner; if to be obstructed in the enjoyment of it were simply a private injury, it would make some difference whether the injury was inflicted only on a few persons or on many. But the peculiar evil of silencing the expression of an opinion is, that it is robbing the human race; posterity as well as the existing generation; those who dissent from the opinion, still more than those who hold it. If the opinion is right, they are deprived of the opportunity of exchanging error for truth: if wrong, they lose, what is almost as great a benefit, the clearer perception and livelier impression of truth, produced by its collision with error. . . .

[Editor's note: Mill goes on to discuss four reasons why there should be freedom of speech, which he then summarizes as follows.]

We have now recognized the necessity to the mental well-being of mankind (on which all their other well-being depends) of freedom of opinion, and freedom of the expression of opinion, on four distinct grounds; which we will now briefly recapitulate.

First, if any opinion is compelled to silence, that opinion may, for aught we can certainly know, be true. To deny this is to assume our own infallibility.

Secondly, though the silenced opinion be an error, it may, and very commonly does, contain a portion of truth; and since the general or prevailing opinion on any subject is rarely or never the whole truth, it is only by the collision of adverse opinions that the remainder of the truth has any chance of being supplied.

Thirdly, even if the received opinion be not only true, but the whole truth; unless it is suffered to be, and actually is, vigorously and earnestly contested, it will, by most of those who receive it, be held in the manner of a prejudice, with little comprehension or feeling of its rational grounds. And not only this, but, fourthly, the meaning of the doctrine itself will be in danger of being lost, or enfeebled, and deprived of its vital effect on the character and conduct: the dogma becoming a mere formal profession, inefficacious for good, but cumbering the ground, and preventing the growth of any real and heartfelt conviction, from reason or personal experience. . . .

CHAPTER 3: OF INDIVIDUALITY, AS ONE OF THE ELEMENTS OF WELL-BEING

Such being the reasons which make it imperative that human beings should be free to form opinions, and to express their opinions without reserve; and such the baneful consequences to the intellectual, and through that to the moral nature of man, unless this liberty is either conceded, or asserted in spite of prohibition; let us next examine whether the same reasons do not require that men should be free to act upon their opinions—to carry these out in their lives, without hindrance, either physical or moral, from their fellow-men, so long as it is at their own risk and peril. This last proviso is of course indispensable. No one pretends that actions should be as free as opinions. On the contrary, even opinions lose their immunity when the circumstances in which they are expressed are such as to constitute their expression a positive instigation to some mischievous act. . . . As it is useful that while mankind are imperfect there should be different opinions, so it is that there should be different experiments of living; that free scope should be given to varieties of character, short of injury to others; and that the worth of different modes of life should be proved practically, when any one thinks fit to try them. It is desirable, in short, that in things which do not primarily concern others, individuality should assert itself. Where, not the person's own character, but the traditions or customs of other people are the rule of conduct, there is wanting one of the principal ingredients of human happiness, and quite the chief ingredient of individual and social progress.

In maintaining this principle, the greatest difficulty to be encountered does not lie in the appreciation of means towards an acknowledged end, but in the indifference of persons in general to the end itself. If it were felt that the free development of individuality is one of the leading essentials of well-being; that it is not only a co-ordinate element with all that is designated by the terms civilization, instruction, education, culture, but is itself a necessary part and condition of all those things; there would be no danger that liberty should be undervalued, and the adjustment of the boundaries between it and social control would present no extraordinary difficulty. But the evil is, that individual spontaneity is hardly recognized by the common modes of thinking as having any intrinsic worth, or deserving any regard on its own account. . . .

He who lets the world, or his own portion of it, choose his plan of life for him, has no need of any other faculty than the ape-like one of imitation. He who chooses his plan for himself, employs all his faculties. He must use observation to see, reasoning and judgment to foresee, activity to gather materials for decision, discrimination to decide, and when he has decided, firmness and self-control to hold to his deliberate decision. And these qualities he requires and exercises exactly in proportion as the part of his conduct which he determines according to his own judgment and feelings is a large one. It is possible that he might be guided in some good path, and kept out of harm's way, without any of these things. But what will be his comparative worth as a human being? It really is of importance, not only what men do, but also what manner of men they are that do it. Among the works of man, which human life is rightly employed in perfecting and beautifying, the first in importance surely is man himself. Supposing it were possible to get

houses built, corn grown, battles fought, causes tried, and even churches erected and prayers said, by machinery—by automatons in human form—it would be a considerable loss to exchange for these automatons even the men and women who at present inhabit the more civilized parts of the world, and who assuredly are but starved specimens of what nature can and will produce. Human nature is not a machine to be built after a model, and set to do exactly the work prescribed for it, but a tree, which requires to grow and develop itself on all sides, according to the tendency of the inward forces which make it a living thing. . . .

CHAPTER 4: OF THE LIMITS TO THE AUTHORITY OF SOCIETY OVER THE INDIVIDUAL

What, then, is the rightful limit to the sovereignty of the individual over himself? Where does the authority of society begin? How much of human life should be assigned to individuality, and how much to society?

Each will receive its proper share, if each has that which more particularly concerns it. To individuality should belong the part of life in which it is chiefly the individual that is interested; to society, the part which chiefly interests society.

Though society is not founded on a contract, and though no good purpose is answered by inventing a contract in order to deduce social obligations from it, every one who receives the protection of society owes a return for the benefit, and the fact of living in society renders it indispensable that each should be bound to observe a certain line of conduct towards the rest. This conduct consists, first, in not injuring the interests of one another; or rather certain interests, which, either by express legal provision or by tacit understanding, ought to be considered as rights; and secondly, in each person's bearing his share (to be fixed on some equitable principle) of the labors and sacrifices incurred for defending the society or its members from injury and molestation. These conditions society is justified in enforcing, at all costs to those who endeavor to withhold fulfilment. Nor is this all that society may do. The acts of an individual may be hurtful to others, or wanting in due consideration for their welfare, without going to the length of violating any of their constituted rights. The offender may then be justly punished by opinion, though not by law. As soon as any part of a person's conduct affects prejudicially the interests of others, society has jurisdiction over it, and the question whether the general welfare will or will not be promoted by interfering with it, becomes open to discussion. But there is no room for entertaining any such question when a person's conduct affects the interests of no persons besides himself, or needs not affect them unless they like (all the persons concerned being of full age, and the ordinary amount of understanding). In all such cases, there should be perfect freedom, legal and social, to do the action and stand the consequences. . . .

The distinction here pointed out between the part of a person's life which concerns only himself, and that which concerns others, many persons will refuse to admit. How (it may be asked) can any part of the conduct of a member of society be a matter of indifference to the other members? No person is an entirely isolated being; it is impossible for a person to do anything seriously or permanently hurtful to himself, without mischief reaching at least to his near connections, and often far beyond them. If he injures his property, he does harm to those who directly or indirectly derived support from it, and usually diminishes, by a greater or less amount, the general resources of the community. If he deteriorates his bodily or mental faculties, he not only brings evil upon all who depended on him for any portion of their happiness, but disqualifies himself for rendering the services which he owes to his fellow creatures generally; perhaps becomes a burden on their affection or benevolence; and if such conduct were very frequent, hardly any offence that is committed would detract more from the general sum of good. Finally, if by his vices or follies a person does no direct harm to others, he is nevertheless (it may be said) injurious by his example; and ought to be compelled to control himself, for the sake of those whom the sight or knowledge of his conduct might corrupt or mislead.

And even (it will be added) if the consequences of misconduct could be confined to the vicious or thoughtless individual, ought society to abandon to their own guidance those who are manifestly unfit for it? If protection against themselves is confessedly due to children and persons under age, is not society equally bound to afford it to persons of mature years who are equally incapable of self-government? If gambling, or drunkenness, or incontinence, or idleness, or uncleanliness, are as injurious to happiness, and as great a hindrance to improvement, as many or most of the acts prohibited by law, why (it may be asked) should not law, so far as is consistent with practicability and social convenience, endeavor to repress these also? And as a supplement to the unavoidable imperfections of law, ought not opinion at least to organize a powerful police against these vices, and visit rigidly with social penalties those who are known to practice them? There is no question here (it may be said) about restricting individuality, or impeding the trial of new and original experiments in living. The only things it is sought to prevent are things which have been tried and condemned from the beginning of the world until now; things which experience has shown not to be useful or suitable to any person's individuality. There must be some length of time and amount of experience after which a moral or prudential truth may be regarded as established: and it is merely desired to prevent generation after generation from falling over the same precipice which has been fatal to their predecessors.

I fully admit that the mischief which a person does to himself may seriously affect, both through their sympathies and their interests, those nearly connected with him and, in a minor degree, society at large. When, by conduct of this sort, a person is led to violate a distinct and assignable obligation to any other person or persons, the case is taken out of the self-regarding class, and becomes amenable to moral disapprobation in the proper sense of the term. If, for example, a man, through intemperance or extravagance, becomes unable to pay his debts, or, having undertaken the moral responsibility of a family, becomes from the same cause incapable of supporting or educating them, he is deservedly reprobated, and might be justly punished; but it is for the breach of duty to his family or creditors, not for the extravagance. If the resources which ought to have been devoted to them, had been diverted from them for the most prudent investment, the moral culpability would have been the same. George Barnwell murdered his uncle to get money for his mistress, but if he had done it to set himself up in business, he would equally have been hanged. Again, in the frequent case of a man who causes grief to his family by addiction to bad habits, he deserves reproach for his unkindness or ingratitude; but so he may for cultivating habits not in themselves vicious, if they are painful to those with whom he passes his life, who from personal ties are dependent on him for their comfort. Whoever fails in the consideration generally due to the interests and feelings of others, not being compelled by some more imperative duty, or justified by allowable self-preference, is a subject of moral disapprobation for that failure, but not for the cause of it, nor for the errors, merely personal to himself, which may have remotely led to it. In like manner, when a person disables himself, by conduct purely self-regarding, from the performance of some definite duty incumbent on him to the public, he is guilty of a social offence. No person ought to be punished simply for being drunk; but a soldier or a policeman should be punished for being drunk on duty. Whenever, in short, there is a definite damage, or a definite risk of damage, either to an individual or to the public, the case is taken out of the province of liberty, and placed in that of morality or law. . . .

But the strongest of all the arguments against the interference of the public with purely personal conduct is that, when it does interfere, the odds are that it interferes wrongly, and in the wrong place. On questions of social morality, of duty to others, the opinion of the public, that is, of an overruling majority, though of wrong, is likely to be still oftener right; because on such questions they are only required to judge of their own interests; of the manner in which some mode of conduct, if allowed to be practice, would effect themselves. But the opinion of a similar majority, imposed as a law on the minority, on questions of self-regarding conduct, is quite as likely to be wrong as right; for in these cases public opinion means, at the best, some people's opinion of what is good or bad for other people; while very often it does not even mean that; the public, with the most perfect indifference, passing over the pleasure or convenience of those whose conduct they censure, and considering only their own preference. There are many who consider as an injury to themselves any conduct which they have a distaste for, and resent it as an outrage to their feelings; as a religious bigot, when charged with disregarding the religious feelings of others, has been known to retort that they disregard his feelings, by persisting in their abominable worship or creed. But there is no parity between the feeling of a person for his own opinion, and the feeling of another who is offended at his holding it; no more than between the desire of a thief to take a purse, and the desire of the right owner to keep it. And a person's taste is as much his own peculiar concern as his opinion or his purse. It is easy for any one to imagine an ideal public which leaves the freedom and choice of individuals in all uncertain matters undisturbed, and only requires them to abstain from modes of conduct which universal experience has condemned. But where has there been seen a public which set any such limit to its censorship? or when does the public trouble itself about universal experience? In its interferences with personal conduct it is seldom thinking of anything but the enormity of acting or feeling differently from itself. . . .

Questions for Reflection

In the preceding reading, Mill expressed the principle that "To individuality should belong the part of life in which it is chiefly the individual that is interested; to society, the part which chiefly interests society." Consider the following list of actions (assume that they are all performed by an adult). Assign each action to one of the following three categories:

a. This action is a matter of personal choice and society should have nothing to say about it.
b. This action affects the interests of society and laws should govern it. (Ignore the question of whether the action currently is illegal or not.)
c. This action should not be illegal, but the person should be criticized, persuaded not to do it, and receive social rebuke.

1. In spite of numerous reports of head injuries from motorcycle accidents, Barlow refuses to wear a safety helmet when he rides his motorcycle.
2. Cassie routinely gets high on hallucinogenic drugs in the privacy of her own home, but never takes them when she is going out somewhere.
3. Williford frequently drives while intoxicated, claiming that he is a better driver than most who are sober.
4. Lucy is in pain from a terminal disease and requests the services of a physician to help her commit suicide.
5. Dale and Britt are a same-sex couple who are sexually intimate.
6. Harriet is a single woman who spends most of her paycheck gambling and often does not have enough money to buy food or the medicine she herself needs.
7. Brad, a single father, spends most of his paycheck gambling and often does not have enough money to buy food or medicine for his children.
8. Chase is married to five women who all live together with him and are fully in favor of their polygamous marriage.

For each one of your judgments, state how you would defend it to someone who disagreed with you. In each case, try to figure out whether Mill would agree with you.

    KARL MARX AND FRIEDRICH ENGELS

The Communist Theory

Karl Marx (1818–1883), the founder of communism, was born in the Rhineland of Germany. He studied at the universities of Bonn and Berlin, hoping to become a lawyer like his father. However, at the University of Berlin he joined a group of political radicals and became caught up in the excitement of the political and philosophical debates of his time. Consequently, he abandoned law for the study of philosophy. He ended up getting a doctorate in philosophy at the University of Jena.

From Karl Marx and Friedrich Engels, *Manifesto of the Communist Party,* trans. by Samuel Moore in 1888 from the original text of 1848.

While Marx was destined to be a philosophy professor, the conservative Prussian government closed this option when it prohibited political radicals such as Marx from teaching in the universities. Consequently, he became a political journalist, but was forced to continually move from city to city and country to country as his journals were banned by various governments. He finally settled in London in 1849, where he remained the rest of his life, working long hours every day writing the philosophical, historical, political, and economic manuscripts that would change the face of the world. The only stable job he ever held was as a European correspondent for the *New York Tribune* from 1851 to 1862. The rest of the time he survived on family donations, loans, and subsidies from his lifelong friend and collaborator, Friedrich Engels.

While people can debate the credibility of Marx's theories, no one can dispute their influence. No philosopher in history can claim to have had an international, organized, and activist following of such proportions. As a result of his theories, governments have been overthrown, maps have been changed, and his name has become a household word. As Marx said in one of his more famous quotes, "the philosophers have only *interpreted* the world, in various ways; the point is to *change* it." Marx's philosophy can be summarized in the following five points.

1. *Economics Rules Everything.* According to Marx, economics is the basis of all other facets of society and culture (including philosophy). It follows from this that those who have economic power control the society. As Marx put it: "The ideas of the ruling class are in every epoch the ruling ideas; . . . The class which has the means of production at its disposal, has control at the same time over the means of mental production."

2. *Class Struggle Is the One Constant throughout History.* According to Marx, the story of history is the story of those who have power and those who do not, a struggle between the exploiters and the exploited. In the modern era, this struggle has been carried on between two classes: the bourgeoisie and the proletariat. The **bourgeoisie** are the capitalists, or the owners of the means of industrial production (such as the factories) and the employers of wage labor. They also include the middle class who benefit from the current economic system. The other half of society is made up of the **proletariat** or the workers, those who own no property and who must survive by selling their labor as a commodity.

3. *Capitalism Survives by Exploiting the Workers.* In Marx's terminology, *capital* is anything that constitutes economic wealth in that it has exchange value, such as money, property, or goods. The *capitalists* are those who control the economic resources of society, such as the factories. **Capitalism** is that political and economic system in which the means of production and economic wealth are privately controlled. In order to maintain an edge over the competition, Marx says the capitalist must increase his profits by paying his workers as little as possible. Marx believed that the type of freedom espoused by liberal philosophers such as John Stuart Mill (reading 67) was really a sham. For the government to allow everyone to do as they wish simply meant that those who were wealthy, owned the factories, and controlled all the political power, were free to exploit the rest.

4. *History Is a Deterministic Process.* Marx refers to the laws of history as "tendencies working with iron necessity towards inevitable results." Thus, the various movements and stages in history are not a matter of happenstance; instead, internal laws are at

work, bringing about a determined outcome. Accordingly, in Marx's theory, the oppressed class does not need to hope for social justice as merely a tentative possibility, because the laws of history are on their side and guarantee the results. Marx said that each era of history goes through three stages. The initial state of affairs (called the *thesis*) develops to a point where it produces its own contradiction (the *antithesis*). The two remain in tension until another state of affairs supersedes them (the *synthesis*). In each round of this triad (called the *dialectic*), the deficiencies of one stage bring forth opposing forces to balance out what is lacking. Thus, conflict and struggle are an inevitable part of history.

5. *Capitalism Will Undermine Itself and Lead to Communism.* Using the terms of Marx's dialectic, capitalism is the *thesis* that produces its own *antithesis,* an ever-growing, international, embittered, and impoverished, but unified class of proletarians (or workers). For this reason, Marx says of the bourgeoisie (or capitalist) class: "What the bourgeoisie, therefore, produces, above all, is its own grave-diggers. Its fall and the victory of the proletariat are equally inevitable." While the capitalists strive to maintain their position, the situation of the workers becomes intolerable. Society becomes like a tire continually being pumped with air until the internal pressure becomes so great it explodes. This leads to the third stage (the *synthesis*) of the final cycle of history. After several transitional phases, history will culminate in communism, where the people themselves will control not only political decisions but also the economic life of the country.

Reading Questions

1. Marx's view of history is that it is a continual succession of conflicts between social and economic classes. What examples does he cite from history to support this thesis? What are the two conflicting forces in our current epoch?
2. How does he describe the bourgeoisie? What crisis faces the bourgeoisie? How do they try to respond to it?
3. How does Marx describe the proletariat? Who has brought them into existence?
4. Why does Marx say the bourgeoisie have produced their own gravediggers?
5. What is the relationship of the Communist party to the proletariat?
6. What will be some of the goals of the proletarian revolution?
7. What will be the effects of the revolution in the most advanced countries? How many of these predictions have come true?
8. What will be the final outcome with respect to class divisions?

CHAPTER 1: BOURGEOIS AND PROLETARIANS

The history of all hitherto existing society is the history of class struggles.

Freeman and slave, patrician and plebeian, lord and serf, guild-masters and journeyman, in a word, oppressor and oppressed stood in constant opposition to one another, carried on an uninterrupted, now hidden, now open fight, a fight that each time ended either in a revolutionary reconstitution of society at large, or in the common ruin of the contending classes.

In the earlier epochs of history we find almost everywhere a complicated arrangement of society into various orders, a manifold gradation of social rank. In ancient Rome we have patricians, knights, plebeians, slaves; in the Middle Ages, feudal lords, vassals, guild-masters, journeymen, apprentices, serfs; in almost all of these classes, again, subordinate gradations.

The modern bourgeois society that has sprouted from the ruins of feudal society has not done away with class antagonisms. It has but established new classes, new conditions of oppression, new forms of struggle in place of the old ones.

Our epoch, the epoch of the bourgeoisie, possesses, however, this distinctive feature: it has simplified the class antagonisms. Society as a whole is more and more splitting up into two great hostile camps, into two great classes directly facing each other—bourgeoisie and proletariat.

From the serfs of the Middle Ages sprang the chartered burghers of the earliest towns. From these burgesses the first elements of the bourgeoisie were developed.

The discovery of America, the rounding of the Cape, opened up fresh ground for the rising bourgeoisie. The East Indian and Chinese markets, the colonization of America, trade with the colonies, the increase in the means of exchange and in commodities generally, gave to commerce, to navigation, to industry, an impulse never before known, and thereby, to the revolutionary element in the tottering feudal society, a rapid development.

The feudal system of industry, in which industrial production was monopolized by closed guilds, now no longer sufficed for the growing wants of the new markets. The manufacturing system took its place. The guild-masters were pushed aside by the manufacturing middle class; division of labor between the different corporate guilds vanished in the face of division of labor in each single workshop.

Meantime the markets kept ever growing, the demand ever rising. Even manufacture no longer sufficed. Thereupon, steam and machinery revolutionized industrial production. The place of manufacture was taken by the giant, modern industry, the place of the industrial middle class, by industrial millionaires—the leaders of whole industrial armies, the modern bourgeois.

Modern industry has established the world market, for which the discovery of America paved the way. This market has given an immense development to commerce, to navigation, to communication by land. This development has, in its turn, reacted on the extension of industry; and in proportion as industry, commerce, navigation, railways extended, in the same proportion the bourgeoisie developed, increased its capital, and pushed into the background every class handed down from the Middle Ages.

We see, therefore, how the modern bourgeoisie is itself the product of a long course of development, of a series of revolutions in the modes of production and of exchange. . . .

The bourgeoisie, wherever it has got the upper hand, has put an end to all feudal, patriarchal, idyllic relations. It has pitilessly torn asunder the motley feudal ties that bound man to his "natural superiors," and has left no other bond between man and man than naked self-interest, than callous "cash payment." It has drowned the most heavenly ecstasies of religious fervor, of chivalrous enthusiasm, of philistine sentimentalism, in the icy water of egotistical calculation. It has resolved personal worth into exchange value, and in place of the numberless indefeasible chartered freedoms has set up that single, unconscionable freedom—Free Trade. In one word, for exploitation, veiled by religious and political illusions, it has substituted naked, shameless, direct, brutal exploitation.

The bourgeoisie has stripped of its halo every occupation hitherto honored and looked up to with reverent awe. It has converted the physician, the lawyer, the priest, the poet, the man of science, into its paid wage laborers.

The bourgeoisie has torn away from the family its sentimental veil, and has reduced the family relation to a mere money relation. . . .

The bourgeoisie cannot exist without constantly revolutionizing the instruments of production, and thereby the relations of production, and with them the whole relations of society. Conservation of the old modes of production in unaltered form was, on the contrary, the first condition of existence for all earlier industrial classes. Constant revolutionizing of production, uninterrupted disturbance of all social conditions, everlasting uncertainty and agitation distinguish the bourgeois epoch from all earlier ones. All fixed, fast-frozen relations with their train of ancient and venerable prejudices and opinions are swept away; all new-formed ones become antiquated before they can ossify. All that is solid melts in air, all that is holy is profaned, and man is at last compelled to face with sober senses his real conditions of life and his relations with his kind.

The need of a constantly expanding market for its products chases the bourgeoisie over the whole surface of the globe. It must nestle everywhere, settle everywhere, establish connections everywhere.

The bourgeoisie has through its exploitation of the world market given a cosmopolitan character to production and consumption in every country. To the great chagrin of reactionaries it has drawn from under the feet of industry the national ground on which it stood. All old-established national industries have been destroyed or are daily being destroyed. They are dislodged by new industries whose introduction becomes a life and death question for all civilized nations; by industries that no longer work up indigenous raw material, but raw material drawn from the remotest zones; industries whose products are consumed, not only at home, but in every quarter of the globe. In place of the old wants, satisfied by the production of the country, we find new wants, requiring for their satisfaction the products of distant lands and climes. In place of the old local and national seclusion and self-sufficiency we have intercourse in every direction, universal inter-dependence of nations. And as in material, so also in intellectual production. The intellectual creations of individual nations become common property. National one-sidedness and narrow-mindedness become more and more impossible, and from the numerous national and local literatures there arises a world literature.

The bourgeoisie, by the rapid improvement of all instruments of production, by the immensely facilitated means of communication, draws all nations, even the most barbarian, into civilization. The cheap prices of its commodities are the heavy artillery with which it batters down all Chinese walls, with which it forces the barbarians' intensely obstinate hatred of foreigners to capitulate. It compels all nations, on pain of extinction, to adopt the bourgeois mode of production; it compels them to introduce what it calls civilization into their midst, i.e., to become bourgeois themselves. In a word, it creates a world after its own image.

The bourgeoisie has subjected the country to the rule of the towns. It has created enormous cities, has greatly increased the urban population as compared with the rural, and has thus rescued a considerable part of the population from the idiocy of rural life. Just as it has made the country dependent on the towns, so it has made barbarian and semi-barbarian countries dependent on the civilized ones, nations of peasants on nations of bourgeois, the East on the West.

More and more the bourgeoisie keeps doing away with the scattered state of the population, of the means of production, and of property. It has agglomerated population, centralized means of production, and has concentrated property in a few hands. The necessary consequence of this was political centralization. Independent, or but loosely connected provinces, with separate interests, laws, governments and systems of taxation, became lumped together into one nation, with one government, one code of laws, one national class interest, one frontier and one customs tariff.

The bourgeoisie during its rule of scarce one hundred years has created more massive and more colossal productive forces than have all preceding generations together. Subjection of nature's forces to man, machinery, application of chemistry to industry and agriculture, steam-navigation, railways, electric telegraphs, clearing of whole continents for cultivation, canalization of rivers, whole populations conjured out of the ground—what earlier century had even a presentiment that such productive forces slumbered in the lap of social labor?

We see, then, that the means of production and of exchange which served as the foundation for the growth of the bourgeoisie were generated in feudal society. At a certain stage in the development of these means of production and of exchange, the conditions under which feudal society produced and exchanged, the feudal organization of agriculture and manufacturing industry, in a word, the feudal relations of property became no longer compatible with the already developed productive forces; they became so many fetters. They had to be burst asunder; they were burst asunder.

Into their place stepped free competition, accompanied by a social and political constitution adapted to it, and by the economic and political sway of the bourgeois class.

A similar movement is going on before our own eyes. Modern bourgeois society with its relations of production, of exchange and of property, a society that has conjured up such gigantic means of production and of exchange, is like the sorcerer who is no longer able to control the powers of the nether world whom he has called up by his spells. For many a decade past the history of industry and commerce is but the history of the revolt of modern productive forces against modern conditions of production, against the property relations that are the conditions for the existence of the bourgeoisie and of its rule. It is enough to mention the commercial crises that by their periodical return put the existence of the entire bourgeois society on trial, each time more threateningly. In these crises a great part not only of the existing products, but also of the previously created productive forces, are periodically destroyed. In these crises there breaks out an epidemic that, in all earlier epochs, would have seemed an absurdity—the epidemic of overproduction. Society suddenly finds itself put back into a state of momentary barbarism; it appears as if a famine, a universal war of devastation had cut off the supply of every means of subsistence; industry and commerce seem to be destroyed. And why? Because there is too much civilization, too much means of subsistence, too much industry, too much commerce. The productive forces at the disposal of society no longer tend to further the development of the conditions of bourgeois property; on the contrary, they have become too powerful for these conditions, by which they are fettered, and no sooner do they overcome these fetters than they bring disorder into the whole of bourgeois society, endanger the existence of bourgeois property. The conditions of bourgeois society are too narrow to comprise the wealth created by them. And how does the bourgeoisie get over these crises? On the one hand by enforced destruction of a mass of productive forces; on the other, by the conquest of new markets and by the more thorough exploitation of the old ones. That is to say, by paving the way for more extensive and more destructive crises, and by diminishing the means whereby crises are prevented.

The weapons with which the bourgeoisie felled feudalism to the ground are now turned against the bourgeoisie itself.

But not only has the bourgeoisie forged the weapons that bring death to itself; it has also called into existence the men who are to wield those weapons—the modern working class, the proletarians.

In proportion as the bourgeoisie, i.e., capital, is developed, in the same proportion is the proletariat, the modern working class, developed—a class of laborers, who live only so long as they find work, and who find work only so long as their labor increases capital. These laborers, who must sell themselves piecemeal, are a commodity like every other article of commerce, and are consequently exposed to all the vicissitudes of competition, to all the fluctuations of the market.

Owing to the extensive use of machinery and to division of labor, the work of the proletarians has lost all individual character, and, consequently, all charm for the workman. He becomes an appendage of the machine, and it is only the most simple, most monotonous, and most easily acquired knack that is required of him. Hence, the cost of production of a workman is restricted almost entirely to the means of subsistence that he requires for his maintenance and for the propagation of his race. But the price of a commodity, and therefore also of labor, is equal to its cost of production. In proportion, therefore, as the repulsiveness of the work increases, the wage decreases. Nay more, in proportion as the use of machinery and division of labor increases, in the same proportion the burden of toil also increases, whether by prolongation of the working hours, by increase of the work exacted in a given time, or by increased speed of the machinery, etc.

Modern industry has converted the little workshop of the patriarchal master into the great factory of the industrial capitalist. Masses of laborers, crowded into the factory, are organized like soldiers. As privates of the industrial army they are placed under the command of a perfect hierarchy of officers and sergeants. Not only are they slaves of the bourgeois class and of the bourgeois state; they are daily and hourly enslaved by the machine, by the overseer, and, above all, by the individual bourgeois manufacturer himself. The more openly this despotism proclaims gain to be its end and aim, the more petty, the more hateful, and the more embittering it is.

The less the skill and exertion of strength implied in manual labor—in other words, the more modern industry develops—the more is the labor of men superseded by that of women. Differences of age and sex have no longer any distinctive social validity for the working class. All are instruments of labor, more or less expensive to use, according to their age and sex.

No sooner has the laborer received his wages in cash, for the moment escaping exploitation by the manufacturer, than he is set upon by the other portions of the bourgeoisie—the landlord, the shopkeeper, the pawnbroker, etc.

The lower strata of the middle class—the small tradespeople, shopkeepers, and retired tradesmen generally, the handicraftsmen and peasants—all these sink gradually into the proletariat, partly because their diminutive capital does not suffice for the scale on which modern industry is carried on and is swamped in the competition with the large capitalists, partly because their specialized skill is rendered worthless by new methods of production. Thus the proletariat is recruited from all classes of the population.

The proletariat goes through various stages of development. With its birth begins its struggle with the bourgeoisie. At first the contest is carried on by individual laborers, then by the workpeople of a factory, then by the operatives of one trade, in one locality, against the individual bourgeois who directly exploits them. They direct their attacks not against the bourgeois conditions of production, but against the instruments of production themselves; they destroy imported wares that compete with their labor, they smash machinery to pieces, they set factories ablaze, they seek to restore by

force the vanished status of the workman of the Middle Ages.

At this stage the laborers still form an incoherent mass scattered over the whole country, and broken up by their mutual competition. If anywhere they unite to form more compact bodies, this is not yet the consequence of their own active union, but of the union of the bourgeoisie, which class, in order to attain its own political ends, is compelled to set the whole proletariat in motion, and is, moreover, still able to do so for a time. At this stage, therefore, the proletarians do not fight their enemies, but the enemies of their enemies, the remnants of absolute monarchy, the landowners, the non-industrial bourgeois, the petty bourgeoisie. Thus the whole historical movement is concentrated in the hands of the bourgeoisie; every victory so obtained is a victory for the bourgeoisie.

But with the development of industry the proletariat not only increases in number; it becomes concentrated in greater masses, its strength grows, and it feels that strength more. The various interests, and conditions of life within the ranks of the proletariat are more and more equalized, in proportion as machinery obliterates all distinctions of labor and nearly everywhere reduces wages to the same low level. The growing competition among the bourgeois and the resulting commercial crises make the wages of the workers ever more fluctuating. The unceasing improvement of machinery, ever more rapidly developing, makes their livelihood more and more precarious; the collisions between individual workmen and individual bourgeois take more and more the character of collisions between two classes. Thereupon the workers begin to form combinations (trade unions) against the bourgeoisie; they club together in order to keep up the rate of wages; they found permanent associations in order to make provision beforehand for these occasional revolts. Here and there the contest breaks out into riots.

Now and then the workers are victorious, but only for a time. The real fruit of their battles lies not in the immediate result but in the ever expanding union of the workers. This union is furthered by the improved means of communication which are created by modern industry, and which place the workers of different localities in contact with one another. It was just this contact that was needed to centralize the numerous local struggles, all of the same character, into one national struggle between classes. But every class struggle is a political struggle. And that union, which the burghers of the Middle Ages, with their miserable highways, required centuries to attain, the modern proletarians, thanks to railways achieve in a few years.

This organization of the proletarians into a class, and consequently into a political party, is continually being upset again by the competition between the workers themselves. But it ever rises up again, stronger, firmer, mightier. It compels legislative recognition of particular interests of the workers by taking advantage of the divisions among the bourgeoisie itself. . . .

Altogether, collisions between the classes of the old society further the course of development of the proletariat in many ways. The bourgeoisie finds itself involved in a constant battle—at first with the aristocracy; later on, with those portions of the bourgeoisie itself whose interests have become antagonistic to the progress of industry; at all times with the bourgeoisie of foreign countries. In all these battles it sees itself compelled to appeal to the proletariat, to ask for its help, and thus to drag it into the political arena. The bourgeoisie itself, therefore, supplies the proletariat with its own elements of political and general education; in other words, it furnishes the proletariat with weapons for fighting the bourgeoisie.

Further, as we have already seen, entire sections of the ruling classes are, by the advance of industry, precipitated into the proletariat, or are at least threatened in their conditions of existence. These also supply the proletariat with fresh elements of enlightenment and progress.

Finally, in times when the class struggle nears the decisive hour, the process of dissolution going on within the ruling class, in fact within the whole range of old society, assumes such a violent, glaring character that a small section of the ruling class cuts itself adrift and joins the revolutionary class, the class that holds the future in its hands. Just as,

therefore, at an earlier period a section of the nobility went over to the bourgeoisie, so now a portion of the bourgeoisie goes over to the proletariat, and in particular, a portion of the bourgeois ideologists who have raised themselves to the level of comprehending theoretically the historical movement as a whole.

Of all the classes that stand face to face with the bourgeoisie today, the proletariat alone is a really revolutionary class. The other classes decay and finally disappear in the face of modern industry; the proletariat is its special and essential product.

The lower middle class, the small manufacturer, the shopkeeper, the artisan, the peasant—all these fight against the bourgeoisie, to save from extinction their existence as fractions of the middle class. They are, therefore, not revolutionary but conservative. Nay more, they are reactionary, for they try to roll back the wheel of history. If by chance they are revolutionary they are so only in view of their impending transfer into the proletariat; they thus defend not their present but their future interests; they desert their own standpoint to adopt that of the proletariat. . . .

The social conditions of the old society no longer exist for the proletariat. The proletarian is without property; his relation to his wife and children has no longer anything in common with bourgeois family relations; modern industrial labor, modern subjection to capital, the same in England as in France, in America as in Germany, has stripped him of every trace of national character. Law, morality, religion are to him so many bourgeois prejudices, behind which lurk in ambush just as many bourgeois interests.

All the preceding classes that got the upper hand sought to fortify their already acquired status by subjecting society at large to their conditions of appropriation. The proletarians cannot become masters of the productive forces of society except by abolishing their own previous mode of appropriation, and thereby also every other previous mode of appropriation. They have nothing of their own to secure and to fortify; their mission is to destroy all previous securities for, and insurances of, individual property.

All previous historical movements were movements of minorities, or in the interest of minorities. The proletarian movement is the self-conscious, independent movement of the immense majority, in the interest of the immense majority. The proletariat, the lowest stratum of our present society, cannot stir, cannot raise itself up, without the whole superincumbent strata of official society being sprung into the air.

Though not in substance, yet in form, the struggle of the proletariat with the bourgeoisie is at first a national struggle. The proletariat of each country must, of course, first of all settle matters with its own bourgeoisie.

In depicting the most general phases of the development of the proletariat we traced the more or less veiled civil war raging within existing society, up to the point where that war breaks out into open revolution, and where the violent overthrow of the bourgeoisie lays the foundation for the sway of the proletariat.

Hitherto, every form of society has been based, as we have already seen, on the antagonism of oppressing and oppressed classes. But in order to oppress a class certain conditions must be assured to it under which it can, at least, continue its slavish existence. The serf, in the period of serfdom, raised himself to membership in the commune, just as the petty bourgeois, under the yoke of feudal absolutism, managed to develop into a bourgeois.

The modern laborer, on the contrary, instead of rising with the progress of industry, sinks deeper and deeper below the conditions of existence of his own class. He becomes a pauper, and pauperism develops more rapidly than population and wealth. And here it becomes evident that the bourgeoisie is unfit any longer to be the ruling class in society and to impose its conditions of existence upon society as an overriding law. It is unfit to rule because it is incompetent to assure an existence to its slave within his slavery, because it cannot help letting him sink into such a state that it has to feed him, instead of being fed by him. Society can no longer live under this bourgeoisie, in other words, its existence is no longer compatible with society.

The essential condition for the existence and sway of the bourgeois class is the formation and augmentation of capital; the condition for capital is wage labor. Wage labor rests exclusively on competition between the laborers. The advance of industry, whose involuntary promoter is the bourgeoisie, replaces the isolation of the laborers, due to competition, by their revolutionary combination, due to association. The development of modern industry, therefore, cuts from under its feet the very foundation on which the bourgeoisie produces and appropriates products. What the bourgeoisie, therefore, produces above all are its own grave-diggers. Its fall and the victory of the proletariat are equally inevitable.

CHAPTER 2: PROLETARIANS AND COMMUNISTS

In what relation do the Communists stand to the proletarians as a whole?

The Communists do not form a separate party opposed to other working class parties.

They have no interests separate and apart from those of the proletariat as a whole.

They do not set up any sectarian principles of their own by which to shape and mold the proletarian movement.

The Communists are distinguished from the other working class parties by this only: 1. In the national struggles of the proletarians of the different countries they point out and bring to the front the common interests of the entire proletariat, independently of all nationality; 2. In the various stages of development which the struggle of the working class against the bourgeoisie has to pass through they always and everywhere represent the interests of the movement as a whole.

The Communists, therefore, are on the one hand, practically, the most advanced and resolute section of the working class parties of every country, that section which pushes forward all others; on the other hand, theoretically, they have over the great mass of the proletariat the advantage of clearly understanding the line of march, the conditions, and the ultimate general results of the proletarian movement.

The immediate aim of the Communists is the same as that of all the other proletarian parties: formation of the proletariat into a class, overthrow of bourgeois supremacy, conquest of political power by the proletariat. . . .

The proletariat will use its political supremacy to wrest by degrees all capital from the bourgeoisie, to centralize all instruments of production in the hands of the state, i.e., of the proletariat organized as the ruling class, and to increase the total of productive forces as rapidly as possible.

Of course, in the beginning this cannot be effected except by means of despotic inroads on the rights of property and on the conditions of bourgeois production; by means of measures, therefore, which appear economically insufficient and untenable, but which, in the course of the movement outstrip themselves, necessitate further inroads upon the old social order, and are unavoidable as a means of entirely revolutionizing the mode of production.

These measures will, of course, be different in different countries.

Nevertheless, in the most advanced countries the following will be pretty generally applicable:

1. Abolition of property in land and application of all rents of land to public purposes.

2. A heavy progressive or graduated income tax.

3. Abolition of all right of inheritance.

4. Confiscation of the property of all emigrants and rebels.

5. Centralization of credit in the hands of the state by means of a national bank with state capital and an exclusive monopoly.

6. Centralization of the means of communication and transport in the hands of the state.

7. Extension of factories and instruments of production owned by the state; the bringing into cultivation of waste lands, and the im-provement of the soil generally in accordance with a common plan.

8. Equal obligation of all to work. Establishment of industrial armies, especially for agriculture.

9. Combination of agriculture with manufacturing industries; gradual abolition of the distinction between town and country by a more equable distribution of the population over the country.

10. Free education for all children in public schools. Abolition of child factory labor in its present form. Combination of education with industrial production, etc.

When in the course of development class distinctions have disappeared and all production has been concentrated in the hands of a vast association of the whole nation, the public power will lose its political character. Political power, properly so called, is merely the organized power of one class for oppressing another. If the proletariat during its contest with the bourgeoisie is compelled by the force of circumstances to organize itself as a class; if by means of a revolution it makes itself the ruling class and, as such, sweeps away by force the old conditions of production, then it will, along with these conditions, have swept away the conditions for the existence of class antagonisms and of classes generally, and will thereby have abolished its own supremacy as a class.

In place of the old bourgeois society, with its classes and class antagonisms, we shall have an association in which the free development of each is the condition for the free development of all. . . .

The Communists disdain to conceal their views and aims. They openly declare that their ends can be attained only by the forcible overthrow of all existing social conditions. Let the ruling classes tremble at a Communist revolution. The proletarians have nothing to lose but their chains. They have a world to win.

WORKINGMEN OF ALL COUNTRIES, UNITE!

Questions for Reflection

1. Marx believed that economics was the basis of all other cultural institutions. Based on this point, work out a Marxist analysis of the economic influences on the worlds of sports, music, religion, education, and politics as they exist in our society today. Do you think the Marxist analysis has captured any of the truth about these features of our contemporary culture? On the other hand, do you think Marx overemphasized the role of economics on society? Can all aspects of human life and culture be explained on the basis of economic motivations?

2. One hundred years after the publication of *The Communist Manifesto,* philosopher Sidney Hook listed the following features of capitalism as described by Marx:

   economic centralization and monopoly, the cycle of boom and depression, unemployment and the effects of technological change, political and economic class wars, excessive specialization and division of labor, the triumph of materialistic and money values on the rest of our culture.*

   How many of these problems of capitalism described by Marx still exist in our society today?

3. Under capitalism, you have the opportunity to form your own corporation and, if it is successful, become a millionaire. Under communism, private, profit-making corporations do not exist and personal wealth is severely restricted. However, people receive a guaranteed income, free education, and free medical care, and the costs of cultural events such as the opera are available to the common person. Very few people in our society are able to become millionaires as a result of our economic freedom. However, everyone would benefit from free education and medical care. Do you think the individual freedom of capitalism is enough to justify the lack of these governmental benefits? Or would it be worth sacrificing some freedoms so that everyone in society would benefit from the government-provided benefits?

4. Contrary to Marx's predictions, the plight of the worker has not gotten worse. Salaries, health and safety standards, the length of the working day, and benefits are all better than they were in Marx's day. However, contemporary Marxist Herbert Marcuse argues that capitalists will make working conditions better only if it serves to increase their profits. Furthermore, he says, by giving workers more materialistic benefits, they have actually made them blind to their true alienation and lack of political power. In spite of the better conditions of the worker, do you think that the capitalist system is still as unjust as the Marxists claim? Or do the improved conditions of the workers demonstrate that Marx was wrong?

---

* Sidney Hook, "*The Communist Manifesto* 100 Years After," *New York Times Magazine,* February 1, 1948, in *Molders of Modern Thought,* ed. Ben B. Seligman (Chicago: Quadrangle Books, 1970), p. 80.

JOHN RAWLS

Contemporary Liberalism

John Rawls (1921–   ) is professor of Philosophy at Harvard University. He has published many influential articles and books in moral and political philosophy. No book has been more in the forefront of current discussions about political philosophy than Rawls's 1971 book *A Theory of Justice*. In this book, Rawls attempts to find a balance between individual liberty and rights on the one hand and society's duties and interest in maintaining an equitable distribution of goods on the other hand. In seeking this balance, Rawls sets out a blueprint of a society in which people are encouraged to succeed and better their position, and yet are guaranteed that no one will be hopelessly left behind.

According to Rawls, an adequate theory of justice must be one that will be acceptable to everyone. But how is this possible? Each person has different needs, interests, abilities, social circumstances, and agendas. Rawls's answer is that people will accept a theory of justice only if they think it is fair. But once again, how can different people in different circumstances agree on what is fair? To solve this problem, Rawls comes up with a clever solution based on a thought experiment. He asks us to imagine that there is as yet no society, but we are all coming together in a state of perfect equality to create a new society and to decide what principles shall govern it. Rawls calls this initial situation the "original position." He further adds that in deciding what principles shall govern our society, we stand behind a "veil of ignorance." For example, you do not know whether your lot in life will be that of someone who is rich or poor, physically abled or physically challenged, intellectually superior or intellectually inferior, white or black, male or female, and so on. Under these circumstances, what sort of society would you choose?

Reading Questions

1. What is Rawls's guiding idea concerning the principles of justice for the basic structure of society?
2. What is the "original position"? How does Rawls describe it? Does it refer to an actual historical state of affairs?
3. What does Rawls mean when he says that the people in the original position who are to choose the principles of justice stand behind a "veil of ignorance"? What is it that they do not know? What is the purpose of the thought experiment of choosing principles of justice behind a veil of ignorance?
4. John Stuart Mill (reading 67) thought that the principle of utility should be the basis of society. The principle of utility states that we should always seek to maximize the greatest amount of good. Why does Rawls think that the principle of utility would not be chosen by people in the original position?

From John Rawls, *A Theory of Justice* (Cambridge: Harvard University Press, 1971).

5. What are the two principles that Rawls claims rationally self-interested persons would choose in the original position? What are the applications of the two principles? Which one has priority? What is the more general conception of justice of which these two principles are a special case? How does Rawls define injustice?

6. What should we do in cases where people have been favored by nature with certain advantages (intelligence, a superior character)?

THE MAIN IDEA OF THE THEORY OF JUSTICE

My aim is to present a conception of justice which generalizes and carries to a higher level of abstraction the familiar theory of the social contract as found, say, in Locke, Rousseau, and Kant. In order to do this we are not to think of the original contract as one to enter a particular society or to set up a particular form of government. Rather, the guiding idea is that the principles of justice for the basic structure of society are the object of the original agreement. They are the principles that free and rational persons concerned to further their own interests would accept in an initial position of equality as defining the fundamental terms of their association. These principles are to regulate all further agreements; they specify the kinds of social cooperation that can be entered into and the forms of government that can be established. This way of regarding the principles of justice I shall call justice as fairness.

Thus we are to imagine that those who engage in social cooperation choose together, in one joint act, the principles which are to assign basic rights and duties and to determine the division of social benefits. Men are to decide in advance how they are to regulate their claims against one another and what is to be the foundation charter of their society. Just as each person must decide by rational reflection what constitutes his good, that is, the system of ends which it is rational for him to pursue, so a group of persons must decide once and for all what is to count among them as just and unjust. The choice which rational men would make in this hypothetical situation of equal liberty, assuming for the present that this choice problem has a solution, determines the principles of justice.

In justice as fairness the original position of equality corresponds to the state of nature in the traditional theory of the social contract. This original position is not, of course, thought of as an actual historical state of affairs, much less as a primitive condition of culture. It is understood as a purely hypothetical situation characterized so as to lead to a certain conception of justice. Among the essential features of this situation is that no one knows his place in society, his class position or social status, nor does any one know his fortune in the distribution of natural assets and abilities, his intelligence, strength, and the like. I shall even assume that the parties do not know their conceptions of the good or their special psychological propensities. The principles of justice are chosen behind a veil of ignorance. This ensures that no one is advantaged or disadvantaged in the choice of principles by the outcome of natural chance or the contingency of social circumstances. Since all are similarly situated and no one is able to design principles to favor his particular condition, the principles of justice are the result of a fair agreement or bargain. For given the circumstances of the original position, the symmetry of everyone's relations to each other, this initial situation is fair between individuals as moral persons, that is, as rational beings with their own ends and capable, I shall assume, of a sense of justice. The original position is, one might say, the appropriate initial status quo, and thus the fundamental agreements reached in it are fair. This explains the propriety of the name "justice as fairness": it conveys the idea that the principles of justice are agreed to in an initial situation that is fair. The name does not mean that the concepts of justice and fairness are the same, any more than the phrase "poetry as metaphor" means that the concepts of poetry and metaphor are the same.

Justice as fairness begins, as I have said, with one of the most general of all choices which persons might make together, namely, with the choice of the first principles of a conception of justice which is to regulate all subsequent criticism and reform of institutions. Then, having chosen a conception of justice, we can suppose that they are to choose a constitution and a legislature to enact laws, and so on, all in accordance with the principles of justice initially agreed upon. Our social situation is just if it is such that by this sequence of hypothetical agreements we would have contracted into the general system of rules which defines it. Moreover, assuming that the original position does determine a set of principles (that is, that a particular conception of justice would be chosen), it will then be true that whenever social institutions satisfy these principles those engaged in them can say to one another that they are cooperating on terms to which they would agree if they were free and equal persons whose relations with respect to one another were fair. They could all view their arrangements as meeting the stipulations which they would acknowledge in an initial situation that embodies widely accepted and reasonable constraints on the choice of principles. The general recognition of this fact would provide the basis for a public acceptance of the corresponding principles of justice. No society can, of course, be a scheme of cooperation which men enter voluntarily in a literal sense; each person finds himself placed at birth in some particular position in some particular society, and the nature of this position materially affects his life prospects. Yet a society satisfying the principles of justice as fairness comes as close as a society can to being a voluntary scheme, for it meets the principles which free and equal persons would assent to under circumstances that are fair. In this sense its members are autonomous and the obligations they recognize self-imposed.

One feature of justice as fairness is to think of the parties in the initial situation as rational and mutually disinterested. This does not mean that the parties are egoists, that is, individuals with only certain kinds of interests, say in wealth, prestige, and domination. But they are conceived as not taking an interest in one another's interests. They are to presume that even their spiritual aims may be opposed, in the way that the aims of those of different religions may be opposed. Moreover, the concept of rationality must be interpreted as far as possible in the narrow sense, standard in economic theory, of taking the most effective means to given ends. I shall modify this concept to some extent . . . but one must try to avoid introducing into it any controversial ethical elements. The initial situation must be characterized by stipulations that are widely accepted.

In working out the conception of justice as fairness one main task clearly is to determine which principles of justice would be chosen in the original position. To do this we must describe this situation in some detail and formulate with care the problem of choice which it presents. These matters I shall take up in the immediately succeeding chapters. It may be observed, however, that once the principles of justice are thought of as arising from an original agreement in a situation of equality, it is an open question whether the principle of utility would be acknowledged. Offhand it hardly seems likely that persons who view themselves as equals, entitled to press their claims upon one another, would agree to a principle which may require lesser life prospects for some simply for the sake of a greater sum of advantages enjoyed by others. Since each desires to protect his interests, his capacity to advance his conception of the good, no one has a reason to acquiesce in an enduring loss for himself in order to bring about a greater net balance of satisfaction. In the absence of strong and lasting benevolent impulses, a rational man would not accept a basic structure merely because it maximized the algebraic sum of advantages irrespective of its permanent effects on his own basic rights and interests. Thus it seems that the principle of utility is incompatible with the conception of social cooperation among equals for mutual advantage. It appears to be inconsistent with the idea of reciprocity implicit in the notion of a well-ordered society. Or, at any rate, so I shall argue.

I shall maintain instead that the persons in the initial situation would choose two rather different principles: the first requires equality in the assignment of basic rights and duties, while the second holds that social and economic inequalities, for example inequalities of wealth and authority, are just only if they result in compensating benefits for everyone, and in particular for the least advantaged members of society. These principles rule out justifying institutions on the grounds that the hardships of some are offset by a greater good in the aggregate. It may be expedient but it is not just that some should have less in order that others may prosper. But there is no injustice in the greater benefits earned by a few provided that the situation of persons not so fortunate is thereby improved. The intuitive idea is that since everyone's well-being depends upon a scheme of cooperation without which no one could have a satisfactory life, the division of advantages should be such as to draw forth the willing cooperation of everyone taking part in it, including those less well situated. Yet this can be expected only if reasonable terms are proposed. The two principles mentioned seem to be a fair agreement on the basis of which those better endowed, or more fortunate in their social position, neither of which we can be said to deserve, could expect the willing cooperation of others when some workable scheme is a necessary condition of the welfare of all. Once we decide to look for a conception of justice that nullifies the accidents of natural endowment and the contingencies of social circumstance as counters in quest for political and economic advantage, we are led to these principles. They express the result of leaving aside those aspects of the social world that seem arbitrary from a moral point of view. . . .

TWO PRINCIPLES OF JUSTICE

I shall now state in a provisional form the two principles of justice that I believe would be chosen in the original position. In this section I wish to make only the most general comments, and therefore the first formulation of these principles is tentative. . . .

The first statement of the two principles reads as follows.

First: each person is to have an equal right to the most extensive basic liberty compatible with a similar liberty for others.

Second: social and economic inequalities are to be arranged so that they are both (a) reasonably expected to be to everyone's advantage, and (b) attached to positions and offices open to all. . . .

By way of general comment, these principles primarily apply, as I have said, to the basic structure of society. They are to govern the assignment of rights and duties and to regulate the distribution of social and economic advantages. As their formulation suggests, these principles presuppose that the social structure can be divided into two more or less distinct parts, the first principle applying to the one, the second to the other. They distinguish between those aspects of the social system that define and secure the equal liberties of citizenship and those that specify and establish social and economic inequalities. The basic liberties of citizens are, roughly speaking, political liberty (the right to vote and to be eligible for public office) together with freedom of speech and assembly; liberty of conscience and freedom of thought; freedom of the person along with the right to hold (personal) property; and freedom from arbitrary arrest and seizure as defined by the concept of the rule of law. These liberties are all required to be equal by the first principle, since citizens of a just society are to have the same basic rights.

The second principle applies, in the first approximation, to the distribution of income and wealth and to the design of organizations that make use of differences in authority and responsibility, or chains of command. While the distribution of wealth and income need not be equal, it must be to everyone's advantage, and at the same time, positions of authority and offices of command must be accessible to all. One applies the second principle by holding positions open, and then, subject to this constraint, arranges social and economic inequalities so that everyone benefits.

These principles are to be arranged in a serial order with the first principle prior to the second. This ordering means that a departure from the institutions of equal liberty required by the first principle cannot be justified by, or compensated for, by greater social and economic advantages. The distribution of wealth and income, and the hierarchies of authority, must be consistent with both the liberties of equal citizenship and equality of opportunity.

It is clear that these principles are rather specific in their content, and their acceptance rests on certain assumptions that I must eventually try to explain and justify. A theory of justice depends upon a theory of society in ways that will become evident as we proceed. For the present, it should be observed that the two principles (and this holds for all formulations) are a special case of a more general conception of justice that can be expressed as follows.

> All social values—liberty and opportunity, income and wealth, and the bases of self-respect—are to be distributed equally unless an unequal distribution of any, or all, of these values is to everyone's advantage.

Injustice, then, is simply inequalities that are not to the benefit of all. Of course, this conception is extremely vague and requires interpretation.

As a first step, suppose that the basic structure of society distributes certain primary goods, that is, things that every rational man is presumed to want. These goods normally have a use whatever a person's rational plan of life. For simplicity, assume that the chief primary goods at the disposition of society are rights and liberties, powers and opportunities, income and wealth. (Later on in Part Three the primary good of self-respect has a central place.) These are the social primary goods. Other primary goods such as health and vigor, intelligence and imagination, are natural goods; although their possession is influenced by the basic structure, they are not so directly under its control. Imagine, then, a hypothetical initial arrangement in which all the social primary goods are equally distributed: everyone has similar rights and duties, and income and wealth are evenly shared. This state of affairs provides a benchmark for judging improvements. If certain inequalities of wealth and organizational powers would make everyone better off than in this hypothetical starting situation, then they accord with the general conception.

Now it is possible, at least theoretically, that by giving up some of their fundamental liberties men are sufficiently compensated by the resulting social and economic gains. The general conception of justice imposes no restrictions on what sort of inequalities are permissible; it only requires that everyone's position be improved. We need not suppose anything so drastic as consenting to a condition of slavery. Imagine instead that men forgo certain political rights when the economic returns are significant and their capacity to influence the course of policy by the exercise of these rights would be marginal in any case. It is this kind of exchange which the two principles as stated rule out; being arranged in serial order they do not permit exchanges between basic liberties and economic and social gains. The serial ordering of principles expresses an underlying preference among primary social goods. When this preference is rational so likewise is the choice of these principles in this order.

In developing justice as fairness I shall, for the most part, leave aside the general conception of justice and examine instead the special case of the two principles in serial order. The advantage of this procedure is that from the first the matter of priorities is recognized and an effort made to find principles to deal with it. One is led to attend throughout to the conditions under which the acknowledgment of the absolute weight of liberty with respect to social and economic advantages, as defined by the lexical order of the two principles, would be reasonable. Offhand, this ranking appears extreme and too special a case to be of much interest; but there is more justification for it than would appear at first sight. Or at any rate, so I shall maintain. . . . Furthermore, the distinction between fundamental rights and liberties and economic and social benefits marks a difference among primary social goods that one should try to exploit. It suggests an important division in the social system. Of course, the distinctions drawn and the ordering proposed are bound to be at best only approximations. There are surely circumstances in which they fail. But it is essential to depict clearly the main lines of a reasonable conception of justice; and under many conditions anyway, the two principles in serial order may serve well enough. When necessary we can fall back on the more general conception.

The fact that the two principles apply to institutions has certain consequences. Several points illustrate this. First of all, the rights and liberties referred to by these principles are those which are defined by the public rules of the basic structure. Whether men are free is determined by the rights and duties established by the major institutions of society. Liberty is a certain pattern of social forms. The first principle simply requires that certain sorts of rules, those defining basic liberties, apply to everyone equally and that they allow the most extensive liberty compatible with a like liberty for all. The only reason for circumscribing the rights defining liberty and making men's freedom less extensive than it might otherwise be is that these equal rights as institutionally defined would interfere with one another.

Another thing to bear in mind is that when principles mention persons, or require that everyone gain from an inequality, the reference is to representative persons holding the various social positions, or offices, or whatever, established by the basic structure. Thus in applying the second principle I assume that it is possible to assign an expectation of well-being to representative individuals holding these positions. This expectation indicates their life prospects as viewed from their social station. In general, the expectations of representative persons depend upon the distribution of rights and duties throughout the basic structure. When this changes, expectations change. I assume, then, that expectations are connected: by raising the prospects of the representative man in one position we presumably increase or decrease the prospects of representative men in other positions. Since it applies to institutional forms, the second principle (or rather the first part of it) refers to the expectations of representative individuals. As I shall discuss below, neither principle applies to distributions of particular goods to particular individuals who may be identified by their proper names. The situation where someone is considering how to allocate certain commodities to needy persons who are known to him is not within the scope of the principles. They are meant to regulate basic institutional arrangements. We must not assume that there is much similarity from the standpoint of justice between an administrative allotment of goods to specific persons and the appropriate design of society. Our common sense intuitions for the former may be a poor guide to the latter.

Now the second principle insists that each person benefit from permissible inequalities in the basic structure. This means that it must be reasonable for each relevant representative man defined by this structure, when he views it as a going concern, to prefer his prospects with the inequality to his prospects without it. One is not allowed to justify differences in income or organizational powers on the ground that the disadvantages of those in one position are outweighed by the greater advantages of those in another. Much less can infringements of liberty be counterbalanced in this way. Applied to the basic structure, the principle of utility would have us maximize the sum of expectations of representative men (weighted by the number of persons they represent, on the classical view); and this would permit us to compensate for the losses of some by the gains of others. Instead, the two principles require that everyone benefit from economic and social inequalities. It is obvious, however, that there are indefinitely many ways in which all may be advantaged when the initial arrangement of equality is taken as a benchmark. How then are we to choose among these possibilities? The principles must be specified so that they yield a determinate conclusion. . . .

. . . Those who have been favored by nature, whoever they are, may gain from their good fortune only on terms that improve the situation of those who have lost out. The naturally advantaged are not to gain merely because they are more gifted, but only to cover the costs of training and education and for using their endowments in ways that help the less fortunate as well. No one deserves his greater natural capacity nor merits a more favorable starting place in society. But it does not follow that one should eliminate these distinctions. There is another way to deal with them. The basic structure can be arranged so that these contingencies work for the good of the least fortunate. . . .

Perhaps some will think that the person with greater natural endowments deserves those assets and the superior character that made their development possible. Because he is more worthy in this sense, he deserves the greater advantages that he could achieve with them. This view, however, is surely incorrect. It seems to be one of the fixed points of our considered judgments that no one deserves his place in the distribution of native endowments, any more than one deserves one's initial starting place in society. The assertion that a man deserves the superior character that enables him to make the effort to cultivate his abilities is equally problematic; for his character depends in large part upon fortunate family and social circumstances for which he can claim no credit. The notion of desert seems not to apply to these cases. Thus the more advantaged representative man cannot say that he deserves and therefore has a right to a scheme of cooperation in which he is permitted to acquire benefits in ways that do not contribute to the welfare of others. There is no basis for his making this claim.

Questions for Reflection

1. If you were in the original position as Rawls describes it and behind the veil of ignorance, would you agree with him that the two principles he states are the ones a rational self-interested person would choose? Can you think of any additional principles that he overlooked?

2. What might be an example of where inequalities of wealth may, nevertheless, make everyone better off than if everyone were equal?

3. Some people in our society are unusually intelligent, athletic, or good-looking (natural gifts) or persistent, highly motivated, or optimistic (superior character). Some philosophers think that such persons have a right to reap society's richest rewards (such as wealth, fame, or opportunities) by making use of their gifts or character traits. But Rawls thinks that such persons do not have an unqualified right to the benefits of nature's gifts. What do you think?

4. How might our society be different if it was structured as Rawls thinks it should be? Would it be a more fair society or less? Would it be a better society or worse?

JOHN HOSPERS

Political Libertarianism

Although John Hospers has written on a wide range of philosophical topics, he is particularly well-known for his advocacy of political libertarianism. His writings on this topic include *Libertarianism* (1971) and *Will Capitalism Survive?* (1980) as well as numerous articles. Hospers was one of the founders of the Libertarian Party and was that party's candidate for president of the United States in 1972. (We previously encountered Hospers's argument against skepticism in reading 29.)

From John Hospers, "What Libertarianism Is," in *The Libertarian Alternative,* ed. Tibor Machan (Chicago: Nelson-Hall, 1974).

Hospers believes that individual freedom and autonomy are of the highest value. Each of us is the owner of our own life. It follows that no other individual or government can interfere with your right to make choices about your life, unless those choices interfere with someone else's rights. Hence, the role of government is solely to protect our right to life, liberty, and property, but not to maximize the public good, nor to force you to act in your own best interests, nor to force you to help others. There is much here that is similar to John Stuart Mill's essay on liberty (reading 67). However, Mill thought that the protection of individual liberty was a means to maximize the greatest amount of good in society. Taking a slightly different approach, Hospers believes that government's sole task is to protect individual liberty and that maximizing the greatest good will be an outcome of this, but not the goal.

Reading Questions

1. How does Hospers define libertarianism?
2. What are the three theses of libertarianism?
3. Why does Hospers think that property rights are equally important as the rights of life and liberty?
4. What is the role of government? What areas should not be a matter of government intrusion?
5. What are the three types of laws? According to Hospers, which of these are legitimate types of laws and which are not?
6. What does Hospers think of the notions of a right to a job, free medical care, free food, and free education?
7. Why does he think that the elimination of welfare would not cause people to be destitute?

The political philosophy that is called libertarianism (from the Latin *libertas,* liberty) is the doctrine that every person is the owner of his own life, and that no one is the owner of anyone else's life: and that consequently every human being has the right to act in accordance with his own choices, unless those actions infringe on the equal liberty of other human beings to act in accordance with their choices.

There are several other ways of stating the same libertarian thesis:

1. *No one is anyone else's master, and no one is anyone else's slave.* Since I am the one to decide how my life is to be conducted just as you decide about yours, I have no right (even if I had the power) to make you my slave and be your master, nor have you the right to become the master by enslaving me. Slavery is *forced* servitude, and since no one

owns the life of anyone else, no one has the right to enslave another. Political theories past and present have traditionally been concerned with who should be the master (usually the king, the dictator, or government bureaucracy) and who should be the slaves, and what the extent of the slavery should be. Libertarianism holds that no one has the right to use force to enslave the life of another, or any portion or aspect of that life.

2. *Other men's lives are not yours to dispose of.* I enjoy seeing operas; but operas are expensive to produce. Opera-lovers often say, "The state (or the city, etc.) should subsidize opera, so that we can all see it. Also it would be for people's betterment, cultural benefit, etc." But what they are advocating is nothing more or less than legalized plunder. They can't pay for the productions themselves, and yet they want to see opera, which involves a large num-

ber of people and their labor; so what they are saying in effect is, "Get the money through legalized force. Take a little bit more out of every worker's paycheck every week to pay for the operas we want to see." But I have no right to take by force from the workers' pockets to pay for what I want.

Perhaps it would be better if he *did* go to see opera—then I should try to convince him to go voluntarily. But to take the money from him forcibly, because in my opinion it would be good for *him,* is still seizure of his earnings, which is plunder.

Besides, if I have the right to force him to help pay for my pet projects, hasn't he equally the right to force me to help pay for his? Perhaps he in turn wants the government to subsidize rock-and-roll, or his new car, or a house in the country? If I have the right to milk him, why hasn't he the right to milk me? If I can be a moral cannibal, why can't he too?

We should beware of the inventors of utopias. They would remake the world according to their vision—with the lives and fruits of the labor of *other* human beings. Is it someone's utopian vision that others should build pyramids to beautify the landscape? Very well, then other men should provide the labor; and if he is in a position of political power, and he can't get men to do it voluntarily, then he must *compel* them to "cooperate"—i.e., he must enslave them.

A hundred men might gain great pleasure from beating up or killing just one insignificant human being; but other men's lives are not theirs to dispose of. "In order to achieve the worthy goals of the next five-year-plan, we must forcibly collectivize the peasants . . ."; but other men's lives are not theirs to dispose of. Do you want to occupy, rent-free, the mansion that another man has worked for twenty years to buy? But other men's lives are not yours to dispose of. Do you want operas so badly that everyone is forced to work harder to pay for their subsidization through taxes? But other men's lives are not yours to dispose of. Do you want to have free medical care at the expense of other people, whether they wish to provide it or not? But this would require them to work longer for you whether they want to or not, and other men's lives are not yours to dispose of. . . .

3. *No human being should be a nonvoluntary mortgage on the life of another.* I cannot claim your life, your work, or the products of your effort as mine. The fruit of one man's labor should not be fair game for every freeloader who comes along and demands it as his own. The orchard that has been carefully grown, nurtured, and harvested by its owner should not be ripe for the plucking for any bypasser who has a yen for the ripe fruit. The wealth that some men have produced should not be fair game for looting by government, to be used for whatever purposes its representatives determine, no matter what their motives in so doing may be. The theft of your money by a robber is not justified by the fact that he used it to help his injured mother.

It will already be evident that libertarian doctrine is embedded in a view of the rights of man. Each human being has the right to live his life as he chooses, compatibly with the equal right of all other human beings to live their lives as they choose.

All man's rights are implicit in the above statement. Each man has the right to life: any attempt by others to take it away from him, or even to injure him, violates this right, through the use of coercion against him. Each man has the right to liberty: to conduct his life in accordance with the alternatives open to him without coercive action by others. And every man has the right to property: to work to sustain his life (and the lives of whichever others he chooses to sustain, such as his family) and to retain the fruits of his labor.

People often defend the rights of life and liberty but denigrate property rights, and yet the right to property is as basic as the other two: indeed, without property rights no other rights are possible. Depriving you of property is depriving you of the means by which you live. . . .

I have no right to decide how *you* should spend your time or your money. I can make that decision for myself, but not for you, my neighbor. I may deplore your choice of life-style, and I may talk with you about it provided you are willing to listen to me. But I have no right to use force to change it. Nor have I the right to decide how you should spend the money you have earned. I may appeal to you to give it to the Red Cross, and you may prefer to go to prize-fights. But that is your decision, and however much I may chafe about it I do not have the right to interfere forcibly with it, for example by robbing you in order to use the money in accordance with *my* choices. (If I have the right to rob you, have you also the right to rob me?)

When I claim a right, I carve out a niche, as it were, in my life, saying in effect, "This activity I must be able to perform without interference from others. For you and everyone else, this is off limits." And so I put up a "no trespassing" sign, which marks off the area of my right. Each individual's right is his "no trespassing" sign in relation to me and others. I may not encroach upon his domain any more than he upon mine, without my consent. Every right entails a duty, true—but the duty is only that of *forbearance*—that is, of *refraining* from violating the other person's right. If you have a right to life, I have no right to take your life; if you have a right to the products of your labor (property), I have no right to take it from you without your consent. The nonviolation of these rights will not guarantee you protection against natural catastrophes such as floods and earthquakes, but it will protect you against the aggressive activities *of other men*. And rights, after all, have to do with one's relations to other human beings, not with one's relations to physical nature.

Nor were these rights created by government; governments—some governments, obviously not all—*recognize* and *protect* the rights that individuals already have. Governments regularly forbid homicide and theft; and, at a more advanced stage, protect individuals against such things as libel and breach of contract. . . .

The *right to property* is the most misunderstood and unappreciated of human rights, and it is one most constantly violated by governments. "Property" of course does not mean only real estate; it includes anything you can call your own—your clothing, your car, your jewelry, your books and papers. . . .

Government has always been the chief enemy of the right to property. The officials of government, wishing to increase their power, and finding an increase of wealth an effective way to bring this about, seize some or all of what a person has earned—and since government has a monopoly of physical force within the geographical area of the nation, it has the power (but not the right) to do this. When this happens, of course, every citizen of that country is insecure: he knows that no matter how hard he works the government can swoop down on him at any time and confiscate his earnings and possessions. A person sees his life savings wiped out in a moment when the tax-collectors descend to deprive him of the fruits of his work; or, an industry which has been fifty years in the making and cost millions of dollars and millions of hours of time and planning, is nationalized overnight. Or the government, via inflation, cheapens the currency, so that hard-won dollars aren't worth anything any more. The effect of such actions, of course, is that people lose hope and incentive: if no matter how hard they work the government agents can take it all away, why bother to work at all, for more than today's needs? Depriving people of property is *depriving them of the means by which they live*—the freedom of the individual citizen to do what he wishes with his own life and to plan for the future. Indeed only if property rights are respected is there any point to planning for the future and working to achieve one's goals. *Property rights are what makes long-range planning possible*—the kind of planning which is a distinctively human endeavor, as opposed to the day-by-day activity of the lion who hunts, who depends on the supply of game tomorrow but has no real insurance against starvation in a day or a week. Without the right to property, the right to life itself amounts to little: how can you sustain your life if you cannot plan ahead? and how can you plan ahead if the fruits of your labor can at any moment be confiscated by government? . . .

"But why have *individual* property rights? Why not have lands and houses owned by everybody together?" Yes, this involves no violation of individual rights, as long as everybody consents to this arrangement and no one is forced to join it. The parties to it may enjoy the communal living enough (at least for a time) to overcome certain inevitable problems: that some will work and some not, that some will achieve more in an hour than others can do in a day, and still they will all get the same income. The few who do the most will in the end consider themselves "workhorses" who do the work of two or three or twelve, while the others will be "freeloaders" on the efforts of these few. But as long as they can get out of the arrangement if they no longer like it, no violation of rights is involved. They got in voluntarily, and they can get out voluntarily; no one has used force.

"But why not say that everybody owns everything? That we *all* own everything there is?"

To some this may have a pleasant ring—but let us try to analyze what it means. If everybody owns everything, then everyone has an equal right to go everywhere, do what he pleases, take what he likes, destroy if he wishes, grow crops or burn them, trample them under, and so on. Consider what it would be like in practice. Suppose you have saved money to buy a house for yourself and your family. Now suppose that the principle, "everybody owns everything," becomes adopted. Well then, why shouldn't every itinerant hippie just come in and take over, sleeping in your beds and eating in your kitchen and not bothering to replace the food supply or clean up the mess? After all, it belongs to all of us, doesn't it? So we have just as much right to it as you, the buyer, have. What happens if we *all* want to sleep in the bedroom and there's not room for all of us? Is it the strongest who wins?

What would be the result? Since no one would be responsible for anything, the property would soon be destroyed, the food used up, the facilities nonfunctional. Beginning as a house that *one* family could use, it would end up as a house that *no one* could use. And if the principle continued to be adopted, no one would build houses any more—or anything else. What for? They would only be occupied and used by others, without remuneration.

Suppose two men are cast ashore on an island, and they agree that each will cultivate half of it. The first man is industrious and grows crops and builds a shelter, making the most of the situation with which he is confronted. The second man, perhaps thinking that the warm days will last forever, lies in the sun, picks coconuts while they last, and does a minimum of work to sustain himself. At the time of harvest, the second man has nothing to harvest, nor does he assist the first man in his labors. But later when there is a dearth of food on the island, the second man comes to the first man and demands half of the harvest as his right. But of course he has no right to the product of the first man's labors. The first man may freely choose to give part of his harvest to the second out of charity rather than see him starve; but that is just what it is—charity, not the second man's right.

How can any of man's rights be violated? Ultimately, only by the use of force. I can make suggestions to you, I can reason with you, entreat you (if you are willing to listen), but I cannot *force* you without violating your rights; only by forcing you do I cut the cord between your free decisions and your actions. Voluntary relations between individuals involve no deprivation of rights, but murder, assault, and rape do, because in doing these things I make you the unwilling victim of my actions. A man's beating his wife involves no violation of rights if she *wanted* to be beaten. *Force is behavior that requires the unwilling involvement of other persons.*

Thus the use of force need not involve the use of physical violence. If I trespass on your property or dump garbage on it, I am violating your property rights, as indeed I am when I steal your watch; although this is not force in the sense of violence, it *is* a case of your being an unwilling victim of my action. Similarly, if you shout at me so that I cannot be heard when I try to speak, or blow a siren in my ear, or start a factory next door which pollutes my land, you are again violating my rights (to free speech, to property); I am, again, an unwilling victim of your actions. Similarly, if you steal a manuscript of mine and publish it as your own, you are confiscating a piece of my property and thus violating my right to keep what is the product of my labor. Of course, if I give you the manuscript with permission to sign your name to it and keep the proceeds, no violation of rights is involved—any more than if I give you permission to dump garbage on my yard.

According to libertarianism, the role of government should be limited to the retaliatory use of force against those who have initiated its use. It should not enter into any other areas, such as religion, social organization, and economics.

GOVERNMENT

Government is the most dangerous institution known to man. Throughout history it has violated the rights of men more than any individual or group of individuals could do: it has killed people, enslaved them, sent them to forced labor and concentration camps, and regularly robbed and pillaged them of the fruits of their expended labor. Unlike individual criminals, government has the power to arrest and try; unlike individual criminals, it can surround and encompass a person totally, dominating every aspect of one's life, so that one has no recourse from it but to leave the country (and in totalitarian nations even that is prohibited). Government throughout history has a much sorrier record than any individual, even that of a ruthless mass murderer. The signs we see on bumper stickers are chillingly accurate: "Beware: the Government Is Armed and Dangerous."

The only proper role of government, according to libertarians, is that of the protector of the citizen against aggression by other individuals. The government, of course, should never initiate aggression; its proper role is as the embodiment of the *retaliatory* use of force against anyone who initiates its use.

If each individual had constantly to defend himself against possible aggressors, he would have to spend a considerable portion of his life in target practice, karate exercises, and other means of self-defense, and even so he would probably be helpless against groups of individuals who might try to kill, maim, or rob him. He would have little time for cultivating those qualities which are essential to civilized life, nor would improvements in science, medicine, and the arts be likely to occur. The function of government is to take this responsibility off his shoulders: the government undertakes to defend him against aggressors and to punish them if they attack him. When the government is effective in doing this, it enables the citizen to go about his business unmolested and without constant fear for his life. To do this, of course, government must have physical power—the police, to protect the citizen from aggression within its borders, and the armed forces, to protect him from aggressors outside. Beyond that, the government should not intrude upon his life, either to run his business, or adjust his daily activities, or prescribe his personal moral code.

Government, then, undertakes to be the individual's protector; but historically governments have gone far beyond this function. Since they already have the physical power, they have not hesitated to use it for purposes far beyond that which was entrusted to them in the first place. Undertaking initially to protect its citizens against aggression, it has often itself become an aggressor—a far greater aggressor, indeed, than the criminals against whom it was supposed to protect its citizens. Governments have done what no private citizen can do: arrest and imprison individuals without a trial and send them to slave labor camps. Government must have power in order to be effective—and yet the very means by which alone it can be effective make it vulnerable to the abuse of power, leading to managing the lives of individuals and even inflicting terror upon them.

What then should be the function of government? In a word, the *protection of human rights*.

1. *The right to life:* libertarians support all such legislation as will protect human beings against the use of force by others, for example, laws against killing, attempting killing, maiming, beating, and all kinds of physical violence.

2. *The right to liberty:* there should be no laws compromising in any way freedom of speech, of the press, and peaceable assembly. There should be no censorship of ideas, books, films, or of anything else by government.

3. *The right to property:* libertarians support legislation that protects the property rights of individuals against confiscation, nationalization, eminent domain, robbery, trespass, fraud and misrepresentation, patent and copyright, libel and slander. . . .

Laws may be classified into three types: (1) laws protecting individuals against themselves, such as laws against fornication and other sexual behavior, alcohol, and drugs; (2) laws protecting individuals against aggressions by other individuals, such as laws against murder, robbery, and fraud; (3) laws requiring people to help one another; for example, all laws which rob Peter to pay Paul, such as welfare.

Libertarians reject the first class of laws totally. Behavior which harms no one else is strictly the individual's own affair. Thus, there should be no laws against becoming intoxicated, since whether or not to become intoxicated is the individual's own decision: but there should be laws against driving while intoxicated, since the drunken driver is a threat to every other motorist on the highway (drunken driving falls into type 2). Similarly, there should be no laws against drugs (except the prohibition of sale of drugs to minors) as long as the taking of these drugs poses no threat to anyone else. Drug addiction is a psychological problem to which no present solution exists. Most of the social harm caused by addicts, other than to themselves, is the result of thefts which they perform in order to continue their habit—and then the *legal* crime is the theft, not the addiction. The actual cost of heroin is about ten cents a shot; if it were legalized, the enormous traffic in illegal sale and purchase of it would stop, as well as the accompanying proselytization to get new addicts (to make more money for the pusher) and the thefts performed by addicts who often require eighty dollars a day just to keep up the habit. Addiction would not stop, but the crimes would: it is estimated that 75 percent of the burglaries in New York City today are performed by addicts, and all these crimes could be wiped out at one stroke through the legalization of drugs. (Only when the taking of drugs could be shown to constitute a threat to *others,* should it be prohibited by law. It is only laws protecting people against *themselves* that libertarians oppose.)

Laws should be limited to the second class only: aggression by individuals against other individuals. These are laws whose function is to protect human beings against encroachment by others; and this, as we have seen, is (according to libertarianism) the sole function of government.

Libertarians also reject the third class of laws totally: no one should be forced by law to help others, not even to tell them the time of day if requested, and certainly not to give them a portion of one's weekly paycheck. Governments, in the guise of humanitarianism, have given to some by taking from others (charging a "handling fee" in the process, which, because of the government's waste and inefficiency, sometimes is several hundred percent). And in so doing they have decreased incentive, violated the rights of individuals and lowered the standard of living of almost everyone.

All such laws constitute what libertarians call *moral cannibalism.* A cannibal in the physical sense is a person who lives off the flesh of other human beings. A *moral* cannibal is one who believes he has a right to live off the "spirit" of other human beings—who believes that he has a moral claim on the productive capacity, time, and effort expended by others.

It has become fashionable to claim virtually everything that one needs or desires as one's *right.* Thus, many people claim that they have a right to a job, the right to free medical care, to free food and clothing, to a decent home, and so on. Now if one asks, apart from any specific context, whether it would be desirable if everyone had these things, one might well say yes. But there is a gimmick attached to each of them: *At whose expense?* Jobs, medical care, education, and so on, don't grow on trees. These are goods and services *produced only by men.* Who then is to provide them, and under what conditions?

If you have a right to a job, who is to supply it? Must an employer supply it even if he doesn't want to hire you? What if you are unemployable, or incurably lazy? (If you say "the government must supply it," does that mean that a job must be created for you which no employer needs done, and that you must be kept in it regardless of how much or little you work?) If the employer is forced to supply it at his expense even if he doesn't need you, then isn't *he* being enslaved to that extent? What ever happened to *his* right to conduct his life and his affairs in accordance with his choices?

If you have a right to free medical care, then, since medical care doesn't exist in nature as wild apples do, some people will have to supply it to you for free: that is, they will have to spend their time and money and energy taking care of you whether they want to or not. What ever happened to *their* right to conduct their lives as they see fit? Or do you have a right to violate theirs? Can there be a right to violate rights?

All those who demand this or that as a "free service" are consciously or unconsciously evading the fact that there is in reality no such thing as free services. All man-made goods and services are the result of human expenditure of time and effort. There is no such thing as "something for nothing" in this world. If you demand something free, you are demanding that other men give their time and effort to you without compensation. If they voluntarily choose to do this, there is no problem; but if you demand that they be *forced* to do it, you are interfering with their right not to do it if they so choose. "Swimming in this pool ought to be free!" says the indignant passerby. What he means is that others should build a pool, others should provide the material, and still others should run it and keep it in functioning order, so that *he* can use it without fee. But what right has he to the expenditure of *their* time and effort? To expect something "for free" is to expect it *to be paid for by others* whether they choose to or not.

Many questions, particularly about economic matters, will be generated by the libertarian account of human rights and the role of government. Should government have a role in assisting the needy, in providing social security, in legislating minimum wages, in fixing prices and putting a ceiling on rents, in curbing monopolies, in erecting tariffs, in guaranteeing jobs, in managing the money supply? To these and all similar questions the libertarian answers with an unequivocal no.

"But then you'd let people go hungry!" comes the rejoinder. This, the libertarian insists, is precisely what would not happen; with the restrictions removed, the economy would flourish as never before. With the controls taken off business, existing enterprises would expand and new ones would spring into existence satisfying more and more consumer needs; millions more people would be gainfully employed instead of subsisting on welfare, and all kinds of research and production, released from the stranglehold of government, would proliferate, fulfilling man's needs and desires as never before. It has always been so whenever government has permitted men to be free traders on a free market. But *why* this is so, and how the free market is the best solution to all problems relating to the material aspect of man's life, is another and far longer story.

Questions for Reflection

1. What basic principles of libertarianism are exemplified in your government? What practices of your government would violate libertarian principles?
2. What would the libertarian say about laws prohibiting the following activities: prostitution, recreational drug use, polygamy, pornography, and gambling? Do you agree with the libertarian position on each of these issues? What principles would you use to support your answer?
3. What would be the similarities and differences between Hospers's view of government and those of Mill or Marx, respectively, in the previous readings?
4. In John Rawls's famous thought experiment (reading 69), he asks us to imagine what it would be like in the "original position" and "behind the veil of ignorance." In other words, imagine that you did not know whether you would be born black or white, male or female, rich or poor, able-bodied or physically challenged. Supposing that you do not know what your situation in life will be, would you rationally choose to live in a libertarian society?
5. Do you agree with Hospers that a completely libertarian government would not only do away with the government-supported welfare system but would eliminate the need for one?

CONTEMPORARY APPLICATION: DOES THE GOVERNMENT HAVE A RIGHT TO PROTECT US FROM OURSELVES?

One does not have to look very long in browsing through newspaper or magazine articles before running across a reference to society's "drug problem." But what is the problem? Some view it along the lines of a medical problem, where the terminology of disease is employed with talk of "epidemics" and "therapies." Others view it as an issue in criminal justice and see it as a problem that needs to be addressed by police, legislators, and judges. In the following reading, James Q. Wilson refers to both of these approaches. However, in the next reading, Thomas Szasz questions whether there is a "problem" at all and views drug usage as a matter of personal morality, individual choices, and lifestyle preferences. Although the two writers have factual disagreements concerning the nature of drug addiction and its effects on society, the writers disagree the most concerning their respective political philosophies. At the heart of their disagreement are differing conceptions of the appropriate extent of individual liberty and governmental authority.

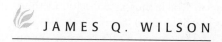

JAMES Q. WILSON

Drug Laws Constitute Justified Paternalism

James Q. Wilson is a professor emeritus of management and public policy at the University of California, Los Angeles. He is the author or coauthor of 12 books, including *Crime and Human Nature* and *The Moral Sense*. In 1972 he was appointed chairman of the National Advisory Council for Drug Abuse Prevention.

  In the following essay, Wilson argues that society has a moral obligation to its citizens to curtail the usage of drugs. He is concerned for the individual user, for he believes that using drugs like cocaine "alters one's soul" and "destroys the user's essential humanity." Hence, he adheres to a disease model of drug usage, referring to it as an "epidemic," and he views the addicts as victims, unable to control themselves, thus justifying paternalistic and therapeutic intervention on the part of society. But Wilson is also concerned about the consequences of drug usage for society at large, rejecting the argument that it harms only the user or that it is a "victimless crime." As you read this essay, see if you can discern the political philosophy underlying it and Wilson's view of the degree to which it is legitimate for the government to exercise its power over the lives of its citizens.

From James Q. Wilson, "Against the Legalization of Drugs," in *Commentary* (February 1990).

Reading Questions

1. What does Wilson think would have happened to heroin usage if we had followed Milton Friedman's advice?
2. What does Wilson think we can learn from Great Britain's experience?
3. What does he think of the claim that drug abuse is a "victimless crime"?
4. How does he answer the question, "Have we lost the war on drugs?"
5. Why does he think that the legalization of recreational drugs will not reduce crime?
6. What are some of the benefits of our current system of making drugs illegal? Why does Wilson think these outweigh the arguments for legalization?
7. What differences does Wilson find between the morality of tobacco addiction and cocaine addiction?
8. How does he respond to critics who claim that it is hypocritical to legalize alcohol but not heroin, cocaine, PCP, and marijuana?
9. How can science help us in coping with addiction?
10. In his closing remarks, why does he think there is less risk and more to gain in supposing he is right than in supposing he is wrong?

In 1972, the President appointed me chairman of the National Advisory Council for Drug Abuse Prevention. Created by Congress, the Council was charged with providing guidance on how best to coordinate the national war on drugs. (Yes, we called it a war then, too.) In those days, the drug we were chiefly concerned with was heroin. When I took office, heroin use had been increasing dramatically. Everybody was worried that this increase would continue. Such phrases as "heroin epidemic" were commonplace.

That same year, the eminent economist Milton Friedman published an essay in *Newsweek* in which he called for legalizing heroin. His argument was on two grounds: as a matter of ethics, the government has no right to tell people not to use heroin (or to drink or to commit suicide); as a matter of economics, the prohibition of drug use imposes costs on society that far exceed the benefits. Others, such as the psychoanalyst Thomas Szasz, made the same argument. . . .

RELIVING THE PAST

Suppose we had taken Friedman's advice in 1972. What would have happened? We cannot be entirely certain, but at a minimum we would have placed the young heroin addicts (and, above all, the prospective addicts) in a very different position from the one in which they actually found themselves. Heroin would have been legal. Its price would have been reduced by 95 percent (minus whatever we chose to recover in taxes). Now that it could be sold by the same people who make aspirin, its quality would have been assured—no poisons, no adulterants. Sterile hypodermic needles would have been readily available at the neighborhood drugstore, probably at the same counter where the heroin was sold. No need to travel to big cities or unfamiliar neighborhoods—heroin could have been purchased anywhere, perhaps by mail order.

There would no longer have been any financial or medical reason to avoid heroin use. Anybody could have afforded it. We might have tried to prevent children from buying it, but as we have learned from our efforts to prevent minors from buying alcohol and tobacco, young people have a way of penetrating markets theoretically reserved for adults. Returning Vietnam veterans would have discovered that Omaha and Raleigh had been converted into the pharmaceutical equivalent of Saigon.

Under these circumstances, can we doubt for a moment that heroin use would have grown exponentially? Or that a vastly larger supply of new users would have been recruited? . . .

But we need not rely on speculation, however plausible, that lowered prices and more abundant supplies would have increased heroin usage. Great Britain once followed such a policy and with almost exactly those results. Until the mid-1960's, British physicians were allowed to prescribe heroin to certain classes of addicts. (Possessing these drugs without a doctor's prescription remained a criminal offense.) For many years this policy worked well enough because the addict patients were typically middle-class people who had become dependent on opiate painkillers while undergoing hospital treatment. There was no drug culture. The British system worked for many years, not because it prevented drug abuse, but because there was no problem of drug abuse that would test the system.

All that changed in the 1960's. A few unscrupulous doctors began passing out heroin in wholesale amounts. One doctor prescribed almost 600,000 heroin tablets—that is, over thirteen pounds—in just one year. A youthful drug culture emerged with a demand for drugs far different from that of the older addicts. As a result, the British government required doctors to refer users to government-run clinics to receive their heroin.

But the shift to clinics did not curtail the growth in heroin use. Throughout the 1960's the number of addicts increased—the late John Kaplan of Stanford estimated by fivefold—in part as a result of the diversion of heroin from clinic patients to new users on the streets. An addict would bargain with the clinic doctor over how big a dose he would receive. The patient wanted as much as he could get, the doctor wanted to give as little as was needed. The patient had an advantage in this conflict because the doctor could not be certain how much was really needed. Many patients would use some of their "maintenance" dose and sell the remaining part to friends, thereby recruiting new addicts. As the clinics learned of this, they began to shift their treatment away from heroin and toward methadone, an addictive drug that, when taken orally, does not produce a "high" but will block the withdrawal pains associated with heroin abstinence.

Whether what happened in England in the 1960's was a mini-epidemic or an epidemic depends on whether one looks at numbers or at rates of change. Compared to the United States, the numbers were small. In 1960 there were 68 heroin addicts known to the British government; by 1968 there were 2,000 in treatment and many more who refused treatment. (They would refuse in part because they did not want to get methadone at a clinic if they could get heroin on the street.) Richard Hartnoll estimates that the actual number of addicts in England is five times the number officially registered. At a minimum, the number of British addicts increased by thirtyfold in ten years; the actual increase may have been much larger.

In the early 1980's the numbers began to rise again, and this time nobody doubted that a real epidemic was at hand. The increase was estimated to be 40 percent a year. By 1982 there were thought to be 20,000 heroin users in London alone. Geoffrey Pearson reports that many cities—Glasgow, Liverpool, Manchester, and Sheffield among them—were now experiencing a drug problem that once had been largely confined to London. The problem, again, was supply. The country was being flooded with cheap, high-quality heroin, first from Iran and then from Southeast Asia.

The United States began the 1960's with a much larger number of heroin addicts and probably a bigger at-risk population than was the case in Great Britain. Even though it would be foolhardy to suppose that the British system, if installed here, would have worked the same way or with the same results, it would be equally foolhardy to suppose that a combination of heroin available from leaky clinics and from street dealers who faced only minimal law-enforcement risks would not have produced a much greater increase in heroin use than we actually experienced. My guess is that if we had allowed either doctors or clinics to prescribe heroin, we would have had far worse results than were produced in Britain, if for no other reason than the vastly larger number of addicts with which we began. We would have had to find some way to police thousands (not scores) of physicians and hundreds (not dozens) of clinics. If the British civil service found it difficult to keep heroin in the hands of addicts and out of the hands of recruits when it was dealing with a few hundred people, how well would the American civil service have accomplished the same tasks when dealing with tens of thousands of people?

BACK TO THE FUTURE

Now cocaine, especially in its potent form, crack, is the focus of attention. Now as in 1972 the government is trying to reduce its use. Now as then some people are advocating legalization. Is there any more reason to yield to those arguments today than there was almost two decades ago?

I think not. If we had yielded in 1972 we almost certainly would have had today a permanent population of several million, not several hundred thousand, heroin addicts. If we yield now we will have a far more serious problem with cocaine.

Crack is worse than heroin by almost any measure. Heroin produces a pleasant drowsiness and, if hygienically administered, has only the physical side effects of constipation and sexual impotence. Regular heroin use incapacitates many users, especially poor ones, for any productive work or social responsibility. They will sit nodding on a street corner, helpless but at least harmless. By contrast, regular cocaine use leaves the user neither helpless nor harmless. When smoked (as with crack) or injected, cocaine produces instant, intense, and short-lived euphoria. The experience generates a powerful desire to repeat it. If the drug is readily available, repeat use will occur. Those people who progress to "bingeing" on cocaine become devoted to the drug and its effects to the exclusion of almost all other considerations—job, family, children, sleep, food, even sex. Dr. Frank Gawin at Yale and Dr. Everett Ellinwood at Duke report that a substantial percentage of all high-dose, binge users become uninhibited, impulsive, hypersexual, compulsive, irritable, and hyperactive. Their moods vacillate dramatically, leading at times to violence and homicide.

Women are much more likely to use crack than heroin, and if they are pregnant, the effects on their babies are tragic. Douglas Besharov, who has been following the effects of drugs on infants for twenty years, writes that nothing he learned about heroin prepared him for the devastation of cocaine. Cocaine harms the fetus and can lead to physical deformities or neurological damage. Some crack babies have for all practical purposes suffered a disabling stroke while still in the womb. The long-term consequences of this brain damage are lowered cognitive ability and the onset of mood disorders. Besharov estimates that about 30,000 to 50,000 such babies are born every year, about 7,000 in New York City alone. There may be ways to treat such infants, but from everything we now know the treatment will be long, difficult, and expensive. Worse, the mothers who are most likely to produce crack babies are precisely the ones who, because of poverty or temperament, are least able and willing to obtain such treatment. In fact, anecdotal evidence suggests that crack mothers are likely to abuse their infants.

The notion that abusing drugs such as cocaine is a "victimless crime" is not only absurd but dangerous. Even ignoring the fetal drug syndrome, crack-dependent people are, like heroin addicts, individuals who regularly victimize their children by neglect, their spouses by improvidence, their employers by lethargy, and their coworkers by carelessness. Society is not and could never be a collection of autonomous individuals. We all have a stake in ensuring that each of us displays a minimal level of dignity, responsibility, and empathy. We cannot, of course, coerce people into goodness, but we can and should insist that some standards must be met if society itself—on which the very existence of the human personality depends—is to persist. Drawing the line that defines those standards is difficult and contentious, but if crack and heroin use do not fall below it, what does? . . .

It is possible that some people will not become heavy users even when the drug is readily available in its most potent form. So far there are no scientific grounds for predicting who will and who will not become dependent. Neither socioeconomic background nor personality traits differentiate between casual and intensive users. Thus, the only way to settle the question of who is correct about the effect of easy availability on drug use, Nadelmann or Gawin and Ellinwood, is to try it and see. But that social experiment is so risky as to be no experiment at all, for if cocaine is legalized and if the rate of its abusive use increases dramatically, there is no way to put the genie back in the bottle, and it is not a kindly genie.

HAVE WE LOST?

Many people who agree that there are risks in legalizing cocaine or heroin still favor it because, they think, we have lost the war on drugs. "Nothing we have done has worked" and the current federal policy is just "more of the same." Whatever the costs of greater drug use, surely they would be less than the costs of our present, failed efforts.

That is exactly what I was told in 1972—and heroin is not quite as bad a drug as cocaine. We did not surrender and we did not lose. We did not win, either. What the nation accomplished then was what most efforts to save people from themselves accomplish: the problem was contained and the number of victims minimized, all at a considerable cost in law enforcement and increased crime. Was the cost worth it? I think so, but others may disagree. What are the lives of would-be addicts worth? I recall some people saying to me then, "Let them kill themselves." I was appalled. Happily, such views did not prevail.

Have we lost today? Not at all. High-rate cocaine use is not commonplace. The National Institute of Drug Abuse (NIDA) reports that less than 5 percent of high-school seniors used cocaine within the last thirty days. Of course this survey misses young people who have dropped out of school and miscounts those who lie on the questionnaire, but even if we inflate the NIDA estimate by some plausible percentage, it is still not much above 5 percent. Medical examiners reported in 1987 that about 1,500 died from cocaine use; hospital emergency rooms reported about 30,000 admissions related to cocaine abuse.

These are not small numbers, but neither are they evidence of a nationwide plague that threatens to engulf us all. Moreover, cities vary greatly in the proportion of people who are involved with co-

caine. To get city-level data we need to turn to drug tests carried out on arrested persons, who obviously are more likely to be drug users than the average citizen. The National Institute of Justice, through its Drug Use Forecasting (DUF) project, collects urinalysis data on arrestees in 22 cities. As we have already seen, opiate (chiefly heroin) use has been flat or declining in most of those cities over the last decade. Cocaine use has gone up sharply, but with great variation among cities. New York, Philadelphia, and Washington, D.C., all report that two-thirds or more of their arrestees tested positive for cocaine, but in Portland, San Antonio, and Indianapolis the percentage was one-third or less.

In some neighborhoods, of course, matters have reached crisis proportions. Gangs control the streets, shootings terrorize residents, and drug-dealing occurs in plain view. The police seem barely able to contain matters. But in these neighborhoods—unlike at Palo Alto cocktail parties—the people are not calling for legalization, they are calling for help. And often not much help has come. Many cities are willing to do almost anything about the drug problem except spend more money on it. The federal government cannot change that; only local voters and politicians can. It is not clear that they will.

It took about ten years to contain heroin. We have had experience with crack for only about three or four years. Each year we spend perhaps $11 billion on law enforcement (and some of that goes to deal with marijuana) and perhaps $2 billion on treatment. Large sums, but not sums that should lead anyone to say, "We just can't afford this any more."

The illegality of drugs increases crime, partly because some users turn to crime to pay for their habits, partly because some users are stimulated by certain drugs (such as crack or PCP) to act more violently or ruthlessly than they otherwise would, and partly because criminal organizations seeking to control drug supplies use force to manage their markets. These also are serious costs, but no one knows how much they would be reduced if drugs were legalized. Addicts would no longer steal to pay black-market prices for drugs, a real gain. But some, perhaps a great deal, of that gain would be offset by the great increase in the number of addicts. These people, nodding on heroin or living in the delusion-ridden high of cocaine, would hardly be ideal employees. Many would steal simply to support themselves, since snatch-and-grab, opportunistic crime can be managed even by people unable to hold a regular job or plan an elaborate crime. Those British addicts who get their supplies from government clinics are not models of law-abiding decency. Most are in crime, and though their per-capita rate of criminality may be lower thanks to the cheapness of their drugs, the total volume of crime they produce may be quite large. Of course, society could decide to support all unemployable addicts on welfare, but that would mean that gains from lowered rates of crime would have to be offset by large increases in welfare budgets.

Proponents of legalization claim that the costs of having more addicts around would be largely if not entirely offset by having more money available with which to treat and care for them. The money would come from taxes levied on the sale of heroin and cocaine.

To obtain this fiscal dividend, however, legalization's supporters must first solve an economic dilemma. If they want to raise a lot of money to pay for welfare and treatment, the tax rate on the drugs will have to be quite high. Even if they themselves do not want a high rate, the politicians' love of "sin taxes" would probably guarantee that it would be high anyway. But the higher the tax, the higher the price of the drug, and the higher the price the greater the likelihood that addicts will turn to crime to find the money for it and that criminal organizations will be formed to sell tax-free drugs at below-market rates. If we managed to keep taxes (and thus prices) low, we would get that much less money to pay for welfare and treatment and more people could afford to become addicts. There may be an optimal tax rate for drugs that maximizes revenue while minimizing crime, bootlegging, and the recruitment of new addicts, but our experience with alcohol does not suggest that we know how to find it.

THE BENEFITS OF ILLEGALITY

The advocates of legalization find nothing to be said in favor of the current system except, possibly, that it keeps the number of addicts smaller than it would otherwise be. In fact, the benefits are more substantial than that.

First, treatment. All the talk about providing "treatment on demand" implies that there is a demand for treatment. That is not quite right. There are some drug-dependent people who genuinely want treatment and will remain in it if offered; they should receive it. But there are far more who want only short-term help after a bad crash; once stabilized and bathed, they are back on the street again, hustling. And even many of the addicts who enroll in a program honestly wanting help drop out after a short while when they discover that help takes time and commitment. Drug-dependent people have very short time horizons and a weak capacity for commitment. These two groups—those looking for a quick fix and those unable to stick with a long-term fix—are not easily helped. Even if we increase the number of treatment slots—as we should—we would have to do something to make treatment more effective.

One thing that can often make it more effective is compulsion. Douglas Anglin of UCLA, in common with many other researchers, has found that the longer one stays in a treatment program, the better the chances of a reduction in drug dependency. But he, again like most other researchers, has found that drop-out rates are high. He has also found, however, that patients who enter treatment under legal compulsion stay in the program longer than those not subject to such pressure. His research on the California civil-commitment program, for example, found that heroin users involved with its required drug-testing program had over the long term a lower rate of heroin use than similar addicts who were free of such constraints. If for many addicts compulsion is a useful component of treatment, it is not clear how compulsion could be achieved in a society in which purchasing, possessing, and using the drug were legal. It could be managed, I suppose, but I would not want to have to answer the challenge from the American Civil Liberties Union that it is wrong to compel a person to undergo treatment for consuming a legal commodity.

Next, education. We are now investing substantially in drug-education programs in the schools. Though we do not yet know for certain what will work, there are some promising leads. But I wonder how credible such programs would be if they were aimed at dissuading children from doing something perfectly legal. We could, of course, treat drug education like smoking education: inhaling crack and inhaling tobacco are both legal, but you should not do it because it is bad for you. That tobacco is bad for you is easily shown; the Surgeon General has seen to that. But what do we say about crack? It is pleasurable, but devoting yourself to so much pleasure is not a good idea (though perfectly legal)? Unlike tobacco, cocaine will not give you cancer or emphysema, but it will lead you to neglect your duties to family, job, and neighborhood? Everybody is doing cocaine, but you should not?

Again, it might be possible under a legalized regime to have effective drug-prevention programs, but their effectiveness would depend heavily, I think, on first having decided that cocaine use, like tobacco use, is purely a matter of practical consequences; no fundamental moral significance attaches to either. But if we believe—as I do—that dependency on certain mind-altering drugs is a moral issue and that their illegality rests in part on their immorality, then legalizing them undercuts, if it does not eliminate altogether, the moral message.

That message is at the root of the distinction we now make between nicotine and cocaine. Both are highly addictive; both have harmful physical effects. But we treat the two drugs differently, not simply because nicotine is so widely used as to be beyond the reach of effective prohibition, but because its use does not destroy the user's essential humanity. Tobacco shortens one's life, cocaine debases it. Nicotine alters one's habits, cocaine alters one's soul. The heavy use of crack, unlike the heavy use of tobacco, corrodes those natural sentiments

of sympathy and duty that constitute our human nature and make possible our social life. To say, as does Nadelmann, that distinguishing morally between tobacco and cocaine is "little more than a transient prejudice" is close to saying that morality itself is but a prejudice.

THE ALCOHOL PROBLEM

Now we have arrived where many arguments about legalizing drugs begin: is there any reason to treat heroin and cocaine differently from the way we treat alcohol?

There is no easy answer to that question because, as with so many human problems, one cannot decide simply on the basis either of moral principles or of individual consequences; one has to temper any policy by a common-sense judgment of what is possible. Alcohol, like heroin, cocaine, PCP, and marijuana, is a drug—that is, a mood-altering substance—and consumed to excess it certainly has harmful consequences: auto accidents, barroom fights, bedroom shootings. It is also, for some people, addictive. We cannot confidently compare the addictive powers of these drugs, but the best evidence suggests that crack and heroin are much more addictive than alcohol.

Many people, Nadelmann included, argue that since the health and financial costs of alcohol abuse are so much higher than those of cocaine or heroin abuse, it is hypocritical folly to devote our efforts to preventing cocaine or drug use. But as Mark Kleiman of Harvard has pointed out, this comparison is quite misleading. What Nadelmann is doing is showing that a *legalized* drug (alcohol) produces greater social harm than *illegal* ones (cocaine and heroin). But of course. Suppose that in the 1920's we had made heroin and cocaine legal and alcohol illegal. Can anyone doubt that Nadelmann would now be writing that it is folly to continue our ban on alcohol because cocaine and heroin are so much more harmful?

And let there be no doubt about it—widespread heroin and cocaine use are associated with all manner of ills. Thomas Bewley found that the mortality rate of British heroin addicts in 1968 was 28 times as high as the death rate of the same age group of non-addicts, even though in England at the time an addict could obtain free or low-cost heroin and clean needles from British clinics. Perform the following mental experiment: suppose we legalized heroin and cocaine in this country. In what proportion of auto fatalities would the state police report that the driver was nodding off on heroin or recklessly driving on a coke high? In what proportion of spouse-assault and child-abuse cases would the local police report that crack was involved? In what proportion of industrial accidents would safety investigators report that the forklift or drill-press operator was in a drug-induced stupor or frenzy? We do not know exactly what the proportion would be, but anyone who asserts that it would not be much higher than it is now would have to believe that these drugs have little appeal except when they are illegal. And that is nonsense.

An advocate of legalization might concede that social harm—perhaps harm equivalent to that already produced by alcohol—would follow from making cocaine and heroin generally available. But at least, he might add, we would have the problem "out in the open" where it could be treated as a matter of "public health." That is well and good, *if* we knew how to treat—that is, cure—heroin and cocaine abuse. But we do not know how to do it for all the people who would need such help. We are having only limited success in coping with chronic alcoholics. Addictive behavior is immensely difficult to change, and the best methods for changing it—living in drug-free therapeutic communities, becoming faithful members of Alcoholics Anonymous or Narcotics Anonymous—require great personal commitment, a quality that is, alas, in short supply among the very persons—young people, disadvantaged people—who are often most at risk for addiction.

Suppose that today we had, not 15 million alcohol abusers, but half a million. Suppose that we already knew what we have learned from our long experience with the widespread use of alcohol. Would we make whiskey legal? I do not know, but I suspect there would be a lively debate. The Surgeon General would remind us of the risks alcohol poses to pregnant women. The National Highway Traffic Safety Administration would point to the likelihood of more highway fatalities caused by drunk drivers. The Food and Drug Administration might find that there is a nontrivial increase in cancer associated with alcohol consumption. At the same time the police would report great difficulty in keeping illegal whiskey out of our cities, officers being corrupted by bootleggers, and alcohol addicts often resorting to crime to feed their habit. Libertarians, for their part, would argue that every citizen has a right to drink anything he wishes and that drinking is, in any event, a "victimless crime."

However the debate might turn out, the central fact would be that the problem was still, at that point, a small one. The government cannot legislate away the addictive tendencies in all of us, nor can it remove completely even the most dangerous addictive substances. But it can cope with harms when the harms are still manageable.

SCIENCE AND ADDICTION

One advantage of containing a problem while it is still containable is that it buys time for science to learn more about it and perhaps to discover a cure. Almost unnoticed in the current debate over legalizing drugs is that basic science has made rapid strides in identifying the underlying neurological processes involved in some forms of addiction. Stimulants such as cocaine and amphetamines alter the way certain brain cells communicate with one another. That alteration is complex and not entirely understood, but in simplified form it involves modifying the way in which a neurotransmitter called dopamine sends signals from one cell to another.

When dopamine crosses the synapse between two cells, it is in effect carrying a message from the first cell to activate the second one. In certain parts of the brain that message is experienced as pleasure. After the message is delivered, the dopamine returns to the first cell. Cocaine apparently blocks this return, or "reuptake," so that the excited cell and others nearby continue to send pleasure messages. When the exaggerated high produced by cocaine-influenced dopamine finally ends, the brain cells may (in ways that are still a matter of dispute) suffer from an extreme lack of dopamine, thereby making the individual unable to experience any pleasure at all. This would explain why cocaine users often feel so depressed after enjoying the drug. Stimulants may also affect the way in which other neurotransmitters, such as serotonin and noradrenaline, operate.

Whatever the exact mechanism may be, once it is identified it becomes possible to use drugs to block either the effect of cocaine or its tendency to produce dependency. There have already been experiments using desipramine, imipramine, bromocriptine, carbamazepine, and other chemicals. There are some promising results.

Tragically, we spend very little on such research, and the agencies funding it have not in the past occupied very influential or visible posts in the federal bureaucracy. If there is one aspect of the "war on drugs" metaphor that I dislike, it is its tendency to focus attention almost exclusively on the troops in the trenches, whether engaged in enforcement or treatment, and away from the research-and-development efforts back on the home front where the war may ultimately be decided.

I believe that the prospects of scientists in controlling addiction will be strongly influenced by the size and character of the problem they face. If the problem is a few hundred thousand chronic, high-dose users of an illegal product, the chances of making a difference at a reasonable cost will be much greater than if the problem is a few million chronic users of legal substances. Once a drug is legal, not only will its use increase but many of those who then use it will prefer the drug to the treatment: they will want the pleasure, whatever the cost to themselves or their families, and they will resist—probably successfully—any effort to wean them away from experiencing the high that comes from inhaling a legal substance.

IF I AM WRONG . . .

No one can know what our society would be like if we changed the law to make access to cocaine, heroin, and PCP easier. I believe, for reasons given, that the result would be a sharp increase in use, a more widespread degradation of the human personality, and a greater rate of accidents and violence.

I may be wrong. If I am, then we will needlessly have incurred heavy costs in law enforcement and some forms of criminality. But if I am right, and the legalizers prevail anyway, then we will have consigned millions of people, hundreds of thousands of infants, and hundreds of neighborhoods to a life of oblivion and disease. To the lives and families destroyed by alcohol we will have added countless more destroyed by cocaine, heroin, PCP, and whatever else a basement scientist can invent.

Human character is formed by society; indeed, human character is inconceivable without society, and good character is less likely in a bad society. Will we, in the name of an abstract doctrine of radical individualism, and with the false comfort of suspect predictions, decide to take the chance that somehow individual decency can survive amid a more general level of degradation?

I think not. The American people are too wise for that, whatever the academic essayists and cocktail-party pundits may say. But if Americans today are less wise than I suppose, then Americans at some future time will look back on us now and wonder, what kind of people were they that they could have done such a thing?

Questions for Reflection

1. Wilson claims that a relevant difference between cocaine use and tobacco use is that cocaine "destroy's the user's essential humanity," while tobacco does not. Do you think, as he does, that the difference between these two addictions is a moral one and not simply a difference in their physical effects? Do you think that if he were consistent he should prohibit tobacco use as well? Or do you agree with him that, in spite

of the harmful effects of tobacco, there is a deep moral difference between tobacco use and cocaine use?

2. According to John Hospers's libertarianism (reading 70), making certain drugs illegal is a case of the government intruding upon our autonomy, trying to protect us from ourselves. Do you agree with Hospers or do you agree with Wilson that making drugs illegal is an appropriate use of the government's power?

3. A large part of Wilson's argument is based on his projections of the negative results of legalizing drugs. How plausible do you find his projections? How plausible do you find the projected benefits of legalizing drugs as envisioned by the advocates of this position?

    THOMAS SZASZ

People Should Be Free to Take Any Drug They Want

Thomas Szasz (1920–   ) is professor of psychiatry emeritus at the State University of New York Upstate Medical University. He is an internationally famous psychiatrist, libertarian activist, and philosopher of medicine who has published hundreds of articles as well as 25 books, including *The Myth of Mental Illness* and *The Manufacture of Madness.* Szasz is best known for arguing that what we call "mental illness" is really a social construct of the medical community and government to control, oppress, and manipulate people who do not conform to society's standards.

In the following essay, Szasz attempts to refute the arguments in favor of governmental paternalism and control with respect to drug usage or "self-medication." Rejecting the notion that drug addiction is a "disease" from which people must be "cured," Szasz argues that drug usage is a personal choice and that adults should be given the freedom to have control over their own lives, even when society deems those choices unwise. As you read his essay, try to formulate his political philosophy and his view of the limits of the government's authority.

Reading Questions

1. What is the definition of drug abuse according to the World Health Organization? Why does Szasz think that this definition illustrates the fact that the issue of drug abuse is a matter of moral judgment rather than a medical or technical issue?

From Thomas Szasz, "The Ethics of Addiction," *Harper's Magazine* (April 1972).

2. According to Szasz, what are the two reasons why the antidrug forces falsify the pharmacological facts about drugs?

3. Why does he reject the argument that drugs should be illegal because they are dangerous?

4. According to Szasz, what are the two reasons why people take drugs? Which reason does he think is the predominant one today? Why does he reject the notion that drug users are "sick" and need to be made "well"?

5. Even though Szasz rests his case for the legalization of drugs on moral and political grounds, what is his economic argument for this position?

6. What sorts of circumstances surrounding drug use does Szasz think are legitimate interests of the government?

7. What are the two methods of legitimizing policy in our society? Why does he think that both methods are arbitrary in making drugs illegitimate?

8. Why does Szasz think that his proposed medical reformation is similar to the Protestant Reformation?

9. How does Szasz argue that self-medication is a fundamental, American right, consistent with the Declaration of Independence and the Constitution?

10. What use does Szasz make of John Stuart Mill's philosophy in defending the legalization of drugs?

To avoid clichés about "drug abuse," let us analyze its official definition. According to the World Health Organization, "Drug addiction is a state of periodic or chronic intoxication detrimental to the individual and to society, produced by the repeated consumption of a drug (natural or synthetic). Its characteristics include: (1) an overpowering desire or need (compulsion) to continue taking the drug and to obtain it by any means, (2) a tendency to increase the dosage, and (3) a psychic (psychological) and sometimes physical dependence on the effects of the drug."

Since this definition hinges on the harm done to both the individual and society, it is clearly an ethical one. Moreover, by not specifying what is "detrimental," it consigns the problem of addiction to psychiatrists who define the patient's "dangerousness to himself and others."

Next, we come to the effort to obtain the addictive substance "by any means." This suggests that the substance must be prohibited, or is very expensive, and is hence difficult for the ordinary person to obtain (rather than that the person who wants it has an inordinate craving for it). If there were an abundant and inexpensive supply of what the "ad-

dict" wants, there would be no reason for him to go to "any means" to obtain it. Thus by the WHO's definition, one can be addicted only to a substance that is illegal or otherwise difficult to obtain. This surely removes the problem of addiction from the realm of medicine and psychiatry, and puts it squarely into that of morals and law.

In short, drug addiction or drug abuse cannot be defined without specifying the proper and improper uses of certain pharmacologically active agents. The regular administration of morphine by a physician to a patient dying of cancer is the paradigm of the proper use of a narcotic; whereas even its occasional self-administration by a physically healthy person for the purpose of "pharmacological pleasure" is the paradigm of drug abuse.

I submit that these judgments have nothing whatever to do with medicine, pharmacology, or psychiatry. They are moral judgments. Indeed, our present views on addiction are astonishingly similar to some of our former views on sex. Until recently, masturbation—or self-abuse, as it was called—was professionally declared, and popularly accepted, as both the cause and the symptom of a variety of illnesses. Even today, homosexuality—called a "sexual perversion"—is regarded as a disease by medical and psychiatric experts as well as by "well-informed" laymen.

To be sure, it is now virtually impossible to cite a contemporary medical authority to support the concept of self-abuse. Medical opinion holds that whether a person masturbates or not is medically irrelevant: and that engaging in the practice or refraining from it is a matter of personal morals or life-style. On the other hand, it is virtually impossible to cite a contemporary medical authority to oppose the concept of drug abuse. Medical opinion holds that drug abuse is a major medical, psychiatric, and public health problem; that drug addiction is a disease similar to diabetes, requiring prolonged (or lifelong) and careful, medically supervised treatment; and that taking or not taking drugs is primarily, if not solely, a matter of medical responsibility.

Thus the man on the street can only believe what he hears from all sides—that drug addiction is a disease, "like any other," which has now reached "epidemic proportions," and whose "medical" containment justifies the limitless expenditure of tax monies and the corresponding aggrandizement and enrichment of noble medical warriors against this "plague."

PROPAGANDA TO JUSTIFY PROHIBITION

Like any social policy, our drug laws may be examined from two entirely different points of view: technical and moral. Our present inclination is either to ignore the moral perspective or to mistake the technical for the moral.

Since most of the propagandists against drug abuse seek to justify certain repressive policies because of the alleged dangerousness of various drugs, they often falsify the facts about the true pharmacological properties of the drugs they seek to prohibit. They do so for two reasons: first, because many substances in daily use are just as harmful as the substances they want to prohibit; second, because they realize that dangerousness alone is

never a sufficiently persuasive argument to justify the prohibition of any drug, substance, or artifact. Accordingly, the more they ignore the moral dimensions of the problem, the more they must escalate their fraudulent claims about the dangers of drugs.

To be sure, some drugs are more dangerous than others. It is easier to kill oneself with heroin than with aspirin. But it is also easier to kill oneself by jumping off a high building than a low one. In the case of drugs, we regard their potentiality for self-injury as justification for their prohibition: in the case of buildings, we do not.

Furthermore, we systematically blur and confuse the two quite different ways in which narcotics may cause death: by a deliberate act of suicide or by accidental overdosage.

Every individual is capable of injuring or killing himself. This potentiality is a fundamental expression of human freedom. Self-destructive behavior may be regarded as sinful and penalized by means of informal sanctions. But it should not be regarded as a crime or (mental) disease, justifying or warranting the use of the police powers of the state for its control.

Therefore, it is absurd to deprive an adult of a drug (or of anything else) because he might use it to kill himself. To do so is to treat everyone the way institutional psychiatrists treat the so-called suicidal mental patient: they not only imprison such a person but take everything away from him—shoelaces, belts, razor blades, eating utensils, and so forth—until the "patient" lies naked on a mattress in a padded cell—lest he kill himself. The result is degrading tyrannization.

Death by accidental overdose is an altogether different matter. But can anyone doubt that this danger now looms so large precisely because the sale of narcotics and many other drugs is illegal? Those who buy illicit drugs cannot be sure what drug they are getting or how much of it. Free trade in drugs, with governmental action limited to safeguarding the purity of the product and the veracity of the labeling, would reduce the risk of accidental overdose with "dangerous drugs" to the same levels that prevail, and that we find acceptable, with respect to other chemical agents and physical artifacts that abound in our complex technological society.

This essay is not intended as an exposition on the pharmacological properties of narcotics and other mind-affecting drugs. However, I want to make it clear that in my view, *regardless* of their danger, all drugs should be "legalized" (a misleading term I employ reluctantly as a concession to common usage). Although I recognize that some drugs—notably heroin, the amphetamines, and LSD, among those now in vogue—may have undesirable or dangerous consequences, I favor free trade in drugs for the same reason the Founding Fathers favored free trade in ideas. In an open society, it is none of the government's business what idea a man puts into his mind; likewise, it should be none of the government's business what drug he puts into his body.

WITHDRAWAL PAINS
FROM TRADITION

It is a fundamental characteristic of human beings that they get used to things: one becomes habituated, or "addicted," not only to narcotics, but to cigarettes, cocktails before dinner, orange juice for breakfast, comic strips, and so forth. It is similarly a fundamental characteristic of living organisms that they acquire increasing tolerance to various chemical agents and physical stimuli: the first cigarette may cause nothing but nausea and headache; a year later, smoking three packs a day may be pure joy. Both alcohol and opiates are "addictive" in the sense that the more regularly they are used, the more the user craves them and the greater his tolerance for them becomes. Yet none of this involves any mysterious process of "getting hooked." It is simply an aspect of the universal biological propensity for *learning*, which is especially well developed in man. The opiate habit, like the cigarette habit or food habit, can be broken—and without any medical assistance—provided the person wants to break it. Often he doesn't. And why, indeed, should he, if he has nothing better to do with his life? Or, as hap-

pens to be the case with morphine, if he can live an essentially normal life while under the influence?

Actually, opium is much less toxic than alcohol. Just as it is possible to be an "alcoholic" and work and be productive, so it is (or, rather, it used to be) possible to be an opium addict and work and be productive. According to a definitive study published by the American Medical Association in 1929, ". . . morphine addiction is not characterized by physical deterioration or impairment of physical fitness . . . There is no evidence of change in the circulatory, hepatic, renal, or endocrine functions. When it is considered that these subjects had been addicted for at least five years, some of them for as long as twenty years, these negative observations are highly significant." In a 1928 study, Lawrence Kolb, an Assistant Surgeon General of the United States Public Health Service, found that of 119 persons addicted to opiates through medical practice, "90 had good industrial records and only 29 had poor ones . . . Judged by the output of labor and their own statements, none of the normal persons had [his] efficiency reduced by opium. Twenty-two of them worked regularly while taking opium for twenty-five years or more; one of them, a woman aged 81 and still alert mentally, had taken 3 grains of morphine daily for 65 years. [The usual therapeutic dose is one-quarter grain, three or four grains being fatal for the nonaddict.] She gave birth to and raised six children, and managed her household affairs with more than average efficiency. A widow, aged 66, had taken 17 grains of morphine daily for most of 37 years. She is alert mentally . . . does physical labor every day, and makes her own living."

I am not citing this evidence to recommend the opium habit. The point is that we must, in plain honesty, distinguish between pharmacological effects and personal inclinations. Some people take drugs to help them function and conform to social expectations; others take them for the very opposite reason, to ritualize their refusal to function and conform to social expectations. Much of the "drug abuse" we now witness—perhaps nearly all of it—is of the second type. But instead of acknowledging that "addicts" are unfit or unwilling to work and be "normal," we prefer to believe that they act as they do because certain drugs—especially heroin, LSD, and the amphetamines—make them "sick." If only we could get them "well," so runs this comforting view, they would become "productive" and "useful" citizens. To believe this is like believing that if an illiterate cigarette smoker would only stop smoking, he would become an Einstein. With a falsehood like this, one can go far. No wonder that politicians and psychiatrists love it.

The concept of free trade in drugs runs counter to our cherished notion that everyone must work and idleness is acceptable only under special conditions. In general, the obligation to work is greatest for healthy, adult, white men. We tolerate idleness on the part of children, women, Negroes, the aged, and the sick, and even accept the responsibility to support them. But the new wave of drug abuse affects mainly young adults, often white males, who are, in principle at least, capable of working and supporting themselves. But they refuse: they "drop out"; and in doing so, they challenge the most basic values of our society.

The fear that free trade in narcotics would result in vast masses of our population spending their days and nights smoking opium or mainlining heroin, rather than working and taking care of their responsibilities, is a bugaboo that does not deserve to be taken seriously. Habits of work and idleness are deep-seated cultural patterns. Free trade in abortions has not made an industrious people like the Japanese give up work for fornication. Nor would free trade in drugs convert such a people from hustlers to hippies. Indeed, I think the opposite might be the case: it is questionable whether, or for how long, a responsible people can tolerate being treated as totally irresponsible with respect to drugs and drug-taking. In other words, how long can we live with the inconsistency of being expected to be responsible for operating cars and computers, but not for operating our own bodies?

Although my argument about drug-taking is moral and political, and does not depend upon showing that free trade in drugs would also have fiscal advantages over our present policies, let me indicate briefly some of its economic implications.

The war on addiction is not only astronomically expensive; it is also counterproductive. On April 1, 1967, New York State's narcotics addiction control program, hailed as "the most massive ever tried in the nation," went into effect. "The program, which may cost up to $400 million in three years," reported *The New York Times,* "was hailed by Governor Rockefeller as 'the start of an unending war.'" Three years later, it was conservatively estimated that the number of addicts in the state had tripled or quadrupled. New York State Senator John Hughes reports that the cost of caring for each addict during this time was $12,000 per year (as against $4,000 per year for patients in state mental hospitals). It's been a great time, though, for some of the ex-addicts. In New York City's Addiction Services Agency, one ex-addict started at $6,500 a year in 1967, and was making $16,000 seven months later. Another started at $6,500 and soon rose to $18,100. The salaries of the medical bureaucrats in charge of these programs are similarly attractive. In short, the detection and rehabilitation of addicts is good business. We now know that the spread of witchcraft in the late Middle Ages was due more to the work of witchmongers than to the lure of witchcraft. Is it not possible that the spread of addiction in our day is due more to the work of addictmongers than to the lure of narcotics?

Let us see how far some of the monies spent on the war on addiction could go in supporting people who prefer to drop out of society and drug themselves. Their "habit" itself would cost next to nothing: free trade would bring the price of narcotics down to a negligible amount. During the 1969–70 fiscal year, the New York State Narcotics Addiction Control Commission had a budget of nearly $50 million, excluding capital construction. Using these figures as a tentative base for calculation, here is what we come to: $100 million will support 30,000 drug addicts at $3,300 per year. Since the population of New York State is roughly one-tenth that of the nation, if we multiply its operating budget for addiction control by ten, we arrive at a figure of $500 million, enough to support 150,000 addicts.

I am not advocating that we spend our hard-earned money in this way I am only trying to show that free trade in narcotics would be more economical for those of us who work, even if we had to support legions of addicts, than is our present program of trying to "cure" them. Moreover, I have not even made use, in my economic estimates, of the incalculable sums we would save by reducing crimes now engendered by the illegal traffic in drugs.

THE RIGHT OF SELF-MEDICATION

Clearly, the argument that marijuana—or heroin, methadone, or morphine—is prohibited because it is addictive or dangerous cannot be supported by facts. For one thing, there are many drugs, from insulin to penicillin, that are neither addictive nor dangerous but are nevertheless also prohibited; they can be obtained only through a physician's prescription. For another, there are many things, from dynamite to guns, that are much more dangerous than narcotics (especially to others) but are not prohibited. As everyone knows, it is still possible in the United States to walk into a store and walk out with a shotgun. We enjoy this right not because we believe that guns are safe but because we believe even more strongly that civil liberties are precious. At the same time, it is not possible in the United States to walk into a store and walk out with a bottle of barbiturates, codeine, or other drugs.

I believe that just as we regard freedom of speech and religion as fundamental rights, so we should also regard freedom of self-medication as a fundamental right. Like most rights, the right of self-medication should apply only to adults; and it should not be an unqualified right. Since these are important qualifications, it is necessary to specify their precise range.

John Stuart Mill said (approximately) that a person's right to swing his arm ends where his neighbor's nose begins. And Oliver Wendell Holmes said that no one has a right to shout "Fire!" in a crowded theater. Similarly, the limiting condition with respect to self-medication should be the inflicting of actual (as against symbolic) harm on others.

Our present practices with respect to alcohol embody and reflect this individualistic ethic. We have the right to buy, possess, and consume alcoholic beverages. Regardless of how offensive drunkenness might be to a person, he cannot interfere with another person's "right" to become inebriated so long as that person drinks in the privacy of his own home or at some other appropriate location, and so long as he conducts himself in an otherwise law-abiding manner. In short, we have a right to be intoxicated—in private. Public intoxication is considered an offense to others and is therefore a violation of the criminal law. It makes sense that what is "right" in one place may become, by virtue of its disruptive or disturbing effect on others, an offense somewhere else.

The right to self-medication should be hedged in by similar limits. Public intoxication, not only with alcohol but with any drug, should be an offense punishable by the criminal law. Furthermore, acts that may injure others—such as driving a car—should, when carried out in a drug-intoxicated state, be punished especially strictly and severely. The right to self-medication must thus entail unqualified responsibility for the effects of one's drug-intoxicated behavior on others. For unless we are willing to hold ourselves responsible for our own behavior, and hold others responsible for theirs, the liberty to use drugs (or to engage in other acts) degenerates into a license to hurt others.

Such, then, would be the situation of adults, if we regarded the freedom to take drugs as a fundamental right similar to the freedom to read and worship. What would be the situation of children? Since many people who are now said to be drug addicts or drug abusers are minors, it is especially important that we think clearly about this aspect of the problem.

I do not believe, and I do not advocate, that children should have a right to ingest, inject, or otherwise use any drug or substance they want. Children do not have the right to drive, drink, vote, marry, or make binding contracts. They acquire these rights at various ages, coming into their full possession at maturity, usually between the ages of eighteen and twenty-one. The right to self-medication should similarly be withheld until maturity.

In short, I suggest that "dangerous" drugs be treated, more or less, as alcohol is treated now. Neither the use of narcotics, nor their possession, should be prohibited, but only their sale to minors. Of course, this would result in the ready availability of all kinds of drugs among minors—though perhaps their availability would be no greater than it is now, but would only be more visible and hence more easily subject to proper controls. This arrangement would place responsibility for the use of all drugs by children where it belongs: on parents and their children. This is where the major responsibility rests for the use of alcohol. It is a tragic symptom of our refusal to take personal liberty and responsibility seriously that there appears to be no public desire to assume a similar stance toward other "dangerous" drugs.

Consider what would happen should a child bring a bottle of gin to school and get drunk there. Would the school authorities blame the local liquor stores as pushers? Or would they blame the parents and the child himself? There is liquor in practically every home in America and yet children rarely bring liquor to school. Whereas marijuana, Dexedrine, and heroin—substances children usually do not find at home and whose very possession is a criminal offense—frequently find their way into the school.

Our attitude toward sexual activity provides another model for our attitude toward drugs. Although we generally discourage children below a certain age from engaging in sexual activities with others, we do not prohibit such activities by law. What we do prohibit by law is the sexual seduction of children by adults. The "pharmacological seduction" of children by adults should be similarly punishable. In other words, adults who give or sell drugs to children should be regarded as offenders. Such a specific and limited prohibition—as against the kinds of generalized prohibitions that we had under the Volstead Act or have now with respect to countless drugs—would be relatively easy to enforce. Moreover, it would probably be rarely violated, for there would be little psychological interest and no economic profit in doing so.

THE TRUE FAITH: SCIENTIFIC MEDICINE

What I am suggesting is that while addiction is ostensibly a medical and pharmacological problem, actually it is a moral and political problem. We ought to know that there is no necessary connection between facts and values, between what is and what ought to be. Thus, objectively quite harmful acts, objects, or persons may be accepted and tolerated—by minimizing their dangerousness. Conversely, objectively quite harmless acts, objects, or persons may be prohibited and persecuted—by exaggerating their dangerousness. It is always necessary to distinguish—and especially so when dealing with social policy—between description and prescription, fact and rhetoric, truth and falsehood.

In our society, there are two principle methods of legitimizing policy: social tradition and scientific judgment. More than anything else, time is the supreme ethical arbiter. Whatever a social practice might be, if people engage in it, generation after generation, that practice becomes acceptable.

Many opponents of illegal drugs admit that nicotine may be more harmful to health than marijuana; nevertheless, they urge that smoking cigarettes should be legal but smoking marijuana should not be, because the former habit is socially accepted while the latter is not. This is a perfectly reasonable argument. But let us understand it for what it is—a plea for legitimizing old and accepted practices, and for illegitimizing novel and unaccepted ones. It is a justification that rests on precedent, not evidence.

The other method of legitimizing policy, ever more important in the modern world, is through the authority of science. In matters of health, a vast and increasingly elastic category, physicians play important roles as legitimizers and illegitimizers. This, in short, is why we regard being medicated by a doctor as drug use, and self-medication (especially with certain classes of drugs) as drug abuse.

This, too, is a perfectly reasonable arrangement. But we must understand that it is a plea for legitimizing what doctors do, because they do it with "good therapeutic" intent; and for illegitimizing what laymen do, because they do it with bad self-abusive ("masturbatory" or mind-altering) intent. This justification rests on the principles of professionalism, not of pharmacology. Hence we applaud the systematic medical use of methadone and call it "treatment for heroin addiction," but decry the occasional nonmedical use of marijuana and call it "dangerous drug abuse."

Our present concept of drug abuse articulates and symbolizes a fundamental policy of scientific medicine—namely, that a layman should not medicate his own body but should place its medical care under the supervision of a duly accredited physician. Before the Reformation, the practice of True Christianity rested on a similar policy—namely, that a layman should not himself commune with God but should place his spiritual care under the supervision of a duly accredited priest. The self-interests of the church and of medicine in such policies are obvious enough. What might be less obvious is the interest of the laity: by delegating responsibility for the spiritual and medical welfare of the people to a class of authoritatively accredited specialists, these policies—and the practices they ensure—relieve individuals from assuming the burdens of responsibility for themselves. As I see it, our present problems with drug use and drug abuse are just one of the consequences of our pervasive ambivalence about personal autonomy and responsibility.

I propose a medical reformation analogous to the Protestant Reformation: specifically, a "protest" against the systematic mystification of man's relationship to his body and his professionalized separation from it. The immediate aim of this reform would be to remove the physician as intermediary between man and his body and to give the layman direct access to the language and contents of the pharmacopoeia. If man had unencumbered access to his own body and the means of chemically altering it, it would spell the end of medicine, at least as we now know it. This is why, with faith in scientific medicine so strong, there is little interest in this kind of medical reform. Physicians fear the loss of their privileges: laymen, the loss of their protections.

Finally, since luckily we still do not live in the utopian perfection of "one world," our technical approach to the "drug problem" has led, and will undoubtedly continue to lead, to some curious attempts to combat it.

Here is one such attempt: the American government is now pressuring Turkey to restrict its farmers from growing poppies (the source of morphine and heroin). If turnabout is fair play, perhaps we should expect the Turkish government to pressure the United States to restrict its farmers from growing corn and wheat. Or should we assume that Muslims have enough self-control to leave alcohol alone, but Christians need all the controls that politicians, policemen, and physicians can bring to bear on them to enable them to leave opiates alone?

LIFE, LIBERTY, AND THE PURSUIT OF HIGHS

Sooner or later we shall have to confront the basic moral dilemma underlying this problem: does a person have the right to take a drug, any drug—not because he needs it to cure an illness, but because he wants to take it?

The Declaration of Independence speaks of our inalienable right to "life, liberty, and the pursuit of happiness." How are we to interpret this? By asserting that we ought to be free to pursue happiness by playing golf or watching television, but not by drinking alcohol, or smoking marijuana, or ingesting pep pills?

The Constitution and the Bill of Rights are silent on the subject of drugs. This would seem to imply that the adult citizen has, or ought to have, the right to medicate his own body as he sees fit. Were this not the case, why should there have been a need for a Constitutional Amendment to outlaw drinking? But if ingesting alcohol was, and is now again, a Constitutional right, is ingesting opium, or heroin, or barbiturates, or anything else, not also such a right? If it is, then the Harrison Narcotic Act is not only a bad law but is unconstitutional as well, because it prescribes in a legislative act what ought to be promulgated in a Constitutional Amendment.

The questions remain: as American citizens, should we have the right to take narcotics or other drugs? If we take drugs and conduct ourselves as responsible and law-abiding citizens, should we have a right to remain unmolested by the government? Lastly, if we take drugs and break the law, should we have a right to be treated as persons accused of crime, rather than as patients accused of mental illness?

These are fundamental questions that are conspicuous by their absence from all contemporary discussions of problems of drug addiction and drug abuse. The result is that instead of debating the use of drugs in moral and political terms, we define our task as the ostensibly narrow technical problem of protecting people from poisoning themselves with substances for whose use they cannot possibly assume responsibility. This, I think, best explains the frightening national consensus against personal responsibility for taking drugs and for one's conduct while under their influence. In 1965, for example, when President Johnson sought a bill imposing tight federal controls over pep pills and goof balls, the bill cleared the House by a unanimous vote, 402 to 0.

The failure of such measures to curb the "drug menace" has only served to inflame our legislators' enthusiasm for them. In October 1970 the Senate passed, again by a unanimous vote (54 to 0), "a major narcotics crackdown bill."

To me, unanimity on an issue as basic and complex as this means a complete evasion of the actual problem and an attempt to master it by attacking and over-powering a scapegoat—"dangerous drugs" and "drug abusers." There is an ominous resemblance between the unanimity with which all "reasonable" men—and especially politicians, physicians, and priests—formerly supported the protective measures of society against witches and Jews, and that with which they now support them against drug addicts and drug abusers.

After all is said and done, the issue comes down to whether we accept or reject the ethical principle John Stuart Mill so clearly enunciated: "The only purpose [he wrote in *On Liberty*] for which power can be rightfully exercised over any member of a civilized community, against his will, is to prevent harm to others. His own good, either physical or moral, is not a sufficient warrant. He cannot rightfully be compelled to do or forbear because it will make him happier, because in the opinion of others, to do so would be wise, or even right . . . In the part [of his conduct] which merely concerns himself, his independence is, of right, absolute. Over himself, over his own body and mind, the individual is sovereign."

By recognizing the problem of drug abuse for what it is—a moral and political question rather than a medical or therapeutic one—we can choose to maximize the sphere of action of the state at the expense of the individual, or of the individual at the expense of the state. In other words, we could commit ourselves to the view that the state, the representative of many, is more important than the individual; that it therefore has the right, indeed the duty, to regulate the life of the individual in the best interests of the group. Or we could commit ourselves to the view that individual dignity and liberty are the supreme values of life, and that the foremost duty of the state is to protect and promote these values.

In short, we must choose between the ethic of collectivism and individualism, and pay the price of either—or of both.

Questions for Reflection

1. How would James Q. Wilson (reading 71) respond to Szasz's argument? Whose arguments do you think are the strongest?
2. What does Szasz mean when he says the issue of drug usage is a moral and political one and not a medical or technical one? How does viewing the issue as a matter of moral judgment strengthen his case?

3. Szasz contrasts the relative legality of alcohol with the criminalization of drugs, claiming that these two policies are inconsistent and hypocritical. Do you agree?
4. Szasz thinks that the consequences to society of legalizing drugs would be minimal and even beneficial, while opponents (such as Wilson) think the consequences would be disastrous. Who do you think is right?

C H A P T E R   8

Postscript: What Is the Meaning of Life?

THE MEANING OF LIFE: WHAT ARE THE ISSUES?

Does life have meaning? If so, what is it? Almost everybody has tried their hand at a jigsaw puzzle at one time or another. Typically, the finished picture is represented on the cover of the box. This is helpful in solving the puzzle, for without a clue as to what you are working toward, the individual pieces are a chaotic and meaningless jumble of colors and shapes. Here is a piece that is blue. Is this the blue of a sky? Of the ocean? Is it part of a cluster of blueberries? Without the big picture, the individual pieces could represent almost anything. The same is true with our lives. Our lives are made up of fragments of experiences and events—some of them are joyous, some are tragic, but most are the mundane details of our daily routine. But do these pieces of our lives contribute to some overall meaning? Do they somehow fit into a bigger picture? What is the meaning of it all?

One way of answering the previous question is to ask, what is the purpose of my life? Or what is the purpose of human life in general? In many activities, an understanding of the purpose or the goal of the activity is important to understand what you are doing. For example, the purpose of football is to get the highest score possible. In contrast, the purpose of golf is to get the lowest score possible. If you were playing an unfamiliar game in which you moved pieces about the board but hadn't a clue as to what the purpose of the game was, you would be in the dark as to whether you were playing well or badly. That is why most philosophers as well as most ordinary people believe that worrying about the meaning of life is so important. Socrates, for one, pointed out that we are all engaged in particular pursuits. Some are artists, some are businesspeople, others are physicians, politicians, or shoemakers. Each particular craft or activity has its own goal and purpose. But Socrates believed that being a human being is itself an activity in which we are engaged. As with any of the other activities we engage in, we can either be excellent or do poorly in the job of being a human being. With respect to our lives, as with any activity, we need to have a clear conception of what human existence is all about. In the reading selections to follow, different philosophers will provide different answers as to the goal of life.

There seem to be two major approaches to the question of the meaning of life. First, (referring back to our jigsaw puzzle metaphor) some philosophers think that there is one grand picture into which the individual pieces of our lives can be fitted. They seek for the MEANING of life (in capital letters). Typically, this is the approach of most religious thinkers who believe that humans were brought into the world to serve some purpose. After all, if you observed an arrangement of colors on a canvas, you would ask "What does it mean?" only if you thought that some artist had purposely created it rather than it being the product of a random explosion of paint pigments. However, the search for some ultimate meaning is not confined exclusively to religious philosophers. There are some philosophers such as Plato or Aristotle who seek for the ultimate purpose of human life without referring to any divine purposes.

The second approach is taken by philosophers who think there is no ultimate meaning to the universe or human life. They see the pieces of our lives as fitting together in various ways to make many interesting and satisfying combinations but without supposing that there is one, pregiven picture that we were all intended to complete. These philosophers contend that life can be worth living in terms of the little meanings (small letters) that we find or create during our journey in life. The first approach says our lives will be meaningful only if we discover the purpose of life, while the second approach says we can live meaningful lives if we individually find purpose in our respective lives.

WHAT ARE MY OPTIONS CONCERNING THE MEANING OF LIFE?

Hedonism claims that the only thing in life that has value is pleasure. Almost everyone agrees that at least some pleasures are among the things in life that are good and worth pursuing for their own sake. Suppose, for example, I asked you why you were listening to a particular selection of music and you replied "I enjoy listening to this type of music." If I then asked you "Why do you do things you enjoy?," the question would make no sense, because the experience of pleasure is a basic good that needs no further justification. Even though everyone finds pleasurable experiences to be an important ingredient in life, what qualifies one as a hedonist is the claim that pleasure is the *only* thing that has value. The most plausible versions of hedonism are those that recognize that not all pleasures are equal in value, for some pleasures are followed by pain (e.g., an alcohol high that is followed by a hangover). Hence, the moderate or prudent hedonist would caution that we should be wise in discerning which pleasures lead to the most satisfying life in the long run, such as intellectual and aesthetic pleasures, and particularly the pleasures of a good friendship. In summary, the hedonist believes that life is meaningful if the sum of our experiences is more pleasurable than not.

Hedonism appeared among the early Greeks, but it is a philosophy that has found many supporters throughout the centuries. One of the most articulate versions of hedonism was developed by the 19th-century British utilitarians, Jeremy Bentham and John Stuart Mill (see reading 58). In the selections that follow, the Greek philosopher Epicurus will represent the voice of hedonism.

Stoicism is a philosophy that was founded by a philosopher in Athens named Zeno (who lived about 336 to 264 B.C.) The Stoics were rivals of the Epicurean hedonists. The Stoics taught that everything in the world is determined down to the smallest detail and events could not be any other way than they are. However, this is not a cold, blind, and impersonal determinism, for the Stoics also taught that the universe is a beautiful, purposeful system that flows from the being of a good and just God. If things are as they must be, and every event is contributing to the overall goodness and purpose of the whole, then the proper attitude toward life is to simply accept what comes our way and, thereby, achieve peace of mind. If everything has a good purpose and is determined, it is as foolish to say "I wish things had not turned out this way" as it is to say "I wish that 2 + 3 did not equal 5." Hence, for the Stoics, the emotions of desire, regret, or fear are irrational, for they assume that things could be different than they are. Even today, we say "Be stoical" when we are advising friends to resign themselves to circumstances they cannot change and to accept what life brings their way. If we achieve this attitude, then we will not be at the mercy of external circumstances, for our lives will be ruled from within. In summary, the meaning of life for the Stoics is to achieve peace of mind by accepting or being resigned to whatever may happen. In the readings, Stoicism will be represented by Epictetus, a former Greek slave in the ancient world.

Theism is the view that the world is governed by a benevolent God. The most influential versions of this worldview are Judaism, Christianity, Islam, and some forms of Hinduism. The theist believes that the world is more than simply a random collection of atoms in motion. Instead, according to the theist, the world was designed by a benevolent, intelligent, and all-powerful God and we humans were created for a purpose: to love and serve God. (Obviously, Stoicism is one version of theism, but they were discussed separately because not all theists would embrace the Stoics' emphasis on determinism and resignation.) The theist's answer to the meaning of life can be summarized by paraphrasing the 17th-century mathematician and philosopher Blaise Pascal: Every human heart contains the empty outline of true happiness—an infinite abyss that can only be filled with the infinite God. In the selection by the Christian writer Leo Tolstoy, he records his struggles to find meaning and how he filled the void Pascal describes.

Atheism is the view that there is no God. If atheism is true, then the human race is an anomalous collection of meaning-seeking creatures who were spewed up by an uncaring and meaningless universe. There is no ultimate meaning to the universe and no pregiven purpose to human life. Furthermore, there is no guarantee that goodness will triumph over evil and there is no hope of life after death. Daunting as all these conclusions may be, most atheists would say life can still be worth living if we give up our vain hopes, lower our expectations, and learn to make the best of things. There is no one "big" Meaning that drops out of the sky; instead, meaning comes in little packages. Meaning can be found in the warmth of a good friendship, in the fulfillment of a satisfying career, in the reward of seeing the world being made a little bit better through our efforts. Think of the sorts of experiences you sometimes have that make you say "This has been a good day!" The atheist might ask, "Can't a meaningful life be built on these sorts of experiences without there being some grandiose, cosmic meaning behind it all?" In the reading by Bertrand Russell, he urges us to bravely face a purposeless universe by uniting with our fellow human beings. In the end, we will have made the best of a grim situation if we are able to say that "we were ready with encouragement, with sympathy, with brave words in which high courage glowed."

Existentialism is a philosophical movement that arose in the 19th century in the writings of two disparate philosophers: Søren Kierkegaard (1813–1855), a passionate Christian, and Friedrich Nietzsche (1844–1900), an equally intense atheist. Their writings were not appreciated in their own time, but like intellectual time bombs, their ideas exploded in the 20th century, and existentialism came to have a wide-ranging influence in philosophy, theology, psychology, literature, and the arts.

Since individualism is one of the major themes of existentialism, there is no common list of doctrines to which all the existentialists subscribe. Nevertheless, some of the themes that are common to all existential thinkers are the priority of (1) subjective choosing over objective reasoning, (2) concrete experience over intellectual

	What Is the Human Condition?	What Is the Meaning of Life?
TABLE 8.1 FIVE ANSWERS CONCERNING THE MEANING OF LIFE		
Hedonism (Epicurus)	We and the rest of the world are made up of matter in motion, governed by pure randomness.	To enjoy life's simple pleasures and avoid pain.
Stoicism (Epictetus)	Everything that happens to us is determined and is as it was meant to be.	To find peace of mind by accepting whatever happens and cultivating an attitude of resignation.
Theism (Leo Tolstoy)	We were created by a benevolent God for a spiritual destiny and no earthly possession or accomplishment will leave us satisfied.	To have faith and be united with the infinite God, achieving the hope of eternal happiness.
Atheism (Bertrand Russell)	We live in a meaningless, purposeless universe that will eventually crush all human hopes and dreams.	To face life bravely, refusing to let our spirits be crushed, and bowing down to no power except our own human ideals and accomplishments, while bonding with our fellow human beings.
Atheistic Existentialism (Jean-Paul Sartre)	We have no pregiven meaning, purpose, or human nature, but we have the freedom to make choices and, thereby, to decide our own meaning.	We must accept the burden of our total freedom and acknowledge the lack of any guidance, and each of us must create our own meaning in ways that are responsible and authentic.

abstractions, (3) individuality over mass culture, (4) human freedom over determinism, and (5) authentic living over inauthenticity. In the final reading of this chapter, we will examine Jean-Paul Sartre's atheistic variety of existentialism. While his diagnosis of the human condition is similar to that of Russell, Sartre emphasizes that meaning is not something that we find, but something that each person must invent for himself or herself. Not only is there no one picture that would solve the jigsaw puzzle of life, but, for Sartre, it is as though the pieces are blank and we are painting their colors. To summarize Sartre's outlook, we have to decide on the meaning of our life's experiences and compose the big picture for ourselves.

Everyone who offers a solution to the meaning of life first presupposes a certain view of the universe and, specifically, a diagnosis of the human condition. Accordingly, Table 8.1 presents the positions represented in the readings and their answers concerning these two issues.

OPENING NARRATIVE: THE PROBLEM OF MEANING

W. H. AUDEN

The Unknown Citizen

W. H. Auden (1907–1973) was born in England and educated at Oxford University. He first achieved literary fame with his 1930 collection, *Poems*. In 1939 he moved to the United States and eventually became an American citizen. He is considered by many to be the greatest English poet of the 20th century and his work has exerted a major influence on succeeding generations of poets on both sides of the Atlantic.

Auden's poem "The Unknown Citizen" is a sarcastic view of modern life and provides an image of the "perfect citizen" from the standpoint of a government bureaucracy. The description of this citizen's life is filled with the details of a normal, average career. But something is missing. There is no sense of any significance or meaning that this life had. What did it all amount to? Is this all that life is about—having a job, having possessions, having the proper opinions? When someone sums up your life, what will be said? Will there be any guiding theme or overarching meaning to your life?

Reading Questions

1. On what basis did the government consider this citizen a "saint"? Is the meaning of the word trivialized here?
2. The account describes the citizen as "normal." From Auden's point of view, is this a compliment or a criticism?
3. As you read through this biography why does the citizen's life seem empty?

(To JS/07/M/378 This Marble Monument Is Erected by the State)
He was found by the Bureau of Statistics to be
One against whom there was no official complaint,
And all the reports on his conduct agree
That, in the modern sense of an old-fashioned word, he was a saint,
For in everything he did he served the Greater Community.
Except for the War till the day he retired
He worked in a factory and never got fired,
But satisfied his employers, Fudge Motors Inc.

Yet he wasn't a scab or odd in his views,
For his Union reports that he paid his dues,
(Our report on his Union shows it was sound)
And our Social Psychology workers found
That he was popular with his mates and liked a drink.
The Press are convinced that he bought a paper every day
And that his reactions to advertisements were normal in every way.
Policies taken out in his name prove that he was fully insured,

---

From W. H. Auden, "The Unknown Citizen," in *Collected Shorter Poems 1927–1957* (New York: Random House, 1966).

And his Health-card shows he was once in a hospital but left it cured.

Both Producers Research and High-Grade Living declare

He was fully sensible to the advantages of the Installment Plan

And had everything necessary to the Modern Man,

A phonograph, a radio, a car and a frigidaire.

Our researchers into Public Opinion are content

That he held the proper opinions for the time of year;

When there was peace, he was for peace: when there was war, he went.

He was married and added five children to the population,

Which our Eugenist says was the right number for a parent of his generation.

And our teachers report that he never interfered with their education.

Was he free? Was he happy? The question is absurd:

Had anything been wrong, we should certainly have heard.

Questions for Reflection

1. If someone were to write your obituary, what would they say? Besides the facts and details concerning your life, what would you want someone to say about you?
2. If the citizen in the poem were to say to you, "I have done well in my career and achieved the approval of my society, but I keep wondering, is this enough?," how would you reply to him?

ALTERNATIVE VISIONS OF LIFE

 EPICURUS

Moderate Hedonism—Enjoy Life's Simple Pleasures

Epicurus (341–270 B.C.) was born seven years after Plato's death. By the time he had reached his mid-30s, he had achieved fame for the philosophy and the way of life that he taught. He purchased a garden at the edge of Athens where he created a very close-knit philosophical commune. The Garden (as the school was called) attracted many followers and was open to all people, the community being made up of both men and women, and included children, slaves, soldiers, and courtesans as well as prominent citizens. Epicurus was noted for his warm affection for his followers, who in turn were deeply devoted to him. Epicureanism proved a very attractive philosophy, and with mis-

---

From Epicurus, *Letter to Menoeceus,* translated by Robert Drew Hicks (1925).

sionary zeal its adherents made so many converts that the philosophy rapidly permeated the Greek-speaking world. The successors of Epicurus made very few changes to his doctrines because the philosophy was taught by means of a catechism (a form of memorized teachings common among religious groups).

Epicurus was a materialist, believing that all reality (including the human soul) was made up of physical atoms. Consequently, he discussed ethical concepts in terms of sensations and psychological states. More specifically, he identified good with pleasure and evil with pain. This position is known as **hedonism** (from the Greek word for pleasure). We encountered this position previously in the utilitarian ethics of John Stuart Mill (reading 58). Most people would say that pleasure is good, but what makes one a hedonist is the more exclusive claim that "pleasure is the only thing that is intrinsically good." Because of Epicurus's emphasis on pleasure, "Epicureanism" has come to be associated with living life in the fast lane or a devotion to gourmet foods, strong drink, and other sensuous, luxurious pleasures. As you read Epicurus's own words, decide for yourself whether this is an accurate characterization of his philosophy.

Reading Questions

1. What does Epicurus say about popular notions of the gods?
2. What should be our attitude toward death? What reasons does he give for his view? Do you agree with his argument?
3. How does Epicurus classify the desires? Make a chart corresponding to his remarks and think of examples of each category.
4. Since pleasure is good, why does he say that some pleasures should not be chosen? Since all pain is evil, why does he say that some pains should not be avoided? Based on Epicurus's reasoning, provide examples of pleasures that should be avoided and pains that should not be avoided.
5. Make a list of all the varieties of pleasures Epicurus values the highest. Given this list, how accurate is the view that Epicureanism is the philosophy that advises us to "eat, drink, and be merry"?

Let no one be slow to seek wisdom when he is young nor weary in the search thereof when he is grown old. For no age is too early or too late for the health of the soul. And to say that the season for studying philosophy has not yet come, or that it is past and gone, is like saying that the season for happiness is not yet or that it is now no more. Therefore, both old and young ought to seek wisdom, the former in order that, as age comes over him, he may be young in good things because of the grace of what has been, and the latter in order that, while he is young, he may at the same time be old, because he has no fear of the things which are to come. So we must exercise ourselves in the things which bring happiness, since, if that be present, we have everything, and, if that be absent, all our actions are directed toward attaining it.

Those things which without ceasing I have declared to you, those do, and exercise yourself in those, holding them to be the elements of right life. First believe that God is a living being immortal and happy, according to the notion of a god indicated by the common sense of humankind; and so believing, you shall not affirm of him anything that is foreign to his immortality or that is repugnant to his blessedness. Believe about him whatever may uphold both his blessedness and his immortality. For truly there are gods, and knowledge of them is evident; but they are not such as the multitude believe, seeing that people do not steadfastly maintain the notions they form respecting them. Not the person who denies the gods worshiped by the multitude, but he who affirms of the gods what the multitude believes about them is truly impious. For the utterances of the multitude about the gods are not true preconceptions but false assumptions; hence it is that the greatest evils happen to the wicked and the greatest blessings happen to the good from the hand of the gods, seeing that they are always favorable to their own good qualities and take pleasure in people like to themselves, but reject as alien whatever is not of their kind.

Accustom yourself to believe that death is nothing to us, for good and evil imply awareness, and death is the privation of all awareness; therefore a right understanding that death is nothing to us makes the mortality of life enjoyable, not by adding to life an unlimited time, but by taking away the yearning after immortality. For life has no terror; for those who thoroughly apprehend that there are no terrors for them in ceasing to live. Foolish, therefore, is the person who says that he fears death, not because it will pain when it comes, but because it pains in the prospect. Whatever causes no annoyance when it is present, causes only a groundless pain in the expectation. Death, therefore, the most awful of evils, is nothing to us, seeing that, when we are, death is not come, and, when death is come, we are not. It is nothing, then, either to the living or to the dead, for with the living it is not and the dead exist no longer. But in the world, at one time people shun death as the greatest of all evils, and at another time choose it as a respite from the evils in life. The wise person does not deprecate life nor does he fear the cessation of life. The thought of life is no offense to him, nor is the cessation of life regarded as an evil. And even as people choose of food not merely and simply the larger portion, but the more pleasant, so the wise seek to enjoy the time which is most pleasant and not merely that which is longest. And he who admonishes the young to live well and the old to make a good end speaks foolishly, not merely because of the desirability of life, but because the same exercise at once teaches to live well and to die

well. Much worse is he who says that it were good not to be born, but when once one is born to pass with all speed through the gates of Hades. For if he truly believes this, why does he not depart from life? It were easy for him to do so, if once he were firmly convinced. If he speaks only in mockery, his words are foolishness, for those who hear believe him not.

We must remember that the future is neither wholly ours nor wholly not ours, so that neither must we count upon it as quite certain to come nor despair of it as quite certain not to come.

We must also reflect that of desires some are natural, others are groundless; and that of the natural some are necessary as well as natural, and some natural only. And of the necessary desires some are necessary if we are to be happy, some if the body is to be rid of uneasiness, some if we are even to live. He who has a clear and certain understanding of these things will direct every preference and aversion toward securing health of body and tranquility of mind, seeing that this is the sum and end of a happy life. For the end of all our actions is to be free from pain and fear, and, when once we have attained all this, the tempest of the soul is laid; seeing that the living creature has no need to go in search of something that is lacking, nor to look for anything else by which the good of the soul and of the body will be fulfilled. When we are pained because of the absence of pleasure, then, and then only, do we feel the need of pleasure. For this reason we call pleasure the alpha and omega of a happy life. Pleasure is our first and kindred good. It is the starting-point of every choice and of every aversion, and to it we come back, inasmuch as we make feeling the rule by which to judge of every good thing. And since pleasure is our first and native good, for that reason we do not choose every pleasure whatever, but often pass over many pleasures when a greater annoyance ensues from them. And often we consider pains superior to pleasures when submission to the pains for a long time brings us as a consequence a greater pleasure. While therefore all pleasure because it is naturally akin to us is good, not all pleasure is worthy of choice, just as all pain is an evil and yet not all pain is to be shunned. It is, however, by measuring one against another, and by looking at the conveniences and inconveniences, that all these matters must be judged. Sometimes we treat the good as an evil, and the evil, on the contrary, as a good. Again, we regard independence of outward things as a great good, not so as in all cases to use little, but so as to be contented with little if we have not much, being honestly persuaded that they have the sweetest enjoyment of luxury who stand least in need of it, and that whatever is natural is easily procured and only the vain and worthless hard to win. Plain fare gives as much pleasure as a costly diet, when once the pain of want has been removed, while bread and water confer the highest possible pleasure when they are brought to hungry lips. To habituate one's self therefore, to a simple and inexpensive diet supplies all that is needful for health, and enables a person to meet the necessary requirements of life without shrinking and it places us in a better condition when we approach at intervals a costly fare and renders us fearless of fortune.

When we say, then, that pleasure is the end and aim, we do not mean the pleasures of the prodigal or the pleasures of sensuality, as we are understood to do by some through ignorance, prejudice, or willful misrepresentation. By pleasure we mean the absence of pain in the body and of trouble in the soul. It is not an unbroken succession of drinking-bouts and of merrymaking, not sexual love, not the enjoyment of the fish and other delicacies of a luxurious table, which produce a pleasant life; it is sober reasoning, searching out the grounds of every choice and avoidance, and banishing those beliefs through which the greatest disturbances take possession of the soul. Of all this the beginning and the greatest good is prudence. For this reason prudence is a more precious thing even than the other virtues, for one cannot lead a life of pleasure which is not also a life of prudence, honor, and justice; nor lead a life of prudence, honor, and justice, which is not also a life of pleasure. For the virtues have grown into one with a pleasant life, and a pleasant life is inseparable from them.

Who, then, is superior in your judgment to such a person? He holds a holy belief concerning the gods, and is altogether free from the fear of death. He has diligently considered the end fixed by nature, and understands how easily the limit of good things can be reached and attained, and how either the duration or the intensity of evils is but slight. Destiny which some introduce as sovereign over all things, he laughs to scorn, affirming rather that some things happen of necessity, others by chance, others through our own agency. For he sees that necessity destroys responsibility and that chance or fortune is inconstant; whereas our own actions are free, and it is to them that praise and blame naturally attach. It were better, indeed, to accept the legends of the gods than to bow beneath destiny which the natural philosophers have imposed. The one holds out some faint hope that we may escape if we honor the gods, while the necessity of the naturalists is deaf to all entreaties. Nor does he hold chance to be a god, as the world in general does, for in the acts of a god there is no disorder; nor to be a cause, though an uncertain one, for he believes that no good or evil is dispensed by chance to people so as to make life happy, though it supplies the starting-point of great good and great evil. He believes that the misfortune of the wise is better than the prosperity of the fool. It is better, in short, that what is well judged in action should not owe its successful issue to the aid of chance.

Exercise yourself in these and kindred precepts day and night, both by yourself and with him who is like to you; then never, either in waking or in dream, will you be disturbed, but will live as a god among people. For people lose all appearance of mortality by living in the midst of immortal blessings.

Questions for Reflection

1. In what ways does your lifestyle conform to Epicurus's vision of life? Is there anything about your lifestyle Epicurus might criticize? Concerning the points on which you disagree, how would you respond to Epicurus?

2. Epicurus's philosophy is a moderate version of hedonism. Hedonism claims that, in the final analysis, "*only* pleasure is good." Do you think this is a plausible claim? Can you think of something that you label as "good" that could not be plausibly thought of as a type of pleasure itself or something that leads to pleasure? If you can think of such an example, how might Epicurus respond?

3. We typically think of "pleasure" as referring specifically to sensory pleasures. In what ways does Epicurus provide a much broader understanding of pleasure beyond simply physical sensations?

4. According to your own account, what role should pleasure play in a life that is lived well?

EPICTETUS

Stoicism—Take Things As They Come

Epictetus (around 50–138), was an enormously influential teacher of Stocism. He was born a Greek slave in Asia Minor but was brought to Rome by his master. He was crippled in slavery (some say from abuse) and was lame the rest of his life. While still a slave, he was given the opportunity to study with one of the leading Stoics of the time. As a result of his instruction in Stoicism and, perhaps, in response to his infirmity, Epictetus's motto was "Bear and forbear." Sometime after the death of the Roman Emperor Nero in 68, Epictetus was given his freedom. Around the year 89, he and other philosophers in Rome were banished from Rome by the Emperor Domitian. Epictetus went to the northwestern part of Greece where he opened his own school. He became quite famous in his own time and his school flourished, attracting many upper-class Romans. Like Socrates, he did not publish anything, but his student Flavius Arrianus recorded his teachings, which include *The Discourses* and the *Enchiridion* (which means "The Manual"). Epictetus's Stoical philosophy can best be summarized in his own words from the *Enchiridion* selection that follows: "Don't demand that things happen as you wish, but wish that they happen as they do happen, and you will go on well."

Reading Questions

1. What sorts of things are in our control and what are not in our control? Why is it important to keep this distinction in mind?

2. What is the problem with having desires? What advice does Epictetus give us concerning desires?

From Epictetus, *Enchiridion,* translated by Elizabeth Carter (1758).

3. What does Epictetus mean when he says that it is not things that disturb us but the notions we form of things? He uses death as an example, but can you think of other examples?
4. What should be our attitude toward sickness, lameness, accidental events, and losses?
5. What does Epictetus mean when he says "you must behave in life as at a dinner party"?
6. What is Epictetus's attitude toward the body and bodily pleasures?
7. This essay could be given the title "Instructions on How to Be Free." What is Epictetus's notion of freedom? How are we to attain true freedom?

---

1. Some things are in our control and others not. Things in our control are opinion, pursuit, desire, aversion, and, in a word, whatever are our own actions. Things not in our control are body, property, reputation, command, and, in one word, whatever are not our own actions.

The things in our control are by nature free, unrestrained, unhindered; but those not in our control are weak, slavish, restrained, belonging to others. Remember, then, that if you suppose that things which are slavish by nature are also free, and that what belongs to others is your own, then you will be hindered. You will lament, you will be disturbed, and you will find fault both with gods and men. But if you suppose that only to be your own which is your own, and what belongs to others such as it really is, then no one will ever compel you or restrain you. Further, you will find fault with no one or accuse no one. You will do nothing against your will. No one will hurt you, you will have no enemies, and you will not be harmed.

Aiming therefore at such great things, remember that you must not allow yourself to be carried, even with a slight tendency, towards the attainment of lesser things. Instead, you must entirely quit some things and for the present postpone the rest. But if you would both have these great things, along with power and riches, then you will not gain even the latter, because you aim at the former too: but you will absolutely fail of the former, by which alone happiness and freedom are achieved.

Work, therefore to be able to say to every harsh appearance, "You are but an appearance, and not absolutely the thing you appear to be." And then examine it by those rules which you have, and first,

and chiefly, by this: whether it concerns the things which are in our own control, or those which are not; and, if it concerns anything not in our control, be prepared to say that it is nothing to you.

2. Remember that following desire promises the attainment of that of which you are desirous; and aversion promises the avoiding that to which you are averse. However, he who fails to obtain the object of his desire is disappointed, and he who incurs the object of his aversion wretched. If, then, you confine your aversion to those objects only which are contrary to the natural use of your faculties, which you have in your own control, you will never incur anything to which you are averse. But if you are averse to sickness, or death, or poverty, you will be wretched. Remove aversion, then, from all things that are not in our control, and transfer it to things contrary to the nature of what is in our control. But, for the present, totally suppress desire: for, if you desire any of the things which are not in your own control, you must necessarily be disappointed; and of those which are, and which it would be laudable to desire, nothing is yet in your possession. Use only the appropriate actions of pursuit and avoidance; and even these lightly, and with gentleness and reservation.

3. With regard to whatever objects give you delight, are useful, or are deeply loved, remember to tell yourself of what general nature they are, beginning from the most insignificant things. If, for example, you are fond of a specific ceramic cup, remind yourself that it is only ceramic cups in general of which you are fond. Then, if it breaks, you will not be disturbed. If you kiss your child, or your

wife, say that you only kiss things which are human, and thus you will not be disturbed if either of them dies. . . .

5. Men are disturbed, not by things, but by the principles and notions which they form concerning things. Death, for instance, is not terrible, else it would have appeared so to Socrates. But the terror consists in our notion of death that it is terrible. When therefore we are hindered, or disturbed, or grieved, let us never attribute it to others, but to ourselves; that is, to our own principles. An uninstructed person will lay the fault of his own bad condition upon others. Someone just starting instruction will lay the fault on himself. Someone who is perfectly instructed will place blame neither on others nor on himself.

6. Don't be prideful with any excellence that is not your own. If a horse should be prideful and say, "I am handsome," it would be supportable. But when you are prideful, and say, "I have a handsome horse," know that you are proud of what is, in fact, only the good of the horse. What, then, is your own? Only your reaction to the appearances of things. Thus, when you behave conformably to nature in reaction to how things appear, you will be proud with reason; for you will take pride in some good of your own. . . .

8. Don't demand that things happen as you wish, but wish that they happen as they do happen, and you will go on well.

9. Sickness is a hindrance to the body, but not to your ability to choose, unless that is your choice. Lameness is a hindrance to the leg, but not to your ability to choose. Say this to yourself with regard to everything that happens, then you will see such obstacles as hindrances to something else, but not to yourself.

10. With every accident, ask yourself what abilities you have for making a proper use of it. If you see an attractive person, you will find that self-restraint is the ability you have against your desire. If you are in pain, you will find fortitude. If you hear unpleasant language, you will find patience. And thus habituated, the appearances of things will not hurry you away along with them.

11. Never say of anything, "I have lost it," but "I have returned it." Is your child dead? It is returned. Is your wife dead? She is returned. Is your estate taken away? Well, and is not that likewise returned? "But he who took it away is a bad man." What difference is it to you who the giver assigns to take it back? While he gives it to you to possess, take care of it; but don't view it as your own, just as travelers view a hotel.

12. If you want to improve, reject such reasonings as these: "If I neglect my affairs, I'll have no income; if I don't correct my servant, he will be bad." For it is better to die with hunger, exempt from grief and fear, than to live in affluence with perturbation; and it is better your servant should be bad, than you unhappy.

Begin therefore from little things. Is a little oil spilt? A little wine stolen? Say to yourself, "This is the price paid for apathy, for tranquillity, and nothing is to be had for nothing." When you call your servant, it is possible that he may not come; or, if he does, he may not do what you want. But he is by no means of such importance that it should be in his power to give you any disturbance.

13. If you want to improve, be content to be thought foolish and stupid with regard to external things. Don't wish to be thought to know anything; and even if you appear to be somebody important to others, distrust yourself. For it is difficult to both keep your faculty of choice in a state conformable to nature, and at the same time acquire external things. But while you are careful about the one, you must of necessity neglect the other.

14. If you wish your children, and your wife, and your friends to live for ever, you are stupid; for you wish to be in control of things which you cannot, you wish for things that belong to others to be your own. So likewise, if you wish your servant to be without fault, you are a fool; for you wish vice not to be vice, but something else. But, if you wish to have your desires undisappointed, this is in your own control. Exercise, therefore, what is in your control. He is the master of every other person who is able to confer or remove whatever that person wishes either to have or to avoid. Whoever, then,

would be free, let him wish nothing, let him decline nothing, which depends on others else he must necessarily be a slave.

15. Remember that you must behave in life as at a dinner party. Is anything brought around to you? Put out your hand and take your share with moderation. Does it pass by you? Don't stop it. Is it not yet come? Don't stretch your desire towards it, but wait till it reaches you. Do this with regard to children, to a wife, to public posts, to riches, and you will eventually be a worthy partner of the feasts of the gods. And if you don't even take the things which are set before you, but are able even to reject them, then you will not only be a partner at the feasts of the gods, but also of their empire. For, by doing this, Diogenes, Heraclitus and others like them, deservedly became, and were called, divine.

16. When you see anyone weeping in grief because his son has gone abroad, or is dead, or because he has suffered in his affairs, be careful that the appearance may not misdirect you. Instead, distinguish within your own mind, and be prepared to say, "It's not the accident that distresses this person, because it doesn't distress another person; it is the judgment which he makes about it." As far as words go, however, don't reduce yourself to his level, and certainly do not moan with him. Do not moan inwardly either.

17. Remember that you are an actor in a drama, of such a kind as the author pleases to make it. If short, of a short one; if long, of a long one. If it is his pleasure you should act a poor man, a cripple, a governor, or a private person, see that you act it naturally. For this is your business, to act well the character assigned you; to choose it is another's. . . .

19. You may be unconquerable, if you enter into no combat in which it is not in your own control to conquer. When, therefore, you see anyone eminent in honors, or power, or in high esteem on any other account, take heed not to be hurried away with the appearance, and to pronounce him happy; for, if the essence of good consists in things in our own control, there will be no room for envy or emulation. But, for your part, don't wish to be a general, or a senator, or a consul, but to be free; and the only way to this is a contempt of things not in our own control.

20. Remember, that not he who gives ill language or a blow insults, but the principle which represents these things as insulting. When, therefore, anyone provokes you, be assured that it is your own opinion which provokes you. Try, therefore, in the first place, not to be hurried away with the appearance. For if you once gain time and respite, you will more easily command yourself. . . .

22. If you have an earnest desire of attaining to philosophy, prepare yourself from the very first to be laughed at, to be sneered by the multitude, to hear them say,." He is returned to us a philosopher all at once," and " Whence this supercilious look?" Now, for your part, don't have a supercilious look indeed; but keep steadily to those things which appear best to you as one appointed by God to this station. For remember that, if you adhere to the same point, those very persons who at first ridiculed will afterwards admire you. But if you are conquered by them, you will incur a double ridicule.

23. If you ever happen to turn your attention to externals, so as to wish to please anyone, be assured that you have ruined your scheme of life. Be contented, then, in everything with being a philosopher; and, if you wish to be thought so likewise by anyone, appear so to yourself, and it will suffice you. . . .

29. In every affair consider what precedes and follows, and then undertake it. Otherwise you will begin with spirit; but not having thought of the consequences, when some of them appear you will shamefully desist. "I would conquer at the Olympic games." But consider what precedes and follows, and then, if it is for your advantage, engage in the affair. You must conform to rules, submit to a diet, refrain from [pastries]; exercise your body, whether you choose it or not, at a stated hour, in heat and cold; you must drink no cold water, nor sometimes even wine. In a word, you must give yourself up to your master, as to a physician. Then, in the combat, you may be thrown into a ditch,

dislocate your arm, turn your ankle, swallow dust, be whipped, and, after all, lose the victory. When you have evaluated all this, if your inclination still holds, then go to war. Otherwise, take notice, you will behave like children who sometimes play like wrestlers, sometimes gladiators, sometimes blow a trumpet, and sometimes act a tragedy when they have seen and admired these shows. Thus you too will be at one time a wrestler, at another a gladiator, now a philosopher, then an orator; but with your whole soul, nothing at all. Like an ape, you mimic all you see, and one thing after another is sure to please you, but is out of favor as soon as it becomes familiar. For you have never entered upon anything considerately, nor after having viewed the whole matter on all sides, or made any scrutiny into it, but rashly, and with a cold inclination. Thus some, when they have seen a philosopher and heard a man speaking like Euphrates (though, indeed, who can speak like him?), have a mind to be philosophers too. Consider first, man, what the matter is, and what your own nature is able to bear. If you would be a wrestler, consider your shoulders, your back, your thighs; for different persons are made for different things. Do you think that you can act as you do, and be a philosopher? That you can eat and drink, and be angry and discontented as you are now? You must watch, you must labor, you must get the better of certain appetites, must quit your acquaintance, be despised by your servant, be laughed at by those you meet; come off worse than others in everything, in magistracies, in honors, in courts of judicature. When you have considered all these things round, approach, if you please; if, by parting with them, you have a mind to purchase apathy, freedom, and tranquillity. If not, don't come here; don't, like children, be one while a philosopher, then a publican, then an orator, and then one of Caesar's officers. These things are not consistent. You must be one man, either good or bad. You must cultivate either your own ruling faculty or externals, and apply yourself either to things within or without you; that is, be either a philosopher, or one of the vulgar.

30. Duties are universally measured by [social] relations. Is anyone a father? If so, it is implied that the children should take care of him, submit to him in everything, patiently listen to his reproaches, his correction. But he is a bad father. Are you naturally entitled, then, to a good father? No, only to a father. Is a brother unjust? Well, keep your own situation towards him. Consider not what he does, but what you are to do to keep your own faculty of choice in a state conformable to nature. For another will not hurt you unless you please. You will then be hurt when you think you are hurt. In this manner, therefore, you will find, from the idea of a neighbor, a citizen, a general, the corresponding duties if you accustom yourself to contemplate the several relations.

31. Be assured that the essential property of piety towards the gods is to form right opinions concerning them, as existing and as governing the universe with goodness and justice. And fix yourself in this resolution, to obey them, and yield to them, and willingly follow them in all events, as produced by the most perfect understanding. For thus you will never find fault with the gods, nor accuse them as neglecting you. And it is not possible for this to be effected any other way than by withdrawing yourself from things not in our own control, and placing good or evil in those only which are. For if you suppose any of the things not in our own control to be either good or evil, when you are disappointed of what you wish, or incur what you would avoid, you must necessarily find fault with and blame the authors. For every animal is naturally formed to fly and abhor things that appear hurtful, and the causes of them; and to pursue and admire those which appear beneficial, and the causes of them. It is impractical, then, that one who supposes himself to be hurt should be happy about the person who, he thinks, hurts him, just as it is impossible to be happy about the hurt itself. Hence, also, a father is reviled by a son, when he does not impart to him the things which he takes to be good; and the supposing empire to be a good made Polynices and Eteocles mutually enemies. On this account the husbandman, the sailor, the merchant, on this account those who lose wives and children, revile the gods. For where interest is, there too is piety placed. So that, whoever is careful

to regulate his desires and aversions as he ought, is, by the very same means, careful of piety likewise. But it is also incumbent on everyone to offer libations and sacrifices and first fruits, conformably to the customs of his country, with purity, and not in a slovenly manner, nor negligently, nor sparingly, nor beyond his ability. . . .

33. Immediately prescribe some character and [type for yourself], which you may keep both alone and in company.

Be for the most part silent, or speak merely what is necessary, and in few words. We may, however, enter, though sparingly, into discourse sometimes when occasion calls for it, but not on any of the common subjects, of gladiators, or horse races, or athletic champions, or feasts, the vulgar topics of conversation; but principally not of men, so as either to blame, or praise, or make comparisons. If you are able, then, by your own conversation bring over that of your company to proper subjects; but, if you happen to be taken among strangers, be silent.

Don't allow your laughter [to] be much, nor on many occasions, nor profuse.

Avoid [taking oaths], if possible, altogether; if not, as far as you are able.

Avoid public and vulgar entertainments; but, if ever an occasion calls you to them, keep your attention upon the stretch, that you may not imperceptibly slide into vulgar manners. For be assured that if a person be ever so sound himself, yet, if his companion be infected, he who converses with him will be infected likewise.

Provide things relating to the body no further than mere use; as meat, drink, clothing, house, family. But strike off and reject everything relating to show and [luxury].

As far as possible, before marriage, keep yourself pure from familiarities with women, and, if you indulge them, let it be lawfully. But don't therefore be troublesome and full of reproofs to those who use these liberties, nor frequently boast that you yourself don't.

If anyone tells you that such a person speaks ill of you, don't make excuses about what is said of you, but answer: "He does not know my other faults, else he would not have mentioned only these."

It is not necessary for you to appear often at public spectacles; but if ever there is a proper occasion for you to be there, don't appear more solicitous for anyone than for yourself; that is, wish things to be only just as they are, and him only to conquer who is the conqueror, for thus you will meet with no hindrance. But abstain entirely from declamations and derision and violent emotions. And when you come away, don't discourse a great deal on what has passed, and what does not contribute to your own [improvement]. For it would appear by such discourse that you were immoderately struck with the show. . . .

When you are going to confer with anyone, and particularly of those in a superior station, represent to yourself how Socrates or Zeno would behave in such a case, and you will not be at a loss to make a proper use of whatever may occur.

When you are going to any of the people in power, represent to yourself that you will not find him at home; that you will not be admitted; that the doors will not be opened to you; that he will take no notice of you. If, with all this, it is your duty to go, bear what happens, and never say [to yourself], " It was not worth so much." For this is vulgar, and like a man dazed by external things.

In parties of conversation, avoid a frequent and excessive mention of your own actions and dangers. For, however agreeable it may be to yourself to mention the risks you have run, it is not equally agreeable to others to hear your adventures. Avoid, likewise, an endeavor to excite laughter. For this is a slippery point, which may throw you into vulgar manners, and, besides, may be apt to lessen you in the esteem of your acquaintance. Approaches to indecent discourse are likewise dangerous. Whenever, therefore, anything of this sort happens, if there be a proper opportunity, rebuke him who makes advances that way; or, at least, by silence and blushing and a forbidding look, show yourself to be displeased by such talk.

34. If you are struck by the appearance of any promised pleasure, guard yourself against being

hurried away by it; but let the affair wait your leisure, and procure yourself some delay. Then bring to your mind both points of time: that in which you will enjoy the pleasure, and that in which you will repent and reproach yourself after you have enjoyed it; and set before you, in opposition to these, how you will be glad and applaud yourself if you abstain. And even though it should appear to you a seasonable gratification, take heed that its enticing, and agreeable and attractive force may not subdue you; but set in opposition to this how much better it is to be conscious of having gained so great a victory.

35. When you do anything from a clear judgment that it ought to be done, never shun the [being seen doing it], even though the world should make a wrong supposition about it; for, if you don't act right, shun the action itself; but, if you do, why are you afraid of those who censure you wrongly? . . .

37. If you have assumed any character [or role] above your strength, you have both made an ill figure in that and [neglected] one which you might have supported.

38. When walking, you are careful not to step on a nail or turn your foot; so likewise be careful not to hurt the ruling faculty of your mind. And, if we were to guard against this in every action, we should undertake the action with the greater safety. . . .

41. It is a mark of want of genius to spend much time in things relating to the body, as to be long in our exercises, in eating and drinking, and in the discharge of other animal functions. These should be done incidentally and slightly, and our whole attention be engaged in the care of the understanding.

42. When any person harms you, or speaks badly of you, remember that he acts or speaks from a supposition of its being his duty. Now, it is not possible that he should follow what appears right to you, but what appears so to himself. Therefore, if he judges from a wrong appearance, he is the person hurt, since he too is the person deceived. For if anyone should suppose a true proposition to be false, the proposition is not hurt, but he who is deceived about it. Setting out, then, from these principles, you will meekly bear a person who reviles you, for you will say upon every occasion, "It seemed so to him."

43. Everything has two handles, the one by which it may be carried, the other by which it cannot. If your brother acts unjustly, don't lay hold on the action by the handle of his injustice, for by that it cannot be carried; but by the opposite, that he is your brother, that he was brought up with you; and thus you will lay hold on it, as it is to be carried.

44. These reasonings are unconnected: "I am richer than you, therefore I am better"; "I am more eloquent than you, therefore I am better." The connection is rather this: "I am richer than you, therefore my property is greater than yours;" "I am more eloquent than you, therefore my style is better than yours." But you, after all, are neither property nor style. . . .

46. Never call yourself a philosopher, nor talk a great deal among the unlearned about theorems, but act conformably to them. Thus, at an entertainment, don't talk how persons ought to eat, but eat as you ought. For remember that in this manner Socrates also universally avoided all ostentation. And when persons came to him and desired to be recommended by him to philosophers, he took and recommended them, so well did he bear being overlooked. So that if ever any talk should happen among the unlearned concerning philosophic theorems, be you, for the most part, silent. For there is great danger in immediately throwing out what you have not digested. And, if anyone tells you that you know nothing, and you are not [hurt by it], then you may be sure that you have begun your business [of being improved]. For sheep don't throw up the grass to show the shepherds how much they have eaten; but, inwardly digesting their food, they outwardly produce wool and milk. Thus, therefore, do you likewise not show theorems to the unlearned, but the actions produced by them after they have been digested. . . .

48. The condition and characteristic of a vulgar person, is, that he never expects either benefit

or hurt from himself, but from externals. The condition and characteristic of a philosopher is, that he expects all hurt and benefit from himself. The marks of [one making progress] are, that he censures no one, praises no one, blames no one, accuses no one, says nothing concerning himself as being anybody, or knowing anything: when he is, in any instance, hindered or restrained, he accuses himself; and, if he is praised, he secretly laughs at the person who praises him; and, if he is censured, he makes no defense. But he goes about with the caution of sick or injured people, dreading to move anything that is set right, before it is perfectly fixed. He suppresses all desire in himself; he transfers his aversion to those things only which thwart the proper use of our own faculty of choice; the exertion of his active powers towards anything is very gentle; if he appears stupid or ignorant, he does not care, and, in a word, he watches himself as an enemy, and one in ambush. . . .

50. Whatever moral rules you have deliberately proposed to yourself. abide by them as they were laws, and as if you would be guilty of impiety by violating any of them. Don't regard what anyone says of you, for this, after all, is no concern of yours. How long, then, will you put off thinking yourself worthy of the highest improvements and follow the distinctions of reason? You have received the philosophical theorems, with which you ought to be familiar, and you have been familiar with them. What other master, then, do you wait for, to throw upon that the delay of reforming yourself? You are no longer a boy, but a grown man. If, therefore, you will be negligent and slothful, and always add procrastination to procrastination, purpose to purpose, and fix day after day in which you will attend to yourself, you will insensibly continue without proficiency, and, living and dying, persevere in being one of the vulgar. This instant, then, think yourself worthy of living as a man grown up, and [as one making progress]. Let whatever appears to be the best be to you an inviolable law. And if any instance of pain or pleasure, or glory or disgrace, is set before you, remember that now is the combat, now the Olympiad comes on, nor can it be put off. By once being defeated and giving way, proficiency is lost, or by the contrary preserved. Thus Socrates became perfect, improving himself by everything. attending to nothing but reason. And though you are not yet a Socrates, you ought, however, to live as one desirous of becoming a Socrates.

51. The first and most necessary topic in philosophy is that of the use of moral theorems, such as, "We ought not to lie;" the second is that of demonstrations, such as, "What is the origin of our obligation not to lie;" the third gives strength and articulation to the other two, such as, ["Why is this a demonstration?"] For what is demonstration? What is consequence? What contradiction? What truth? What falsehood? The third topic, then, is necessary on the account of the second, and the second on the account of the first. But the most necessary, and that whereon we ought to rest, is the first. But we act just on the contrary. For we spend all our time on the third topic, and employ all our diligence about that, and entirely neglect the first. Therefore, at the same time that we lie, we are immediately prepared to show how it is demonstrated that lying is not right.

52. Upon all occasions we ought to have these maxims ready at hand:

> Conduct me, Jove, and you, O Destiny,
> Wherever your decrees have fixed my station.
> I follow cheerfully; and, did I not,
> Wicked and wretched, I must follow still.
> (Cleanthes)

> Whoever yields properly to Fate, is deemed
> Wise among men, and knows the laws of
> heaven.
> (Euripides)

And this third:

> O Crito, if it thus pleases the gods, thus let it be.
> Anytus and Melitus may kill me indeed, but hurt me they cannot.
> (Socrates)

Questions for Reflection

1. In paragraph 17, Epictetus says that we are characters in a drama that is not of our own making. Who do you think he believes is the author of the drama of life? What are the advantages of thinking of your life as a story written by someone else? What are the disadvantages of thinking about yourself this way?

2. In surveying all the Greek philosophies of their time, the early Christians saw Stoicism as one of the philosophies that came closest to their own viewpoint. Why do you think the Christians had such a high regard for the Stoics?

3. Compare Epicurus's version of hedonism with Epictetus's Stoicism. On what points might they agree? What are the major differences between their philosophies? If you had to choose between the two philosophies, which one provides the best guidance for life?

4. Are there times in your life when you faced some disappointment or crisis and you followed the advice: "Be Stoical about it. Let it go. Don't worry. Five years from now you won't even remember it"? Did this response make it easier to cope with your situation? To what degree do you think you would be more free, unencumbered, unaffected by external circumstances, and more in charge of your life if you consistently followed Epictetus's advice? What would be the negative consequences (if any) of being a consistent Stoic?

5. Some have criticized the Stoics because they make apathy or philosophical detachment into a virtue. For example, the philosopher Bertrand Russell said that there is "a certain coldness in the Stoic conception of virtue. Not only bad passions are condemned, but all passions." With the emphasis on detachment and passive acceptance, could a Stoic be a good parent, a good lover, a social reformer? Are these legitimate criticisms? How would Epictetus reply?

LEO TOLSTOY

Theism—Meaning Is Found in an Infinite God

Count Leo Tolstoy (1828–1910) was born in central Russia and, though he traveled widely, he spent most of his life in Russia. His epic novels, especially *War and Peace* and *Anna Karenina,* as well as his short stories and essays, have earned him the title of one of Russia's best-known and beloved authors.

At age 50, a spiritual crisis led to a search for the meaning of life that culminated in his embracing the simple Christianity of the Gospels, which he believed was exemplified in the lives of the Russian peasants. From this time until his death he was preoc-

From Leo Tolstoy, *Confession,* translated by David Patterson (New York: W. W. Norton, 1983).

cupied primarily with moral and social reform. The religious and ethical teachings of this period of his life were expressed in a number of essays, stories, and pamphlets, most of which were banned from publication in Russia by government censors. Even after his conversion, he continued to write stories that not only expressed his moral concerns, but also are considered to be some of his notable literary achievements. The following selection is from *My Confession,* written in the years 1879–1882, which details Tolstoy's spiritual journey and represents the theistic answer concerning the meaning of life.

Reading Questions

1. Tolstoy says that he once thought the only truth was that the goal of life was to "live for whatever is best for ourselves and our family." What happened to him that unsettled this comfort?
2. What are the profound questions he faced that he could not answer?
3. Why did he feel that his life was a "stupid and evil practical joke" played on him by somebody?
4. What are the two drops of honey in Tolstoy's life that once gave him pleasure? Why does he no longer experience them as sweet?
5. Why is Tolstoy dissatisfied with the answers provided by the sciences concerning the meaning of life?
6. After finding no satisfying answers among the intellectuals, why does Tolstoy turn to the working class in his search for meaning?
7. What is the solution to the meaning of life that Tolstoy eventually embraces? Why does he think that it is the correct answer?

In spite of the fact that during these fifteen years I regarded writing as a trivial endeavor, I continued to write. I had already tasted the temptations of authorship, the temptations of enormous monetary rewards and applause for worthless work, and I gave myself up to it as a means of improving my material situation and as a way of stifling any questions in my soul concerning the meaning of my life and of life in general.

As I wrote I taught what to me was the only truth: that we must live for whatever is best for ourselves and our family.

And so I lived. But five years ago something very strange began to happen to me. At first I began having moments of bewilderment, when my life would come to a halt, as if I did not know how to live or what to do; I would lose my presence of mind and fall into a state of depression. But this passed, and I continued to live as before. Then the moments of bewilderment recurred more fre-

quently, and they always took the same form. Whenever my life came to a halt, the questions would arise: Why? And what next?

At first I thought these were pointless and irrelevant questions. I thought that the answers to them were well known and that if I should ever want to resolve them, it would not be too hard for me; it was just that I could not be bothered with it now, but if I should take it upon myself, then I would find the answers. But the questions began to come up more and more frequently, and their demands to be answered became more and more urgent. And like points concentrated into one spot, these questions without answers came together to form a single black stain.

It happened with me as it happens with everyone who contracts a fatal internal disease. At first there were the insignificant symptoms of an ailment, which the patient ignores; then these symptoms recur more and more frequently, until they merge into one continuous duration of suffering. The suffering increases, and before he can turn around the patient discovers what he already knew: the thing he had taken for a mere indisposition is in fact the most important thing on earth to him, is in fact death.

This is exactly what happened to me. I realized that this was not an incidental ailment but something very serious, and that if the same questions should continue to recur, I would have to answer them. And I tried to answer them. The questions seemed to be such foolish, simple, childish questions. But as soon as I laid my hands on them and tried to resolve them, I was immediately convinced, first of all, that they were not childish and foolish questions but the most vital and profound questions in life, and, secondly, that no matter how much I pondered them there was no way I could resolve them. Before I could be occupied with my Samara estate, with the education of my son, or with the writing of books, I had to know why I was doing these things. As long as I do not know the reason why, I cannot do anything. In the middle of my concern with the household, which at the time kept me quite busy, a question would suddenly come into my head: "Very well, you will have 6,000 desyatins [16,200 acres] in the Samara province, as well as 300 horses; what then?" And I was completely taken aback and did not know what else to think. As soon as I started to think about the education of my children, I would ask myself, "Why?" Or I would reflect on how the people might attain prosperity, and I would suddenly ask myself, "What concern is it of mine?" Or in the middle of thinking about the fame that my works were bringing me I would say to myself, "Very well, you will be more famous than Gogol, Pushkin, Shakespeare, Molière, more famous than all the writers in the world—so what?"

And I could find absolutely no reply. . . .

And this was happening to me at a time when, from all indications, I should have been considered a completely happy man; this was when I was not yet fifty years old. I had a good, loving, and beloved wife, fine children, and a large estate that was growing and expanding without any effort on my part. More than ever before I was respected by friends and acquaintances, praised by strangers, and I could claim a certain renown without really deluding myself. Moreover, I was not physically and mentally unhealthy; on the contrary, I enjoyed a physical and mental vigor such as I had rarely encountered among others my age. Physically, I could keep up with the peasants working in the fields; mentally, I could work eight and ten hours at a stretch without suffering any aftereffects from the strain. And in such a state of affairs, I came to a point where I could not live; and even though I feared death, I had to employ ruses against myself to keep from committing suicide.

I described my spiritual condition to myself in this way: my life is some kind of stupid and evil practical joke that someone is playing on me. In spite of the fact that I did not acknowledge the existence of any "Someone" who might have created me, the notion that someone brought me into the world as a stupid and evil joke seemed to be the most natural way to describe my condition.

I could not help imagining that somewhere there was someone who was now amusing himself, laughing at me and at the way I had lived for thirty or forty years, studying, developing, growing in body and soul; laughing at how I had now completely matured intellectually and had reached that summit from which life reveals itself only to stand there like an utter fool, clearly seeing that there is nothing in life, that there never was and never will be. "And it makes him laugh . . ."

But whether or not there actually was someone laughing at me did not make it any easier for me. I could not attach a rational meaning to a single act in my entire life. The only thing that amazed me was how I had failed to realize this in the very beginning. All this had been common knowledge for so long. If not today, then tomorrow sickness and death will come (indeed, they were already approaching) to everyone, to me, and nothing will remain except the stench and the worms. My deeds, whatever they may be, will be forgotten sooner or later, and I myself will be no more. Why, then, do anything? How can anyone fail to see this and live? That's what is amazing! It is possible to live only as long as life intoxicates us; once we are sober we cannot help seeing that it is all a delusion, a stupid delusion! Nor is there anything funny or witty about it; it is only cruel and stupid.

There is an old Eastern fable about a traveler who was taken by surprise in the steppes by a raging wild beast. Trying to save himself from the beast, the traveler jumps into a dried-up well; but at the bottom of the well he sees a dragon with its jaws open wide, waiting to devour him. The unhappy man does not dare climb out for fear of being killed by the wild beast, and he does not dare jump to the bottom of the well for fear of being devoured by the dragon. So he grabs hold of a branch of a wild bush growing in the crevices of the well and clings to it. His arms grow weak, and he feels that soon he must fall prey to the death that awaits him on either side. Yet he still holds on, and while he is clinging to the branch he looks up to see two mice, one black and one white, evenly working their way around the branch of the bush he is hanging from, gnawing on it. Soon the bush will give way and break off, and he will fall into the jaws of the dragon. The traveler sees this and knows that he will surely die. But while he is still hanging there he looks around and sees some drops of honey on the leaves of the bush, and he stretches out his tongue and licks them. Thus I cling to the branch of life, knowing that inevitably the dragon of death is waiting, ready to tear me to pieces; and I cannot understand why this torment has befallen me. I try to suck the honey that once consoled me, but the honey is no longer sweet. Day and night the black mouse and the white mouse gnaw at the branch to which I cling. I clearly see the dragon, and the honey has lost all its sweetness. I see only the inescapable dragon and the mice, and I cannot turn my eyes from them. This is no fairy tale but truth, irrefutable and understood by all.

The former delusion of the happiness of life that had concealed from me the horror of the dragon no longer deceives me. No matter how much I tell myself that I cannot understand the meaning of life, that I should live without thinking about it, I cannot do this because I have done it for too long already. Now I cannot help seeing the days and nights rushing toward me and leading me to death. I see only this, and this alone is truth. Everything else is a lie.

The two drops of honey which more than anything else had diverted my eyes from the cruel truth were my love for my family and my writing, which I referred to as art; yet this honey had lost its sweetness for me.

"My family . . . ," I said to myself. But my family, my wife and children, are people too. They are subject to the same conditions as I: they must either live in the lie or face the terrible truth. Why should they live? Why should I love them? Why care for them, bring them up, and watch over them? So that they can sink into the despair that eats away at me, or to turn them over to stupidity? If I love them, then I cannot hide the truth from them. Every step they take in knowledge leads them to this truth. And the truth is death.

"Art, literature . . . ?" Under the influence of success and praise from others I had persuaded myself for a long time that this was something that may be done in spite of the approaching death that will annihilate everything—myself, my works, and the memory of them. But I soon saw that this, too, was a delusion. It became clear to me that art is an ornamentation of life, something that lures us into life. But life had lost its charm for me, so how was I to charm others? As long as I was not living my own life but the life of another that was carrying me along on its crest, as long as I believed that life had a meaning, even though I could not express it, the reflection of every kind of life through literature and the arts gave me pleasure; I enjoyed looking at life in the mirror of art. But when I began to search for the meaning of life, when I began to feel the need to live, this mirror became either tormenting or unnecessary, superfluous and ludicrous. It was no longer possible for me to be consoled by what I saw in the mirror, for I could see that my situation was stupid and despairing. It was good for me to rejoice when in the depths of my soul I believed that my life had meaning. Then this play of lights and shades, the play of the comical, the tragic, the moving, the beautiful, and the terrible elements in life had comforted me. But when I saw that life was meaningless and terrible the play in the mirror could no longer amuse me. No matter how sweet the honey, it could not be sweet to me, for I saw the dragon and the mice gnawing away at my support.

But it did not stop here. Had I simply understood that life has no meaning, I might have been able to calmly accept it; I might have recognized that such was my lot. But I could not rest content at this. Had I been like a man who lives in a forest from which he knows there is no way out, I might have been able to go on living; but I was like a man lost in the forest who was terrified by the fact that he was lost, like a man who was rushing about, longing to find his way and knowing that every step was leading him into deeper confusion, and yet who could not help rushing about.

This was the horror. And in order to be delivered from this horror, I wanted to kill myself. I felt a horror of what awaited me; I knew that this horror was more terrible than my present situation, but I could not keep it away and I did not have the patience to wait for the end. No matter how convincing the argument as that a blood vessel in the heart would burst anyway or that something else would rupture and it would be all over, I could not patiently await the end. The horror of the darkness was too great, and I wanted to be free of it as quickly as possible by means of a rope or a bullet. It was this feeling, more powerful than any other, that was leading me toward suicide. . . .

In my search for answers to the question of life I felt exactly as a man who is lost in a forest.

I came to a clearing, climbed a tree, and had a clear view of the endless space around me. But I could see that there was no house and that there could be no house; I went into the thick of the forest, into the darkness, but again I could see no house—only darkness.

Thus I wandered about in the forest of human knowledge. On one side of me were the clearings of mathematical and experimental sciences, revealing to me sharp horizons; but in no direction could I see a house. On the other side of me was the darkness of the speculative sciences, where every step I took plunged me deeper into darkness, and I was finally convinced that there could be no way out.

When I gave myself over to the bright light of knowledge, I was only diverting my eyes from the question. However clear and tempting the horizons that opened up to me might have been, however tempting it was to sink into the infinity of this knowledge, I soon realized that the clearer this knowledge was, the less I needed it, the less it answered my question.

"Well," I said to myself, "I know everything that science wants so much to know, but this path will not lead me to an answer to the question of the meaning of my life." In the realm of speculative science I saw that in spite of—or rather precisely because of—the fact that this knowledge was designed to answer my question, there could be no answer other than the one I had given myself: What is the meaning of my life? It has none. Or: What will come of my life? Nothing. Or: Why does everything that is exist, and why do I exist? Because it exists.

From one branch of human knowledge I received an endless number of precise answers to questions I had not asked, answers concerning the chemical composition of the stars, the movement of the sun toward the constellation Hercules, the origin of the species and of man, the forms of infinitely small atoms, and the vibration of infinitely small and imponderable particles of ether. But the answer given by this branch of knowledge to my question about the meaning of my life was only this: you are what you call your life; you are a temporary, random conglomeration of particles. The thing that you have been led to refer to as your life is simply the mutual interaction and alteration of these particles. This conglomeration will continue for a certain period of time; then the interaction of these particles will come to a halt, and the thing you call your life will come to an end and with it all your questions. You are a little lump of something randomly stuck together. The lump decomposes. The decomposition of this lump is known as your life. The lump falls apart, and thus the decomposition ends, as do all your questions. Thus the clear side of knowledge replies, and if it strictly follows its own principles, there is no more to be said.

It turns out, however, that such an answer does not constitute a reply to the question. I must know the meaning of my life, but to say that it is a particle of infinity not only fails to give it any meaning but destroys all possible meaning.

The experimental, exact side of knowledge may strike some vague agreement with the speculative side, saying that the meaning of life lies in development and in the contributions made to this development. But given the inaccuracy and obscurity of such a remark, it cannot be regarded as an answer.

Whenever it holds strictly to its own principles in answering the question, the speculative side of knowledge has always come up with the same reply down through the centuries: the universe is something that is infinite and incomprehensible. Human life is an inscrutable part of this inscrutable "whole." . . .

For a long time I lived in this state of madness which, if not in word then in deed, is especially pronounced among the most liberal and most learned of men. I do not know whether it was due to the strange sort of instinctive love I had for the working people that I was compelled to understand them and to see that they are not as stupid as we think; or whether it was my sincere conviction that I knew nothing better to do than to hang myself that led me to realize this: if I wanted to live and to understand the meaning of life, I had to seek this meaning not among those who have lost it and want to destroy themselves but among the millions of people, living and dead, who created life and took upon themselves the burden of their lives as well as our own. So I looked around at the huge masses of simple people, living and dead, who were neither learned nor wealthy, and I saw something quite different. I saw that all of these millions of people who have lived and still live did not fall into my category, with only a few rare exceptions. I could not regard them as people who did not understand the question because they themselves put the question with unusual clarity and answered it. Nor could I regard them as Epicureans, since their lives are marked more by deprivation and suffering than by pleasure. And even less could I regard them as people who carried on a meaningless life in an irrational manner, since they could explain every act of their lives, even death itself. And they looked upon killing oneself as the greatest of evils. It turned out that all of humanity had some kind of knowledge of the meaning of life which I had overlooked and held in contempt. It followed that rational knowledge

does not give meaning to life, that it excludes life; the meaning that millions of people give to life is based on some kind of knowledge that is despised and considered false.

As presented by the learned and the wise, rational knowledge denies the meaning of life, but the huge masses of people acknowledge meaning through an irrational knowledge. And this irrational knowledge is faith, the one thing that I could not accept. This involves the God who is both one and three, the creation in six days, devils, angels and everything else that I could not accept without taking leave of my senses.

My position was terrible. I knew that I could find nothing in the way of rational knowledge except a denial of life; and in faith I could find nothing except a denial of reason, and this was even more impossible than a denial of life. According to rational knowledge, it followed that life is evil, and people know it. They do not have to live, yet they have lived and they do live, just as I myself had lived, even though I had known for a long time that life is meaningless and evil. According to faith, it followed that in order to understand the meaning of life I would have to turn away from reason, the very thing for which meaning was necessary.

I ran into a contradiction from which there were only two ways out: either the thing that I had referred to as reason was not as rational as I had thought, or the thing that I took to be irrational was not as irrational as I had thought. And I began to examine the course of the arguments that had come of my rational knowledge.

As I looked more closely at this course, I found it to be entirely correct. The conclusion that life is nothing was unavoidable; but I detected a mistake. The mistake was that my thinking did not correspond to the question I had raised. The question was: Why should I live? Or: Is there anything real and imperishable that will come of my illusory and perishable life? Or: What kind of meaning can my finite existence have in this infinite universe? In order to answer this question, I studied life.

It was obvious that the resolution of all the possible questions of life could not satisfy me because my question, no matter how simple it may seem at first glance, entails a demand to explain the finite by means of the infinite and the infinite by means of the finite.

I asked, "What is the meaning of my life beyond space, time, and causation?" And I answered, "What is the meaning of my life within space, time, and causation?" After a long time spent in the labor of thought, it followed that I could reply only that my life had no meaning at all.

Throughout my reasoning I was constantly comparing the finite to the finite and the infinite to the infinite; indeed, I could not do otherwise. Thus I concluded and had to conclude that force is force, matter is matter, will is will, infinity is infinity, nothing is nothing; and I could not get beyond that.

It was something similar to what happens in mathematics when we are trying to figure out how to solve an equation and all we can get is an identity. The method for solving the equation is correct, but all we get for an answer is $a = a$, or $x = x$, or $o = o$. The same thing was happening with my reasoning in regard to the question concerning the significance of my life. The answers that all the sciences give to this question are only identities.

And in reality a strictly rational knowledge begins, in the manner of Descartes, with an absolute doubt of everything. Strictly rational knowledge casts aside any knowledge based on faith and reconstructs everything anew according to the laws of reason and experiment; it can give no answer to the question of life other than the one I had received—an indefinite one. It seemed to me only at first that knowledge gave a positive answer, the answer of Schopenhauer: life has no meaning, it is an evil. But as I looked into the matter I realized that this is not a positive answer and that only my emotions had taken it to be so. Strictly expressed, as it is expressed by the Brahmins, by Solomon, and by Schopenhauer, the answer is only a vague one or an identity; $o = o$, life that presents itself to me as nothing is nothing. Thus philosophical knowledge denies nothing but merely replies that it cannot decide this question and that from its point of view any resolution remains indefinite.

Having understood this, I realized that I could not search for an answer to my question in rational knowledge. The answer given by rational knowledge is merely an indication that an answer can be obtained only by formulating the question differently, that is, only when the relationship between the finite and the infinite is introduced into the question. I also realized that no matter how irrational and unattractive the answers given by faith, they have the advantage of bringing to every reply a relationship between the finite and the infinite, without which there can be no reply. However I may put the question of how I am to live, the answer is: according to the law of God. Is there anything real that will come of my life? Eternal torment or eternal happiness. What meaning is there which is not destroyed by death? Union with the infinite God, paradise.

Thus in addition to rational knowledge, which before had seemed to be the only knowledge, I was inevitably led to recognize a different type of knowledge, an irrational type, which all of humanity had: faith, which provides us with the possibility of living. As far as I was concerned, faith was as irrational as ever, but I could not fail to recognize that it alone provides humanity with an answer to the question of life, thus making it possible to live.

Rational knowledge led me to the conclusion that life is meaningless; my life came to a halt, and I wanted to do away with myself. As I looked around at people, I saw that they were living, and I was convinced that they knew the meaning of life. Then I turned and looked at myself; as long as I knew the meaning of life, I lived. As it was with others, so it was with me: faith provided me with the meaning of life and the possibility of living.

Upon a further examination of the people in other countries, of my contemporaries, and of those who have passed away, I saw the same thing. Wherever there is life, there is faith; since the origin of mankind faith has made it possible for us to live, and the main characteristics of faith are everywhere and always the same.

No matter what answers a given faith might provide for us, every answer of faith gives infinite meaning to the finite existence of man, meaning that is not destroyed by suffering, deprivation, and death. Therefore, the meaning of life and the possibility of living may be found in faith alone. I realized that the essential significance of faith lies not only in the "manifestation of things unseen" and so on, or in revelation (this is simply a description of one of the signs of faith); nor is it simply the relation between man and God (faith must first be determined and then God, not the other way around), or agreeing with what one has been told, even though this is what it is most often understood to be. Faith is the knowledge of the meaning of human life, whereby the individual does not destroy himself but lives. Faith is the force of life. If a man lives, then he must have faith in something. If he did not believe that he had something he must live for, then he would not live. If he fails to see and understand the illusory nature of the finite, then he believes in the finite; if he understands the illusory nature of the finite, then he must believe in the infinite. Without faith it is impossible to live. . . .

. . . In order for all humankind to live, to sustain life and instill it with meaning, these millions must all have a different, more genuine concept of faith. Indeed, it was not that Solomon, Schopenhauer, and I did not kill ourselves that convinced me of the existence of faith but that these millions have lived and continue to live, carrying the Solomons and me on the waves of their lives.

And I began to grow closer to the believers from among the poor, the simple, the uneducated folk, from among the pilgrims, the monks, the Raskolniks [dissenters], the peasants. The beliefs of those from among the people, like those of the pretentious believers from our class, were Christian. Here too there was much superstition mixed in with the truths of Christianity, but with this difference: the superstitions of the believers from our class were utterly unnecessary to them, played no role in their lives, and were only a kind of epicurean diversion, while the superstitions of the believers from the laboring people were intertwined with their lives to such a degree that their lives could not be conceived without them: their superstitions were a necessary condition for their lives. The whole life of the believers from our class was in opposition to their faith, while the whole life of the believers from the working people was a confirmation of that meaning of life which was the substance of their faith. So I began to examine the life and the teachings of these people, and the closer I looked, the more I was convinced that theirs was the true

faith, that their faith was indispensable to them and that this faith alone provided them with the meaning and possibility of life. Contrary to what I saw among the people of our class, where life was possible without faith and scarcely one in a thousand was a believer, among these people there was scarcely one in a thousand who was not a believer. Contrary to what I saw among the people of our class, where a lifetime is passed in idleness, amusement, and dissatisfaction with life, these people spent their lives at hard labor and were less dissatisfied with life than the wealthy. Contrary to the people of our class who resist and are unhappy with the hardship and suffering of their lot, these people endure sickness and tribulation without question or resistance—peacefully, and in the firm conviction that this is as it should be, cannot be otherwise, and is good. Contrary to the fact that the greater our intellect, the less we understand the meaning of life and the more we see some kind of evil joke in our suffering and death, these people live, suffer, and draw near to death peacefully and, more often than not, joyfully. Contrary to peaceful death—death without horror and despair, which is the rarest exception in our class—it is the tormenting, unyielding, and sorrowful death that is the rarest exception among the people. And these people, who are deprived of everything that for Solomon and me constituted the only good in life, yet who nonetheless enjoy the greatest happiness, form the overwhelming majority of mankind. I looked further still around myself. I examined the lives of the great masses of people who have lived in the past and live today. Among those who have understood the meaning of life, who know how to live and die, I saw not two or three or ten but hundreds, thousands, millions. And all of them, infinitely varied in their customs, intellects, educations, and positions and in complete contrast to my ignorance, knew the meaning of life and death, labored in peace, endured suffering and hardship, lived and died, and saw in this not vanity but good.

I grew to love these people. The more I learned about the lives of those living and dead about whom I had read and heard, the more I loved them and the easier it became for me to live. I lived this way for about two years, and a profound transformation came over me, one that had been brewing in me for a long time and whose elements had always been a part of me. The life of our class, of the wealthy and the learned, was not only repulsive to me but had lost all meaning. The sum of our action and thinking, of our science and art, all of it struck me as the overindulgences of a spoiled child. I realized that meaning was not to be sought here. The actions of the laboring people, of those who create life, began to appear to me as the one true way. I realized that the meaning provided by this life was truth, and I embraced it.

Questions for Reflection

1. Tolstoy seems to think that rational knowledge will lead to the conclusion that life is meaningless, whereas faith is a kind of irrational knowledge. However, those philosophers who provided rational arguments for the existence of God in Chapter 2 did not think faith was irrational. Is Tolstoy creating a false dichotomy, asking us to choose either reason and meaninglessness on the one hand or an irrational faith and meaning on the other hand?

2. In this very moving account, Tolstoy arises out of despair to find meaning in a living faith. It certainly worked for him and gave him emotional satisfaction. But is emotional satisfaction enough? Do we really want to be emotionally satisfied by an illusion? Isn't it important that our hopes and meaning be based on what is true and real? Karl Marx said that religion is the opiate of the people. Has Tolstoy merely discovered a psychological opiate that makes him feel good about his life? Has he ignored the issue of the truth of his faith? Or was the 17th-century philosopher Blaise Pascal correct when he said "the heart has its reasons that reason itself does not know"? What do you think?

3. Tolstoy was convinced by the faith of simple working folk who experienced great suffering, but whose lives, nevertheless, were full of peace, joy, and meaning. For Tolstoy and these Russian peasants, the meaning of life was found by embracing Christianity. But if Tolstoy had looked long enough he would find similar lives of peace and joy among Hindus, Buddhists, and even atheists. Though they lack Tolstoy's faith, most atheists do not necessarily experience his despair, nor do they live aimlessly, lacking the courage to take their own lives. Because of his own psychological constitution, has Tolstoy too quickly assumed that he has found the *only* solution to the meaning of life?

4. What (if anything) moved you about Tolstoy's narrative? Did you identify with any of the phases of his journey? Did you gain any insights? Is there anything in your own experience that contradicts his? If you are visiting an unfamiliar city, you can find your way about by learning from the experience of one who has been there. But is the same true about the meaning of life? Is another person's experience irrelevant in deciding how to live your life? Or is there something that can be learned from biographies?

BERTRAND RUSSELL

Atheism—Finding Meaning in a World without God

Bertrand Russell (1872–1970) was born into an aristocratic British family. (He inherited the title of Earl Russell in 1931.) His parents died when he was three and even though they were freethinkers, he ended up being raised by his fervently religious grandmother. When he was a teenager, he wrestled intensely with the intellectual credibility of theism and abandoned it by the time he was 18. The rest of his life he was an outspoken critic of all forms of religious belief.

Russell was never reticent about speaking his mind, and throughout his life his iconoclastic and liberal opinions caused a stir wherever he went. He was fired from two academic positions because of his controversial views on politics and sexual morality. His confrontational political protests also landed him in jail several times. Even at the age of 89, he was still going strong and was jailed for leading a protest against nuclear arms in London.

In spite of these troubles, Russell was a respected international figure because of his groundbreaking work in logic and philosophy. Throughout his long career, Russell received many distinguished honors, including the Nobel Prize for literature in 1950. In addition to numerous articles, he wrote over 90 books, both technical and popular, on a wide range of topics. Russell died in 1970, two years short of living a century.

Even though Russell was irreligious, he gave the following essay the ironic title "A Free Man's Worship." He argues that even an atheist can have a sense of worship but only by making our own, human ideals the object of our awe and commitment. The essay remains one of Russell's most popular and most reprinted writings and is an eloquent attempt to articulate the meaning of human existence in the face of an uncaring universe.

Reading Questions

1. After presenting an absurd version of the story of creation, why does Russell say that the world which science presents for our belief is "even more purposeless, more void of meaning"?
2. In what sense are humans free? In what sense are we superior to the forces of nature that control us?
3. What is Russell's attitude toward those, religious and nonreligious, who worship force or power?
4. Why does he say "a spirit of fiery revolt" is necessary to assert our freedom? Freedom from what?
5. Why does he think that resignation is a virtue? Resignation to what? What more is required beyond passive resignation to achieve wisdom?

From Bertrand Russell, "A Free Man's Worship," originally published in the *Independent Review* in 1903.

6. What is Russell referring to when he uses the symbol of the "temple"? What is the "cavern of darkness" that precedes it?
7. In Russell's view of our journey through life, what role does our relationship with our fellow human beings play?
8. In the closing paragraph, what does Russell mean when he says we must "worship at the shrine that [our] own hands have built"?
9. This essay has all the emotion and rhythms of a revivalistic sermon. Why do you suppose Russell gives it such a religious tone, including the insertion of the word *worship* in the title? How does Russell characterize the "free man" (or woman) throughout this essay?

To Dr. Faustus in his study Mephistopheles told the history of the Creation, saying:

"The endless praises of the choirs of angels had begun to grow wearisome; for, after all, did he not deserve their praise? Had he not given them endless joy? Would it not be more amusing to obtain undeserved praise, to be worshipped by beings whom he tortured? He smiled inwardly, and resolved that the great drama should be performed.

"For countless ages the hot nebula whirled aimlessly through space. At length it began to take shape, the central mass threw off planets, the planets cooled, boiling seas and burning mountains heaved and tossed, from black masses of cloud hot sheets of rain deluged the barely solid crust. And now the first germ of life grew in the depths of the ocean, and developed rapidly in the fructifying warmth into vast forest trees, huge ferns springing from the damp mould, sea monsters breeding, fighting, devouring, and passing away. And from the monsters, as the play unfolded itself, Man was born, with the power of thought, the knowledge of good and evil, and the cruel thirst for worship. And Man saw that all is passing in this mad, monstrous world, that all is struggling to snatch, at any cost, a few brief moments of life before Death's inexorable decree. And Man said: 'There is a hidden purpose, could we but fathom it, and the purpose is good; for we must reverence something, and in the visible world there is nothing worthy of reverence.' And Man stood aside from the struggle, resolving that God intended harmony to come out of chaos by human efforts. And when he followed the instincts which God had transmitted to him from his ancestry of beasts of prey, he called it Sin, and asked God to forgive him. But he doubted whether he could be justly forgiven, until he invented a divine Plan by which God's wrath was to have been appeased. And seeing the present was bad, he made it yet worse, that thereby the future might be better. And he gave God thanks for the strength that enabled him to forgo even the joys that were possible. And God smiled; and when he saw that Man had become perfect in renunciation and worship, he sent another sun through the sky, which crashed into Man's sun; and all returned again to nebula.

"'Yes,' he murmured, 'it was a good play; I will have it performed again.'"

Such, in outline, but even more purposeless, more void of meaning, is the world which Science presents for our belief. Amid such a world, if anywhere, our ideals henceforward must find a home. That Man is the product of causes which had no prevision of the end they were achieving; that his origin, his growth, his hopes and fears, his loves and his beliefs, are but the outcome of accidental collocations of atoms; that no fire, no heroism, no intensity of thought and feeling, can preserve an individual life beyond the grave; that all the labours of the ages, all the devotion, all the inspiration, all the noonday brightness of human genius, are destined to extinction in the vast death of the solar system, and that the whole temple of Man's achievement must inevitably be buried beneath the debris of a universe in ruins—all these things, if not quite beyond dispute, are yet so nearly certain, that no philosophy which rejects them can hope to stand. Only within the scaffolding of these truths, only on the firm foundation of unyielding despair, can the soul's habitation henceforth be safely built.

How, in such an alien and inhuman world, can so powerless a creature as Man preserve his aspirations untarnished? A strange mystery it is that Nature, omnipotent but blind, in the revolutions of her secular hurryings through the abysses of space, has brought forth at last a child, subject still to her power, but gifted with sight, with knowledge of good and evil, with the capacity of judging all the works of his unthinking Mother. In spite of Death, the mark and seal of the parental control, Man is yet free, during his brief years, to examine, to criticise, to know, and in imagination to create. To him alone, in the world with which he is acquainted, this freedom belongs; and in this lies his superiority to the resistless forces that control his outward life.

The savage, like ourselves, feels the oppression of his impotence before the powers of Nature; but having in himself nothing that he respects more than Power, he is willing to prostrate himself before his gods, without inquiring whether they are worthy of his worship. Pathetic and very terrible is the long history of cruelty and torture, of degradation and human sacrifice, endured in the hope of placating the jealous gods: surely, the trembling believer thinks, when what is most precious has been freely given, their lust for blood must be appeased, and more will not be required. The religion of Moloch—as such creeds may be generically called—is in essence the cringing submission of the slave, who dare not, even in his heart, allow the thought that his master deserves no adulation. Since the independence of ideals is not yet acknowledged, Power may be freely worshipped, and receive an unlimited respect, despite its wanton infliction of pain.

But gradually, as morality grows bolder, the claim of the ideal world begins to be felt; and worship, if it is not to cease, must be given to gods of another kind than those created by the savage. Some, though they feel the demands of the ideal, will still consciously reject them, still urging that naked Power is worthy of worship. Such is the attitude inculcated in God's answer to Job out of the whirlwind: the divine power and knowledge are paraded, but of the divine goodness there is no hint. Such also is the attitude of those who, in our own day, base their morality upon the struggle for survival, maintaining that the survivors are necessarily the fittest. But others, not content with an answer so repugnant to the moral sense, will adopt the position which we have become accustomed to regard as specially religious, maintaining that, in some hidden manner, the world of fact is really harmonious with the world of ideals. Thus Man creates God, all-powerful and all-good, the mystic unity of what is and what should be.

But the world of fact, after all, is not good; and, in submitting our judgment to it, there is an element of slavishness from which our thoughts must be purged. For in all things it is well to exalt the dignity of Man, by freeing him as far as possible from the tyranny of non-human Power. When we have realised that Power is largely bad, that man, with his knowledge of good and evil, is but a helpless atom in a world which has no such knowledge, the choice is again presented to us: Shall we worship Force, or shall we worship Goodness? Shall our God exist and be evil, or shall he be recognised as the creation of our own conscience?

The answer to this question is very momentous, and affects profoundly our whole morality. The worship of Force, to which Carlyle and Nietzsche and the creed of Militarism have accustomed us, is the result of failure to maintain our own ideals against a hostile universe: it is itself a prostrate submission to evil, a sacrifice of our best to Moloch. If strength indeed is to be respected, let us respect rather the strength of those who refuse that false "recognition of facts" which fails to recognise that facts are often bad. Let us admit that, in the world we know, there are many things that would be better otherwise, and that the ideals to which we do and must adhere are not realised in the realm of matter. Let us preserve our respect for truth, for beauty, for the ideal of perfection which life does not permit us to attain, though none of these things meet with the approval of the unconscious universe. If Power is bad, as it seems to be, let us reject it from our hearts. In this lies Man's true freedom: in determination to worship only the God created by our own love of the good, to respect only the heaven which inspires the insight of our best moments. In action, in desire, we must submit perpetually to the tyranny of outside forces; but in thought, in aspiration, we are free, free from our fellow-men, free from the petty planet on which our bodies impotently crawl, free even, while we live, from the tyranny of death. Let us learn, then, that energy of faith which enables us to live constantly in the vision of the good; and let us descend, in action, into the world of fact, with that vision always before us.

When first the opposition of fact and ideal grows fully visible, a spirit of fiery revolt, of fierce hatred of the gods, seems necessary to the assertion of freedom. To defy with Promethean constancy a hostile universe, to keep its evil always in view, always actively hated, to refuse no pain that the malice of Power can invent, appears to be the duty of all who will not bow before the inevitable. But indignation is still a bondage, for it compels our thoughts to be occupied with an evil world; and in the fierceness of desire from which rebellion springs there is a kind of self-assertion which it is necessary for the wise to overcome. Indignation is a submission of our thoughts, but not of our desires; the Stoic freedom in which wisdom consists is found in the submission of our desires, but not of our thoughts. From the submission of our desires springs the virtue of resignation; from the freedom of our thoughts springs the whole world of art and philosophy, and the vision of beauty by which, at last, we half reconquer the reluctant world. But the vision of beauty is possible only to unfettered contemplation, to thoughts not weighted by the load of eager wishes; and thus Freedom comes only to those who no longer ask of life that it shall yield them any of those personal goods that are subject to the mutations of Time.

Although the necessity of renunciation is evidence of the existence of evil, yet Christianity, in preaching it, has shown a wisdom exceeding that of the Promethean philosophy of rebellion. It must be admitted that, of the things we desire, some, though they prove impossible, are yet real goods; others, however, as ardently longed for, do not form part of a fully purified ideal. The belief that what must be renounced is bad, though sometimes false, is far less often false than untamed passion supposes; and the creed of religion, by providing a reason for proving that it is never false, has been the means of purifying our hopes by the discovery of many austere truths.

But there is in resignation a further good element: even real goods, when they are unattainable, ought not to be fretfully desired. To every man comes, sooner or later, the great renunciation. For the young, there is nothing unattainable; a good thing desired with the whole force of a passionate will, and yet impossible, is to them not credible. Yet, by death, by illness, by poverty, or by the voice of duty, we must learn, each one of us, that the world was not made for us, and that, however beautiful may be the things we crave, Fate may nevertheless forbid them. It is the part of courage, when misfortune comes, to bear without repining the ruin of our hopes, to turn away our thoughts from vain regrets. This degree of submission to Power is not only just and right: it is the very gate of wisdom.

But passive renunciation is not the whole of wisdom; for not by renunciation alone can we build a temple for the worship of our own ideals. Haunting foreshadowings of the temple appear in the realm of imagination, in music, in architecture, in the untroubled kingdom of reason, and in the golden sunset magic of lyrics, where beauty shines and glows, remote from the touch of sorrow, remote from the fear of change, remote from the failures and disenchantments of the world of fact. In the contemplation of these things the vision of heaven will shape itself in our hearts, giving at once a touchstone to judge the world about us, and an inspiration by which to fashion to our needs whatever is not incapable of serving as a stone in the sacred temple.

Except for those rare spirits that are born without sin, there is a cavern of darkness to be traversed before that temple can be entered. The gate of the cavern is despair, and its floor is paved with the gravestones of abandoned hopes. There Self must die; there the eagerness, the greed of untamed desire must be slain, for only so can the soul be freed from the empire of Fate. But out of the cavern the

Gate of Renunciation leads again to the daylight of wisdom, by whose radiance a new insight, a new joy, a new tenderness, shine forth to gladden the pilgrim's heart.

When, without the bitterness of impotent rebellion, we have learnt both to resign ourselves to the outward rules of Fate and to recognise that the non-human world is unworthy of our worship, it becomes possible at last so to transform and refashion the unconscious universe, so to transmute it in the crucible of imagination, that a new image of shining gold replaces the old idol of clay. In all the multiform facts of the world—in the visual shapes of trees and mountains and clouds, in the events of the life of man, even in the very omnipotence of Death—the insight of creative idealism can find the reflection of a beauty which its own thoughts first made. In this way mind asserts its subtle mastery over the thoughtless forces of Nature. The more evil the material with which it deals, the more thwarting to untrained desire, the greater is its achievement in inducing the reluctant rock to yield up its hidden treasures, the prouder its victory in compelling the opposing forces to swell the pageant of its triumph. Of all the arts, Tragedy is the proudest, the most triumphant; for it builds its shining citadel in the very centre of the enemy's country, on the very summit of his highest mountain; from its impregnable watchtowers, his camps and arsenals, his columns and forts, are all revealed; within its walls the free life continues, while the legions of Death and Pain and Despair, and all the servile captains of tyrant Fate, afford the burghers of that dauntless city new spectacles of beauty. Happy those sacred ramparts, thrice happy the dwellers on that all-seeing eminence. Honour to those brave warriors who, through countless ages of warfare, have preserved for us the priceless heritage of liberty, and have kept undefiled by sacrilegious invaders the home of the unsubdued.

But the beauty of Tragedy does but make visible a quality which, in more or less obvious shapes, is present always and everywhere in life. In the spectacle of Death, in the endurance of intolerable pain, and in the irrevocableness of a vanished past, there is a sacredness, an overpowering awe, a feeling of the vastness, the depth, the inexhaustible mystery of existence, in which, as by some strange marriage of pain, the sufferer is bound to the world by bonds of sorrow. In these moments of insight, we lose all eagerness of temporary desire, all struggling and striving for petty ends, all care for the little trivial things that, to a superficial view, make up the common life of day by day; we see, surrounding the narrow raft illumined by the flickering light of human comradeship, the dark ocean on whose rolling waves we toss for a brief hour; from the great night without, a chill blast breaks in upon our refuge; all the loneliness of humanity amid hostile forces is concentrated upon the individual soul, which must struggle alone, with what of courage it can command, against the whole weight of a universe that cares nothing for its hopes and fears. Victory, in this struggle with the powers of darkness, is the true baptism into the glorious company of heroes, the true initiation into the overmastering beauty of human existence. From that awful encounter of the soul with the outer world, enunciation, wisdom, and charity are born; and with their birth a new life begins. To take into the inmost shrine of the soul the irresistible forces whose puppets we seem to be—Death and change, the irrevocableness of the past, and the powerlessness of Man before the blind hurry of the universe from vanity to vanity—to feel these things and know them is to conquer them.

This is the reason why the Past has such magical power. The beauty of its motionless and silent pictures is like the enchanted purity of late autumn, when the leaves, though one breath would make them fall, still glow against the sky in golden glory. The Past does not change or strive; like Duncan, after life's fitful fever it sleeps well; what was eager and grasping, what was petty and transitory, has faded away, the things that were beautiful and eternal shine out of it like stars in the night. Its beauty, to a soul not worthy of it, is unendurable; but to a soul which has conquered Fate it is the key of religion.

The life of Man, viewed outwardly, is but a small thing in comparison with the forces of Nature. The slave is doomed to worship Time and Fate and Death, because they are greater than anything he finds in himself, and because all his thoughts are of things which they devour. But, great as they are, to think of them greatly, to feel their passionless splendour, is greater still. And such thought makes us free men; we no longer bow before the inevitable in Oriental subjection, but we absorb it, and make it a part of ourselves. To abandon the struggle for private happiness, to expel all eagerness of temporary desire, to burn with passion for eternal things—this is emancipation, and this is the free man's worship. And this liberation is effected by a contemplation of Fate; for Fate itself is subdued by the mind which leaves nothing to be purged by the purifying fire of Time.

United with his fellow-men by the strongest of all ties, the tie of a common doom, the free man finds that a new vision is with him always, shedding over every daily task the light of love. The life of Man is a long march through the night, surrounded by invisible foes, tortured by weariness and pain, towards a goal that few can hope to reach, and where none may tarry long. One by one, as they march, our comrades vanish from our sight, seized by the silent orders of omnipotent Death. Very brief is the time in which we can help them, in which their happiness or misery is decided. Be it ours to shed sunshine on their path, to lighten their sorrows by the balm of sympathy, to give them the pure joy of a never-tiring affection, to strengthen failing courage, to instil faith in hours of despair. Let us not weigh in grudging scales their merits and demerits, but let us think only of their need—of the sorrows, the difficulties, perhaps the blindnesses, that make the misery of their lives; let us remember that they are fellow-sufferers in the same darkness, actors in the same tragedy as ourselves. And so, when their day is over, when their good and their evil have become eternal by the immortality of the past, be it ours to feel that, where they suffered, where they failed, no deed of ours was the cause; but wherever a spark of the divine fire kindled in their hearts, we were ready with encouragement, with sympathy, with brave words in which high courage glowed.

Brief and powerless is Man's life; on him and all his race the slow, sure doom falls pitiless and dark. Blind to good and evil, reckless of destruction, omnipotent matter rolls on its relentless way; for Man, condemned to-day to lose his dearest, to-morrow himself to pass through the gate of darkness, it remains only to cherish, ere yet the blow falls, the lofty thoughts that ennoble his little day; disdaining the coward terrors of the slave of Fate, to worship at the shrine that his own hands have built; undismayed by the empire of chance, to preserve a mind free from the wanton tyranny that rules his outward life; proudly defiant of the irresistible forces that tolerate, for a moment, his knowledge and his condemnation, to sustain alone, a weary but unyielding Atlas, the world that his own ideals have fashioned despite the trampling march of unconscious power.

Questions for Reflection

1. In what ways is Russell's response to life similar to that of the Stoics? In what ways is it different?

2. Suppose you were to agree with Russell's initial starting-point that there is no God and that, in the final analysis, humans are nothing more than an "accidental collocation of atoms." Would you then also agree with his pessimistic assessment of the human situation?

3. Some may be tempted to say that Russell's picture of the human situation is too pessimistic and that it should be rejected for that reason. But is the fact that it is a pessimistic picture a sufficient basis for saying it is false? Should we accept a view of the universe and of human life simply because it is comfortable and makes us feel good? Should we reject a philosophy simply because we find it depressing? What role should the degree of subjective satisfaction that an idea brings play in deciding what is true and real?

4. Russell's picture is very pessimistic, claiming that everything humanity values is "destined to extinction in the vast death of the solar system." Nevertheless, what is it, do you suppose, that gives Russell his reason for living? What is it that makes life meaningful for him? Do you agree or disagree with him that this is a sufficient basis for living a meaningful life?

 JEAN-PAUL SARTRE

Existentialism—We Must Each Create Our Own Meaning

Jean-Paul Sartre (1905–1980) was born in Paris and lived most of his life there. After receiving an education at one of France's most prestigious universities, he began his career by teaching philosophy. However, his rise to fame as a writer began in 1938 when he published *Nausea,* his first novel and a best-seller. Eventually, Sartre resigned his professorship and for the rest of his life was able to live on his literary income alone. When World War II broke out, Sartre was called into military service, but was captured and confined to a Nazi prison camp for approximately a year. While there, he wrote and produced plays for his fellow prisoners. He was allowed to return to Paris because of poor health, but he immediately became active in the underground movement of the French Resistance, writing for a number of anti-Nazi newspapers. In 1943, he published his philosophical masterpiece, *Being and Nothingness: A Phenomenological Essay on Ontology*. It has been called "the principle text of modern existentialism." In recognition of his many novels and plays, Sartre was awarded the Noble Prize for Literature in 1964, but he refused to accept the honor and the substantial cash prize because he did not want to become a tool of the establishment. On April 15, 1980, Sartre died of heart failure. As the hearse bearing his body drove to the cemetery, a crowd of about 50,000 people, most of them students, accompanied it through the streets of Paris.

The following essay on "Existentialism and Humanism" is one of Sartre's best-known and most reprinted essays. As Sartre points out, there are two kinds of existentialism: religious and atheistic. While he frequently uses the phrase "we existentialists," it is important to note that many of his points apply only to the atheistic variety of this philosophical movement. In the beginning of the essay he discusses the relationship between existence and essence. The essence of something is its defining characteristic or basic nature. For example, before a building is constructed an architect draws up the blueprints. These define what the building is, how it will function, and what purpose it will serve. However, according to Sartre, if there is no God, then you (unlike the

From Jean-Paul Sartre, *Existentialism and Humanism,* translated by Philip Mairet (New York: Haskell House, 1948).

building) have no essence. You must choose who you are and what will be your purpose. Many previous atheists reveled in the idea that if there is no God then we are totally free to be what we choose to be. Sartre, however, believes that this is a burdensome freedom and an awesome responsibility that leads to feelings of anguish, abandonment, and despair. Nevertheless, he says, if we honestly face our predicament we will realize that his philosophy is genuinely optimistic, for it asserts human freedom, dignity, and responsibility.

Reading Questions

1. What are the two kinds of existentialists? Which kind is Sartre?
2. According to the theistic view, how is the creation of humanity like the making of a paper-knife? What is the relationship between existence and essence in these two cases?
3. According to atheistic existentialism, what is the relationship between existence and essence in the case of humanity? What does Sartre say about human nature? Why? How does his view differ from the theistic view?
4. What does Sartre mean when he says we choose ourselves? Why does he think this also means that we choose for all humanity as well?
5. What does Sartre mean by anguish, abandonment, and despair? Why does he think these terms characterize the human situation?
6. According to Sartre, what are the consequences of asserting that God does not exist?
7. What does Sartre mean by saying "man is condemned to be free"? Why is our freedom a problem?
8. Consider the case of the student choosing between going to war and staying with his mother. Why does Sartre say that objective ethical principles (those of the Christian or the Kantian, for example) provide no guidance to him in making his decision?
9. Do you agree with Sartre that your feelings are formed by your actions and cannot be a guide to action?

What, then, is this that we call existentialism?

Most of those who are making use of this word would be highly confused if required to explain its meaning. For since it has become fashionable, people cheerfully declare that this musician or that painter is "existentialist." A columnist in *Clartés* signs himself "The Existentialist," and, indeed, the word is now so loosely applied to so many things that it no longer means anything at all. It would appear that, for the lack of any novel doctrine such as that of surrealism, all those who are eager to join in the latest scandal or movement now seize upon this philosophy in which, however, they can find nothing to their purpose. For in truth this is of all teachings the least scandalous and the most austere: it is intended strictly for technicians and philosophers. All the same, it can easily be defined.

The question is only complicated because there are two kinds of existentialists. There are, on the one hand, the Christians, amongst whom I shall name [Karl] Jaspers and Gabriel Marcel, both professed Catholics; and on the other the existential atheists, amongst whom we must place Heidegger as well as the French existentialists and myself. What they have in common is simply the fact that they believe that *existence* comes before *essence*—or, if you will, that we must begin from the subjective. What exactly do we mean by that? If one considers an article of manufacture as, for example, a book or a paper-knife—one sees that it has been made by an artisan who had a conception of it; and he has paid attention, equally, to the conception of a paper-knife and to the pre-existent technique of production which is a part of that conception and is, at bottom, a formula. Thus the paper-knife is at the same time an article producible in a certain manner and one which, on the other hand, serves a definite purpose, for one cannot suppose that a man would produce a paper-knife without knowing what it was for. Let us say, then, of the paper-knife that its essence—that is to say the sum of the formulae and the qualities which made its production and its definition possible—precedes its existence. The presence of such-and-such a paper-knife or book is thus determined before my eyes. Here, then, we are viewing the world from a technical standpoint, and we can say that production precedes existence.

When we think of God as the creator, we are thinking of him, most of the time, as a supernal artisan. Whatever doctrine we may be considering, whether it be a doctrine like that of Descartes, or of Leibnitz himself, we always imply that the will follows, more or less, from the understanding or at least accompanies it, so that when God creates he knows precisely what he is creating. Thus, the conception of man in the mind of God is comparable to that of the paper-knife in the mind of the artisan: God makes man according to a procedure and a conception, exactly as the artisan manufactures a paper-knife, following a definition and a formula. Thus each individual man is the realization of a certain conception which dwells in the divine understanding. In the philosophic atheism of the eighteenth century, the notion of God is suppressed, but not, for all that, the idea that essence is prior to existence; something of that idea we still find everywhere, in Diderot, in Voltaire and even in Kant. Man possesses a human nature; that "human nature," which is the conception of human being, is found in every man; which means that each man is a particular example of a universal conception, the conception of Man. In Kant, this universality goes so far that the wild man of the woods, man in the state of nature and the bourgeois are all contained in the same definition and have the same fundamental qualities. Here again, the essence of

man precedes that historic existence which we confront in experience.

Atheistic existentialism, of which I am a representative, declares with greater consistency that if God does not exist there is at least one being whose existence comes before its essence, a being which exists before it can be defined by any conception of it. That being is man or, as Heidegger has it, the human reality. What do we mean by saying that existence precedes essence? We mean that man first of all exists, encounters himself, surges up in the world—and defines himself afterwards. If man as the existentialist sees him is not definable, it is because to begin with he is nothing. He will not be anything until later, and then he will be what he makes of himself. Thus, there is no human nature, because there is no God to have a conception of it. Man simply is. Not that he is simply what he conceives himself to be, but he is what he wills, and as he conceives himself after already existing—as he wills to be after that leap towards existence.

Man is nothing else but that which he makes of himself. That is the first principle of existentialism. And this is what people call its "subjectivity," using the word as a reproach against us. But what do we mean to say by this, but that man is of a greater dignity than a stone or a table? For we mean to say that man primarily exists—that man is, before all else, something which propels itself towards a future and is aware that it is doing so. Man is, indeed, a project which possesses a subjective life, instead of being a kind of moss, or a fungus or a cauliflower. Before that projection of the self nothing exists; not even in the heaven of intelligence: man will only attain existence when he is what he purposes to be. Not, however, what he may wish to be. For what we usually understand by wishing or willing is a conscious decision taken—much more often than not—after we have made ourselves what we are. I may wish to join a party, to write a book or to marry—but in such a case what is usually called my will is probably a manifestation of a prior and more spontaneous decision. If, however, it is true that existence is prior to essence, man is responsible for what he is. Thus, the first effect of existentialism is that it puts every man in possession of himself as he is, and places the entire responsibility for his existence squarely upon his own shoulders. And, when we say that man is responsible for himself, we do not mean that he is responsible only for his own individuality, but that he is responsible for all men.

The word "subjectivism" is to be understood in two senses, and our adversaries play upon only one of them. Subjectivism means, on the one hand, the freedom of the individual subject and, on the other, that man cannot pass beyond human subjectivity. It is the latter which is the deeper meaning of existentialism. When we say that man chooses himself, we do mean that every one of us must choose himself; but by that we also mean that in choosing for himself he chooses for all men. For in effect, of all the actions a man may take in order to create himself as he wills to be, there is not one which is not creative, at the same time, of an image of man such as he believes he ought to be. To choose between this or that is at the same time to affirm the value of that which is chosen; for we are unable ever to choose the worse. What we choose is always the better; and nothing can be better for us unless it is better for all.

If, moreover, existence precedes essence and we will to exist at the same time as we fashion our image, that image is valid for all and for the entire epoch in which we find ourselves. Our responsibility is thus much greater than we had supposed, for it concerns mankind as a whole. If I am a worker, for instance, I may choose to join a Christian rather than a Communist trade union. And if, by that membership, I choose to signify that resignation is, after all, the attitude that best becomes a man, that man's kingdom is not upon this earth, I do not commit myself alone to that view. Resignation is my will for everyone, and my action is, in consequence, a commitment on behalf of all mankind. Or if, to take a more personal case, I decide to marry and to have children, even though this decision proceeds simply from my situation, from my passion or my desire, I am thereby committing not only myself, but humanity as a whole, to the practice of monogamy. I am thus responsible for myself and for all men, and I am creating a certain image of man as I would have him to be. In fashioning myself I fashion man.

This may enable us to understand what is meant by such terms—perhaps a little grandiloquent—as anguish, abandonment and despair. As you will soon see, it is very simple. First, what do we mean by anguish? The existentialist frankly states that man is in anguish. His meaning is as follows— When a man commits himself to anything, fully realizing that he is not only choosing what he will be, but is thereby at the same time a legislator deciding for the whole of mankind—in such a moment a man cannot escape from the sense of complete and profound responsibility. There are many, indeed, who show no such anxiety. But we affirm that they are merely disguising their anguish or are in flight from it. Certainly, many people think that in what they are doing they commit no one but themselves to anything: and if you ask them, "What would happen if everyone did so?" they shrug their shoulders and reply, "Everyone does not do so." But in truth, one ought always to ask oneself what would happen if everyone did as one is doing; nor can one escape from that disturbing thought except by a kind of self-deception.

The man who lies in self-excuse, by saying "Everyone will not do it" must be ill at ease in his conscience, for the act of lying implies the universal value which it denies. By its very disguise his anguish reveals itself. This is the anguish that Kierkegaard called "the anguish of Abraham." You know the story: An angel commanded Abraham to sacrifice his son: and obedience was obligatory, if it really was an angel who had appeared and said, "Thou, Abraham, shalt sacrifice thy son." But anyone in such a case would wonder, first, whether it was indeed an angel and secondly, whether I am really Abraham. Where are the proofs? A certain mad woman who suffered from hallucinations said that people were telephoning to her, and giving her orders. The doctor asked, "But who is it that speaks to you?" She replied: "He says it is God." And what, indeed, could prove to her that it was God? If an angel appears to me, what is the proof that it is an angel; or, if I hear voices, who can prove that they proceed from heaven and not from hell, or from my own subconsciousness or some pathological condition? Who can prove that they are really addressed to me?

Who, then, can prove that I am the proper person to impose, by my own choice, my conception of man upon mankind? I shall never find any proof whatever; there will be no sign to convince me of it. If a voice speaks to me, it is still I myself who must decide whether the voice is or is not that of an angel. If I regard a certain course of action as good, it is only I who choose to say that it is good and not bad. There is nothing to show that I am Abraham: nevertheless I also am obliged at every instant to perform actions which are examples. Everything happens to every man as though the whole human race had its eyes fixed upon what he is doing and regulated its conduct accordingly. So every man ought to say, "Am I really a man who has the right to act in such a manner that humanity regulates itself by what I do." If a man does not say that, he is dissembling his anguish.

Clearly, the anguish with which we are concerned here is not one that could lead to quietism or inaction. It is anguish pure and simple, of the kind well known to all those who have borne responsibilities. When, for instance, a military leader takes upon himself the responsibility for an attack and sends a number of men to their death, he chooses to do it and at bottom he alone chooses. No doubt under a higher command, but its orders, which are more general, require interpretation by him and upon that interpretation depends the life of ten, fourteen or twenty men. In making the decision, he cannot but feel a certain anguish. All leaders know that anguish. It does not prevent their acting, on the contrary it is the very condition of their action, for the action presupposes that there is a plurality of possibilities, and in choosing one of these, they realize that it has value only because it is chosen. Now it is anguish of that kind which existentialism describes, and moreover, as we shall see, makes explicit through direct responsibility towards other men who are concerned. Far from being a screen which could separate us from action, it is a condition of action itself.

And when we speak of "abandonment"—a favorite word of Heidegger—we only mean to say that God does not exist, and that it is necessary to draw the consequences of his absence right to the end. The existentialist is strongly opposed to a certain type of secular moralism which seeks to suppress God at the least possible expense. Towards 1880, when the French professors endeavored to formulate a secular morality, they said something like this: God is a useless and costly hypothesis, so we will do without it. However, if we are to have morality, a society and a law-abiding world, it is essential that certain values should be taken seriously; they must have an *à priori* existence ascribed to them. It must be considered obligatory *à priori* to be honest, not to lie, not to beat one's wife, to bring up children and so forth; so we are going to do a little work on this subject, which will enable us to show that these values exist all the same, inscribed in an intelligible heaven although, of course, there is no God. In other words—and this is, I believe, the purport of all that we in France call radicalism—nothing will be changed if God does not exist; we shall rediscover the same norms of honesty, progress and humanity, and we shall have disposed of God as an out-of-date hypothesis which will die away quietly of itself.

The existentialist, on the contrary, finds it extremely embarrassing that God does not exist, for there disappears with Him all possibility of finding values in an intelligible heaven. There can no longer be any good *à priori*, since there is no infinite and perfect consciousness to think it. It is nowhere written that "the good" exists, that one must be honest or must not lie, since we are now upon the plane where there are only men. Dostoevsky once wrote "If God did not exist, everything would be permitted"; and that, for existentialism, is the starting point. Everything is indeed permitted if God does not exist, and man is in consequence forlorn, for he cannot find anything to depend upon either within or outside himself. He discovers forthwith, that he is without excuse.

For if indeed existence precedes essence, one will never be able to explain one's action by reference to a given and specific human nature; in other words, there is no determinism—man is free, man is freedom. Nor, on the other hand, if God does not exist, are we provided with any values or commands that could legitimize our behavior. Thus we have neither behind us, nor before us in a luminous realm of values, any means of justification or excuse. We are left alone, without excuse.

That is what I mean when I say that man is condemned to be free. Condemned, because he did not create himself, yet is nevertheless at liberty, and from the moment that he is thrown into this world he is responsible for everything he does. The existentialist does not believe in the power of passion. He will never regard a grand passion as a destructive torrent upon which a man is swept into certain actions as by fate, and which, therefore, is an excuse for them. He thinks that man is responsible for his passion. Neither will an existentialist think that a man can find help through some sign being vouchsafed upon earth for his orientation: for he thinks that the man himself interprets the sign as he chooses. He thinks that every man, without any support or help whatever, is condemned at every instant to invent man. As Ponge has written in a very fine article, "Man is the future of man." That is exactly true. Only, if one took this to mean that the future is laid up in Heaven, that God knows what it is, it would be false, for then it would no longer even be a future. If, however, it means that, whatever man may now appear to be, there is a future to be fashioned, a virgin future that awaits him—then it is a true saying. But in the present one is forsaken.

As an example by which you may the better understand this state of abandonment, I will refer to the case of a pupil of mine, who sought me out in the following circumstances. His father was quarreling with his mother and was also inclined to be a "collaborator"; his elder brother had been killed in the German offensive of 1940 and this young man, with a sentiment somewhat primitive but generous, burned to avenge him. His mother was living alone with him, deeply afflicted by the semi-treason of his father and by the death of her eldest son, and her one consolation was in this young man. But he, at this moment, had the choice between going to England to join the Free French Forces or of staying near his mother and helping her to live. He fully realised that this woman lived only for him and that his disappearance—or perhaps his death—would plunge her into despair. He also realised that, concretely and in fact, every action he

performed on his mother's behalf would be sure of effect in the sense of aiding her to live, whereas anything he did in order to go and fight would be an ambiguous action which might vanish like water into sand and serve no purpose. For instance, to set out for England he would have to wait indefinitely in a Spanish camp on the way through Spain; or, on arriving in England or in Algiers he might be put into an office to fill up forms. Consequently, he found himself confronted by two very different modes of action; the one concrete, immediate, but directed towards only one individual; and the other an action addressed to an end infinitely greater, a national collectivity, but for that very reason ambiguous—and it might be frustrated on the way. At the same time, he was hesitating between two kinds of morality; on the one side the morality of sympathy, of personal devotion and, on the other side, a morality of wider scope but of more debatable validity. He had to choose between those two.

What could help him to choose? Could the Christian doctrine? No. Christian doctrine says: Act with charity, love your neighbor, deny yourself for others, choose the way which is hardest, and so forth. But which is the harder road? To whom does one owe the more brotherly love, the patriot or the mother? Which is the more useful aim, the general one of fighting in and for the whole community, or the precise aim of helping one particular person to live? Who can give an answer to that *à priori?* No one. Nor is it given in any ethical scripture. The Kantian ethic says, Never regard another as a means, but always as an end. Very well; if I remain with my mother, I shall be regarding her as the end and not as a means: but by the same token I am in danger of treating as means those who are fighting on my behalf; and the converse is also true, that if I go to the aid of the combatants I shall be treating them as the end at the risk of treating my mother as a means.

If values are uncertain, if they are still too abstract to determine the particular, concrete case under consideration, nothing remains but to trust in our instincts. That is what this young man tried to do; and when I saw him he said, "In the end, it is feeling that counts; the direction in which it is really pushing me is the one I ought to choose. If I feel that I love my mother enough to sacrifice everything else for her—my will to be avenged, all my longings for action and adventure—then I stay with her. If, on the contrary, I feel that my love for her is not enough, I go." But how does one estimate the strength of a feeling? The value of his feeling for his mother was determined precisely by the fact that he was standing by her. I may say that I love a certain friend enough to sacrifice such or such a sum of money for him, but I cannot prove that unless I have done it. I may say, "I love my mother enough to remain with her," if actually I have remained with her. I can only estimate the strength of this affection if I have performed an action by which it is defined and ratified. But if I then appeal to this affection to justify my action, I find myself drawn into a vicious circle.

Moreover, as Gide has very well said, a sentiment which is play-acting and one which is vital are two things that are hardly distinguishable one from another. To decide that I love my mother by staying beside her, and to play a comedy the upshot of which is that I do so—these are nearly the same thing. In other words, feeling is formed by the deeds that one does; therefore I cannot consult it as a guide to action. And that is to say that I can neither seek within myself for an authentic impulse to action, nor can I expect, from some ethic, formulae that will enable me to act. You may say that the youth did, at least, go to a professor to ask for advice. But if you seek counsel—from a priest, for example—you have selected that priest; and at bottom you already knew, more or less, what he would advise. In other words, to choose an adviser is nevertheless to commit oneself by that choice. If you are a Christian, you will say, Consult a priest; but there are collaborationists, priests who are resisters and priests who wait for the tide to turn: which will you choose? Had this young man chosen a priest of the resistance, or one of the collaboration, he would have decided beforehand the kind of advice he was to receive. Similarly, in coming to me, he knew what advice I should give him, and I had but one reply to make. You are free, therefore choose—that is to say, invent. No rule of general morality can show you what you ought to do: no signs are vouchsafed in this world. The Catholics

will reply, "Oh, but they are!" Very well; still, it is I myself, in every case, who have to interpret the signs.

While I was imprisoned, I made the acquaintance of a somewhat remarkable man, a Jesuit, who had become a member of that order in the following manner. In his life he had suffered a succession of rather severe setbacks. His father had died when he was a child, leaving him in poverty, and he had been awarded a free scholarship in a religious institution, where he had been made continually to feel that he was accepted for charity's sake, and, in consequence, he had been denied several of those distinctions and honors which gratify children. Later, about the age of eighteen, he came to grief in a sentimental affair; and finally, at twenty-two—this was a trifle in itself, but it was the last drop that overflowed his cup—he failed in his military examination. This young man, then, could regard himself as a total failure: it was a sign—but a sign of what? He might have taken refuge in bitterness or despair. But he took it—very cleverly for him—as a sign that he was not intended for secular success, and that only the attainments of religion, those of sanctity and of faith, were accessible to him. He interpreted his record as a message from God, and became a member of the Order. Who can doubt but that this decision as to the meaning of the sign was his, and his alone? One could have drawn quite different conclusions from such a series of reverses—as, for example, that he had better become a carpenter or a revolutionary. For the decipherment of the sign, however, he bears the entire responsibility. That is what "abandonment" implies, that we ourselves decide our being. And with this abandonment goes anguish.

As for "despair," the meaning of this expression is extremely simple. It merely means that we limit ourselves to a reliance upon that which is within our wills, or within the sum of the probabilities which render our action feasible. Whenever one wills anything, there are always these elements of probability. If I am counting upon a visit from a friend, who may be coming by train or by tram, I presuppose that the train will arrive at the appointed time, or that the tram will not be derailed. I remain in the realm of possibilities; but one does not rely upon any possibilities beyond those that are strictly concerned in one's action. Beyond the point at which the possibilities under consideration cease to affect my action, I ought to disinterest myself. For there is no God and no prevenient design, which can adapt the world and all its possibilities to my will. When Descartes said, "Conquer yourself rather than the world," what he meant was, at bottom, the same—that we should act without hope. . . .

Quietism is the attitude of people who say, "let others do what I cannot do." The doctrine I am presenting before you is precisely the opposite of this, since it declares that there is no reality except in action. It goes further, indeed, and adds, "Man is nothing else but what he purposes, he exists only in so far as he realizes himself, he is therefore nothing else but the sum of his actions, nothing else but what his life is." Hence we can well understand why some people are horrified by our teaching. For many have but one resource to sustain them in their misery, and that is to think, "Circumstances have been against me, I was worthy to be something much better than I have been. I admit I have never had a great love or a great friendship; but that is because I never met a man or a woman who were worthy of it; if I have not written any very good books, it is because I had not the leisure to do so; or, if I have had no children to whom I could devote myself it is because I did not find the man I could have lived with. So there remains within me a wide range of abilities, inclinations and potentialities, unused but perfectly viable, which endow me with a worthiness that could never be inferred from the mere history of my actions."

But in reality and for the existentialist, there is no love apart from the deeds of love; no potentiality of love other than that which is manifested in loving; there is no genius other than that which is expressed in works of art. The genius of Proust is the totality of the works of Proust; the genius of Racine is the series of his tragedies, outside of which there is nothing. Why should we attribute to Racine the capacity to write yet another tragedy when that is precisely what he did not write? In life, a man commits himself, draws his own portrait and there is nothing but that portrait. No doubt this thought may seem comfortless to one who has not made a success of his life. On the other hand, it puts everyone in a position to understand that reality alone is reliable; that dreams, expectations and hopes serve to define a man only as deceptive dreams, abortive hopes, expectations unfulfilled; that is to say, they define him negatively, not positively. Nevertheless, when one says, "You are nothing else but what you live," it does not imply that an artist is to be judged solely by his works of art, for a thousand other things contribute no less to his definition as a man. What we mean to say is that a man is no other than a series of undertakings, that he is the sum, the organization, the set of relations that constitute these undertakings. . . .

You can see from these few reflections that nothing could be more unjust than the objections people raise against us. Existentialism is nothing else but an attempt to draw the full conclusions from a consistently atheistic position. Its intention is not in the least that of plunging men into despair. And if by despair one means—as the Christians do—any attitude of unbelief, the despair of the existentialists is something different. Existentialism is not atheist in the sense that it would exhaust itself in demonstrations of the non-existence of God. It declares, rather, that even if God existed that would make no difference from its point of view. Not that we believe God does exist, but we think that the real problem is not that of His existence; what man needs is to find himself again and to understand that nothing can save him from himself, not even a valid proof of the existence of God. In this sense existentialism is optimistic. It is a doctrine of action, and it is only by self-deception, by confounding their own despair with ours that Christians can describe us as without hope.

Questions for Reflection

1. Sartre's advice in making ethical decisions is "You are free, therefore choose—that is to say, invent." Do you think this is an adequate ethical principle? Do you agree with Sartre that, in the final analysis, there are no other alternatives? Kant would ask, "Can this principle be universalized? Can we rationally wish that everyone would follow this principle in making ethical decisions?" What do you think?

2. Sartre claims that individuals are nothing more than the sum of their actions—that, for example, there is no love apart from the deeds of love. Do you agree with this?

3. Do you agree with Sartre's claim that even if God existed it would make no difference to our situation, because ultimately the burden of making choices would still rest fully on our shoulders? How does he illustrate this point with the example of the young man choosing between his mother and the war and the example of the man who felt called to be a Jesuit priest?

4. What in Sartre's philosophy of life leads to despair? Why does he, nevertheless, claim that his version of existentialism is an optimistic philosophy?

Credits

Chapter 2

p. 56 From *Basic Writings of St. Thomas Aquinas,* ed. Anton C. Pegis, Hackett Publishing Company, 1997. Reprinted by permission of Hackett Publishing Company, Inc. All rights reserved.

p. 59 From Richard Taylor, *Metaphysics,* fourth edition, Prentice-Hall, 1974. Copyright © 1974 by Prentice-Hall, Inc. Reprinted with permission from Prentice-Hall, Inc., Upper Saddle River, NJ.

p. 66 From William Rowe, *Philosophy of Religion: An Introduction,* third edition, Wadsworth, 2001.

p. 90 From St. Anselm, *Proslogium* and Gaunilo, *In Behalf of the Fool* in *St. Anselm: Basic Writings,* trans. S. W. Deane, Open Court Publishing Company. Copyrighted by The Open Court Publishing Co. 1903. Second copyright © by The Open Court Publishing Co. 1962.

p. 93 From Michael Martin, *Atheism: A Philosophical Justification,* Temple University Press, 1990.

p. 101 From Albert Camus, *The Plague,* trans. Stuart Gilbert, Random House, 1948.

p. 106 From B. C. Johnson, *The Atheist Debater's Handbook,* Prometheus Books, © 1981 by B. C. Johnson. Reprinted with permission of the publisher.

p. 111 From John Hick, *Philosophy of Religion,* Prentice Hall, 1963.

p. 130 From Michael Scriven, *Primary Philosophy,* McGraw-Hill, 1966.

p. 137 From *New Essays in Philosophical Theology,* ed. Antony Flew and Alasdair MacIntyre, SCM Press, 1955. Copyright © 1955 by Antony Flew and Alasdair MacIntyre; renewed 1983. Reprinted with permission of Scribner, an imprint of Simon & Schuster Adult Publishing Group.

p. 146 From Richard Dawkins, "Is Science a Religion?" Reprinted from *The Humanist Magazine,* 1997.

p. 151 From Paul Davies, "The Unreasonable Effectiveness of Science." Reprinted from *Evidence of Purpose,* ed. John Marks Templeton, *Continuum,* 1994.

Chapter 3

p. 168 From René Descartes, *Meditations on First Philosophy,* third edition, trans. Donald Cress, Hackett Publishing Company, 1993. Reprinted by permission of Hackett Publishing Company, Inc. All rights reserved.

p. 219 From Alison M. Jaggar, "Love and Knowledge: Emotion in Feminist Epistemology." Reprinted from *Inquiry* vol 32:2, pp. 151–176, by permission of Scandinavian University Press, Oslo, Norway, and the author.

p. 236 From O. K. Bouwsma, *Philosophical Essays,* University of Nebraska Press, 1965.

p. 243 From John Hospers, *an Introduction to Philosophical Analysis,* second edition, Prentice-Hall, 1967.

p. 252 From Steven Weinberg, "The Revolution That Didn't Happen." Reprinted from *The New York Review of Books,* October 8, 1998.

p. 261 From Richard Rorty, "Science as Solidarity." Reprinted from *The Rhetoric of the Human Sciences: Language and Argument in Scholarship and Public Affairs,* ed. John S. Nelson, Allan Megill, and Donald N. McCloskey, University of Wisconsin Press, 1987.

Chapter 4

p. 276 From Daniel Dennett, "Where Am I?" Reprinted from *Brainstorms: Philosophical Essays on Mind and Psychology.* Copyright © 1978 by Bradford Books, Publishers. All rights reserved. Reprinted by permission of MIT Press.

p. 287 From René Descartes, *Meditations on First Philosophy,* third edition, trans. Donald Cress, Hackett Publishing Company, 1993. Reprinted by permission of Hackett Publishing Company, Inc. All rights reserved.

p. 291 From Gilbert Ryle, *The Concept of Mind*. Copyright 1949 by Gilbert Ryle. Reprinted by permission of Harper-Collins Publishers.

p. 299 From Paul Churchland, *Matter and Consciousness*, MIT Press, 1984. Reprinted by permission of the author and publisher.

p. 305 From David Chalmers, "The Puzzle of Conscious Experience," *Scientific American*, December 1995. Copyright © 1995 by Scientific American, Inc. All rights reserved. With permission from the publisher.

p. 324 From Jeffrey Olen, *Persons and Their World*, McGraw-Hill, 1983.

p. 334 From Linda Badham, "A Naturalistic Case for Extinction." Reprinted from *Death and Immortality in the Religions of the World*, ed. Paul and Linda Badham. Copyright © 1987 by Paragon House Publishers. Reprinted by permission.

p. 343 From Christopher Evans, *The Micro Millennium*, Viking Press, 1979.

p. 354 From John Searle, *Minds, Brains, and Science*, Harvard University Press, 1984.

p. 362 From Terry Bisson, "They're Made Out of Meat," in *Omni*, April 1991. Copyright © 1991 by Terry Bisson. Reprinted by permission of the author and his literary agent Susan Ann Protter.

Chapter 5

p. 369 From Jonathan Harrison, "Tom & Jerry or What Price Pelagius?" *Religious Studies*, 17 (December 1981). Reprinted with the permission of Cambridge University Press.

p. 381 From C. A. Campbell, *On Selfhood and Godhood*, George Allen & Unwin, 1957. Reprinted with permission from HarperCollins Publishers, Ltd., United Kingdom.

p. 388 From W. T. Stace, *Religion and the Modern Mind*. Copyright 1952 by W. T. Stace, renewed © 1980 by Blanche Stace. Reprinted by permission of HarperCollins Publishers Inc.

p. 395 From B. F. Skinner, "A Lecture on 'Having' a Poem," in *Cumulative Record: A Selection of Papers*, third edition, Appleton-Century Crofts, 1972. Reprinted with permission from the B. F. Skinner Foundation.

p. 400 From C. S. Lewis, "The Humanitarian Theory of Punishment," in *God in the Dock*, William B. Eerdmans, 1970. Copyright © 1940 C. S. Lewis Pte. Ltd. Extract reprinted by permission.

p. 405 From Clarence Darrow, "The Crime of Compulsion," in *Attorney for the Damned*, ed. Arthur Weinberg, Simon and Schuster, 1957.

Chapter 6

p. 421 From Ruth Benedict, "Anthropology and the Abnormal," *The Journal of General Psychology* 10, 1934. Reprinted with permission of the Hellen Dwight Reid Educational Foundation. Published by Heldref Publications, 1319 Eighteenth St., N.W., Washington, D.C. 20036-1802. Copyright © 1934 Heldref Publications.

p. 427 From James Rachels, *The Elements of Moral Philosophy*, second edition, McGraw-Hill, 1993.

p. 462 From Ayn Rand, "The Ethics of Emergencies," in *The Virtue of Selfishness: A New Concept of Egoism*, Signet Books, 1964.

p. 468 From Alison M. Jaggar, "Feminist Ethics," in *Encyclopedia of Ethics*, vol. 1, eds. Lawrence C. Becker and Charlotte B. Becker, Routledge, 2001.

p. 482 From Judith Jarvis Thomson, "A Defense of Abortion," in *Philosophy and Public Affairs*, vol. 1, no. 1 (1971). Copyright © 1971 by Princeton University Press. Reprinted by Permission of Princeton University Press.

p. 489 From Sidney Callahan, "Abortion and the Sexual Agenda," in *Commonweal*, April 25, 1986. Copyright © 1986, 1996 Commonweal Foundation. Used with Permission.

Chapter 7

p. 504 From Richard Taylor, Freedom, *Anarchy, and the Law: An Introduction to Political Philosophy*, second edition, Prometheus Books, 1982.

p. 514 From Martin Luther King Jr., "Letter from Birmingham Jail." Copyright 1963 Dr. Martin Luther King Jr., copyright renewed 1986 Coretta Scott King. Reprinted by arrangement with the Estate of Martin Luther King Jr., c/o Writers House as agent for the proprietor New York, NY.

p. 544 From John Rawls, *A Theory of Justice*, Cambridge, Mass.: The Belknap Press of Harvard University Press, copyright © 1971, 1999 by the President and Fellows of Harvard College. Reprinted by permission of the publisher.

p. 550 From John Hospers, "What Libertarianism Is," in *The Libertarian Alternative*, ed. Tibor Machan, Nelson-Hall, 1974.

p. 558 From James Q. Wilson, "Against the Legalization of Drugs," in *Commentary*, 89, no. 2, February 1990. Reprinted by permission of the publisher. All rights reserved.

p. 567 From Thomas Szasz, "The Ethics of Addiction," *Harper's Magazine*, 244, April 1972. Copyright © 1972 by Harper's Magazine. All rights reserved. Reproduced from the April issue by special permission.

Chapter 8

p. 581 From W. H. Auden, "The Unknown Citizen," in *Collected Shorter Poems 1927–1957,* Random House, 1966. Copyright 1940 and renewed 1968 by W. H. Auden. Reprinted by permission of Random House.

p. 595 From Leo Tolstoy, *Confession,* trans. David Patterson, W.W. Norton, 1983.

p. 610 From Jean-Paul Sartre, *Existentialism and Humanism,* trans. Philip Mairet. Reprinted with permission of Haskell House Publishers Ltd.